EDMUND WILSON

Edmund Wilson

LITERARY ESSAYS AND REVIEWS
OF THE 1930s & 40s

The Triple Thinkers
The Wound and the Bow
Classics and Commercials
Uncollected Reviews

THE LIBRARY OF AMERICA

Volume compilation, notes, and chronology copyright © 2007 by
Literary Classics of the United States, Inc., New York, N.Y.
All rights reserved.
No part of this book may be reproduced commercially
by offset-lithographic or equivalent copying devices without
the permission of the publisher.

The Triple Thinkers copyright © 1948 by Edmund Wilson; renewed
1975 by Elena Wilson. *The Wound and the Bow* copyright © 1978 by
Edmund Wilson. *Classics and Commercials* copyright © 1950 by
Edmund Wilson; renewed 1977 by Elena Wilson. "Return of
Ernest Hemingway" copyright © 1940, renewed 1968 by Edmund
Wilson. "Doubts and Dreams" copyright © 1944, renewed 1971 by
Edmund Wilson. "Faintness of the *Age of Thunder* and Power of
The Folded Leaf" copyright © 1945, renewed 1972 by Edmund
Wilson. "Theodore Dreiser's Quaker and Graham Greene's
Priest" copyright © 1946, renewed 1973 by Elena Wilson.
"Henry James and Auden in America" copyright
© 1946, renewed 1973 by Elena Wilson.

Reprinted by permission of Farrar, Straus and Giroux, LLC.

The paper used in this publication meets the
minimum requirements of the American National Standard for
Information Sciences—Permanence of Paper for Printed
Library Materials, ANSI z39.48—1984.

Distributed to the trade
in the United States by Penguin Putnam Inc.
and in Canada by Penguin Books Canada Ltd.

Library of Congress Control Number: 2007928899
ISBN 978-1-59853-014-8
———
First Printing
The Library of America—177

Manufactured in the United States of America

LEWIS M. DABNEY
WROTE THE CHRONOLOGY AND NOTES
FOR THIS VOLUME

Edmund Wilson's
Literary Essays and Reviews of the 1930s & 40s
is published with support from

THE GEOFFREY C. HUGHES FOUNDATION

and will be kept in print by its gift to
the Guardians of American Letters Fund,
established by The Library of America
to ensure that every volume in the series
will be permanently available.

Contents

THE TRIPLE THINKERS

Twelve Essays on Literary Subjects

What is the artist if he is not a triple thinker?
FLAUBERT TO LOUISE COLET

CONTENTS

FOREWORD

This volume contains nine of the ten essays published under the same title in 1938, with three new ones: *Morose Ben Jonson*, *'Mr. Rolfe,'* and *The Historical Interpretation of Literature*. The old essays have been revised—in some cases, completely rewritten. I have never changed seriously the substance of what I wrote in the first edition, but I have sometimes allowed myself references to books which had not then been published— as when I have given Joyce's *Work in Progress* its eventual title of *Finnegans Wake* or mentioned Auden's preface to the new edition of Henry James's *The American Scene*. When I have wanted to note a new event or to add a new idea, I have put it in a postscript or a footnote.

I may take this occasion to comment on certain criticisms that have been made of these essays and of those in *The Wound and the Bow*. It has sometimes been complained in connection with my studies of Dickens and Housman that, because I have had little to say about the humor of the former or the poetry of the latter, I must entirely have failed to appreciate the genius of my subjects. Now, my purpose has always been to try to contribute something new: I have aimed either to present some writer who was not well enough known or, in the case of a familiar writer, to call attention to some neglected aspect of his work or his career. I did not feel that there was anything fresh to say about either the humor of *Pickwick* or the pathos of the *Shropshire Lad*. I thought that I could assume that they were already well known to anyone with enough interest in literature to read a volume of literary criticism. But the classical scholarship of Housman in its bearing on his poetry and his personality and the social and moral criticism embodied in Dickens' later novels have not had justice done them. On the other hand, in the case of a writer like Pushkin or John Jay Chapman, I had to introduce him to a public who knew almost nothing about him, so I have started from the beginning and described his most obvious qualities.

Another objection is perhaps more valid. I have occasionally been accused of conveying a too favorable impression of certain rather imperfect works—notably, Dickens' later novels and Flaubert's *L'Education sentimentale*—by retelling them in such a way as to conjure out of sight their demerits. Well, it is true that it is pleasantly possible to go through a book that one has read before, skimming over the boring parts or disregarding some fundamental weakness, and that one can sometimes in this way arrive at the book that the author *intended* to write but did not quite fill in or rise to, and enjoy it as one could not do otherwise. When I reread *Our Mutual Friend*, for example, probably the weakest of Dickens' social novels, it is true that I leapt over the love scenes and the less successful grotesques, and got for the first time a good view of the general structure of the novel and the purport of its complicated parable, in such a way as is not always easy with even the best of Dickens, who so energetically plays on our interest with first one, then another, of his entertaining groups that we may miss the plan and the point. And so with *L'Education sentimentale*, if one can manage to displace one's attention from the hero, Frédéric Moreau, so that one is no longer bothered by his two-dimensional flatness and his lack of human development, one can survey for the first time the big canvas which Flaubert has animated, but to the historical and esthetic values of which—it is a real and grave fault—Frédéric tends to act as a non-conductor.

When I was writing about James, however, I did not review in this selective way the three long later novels that I had read first twenty years before; and it may be that, if I had done so, I should have given a somewhat different account. In looking into them again just now, I seemed sometimes to catch sight of qualities which I had not appreciated in my college days—at an age when James's lack of real 'love interest' is likely to prejudice one against him—and to which I feared I might not have done justice. But there is really no way of considering a book independently of one's special sensations in reading it on a particular occasion. In this as in everything else one must allow for a certain relativity. In a sense, one can never read the book that the author originally wrote, and one can never read the same book twice.

1948

Mr. More and the Mithraic Bull*

I MET Mr. Paul Elmer More several times, but had an extended conversation with him only once. I wrote down a record of it at the time and give it here, as I wrote it then, embedded in a Princeton weekend.

I was taken to Mr. More's house by Dean Gauss, who was one of his closest friends at Princeton. Dean Gauss, on this Saturday afternoon, had a special reason for wanting to consult him.

At that time—this visit took place in the December of 1929 —compulsory chapel had been partially abolished at Princeton, but it had been found desirable to make the students attend half the chapel services on Sundays in order to keep them in town over the weekends. Those students who professed unorthodox views—and who were often, as it turned out, the same ones that wanted to spend Saturday nights in Philadelphia or New York—were obliged to attend non-sectarian religious discussions which took place on Sunday evenings and were conducted by members of the faculty in rotation.

That month it had been Dean Gauss's turn, and he had begun on his first evening by attempting to find out how much the students knew about or were interested in religion. It had turned out that, though several boys believed in Heaven, nobody believed in the Devil; and when he had chalked up a list of theological words beginning with *infralapsarian* and *supralapsarian* and ending with *theism* and *deism*, it had been obvious that nobody knew anything about any of them. In dismissing the class, he had invited them to hand in questions which might stimulate discussion; and the sole response to this had been a letter written in Latin by a freshman and expressing a desire to learn something about Mithraism. Dean Gauss had decided to brush up on the subject by calling on Mr. More, who had the history of religions at his fingertips.

Mr. More had at that time just built himself a new house in

*Written on the occasion of Paul Elmer More's death, March 9, 1937.

the new residential section of Princeton near the Graduate
School, and we approached it along a rainy new-laid pavement.
The sitting room, where we waited a few moments, was comfortable but rather somber. With its walls densely lined with
books, it was pre-eminently the room of a scholar—though
there were a few carefully chosen articles of ornament: two
small panes of Dutch stained glass, for example, which Mr.
More had brought back from Europe and had had inlaid in the
glass of a large window at the further end of the room.

But Mr. More did not make us wait long: he appeared almost
at once, brisk enough, and greeted us with an alertness and an
evident pleasure at having people come to see him, very attractive in a man of sixty-five. He was short and had picked up
some of the plumpness that goes with a sedentary occupation.
He had a Roman nose, a pale gray eye and an iron lock of hair
on his forehead—in general, a peculiar iron-gray aspect. There
was in his face much strength and some nobility, but a curious
absence of color.

Affably he attended to the tea and began talking about T. S.
Eliot, whom he had suggested inviting to Princeton to lecture.
I was surprised to see how much he admired Eliot. He told
us, in reply to our questions, that Eliot was 'tall and thin, quite
strikingly good-looking,' and that he, More, had gone to
Eliot's house in London and had met people there. He explained to us that Eliot's grandfather had been chancellor of
Washington University in St. Louis at the time when he, More,
had been a student there, so that he had already known the
poet's family. And as he went on, I came to realize that it was
for him a matter of deep gratification to have made the acquaintance of another writer of high intellectual distinction
who had come like More himself out of that old Middle-
Western world, who had the freedom of that literary life of
Europe from which More's provincialism had largely shut him
out, and who had been kind enough to bring More into contact with it—a man who, with all his brilliant reputation, his
position as a god of the young, was yet a scholar and a serious
critic, preoccupied with problems of morality, and striving,
although by a different route, just as More himself was, to find
his way back to the Christian religion.

We talked about Eliot's influence among the students, and

More demurred over Eliot's poetry. I asked him whether he didn't admire *The Waste Land*. 'Well, one can see,' he conceded, 'that it's written by a man of parts.' But it seemed to be *The Hippopotamus* which presented the most serious difficulties. 'I must say that it reads aloud very well,' he confessed; but he couldn't understand what Eliot meant by it. I suggested that it was a satire on the Church. 'But,' Mr. More protested, 'I can't understand how Eliot reconciles that with his present position.' I reminded him that Eliot had written the poem a good many years before; but Mr. More only shook his head and repeated that he could not reconcile those two things. Nor could he follow Eliot's enthusiasm for Baudelaire: 'It seems to me that he finds in Baudelaire . . . things that aren't there.' I admitted that there might be something in that, but asked him why he could not admire Baudelaire. 'Why,' he replied—he had an abrupt hesitation, as over the difficulty of dealing urbanely with a subject about which he felt so strongly, with an author of whom he so greatly disapproved, and upon whom, if he had been writing an essay, he would certainly have visited his stinging indignation—'I'm old-fashioned about Baudelaire. I recognize his power—and his significance in his time—but as a guide to life—!' He stopped, and neither Gauss nor I tried to debate the matter further.

It was the moment of the great controversy over Humanism, and we tried to draw him out on this subject. I had been hearing from a friend at Harvard of the belief of the fanatical Babbitt that his doctrine was gradually but surely taking possession of all the ablest minds of the time, and of the legend, circulated among his students, that the old man had a great map in his study and stuck a thumb-tack into it at every point where a Humanist center was supposed to have sprung up. But Mr. More was much more sensible and less pretentious. When Gauss asked him whether he felt it was true that a great tide of Humanism was rising: 'Well,' he replied, 'I'd rather say that it was having a great splurge just now, but it's partly based on misunderstanding.' Yet he spoke with evident satisfaction of an article on Stuart P. Sherman which Seward Collins had recently published in the *Bookman*. Sherman had been the favorite disciple who had turned renegade to the Humanist band —the split had come when Sherman praised Whitman—and

Seward Collins had now repudiated Sherman. 'It seems,' remarked Mr. More, 'as if something like a conversion had taken
place there.'

Gauss and More discussed their first acquaintance. The
Dean in those now remote days had been an eager young journalist and poet, just back from the Paris of the nineties, with
long yellow hair and a flowing Latin Quarter tie, and he had
written a furious letter of protest to More over a review of
some French life of Sainte-Beuve which the latter had published in the *Nation*. 'It wasn't a slating, was it?' said More,
almost chuckling at the memory of past ferocity. 'It was just a
bit—contemptuous.' He had answered Gauss's letter and received a second letter equally violent. Then he had invited
Gauss to lunch and had found him, he said, quite amiable and
mild. One of the great sources of More's strength, I realized,
lay in the fact that he always knew precisely what he thought
and was always ready to face anybody down, uncompromisingly and promptly. I looked at Gauss: his golden locks were
gone and had left a prodigiously high domed bald forehead.
With his fine profile of a blond South German Dante, in his
Princetonian soft shirt and tweed golf suit, he sat today, lying
back in his chair, the great expounder of French romanticism,
hobnobbing with the great anti-romantic. So much subtler a
mind than More, with so much wider a range of imaginative
sympathy, and correspondingly so much less fixed in his opinions, he looked out coolly through his eyeglasses without rims
on those prejudices and principles of More's which years ago
had aroused his indignation. The amenities and responsibilities
of Princeton had dimmed the flamboyance of his romanticism.
But Paul Elmer More, still just as positive, still nearly as narrow as then, sat attentively forward in his chair, still ready to
face anybody down.

Dean Gauss now remembered Mithra and asked for light
from Mr. More on the subject. Mr. More, who had the pride
of learning, replied with immediate gusto: 'Why, I don't
suppose I know any more about Mithraism than you do,
Christian!'—At this moment there came into the room a sister
of Mr. More's, who lived with him. She was a pleasant old lady,
with none of her brother's asperity—dressed in black and very

deaf. She had just been going through her bureau-drawers, she said—'And it's so hard to know what to throw away! It's really not worth the trouble trying to sort things!' Mr. More admitted rather perfunctorily and speaking loudly in order to make her hear, that this did constitute a perplexing problem, and quickly brought the conversation back to Mithra.

'Well,' he demanded in a brisk businesslike manner, pouring his sister a cup of tea, 'what d'ye want to know about Mithraism, Christian?' His voice, nasal, clear and Middle-Western, had a suggestion, not unattractive, of the homely plain-spoken manner of the old successful American merchant or banker. 'The Mithraic bee,' began Gauss, 'was a symbol of immortality—' 'I've never heard of that,' Mr. More caught him up. 'Where'd you find that?' 'I can't remember where,' replied Gauss. 'That's what I wanted to ask you. I read it years ago in some book and I can't remember now what it was. I thought you might know.' But Mr. More did not know: he mentioned all the books he had read that dealt with Mithraism and said that there was nothing in any of them about it. What he knew, it was plain, he knew: he needed to consult no index. 'I suppose,' Dean Gauss pursued, 'that the bee came to stand for immortality through the belief that bees were bred spontaneously in the carcasses of dead animals. It was really the carrion-fly. Virgil talks about it in the *Georgics*.' 'The "out of the strong came forth sweetness" of the Bible,' put in Mr. More. 'Yes,' said Gauss. 'Clovis was a Mithraist—' 'That I didn't know,' said Mr. More. 'Yes, Clovis was a Mithraist,' the Dean pursued, 'and his emblem before his conversion was the bee.' 'Is that a guess?' demanded Mr. More. 'No,' said the Dean. 'I read it all somewhere, but I can't remember where.' Clovis's bee, which Mr. More had never heard of and as to which, failing definite authority, he was not prepared to indulge in speculation, seemed to have made him a shade impatient. He delivered, however, a short lecture on what he did know about Mithraic myths; and it was amazing how much he knew and how accurately he was able to retail it. He traced Mithra, the God of Light, from the Vedic hymns into Persian mythology, and from the Orient into Greece, indicating his various transformations with confidence, lucidity and logic, but with a curious effect of his having retained them as ideas without their passing through the picture-making imagination. And yet the Mithra he described was alive, devoid of mystery, form or color though he was. It reminded me of a book called *Error's Chains*, which I had used to look at in my grandfather's library and which had had many illustrations of the heathen gods, old line drawings done from paintings and statues.—Miss More was sitting beside me on the couch and could not hear the general conversation, so we talked separately from time to time while the discussion of Mithraism proceeded. 'You might just as well take it all out and burn it up!' she declared, still thinking of her bureau-drawers. 'When it's been accumulating as long as that, it's not worth the trouble to go through it and pick things out to save!'

At this point Mr. Frank Jewett Mather arrived. He was a cheerful little man in a checked vest and spats, with the cocky pointed mustache of an old beau and the rosiness of a child. And he turned out to know a lot about Mithraism. He told us that it had had a great success with the Roman soldiers because it had promised them a sure immortality, and that it had developed in the third century into a serious competitor to Christianity.—Mr. More's sister suddenly got up: 'I'm going to burn up all that old stuff!' she announced, with the air of one who has finally arrived at a thoroughly satisfactory resolution —and she said good-by and went upstairs.—Mr. Mather explained in detail the symbolism of Mithraic art. There was a Mithraic bull in the Museum, he said, which he had bought and brought back from Europe and which was one of the best things the Museum had. 'I didn't know that,' said Gauss with interest. 'I must go over and see it.' 'It's the best Mithraic bull on this side,' said Mather. 'The only really first-rate one.' It was a marble relief of the Sun-God holding a bull by the horns; there was a dog which was leaping at the throat of the bull and a snake which was attacking his testicles; the snake and the dog were Evil and Darkness. 'Let's go over and see it!' the Dean proposed to me.

Mr. More now reverted to the days of the *Nation*. He told us that Oswald Garrison Villard had sometimes disapproved of what he wrote but had always had somebody else speak to him about it. Mr. More seemed frankly delighted at this evidence that Villard had found him formidable. 'Afraid the "inner check" wouldn't work!' Frank Mather impishly put in. But Mr. More possessed no technique to deal with people who made jokes about Humanism and did not deign to reply to this. 'Who originated the term "inner check"? Was it you or Babbitt?' asked Mather. 'I was the first to use it,' said More. 'In the *Shelburne Essays*. But Babbitt has made much more of it than I have.' And he added, after a moment's pause: 'I think the phrase occurs once in Emerson.'

In the course of the conversation that followed, Mr. Mather ventured to remark that he didn't see how Humanism was going to get us very far by going back to the Council of Chalcedon. Mr. More was then nearing the completion of his series of volumes on Greek philosophy and Christianity. A man of true spiritual vocation, unable to remain a simple rationalist but prevented by a Protestant education and an obstinate hard-headed common sense from finding a basis in the mysticism of Rome, he had devoted long and diligent years to establishing an historical tradition which would justify his peculiar point of view. At that time he had just published the volume which brought the line of development to its climax with the promulgation at Chalcedon in the fifth century of the dogma of the Incarnation—a doctrine which, in laying down the dual nature of Christ, in representing him as both human and divine, had seemed to Mr. More to make it possible for him to preserve the philosophy of Plato, so attractive to his intellectual and esthetic side, and at the same time not to cut himself loose from the supernatural authority of religion. So he made no reply to this gibe—but presently, with a touch of severity, accused Mather of being 'a half-way Platonist like Santayana.' He seemed to me that day very clear-cut against the background of the college community. He was himself not really typical of the American academic world: he was an independent scholar, who had denounced in the most vigorous language the lack of sincerity and the incompetence of the colleges. He stood out, not merely through his distinction of learning, his Greek and Sanskrit and Hebrew and Persian and the rest, but by reason of his unremitting seriousness, his stubborn insistence on the importance of maintaining in one's relation to literature a position which should be realistic in the sense that it would never lose contact with moral problems as he himself understood

them, his refusal to allow himself to be seduced by purely esthetic or intellectual satisfactions. Gauss told him about a student at one of the Sunday-night meetings who had put himself
down as a 'synthetic hedonist'; More smiled, but said, 'I wonder what he meant.'

We discussed an exhibition of modern art then on view in
New York. Gauss thought Seurat essentially classical, but
Mather insisted that he was decadent: Seurat's figures, he said,
seemed to be perfectly realized, but actually they were hanging
in the air, like the characters of Proust or Henry James, with
no real connection with anything. And this led us to contemporary writing. Mr. More, who in a recent essay had allowed
his intolerance of his contemporaries to go to lengths of positive ill temper in characterizing as 'an explosion in a cesspool'
Dos Passos's *Manhattan Transfer*, conceded now, with an
evident desire to be fair, that he 'recognized the element of
protest in Dos Passos and Joyce.' I said that, though there
was protest in Dos Passos, I did not believe there was any in
Joyce, and thus unfortunately deprived Mr. More of his only
excuse for being polite about *Ulysses*. He was afterwards to give
more serious consideration to such writers as Joyce and Proust.
His last volume of *Shelburne Essays* contained papers on these
two novelists, which, uncongenial to More though the subjects
were, show more grasp of what is really at issue in their books
than most of the stuff which has been written to exalt them.
The moralist in Paul Elmer More, who had always been at war
with the poet and who had scored over him so crushing a victory, could usually be counted upon to formulate clearly—
though of course a clear formulation may misrepresent a poet
—the case of any writer, however abhorrent, who had a serious
moral basis, even though the provincial prig who inseparably
accompanied the moralist might prevent him from appreciating the artist's achievement. But at that time I do not think
he had read *Ulysses*; and I myself was a little touchy on the subject, as my attention had just been called by Gauss to an editorial in *The New York Times* that morning in which one of their
anonymous writers had ridiculed an article of mine on Joyce.
Now I was further dismayed, as it seemed to me that these
three men, in their fields of literature and art certainly among

the ablest in the country, were themselves disposed to outlaw from literature the greatest literary artist then alive. The same confounded old academic inertia! I thought; the same old proprietary interest in the classics, which made them unwilling to believe that anything new could have great value! I remembered how thirteen years before it had been the same thing about Bernard Shaw, then already practically a classic. Dean Gauss had read *Ulysses*, but had not liked it much; and, though it turned out that Mather, the old rascal, had investigated Mrs. Bloom's soliloquy, he would not commit himself on the subject. Paul Elmer More, who, as I say, had evidently not yet read Joyce, began by trying to handle the matter without heat, but when I talked about the Homeric parallel—at the suggestion of such a fellow as Joyce's having the effrontery to associate himself with one of the major Greek classics—his arrogance suddenly started up from behind his deliberate urbanity, and he sharply cut down on the discussion—(it had also been a question of whether the characters in *Ulysses* were 'purposive' or mere passive recorders of impressions): 'But Homer's Ulysses knew what he wanted. He didn't need special explanations!' It seemed to me that there were so many misconceptions lodged behind this remark of Mr. More's that I had difficulty in knowing how to deal with it. The conversation became rather confused and took on a slightly acrimonious accent. Somebody changed the subject, and Mr. More proposed showing us his new house.

We went upstairs. On one side of the hallway which led to Mr. More's study was a bookcase entirely filled with detective stories, which I was told he systematically graded with A's, B's, C's and D's. On the shelves of his study were Plato and Plotinus and the Fathers of the Church. Frank Mather mischievously inquired where the Acts of the Council of Chalcedon were kept, and More as usual made no reply. The study was a small unpretentious room at the very top of the house: it had one large Morris chair and a table and a desk. On the walls hung two framed photographs, yellowish-brownish: one of Perugino's *Crucifixion* and the other of two battered Greek torsos, with both arms and legs broken off, awkwardly reclining together. They faced one another across the room, the Christian world and the Greek, and seemed to neutralize one another.

Then we descended and took our leave. Still chafing at
More's attitude toward Joyce, I asked him, just as we were
going out the door, whether he had ever read Eliot on *Ulysses*.
He replied that he had not, and I told him that Eliot considered *Ulysses* a work of the highest importance. His whole attitude toward Eliot, so friendly before seemed, as if by reflex
action, to stiffen. 'I don't see,' he retorted, 'what *Ulysses* has to
do with Royalism, Anglo-Catholicism and Classicism!'—and
added, 'That young man has a screw loose somewhere!'
'Would you agree with Huneker,' said Mather, 'that it's impossible for the same person really to like both Raphael and
Goya?' 'I don't think,' Mr. More replied, 'that that pair is particularly well chosen; but I should say that a capacity for enjoying certain authors made it impossible to enjoy Dante or
Shakespeare or Milton—or rather, I should say that, if a man
liked certain things and claimed to enjoy Shakespeare and
Dante, it would be impossible that he should really appreciate
them!'

On this implacable dictum we went.

The next day I took a walk on the campus. It was dreary,
misty and damp. I remembered the Mithraic bull and decided
to look it up in the Museum. There it was, sure enough, right
opposite the front door as I went in, shining in the dim
afternoon: the white marble relief of Mithra, a naked youth in
a peaked Phrygian cap, clasping the sacred bull, which had the
dog and the snake that were Darkness and Evil threatening its
throat and its balls. But the Sun-God was to kill the bull, and
thereby to conquer the darkness and to make himself the creator of life, all the multiform life of the earth, which was to
spring from the bull's ebbing blood. There they hung—once
the light of those pagan caves to which the soldiers from their
doomed legions had crept, once the Apollonian rivals of the
Crucified—there they hung in the Princeton Museum on a
Sunday afternoon! I went on to the glass-cases inside, but—
Roman busts, Egyptian gods, Greek marbles—almost everything was a reproduction and gave me the impression of being
denatured and canned. The afternoon light was gray, the rooms
were becoming chill. I turned back and stood before the
Mithra, which—round and complete and glowing—seemed

the only thing alive in the Museum. I remembered with what amazement, a wonder that became exaltation, I had come upon the Apollo Belvedere when I had first visited Rome as a child—how I had turned back to stare at its beauty.

I went over to the University Library and sat down and wrote the *Times* a caustic letter about their sneering editorial on Joyce.

Then I went to see if Gauss were free. He had been busy all the afternoon and had evidently had a great many people: Sunday visitors, college officials, protesting parents of students whom he had disciplined. He always gave his closest attention to anything that was submitted for his decision and dealt with it according to his most scrupulous judgment; and I thought his mind was tired. And now he had to prepare his talk for the evening religious meeting. But he revived when I told him that I had been to see the bull and was all for going to the Museum at once. He got his hat and coat and stick, and we set out.

'It's curious,' he mused on the way, 'how closely it paralleled Christianity. They had a sacrifice, a communion and an atonement. The bull was killed in a cave, and that symbolized the resurrection.'—He spoke of his affection for More and told me a curious story. When More had come back recently from Italy, he had announced with gratification and assurance that he had discovered the finest picture in Florence. Gauss had said to him: 'I'll bet I can guess what it is! Don't tell me— I'll bet I can guess what you think is the finest picture in Florence!'—and he guessed Perugino's *Crucifixion*. He was right; More had been quite taken aback. 'But how did you know?' I asked. 'Why should he have liked that picture particularly?' 'Why, you see Christ way up there—so far above the world.'

But when we got to the Museum, it was dark, and we found that the front door had been locked. We squinted at the marble through the glass, but it was scarcely visible now: we could make out only a whitish blur at the bottom of the cavernous entrance hall. We walked around the building and found a side-door unlocked and went in. Obstinately, we climbed stairs, explored galleries, invaded classrooms and studios for classes, with their chalky plaster casts of famous statues; but all the doors into the Museum proper turned out to be locked tight for the night. A late student in one of the classrooms suggested that we might try to find the curator; but the curator was not in his office, and all the other offices were dark.

We walked back across the campus and parted. The Dean had to go to the library to look up some more about Mithra, and I remained in his office to type out my letter on Joyce.

The visit long haunted my memory, and now the news of Mr. More's death has brought it back into my mind: the empty academic week end, the new suburban house, the meetings for the discussion of religion designed to bring the students back to town, the Acts of the Council of Chalcedon, the nice old lady with her firm resolution to burn all that old stuff up, the argument over Joyce, More himself with his lifelong consecration to that great world of culture and thought which he had succeeded in making real to others but which he could never quite rejoin himself, and Gauss and I peering at Mithra through the glass.

Is Verse a Dying Technique?

THE more one reads the current criticism of poetry by poets and their reviewers, the more one becomes convinced that the discussion is proceeding on false assumptions. The writers may belong to different schools, but they all seem to share a basic confusion.

This confusion is the result of a failure to think clearly about what is meant by the words 'prose,' 'verse,' and 'poetry'—a question which is sometimes debated but which never gets straightened out. Yet are not the obvious facts as follows?

What we mean by the words 'prose' and 'verse' are simply two different techniques of literary expression. Verse is written in lines with a certain number of metrical feet each; prose is written in paragraphs and has what we call rhythm. But what is 'poetry,' then? What I want to suggest is that 'poetry' formerly meant one kind of thing but that it now means something different, and that one ought not to generalize about 'poetry' by taking all the writers of verse, ancient, medieval and modern, away from their various periods and throwing them together in one's mind, but to consider both verse and prose in relation to their functions at different times.

The important thing to recognize, it seems to me, is that the literary technique of verse was once made to serve many purposes for which we now, as a rule, use prose. Solon, the Athenian statesman, expounded his political ideas in verse; the *Works and Days* of Hesiod are a shepherd's calendar in verse; his *Theogony* is versified mythology; and almost everything that in contemporary writing would be put into prose plays and novels was versified by the Greeks in epics or plays.

It is true that Aristotle tried to discriminate. 'We have no common name,' he wrote, 'for a mime of Sophron or Xenarchus and a Socratic conversation; and we should still be without one even if the imitation in the two instances were in trimeters or elegiacs or some other kind of verse—though it is the way with people to tack on "poet" to the name of a meter, and talk of elegiac-poets and epic-poets, thinking that they call them poets not by reason of the imitative nature of their work, but indiscriminately by reason of the meter they write in. Even if a theory of medicine or physical philosophy be put forth in a metrical form, it is usual to describe the writer in this way; Homer and Empedocles, however, have really nothing in common apart from their meter; so that, if the one is to be called a poet, the other should be termed a physicist rather than a poet.'

But he admitted that there was no accepted name for the creative—what he calls the 'imitative'—art which had for its mediums both prose and verse; and his posterity followed the custom of which he had pointed out the impropriety by calling anything in meter a 'poem.' The Romans wrote treatises in verse on philosophy and astronomy and farming. The 'poetic' of Horace's *Ars Poetica* applies to the whole range of ancient verse—though Horace did think it just as well to mingle the 'agreeable' with the 'useful'—and this essay in literary criticism is itself written in meter. 'Poetry' remained identified with verse; and since for centuries both dramas and narratives continued largely to be written in verse, the term of which Aristotle had noticed the need—a term for imaginative literature itself, irrespective of literary techniques—never came into common use.

But when we arrive at the nineteenth century, a new conception of 'poetry' appears. The change is seen very clearly in the doubts which began to be felt as to whether Pope were really a poet. Now, it is true that a critic like Johnson would hardly have assigned to Pope the position of pre-eminence he does at any other period than Johnson's own; but it is *not* true that only a critic of the latter part of the eighteenth century, a critic of an 'age of prose,' would have considered Pope a poet. Would not Pope have been considered a poet in any age before the age of Coleridge?

But the romantics were to redefine 'poetry.' Coleridge, in the *Biographia Literaria*, denies that any excellent work in meter may be properly called a 'poem.' 'The final definition . . .' he says, 'may be thus worded. A poem is that species of composition which is opposed to works of science by proposing for its *immediate* object pleasure, not truth; and from all other species —(having *this* object in common with it)—it is discriminated by proposing to itself such delight from the *whole* as is com-

patible with a distinct gratification from each component part.'
This would evidently exclude the *Ars Poetica* and the *De Rerum
Natura*, whose immediate objects are as much truth as pleasure. What is really happening here is that for Coleridge the
function of 'poetry' is becoming more specialized. Why? Coleridge answers this question in formulating an objection which
may be brought against the first part of his definition: 'But the
communication of pleasure may be the immediate object of a
work not metrically composed; and that object may have been
in a high degree attained, as in novels and romances.' Precisely; and the novels and romances were formerly written in
verse, whereas they are now usually written in prose. In Coleridge's time, tales in verse were more and more giving place to
prose novels. Before long, novels in verse such as *Aurora Leigh*
and *The Ring and the Book* were to seem more or less literary
oddities. 'Poetry,' then, for Coleridge, has become something
which, unless he amends his definition, may equally well be
written in prose: Isaiah and Plato and Jeremy Taylor will, as he
admits, be describable as 'poetry.' Thereafter, he seems to
become somewhat muddled; but he finally arrives at the conclusion that the 'peculiar property of poetry' is 'the property of
exciting a more continuous and equal attention than the language of prose aims at, whether colloquial or written.'

The truth is that Coleridge is having difficulties in attempting
to derive his new conception of poetry from the literature of
the past, which has been based on the old conception. Poe,
writing thirty years later, was able to get a good deal further.
Coleridge had said—and it seems to have been really what he
was principally trying to say—that 'a poem of any length
neither can be, nor ought to be, all poetry.' (Yet are not the
Divine Comedy and Shakespeare's tragedies 'all poetry'? Or
rather, in the case of these masterpieces, is not the work as a
whole really a 'poem,' maintained, as it is, at a consistently
high level of intensity and style and with the effects of the different parts dependent on one another?) Poe predicted that
'no very long poem would ever be popular again,' and made
'poetry' mean something even more special by insisting that it
should approach the indefiniteness of music. The reason why
no very long poem was ever to be popular again was simply
that verse as a technique was then passing out of fashion in

every department of literature except those of lyric poetry and the short idyl. The long poems of the past—Shakespeare's plays, the *Divine Comedy*, the Greek dramatists and Homer—were going to continue to be popular; but writers of that caliber in the immediate future were not going to write in verse.

Matthew Arnold was to keep on in Coleridge's direction, though by a route somewhat different from Poe's. He said, as we have heard so repeatedly, that poetry was at bottom a criticism of life; but, though one of the characteristics which true poetry might possess was 'moral profundity,' another was 'natural magic,' and 'eminent manifestations of this magical power of poetry' were 'very rare and very precious.' 'Poetry' is thus, it will be seen, steadily becoming rarer. Arnold loved quoting passages of natural magic and he suggested that the lover of literature should carry around in his mind as touchstones a handful of such topnotch passages to test any new verse he encountered. His method of presenting the poets makes poetry seem fleeting and quintessential. Arnold was not happy till he had edited Byron and Wordsworth in such a way as to make it appear that their 'poetry' was a kind of elixir which had to be distilled from the mass of their work—rather difficult in Byron's case: a production like *Don Juan* does not really give up its essence in the sequences excerpted by Arnold.

There was, to be sure, some point in what Arnold was trying to do for these writers: Wordsworth and Byron both often wrote badly and flatly. But they would not have lent themselves at all to this high-handed kind of anthologizing if it had not been that, by this time, it had finally become almost impossible to handle large subjects successfully in verse. Matthew Arnold could have done nothing for Dante by reducing him to a little book of extracts—nor, with all Shakespeare's carelessness, for Shakespeare. The new specialized idea of poetry appears very plainly and oddly when Arnold writes about Homer: the *Iliad* and the *Odyssey*, which had been for the Greeks fiction and scripture, have come to appear to this critic long stretches of ancient legend from which we may pick out little crystals of moral profundity and natural magic.

And in the meantime the ideas of Poe, developed by the Symbolists in France, had given rise to the *Art poétique* of Verlaine, so different from that of Horace: 'Music first of all . . . no

Color, only the *nuance*! . . . Shun Point, the murderer, cruel
Wit and Laughter the impure . . . Take eloquence and wring
its neck! . . . Let your verse be the luck of adventure flung to
the crisp morning wing that brings us a fragrance of thyme and
mint—and all the rest is literature.'

Eliot and Valéry followed. Paul Valéry, still in the tradition
of Poe, regarded a poem as a specialized machine for producing a certain kind of 'state.' Eliot called poetry a 'superior
amusement,' and he anthologized, in both his poems and his
essays, even more fastidiously than Arnold. He, too, has his favorite collection of magical and quintessential passages; and he
possesses an uncanny gift for transmitting to them a personal
accent and imbuing them with a personal significance. And as
even those passages of Eliot's poems which have not been imitated or quoted often seemed to have been pieced together
out of separate lines and fragments, so his imitators came to
work in broken mosaics and 'pinches of glory'—to use E. M.
Forster's phrase about Eliot—rather than with conventional
stanzas.

The result has been an optical illusion. The critic, when he
read the classic, epic, eclogue, tale or play, may have grasped it
and enjoyed it as a whole; yet when the reader reads the comment of the critic, he gets the impression, looking back on the
poem, that the *Divine Comedy*, say, so extraordinarily sustained
and so beautifully integrated, is remarkable mainly for Eliot-
like fragments. Once we know Matthew Arnold's essay, we
find that the ἀνήριθμον γέλασμα of Aeschylus and the 'daffodils that come before the swallow dares' of Shakespeare tend
to stick out from their contexts in a way that they hardly deserve to. Matthew Arnold, unintentionally and unconsciously,
has had the effect of making the poet's 'poetry' seem to be
concentrated in the phrase or the line.

Finally, Mr. A. E. Housman, in his lecture on *The Name and
Nature of Poetry*, has declared that he cannot define poetry.
He can only become aware of its presence by the symptoms he
finds it producing: 'Experience has taught me, when I am
shaving of a morning, to keep watch over my thought, because
if a line of poetry strays into my memory, my skin bristles
so that the razor ceases to act. This particular symptom is
accompanied by a shiver down the spine; there is another

which consists in a constriction of the throat and a precipita-
tion of water to the eyes; and there is a third which I can only
describe by borrowing a phrase from one of Keats's last letters,
where he says, speaking of Fanny Brawne, "everything that reminds me of her goes through me like a spear." The seat of
this sensation is the pit of the stomach.'

One recognizes these symptoms; but there are other things,
too, which produce these peculiar sensations: scenes from
prose plays, for example (the final curtain of *The Playboy of the
Western World* could make one's hair stand on end when it was
first done by the Abbey Theater), passages from prose novels
(Stephen Daedalus' broodings over his mother's death in the
opening episode of *Ulysses* and the end of Mrs. Bloom's soliloquy), even scenes from certain historians, such as Mirabeau's
arrival in Aix at the end of Michelet's *Louis XVI*, even passages in a philosophical dialogue: the conclusion of Plato's
Symposium. Though Housman does praise a few long English
poems, he has the effect, like these other critics, of creating the
impression that 'poetry' means primarily lyric verse, and this
only at its most poignant or most musical moments.

Now all that has been said here is, of course, not intended to
belittle the value of what such people as Coleridge and Poe,
Arnold and Eliot have written on the subject of poetry. These
men are all themselves first-class poets; and their criticism is
very important because it constitutes an attempt to explain
what they have aimed at in their own verse, of what they have
conceived, in their age, to be possible or impossible for their
medium.

Yet one feels that in the minds of all of them a certain confusion persists between the new idea of poetry and the old—
between Coleridge's conception, on the one hand, and
Horace's, on the other; that the technique of prose is inevitably
tending more and more to take over the material which had
formerly provided the subjects for compositions in verse, and
that, as the two techniques of writing are beginning to appear,
side by side or combined, in a single work, it is becoming more
and more impossible to conduct any comparative discussion of
literature on a basis of this misleading division of it into the departments of 'poetry' and of 'prose.'

One result of discussion on this basis, especially if carried on by verse-writers, is the creation of an illusion that contemporary 'poets' of relatively small stature (though of however authentic gifts) are the true inheritors of the genius and carriers-on of the tradition of Aeschylus, Sophocles and Virgil, Dante, Shakespeare and Milton. Is it not time to discard the word 'poetry' or to define it in such a way as to take account of the fact that the most intense, the most profound, the most beautifully composed and the most comprehensive of the great works of literary art (which for these reasons are also the most thrilling and give us most prickly sensations while shaving) have been written sometimes in verse technique, sometimes in prose technique, depending partly on the taste of the author, partly on the mere current fashion. It is only when we argue these matters that we become involved in absurdities. When we are reading, we appraise correctly. Matthew Arnold cites examples of that 'natural magic' which he regards as one of the properties of 'poetry' from Chateaubriand and Maurice de Guérin, who did not write verse but prose, as well as from Shakespeare and Keats; and he rashly includes Molière among the 'larger and more splendid luminaries in the poetical heaven,' though Molière was scarcely more 'poetic' in any sense except perhaps that of 'moral profundity' when he wrote verse than when he wrote prose and would certainly not have versified at all if the conventions of his time had not demanded it. One who has first come to Flaubert at a sensitive age when he is also reading Dante may have the experience of finding that the paragraphs of the former remain in his mind and continue to sing just as the lines of the latter do. He has got the prose by heart unconsciously just as he has done with favorite passages of verse; he repeats them, admiring the form, studying the choice of words, seeing more and more significance in them. He realizes that, though Dante may be greater than Flaubert, Flaubert belongs in Dante's class. It is simply that by Flaubert's time the Dantes present their visions in terms of prose drama or fiction rather than of epics in verse. At any other period, certainly, *La Tentation de Saint Antoine* would have been written in verse instead of prose.

And if one happens to read Virgil's *Georgics* not long after having read Flaubert, the shift from verse to prose technique gets the plainest demonstration possible. If you think of Virgil with Tennyson, you have the illusion that the Virgilian poets are shrinking; but if you think of Virgil with Flaubert, you can see how a great modern prose-writer has grown out of the great classical poets. Flaubert somewhere—I think, in the Goncourt journal—expresses his admiration for Virgil; and, in method as well as in mood, the two writers are often akin. Flaubert is no less accomplished in his use of words and rhythms than Virgil; and the poet is as successful as the novelist in conveying emotion through objective statement. The *Georgics* were seven years in the writing, as *Madame Bovary* was six. And the fact that—in *Madame Bovary* especially—Flaubert's elegiac feeling as well as his rural settings run so close to the characteristic vein of Virgil makes the comparison particularly interesting. Put the bees of the *Georgics*, for example, whose swarming Virgil thus describes:

> *aethere in alto*
> *Fit sonitus, magnum mixtae glomerantur in orbem*
> *Praecipitesque cadunt*

beside the bees seen and heard by Emma Bovary on an April afternoon: 'quelquefois les abeilles, tournoyant dans la lumière, frappaient contre les carreaux comme des balles d'or rebondissantes.' Put

> *Et iam summa procul villarum culmina fumant,*
> *Maioresque cadunt altis de montibus umbrae*

beside: 'La tendresse des anciens jours leur revenait au cœur, abondante et silencieuse comme la rivière qui coulait, avec autant de mollesse qu'en apportait le parfum des seringas, et projetait dans leurs souvenirs des ombres plus démesurées et plus mélancoliques que celles des saules immobiles qui s'allongeaient sur l'herbe.' And compare Virgil's sadness and wistfulness with the sadness and nostalgia of Flaubert: the melancholy of the mountainous pastures laid waste by the cattle plague:

> *desertaque regna*
> *Pastorum, et longe saltus lateque vacantes*

with the modern desolations of Paris in *L'Education sentimentale*: 'Les rues étaient désertes. Quelquefois une charrette

lourde passait, en ébranlant les pavés,' etc.; or Palinurus, fallen
into the sea, swimming with effort to the coast of Italy, but
only to be murdered and left there 'naked on the unknown
sand,' while his soul, since his corpse lies unburied, must forever be excluded from Hades, or Orpheus still calling Eurydice
when his head has been torn from his body, till his tongue has
grown cold and the echo of his love has been lost among the
river banks—compare these with Charles Bovary, a schoolboy,
looking out on fine summer evenings at the sordid streets of
Rouen and sniffing for the good country odors 'qui ne venaient pas jusqu'à lui'—('tendebantque manus ripae ulterioris
amore')—or with the scene in which Emma Bovary receives
her father's letter and remembers the summers of her girlhood,
with the galloping colts and the bumping bees, and knows that
she has spent all her illusions in maidenhood, in marriage, in
adultery, as a traveler leaves something of his money at each of
the inns of the road.

We find, in this connection, in Flaubert's letters the most
explicit statements. 'To desire to give verse-rhythm to prose,
yet to leave it prose and very much prose,' he wrote to Louise
Colet (March 27, 1853), 'and to write about ordinary life as histories and epics are written, yet without falsifying the subject,
is perhaps an absurd idea. Sometimes I almost think it is. But it
may also be a great experiment and very original.' The truth is
that Flaubert is a crucial figure. He is the first great writer in
prose deliberately to try to take over for the treatment of ambitious subjects the delicacy, the precision and the intensity
that have hitherto been identified with verse. Henrik Ibsen, for
the poetic drama, played a role hardly less important. Ibsen
began as a writer of verse and composed many short and non-
dramatic poems as well as *Peer Gynt* and *Brand* and his other
plays in verse, but eventually changed over to prose for the
concentrated Sophoclean tragedies that affected the whole
dramatic tradition. Thereafter the dramatic 'poets'—the Che-
khovs, the Synges and the Shaws (Hauptmann had occasional
relapses)—wrote almost invariably in prose. It was by such that
the soul of the time was given its dramatic expression: there
was nothing left for Rostand's alexandrines but fireworks and
declamation.

In the later generation, James Joyce, who had studied

Flaubert and Ibsen as well as the great classical verse-masters, set out to merge the two techniques. Dickens and Herman Melville had occasionally resorted to blank verse for passages which they meant to be elevated, but these flights had not matched their context, and the effect had not been happy. Joyce, however, now, in *Ulysses*, has worked out a new medium of his own which enables him to exploit verse metrics in a texture which is basically prose; and he has created in *Finnegans Wake* a work of which we cannot say whether it ought, in the old-fashioned phraseology, to be described as prose or verse. A good deal of *Finnegans Wake* is written in regular meter and might perfectly well be printed as verse, but, except for the interpolated songs, the whole thing is printed as prose. As one reads it, one wonders, in any case, how anything could be demanded of 'poetry' by Coleridge with his 'sense of novelty and freshness with old and familiar objects,' by Poe with his indefiniteness of music, by Arnold with his natural magic, by Verlaine with his nuance, by Eliot with his unearthliness, or by Housman with his bristling of the beard, which the *Anna Livia Plurabelle* chapter (or canto) does not fully supply.

If, then, we take literature as a whole for our field, we put an end to many futile controversies—the controversies, for example, as to whether or not Pope is a poet, as to whether or not Whitman is a poet. If you are prepared to admit that Pope is one of the great English writers, it is less interesting to compare him with Shakespeare—which will tell you something about the development of English verse but not bring out Pope's peculiar excellence—than to compare him with Thackeray, say, with whom he has his principal theme—the vanity of the world—in common and who throws into relief the more passionate pulse and the solider art of Pope. And so the effort to apply to Whitman the ordinary standards of verse has hindered the appreciation of his careful and exquisite art.

If, in writing about 'poetry,' one limits oneself to 'poets' who compose in verse, one excludes too much of modern literature, and with it too much of life. The best modern work in verse has been mostly in the shorter forms, and it may be that our lyric poets are comparable to any who have ever lived, but we have had no imaginations of the stature of Shakespeare or

Dante who have done their major work in verse. The horizon and even the ambition of the contemporary writer of verse has narrowed with the specialization of the function of verse itself. (Though the novelists Proust and Joyce are both masters of what used to be called 'numbers,' the verses of the first are negligible and those of the second minor.)

Would not D. H. Lawrence, for example, if he had lived a century earlier, probably have told his tales, as Byron and Crabbe did: in verse? Is it not just as correct to consider him the last of the great English romantic poets as one of the most original of modern English novelists? Must we not, to appreciate Virginia Woolf, be aware that she is trying to do the kind of thing that the writers of verse have done even more than she is trying to do what Jane Austen or George Eliot were doing?

Recently the techniques of prose and verse have been getting mixed up at a bewildering rate—with the prose technique steadily gaining. You have had the verse technique of Ezra Pound gradually changing into prose technique. You have had William Faulkner, who began by writing verse, doing his major work in prose fiction without ever quite mastering prose, so that he may at any moment upset us by interpolating a patch of verse. You have had Robinson Jeffers, in narrative "poems" which are as much novels as some of Lawrence's, reeling out yards of what are really prose dithyrambs with a loose hexametric base; and you have had Carl Sandburg, of *The People, Yes*, producing a queer kind of literature which oscillates between something like verse and something like the paragraphs of a newspaper 'column.'

Sandburg and Pound have, of course, come out of the old *vers libre*, which, though prose-like, was either epigrammatic or had the rhythms of the Whitmanesque chant. But since the Sandburg-Pound generation, a new development in verse has taken place. The sharpness and the energy disappear; the beat gives way to a demoralized weariness. Here the 'sprung-rhythm' of Gerard Manley Hopkins has sometimes set the example. But the difference is that Hopkins' rhythms convey agitation and tension, whereas the rhythms of MacNeice and Auden let down the taut traditions of lyric verse with an effect that is often comic and probably intended to be so—these poets are not far at moments from the humorous rhymed prose of Ogden Nash. And finally—what is very strange to see—Miss Edna St. Vincent Millay in *Conversation at Midnight*, slackening her old urgent pace, dimming the ring of her numbers, has given us a curious example of metrics in full dissolution, with the stress almost entirely neglected, the lines running on for paragraphs and even the rhymes sometimes fading out. In some specimens of this recent work, the beat of verse has been so slurred and muted that it might almost as well have been abandoned. We have at last lived to see the day when the ballads of Gilbert and Hood, written without meter for comic effect in long lines that look and sound like paragraphs, have actually become the type of a certain amount of serious poetry.

You have also the paradox of Eliot attempting to revive the verse-drama with rhythms which, adapting themselves to the rhythms of colloquial speech, run sometimes closer to prose. And you have Mr. Maxwell Anderson trying to renovate the modern theater by bringing back blank verse again—with the result that, once a writer of prose dialogue distinguished by some color and wit, he has become, as a dramatic poet, banal and insipid beyond belief. The trouble is that no verse technique is more obsolete today than blank verse. The old iambic pentameters have no longer any relation whatever to the tempo and language of our lives. Yeats was the last who could write them, and he only because he inhabited, in Ireland and in imagination, a grandiose anachronistic world. You cannot deal with contemporary events in an idiom which was already growing trite in Tennyson's and Arnold's day; and if you try to combine the rhythm of blank verse with the idiom of ordinary talk, you get something—as in Anderson's *Winterset*—which lacks the merits of either. Nor can you try to exploit the worked-out rhythm without also finding yourself let in for the antiquated point of view. The comments on the action in *Winterset* are never the expression of sentiments which we ourselves could conceivably feel in connection with the events depicted: they are the echoes of Greek choruses and Elizabethan soliloquies reflecting upon happenings of a different kind.

Thus if the poets of the Auden-MacNeice school find verse turning to prose in their hands, like the neck of the flamingo in Lewis Carroll with which Alice tried to play croquet, Mr.

Anderson, returning to blank verse, finds himself in the more awkward predicament of the girl in the fairy tale who could never open her mouth without having a toad jump out.

But what has happened? What, then, is the cause of this disuse into which verse technique has been falling for at least the last two hundred years? And what are we to expect in the future? Is verse to be limited now to increasingly specialized functions and finally to go out altogether? Or will it recover the domains it has lost?

To find out, if it is possible to do so, we should be forced to approach this change from the anthropological and sociological points of view. Is verse a more primitive technique than prose? Are its fixed rules like the syntax of languages, which are found to have been stiffer and more complicated the further back one goes? Aside from the question of the requirements of taste and the self-imposed difficulties of form which have always, in any period, been involved in the production of great works of art, does the easy flexibility, say, of modern English prose bear to the versification of Horace the same relation that English syntax bears to Horace's syntax, or that Horace's bears to that of the Eskimos?

It seems obvious that one of the important factors in the history of the development of verse must have been its relations with music. Greek verse grew up in fusion with music: verse and music were learned together. It was not till after Alexander the Great that prosody was detached from harmony. The Greek name for 'prose' was 'bare words'—that is, words divorced from music. But what the Romans took over and developed was a prosody that was purely literary. This, I believe, accounts for the fact that we seem to find in Greek poetry, if we compare it with Latin poetry, so little exact visual observation. Greek poetry is mainly for the ear. Compare a landscape in one of the choruses of Sophocles or Aristophanes with a landscape of Virgil or Horace: the Greeks are *singing* about the landscape, the Romans are fixing it for the eye of the mind; and it is Virgil and Horace who lead the way to all the later picture poetry down to our own Imagists. Again, in the Elizabethan age, the English were extremely musical: the lyrics of Campion could hardly have been composed apart from their musical settings; and Shakespeare is permeated with music. When Shakespeare wants to make us see something, he is always compelling and brilliant; but the effect has been lique- fied by music so that it sometimes gives a little the impression of objects seen under water. The main stream of English poetry continues to keep fairly close to music through Milton, the musician's son, and even through the less organ-voiced Dryden. What has really happened with Pope is that the musi- cal background is no longer there and that the ocular sense has grown sharp again. After this, the real music of verse is largely confined to lyrics—songs—and it becomes more and more of a trick to write them so that they seem authentic—that is, so that they sound like something sung. It was the aim of the late-nineteenth-century Symbolists, who derived their theory from Poe, to bring verse closer to music again, in opposition to the school of the Parnassians, who cultivated an opaque ob- jectivity. And the excellence of Miss Millay's lyrics is obviously connected with her musical training, as the metrical parts of Joyce—such as the Sirens episode in *Ulysses*, which attempts to render music, the response to a song of its hearer—are obvi- ously associated with his vocal gifts. (There is of course a kind of poetry which produces plastic effects not merely by picture- making through explicit descriptions or images, but by giving the language itself—as Allen Tate is able to do—a plastic qual- ity rather than a musical one.)

We might perhaps see a revival of verse in a period and in a society in which music played a leading role. It has long played a great role in Russia; and in the Soviet Union at the present time you find people declaiming poetry at drinking parties or while traveling on boats and trains almost as readily as they burst into song to the accordion or the balalaika, and flocking to poetry-readings just as they do to concerts. It is possible that the Russians at the present time show more of an appetite for 'poetry,' if not always for the best grade of literature, than any of the Western peoples. Their language, half-chanted and strongly stressed, in many ways extremely primitive, provides by itself, as Italian does, a constant stimulus to the writing of verse.

Here in the United States, we have produced some of our

truest poetry in the folk-songs that are inseparable from their tunes. One is surprised, in going through the collections of American popular songs (of Abbé Niles and W. C. Handy, of Carl Sandburg, of the various students trained by Professor Kittredge), which have appeared during the last ten or fifteen years, to discover that the peopling of the continent has had as a by-product a body of folk-verse not unworthy of comparison with the similar material that went to make Percy's *Reliques.* The air of the popular song will no doubt be carrying the words that go with it into the 'poetry' anthologies of the future when many of the set-pieces of 'poetry,' which strain to catch a music gone with Shakespeare, will have come to seem words on the page, incapable of reverberation or of flight from between the covers.

Another pressure that has helped to discourage verse has undoubtedly been the increased demand for reading matter which has been stimulated by the invention of the printing press and which, because ordinary prose is easier to write than verse, has been largely supplied by prose. Modern journalism has brought forth new art-forms; and you have had not only the masterpieces of fiction of such novelists as Flaubert and Joyce, who are also consummate artists in the sense that the great classical poets were, but also the work of men like Balzac and Dickens which lacks the tight organization and the careful attention to detail of the classical epic or drama, and which has to be read rapidly in bulk. The novels of such writers are the epics of societies: they have neither the concision of the folk-song nor the elegance of the forms of the court; they sprawl and swarm over enormous areas like the city populations they deal with. Their authors, no longer schooled in the literary tradition of the Renaissance, speak the practical everyday language of the dominant middle class, which has destroyed the Renaissance world. Even a writer like Dostoevsky rises out of this weltering literature. You cannot say that his insight is less deep, that his vision is less noble or narrower, or that his mastery of his art is less complete than that of the great poets of the past. You can say only that what he achieves he achieves by somewhat different methods.

The technique of prose today seems thus to be absorbing

the technique of verse; but it is showing itself quite equal to that work of the imagination which caused men to call Homer 'divine': that re-creation, in the harmony and logic of words, of the cruel confusion of life. Not, of course, that we shall have Dante and Shakespeare redone in some prose form any more than we shall have Homer in prose. In art, the same things are not done again or not done again except as copies. The point is that literary techniques are tools, which the masters of the craft have to alter in adapting them to fresh uses. To be too much attached to the traditional tools may be sometimes to ignore the new masters.

1948. The recent work of W. H. Auden has not shown a running-to-seed of the tendencies mentioned above, but has on the contrary taken the direction of returning to the older tradition of serviceable and vigorous English verse. His *New Year Letter* must be the best specimen of purely didactic verse since the end of the eighteenth century, and the alliterative Anglo-Saxon meter exploited in *The Age of Anxiety* has nothing in common with prose. It may, however, be pointed out, for the sake of my argument above, that in the speech of the girl over the sleeping boy in the fifth section of the latter poem, the poet has found it easy to slip into the rhythms and accents of Mrs. Earwicker's half-prose soliloquy at the end of *Finnegans Wake*.

In Honor of Pushkin

I. Evgeni Onegin*

ANYONE who has read criticism by foreigners, even well-informed criticism, of the literature of his own country knows what a large part of it is likely to be made up of either banalities or errors. In the case of a novice at Russian like the writer, this danger is particularly great; and I shall probably be guilty of many sins in the eyes of Russian readers who should happen to see this essay. But Pushkin, the hundredth anniversary of whose death is being celebrated this year by the Soviets, has in general been so little appreciated in the English-speaking countries that I may, perhaps, be pardoned for however imperfect an attempt to bring his importance home to English-speaking readers. And Evgeni Onegin, who has played such a role for the Russian imagination, really belongs among those figures of fiction who have a meaning beyond their national frontiers for a whole age of Western society. The English Hamlet was as real, and as Russian, to the Russians of the generations that preceded the Revolution as any character in Russian literature. Let us receive Evgeni Onegin as a creation equally real for us.

It has always been difficult for Westerners—except perhaps for the Germans, who seem to have translated him more successfully than anyone else—to believe in the greatness of Pushkin. We have always left him out of account. George Borrow, who visited Russia in the course of his work for the Bible Society, published some translations of Pushkin in 1835; but the conventional world of literature knew little or nothing about him. Three years after Pushkin's death (and when Lermontov's career was nearly over), Carlyle, in *Heroes and Hero Worship*, described Russia as a 'great dumb monster,' not yet matured to the point where it finds utterance through the 'voice of genius.' Turgenev struggled vainly with Flaubert to make him recognize Pushkin's excellence; and even Renan was so ignorant of Russian literature that it was possible for him to declare

*Written for the centenary of Pushkin's death, January 29, 1937.

35

on Turgenev's death that Russia had at last found her voice. Matthew Arnold, in writing about Tolstoy, remarked complacently that 'the crown of literature is poetry' and that the Russians had not yet had a great poet; and T. S. Eliot, not long ago, in a discussion of the importance of Greek and Latin, was insisting on the inferior educational value of what he regarded as a merely modern literature like Russian, because 'half a dozen great novelists'—I quote from memory—'do not make a culture.' Even today we tend to say to ourselves, 'If Pushkin is really as good as the Russians think he is, why has he never taken his place in world literature as Dante and Goethe have, and as Tolstoy and Dostoevsky have?'

The truth is that Pushkin *has* come through into world literature—he has come through by way of the Russian novel. Unlike most of the poets of his period, he had the real dramatic imagination, and his influence permeates Russian fiction —and theater and opera as well. Reading Pushkin for the first time, for a foreigner who has already read later Russian writers, is like coming for the first time to Voltaire after an acquaintance with later French literature: he feels that he is tasting the pure essence of something which he has found before only in combination with other elements. It is a spirit whose presence he has felt and with whom in a sense he is already familiar, but whom he now first confronts in person.

For the rest, it is true that the poetry of Pushkin is particularly difficult to translate. It is difficult for the same reason that Dante is difficult: because it says so much in so few words, so clearly and yet so concisely, and the words themselves and their place in the line have become so much more important than in the case of more facile or rhetorical writers. It would require a translator himself a poet of the first order to reproduce Pushkin's peculiar combination of intensity, compression and perfect ease. A writer like Pushkin may easily sound 'flat,' as he did to Flaubert in French, just as Cary's translation of Dante sounds flat. Furthermore, the Russian language, which is highly inflected and able to dispense with pronouns and prepositions in many cases where we have to use them and which does without the article altogether, makes it possible for Pushkin to pack his lines (separating modifiers from substantives, if need be) in a way which renders the problem of translating him closer to that of translating a tightly articulated Latin poet like Horace than any modern poet that we know. Such a poet in translation may sound trivial just as many of the translations of Horace sound trivial—because the weight of the words and the force of their relation have been lost with the inflections and the syntax.

So that, failing any adequate translation, we have tended, if we have thought about Pushkin at all, to associate him vaguely with Byronism: we have heard that *Evgeni Onegin* is an imitation of *Don Juan*. But this comparison is very misleading. Pushkin was a great artist: he derived as much from André Chénier as from Byron. *Don Juan* is diffuse and incoherent, sometimes brilliant, sometimes silly; it has its unique excellence, but it is the excellence of an improvisation. Byron said of some of the cantos that he wrote them on gin, and essentially it is a drunken monologue by a desperately restless, uncomfortable man, who does not know what is the matter with him or what he ought to do with himself, who wants to tell stories about other things or to talk about himself in such a way as to be able to laugh and curse and grieve without looking into anything too closely. Byron's achievement, certainly quite remarkable, is to have raised the drunken monologue to a literary form. But the achievement of Pushkin is quite different. He had, to be sure, learned certain things from Byron—for example, the tone of easy negligence with which *Evgeni Onegin* begins and the habit of personal digression; but both of these devices in Pushkin are made to contribute to a general design. *Evgeni Onegin* is the opposite of *Don Juan* in being a work of unwavering concentration. Pushkin's 'novel in verse' came out of Pushkin's deepest self-knowledge and was given form by a long and exacting discipline. The poet had adopted a compact speech and a complicated stanza-form as different as possible from Byron's doggerel; and he worked over the three hundred and eighty-nine stanzas which fill about two hundred pages through a period of eight years (1823–31) and was still, with every successive edition, revising them and cutting them down up to the time of his death.

One can convey a much more accurate impression of what Pushkin's actual writing is like by comparing him to Keats than to Byron. There are passages in *Evgeni Onegin*, such as those

that introduce the seasons, which have a felicity and a fullness
of detail not unlike Keats's *Ode to Autumn*—or, better perhaps, the opening of *The Eve of St. Agnes*, which resembles
them more closely in form:

> St. Agnes' Eve—Ah, bitter chill it was!
> The owl, for all his feathers, was a-cold;
> The hare limp'd trembling through the frozen grass,
> And silent was the flock in woolly fold:
> Numb were the Beadsman's fingers while he told
> His rosary, and while his frosted breath,
> Like pious incense from a censer old,
> Seem'd taking flight for heaven without a death,
> Past the sweet Virgin's picture, while his prayer he saith.

Here is Pushkin's description of the coming of winter:

'Already now the sky was breathing autumn, already the dear sun
more seldom gleamed, shorter grew the day, the forest's secret
shadow was stripped away with sighing sound, mist lay upon the
fields, the caravan of loud-tongued geese stretched toward the south:
drew near the duller season; November stood already at the door.

'Rises the dawn in cold murk; in the fields the sound of work is still;
the wolf with his hungry mate comes out upon the road; sniffing, the
road-horse snorts—and the traveler who is wise makes full speed up
the hill; the herdsman now at last by morning light no longer drives
his cattle from the byre; at mid-day to their huddle his horn no longer
calls them; inside her hut, the farm girl, singing, spins, while—friend
of winter nights—her little flare of kindling snaps beside her.

'And now the heavy frosts are snapping and spread their silver
through the fields . . . smoother than a smart parquet glistens the
ice-bound stream. The merry mob of little boys with skates cut
ringingly the ice; on small red feet the lumbering goose, hoping to
float on the water's breast, steps carefully but slips and topples; gaily
the first snow flashes and whirls about, falling in stars on the bank.'

If you can imagine this sort of thing, which I have translated
more or less literally, done in something like Keats's marrowy
line, you will get some idea of what Pushkin is like. He can make
us see and hear things as Keats can, but his range is very much
greater: he can give us the effect in a few lines of anything
from the opening of a bottle of champagne or the loading and
cocking of pistols for a duel to the spinning and skipping of a

ballet girl—who 'flies like fluff from Aeolus' breath'—or the falling of the first flakes of snow. And as soon as we put *The Eve of St. Agnes* (published in 1820) beside *Evgeni Onegin*, it seems to us that Keats is weakened by an element of the conventionally romantic, of the mere storybook picturesque. But Pushkin can dispense with all that: here everything is sharp and real. No detail of country life is too homely, no phase of city life too worldly, for him to master it by the beauty of his verse. Artistically, he has outstripped his time; and neither Tennyson in *In Memoriam* nor Baudelaire in *Les Fleurs du Mal* was ever to surpass Pushkin in making poetry of classical precision and firmness out of a world realistically observed.

I should note also—what I have never seen mentioned—that the passages of social description often sound a good deal more like Praed than like Byron. It is not likely that Pushkin was influenced by Praed, since Praed's poems began to appear in *Knight's Quarterly* only in 1823, the year that *Onegin* was begun, and his characteristic vein of *vers de société* seems to date only from 1826, in which year Pushkin completed his sixth chapter. But the stanza in Chapter Two, with its epitaph, on the death of Tatyana's father might have been imitated from Praed's poem *The Vicar*, and if you can imagine Praed's talent raised to a higher power and telling a long story in his characteristically terse and witty stanzas (Pushkin's measure is shorter than Byron's, a rapid tetrameter like Praed's), you will be closer to Pushkin than *Don Juan* will take you:

> *Good night to the Season!—the dances,*
>   *The fillings of hot little rooms,*
> *The glancings of rapturous glances,*
>   *The fancyings of fancy costumes;*
> *The pleasures which Fashion makes duties,*
>   *The praisings of fiddles and flutes,*
> *The luxury of looking at Beauties,*
>   *The tedium of talking to Mutes;*
> *The female diplomatists, planners*
>   *Of matches for Laura and Jane;*
> *The ice of her Ladyship's manners,*
>   *The ice of his Lordship's champagne.*

To have written a novel in verse, and a novel of contemporary

manners, which was also a great poem was Pushkin's unprecedented feat—a feat which, though anticipated on a smaller
scale by the tales in verse of Crabbe and several times later attempted by nineteenth-century poets, was never to be repeated.
And when we think of *Evgeni Onegin* in connection with *Don
Juan* or *The Ring and the Book* or *Aurora Leigh* or *Evangeline*,
we find that it refuses to be classed with them. Pushkin's genius,
as Maurice Baring has said, has more in common with the
genius of Jane Austen than with the general tradition of the
nineteenth-century novel. It is classical in its even tone of
comedy which is at the same time so much more serious than
the tragedies of Byron ever are, in its polishing of the clear and
rounded lens which focuses the complex of human relations.

But Pushkin is much more vigorous than Jane Austen: the
compression and rigor of the verse cause the characters to
seem to start out of the stanzas. And he deals with more violent emotions. *Evgeni Onegin* is occupied with Byronism in a
different way than that of deriving from Byron: it is among
other things an objective study of Byronism. Both in the poem
itself and in a letter that Pushkin wrote while he was working
on it, he makes significant criticisms of Byron. 'What a man
this Shakespeare is!' he exclaims. 'I can't get over it. How small
the tragic Byron seems beside him!—that Byron who has been
able to imagine but a single character: his own . . . Byron
simply allots to each of his characters some characteristic of his
own: his pride to one, his hatred to another, his melancholy to
a third, etc., and thus out of a character which is in itself rich,
somber and energetic, he makes several insignificant characters; but that is not tragedy.' And in *Evgeni Onegin*, he speaks
of Byron's 'hopeless egoism.' Pushkin has been working away
from his early romantic lyricism toward a Shakespearean dramatization of life, and now he is to embody in objective creations,
to show involved in a balanced conflict, the currents of the age
which have passed through him. Evgeni Onegin is presented
quite differently from any of the romantic heroes of Byron or
Chateaubriand or Musset: when Byron dropped the attitudes
of Childe Harold, the best he could do with Don Juan was to
give him the innocence of Candide. Evgeni differs even from
his immediate successor and kinsman, Lermontov's Hero of
Our Time—because Lermontov, though he tells his story with

the distinctive Russian realism absent in the other romantic writers, is really involved to a considerable degree with the attitudes of his hero; whereas Pushkin, in showing us Evgeni, neither exalts him in the perverse romantic way nor yet, in exposing his weakness, hands him over to conventional morality. There is, I think, but one creation of the early nineteenth century who is comparable to Evgeni Onegin: Stendhal's Julien Sorel; and the poem is less akin to anything produced by the romantic poets than it is to *Le Rouge et le Noir* and *Madame Bovary*.

Our first glimpse of Pushkin's hero is not an ingratiating one: he has just been summoned to the bedside of a dying uncle, whose estate he is going to inherit, and he is cursing at the tiresome prospect of sitting around till the old man dies. But the scene is shifted at once to his previous life in St. Petersburg. He has been a young man about town, who has had everything society can give him. We see him at the restaurant, the opera, the ball; in one masterly passage we are shown him falling asleep after a round of the pleasures of the capital while the Petersburg of the merchants and cabmen and peddlers is just waking up for the day. But Evgeni is intelligent: he gets tired of his friends, tired of his love affairs. He is infected with the 'English spleen' and grows languid and morose like Childe Harold. He shuts himself up to write, but he finds it terribly hard and gives it up. Then his uncle dies, and he inherits the estate and goes to live in the country.

The country bores him, too. Being a man of liberal ideas, he tries to lighten the lot of his serfs, and the neighbors decide he is a dangerous fellow. Then there appears in the neighborhood a young man named Lensky with whom Evgeni finds he has something in common. Lensky has just come back from Göttingen and is saturated with German idealism; and he is a poet in the German-romantic vein. Evgeni thinks him callow and naïve, but tries not to throw cold water on his illusions. He likes Lensky, and they go riding and have long arguments together.

Lensky is in love in the most idealistic fashion with a girl whom he has known since childhood and to whom he has always been faithful. She is pretty but entirely uninteresting: Pushkin tells us that she is just like the heroines of all the popular love stories of the day. Lensky goes to see her every evening—she lives with her sister and her widowed mother on a nearby estate—and one day takes Evgeni with him. Evgeni has sarcastically told Lensky in advance what the refreshments and the conversation will be like—the Larins will be just a 'simple Russian family'; and on the drive back home he remarks that the face of Lensky's worshiped sweetheart is lifeless, red, and round 'like this silly moon over this silly horizon,' and remarks that if *he* were a poet like Lensky, he would have preferred the older sister, who had sat sadly by the window and said nothing.

This older sister, Tatyana, is 'wild, melancholy, silent, and shy' and not so pretty as Olga. As a child, she hadn't liked games and hadn't been fond of dolls; she had thought it was funny to mimic her mother by lecturing her doll on how young ladies ought to comport themselves. Now her head is full of Richardson and Rousseau, and she likes to get up before dawn and watch the stars fade and the distance grow bright and feel the morning wind. And now, from the first moment she sees him, she falls furiously in love with Evgeni. She waits for a time in silence; then, as Evgeni does not come to call again, she sits down and writes him a letter, in which, painfully, uncontrollably, innocently, she confesses to him her love. This chapter, which deals with Tatyana's letter, is one of the great descriptions of first love in literature. Pushkin renews for us as we read all the poignancy and violence of those moments when for the first time the emotional forces of youth are released by another human being and try to find their realization through him. All the banal and deluded things that young people say and feel— that Evgeni is the one man in the world for her, the man for whom she has been waiting all her life, that he has been appointed by God to be her protector, that she is all alone and that no one understands her—poor Tatyana believes them all and puts them all into her letter; and Pushkin has succeeded in giving them to us in all their banality and deludedness, with no romantic sentimentalization, and yet making them move us profoundly. We enter into the emotions of Tatyana as we do into those of Juliet, yet at the same time Pushkin has set the whole picture in a perspective of pathetic irony which is not in that early play of Shakespeare's: there is nothing to indicate that Shakespeare's lovers might not have been ideally happy if it had not been for the family feud; but, in the case of Tatyana, we know from the first moment that her love is hopelessly misplaced in Evgeni. And the whole thing is set off and rooted in life by a series of marvelous touches—Tatyana's conversation with the nurse, the song she hears the serf-girls singing—and saturated with the atmosphere of the country estate where Tatyana has spent her whole life and where—so amazing is Pushkin's skill at evoking a complete picture through suggestion, needing only a few hundred lines where a novelist would take as many pages—we feel by the time she leaves it that we have lived as long as she.

Evgeni does not answer the letter, but two days afterwards he comes to see her. The role of the seducer is *passé*: it went out with periwigs and red heels; and for Evgeni the time for great passions is past: it is too much trouble to do anything about Tatyana. He conducts himself honorably, he talks to her kindly. He tells her that, if he had any desire for family life, she would certainly be the woman he would choose for a wife. But he was not created for happiness, such satisfactions are foreign to his soul. As a husband, he would be gloomy and disagreeable, and he would eventually cease to love her. He makes quite a long speech about it. And he tells her that she ought to learn to control herself: another man might not understand as he does. Tatyana listens silently, in tears. He gives her his arm and leads her back to the house.

But now Evgeni takes an unexpected turn. The Larins give a big evening party to celebrate Tatyana's Saint's Day. Evgeni goes and sits opposite Tatyana and realizes that she is still in love with him and frightened to death in his presence. He thinks that he is angry with Lensky because the party has turned out a bore and Lensky has brought him there on false pretenses. He has for months been watching Lensky moon over Olga with his eternal romantic devotion which treats the beloved object with a reverence almost religious and never makes any practical advances; and he sets out now to annoy the young poet by getting Olga away from him for the evening. Evgeni makes Olga dance with him repeatedly, pays her animated attentions—to which, as she is incapable of saying no, she almost automatically responds. Lensky is deeply hurt and furious; he leaves the party and goes straight home and writes Evgeni a note calling him out.

Evgeni's first impulse, when he receives the challenge, is to set things right with Lensky, not to let the young man make a fool of himself. But then he is moved, as he tells himself, by the fear of public opinion: the second by whom Lensky has sent the challenge, though a thoroughly disreputable individual, is an old-fashioned fancier and promoter of duels. The night before they are to meet, Lensky sits up till morning writing poetry. Evgeni sleeps sound and late; he arrives on the field with his French valet, whom he insolently presents as his second. He and Lensky take their four paces away from one another. But Evgeni, while he walks, is quietly raising his pistol, so that, the moment he turns around, he is able to shoot Lensky before the latter has had a chance to aim. Lensky falls: in a remarkable simile, characteristically realistic and exact, Pushkin tells us how the young man's heart, in which a moment before all the human passions were dwelling, becomes suddenly like an abandoned house blinded and dark and silent, with the windows covered with chalk and the owner gone away. Evgeni has killed in the most cowardly fashion a man whose friend he had believed himself to be and whom he had thought he did not want to kill. Now at last we are sure of what Pushkin, who has always given us Evgeni's version of his own motives, has only so far in various ways suggested: that, for all Lensky's obtuseness and immaturity, Evgeni has been jealous of him, because Lensky has been able to feel for Olga an all-absorbing emotion whereas Evgeni, loved so passionately by Tatyana, has been unable to feel anything at all. Lensky, the author now tells us, might or might not have become a good poet; but the point is, as he lets us know without telling us, that it is the poet in Lensky whom Evgeni has hated. Evgeni had wanted to write; but when he had sat down with the paper before him, he had found it was too much trouble.

After the duel, Evgeni leaves the countryside. Lensky is soon forgotten by Olga. She says yes to an uhlan, who takes her off when he goes to join his regiment. Tatyana is left alone. She walks over to Evgeni's house and gets the caretaker to let her in; and there she returns day after day and reads the books—so much more up to date than Richardson and Rousseau—which she has found in Evgeni's library. There are a picture of Byron on the wall and a little iron statue of Napoleon; and, for the first time, Tatyana reads Byron, as well as several fashionable novels which reflect the fashionable attitudes of the day. Evgeni has marked them and made notes in the margin: and now his lecture to her after her letter begins to have the sound of an echo of all the things he has read.

But Tatyana continues to languish, doesn't get married. Her mother decides to take her to Moscow. There follows a wonderful description of the Larin family traveling to Moscow. Pushkin, with his infinite sympathy and his equally universal detachment, puts on record characteristics and customs of the Russians which are still striking to a foreigner today. The Larins set several dates to get off, but they never get off on those dates. Then at last they do get off and get there. Now the leafy and mazy and timeless estate is far behind Tatyana, and she sees the gold crosses of the churches and then the people and shops and palaces of Moscow. The shift from country to town is beautifully handled by Pushkin; and there is nothing in fiction more remarkable in its way than the account of Tatyana's first days in Moscow. It is the forerunner of the social scenes in *War and Peace*, and Natasha Rostova and her family seem related to Tatyana and hers, just as Tolstoy's Moscow originals must have been to Pushkin's. The Moscow cousin, to whose house Tatyana and her mother first go and where an old Kalmuck in a ragged caftan and spectacles lets them in, had been in love before she was married with a dandy whom she had thought another Sir Charles Grandison; and now the first thing she says to Tatyana's mother, in whom she had used to confide, is, 'Cousin, do you remember Grandison?' 'What Grandison? Oh, Grandison!—of course, I remember: where is he?' 'He's living in Moscow now; he came to see me at Christmas; he married off his son not long ago.'—But the fashion of the younger generation—we are not told whether or not Tatyana makes this reflection—is for Byron instead of Grandison.

Tatyana cannot at first take her place in this world. Her cousins, though urban, are nice; they look her over and decide she is nice. They confide in her, but she cannot return their confidences: she moves among them detached, distracted. She goes to dinner to be shown to her grandparents: '"How Tanya has grown!" they say. "Wasn't it just the other day I christened you? and *I* used to carry you in my arms! And *I* boxed your ears! And *I* used to feed you gingerbread!" And the old ladies in chorus would keep repeating: "How our years fly by!"—But they—in them she could see no change; it was all on the same old pattern: her aunt, the Princess Helena, still had the same tulle bonnet, Lukerya Lvovna still powdered herself just as much, Lyubov Petrovna still told the same lies, Ivan Petrovich was still just as silly, Semen Petrovich was still just as stingy, Pelagya Nikolavna still had the same friend, M. Finemouche, and the same Pomeranian and the same husband; and her husband was just as punctual at his club and just as meek and just as deaf as ever, and still ate and drank enough for two.' One night at a ball, her solicitous aunt whispers to her to look to the left. An important-looking general is staring at her. 'Who?' she asks. 'That fat general?'

When Evgeni returns from his travels and goes into society again, he sees at a ball an extraordinarily smart lady who combines perfect naturalness with great dignity, whom everybody wants to speak to and to whom everybody defers; and he gasps at her resemblance to Tatyana. He inquires who she is of a man he knows. 'My wife,' the friend replies. It is Tatyana, now a princess; the man is the pompous general. Tatyana meets Evgeni without batting an eyelash: she asks him whether he has been long in St. Petersburg and whether he doesn't come from her part of the world.

Evgeni pays her court, follows her everywhere; but she refuses to recognize him. He writes her a letter, which is the counterpart of hers: now the roles are reversed—it is he who is putting himself at her mercy. She doesn't answer: he writes again and again. Then he shuts himself up in his house, cuts himself off from society and gives himself up to serious reading: history and moral philosophy. But Lensky gets between him and the page, and he hears a voice that says, 'What, killed?' and he sees all the malicious gossips and the mean cowards and the young jilts and bitches whom he has known in Petersburg society and whom he has wanted to get away from and forget, and he sees Tatyana in the country house, sitting silent beside the window, as on the day when he first called.

Suddenly, one day when the winter snow is melting, he gets into his sleigh and drives off to her house. There is no one in the hall: he walks in. He finds her reading his letters. He throws himself at her feet. She looks at him without anger or surprise; she sees how sick and pitiful he is; the girl who loved him so in the country wakens again in her heart; she does not take her hand from his lips. Then, after a moment, she makes him get up. 'I must be frank with you,' she tells him. 'Do you remember in the orchard how submissively I listened to your rebuke? Now it's my turn. I was younger then, and better. I loved you, and you were severe with me. The love of a humble country girl was not exciting for you. Good heavens! my blood still chills when I remember the cold look and the sermon you gave me. You didn't like me then in the country, and why do you run after me now? Because I'm rich and well known? because my husband has been wounded on the battlefield? because we're in favor at court? Isn't it because my shame would now be known to everybody, and would give you a reputation as a rake? Don't you think I would a thousand times rather be back with the orchard and my books and the places where I first saw you and the graveyard with my nurse's grave, than play this role in this noisy masquerade? But it's too late to do anything now. From the moment when you wouldn't have me, what did it matter to me what became of me? And now you're a man of honor; and although I love you still—why should I pretend?—I've given myself to another and I shall always be faithful to him.'

She goes; and Evgeni stands thunderstruck, and then he hears the clank of the general's spurs. And there Pushkin leaves him.

The truth about Evgeni's fatal weakness has for the first time been fully driven home in Tatyana's speech: he has never been able to judge for himself of the intrinsic value of anything; all his values are social values; he has had enough independence, he has been enough superior to his associates, to be dissatisfied with the life of society, but, even in his disaffection, he has only been able to react into the disaffected attitude that is fashionable; his misanthropy itself has been developed in terms of what people will think of him, and, even trying to escape to the country, he has brought with him the standards of society.

He had had enough sense of real values to know that there was something in Tatyana, something noble about her passion for him, to recognize in his heart that it was she who was the true unquiet brooding spirit, the true rebel against the conventions, where his quarrel with the world had been half a pose; but he had not had quite enough to love her just as she was: he had only been able to shoot Lensky.

Pushkin has put into the relations between his three central characters a number of implications. In one sense, they may be said to represent three intellectual currents of the time: Evgeni is Byronism turning worldly and dry; Lensky, with his Schiller and Kant, German romantic idealism; Tatyana, that Rousseauist Nature which was making itself heard in romantic poetry, speaking a new language and asserting a new kind of rights. And from another point of view they represent different tendencies in Russia itself: both Evgeni and Lensky are half foreigners, they think in terms of the cultures of the West, whereas Tatyana, who has spent her whole life on the wild old feudal estate, is for Pushkin the real Russia. Tatyana, like Pushkin, who said he owed so much to the stories of his Russian nurse, has always loved old wives' tales and is full of country superstitions. Before the fatal Saint's-Day party and after her conversation with Onegin, she has an ominous dream, which is recounted at length. Tatyana's subconscious insight, going to the bottom of the situation and clothing it with the imagery of folk-tales, reveals to her a number of things which the others do not yet know about themselves: that there is something bad about Evgeni and that there is an antagonism between him and Lensky; in her dream, she sees Onegin stab Lensky. It is the sensitive though naïve Russian spirit, always aware of the hidden realities, with which Tolstoy and Dostoevsky were later on still attempting to make contact in their reaction against Western civilization. Yet with Pushkin, as Gide says of Dostoevsky, the symbols are perfectly embodied in the characters; they never deform the human being or convert him into an uninteresting abstraction. *Evgeni Onegin* has been popular because it has for generations been read by young Russians as a story—a story in which the eternal reasoning male is brought up against the eternal instinctive woman—like Eliza-

beth Bennet and Mr. Darcy; and in which the modest heroine
—who, besides, is Cinderella and will end up expensively
dressed and with the highest social position—gets morally all
the best of it.

But there is still another aspect which the characters in
Evgeni Onegin present. Pushkin speaks, at the end, of the years
which have elapsed since he first saw Evgeni dimly, before the
'free novel' which was to shape itself could be discerned
'through the magic crystal.' This magic crystal was Pushkin's
own mind, which figures in the poem in a peculiar way. The
poet, when he talks about himself, is not willful and egoistic
like Byron; his digressions, unlike Byron's or Sterne's, always
contribute to the story: they will begin by sounding like asides,
in which the author is merely growing garrulous on the subject of some personal experience, but they will eventually turn
out to merge into the experience of one of his characters,
which he has been filling-in in this indirect way. Yet the crystal
sphere is always there: it is inside it that we see the drama.
Pushkin, throughout this period, had been tending to get
away from his early subjective lyricism and to produce a more
objective kind of art. After *Evgeni Onegin*, he was to write
principally stories in prose. And in *Evgeni Onegin* it is almost
as if we had watched the process—as we can see in the life-cell
the nucleus splitting up into its separate nuclei and each concentrating its filaments and particles about it—by which the
several elements of his character, the several strands of his experience, have taken symmetry about the foci of distinct characters. Pushkin had finally transfused himself into a dramatic
work of art as none other of his romantic generation had done
—for his serenity, his perfect balance of tenderness for human
beings with unrelenting respect for reality, show a rarer quality
of mind than Stendhal's.

Yet *Evgeni Onegin*, for all its lucidity, all its objectification,
has behind it a conflict no less desperate than those which the
other romantics were presenting so much more hysterically.
Though Pushkin had triumphed as an artist as Byron was
never able to do, he is otherwise a figure more tragic than the
man who died at Missolonghi. For, after all, the chief disaster
of *Evgeni Onegin* is not Evgeni's chagrin or Lensky's death: it
is that Tatyana should have been caught up irrevocably by that

empty and tyrannical social world from which Evgeni had tried to escape and which she had felt and still feels so alien. Pushkin married, the same year that *Onegin* was finished, a young and pleasure-loving wife who submerged him in the expenses of social life; and before he was out of his thirties, he got himself killed in a duel by a man whom he suspected of paying her attentions. It was as if in those generations where Byron, Shelley, Keats, Leopardi and Poe were dead in their twenties or thirties or barely reached forty, where Coleridge and Wordsworth and Beddoes and Musset burned out while still alive, where Lermontov, like Pushkin, was killed in a duel, before he was twenty-seven—it was as if in that great age of the bourgeois ascendancy—and even in still feudal Russia—it were impossible for a poet to survive. There was for the man of imagination and moral passion a basic maladjustment to society in which only the student of society—the social philosopher, the historian, the novelist—could find himself and learn to function. And to deal with the affairs of society, he had to learn to speak its language: that is, giving up the old noble language, he had—as Goethe and Hugo did, and as Pushkin did just before he died—to train himself to write in prose.

Yet Pushkin, who had done for the Russian language what Dante had done for Italian and who had laid the foundations of Russian fiction, had, in opposing the natural humanity of Tatyana to the social values of Evgeni, set a theme which was to be developed through the whole of Russian art and thought, and to give it its peculiar power. Lenin, like Tolstoy, could only have been possible in a world where this contrast was acutely felt. Tatyana, left by Pushkin with the last word, was actually to remain triumphant.

II. THE BRONZE HORSEMAN

In attempting a new translation of A. S. Pushkin's great poem, *The Bronze Horseman*, it may be useful to make a few explanations.

The poem deals with the tragic contradiction between the right to peace and happiness of the ordinary man and the right to constructive domination of the state. (The Bronze Horseman, which symbolizes the latter, is Falconet's well-known statue of Peter the Great, which has figured in several Soviet films.) What is present to the minds of Russian readers but what may not be equally familiar to foreign ones is the background of the history of St. Petersburg. This new capital was built by Peter the Great—the 'He' of the first part of the poem —at the beginning of the eighteenth century, on the swampy shores and islands of the Neva. The difficulties involved in the feat were prodigious, and neither then nor with a view to the future did Peter stint himself in the expenditure of human life. Of the artisans whom he compelled to come north to lay the foundations of the city, thousands died of hardship and disease; and the city, in its unnatural location, was at the mercy of terrible floods caused by the breaking-up of the ice of Lake Ladoga just east of it or—as on the occasion described in the poem—by the west wind blowing back the Neva. There had been one such flood in 1777, there was another in 1824, and they continued after Pushkin's time.

Pushkin contributed anonymously to the victims of 1824, and it is with this disaster that *The Bronze Horseman* deals. But the poem was not written until 1833. The poet, who had spent seven of the best years of his youth in exile and under surveillance as a result of his revolutionary verses and who, finally allowed to return to St. Petersburg, was still obliged to submit all his writings and movements to the obstructive control of the Tsar, knew well what it was to have one's life in the hands of a ruthless authority. And he had recently married a young wife who was bringing him into the circle of the Court, where the obligations imposed by the Tsar were weighing on him more heavily than ever and where, it has been supposed, the attentions of the Tsar to his wife were one of the factors in the sequence of events which drove Pushkin, hardly more than three years later, to issue the challenge to his fatal duel.

In *The Bronze Horseman*, as in *Evgeni Onegin*, we can see very clearly the process by which the creations which Pushkin in the beginning has identified more or less with himself become detached from the author, turn into sharply outlined characters and dramatize the impulse which engendered them in a purely objective way. The original intention of Pushkin had been to continue *Evgeni Onegin*. In this sequel Evgeni was to have played some role in connection with the Decembrist revolt of 1825, in consequence of which so many of Pushkin's friends had been executed or sent to Siberia. He wrote this tenth canto in cipher and then, still fearing that it might get him into trouble, burned most of the manuscript. Then he embarked on an entirely new poem in the same stanza-form as *Evgeni Onegin* and with a hero whose first name was still Evgeni, but whose family name was different and who was in fact a quite different person. The new Evgeni is the descendant of an illustrious old boyar family—Pushkin begins with a long genealogy—whose possessions and credit have terribly dwindled. Evgeni himself is a clerk; and Pushkin in his original draft conducted a long argument with imaginary opponents over his right to choose so humble a personage, in defiance of the romantic fashion, as the hero of a narrative poem. The situation of the new Evgeni was a caricature of Pushkin's own. He himself was the descendant of boyars—the early Pushkins had been among the electors of the first Romanov—and now he found himself a socially insignificant person in a *haut monde* where neither his ancient blood nor his genius as a poet was much respected. He had been put under a terrible strain since his marriage to keep up his establishment from his literary earnings.

And, as Pushkin begins to develop his real theme, the new Evgeni evolves entirely out of the *Evgeni Onegin* frame. Pushkin drops the genealogy, the *vers de société* stanza-form, the amusing man-of-the-world digressions. He drops the imaginary argument, of which he has apparently gotten the better. The former family glories of the hero, which we are told he spends no time regretting, are alluded to in half a dozen lines; and the poet in two words says curtly that Evgeni avoids the nobility. The life of upper-class St. Petersburg figures only in an introduction, in which Pushkin describes its attractions in his own conventional character; and his deeper feelings have obviously been canalized in the character of the unfortunate desk-worker who hopes to own two chairs and a table. Indeed, Pushkin has used already in regard to himself, in one of the rejected parts of *Evgeni Onegin*, exactly the same phrases about wanting only to be master in his own house with a pot of cabbage soup, which he now assigns to the second Evgeni. At the beginning of *Evgeni Onegin*, we see Evgeni, the Petersburg dandy, returning home after a night of gaiety just as the common people of the capital are getting up and going about their tasks. The new Evgeni is now one of these common people: Pushkin has dropped even the literary avocations which he gave him in his original version. And he has made out of Evgeni's collision with the power and pride of St. Petersburg a poem which has been put by Russian critics beside the longer masterpiece that preceded it—which has indeed been described by D. S. Mirsky as probably the greatest Russian poem ever written.

It would be impossible to reproduce in English the peculiar poetic merits of *The Bronze Horseman*. The terseness and compactness of Pushkin's style, which constitute one of the chief difficulties of translating him, reach a point in this poem where, as Mirsky says, 'the words and their combinations' are 'charged to breaking-point with all the weight of meaning they can bear.' The two terrific themes of violence: the oppressive power of the city, made solid in stone and metal, the liquid force and fury of the flood, are embodied in language of a density and energy which are hardly to be found in English outside the first books of *Paradise Lost*:

> *He scarce had finisht, when such murmur fill'd*
> *Th' assembly, as when hollow rocks retain*
> *The sound of blust'ring winds, which all night long*
> *Had rous'd the sea, now with hoarse cadence lull*
> *Sea-faring men o'er watcht . . .*

Or,

> *Rocks, caves, lakes, fens, bogs, dens, and shades of death . . .*

Yet I believe it is worth while to make an attempt to present *The Bronze Horseman* in English. There has, so far as I know, been only one English translation—that of Professor Oliver Elton, included by Mr. Avrahm Yarmolinsky in his *Poems, Prose and Plays of Pushkin*. This translation is a very respectable performance: it has certain merits which mine cannot pretend to. Professor Elton, following Pushkin's rhymed verse, has been able to succeed far better than I in catching the tumult and movement of the poem, and he has occasionally struck off a fine Pushkinian line; but he has blurred the effect of the whole by diluting it with a kind of stock romantic verbiage.

I have tried the experiment of translating the poem into prose with an iambic base. This at least makes it possible to avoid the woolliness which is the bane of translations of Pushkin —who is the least woolly of poets—since one is not obliged to pad out the spare and rapid phrases of the original with half-a-dozen words or more for every two of the text and with adjectives and images which are not Pushkin's. (I have used a different text from Professor Elton's: that of P. E. Shchegolev.)

But the main point is that this tale in verse is certainly one of the most enlightening things ever written about Russia by a Russian. It is not only in the portrayal of chaos, the resounding accents of power, that Pushkin is comparable to Milton. Pushkin's poor clerk Evgeni, too, is defying Eternal Order. But his defiance no longer appears under the aspect of a theological struggle; it is the great theme of the nineteenth century: the struggle of the individual with society—the theme of which, in terms of the bourgeois world, the great artistic presentation is in Ibsen. But Pushkin had dramatized it in terms of a society partly modernized and yet basically and belatedly feudal. Evgeni has lost his position as a gentleman through the incompetence of his father as a landlord (this appears from the genealogical fragment which Pushkin broke off and published separately), but he has not become a middle-class man. He is the pettiest of *petits bourgeois*; with his two chairs and his pot of cabbage soup, he has been reduced practically to a working-class level. The distance between him and the Statue, and what the Statue represents, is immense. He will be crushed, and his protest will never be heard—or rather, it would never have been heard if it had not been transmitted by Pushkin, whose poet's vocation it was to hear and to give a voice to the voiceless.

The Tsar was to do his best to prevent it from being heard: *The Bronze Horseman* was suppressed by the censorship and not published till after Pushkin's death. And one wonders, in reading it today, what repercussions it may have in Soviet Russia. After all, the construction of the White Sea canal has been accomplished by forced labor not much different from the forced labor with which Peter the Great built St. Petersburg;

and, after all, Peter the Great is the figure to whom the laureates of Stalin most willingly compare him and to whom he is said to be most willing to be compared. The dissident and the irreverent, like Evgeni, hear behind them a horseman, not of bronze but of steel, and no matter where they go, they cannot escape him; he drives them into the prisons of the GPU just as surely as he drove Evgeni into the Gulf of Finland; and just as Evgeni took off his hat and slunk aside where he had formerly hissed a threat, so the guilt of simple opposition puts them ultimately at the mercy of the 'Idol' and compels them to confess to crimes which they have unquestionably never committed. Between the power that builds the State and the Idol that represents it, on the one hand, and the ordinary man, on the other, the distance is still very great.

Not of course that Soviet Russia is not an advance beyond Tsarist Russia. The gains of the Revolution and the potentialities of its program should be no more destructible by the policies of however narrow and harsh an administration than the gains of the American Revolution and the potentialities of our republic were destroyed by Harding and Hoover. And not, on the other hand, that government of any sort, whether tsarist or capitalist or socialist, may not give rise to the same kind of conflict between the individual and the corporate interest which Pushkin presents in this poem. But it is well to remember nowadays that the attempt to establish socialism in Russia has had to be carried out in a society conditioned by despotism.

It is also well to remember that Pushkin makes Evgeni's defiance take place in Senate Square, the scene of the Decembrist revolt, which occurred the year after the flood; and that, however discouraged the poet may have been by the suppression of the revolt and by his own eclipse, that defiance was ultimately made good—in November, 1917.

THE BRONZE HORSEMAN
A Petersburg Tale

The incident described in this tale is based on fact. The details are taken from contemporary magazines. The curious may verify them from the material compiled by V. I. Berkh.—Foreword by Pushkin.

Beside the desolate waves stood *He*, and, thronged with mighty thoughts, stared out. Before him, broad, the river rushed along; a poor skiff plied upon it, solitary. Along the mossy marshy bank, the cabins, here and there, showed black: roofs for the wretched Finn; and forests, never brightened by the mist-enshrouded sun, were roaring all around.

Thought *He*: 'We shall from hence strike terror to the Swede. Here shall a town be reared to that arrogant neighbor's woe. Here, for our greatness, Nature has ordained that we shall break a window through to Europe; shall stand with foot set firm beside the sea. Hither, by waters they have never known, all flags shall come to be our guests, and we shall glory in our scope.'

A hundred years went by, and that young city, of northern lands the beauty and the marvel, from dark of forests, damp of bogs, rose up in all its grandeur and its pride; where once the Finnish fisher, Nature's sullen stepchild, had all alone beside low-lying shores let down his ragged nets, today by bustling docks, crowd, strong and shapely, bulks of tower and palace; ships swarm from all earth's ends to that rich port; Neva has clothed herself in stone; bridges have spanned her waters; her isles with groves dark-green are covered over; and now before the younger capital, old Moscow dims—as, before the new Tsarina, the widow of the purple.

I love thee, masterpiece of Peter—I love thine aspect, grace-ful and severe, Neva's mighty stream, her granite banks, stiff lace of iron fences, the limpid dusk and moonless radiance of nights so full of thought, when lampless in my room I write and read, and sleeping masses of deserted streets show clear, and the Admiralty's needle gleams, and, never suffering the shade of night to dim the golden sky, one glow makes haste to take the other's place, leaves night but half an hour. I love thy cruel winters, the frost and moveless air, the racing of the sleighs beside broad Neva, the girls with faces brighter bit than roses, the balls with all their glitter, stir and chatter, and bachelor feasts, with fizz of foaming goblets and azure flame of punch. I love the warlike liveliness of playing-fields of Mars, monotonous beauty of the Horse and Foot in ranks that sway in rhythm, streaming triumphant banners, the glinting of their bronze war-riddled helmets. I love, O martial capital, thy fort's loud smoke and thunder, when the Empress of the North gives the Imperial house a son, or Russia greets, exulting, her foeman's fresh defeat, or Neva, breaking through the dark blue ice, forth sweeps it to the sea and, smelling spring days, rejoices.

Be splendid, Peter's City, and stand, like Russia, strong—for lo, the very conquered element has made her peace with thee at last; their ancient hate and bondage may the Finnish waves forget, nor vex with impotent anger Peter's eternal sleep!

A dreadful time there *was*—of that I tell. And may my story, friends, be but, for you, a grisly fireside tale, no legend of bad omen . . .

I

On Petrograd, all clouded over, November breathed the autumn cold. Splashing with loud waves against her handsome banks, Neva threshed about, a sick man on his restless bed. The hour was late and dark; angry, the rain against the window beat, the dolorous wind drove howling. That evening from the house of friends returned the young Evgeni. We shall call our hero so: the name rings nicely; my pen is friendly to it from of old. No need to give his surname—though in former times it may have shone, and sounded from the pen of Karamzin among our country's annals; today the world of gossip has forgot it. Our hero lodges in a little room. He works somewhere or other, shuns the gentry, pines after neither his departed relatives nor old days now forgotten.

And so, come home, he shook his overcoat, undressed and went to bed, but long he could not sleep, disturbed by divers thoughts. What thoughts? That he was poor; that he had to work for decent independence; that God might make him cleverer and richer; that there were certain lucky idle fellows, who loafed and took no thought and found life light enough!;

that he must wait two years perhaps to get promotion; that the river was all bloated, that the weather got no better; that the bridges might perhaps be taken up, and that in that case his Parasha would surely miss him . . . Here he was filled with ardent tenderness, his fancy, like a poet's, soared away.

Get married? Well, why not? Why not, indeed? 'I shall make myself a modest little corner and there I shall give Parasha peace. A bed, two chairs, a pot of cabbage soup, and I the master of the house . . . What more should I want? We shall coddle no caprices; I shall take Parasha out for country walks on summer Sundays; humble I'll be and sly: they'll give me a snug berth; Parasha will keep house, bring up the children . . . And so we'll live and so go down to death, still hand in hand, and be buried by our grandsons . . .'

So he mused. And yet that night he was melancholy, and he wished that the wind would not sound so dreary, that the rain would not sound so angry, as it beat against the pane.

Sleepy, he closed his eyes at last. And lo! the dark of that foul night is thinning, and pale day is at hand . . . Ah, dreadful day!

All night had Neva plunged against the storm to reach the sea, but, worsted by that fury, she now could fight no more . . . At morning to her shores the people flocked in crowds, in wonder at the spray, the mountainous swell, the foam of raging waters. But Neva, by the Gulf winds' driving taxed now beyond her force, fell back in rage and tumult; flooded the islands; fiercer and fiercer grew; reared up and roared; like a caldron, boiled, breathed steam; and, frenzied, fell at last upon the town. All fled before her—all was left abandoned—and now the waves were breaking through the streets, and now invading basements; Neva's canals were all one sea with her, and like a Triton, Petropol emerged, waist-deep in water.

A siege! A storming! Waves, like savage beasts, climb to the windows. Boats, pell-mell borne along, strike the glass with their sterns. Bridges swept loose by the deluge, fragments of cabins, timbers, roofs, the thrifty merchant's wares, the wretched chattels of the poor, the wheels of city droshkies, the coffins from the graveyard, washed afloat—all these drift through the town!

The people see the wrath of God and wait their execution.
Alas! all ruined: roof and food! Where will it end?

The late Tsar in that terrible year still gloriously ruled Russia. Distressed and baffled now, he sought the balcony and spoke: 'To tsars it is not given to curb the elements, for they belong to God.' With mournful brooding eyes, he watched the dreadful work. The public squares were lakes, and into them the streets were pouring rivers. The palace seemed a dismal isle. The Tsar's command went forth: his generals, far and wide, through stormy waters on a perilous course, plunged through the streets and sought to save the people, gone mad with panic, drowning in their houses.

Now at this time in Peter's Square, where a new corner-house had risen, where on the perron high, lifelike with lifted paw, two ornamental lions stand—astride one marble beast, hatless, with arms tight folded, rigid and deathly pale, Evgeni perched. Not for himself, poor fellow, did he fear. He did not notice how the greedy billows rose till they lapped his soles nor how his face was dashed with rain nor how the wildly howling wind had suddenly snatched his hat. His eyes were fixed far out in one strained desperate stare. *There* reared and raged the waves, like mountains, from the outraged deep; *there* raved the storm, *there* broken things were tossed . . . And *there*—God! God!—alas! within the billows' reach, by the Gulf's very brink—the paintless fence, the willow, the little flimsy house—and they, the widow and her daughter, *there*— his dear Parasha, all his hope . . . Or is it all a dream that he beholds? Or is our life, then, nothingness—as empty as a dream, Fate's mockery of man? As if bewitched, fast rooted to the marble, he can't dismount! About him stretches water— water now and nothing else. And, back turned toward him, steady on its height above defiant Neva, rears on its steed of bronze, with outstretched arm, the idol.

II

But now, with ruin sated, with insolent uproar spent, Neva crept back, well pleased to have wreaked her fury and heedlessly abandoning her booty. So, with his villainous band invading town, the ruffian breaks in, wrecks, ransacks, cuts throats:

cries, grindings, violence, oaths, alarms and howls! . . . And, burdened with their plunder, fearing pursuit and tired, the robbers hurry home and drop their loot along the road.

The water sank, the pavements cleared again, and my Evgeni hastes with fainting spirit, hoping, fearing, yearning, to the river scarce grown tame. But, still exulting fiercely in the fullness of their triumph, still wickedly the waters boil; still does the foam o'erspread them, and like a warhorse running from a battle, heavily Neva breathes. Evgeni looks: he sees a boat, a godsend; he runs, calls out to the boatman—he, careless of danger, is ready enough to take him across the terrible waters for ten kopecks.

And long the practiced oarsman contends with the tossing waves, and momently the skiff with its rash sailors seems like to plumb the abyss between their ranks—and now at last it makes the land.

The poor wretch runs along the familiar street to find the familiar place. He looks—oh, dreadful sight!—he knows it not. All lies a heap before him; part tumbled down, part swept away; some of the little houses knocked awry, some quite destroyed, some shifted by the waves—and all about, as on a field of battle, bodies are strewn. Evgeni rushes headlong—uncomprehending, faint with horror—where Fate awaits him with the unseen tidings as if with a sealed letter. And now he is in that last outlying suburb, and here's the Gulf, and here's the house hard by it . . . What's this? . . . He stops—goes back, returns. He stares . . . advances . . . stares again. Here is the place their house stood; here is the willow. Here were the gates—so they've been carried off. But where's the house? And, full of black foreboding, he prowls and prowls about, talks loudly to himself—then suddenly, striking his brow, he bursts out laughing.

Night's darkness fell upon the frightened town; and long the people did not sleep, but talked of the day just past.

The morning's ray, from pale and haggard clouds, shone on a quiet capital and found no trace of yesterday's disaster; with royal purple now the hurt was overspread. And all took up the old routine. Already through the streets, now clear again, with cold indifference flowed the crowd. The clerks, quitting their lodgings, went to their desks. Hardy trade, not downed, explored his cellars, plundered by the river, preparing to revenge his heavy losses out of his neighbor's pocket. And people took the boats out of the courtyards.

And Khostov, poet, favorite of the heavens, already sang in verses never to die the griefs of Neva's shores.

But ah, my poor Evgeni . . . alas! his baffled wits gave way before these blows. The mutinous roar of Neva and the winds were now resounding in his ears. Possessed by dreadful thoughts he could not utter, he strayed from place to place. Some dream was preying on him. A week, and then a month had passed—he never from that day went home. His empty lodging, when the lease expired, the landlord rented out to a poor poet. Evgeni never came to claim his things. The world forgot him soon. All day he tramped, at night slept on the docks; his food was morsels handed out from windows. His shabby clothes were torn and wearing out. The cruel children stoned him as he passed. Often he felt the coachmen's whips, for all was thoroughfare to him alike—courtyard or street, he never paid attention, always submerged in some strange inner terror. And so he dragged his miserable life, not beast nor man, not this nor that, no dweller on the earth nor yet departed spirit . . .

One night he slept on a landing of the Neva. The summer days inclined toward fall. A foul wind blew. The dark surf dashed on the wharf, muttering grief and beating the smooth steps, like a suppliant at the door of a deaf court. The poor wretch fell asleep. The dark had come; the rain was dripping down; the wind was dreary; from far away the sentry through the thickness of the night returned its cry . . . Evgeni leapt from sleep; his horror had come on him; quickly he rose and started on his wandering. Then suddenly he stopped and, standing very still, his face aghast with terror, began to gaze about. The great house with its columns rose before him. And on the perron high, lifelike with lifted paw, the ornamental lions stood; and right before him, from its fenced-in rock, with outstretched arm, uprearing in the darkness, the idol sat its copper steed.

A shudder shook Evgeni. His thoughts grew terribly clear. He knew this place where the flood had had its sport, where the waves had flocked like beasts of prey about him, ruthless,

in full rebellion—and he knew these lions and this square, and
him he knew who, fixed and still forever, held high in the murk
of night his copper head—himself whose fateful will had based
the city on the sea . . . How dreadful now in all-enveloping
mist! What power of thought upon his brow! What force
within! And in that steed what fire! Where dost thou gallop,
haughty steed? And where wilt thou plant thy hoof? O thou
who, in thy might, didst master Destiny! Didst not just so,
aloft, above the very precipice, with iron curb make Russia rear?

The poor crazed fellow prowled about the pedestal, cast
wild looks on the image of the lord of half the world. His chest
grew tight. He pressed his brow against the cold grate; his eyes
blurred with mist; a flame flashed through his heart; his blood
boiled up. Somber he stood before the arrogant statue, and,
clinching teeth and fists, possessed by some black force: 'Good!
wonderworking builder!' with quivering hate, he hissed.
'You'll reckon with me yet!'—And headlong took to flight.
The terrible Tsar, on the instant hot with wrath, had seemed
all soundlessly to turn his head.

And through the empty square he plunges wildly, and hears
behind—like rattling thunderclap—against the pounded pave
a heavy-ringing gallop. And, dark in the pale moon, one arm
flung up, the Copper Horseman comes behind, his charger's
gallop ringing brass; and all night long, turn where Evgeni
will, the Copper Horseman's clattering hoofbeats hammer—
pursuing, still impend.

Thereafter, if he chanced upon the Square, his face, dismayed, would darken. Quick he would press his hand against
his heart as if to calm its fluttering, remove his shabby cap, cast
down his gaze and slink away.

A little isle there is that lies offshore. Sometimes the fisher
moors there with his net, belated at the haul, and cooks his
humble supper, or some dreaming Sunday boatman puts in at
the desert place. No blade of grass has ever sprouted there.
But there the sportive flood had brought a flimsy cottage. Like
a blackened bush it showed above the water. Last spring they
took it up aboard a barque. It was empty, all a wreck; but on its
threshold they dragged up my madman, and there for Charity's sake they buried his cold corpse.

A. E. Housman

The Voice, Sent Forth, Can Never Be Recalled

WHEN A. E. Housman's *Introductory Lecture* delivered in 1892 'Before the Faculties of Arts and Laws and of Science in University College, London' was reprinted in 1933, Housman characteristically wrote of it as follows: 'The Council of University College, not I, had the lecture printed.' He described it as 'rhetorical and not wholly sincere' and put upon the title page, *Nescit vox missa reverti.*

The little essay is curious in largely evading the questions it raises and taking the direction of a piece of special pleading for the author's own pursuits. Both the sciences and the arts, says Housman, are ordinarily defended by arguments which make their interests appear mutually antagonistic. But the arguments on both sides are mistaken. Science is said to be useful; but what is the use, for example, of a great deal of astronomical research? And the businessmen who make practical use of the results of scientific study are usually not scientists at all. (They do make use of them, nevertheless; and the results of the most gratuitous researches are always likely to turn out to be useful.) The Humanities, on the other hand, are supposed to 'transform and beautify our inner nature by culture.' Yet the proportion of the human race capable of being benefited by classical studies is certainly very small, and these 'can attain the desired end without that minute and accurate study of the classical tongues which affords Latin professors their only excuse for existing.' Not even the great critics of the classics are genuine classical scholars: 'When it comes to literary criticism, heap up in one scale all the literary criticism that the whole nation of professed scholars ever wrote, and drop into the other the thin green volume of Matthew Arnold's *Lectures on Translating Homer*, which has long been out of print because the British public does not care to read it, and the first scale, as Milton says, will straight fly up and kick the beam.' (We shall look into the assumptions here in a moment.)

63

The arts and the sciences alike are only to be defended, says Housman, on the ground that the desire for knowledge is one of the normal human appetites, and that men suffer if they do not have it gratified. And 'once we have recognized that knowledge in itself is good for man, we shall need to invent no pretexts for studying this subject or that; we shall import no extraneous considerations of use or ornament to justify us in learning one thing rather than another. If a certain department of knowledge specially attracts a man, let him study that, and study it because it attracts him; and let him not fabricate excuses for that which requires no excuse, but rest assured that the reason why it most attracts him is that it is best for him.'

This is certainly true in so far as it means that we should follow the direction of our aptitudes; but it seems to imply that there is no difference in value between one department of learning and another or between the different points of view from which the various kinds of research can be conducted. There is no conception in Housman's mind, as there would have been in Whitehead's, for example, of relating the part to the whole, understanding the organism through the cell. Knowledge seems to be regarded by Housman as a superior sort of pastime—'good for man' because it gives him pleasure and at most because 'it must in the long run be better for a man to see things as they are than to be ignorant of them; just as there is less fear of stumbling or of striking against corners in the daylight than in the dark.' (*The thoughts of others Were light and fleeting, Of lovers' meeting Or luck or fame; Mine were of trouble And mine were steady, So I was ready When Trouble came.'*) The disillusionment of western man in regard to his place in the universe, finding 'that he has been deceived alike as to his origin and his expectations, that he neither springs of the high lineage he fancied, nor will inherit the vast estate he looked for,' is described in an eloquent passage; and the activities of the 'Arts and Laws and Science' are finally characterized as 'the rivalry of fellow soldiers in striving which can most victoriously achieve the common end of all, to set back the frontier of darkness.'

In other words, there is no role for creation in Housman's scheme of things. Indeed, if one had read only his poetry, one might be surprised to find that he even believed that it was possible or of any importance to set back the frontier of darkness. In this poetry, we find only the realization of man's smallness on his turning globe among the other revolving planets and of his own basic wrongness to himself, his own inescapable anguish. No one, it seems, can do anything about this universe which 'ails from its prime foundation': we can only, like Mithridates, render ourselves immune to its poisons by compelling ourselves to absorb them in small quantities in order that we may not succumb to the larger doses reserved for us by our fellows, or face the world with the hard mask of stoicism, 'manful like the man of stone.' For the rest, 'let us endure an hour and see injustice done.' And now we learn that for Housman knowledge itself meant at most the discovery of things that were already there—of those sharp corners which it was just as well not to bump into, of facts that were as invariable and as inert as the astronomical phenomena which are always turning up in his poems and which form the subject of the poem of Manilius to which he devoted so much of his life. He does not look to the sciences and arts for the births of new worlds of thought, of new possibilities for men themselves. It is characteristic of him that he should speak, in this essay, of Milton as a greater artist than Shakespeare, of Shakespeare, in fact, as not 'a great artist'—as if the completeness and richness of Shakespeare's dramatic imagination, a kind of genius which Milton, by comparison, seems hardly to possess at all, were not important enough to be taken into account in estimating his greatness as an artist—as if those stretches of *Paradise Lost* where everything is dead but the language were not the result of artistic deficiency. Again, the creation of life has no place in the universe of Housman.

Housman's practice in his own field of scholarship is an astonishing proof of this. The modern English classical scholar of the type of A. W. Verrall or Gilbert Murray is a critic not merely of texts but of the classics in their quality as literature and of literature in its bearing on history. This school on one of its sides sometimes merges with the anthropology of J. G. Frazer; and it deals with ancient Greece and Rome in relation to the life of its own time, restates them in terms of its own time. The danger, of course, with a Verrall or a Murray is that,

with something of the poet's imagination himself, he may give
way, in the case of Greek drama, for example, to inventing new
plays of his own and trying to foist them on Euripides or
Aeschylus. With Housman we do not run this danger. Housman is the opposite kind of scholar; he is preoccupied with the
emendation of texts. He could never have been guilty of the
extravagances of a Gilbert Murray or a Verrall, but he was not
capable of their kind of illumination. Note his assumption, in
the passage quoted above, that 'the minute and accurate study
of the classical tongues,' with which he himself is exclusively
preoccupied, 'affords Latin professors their only excuse for existing.' Have those classical scholars who write history, who
write criticism, who make translations—Gibbon and Renan and
Verrall and Murray and Jowett and Mackail (to take in the
whole field of the classics)—no excuse for existing, then? Is it
so certain that, if their literary criticism were put into the scales
with Matthew Arnold on Homer, the scholars would kick the
beam? Or are such persons not scholars at all? In either case, it
is plain that, for Housman, their activities lie outside the pe-
riphery of the sphere which he has chosen for himself.

Not, however, that Housman in this limited sphere has left
the poet of *The Shropshire Lad* behind him. On the contrary,
the peculiar genius which won him a place beside Porson and
Bentley, which established him in his own time as almost
supreme, with, apparently, only Wilamowitz as a rival, was derived from his ability to combine with the most 'minute and
accurate' mastery of language a first-hand knowledge of how
poets express themselves. 'The task of editing the classics,' he
wrote in his preface to Juvenal, 'is continually attempted by
scholars who have neither enough intellect nor enough literature. Unless a false reading chances to be unmetrical or un-
grammatical they have no means of knowing that it is false.'
And he himself seemed able with a miraculous sureness to give
the authors back their lines as they had written them. So, for
example, despite a unanimity of manuscripts which read 'Omnis ab hac cura mens relavata mea est,' Housman restored to
Ovid from an inscription one of the latter's characteristic turns
of style: 'Omnis ab hac cura cura levata mea est.' (*'And set you
at your threshold down, Townsman of a stiller town'*; *'Runners
whom renown outran And the name died before the man'*; *'By*

Sestos tower, in Hero's town, On Hero's heart Leander lies.') So, slightly emending the text, he turned a meaningless accepted reading of Juvenal, 'Perditus ac vilis sacci mercator olentis,' into a characteristically vivid satiric stroke: 'Perditus ac similis sacci mercator olentis'—the money-chasing merchant, on a stormy voyage, turns as yellow as his bag of saffron. (*They shook, they stared as white's their shirt: Them it was their poison hurt.'*) So, without even an emendation and simply by indicating a new relation between three words of Virgil's, he was able to save Virgil's style in a phrase—*fallax herba veneni*—which had always up to then been read as if it had been written with neither style nor grammar: substituting for 'the deceitful plant of poison,' 'the plant that dissimulates its venom.' (*'And bear from hill and valley The daffodil away That dies on Easter day'; 'Lie long, high snowdrifts in the hedge That will not shower on me'; 'Snap not from the bitter yew His leaves that live November through.'*) Several of his readings, I understand, have been confirmed by the subsequent discovery of manuscripts which Housman had never seen.

To this rescue of the Greek and Roman poets from the negligence of the Middle Ages, from the incompetence and insensitivity of the scholars, A. E. Housman brought an unremitting zeal which may almost be described as a passion. It has been said of the theorems of Newton that they cause the pulse to beat faster as one follows them. But the excitement and satisfaction afforded by the classical commentary of Housman must be unique in the history of scholarship. Even the scraping of the rust from an old coin is too tame an image to convey the experience of pursuing one of his arguments to its climax. It is as if, from the ancient author, so long dumb with his language itself, his very identity blurred or obliterated, the modern classicist were striking a new spark of life—as if the poet could only find his tongue at the touch across Time of the poet. So far is Housman the scholar a giver of life—yet it is only as re-creator. He is only, after all, again, discovering things that were already there. His findings do not imply a new vision.

It was a queer destiny, and one that cramped him—if one should not say rather that he had cramped himself. (Not to dispute, however, with Housman, who thought that human beings were all but helpless, the problem of natural fate and free will.)

The great work of A. E. Housman's life in the field of classical scholarship was his edition of the five books of Manilius, the publication of which alone extended from 1903 to 1930. We are told in a memoir of Housman by his colleague, Professor A. S. F. Gow of Cambridge, that Housman regarded Manilius as 'a facile and frivolous poet, the brightest facet of whose genius was an eminent aptitude for doing sums in verse.' And the layman may be disposed to assume that by Housman's time the principal Latin poets had already been covered so completely that there was nobody left except third-rate ones like Manilius. But it turns out from Professor Gow that Housman's real favorite was Propertius, and that he had done a great deal of valuable work on him and had at one time contemplated a complete edition. Professor Gow says that presumably Housman saw in Manilius and Lucan (Lucan he seems also to have despised) 'more opportunity than in Propertius of displaying his special gifts, and more hope of approaching finality in the solution of the problems presented,' but adds that he 'cannot help regretting that he [Housman] abandoned a great and congenial poet on whom so much time had already been lavished.'

The elegist of *The Shropshire Lad*, then, deliberately and grimly chose Manilius when his real interest was in Propertius. There is an element of perversity, of self-mortification, in Housman's career all along. (Gow tells how up to the time of his death 'he would be found reading every word of books whose insignificance must have been apparent in ten pages, and making remorseless catalogues of their shortcomings.') And his scholarship, great as it is in its way, is poisoned in revenge by the instincts which it seems to be attempting to destroy, so that it radiates more hatred for his opponents than love for the great literature of antiquity. Housman's papers on classical subjects, which shocked the sense of decorum of his colleagues, are painful to the admirers of his poetry. The bitterness here *is* indecent as in his poetry it never is. In a prose, old-fashioned and elaborate, which somewhat resembles Pope's, he will attack the German professors who have committed the unpardonable sin of editing the Latin authors inadequately with sentences that coil and strike like rattlesnakes, or that wrap themselves around their victims and squeeze them to death like boa constrictors. When English fails, he takes to scurrilous Latin. And the whole thing is likely at any moment to give way to some morose observation on the plight of the human race: 'To believe that wherever a best *ms* gives possible readings it gives true readings, and that only when it gives impossible readings does it give false readings, is to believe that an incompetent editor is the darling of Providence, which has given its angels charge over him lest at any time his sloth and folly should produce their natural results and incur their appropriate penalty . . . How the world is managed, and why it was created, I cannot tell; but it is no feather-bed for the repose of sluggards.' And not only, he continues, has the notion been imposed that 'inert adhesion to one authority is methodical criticism,' but 'rational criticism has been branded with a term of formal reprobation.' 'But still there is a hitch. Competent editors exist; and side by side with those who have embraced "the principles of criticism," there are those who follow the practice of critics: who possess intellects, and employ them on their work. Consequently their work is better done, and the contrast is mortifying. This is not as it should be. As the wise man dieth, so dieth the fool: why then should we allow them to edit the classics differently? If nature, with flagitious partiality, has given judgment and industry to some men and left other men without them, it is our evident duty to amend her blind caprice; and those who are able and willing to think must be deprived of their unfair advantage by stringent prohibitions. In Association football you must not use your hands, and similarly in textual criticism you must not use your brains. Since we cannot make fools behave like wise men, we will insist that wise men should behave like fools: by these means only can we redress the injustice of nature and anticipate the equality of the grave.'

And here is the somber and threatening, the almost Isaian, utterance to which he is moved by the failure of one of the compilers of a German-Latin dictionary to include in the article on *aelurus*, the Latinized Greek word for *cat*, any mention of an instance of its occurrence arrived at by emendation in Juvenal and believed by Housman to be the first extant:

'Everyone can figure to himself the mild inward glow of pleasure and pride which the author of this unlucky article felt
while he was writing it and the peace of mind with which he
said to himself, when he went to bed that night, "Well done,
thou good and faithful servant." This is the felicity of the
house of bondage, and of the soul which is so fast in prison
that it cannot go forth; which commands no outlook on the
past or the future, but believes that the fashion of the present,
unlike all fashions heretofore, will endure perpetually and that
its own flimsy tabernacle of second-hand opinions is a habitation for everlasting.'

Even when Housman is saying something positive the emotion is out of proportion to its object: he speaks feverishly,
seems unnaturally exalted. Here is a passage on Bentley from
the preface to the first volume of his Manilius: '*Lucida tela
diei:* these are the words that come into one's mind when one
has halted at some stubborn perplexity of reading or interpretation, has witnessed Scaliger and Gronovius and Huetius
fumble at it one after another, and then turns to Bentley and
sees Bentley strike his finger on the place and say *thou ailest
here, and here* . . . The firm strength and piercing edge and
arrowy swiftness of his intellect, his matchless facility and
adroitness and resource, were never so triumphant as where
defeat seemed sure; and yet it is other virtues that one most
admires and welcomes as one turns from the smoky fire of
Scaliger's genius to the sky and air of Bentley's: his lucidity, his
sanity, his great and simple and straightforward fashion of
thought.' Transferring Arnold's words for Goethe to Bentley
is not perhaps comparing great things with small, but in the
substitution for the 'physician of the Iron Age' of the physician
of mangled texts, there is a narrowing of scope almost comic.
The preface to the first book of Manilius, from which the
above passage has been quoted, magnificent as it is in its way,
has also something monstrous about it.

Yet some acquaintance with the classical work of Housman
greatly increases one's estimate of his stature. One encounters
an intellectual pride almost Dantesque or Swiftian. 'You would
be welcome to praise me,' he writes, 'if you did not praise one
another'; and 'the reader whose good opinion I desire and have
done my utmost to secure is the next Bentley or Scaliger who

may chance to occupy himself with Manilius.' His arrogance is perhaps never more ferocious than when he is judging himself severely: when a friend who had ventured to suggest the publication of a paper on Swinburne which Housman had read before a college literary society had been told by Housman that he was leaving directions to have it destroyed after his death and had retorted that if the writer really thought it so bad, he would already himself have destroyed it, Housman replied: 'I do not think it bad: I think it not good enough for me.' And he put on the title page of his edition of Juvenal, *editorum in usum edidit*, to indicate that this feat of erudition —according to his own announcement, unprecedented—was merely intended as a hint to future scholars who might tackle the subject as to how they might accomplish their task in a thoroughgoing fashion.

Is this the spectacle of a great mind crippled? Certainly it is the spectacle of a mind of remarkable penetration and vigor, of uncommon sensibility and intensity, condemning itself to duties which prevent it from rising to its full height. Perhaps it is the case of a man of genius who has never been allowed to come to growth. Housman's anger is tragic like Swift's. He is perhaps more pitiable than Swift, because he has been compelled to suppress himself more completely. Even when Swift had been exiled to Ireland, he was able to take out his fury in crusading against the English. But A. E. Housman, giving up Greek in order to specialize in Latin because he 'could not attain to excellence in both,' giving up Propertius, who wrote about love, for Manilius, who did not even deal with human beings, turning away from the lives of the Romans to rivet his attention to the difficulties of their texts, can only flatten out small German professors with weapons which would have found fit employment in the hands of a great reformer or a great satirist. He is the hero of *The Grammarian's Funeral*— the man of learning who makes himself impressive through the magnitude, not the importance, of his achievement. After all, there was no need for another Bentley.

It is only in the Latin verses—said to have been called by Murray the best since the ancient world—which Housman prefixed to his Manilius, in his few translations from Latin and Greek, and in his occasional literary essays, that the voice of

the Shropshire Lad comes through—that voice which, once
sped on its way, so quickly pierced to the hearts and the minds
of the whole English-speaking world and which went on vibrating for decades, disburdening hearts with its music that
made loss and death and disgrace seem so beautiful, while poor
Housman, burdened sorely forever, sat grinding and snarling
at his texts. Would he have called back that voice if he could, as
he recalled, or tried to recall, so much else? There are moments when his ill humor and his pedantry, his humility which
is a perverse kind of pride, almost make us think that he would.

At this point Professor Gow is able to throw some further
light on his friend. It seems that Housman had marked the following passage from Colonel Lawrence's *Seven Pillars of Wisdom*, which he had come across in a review:

'There was my craving to be liked—so strong and nervous
that never could I open myself friendly to another. The terror
of failure in an effort so important made me shrink from
trying; besides, there was the standard; for intimacy seemed
shameful unless the other could make the perfect reply, in the
same language, after the same method, for the same reasons.

'There was a craving to be famous; and a horror of being
known to like being known. Contempt for my passion for distinction made me refuse every offered honor. I cherished my
independence almost as did a Beduin, but my impotence of vision showed me my shape best in painted pictures, and the
oblique overheard remarks of others best taught me my created impression. The eagerness to overhear and oversee myself
was my assault upon my own inviolate citadel.'

Housman had written in the margin, 'This is me.' Both had
been compelled by their extreme sensibility to assume in the
presence of their fellows eccentric or repellent masks. Both had
been led by extreme ambition to perform exploits which did
not do them justice, exploits which their hearts were but half
in: Professor Gow says that Housman's prime motive in undertaking his edition of Manilius was the ambition to 'build' himself 'a monument.' And just as Lawrence was always losing the
manuscripts of his books, limiting their circulation, making the
pretense of suppressing them altogether, so Housman kept his
poems out of anthologies, made the gestures of a negative at-

titude in regard to the reprinting of his other writings, and left instructions that his classical papers, of which Gow says there are something like a hundred, should never be collected in a volume (instructions which it is to be hoped will be disobeyed).

Both were products of the English universities; and it would take an Englishman properly to account for them. But their almost insane attempts to conceal their blazing lights under bushels are recognizable as exaggerations of the Englishman's code of understatement in connection with his achievements and conquests. And both obviously belong to the monastic order of English university ascetics. The company to which Housman refers himself is that of Walter Pater, Lewis Carroll, Edward FitzGerald and Gerard Manley Hopkins—and, earlier, Thomas Gray. Hopkins, converted at Oxford, entered the Jesuit order; Pater and Dodgson stayed on there as dons; Fitz-Gerald and Gray, when they had finished at Cambridge, continued to haunt the place: they remained men of the monastery all their lives. Are their humility, which seems imposed by moral principles, their shyness in relation to the extra-collegiate world, derived from the ages when learning was the possession of pious brotherhoods and shut away between the walls of foundations?

Certainly their failure to develop emotionally is due to that semi-monastic training. All seem checked at some early stage of growth, beyond which the sensibility and the intellect—even, in Lawrence's case, the ability to manage men—may crystallize in marvelous forms, but after which there is no natural progress in the experience of human relationships. Their works are among the jewels of English literature rather than among its great springs of life; and Alice and the Shropshire Lad and Marius the Epicurean are all the beings of a looking-glass world, either sexless or with an unreal sex which turns only toward itself in the mirror of art. Isn't the state of mind indicated by Lawrence in the first of the paragraphs quoted above essentially an adolescent one? We are told, in a recent memoir, that Housman used to rail against marriage and child-bearing. 'My father and my mother,' he makes one of his hanged heroes say, 'They had a likely son, And I have none.'

It would not be true to say of Housman, as it would be of FitzGerald or Gray, that his achievement has been merely to state memorably certain melancholy commonplaces of human existence without any real presentation of that existence as we live it through. There *is* immediate emotional experience in Housman of the same kind that there is in Heine, whom he imitated and to whom he has been compared. But Heine, for all his misfortunes, moves at ease in a larger world. There is in his work an exhilaration of adventure—in travel, in love, in philosophy, in literature, in politics. Doleful though his accents may sometimes be, he always lets in air and light to the mind. But Housman is closed from the beginning. His world has no opening horizons; it is a prison that one can only endure. One can only come the same painful cropper over and over again and draw from it the same bitter moral.

And Housman has managed to grow old without in a sense ever knowing maturity. He has somehow never arrived at the age when the young man decides at last to summon all his resources and try to make something out of this world he has never made.

The Politics of Flaubert

GUSTAVE FLAUBERT has figured for decades as the great glorifier and practitioner of literary art at the expense of human affairs both public and personal. We have heard about his asceticism, his nihilism, his consecration to the search for *le mot juste*. His admirers have tended to praise him on the same assumption on which his critics have found him empty and sterile: the assumption that he had no moral or social interests. At most, *Madame Bovary* has been taken as a parable of the romantic temperament.

Really Flaubert owed his superiority to those of his contemporaries—Gautier, for example, who professed the same literary creed—to the seriousness of his concern with the large questions of human destiny. It was a period when the interest in history was intense; and Flaubert, in his intellectual tastes as well as in his personal relations, was almost as close to the historians Michelet, Renan and Taine, and to the biographical critic Sainte-Beuve, as to Gautier and Baudelaire. In the case of Taine and Sainte-Beuve, he came to deplore their preoccupation in their criticism with the social aspects of literature at the expense of all its other values; but he himself seems always to see humanity in social terms and historical perspective. His point of view may be gauged pretty accurately from his comments in one of his letters on Taine's *History of English Literature*: 'There is something else in art beside the milieu in which it is practiced and the physiological antecedents of the worker. On this system you can explain the series, the group, but never the individuality, the special fact which makes him this person and not another. This method results inevitably in leaving *talent* out of consideration. The masterpiece has no longer any significance except as an historical document. It is the old critical method of La Harpe exactly turned around. People used to believe that literature was an altogether personal thing and that books fell out of the sky like meteors. Today they deny that the will and the absolute have any reality at all. The truth, I believe, lies between the two extremes.'

But it was also a period in France—Flaubert's lifetime, 1820–81—of alternating republics and monarchies, of bogus emperors and defeated revolutions, when political ideas were in much confusion. The French historians of the Enlightenment tradition, which was the tradition of the Revolution, were steadily becoming less hopeful; and a considerable group of the novelists and poets held political and social issues in contempt and staked their careers on art as an end in itself: their conception of their relation to society was expressed in their damnation of the bourgeois, who gave his tone to all the world, and their art was a defiance of him. The Goncourts in their journal have put the attitude on record: 'Lying phrases, resounding words, hot air—that's just about all we get from the political men of our time. Revolutions are a simple *déménagement* followed by the moving-back of the same ambitions, corruptions and villainies into the apartment which they have just been moved out of—and all involving great breakage and expense. No political morals whatever. When I look about me for a disinterested opinion, I can't find a single one. People take risks and compromise themselves on the chance of getting future jobs . . . You are reduced, in the long run, to disillusion, to a disgust with all beliefs, a tolerance of any power at all, an indifference to political passion, which I find in all my literary friends, and in Flaubert as in myself. You come to see that you must not die for any cause, that you must live with any government that exists, no matter how antipathetic it may be to you—you must believe in nothing but art and profess only literature. All the rest is a lie and a booby-trap.' In the field of art, at least, it was possible, by heroic effort, to prevent the depreciation of values.

This attitude, as the Goncourts say, Flaubert fully shared. 'Today,' he wrote Louise Colet in 1853, 'I even believe that a thinker (and what is an artist if he is not a triple thinker?) should have neither religion nor fatherland nor even any social conviction. It seems to me that absolute doubt is now indicated so unmistakably that it would almost amount to an absurdity to take the trouble to formulate it.' And: 'The citizens who work themselves up for or against the Empire or the Republic,' he wrote George Sand in 1869, 'seem to be just about as useful as the ones who used to argue about efficacious grace and efficient grace.' Nothing exasperated him more—and we may sympathize with him today—than the idea that the soul is to be saved by the profession of correct political opinions.

Yet Flaubert is an idealist on a grandiose scale. 'The idea' which turns up in his letters of the fifties—'genius like a powerful horse drags humanity at her tail along the roads of the idea,' in spite of all that human stupidity can do to rein her in —is evidently, under its guise of art, none other than that Hegelian 'Idea' which served Marx and so many others under a variety of different guises. There are great forces in humanity, Flaubert feels, which the present is somehow suppressing but which may some day be gloriously set free. 'The soul is asleep today, drunk with the words she has listened to, but she will experience a wild awakening, in which she will give herself up to the ecstasies of liberation, for there will be nothing more to constrain her, neither government nor religion, not a formula; the republicans of all shades of opinion seem to me the most ferocious pedagogues, with their dreams of organizations, of legislations, of a society constructed like a convent.'

When he reasons about society—which he never does except in his letters—his conceptions seem incoherent. But Flaubert, who believed that the artist should be triply ('to the n*th* degree') a thinker and who had certainly one of the great minds of his time, was the kind of imaginative writer who works directly in concrete images and does not deal at all in ideas. His informal expressions of his general opinions are as unsystematized and impromptu as his books are well-built and precise. But it is worth while to quote a few from his letters, because, though he never came anywhere near to expounding a social philosophy—when George Sand accused him of not having one, he admitted it—they do indicate the instincts and emotions which are the prime movers in the world of his art.

Flaubert is opposed to the socialists because he regards them as materialistic and because he dislikes their authoritarianism, which he says derives straight from the tradition of the Church. Yet they have 'denied *pain*, have blasphemed three-quarters of modern poetry, the blood of Christ, which quickens in us.' And: 'O socialists, there is your ulcer: the ideal is lacking to you; and that very matter which you pursue slips through your fingers like a wave; the adoration of humanity for itself and by itself (which brings us to the doctrine of the useful in Art, to the theories of public safety and reason of state, to all the injustices and all the intolerances, to the immolation of the right, to the leveling of the Beautiful), that cult of the belly, I say, breeds wind.' One thing he makes clear by reiteration through the various periods of his life: his disapproval of the ideal of equality. What is wanted, he keeps insisting, is 'justice'; and behind this demand for justice is evidently Flaubert's resentment, arising from his own experience, against the false reputations, the undeserved rewards and the stupid repressions of the Second Empire. And he was skeptical of popular education and opposed to universal suffrage.

Yet among the men of his time whom Flaubert admired most were democrats, humanitarians and reformers. 'You are certainly the French author,' he wrote Michelet, 'whom I have read and reread most'; and he said of Victor Hugo that Hugo was the living man 'in whose skin' he would be happiest to be. George Sand was one of his closest friends: *Un Cœur simple* was written for her—apparently in answer to her admonition that art was 'not merely criticism and satire' and to show her that he, too, had a heart.

When we come to Flaubert's books themselves, we find a much plainer picture of things.

It is not true, as is sometimes supposed, that he disclaimed any moral intention. He deliberately refrained in his novels from commenting on the action in his own character: 'the artist ought not to appear in his work any more than God in nature.' But, like God, he rules his universe through law; and the reader, from what he hears and sees, must infer the moral system.

What *are* we supposed to infer from Flaubert's work? His general historical point of view is, I believe, pretty well known. He held that 'the three great evolutions of humanity' had been 'paganisme, christianisme, muflisme [muckerism],' and that Europe was in the third of these phases. Paganism he depicted in *Salammbô* and in the short story *Hérodias*. The Carthaginians of *Salammbô* had been savage and benighted barbarians: they had worshiped serpents, crucified lions, sacrificed their children to Moloch, and trampled armies to death with herds of elephants; but they had slaughtered, lusted and agonized superbly. Christianity is represented by the two legends of saints, *La Tentation de Saint Antoine* and *La Légende de Saint Julien l'Hospitalier*. The Christian combats his lusts, he expiates human cruelty; but this attitude, too, is heroic: Saint Anthony, who inhabits the desert, Saint Julien, who lies down with the leper, have pushed to their furthest limits the virtues of abnegation and humility. But when we come to the *muflisme* of the nineteenth century—in *Madame Bovary* and *L'Education sentimentale*—all is meanness, mediocrity and timidity.

The villain here is, of course, the bourgeois; and it is true that these two novels of Flaubert ridicule and damn the contemporary world, taking down its pretentions by comparing it with Carthage and the Thebaid. But in these pictures of modern life there is a complexity of human values and an analysis of social processes which does not appear in the books that deal with older civilizations; and this social analysis of Flaubert's has, it seems to me, been too much disregarded—with the result that *L'Education sentimentale*, one of his most remarkable books, has been rather underestimated.

In *Madame Bovary*, Flaubert is engaged in criticizing that very longing for the exotic and the faraway which played such a large part in his own life and which led him to write *Salammbô* and *Saint Antoine*. What cuts Flaubert off from the other romantics and makes him primarily a social critic is his grim realization of the futility of dreaming about the splendors of the Orient and the brave old days of the past as an antidote to bourgeois society. Emma Bovary, the wife of a small country doctor, is always seeing herself in some other setting, imagining herself someone else. She will not face her situation as it is, and the result is that she is eventually undone by the realities she has been trying to ignore. The upshot of all Emma's yearnings for a larger and more glamorous life is that her poor little daughter, left an orphan by Emma's suicide and the death of her father, is sent to work in a cotton mill.

The socialist of Flaubert's time might perfectly have approved of this: while the romantic individualist deludes himself with unrealizable fantasies, in the attempt to evade bourgeois society, and only succeeds in destroying himself, he lets humanity fall a victim to the industrial-commercial processes, which, unimpeded by his dreaming, go on with their deadly work.

Flaubert had more in common with, and had perhaps been influenced more by, the socialist thought of his time than he would ever have allowed himself to confess. In his novels, it is never the nobility—indistinguishable for mediocrity from the bourgeoisie—but the peasants and working people whom he habitually uses as touchstones to show up the pretensions of the bourgeois. One of the most memorable scenes in *Madame Bovary* is the agricultural exhibition at which the pompous local dignitaries award a medal to an old farm servant for forty-five years of service on the same farm. Flaubert has told us about the bourgeois at length, made us listen to a long speech by a town councilor on the flourishing state of France; and now he describes the peasant—scared by the flags and drums and by the gentlemen in black coats, and not understanding what is wanted of her. Her long and bony hands, with which she has worked all her life in stable dust, lye and greasy wool, still seem dirty, although she has just washed them, and they hang at her sides half open, as if to present a testimony of toil. There is no tenderness or sadness in her face: it has a rigidity almost monastic. And her long association with animals has given her something of their placidity and dumbness. 'So she stood up before those florid bourgeois, that half-century of servitude.' And the heroine of *Un Cœur simple*, a servant who devotes her whole life to the service of a provincial family and gets not one ray of love in return, has the same sort of dignity and pathos.

It is, however, in *L'Education sentimentale* that Flaubert's account of society comes closest to socialist theory. Indeed, his presentation here of the Revolution of 1848 parallels in so striking a manner Marx's analysis of the same events in *The Eighteenth Brumaire of Louis Napoleon* that it is worth while to focus together the diverse figures of Flaubert and Marx in order to recognize how two of the most searching minds of the century, pursuing courses so apparently divergent, arrived at almost identical interpretations of the happenings of their own time.

When we do this, we become aware that Marx and Flaubert

started from very similar assumptions and that they were actuated by moral aims almost equally uncompromising. Both implacably hated the bourgeois, and both were resolved at any cost of worldly success to keep outside the bourgeois system. And Karl Marx, like Flaubert, shared to some degree the romantic bias in favor of the past. The author of *Das Kapital* can hardly, of course, be said to have had a very high opinion of any period of human history; but in comparison with the capitalist nineteenth century, he did betray a certain tenderness for Greece and Rome and the Middle Ages. He pointed out that the slavery of the ancient world had at least purchased the 'full development' of the masters, and that a certain Antipater of Thessalonica had joyfully acclaimed the invention of the water wheel for grinding corn because it would set free the female slaves who had formerly had to do this work, whereas the bourgeois economists had seen in machinery only a means for making the workers work faster and longer in order 'to transform a few vulgar and half-educated upstarts into "eminent cotton spinners," "extensive sausage makers" and "influential blacking dealers."' And he had also a soft spot for the feudal system before the nobility had revolted against the Crown and while the rights of all classes, high and low, were still guaranteed by the king. Furthermore, the feudal lords, he insisted, had spent their money lavishly when they had it, whereas it was of the essence of capitalism that the capitalist saved his money and invested it, only to save and reinvest the profits.

Karl Marx's judgment on his age was the *Communist Manifesto*. Let us examine the implications of Flaubert's political novel. The hero of *L'Education sentimentale*, Frédéric Moreau, is a sensitive and intelligent young man equipped with a moderate income; but he has no stability of purpose and is capable of no emotional integrity. He becomes aimlessly, will-lessly, involved in love affairs with different types of women and he is unable to make anything out of any of them: they simply get in each other's way till in the end he is left with nothing. Frédéric is most in love from the very beginning of the story with the virtuous oval-faced wife of a sort of glorified drummer, who is engaged in more or less shady business enterprises; but, what with his timidity and her virtue, he never gets anywhere with her—even though she loves him in return—and leaves her in the hands of the drummer. Flaubert makes it plain to us, however, that Frédéric and the vulgar husband at bottom represent the same thing: Frédéric is only the more refined as well as the more incompetent side of the middle-class mediocrity of which the dubious promoter represents the more flashy and active aspect. And so in the case of the other characters, the journalists and the artists, the members of the various political factions, the remnants of the old nobility, Frédéric finds the same shoddiness and lack of principle which are gradually revealed in himself—the same qualities which render so odious to him the banker M. Dambreuse, the type of the rich and powerful class. M. Dambreuse is always ready to trim his sails to any political party, monarchist or republican, which seems to have a chance of success. 'Most of the men who were there,' Flaubert writes of the guests at the Dambreuse house, 'had served at least four governments; and they would have sold France or the human race in order to guarantee their fortune, to spare themselves an anxiety or a difficulty, or even from simple baseness, instinctive adoration of force.' 'Je me moque des affaires!' cries Frédéric when the guests at M. Dambreuse's are complaining that criticism of the government hurts business; but he cannot give up going to the house, because he always hopes to profit by Dambreuse's investments and influence.

The only really sympathetic characters in *L'Education sentimentale* are, again, the representatives of the people. Rosanette, Frédéric's mistress, is the daughter of poor workers in the silk mills, who sold her at fifteen as mistress to an old bourgeois. Her liaison with Frédéric is a symbol of the disastrously unenduring union between the proletariat and the bourgeoisie, of which Karl Marx had written in *The Eighteenth Brumaire*. After the suppression of the workers' insurrection during the June days of '48, Rosanette gives birth to a weakly child, which dies at the same time that Frédéric is already arranging a love affair with the dull wife of the banker. Frédéric believes that Mme Dambreuse will be able to advance his interests. And bourgeois socialism gets a very Marxist treatment —save in one respect, which we shall note in a moment—in the character of Sénécal, who is eternally making himself unpleasant about communism and the welfare of the masses, for which he is ready to fight to the last barricade. When, later,

Sénécal gets a job as foreman in a pottery factory, he at once becomes a harsh little tyrant; and as soon as it begins to appear, after the putting-down of the June riots, that the reaction is sure to triumph, he decides, like certain radicals turned fascists, that the strong centralization of the government is already a kind of communism and that authority is in itself a great thing.

You have, on the other hand, the clerk Dussardier, a strapping and obtuse fellow, who is one of the few honest characters in the book. When we first see him, he has just knocked down a policeman in a political brawl on the street. Later, when the National Guard, of which Dussardier is a member, turns against the proletariat in the interests of law and order, Dussardier fells one of the insurgents from the top of a barricade and gets at the same time a bullet in the leg, thereby becoming a great hero of the bourgeois. But the poor fellow himself is unhappy. The boy that he had knocked down had wrapped the tricolor around him and shouted to the National Guard: 'Are you going to fire on your brothers?' Dussardier is not at all sure that he ought not to have been on the other side. His last appearance is at the climax of the story, constitutes, indeed, the climax: he turns up in a proletarian street riot, which the cavalry and the police are putting down. Dussardier refuses to move, crying 'Vive la République!'; and Frédéric comes along just in time to see one of the policemen kill him. Then he recognizes this policeman: it is the socialist, Sénécal.

L'Education sentimentale, unpopular when it first appeared, is likely, if we read it in youth, to prove baffling and even repellent. The title may have given the impression that we are going to get a love story, but the love affairs turn out invariably to be tepid or incomplete, and one finds oneself depressed or annoyed. Is it a satire? The characters are too close to life, and a little too well rounded, for satire. Yet they are not quite vitalized enough, not quite responsive enough, to seem the people of a straight novel. But we find that it sticks in our crop. If it is true, as Bernard Shaw has said, that *Das Kapital* makes us see the nineteenth century 'as if it were a cloud passing down the wind, changing its shape and fading as it goes,' so that we are afterwards never able to forget that 'capitalism,

with its wage slavery, is only a passing phase of social development, following primitive communism, chattel slavery and
feudal serfdom into the past'—so Flaubert's novel plants deep
in our mind an idea which we never quite get rid of: the suspicion that our middle-class society of manufacturers, businessmen and bankers, of people who live on or deal in investments,
so far from being redeemed by its culture, has ended by
cheapening and invalidating all the departments of culture, political, scientific, artistic and religious, as well as corrupting and
weakening the ordinary human relations: love, friendship and
loyalty to cause—till the whole civilization seems to dwindle.

But fully to appreciate the book, one must have had time to
see something of life and to have acquired a certain interest in
social and political dramas as distinct from personal ones. If
one rereads it in middle age, one finds that the author's tone
no longer seems quite so acrid, that one is listening to a muted
symphony of which the varied instrumentation and the pattern, the marked rhythms and the melancholy sonorities, had
been hardly perceptible before. There are no hero, no villain,
to arouse us, no clowns to entertain us, no scenes to wring our
hearts. Yet the effect is deeply moving. It is the tragedy of nobody in particular, but of the poor human race itself reduced
to such ineptitude, such cowardice, such commonness, such
weak irresolution—arriving, with so many fine notions in its
head, so many noble words on its lips, at a failure which is all
the more miserable because those who have failed in their roles
have even forgotten what roles they were cast for. We come to
understand the statement of Mr. Ford Madox Ford that he has
found it is not too much to read the book fourteen times.
Though *L'Education sentimentale* is less attractive on the surface and less exciting as a story than *Madame Bovary*, it is
certainly the book of Flaubert's which is most ambitiously
planned and into which he has tried to put most. And once we
have got the clue to the immense and complex drama which
unrolls itself behind the half-screen of the detached and monotonous style, we find it as absorbing and satisfying as a great
play or a great piece of music.

The one conspicuous respect in which Flaubert's point of
view on the events of 1848 *diverges* from that of Marx has been
thrown into special relief by the events of our own time. For

Marx, the evolution of the socialist into a proletarian-persecuting policeman would have been blamed on the bourgeois in Sénécal; for Flaubert, it is a development of socialism implicit in socialist beginnings. He distrusted, as I have shown above, the authoritarian aims of the socialists. It is Flaubert's conception that Sénécal, given his bourgeois hypocrisy, is still carrying out a socialist principle—or rather, that his behavior as a policeman and his yearnings toward socialist control are both derived from his impulse toward despotism.

We may not be prepared to conclude that the evolution of Sénécal represents the whole destiny of socialism, but we must recognize that Flaubert had here brought to attention a danger of which Marx was not aware. We have had the opportunity to see how even a socialism which has come to power as the result of a proletarian revolution can breed a political police of almost unprecedented ruthlessness—how the example of Marx himself, with his emphasis on dictatorial control rather than on democratic processes, has contributed to produce this disaster. Flaubert, who believed that the artist should rid himself of social convictions, has gauged the tendencies of a political doctrine as the greatest of doctrinaires could not; and here the attitude he proposed has been justified.

The war of 1870 was a terrible shock to Flaubert: the nervous disorders of his later years have been attributed to it. He had the Prussians in his house at Croisset and had to bury his manuscripts. When he made a trip to Paris after the Commune, he came back to the country deeply shaken. 'This would never have happened,' he said when he saw the wreck of the Tuileries, 'if they had only understood *L'Education sentimentale.*' What Flaubert meant, no doubt, was that if the French had seen the falsity of their politics, they would never have fought about them so fiercely. 'Oh, how tired I am,' he writes George Sand, 'of the ignoble worker, the inept bourgeois, the stupid peasant and the odious ecclesiastic.'

But in his letters of this period, which are more violent than ever, we see him taking a new direction. The effect of the Commune on Flaubert, as on so many of the other French intellectuals, was to bring out in him the class-conscious bourgeois. Basically bourgeois his life had always been, with his

mother and his little income. He had, like Frédéric Moreau
himself, been 'cowardly in his youth,' he wrote George Sand.
'I was *afraid* of life.' And, even moving amongst what he regarded as the grandeurs of the ancient world, he remains a
moderate Frenchman of the middle nineteenth century, who
seems to cultivate excess, systematically and with a certain self-
consciousness, in the hope of horrifying other Frenchmen.
Marcel Proust has pointed out that Flaubert's imagery, even in
books which do not deal with the bourgeois, tends to be
rather banal. It was the enduring tradition of French classicism
which had saved him from the prevailing shoddiness: by discipline and objectivity, by heroic application to the mastery of
form, he had kept the enemy at a distance. But now when a
working-class government had held Paris for two months and
a half and had wrecked monuments and shot bourgeois
hostages, Flaubert found himself as fierce against the Communards as any respectable 'grocer.' 'My opinion is,' he wrote
George Sand, 'that the whole Commune ought to have been
sent to the galleys, that those sanguinary idiots ought to have
been made to clean up the ruins of Paris, with chains around
their necks like convicts. That would have wounded *humanity*,
though. They treat the mad dogs with tenderness, but not the
people whom they have bitten.' He raises his old cry for 'justice.' Universal suffrage, that 'disgrace to the human spirit,'
must first of all be done away with; but among the elements of
civilization which must be given their due importance he now
includes 'race and even money' along with 'intelligence' and
'education.'

For the rest, certain political ideas emerge—though, as usual,
in a state of confusion. 'The mass, the majority, are always idiotic. I haven't got many convictions, but that one I hold very
strongly. Yet the mass must be respected, no matter how inept
it is, because it contains the germs of an incalculable fecundity.
Give it liberty, but not power. I don't believe in class distinctions any more than you do. The castes belong to the domain
of archeology. But I do believe that the poor hate the rich and
that the rich are afraid of the poor. That will go on forever. It
is quite useless to preach the gospel of love to either. The most
urgent need is to educate the rich, who are, after all, the
strongest.' 'The only reasonable thing to do—I always come

back to that—is a government of mandarins, provided that the
mandarins know something and even that they know a great
deal. The people is an eternal minor, and it will always (in the
hierarchy of social elements) occupy the bottom place, because
it is unlimited number, mass. It gets us nowhere to have large
numbers of peasants learn to read and no longer listen to their
priest; but it is infinitely important that there should be a great
many men like Renan and Littré who can live and be listened
to. Our salvation now is in a *legitimate aristocracy*, by which I
mean a majority which will be made up of something other
than numerals.' Renan himself and Taine were having recourse
to similar ideas of the salvation of society through an 'élite.' In
Flaubert's case, it never seems to have occurred to him that his
hierarchy of mandarins and his project for educating the rich
were identical with the notions of Saint-Simon, which he had
rejected with scorn years before on the ground that they were
too authoritarian. The Commune has stimulated in Flaubert a
demand for his own kind of despotism.

He had already written in 1869: 'It's no longer a question of
imagining the best form of government possible, because they
are all alike, but of making sure that science prevails. That is
the most urgent problem. Everything else will inevitably follow. The purely intellectual type of man has done more for the
human race than all the Saint Vincent de Pauls in the world!
And politics will remain idiotic forever so long as it does not
derive from science. The government of a country ought to be
a department of the Institute, and the least important of all.'
'Politics,' he reiterated in 1871, 'must become a positive science, as war has already become'; and, 'The French Revolution must cease to be a dogma and become part of the domain
of science, like all the rest of human affairs.' Marx and Engels
were not reasoning otherwise; but they believed, as Flaubert
could not do, in a coming-of-age of the proletariat which
would make possible the application of social science. To
Flaubert the proletariat made a certain pathetic appeal, but it
seemed to him much too stupid to act effectively in its own behalf; the Commune threw him into such a panic that he reviled
the Communards as criminals and brutes. At one moment he
writes to George Sand: 'The International may end by winning
out, but not in the way that it hopes, not in the way that

people are afraid of'; and then, two days later, 'the International will collapse, because it is on the wrong path. No ideas, nothing but envy!'

Finally, he wrote her in 1875: 'The words "religion" or "Catholicism," on the one hand, "progress," "fraternity," "democracy," on the other, no longer answer the spiritual needs of the day. The dogma of equality—a new thing—which the radicals have been crying up, has been proved false by the experiments of physiology and by history. I do not at the present time see any way of setting up a new principle, any more than of still respecting the old ones. So I search unsuccessfully for the central idea from which all the rest ought to depend.'

In the meantime, his work becomes more misanthropic. 'Never, my dear old chap,' he had written Ernest Feydeau, 'have I felt so colossal a disgust for mankind. I'd like to drown the human race under my vomit.' His political comedy, *Le Candidat*, produced in 1874, is the only one of his works which does not include a single character for whom one can feel any sympathy. The rich parvenu who is running for deputy not only degrades himself by every form of truckling and trimming in order to win the election, but sacrifices his daughter's happiness and allows himself to be cuckolded by his wife. The audiences would not have it; the actor who played the candidate came off the stage in tears. And, reading the play today, one cannot but agree with the public. It has some amusing and mordant passages, but one's gorge rises against it.

Flaubert then embarked on *Bouvard et Pécuchet*, which occupied him—with only one period of relief, when he indulged his suppressed kindliness and idealism in the relatively human *Trois Contes*—for most of the rest of his life. Here two copyists retire from their profession and set out to cultivate the arts and sciences. They make a mess of them all. The book contains an even more withering version of the events of 1848, in which the actors and their political attitudes are reduced to the scale of performing fleas. (There is one bitter scene, however, which has a terrible human force: that in which, the revolution having failed and the reaction having entrusted to the clergy the supervision of public education, the village priest visits the village schoolmaster, a freethinker who has been on the revolutionary side, and compels him, by threatening to dismiss him from the job which he needs to support his children, to consent to betray his principles by teaching catechism and sacred history.) When Bouvard and Pécuchet find at last that everything has 'cracked in their hands,' they go back to copying again. Flaubert did not live to finish the book; but he had already compiled some of the materials which he had intended to use in the second part: a collection of ridiculous statements and idiotic sentiments that Bouvard and Pécuchet were to find in the works they should copy.

This last uncompleted novel has somewhat mystified those critics who have taken it for an attack on the bourgeois like *L'Education sentimentale*—though there would not have been much point in Flaubert's simply doing the same thing again in a smaller and drier way. But M. René Dumesnil, one of the principal authorities on Flaubert, believes that *Bouvard et Pécuchet* was to have had a larger application. The anthology of 'idées reçues' was to have been not merely a credo of the bourgeois: it was to have included, also, many lapses by distinguished men of the past as well as the present, of writers, in certain cases, whom Flaubert immensely admired, and some passages, even, from Flaubert himself (in the first part of the book, it is obvious that the author is caricaturing his own ideas along with those of everybody else). Bouvard and Pécuchet, having realized the stupidity of their neighbors and discovered their own limitations, were to be left with a profound impression of the general imbecility and ignorance. They were themselves to assemble this monument to the inanity of the human mind.

If this be true—and the papers left by Flaubert seem to make his intention clear—he had lifted the blame from a social class and for the first time written a work of the type of *Gulliver's Travels*: a satire on the human race. The bourgeois has ceased to preach to the bourgeois: as the first big cracks begin to show in the structure of the nineteenth century, he shifts his complaint to the incompetence of humanity, for he is unable to believe in, or even to conceive, any non-bourgeois way out.

The Ambiguity of Henry James

A DISCUSSION of Henry James's ambiguity may appropriately begin with *The Turn of the Screw*. This story, which seems to have proved more fascinating to the general reading public than anything else of James's except *Daisy Miller*, perhaps conceals another horror behind the ostensible one. I do not know who first suggested this idea; but I believe that Miss Edna Kenton, whose insight into James is profound, was the first to write about it,* and the water-colorist Charles Demuth did a set of illustrations for the tale that were evidently based on this interpretation.

The theory is, then, that the governess who is made to tell the story is a neurotic case of sex repression, and that the ghosts are not real ghosts but hallucinations of the governess.

Let us see how the narrative runs. This narrative is supposed to have been written by the governess herself, but it begins with an introduction in which we are told something about her by a man whose sister's governess she had been after the time of the story. The youngest daughter of a poor country parson, she struck him, he explains, as 'awfully clever and nice . . . the most agreeable woman I've ever known in her position' and 'worthy of any whatever.' (Now, it is a not infrequent trick of James's to introduce sinister characters with descriptions that at first sound flattering, so this need not throw us off.) Needing work, she had come up to London to answer an advertisement and had found someone who wanted a governess for an orphaned nephew and niece. 'This prospective patron proved a gentleman, a bachelor in the prime of life, such a figure as had never risen, save in a dream or an old novel, before a fluttered, anxious girl out of a Hampshire vicarage.' It is made clear that the young woman has become thoroughly infatuated with her employer. He is charming to her and lets her have the job on condition that she will take all the responsibility and never bother him about the children;

---

*In *The Arts*, November, 1924. This issue contains also photographs of the Demuth illustrations.

and she goes down to the house in the country where they have been left with a housekeeper and some other servants.

The boy, she finds, has been sent home from school for reasons into which she does not inquire but which she colors, on no evidence at all, with a significance somehow ominous. She learns that her predecessor left, and that the woman has since died, under circumstances which are not explained but which are made in the same way to seem queer. The new governess finds herself alone with the good but illiterate housekeeper and the children, who seem innocent and charming. As she wanders about the estate, she thinks often how delightful it would be if one should come suddenly round the corner and see the master just arrived from London: there he would stand, handsome, smiling, approving.

She is never to meet her employer again, but what she does meet are the apparitions. One day when his face has been vividly in her mind, she comes out in sight of the house and, looking up, sees the figure of a man on a tower, a figure which is not the master's. Not long afterwards, the figure appears again, toward the end of a rainy Sunday. She sees him at closer range and more clearly: he is wearing smart clothes but is obviously not a gentleman. The housekeeper, meeting the governess immediately afterwards, behaves as if the governess herself were a ghost: 'I wondered why she should be scared.' The governess tells her about the apparition and learns that it answers the description of one of the master's valets, who had stayed down there and who had sometimes stolen his clothes. The valet had been a bad character, had used 'to play with the boy . . . to spoil him'; he had finally been found dead, having apparently slipped on the ice coming out of a public house—though one couldn't say he hadn't been murdered. The governess cannot help believing that he has come back to haunt the children.

Not long afterwards, she and the little girl are out on the shore of a lake, the child playing, the governess sewing. The latter becomes aware of a third person on the opposite side of the lake. But she looks first at little Flora, who is turning her back in that direction and who, she notes, has 'picked up a small flat piece of wood, which happened to have in it a little hole that had evidently suggested to her the idea of sticking in another fragment that might figure as a mast and make the thing a boat. This second morsel, as I watched her, she was very markedly and intently attempting to tighten in its place.' This somehow 'sustains' the governess so that she is able to raise her eyes: she sees a woman 'in black, pale and dreadful.' She concludes that it is the former governess. The house-keeper, questioned, tells her that this woman, although a lady, had had an affair with the valet. The boy had used to go off with the valet and then lie about it afterwards. The governess concludes that the boy must have known about the valet and the woman—the boy and girl have been corrupted by them.

Observe that there is never any reason for supposing that anybody but the governess sees the ghosts. She believes that the children see them, but there is never any proof that they do. The housekeeper insists that she does not see them; it is apparently the governess who frightens her. The children, too, become hysterical; but this is evidently the governess' doing. Observe, also, from the Freudian point of view, the signifi-cance of the governess' interest in the little girl's pieces of wood and of the fact that the male apparition first takes shape on a tower and the female apparition on a lake. There seems here to be only a single circumstance which does not fit into the hypothesis that the ghosts are mere fancies of the gov-erness: the fact that her description of the masculine ghost at a time when she knows nothing of the valet should be identifi-able as the valet by the housekeeper. And when we look back, we see that even this has perhaps been left open to a double in-terpretation. The governess has never heard of the valet, but it has been suggested to her in a conversation with the house-keeper that there has been some other male about who 'liked everyone young and pretty,' and the idea of this other person has been ambiguously confused with the master and with the master's possible interest in her, the present governess. And may she not, in her subconscious imagination, taking her cue from this, have associated herself with her predecessor and conjured up an image who wears the master's clothes but who (the Freudian 'censor' intervening) looks debased, 'like an ac-tor,' she says (would he not have to stoop to love her)? The apparition had 'straight, good features' and his appearance is described in detail. When we look back, we find that the master's appearance has never been described at all: we have merely been told that he was 'handsome,' and it comes out in the talk with the housekeeper that the valet was 'remarkably handsome.' It is impossible for us to know how much the phantom resembles the master—the governess, certainly, would never tell.

The new apparitions now begin to be seen at night, and the governess becomes convinced that the children get up to meet them, though they are able to give plausible explanations of the behavior that has seemed suspicious. The housekeeper now says to the governess that, if she is seriously worried about all this, she ought to report it to the master. The governess, who has promised not to bother him, is afraid he would think her insane; and she imagines 'his derision, his amusement, his contempt for the breakdown of my resignation at being left alone and for the fine machinery I had set in motion to attract his attention to my slighted charms.' The housekeeper, hearing this, threatens to send for the master herself; the governess threatens to leave if she does. After this, for a considerable period, the visions no longer appear.

But the children become uneasy: they wonder when their uncle is coming, and they try to communicate with him—but the governess suppresses their letters. The boy finally asks her frankly when she is going to send him to school, intimates that if he had not been so fond of her, he would have complained to his uncle long ago, declares that he will do so at once.

This upsets her: she thinks for a moment of leaving, but decides that this would be deserting them. She is now, it seems, in love with the boy. Entering the schoolroom, after her conversation with him, she finds the ghost of the other governess sitting with her head in her hands, looking 'dishonored and tragic,' full of 'unutterable woe.' At this point the new governess feels—the morbid half of her split personality is now getting the upper hand of the other—that it is she who is intruding upon the ghost: 'You terrible miserable woman!' she cries. The apparition disappears. She tells the housekeeper, who looks at her oddly, that the soul of the woman is damned and wants the little girl to share her damnation. She finally agrees to write to the master, but no sooner has she sat down to the paper than she gets up and goes to the boy's bedroom, where she finds him lying awake. When he demands to go back to school, she embraces him and begs him to tell her why he was sent away; appealing to him with what seems to her desperate tenderness but in a way that disquiets the child, she insists that all she wants is to save him. There is a sudden gust of wind—it is a stormy night outside—the casement rattles, the boy shrieks. She has been kneeling beside the bed: when she gets up, she finds the candle extinguished. 'It was I who blew it, dear!' says the boy. For her, it is the evil spirit disputing her domination. She cannot imagine that the boy may really have blown out the candle in order not to have to tell her with the light on about his disgrace at school. (Here, however, occurs a detail which is less easily susceptible of double explanation: the governess has *felt* a 'gust of frozen air' and yet sees that the window is 'tight.' Are we to suppose she merely fancied that she felt it?)

The next day, the little girl disappears. They find her beside the lake. The young woman for the first time now speaks openly to one of the children about the ghosts. 'Where, my pet, is Miss Jessel?' she demands—and immediately answers herself: 'She's there, she's there!' she cries, pointing across the lake. The housekeeper looks with a 'dazed blink' and asks where she sees anything; the little girl turns upon the governess 'an expression of hard, still gravity, an expression absolutely new and unprecedented and that appeared to read and accuse and judge me.' The governess feels her 'situation horribly crumble' now. The little girl breaks down, becomes feverish, begs to be taken away from the governess; the housekeeper sides with the child and hints that the governess had better go. But the young woman forces her, instead, to take the little girl away; and she tries to make it impossible, before their departure, for the children to see one another.

She is now left alone with the boy. A strange and dreadful scene ensues. 'We continued silent while the maid was with us —as silent, it whimsically occurred to me, as some young couple who, on their wedding-journey, at the inn, feel shy in the presence of the waiter.' When the maid has gone, and she presses him to tell her the reason for his expulsion from school, the boy seems suddenly afraid of her. He finally confesses that he 'said things'—to 'a few,' to 'those he liked.' It all sounds sufficiently harmless: there comes to her out of her 'very pity the appalling alarm of his being perhaps innocent. It was for the instant confounding and bottomless, for if he *were* innocent, what then on earth was I?' The valet appears at the window—it is 'the white face of damnation.' (But is it really the spirits who are damned or the governess who is slipping to damnation herself?) She is aware that the boy does not see it. 'No more, no more, no more!' she shrieks to the apparition. 'Is she *here?*' demands the boy in panic. (He has, in spite of the governess' efforts, succeeded in seeing his sister and has heard from her of the incident at the lake.) No, she says, it is not the woman: 'But it's at the window—straight before us. It's *there!*' . . . 'It's *he?*' then. Whom does he mean by 'he'? '"Peter Quint—you devil!" His face gave again, round the room, its convulsed supplication. "Where?"' 'What does he matter now, my own?' she cries. 'What will he *ever* matter? *I* have you, but he has lost you forever!' Then she shows him that the figure has vanished: 'There, *there!*' she says, pointing toward the window. He looks and gives a cry; she feels that he is dead in her arms. From the governess' point of view, the final disappearance of the spirit has proved too terrible a shock for the child and 'his little heart, dispossessed, has stopped'; but if we study the dialogue from the other point of view, we see that he must have taken her 'There, *there!*' as an answer to his own 'Where?' Instead of persuading him that there is nothing to be frightened of, she has, on the contrary, finally convinced him either that he has actually seen or that he is just about to see some horror. He gives 'the cry of a creature hurled over an abyss.' She has literally frightened him to death.

When one has once got hold of the clue to this meaning of *The Turn of the Screw*, one wonders how one could ever have missed it. There is a very good reason, however, in the fact that nowhere does James unequivocally give the thing away: almost everything from beginning to end can be read equally in either of two senses. In the preface to the collected edition, however, as Miss Kenton has pointed out, James does seem to want to give a hint. He asserts that *The Turn of the Screw* is 'a fairy-tale pure and simple'—but adds that the apparitions are of the order of those involved in witchcraft cases rather than of those in cases of psychic research. And he goes on to tell of his

reply to one of his readers who objected that he had not characterized the governess sufficiently. At this criticism, he says,
'One's artistic, one's ironic heart shook for the instant almost
to breaking'; and he answered: 'It was "*déjà très-joli*" . . .
please believe, the general proposition of our young woman's
keeping crystalline her record of so many intense anomalies
and obscurities—*by which I don't of course mean her explanation of them, a different matter* . . . She has "authority,"
which is a good deal to have given her . . .' The italics above
are mine: these words seem impossible to explain except on
the hypothesis of hallucination (though this is hardly consistent with the intention of writing 'a fairy-tale pure and simple').
And note too, that in the collected edition James has not included *The Turn of the Screw* in the volume with his other
ghost stories but with stories of another kind: between *The
Aspern Papers* and *The Liar*—the first a study of a curiosity
which becomes a mania and menace (to which we shall revert
in a moment), the second a study of a pathological liar, whose
wife protects his lies against the world, acting with very much
the same sort of 'authority' as the governess in *The Turn of the
Screw*.

   When we look back in the light of these hints, we are inclined
to conclude from analogy that the story is primarily intended
as a characterization of the governess: her somber and guilty
visions and the way she behaves about them seem to present,
from the moment we examine them from the obverse side of
her narrative, an accurate and distressing picture of the poor
country parson's daughter, with her English middle-class class-
consciousness, her inability to admit to herself her natural
sexual impulses and the relentless English 'authority' which
enables her to put over on inferiors even purposes which are
totally deluded and not at all in the other people's best interests.
Remember, also, in this connection, the peculiar psychology of
governesses, who, by reason of their isolated position between
the family and the servants, are likely to become ingrown and
morbid. One has heard of actual cases of women who have
frightened a household by opening doors or smashing mirrors
and who have succeeded in torturing parents by mythical stories of kidnappers. The traditional 'poltergeist' who breaks
crockery and upsets furniture has been for centuries a recurring

phenomenon. First a figure of demonology, he later became an object of psychic research, and is now a recognized neurotic type.

Once we arrive at this conception of *The Turn of the Screw*, we can see in it a new significance in its relation to Henry James's other work. We find now that it is a variation on one of his familiar themes: the thwarted Anglo-Saxon spinster; and we remember unmistakable cases of women in James's fiction who deceive themselves and others about the origins of their aims and emotions. One of the most obvious examples is that remarkable and too little read novel, *The Bostonians*. The subject of *The Bostonians* is the struggle for the daughter of a poor evangelist between a young man from the South who wants to marry her and a well-to-do Boston lady with a Lesbian interest in her. The strong-minded and strong-willed spinster is herself apparently quite in the dark as to the real character of her feeling for the girl: she is convinced that her desire to dominate her, to have her always living with her, to teach her to make speeches on women's rights and to prevent the young Southerner from marrying her, is a disinterested ardor for the Feminist cause. But the reader is not left in doubt; and Olive Chancellor is shown us in a setting of other self-deluded New England idealists.

There is a theme of very much the same kind in the short story called *The Marriages*, which amused R. L. Stevenson so hugely. But here the treatment is frankly comic. A young and rather stupid girl, described as of the unmarriageable type, but much attached to her widower father and obsessed by the memory of her mother, undertakes to set up an obstacle to her father's proposed second marriage. Her project, which she carries out, is to go to his fiancée and tell this lady that her father is an impossible character who had made her late mother miserable. She thus breaks up the projected match; and when her brother calls her a raving maniac, she is not in the least disquieted in her conviction that, by frustrating her father, she has proved faithful in her duty to her mother.

James's world is full of these women. They are not always emotionally perverted. Sometimes they are apathetic—like the charming Francie Dosson of *The Reverberator*, who, though men are always falling in love with her, seems not really ever to have grasped what courtship and marriage mean and is apparently quite content to go on all the rest of her life eating *marrons glacés* with her family in a suite in a Paris hotel. Or they are longing, these women, for affection but too inhibited or passive to obtain it for themselves, like the pathetic Milly Theale of *The Wings of the Dove*, who wastes away in Venice and whose doctor recommends a lover.

II

James's men are not precisely neurotic; but they are the masculine counterparts of his women. They have a way of missing out on emotional experience, either through timidity or prudence or through heroic renunciation.

The extreme and fantastic example is the hero of *The Beast in the Jungle*, who is finally crushed by the realization that his fate is to be the man in the whole world to whom nothing at all is to happen. Some of these characters are presented ironically: Mr. Acton of *The Europeans*, so smug and secure in his clean-swept house, deciding not to marry the baroness who has proved such an upsetting element in his little New England community, is an amusing and accurate portrait of a certain kind of careful Bostonian. Others are made sympathetic, such as the starved Lambert Strether of *The Ambassadors*, who comes to Paris too late in life.

Sometimes, however, the effect is ambiguous. Though the element of irony in Henry James is often underestimated by his readers, there are stories which leave us in doubt as to whether or not the author could foresee how his heroes would strike the reader. Is the fishy Bernard Longueville, for example, of the early novel called *Confidence* really intended for a sensitive and interesting young man or is he a prig in the manner of Jane Austen? This is not due to a beginner's uncertainty, for some of James's later heroes make us uneasy in a similar way. The very late short story *Flickerbridge*, in which a young American painter decides not to marry a young newspaper woman (the men are always deciding *not* to marry the women in Henry James) because he fears that she will spoil by publicizing it a delightful old English house, the property of a cousin of hers, which she herself has not yet seen but at which he has enjoyed visiting—this story is even harder to swallow, since it is all too evident here that the author approves of his hero.

But what are we to think of *The Sacred Fount*? This short novel, surely James's most curious production, inspired when it first appeared a parody by Owen Seaman which had a certain historical significance because the book seemed to mark the point at which James, for the general public, had definitely become unassimilable, and therefore absurd or annoying. *The Sacred Fount* was written not long after *The Turn of the Screw* and is a sort of companionpiece to it. Here we have the same setting of an English country house, the same passages of a strange and sad beauty, the same furtive subversive happenings in an atmosphere of clarity and brightness, the same dubious central figure, the same almost inscrutable ambiguity. As in the case of *The Turn of the Screw*, the fundamental question presents itself and never seems to get properly answered: What is the reader to think of the protagonist?—who is here a man instead of a woman.

It would be tedious to analyze *The Sacred Fount* as I have done *The Turn of the Screw*—and it would prove, I think, somewhat more difficult. The book is not merely mystifying but maddening. Yet I believe that if one got to the bottom of it, a good deal of light would be thrown on the author. Rebecca West, in her little book on James, has given a burlesque account of this novel as the story of how 'a week-end visitor spends more intellectual force than Kant can have used on *The Critique of Pure Reason* in an unsuccessful attempt to discover whether there exists between certain of his fellow-guests a relationship not more interesting among these vacuous people than it is among sparrows.' This visitor, who himself tells the story, observes that, among the other guests, a man and a woman he knows, both of them middle-aged, appear to have taken a new lease on life, whereas a younger man and woman appear to have been depleted. He evolves a theory about them: he imagines that the married couples have been forming new combinations and that the younger man and woman have been feeding the older pair from the sacred fount of their youth at the price of getting used up themselves.

This theory seems rather academic—and does James really mean us to accept it? Do not the narrator's imaginings serve to characterize the narrator just as the governess' ghosts serve to characterize the governess? As this detached and rather eerie individual proceeds to spy on and question his friends in order to find out whether the facts fit his hypothesis, we decide, as we do with *The Turn of the Screw*, that there are two separate stories to be kept distinct: a romance which the narrator is spinning and a reality which we are supposed to divine from what he tells us about what actually happens. We remember the narrator of *The Aspern Papers*, another prying and importunate fellow, who is finally foiled and put to rout by the old lady whose private papers he is trying by fraud to get hold of. In the case of *The Aspern Papers*, there is no uncertainty whatever as to what we are to think of the narrator: the author is quite clear that the papers were none of the journalist's business and that the rebuff he received served him right. Now, the amateur detective of *The Sacred Fount* is also foiled and rebuffed, and in very much the same manner, by one of his recalcitrant victims. 'My poor dear, you *are* crazy, and I bid you good-night!' she says to him at the end of the story. 'Such a last word,' the narrator remarks, 'the word that put me altogether nowhere—was too inacceptable not to prescribe afresh that prompt test of escape to other air for which I had earlier in the evening seen so much reason. I *should* certainly never again, on the spot, quite hang together, even though it wasn't really that I hadn't three times her method. What I too fatally lacked was her tone.' But *why* did he lack her tone?—*why* would he not hang together? What view are we supposed to take of the whole exploit of this singular being?

Mr. Wilson Follett, the only writer, so far as I know, who has given special attention to *The Sacred Fount*,* believes that the book is a parable—even a conscious parody—of James's own role as an artist. The narrator may or may not have been right as to the actual facts of the case. The point is that, in elaborating his theory, he has constructed a work of art, and that you cannot test the validity of works of art by checking them

* *Henry James's 'Portrait of Henry James'* in the *New York Times Book Review*, August 23, 1936. (Since my own essay was first written, Mr. Edward Sackville West, in the *New Statesman and Nation* of October 4, 1947, has taken issue with the views here expressed in the best defense of this book I have seen.)

against actuality. The kind of reality that art achieves, made up of elements abstracted from experience and combined in a new way by the artist, would be destroyed by a collision with the actual, and the artist would find himself blocked.

Now it may very well be true that James has put himself into *The Sacred Fount*—that he has intended some sort of fable about the brooding imaginative mind and the material with which it works. But it seems to me that Mr. Follett's theory assumes on James's part a conception of artistic truth which would hardly be worthy of him. After all, the novelist must pretend to know what people are actually up to, however much he may rearrange actuality; and it is not clear in *The Sacred Fount* whether the narrator really knows what he is talking about. If the book is, then, merely a parody, what is the point of the parody? Why should James have represented the artist as defeated by the breaking-in of life?

The truth is, I believe, that Henry James was not clear about the book in his own mind. Already, with *The Turn of the Screw*, he has carried his ambiguous procedure to a point where we almost feel that the author does not want the reader to get through to the hidden meaning. See his curious replies in his letters to correspondents who write him about the story: when they challenge him with leading questions, he seems to give evasive answers, dismissing the tale as a mere 'pot-boiler,' a mere *jeu d'esprit*. There was no doubt in *The Bostonians*, for example, as to what view the reader was intended to take of such a character as Olive Chancellor: Olive, though tragic perhaps, is definitely unhealthy and horrid, and she is vanquished by Basil Ransom. But James does leave his readers uncomfortable as to what they are to think of the governess. And now, in *The Sacred Fount*, we do not know whether the week-end guest, though he was unquestionably obnoxious to the other guests, is intended to be taken as one of the élite, a fastidious, highly civilized sensibility, or merely as a little bit cracked and a bore. The man who tried to get the Aspern papers was a fanatic, a cad and a nuisance; but many of James's inquisitive observers who never take part in the action are presented as superior people, and Henry James had confessed to being an inquisitive observer himself. Ambiguity was certainly growing on him. It was eventually to pass all bounds in those scenes in his later novels (of which the talks in *The Turn of the Screw* between the housekeeper and the governess are only comparatively mild examples) in which he compels his characters to carry on long conversations with each of the interlocutors always mistaking the other's meaning and neither ever yielding to the impulse to say one of the obvious things that would clear the situation up.

What if the hidden theme of *The Sacred Fount* is simply sex again? What if the real sacred fount, from which the narrator's acquaintances have been drawing their new vitality, is love, sexual love, instead of youth? They have something which he has not had, know something which he does not know; and, lacking the clue of experience, he can only misunderstand them and elaborate pedantic hypotheses; while they, having the forces of life on their side, are in a position to frighten him away. This theory may be dubious, also; but there is certainly involved in *The Sacred Fount*, whether or not Henry James quite meant to put it there, the conception of a man shut out from love, condemned to peep at other people's activities and to speculate about them rather barrenly, who will be shocked and put to rout when he touches the live current of human relations.

Hitherto, as I have said, it has usually been plain what James wanted us to think of his characters; but now there appears in his work a relatively morbid element which is not always handled objectively and which seems to have invaded the storyteller himself. It is as if at this point he had taken to dramatizing the frustrations of his own life without quite being willing to confess it, without fully admitting it even to himself.

But before we go further with this line of inquiry, let us look at Henry James in another connection.

III

Who *are* these characters of James's about whom we come to be less certain as to precisely what we ought to think?

The type of Henry James's observers and sometimes of his heroes is the cultivated American bourgeois, like Henry James himself, who lives on an income derived from some form of business activity, usually left rather vague, but who has rarely played any part in the efforts which have created the business.

These men turn their backs on the commercial world; they disdain its vulgarity and dullness, and they attempt to enrich their experience through the society and art of Europe. But they bring to these the bourgeois qualities of timidity, prudence, primness, the habits of mind of a puritan morality, which, even when they wish to be men of the world, make it too easy for them to be disconcerted. They wince alike at the brutalities of the aristocracy and at the coarseness of the working class; they shrink most of all from the 'commonness' of the less polished bourgeoisie, who, having acquired their incomes more recently, are not so far advanced in self-improvement. The women have the corresponding qualities: they are innocent, conventional and rather cold—sometimes they suffer from Freudian complexes or a kind of arrested development, sometimes they are neglected or cruelly cheated by the men to whom they have given their hearts. And even when James's central characters are English, they assimilate themselves to these types.

It is enlightening in this connection to compare James's point of view with Flaubert's. The hero of *L'Education sentimentale* is a perfect Henry James character: he is sensitive, cautious, afraid of life; he lives on a little income and considers himself superior to the common run. But Flaubert's attitude toward Frédéric Moreau is devastatingly ironic. Frédéric has his aspects of pathos, his occasional flashes of spirit: but Flaubert is quite emphatic in his final judgment of Frédéric. He considers Frédéric a worm.

Now, James has his own kind of irony, but it is not Flaubert's kind. Frédéric Moreau, in a sense, is the hero of many of James's novels, and you can see how the American's relation to him usually differs from the Frenchman's if you compare certain kinds of scenes which tend to recur in Henry James with certain scenes in *L'Education sentimentale* of which they sometimes seem like an echo: those ominous situations in which we find the sensitive young man either immersed in some sort of gathering or otherwise meeting successively a number of supposed friends, more worldly and unscrupulous persons, who are obviously talking over his head, acting behind his back, without his being able, in his innocence, quite to make out what they are up to. You have this same situation, as I say, in James and in Flaubert; but the difference is that, whereas with James the young man is made wondering and wistful and is likely to turn out a pitiful victim, with Flaubert he is quietly and cruelly made to look like a fool and is as ready to double-cross these other people who seem to him so inferior to himself as they are to double-cross him.

In this contrast between Flaubert's treatment of Frédéric Moreau and James's treatment of, say, Hyacinth Robinson in *The Princess Casamassima* is to be found perhaps one of the reasons for James's resentment of Flaubert. James had known Flaubert, had read him when young, had obviously been impressed by his work; he had it in common with the older man that he wanted to give dignity and integrity to the novel of modern life by imposing on it rigorous esthetic form. Yet there is something about Flaubert that sticks in his crop, and he keeps up a sort of running quarrel with him, returning to the subject again and again in the course of his critical writing. But though it is plain that James cannot help admiring the author of *Madame Bovary*, he usually manages before he has done to give the impression of belittling him—and he is especially invidious on the subject of *L'Education sentimentale*. His great complaint is that Flaubert's characters are intrinsically so ignoble that they do not deserve to be treated at length or to have so much art expended on them and that there must have been something wrong with Flaubert for him ever to have supposed that they did. James does not seem to understand that Flaubert *intends* all his characters to be 'middling' and that the greatness of his work arises from the fact that it constitutes a criticism of something bigger than they are. James praises the portrait of Mme Arnoux: let us thank God, at least, he exclaims, that Flaubert was able here to command the good taste to deal delicately with a fine-grained woman! He does not seem to be aware that Mme Arnoux is treated as ironically as any of the other characters—that the virtuous bourgeois wife with her inhibitions and superstitions is pathetic only as a part of the failure of a civilization. Henry James mistakes Mme Arnoux for a refined American woman and he is worried because Frédéric isn't one of his own American heroes, quietly vibrating and scrupulously honorable. Yet it probably makes him uncomfortable to feel that Flaubert is flaying remorselessly the squeamish young man of this type; and it may be that

Henry James's antagonism to Flaubert has something to do with the fact that the latter's all-permeating criticism of the pusillanimity of the bourgeois soul has touched Henry James himself. The protagonists of the later James are always regretting having lived too meagerly; and James distills from these non-participants all the sad self-effacing nobility, all the fine wan beauty, they are good for. Flaubert extracts something quite different from Frédéric Moreau—a kind of acrid insecticide: when Frédéric and his friend, both middle-aged by now, recall at the end of the book their first clumsy and frightened visit to a brothel as the best that life has had to offer them, it is a damnation of their whole society.

But there was another kind of modern society which Gustave Flaubert did not know and which Henry James did. Henry James was himself that new anomalous thing, an American. He had, to be sure, lived a good deal in Europe both in childhood and early manhood, and he had to a considerable extent become imbued with the European point of view—so that the monuments of antiquity and feudalism, the duchesses and princesses and princes who seem to carry on the feudal tradition, are still capable of having the effect for him of making modern life look undistinguished. But the past, in the case of James, does not completely dwarf the present, as the vigil of Flaubert's Saint Anthony and the impacts of his pagan armies diminish Frédéric Moreau. The American in Henry James asserts himself insistently against Europe. After all, Frédéric Moreau and the respectable Mme Arnoux are the best people of Albany and Boston!—but in America they are not characters in Flaubert. Their scruples and renunciations have a real moral value here—for Frédéric Moreau at home possesses a real integrity; and when these best people come over to Europe, they judge the whole thing in a quite new way. James speaks somewhere of his indignation at an Englishwoman's saying to him in England, in connection with something they were discussing: 'That is true of the aristocracy, but in one's own class it is quite different.' As an American and the grandson of a millionaire, it had never occurred to James that anyone could consider him a middle-class person. When Edith Wharton accused him in his later years of no longer appreciating Flaubert and demanded of him why Emma Bovary, the choice of whom as a heroine he had always deplored, was not just as good a subject for fiction as Tolstoy's Anna Karenina, he replied: 'Ah, but one paints the fierce passions of a luxurious aristocracy; the other deals with the petty miseries of a little bourgeoise in a provincial town!' But if Emma Bovary is small potatoes, what about Daisy Miller? Why, Daisy Miller is an American girl! Emma Bovary has her longings and her debts and her adulteries, but she is otherwise a conventional person, she remains in her place in the social scheme even when she dreams of rising out of it. So great is the prestige for her of the local nobility that when she goes to the château for the ball, the very sugar in the sugar bowl seems to her whiter and finer than the sugar she has at home; whereas a girl like Daisy Miller as well as one like Isabel Archer represents a human species that had been bred outside of Europe and that cannot be accommodated or judged inside the European frame. When this species comes back to Europe, it tends to disregard the social system. Europe is too much for Daisy Miller: she catches cold in the Coliseum, where according to European conventions she oughtn't to have been at that hour. But the great popularity of her story was certainly due to the fact that her creator had somehow conveyed the impression that her spirit went marching on.

There evidently went on in the mind of James a debate that was never settled between the European and the American points of view; and this conflict may have had something to do with his inability sometimes to be clear as to what he wants us to think of a certain sort of person. It is quite mistaken to talk as if James had uprooted himself from America in order to live in England. He had traveled so much from his earliest years that he had never had real roots anywhere. His father had himself been a wandering intellectual, who had oscillated back and forth between Europe and the United States; and even in America the Jameses were always oscillating between New York and Boston. They were not New Englanders even by ancestry, but New Yorkers of Irish and Scotch-Irish stock, and they had none of the tight New England local ties—they always came to Boston from a larger outside world and their point of view about it was objective and often rather ironical. To this critical attitude on Henry's part was probably partly due the failure of *The Bostonians*; and this failure seems to mark the moment of his abandonment of his original ambition of becoming the American Balzac, as it does that of his taking up his residence in England and turning, for the subjects of his fiction, from the Americans to the English. He had been staying for some time in London, and he found he liked living in London better than in New York or New England, better than in Paris or Rome. His parents in the States had just died, and his sister came over to join him.

IV

And this brings us to what seems to have been the principal crisis in Henry James's life and work. We know so little about his personal life from any other source than himself, and even in his memoirs and letters he tells us so little about his emotions, that it is impossible to give any account of it save as it reflects itself in his writings.

Up to the period of his playwriting, his fiction has been pretty plain sailing. He has aimed to be a social historian, and, in a limited field, he has succeeded. His three long novels of the later eighties—*The Bostonians, The Princess Casamassima* and *The Tragic Muse*—are, indeed, as social history, his most ambitious undertakings, and from the conventional point of view—that of the reporting of the surface of life—by far his most successful. The first hundred pages of *The Bostonians*, with the arrival of the young Southerner in Boston and his first contacts with the Boston reformers, is, in its way, one of the most masterly things that Henry James ever did. *The Princess Casamassima*, with its opening in the prison and its revolutionary exiles in London, deals with issues and social contrasts of a kind that James had never before attempted. The familiar criticism of Henry James—the criticism made by H. G. Wells: that he had no grasp of politics or economics—does not, in fact, hold true of these books. Here his people do have larger interests and functions aside from their personal relations: they have professions, missions, practical aims; and they also engage in more drastic action than in his novels of any other period. Basil Ransom pursues Verena Tarrant and rescues her from the terrible Olive Chancellor; Hyacinth Robinson pledges himself to carry out a political assassination, then commits suicide instead; Miriam Rooth makes her career as a great actress. One finds in all three of these novels a will to participate in life, to play a responsible role, quite different from the passive ones of the traveler who merely observes or the victim who merely suffers, that had seemed characteristic of James's fiction. Up to a point these books are brilliant.

But there is a point—usually about half way through—at which every one of these novels begins strangely to run into the sands; the excitement of the story lapses at the same time as the treatment becomes more abstract and the color fades from the picture. The ends are never up to the beginnings. This is most obvious—even startling—in *The Tragic Muse*, the first volume of which, as we read it, makes us think that it must be James's best novel, so solid and alive does it seem. Here are areas of experience and types of a kind that James has never before given us: a delicately comic portrait of a retired parliamentarian, which constitutes, by implication, a criticism of British Liberal politics; a really charged and convincing scene between a man and a woman (Nick Dormer and Julia Dallow) in place of the mild battledore-and-shuttlecock that we are accustomed to getting from James; and, in Miriam Rooth, the Muse, a character who comes nearer to carrying the author out of the bounds of puritan scruples and prim prejudices on to the larger and more dangerous stage of human creative effort than any other he has hitherto drawn. Here at last we are among complete people, who have the appetites and ambitions that we recognize—and in comparison, the characters of his earlier works only seem real in a certain convention. Then suddenly the story stops short: after the arrival of Miriam in London, *The Tragic Muse* is almost a blank. Of the two young men who have been preoccupied with Miriam, one renounces her because she will not leave the stage and the other doesn't, apparently, fall in love with her. Miriam herself, to be sure, makes a great success as an actress, but we are never taken into her life, we know nothing at first hand of her emotions. The only decisions that are looming are negative ones, and the author himself seems to lose interest.

These earlier chapters of *The Tragic Muse* are the high point of the first part of James's career, after which something snaps. He announces that he will write no more long novels, but only fiction of shorter length; and it may be that he has become aware of his failure in his longer novels to contrive the mounting-up to a climax of intensity and revelation which, in order to be effective, this kind of full-length fiction demands. At any rate, he applied himself to writing plays, and for five years he produced little else; but one wonders when one reads these plays—in the two volumes he called *Theatricals*—why James should have sacrificed not only his time but also all the strength of his genius for work that was worse than mediocre. He had had reason to complain at this period that he had difficulty in selling his fiction, and he confessed that his plays were written in the hope of a popular success, and that they were intended merely as entertainment and were not to be taken too seriously—seeking to excuse that which 'would otherwise be inexplicable' by invoking 'the uttermost regions of dramatic amiability, the bland air of the little domestic fairy-tale.' Yet the need for money and even for fame is surely an insufficient explanation for the phenomenon of a novelist of James's gifts almost entirely abandoning the art in which he has perfected himself to write plays that are admittedly trivial.

That there was something insufficient and unexplained about James's emotional life seems to appear unmistakably from his novels. I believe that it may be said that there have not been up to this point any consummated love affairs in his fiction—that is, none among the principal characters and while the action of the story is going on; and this deficiency must certainly have contributed to his increasing loss of hold on his readers. It is not merely that he gave in *The Bostonians* an unpleasant picture of Boston, and in *The Tragic Muse*, on the whole, a discouraging picture of the English; it is not merely that *The Princess Casamassima* treated a social-revolutionary subject from a point of view that was non-political and left neither side a moral advantage. It was not merely that he was thus at this period rather lost between America and England. It was also that you cannot enchant an audience with stories about men wooing women in which the parties either never get together or are never seen functioning as lovers. And you will particularly dampen your readers with a story—*The Tragic Muse*—which deals with two men and a girl but in which neither man ever gets her. There is, as I have said, in *The*

Tragic Muse, one of his more convincing man-and-woman relationships. Julia Dallow is really female and she behaves like a
woman with Nick Dormer; but here the woman's political ambitions get between Nick and her, so that this, too, never comes
to anything: here the man, again, must renounce. (In Henry
James's later novels, these healthily female women—Kate Croy
and Charlotte Stant—are to take on a character frankly sinister.) Years later, Henry James explained in his preface to *The
Tragic Muse* that the prudery, in the eighties, of the American
magazines had made it impossible for Miriam Rooth to follow
the natural course of becoming Nick Dormer's mistress; and
certainly the skittishness of a public that was scandalized by
Jude the Obscure is not to be underestimated. But, after all,
Hardy did write about Jude, and Meredith about Lord
Ormont and his Aminta, and let the public howl; and it might
well have enhanced Henry James's reputation—to which he
was by no means indifferent—if he had done the same thing
himself. Problems of sexual passion in conflict with convention
and law were beginning to be subjects of burning interest. But
it is probable that James had by this time—not consciously,
perhaps, but instinctively—come to recognize his unfittedness
for dealing with them and was far too honest to fake.

One feels about the episode of his playwriting that it was an
effort to put himself over, an effort to make himself felt, as he
had never succeeded in doing. His brother William James wrote
home in the summer of 1889, at the beginning of this playwriting period, that Henry, beneath the 'rich sea-weeds and
rigid barnacles and things' of 'strange heavy alien manners and
customs' with which he had covered himself like a 'marine
crustacean,' remained the 'same dear old, good, innocent and
at bottom very powerless-feeling Harry.' He had seriously injured his back in an accident in his boyhood, and it was necessary for him still, in his forties, to lie down for regular rests.
And now it is as if he were trying to put this 'broken back,' as
he once called it, into making an impression through the
drama as he had never been able to put it into a passion. His
heroine Miriam Rooth has just turned away from the Philistine
English world which rejects her and taken into the theater the
artist's will with which she is to conquer that world; and her
creator is now to imitate her.

But his plays were either not produced or not well received. At the first night of *Guy Domville* (January 5, 1895), he ran foul of a gallery of hooligans, who booed and hissed him when he came before the curtain. Their displeasure had evidently been partly due to a feeling of having been let down by one of James's inevitable scenes of abdication of the lover's role: the hero, at the end of the play, had rejected a woman who adored him and an estate he had just inherited in order to enter the Church. These five years of unsuccessful playwriting had put Henry James under a strain, and this was the final blow. When he recovers from his disappointment, he is seen to have passed through a crisis.

Now he enters upon a new phase, of which the most obvious feature is a subsidence back into himself. And now sex *does* appear in his work—even becoming a kind of obsession—in a queer and left-handed way. We have *The Turn of the Screw* and *The Sacred Fount*; *What Maisie Knew* and *In the Cage*. There are plenty of love affairs now and plenty of irregular relationships, but there are always thick screens between them and us; illicit appetites, maleficent passions, now provide the chief interest, but they are invariably seen from a distance.

For the Jamesian central observer who has become a special feature of his fiction—the reflector by whose consciousness is registered all that we know of events—has undergone a diminution. This observer is less actively involved and is rarely a complete and a full-grown person: we have a small child who watches her elders, a female telegraph operator who watches the senders of telegrams and lives vicariously through them, a week-end guest who seems not to exist in any other capacity whatever except that of week-end guest and who lives vicariously through his fellow guests. The people who surround this observer tend to take on the diabolic values of the specters of *The Turn of the Screw*, and these diabolic values are almost invariably connected with sexual relations that are always concealed and at which we are compelled to guess. The innocent Nanda Brookenham of *The Awkward Age*, a work of the same period and group, is hemmed in by a whole host of goblins who beckon and hint and whisper and exhale a creepy atmosphere of scandal. It has for the time become difficult for James to sustain his old objectivity: he has relapsed into a dreamy interior world, where values are often uncertain and where it is not even possible any longer for him to judge his effect on his audience—on the audience which by this time has shrunk to a relatively small band of initiated readers. One is dismayed, in reading his comments on *The Awkward Age*, which he regarded as a technical triumph, to see that he was quite unaware of the inhuman aspect of the book which makes it a little repellent. The central figure of *The Sacred Fount* may perhaps have been presented ironically; but James evidently never suspected how the ordinary reader would feel about this disemboweled gibbering crew who hover around Nanda Brookenham with their shadowy sordid designs.

This phase of Henry James's development is also distinguished by a kind of expansion of the gas of the psychological atmosphere—an atmosphere which has now a special flavor. With *What Maisie Knew*, James's style, as Ford Madox Ford says, first becomes a little gamey. He gets rid of some of his old formality and softens his mechanical hardness; and, in spite of the element of abstraction which somewhat dilutes and dims his writing at all periods, his language becomes progressively poetic.

With all this, his experience of playwriting has affected his fiction in a way which does not always seem quite to the good. He had taken as models for his dramatic work the conventional 'well made' French plays of the kind that Bernard Shaw was ridiculing as 'clock-work mice'; and when he took to turning his plays into novels (*Covering End* and *The Outcry*), their frivolity and artificiality became even more apparent (it was only in *The Other House*, which he also made into a novel, that he had dared to be at all himself, and had produced a psychological thriller that had something in common with *The Turn of the Screw*; *Guy Domville*, too, was evidently more serious, but the text has never been published). Even after he had given up the theater, he went on casting his novels in dramatic form—with the result that *The Awkward Age*, his supreme effort in this direction, combines a lifeless trickery of logic with the equivocal subjectivity of a nightmare.

In this period also originates a tendency on James's part to exploit his sleight-of-hand technique for the purpose of diverting attention from the inadequacies of his imagination. This has imposed on some of James's critics and must of course have imposed on James himself. One can see from his comments at various periods how a method like that of Tolstoy became more and more distasteful to him. Tolstoy, he insisted, was all over the shop, never keeping to a single point of view but entering the minds of all his characters and failing to exercise sufficiently the principle of selection, and James was even reckless enough, in his preface to *The Tragic Muse*, to class *War and Peace* with *Les Trois Mousquetaires* and *The Newcomes*, as 'large loose baggy monsters, with . . . queer elements of the accidental and the arbitrary'—though the truth was, of course, that Tolstoy had spent six years on his novel, had reduced it by a third of its original length and made of every little scene a masterpiece of economy and relevance. He speaks in the same preface of the difficulty he has found himself in handling a complex subject—though it is only a problem here of going into the minds of two of the characters. The truth is, of course, that the question of whether or not the novelist enters into a variety of points of view has nothing necessarily to do with his technical mastery of his materials or even with his effect of concentration. Precisely one trouble with *The Tragic Muse* is that James does not get inside Miriam Rooth; and if he fails even to try to do so, it is because, in his experience of the world and his insight into human beings, he is inferior to a man like Tolstoy. So, in *The Wings of the Dove*, the 'messengering,' as the drama courses say, of Kate Croy's final scene with Merton Densher is probably due to James's increasing incapacity for dealing directly with scenes of emotion rather than to the motives he alleges. And so his recurring complaint that he is unable to do certain things because he can no longer find space within his prescribed limits has the look of another excuse. Henry James never seems aware of the amount of space he is wasting through the long abstract formulations that do duty for concrete details, the unnecessary circumlocutions and the gratuitous meaningless verbiage—the *as it were's* and *as we may say's* and all the rest—all the words with which he pads out his sentences and which themselves are probably symptomatic of a tendency to stave off his main problems, since they are a part of the swathing process with which he makes his embarrassing subjects always seem to present smooth contours.

V

But after this a new process sets in. In *The Ambassadors*, *The Wings of the Dove* and *The Golden Bowl*, the psychological atmosphere thickens and fills up the structure of the novel, so carefully designed and contrived, with the fumes of the Jamesian gas; and the characters, though apprehended as recognizable human entities, loom obscurely through a phantasmagoria of dream-like similes and metaphors that seem sometimes, as Miss West has said, more vivid and solid than the settings.

But a positive element reappears. The novels of *The Awkward Age* period were written not merely from an international limbo between Europe and the United States but in the shadow of defeat and self-doubt. Yet in these queer and neurotic stories (some of them, of course—*The Turn of the Screw* and *What Maisie Knew*—among James's masterpieces) moral values begin to reassert themselves. These present themselves first in an infantile form, in Maisie Farrange and in Nanda Brookenham, whose innocence is a touchstone for the other characters. Then, in the longer novels that follow, embodied in figures of a more mature innocence, they come completely to dominate the field. These figures are now always Americans. We have returned to the pattern of his earlier work, in which the typical dramatic conflict took place between glamorous people who were worldly and likely to be wicked, and people of superior scruples who were likely to be more or less homely, and in which the glamorous characters usually represented Europe and the more honorable ones the United States. In those earlier novels of James, it had not been always—as in *The Portrait of a Lady*—the Americans who were left with the moral advantage; the Europeans—as in the story with that title—had been sometimes made the more sympathetic. But in these later ones it is always the Americans who command admiration and respect—where they are pitted against a fascinating Italian prince, a charming and appealing French lady, and a formidable group of rapacious English. Yes: there *was* a beauty and there was also a power in the goodness of these naïve but sensitive people—there *were* qualities which did not figure in Flaubert's or Thackeray's picture. This *was* something new in the world which did not fit into the formulas of Europe. What if poor Lambert Strether *had* missed in Woollett, Mass., many things he would have enjoyed in Paris: he had brought to Paris something it lacked. And the burden of James's biography of William Wetmore Story, which came out at the same time as these novels, the early years of the century—rather different from that of his study of Hawthorne, published in 1880—is that artists like Story who left Boston for Europe eventually found themselves in a void and might better have stayed at home.

And now Henry James revisits America, writes *The American Scene*, and, for the first time since the rejected *Bostonians*, lays the scene of a novel—*The Ivory Tower*, which he dropped and did not live to finish—entirely in the United States.

In another unfinished novel, the fantasia called *The Sense of the Past*, he makes a young contemporary American go back into eighteenth-century England. Here the Jamesian ambiguity serves an admirable artistic purpose. Is it the English of the past who are ghosts or the American himself who is only a dream?—will the moment come when *they* will vanish or will he himself cease to exist? And, as before, there is a question of James's own asking at the bottom of the ambiguity: Which is real—America or Europe?—a question which was apparently to be answered by the obstinate survival of the American in the teeth of the specters who would drag him back. (It is curious, by the way, to compare *The Sense of the Past* with Mark Twain's *Connecticut Yankee*: the two books have a good deal in common.)

Yes: in spite of the popular assumption, founded on his expatriation and on his finally becoming a British citizen, it is the ideals of the United States which triumph in James's work. His warmest tributes to American genius come out of these later years. Though he could not, in *Notes of a Son and Brother*, resist the impulse to remove references to Lincoln as 'old Abe' from William James's early letters of the wartime, this autobiographical novel contains pages on Lincoln's death of a touching appreciation and pride. 'It was vain to say,' he writes of Andrew Johnson, of whom he declares that the American people felt him unworthy to represent them, 'that we had deliberately invoked the "common" in authority and must drink the wine we had drawn. No countenance, no salience of aspect

nor composed symbol, could superficially have referred itself
less than Lincoln's mold-smashing mask to any mere matter-
of-course type of propriety; but his admirable unrelated head
had itself revealed a type—as if by the very fact that what made
in it for roughness of kind looked out only less than what
made in it for splendid final stamp; in other words for com-
manding Style.' And of the day when the news reached
Boston: 'I was fairly to go in shame of its being my birthday.
These would have been the hours of the streets if none others
had been—when the huge general gasp filled them like a great
earth-shudder and people's eyes met people's eyes without the
vulgarity of speech. Even this was, all so strangely, part of the
lift and the swell, as tragedy has but to be of a pure enough
strain and a high enough connection to sow with its dark hand
the seed of greater life. The collective sense of what had occurred was of a sadness too noble not somehow to inspire, and
it was truly in the air that, whatever we had as a nation produced or failed to produce, we could at least gather round this
perfection of classic woe.' In *The American Scene*, he writes of
Concord: 'We may smile a little as we "drag in" Weimar, but I
confess myself, for my part, much more satisfied than not by
our happy equivalent, "in American money," for Goethe and
Schiller. The money is a potful in the second case as in the first,
and if Goethe, in the one, represents the gold and Schiller the
silver, I find (and quite putting aside any bimetallic prejudice)
the same good relation in the other between Emerson and
Thoreau. I open Emerson for the same benefit for which I
open Goethe, the sense of moving in large intellectual space,
and that of the gush, here and there, out of the rock, of the
crystalline cupful, in wisdom and poetry, in *Wahrheit* and
Dichtung; and whatever I open Thoreau for (I needn't take
space here for the good reasons) I open him oftener than I
open Schiller.' Edith Wharton says that he used to read Walt
Whitman aloud 'in a mood of subdued ecstasy' and with
tremendous effect on his hearers.

James's visit to the United States in 1904–05, after nearly a
quarter of a century's absence, had been immensely exciting to
him. He had plunged into his sensations with a gusto, explored everything accessible with a voracity and delivered himself of positive ideas (the presence and the opinions of William

must partly have stimulated this, as a passage in Henry's note-
books suggests) at a rate that seems almost to transform the
personality of the modest recluse of Lamb House, with his addiction to the crepuscular and the dubious. One realizes now
for the first time, as he was realizing for the first time himself,
how little of America he had seen before. He had never been
West or South. He had known only New York, Boston and
Newport. But he now traveled all the way south to Florida and
all the way west to California, apparently almost drunk with
new discoveries and revelations. His account of his trip in *The
American Scene*, published in 1907, has a magnificent solidity
and brilliance quite different from the vagueness of impressionism which had been making the backgrounds of his novels
a little unsatisfactory; and the criticism of the national life shows
an incisiveness, a comprehensiveness, a sureness in knowing his
way about, a grasp of political and economic factors, that one
might not have expected of Henry James returning to Big
Business America. It is probably true that James—as W. H.
Auden has suggested—had never approached Europe with anything like the same boldness. In Italy, France, or England, he
had been always a 'passionate pilgrim' looking for the picturesque. But with long residence abroad, as he tells us, the romance and the mystery had evaporated, and America, of which
he had been hearing such sensational if sometimes dismaying
news, had in its turn been coming to seem romantic. What is
exhilarating and most surprising is the old-fashioned American
patriotism which—whether he is admiring or indignant—
throbs in every pulse of *The American Scene*. It would be difficult to understand why James should have been credited in the
United States with being an immoderate Anglophile—even if
the implications of *The Wings of the Dove* had been missed—
after *The American Scene* had appeared, if one did not have to
allow for the shallowness of professional criticism and the stupid indifference of the public that marked that whole period in
the United States. The truth is that he returns to America with
something like an overmastering homesickness that makes
him desire to give it the benefit of every doubt, to hope for the
best from what shocks or repels him. He is not at the mercy of
his wincings from the elements that are alien and vulgar. The
flooding-in of the new foreign population, though he has to

make an effort to accept it, does not horrify him or provoke him to sneers, as it did that professional explorer but professional Anglo-Saxon, Kipling—after all, the James family themselves had not been long in the United States and were so nearly pure Irish that Henry speaks of their feeling a special interest in the only set of their relatives that represented the dominant English blood. He thinks it a pity that the immigrants should be standardized by barren New York, but he is gratified at the evidence that America has been able to give them better food and clothing. The popular consumption of candy, in contrast to the luxury and privilege that sweets have always been in Europe, seems to please him when he attends the Yiddish theater. He is angry over the ravages of commercialism—the exploitation of real-estate values and the destruction of old buildings and landmarks that followed the Civil War—but he is optimistic enough to hope that the time is approaching when the national taste will have improved sufficiently to check this process. And in the meantime at Mount Vernon he feels awe at the memory of Washington, invokes in the Capitol the American eagle as a symbol of the republican idealism, and writes one of the most eloquent and most moving pages to be found in the whole range of his work in celebration of the Concord bridge and the shot heard round the world. It is as if, after the many books which James had written in countries not native to him, under the strain of maintaining an attitude that should be rigorously international, yet addressing himself to an audience that rarely understood what he was trying to do and in general paid little attention to him—it is as if, after a couple of decades of this, his emotions had suddenly been given scope, his genius for expression liberated, as if his insight had been confronted with a field on which it could play without diffidence; and he produced in *The American Scene*, one of the very best books about modern America.

The point is that James's career—given his early experience of Europe—had inevitably been affected by the shift in American ambitions which occurred after the Civil War. It has been shown by Mr. Van Wyck Brooks in his literary history of the United States how the post-Revolutionary American had been stimulated—much like the Russian of the first years of the Soviet regime—to lay the foundations for a new humanity, set free from the caste-barriers and the poverties of Europe, which should return to the mother-continent only to plunder her for elements of culture that might be made to serve the new aim; but how, with the growth of industry, the ascendancy of business ideals, the artists and the other intellectuals found it difficult to function at home and discouraged with the United States, more and more took refuge in Europe. James explains, in *The American Scene*, that the residence abroad of Americans like himself, of small incomes and non-acquisitive tastes, had by this time become merely a matter of having found oneself excreted by a society with whose standards of expenditure one was not in a position to keep up, at the same time that one could not help feeling humiliated at being thrust by it below the salt. But though his maturity belonged to this second phase, he had grown up during the first—the brothers of his grandmother James had fought in the Revolution and been friends of Lafayette and Washington, and his James grandfather had come to America from Ireland and made a fortune of three million dollars—and he had never lost the democratic idealism, the conviction of having scored a triumph and shown the old world a wonder, that were characteristic of it. This appears at the beginning of James's career in the name of 'the American,' Newman, and at the end in his magnificent phrase about Lincoln's 'mold-smashing mask.'

VI

But Henry James is a reporter, not a prophet. With less politics even than Flaubert, he can but chronicle the world as it passes, and in his picture the elements are mixed. In the Americans of Henry James's later novels (those written before his return)— the Milly Theales, the Lambert Strethers, the Maggie Ververs —he shows us all that was magnanimous, reviving and warm in the Americans at the beginning of the new century along with all that was frustrated, sterile, excessively refined, depressing —all that they had in common with the Frédéric Moreaus and with the daughters of poor English parsons. Here they are with their ideals and their blights: Milly Theale, for example, quite real at the core of her cloudy integument, probably the best portrait in fiction of a rich New Yorker of the period. It is the period of the heyday of Sargent; but compare such figures of

James's with the fashionable paintings of Sargent, truthful though these are in their way, and see with what profounder insight as well as with what superior delicacy Henry James has caught the monied distinction of the Americans of this race.

But between the first blooming and the second something tragic has happened to these characters. What has become of Christopher Newman? What has become of Isabel Archer? They are Lambert Strether and Milly Theale—the one worn out by Woollett, Mass., the other overburdened with money and dying for lack of love. Neither finds any fulfilment in Europe, neither ever gets his money's worth. Maggie Verver has her triumph in the end, but she, too, is much too rich for comfort. These people look wan and they are more at sea than the people of the earlier novels. They have been tumbled along or been ground in the sand by the surf of commercial success that has been running in the later part of the century, and in either case are very much the worse for it. It seems to me foolish to reproach Henry James for having neglected the industrial background. Like sex, we never get very close to it, but its effects are a part of his picture. James's tone is more often old-maidish than his sense of reality is feeble; and the changes in American life that have been going on during his absence are implied in these later books.

When he revisits the States at last, he is aroused to a new effort in fiction as well as to the reporting of *The American Scene*. The expatriate New Yorker of *The Jolly Corner* comes back to the old house on Fifth Avenue to confront the apparition of himself as he would have been if he had stayed and worked 'downtown.' 'Rigid and conscious, spectral yet human, a man of his own substance and stature waited there to measure himself with his power to dismay.' At first this *alter ego* covers its face with its hands; then it advances 'as for aggression, and he knew himself give ground. Then harder pressed still, sick with the force of his shock, and falling back as under the hot breath and the sensed passion of a life larger than his own, a rage of personality before which his own collapsed, he felt the whole vision turn to darkness and his very feet give way.' He faints.

Yet at contact with this new America which is extravagant at the same time as ugly, the old Balzac in James revives. I do not know why more has not been made in the recent discussion of James—especially by the critics of the Left, who are so certain that there is nothing in him—of the unfinished novel called *The Ivory Tower*. The work of James's all but final period has been 'poetic' rather than 'realistic'; but now he passes into a further phase in which the poetic treatment is applied to what is for James a new kind of realism. The fiction of his latest period is occupied in a special way with the forgotten, the poor and the old, even—what has been rare in James—with the uncouth, the grotesque. It is perhaps the reflection of his own old age, his own lack of worldly success, the strange creature that he himself has become. This new vein had already appeared in the long short story *The Papers*, with its fantastically amusing picture of the sordid lives of journalists in London; and he later wrote *Fordham Castle*, in which he said he had tried to do something for the parents of the Daisy Millers whose children had left them behind—a curious if not very successful glimpse of the America of Sinclair Lewis; and *The Bench of Desolation*, the last story but one that he published, surely one of the most beautifully written and wonderfully developed short pieces in the whole range of James's work: a sort of prose poem of loneliness and poverty among the nondescript small shopkeepers and retired governesses of an English seaside resort.

But in the meantime the revelation of Newport, as it presented itself in the nineteen hundreds—so different from the Newport which James had described years ago in *An International Episode*—stimulates him to something quite new: a kind of nightmare of the American *nouveaux riches*. Here his appetite for the varied forms of life, his old interest in social phenomena, seem brusquely to wake him up from revery. The appearances of things become vivid again. To our amazement, there starts into color and relief the America of the millionaires, at its crudest, corruptest and phoniest: the immense amorphous mansions, complicated by queer equipment which seems neither to have been purchased by personal choice nor humanized by personal use; the old men of the Rockefeller-Frick generation, landed, with no tastes and no interests, amidst a limitless magnificence which dwarfs them; the silly or clumsy young people of the second generation with their dubious relationships, their enormous and meaningless parties, their touching longings and resolute strivings for an elegance and cultivation which they have no one to guide them in acquiring. The specter of *The Jolly Corner* appeared to the expatriate American 'quite as one of those expanding fantastic images projected by the magic lantern of childhood'; and in somewhat the same way, for the reader of James, with the opening of *The Ivory Tower*, there emerges the picture of old Abner Gaw, a kind of monster from outside the known Jamesian world, sitting and rocking his foot and looking out on the sparkling Atlantic while he waits for his business partner to die. *The Ivory Tower*, in dealing with the newest rich, is comic and even homely; but it is also, like all this later work of Henry James, poetic in that highest sense that its characters and scenes and images shine out with the incandescence which shows them as symbols of phases through which the human soul has passed. The moral of the novel—which seems quite plain from the scenario left by James—is also of particular interest. The ivory tower itself, a fine piece of Chinese carving, is to represent, for the young American who has just returned from Europe and inherited his uncle's fortune, that independence of spirit, that private cultivation of sensations and that leisure for literary work, which the money is to make possible for him; but it fatally contains, also, the letter in which Abner Gaw, out of vindictiveness toward the partner who has double-crossed him, has revealed all the swindles and perfidies by which the fortune has been created. So that the cosmopolitan nephew (he has always had a *little* money) is finally to be only too glad to give up the independence with the fortune.

Henry James dropped *The Ivory Tower* when the war broke out in 1914, because he felt it was too remote from the terrible contemporary happenings. These events seem to have presented themselves to James as simply a critical struggle between, on the one hand, French and English civilization and, on the other, German barbarity. He had believed in and had invoked rather vaguely the possible salutary effect for the world of an influential group of international élite made up of the kind of people with whom he associated and whom he liked to depict in his novels; but now he spoke of the past as 'the age of the mistake,' the period when people had thought that the affairs of the world were sufficiently settled for such an élite to flourish. He was furiously nationalistic, or at least furiously pro-Ally. He railed against Woodrow Wilson for his delay in declaring war, and he applied in 1915, in a gesture of rejection and allegiance, to become a British subject. 'However British you may be, I am more British still!' he is said to have exclaimed to Edmund Gosse, when the process had been completed—something which, Gosse is supposed to have remarked, 'nobody wanted him to be.' He had hitherto refrained from this step, feeling, as we gather from *The American Scene*, some pride and some advantage in his status as a citizen of the United States. But he had been thrown off his balance again, had been swung from his poise of detachment, always a delicate thing to maintain and requiring special conditions. It never occurred to James that he had been, in *The Ivory Tower*, much closer to contemporary realities than he was when he threw up his hat and enlisted in a holy war on Germany; that the partnership of Betterman and Gaw was not typical merely of the United States but had its European counterparts—any more than it was present to him now that the class antagonisms of *The Princess Casamassima*, his response to the depression of the eighties, must inevitably appear again and that the events he was witnessing in Europe were partly due to that social system whose corruption he had been consciously chronicling, and were expediting the final collapse which he had earlier half-predicted.

But as Hyacinth Robinson had died of the class struggle, so Henry James died of the war. He was cremated, and a funeral service was held—on March 3, 1916—at Chelsea Old Church in London; but his ashes, as he had directed, were brought to the United States and buried in the Cambridge cemetery beside his parents and sister and brother. One occasionally, however, finds references to him which assume that he was buried in England—just as one sometimes also finds references which assume that he was born in New England—so that even Henry James's death has been not without a suggestion of the equivocal.

The English had done him the honor, not long before he died, of awarding him the Order of Merit. But I do not think that anybody has yet done full justice to his genius as an international critic of manners, esthetic values and morals. The strength of that impartial intelligence of which his hesitating and teasing ambiguity sometimes represented a weakness had prompted him to find his bearings among social gravitational fields which must at the time have seemed almost as bewildering as the astronomical ones with which the physics of relativity were just beginning to deal. It had fortified him to meet and weather the indifference or ridicule of both the two English-speaking peoples to whom he had addressed himself and whose historian he had trained himself to be; and it had stimulated him, through more than half a hundred books, a long life of unwearying labor, to keep recreating himself as an artist and even to break new ground at seventy.

For Henry James *is* a first-rank writer in spite of certain obvious deficiencies. His work is incomplete as his experience was; but it is in no respect second-rate, and he can be judged only in company with the greatest. I have been occupied here with the elements that travail or contend or glow beneath the surface of his even fiction, and my argument has not given me occasion to insist, as ought to be done in any 'literary' discussion of James, on his classical equanimity in dealing with diverse forces, on his combination, equally classical, of hard realism with formal harmony. These are qualities—I have tried to describe them in writing about Pushkin—which have always been rather rare in American and English literature and of which the fiction of James is one of the truest examples.

———

1948. I have left my description of *The Turn of the Screw* mainly as I originally wrote it. In going over it again, however, it has struck me that I forced a point in trying to explain away the passage in which the housekeeper identifies, from the governess' description, the male apparition with Peter Quint. The recent publication of Henry James's note-books seems, besides, to make it quite plain that James's conscious intention, in *The Turn of the Screw*, was to write a *bona fide* ghost story; and it also becomes clear that the theme of youth feeding age was to have been the real subject of *The Sacred Fount*. I should today restate my thesis as follows:

At the time that James wrote these stories, his faith in himself had been somewhat shaken. Though he had summoned the whole force of his will and brought his whole mind to bear on writing plays, he had not made connections with the theater. The disastrous opening night of *Guy Domville* had occurred on January 5, 1895. On the evening of January 10, we learn from an entry in the note-books, James had heard from Archbishop Benson the story that suggested *The Turn of the Screw*. On January 23, he writes: 'I take up my *own* old pen again—the pen of all my old unforgettable efforts and sacred struggles. To myself—today—I need say no more. Large and full and high the future still opens. It is now indeed that I may do the work of my life. And I will . . . I have only to face my problems.' *The Turn of the Screw* was begun in the fall of 1897 (*The Spoils of Poynton* and *What Maisie Knew* had been written in between). Now, to fail as James had just done is to be made to doubt one's grasp of reality; and the doubts that some readers feel as to the soundness of the governess' story are, I believe, the reflection of James's doubts, communicated unconsciously by James himself (in sketching out his stories in his note-books—as for *The Friends of the Friends*, described below —he sometimes shifts over without a break from a first person which refers to himself to a first person which refers to the imaginary teller). An earlier story, *The Path of Duty*, published in 1884, is perhaps the most obvious example of James's interest in cases of self-deception and his trick of presenting them from their own points of view; and it is given a special relevance to the problem of *The Turn of the Screw* by the entry about it in the note-books. This entry is simply a notation of a curious piece of gossip which James had heard in London, with a discussion of the various ways in which it could be treated in fiction; but the story that James afterwards wrote depends for its effectiveness on an element which James does not mention there. The original anecdote is used, but it here gets another dimension from the attitude of the woman who is supposed to be telling it. This American lady in London is enamored of an attractive nobleman in line for a desirable baronetcy, with whom she is on fairly close terms but who takes no serious interest in her. She therefore intervenes in a mischievous way, under the pretense of keeping him to the 'path of duty,' to prevent him from marrying the woman he loves and induce him to marry one he doesn't—a situation in

which everybody else is to be left as dissatisfied as she is. She
has never admitted to herself her real motives for what she is
doing, and they gradually dawn on the reader in the form of
intermittent suspicions like the suspicions that arise in one's
mind in reading *The Turn of the Screw*. But in the case of *The
Path of Duty*, we are quite clear as we finish the story, as to
what role the narrator has actually played. She has written her
account, we realize, though ostensibly to satisfy a friend who
has been asking her about the episode, really as a veiled confession; and then she has decided to withhold it, ostensibly to
shield the main actors, but really to shield herself. Here James,
having noted down an anecdote, as he was also to do for *The
Turn of the Screw* and had already done with the notion that
was to be used in *The Sacred Fount*, has produced a psychological study for which the anecdote is only a pretext. Another
story, *The Friends of the Friends*, the idea for which James first
noted in the December of 1895 and which he immediately
afterwards wrote, also offers a clue to the process which I
believe was at work in *The Turn of the Screw*. *The Friends of the
Friends* is a ghost story, which involves, like *The Marriages* and
The Path of Duty, a mischievous intervention prompted by interested motives on the part of a woman narrator; and the
ghost is presumably a product of this narrator's neurotic jealousy. *Maud-Evelyn*, a story written later and first published in
1900, though the first suggestion of it seems also to occur in
the note-books of 1895, presents a young man who from interested motives lends himself to the spiritualistic self-deceptions
of parents who have lost their daughter. One is led to conclude
that, in *The Turn of the Screw*, not merely is the governess self-
deceived, but that James is self-deceived about her.

A curious feature of these note-books is the tone that Henry
James takes in collecting his materials and outlining his plots.
It is not, as with the notes of most writers, as if James were sitting in the workshop of his mind, alone and with no consciousness of an audience, but exactly as if he were addressing
a letter to a friend who took a keen interest in his work but
with whom he is not sufficiently intimate to discuss his personal affairs. He calls himself *mon bon* and *caro mio*—'Causons,
causons, mon bon,' he will write—and speaks to himself with
polite depreciation—referring to 'the narrator of the tale, as I

may in courtesy call it.' But, though he talks to himself a good deal—and sometimes very excitedly and touchingly—about his relation to his work, his 'muse,' he never notes down personal emotions in relation to anything else as possible subjects for fiction. One comes to the conclusion that Henry James, in a special and unusual way, was what is nowadays called an 'extrovert'—that is, he did not brood on himself and analyze his own reactions, as Stendhal, for example, did, but always dramatized his experience immediately in terms of imaginary people. One gets the impression here that James was not introspective. Nor are his characters really so. They register, as James himself registered, a certain order of perceptions and sensations; but they justify to some degree the objection of critics like Wells that his psychology is superficial—though it would be more correct to put it that, while his insight is not necessarily superficial, his 'psychologizing' tends to be so. What we are told is going on in the characters' heads is a sensitive reaction to surfaces which itself seems to take place on the surface. We do not often see them grappling with their problems in terms of concrete ambitions or of intimate relationships. What we see when we are supposed to look into their minds is something as much arranged by James to conceal, to mislead and to create suspense as the actual events presented. These people, so far as the 'psychologizing' goes, are not intimate even with themselves. They talk to themselves about what they are doing and what is happening to them even a good deal less frankly than James talks to himself about them, and that is already with the perfect discretion of an after-dinner conversation between two gentlemanly diners-out. As Henry James gets further away—beginning with *What Maisie Knew*—from the realism of his earlier phases, his work—as Stephen Spender has said in connection with *The Golden Bowl*—becomes all a sort of ruminative poem, which gives us not really a direct account of the internal workings of his characters, but rather James's reflective feelings, the flow of images set off in his mind, as he peeps not impolitely inside them. Not, however, that his sense of life—of personal developments and impacts—is not often profound and sure. The point is merely that it is not always so, and that the floor of the layer of consciousness that we are usually allowed to explore sometimes rings rather hollow.

Where motivations are rarely revealed, we cannot always tell how much the author knows; and it is on this account that arguments occur—and not only in the case of *The Turn of the Screw* but also in that of *The Golden Bowl*—as to what is supposed to be happening in a given situation or as to what kind of personalities the characters are supposed to be. Carefully though, from one point of view, the point of view of technical machinery, Henry James always planned his novels, he seems sometimes to falter and grope in dealing with their human problems. The habits he imposed on himself in his attempt to write workable plays was unfortunate in this connection. The unperformed comedies that he published in the two volumes of *Theatricals*, which are almost the only things he wrote that can really be called bad, show a truly appalling self-discipline in sterile and stale devices and artificial motivations. In the stage world of Henry James, young men are always prepared to marry, regardless of personal taste or even of close acquaintance, from an interest in a property or an inheritance, or because they have been told that they have compromised girls or simply because women have proposed to them; and an element of this false psychology was afterwards carried by James through the whole of his later fiction along with his stage technique. It is true that in this later fiction there is a good deal of illicit passion, as had not been the case in his plays; but his adulteries seem sometimes as arbitrary as the ridiculous engagements of *Theatricals*. They are not always really explained, we cannot always be sure they are really there, that the people have been to bed together. But, on the other hand, we sometimes feel the presence, lurking like 'the beast in the jungle,' of other emotional factors with which the author himself does not always appear to have reckoned.

I once gave *The Turn of the Screw* to the Austrian novelist Franz Höllering to see what impression he would get of it. It did not occur to him that it was not a real ghost story, but he said to me, after he had read it: 'The man who wrote that was a *Kinderschänder*'; and I remembered that in all James's work of this period—which extends from *The Other House* through *The Sacred Fount*—the favorite theme is the violation of innocence, with the victim in every case (though you have in *The*

Turn of the Screw a boy as well as a girl) a young or a little girl. In *The Other House* a child is murdered; in *What Maisie Knew* and *The Awkward Age*, a child and a young virgin are played upon by forces of corruption which, though they do not destroy the girls' innocence, somewhat harm them or dislocate their emotions by creating abnormal relationships; in *The Turn of the Screw*, whichever way you take it, the little girl is either hurt or corrupted. (The candid and loyal young heroines of *The Spoils of Poynton* and *In the Cage*, though they can hardly be said to be violated, are both, in their respective ways, represented as shut out from something.) This, of course, in a sense, is an old theme for James: *Washington Square* and *The Portrait of a Lady* were studies in innocence betrayed. But there is something rather peculiar, during this relatively neurotic phase, in his interest in and handling of this subject. The real effectiveness of all these stories derives, not from the conventional pathos of a victim with whom we sympathize but from the excitement of the violation; and if we look back to Henry James's first novel, *Watch and Ward*, serialized when he was twenty-eight, we find a very queer little tale about a young man of twenty-six who becomes the guardian of a girl of ten and gradually falls in love with her but is for a long time debarred from marrying her, when she comes of age to marry, by a complication of scruples and misunderstandings. The relationship clearly connects itself with the relationship, in *The Awkward Age*, between Nanda and Mr. Langdon, in which, also, the attitude of the pseudo-father is given a flavor of unavowed sex. We are not in a position to explain, on any basis of early experience, this preoccupation of James with immature girls who are objects of desire or defilement; but it seems clear what symbolic role they played from time to time in his work. He seems early to have 'polarized' with his brother William in an opposition of feminine and masculine. This appears in a significant anecdote which he tells in his autobiography about William's having left him once to go to play, as he said, with 'boys that curse and swear'; and in his description of his feeling from the first that William was 'occupying a place in the world to which I couldn't at all aspire—to any approach to which in truth I seem to myself ever conscious of having signally forfeited a title'; and one finds it in their correspondence and in everything one has heard of their relations. There was always in Henry James an innocent little girl whom he cherished and loved and protected and yet whom he later tried to violate, whom he even tried to kill. He must have felt particularly help-less, particularly unsuited for the battle with the world, partic-ularly exposed to rude insult, after the failure of his dramatic career, when he retreated into his celibate solitude. The maiden innocent of his early novels comes to life again; but he now does not merely pity her, he does not merely adore her: in his impotence, his impatience with himself, he would like to de-stroy or rape her. The real dramatic and esthetic values of the stories that he writes at this period are involved with an equiv-ocal blending of this impulse and an instinct of self-pity. (The conception of *innocence excluded* is a reaction to the same situ-ation: Fleda Vetch, in *The Spoils of Poynton*, misses marrying the man she loves and misses inheriting the spoils, which in any case go up in flames; the girl in the telegraph office finds that it is not she who is 'in the cage' but the dashing young captain whose amours she has fascinatedly watched from afar —just as James must have had to decide that the worldly suc-cess he had tried for was, after all, not worth having. So the in-nocents in certain of the other stories, too, are left with a moral advantage.) This is not in the least, on the critic's part, to pretend to reduce the dignity of these stories by reading into them the embarrassments of the author. They do contain, I believe, a certain subjective element which hardly appears to the same degree elsewhere in James's mature work; but he has expressed what he had to express—disappointments and dis-satisfactions that were poignantly and not ignobly felt—with dramatic intensity and poetic color. These are fairy-stories, but fairy-stories that trouble, that get a clear and luminous music out of chords very queerly combined. They are unique in liter-ature, and their admirable style and form are not quite like anything else even in the work of James. In *The Wings of the Dove*, of course, which follows *The Awkward Age*, he is still oc-cupied with violated innocence, but now his world is firm again on its base, and we are back on the international stage of *The Portrait of a Lady*. Milly Theale, though languishing and fatally ill, is a real and full-grown woman dealing with a practical conspiracy, not a tender little girl or *jeune fille* jeopardized by an ambiguous dream.*

*The immaturity of the heroines in James serves sometimes to provide one of his many pretexts for making it impossible for the heroes to marry them. The whole question of the motif of impotence in James has been discussed very suggestively and interestingly—though on the basis of an incomplete acquaintance with Henry James's work—in a paper called *The Ghost of Henry James: A Study in Thematic Apperception* by Dr. Saul Rosenzweig (*Character and Personality*, December 1943). Dr. Rosenzweig suggests that the accident in which Henry James sprained his back at eighteen—'a horrid even if an obscure hurt,' as James himself calls it—and from which he suffered, sometimes acutely, all the rest of his life, may have been partly neurotic not only in its results but even in its origin—since it offers a strangely close parallel with the accident in which the elder Henry James had lost his leg—also in extinguishing a fire—at the age of thirteen. The son's accident had occurred, as he tells us himself, at the beginning of the Civil War and put it out of the question for him to answer Lincoln's first call for volunteers. Dr. Rosenzweig has brought to light a very early story of James, the first he ever published: *The Story of a Year*, which appeared in the *Atlantic Monthly* in March 1865. Here you have a young man of the North who, just before going off to the war, becomes engaged to a girl but makes her promise that, if he should die, she will forget him and marry someone else. She dreams, when he has gone, that she is walking in a wood with a man who calls her wife and that they find a dead man covered with wounds. They lift the corpse up to bury it, and it opens its eyes and says 'Amen'; they stamp down the dirt of the grave. The lover is actually wounded, lingers for some time between life and death, and then dies, leaving the fiancée to marry another man. Another factor in the story is the young man's mother, who comes between him and the girl, being unwilling to have him marry her and trying to prevent her seeing him after he has been brought home wounded —Henry James, it seems, was his mother's favorite child. Dr. Rosenzweig might also have cited another early short story, *An Extraordinary Case* (1868), in which another returned soldier, suffering from an unspecified ailment, loses his girl to another man and dies.

One can agree with Dr. Rosenzweig that a castration theme appears here— one recognizes it as the same that figures through the whole of James's work; but that work does not bear out the contention put forward by Dr. Rosenzweig that James was to suffer all his life from unallayed feelings of guilt for not having taken part in the war. The only real pieces of evidence that Dr. Rosenzweig is able to produce are the short story, *Owen Wingrave*, which deals with the deliberate pacifism of a young man from a military family and leaves the moral advantage all with the pacifist, who dies in the cause of peace; and Henry James's excitement at the beginning of World War I and his memories at this time of the Civil War. He must certainly be right, however, in assuming that well before the age when *The Story of a Year* was written, a state of mind in which 'aggression and sexuality were repressed' had been 'established as a *modus vivendi*.' One of James's most curious symbols for his chronic inhibition occurs in a very early story called first *Théolinde*, then *Rose-Agathe*, in

It is of course no longer true, as is implied in the above essay, that the stature and merits of James are not fully appreciated in the English-speaking world. Since the centenary of James's birth in 1943, he has been celebrated, interpreted, reprinted, on a scale which, I believe, is unprecedented for a classical American writer. There have contributed to this frantic enthusiasm perhaps a few rather doubtful elements. A novelist whose typical hero invariably decides not to act, who remains merely an intelligent onlooker, appeals for obvious reasons to a period when many intellectuals, formerly romantic egoists or partisans of the political Left, have been resigning themselves to the role of observer or of passive participant in activities which cannot command their whole allegiance. The stock of Henry James has gone up in the same market as that of Kafka, and the recent apotheosis of him has sometimes been conducted as uncritically as the prayers and contemplations of the Kafka cult. At the same time, in a quite different way, he has profited from—or, at any rate, been publicized by—the national propaganda movement which has been advertising American civilization under stimulus of our needs in the war and our emergence into the international world. The assumption seems to be that Henry James is our counterpart to Yeats, Proust and Joyce, and he has been tacitly assigned to high place in the official American Dream along with 'Mr. Jefferson,' the *Gettysburg Address*, Paul Bunyan, the Covered Wagon, and Mom's Huckleberry Pie. He will doubtless be translated for the Japanese, who were fascinated before the war by the refinements of Paul Valéry and Proust.*

Yet we do well to be proud of him, and there are very good reasons for young people to read him straight through, as—incredible though it would have sounded at the time he was still alive—they seem more and more to be doing. Henry James stands out today as unique among our fiction writers of the nineteenth century in having devoted wholeheartedly to liter-

---

which a man falls in love with a dummy in a Parisian hairdresser's window and finally buys her and takes her home to live with. The wax dummy is cut off at the waist.

*Since writing this, I have found in a book catalogue—along with a Japanese translation of *Ulysses*—a volume of James's short stories translated into Japanese (1924), and a Japanese book about James (1934).

ature the full span of a long life and brought to it first-rate abilities. Beside James's half century of achievement, with its energy, continuity and variety, the production of Hawthorne looks furtive and meager and the work of Poe's brief years fragmentary. Alone among our novelists of the past, Henry James managed to master his art and to practice it on an impressive scale, to stand up to popular pressures so as not to break down or peter out, and to build up what the French call an *œuvre*.

John Jay Chapman

The Mute and the Open Strings

M R. M. A. DeWolfe Howe has done an excellent job with the letters and papers of the late John Jay Chapman.* Mr. Howe enjoyed the advantages of having known Chapman personally and of already being thoroughly at home in the latter's period and circle.

One's only complaint about Mr. Howe's book is that there is not anywhere near enough of it. I understand that he was induced by his publishers to cut down his original manuscript; and this seems to me to have been a mistake. Anybody interested in Chapman at all would be able to read a book twice as long as the present one. My own impression from what is here published is that John Jay Chapman was probably the best letter-writer that we have ever had in this country. And it seems to me a pity that Mr. Howe did not include the whole text of the autobiographical document which Chapman prepared not long before his death, instead of only selections from it. My hope and belief is, in fact, that the future will be sufficiently interested in Chapman to print and read his letters as eagerly as has been done with Horace Walpole's—as well as to go back to his published works as we have done to those of Thoreau.

Yet at the present time hardly one reader in a million has heard of even the name of John Jay Chapman. His later books have had no circulation, and most of his earlier ones are out of print. How, then, is it possible to attach so much importance to a writer who has been persistently ignored by the historians of American literature and who has been read by almost nobody, even during these last twenty years when so much rummaging has been going on in the attic of our literary history? How has it been possible thus for a writer who was at one time a conspicuous figure and who is still valued so highly by a few readers, to become completely invisible to the general reading public even while he was still living and writing?

*John Jay Chapman and His Letters.

This essay will attempt to answer that question, on which Mr. Howe's biography has thrown a great deal of light.

I

Perhaps our most vivid impression as we read about Chapman in this book—especially through the first half of his life—is that we have encountered a personality who does not belong in his time and place and who by contrast makes us aware of the commonness, the provinciality and the timidity of most of his contemporaries. 'Yes,' we say to ourselves in our amazement, 'people ought to be more like this!'

When John Jay Chapman was twenty five and studying law at Harvard—it was the winter of 1886–7—he made the acquaintance of the half-Italian niece of the Brimmer family of Boston: 'a swarthy, fiery large-eyed girl, who looked like the younger Sibyl of Michael Angelo' and 'had the man-minded seriousness of women in classic myths, the regular brow, heavy dark hair, free gait of the temperament that lives in heroic thought and finds the world full of chimeras, of religious mysteries, sacrifice, purgation'—such a woman as had hardly existed outside 'the imagination of Aeschylus and the poets.'

'I had never abandoned my reading of Dante'—it would be a pity not to give it in his own words—'and it somehow came about that I read Dante with Minna. There was a large airy room at the top of the old Athenaeum Library in Boston whose windows looked out on the churchyard. It was a bare and quiet place: no one ever came there. And during the winter we read Dante there together, and in the course of this she told me of her early life in Milan. There were five children, three of them boys, and there were tempestuous quarrels between the parents. I saw that it was from her mother that she had inherited her leonine temperament. The mother had been a fury. I could see this, though she did not say it . . . The Dante readings moved gradually like a cloud between me and the law, between me and the rest of life. It was done with few words. I had come to see that she was in love with someone. It never occurred to me that she might be in love with me. An onlooker might have said, "You loved her for the tragedies of her childhood and she loved you that you did pity them."

'The case was simple, but the tension was blind and terrible. I was completely unaware that I was in love.'

But he did come to be aware that something was making her unhappy, and he decided that 'an acquaintance of hers, a friend in whom she had little interest,' had been trifling with her affections. One evening at 'the most innocent kind of party that you can imagine at a country house,' he suddenly, without conscious premeditation, invited the man outside and beat him.

'The next thing I remember is returning late at night to my room. At that time I was rooming alone in a desolate side-street in Cambridge. It was a small, dark, horrid little room. I sat down. There was a hard-coal fire burning brightly. I took off my coat and waistcoat, wrapped a pair of suspenders tightly on my left forearm above the wrist, plunged the left hand deep in the blaze and held it down with my right hand for some minutes. When I took it out, the charred knuckles and finger bones were exposed. I said to myself, "This will never do." I took an old coat, wrapped it about my left hand and arm, slipped my right arm into an overcoat, held the coat about me and started for Boston in the horsecars. On arriving at the Massachusetts General Hospital I showed the trouble to a surgeon, was put under ether, and the next morning waked up without the hand and very calm in my spirits. Within a few days I was visited by the great alienist, Dr. Reginald Heber Fitz, an extremely agreeable man. He asked me among other things whether I was insane. I said, "That is for you to find out." He reported me as sane. I took no interest in the scandal which my two atrocious acts must have occasioned.'

He knew now that he was in love with Minna and that it was he whom Minna loved. 'Do you know, Minna,' he wrote her, before they were married, in the summer of the same year, 'the one time in my life during which I lived was that twenty days of pain. I read *Henry Esmond*, Dickens' *Christmas Stories*, one morning—I never shall forget them—*Mr. Barnes of New York*. Every word of it is glowing with life and love. There was fire in everything I touched—the fire of the activity of that part of me which was meant to be used, which got suppressed all my life till it broke. The depth of the intentions and remote unkempt wells of life and feeling. Browning I used to read anywhere . . . Somehow I have known the meaning of things, if not for long, and all the while I thought I need rest, I need sleep. You see life is an experiment. I had not the least idea but what [if] I met you all this would run the other way and the pain turn into pleasure. I thought I had opened life forever—what matter if the entrance was through pain.'

And later, three years after they were married, he wrote her in an extraordinary love letter on one of his business trips to the West: 'It was not a waste desert in Colorado. It is not a waste time, for you are here and many lives packed into one life, and the green shoot out of the heart of the plant, springing up blossoms in the night, and many old things have put on immortality and lost things have come back knocking within, from before the time I was conceived in the womb, there were you, also. And what shall we say of the pain! it was false—and the rending, it was unnecessary. It was the breaking down of the dams that ought not to have been put up—but being up it was the sweeping away of them that the waters might flow together.'

They lived in New York, where he had been born. Chapman practiced and hated law. He was, on the other hand, passionately interested in politics. He had been a member of the City Reform Club, founded by Theodore Roosevelt and others, almost from its beginning in 1882; and later became president of the Good Government Club, which had grown out of the City Reform Club. The Good Government Club had been founded by another Harvard man, Edmond Kelly, for the purpose of fighting Tammany Hall. When Kelly found out that it was impossible to recruit the working-class to his movement, he gave it up and became a socialist. But Chapman and another Harvard man assumed the leadership of the Good Government movement, and from 1895 through 1900 he had an odd and very interesting career as a non-socialist political radical.

In the election of 1895, the 'Goo-Goo's,' unable to agree with the Republicans on a common ticket against Tammany, ran a campaign of their own and were defeated; and in all this John Jay Chapman played a spirited and provocative part. He made speeches from the cart-tail in the streets and created a great impression by getting down and manhandling hecklers who were trying to break him up—he was a man of formidable build—then going back and finishing his speech and

afterwards buying his opponents drinks; and he was able, also,
to upset the routine of such accepted professional reformers as
Joseph Choate and Godkin of the *Post*. His announced policy
at political dinners was 'to say nothing that he would not regret'; and he is reported to have been the only person who
ever caused the venerable and cultivated Choate to lose his
urbanity in public—by pointing out to him that the anti-
Tammany organization to which Mr. Choate belonged had
been guilty of a deal with the enemy. John Jay Chapman did
not understand politics even as the political reformers did. He
combined the extreme exhilaration of hope with the utmost
contempt of compromise. He had at this period what the poet
Yeats calls 'the purity of a natural force,' and he disturbed and
frightened people.

But he was presently to collide with another personality, with
whom he had supposed himself to be traveling, but of whom
he turned out to be crossing the path. In the autumn of 1898,
John Jay Chapman was one of the leaders of a group of political Independents who wanted to nominate Theodore Roosevelt for the governorship of New York. Chapman had an
interview with Roosevelt: the latter accepted the nomination
and continued to affirm his willingness to be run by the Independents even after the Republican Party had offered to nominate him, too. But, in the meantime, the Independents had
drawn up a whole Independent ticket; and the Republican boss,
Tom Platt, told Roosevelt that if he wanted the Republicans to
run him, he would have to throw over the Independents—
which Roosevelt immediately did. Chapman had been so un-
wary as to fail to extract a written promise from Roosevelt,
because he had supposed a gentleman's word was enough. He
had happened to start down to Oyster Bay to call on his supposed candidate just before the news of the defection broke in
New York; and when he got there, he found there was no train
back, so that he had to spend the evening with Roosevelt. It
seems to have been a harrowing occasion, 'for I was not going
home leaving any mist or misunderstandings in the air as to
how the Good Government Club group viewed the situation.
But I went further. I unloaded the philosophy of agitation
upon Roosevelt and pictured him as the broken-backed half-
good man, the successor of the doughface and Northern man

with Southern principles of Civil War times, the trimmer who wouldn't break with his party and so, morally speaking, it ended by breaking him.'

Chapman knew very well what Roosevelt had promised him; and the incident gave him seriously to think. He observed that Roosevelt presently persuaded himself that he had never understood the original proposal; and that he thereafter became very vociferous over the damage done progressive movements by fanatics on their 'lunatic fringe.' Chapman had been publishing since March 1897 a review called the *Political Nursery* (originally, simply the *Nursery*), and he now used it to attack Roosevelt's subsequent activities and those of the reformist mayor, Seth Low, formerly a candidate of the Independents. It was the McKinley-Roosevelt era of American imperialist expansion, and Chapman fought the policy of the United States in Cuba and in the Philippines, as well as denounced the British in South Africa.

This review, which he carried on through January 1901, is one of the best written things of the kind which has ever been published anywhere. Chapman wrote most of it himself, and he dealt with philosophical and literary, as well as with political, subjects. Here he began the characteristic practice which William James described when he wrote of him: 'He just looks at things and tells the truth about them—a strange thing even to *try* to do, and he doesn't always succeed.' But he did succeed pretty often, and he is at his best during this early period. As I have not the files of the *Political Nursery* by me, I shall quote some portraits and comments from the letters of his later as well as of his earlier years.

Of James Russell Lowell, he wrote in 1896:

'I don't dislike the man. I think him a fine man, a little dandified and genteel perhaps, but still a good story character. His poetry is nothing but a fine talent, a fine ear, a fine facility— too much morality and an incredible deftness at imitating everybody from Milton down. I cannot read his poems with any comfort—but his early essays I still think the best things he ever did, witty, snappy, "smart" to a degree, and quite natural— they are the only things he ever did that were quite natural. In later life he got all barnacled with quotations and leisure. He pulls out pocket-books and gold snuff boxes and carbuncled

cigarette-cases, and emerald eye-glasses, and curls and poma-
tums himself and looks in pocket looking glasses, and
smoothes his Vandyke beard and is a literary fop—f-o-p, fop.
Too much culture—overnourished as Waddy Longfellow says
—too many truffled essays and champagne odes and lobster
sonnets, too much Spanish olives, potted proverbs—a gouty
old cuss in his later essays. But in '54–'65 he wrote rapidly and
most clearly. Belles Lettres is the devil after all. It spoils a man.
His prefaces—sometimes very nice, in spirit—but his later
prefaces are so expressive— O my! so expressive of hems and
haws and creased literary trousers. I feel like running him in
the belly and singing out Hulloo! old cockolorum.'

Of President Eliot of Harvard (1898):

'Read the essays of (Pres.) Eliot. There's no offense in them.
Two by six. Everything in Massachusetts is deal boards. You
can put every man in a box—Smug, Smug. He has a good
word for poetry too. It's the Dodgedom of Culture. My God,
how I hate it. He's the very highest type of a most limited and
inspiring pork-chopism. My God, he is hopeful—calls his book
American Contributions to Civilization—thinks we don't
understand small parks and drainage—but will learn and are
doing nicely. Has a chapter on "the pleasures of life." It's all
one size. Every word in this work is the same size. The Puritans
—the war—the problems of labor and capital—education—all
excite the same emotion—i.e. that of a woodchuck eating a
carrot.'

Of Eliot and J. Pierpont Morgan (1907):

'Pierpont Morgan is the actual apex as well as the type, of
the commercial perversions of the era. The political corruption, etc., the power behind all . . . Now then, at the dedication of the New Medical School, Eliot goes about in a cab with
Pierpont, hangs laurel wreaths on his nose, and gives him his
papal kiss. Now what I want to know is this—what has Eliot
got to say to the young man entering business or politics who
is about to be corrupted by Morgan and his class? How eloquently can Eliot present the case for honesty? Can he say anything that will reverberate through the chambers of that young
man's brain more loudly than that kiss?

'If Eliot is a great man, I want a small man.'

Of Roosevelt and Wilson (1930):

'I have just read in type-writing a book about Roosevelt—which ought to be called the Night Side of T. R.; for it is wholly malignant—and to that extent ineffective. But it's true. He was very nearly mad at times—and broke down his mind by his egotism and mendacity. I had a quarrel with him—political, and personal, and deadly. He was a great genius for handling a situation, and with men, in such a way as to get credit—but he was a damned scoundrel. His genius was to flash a light, put someone down a well, raise a howl to heaven about honesty, and move on to the next thing. Such a genius for publicity as never was—and our people being boy-minded and extremely stupid found him lovely. His feebleness of intellect appears in his writings—which are dull and bombastic—and I doubt whether he will go down as a great man. He's more like a figure out of Dumas. Wilson, a character more odious still, will go down to history as the father of the League of Nations. Drat him! His writings also are dull and he also had the power of hypnotizing men. They idolized him—even those who didn't like him—obeyed—worshiped.

'Apropos—aren't great men apt to be horrid?'

In 1898, he published a volume of literary papers called *Emerson and Other Essays*. In this collection and in the *Political Nursery*, he wrote a commentary on authors then popular —Stevenson, Kipling, Browning, etc.—of which in our day the acumen seems startling. I cannot remember any other American critic of that period—except, in his more specialized field and his more circumlocutionary way, Henry James—who had anything like the same sureness of judgment, the same freedom from current prejudices and sentimentalities. Chapman was then, as, it seems to me, he was to remain, much our best writer on literature of his generation—who made the Babbitts and the Mores and the Brownells, for all the more formidable rigor of their systems and the bulkier mass of their work, look like colonial schoolmasters.

It is worth while to rescue a passage from one of his more ephemeral papers—an article on Kipling in the *Political Nursery* of April 1899—for its statement of his organic ideal for literature:

'Permanent interest cannot attach to anything which does not consist, from rind to seeds, of instructive truth. A thing must be interesting from every point of view, as history, as poetry, as philosophy; good for a sick man, just the thing for Sunday morning. It must be true if read backwards, true literally and true as a parable, true in fragments and true as a whole. It must be valuable as a campaign document, and it must make you laugh or cry at any time, day or night. Lasting literature has got to be so very good as to fulfill all these conditions. Kipling's work does not do so since the time he began making money out of it.'

But the long study of Emerson had a special importance. It was something other than a mere essay on Emerson. It was rather an extension of Emerson, a re-creation of Emerson for a new generation, for it was really an expression—the first full expression—of Chapman's own point of view. And what Chapman got out of Emerson was something entirely different from the gentle and eupeptic personality—though that was a part of the real Emerson, too—of Van Wyck Brooks's recent portrayals. What Chapman got out of Emerson was a sort of beneficent Nietzscheanism, as electrical as Nietzsche's but less rhetorical. It had seemed to him at college, Chapman wrote, 'as if Emerson were a younger brother of Shakespeare . . . I was intoxicated with Emerson. He let loose something within me which made me in my own eyes as good as anyone else.' It was Emerson who had first made it possible for him to say to himself: 'After all, it is just as well that there should be *one* person like *me* in the world.' John Jay Chapman was thus a continuator of the individualist tradition of Emerson, which is also the tradition of Thoreau. (Chapman speaks of Thoreau less often, though it seems to me that he is in some ways even more closely akin to him.) He had carried this tradition to New York—for, in spite of the influence on his thought of Cambridge and Concord and Boston, he was distinctly to remain a New Yorker; and in his hands it was to undergo here an interesting variation.

'As I look back over my past,' he writes, 'the figure of Emerson looms up in my mind as the first modern man, and the city of Boston as the first living civilization which I knew. New York is not a civilization; it is a railway station.' Yet the New Yorker, though beside the New Englanders, with their Concord flavor and color, he may seem a little abstract and steely (as Henry James does, also, beside Hawthorne), is the man of a larger world. He was to bring against Emerson a new criticism. 'Our people are as thin-skinned as babies,' he wrote in one of his lectures, 'and the Massachusetts crowd has never been criticized.' No one had ventured to stand up to Emerson on the issue of the sexual emotions since Walt Whitman had walked with him on Boston Common and, after listening to all his remonstrances against the *Children of Adam* section of *Leaves of Grass*, had replied that he couldn't answer Emerson's arguments, but that he felt sure of being right just the same. 'If an inhabitant of another planet,' wrote Chapman, 'should visit the earth, he would receive, on the whole, a truer notion of human life by attending an Italian opera than he would by reading Emerson's volumes. He would learn from the Italian opera that there were two sexes; and this, after all, is probably the fact with which the education of such a stranger ought to begin. In a review of Emerson's personal character and opinions, we are thus led to see that his philosophy, which finds no room for the emotions, is a faithful exponent of his own and of the New England temperament, which distrusts and dreads the emotions. Regarded as a sole guide to life for a young person of strong conscience and undeveloped affections, his works might conceivably be even harmful because of their unexampled power of purely intellectual stimulation.'

And he was to take the Thoreauvian intransigence into society instead of into solitude. John Jay Chapman's attitude toward politics is to develop with a curious logic, which is set forth in two other remarkable books: *Causes and Consequences* (1898) and *Practical Agitation* (1900). *Causes and Consequences* is one of the most powerful tracts ever written on the debasement of our politics and government by unscrupulous business interests. It begins with a pungent fable about the gradual but complete domination of a small American town by a railroad which passes through it. This, says Chapman, when he has told his story, is the whole history of America since the Civil War. And he shows the results of this process in the general cultural life with a force which was not later surpassed by Mencken or Van Wyck Brooks:

'We have seen that the retailer in the small town could not afford to think clearly upon the political situation. But this was a mere instance, a sample of his mental attitude. He dare not face any question. He must shuffle, qualify and defer. Here at last we have the great characteristic which covers our continent like a climate—intellectual dishonesty. This state of mind does not merely prevent a man having positive opinions. The American is incapable of taking a real interest in anything. The lack of passion in the American—noticeable in his books and in himself—comes from the same habitual mental distraction; for passion is concentration. Hence also the flippancy, superficiality and easy humor for which we are noted. Nothing except the dollar is believed to be worthy the attention of a serious man. People are even ashamed of their tastes. Until recently, we thought it effeminate for a man to play on the piano. When a man takes a living interest in anything, we call him a "crank." There is an element of self-sacrifice in any honest intellectual work which we detect at once and score with contumely.

'It was not solely commercial interest that made the biographers of Lincoln so thrifty to extend and veneer their books. It was that they themselves did not, could not, take an interest in the truth about him. The second-rate quality of all our letters and verse is due to the same cause. The intellectual integrity is undermined. The literary man is concerned for what "will go," like the reformer who is half politician. The attention of everyone in the United States is on someone else's opinion, not on truth.'

What is one to do in such a world? The diagnosis of *Causes and Consequences* is followed by a program of action in *Practical Agitation*; but Chapman's practical agitation is of a special and unexpected kind. As a result of his experience as a reformer, he has ceased to believe in the possibility of organized political reform under the American conditions of the time. One of the most amusing and searching passages of *Practical Agitation* describes the rapid absorption and the complete neutralization of a reform movement by the forces it has set out to correct. The commercial solidarity of society has rendered such crusading futile.

Once arrived at such a recognition, one might expect a man like Chapman to turn socialist; but his position on socialism is stated as follows:

'The function of Socialism is clear. It is a religious reaction going on in an age which thinks in terms of money. We are very nearly at the end of it, because we are very nearly at the end of the age. Some people believe they hate the wealth of the millionaire. They denounce corporations and trusts, as if these things hurt them. They strike at the symbol. What they really hate is the irresponsible rapacity which these things typify, and which nothing but moral forces will correct. In so far as people seek the cure in property-laws they are victims of the plague. The cure will come entirely from the other side; for as soon as the millionaires begin to exert and enjoy the enormous power for good which they possess, everybody will be glad they have the money.'

He does not, therefore, believe much in economics:

'The economic laws are valuable and suggestive, but they are founded on the belief that a man will pursue his own business interests exclusively. This is never entirely true even in trade, and the doctrines of the economists become more and more misleading when applied to fields of life where the money motive becomes incidental. The law of supply and demand does not govern the production of sonnets.'

But, 'when you see cruelty going on before you, you are put to the alternative of interposing to stop it, or of losing your sensibility.'

What then? Here is where Emerson comes in. 'If a soul,' he wrote, 'be taken and crushed by democracy till it utter a cry, that cry will be Emerson.' And: 'The thing seems to me about this,' he wrote in a letter of this time, after finishing an essay on the *Social Results of Commercialism*—'Emerson made coherent. It's all Emerson. I should have had neither the ideas reduced so clearly nor the public to understand them if it hadn't been for Emerson. I can't imagine what I should have been if it hadn't been for Emerson.' For he is thrown back on the individual conscience. Here is the situation with which the citizen finds himself confronted:

'Remember . . . that there is no such thing as abstract truth. You must talk facts, you must name names, you must impute motives. You must say what is in your mind. It is the only means you have of cutting yourself free from the body of this death. Innuendo will not do. Nobody minds innuendo. We live and breathe nothing else. If you are not strong enough to face the issue in private life, do not dream that you can do anything for public affairs. This, of course, means fight, not tomorrow, but now. It is only in the course of conflict that anyone can come to understand the system, the habit of thought, the mental condition, out of which all our evils arise. The first difficulty is to see the evils clearly; and when we do see them it is like fighting an atmosphere to contend against them. They are so universal and omnipresent that you have no terms to name them by. You must burn a disinfectant.'

And one can take only individual action:

'You yourself cannot turn Niagara; but there is not a town in America where one single man cannot make his force felt against the whole torrent. He takes a stand on a practical matter. He takes action against some abuse. What does this accomplish? Everything. How many people are there in your town? Well, every one of them gets a thrill that strikes deeper than any sermon he ever heard. He may howl, but he hears. The grocer's boy, for the first time in his life, believes that the whole outfit of morality has any place in the practical world.'

There can have been few codes of morality ever formulated so individualistic as John Jay Chapman's:

'If you want a compass at any moment in the midst of some difficult situation, you have only to say to yourself, "Life is larger than this little imbroglio. I shall follow my instinct." As you say this, your compass swings true. You may be surprised to find what course it points to. But what it tells you to do will be practical agitation.'

This code, with high courage and immense energy, he attempted to put into practice. These were intent and tumultuous years, during which he was shaken by many emotions. At the beginning of 1897, after the birth of their second son, his wife suddenly and unexpectedly died while he was reading to her aloud as she lay in bed. The next year he married his friend, Elizabeth Chanler. Through all this he had been speaking, writing, organizing, getting out his paper, practicing law and leading an active social life—while the immovable magnitude of the forces against him was gradually but inexorably becoming clear to him. 'My own family and connections,' he wrote, 'being a lot of well-meaning bourgeois, are horrified at me. But I enjoy it.' Yet, 'Politics takes physique,' he wrote at another time, 'and being odious takes physique. I feel like Atlas, lifting the entire universe. I hate this community and despise 'em—and fighting, fighting, fighting, fighting an atmospheric pressure gets tiresome.' When his friends expressed apprehension: 'As for insanity,' he replied, 'why, I was once examined for insanity by the two most distinguished physicians in Boston [at the time when he had burned off his hand]. It has no terrors. I talked to them like Plato.'

In the summer of 1900, he went out to attend a convention in Indianapolis which nominated 'Gold Democrat' candidates to run against both McKinley and Bryan; and he worked hard to organize a 'National Party,' the candidates proposed for which refused to run. That winter, after an attack of grippe, at the time when his wife was expecting a baby, he suddenly broke down in the midst of a speech in a small town in Pennsylvania. 'Too much will and self-will,' he wrote his mother.

He retreated to a darkened room. For a year he did not leave his bed, and when he was finally able to get up, remained for two or three years longer under the delusion that he was unable to walk without crutches. Turned in on his own blackness, the sight of a beautiful sunset or the interior of an Italian church, which he had been induced to come out to see, would excite him to the point of collapse.

II

The second half of John Jay Chapman's life is quite distinct from the first. In the August of 1903, one of his sons by his first wife Minna was drowned in an Austrian river; and the shock seems to have brought him to himself. He went back to the United States without his crutches.

He recovered, and thereafter for thirty years led the life of a well-to-do country squire at Barrytown on the Hudson. His second wife's family, the Chanlers, were among the most adventurous and gifted of that special race, the Hudson River gentry; and John Jay Chapman took his place in their world. Chapman's father had been president of the New York Stock Exchange, but had lost heavily in the panic of the seventies, so that John Jay had had partly to put himself through college by tutoring, and he seems to have had a certain amount of difficulty in supporting his family on his earnings from the law. In his youth he had had a variety of social experience which verged at moments on the picaresque. In the course of a trip to Europe after his graduation from Harvard, he had gone to visit an aunt who had married the German minister to Russia and had attended a ball at the Winter Palace, where he saw through the eyes of Tolstoy the Grand Dukes and 'the gorgeous ministers holding glittering staves' and the 'consoling duplicities' of the diplomats, and rescued a pair of toboggans which seemed about to become untied on a chute by throwing himself between them and holding them together while he was dragged on his belly to the bottom; and not long afterwards, when he had returned to America, he went to Canada and hired himself out as a farm-hand: he 'did chores, digged holes for posts, picked cherries on a ladder' till his 'head swam' and 'the landscape reeled,' but was so bad at it that one farmer refused to pay him, and he finally came back to his family in such a condition of raggedness and shagginess that they were unable to recognize him; his whole exploit had netted him a dollar.

On the eve of his second marriage, he had been troubled by apprehensions at the prospect of being well-to-do. 'The first thing you know we'll be drowned in possessions,' he wrote at that time to Miss Chanler, 'and then by thinking of our horses' health. It is not so easy to keep the keen vision which an empty stomach lends, if you have footmen. I fear a footman. I tremble before a man with hot water . . . Let's keep the New Testament open before us. The losing of wrath is to be feared . . . If I become classed with men at ease about money, the Lord protect me. It is a steel corselet against the heart of mankind and the knowledge of life.' And there are indications in his later letters that he continued to shrink from allowing himself to be 'classed with men at ease about money.' 'I take rides on the busses—for 4d.,' he wrote a friend from London. 'You can go at the rate of 10 m. per hour for half an hour. These things recall London—and student days. The cheap things give one most pleasure—when one is old and rich like me.' And: 'The food of the rich is disgusting to me . . . messes. Last night I had to go to Childs and eat cornbeef hash and poached eggs, which pulled me round.'

Yet he is haunted by ideas of his affinities with royalty and aristocracy. 'I never saw children like them,' he wrote of his sons by his first wife. 'They are King's children in disguise, and I am a stepfather to them.' And, during a visit to an Italian noble, 'I am having some gold fringe put on my pants and I have assumed the title of Monsignore. It is amazing how easily gentility sits on me. I believe some people are just naturally swells—you know what I mean—and fit well in palaces and eat good food naturally and without effort. I remember the first royal palace I saw—seemed to me—gave me a feeling—just like the old homestead. I often think that Grandma Jones used to say, "the Chapmans were once Kings." Dear old Grandpa, with his old cotton socks, wouldn't he be proud if he could see me he-hawing and chaw-chawing with Roman princes!' His plays are full of princes and counts and kings. He had himself something of a kingly presence, especially adorned with the magnificent beard with which he had emerged from his illness. And it is impossible to escape the impression that the comfort and security of his later years did to some degree dull his responses and cut him off from the active world. He suc-cumbed to the Hudson Valley in becoming one of its principal ornaments—to Dutchess County, with its cupolaed castles on their towering dark-wooded hills, which do their best to give work or give alms to the humble feudal villages on the river-bank, to the thunderstorms that seem to crack the firmament and the heavy and slumbrous summers, to the tradition of public responsibility which Hamilton Fish shares with Franklin D. Roosevelt, to the culture which, where it occurs, is likely to range so much more widely and to seem to have so much more authenticity than that of most wealthy communities in America, and to the naturalness and amiability which merge quietly and not unpleasantly with smugness—and all, as it were, walled-in from the rest of the United States and alone with the noble river.

The young John Jay Chapman had plunged into the thick of the conflicts of his time. *Emerson* and *Causes and Consequences* had been talked about and read, had had their influence. In both his political and his literary writing, he had dealt with matters of current interest. But now, in his second period, he seems to have withdrawn from contemporary life, and tends to confine himself to history and the classics. He seems almost to be talking to himself, he seems hardly to expect or hope for an audience; and so people cease to listen to him. The second half of Chapman's career must inevitably be surprising and depressing, though not entirely disappointing, to one who has been stirred by the first. Though he had been able to throw away his crutches, he was to remain, in a deeper sense, a crippled man all the rest of his life. Yet the alternative to survival on these terms would, one supposes, have been madness or death; and it is the proof of the authenticity of his genius that, throughout this long period when he is turned toward the past, when, as a rule, he emerges into the present to raise only trivial or unreal issues, he keeps his power not merely to charm but also sometimes to stimulate.

The Americans who graduated from college in the eighties had to contend with a world that broke most of them. One can see the situation very clearly if one compares the men of the eighties even with those of the seventies. In the seventies, the universities were still turning out admirable professional men, who had had the old classical education, a culture much wider than their profession and the tradition of political idealism and public conscience which had presided at the founding of the Republic. The world which they had found when they got out had not yet become different enough from the world for which their education had fitted them so that they were not able, on the terms of that old education, to make for themselves positions of dignity in it. But by the later years of the eighties, the industrial and commercial development which followed the Civil War had reached a point where the old education was no longer an equipment for life. It had, in fact, become a troublesome handicap. The best of the men who had taken it seriously were launched on careers of tragic misunderstanding. They could no longer play the role in the professions of a trained and public-spirited caste: the new society did not recognize them. The rate of failure and insanity and suicide in some of the college 'classes' of the eighties shows an appalling demoralization.

Some set themselves to learn the new methods and choked their scruples and did their best to cash in; but John Jay Chapman—who had John Jay among his ancestors—was too honest, too fastidious, too proud, and too violently impulsive, for this. Others compromised shrewdly, like Roosevelt; but the merest suggestion of compromise seems at that period to have driven Chapman into a frenzy. Almost all were compelled to accept in some way the values of the world of business; but how little this was possible for Chapman is indicated in one of his late letters when he insists that, let people say what they please, business can never be a profession. (I have heard a college man of as late as the nineties, who had spent fifty years with an importing firm, tell of his feelings of humiliation when he first started in to work there at a time when the business men, on their side, were supposed to have no use for college graduates. By the second decade of our century, probably the majority of college students had no higher object, on graduating, than to qualify for selling bonds or to slip behind some desk in a family concern and present a well-brushed appearance; and the movement for business courses in the colleges and the talk of the university as a 'big business' were already well under way.)

Given the fineness of Chapman's equipment, the overpowering nature of his emotions and the relentless clarity of his insight—and given the inescapable conviction of his superiority which made him, for all the ardor of his patriotism, talk about 'a soul crushed by democracy'—there was nothing for him to do but break. And the permanent psychological damage which he had inflicted upon himself by beating his head against the gilt of the Gilded Age was as much one of the scars of the heroism of his passionate and expiatory nature as the hand he had burnt off in his youth.

Let us see how he occupies himself. He begins by writing little plays for children—then, later, tries longer plays. *The Treason and Death of Benedict Arnold* (1910) is perhaps the best of these and has a certain personal interest—with its Coriolanian picture of a man of touchy pride and strong self-will driving through a perverse course of action, which will bring him, among his enemies, honor but no comfort and which will separate him forever from the cause for which he has fought:

> *They must pet me then,*
> *To show that loyal treason reaps reward.*
> *'Twas policy, not liking for my face,*

That made King George so sweet.
What in this world of savage Englishmen,
Strange monsters that they are, have you and I
Found of a country? Friends, good hearts and true;
But alien as the mountains of the moon,
More unrelated than the Polander,
Are Englishmen to us. They are a race,
A selfish, brawling family of hounds,
Holding a secret contract on each fang,
'For us,' 'for us,' 'for us.' They'll fawn about;
But when the prey's divided;—Keep away!
I have some beef about me and bear up
Against an insolence as basely set
As mine own infamy; yet I have been
Edged to the outer cliff. I have been weak,
And played too much the lackey. What am I
In this waste, empty, cruel, land of England,
Save an old castaway,—a buccaneer,—
The hull of derelict Ambition,—
Without a mast or spar, the rudder gone,
A danger to mankind!

But, on the whole, as his biographer says, Chapman is unable to transmit to his characters his own power of self-dramatization. He shrank from and had little comprehension of the new dramatic forms of Ibsen and Shaw, as he shrank from the world they reflected. The companion of Shakespeare and Aeschylus, he followed their methods as a matter of course, with results which are not hopelessly academic only because he could not help getting some reality into everything that he wrote. His plays were mostly in verse; and his verse—he also made some translations from the Greeks and published a certain amount of miscellaneous poetry—is usually only effective when it approximates to the qualities of his prose. There are a few exceptions to this, such as his fine translations from Dante; but the poet that there undoubtedly was in Chapman—perhaps some Puritan heritage had its blighting effect here—found expression chiefly in preaching. As a moralist, John Jay Chapman is a highly successful artist; and it is mainly as a moralist now that he will continue to hold our attention.

With his illness, there emerges a new point of view—really a sort of rarefication of his earlier one. It was before the days of psychoanalysis, and he had been helped through his breakdown by 'faith healers.' In a peculiar and personal way, he now becomes religious. 'There was never anyone with more practical notions, or less under the belief that he was religious in his aims, than I,' he wrote to a friend in 1922 of his early political experience. 'I wanted to attack practical evils—find out about them anyway, affront and examine them, understand them—and I set out by experiment and analysis to deal with them as a workaday problem. And gradually under inspection and ratiocination they turned into spiritual things—mystical elements, and went back into the envelope of religious truth. Nothing else but religious truth was involved. It happened to me apropos of reform movements, to the next man in medicine, to the next in hygiene, in education, in literary work—(look at Winston Churchill). Surely all of us were toys in a shop, and were being turned by the same dynamo—we all approach more nearly all the time to a common frame of mind and temperament—a common sense of helplessness—we who were going to be so powerful and triumphant.' He had announced his new attitude in 1913 at the end of his book on William Lloyd Garrison: 'At first,' he says, 'we desire to help vigorously, and we do all in our power to assist mankind. As time goes on, we perceive more and more clearly that the advancement of the world does not depend upon us, but that we, rather, are bound up in it, and can command no foothold of our own. At last we see that our very ambitions, desires and hopes in the matter are a part of the Supernal Machinery moving through all things, and that our souls can be satisfied and our power exerted only in so far as we are taken up into that original motion, and merged in that primal power. Our minds thus dissolve under the grinding analysis of life, and leave behind nothing except God. Towards him we stand and look: and we, who started out with so many gifts for men, have nothing left in our satchel for mankind except a blessing.'

To one who, like the present writer, is fundamentally unsympathetic with all modern manifestations of religion, the books of John Jay Chapman on this subject—*Notes on Religion* (1922) and *Letters and Religion* (1924)—seem genuine and impressive in a way that most other such recent writings do not. There have been lately in fashion among literary people two main ways of being religious: one historical, philosophical and ritualistic—the convert turns to the Catholic Church; the other through a substitute pseudo-religion, like that proposed by H. G. Wells. But in the flashes of revelation that were intermittently noted by Chapman, we seem to touch a live spiritual experience as we do not often do with these writers. It is, of course, intensely Protestant: it is Emersonianism again. We are not to look for direction to any established church; each is to trust his own instinct and to interpret the Scriptures for himself:

'Christianity accomplishes itself; and this not through a grand, frontal attack on humanity, but rather through the story and sayings of Christ which dart through the earth, pierce men's ears and heal them, run like elixirs through the languages and habits of men. They are couriers, arrows that live in the ether and need no inns or baiting-places between their flights. The sayings have inexhaustible meanings, and many depths of meaning which the comfortable people of the world cannot hope to fathom—meanings that lie in ambush in the texts, and enter men's hearts in the wake of grief. A man must have been disgraced and in jail to know many of them.' Yet the instincts of individuals are to unite in communion the whole of mankind. With the capacity for deep humility and the sympathy with American life which saved his sense of superiority from snobbery, he was able to interest himself in philanthropies and popular churches:

'I believe that if we could see the invisible church as it actually exists in the interlacing of all men in God and with each other through the force that makes them live, the alarm of those who are fostering religion for fear it will die out would appear ridiculous. Even the half-charlatan, half-illiterate American religious cults deserve our interest and respect.'

'The new American mysticism, for all its eccentricities, dropped an anchor for a generation that had been living in continuous flotation; and being at anchor, the waves of life began to play against the souls of that generation, and beat them into faith. The breakdown of the older ecclesiastical authorities proved a blessing. All the barriers, the interpretations, the shopworn catechisms, the churchy miasmas of many centuries, had been blown away, and the bare text of the New Testament began to convert a new generation and to bring them rest. The new faith was purest in the most humble, as has been the case with all Christian revivals.'

The later Chapman is a lesser Tolstoy, fighting out on his estate on the Hudson the same kind of long war with his conscience which Tolstoy fought at Yasnaya Polyana. And we feel about him somewhat as the contemporaries of Tolstoy seem to have felt about him: that, whatever his inconsistencies and his crusadings for mistaken causes, his spirit and example were a force of incalculable value.

'Truly,' he wrote in one of his letters, 'it is the decay in the American brain that is the real danger, and in my narrow philosophy I see the only cure in self-expression, passion, feeling —spiritual reality of some sort. We're about dead spiritually— that's my illusion.' William James, the one of Chapman's contemporaries who probably appreciated him most, called him 'a profound moralist.' 'I have a notion,' he once wrote James, 'that I could tell you what is the matter with pragmatism—if you would only stand still. A thing is not truth till it is so strongly believed in that the believer is convinced that its existence does not depend upon him. This cuts off the pragmatist from knowing what truth is.' And: 'It is utter nonsense,' he wrote another correspondent, 'this great passion and little passion—this upper clef and lower clef. All life is nothing but passion. From the great passion of love to the regard for a passing stranger is all one diapason, and is the same chord. The whole of it vibrates no matter where you touch it—tho' in different degrees.' His ideal of practical agitation has in his later phase subsided to this: 'I am saying things which will some day be thought of, rather than trying to get the attention of anyone.' 'It is an accident when I *do* right, but I *am* right,' he once declared.

This rightness was due to some influence which took possession of him and was stronger than he. We may be puzzled at first by the language in which he writes to Minna Timmins, his future wife, after the experience of burning off his hand: 'I do think there was something Promethean in it, in the capacity to yield.' What fire had Chapman snatched from Heaven? And is it Promethean to yield? He means that a divine revelation had caused him to mutilate himself—the revelation of his love for Minna, which was unable to break through into his consciousness and to assert its authority over him save by compelling him to recognize, and hence to punish himself for, his mistake. And he wrote later on to Miss Chanler: 'I . . . have broken and battered down the doors of silence once and forever years ago, and go about the world escaped from that prison, I thank the powers of life.' Yet he must break out of prison again and again; and his language is always that of giving himself up to something that invades him from outside: 'I'll tell you my philosophy—that there's only one real joy in life . . . —the joy of casting at the world the stone of an unknown world.' His first love, his first wife and her children, with their fierce natures and their sudden or violent deaths, is itself like a power that seizes upon him, a current for which he acts as conductor and which will leave him partially shattered. And when it is not love, he calls it God.

Besides these religious *pensées*, Chapman publishes during this period several volumes of essays, literary, historical and social, and some memoirs of New York and Boston. He perfects himself now as a writer: in these books, the 'style all splinters,' of which William James wrote at the time of *Practical Agitation*, is hammered out into an instrument of perfect felicity, economy, limpidity, precision and point. Some of his most beautiful prose is in his very latest writings. And he can still take our breath away by laying hold of the root of some subject, by thrusting through, with a brusque direct gesture, all the familiar conventions and pretensions with which it has been enclosed.

In his relation to the literary classics, he was that almost unprecedented phenomenon, a highly intelligent and well-educated American who paid almost no attention to European criticism and scholarship. Well as he knew Europe, he was never afflicted with the nostalgia for it which seized so many of the cultivated Americans of his time. In his opinions on European culture, he was as naturally and uncompromisingly American as Walt Whitman or Mark Twain. The accepted apparatus of learning he either quarreled with or disregarded—characterizing, for example, the taking-over of Greek literature by the mandarins of the English universities as an incident in the expansion of the British Empire.

To Chapman, the great writers of the past were neither a pantheon nor a vested interest. He approached them open-mindedly and boldly, very much as he did living persons who he thought might entertain or instruct him. Not that he judged them by contemporary standards; but he would go straight to them across the ages in the role of an independent traveler, who was willing to pay his toll to the people that kept the roads but wished to linger with them as little as possible. He sometimes committed blunders: he got the relationships mixed up in the *Antigone*, and he never grasped the simple enough principles which govern, in the *Divine Comedy*, the assignment of the souls to the different worlds—complaining that Dante's arrangements involved a good deal of injustice. 'You know,' he says in a letter, 'I've never known the literature of the subjects I wrote on. I never knew the Emerson literature—except Emerson himself.' But Chapman has at least always got there and had a good look at the man; and he can always tell you about him something that you have not heard before. To me, Chapman's flashlighting and spotlighting in his studies of the Greeks, Dante, Shakespeare and Goethe (this last left unpublished at his death and unfortunately not yet published) are among the few real recent contributions to the knowledge of these familiar subjects. He cannot help bumping into aspects which, though they bulk very large in these authors, have so often been ignored or evaded that many people have never noticed they were there. He saw the basic barbarity of Greek tragedy, which he denounced Gilbert Murray for sentimentalizing; he saw the importance of the pederasty of Plato: Diotima, he writes, is 'an odious creature, being a man in disguise'; he saw, through all the Dante commentaries, how impossible it is to interpret Dante in terms of medieval theology.

Here are passages from some of the latest of these essays, which show the freshness of Chapman's mind in his sixties:

'Plato soothes and rests. He takes the mind off its troubles and supplies it with imaginative solutions for problems which do not press. To read him is a solace and to write commentaries on him is an entrancing and enduring preoccupation. He is the patron saint of those who sit in armchairs and speculate.

His wealth of information, myth and anecdote, the amenity and fluidity of his procedure, endear him to all book-lovers. He is enshrined in a civilization which will interest the world as long as intelligent men shall be born into it. Even the limitations and defects of the Athenians are stimulating. "Athens," we say, and surrender ourselves to romance. We sleep while awake; and if you point out that Plato deceives us by intellectual legerdemain which cheats the mind, nay, if you should prove it, this will make you no friends; for, as Mr. Barnum discovered to his profit many centuries later, the public likes to be fooled. A vision of truth which does not call upon us to get out of our armchair—why, this is the desideratum of mankind.'

'Dante's frailty is the source of his power. Had he been truly a medieval theologian, or philosopher, or moralist, or historian, he would today be as dead as the rest of them . . . [His philosophy] is full of whimsies and cobwebs, private significances and key-words; and there is no philosophic instrument of thought which he does not distort as he touches it—even as all poets do, and must do.' 'The conceptions of Greek mythology spring out of a Supermind which harmonizes the fantasies of childhood with the thought of mature age. They are embedded in the ganglia of the brain as music is: no explanation touches them. They defy analysis, and Dante himself fails to interpret them: his metaphysics will not stick to them.' 'To raise the question whether Dante was technically or virtually a heretic . . . is to miss the human and important point of the whole question. Dante's attitude toward the Empire and the Papacy was that of a super-autocrat who is above both of them, and holds a commission from on high to regulate the affairs of each.' 'The truth is that one must gather Dante's meanings, as one gathers the meanings of other men, by putting two and two together, not by drawing pictures of his Supposed Universe, and then hanging his phrases on them as on a Christmas Tree.' 'He had invented the *terza rima*, a form in which a continuous lyric can float and be indefinitely sustained upon the narrative below it.'

What a pity, one is moved to exclaim, that John Jay Chapman remained a dilettante! Yet 'dilettante' is not the proper word for one who worked at his writing so diligently and so seriously. And his literary essays, after all, are only a part of his general commentary, which possesses a sort of center of its own, independent of the various subjects treated.

Aside from this purely literary activity, he carried on a certain amount of agitation, sporadically and in behalf of a strange diversity of causes. His rejection of economics, his failure, when he had recognized political corruption as a mere by-product of the industrial-commercial system, to study the mechanics and the history of that system, had left him without bearings in the political world.

First of all, he went back to the Civil War—he was very proud of one of his grandmothers, who had been a prominent Abolitionist—and in his book on William Lloyd Garrison fought the battle of slavery all over again with a spirit that would have been employed more usefully in fighting the battle of labor. It was the period of the rise of Bill Haywood's Wobblies, of the growth of Eugene Debs's Socialist Party, of Lincoln Steffens' muck-raking movement.

On August 13, 1911, a Negro who had shot and killed a special officer of the Worth Brothers Steel Company in Coatesville, Pennsylvania, was burned alive by a mob under circumstances of special horror. Chapman, who was full of the Civil War, brooded upon this incident till he 'felt as if the whole country would be different if any one man did something in penance, and so I went to Coatesville and declared my intention of holding a prayer meeting to the various business men I could buttonhole.' He had difficulty in getting a hall, but finally, four days after the anniversary of the lynching, succeeded in finding a place to speak. The address he delivered was strange and moving. He said that, when he had read in the papers how 'hundreds of well-dressed American citizens' had stood by and watched the torture of the Negro, he had seemed to see into 'the unconscious soul' of America. And what he had seen there was death—'the paralysis of the nerves about the heart in a people habitually and unconsciously given over to selfish aims.' They had 'stood like blighted things, like ghosts about Acheron, waiting for someone or something to determine their destiny for them.' It was the old wickedness, not yet purged, of the slave trade, and all America was to blame for it. They could but open their hearts to God and pray

that new life might flow into them.—The only persons who attended the meeting were an educated Negro woman from
Boston and a stool pigeon sent by the police.

The World War, when it first broke out, aroused him to a
new burst of agitation. He was in Europe in August 1914, and
went immediately to Balfour, Haldane and Sir Edward Grey,
and told them that it was of vital importance, in order to elicit
the sympathy of the world, that the Allies should declare their
aims to be non-aggressive and announce their intention, in the
event of their victory, of calling a world disarmament congress;
and he seems to have been deceived by the intelligence and
kindness with which these statesmen heard him out. Later, he
went to Wilson and urged him to elicit such a declaration. He
also published a book, *Deutschland über Alles* (1914), in which
he pointed out the propaganda methods by which the Germans had been worked up to the war, and advised the United
States to stay out. 'If America should enter the war, the world
would lose the benevolence and commonsense which we now
possess, and which is a strong factor in the whole situation.
You and I would, in that case, become partisans, cruel, excited
and bent on immediate results.'

In the meantime, however, his son Victor, one of his children by his first wife, had, against his father's wishes, enlisted
in the Foreign Legion and had later become one of the most
daring pilots of the Lafayette Escadrille. He was killed—the
first American aviator to die—on June 23, 1916; and his father
now fell a victim to that war psychology which he had foreseen
and dreaded for the country. Chapman was even betrayed
temporarily into applauding his old enemy Roosevelt, whose
pro-Ally bellowings and pawings of the ground were certainly
no more to be taken seriously than the other Rooseveltian impostures which Chapman had so relentlessly exposed. Later, in
1920, when Siegfried Sassoon came to New York, and read his
poems and made an anti-war speech at the Cosmopolitan
Club, the former opponent of wartime fanaticism—who, no
doubt, felt it a duty to speak for his dead son—got up and
aroused consternation and hisses by denouncing what he characterized as a philosophy of fear and self-pity. The next day he
tried to call on Sassoon and finally wrote him a letter: 'Sorry to
miss you this morning. It was a suffering occasion last night. I

think I suffered as much as you did. If you will do it, why, you must.' Had he remembered his early gospel of the value of the individual gesture and reflected that the young Sassoon had, after all, only been doing what he himself had done when, for example, at that political dinner in 1895, he had spoken out in a way that had made old Mr. Choate turn pale?

The most wrongheaded of all his crusades, but the one to which he devoted most energy, was his attack on the Roman Catholic Church. He had received no doubt a terrifying impression of the bad influence of the Catholics in Boston; but he exaggerated its importance in the United States as a whole, and he had become, by 1925, so almost monomaniacally obsessed by it that it was thought best for him to go abroad to distract his mind from the subject and avoid another breakdown.* At one period he was inclined to believe—in spite of the admiration for Jewish culture which had caused him once to call himself a 'Hebraist'—that the Jews, also, were coming to be a sinister influence, and he even contributed a sonnet, anti-Catholic and anti-Semitic, to the organ of the Ku Klux Klan. ('The Jews,' he had written in 1897, 'have in my experience more faith than the Christians. They have clever heads, better hearts, and more belief in the power of good every way. They gave to the world all the religion it has got and are themselves the most religious people in it. I work with them day and night and most of the time is spent in prying up some Christian to do a half day's work.')

For two years he and Mrs. Chapman conducted a clubroom for young people in the Hell's Kitchen section of New York. On one occasion, two boys whom he had had to put out, came back and blew kerosene in his beard and tried to set it afire. When they had failed, he handed them a handkerchief and told them to wipe themselves off.

Besides all this, he was continually agitating against the influence of big business at Harvard and harrying with scolding letters the Head Master of St. Paul's School, as well as old friends in positions of prominence of whose activities he disapproved. One of his correspondents, Mr. T. B. Wells, the

*Since this was written, the Catholic Church has become in the United States a formidable pressure group, exercising the retrograde and repressive force that Chapman at that time ascribed to it.

editor of *Harper's Magazine*, was finally goaded to ask what
Chapman himself had accomplished any more than 'a lot of
other brilliant fellows who did not make full use of their talents' to give him the right to call everyone else to account over
the way they handled their jobs. And it is true that one feels a
touch of envy in his tone toward men like Shaw and Wells,
even toward William James, whom he undoubtedly liked and
admired—who were doing a kind of work that one would
think he might have applauded. There is even an occasional accent of the ignorant and cutting Boston snootiness that he had
disliked and ridiculed. As one goes through his later letters—as
in reading his work of this period—one is made more and
more uncomfortable by the feeling that one has been shut up
in a chamber from which the air is being gradually withdrawn
—shut in with a chafing spirit who, baffled of finding an outlet, is sometimes furious and sometimes faint. Then suddenly
one recoils and stands outside the cell: one sees how Chapman's outlook has narrowed. One remembers all the things
that have happened in the world of which there is almost no
mention in these letters—almost the whole significant life of
the time; and one realizes that Chapman's interests have come
to be almost entirely confined to the horizons of his old Harvard circle. It is all Harvard College and St. Paul's School,
Porcellian Club and Tavern Club. He writes to Dr. Drury of
St. Paul's and E. S. Martin of *Life* as if they were among the
great molders of thought of their age. We have the suspicion
that even William James, as distinct from Wells and Shaw, is
only admitted to the sphere of Chapman's interest because he,
too, belongs to Harvard. It is the lost traveler's dream under
the hill—the old conception of the caste of trained 'college
men' who were to preside over the arts and professions. It is
the same point of view—we had not recognized it at first—
that seemed so fatuous, that became so unconsciously comic,
in Owen Wister's memoirs of Roosevelt. Mr. Wister, whose
claim to celebrity consists in his having written novels, is wonderful when, after telling of his acquaintance with various per-
sonages of Philadelphia and Harvard of whom we have never
heard, he says that, 'Huysmans (if I recall the right name) had
recently published a novel, in which were described the rites of
the Black Mass'—and he is even more wonderful when, after a

life 'chiefly passed,' as he says, 'among the Alexander Cassatts, the George Baers and the Weir Mitchells' of Philadelphia, he goes West and discovers Coxey's army and the stoppage of trains due to the Pullman strike, and is obliged to spend two dreadful nights sleeping on the floor of a boat from San Pedro. But this failure of response to contemporary events, either artistic or economic is, in Chapman's case, simply depressing. Owen Wister thinks them still important, Olympians who dominate the world—Roosevelt and Henry Adams and Henry Cabot Lodge and the rest. John Jay Chapman has no illusions about them, but he has to go on nagging at them and abusing them. He does not seem to realize that they have all been either absorbed or left behind by a new world never contemplated by old Harvard. He himself—for all the piercing intuitions which still at moments strike through age and class—has been left behind by that world.

He believed in these later days that the society of the period after the war was on the eve of a great religious reawakening:

'Who shall say that this present era, when all the idols are broken, all the great traditions dead, and the fine arts have become mere wandering lights, while the mind of man seems to have passed into a tunnel of transition—who shall say that these apparent extinguishments and this twilight are not necessary? Our present incredulity as to all the explanations of life is very favorable to a direct vision of life itself. The floods have carried away our mills, and a thunderstorm has destroyed the wiring of our houses; but the powers of gravity and electricity are not abolished for a moment. The contrivances on which we had set so much store served but to obscure the phenomena. Like Job in the wreck of his homestead, we have been humbled. The war humbled that spirit which had ruled the nineteenth century. In scale the drama differed from the Book of Job, but in plot it was similar.

'In the meantime, though the arts have lost their message, religion stalks in upon us. The auld wives' tales about prayer and healing, which during many centuries had been regarded as ecstatic parables, are now taken literally: we live in them. This tunnel into which the age is running is one of the clairvoyant periods of history in which men are seen as trees walking. The actual world does not disappear, nor is it relegated to a life to come, or disparaged, or condemned as evil. It remains perfectly real, and yet visibly penetrated by the rays of an inner universe which are at play everywhere.'

One used to see him, during those years, in New York, in company a figure of a distinction almost exotic for the United States, with his fine manners, his sensitive intelligence, his clothes with their attractive suggestion of the elegance of another era, his almost Jove-like beard and brow, his deep and genial laugh; or for a moment under a quite different aspect, when one had happened to meet him in the street: walking alone, head drooping and brooding, with his muffler around his neck, in his face dreadful darkness and sadness and fear, as if he were staring into some lidless abyss.

He died, after an operation, on November 4, 1933. He had loved music, and when he was a student at Harvard had had what he described as 'an obsession, a sort of self-willed mania for learning to play the violin, for which I had no talent.' He had worked at it two years, but his fellow students had discouraged him by throwing coal scuttles at his door and hanging alarm-clocks outside his windows. After his father's financial failure, he wrote home, 'I shall sell the violin: it's no halfway business.' But at the time he was recovering from his breakdown, he had taken up the study of harmony and tried to compose a little. Now two days before his death, writes Mrs. Chapman, he kept murmuring, 'A soldier lay dying, a soldier lay dying.' 'I bent over him to catch the words, and he repeated the first four lines of "A soldier of the Legion lay dying in Algiers," adding, "*But there is lack of nothing here*," in a voice of deep feeling.' But later, when semi-conscious, he began saying, 'plucking at my fingers, "I want to take it away, I want to take it away!" "What?" I asked. "The pillow?" "No," he said. "The mute, the mute. I want to play on the open strings."'

Bernard Shaw at Eighty

TIME has shifted our point of view on Bernard Shaw, yet he is still worth our contemplation. Let us cast a look back over his career.

George Bernard Shaw was born in Dublin, July 26, 1856, the son of shabby-genteel parents who had connections with the Irish nobility. The elder Shaw became an alcoholic, and the boy had to go to work as a clerk at the age of fifteen. Mrs. Shaw finally left her husband and went to London, where she made a living by teaching music. Her son came to live with her when he was twenty and wrote novels which he was unable to sell and picked up through journalism such money as he could. He remained with his mother till he was forty-two.

In the fall of 1882 he happened to attend a lecture on land nationalization delivered by Henry George in London. The result was a revelation: 'It flashed on me,' he writes, 'that "the conflict between religion and science" . . . the overthrow of the Bible, the higher education of women, Mill on Liberty and all the rest of the storm that raged around Darwin, Tyndall, Huxley, Spencer and the rest, on which I had brought myself up intellectually, was a mere middle-class business . . . The importance of the economic basis dawned on me.' He read George's *Progress and Poverty*—then someone told him to read *Das Kapital*. 'Karl Marx,' he once said, 'made a man of me.'

The result of the depression of the eighties was a revival of socialist agitation. Bernard Shaw became a socialist and spoke in halls, on street corners, in Hyde Park. The 'insurrectionism' of the period reached a climax in the 'Bloody Sunday' of November 1887, when the socialists, at the head of a working-class demonstration, invaded Trafalgar Square and were routed by the police. After this, business revived and took up the slack of unemployment, and the agitation quieted down.

In the meantime, Shaw had attached himself to the socialist statistician, Sidney Webb, and with others they had founded the Fabian Society, which had 'agreed to give up the delightful ease of revolutionary heroics and take to the hard work of practical reform on ordinary parliamentary lines.' Webb was a civil servant with a post in the colonial office and later a member of the London County Council; Shaw became a vestryman, then a borough councilor. The Fabians continued to treat Marx with respect, but the polite and reasonable criticism to which they subjected him was designed to discredit some of his main assumptions. Marx had asserted that the value of commodities was derived from the labor which had gone to produce them; and the Fabians, by elaborating a counter-theory that made value depend on demand, shifted the emphasis from the working class to the 'consumer.' They also repudiated the class war, showed that it would never occur. Socialist nationalization was to be accomplished by a corps of experts who should 'permeate' government and business, quietly invading Whitehall and setting up state departments which, unassisted by the action of the masses, should put socialist ideas into effect. Shaw boasted that the Fabians had made socialism respectable.

This variation of Marxism in England was natural to the place and time. A period of prosperity during the seventies had deflated the Chartist agitation (I am indebted to Mr. Mark Starr for a Marxist analysis of Fabian Marxism); and it was not until the eighties, when British commercial domination was being challenged by the United States and Germany, that the dangers of the capitalist system began to become generally plain. But now attention was principally directed toward the evils of competition. The development of large-scale industry was eliminating competition and making municipal ownership seem desirable, not only to the lower layers of the middle class, but even to private enterprise itself, which benefited from good housing and cheap tram-lines. The professional middle class were in a position to see the value of nationalization, and the working class had not yet discovered that for them there was not very much difference between being exploited by a private employer and being exploited by a government that was controlled by the propertied classes. The Fabians looked no further than their reforms.

In Bernard Shaw's case, this compromise Marxism played in with the elements of his character and influenced its subsequent development. Coming to London, as he has recently told us, with a conviction of his own superiority and a snobbish family tradition, but with no money and no social experience, Shaw was himself one of the dispossessed, and the socialist criticism of the class system based on property strongly recommended itself to him. Yet at the same time that in all good faith he was working to destroy that system, there is apparent in his career a tendency in the inverse direction to this. At the same time that he was spurred by a moral need to work for a future society consistent with his sense of justice, he was spurred, also, by a social need to vindicate his rightful position in the society in which he lived. He has told us that his father's bad habits had caused his family to be dropped socially in Dublin and that when he first came to London he was so shy that he would not accept dinner invitations and would 'sometimes walk up and down the Embankment for twenty minutes or more before venturing to knock at the door' of a house to which he had been asked. He goes on to say, 'The house and its artistic atmosphere were most congenial to me; and I liked all the Lawsons; but I had not mastered the art of society at that time and could not bear making an inartistic exhibition of myself; so I soon ceased to plague them.' There has always been thus in Shaw a certain amount of social snobbery mixed up with his intellectual snobbery.

The confusion produced in his thought by these two conflicting tendencies is curiously illustrated in a passage from his autobiographical preface to the collected edition of his works: 'Finding one's place may be made very puzzling,' he writes, 'by the fact that there is no place in ordinary society for extraordinary individuals. For the worldly wiseman, with common ambitions, the matter is simple enough: money, title, precedence, a seat in parliament, a portfolio in the cabinet, will mean success both to him and to his circle. But what about people like St. Francis and St. Clare? Of what use to them are the means to live the life of the country house and the West End mansion? They have literally no business in them, and must necessarily cut an unhappy and ridiculous figure there. They have to make a society of Franciscans and Poor Clares for themselves before they can work or live socially. It is true that those who are called saints are not saintly all the time and in everything. In eating and drinking, lodging and sleeping, chatting and playing: in short, in everything but working out their destiny as saints, what is good enough for a plowman is good enough for a poet, a philosopher, a saint or a higher mathematician. But Hodge's work is not good enough for Newton, nor Falstaff's conversation holy enough for Shelley. Christ adapted himself so amicably to the fashionable life of his time in his leisure that he was reproached for being a gluttonous man and a winebibber, and for frequenting frivolous and worthless sets. But he did not work where he feasted, nor flatter the Pharisees, nor ask the Romans to buy him with a sinecure. He knew when he was being entertained, well treated, lionized: not an unpleasant adventure for once in a way; and he did not quarrel with the people who were so nice to him. Besides, to sample society is part of a prophet's business: he must sample the governing class above all, because his inborn knowledge of human nature will not explain the anomalies produced in it by Capitalism and Sacerdotalism. But he can never feel at home in it.'

But which is true: that the St. Francis or the St. Clare can't 'live socially' till they have 'made a society of Franciscans and Poor Clares' or that 'in eating and drinking, lodging and sleeping, chatting and playing,' 'what is good enough for a plowman is good enough for a saint'? And as for Shaw's description of Christ, it evokes an incongruous picture: what one sees is the preacher of the Sermon on the Mount very much pleased with himself on the beach at the Riviera or playing Santa Claus at Lady Astor's Christmas party.

And other influences, from his early education, came to deflect the straight line of his socialism.

The escapades of the romantic hero, from Childe Harold through Don César de Bazan, with his 'Tant pis! C'est moi!,' to Siegfried, had been a protest against the meanness and dullness of the commercial bourgeois world; but this revolt was itself merely a further phase of the tradition of individual assertion which, deriving from the Protestant conscience, had produced the anarchic individualism of the competitive commercial system. The romantic, like the old-fashioned capitalist, proclaimed the power of the personal will in defiance of society and God.

William Archer tells us that the first time he ever saw Shaw, the latter was sitting in the British Museum studying alternately the French translation of *Das Kapital* and the score of *Tristan und Isolde*. When Shaw first came before the public, he fell instinctively into dramatizing himself as a semi-romantic character—and this in spite of the fact that he was managing to figure at the same time as the arch-enemy and blasphemer of romanticism. The impulse to satirize romanticism implies, as in the case of Flaubert, a strong predisposition toward it; and the exploded romantic, Captain Brassbound, is offset by the Devil's Disciple. It is true that Shaw's conscious intention was to ridicule and shame his audience out of exclusive preoccupation with the emotions of their personal lives—especially, with romantic love—and to interest them in the problems of society. Here is the fine and well-known passage from *Man and Superman*, in which he defends what he calls the 'artist-philosophers' against the 'mere artists': 'This is the true joy in life, the being used for a purpose recognized by yourself as a mighty one; the being thoroughly worn out before you are thrown on the scrap heap; the being a force of Nature instead of a feverish selfish little clod of ailments and grievances complaining that the world will not devote itself to making you happy.' Yet is this not, too, a kind of romanticism—romanticism *par excellence*? The ego has now, to be sure, identified itself with a force of Nature, but this simply makes the ego seem godlike. There is nothing to guarantee that it will respect either the feelings or the interests of others. The ideal artist-philosopher of Bernard Shaw has always a strong social conscience, and his heroes are likely to be philosopher-statesmen or social prophets or saviors of society; but there is nothing to guarantee that they shall be, in the socialist sense, genuine popular leaders, deriving their power from, as well as guiding, the dispossessed: they may be simply despot-heroes—as Shaw's Julius Caesar actually is—acting in the right of their own superiority and giving people what they know to be good for them.

And finally, of course, Bernard Shaw was not only a political prophet struggling for socialist ideas, but an artist trying to realize himself through art. There was a poet in Shaw, still partly suppressed, or at any rate terribly overtaxed, by the round of political meetings, the functions of vestryman and borough councilor, and the years of theatergoing and weekly article-writing about the theater, which he had come to judge almost exclusively in terms of the sort of thing that he wanted to do himself. His own plays he had been writing in note-books while traveling on the tops of buses between one engagement and another. Now in 1898, when he was forty-two, he had what seems to have been a general collapse as the result of a bad fall and a serious injury to his foot. When he recovered, he married an Irish lady, well-to-do but belonging like Shaw to the general 'advanced' movement, who gave him for apparently the first time in his life a comfortable place to live and took the most excellent care of him. Thereafter, he was able to give up the journalism on which he had depended for a living and to devote all his best energies to his plays. He remained a public man, but he spoke no more at dockers' strikes.

By 1905 he was writing *Major Barbara*, in which the type of Christian sainthood, an aristocratic Salvation Army worker, is confronted with a self-made munitions manufacturer, the type of successful capitalism; and ending the play with an alliance between them. In his preface, he made out a ringing case for the man who recognizes poverty as the worst of all the evils and consequently the worst of all the sins, and who saves himself from it at any cost. *Major Barbara* contains one of the best expositions of the capitalist point of view ever written. Bernard Shaw, like his hero, Andrew Undershaft, had come by that time to know what it was to make one's way in capitalist society and to occupy a position of power. He had himself become the type of the critic, who, by scolding the bourgeoisie, makes good with it and becomes one of its idols. He was gradually, for all the scandal of his début, turning into a dependable member of the British propertied classes; and he was to end as an esteemed public figure in a country where an aristocratic governing class was still able to contribute to public life a certain distinction and glamor.

II

The real Shaw has thus never been the single-minded crusader that people at one time used to think him. Except for a limited period during the eighties and early nineties—when he wrote his only straight socialist plays, *Widowers' Houses* and *Mrs. Warren's Profession*—he has never really been a practicing

socialist. And I am inclined to believe that the future will exactly reverse the opinion which his contemporaries have usually had of him. It used always to be said of Shaw that he was
primarily not an artist, but a promulgator of certain ideas. The
truth is, I think, that he is a considerable artist, but that his
ideas—that is, his social philosophy proper—have always been
confused and uncertain. As he has grown older and as the world
has been shaken out of the pattern to which he had adapted his
attitudes, the inadequacy of those attitudes has been exposed.

One is struck, as one goes through the volumes of the collected edition of Shaw, which includes a good deal of his journalism, by the fact that, though his writing on musical and
theatrical and literary subjects remains remarkably fresh, the
pieces on public affairs and on social questions in general prove
very much less satisfactory than one had remembered their
seeming when they first came out. There are passages of admirable exposition and passages of wonderful eloquence—
some of which, such as the peroration to *The Intelligent
Woman's Guide to Socialism and Capitalism*, will probably
always stand among the classics of socialist literature. But the
political writing of Shaw does not drive you into taking up a
position as the greatest socialist writing does: indeed, before
he has finished—and he is likely to go on talking too long—he
has often seemed to compromise the points which you had
imagined he was trying to make, and has produced, with much
earnestness and emphasis, an impression rather blurred by
rhetoric. Both his intelligence and his sense of justice have prevented him from assailing the capitalist system with such intolerant resentment and unscrupulous methods as Voltaire trained
on the Church. With Voltaire, it *is* the crusader that counts;
with Shaw, it is the dramatic poet.

The volume which covers the wartime exposes Bernard
Shaw's contradictions in a particularly striking manner.
Though he was perfectly familiar with the Marxist theory of
capitalist expansion and aggression, and had expounded it on
many occasions, he had always been liable to fits of admiration
for the exploits of the British Empire. Irishman though he
was, he had never been an Irish patriot; and, critical though
he was of the English, he had in *John Bull's Other Island*—
which was written for but declined by Abbey Theater—backed

them against the Irish on account of what he regarded as their superior enterprise and practicality. And though he denounced the Denshawai massacre in Egypt, he supported the British against the Boers at the time of the South African war, because the Boers represented for him a backward civilization and the British a progressive one. When the civilizing forces of the various nations had finally collided in 1914, it was Lenin, the revolutionary exile, not Shaw, the successful British citizen, who wrote *Imperialism: The Last Stage of Capitalism.*

What Bernard Shaw did write was *Common Sense About the War*, which, although it raised a terrible outcry in the fall of 1914 on the part of certain elements of the British public who thought that Shaw ought to be put in the Tower, seems today rather a double-facing document. Shaw, to be sure, makes a certain amount of effort still to keep before the minds of his readers the socialist interpretation of the War. 'Will you,' he writes, 'now at last believe, O stupid British, German and French patriots, what the Socialists have been telling you for so many years: that your Union Jacks and tricolors and Imperial Eagles ("where the carcase is, there will the eagles be gathered") are only toys to keep you amused, and that there are only two real flags in the world henceforth: the red flag of Democratic Socialism and the black flag of Capitalism, the flag of God and the flag of Mammon? What earthly or heavenly good is done when Tom Fool shoots Hans Narr? The plain fact is that if we leave our capital to be dealt with according to the selfishness of the private man he will send it where wages are low and workers enslaved and docile: that is, as many thousand miles as possible from the Trade Unions and Trade Union rates and parliamentary Labour parties of civilization; and Germany, at his sordid behest, will plunge the world into war for the sake of disgracing herself with a few rubber plantations, poetically described by her orators and journalists as "a place in the sun." When you do what the Socialists tell you by keeping your capital jealously under national control and reserving your shrapnel for the wasters who not only shirk their share of the industrial service of their country, but intend that their children and children's children shall be idle wasters like themselves, you will find that not a farthing of our capital will go abroad as long as there is a British slum to be cleared and rebuilt or a hungry, ragged and ignorant British child to be fed, clothed and educated.'

This sounds spirited enough by itself, yet the burden of *Common Sense About the War* is that the war must be supported and vigorously prosecuted. Shaw afterwards visited and wrote about the front at the invitation of Sir Douglas Haig and even did some work for the propaganda department of the government. In his discussion of compulsory military service in *Common Sense About the War*, he defends his position as follows: 'In my own case, the question of conscientious objection did not arise: I was past military age. I did not counsel others to object, and should not have objected myself if I had been liable to serve: for intensely as I loathed the war, and free as I was from any illusion as to its character, and from the patriotic urge (patriotism in my native county taking the form of an implacable hostility to England), I knew that when war is once let loose, and it becomes a question of kill or be killed, there is no stopping to argue about it: one must just stand by one's neighbors and take a hand with the rest. If England had adopted me, as some of my critics alleged in their attempts to convict me of gross ingratitude, I could have pleaded that she must take the consequences without claiming any return; but as I had practically adopted England by thrusting myself and my opinions on her in the face of every possible rebuff, it was for me to take the consequences, which certainly included an obligation to help my reluctant ward in her extremity as far as my means allowed.'

Frank Harris, in his book about Shaw, reproached him for supporting the war; and Shaw retorted in a postscript that Harris 'could not stop to ask himself the first question . . . of the intellectually honest judicious critic, "What else could I have done had it been my own case?"' Yet surely there were other courses open to a man of Shaw's opinions. He could have expressed his disapproval and shut up, as John Morley and others did. But it is impossible for Shaw to shut up, and he went on talking incessantly through the whole four years of slaughter. Much of what he had to say was intelligent, and it required some courage to say it. Compared with most of the British writers, he seemed at the time to an American remarkably cool and sagacious. The atmosphere was feverish with panic and stupefying with the fumes of propaganda, and Shaw did do something to clear the air for a discussion of the origin and aims of the war. But when we reread what he wrote today, he looks a little foolish. The old socialist has gone down into the mêlée and sacrificed something of his moral dignity: we hear him remonstrating, scolding, exhorting, making fun of the politicians and at the same time lending a hand to the government, pleading for the conscientious objectors and at the same time 'joy-riding at the front'—and doing everything with equal cocksureness.

Before the Peace Conference, he had great hopes of Wilson. Before the Washington Disarmament Conference, he was cynical. Later, he spoke a kind word for the League of Nations. And in the meantime the Russian Revolution had set him off on a different tack. He would alternately lecture Lenin and Trotsky on the futility of what they were trying to do and applaud them for succeeding in doing it: he was alternately a middle-class socialist using Fabianism against the Marxists and a Marxist using Lenin and Trotsky against the British governing class. (It is interesting to note that Lenin characterized him as 'a good man fallen among Fabians,' and that Trotsky, of whom Shaw wrote enthusiastically as 'the Prince of Pamphleteers,' expressed the wish, apropos of his own exclusion from England, that 'the Fabian fluid that ran in [Bernard Shaw's] veins' might have 'been strengthened by even so much as five per cent of the blood of Jonathan Swift.' It is amusing to see Trotsky's indignation in his *Where Is Britain Going?* over Shaw's cavalier suggestion that Marx had been superseded by H. G. Wells's *Outline of History*. Trotsky had gone to the trouble of procuring and looking into Wells.)

In his political utterances since the war, it is hardly too much to say that Bernard Shaw has behaved like a jackass. In the autumn of 1927, he was staying in Italy on the Lago Maggiore and throwing bouquets at Mussolini. It was his old admiration for the romantic hero, his old idealization—which was as likely to be set off by an imperialist as a Marxist theme—of the practical Caesarean statesman who makes people stand around. Mussolini had, according to Shaw, 'achieved a dictatorship in a great modern state without a single advantage, social, official or academic, to assist him, after marching to Rome with a

force of Black Shirts which a single disciplined regiment
backed by a competent government could have routed at any
moment . . . After the war the government of Italy' had
been 'so feeble that silly Syndicalists were seizing factories, and
fanatical devotees of that curious attempt at a new Catholic
church called the Third International were preaching a *coup
d'état* and a Crusade in all directions, and imagining that this
sort of thing was Socialism and Communism. Mussolini, without any of Napoleon's prestige, has done for Italy what
Napoleon did for France, except that for the Duc d'Enghien
you must read Matteotti.' When Gaetano Salvemini reminded
Shaw that, so far from being 'without a single advantage,'
Mussolini had had behind him 'the money of the banks, the
big industrialists and the landowners,' and that his Black Shirts
had been 'equipped with rifles, bombs, machine-guns, and
motor-lorries by the military authorities, and assured of im-
punity by the police and the magistracy, while their adversaries
were disarmed and severely punished if they attempted resistance,' Shaw's rebuttal was almost unbelievable: Why, he demanded, had Mussolini been able to command the support of
the army officers and capitalists 'instead of Signors Salvemini,
Giolitti, Turati, Matteotti and their friends, in spite of the fact
that he was farther to the Left in his political opinions than any
of them? The answer, as it seems to me, is that he combined
with extreme opinions the knowledge that the first duty of any
Government, no matter what its opinions are, is to carry on,
and make its citizens carry on, liberty or no liberty, democracy
or no democracy, socialism or no socialism, capitalism or no
capitalism. Until Salvemini and his friends convince Italy that
they understand this necessity as well as Mussolini does they
will never shake his hold on the situation. To rail at him as
Shelley railed at Castlereagh and Eldon, Marx at Napoleon III
and Thiers, Kautsky at Lenin, is to play the amusing but inglo-
rious part of Thersites.' Now a dramatist in his capacity of
dramatist may make out a very interesting case for a Castlereagh or a Napoleon III; but why should Shaw in his capacity
as a political writer take the part of such politicians against
their philosophical opponents? He is himself of the company
of Shelley and Marx—the company of the poets and prophets;
and railing at the Castlereaghs and Napoleons—of which Shaw

himself has done plenty on occasion—is by no means the least valuable of their functions. The analogy between these other cases and Kautsky complaining of Lenin is certainly a silly and dishonest one.

That spring he had finished a long treatise—*The Intelligent Woman's Guide*—in which he had made a more comprehensive effort than he had ever done in his socialist days in the eighties to analyze capitalist society and to argue the case for socialism. Perhaps the book should have been written in the eighties. Ramsay Macdonald and Sidney Webb had come to power with the Labour Government in 1924, and Macdonald had not yet definitely sold out; and the whole story is repeated in general in the familiar Fabian terms—to which Shaw, without Fabian sanction, had added equality of income as a prime item of his socialist program. Through many pages of swift exposition, perhaps Shaw's most precise and limpid writing, which, together with the magnificent close, give the book an enduring value, he makes his way to conclusions that perplex us in proportion as the reasoning becomes more fine-spun and that do not seem finally to land us in any very realistic relation to the England of after the war. 'A series of properly prepared nationalizations may not only be understood and voted for by people who would be quite shocked if they were called Socialists, but would fit in perfectly with the habits of the masses who take their bread as it comes and never think about anything of a public nature.' And in the meantime the road to socialism remains for a good part of the way—through 'nationalizations, expropriative taxation and all the constructive political machinery'—identical with the road to state capitalism. So that Lenin, says Shaw, had been quite in the wrong when he had denounced the methods of the Fabians as state capitalism.

But Lenin had been aware of the psychological pitfalls in the approach of the Fabians toward socialism—pitfalls which no amount of lucid explanation was able to get them over and which Shaw continued to stumble into himself. From the moment that you propose to benefit people from the point of view of imposing upon them what is best for them rather than of showing them the way to what they ought to have and awaiting the moment when they will know that they must have it, what is to prevent your slipping—the post-Lenin period in Russia has proved it as much as the Ramsay Macdonald Labour Government—into imposing upon the people something which will benefit you yourself?

I shall not here pursue the story of the subsequent career of the Fabians, as I want to show further on how it was reflected in Bernard Shaw's later plays. But I will note here that in 1931 he visited Soviet Russia in company with the Tory Lady Astor and with the liberal Marquess of Lothian, had an audience with Stalin, at which, as he said, they treated Stalin like 'a friendly emperor,' and, on his return, began loudly endorsing Russia and especially scolding the United States for not following the Soviet example. Later, in his *Preface on Bosses* in his volume of plays of 1936, he was back praising Mussolini again and even throwing a few kind words to Hitler, whom he described as 'not a stupid German' (did Bernard Shaw prefer a crazy Austrian?) and whose persecution of the Jews he characterized considerately as 'a craze, a complex, a bee in his bonnet, a hole in his armor, a hitch in his statesmanship, one of those lesions which sometimes prove fatal.' Of the systematic persecution by the Nazis of Communists, Socialists and Pacifists, of everybody—including critics and artists—who belonged to Bernard Shaw's own camp, he had nothing whatever to say save to mention it and minimize it in passing as 'plundering raids and *coups d'état* against inconvenient Liberals or Marxists.' At the time of the Ethiopian War, he came out strongly for Mussolini on the same grounds on which he had formerly defended the behavior of the British in South Africa, and insisted that the League of Nations, on behalf of which in 1928 he had written a Fabian pamphlet, should never have tried to interfere.

Thus in this period of disastrous dictatorships, when it was very important for a socialist to keep clear in the eyes of the public the difference between the backing and aims of Lenin and the backing and aims of Mussolini, Bernard Shaw has done a good deal to confuse them and, parliamentary socialist though he claims to be, to exalt the ideal of the dictator. When the socialist dictatorship of Lenin gave way to the despotism of Stalin, Shaw did not seem to know the difference, but applauded the suppression of the old Leninists, on the ground that most professional revolutionists ought to be shot the morning after the revolution, and, on the principle that the socially harmful had to be got out of the way, gave his blessing to the Russian concentration camps, with their millions of political prisoners.

All this he has handled, of course, with his marvelous cleverness and style. Analyzing everybody perpetually, he is a great master of the smoke-screen against criticism. It is done partly by sheer personal hypnotism and Irish gift of gab. Before you arrive at any book of Bernard Shaw's—from *What I Really Wrote About the War* to his correspondence with Ellen Terry— you have almost invariably been told what to think of it in a preface by which Shaw has protected himself against your possible perception of his weakness. If you submit to his spell, you will allow him to manipulate the lights in such a way that, by the time the curtain goes up, you find Shaw looking noble in the center of the stage with everything else left in semi-obscurity, and yourself with your discriminatory powers in a temporary state of suspension, under the illusion that you must either accept or reject him. (Of late the exhibitionistic vanity which seemed dashing in his early days when he was assailing the philistines with such spirit has come to be tiresome and even repellent—as, for example, when his comment on the death of one of his distinguished contemporaries takes the form of the irrelevant reflection, 'I'll be dead very soon myself!')

But there has been also an odd kind of trickery involved in the whole of Bernard Shaw's career. It depends on a technique which he has mastered of functioning on three distinct planes and of shifting from one to another. His air of certainty, his moralist's tone, his well-drilled sentences, his regular emphasis, all go to create an impression of straightforwardness. But actually the mind of Shaw is always fluctuating between various emotions which give rise to various points of view.

The mechanics seem to be somewhat as follows: At the bottom of Shaw is a commonsense sphere of practical considerations; above this is a plane of socialism, of the anticipated reorganization of society in the interest of ideal values; and above this, a poet-philosopher's ether from which he commands a longer view of life *sub specie aeternitatis* and where the poet allows himself many doubts which neither the socialist nor the bourgeois citizen can admit. Shaw has never really taken up his residence for any great length of time on any one of these three planes of thinking. The socialist, for example, denounces war; but when England actually goes to war, the respectable householder backs her. The moralist denounces marriage; but the conventional married man always advises young people to get married. The socialist takes sword in hand to battle for a sounder society based on a redistribution of income; and the long-view philosopher-poet comes to sap the socialist's faith with misgivings as to the capacity for intellect and virtue of the material of common humanity as contrasted with philosopher-poets. The poet gets a good way above the earth in the ecstasy of imaginative vision; but the socialist reminds him that it is the duty of art to teach a useful social lesson, and the householder damps the fires of both by admonishing them that the young people in the audience oughtn't to be told anything that will get them into trouble. The result is that reading Shaw is like looking through a pair of field glasses of which the focus is always equally sharp and clear but the range may be changed without warning.

So adroit are Shaw's transitions that we are usually unaware of what has happened; and when we have come to be conscious of them, we wonder how much Shaw is aware. It is curious to go back over his work and see him juggling with his various impersonations: the socialist, the fascist, the saint, the shrewd businessman, the world genius, the human being, the clever journalist who knows how to be politic, the popular speaker who knows how to be tactful. It is quite as if they were the characters in a comedy, each of whom he can pick up where he has dropped him and have him go on with his part.

III

But comedies are best presented in the theater; and in the theater Shaw's conflicts of impulse, his intellectual flexibility and his genius for legerdemain—all the qualities that have had the effect of weakening his work as a publicist—have contributed to his success as an artist.

One of the prime errors of recent radical criticism has been the assumption that great novels and plays must necessarily be written by people who have everything clear in their minds. People who have everything clear in their minds, who are not capable of identifying themselves imaginatively with, who do not actually embody in themselves, contrary emotions and points of view, do not write novels or plays at all—do not, at any rate, write good ones. And—given genius—the more violent the contraries, the greater the works of art.

Let us consider Shaw as an artist.

Bernard Shaw's great role in the theater has been to exploit the full possibilities of a type of English comedy which had first been given its characteristic form during the seventies of the nineteenth century in the comedies of W. S. Gilbert. The comedy of the Restoration, which had culminated in Congreve, had been the product of an aristocratic society, which depended for its ironic effects on the contrast between artificial social conventions and natural animal instincts, between fine manners and fine intelligence, on the one hand, and the crudest carnal appetites, on the other. The comedy of the nineteenth century—setting aside Oscar Wilde—depended on the contrast between the respectable conventions of a pious middle-class society and the mean practical realities behind them, between the pretension to high moral principles and the cold complacency which underlay it. As with the dramatists of the Restoration, it was always the pursuit of pleasure that emerged from behind the formalities, so, in the comedies of Gilbert which preceded his Savoy operas and of which the most famous and successful was *Engaged* (1877), it is always the greed for money that extrudes from behind the screen of noble words and discreet behavior. 'Dear papa,' says the Victorian young lady in one of the scenes of *Engaged*, when she has just heard of the failure of a bank in which the fortune of her fiancé was invested, 'I am very sorry to disappoint you, but unless your tom-tit is very much mistaken, the Indestructible was registered under the Joint Stock Companies Act of '62 and in that case the stockholders are jointly and severally liable to the whole extent of their available capital. Poor little Minnie don't pretend to have a business head; but she is not quite such a little donkey as that, dear papa!' The characters of Gilbert's comedies, who talk the language of Victorian fiction, are never for a moment betrayed by emotion into allowing themselves to be diverted from the main chance; and the young men are perfectly ready, not from appetite but from sheer indifference, to make equally passionate professions to any number of young ladies at the same time. It is not far from the Symperson family and Cheviot Hill of *Engaged* to Shaw's *The Philanderer* and *Widowers' Houses.*

But neither Gilbert nor Dickens nor Samuel Butler—those two other great satirists of the money-minded English, to whom, also, Shaw is indebted—could teach him to analyze society in terms of economic motivation or to understand and criticize the profit system. This he learned to do from Karl Marx, whose work during his English residence, the period when *Das Kapital* was written, was itself of course a product of and an ironical protest against English nineteenth-century civilization. Bernard Shaw thus brought something quite new into English imaginative literature. His study of economics had served him, as he said, for his plays as the study of anatomy had served Michael Angelo. And with economic insight and training he joined literary qualities of a kind that had never yet appeared in combination with them—qualities, in fact, that, since the century before, had been absent from English literature entirely.

The Irish of Bernard Shaw's period enjoyed, in the field of literature, certain special advantages over the English, due to the fact that, since Irish society was still mainly in the pre-industrial stage, they were closer to eighteenth-century standards. If we compare Shaw, Yeats and Joyce to, say, Galsworthy, Wells and Bennett, we are struck at once by the extent to which these latter writers have suffered from their submergence in the commercial world. In their worst phases of sentimentality and philistinism, there is almost nothing to choose between them and the frankly trashy popular novelist; whereas the Irish have preserved for English literature classical qualities of hardness and elegance.

Bernard Shaw has had the further advantage of a musical education. 'Do not suppose for a moment,' he writes, 'that I learnt my art from English men of letters. True, they showed me how to handle English words; but if I had known no more than that, my works would never have crossed the Channel. My masters were the masters of a universal language; they were, to go from summit to summit, Bach, Handel, Haydn, Mozart, Beethoven and Wagner . . . For their sakes, Germany stands consecrated as the Holy Land of the capitalistic age.' Einstein has said that Shaw's plays remind him of Mozart's music: every word has its place in the development. And if we allow for some nineteenth-century prolixity, we can see in Shaw's dramatic work a logic and grace, a formal precision, like that of the eighteenth-century composers.

Take *The Apple Cart*, for example. The fact that Shaw is here working exclusively with economic and political materials has caused its art to be insufficiently appreciated. If it had been a sentimental comedy by Molnar, the critics would have applauded its deftness; yet Shaw is a finer artist than any of the Molnars or Schnitzlers. The first act of *The Apple Cart* is an exercise in the scoring for small orchestra at which Shaw is particularly skillful. After what he has himself called the overture before the curtain of the conversation between the two secretaries, in which the music of King Magnus is foreshadowed, the urbane and intelligent King and the 'bull-roarer Boanerges' play a duet against one another. Then the King plays a single instrument against the whole nine of the cabinet. The themes emerge: the King's disinterestedness and the labor government's sordid self-interest. The development is lively: the music is tossed from one instrument to another, with, to use the old cliché, a combination of inevitableness and surprise. Finally, the King's theme gets a full and splendid statement in the long speech in which he declares his principles: 'I stand for the great abstractions: for conscience and virtue; for the eternal against the expedient; for the evolutionary appetite against the day's gluttony,' etc. This silver voice of the King lifts the movement to a poignant climax; and now a dramatic reversal carries the climax further and rounds out and balances the harmony. Unexpectedly, one of the brasses of the ministry takes up the theme of the King and repeats it more passionately and loudly: 'Just so! . . . Listen to me, sir,' bursts out the Powermistress, 'and judge whether I have not reason to feel everything you have just said to the very marrow of my bones. Here am I, the Powermistress Royal. I have to organize and administer all the motor power in the country for the good of the country. I have to harness the winds and the tides, the oils and the coal seams.' And she launches into an extraordinary tirade in which the idea of political disinterestedness is taken out of the realm of elegant abstraction in which it has hitherto remained with the King and reiterated in terms of engineering: 'every little sewing machine in the Hebrides, every dentist's drill in Shetland, every carpet sweeper in Margate,' etc. This ends on crashing chords, but immediately the music of the cabinet snarlingly reasserts itself. The act ends on the light note of the secretaries.

This music is a music of ideas—or rather, perhaps, it is a music of moralities. Bernard Shaw is a writer of the same kind as Plato. There are not many such writers in literature—the *Drames philosophiques* of Renan would supply another example —and they are likely to puzzle the critics. Shaw, like Plato, repudiates as a dangerous form of drunkenness the indulgence in literature for its own sake; but, like Plato, he then proceeds, not simply to expound a useful morality, but himself to indulge in an art in which moralities are used as the motifs. It is partly on this account, certainly, that Bernard Shaw has been underrated as an artist. Whether people admire or dislike him, whether they find his plays didactically boring or morally stimulating, they fail to take account of the fact that it is the enchantment of a highly accomplished art which has brought them to and kept them in the playhouse. It is an art that has even had the power to preserve such pieces as *Getting Married*, of which the 1908 heresies already seemed out of date twenty or thirty years later but of which the symphonic development still remains brilliant and fresh. So far from being relentlessly didactic, Shaw's mind has reflected in all its complexity the intellectual life of his time; and his great achievement is to have reflected it with remarkable fidelity. He has *not* imposed a cogent system, but he has worked out a vivid picture. It is, to be sure, not a passive picture, like that of Santayana or Proust: it is a picture in which action plays a prominent part. But it does not play a consistent part: the dynamic principle in Shaw is made to animate a variety of forces.

Let us see what these forces are and to what purpose they interact.

IV

What are the real themes of Bernard Shaw's plays?

He has not been a socialist dramatist in the sense that, say, Upton Sinclair has been a socialist novelist. His economics have served him, it is true, as anatomy served Michael Angelo; but to say that is to give as little idea of what kind of characters he creates and what his plays are about as it would of the figures of the sculptor to say that they were produced by an artist who understood the skeleton and the muscles. It is quite wrong to assume, as has sometimes been done, that the possession of the social-economic intelligence must imply that the writer who has it writes tracts for social reform.

Shaw is himself partly responsible for this assumption. In his early days, when he *was* a social reformer, he wrote books about Wagner and Ibsen which introduced them to the English-speaking public as primarily social reformers, too. There is of course a social revolutionist, a man of 1848, in Wagner, and a critic of bourgeois institutions in Ibsen. But Bernard Shaw, in his brilliant little books, by emphasizing these aspects of their work at the expense of everything else, seriously misrepresents them. He appreciates Siegfried and Brunhilde in their heroic and rebellious phases; but Wagner's tragedies of love he pooh-poohs; and it is sometimes just when Ibsen is at his strongest— as in *Brand* or *Rosmersholm*—that Bernard Shaw is least satisfactory on him, because the tragic spirit of Ibsen does not fit into Shaw's preconception. In Ibsen's case, Shaw is particularly misleading, because Ibsen disclaimed again and again any social-reforming intentions. His great theme, characteristic though it is of nineteenth-century society, is not a doctrine of social salvation: it is the conflict between one's duty to society as a unit in the social organism and the individual's duty to himself. Ibsen treats this theme over and over but in a number of different ways, sometimes emphasizing the validity of social claims as opposed to the will of the individual (*Little Eyolf*), sometimes showing them as unjustified and oppressive (*Ghosts*); sometimes showing the individual undone by self-indulgence or perverse self-assertion (*Peer Gynt* and *Brand*), sometimes showing him as noble and sympathetic (the hero and heroine of *Rosmersholm*); sometimes dramatizing the two poles of conduct in the career of a single individual, like Dr. Stockman in *An Enemy of the People*, who begins by trying to save society but who later, when society turns against him, is driven back into an individualistic vindication of the social conscience itself with the realization that 'the strongest man is he who stands most alone.' But the conflict is always serious; and it usually ends in disaster. Rarely—*A Doll's House* is the principal example—does it result in a liberation. Ibsen is hardly ever a social philosopher: he goes no further than the conflict itself.

Now is there any such basic theme in Bernard Shaw? Has he been creating a false impression not only about Ibsen but also about himself? Certainly the prefaces he prefixes to his plays do not really explain them any more than *The Quintessence of Ibsenism* really explains Ibsen.

The principal pattern which recurs in Bernard Shaw—aside from the duel between male and female, which seems to me of much less importance—is the polar opposition between the type of the saint and the type of the successful practical man. This conflict, when it is present in his other writing, has a blurring, a demoralizing effect, as in the passage on Saint Francis *et al.* which I quoted at the beginning of this essay; but it is the principle of life of his plays. We find it in its clearest presentation in the opposition between Father Keegan and Tom Broadbent in *John Bull's Other Island* and between Major Barbara and Undershaft—where the moral scales are pretty evenly weighted and where the actual predominance of the practical man, far from carrying ominous implications, produces a certain effect of reassurance: this was apparently the period—when Bernard Shaw had outgrown his early battles and struggles and before the war had come to disturb him—of his most comfortable and self-confident exercise of powers which had fully matured. But these opposites have also a tendency to dissociate themselves from one another and to feature themselves sometimes, not correlatively, but alternatively in successive plays. In *The Devil's Disciple* and *The Shewing-up of Blanco Posnet*, the heroes are dashing fellows who have melodramatic flashes of saintliness; their opponents are made comic or base. *Caesar and Cleopatra* is a play that glorifies the practical man;

Androcles and the Lion is a play that glorifies the saint. So is *Saint Joan*, with the difference that here the worldly antagonists of the saint are presented as intelligent and effective.

Certainly it is this theme of the saint and the world which has inspired those scenes of Shaw's plays which are most moving and most real on the stage—which are able to shock us for the moment, as even the 'Life Force' passages hardly do, out of the amiable and objective attention which has been induced by the bright play of the intelligence. It is the moment when Major Barbara, brought at last to the realization of the power of the capitalist's money and of her own weakness when she hasn't it to back her, is left alone on the stage with the unregenerate bums whose souls she has been trying to save; the moment when Androcles is sent into the arena with the lion; the moment in the emptied courtroom when Joan has been taken out to be burned and the Bishop and the Earl of Warwick are trying each to pin the responsibility on the other. It is the scene in *Heartbreak House* between Captain Shotover and Hector, when they give voice to their common antagonism toward the forces that seem to have them at their mercy: 'We must win powers of life and death over them . . . There is enmity between our seed and their seed. They know it and act on it, strangling our souls. They believe in themselves. When we believe in ourselves, we shall kill them . . . We kill the better half of ourselves every day to propitiate them.' It is the scene in *Back to Methuselah* when the Elderly Gentleman declares to the Oracle: 'They have gone back to lie about your answer [the political delegation with whom he has come]. I cannot go with them. I cannot live among people to whom nothing is real!'—and when she shows him her face and strikes him dead.

But now let us note—for the light they throw on Bernard Shaw in his various phases—the upshots of these several situations. In *Major Barbara*, the Christian saint, the man of learning, and the industrial superman form an alliance from which much is to be hoped. In *Androcles and the Lion*, written in 1913, in Shaw's amusing but least earnest middle period, just before the war, Androcles and the lion form an alliance, too, of which something is also to be hoped, but go out arm in arm after a harlequinade on the level of a Christmas pantomime. In

Heartbreak House, which was begun in 1913 and not finished till 1916, the declaration of war by the unworldlings takes place in the midst of confusion and does not lead to any action on their part.

In *Back to Methuselah*, of the postwar period, the Elderly Gentleman is blasted by the Oracle in a strange scene the implications of which we must stop to examine a moment. The fate of the Elderly Gentleman is evidently intended by Shaw to have some sort of application to himself: though a member of a backward community in which people have not yet achieved the Methuselah-span of life, he differs from his fellows at least in this: that he finds he cannot bear any longer to live among people to whom nothing is real. So the Oracle shrivels him up with her glance.

But what is this supposed to mean? What *is* this higher wisdom which the Elderly Gentleman cannot contemplate and live? So far as the reader is concerned, the revelation of the Oracle is a blank. The old system of Bernard Shaw, which was plausible enough to pass before the war, has just taken a terrible blow, and its grotesque and gruesome efforts to pull itself together and function give the effect of an umbrella, wrecked in a storm, which, when the owner tries to open it up, shows several long ribs of steel sticking out. The Life Force of the man and woman in *Man and Superman* no longer leads either to human procreation or social-revolutionary activity. The Life Force has been finally detached from socialism altogether. In the *Intelligent Woman's Guide*, Shaw will reject the Marxist dialectic as a false religion of social salvation; but the Life Force is also a religious idea, which we have always supposed in the past to be directed toward social betterment, and now, in *Back to Methuselah*, we find that it has misfired with socialism. Socialism has come and gone; the planet has been laid waste by wars; the ordinary people have all perished, and there is nobody left on earth but a race of selected supermen. And now the race of superior human beings, which was invoked in *Man and Superman* as the prime indispensable condition for any kind of progress whatever but which was regarded by Shaw at that time as producible through eugenic breeding, has taken here a most unearthly turn. It has always been through the superman idea that Shaw has found it possible to escape from the implications of his socialism; and he now no longer even imagines that the superior being can be created by human idealism through human science. The superior beings of *Back to Methuselah* are people who live forever; but they have achieved this superiority through an unconscious act of the will. When they have achieved it, what the Life Force turns out to have had in store for them is the mastery of abstruse branches of knowledge and the extra-uterine development of embryos. Beyond this, there is still to be attained the liberation of the spirit from the flesh, existence as a 'whirlpool in pure force.' 'And for what may be beyond, the eyesight of Lilith is too short. It is enough that there is a beyond.'

Humanity, in *Back to Methuselah*, has dropped out for the moment altogether. The long-livers of the period of progress contemporary with the Elderly Gentleman are not the more 'complete' human beings, with lives richer and better rounded, which Marx and Engels and Lenin imagined for the 'classless society': they are Shavian super-prigs who say the cutting and dampening things which the people have always said in Shaw's plays but who have been abstracted here from the well-observed social setting in which Shaw has always hitherto presented them. And the beings of the later epoch are young people playing in an Arcadia and ancients immersed in cogitations, alike—both cogitations and Arcadia—of the bleakest and most desolating description. There is in *Back to Methuselah* nothing burning or touching, and there is nothing genuinely thrilling except the cry of the Elderly Gentleman; and that, for all the pretense of revelation, is answered by a simple extinction.

In the *Tragedy of an Elderly Gentleman*, the Elderly Gentleman is frightened, but his tragedy is not a real tragedy. *Saint Joan* (1924) is an even more frightened play, and, softened though it is by the historical perspective into which Shaw manages to throw it through his epilogue, it was the first genuine tragedy that Shaw had written. The horror of *Back to Methuselah* is a lunar horror; the horror of *Saint Joan* is human. The saint is suppressed by the practical man; and even when she comes back to earth, though all those who exploited or destroyed her are now obliged to acknowledge her holiness, none wants her to remain among them: each would do the same thing again. Only the soldier who had handed her the cross at the stake is willing to accept her now, but he is only a poor helpless clown condemned to the dungeon of the flesh.

v

Back to Methuselah is a flight into the future; *Saint Joan* is a flight into the past. But with *Heartbreak House* Bernard Shaw had already begun a series of plays in which he was to deal with the postwar world and his own relation to it in terms of contemporary England—a section of his work which, it seems to me, has had too little appreciation or comprehension.

Heartbreak House has the same sort of setting and more or less the same form as such Shavian conversations as *Getting Married* and *Misalliance*; but it is really something new for Shaw. There is no diagram of social relations, no tying-up of threads at the end. *Heartbreak House*, Shaw says in his preface, is 'cultured leisured Europe before the War'; but the play, he told Archibald Henderson, 'began with an atmosphere and does not contain a word that was foreseen before it was written,' and it is the only one of his plays which he has persistently refused to explain. 'How should *I* know?' he replied, when he was asked by his actors what it meant. 'I am only the author.' Heartbreak House, built like a ship, with its old drunken and half-crazy master, the retired adventurer Captain Shotover, is cultured and leisured England; but the characters are no longer pinned down and examined as social specimens: in an atmosphere heavily charged, through a progression of contacts and collisions, they give out thunder and lightning like storm-clouds. Brooding frustrations and disillusions, childlike hurts and furious resentments, which have dropped the old Shavian masks, rush suddenly into an utterance which for the moment has burst out of the old rationalistic wit. For once, where Bernard Shaw has so often reduced historical myths to the sharp focus of contemporary satire, he now raises contemporary figures to the heroic proportions of myth.—An air-raid brings down the final curtain: Heartbreak House has at last been split wide. The capitalist Mangan gets killed, and there is a suggestion that they may all be the better for it.

But in 1924 the Labour Party came to power, with Ramsay Macdonald as Prime Minister. Macdonald had been a member of the Executive Committee of the Fabian Society, and he brought with him two other Fabians, Sidney Webb and Sydney Olivier, who took the portfolios of Minister of Labour and Secretary of State for India. When Macdonald was re-elected in 1929, he was accompanied by no less than twenty Fabians, of whom eight were cabinet members. The Fabians had now achieved the aim which was to have been the condition for the success of their ideas: they had 'interpenetrated' the government. But in the meantime the competition of the British Empire with the German had culminated in a four years' war; and in England after the war, with the top manhood of her society slaughtered and the lower classes laid off from their wartime jobs, and with English commercial domination further damaged by the United States, the influence of the Fabians could do little to bridge over the abyss which had been blasted between the extremes of the British class society. The best measures of the Labour Government were able to accomplish no more than just to keep the unemployed alive; and when the capitalists began to feel the pinch, they openly took over control. Ramsay Macdonald, in 1931, became Prime Minister in a Nationalist government and cleared his socialists out of office.

At the moment of the second accession of the Labour Party to power, Shaw had written *The Apple Cart*, in which Macdonald is caricatured as Proteus, the Prime Minister of a labor government. This government is represented as really controlled by Breakages, Limited, a great monopoly which opposes industrial progress for the reason that it has an interest in perpetuating the inferior and less durable machinery that requires more frequent repairs. But one finds in *The Apple Cart* no comment on the Fabianism, which, after all, has been partly responsible for Proteus: the blame is laid at the door, not of that socialism by interpenetration which has ended by itself being interpenetrated, but of something which Shaw calls 'democracy'; and what is opposed to the corrupt socialism of Proteus is not socialism of a more thoroughgoing kind, but the super-constitutional-monarch, King Magnus. Again, Shaw has given the slip to his problems through recourse to the cult of the superior person.

Yet in 1931, after the final collapse of the Labour Government, Bernard Shaw visited Russia and, by applauding the Soviet system, incurred unpopularity in England for the first time since the war. In the same year, he wrote *Too True to Be Good*, a curious 'political extravaganza,' in which he turns back upon and criticizes his own career. Here the theme of the bourgeois radical of the eighties, disillusioned with himself under stress of the disasters of the twentieth century, is treated in the same vein, with the same kind of idealist poetry, now grown frankly elegiac and despairing, which Shaw had opened in *Heartbreak House* and which had made the real beauty of *The Apple Cart*.

A rich young English girl of the upper middle class is languishing with an imaginary illness in a gloomy Victorian chamber, fussed over by a Victorian mother. Into this sickroom erupt two rebels: a young preacher and a former chambermaid, who is an illegitimate child of the aristocracy. The chambermaid has been masquerading as the heiress's trained nurse, and she and the preacher have a plot to steal the heiress's pearl necklace. The girl comes to from her megrims and puts up an unexpected struggle. The preacher becomes interested in his victim and says that he has always wondered why she does not steal the necklace herself. Why doesn't she take it and go and do what she pleases, instead of staying home with her mother, moping and fancying herself sick? Why doesn't she let him and his accomplice sell the necklace for her, taking 25 per cent of the price apiece and giving her the other 50? The girl enthusiastically agrees, and while she is getting dressed to go with them, the preacher jumps up on the bed and delivers one of those live-your-own-life sermons with which Shaw, in the nineties, made his first success. Then he is off—in the excitement of his rhetoric, at first forgetting the necklace, which the heiress has to remind him they need.

All three sail away together to an imaginary Balkan country reminiscent of *Arms and the Man*, where they are able to do whatever they like but where their revolt turns out to lead to nothing and eventually to bore them to death. Shaw has evidently put into *Too True to Be Good* a sort of recapitulation of his earlier themes, the shams of bourgeois society: the capitalistic doctor of *The Doctor's Dilemma* is as much a fraud as ever; the pompous British military officer, though retaining an air of authority, has practically ceased even to pretend to be anything other than a fraud and is quite willing to leave the command to a private (drawn from Lawrence of Arabia), if he can only be left in peace with his water-colors; the old-fashioned materialist-atheist who is also the most rigorous of moralists, of the type of Roebuck Ramsden in *Man and Superman*, has lived through into a world where his morality has no power to prevent his son's turning thief, etc. Finally everyone except the preacher sets out for the 'Union of Sensible Republics.'

The preacher is left alone on the shore, abandoned between two worlds. He had come too late for the old and too early for the new. He had had the courage once to steal a necklace but he hadn't carried through his idea. He had given it back to the owner and they had made common cause together: the liberated bourgeois girl had gotten 50 per cent of the price, the radicals only 25 apiece. In this last scene, the darkness comes, the clouds gather; the morale of the preacher breaks down. He can only go on explaining and exhorting, whether or not he has anything to say. A keen wind is blowing in, and it may be the breath of life, but it is too fierce for him to bear.

This, Shaw tells us, is a political fable; and now he is to return to politics proper. In *On the Rocks* (1933), he appears to drive himself into a corner as he has never before done and then comes out with a political position which still manages to be somewhat equivocal.

The first act shows a liberal Prime Minister, hard beset during a period of depression. Pall Mall and Trafalgar Square are full of excited crowds. The Prime Minister, on the verge of a breakdown, can think of nothing to do except to call out the police against them, but he is dissuaded by the Police Commissioner himself and finally induced to go away for a rest. He has just been visited by a labor delegation who have impressed him with the importance of Marxism, and he takes volumes of Marx and Lenin away with him.

When the curtain goes up on the second act, the Prime Minister has read Marx and Lenin; but the effect upon him is unexpected. He has gained an insight into economic motivation, an understanding of the technique of making use of it; but he has not been converted to socialism: he has worked out, on the contrary, an exceedingly clever scheme for preserving the capitalist state through a program, essentially fascist, of partial nationalization and taxation of unearned incomes. He will conciliate the various social groups which would normally be antagonistic by promising a concession to each. The plan seems bidding fair to succeed when it runs aground on Sir Dexter Rightside, the Liberal Prime Minister's Tory colleague in a coalition National Government. Sir Dexter represents the blind conservatism which sticks to the *status quo* through sheer obstinacy and inability to imagine anything else: he threatens to put colored shirts on 'fifty thousand patriotic young Londoners' and to call them into the streets against the proposed program of the government. The Prime Minister has to give up his attempt, but he is now forced to face his situation: 'Do you think I didn't know,' he confesses to his wife, 'in the days of my great speeches and my roaring popularity, that I was only whitewashing the slums? I couldn't help knowing as well as any of those damned Socialists that though the West End of London was chockful of money and nice people all calling one another by their Christian names, the lives of the millions of people whose labor was keeping the whole show going were not worth living; but I was able to put it out of my mind because I thought it couldn't be helped and I was doing the best that could be done. I know better now! I know that it can be helped, and how it can be helped. And rather than go back to the old whitewashing job, I'd seize you tight around the waist and make a hole in the river with you . . . Why don't I lead the revolt against it all? Because I'm not the man for the job, darling . . . And I shall hate the man who will carry it through for his cruelty and the desolation he will bring on us and our like.'

The shouting of the crowd and the crash of glass is suddenly heard outside. The people have broken into Downing Street. The police begin to club them and ride them down. The people sing, 'England, arise!'

Sir Arthur Chavender's more or less liberal fascism has been defeated by the reactionary fascism of his Tory colleague in the National Government, with whom he is indissolubly united. (There is no question any longer of the superior man: King Magnus has disappeared from the scene.) There is a third point of view, opposed to both, but this, also, sounds rather fascist. Old Hipney, the disillusioned labor veteran, who speaks for the dissatisfied classes, seems to be looking for a Man on

Horseback, too: 'Adult suffrage: that was what was to save us all. My God! It delivered us into the hands of our spoilers and oppressors, bound hand and foot by our own folly and ignorance. It took the heart out of old Hipney; and now I'm for any Napoleon or Mussolini or Lenin or Chavender that has the stuff in him to take both the people and the spoilers and oppressors by the scruffs of their silly necks and just sling them into the way they should go with as many kicks as may be needful to make a thorough job of it.' But Chavender declines the job; and the people begin throwing bricks.

The conclusion we are apparently to draw is that parliamentary fascism must fail; and that we may then get either a Lenin or a Mussolini. Is this also a final confession of the failure of Fabianism, which depended on parliament, too?

In any case, at the end of this play, we have come in a sense to the end of Shaw. With the eruption of the uprising, we should be plunged into a situation which could no longer be appropriately handled by the characteristic methods of his comedy. He is still splendid when he is showing the bewilderment of the liberal governing-class prime minister: it is surprising how he is still able to summon his old flickering and piercing wit, his old skill at juggling points of view, to illuminate a new social situation—how quick and skillful he is at describing a new social type: the communist viscount, with his brutal language, which shocks his proletarian allies. But with the shouts and the broken glass, we are made to take account of the fact that Shaw's comedy, for all its greater freedom in dealing with social conditions, is almost as much dependent on a cultivated and stable society as the comedy of Molière, who had his place in the royal dining-room and depended on Louis's favor for the permission to produce his plays. Shaw, as much as Molière, must speak the same language as his audience; he must observe the same conventions of manners. And further than *On the Rocks*—in depicting the realities of the present—we feel that he cannot go.

Then we realize that, after a detour of the better part of half a century, of almost the whole of his artistic career, Shaw has only returned to that Bloody Sunday of 1887 when the Socialists had headed a demonstration and been driven away by the police; and we remember, apropos of Molière, that the most celebrated of British dramatists for a long time found it impossible to get a theater in London for *On the Rocks*.

Shaw's most recent pieces are weaker. *The Simpleton of the Unexpected Isles* (1934) is the only play of the author's which has ever struck me as silly. In it, the Day of Judgment comes to the British Empire, and the privilege of surviving on earth is made to depend upon social utility. But, by setting up a purely theocratic tribunal, Shaw deprives this scene of social point: the principle of selection is so general that it might be applied by the fascists as readily as by the socialists, at the same time that the policy of wholesale extinction seems inspired by an admiration for the repressive tactics of both. The play ends with a salute to the unknown future, which, like the vision of infinity of *Back to Methuselah*, seems perfectly directionless. *The Millionairess* (1936) makes a farce out of the notion that a natural boss, deprived of adventitious authority, will inevitably gravitate again to a position where he can bully and control people, and sounds as if it had been suggested by the later phases of Stalin.

Here it cannot be denied that Bernard Shaw begins to show signs of old age. As the pace of his mind slackens and the texture of his work grows looser, the contradictory impulses and principles which have hitherto provided him with drama begin to show gaping rifts. In his *Preface on Bosses* to *The Millionairess*, he talks about 'beginning a Reformation well to the left of Russia,' but composes the panegyric on Mussolini, with the respectful compliments to Hitler, to which I have already referred.

Yet the openings—the prologue to *The Simpleton*, with its skit on the decay of the British Empire and the knockabout domestic agonies of the first act or two of *The Millionairess*—still explode their comic situations with something of the old energy and wit; and the one-acter, *The Six of Calais*, though it does not crackle quite with the old spark, is not so very far inferior to such an earlier trifle as *How He Lied to Her Husband*. It is interesting to note—what bears out the idea that Shaw is at his best as an artist—that the last thing he is to lose, apparently, is his gift for pure comic invention, which has survived, not much dimmed, though we may tire of it, since the days of *You Never Can Tell*.

And he has also maintained his integrity as a reporter of the processes at work in his time—in regard to which his point of view has never been doctrinaire but always based on observation and feeling. He has not acted a straight role as a socialist; a lot of his writing on public affairs has been nonsense. But his plays down to the very end have been a truthful and continually developing chronicle of a soul in relation to society. Professionally as well as physically—he has just turned eighty-one as I write—he is outliving all the rest of his generation.

Nor can it be said that the confusions of his politics have invalidated his social criticism. Of his educative and stimulative influence it is not necessary today to speak. The very methods we use to check him have partly been learned in his school.

Marxism and Literature

1. Let us begin with Marx and Engels. What was the role assigned to literature and art in the system of Dialectical Materialism? This role was much less cut-and-dried than is nowadays often supposed. Marx and Engels conceived the forms of human society in any given country and epoch as growing out of the methods of production which prevailed at that place and time; and out of the relations involved in the social forms arose a 'superstructure' of higher activities such as politics, law, religion, philosophy, literature and art. These activities were not, as is sometimes assumed, wholly explicable in terms of economics. They showed the mold, in ways direct or indirect, of the social configuration below them, but each was working to get away from its roots in the social classes and to constitute a professional group, with its own discipline and its own standards of value, which cut across class lines. These departments 'all react upon one another and upon the economic base. It is not the case that the economic situation is the sole active cause and everything else only a passive effect. But there is a reciprocal interaction within a fundamental economic necessity, which in the last instance always asserts itself' (Engels to Hans Starkenburg, January 25, 1894). So that the art of a great artistic period may reach a point of vitality and vision where it can influence the life of the period down to its very economic foundations. Simply, it must cease to flourish with the social system which made it possible by providing the artist with training and leisure, even though the artist himself may have been working for the destruction of that system.

2. Marx and Engels, unlike some of their followers, never attempted to furnish social-economic formulas by which the validity of works of art might be tested. They had grown up in the sunset of Goethe before the great age of German literature was over, and they had both set out in their youth to be poets; they responded to imaginative work, first of all, on its artistic merits. They could ridicule a trashy writer like Eugène Sue for what they regarded as his *petit bourgeois* remedies for the

miseries of contemporary society (*The Holy Family*); they could become bitter about Ferdinand Freiligrath, who had deserted the Communist League and turned nationalist in 1870 (Marx to Engels, August 22, 1870). And Marx could even make similar jibes at Heine when he thought that the latter had stooped to truckling to the authorities or when he read the expressions of piety in his will (Marx to Engels, December 21, 1866 and May 8, 1856). But Marx's daughter tells us that her father loved Heine 'as much as his work and was very indulgent of his political shortcomings. He used to say that the poets were originals, who must be allowed to go their own way, and that one shouldn't apply to them the same standards as to ordinary people.' It was not characteristic of Marx and Engels to judge literature—that is, literature of power and distinction—in terms of its purely political tendencies. In fact, Engels always warned the socialist novelists against the dangers of *Tendenz-Literatur* (Engels to Minna Kautsky, November 26, 1885; and to Margaret Harkness, April 1888). In writing to Minna Kautsky about one of her novels, he tells her that the personalities of her hero and heroine have been dissolved in the principles they represent. 'You evidently,' he says, 'felt the need of publicly taking sides in this book, of proclaiming your opinions to the world . . . But I believe that the tendency should arise from the situation and the action themselves without being explicitly formulated, and that the poet is not under the obligation to furnish the reader with a ready-made historical solution for the future of the conflict which he describes.' When Ferdinand Lassalle sent Marx and Engels his poetic tragedy, *Franz von Sickingen*, and invited them to criticize it, Marx replied that, 'setting aside any purely critical attitude toward the work,' it had on a first reading affected him powerfully—characteristically adding that upon persons of a more emotional nature it would doubtless produce an even stronger effect; and Engels wrote that he had read it twice and had been moved by it so profoundly that he had been obliged to lay it aside in order to arrive at any critical perspective. It was only after pulling themselves together and making some purely literary observations that they were able to proceed to discuss, from their special historical point of view, the period with which the drama dealt and to show how Lassalle's own political position had led him to mistake the role of his hero. Aeschylus Marx loved for his grandeur and for the defiance of Zeus by Prometheus; Goethe they both immensely admired: Engels wrote of him as a 'colossal' and 'universal' genius whose career had been marred by an admixture in his character of the philistine and the courtier (*German Socialism in Verse and Prose*); Shakespeare Marx knew by heart and was extremely fond of quoting, but never—despite the long, learned and ridiculous essays which have appeared in the Soviet magazine, *International Literature*—attempted to draw from his plays any general social moral. So far, indeed, was Marx from having worked out a systematic explanation of the relation of art to social arrangements that he could assert, apropos of Greek art, in his *Introduction to the Critique of Political Economy*, that 'certain periods of highest development of art stand in no direct connection with the general development of society, nor with the material basis and the skeleton structure of its organization.'

3. With Marx and Engels there is not yet any tendency to specialize art as a 'weapon.' They were both too much under the influence of the ideal of the many-sided man of the Renaissance, of the 'complete' man, who, like Leonardo, had been painter, mathematician and engineer, or, like Machiavelli, poet, historian and strategist, before the division of labor had had the effect of splitting up human nature and limiting everyone to some single function (Engels' preface to his *Dialectic and Nature*). But with Lenin we come to a Marxist who is specialized himself as an organizer and fighter. Like most Russians, Lenin was sensitive to music; but Gorky tells us that on one occasion, after listening to Beethoven's Appassionata Sonata and exclaiming that he 'would like to listen to it every day: it is marvelous superhuman music—I always think with pride . . . what marvelous things human beings can do,' he screwed up his eyes and smiled sadly and added: 'But I can't listen to music too often. It affects your nerves, makes you want to say stupid, nice things, and stroke the heads of people who could create such beauty while living in this vile hell. And now you mustn't stroke anyone's head—you might get your hand bitten off.' Yet he was fond of fiction, poetry and the

theater, and by no means doctrinaire in his tastes. Krupskaya tells how, on a visit to a Youth Commune, he asked the young people, 'What do you read? Do you read Pushkin?' '"Oh, no!" someone blurted out. "He was a bourgeois. Mayakovsky for us." Ilyitch smiled. "I think Pushkin is better."' Gorky says that one day he found Lenin with *War and Peace* lying on the table: '"Yes, Tolstoy. I wanted to read over the scene of the hunt, then remembered that I had to write a comrade. Absolutely no time for reading." . . . Smiling and screwing up his eyes, he stretched himself deliciously in his armchair and, lowering his voice, added quickly, "What a colossus, eh? What a marvelously developed brain! Here's an artist for you, sir. And do you know something still more amazing? You couldn't find a genuine *muzhik* in literature till this count came upon the scene."' In his very acute essays on Tolstoy, he deals with him much as Engels deals with Goethe—with tremendous admiration for Tolstoy's genius, but with an analysis of his non-resistance and mysticism in terms not, it is interesting to note, of the psychology of the landed nobility, but of the patriarchal peasantry with whom Tolstoy had identified himself. And Lenin's attitude toward Gorky was much like that of Marx toward Heine. He suggests in one of his letters that Gorky would be helpful as a journalist on the side of the Bolsheviks, but adds that he mustn't be bothered if he is busy writing a book.

4. Trotsky is a literary man as Lenin never was, and he published in 1924 a most remarkable little study called *Literature and Revolution*. In this book he tried to illuminate the problems which were arising for Russian writers with the new society of the Revolution. And he was obliged to come to grips with a question with which Marx and Engels had not been much concerned—the question of what Mr. James T. Farrell in his book, *A Note on Literary Criticism*, one of the few sensible recent writings on this subject, calls 'the carry-over value' of literature. Marx had assumed the value of Shakespeare and the Greeks and more or less left it at that. But what, the writers in Russia were now asking, was to be the value of the literature and art of the ages of barbarism and oppression in the dawn of socialist freedom? What in particular was to be the status of the

culture of that bourgeois society from which socialism had just emerged and of which it still bore the unforgotten scars? Would there be a new proletarian literature, with new language, new style, new form, to give expression to the emotions and ideas of the new proletarian dictatorship? There had been in Russia a group called the Proletcult, which aimed at monopolizing the control of Soviet literature; but Lenin had discouraged and opposed it, insisting that proletarian culture was not something which could be produced synthetically and by official dictation of policy, but only by natural evolution as a 'development of those reserves of knowledge which society worked for under the oppression of capitalism, of the landlords, of the officials.' Now, in *Literature and Revolution*, Trotsky asserted that 'such terms as "proletarian literature" and "proletarian culture" are dangerous, because they erroneously compress the culture of the future into the narrow limits of the present day.' In a position to observe from his Marxist point of view the effects on a national literature of the dispossession of a dominant class, he was able to see the unexpected ways in which the presentments of life of the novelists, the feelings and images of the poets, the standards themselves of the critics, were turning out to be determined by their attitudes toward the social-economic crisis. But he did not believe in a proletarian culture which would displace the bourgeois one. The bourgeois literature of the French Revolution had ripened under the old regime; but the illiterate proletariat and peasantry of Russia had had no chance to produce a culture, nor would there be time for them to do so in the future, because the proletarian dictatorship was not to last: it was to be only a transition phase and to lead the way to 'a culture which is above classes and which will be the first truly human culture.' In the meantime, the new socialist literature would grow directly out of that which had already been produced during the domination of the bourgeoisie. Communism, Trotsky said, had as yet no artistic culture; it had only a political culture.

5. All this seems to us reasonable enough. But, reasonable and cultured as Trotsky is, ready as he is to admit that 'one cannot always go by the principles of Marxism in deciding whether to

accept or reject a work of art,' that such a work 'should be judged in the first place by its own law—that is, by the law of art,' there is none the less in the whole situation something which is alien to us. We are not accustomed, in our quarter of the world, either to having the government attempt to control literature and art or to having literary and artistic movements try to identify themselves with the government. Yet Russia, since the Revolution, has had a whole series of cultural groups which have attempted to dominate literature either with or without the authority of the government; and Trotsky himself, in his official position, even in combating these tendencies, cannot avoid passing censure and pinning ribbons. Sympathizers with the Soviet regime used to assume that this state of affairs was inseparable from the realization of socialism: that its evils would be easily outgrown and that in any case it was a great thing to have the government take so lively an interest in culture. I believe that this view was mistaken. Under the Tsar, imaginative literature in Russia played a role which was probably different from any role it had ever played in the life of any other nation. Political and social criticism, pursued and driven underground by the censorship, was forced to incorporate itself in the dramatic imagery of fiction. This was certainly one of the principal reasons for the greatness during the nineteenth century of the Russian theater and novel, for the mastery by the Russian writers—from Pushkin's time to Tolstoy's—of the art of implication. In the fifties and sixties, the stories of Turgenev, which seem mild enough to us today, were capable of exciting the most passionate controversies—and even, in the case of *A Sportsman's Sketches*, causing the dismissal of the censor who had passed it—because each was regarded as a political message. Ever since the Revolution, literature and politics in Russia have remained inextricable. But after the Revolution the intelligentsia themselves were in power; and it became plain that in the altered situation the identification of literature with politics was liable to terrible abuses. Lenin and Trotsky, Lunacharsky and Gorky, worked sincerely to keep literature free; but they had at the same time, from the years of the Tsardom, a keen sense of the possibility of art as an instrument of propaganda. Lenin took a special interest in the moving pictures from the propaganda point of view; and the first Soviet

films, by Eisenstein and Pudovkin, were masterpieces of implication, as the old novels and plays had been. But Lenin died;
Trotsky was exiled; Lunacharsky died. The administration of
Stalin, unliterary and uncultivated himself, slipped into depending more and more on literature as a means of manipulating a people of whom, before the Revolution, 70 or 80 per
cent had been illiterate and who could hardly be expected to
be critical of what they read. Gorky seems to have exerted
what influence he could in the direction of liberalism: to him
was due, no doubt, the liquidation of RAPP, the latest device
for the monopoly of culture, and the opening of the Soviet
canon to the best contemporary foreign writing and the classics. But though this made possible more freedom of form and
a wider range of reading, it could not, under the dictatorship
of Stalin, either stimulate or release a living literature. Where
no political opposition was possible, there was possible no political criticism; and in Russia political questions involve vitally
the fate of society. What reality can there be for the Russians,
the most socially-minded writers on earth, in a freedom purely
'esthetic'? Even the fine melodramatic themes of the post-
revolutionary cinema and theater, with their real emotion and
moral conviction, have been replaced by simple trash not very
far removed from Hollywood, or by dramatized exemplifica-
tions of the latest 'directive' of Stalin which open the night
after the speech that has announced the directive. The recent
damning of the music of Shostakovich on the ground that the
commissars were unable to hum it seems a withdrawal from
the liberal position. And it is probable that the death of Gorky,
as well as the imprisonment of Bukharin and Radek, have removed the last brakes from a precipitate descent, in the artistic
as well as the political field, into a nightmare of informing and
repression. The practice of deliberate falsification of social and
political history which began at the time of the Stalin-Trotsky
crisis and which has now attained proportions so fantastic that
the government does not seem to hesitate to pass the sponge
every month or so over everything that the people have previously been told and to present them with a new and contradictory version of their history, their duty, and the characters and
careers of their leaders—this practice cannot fail in the end to
corrupt every department of intellectual life, till the serious,

the humane, the clear-seeing must simply, if they can, remain silent.

6. Thus Marxism in Russia for the moment has run itself into a blind alley—or rather, it has been put down a well. The Soviets seem hardly at the present time to have retained even the Marxist political culture, even in its cruder forms—so that we are relieved from the authority of Russia as we are deprived of her inspiration. To what conclusions shall we come, then, at this time of day about Marxism and literature—basing our views not even necessarily upon texts from the Marxist Fathers, but upon ordinary commonsense? Well, first of all, that we can go even further than Trotsky in one of the dicta I have quoted above and declare that Marxism by itself can tell us nothing whatever about the goodness or badness of a work of art. A man may be an excellent Marxist, but if he lacks imagination and taste he will be unable to make the choice between a good and an inferior book both of which are ideologically unexceptionable. What Marxism *can* do, however, is throw a great deal of light on the origins and social significance of works of art. The study of literature in its relation to society is as old as Herder—and even Vico. Coleridge had flashes of insight into the connection between literary and social phenomena, as when he saw the Greek state in the Greek sentence and the individualism of the English in the short separate statements of Chaucer's Prologue. But the great bourgeois master of this kind of criticism was Taine, with his *race* and *moment* and *milieu*; yet Taine, for all his scientific professions, responded artistically to literary art, and responded so vividly that his summings-up of writers and re-creations of periods sometimes rival or surpass their subjects. Marx and Engels further deepened this study of literature in relation to its social background by demonstrating for the first time inescapably the importance of economic systems. But if Marx and Engels and Lenin and Trotsky are worth listening to on the subject of books, it is not merely because they created Marxism, but also because they were capable of literary appreciation.

7. Yet the man who tries to apply Marxist principles without real understanding of literature is liable to go horribly wrong.

For one thing, it is usually true in works of the highest order that the purport is not a simple message, but a complex vision of things, which itself is not explicit but implicit; and the reader who does not grasp them artistically, but is merely looking for simple social morals, is certain to be hopelessly confused. Especially will he be confused if the author *does* draw an explicit moral which is the opposite of or has nothing to do with his real purport. Friedrich Engels, in the letter to Margaret Harkness already referred to above, in warning her that the more the novelist allows his political ideas to 'remain hidden, the better it is for the work of art,' says that Balzac, with his reactionary opinions, is worth a thousand of Zola, with all his democratic ones. (Balzac was one of the great literary admirations of both Engels and Marx, the latter of whom had planned to write a book on him.) Engels points out that Balzac himself was, or believed himself to be, a legitimist engaged in deploring the decline of high society; but that actually 'his irony is never more bitter, his satire never more trenchant, than when he is showing us these aristocrats . . . for whom he felt so profound a sympathy,' and that 'the only men of whom he speaks with undissimulated admiration are his most determined political adversaries, the republican heroes of the Cloître-Saint-Merri, the men who at that period (1830–1836) truly represented the popular masses.' Nor does it matter necessarily in a work of art whether the characters are shown engaged in a conflict which illustrates the larger conflicts of society or in one which from that point of view is trivial. In art—it is quite obvious in music, but it is also true in literature—a sort of law of moral interchangeability prevails: we may transpose the actions and the sentiments that move us into terms of whatever we do or are ourselves. Real genius of moral insight is a motor which will start any engine. When Proust, in his wonderful chapter on the death of the novelist Bergotte, speaks of those moral obligations which impose themselves in spite of everything and which seem to come through to humanity from some source outside its wretched self (obligations 'invisible only to fools—and are they really to them?'), he is describing a kind of duty which he felt only in connection with the literary work which he performed in his dark and fetid room; yet he speaks for every moral, esthetic or intellectual passion which holds the expediencies of the world in contempt. And the hero of Thornton Wilder's *Heaven's My Destination*, the traveling salesman who tries to save souls in the smoking car and writes Bible texts on hotel blotters, is something more than a symptom of Thornton Wilder's religious tendencies: he is the type of all saints who begin absurdly; and Wilder's story would be as true of the socialist Upton Sinclair as of the Christian George Brush. Nor does it necessarily matter, for the moral effect of a work of literature, whether the forces of bravery or virtue with which we identify ourselves are victorious or vanquished in the end. In Hemingway's story *The Undefeated*, the old bull-fighter who figures as the hero is actually humiliated and killed, but his courage has itself been a victory. It is true, as I. Kashkin, the Soviet critic, has said, that Hemingway has written much about decadence, but in order to write tellingly about death you have to have the principle of life, and those that have it will make it felt in spite of everything.

8. The Leftist critic with no literary competence is always trying to measure works of literature by tests which have no validity in that field. And one of his favorite occupations is giving specific directions and working out diagrams for the construction of ideal Marxist books. Such formulas are of course perfectly futile. The rules observed in any given school of art become apparent, not before but after, the actual works of art have been produced. As we were reminded by Burton Rascoe at the time of the Humanist controversy, the esthetic laws involved in Greek tragedy were not formulated by Aristotle until at least half a century after Euripides and Sophocles were dead. And the behavior of the Marxist critics has been precisely like that of the Humanists. The Humanists knew down to the last comma what they wanted a work of literature to be, but they never— with the possible exception, when pressed, of *The Bridge of San Luis Rey*, about which they had, however, hesitations— were able to find any contemporary work which fitted their specifications. The Marxists did just the same thing. In an article called *The Crisis in Criticism* in the *New Masses* of February 1933, Granville Hicks drew up a list of requirements which the ideal Marxist work of literature must meet. The primary func-

tion of such a work, he asserted, must be to 'lead the proletarian reader to recognize his role in the class struggle'—and it
must therefore (1) 'directly or indirectly show the effects of the
class struggle'; (2) 'the author must be able to make the reader
feel that he is participating in the lives described'; and, finally,
(3) the author's point of view must 'be that of the vanguard of
the proletariat; he should be, or should try to make himself,
a member of the proletariat.' This formula, he says, 'gives us
. . . a standard by which to recognize the perfect Marxian
novel'—and adds 'no novel as yet written perfectly conforms
to our demands.' But the doctrine of 'socialist realism' promulgated at the Soviet Writers' Congress of August 1934 was
only an attempt on a larger scale to legislate masterpieces into
existence—a kind of attempt which always indicates sterility on
the part of those who engage in it, and which always actually
works, if it has any effect at all, to legislate existing good literature *out of* existence and to discourage the production of any
more. The prescribers for the literature of the future usually
cherish some great figure of the past whom they regard as
having fulfilled their conditions and whom they are always
bringing forward to demonstrate the inferiority of the literature of the present. As there has never existed a great writer
who really had anything in common with these critics' conception of literature, they are obliged to provide imaginary versions of what their ideal great writers are like. The Humanists
had Sophocles and Shakespeare; the socialist realists had Tolstoy. Yet it is certain that if Tolstoy had had to live up to the
objectives and prohibitions which the socialist realists proposed he could never have written a chapter; and that if Babbitt and More had been able to enforce against Shakespeare
their moral and esthetic injunctions he would never have written a line. The misrepresentation of Sophocles, which has involved even a tampering with his text in the interests not
merely of Humanism but of academic classicism in general, has
been one of the scandalous absurdities of scholarship. The
Communist critical movement in America, which had for its
chief spokesman Mr. Hicks, tended to identify their ideal with
the work of John Dos Passos. In order to make this possible, it
was necessary to invent an imaginary Dos Passos. This ideal
Dos Passos was a Communist, who wrote stories about the

proletariat, at a time when the real Dos Passos was engaged in
bringing out a long novel about the effects of the capitalist system on the American middle class and had announced himself
—in the *New Republic* in 1930—politically a 'middle-class liberal.' The ideal Dos Passos was something like Gorky without
the mustache—Gorky, in the meantime, having himself undergone some transmogrification at the hands of Soviet publicity
—and this myth was maintained until the Communist critics
were finally compelled to repudiate it, not because they had
acquired new light on Dos Passos, the novelist and dramatist,
but because of his attitude toward events in Russia.

9. The object of these formulas for the future, as may be seen
from the above quotations from Mr. Hicks, is to make of art
an effective instrument in the class struggle. And we must deal
with the dogma that 'art is a weapon.' It is true that art may be
a weapon; but in the case of some of the greatest works of art,
some of those which have the longest carry-over value, it is difficult to see that any important part of this value is due to their
direct functioning as weapons. The *Divine Comedy*, in its political aspect, is a weapon for Henry of Luxemburg, whom Dante
—with his medieval internationalism and his lack of sympathy
for the nationalistic instincts which were impelling the Italians
of his time to get away from their Austrian emperors—was so
passionately eager to impose on his countrymen. Today we
may say with Carducci that we would as soon see the crown of
his 'good Frederick' rolling in Olona vale: 'Jove perishes; the
poet's hymn remains.' And, though Shakespeare's *Henry IV*
and *Henry V* are weapons for Elizabethan imperialism, their
real center is not Prince Hal but Falstaff; and Falstaff is the
father of *Hamlet* and of all Shakespeare's tragic heroes, who,
if they illustrate any social moral—the moral, perhaps, that
Renaissance princes, supreme in their little worlds, may go
to pieces in all kinds of terrible ways for lack of a larger social
organism to restrain them—do so evidently without Shakespeare's being aware of it. If these works may be spoken of as
weapons at all, they are weapons in the more general struggle
of modern European man emerging from the Middle Ages
and striving to understand his world and himself—a function
for which 'weapon' is hardly the right word. The truth is that

there is short-range and long-range literature. Long-range literature attempts to sum up wide areas and long periods of human experience, or to extract from them general laws; short-range literature preaches and pamphleteers with the view to an immediate effect. A good deal of the recent confusion of our writers in the Leftist camp has been due to their not understanding, or being unable to make up their minds, whether they are aiming at long-range or short-range writing.

10. This brings us to the question of what sort of periods are most favorable for works of art. One finds an assumption on the Left that revolutionary or pre-revolutionary periods are apt to produce new and vital forms of literature. This, of course, is very far from the truth in the case of periods of actual revolution. The more highly developed forms of literature require leisure and a certain amount of stability; and during a period of revolution the writer is usually deprived of both. The literature of the French Revolution consisted of the orations of Danton, the journalism of Camille Desmoulins and the few political poems that André Chenier had a chance to write before he was guillotined. The literature of the Russian Revolution was the political writing of Lenin and Trotsky, and Alexander Blok's poem, *The Twelve*, almost the last fruit of his genius before it was nipped by the wind of the storm. As for pre-revolutionary periods in which the new forces are fermenting, they *may* be great periods for literature—as the eighteenth century was in France and the nineteenth century in Russia (though here there was a decadence after 1905). But the conditions that make possible the masterpieces are apparently not produced by the impending revolutions, but by the phenomenon of literary technique, already highly developed, in the hands of a writer who has had the support of long-enduring institutions. He may reflect an age of transition, but it will not necessarily be true that his face is set squarely in the direction of the future. The germs of the Renaissance are in Dante and the longing for a better world in Virgil, but neither Dante nor Virgil can in any real sense be described as a revolutionary writer: they sum up or write elegies for ages that are passing. The social organisms that give structure to their thought—the Roman Empire and the Catholic Church—are already showing

signs of decay. It is impossible, therefore, to identify the highest creative work in art with the most active moments of creative social change. The writer who is seriously intent on producing long-range works of literature should, from the point of view of his own special personal interests, thank his stars if there is no violent revolution going on in his own country in his time. He may disapprove of the society he is writing about, but if it were disrupted by an actual upheaval he would probably not be able to write.

11. But what about 'proletarian literature' as an accompaniment of the social revolution? In the earlier days of the Communist regime in Russia, one used to hear about Russian authors who, in the effort to eliminate from their writings any vestige of the bourgeois point of view, had reduced their vocabulary and syntax to what they regarded as an A B C of essentials—with the result of becoming more unintelligible to the proletarian audience at whom they were aiming than if they had been Symbolist poets. (Indeed, the futurist poet Mayakovsky has since that time become a part of the Soviet canon.) Later on, as I have said, Soviet culture followed the road that Trotsky recommended: it began building again on the classics and on the bourgeois culture of other countries and on able revolutionary Russian writers who had learned their trade before the Revolution. 'Soviet publishers'—I quote from the Russian edition of *International Literature*, issue 2 of 1936—'are bringing out Hemingway and Proust not merely in order to demonstrate "bourgeois decay." Every genuine work of art—and such are the productions of Hemingway and Proust —enriches the writer's knowledge of life and heightens his esthetic sensibility and his emotional culture—in a word, it figures, in the broad sense, as a factor of educational value. Liberated socialist humanity inherits all that is beautiful, elevating and sustaining in the culture of previous ages.' The truth is that the talk in Soviet Russia about proletarian literature and art has resulted from the persistence of the same situation which led Tolstoy under the old regime to put on the muzhik's blouse and to go in for carpentry, cobbling and plowing: the difficulty experienced by an educated minority, who were only about 20 per cent of the people, in getting in

touch with the illiterate majority. In America the situation is quite different. The percentage of illiterates in this country is only something like 4 per cent; and there is relatively little difficulty of communication between different social groups. Our development away from England, and from the old world generally, in this respect—in the direction of the democratization of our idiom—is demonstrated clearly in H. L. Mencken's *The American Language*; and if it is a question of either the use for high literature of the language of the people or the expression of the dignity and importance of the ordinary man, the country which has produced *Leaves of Grass* and *Huckleberry Finn* has certainly nothing to learn from Russia. We had created during our pioneering period a literature of the common man's escape, not only from feudal Europe, but also from bourgeois society, many years before the Russian masses were beginning to write their names. There has been a section of our recent American literature of the last fifteen years or so—the period of the boom and the depression—which has dealt with our industrial and rural life from the point of view of the factory hand and the poor farmer under conditions which were forcing him to fight for his life, and this has been called proletarian literature; but it has been accompanied by books on the white-collar worker, the storekeeper, the well-to-do merchant, the scientist and the millionaire in situations equally disastrous or degrading. And this whole movement of critical and imaginative writing—though with some stimulus, certainly, from Russia—had come quite naturally out of our literature of the past. It is curious to observe that one of the best of the recent strike novels, *The Land of Plenty* by Robert Cantwell, himself a Westerner and a former mill worker, owes a good deal to Henry James.

12. Yet when all these things have been said, all the questions have not been answered. All that has been said has been said of the past; and Marxism is something new in the world: it is a philosophical system which leads directly to programs of action. Has there ever appeared before in literature such a phenomenon as M. André Malraux, who alternates between attempts, sometimes brilliant, to write long-range fiction on revolutionary themes, and exploits of aviation for the cause of

revolution in Spain? Here creative political action and the more complex kind of imaginative writing have united at least to the extent that they have arisen from the same vision of history and have been included in the career of one man. The Marxist vision of Lenin—Vincent Sheean has said it first—has in its completeness and its compelling force a good deal in common with the vision of Dante; but, partly realized by Lenin during his lifetime and still potent for some years after his death, it was a creation, not of literary art, but of actual social engineering. It is society itself, says Trotsky, which under communism becomes the work of art. The first attempts at this art will be inexpert and they will have refractory material to work with; and the philosophy of the Marxist dialectic involves idealistic and mythological elements which have led too often to social religion rather than to social art. Yet the human imagination has already come to conceive the possibility of re-creating human society; and how can we doubt that, as it acquires the power, it must emerge from what will seem by comparison the revolutionary 'underground' of art as we have always known it up to now and deal with the materials of actual life in ways which we cannot now even foresee? This is to speak in terms of centuries, of ages; but, in practicing and prizing literature, we must not be unaware of the first efforts of the human spirit to transcend literature itself.

Morose Ben Jonson

WHEN Swinburne published his study of Ben Jonson hardly sixty years ago, he indignantly called attention to the fact that English scholarship, which had shown such devotion to the texts of the Greek and Latin classics, should never, in two centuries and a half, have produced a decent edition of so important an English writer. That complaint can no longer be made—though the definitive edition of Jonson by C. H. Herford and Percy and Evelyn Simpson, brought out by the Oxford University Press, has been slow in appearing and is not yet complete. The first two volumes were published in 1925, and the eighth has only just come out. This, containing Jonson's poems and prose, is the last instalment of the text of Jonson, but it is to be followed by two volumes of commentaries, which ought to be particularly valuable, since no writer is more full of allusions, both topical and learned, than Jonson, and his work has never been properly annotated. There has not appeared, from this point of view and from that of clearing up the text, a serious edition of Jonson since that of William Gifford in 1816. This new one is a model of scholarship, handsomely printed and interestingly illustrated—in some cases, with hitherto unpublished drawings made by Inigo Jones for the décors and costumes of Jonson's masques.

Except, however, for the first two volumes, which assemble biographical materials and contain historical and critical essays on Jonson's various works, the Herford-Simpson edition is not especially to be recommended to the ordinary non-scholarly reader who may want to make the acquaintance of Jonson. It presents the original text with the seventeenth-century punctuation and spelling and with no glossary and no notes except textual ones. The books are, besides, expensive, and the earlier volumes are now hard to get—so the approach to this beetling author remains, as it has always been, rather forbidding and fraught with asperities. The best reprinting of the Gifford edition is also expensive and out of print. The three volumes of selections in the Mermaid Series are full of perplexing misprints, which drop out words or substitute wrong ones, and equipped with inadequate notes that turn up often on the wrong pages. The two volumes in the Everyman's Series include only Jonson's plays, and they are printed in a small dense type that makes them uncomfortable reading; there is a glossary, but it is incomplete. The only breach that I know in the hedge that seems to have sprung up around Jonson, as if his editors had somehow been influenced by their bristling and opaque subject, has been made by Mr. Harry Levin in his *Selected Works of Ben Jonson* (published by Random House). Here, in a clear readable text of his own and with a brilliant introduction, Mr. Levin has got together most of the best of Jonson for a compact and well-printed volume. There is an obstacle, though, even here, for he has furnished no notes and no glossary, and with Jonson, the explanation of a literary reference or the key to a phrase of slang is often absolutely indispensable for the understanding of a passage.

But it is not merely that Jonson's text itself has been a little hard to get at. It is rather that lack of demand has not stimulated popular editions. *Volpone* can still hold an audience—though it took a German adaptation to bring it back into fashion; and *The Alchemist* has been recently done both in New York and in London; but, among a thousand people, say, who have some knowledge and love of Shakespeare, and even some taste for Webster and Marlowe, I doubt whether you could find half a dozen who have any enthusiasm for Jonson or who have seriously read his plays. T. S. Eliot, admitting the long neglect into which Ben Jonson's work had fallen, put up, in *The Sacred Wood*, a strong plea for Jonson as an artist, and thus made a respect for this poet *de rigueur* in literary circles. But one's impression is that what people have read has been, not Jonson, but Eliot's essay. The dramatist himself, a great master for the age that followed his own, is still for ours mostly a celebrated name, whose writings are left unexplored. What I want to do here is to attack the problem of Jonson's unpopularity from what I believe to be a new point of view, and to show that his failure as a drawing attraction, in either the theater or the study, is bound up in a peculiar way with his difficulties as an artist.

*

It is a fault of Eliot's essay, so expert in its appreciation of the best-woven passages of Jonson's verse, that it minimizes his glaring defects. If you read it without reading Jonson, you will get a most plausible picture of a special kind of great writer, but this picture is not exactly Jonson. What is suppressed is all that Bernard Shaw meant when, telling off the Elizabethan dramatists, he characterized Ben Jonson as a 'brutal pedant'; and, in grappling with Jonson's shortcomings, we cannot perhaps do better than begin by facing squarely those qualities which made it impossible for Shaw—who admired, though he patronized, Shakespeare—to take seriously the comic writer who had, up to Shaw's own appearance, achieved the greatest reputation in English dramatic literature. The point is that Shakespeare, like Shaw, however much they differ in their philosophies, has an immense range, social and moral, in understanding a variety of people. To an intelligent and sensitive man of any school of thought, Shakespeare appears sensitive and intelligent. But Ben Jonson, after Shakespeare, seems neither. Though he attempts a variety of characters, they all boil down to a few motivations, recognizable as the motivations of Jonson himself and rarely transformed into artistic creations. Shakespeare expands himself, breeds his cells as organic beings, till he has so lost himself in the world he has made that we can hardly recompose his personality. Jonson merely splits himself up and sets the pieces—he is to this extent a dramatist —in conflict with one another; but we have merely to put these pieces together to get Jonson, with little left over. In the theater, he aims at several styles, as he tries for a multiplicity of characters, but the variety here, too, is mainly a mere technical matter of metrics and vocabulary, where Shakespeare can summon voices that seem to come from real human throats.

Jonson also lacks natural invention, and his theater has little organic life. His plots are incoherent and clumsy; his juxtapositions of elements are too often like the 'mechanical mixtures' of chemistry that produce no molecular reactions. His chief artifices for making something happen are to introduce his characters in impossible disguises and to have them play incredible practical jokes. Nor has he any sense of movement or proportion; almost everything goes on too long, and while it continues, it does not develop. Nor is his taste in other matters reliable. His puns, as Dryden complained, are sometimes of a stunning stupidity; and when he is dirty, he is, unlike Shakespeare, sometimes disgusting to such a degree that he makes one sympathetic with the Puritans in their efforts to clean up the theater. His reading of Greek and Latin, for all the boasting he does about it, has served him very insufficiently for the refinement and ordering of his work, and usually appears in his plays as either an alien and obstructive element or, when more skilfully managed, as a padding to give the effect of a dignity and weight which he cannot supply himself. He is much better when he lets himself go in a vein that is completely unclassical.

It is surely, then, misleading for Eliot to talk of Jonson's 'polished surface,' to call him a 'great creative mind,' who 'created his own world,' and not to warn you of the crudities and aridities, the uncertainty of artistic intention and the flat-footed dramatic incompetence, that you will run into when you set out to read him. None of his plays, with the exception of *The Alchemist*, really quite comes off as a whole. The three others of the best four of his comedies, though they all suffer from the faults I have mentioned, have elements of genuine humor and passages of admirable writing. But the story of *The Silent Woman* is revolting in its forced barbarity (Jonson's murderous practical jokes have their only analogue in literature in the booby-traps of Rudyard Kipling); *Volpone*, which reaches at moments a kind of heroic magnificence in exploiting its sordid and cruel themes, suffers, also, though somewhat less, from being based upon practical joking, and it is badly let down at the end by an improbable conventional conclusion; and, as for *Bartholomew Fair*, with some terribly funny scenes and a rich pageant of London low-life, there is in it so much too much of everything that the whole thing becomes rather a wallow of which the Pig-Woman and her pigs are all too truly the symbol. Contrast it with Hogarth's *Southwark Fair* (the product, to be sure, of a more disciplined age), equally confused and crowded, but so much better composed, so much sharper and firmer in outline. With *The Alchemist*, Jonson did ring the bell. This comedy is concentrated and well-constructed. There is no element of false morality to blur Jonson's acrid relish of the confidence games of his rogues: the cynicism is carried right through. The verse, which invests with style, which raises to distinction and glitter till it gives a ring almost like poetry, the slang of the underworld and the jargon of its various chicaneries, is an original achievement of Jonson's, which is only sustained in this one play. And, though there are one or two labored devices, the invention is more resourceful and the dialogue more spontaneous than in any of Jonson's other comedies. Yet this play, one of the funniest in English, is not really an example of high comedy as either a play of Molière's or a play of Aristophanes' is. Ben Jonson is not enough of a critic— that is, he has not enough intelligence—for either Molière's kind of interest in character and human relations or Aristophanes' kind of interest in institutions and points of view. *The Alchemist* is a picaresque farce, fundamentally not different from the Marx brothers. And it shows Jonson's poverty of themes that, when he had earlier attempted a tragedy, he should have arrived at a similar story. *Sejanus*, which takes us to the Roman Senate and inside the court of Tiberius, is also a chronicle of the intrigues of rogues who begin by working together but later sell each other out.

This is a too offhand summary of Jonson's work, but I want to get at him in another way.

Ben Jonson seems an obvious example of a psycholgical type which has been described by Freud and designated by a technical name, *anal erotic*, which has sometimes misled the layman as to what it was meant to imply. Let me introduce it simply by quoting from the account of it in a handbook of psychoanalysis, *The Structure and Meaning of Psychoanalysis* by William Healy, A. F. Bronner and A. M. Bowers. The three main characteristics of this type are here paraphrased from Freud as follows: '(a) orderliness . . . in an over-accentuated form, pedantry; (b) parsimony, which may become avarice; (c) obstinacy, which may become defiance and perhaps also include irascibility and vindictiveness.' Now, Jonson had all these qualities. He was a pedant, whose cult of the classics had little connection with his special kind of genius. There is something of the 'compulsive,' in the neurotic sense, about his constant citing of precedents and his working into the speeches of his plays passages, sometimes not translated, from the Greek and Latin authors (though it was common for the Elizabethans to stick in scraps from Seneca or Ovid), as if they were charms against failure. That he always did fear failure is evident; and the arrogance, irritability and stubbornness which are also characteristic of this Freudian type have obviously, in Jonson's case, their origin in a constant anxiety as to the adequacy of his powers. The more he defies his audience, vindicates himself against his critics (though at the same time he puts himself to special pains to propitiate the vulgar with vulgarity and to impress the learned with learning), in his innumerable prologues, inductions, interludes between the acts, epilogues, dramatic postscripts and apologies added to the printed texts—the more he protests and explains, declaims at unconscionable length his indifference to and scorn of his detractors, the more we feel that he is unquiet, not confident. He is offsetting his internal doubts by demonstrations of self-assertion.

The hoarding and withholding instinct which is the third of the key traits of this type Jonson also displays to a high degree. This tendency is supposed to be based on an attitude toward the excretatory processes acquired in early childhood. Such people, according to Freud, have an impulse to collect and accumulate; they feel that doing so gives them strength and helps them to resist the pressures that their elders are bringing to bear on them. Sometimes they simply concentrate on storing up; sometimes they expend in sudden bursts. They are likely to have a strong interest in food both from the deglutitionary and the excretatory points of view; but the getting and laying by of money or of some other kind of possession which may or may not seem valuable to others is likely to substitute itself for the infantile preoccupation with the contents of the alimentary tract. Now, Jonson certainly exemplified this tendency, and he exhibited it in a variety of ways. His learning is a form of hoarding; and allied to it is his habit of collecting words. He liked to get up the special jargons of the various trades and professions and unload them in bulk on the public—sometimes with amusing results, as in the case of the alchemical and astrological patter reeled off by the crooks of *The Alchemist*, and even of the technique of behavior of the courtiers in *Cynthia's Revels*, but more often, as with the list of cosmetics recommended by Wittipol in *The Devil Is an Ass* and, to my taste, with the legal Latin of the divorce scene in *The Silent Woman*, providing some of his most tedious moments. The point is that Ben Jonson depends on the exhibition of stored-away knowledge to compel admiration by itself. And the hoarding and withholding of money is the whole subject of that strange play *Volpone*. Volpone is not an ordinary miser: he is a Venetian 'magnifico,' whose satisfaction in his store of gold is derived not merely from gloating alone but also, and more excitingly, from stimulating others to desire it, to hope to inherit it from him, and then frustrating them with the gratuitous cruelty which has been noted as one of the features of the aggressive side of this Freudian type. The practical jokes in Jonson have usually this sadistic character, and the people who perpetrate them are usually trying either to get something for themselves or to keep someone else from getting something. The many kinds of frauds and sharpers—from pickpockets to promoters —who figure in Jonson's plays as prominently as the practical jokers are occupied with similar aims; and Subtle and Face, in *The Alchemist*, lurk closeted, like Volpone, in a somber house, where they are hoarding their cleverness, too, and plotting their victims' undoing.

I am not qualified to 'analyze' Jonson in the light of this Freudian conception, and I have no interest in trying to fit him into any formulation of it. I am not even sure that the relation between the workings of the alimentary tract and the other phenomena of personality is, as Freud assumes, a relation of cause and effect; but I am sure that Freud has here really seized upon a nexus of human traits that are involved with one another and has isolated a recognizable type, and it seems to me to leap to the eyes that Jonson belongs to this type. I shall fill in the rest of my picture with the special characteristics of Jonson, which are consistent with the textbook description and which in some cases strikingly illustrate it.

Ben Jonson's enjoyment of tavern life and his great reputation for wit have created, among those who do not read him, an entirely erroneous impression of high spirits and joviality; but his portraits show rather the face of a man who habitually worries, who is sensitive and holds himself aloof, not yielding himself to intimate fellowship. In many of his plays there

figures an unsociable and embittered personage who sometimes represents virtue and censors the other characters, but is
in other cases presented by Jonson as a thoroughly disagreeable person and the butt of deserved persecution. Such, in the
second of these categories, are Macilente in *Every Man Out
of His Humour*, Morose in *The Silent Woman*, Surly in *The
Alchemist* and Wasp in *Bartholomew Fair*. The most conspicuous of these is Morose, and Jonson's treatment of him is particularly significant. The dramatist, on a visit to the country, had
encountered a local character who gave him an idea for a play.
This was a man who had a morbid aversion to noise. Now,
Jonson seems never to have inquired the reason, never to have
tried to imagine what the life of such a man would be really
like; nor could he ever have been conscious of what it was in
himself that impelled him to feel so vivid an interest in him.
According to his usual custom, he simply put him on the stage
as a 'humour,' an eccentric with an irrational horror of any
kind of sound except that of his own voice, who lives in a room
with a double wall and the windows 'close shut and caulked' in
a street too narrow for traffic, and who, declaring that 'all dis-
courses but mine own' seem to him 'harsh impertinent, and
irksome,' makes his servants communicate with him by signs.
And the only way that Jonson can find to exploit the possibilities of this neurotic is to make him the agonized victim of a
group of ferocious young men, who hunt him in his burrow
like a badger, and trick him into marrying a 'silent woman,'
who, immediately after the ceremony—while her sponsors raise
a hideous racket—opens fire on him with a frenzy of chatter,
and turns out in the end to be a boy in disguise. But Morose
himself is cruel through meanness: he has merited the worst he
can suffer. He has wanted to disinherit his nephew, and has
consigned him, in a venomous outburst, to the direst humiliation and poverty. Through Morose and through the characters
like him, Ben Jonson is tormenting himself for what is negative
and recessive in his nature. In *Volpone*, the withholder is
punished only after he has had his fling at the delight of tormenting others. Miserliness, unsociability, a self-sufficient and
systematic spite—these are among Jonson's dominant themes:
all the impulses that grasp and deny. In the final scene of *Cyn-*

thia's Revels, the last play of Jonson's first period, he makes
Cynthia rhetorically demand:

> *When hath Diana, like an envious wretch,*
> *That glitters only to his soothed self,*
> *Denying to the world the precious use*
> *Of hoarded wealth, withheld her friendly aid?*

Yet Cynthia is Diana, and Diana is a virgin queen, who has herself forbidden love to her court; and the attitude which she is
here repudiating is to supply almost all the subjects for the rest
of Jonson's plays, among them all of his best. In these four
lines, you have the whole thing in the words that come to his
pen: envy, denial, hoarding, withholding. The first of these is
very important. (Envy then meant hatred and spite as well as
jealousy of what others have, but I am dealing with it here in
its modern sense, which is usually the sense of Jonson.) In several of the earlier plays, it has been one of the chief motivations. In those you have had, on the one hand, the worthy and
accomplished scholar—Horace of *The Poetaster*, Crites of *Cynthia's Revels*—who is envied by lesser men; and, on the other
hand, the poor and exacerbated wit—Macilente in *Every Man
Out of His Humour*—who envies lesser men. But both are aspects of the same personality; both are identified with Jonson
himself. Whether the injury done the superior man consists of
being slandered by fools or by the fools' being better off than
he, it is the only fulfilment of the play that he is granted his just
revenge, and he scores off his victims with a cruelty almost
equal to that of Volpone frustrating his mercenary friends.

With this, there is no love in Jonson's plays to set against
these negative values. The references to seduction, frequent
though they are, in both his plays and his personal poems, suggest nothing but the coldest of appetites, and often show more
gratification at the idea of cuckolding a husband than at that of
enjoying a woman. In the plays, two sexual types recur, neither
of whom finds any satisfaction in sex. Jonson said of his wife,
from whom he separated, that she had been 'a shrew, yet honest'; and the only women in his plays that have even a sem-
blance of life are shrews of the most pitiless breed. The typical
wife in Jonson is always ready to doublecross her husband, and

she does not want to allow him a moment of self-confidence or tranquillity: whatever the man does must be wrong; yet she may cherish at the same time an illusion that there waits for her somewhere a lover who can give her what she desires and deserves, and the appearance of a tenth-rate courtier may be enough to turn her head. The recurrent male type is a man who is insanely jealous of his wife but, paradoxically, is willing to prostitute her. The rival of the obsessive jealousy is always an obsessive greed either for money, as in the case of Corvino of *Volpone*, or, as in the case of Fitzdottrel of *The Devil Is an Ass*, for some other material advantage which the husband will enjoy by himself: Fitzdottrel likes to dress up and be seen on public occasions, but he never takes his wife with him. We may suspect, reading Jonson today, a connection between the impotence of these husbands to spend any real love on their wives and their fears that they are going to lose them. We may reflect that the self-centered husband might produce the shrewish wife, or that, living with a shrewish wife, a man might grow more self-centered, if he did not, as usually happens with the unfortunate husbands of Jonson's plays, become totally demoralized. But Jonson had nothing of Shakespeare's grasp of organic human character or situation. It is interesting to contrast these bitches with the heroine of *The Taming of the Shrew*. Katharina's bad temper with men is accompanied by a deep conviction that no man can really want to marry her: it is a defiant assertion of self-respect. And so the jealousy of Othello (if not of Leontes) is explained by his consciousness, as a Moor in Venice, living among cleverer people who feel his color as a bar to close fellowship, of being at a disadvantage with the race to which his wife belongs. Whereas Jonson's two depressing stock figures do not afford very much insight into the causes of the traits they exemplify. Turning up again and again with a monotony of which Shakespeare was incapable, they obviously represent phenomena which Jonson has known at first hand and on which he cannot help dwelling: two more aspects of that negative soul that he is impelled to caricature. Yet sometimes, with his special experience, he can make them reveal themselves—as in the self-torturing Proustian soliloquies of Kiteley in *Every Man in His Humour*—in a way that strips off the skin to show, not what is in the depths, but what is just below the surface.

Jonson's positive ideal of womanhood may be summed up in the well-known lyric that begins, *'Have you seen but a bright lily grow, Before rude hands have touched it?,'* and ends *'O so white! O so soft! O so sweet is she!'* It is something quite remote and unreal which he is unable—when he tries, which is seldom, as in the Celia of *Volpone*—to bring to life in his plays, and, though the poems inspired by it are neat and agreeable enough, they have no human tenderness in them, let alone human passion. The touches in Jonson's poetry that come closest to lyric feeling are invariably evocations of coldness: *'Like melting snow upon a craggy hill . . . Since nature's pride is now a withered daffodil,'* or *'Except Love's fires the virtue have To fright the frost out of the grave,'* (from a poem in which the same stanza begins with the incredibly prosaic couplet: *'As in a ruin, we it call One thing to be blown up or fall . . .'*). And we may cite from the masque called *The Vision of Delight* the lines that remained in the memory of Joyce's Stephen Dedalus: *'I was not wearier where I lay By frozen Tithon's side tonight'* . . . ; as well as the passage from the prose *Discoveries* which Saintsbury selected for praise: 'What a deal of cold business doth a man misspend the better part of life in!—in scattering compliments, tendering visits, gathering and venting news, following feasts and plays, making a little winter-love in a dark corner.' At the end of *Cynthia's Revels*, Cupid tries to shoot Cynthia's courtiers and make them fall in love with one another, but he finds that his bow is powerless: they have been drinking from the fount of Self-Love, in which Narcissus admired himself, and they are impervious to his shafts. When Diana is told of his presence, she sends him packing at once. Few lovers are united by Jonson. Is there indeed a case in all his work? And in Jonson's latest plays, the heroines undergo a transformation that makes Cynthia seem relatively human. The Lady Pecunia of *The Staple of News*, surrounded by her female retinue, Mortgage, Statute, Band and Wax, is simply a figure in a financial allegory; and so is Mistress Steel, the Magnetic Lady. Both are heiresses, kept close by guardians and sought by baffled suitors. The feminine principle here has been turned by the instinct for hoarding into something metallic, unyielding. The woman has lost all her womanhood: she is literally the hoarded coin. This evidently appeared to Ben Jonson a perfectly natural pleasantry, but it is quite enough to account for the failure, in his time, of these pieces, and for the distaste that we feel for them today.

To these stock characters of Jonson's theater should be added another that evidently derives from the playwright's social situation as well as from his psychology of hoarding. Ben Jonson, from his own account, was the son of a Scotch gentleman who had possessed some little fortune, but who had been thrown into prison, presumably for his Protestant leanings, in the reign of Bloody Mary, and had had his property confiscated. He died before Ben was born, and Ben's mother married a master bricklayer. Young Ben went to Westminster school, under the patronage of one of the masters, whose attention had been attracted by the boy's exceptional abilities, and may have started in at Cambridge on a scholarship; but he was obliged, apparently through poverty, to give up his studies there, and was set to learn the bricklayer's trade, which he loathed and from which he escaped by enlisting to fight in Flanders. Now, one of Jonson's favorite clowns, who varies little from play to play, is a young heir who is an utter numbskull and who, just having come into his money, begins throwing it away by the handful and soon finds himself fleeced by sharpers. This figure, too, in a different way from the envied or the envious man, is obviously the creation of Jonson's own envy, stimulated, no doubt, from two sources—first, the grievance of the man of good birth unjustly deprived of his patrimony, and, second, the sulky resentment of the man who can only withhold against the man who can freely lavish.

Jonson's hardships and uncertainty in his earlier years—when he can never have known anything but poverty—must have spurred him to desperate efforts to ballast and buttress himself. (For, as I have said, I do not necessarily accept the view of Freud that the training of the excretory functions must precede the development of other traits which exhibit resistance through hoarding, though it seems certain that, in personalities like Jonson's, these various traits are related.) He had acquired classical learning where he could not acquire money; and it was to remain for him a reservoir of strength, a basis of social position, to which he was to go on adding all his life. But his habit of saving and holding back—did his Scotch ancestry figure here, too?—had an unfortunate effect on his work, as well as on his personal relations, in that it made it very difficult for him fully to exploit his talents. It is not that the audiences of Jonson's day, the readers who have come to him since, have been unwilling to give themselves to his talents, but that his talents, authentic though they were, have not given themselves to us—or rather, that they were able to give themselves for only a limited period and then only at the expense of much effort. Ben Jonson, at his best, writes brilliantly; he has a genuine dramatic imagination. But it is hard for him to pump up his powers to work that will display their capacities. His addiction to wine—'drink,' Drummond said, 'is one of the elements in which he liveth'—was, I believe, bound up with the problem of getting himself to the point of high-pressure creative activity. He explained the strength of *Volpone* on the basis of its having been written at the time when he had just received a gift of ten dozen of sack; asserted that a passage in *Catiline* had suffered from having been composed when he was drinking watered wine; and apologized for the weakness of his later plays on the ground that he and his 'boys'—by which he meant his drinking companions—had been getting bad wine at their tavern. This shows that he drank while he was writing; and it is possible that liquor, though effective in helping him to keep up his high vein, may also have been to blame for the badness of some of his work. There are at times a peculiar coarseness in the texture of Jonson's writing, a strained falseness in his comic ideas, which, intolerable to a sober mind, may very well have seemed inspired to a constipated writer well primed with sack.

What Jonson was aiming at—from *Cynthia's Revels*, say— was a majesty and splendor of art which should rival the classics he venerated and the work of his more dashing contemporaries, with their rhetoric, color and spirit. But it is hard to be noble and grand with material so negative, so sour, as that which Jonson's experience had given him. To write in blank verse that is also poetry of the imbecile ambitions and the sordid swindles which furnish the whole subject of *The Al-chemist* was a feat that even Ben Jonson was never to achieve but once. When he attempts a Roman tragedy, as in *Catiline* or *Sejanus*, his Romans are mostly the envious rogues, the merciless prigs and the treacherous sluts with whom we are familiar in his comedies, and they make a more unpleasant impression for not being humorously treated. When Jonson attempts Renaissance splendor, he always gives it an element of the factitious as well as an element of the vulgar, which, as Mr. Levin says, have the effect of making it look ridiculous. The dreams of Sir Epicure Mammon bring a kind of hard glow to the writing, but his banquets and his beds and his mirrors are imaginary like the gold that is to buy them: they never get on to the stage as does the 'alchemist's' fusty lair. And with *Volpone*, the great difficulty is that the mean motivations of the characters have no intimate connection with the background, the house of a rich Venetian. Volpone is simply another of Jonson's hateful and stingy men, who behaves as if he were envious of others, without being provided by Jonson with any real reason for envy. The magnificence of Jonson's grandees, like the purity of his women, is a value that is always unreal and that can never make a satisfactory counterweight to a poverty and a squalor that are actual and vividly rendered. One has to go to the later French naturalists who were influenced by both Flaubert and Zola to find anything comparable to the poetry which Jonson was able to extract from all the cheap and dirty aspects of London: the 'poor spoonful of dead wine, with flies in't'; the gingerbread made of 'stale bread, rotten eggs, musty ginger and dead honey'; the rogue out of luck,

> *at Pie Corner,*
> *Taking your meal of steam in, from cooks' stalls,*
> *Where, like the father of hunger, you did walk*
> *Piteously costive, with your pinched horn-nose,*
> *And your complexion of the Roman wash*
> *Stuck full of black and melancholic worms,*
> *Like powder-corns shot at th' artillery-yard;*

the theater pick-ups, 'lean playhouse poultry,' as described by fat Ursula of the pig-roasting booth, 'that has the bony rump sticking out like the ace of spades or the point of a partizan, that every rib of 'em is like the tooth of a saw; or will so grate 'em [their customers] with their hips and shoulders as—take 'em altogether—they were as good lie with a hurdle.' It is the peculiar beauty of *The Alchemist* that the visions of splendor here are all, frankly, complete illusions created out of sordid materials by rogues in the minds of dupes. The poor stupid whore Doll has to impersonate the Queen of Faery and a great lady in romantic circumstances. A more humane writer might have extracted some pathos from this; but Jonson does get an esthetic effect that is quite close to the Flaubertian chagrin.

But, in *Volpone*, where real gold is involved, we are never allowed to see it. The German adaptation of this play made by Stefan Zweig and done here by the Theater Guild, which has also been used as a basis for the current French film, is an improvement on Jonson's original in one very important respect. It shows us what we want we see, what, subconsciously, we have come to demand: the spending, the liberation of Volpone's withheld gold—when Mosca, to everyone's relief, finally flings it about the stage in fistfuls. But Ben Jonson cannot squander his gold, his gold which he has never possessed; he can only squander excrement. Karl Abraham, one of the psychologists quoted in the book referred to above, 'cites, in proof of the close association between sadistic and anal impulses instances in his experiences with neurotics when an explosive bowel evacuation has been a substitute for a discharge of anger or rage, or has accompanied it.' Certainly Jonson seems to explode in this fashion. The directness with which he gives way to the impulse is probably another cause of his chronic unpopularity. The climax of *The Poetaster* is the administering of emetic pills, the effects of which take, in this case, the form of a poetic joke. The comic high point of *The Alchemist* comes with the locking of one of the characters in a privy, where he will be overcome by the smell. This whole malodorous side of Jonson was given its fullest and most literal expression in the poem called *The Famous Voyage* which was too much for even Gifford and Swinburne, in which he recounts a nocturnal expedition made by two London blades in a wherry through the roofed-over tunnel of Fleet Ditch, which was the sewer for the public privies above it. A hardly less literal letting-go is the whole play of *Bartholomew Fair*, which followed the more pretentious work

(from *Sejanus* through *Catiline*) that we have just been discussing. It is Ben Jonson's least strained and inhibited play,
and one of his most successful. He drops verse for colloquial
prose; he forgets about classical precedents. He dumps out
upon his central group of characters, for the most part pusil-
lanimous examples of the lower middle class, puritan parsons
and petty officials, with, of course, a young spendthrift from
the country, what must have been a lifetime's accumulation of
the billingsgate and gutter practices of the pickpockets, booth-
keepers, peddlers, pimps, ballad-singers and professional
brawlers of the Elizabethan underworld. This comedy, novel
in its day, anticipates both Hogarth and Dickens; but Jonson's
impulse to degrade his objects is something not shared by
either. Hogarth and Dickens both, for all their appetite for
rank vulgarity, are better-humored and more fastidious. The
flood of abusive language let loose by the infuriated Pig-
Woman, well-written and funny though it is, is outpouring for
outpouring's sake: it effects no dramatic move and has in itself
no rhetorical development; and the even more filthy travesty
of Marlowe's *Hero and Leander* in terms of bankside muck has
an ugliness which makes one suspect that Jonson took an ugly
delight in defiling a beautiful poem which he could not hope
to rival. Yet we cannot but succumb—in certain scenes, at least
—to the humor of *Bartholomew Fair*. The tumult of Ursula's
booth and her devotion to her roasting pigs, the monumental
pocket-picking episode that moves to its foreseen conclusion
almost with the inevitability of tragedy—these somehow create
more sympathy (always for the characters outside the law) than
anything else in Jonson's plays.

And Ben Jonson is somehow a great man of letters, if he is
not often a great artist. His very failure to make the best of his
gifts had the result of his leaving a body of work full of hints—
unrealized ambitions, undeveloped beginnings—which later
writers were able to exploit in a way that it was hardly possible
for them to do with the work of Shakespeare, which *was* realized, consummate, complete. The most astonishing variety of
writers owe quite different kinds of debts to Jonson. It is as if
they had found means to deliver, in viable forms of art, the

genius that Jonson had had to withhold. Gifford was certainly right in supposing that Milton owed something to such passages as the opening of *Volpone*, in which the hoarder invokes his gold. The whole comedy of Congreve and Wycherley seems to have grown out of the cynical men-about-town, with their bravura-pieces of wit, in *The Silent Woman*; and Swift must have picked up from Jonson, not only the title of *A Tale of a Tub*, but also the style and tone of his series of poems to Stella, which are so much like certain of those in Jonson's series, *A Celebration of Charis*, as well as his general vein of morosely humorous realism, exemplified in *The Lady's Dressing Room* and *A Description of a City Shower*. The comedy of humors eventually led to the one-idea characters of Peacock, which led, later, to those of Aldous Huxley; and it must have contributed to the novels of Dickens, who loved to act Bobadil in *Every Man in His Humour*. Though Tennyson was under the impression that he himself had invented the stanza-form that he made famous in *In Memoriam*, it had already been used by Jonson in his *Elegy* (*XXII* of *Underwoods*), the tone of which is quite close to Tennyson in his elegiac vein, and in the second of the choruses to *Catiline*, which suggests such weightier use of the meter as one finds in the dedication to Queen Victoria or in the dedication of *Demeter* to Lord Dufferin. And there are touches in Lewis Carroll that seem reminiscent of Jonson: '*I passed by the garden and marked with one eye How the Owl and the Panther were sharing the pie,*' recalls a long nonsense speech in *The Vision of Delight*: '*Yet would I take the stars to be cruel If the crab and the rope-maker ever fight duel,*' etc.; and Sir Politic Would-be of *Volpone*, with his succession of ridiculous inventions, of which he likes to boast, 'Mine own device,' is a forerunner of the White Knight. In the first decades of our own century, that very first-rate comic writer, Ronald Firbank, with how little direct contact one cannot tell, represents a very late development of Ben Jonson's typical methods—eviscerated personalities and monstrous motivations labeled with bizarre names—which, though it shows perhaps a certain decadence, keeps also a good deal of vigor. And James Joyce, who told his friend Frank Budgen that Ben Jonson was one of the only four writers that he had ever read completely through, seems to have had in common with Jonson some of the traits of his psychological type, and may be said to have followed his example—failing, sometimes, from faults like Jonson's—rather, perhaps, than to have exploited to better effect any special aspect of Jonson's work. Joyce, too, hoarded words and learning and attempted to impress his reader by unloading his accumulations; he, too, has his co-prophilic side and his husbands who acquiesce, at the same time that they torture themselves, in the sleepings-abroad of their wives; he, too, is defiant and arrogant, self-consciously resistant to pressures, and holds himself apart and aloof.

It would be interesting, from this point of view, to compare Ben Jonson at length with Gogol as well as with Joyce. Undoubtedly Gogol is a case even more narrowly developed than Jonson of the type in question here. He, too, likes to store up words—his note-books were full of the jargons of special trades and milieux; and he voids them in long dense sentences that agglutinate as massive paragraphs. His characters, in *Dead Souls*, are themselves almost always collectors, and they sometimes collect sheer rubbish—like Manilov, who saves all his old pipe-ashes. Gogol loves to write about eating, he has little sensual interest in women. His comedy *The Inspector General*, farcical, at once gross and inhuman, has something in common with Jonson's comedies; and, like Jonson, he is powerless to lift himself—in the unfinished later instalments of *Dead Souls* —out of the satirical comedy of roguery into a sterner and less turbid medium. The virtuous judge and the altruistic landowner of the second part of *Dead Souls* are as obviously maniacs as the misers and boors of the first part—as the senators, conspirators and emperors of Jonson's Roman plays are just as much 'compulsive' one-track minds as the characters of his comedy of 'humours.' So Joyce, with greater genius and wider range than either Jonson or Gogol, cannot seem to function comfortably and freely except when he has given himself, as in his two most ambitious books, the latitude of a comic frame: his protagonists are comic figures, humiliated, persecuted, rueful, and their epics are systematic ironies, in which their heroic pretensions never wholly emerge from the mud. Gogol and Joyce, too, both share with Jonson his ideal of feminine sweetness and purity—seen only in wistful glimpses—that floats somewhere above and divorced from the smelly and dirty earth. With this motif Gogol succeeds least well: the lovely face fleetingly seen in the coach by Chichikov of *Dead Souls*, the maidenly pensionnaire who strikes him dumb at the ball; Jonson, a little better in the lyrics mentioned above; Joyce, with triumphant success in the vision of the wading girl that makes the climax of *A Portrait of the Artist*.

Later years did not mellow Jonson. When he visited Drummond at forty-five, with most of his best work behind him, he was still running down his contemporaries and asserting his own merits as peevishly as in the days when he had written *The Poetaster*; and at a supper given for him by his younger admirers the year before his death, he painfully embarrassed his friends by inordinately praising himself and vilifying his fellow poets. He could never afford to be generous, because he had never achieved what he wanted; and one suspects that, even in the case of such a lesser contemporary as Marston, Jonson's hateful hostility toward him had in it an element of envy of that touch of sublimity and magic which Marston was able to manage and which was quite beyond Jonson's reach. To Drummond he even grumbled about Shakespeare; and his reference to *The Tempest* in *Bartholomew Fair* betrays how much it must have irked him to see his friend, a much older man, find suddenly a new field for his genius in a form so close to that of the masque, in which Jonson had worked for years without ever striking more than an occasional spark from his pedantic made-to-order prettiness. It is therefore all the more a proof of the deep devotion he cherished for the art that they both practiced that he should have put on record so roundly his high opinion of Shakespeare—and not only of Shakespeare, but also of Donne. In his elegy on Shakespeare especially, in estimating him above all their contemporaries and setting him beside the greatest of the ancients, he does justice to all that is noblest in his own aspiring nature, which had to drag so much dead weight, all that is soundest and most acute in his own cramped but virile intellect. The one thing he really loved was literature, and, having served it as well as he could, no touchiness of personal pride could keep him from honoring one who had been fitted to serve it better precisely by the qualification, among others, of possessing, as Jonson said, 'an open and free nature,' so that he 'flowed with that facility that sometimes it was necessary he should be stopped.'

1948

'Mr. Rolfe'

THE first days of my first fall at prep school were passed in complete confusion. We were always being shrieked at by bells, which uprooted us from what we were doing and compelled us to report somewhere else. We had to get there while the bell was still ringing, and I used to be swamped by the mob of boys pouring in and out of the classrooms and pushing along the corridors and porches, and finally arrive late in a panic.

One of the places in which I used to land was a room that was larger than the others and that had white classical busts above the blackboards and a dais for the master's desk. This was the room to which I went for Greek, and I realized at the first recitation that what occurred there was of a special nature. The master, who was tall and well-dressed and who loomed taller from sitting on the dais, had an aspect, an accent and a manner unfamiliar to the point of seeming foreign. He was blond, with drooping-lidded blue eyes and a high-domed oval head, which was very inadequately thatched with strands of thin yellow hair, and he wore a yellow drooping mustache of the kind that was supposed then to be English and which reminded me of a character called Mr. Batch who figured in the funny papers. His eyebrows were of the kind that arch away from one another like a pair of quotation marks and had the perpetually lifted look which conventionally indicates distress but also comports with irony, and his mustache concealed his mouth, so that his expression remained enigmatic, and you could never be sure whether he were smiling at you kindly or withering you with mock sweetness.

At any rate, as soon as he entered, he dominated the room to the last row of seats. From the moment he sat down at his desk, rearing his neck and his back very straight and setting out his book before him with a kind of sober directness that was a part of his approach to his subject, he kept the class in a state of tension as if they were witnessing a performance in which—and all too often without knowing their lines—they themselves were to be called upon to take part.

233

The first characteristics of Mr. Rolfe's which impressed a new boy in his class were the wittiness, pungency and promptitude of his sarcasm and the mercilessness of his demands. He put you on the spot for your assignment as none of the other masters did; he would not allow you to slide over anything, and it seemed that he would not help you; if you failed, he made you feel by some caustic touch a criticism of your classroom personality. He evidently made tacit but definite assumptions about the classroom personalities of us all—I was supposed to be moony and inattentive—which one might feel did one less than justice. He had a way of going around the class in pursuit of the answer to some question—designating us as 'First little gentleman . . . Second little gentleman,' and so forth, and pointing at us with the butt of his pencil—which could put one at a distance and be paralyzing. And there were also his special drawl, which could be musical and yet so mocking, and his queer but distinguished accent. I knew that he was not an Englishman, in spite of his British mustache and though he pronounced words like *bath* and *advanced* with what was called the 'broad *a*.' *Afterwards*, when it came at the end of a sentence, he pronounced *ahfterwúrds*, with the accent on the last syllable. It seemed impossible to appeal to him outside of class or to establish with him the personal relation by which boys seek to protect themselves from masters, and one got to be afraid of being snubbed. If anyone were rash enough to ask him whether Xenophon, which we were to start next term, or the verbs in $-\mu\iota$, which were looming as the next ordeal in the grammar, were as hard as they were rumored to be, he would answer, glancing away: 'Oh, very difficult! almost impossible.'

I had been rather badly trained at my previous school, and I at once resented Mr. Rolfe. I took to brooding outside of class over his sarcasms; and there were days when I was obsessed by his image and some brief derisive remark of which I had been the victim that morning. The Greek class both excited and scared me.

One night I went to see him in his rooms. He had invited us to come to him for help, and I had finally picked up courage to do so. He was engaged with someone else when I came in, and I shyly glanced about the room and then bent over the books on the table. The incident must have been one of those which sharply and suddenly mark the emergence of some new element into consciousness, because whenever I dream of going back to school and calling on Mr. Rolfe, I never find him in his later rooms where I often went to see him, but always in these earlier ones where I could only have gone a few times and in which, when awake, I never place him. These rooms were the rooms of a bachelor but not those of a bachelor schoolmaster: in their relative elegance and luxury, they reminded me rather of the apartment inhabited by a bachelor uncle; and Mr. Rolfe was sitting back on a couch and giving attention to the passages presented to him less like a master after class than like a gentleman receiving at his ease. In the bookrack, with their titles upturned, I saw volumes of Bernard Shaw, and this somewhat startled and shocked me. I had, at fourteen, not yet read Shaw; but I had heard he was a perverse cynic, who considered himself superior to other people and who liked to wound his reader's sensibilities.

Mr. Rolfe, when my turn came to talk to him, answered my questions with his usual aloofness; and I went out of the room convinced that he was a disciple of Bernard Shaw, and that his brilliant performance in the classroom at the expense of us poor Fourth-Formers had something to do with the scandalous plays and the arrogant personality of which I had been hearing such disturbing accounts. I thought that I had conceived an antagonism, bitter and forever intransigent, against Mr. Rolfe and Shaw.

I began to like Greek, however, which I was only just beginning that year. The truth was that, in spite of his sarcasm, Mr. Rolfe shed on everything he dealt with a peculiar imagination and charm, and that this held you even while you resented him. My feeling about Greek was becoming quite different from my feeling about Latin, which I had not been taught especially well and which seemed to me something technical like algebra, with almost no relation to literature or human speech. The Greek words as he pronounced them or wrote them on the board in his clear and beautiful hand took on an esthetic value; and when you came to understand his attitude, the recitation turned into a kind of game, which, though taxing, had its rewards and its amusements.

I came to see that he was not really cruel. Though severe in his conception of his duty toward his students and of their duty toward their work, he was not really the sort of master who takes a joy in humiliating his class. He never failed to acknowledge good work, though he liked to express his approval in Greek; and he told me one day, in his drawl that always sounded ironic, that if I continued as I had been doing I might get to be his favorite pupil. I decided, thinking it over, that he had meant it; but this won me no indulgence or tenderness, and he would curtly correct my vagaries. It was characteristic of Mr. Rolfe, who aimed to do so much more for his pupils than get them through their college examinations, that he should one day have explained to us in passing the theory of the lost *digamma*, which he described as 'a little thing like a tuning fork'; and it was characteristic of me, with my interest in literary *arcana*, that I should then have become fascinated by the letters that had been dropped out of the Greek alphabet. It was suggested to me by Mr. Rolfe that I should do better if I concentrated on those they had retained.

And I came to understand that his rigor was really in the interests of Greek. I have found out from later experience that it requires a rare blend of qualities for a man or a woman to teach Greek well: he must have a real taste for Greek (which seems rarer than a taste for Latin), a real feeling for its luminosity and subtlety, its nobility and naiveté, a lively imaginative picture of the civilization behind it; and he must, at the same time, be capable of insisting on the high degree of intellectual discipline that is needed to keep the class up to the effort demanded by the difficulties of the subject—difficulties which do not consist merely of the more or less automatic application of formulas one has learned, but involve, along with accurate memory, a certain precision of feeling, in which one can be trained by an adept but which cannot be learned by rote. Mr. Rolfe was the perfect Hellenist. He made you get everything exactly right, and this meant a good deal of drudgery. But one was also always made to feel that there was something worth having there behind the numbered paragraphs and paradigms of Goodwin's Greek grammar, the grim backs and fatiguing notes of the Ginn texts 'for the use of schools'—something exhilarating in the air of the classroom, human, heroic and shining. The prospect of knowing this marvelous thing lent the details excitement—and so it did the daily contest between Mr. Rolfe and you, which eventually became quite jolly. You felt that he was not unkind, that he merely wanted people to learn Greek, that teaching people Greek was an exalted aim to which he had devoted his life, and that he only became really unpleasant with students who did not want to learn it.

I therefore began working hard to keep myself on the right side of his severity. Besides the appetite I had acquired for Greek, I was stimulated also by the fact that I had grown to enjoy his wit. The truth was that I myself had a satirical turn which I was just beginning then to learn to exploit, and that I had never before met in the flesh a real past master of mockery. Hence my resentment, and hence my admiration. I was soon reading Bernard Shaw.

II

The Hill School in 1909 represented a combination of elements which must have made it unique among prep schools. It had been founded by the Reverend Matthew Meigs, a Presbyterian minister from Connecticut, who had settled in Pottstown, Pennsylvania, and started a small school in an old stone house on a hill. In my time it was run by John Meigs, his son, who had extraordinarily enlarged and improved it and made for it a great reputation.

John Meigs, whom we always called 'Professor,' was not really, however, a schoolmaster. He had taken on his father's school and accepted it as a career with reluctance; but once he had done so, he had worked at it tremendously. He had no endowments and no wealthy patrons; and he had at first kept all the accounts, written out all the letters in longhand, and taught twenty-five hours a week as well as personally handled the discipline, the records and the relations with parents. He had created a big school out of small beginnings—just as a boy from a Pennsylvania farm like Henry C. Frick had bought up coke-ovens and created an industry; and, in spite of his New England origins, I have always assimilated John Meigs to the Pennsylvania Dutch of that countryside of the extreme western corner of Montgomery County. A short, stocky man with a wide straight mouth and a square head that was made to

seem even more cubelike by a nose flattened out like a boxer's
—broken at football, I think—he resembled a successful manufacturer who had made himself something of a man of the
world. He had gone to college at Lafayette instead of at Yale
or Harvard; and the school had certain qualities of the back
Pennsylvania of solid farmhouses and brick-streeted towns
rather than of the Eastern seaboard, of Sewickley rather than
Philadelphia. Professor had a certain smartness, but it was the
smartness of a local man of substance, and not at all like the
Episcopalian smartness that one sometimes found in the headmaster of the quite different New England schools. His hair,
which was silver and parted in the middle, curled crisply at the
corners of his forehead, and he liked to wear a bright red tie,
and sometimes a flower in his buttonhole, with a spotless
white vest. As he would walk down from the platform after
prayers, leading the rest of the school, stepping so firmly and
yet jauntily, he was a figure that inspired confidence and in
whom one could feel pride.

In the state he was a man of some consequence, quite active
in local politics. He had, as one of the masters has told me
since, no real interest in education whatever. But he did possess qualities which enabled him to organize a first-rate school.
He had certainly a touch of the brutality characteristic of industrial Pennsylvania, but with it went the independence of
the man who has built up his own business, and a downright
and four-square directness in his dealings with students, parents and faculty. The school was financially sound as I imagine
few prep schools have been, and quite free from the tremors
and depressions that reflect the inability to raise funds. Nor
were there, as far as I was aware, any of those moral leaks
which cause favoritism, ill-feeling and inefficiency.

The efficiency of the Hill was perfect—as perfect as Bethlehem Steel. It was a legend at the time that no student who had
been graduated from the Hill ever failed to get into college,
because the drill we were given was so stiff and the tests we
had to pass so difficult that entrance examinations became
child's play; and it was true that we mostly landed in the top
sections of the college courses. But this system had its disagreeable side. Every moment of our time was disposed of; our
whole life was regulated by bells; and—till we reached the

Sixth Form, at any rate—we had hardly an hour of leisure. The intention was beneficent, of course; but the remorseless paternalism of the Hill had something of the suffocating repressive effect of the Pennsylvania mill-town in which the company owns the workers' houses, controls their contacts with the outside world, and runs the banks, the schools and the stores. Save for walks in the country and excursions into town, for both of which we had to get permission, we were confined to the Hill grounds, which rose like a segregated plateau in the midst of the little steel town—the narrow and cobbled streets where the greenery showed meager in spring, the slag pits and the blast furnaces that startled new boys and kept them awake at night by blazes that would light up the whole room.

The same ideals in John Meigs, however, which had produced this iron regime had secured for the Hill School some admirable things. He had spared no pains or expense to provide the best equipment obtainable: the staff as well as the plant were as good as they could possibly be. The buildings, the gymnasium, the tennis courts, the swimming pool, the showers, the ballfields somewhat offset the drabness of our surroundings. And the masters, to keep us up to scratch, had to be first-rate too. Yet, here, I believe, Professor must have been aiming at something beyond efficiency and may have displayed a certain creativeness, for he did get very able men who, though quite different from one another, evidently worked well together and felt a genuine interest in the school. In talking afterwards to boys from other schools, I never found the same enthusiasm for their masters that the Hill graduates had for theirs. Some of them, I came to realize, were quite above the usual prep-school level and would have adorned any university. Alfred Rolfe was one of these. It was characteristic of Meigs, with his ambition to have the best of everything, that he should have installed, to teach Greek, an accomplished New Englander in the best tradition.

III

For that was what Mr. Rolfe was—a New Englander. And it was that about him that had seemed to me foreign.

He was moreover a special kind of New Englander: he came from Concord, Mass.; and this, as I afterwards observed, was quite distinct from being a Bostonian (and Mr. Rolfe had gone to Amherst, not Harvard). He had that quality of homeliness and freshness that one finds in a Concordian like Thoreau, combined, as it was in Thoreau, with a sharp mind and a fine sensibility. The Yankee accent and rustic expressions with which he sometimes roughened his speech were a feature he knew how to make use of to set off his natural elegance, just as his very large feet and hands were somehow made to play a part in the grace with which he went about his business, and as the touches of gruffness and brusqueness that had the sea captains of New England behind them gave his urbanity a greater authority. All this side of him, in fact, was the rocklike base on which the flowers of Hellenism flourished: the sophistication of his comic sense, his exquisite literary taste, and the benignant incandescence of his mind. Alfred Rolfe has been my only personal contact with the Concord of the great period, and I feel that if I had not known him, I should never really have known what it was, and what a high civilization it represented. For there was nothing about Mr. Rolfe either of the schoolmaster or of the provincial. He had in his early years studied in Germany, but he cared little for travel or cities, and now spent every school year in Pottstown and every summer in Concord; yet he seemed to enjoy, just as Emerson did, the freedom of the great social world as well as of the great world of literature. His brother, Henry Winchester Rolfe, was also a classical scholar. I later read a book of his on Petrarch and discovered that my friend Rolfe Humphries, the Latinist and poet, had been named after him.

The manners that we tended to learn at the Hill were a little on the heavy and flat side; and Mr. Rolfe, for all his dignity, moved among us with a charming ease and what can only be called a kind of blitheness. He was tall but not very well built: besides large feet and hands, he had shoulders that were narrow and sloping. He stooped and thrust forward his head as he walked; and in the skirted black frock-coat and striped trousers which were *de rigueur* for Sunday chapel, he would look like some long-legged great auk as he stalked back to his rooms after service. Yet he was one of the real ornaments of the school, perhaps its principal ornament.

He was an admirable after-dinner speaker and always in demand for banquets. He cultivated the dry, solemn, drawling manner which Mark Twain had made the fashion but which became very New England in his hands. His face, when he was not in conversation, tended to lapse into a Saint Bernard sadness, and he liked to exploit this for comic effect. He was wonderful at 'morning exercises,' where the reading of profane literature had been substituted for passages from the Bible. His fine voice, deep, resonant and rich, was not the voice of a school elocutionist who likes to play-act for his students, but always remained personal and in some special way colloquial: what it was rich in were nuances of humor and perceptions of the values of style. And the rhythms of poetry to Mr. Rolfe seemed something natural and dear; it was as if they represented a dreaminess which, for all his Yankee commonsense, was a part of his everyday life and did not require a condition of trance. The first time that you heard him read aloud a passage of Homer in class, you knew what Homer was as poetry, and no amount of construing and syntactical analysis could blur the effect of that rhythm. We used also to read Browning's plays with him, for fun, between chapel and midday dinner on Sunday, and he would easily disentangle the speeches of such things as *A Blot on the 'Scutcheon* and get out of them their own kind of music. Sometimes at morning exercises he would read from the New England writers, and he would give them a kind of distinction which I had not known was there. In those days we had been brought up on the New Englanders, and by the time we came to read for ourselves we had decided they were childish and a bore. But Mr. Rolfe could put, say, Oliver Wendell Holmes, whom I did not at that time think amusing, in an attractively different light. When he did scenes from *The Autocrat of the Breakfast-Table*, he really made you hear the people in that ideal Boston boardinghouse: you felt that he had boarded there himself, and that the quality of the talk in its way had been good. His rendering of *The Wonderful One-Hoss Shay* was one of his most brilliant performances. When the deacon swore as deacons do with an 'I dew vum' or an 'I tell *yeou*,' the voice of the old man would come through with a sudden dramatic realism that startled us and made us laugh.

He had certainly the sense of audience. When, in the

absence of Professor and Mrs. Meigs, he would preside at our meals in the big dining-room, one felt his presence even here as one did during a recitation. While he would be waiting for the boys to assemble, he would stand up with folded arms, joking with the Sixth-Formers beside him; then he would press the buzzer and say the brief grace—'Bless, O Father, thy gifts to our use and us to thy service: for Christ's sake. Amen'—in which, many times though I heard it, the words never seemed merely a rite, but something said and felt. At the end of the meal, when it would sometimes happen that a general silence fell as we waited for the buzzer to release us, he would mutter some amusing remark which would be caught by the whole room and bring a laugh; if the buzzer stuck, as it sometimes did, he would make it a whole little comedy and would send us out quite lighthearted from the then rather close and crowded dining-room and its Pennsylvania Dutch food.

There was a moment, I remember, when Mr. Rolfe had read something that impressed him about the importance of pulling in one's stomach in order to carry oneself correctly, and when he would preach this to us half-humorously as he attempted to practice it himself. As I watched him one day in the dining-room, throwing back his shoulders and drawing in his chin, which was round and rather recessive, I thought of his luxurious lounging on his comfortable couch and armchair. And there was also his gesture which was so much of a betrayal of his effortful and Spartan pose: a wandering of his hand to his necktie and breast, as a woman fingers a necklace, which came from the something poetic—the something almost romantic—in him. I remembered how he had warned us once in class that it was impossible to study properly when sunk in an easy chair; and I realized that in Mr. Rolfe a certain strain of the sybarite co-existed with rectitude and discipline. I recognized it thus very early because I was unmistakably myself on the sybaritic side. I incurably disliked athletics, carried myself very badly and loved to read in bed. And at this moment I became aware, though I did not formulate the perception, that what made Mr. Rolfe interesting and gave him a sort of rarity was his having reached just that point when a tough and well-tried stock first gets the freedom to smile and to play, to work at belles-lettres for their own sake.

At some point in our early stages of Greek Mr. Rolfe had handed us over for a term or two to his assistant; and by the time I got back to him again, I was no longer so much afraid of him. The Greek class still imposed a certain tension, but it stimulated for those students who had literary tastes a genuine interest in Greek. Mr. Rolfe worked us awfully hard, harder than any other master, but we did feel that we were getting Homer and not just boning assignments. We had to scan every line and understand every form, and we had to translate every word into an English not unworthy of the original. It was as serious to give clumsy equivalents as to miss out on a case or a mood, and would bring down on us his tartest derision. He accepted as a standard for the proper tone of a successful Homeric translation the passage by Dr. Hawtrey cited by Matthew Arnold in his essay on translating Homer: 'Clearly the rest I behold of the dark-eyed sons of Achaia'—and made us commit it to memory.

With all his exacting demands, he had many entertaining devices for relieving the dryness of our drudgery. We were encouraged to think of ὀδύρομαι as 'oh, dear! oh, my!'; we were taught that when γάρ begins a sentence it is always pronounced 'yar,' on the principle on which children are told that a guinea pig's eyes will fall out if you hold it up by its tail; and we were made to learn the speeches of the trial of Orontas in Xenophon and act it out in class. At the end, when Orontas was led into the tent and put to death in a mysterious manner, the boy who played him was taken out into the hall and grisly sounds were heard. Mr. Rolfe shied so naturally away from the tone of the textbook and the classroom that it was difficult for him to remember the wording of the rules as they were given in the book. There is a principle of Homeric versification which was formulated by Goodwin somewhat as follows: 'The penthemimeral caesura gives the line an anapaestic movement, from which it is often recalled by the bucolic diaeresis.' We would be called upon to demonstrate this by rapping it out on our seat-arms with pencils; but Mr. Rolfe, when he cited the rule, would resist the language of the grammar, by stumbling over the second part and turning the 'from which it is often recalled' into 'from which it is frequently rescued.' The whole thing got thus a faint comic flavor; and this little involuntary touch has always remained in my mind as an example of his putting in its place of the academic side of his subject.

The impulse to parody was strong in him, though he usually indulged it quite casually. When Tennyson's *Enoch Arden* was read once at morning exercises, he suggested that the end of the poem really needed another line:

> *So past the strong heroic soul away.*
> *And when they buried him the little port*
> *Had seldom seen a costlier funeral;*
> And Annie wore her best black bombazine.

I was thus tremendously flattered when he complimented me on a parody of Browning which I had published in the school magazine. And later, when another Hill boy and I had invented, as freshmen at college, an imaginary figure of speech, I was surprised at the amusement it seemed to afford him when we told him about it on a visit. '*Thypsis . . . thypsis*,' he murmured to himself at some later moment of the conversation.

In my last year of school, when I lived above him, I used to go and read in his rooms. It was one of the paradoxes of the Hill, which excelled in literary activity, that Professor, in installing his extraordinary equipment, should almost completely have neglected the library. He must have conceived of books as something to be fed us in calculated doses by the masters in the different departments. He could never have had any interest in making literature generally available, for the two or three small rooms called the library contained almost nothing up to date, and they were full of ancient textbooks and works of reference that had belonged to the Reverend Matthew Meigs and went back to the eighteenth and seventeenth centuries. There were not even good editions of the classics, and I almost put my eyes out my first year at school on a copy of *Vanity Fair* in double columns of microscopic type. (This deficiency was long ago remedied: the library, I am told, is now first-rate.) But at least half a dozen of the masters had considerable private libraries, which they encouraged us to use. And Mr. Rolfe's was among the most interesting, as it was certainly much the handsomest. He went in for well-bound sets, and he kept up with contemporary literature as no other of the masters did. The new volumes of Chesterton and Shaw always appeared on his table, and I sat on his couch and read them. Sometimes he would come in, greet me briefly, put on his pince-nez, sit down in his large armchair and silently correct his papers.

I was still shy with him: for all his humor, he was one of the most remote of the masters. With his conviction of intellectual superiority and a sensitive personal pride, there was one thing that was quite impossible for him—a capacity that makes life easier for schoolmasters: he could not be a good fellow with the boys, he could not meet them on their own level. The masters who lived in the Sixth Form Flat took turns keeping order in the halls, and most of them could do it quite amiably; but it went against the grain with Mr. Rolfe. When one of our bedtime roughhouses became too long and too loud, he would suddenly appear in his bathrobe like the Statue in *Don Giovanni* and freeze us to the marrow. A few cutting words would silence us and send us rather sulky to bed. His rebuke had been so evidently hostile that it made us feel hostile, too. But I who admired him so much was embarrassed by what I felt was the indecency of his having to do this kind of thing at all. I felt that he hated our seeing him in his bathrobe, that he ought never to be seen in a bathrobe; and I pictured him lying in bed, as I so loved to do at home, enjoying some book from the well-stocked bookcase which I had seen through the doorway beside his bed without being able to make out the contents. How he must have loathed and resented being distracted by our scuttlings and shrieks, and obliged to climb two flights of stairs and pit himself against ribald and breathless boys. He liked to live in his rooms like a man at his club.

One day I had a glimpse, my only glimpse, of Mr. Rolfe's pre-school personality. It turned out that some cousins of mine had known him at the end of the eighties when he was studying Greek in Dresden. They had stayed at the same pension with him, and they said that he had been wonderful in those days—so charming and so funny. My mother and aunt came up one week-end, and he produced an old photograph of a group in which he and my cousins figured. They had been playing charades in the pension and had had themselves taken in their costumes. He had said sadly of my pretty dark cousin Bessie, my mother afterwards told me—for I had not been present at the conversation: 'So poor Bessie is dead!' I wondered whether he had ever been in love. He was now such a complete old bachelor that this was almost impossible to imagine. I remembered that when he was clowning in his after-dinner speeches he sometimes made fun of his homeliness.

IV

Against one element of life at the Hill School Mr. Rolfe, by his very tone and presence, provided a constant correction. The Hill had an evangelical side which it required some stubbornness to stand up to. This was mainly, I have always understood, due to the influence of Mrs. Meigs—always known as Mrs. John—a very earnest and capable woman related to the theological Dwights of New Haven. The school had passed through a series of disasters—three fires as well as a typhoid epidemic in which a hundred students and masters had been ill; and it may be that this had had the effect of stimulating in the Meigses a desperate faith in and dependence on God. But what I was aware of at the time when I was in school was simply that we were worked on systematically by a rotation of visiting evangelists. We had to go not only to chapel, but also—under irresistible pressure—to the meetings of a school Y.M.C.A.; and we were always being called together to listen to special exhortations.

At the bottom of the scale of our speakers was the reformed debauchee and bad egg who testified to the miracle of his salvation. He always had what the stage calls a 'straight man' with him, who gave him his cue and showed him off, with an attitude that fell between that of a man with a trained ape and the 'feeder' of a team of comics. These bums who had been saved used to seem to me still very unpleasant people, who had, before seeing the light, evidently reached such a state of corruption that their new respectability looked precarious, and one listened rather apprehensively to their boasts about their present state of grace as if one feared they might go to pieces as soon as the performance was over.

Then there was a man who had made a specialty of preaching to boys' schools and colleges and whose line was a lachrymose and mealy-mouthed virility. He used to read us Kipling in a way that did much to disgust me with that writer, and announce that he would be accessible in a certain room the next morning and would be glad to discuss with any boy any kind of problem whatever. An imitation of 'Weeping Bob's' speeches had long been current among old Hill men and is one of the things that bind them together. 'Moys,' he used to say in his deep adhesive voice, 'I want to speak to you first of all amout the use of foul and filthy language. Moys: they have a nog up in Alaska that they call the mlue-mlack nog. He is known as the mlue-mlack nog because the insine of his mouth is mlue-mlack. And I want to say to any moy who has the impulse to innulge in foul language that, if he gives way to this impulse and hamitually uses oaths and innecent expressions, the insine of his mouth—spir-it-u-ally speaking—*will mecome mlue-mlack like the mouth of the mlue-mlack nog!*'

A more sophisticated level was represented by a liberal preacher from New York. He was well-dressed in a secular way, and dynamic, free-spoken and pear-shaped. His line was to shock and be witty, to be modern in the interests of the evangelist's God. He was also of course social-minded, and I remember a characteristic touch by which he hoped to make us feel, and to convince himself that he felt, a warm sympathy for the laboring classes: 'Coming up on the train today, I sat opposite an Italian workman. He was dressed in his work-clothes; he had been sweating; but there was nothing dirty about him except the grime of his work. I caught his breath and it smelled of garlic, but it was a good breath; it was wholesome, not foul.' And then of course there were the two-fisted missionaries who shook us down for funds to Christianize and modernize China.

At the center of all this activity stood a kind of special Hill School myth of sin and regeneration. The legend that was handed on from one class at the Hill to another had it that Professor in his college days had been a very fast young fellow, who was known as 'Cigarette Jack,' and that Mrs. John had snatched him as what used to be called a brand from the burning and had made him into the man we knew. This may very well not have been accurate, but it was what we had come to believe: it was like the miraculous conversion from which a cult or an order dates. It was the archetype of the spiritual drama which we seemed to be expected to enact. The hero of this sacred drama was an able and promising boy, well-fitted to be a leader of men, who at college succumbed to temptation: he gambled, he smoked, he drank; he went with a class of women who were not so much bad as misguided. But he was caught on the edge of the abyss and saved for the life of service. I am afraid that there was a little the impression created that you had to have taken the dip toward perdition or you could not make the plane of the élite. The Sixth Form was searched, as it were, every spring for candidates for this sacrificial role. Mrs. John saw every member separately and probed into the state of his soul in a solemn heart-to-heart talk that usually took place in a room on the top floor of the Meigses' house, which was significantly called 'the Sky Parlor.' I have heard the most grueling accounts of the scenes that sometimes occurred at these interviews; but I myself was not a good prospect, and when it came my turn to go, I found that Mrs. John had forgotten the appointment. She was writing at her desk and was surprised to see me; but she made me sit down and told me gently that the literary type of boy had his temptations, too—the temptation, for example, to become so much absorbed in his intellectual interests that he neglected his relation to his fellows, and she prayed with me a moment and let me go. I walked back to my room relieved and yet feeling a little let down that I had not been considered susceptible to the more exciting kind of temptation.

There was a terrible taboo on sex, which was turned into something frightening. Though I was used, before I came to the Hill, to the adolescent folk-lore and gossip of boys of my own age, my speech and my mind had become so purged by the end of my school career that I was shocked when I heard, after leaving, that Mr. Rolfe had once told the story of the man who had started in church when the Seventh Commandment was read and muttered, 'Oh, now I know where I left my umbrella!'

It was true that the boys from Hill had the reputation of slipping at college, and Mrs. John was attempting to fortify them, but her influence worked, also, the other way. If a boy were not naturally serious-minded (as, I must say, a good many were—in which case they had a decided advantage over boys from most other schools), he might forget about the life of service when the restraints of Hill had been removed; but the pattern of the school myth might have been stamped on his mind so strongly that he would be plunged into despair or disorder by the first drinking party or pick-up. (This is no longer true today: the evangelism has disappeared and the paternalism been very much modified.)

I do not know what Mr. Rolfe thought of all this side of Hill; I do not know even what his religious beliefs were. He might have been a liberal Congregationalist or a conventional Episcopalian. He never talked about religion, and when he presided at chapel, he read the Bible in such a way as to make it seem noble and beautiful just as he did Homer. I particularly remember his giving us the last chapter of *Ecclesiastes*, which did not interest our moralistic evangelists. When he prayed, it was never for salvation, but simply for moral stimulus to enable us to deal with our work or get along with our fellows.

V

My own Presbyterian religious training had involved a certain amount of churchgoing and had more or less familiarized me with the Bible, but I had never known what it was to feel faith as something vital; and from the moment I had begun to think about such things for myself, my reactions toward religion had been negative. Under the constant stimulation of the Hill School, however, I tried hard to keep God in my cosmos. I was unable to accept as real for myself—that is, as having serious claims on me—anything that I could not recognize as a part of my own experience, so I had to try to translate my moments of exalted or expansive feeling into terms of the religious illumination about which I was constantly hearing—just as I imagine the eighteenth-century Deists, who had drawn all the rationalistic conclusions, attempted still to provide a Deity who would be somehow the fountainhead of reason. But the fact irreducibly remained that I didn't have the revelatory experience, that I didn't even want it; that my attitude toward our repertoire of dervishes seemed inevitably to become more humorous, and that what had at first been a certain awed respect for this side of the activity of Hill began to give way to the conviction that it was all in awful taste.

One day in my Sixth Form year, when I was coming back to

school on the train, I did at last have a sort of revelation, which was, however, as it were, in reverse. I always had to change in Philadelphia, and, as I usually had to wait for my train, I had got into the habit of killing time in Wanamaker's book department. There I bought one by one all the volumes of Bernard Shaw and even, when there were no more to buy—at the moment I graduated—Archibald Henderson's enormous biography. But I had not yet got to this, and on the occasion of which I speak was reading *Major Barbara*. At the end of the preface about money and religion, I came to the following words: 'At present there is not a single credible established religion in the world.' For a moment I was jolted a little; but I looked out the window at the landscape, rather muddy and sordid with winter, and had to recognize that this was true, that I knew perfectly well it was true, and that I ought to have admitted it before; and the flickering childish faith to which I had been giving artificial respiration expired then and there. I have never thought of religion since save as a delusion entertained by other people which one has to try to allow for and understand. On the train another Hill boy had sat down beside me, and I had reluctantly suspended my reading to have a little conversation with him. He was the simple and candid type. He was built stoutly and went in for football and took the Y.M.C.A. seriously. I derived an ironic pleasure from the reflection that, whereas for him our ridiculous prep-school revivalism would still have the power to plunge him into struggles, earnest labors, sleepless nights, my faith had passed quietly out on the stretch between Norristown and Phoenixville, between two passages of banal conversation in which I had descended affably to the level of my companion. I felt as I had never felt before that such people as he were barbarians.

Professor Meigs had died that autumn—the ordeal of the typhoid epidemic was thought to have weakened his heart; and Mr. Rolfe took over as headmaster. The alumni gave a chapel as memorial, and we were using it by the spring of our commencement. We were to have for our last Sunday service of the year a very famous New York preacher whom we had never heard before. It was as if he were the climax and crown of our whole circus procession of evangelists. But this high point of the theological hierarchy marked for me the nadir of faith. I had heard a great deal about this man. He had long been a public figure. He had been associated with Henry Ward Beecher, and later with Theodore Roosevelt. He was one of those preachers of the turn of the century who had been trying to bring the Christianity of the churches into contact with industrial and social problems; he had published several books on the subject, and even, late in life, turned journalist. I had therefore, I think, been prepared for something a little more stimulating than the figure that appeared in the chapel. He was, to be sure, seventy-seven, but he looked even older—he was the oldest-looking person I had ever seen. He had a beard that was long and stringy and that grew out all around his face. It was the kind of undisciplined beard that we associate with Hebrew prophets, but this old man had none of the fire of the prophet. His eyes under their straggling eyebrows had a grayness almost of blindness, and even his skin was gray. His rather long bottle-ended nose had pores so enormous that you could see them plainly as he passed by the pews up the aisle, supported on either side by one of the adoring Meigs ladies and looking as limp in his long black robe as a Punch-and-Judy puppet from which the showman's hand has been removed. I remembered the scene years later when I saw the Diaghilev ballet do Stravinsky's *L'Oiseau de feu*: the figure of Kashchey the Deathless, the enchanter of the Russian fairy-tales, in his flimsy and hirsute senility, reeling back and forth across the stage as the egg that contains his life is tossed from hand to hand, and finally, as it cracks, collapsing into the arms of his faithful attendants while the captives stream out of his castle— this vision has blended in my memory with the image of that Sunday morning service.

It may be that the religious basis of the school had already been somewhat weakened by the breakdown and death of Professor and by the conduct of public ceremonies by the moderate Mr. Rolfe, whose authority was mainly cultural; it may be that this spokesman of the Church at grips with social problems would have seemed a little less deliquescent if Professor had been there behind him. But the whole thing made an unpleasant impression.

The sermon itself was feeble. The subject was immortality— another link with the imperishable Kashchey, who eventually went to pieces; and this old man, who had prided himself on his modernism, announced in a quavering voice that, though we boys with our lives still before us, might not at this time be disposed to give much serious thought to the life after death, this would come, when we got to be old, to seem 've-ery impo-ortant indeed.' This finished immortality for me—since, if your reason, I told myself, had convinced you in your years of vigor that there existed not a shred of evidence for the survival of the human soul, it was an act of weak-mindedness and cowardice to give in to this primitive myth when you had got to the end of your rope and were about to be extinguished yourself.

I argued the question with a friend of mine, a boy of much intellectual ability, who was related to Mrs. Meigs and whose principles were quite in the tradition of the theology of the Dwights. Some time after our argument, he suddenly renewed it: 'Of course you know,' he said, 'that even if there were no immortality, it would be fatal for the human race to take the belief in it away from people.' I had not yet heard the famous saying about how much difference it makes whether you put truth in the first or the second place; but I knew then, as I left school for college, that the code I was evolving for myself could never have much in common with the official morality of Hill.

VI

Mr. Rolfe ran the school for a time, though I imagine he much preferred teaching. I continued to see him occasionally, and I found that my admiration for him held up as few schoolboy admirations do. I used at first to send him books at Christmas, and when he wrote to thank me for them, he never made the polite pretence of having enjoyed them beyond their merits. He acknowledged Compton Mackenzie's *Youth's Encounter*, about which I had written him a hyperbolic letter, with what I thought was the pointed suggestion that 'μηδὲν ἄγαν is a good motto.' I imagine that my own writings after I got out of college were not of a kind that he particularly approved. When I saw him, he used to kid me in a way that I thought rather old fogyish about the then excellent liberal weekly on which I had a job in the twenties.

The *bête noir* of his later years was progressive education. He used to compose little poems on the subject and was very amusing about it. I had a sort of idea at first that I ought to be on the other side, since my magazine supported John Dewey, but the more I read of Mr. Rolfe's satire, which reached me through the Hill School alumni bulletin, the more I felt that there was something to be said for his position. Wasn't it true that, in order to train children to do anything really well, you had to break them to an exacting discipline as he had done with us in Greek? Without that you couldn't do anything with Greek—you couldn't do anything with anything. How great were the chances that a schoolboy could be counted on to choose what he needed?—my father had made me take Greek, I was too young to know anything about it—or to acquire this discipline through natural bent? Mr. Rolfe may to some extent, of course, have misunderstood and misrepresented what was proposed for progressive education; but when I came later on to see something of the teaching both in progressive institutions and in the ordinary kind, I was appalled by the slackness of the training. Where would our American railroads and ships and buildings and bridges and bathrooms be if the techniques of engineering were taught as the arts and humanities are—so that students are graduated from college, and not merely from progressive colleges, and even take M.A. degrees, without having any idea of the top human achievements in their fields, without, often, being able to express themselves in decent English?

It did not really help to point out that much of our old-fashioned teaching was uninspired. As far as inspiration went, Mr. Rolfe could not teach us an irregular declension without lending its cadences poetry; and one felt that it was doubtful whether progressive education would increase the number of inspired teachers. On the other hand, it probably did tend to make people trust unduly to vague ideas and currents of feeling, to the Rousseauist supposed natural instinct to do well if left to oneself. This trust in the impulses of humanity is perhaps only a transference from the heavens to our hearts of the old idea of Providence; and whatever kind of God Mr. Rolfe believed in, this God, like that of A. E. Housman, had not arranged the world so that anything could be accomplished without somebody in particular doing it and doing it with conscious effort. *You* had to find out about Homer by digging in the Greek lexicon and grammar: you couldn't find out about it by reading an outline of literature written by somebody else; and *he* had to teach you Greek: Greek wouldn't teach itself. He did not depend for this purpose on the natural rectitude of our inclinations—either his own or ours—any more than he did on the evangelistic Christ who was supposed to come to your rescue and give you a bracer of salvation, as the victims of dementia praecox are supposed to be roused to normality by the jolt of a shot of insulin.

Mr. Rolfe of course thus represented both the American individualistic tradition which has cultivated the readiness to think and act for oneself without looking to God or the State as something outside oneself, and the older humanistic tradition: the belief in the nobility and beauty of what man as man has accomplished, and the reverence for literature as the record of this. I had been exposed at the Hill to this humanistic spirit at the same time as to the inspirational religion which has always remained linked in my mind with the industrial background of Pottstown; and the humanism had continued to serve me when the religion had come to seem false. The thing that glowed for me through Xenophon and Homer in those classrooms of thirty years ago has glowed for me ever since.

And at the Hill Mr. Rolfe himself long survived the fading-out of that evangelism. There was a time when I tended to think of him as drying up and growing crabbed at school; but I ran into him one day at Columbia, where he was supervising examinations, and was struck by his kindliness and the attractiveness of his face, which seemed to have grown terribly sad. In the crowd of assembled teachers from a variety of schools and colleges, he still stood out as a distinguished figure who did not seem to belong to that company. An old Hill friend has written me recently of seeing him a few years ago: 'I sat next to him at luncheon. He was then eighty years old and told me that the doctors had said he was in perfect health except for low blood pressure. I told him to drink burgundy or bourbon, and he said that I seemed to speak with authority and experience. He said grace, and when I told him it was a *new* grace, he said he'd be glad to sound the buzzer again and deliver the old grace for dessert.' I wrote to Mr. Rolfe when I heard that he was retiring from Hill. In answering, he explained that he still expected to take a few classes, 'but I shall have plenty of time to write, if I can think of anything to write about . . . I am sorry about Greek,' he said. 'I used to think it would last my day, but it hasn't quite done so'; and he wished me good luck in Greek.

He died last June in Concord, and it is hard to imagine him gone: I had thought of him as a permanent element, a kind of human classic, who persisted through the changes at the Hill and the wars and revolutions of the world. After all, there had always been Mr. Rolfe; and suddenly, as I write this memoir, it seems to me that the stream he was following flowed out of a past that is now remote: from Emerson with his self-dependence, and *The Wonderful One-Hoss Shay* with its satire on the too-perfect Calvinist system; from the days when people went to Germany to hear Wagner and study Greek; from Matthew Arnold, from Bernard Shaw—now almost an old-fashioned classic like Arnold. And I am glad to renew my sense of Alfred Rolfe's contribution to it, as I realize that I myself have been trying to follow and feed it at a time when it has been running low. Its tradition antedates our Christian religion and has in many men's minds survived it, as one may hope it will, also, the political creeds, with their secular evangelism, that are taking the Church's place.

1942

The Historical Interpretation of Literature*

I WANT to talk about the historical interpretation of literature
—that is, about the interpretation of literature in its social,
economic and political aspects.

To begin with, it will be worth while to say something about
the kind of criticism which seems to be furthest removed from
this. There is a kind of comparative criticism which tends to be
non-historical. The essays of T. S. Eliot, which have had such
an immense influence in our time, are, for example, fundamentally non-historical. Eliot sees, or tries to see, the whole of
literature, so far as he is acquainted with it, spread out before
him under the aspect of eternity. He then compares the work
of different periods and countries, and tries to draw from it
general conclusions about what literature ought to be. He
understands, of course, that our point of view in connection
with literature changes, and he has what seems to me a very
sound conception of the whole body of writing of the past as
something to which new works are continually being added,
and which is not thereby merely increased in bulk but modified as a whole—so that Sophocles is no longer precisely what
he was for Aristotle, or Shakespeare what he was for Ben Jonson or for Dryden or for Dr. Johnson, on account of all the
later literature that has intervened between them and us. Yet at
every point of this continual accretion, the whole field may be
surveyed, as it were, spread out before the critic. The critic tries
to see it as God might; he calls the books to a Day of Judgment. And, looking at things in this way, he may arrive at interesting and valuable conclusions which could hardly be reached
by approaching them in any other way. Eliot was able to see,
for example—what I believe had never been noticed before—
that the French Symbolist poetry of the nineteenth century
had certain fundamental resemblances to the English poetry of
the age of Donne. Another kind of critic would draw certain
historical conclusions from these purely esthetic findings, as
the Russian D. S. Mirsky did; but Eliot does not draw them.

Another example of this kind of non-historical criticism, in a

*A lecture delivered at Princeton University, October 23, 1940.

somewhat different way and on a somewhat different plane, is the work of the late George Saintsbury. Saintsbury was a connoisseur of wines; he wrote an entertaining book on the subject. And his attitude toward literature, too, was that of the connoisseur. He tastes the authors and tells you about the vintages; he distinguishes the qualities of the various wines. His palate was as fine as could be, and he possessed the great qualification that he knew how to take each book on its own terms without expecting it to be some other book and was thus in a position to appreciate a great variety of kinds of writing. He was a man of strong social prejudices and peculiarly intransigent political views, but, so far as it is humanly possible, he kept them out of his literary criticism. The result is one of the most agreeable and most comprehensive commentaries on literature that have ever been written in English. Most scholars who have read as much as Saintsbury do not have Saintsbury's discriminating taste. Here is a critic who has covered the whole ground like any academic historian, yet whose account of it is not merely a chronology but a record of fastidious enjoyment. Since enjoyment is the only thing he is looking for, he does not need to know the causes of things, and the historical background of literature does not interest him very much.

There is, however, another tradition of criticism which dates from the beginning of the eighteenth century. In the year 1725, the Neapolitan philosopher Vico published *La Scienza Nuova*, a revolutionary work on the philosophy of history, in which he asserted for the first time that the social world was certainly the work of man, and attempted what is, so far as I know, the first social interpretation of a work of literature. This is what Vico says about Homer: 'Homer composed the *Iliad* when Greece was young and consequently burning with sublime passions such as pride, anger and vengeance—passions which cannot allow dissimulation and which consort with generosity; so that she then admired Achilles, the hero of force. But, grown old, he composed the *Odyssey*, at a time when the passions of Greece were already somewhat cooled by reflection, which is the mother of prudence—so that she now admired Ulysses, the hero of wisdom. Thus also, in Homer's youth, the Greek people liked cruelty, vituperation, savagery, fierceness, ferocity;

whereas, when Homer was old, they were already enjoying the luxuries of Alcinoüs, the delights of Calypso, the pleasures of Circe, the songs of the sirens and the pastimes of the suitors, who went no further in aggression and combat than laying siege to the chaste Penelope—all of which practices would appear incompatible with the spirit of the earlier time. The divine Plato is so struck by this difficulty that, in order to solve it, he tells us that Homer had foreseen in inspired vision these dissolute, sickly and disgusting customs. But in this way he makes Homer out to have been but a foolish instructor for Greek civilization, since, however much he may condemn them, he is displaying for imitation these corrupt and decadent habits which were not to be adopted till long after the foundation of the nations of Greece, and accelerating the natural course which human events would take by spurring the Greeks on to corruption. Thus it is plain that the Homer of the *Iliad* must have preceded by many years the Homer who wrote the *Odyssey*; and it is plain that the former must belong to the northeastern part of Greece, since he celebrates the Trojan War, which took place in his part of the country, whereas the latter belongs to the southeastern part, since he celebrates Ulysses, who reigned there.'

You see that Vico has here explained Homer in terms both of historical period and of geographical origin. The idea that human arts and institutions were to be studied and elucidated as the products of the geographical and climatic conditions in which the people who created them lived, and of the phase of their social development through which they were passing at the moment, made great progress during the eighteenth century. There are traces of it even in Dr. Johnson, that most orthodox and classical of critics—as, for example, when he accounts for certain characteristics of Shakespeare by the relative barbarity of the age in which he lived, pointing out, just as Vico had done, that 'nations, like individuals, have their infancy.' And by the eighties of the eighteenth century Herder, in his *Ideas on the Philosophy of History*, was writing of poetry that it was a kind of 'Proteus among the people, which is always changing its form in response to the languages, manners, and habits, to the temperaments and climates, nay even to the accents of different nations.' He said—what could still seem startling even so late as that—that 'language was not a divine communication, but something men had produced themselves.' In the lectures on the philosophy of history that Hegel delivered in Berlin in 1822–23, he discussed the national literatures as expressions of the societies which had produced them—societies which he conceived as great organisms continually transforming themselves under the influence of a succession of dominant ideas.

In the field of literary criticism, this historical point of view came to its first complete flower in the work of the French critic Taine, in the middle of the nineteenth century. The whole school of historian-critics to which Taine belonged— Michelet, Renan, Sainte-Beuve—had been occupied in interpreting books in terms of their historical origins. But Taine was the first of these to attempt to apply such principles systematically and on a large scale in a work devoted exclusively to literature. In the Introduction to his *History of English Literature*, published in 1863, he made his famous pronouncement that works of literature were to be understood as the upshot of three interfusing factors: *the moment, the race and the milieu*. Taine thought he was a scientist and a mechanist, who was examining works of literature from the same point of view as the chemist's in experimenting with chemical compounds. But the difference between the critic and the chemist is that the critic cannot first combine his elements and then watch to see what they will do: he can only examine phenomena which have already taken place. The procedure that Taine actually follows is to pretend to set the stage for the experiment by describing the moment, the race and the milieu, and then to say: 'Such a situation demands such and such a kind of writer.' He now goes on to describe the kind of writer that the situation demands, and the reader finds himself at the end confronted with Shakespeare or Milton or Byron or whoever the great figure is—who turns out to prove the accuracy of Taine's prognosis by precisely living up to this description.

There was thus a certain element of imposture in Taine; but it was the rabbits he pulled out that saved him. If he had really been the mechanist that he thought he was, his work on literature would have had little value. The truth was that Taine loved literature for its own sake—he was at his best himself a brilliant artist—and he had very strong moral convictions which give his writing emotional power. His mind, to be sure, was an analytic one, and his analysis, though terribly oversimplified, does have an explanatory value. Yet his work was what we call creative. Whatever he may say about chemical experiments, it is evident when he writes of a great writer that the moment, the race and the milieu have combined, like the three sounds of the chord in Browning's poem about Abt Vogler, to produce not a fourth sound but a star.

To Taine's set of elements was added, dating from the middle of the century, a new element, the economic, which was introduced into the discussion of historical phenomena mainly by Marx and Engels. The non-Marxist critics themselves were at the time already taking into account the influence of the social classes. In his chapters on the Norman conquest of England, Taine shows that the difference between the literatures produced respectively by the Normans and by the Saxons was partly the difference between a ruling class, on the one hand, and a vanquished and repressed class, on the other. And Michelet, in his volume on the Regency, which was finished the same year that the *History of English Literature* appeared, studies the *Manon Lescaut* of the Abbé Prévost as a document representing the point of view of the small gentry before the French Revolution. But Marx and Engels derived the social classes from the way that people made or got their livings— from what they called the *methods of production*; and they tended to regard these economic processes as fundamental to civilization.

The Dialectical Materialism of Marx and Engels was not really so materialistic as it sounds. There was in it a large element of the Hegelian idealism that Marx and Engels thought they had got rid of. At no time did these two famous materialists take so mechanistic a view of things as Taine began by professing; and their theory of the relation of works of literature to what they called the *economic base* was a good deal less simple than Taine's theory of the moment, the race and the milieu. They thought that art, politics, religion, philosophy and literature belonged to what they called the *superstructure* of human activity; but they saw that the practitioners of these various professions tended also to constitute social groups, and that they were always pulling away from the kind of solidarity based on economic classes in order to establish a professional solidarity of their own. Furthermore, the activities of the superstructure could influence one another, and they could influence the economic base. It may be said of Marx and Engels in general that, contrary to the popular impression, they were tentative, confused and modest when it came down to philosophical first principles, where a materialist like Taine was cocksure. Marx once made an attempt to explain why the poems of Homer were so good when the society that produced them was from his point of view—that is, from the point of view of its industrial development—so primitive; and this gave him a good deal of trouble. If we compare his discussion of this problem with Vico's discussion of Homer, we see that the explanation of literature in terms of a philosophy of social history is becoming, instead of simpler and easier, more difficult and more complex.

Marx and Engels were deeply imbued, moreover, with the German admiration for literature, which they had learned from the age of Goethe. It would never have occurred to either of them that *der Dichter* was not one of the noblest and most beneficent of humankind. When Engels writes about Goethe, he presents him as a man equipped for 'practical life,' whose career was frustrated by the 'misery' of the historical situation in Germany in his time, and reproaches him for allowing himself to lapse into the 'cautious, smug and narrow' philistinism of the class from which he came; but Engels regrets this, because it interfered with the development of the 'mocking, defiant, world-despising genius,' 'der geniale Dichter,' 'der gewaltige Poet,' of whom Engels would not even, he says, have asked that he should have been a political liberal if Goethe had not sacrificed to his bourgeois shrinkings his truer esthetic sense. And the great critics who were trained on Marx—Franz Mehring and Bernard Shaw—had all this reverence for the priesthood of literature. Shaw deplores the absence of political philosophy and what he regards as the middle-class snobbery in Shakespeare; but he celebrates Shakespeare's poetry and his dramatic imagination almost as enthusiastically as Swinburne does, describing even those potboiling comedies, *Twelfth Night*

and *As You Like It*—the themes of which seem to him most
trashy—as 'the Crown Jewels of English dramatic poetry.'
Such a critic may do more for a writer by showing him as a real
man dealing with a real world at a definite moment of time
than the impressionist critic of Swinburne's type who flourished in the same period of the late nineteenth century. The
purely impressionist critic approaches the whole of literature as
an exhibit of belletristic jewels, and he can only write a rhap-
sodic catalogue. But when Shaw turned his spotlight on
Shakespeare as a figure in the Shavian drama of history, he invested him with a new interest as no other English critic had
done.

The insistence that the man of letters should play a political
role, the disparagement of works of art in comparison with political action, were thus originally no part of Marxism. They
only became associated with it later. This happened by way of
Russia, and it was due to special tendencies in that country
that date from long before the Revolution or the promulgation of Marxism itself. In Russia there have been very good
reasons why the political implications of literature should particularly occupy the critics. The art of Pushkin itself, with its
marvelous power of implication, had certainly been partly created by the censorship of Nicholas I, and Pushkin set the tradition for most of the great Russian writers that followed him.
Every play, every poem, every story, must be a parable of
which the moral is *implied*. If it were stated, the censor would
suppress the book as he tried to do with Pushkin's *Bronze
Horseman*, where it was merely a question of the packed implications protruding a little too plainly. Right down through the
writings of Chekhov and up almost to the Revolution, the
imaginative literature of Russia presents the peculiar paradox
of an art that is technically objective and yet charged with social messages. In Russia under the Tsar, it was inevitable that
social criticism should lead to political conclusions, because
the most urgent need from the point of view of any kind of improvement was to get rid of the tsarist regime. Even the neo-
Christian moralist Tolstoy, who pretended to be non-political,
was to exert a subversive influence, because his independent
preaching was bound to embroil him with the Church, and

the Church was an integral part of the tsardom. Tolstoy's pamphlet called *What Is Art?*, in which he throws overboard Shakespeare and a large part of modern literature, including his own novels, in the interest of his intransigent morality, is the example which is most familiar to us of the moralizing Russian criticism; but it was only the most sensational expression of a kind of approach which had been prevalent since Belinsky and Chernyshevsky in the early part of the century. The critics, who were usually journalists writing in exile or in a contraband press, were always tending to demand of the imaginative writers that they should dramatize bolder morals.

Even after the Revolution had destroyed the tsarist government, this state of things did not change. The old habits of censorship persisted in the new socialist society of the Soviets, which was necessarily made up of people who had been stamped by the die of the despotism. We meet here the peculiar phenomenon of a series of literary groups that attempt, one after the other, to obtain official recognition or to make themselves sufficiently powerful to establish themselves as arbiters of literature. Lenin and Trotsky and Lunacharsky had the sense to oppose these attempts: the comrade-dictators of Proletcult or Lev or Rapp would certainly have been just as bad as the Count Benckendorff who made Pushkin miserable, and when the Stalin bureaucracy, after the death of Gorky, got control of this department as of everything else, they instituted a system of repression that made Benckendorff and Nicholas I look like Lorenzo de' Medici. In the meantime, Trotsky, who was Commissar of War but himself a great political writer with an interest in belles-lettres, attempted, in 1924, apropos of one of these movements, to clarify the situation. He wrote a brilliant and valuable book called *Literature and Revolution*, in which he explained the aims of the government, analyzed the work of the Russian writers, and praised or rebuked the latter as they seemed to him in harmony or at odds with the former. Trotsky is intelligent, sympathetic; it is evident that he is really fond of literature and that he knows that a work of art does not fulfill its function in terms of the formulas of party propaganda. But Mayakovsky, the Soviet poet, whom Trotsky had praised with reservations, expressed himself in a famous joke when he was asked what he thought of Trotsky's book—a pun which implied that a Commissar turned critic was inevitably a Commissar still*; and what a foreigner cannot accept in Trotsky is his assumption that it is the duty of the government to take a hand in the direction of literature.

This point of view, indigenous to Russia, has been imported to other countries through the permeation of Communist influence. The Communist press and its literary followers have reflected the control of the Kremlin in all the phases through which it has passed, down to the wholesale imprisonment of Soviet writers which has been taking place since 1935. But it has never been a part of the American system that our Republican or Democratic administration should lay down a political line for the guidance of the national literature. A recent gesture in this direction on the part of Archibald MacLeish, who seems a little carried away by his position as Librarian of Congress, was anything but cordially received by serious American writers. So long as the United States remains happily a non-totalitarian country, we can very well do without this aspect of the historical criticism of literature.

Another element of a different order has, however, since Marx's time been added to the historical study of the origins of works of literature. I mean the psychoanalysis of Freud. This appears as an extension of something which had already got well started before, which had figured even in Johnson's *Lives of the Poets*, and of which the great exponent had been Sainte-Beuve: the interpretation of works of literature in the light of the personalities behind them. But the Freudians made this interpretation more exact and more systematic. The great example of the psychoanalysis of an artist is Freud's own essay on Leonardo da Vinci; but this has little critical interest: it is an attempt to construct a case history. One of the best examples I know of the application of Freudian analysis to literature is in Van Wyck Brooks's book, *The Ordeal of Mark Twain*, in which Mr. Brooks uses an incident of Mark Twain's boyhood as a key to his whole career. Mr. Brooks has since repudiated the method he resorted to here, on the ground that no one but an

---

*Первый блин лег наркомом, *The first pancake lies like a narkom* (people's commissar)—a parody of the Russian saying, Первый блин лег комом, *The first pancake lies like a lump.*

analyst can ever know enough about a writer to make a valid psychoanalytic diagnosis. This is true, and it is true of the method that it has led to bad results where the critic has built a Freudian mechanism out of very slender evidence, and then given us what is really merely a romance exploiting the supposed working of this mechanism, in place of an actual study that sticks close to the facts and the documents of the writer's life and work. But I believe that Van Wyck Brooks really had hold of something important when he fixed upon that childhood incident of which Mark Twain gave so vivid an account to his biographer—that scene at the deathbed of his father when his mother had made him promise that he would not break her heart. If it was not one of those crucial happenings that are supposed to determine the complexes of Freud, it has certainly a typical significance in relation to Mark Twain's whole psychology. The stories that people tell about their childhood are likely to be profoundly symbolic even when they have been partly or wholly made up in the light of later experience. And the attitudes, the compulsions, the emotional 'patterns' that recur in the work of a writer are of great interest to the historical critic.

These attitudes and patterns are embedded in the community and the historical moment, and they may indicate its ideals and its diseases as the cell shows the condition of the tissue. The recent scientific experimentation in the combining of Freudian with Marxist method, and of psychoanalysis with anthropology, has had its parallel development in criticism. And there is thus another element added to our equipment for analyzing literary works, and the problem grows still more complex.

The analyst, however, is of course not concerned with the comparative values of his patients any more than the surgeon is. He cannot tell you why the neurotic Dostoevsky produces work of immense value to his fellows while another man with the same neurotic pattern would become a public menace. Freud himself emphatically states in his study of Leonardo that his method can make no attempt to account for Leonardo's genius. The problems of comparative artistic value still remain after we have given attention to the Freudian psychological factor just as they do after we have given attention to the Marxist economic factor and to the racial and geographical factors. No matter how thoroughly and searchingly we may have scrutinized works of literature from the historical and biographical points of view, we must be ready to attempt to estimate, in some such way as Saintsbury and Eliot do, the relative degrees of success attained by the products of the various periods and the various personalities. We must be able to tell good from bad, the first-rate from the second-rate. We shall not otherwise write literary criticism at all, but merely social or political history as reflected in literary texts, or psychological case histories from past eras, or, to take the historical point of view in its simplest and most academic form, merely chronologies of books that have been published.

And now how, in these matters of literary art, do we tell the good art from the bad? Norman Kemp Smith, the Kantian philosopher, whose courses I was fortunate enough to take at Princeton twenty-five years ago, used to tell us that this recognition was based primarily on an emotional reaction. For purposes of practical criticism this is a safe assumption on which to proceed. It is possible to discriminate in a variety of ways the elements that in any given department go to make a successful work of literature. Different schools have at different times demanded different things of literature: *unity, symmetry, universality, originality, vision, inspiration, strangeness, suggestiveness, improving morality, socialist realism*, etc. But you could have any set of these qualities that any school of writing has called for and still not have a good play, a good novel, a good poem, a good history. If you identify the essence of good literature with any one of these elements or with any combination of them, you simply shift the emotional reaction to the recognition of the element or elements. Or if you add to your other demands the demand that the writer must have *talent*, you simply shift this recognition to the talent. Once people find some grounds of agreement in the coincidence of their emotional reactions to books, they may be able to discuss these elements profitably; but if they do not have this basic agreement, the discussion will make no sense.

But how, you may ask, can we identify this élite who know what they are talking about? Well, it can only be said of them that they are self-appointed and self-perpetuating, and that they will compel you to accept their authority. Impostors may try to put themselves over, but these quacks will not last. The implied position of the people who know about literature (as is also the case in every other art) is simply that they know what they know, and that they are determined to impose their opinions by main force of eloquence or assertion on the people who do not know. This is not a question, of course, of professional workers in literature—such as editors, professors and critics, who very often have no real understanding of the products with which they deal—but of readers of all kinds in all walks of life. There are moments when a first-rate writer, unrecognized or out of fashion with the official chalkers-up for the market, may find his support in the demand for his work of an appreciative cultivated public.

But what is the cause of this emotional reaction which is the critic's divining rod? This question has long been a subject of study by the branch of philosophy called esthetics, and it has recently been made a subject of scientific experimentation. Both these lines of inquiry are likely to be prejudiced in the eyes of the literary critic by the fact that the inquiries are sometimes conducted by persons who are obviously deficient in literary feeling or taste. Yet one should not deny the possibility that something of value might result from the speculations and explorations of men of acute minds who take as their given data the esthetic emotions of other men.

Almost everybody interested in literature has tried to explain to himself the nature of these emotions that register our approval of artistic works; and I of course have my own explanation.

In my view, all our intellectual activity, in whatever field it takes place, is an attempt to give a meaning to our experience —that is, to make life more practicable; for by understanding things we make it easier to survive and get around among them. The mathematician Euclid, working in a convention of abstractions, shows us relations between the distances of our unwieldy and cluttered-up environment upon which we are able to count. A drama of Sophocles also indicates relations between the various human impulses, which appear so confused and dangerous, and it brings out a certain justice of Fate

—that is to say, of the way in which the interaction of these impulses is seen in the long run to work out—upon which we can also depend. The kinship, from this point of view, of the purposes of science and art appears very clearly in the case of the Greeks, because not only do both Euclid and Sophocles satisfy us by making patterns, but they make much the same kind of patterns. Euclid's *Elements* takes simple theorems and by a series of logical operations builds them up to a climax in the square on the hypotenuse. A typical drama of Sophocles develops in a similar way.

Some writers (as well as some scientists) have a different kind of explicit message beyond the reassurance implicit in the mere feat of understanding life or of molding the harmony of artistic form. Not content with such an achievement as that of Sophocles—who has one of his choruses tell us that it is better not to be born, but who, by representing life as noble and based on law, makes its tragedy easier to bear—such writers attempt, like Plato, to think out and recommend a procedure for turning it into something better. But other departments of literature—lyric poetry such as Sappho's, for example—have *less* philosophical content than Sophocles. A lyric gives us nothing but a pattern imposed on the expression of a feeling; but this pattern of metrical quantities and of consonants and vowels that balance has the effect of reducing the feeling, however unruly or painful it may seem when we experience it in the course of our lives, to something orderly, symmetrical and pleasing; and it also relates this feeling to the more impressive scheme, works it into the larger texture, of the body of poetic art. The discord has been resolved, the anomaly subjected to discipline. And this control of his emotion by the poet has the effect at second-hand of making it easier for the reader to manage his own emotions. (Why certain sounds and rhythms gratify us more than others, and how they are connected with the themes and ideas that they are chosen as appropriate for conveying, are questions that may be passed on to the scientist.)

And this brings us back again to the historical point of view. The experience of mankind on the earth is always changing as man develops and has to deal with new combinations of elements; and the writer who is to be anything more than an echo of his predecessors must always find expression for something which has never yet been expressed, must master a new set of phenomena which has never yet been mastered. With each such victory of the human intellect, whether in history, in philosophy or in poetry, we experience a deep satisfaction: we have been cured of some ache of disorder, relieved of some oppressive burden of uncomprehended events.

This relief that brings the sense of power, and, with the sense of power, joy, is the positive emotion which tells us that we have encountered a first-rate piece of literature. But stay! you may at this point warn: are not people often solaced and exhilarated by literature of the trashiest kind? They are: crude and limited people do certainly feel some such emotion in connection with work that is limited and crude. The man who is more highly organized and has a wider intellectual range will feel it in connection with work that is finer and more complex. The difference between the emotion of the more highly organized man and the emotion of the less highly organized one is a matter of mere gradation. You sometimes discover books —the novels of John Steinbeck, for example—that seem to mark precisely the borderline between work that is definitely superior and work that is definitely bad. When I was speaking a little while back of the genuine connoisseurs who establish the standards of taste, I meant, of course, the people who can distinguish Grade A and who prefer it to the other grades.

THE WOUND
AND THE BOW

Seven Studies in Literature

I bleed by the black stream
For my torn bough!
JAMES JOYCE

I

Dickens: The Two Scrooges

To the Students of English 354,
University of Chicago, Summer, 1939

O F all the great English writers, Charles Dickens has received in his own country the scantiest serious attention from either biographers, scholars, or critics. He has become for the English middle class so much one of the articles of their creed—a familiar joke, a favorite dish, a Christmas ritual—that it is difficult for British pundits to see in him the great artist and social critic that he was. Dickens had no university education, and the literary men from Oxford and Cambridge, who have lately been sifting fastidiously so much of the English heritage, have rather snubbingly let him alone. The Bloomsbury that talked about Dostoevsky ignored Dostoevsky's master, Dickens. What happens when the London of Lytton Strachey does take Dickens up is shown in Hugh Kingsmill's book, *The Sentimental Journey*, in which the man who was called by Taine 'the master of all hearts' is made into one of those Victorian scarecrows with ludicrous Freudian flaws—so infantile, pretentious, and hypocritical as to deserve only a perfunctory sneer.

Since Forster's elaborate memoir, which even in the supplemented edition of Ley has never been a real biography, no authoritative book about Dickens has been published. Some of the main facts about his life have till recently been kept from the public, and now that they have finally come out they have usually been presented either by doddering Dickens-fanciers or through the medium of garrulous memoirs. Mr. Ralph Straus and Mr. T. A. Jackson have recently published studies of Dickens—the one from the psychological, the other from the Marxist, point of view—which attempt a more searching treatment; but though they contain some valuable insights, neither is really first-rate, for neither handles surely enough or carries to fundamental findings the line which it undertakes. The typical

Dickens expert is an old duffer who, as Mr. Straus has said, is primarily interested in proving that Mr. Pickwick stopped at a certain inn and slept in a certain bed.

As for criticism, there has been in English one admirable critic of Dickens, George Gissing, whose prefaces and whose book on Dickens not only are the best thing on Dickens in English but stand out as one of the few really first-rate pieces of literary criticism produced by an Englishman of the end of the century. For the rest, you have mainly G. K. Chesterton, who turned out in his books on Dickens some of the best work of which he was capable and who said some excellent things, but whose writing here as elsewhere is always melting away into that peculiar pseudo-poetic booziness which verbalizes with large conceptions and ignores the most obtrusive actualities. Chesterton celebrated the jolly Dickens; and Bernard Shaw offset this picture by praising the later and gloomier Dickens and insisting on his own debt to the author of *Little Dorrit* at a time when it was taken for granted that he must derive from such foreigners as Ibsen and Nietzsche.

Chesterton asserted that time would show that Dickens was not merely one of the Victorians, but incomparably the greatest English writer of his time; and Shaw coupled his name with that of Shakespeare. It is the conviction of the present writer that both these judgments were justified. Dickens—though he cannot of course pretend to the rank where Shakespeare has few companions—was nevertheless the greatest dramatic writer that the English had had since Shakespeare, and he created the largest and most varied world. It is the purpose of this essay to show that we may find in Dickens' work today a complexity and a depth to which even Gissing and Shaw have hardly, it seems to me, done justice—an intellectual and artistic interest which makes Dickens loom very large in the whole perspective of the literature of the West.

I

The father of Charles Dickens' father was head butler in the house of John Crewe (later Lord Crewe) of Crewe Hall, Member of Parliament for Chester; and the mother of his father was a servant in the house of The Marquess of Blandford in Grosvenor Square, who was Lord Chamberlain to the House-

hold of George III. This grandmother, after her marriage, became housekeeper at Crewe Hall, and it is assumed that it was
through the patronage of her employer that her son John
Dickens was given a clerkship in the Navy Pay Office.

John Dickens began at £70 a year and was in time increased
to £350. But he had always had the tastes of a gentleman. He
was an amiable fellow, with an elegant manner and a flowery
vein of talk, who liked to entertain his friends and who could
not help creating the impression of a way of life beyond his
means. He was always in trouble over bills.

When Charles, who had been born (February 7, 1812) at
Portsmouth and had spent most of his childhood out of London at Portsmouth, Portsea and Chatham, who had had a
chance to go to the theater and to read the *Arabian Nights*
and the eighteenth century novelists, and had been taught by
a tutor from Oxford, came up to London at the age of nine to
join his parents, who had been obliged to return there, he was
terribly shocked to find them, as a consequence of his father's
debts, now living in a little back garret in one of the poorest
streets of Camden Town. On February 20, 1824, when Charles
was twelve, John Dickens was arrested for debt and taken to
the Marshalsea Prison, announcing, as he left the house: 'The
sun has set upon me forever!' At home the food began to run
low; and they had to pawn the household belongings till all but
two rooms were bare. Charles even had to carry his books, one
by one, to the pawnshop. It was presently decided that the
boy should go to work at six shillings a week for a cousin who
manufactured blacking; and through six months, in a rickety
old house by the river, full of dirt and infested with rats, he
pasted labels on blacking bottles, in the company of riverside
boys who called him 'the little gentleman.' He wanted terribly
to go on with his schooling, and couldn't grasp what had happened to him. The whole of the rest of the family moved into
the Marshalsea with his father; and Charles, who had a lodging
near them, went to the jail after work every evening and ate
breakfast with them every morning. He was so ashamed of the
situation that he would never allow his companion at the
blacking warehouse, whose name was Bob Fagin, to go with
him to the door of the prison, but would take leave of him and
walk up the steps of a strange house and pretend to be going

in. He had had a kind of nervous fits in his earlier childhood, and now these began to recur. One day at work he was seized with such an acute spasm that he had to lie down on some straw on the floor, and the boys who worked with him spent half the day applying blacking bottles of hot water to his side.

John Dickens inherited a legacy in May and got out of jail the twenty-eighth; but he let Charles keep on working in the warehouse. The little boys did their pasting next to the window in order to get the light, and people used to stop to look in at them because they had become so quick and skilful at it. This was an added humiliation for Charles; and one day when John Dickens came there, he wondered how his father could bear it. At last—perhaps, Dickens thought, as a result of what he had seen on this visit—John quarreled with Charles's employer, and took the boy out of the warehouse and sent him to school.

These experiences produced in Charles Dickens a trauma from which he suffered all his life. It has been charged by some of Dickens' critics that he indulged himself excessively in self-pity in connection with these hardships of his childhood; it has been pointed out that, after all, he had only worked in the blacking warehouse six months. But one must realize that during those months he was in a state of complete despair. For the adult in desperate straits, it is almost always possible to imagine, if not to contrive, some way out; for the child, from whom love and freedom have inexplicably been taken away, no relief or release can be projected. Dickens' seizures in his blacking-bottle days were obviously neurotic symptoms; and the psychologists have lately been telling us that lasting de-pressions and terrors may be caused by such cuttings-short of the natural development of childhood. For an imaginative and active boy of twelve, six months of despair are quite enough. 'No words can express,' Dickens wrote of his first introduction to the warehouse, in a document he gave to Forster, 'the secret agony of my soul as I sunk into this companionship; compared these every day associates with those of my happier childhood; and felt my early hopes of growing up to be a learned and dis-tinguished man crushed in my breast. The deep remembrance of the sense I had of being utterly neglected and hopeless; of the shame I felt in my position; of the misery it was to my young heart to believe that, day by day, what I had learned, and thought, and delighted in, and raised my fancy and my emulation up by, was passing away from me, never to be brought back any more; cannot be written. My whole nature was so penetrated with the grief and humiliation of such considerations, that even now, famous and caressed and happy, I often forget in my dreams that I have a dear wife and children; even that I am a man; and wander desolately back to that time of my life.'

He never understood how his father could have abandoned him to such a situation. 'I know my father,' he once told Forster, 'to be as kind-hearted and generous a man as ever lived in the world. Everything that I can remember of his conduct to his wife, or children, or friends, in sickness or affliction is beyond all praise. By me, as a sick child, he has watched night and day, unweariedly and patiently, many nights and days. He never undertook any business, charge or trust that he did not zealously, conscientiously, punctually, honorably discharge. His industry has always been untiring. He was proud of me, in his way, and had a great admiration of [my] comic singing. But, in the case of his temper, and the straitness of his means, he appeared to have lost utterly at this time the idea of educating me at all, and to have utterly put from him the notion that I had any claim upon him, in that regard, whatever.' And Charles never forgave his mother for having wanted to keep him working in the warehouse even after his father had decided to take him out. 'I never afterwards forgot,' he wrote of her attitude at this time. 'I never shall forget, I never can forget.'

Of those months he had never been able to bring himself to speak till, just before conceiving *David Copperfield*, he wrote the fragment of autobiography he sent to Forster; and, even after he had incorporated this material in an altered form in the novel, even his wife and children were never to learn about the realities of his childhood till they read about it after his death in Forster's *Life*. But the work of Dickens' whole career was an attempt to digest these early shocks and hardships, to explain them to himself, to justify himself in relation to them, to give an intelligible and tolerable picture of a world in which such things could occur.

Behind the misfortune which had humiliated Charles was the misfortune which had humiliated his father. John Dickens was a good and affectionate man, who had done the best he was able within the limits of his personality and who had not deserved to be broken. But behind these undeserved misfortunes were sources of humiliation perhaps more disturbing still. The father of Charles Dickens' mother, also a £350-a-year clerk in the Navy Pay Office, with the title of Conductor of Money, had systematically, by returning false balances, embezzled funds to the amount of £5689 3s. 3d. over a period of seven years; and when the fraud was discovered, had fled. And the background of domestic service was for an Englishman of the nineteenth century probably felt as more disgraceful than embezzlement. Certainly the facts about Dickens' ancestry were kept hidden by Dickens himself and have, so far as I know, only been fully revealed in the memoir by Miss Gladys Storey, based on interviews with Mrs. Perugini, Dickens' last surviving daughter, which was published in England in the summer of 1939.

But all these circumstances are worth knowing and bearing in mind, because they help us to understand what Dickens was trying to say. He was less given to false moral attitudes or to fear of respectable opinion than most of the great Victorians; but just as through the offices of his friends and admirers his personal life has been screened from the public even up to our own day, in a way that would have been thought unjustified in the case of a Keats or a Byron of the earlier nineteenth century, so the meaning of Dickens' work has been obscured by that element of the conventional which Dickens himself never quite outgrew. It is necessary to see him as a man in order to appreciate him as an artist—to exorcise the spell which has bewitched him into a stuffy piece of household furniture and to give him his proper rank as the poet of that portièred and upholstered world who saw clearest through the coverings and the curtains.

II

If one approaches his first novel, *Pickwick Papers*, with these facts of Dickens' biography in mind, one is struck by certain features of the book which one may not have noticed before.

Here the subject has been set for Dickens. He was supposed to provide some sort of text for a series of comic sporting plates by Seymour—something in the vein of Surtees' *Jorrocks*. As soon, however, as Dickens' scheme gives him a chance to get away from the sporting plates and to indulge his own pre-occupations, the work takes a different turn.

There are in *Pickwick Papers*, especially in the early part, a whole set of interpolated short stories which make a contrast with the narrative proper. These stories are mostly pretty bad and deserve from the literary point of view no more attention than they usually get; but, even allowing here also for an ele-ment of the conventional and popular, of the still-thriving school of Gothic horror, we are surprised to find rising to the surface already the themes which were to dominate his later work.

The first of these interludes in *Pickwick* deals with the death of a pantomime clown, reduced through drink to the direst misery, who, in the delirium of his fever, imagines that he is about to be murdered by the wife whom he has been beating. In the second story, a worthless husband also beats his wife and sets an example of bad conduct to his son; the boy commits a robbery, gets caught and convicted—in prison remains obdu-rate to his mother's attempts to soften his sullen heart; she dies, he repents, it is too late; he is transported, returns after seven-teen years and finds no one to love or greet him; he stumbles at last upon his father, now a sodden old man in the work-house; a scene of hatred and violence ensues: the father, filled with terror, strikes the son across the face with a stick, the son seizes the father by the throat, and the old man bursts a blood-vessel and falls dead. The third story is a document by a mad-man, which, like the delirium of the dying clown, gives Dickens an opportunity to exploit that vein of hysterical fancy which was to find fuller scope in *Barnaby Rudge* and which was there to figure for him the life of the imagination itself. The narrator has lived in the knowledge that he is to be the victim of hered-itary insanity. At last he feels that he is going mad, but at the same moment he inherits money: men fawn upon him and praise him now, but he secretly rejoices in the sense that he is not one of them, that he is fooling them. He marries a girl, who loves another but who has been sold to him by her father and brothers; seeing his wife languish away and coming to understand the situation, fearing also lest she may hand on the family curse, he tries to kill her in her sleep with a razor; she wakes up but dies of the shock. When one of her brothers comes to reproach him, the madman throws him down and chokes him; runs amuck and is finally caught.

But it is in *The Old Man's Tale About the Queer Client* (Chapter XXI) that Dickens' obsessions appear most plainly. Here at the threshold of Dickens' work we are confronted with the Marshalsea Prison. A prisoner for debt, a 'healthy, strong-made man, who could have borne almost any fatigue of active exertion,' wastes away in his confinement and sees his wife and child die of grief and want. He swears to revenge their deaths on the man who has put him there. We have another long passage of delirium, at the end of which the prisoner comes to, to learn that he has inherited his father's money. At a seaside resort where he has been living, he sees a man drowning one evening: the father of the drowning man stands by and begs the ex-prisoner to save his son. But when the wronged man recognizes his father-in-law, the scoundrel who sent him to prison and who allowed his own daughter and grandson to die, he retaliates by letting the boy drown; then, not content with this, he buys up, at 'treble and quadruple their nominal value,' a number of loans which have been made to the old man. These loans have been arranged on the understanding that they are renewable up to a certain date; but the wronged man, taking advantage of the fact that the agreement has never been put on paper, proceeds to call them in at a time when his father-in-law has 'sustained many losses.' The old man is dispossessed of all his property and finally runs away in order to escape prison; but his persecutor tracks him down to a 'wretched lodging'—note well: 'in Camden Town'—and there finally reveals himself and announces his implacable intention of sending his persecutor to jail. The old man falls dead from shock, and the revenger disappears.

In the meantime, the same theme has been getting under way in the main current of the comic novel. Mr. Pickwick has been framed by Dodson and Fogg, and very soon—another wronged man—he will land in the debtors' prison, where a good many of the other characters will join him and where the whole book will deepen with a new dimension of seriousness. The hilarity of the scene in court, in which Mr. Pickwick is convicted of trifling with Mrs. Bardell's affections—a scene openly borrowed from *Jorrocks* but wonderfully transformed by Dickens, and as brilliant as the story of the fiendish revenge on the fiendish father-in-law is bathetic—may disguise from the reader the significance which this episode had for Dickens. Here Dickens is one of the greatest of humorists: it is a laughter which is never vulgar but which discloses the vulgarity of the revered—a laughter of human ecstasy that rises like the phœnix from the cinders to which the dismal denizens of the tribunals have attempted to reduce decent human beings. It represents, like the laughter of Aristophanes, a real escape from institutions.

I shall make no attempt to discuss at length the humor of the early Dickens. This is the aspect of his work that is best known, the only aspect that some people know. In praise of Dickens' humor, there is hardly anything new to say. The only point I want to make is that the humor of Dickens does differ from such humor as that of Aristophanes in being unable forever to inhabit an empyrean of blithe intellectual play, of charming fancies and biting good sense. Dickens' laughter is an exhilaration which already shows a trace of the hysterical. It leaps free of the prison of life; but gloom and soreness must always drag it back. Before he has finished *Pickwick* and even while he is getting him out of jail and preparing to unite the lovers, the prison will close in again on Dickens. While he is still on the last instalments of *Pickwick*, he will begin writing *Oliver Twist*—the story of a disinherited boy, consigned to a workhouse which is virtually a jail and getting away only to fall into the hands of a gang of burglars, pickpockets and prostitutes.

And now we must identify the attitudes with which Dickens' origins and his early experiences had caused him to meet mankind. The ideal of *Pickwick Papers* is a kindly retired business man, piloted through a tough and treacherous world by a shrewd servant of watchful fidelity, who perfectly knows his place: Mr. Pickwick and Sam Weller. But this picture, though real enough to its creator, soon gives way to the figure of a parentless and helpless child—a figure of which the pathos will itself be eclipsed by the horror of the last night in the condemned cell of a betrayer of others to the gallows, and by the headlong descent into hell of a brute who clubs his girl to death and who, treed like a cat by the pursuing mob, hangs himself in trying to escape.

III

Edmund Yates described Dickens' expression as 'blunt' and 'pleasant,' but 'rather defiant.'

For the man of spirit whose childhood has been crushed by the cruelty of organized society, one of two attitudes is natural: that of the criminal or that of the rebel. Charles Dickens, in imagination, was to play the rôles of both, and to continue up to his death to put into them all that was most passionate in his feeling.

His interest in prisons and prisoners is evident from the very beginning. In his first book, *Sketches by Boz*, he tells how he used to gaze at Newgate with 'mingled feelings of awe and respect'; and he sketches an imaginary picture of a condemned man's last night alive, which he is soon to elaborate in *Oliver Twist*. Almost the only passage in *American Notes* which shows any real readiness on Dickens' part to enter into the minds and feelings of the people among whom he is traveling is the fantasy in which he imagines the effects of a sentence of solitary confinement in a Philadelphia jail. He visited prisons wherever he went, and he later found this cruel system imitated in the jail at Lausanne. Dickens was very much gratified when the system was finally abandoned as the result of the prisoners' going mad just as he had predicted they would. He also wrote a great deal about executions. One of the vividest things in *Pictures from Italy* is a description of a guillotining; and one of the most impressive episodes in *Barnaby Rudge* is the narration —developed on a formidable scale—of the hanging of the leaders of the riots. In 1846, Dickens wrote letters to the press in protest against capital punishment for murderers, on the ground among other grounds that this created sympathy for the culprits; in 1849, after attending some executions in London with Forster, he started by writing to *The Times* an agitation which had the effect of getting public hangings abolished. Even in 1867, in the course of his second visit to America, 'I have been tempted out,' Dickens wrote Forster, 'at three in the morning to visit one of the large police station-houses, and was so fascinated by the study of a horrible photograph-book of thieves' portraits that I couldn't put it down.'

His interest in the fate of prisoners thus went a good deal farther than simple memories of the debtors' prison or notes of a court reporter. He identified himself readily with the thief, and even more readily with the murderer. The man of powerful will who finds himself opposed to society must, if he cannot upset it or if his impulse to do so is blocked, feel a compulsion to commit what society regards as one of the capital crimes against itself. With the antisocial heroes of Dostoevsky, this crime is usually murder or rape; with Dickens, it is usually murder. His obsession with murderers is attested by his topical pieces for *Household Words*; by his remarkable letter to Forster on the performance of the French actor Lemaître in a play in which he impersonated a murderer; by his expedition, on his second visit to America, to the Cambridge Medical School for the purpose of going over the ground where Professor Webster had committed a murder in his laboratory and had continued to meet his courses with parts of the body under the lid of his lecture-table. In Dickens' novels, this theme recurs with a probing of the psychology of the murderer which becomes ever more convincing and intimate. Leaving the murderers of the later Dickens till we come to his later books, we may, however, point out here that the crime and flight of Jonas Chuzzlewit already show a striking development beyond the cruder crime and flight of Sikes. The fantasies and fears of Jonas are really, as Taine remarked, the picture of a mind on the edge of insanity. What is valid and impressive in this episode is the insight into the consciousness of a man who has put himself outside human fellowship—the moment, for example, after the murder when Jonas is 'not only fearful *for* himself but *of* himself' and half-expects, when he returns to his bedroom, to find himself asleep in the bed.

At times the two themes—the criminal and the rebel—are combined in a peculiar way. *Barnaby Rudge*—which from the point of view of Dickens' comedy and character-drawing is the least satisfactory of his early books—is, up to *Martin Chuzzlewit*, the most interesting from the point of view of his deeper artistic intentions. It is the only one of these earlier novels which is not more or less picaresque and, correspondingly, more or less of an improvisation (though there is a certain amount of organization discernible in that other somber book, *Oliver Twist*); it was the only novel up to that time which Dickens had been planning and reflecting on for a long time before he wrote it: it is first mentioned in 1837, but was not written till 1841. Its immediate predecessor, *The Old Curiosity Shop*, had been simply an impromptu yarn, spun out—when Dickens discovered that the original scheme of *Master Humphrey's Clock* was not going over with his readers—from what was to have been merely a short story; but *Barnaby Rudge* was a deliberate attempt to find expression for the emotions and ideas that possessed him

The ostensible subject of the novel is the anti-Catholic insurrection known as the 'Gordon riots' which took place in London in 1780. But what is obviously in Dickens' mind is the Chartist agitation for universal suffrage and working-class representation in Parliament which, as a result of the industrial depression of those years, came to a crisis in 1840. In Manchester the cotton mills were idle, and the streets were full of threatening jobless men. In the summer of 1840 there was a strike of the whole North of England, which the authorities found it possible to put down only by firing into the working-class crowds; this was followed the next year by a brickmakers' strike, which ended in bloody riots. Now the immediate occasion for the Gordon riots had been a protest against a bill which was to remove from the English Catholics such penalties and disabilities as the sentence of life imprisonment for priests who should educate children as Catholics and the disqualifications of Catholics from inheriting property; but the real causes behind the demonstration have always remained rather obscure. It seems to indicate an indignation more violent than it is possible to account for by mere anti-Catholic feeling that churches and houses should have been burnt wholesale, all the prisons of London broken open, and even the Bank of England attacked, and that the authorities should for several days have done so little to restrain the rioters; and it has been supposed that public impatience at the prolongation of the American War, with a general desire to get rid of

George III, if not of the monarchy itself, must have contributed to the fury behind the uprising.

This obscurity, at any rate, allowed Dickens to handle the
whole episode in an equivocal way. On the surface he repro-
bates Lord George Gordon and the rioters for their fanatical
or brutal intolerance; but implicitly he is exploiting to the limit
certain legitimate grievances of the people: the neglect of the
lower classes by a cynical eighteenth-century aristocracy, and
especially the penal laws which made innumerable minor offenses punishable by death. The really important theme of the
book—as Dickens shows in his preface, when he is discussing
one of the actual occurrences on which the story is based—is
the hanging under the Shop-lifting Act of a woman who has
been dropped by her aristocratic lover and who has forged
notes to provide for her child. This theme lies concealed, but it
makes itself felt from beginning to end of the book. And as
Pickwick, from the moment it gets really under way, heads by
instinct and, as it were, unconsciously straight for the Fleet
prison, so *Barnaby Rudge* is deliberately directed toward Newgate, where, as in *Pickwick* again, a group of characters will be
brought together; and the principal climax of the story will
be the orgiastic burning of the prison. This incident not only
has nothing to do with the climax of the plot, it goes in spirit
quite against the attitude which Dickens has begun by announcing. The satisfaction he obviously feels in demolishing
the sinister old prison, which, rebuilt, had oppressed him in
childhood, completely obliterates the effect of his right-minded
references in his preface to 'those shameful tumults,' which
'reflect indelible disgrace upon the time in which they occurred, and all who had act or part in them.' In the end, the
rioters are shot down and their supposed instigators hanged;
but here Dickens' *parti pris* emerges plainly: 'Those who suffered as rioters were, for the most part, the weakest, meanest
and most miserable among them.' The son of the woman
hanged for stealing, who has been one of the most violent of
the mob and whose fashionable father will do nothing to save
him, goes to the scaffold with courage and dignity, cursing his
father and 'that black tree, of which I am the ripened fruit.'

Dickens has here, under the stimulus of the Chartist

agitation, tried to give his own emotions an outlet through an historical novel of insurrection; but the historical episode, the contemporary moral, and the author's emotional pattern do not always coincide very well. Indeed, perhaps the best thing in the book is the creation that most runs away with the general scheme that Dickens has attempted. Dennis the hangman, although too macabre to be one of Dickens' most popular characters, is really one of his best comic inventions, and has more interesting symbolic implications than Barnaby Rudge himself. Dennis is a professional executioner, who has taken an active part in the revolt, apparently from simple motives of sadism. Knowing the unpopularity of the hangman, he makes an effort to keep his identity a secret; but he has found this rather difficult to do, because he sincerely loves his profession and cannot restrain himself from talking about it. When the mob invades Newgate, which Dennis knows so well, he directs the liberation of the prisoners; but in the end he slips away to the condemned cells, locks them against the mob and stands guard over the clamoring inmates, cracking them harshly over the knuckles when they reach their hands out over the doors. The condemned are his vested interest, which he cannot allow the rebels to touch. But the momentum of the mob forces the issue, breaks through and turns the criminals loose. When we next encounter Dennis, he is a stool pigeon, turning his former companions in to the police. But he is unable to buy immunity in this way; and he is finally hanged himself. Thus this hangman has a complex value: he is primarily a sadist who likes to kill. Yet he figures as a violator as well as a protector of prisons. In his rôle of insurgent, he attacks authority; in his rôle of hangman, makes it odious. Either way he represents on Dickens' part a blow at whose institutions which the writer is pretending to endorse. There is not, except in a minor way, any other symbol of authority in the book.

The formula of *Barnaby Rudge* is more or less reproduced in the other two novels of Dickens that deal with revolutionary subjects—which, though they belong to later periods of Dickens' work, it is appropriate to consider here. In *Hard Times* (1854), he manages in much the same way to deal sympathetically with the working-class protest against intolerable industrial conditions at the same time that he lets himself out from supporting the trade-union movement. In order to be able to do this, he is obliged to resort to a special and rather implausible device. Stephen Blackpool, the honest old textile worker who is made to argue the cause of the workers before the vulgar manufacturer Bounderby, refuses to join the union because he has promised the woman he loves that he will do nothing to get himself into trouble. He thus finds himself in the singular position of being both a victim of the blacklist and a scab. The trade-union leadership is represented only—although with a comic fidelity, recognizable even today, to a certain type of labor organizer—by an unscrupulous spell binder whose single aim is to get hold of the workers' pennies. Old Stephen, wandering away to look for a job somewhere else, falls into a disused coal-pit which has already cost the lives of many miners, and thus becomes a martyr simultaneously to the employers and to the trade-union movement. In *A Tale of Two Cities* (1859), the moral of history is not juggled as it is in *Barnaby Rudge,* but the conflict is made to seem of less immediate reality by locating it out of England. The French people, in Dickens' picture, have been given ample provocation for breaking loose in the French Revolution; but once in revolt, they are fiends and vandals. The vengeful Madame Defarge is a creature whom—as Dickens implies—one would not find in England, and she is worsted by an Englishwoman. The immediate motive behind *A Tale of Two Cities* is no doubt, as has been suggested and as is intimated at the beginning of the last chapter, the English fear of the Second Empire after Napoleon III's Italian campaign of 1859: Dickens' impulse to write the book closely followed the attempt by Orsini to assassinate Napoleon III in the January of '58. But there is in this book as in the other two—though less angrily expressed—a threat. If the British upper classes, Dickens seems to say, will not deal with the problem of providing for the health and education of the people, they will fall victims to the brutal mob. This mob Dickens both sympathizes with and fears.

Through the whole of his early period, Dickens appears to have regarded himself as a respectable middle-class man. If

Sam Weller, for all his outspokenness, never oversteps his rôle of valet, Kit in *The Old Curiosity Shop* is a model of deference toward his betters who becomes even a little disgusting.

When Dickens first visited America, in 1842, he seems to have had hopes of finding here something in the nature of that classless society which the foreign 'fellow travelers' of yesterday went to seek in the Soviet Union; but, for reasons both bad and good, Dickens was driven back by what he did find into the attitude of an English gentleman, who resented the American lack of ceremony, was annoyed by the American publicity, and was pretty well put to rout by the discomfort, the poverty and the tobacco-juice which he had braved on his trip to the West. Maladjusted to the hierarchy at home, he did not fit in in the United States even so well as he did in England: some of the Americans patronized him, and others were much too familiar. The mixed attitude—here seen at its most favorable to us—which was produced when his British ideas intervened to rein in the sympathy which he tended to feel for American innovations, is well indicated by the passage in *American Notes* in which he discusses the factory-girls of Lowell. These girls have pianos in their boarding-houses and subscribe to circulating libraries, and they publish a periodical. 'How very preposterous!' the writer imagines an English reader exclaiming. 'These things are above their station.' But what is their station? asks Dickens. 'It is their station to work,' he answers. 'And they *do* work. . . . For myself, I know no station in which, the occupation of today cheerfully done and the occupation of tomorrow cheerfully looked to, any one of these pursuits is not most humanizing and laudable. I know no station which is rendered more endurable to the person in it, or more safe to the person out of it, by having ignorance for its associate. I know no station which has a right to monopolize the means of mutual instruction, improvement and rational entertainment; or which has ever continued to be a station very long after seeking to do so.' But he remarks that 'it is pleasant to find that many of [the] Tales [in the library] are of the Mills, and of those who work in them; that they inculcate habits of self-denial and contentment, and teach good doctrines of enlarged benevolence.' The main theme of *Nicholas*

Nickleby is the efforts of Nicholas and his sister to vindicate their position as gentlefolk.

But there is also another reason why these political novels of Dickens are unclear and unsatisfactory. Fundamentally, he was not interested in politics. As a reporter, he had seen a good deal of Parliament, and he had formed a contemptuous opinion of it which was never to change to the end of his life. The Eatanswill elections in *Pickwick* remain the type of political activity for Dickens; the seating of Mr. Veneering in Parliament in the last of his finished novels is hardly different. The point of view is stated satirically in Chapter XII of *Bleak House*, in which a governing class group at a country house are made to discuss the fate of the country in terms of the political activities of Lord Coodle, Sir Thomas Doodle, the Duke of Foodle, the Right Honorable William Buffy, M.P., with his associates and opponents Cuffy, Duffy, Fuffy, etc., while their constituents are taken for granted as 'a certain large number of supernumeraries, who are to be occasionally addressed, and relied upon for shouts and choruses, as on the theatrical stage.' A little later (September 30, 1855), he expresses himself explicitly in the course of a letter to Forster: 'I really am serious in thinking—and I have given as painful consideration to the subject as a man with children to live and suffer after him can honestly give to it—that representative government is become altogether a failure with us, that the English gentilities and subserviences render the people unfit for it, and that the whole thing has broken down since that great seventeenth-century time, and has no hope in it.'

In his novels from beginning to end, Dickens is making the same point always: that to the English governing classes the people they govern are not real. It is one of the great purposes of Dickens to show you these human actualities who figure for Parliament as strategical counters and for Political Economy as statistics; who can as a rule appear only even in histories in a generalized or idealized form. What does a workhouse under the Poor Laws look like? What does it feel like, taste like, smell like? How does the holder of a post in the government look? How does he talk? what does he talk about? how will he treat you? What is the aspect of the British middle class at each of the various stages of its progress? What are the good ones like and what are the bad ones like? How do they affect you, not merely to meet at dinner, but to travel with, to work under, to live with? All these things Dickens can tell us. It has been one of the principal functions of the modern novel and drama to establish this kind of record; but few writers have been able to do it with any range at all extensive. None has surpassed Dickens.

No doubt this concrete way of looking at society may have serious limitations. Dickens was sometimes actually stupid about politics. His lack of interest in political tactics led him, it has sometimes been claimed, to mistake the actual significance of the legislation he was so prompt to criticize. Mr. T. A. Jackson has pointed out a characteristic example of Dickens' inattention to politics in his report of his first trip to America. Visiting Washington in 1842, he registers an impression of Congress very similar to his impressions of Parliament ('I may be of a cold and insensible temperament, amounting to iciness, in such matters'); and he indulges in one of his gushings of sentiment over 'an aged, gray-haired man, a lasting honor to the land that gave him birth, who has done good service to his country, as his forefathers did, and who will be remembered scores upon scores of years after the worms bred in its corruption are so many grains of dust—it was but a week since this old man had stood for days upon his trial before this very body, charged with having dared to assert the infamy of that traffic which has for its accursed merchandise men and women, and their unborn children.' Now this aged gray-haired man, Mr. Jackson reminds us, was none other than John Quincy Adams, who, far from being on his trial, was actually on the verge of winning in his long fight against a House resolution which had excluded petitions against slavery, and who was deliberately provoking his adversaries for purposes of propaganda. Dickens did not know that the antislavery cause, far from being hopeless, was achieving its first step toward victory. (So on his second visit to America—when, however, he was ill and exhausted—his interest in the impeachment of Andrew Johnson seems to have been limited to 'a misgiving lest the great excitement . . . will damage our receipts' from his readings.) Yet his picture of the United States in 1842, at a period of brave boastings and often squalid or meager realities, has a unique and permanent value. Macaulay complained that Dickens did not understand the Manchester school of utilitarian economics which he criticized in *Hard Times*. But Dickens' criticism does not pretend to be theoretical: all he is undertaking to do is to tell us how practising believers in Manchester utilitarianism behave and how their families are likely to fare with them. His picture is strikingly collaborated by the autobiography of John Stuart Mill, who was brought up at the fountainhead of the school, in the shadow of Bentham himself. In Mill, choked with learning from his childhood, overtrained on the logical side of the mind, and collapsing into illogical despair when the lack began to make itself felt of the elements his education had neglected, the tragic moral of the system of Gradgrind is pointed with a sensational obviousness which would be regarded as exaggeration in Dickens.

This very distrust of politics, however, is a part of the rebellious aspect of Dickens. Dickens is almost invariably *against* institutions: in spite of his allegiance to Church and State, in spite of the lip-service he occasionally pays them, whenever he comes to deal with Parliament and its laws, the courts and the public officials, the creeds of Protestant dissenters and of Church of England alike, he makes them either ridiculous or cruel, or both at the same time.

IV

In the work of Dickens' middle period—after the murder in *Martin Chuzzlewit*—the rebel bulks larger than the criminal.

Of all the great Victorian writers, he was probably the most antagonistic to the Victorian Age itself. He had grown up under the Regency and George IV; had been twenty-five at the accession of Victoria. His early novels are freshened by breezes from an England of coaching and village taverns, where the countryside lay just outside London; of an England where jokes and songs and hot brandy were always in order, where every city clerk aimed to dress finely and drink freely, to give an impression of open-handedness and gallantry. The young Dickens of the earliest preserved letters, who invites his friends to partake of 'the rosy,' sounds not unlike Dick Swiveller. When Little Nell and her grandfather on their wanderings spend a

night in an iron foundry, it only has the effect of a sort of Ni-
belungen interlude, rather like one of those surprise grottoes
that you float through when you take the little boat that threads
the tunnel of the 'Old Mill' in an amusement park—a luridly
lighted glimpse on the same level, in Dickens' novel, with the
waxworks, the performing dogs, the dwarfs and giants, the village church. From this point it is impossible, as it was impossible for Dickens, to foresee the full-length industrial town
depicted in *Hard Times*. In that age the industrial-commercial
civilization had not yet got to be the norm; it seemed a disease
which had broken out in spots but which a sincere and cheerful treatment would cure. The typical reformers of the period
had been Shelley and Robert Owen, the latter so logical a
crank, a philanthropist so much all of a piece, that he seems to
have been invented by Dickens—who insisted that his Cheery-
ble brothers, the philanthropic merchants of *Nicholas Nickleby*,
had been taken from living originals.

But when Dickens begins to write novels again after his return from his American trip, a new kind of character appears in
them, who, starting as an amusing buffoon, grows steadily
more unpleasant and more formidable. On the threshold of
Martin Chuzzlewit (1843–45: the dates of its appearance in
monthly numbers), you find Pecksniff, the provincial architect;
on the threshold of *Dombey and Son* (1846–48), you find
Dombey, the big London merchant; and before you have got
very far with the idyllic *David Copperfield* (1849–50), you find
Murdstone, of Murdstone and Grimby, wine merchants. All
these figures stand for the same thing. Dickens had at first
imagined that he was pillorying abstract faults in the manner
of the comedy of humors: Selfishness in *Chuzzlewit*, Pride in
Dombey. But the truth was that he had already begun an indictment against a specific society: the self-important and moralizing middle class who had been making such rapid progress
in England and coming down like a damper on the bright fires
of English life—that is, on the spontaneity and gaiety, the
frankness and independence, the instinctive human virtues,
which Dickens admired and trusted. The new age had brought
a new kind of virtues to cover up the flourishing vices of cold
avarice and harsh exploitation; and Dickens detested these
virtues.

The curmudgeons of the early Dickens—Ralph Nickleby and Arthur Gride, Anthony and Jonas Chuzzlewit (for *Martin Chuzzlewit* just marks the transition from the early to the middle Dickens)—are old-fashioned moneylenders and misers of a type that must have been serving for decades in the melodramas of the English stage. In Dickens their whole-hearted and outspoken meanness gives them a certain cynical charm. They are the bad uncles in the Christmas pantomime who set off the jolly clowns and the good fairy, and who, as everybody knows from the beginning, are doomed to be exposed and extinguished. But Mr. Pecksniff, in the same novel with the Chuzzlewits, already represents something different. It is to be characteristic of Pecksniff, as it is of Dombey and Murdstone, that he does evil while pretending to do good. As intent on the main chance as Jonas himself, he pretends to be a kindly father, an affectionate relative, a pious churchgoer; he is the pillar of a cathedral town. Yet Pecksniff is still something of a pantomime comic whom it will be easy enough to unmask. Mr. Dombey is a more difficult problem. His virtues, as far as they go, are real: though he is stupid enough to let his business get into the hands of Carker, he does lead an exemplary life of a kind in the interests of the tradition of his house. He makes his wife and his children miserable in his devotion to his mercantile ideal, but that ideal is at least for him serious. With Murdstone the ideal has turned sour: the respectable London merchant now represents something sinister. Murdstone is not funny like Pecksniff; he is not merely a buffoon who masquerades: he is a hypocrite who believes in himself. And where Dombey is made to recognize his error and turn kindly and humble in the end, Mr. Murdstone and his grim sister are allowed to persist in their course of working mischief as a matter of duty.

In such a world of mercenary ruthlessness, always justified by rigorous morality, it is natural that the exploiter of others should wish to dissociate himself from the exploited, and to delegate the face-to-face encounters to someone else who is paid to take the odium. Karl Marx, at that time living in London, was demonstrating through these middle years of the century that this system, with its falsifying of human relations and its wholesale encouragement of cant, was an inherent and irremediable feature of the economic structure itself. In Dickens, the Mr. Spenlow of *David Copperfield*, who is always blaming his mean exactions on his supposedly implacable partner, Mr. Jorkins, develops into the Casby of *Little Dorrit*, the benignant and white-haired patriarch who turns over the rackrenting of Bleeding Heart Yard to his bull-terrier of an agent, Pancks, while he basks in the admiration of his tenants; and in *Our Mutual Friend*, into Fledgeby, the moneylender who makes his way into society while the harmless old Jew Riah is compelled to play the cruel creditor.

With Dickens' mounting dislike and distrust of the top layers of that middle-class society with which he had begun by identifying himself, his ideal of middle-class virtue was driven down to the lower layers. In his earlier novels, this ideal had been embodied in such patrons and benefactors as Mr. Pickwick, the retired business man; the substantial and warm-hearted Mr. Brownlow, who rescued Oliver Twist; and the charming old gentleman, Mr. Garland, who took Kit Nubbles into his service. In *David Copperfield* the lawyer Wickfield, who plays a rôle in relation to the hero somewhat similar to those of Brownlow and Garland, becomes demoralized by too much port and falls a victim to Uriah Heep, the upstart Pecksniff of a lower social level. The ideal—the domestic unit which preserves the sound values of England—is located by Dickens through this period in the small middle-class household: Ruth Pinch and her brother in *Martin Chuzzlewit*; the bright hearths and holiday dinners of the *Christmas Books*; the modest home to which Florence Dombey descends from the great house near Portland Place, in happy wedlock with the nephew of Sol Gills, the ships'-instrument-maker.

It is at the end of *Dombey and Son*, when the house of Dombey goes bankrupt, that Dickens for the first time expresses himself explicitly on the age that has come to remain:

'The world was very busy now, in sooth, and had a deal to say. It was an innocently credulous and a much ill-used world. It was a world in which there was no other sort of bankruptcy whatever. There were no conspicuous people in it, trading far and wide on rotten banks of religion, patriotism, virtue, honor. There was no amount worth mentioning of mere paper in circulation, on which anybody lived pretty handsomely, promising to pay great sums of goodness with no effects. There were no shortcomings anywhere, in anything but money. The world was very angry indeed; and the people especially who, in a worse world, might have been supposed to be bankrupt traders themselves in shows and pretences, were observed to be mightily indignant.'

And now—working always through the observed interrelations between highly individualized human beings rather than through political or economic analysis—Dickens sets out to trace an anatomy of that society. *Dombey* has been the first attempt; *Bleak House* (1852–53) is to realize this intention to perfection; *Hard Times,* on a smaller scale, is to conduct the same kind of inquiry.

For this purpose Dickens invents a new literary *genre* (unless the whole mass of Balzac is to be taken as something of the sort): the novel of the social group. The young Dickens had summed up, developed and finally outgrown the two traditions in English fiction he had found: the picaresque tradition of Defoe, Fielding and Smollett, and the sentimental tradition of Goldsmith and Sterne. People like George Henry Lewes have complained of Dickens' little reading; but no artist has ever absorbed his predecessors—he had read most of them in his early boyhood—more completely than Dickens did. There is something of all these writers in Dickens and, using them, he has gone beyond them all. In the historical novel *Barnaby Rudge*—a detour in Dickens' fiction—he had got out of Scott all that Scott had to give him. He was to profit in *Hard Times* by Mrs. Gaskell's industrial studies. But in the meantime it was Dickens' business to create a new tradition himself.

His novels even through *Martin Chuzzlewit* had had a good deal of the looseness of the picaresque school of *Gil Blas,* where the episodes get their only unity from being hung on the same hero, as well as the multiple parallel plots, purely mechanical combinations, that he had acquired from the old plays —though he seems to have been trying more intensively for a unity of atmosphere and feeling. But now he is to organize his stories as wholes, to plan all the characters as symbols, and to invest all the details with significance. *Dombey and Son* derives a new kind of coherence from the fact that the whole novel is made to center around the big London business house: you have the family of the man who owns it, the manager and his family, the clerks, the men dependent on the ships that export its goods, down to Sol Gills and Captain Cuttle (so *Hard Times* is to get its coherence from the organism of an industrial town).

In *Bleak House*, the masterpiece of this middle period, Dickens discovers a new use of plot, which makes possible a tighter organization. (And we must remember that he is always working against the difficulties, of which he often complains, of writing for monthly instalments, where everything has to be planned beforehand and it is impossible, as he says, to 'try back' and change anything, once it has been printed.) He creates the detective story which is also a social fable. It is a *genre* which has lapsed since Dickens. The detective story—though Dickens' friend Wilkie Collins preserved a certain amount of social satire—has dropped out the Dickensian social content; and the continuators of the social novel have dropped the detective story. These continuators—Shaw, Galsworthy, Wells— have of course gone further than Dickens in the realistic presentation of emotion; but from the point of view of dramatizing social issues, they have hardly improved upon *Bleak House*. In Shaw's case, the Marxist analysis, with which Dickens was not equipped, has helped him to the tighter organization which Dickens got from his complex plot. But in the meantime it is one of Dickens' victories in his rapid development as an artist that he should succeed in transforming his melodramatic intrigues of stolen inheritances, lost heirs and ruined maidens—with their denunciatory confrontations that always evoke the sound of fiddling in the orchestra—into devices of artistic dignity. Henceforth the solution of the mystery is to be also the moral of the story and the last word of Dickens' social 'message.'

Bleak House begins in the London fog, and the whole book is permeated with fog and rain. In *Dombey* the railway locomotive —first when Mr. Dombey takes his trip to Leamington, and later when it pulls into the station just at the moment of Dombey's arrival and runs over the fugitive Carker as he steps back to avoid his master—figures as a symbol of that progress of commerce which Dombey himself represents; in *Hard Times* the uncovered coal-pit into which Stephen Blackpool falls is a symbol for the abyss of the industrial system, which swallows up lives in its darkness. In *Bleak House* the fog stands for Chancery, and Chancery stands for the whole web of clotted antiquated institutions in which England stifles and decays. All the principal elements in the story—the young people, the proud Lady Dedlock, the philanthropic gentleman John Jarndyce, and Tom-all-Alone's, the rotting London slum—are involved in the exasperating Chancery suit, which, with the fog-bank of precedent looming behind it like the Great Boyg in *Peer Gynt*, obscures and impedes at every point the attempts of men and women to live natural lives. Old Krook, with his legal junkshop, is Dickens' symbol for the Lord Chancellor himself; the cat that sits on his shoulder watches like the Chancery lawyers the caged birds in Miss Flite's lodging; Krook's death by spontaneous combustion is Dickens' prophecy of the fate of Chancery and all that it represents.

I go over the old ground of the symbolism, up to this point perfectly obvious, of a book which must be still, by the general public, one of the most read of Dickens' novels, because the people who like to talk about the symbols of Kafka and Mann and Joyce have been discouraged from looking for anything of the kind in Dickens, and usually have not read him, at least with mature minds. But even when we think we do know Dickens, we may be surprised to return to him and find in him a symbolism of a more complicated reference and a deeper implication than these metaphors that hang as emblems over the door. The Russians themselves, in this respect, appear to have learned from Dickens.

Thus it is not at first that we recognize all the meaning of the people that thrive or survive in the dense atmosphere of *Bleak House*—an atmosphere so opaque that the somnolent ease at the top cannot see down to the filth at the bottom. And it is an atmosphere where nobody sees clearly what kind of race of beings is flourishing between the bottom and the top. Among the middle ranks of this society we find persons who appear with the pretension of representing Law or Art, Social Elegance, Philanthropy, or Religion—Mr. Kenge and Mr. Vholes, Harold Skimpole, Mr. Turveydrop, Mrs. Pardiggle and Mrs. Jellyby, and Mr. and Mrs. Chadband—side by side with such a sordid nest of goblins as the family of the moneylender Smallweed. But presently we see that all these people are as

single-mindedly intent on selfish interests as Grandfather Smallweed himself. This gallery is one of the best things in Dickens.
The Smallweeds themselves are artistically an improvement on
the similar characters in the early Dickens: they represent, not
a theatrical convention, but a real study of the stunted and de-
graded products of the underworld of commercial London.
And the two opposite types of philanthropist: the moony Mrs.
Jellyby, who miserably neglects her children in order to dream
of doing good in Africa, and Mrs. Pardiggle, who bullies both
her children and the poor in order to give herself a feeling of
power; Harold Skimpole, with the graceful fancy and the talk
about music and art that ripples a shimmering veil over his systematic sponging; and Turveydrop, the Master of Deport-
ment, that parody of the magnificence of the Regency, behind
his rouge and his padded coat and his gallantry as cold and as
inconsiderate as the Chadbands behind their gaseous preachments. Friedrich Engels, visiting London in the early forties,
had written of the people in the streets that they seemed to
'crowd by one another as if they had nothing in common,
nothing to do with one another, and as if their only agreement
were the tacit one that each shall keep to his own side of the
pavement, in order not to delay the opposing streams of
the crowd, while it never occurs to anyone to honor his fellow
with so much as a glance. The brutal indifference, the unfeeling
isolation of each in his private interest, becomes the more repellent the more these individuals are herded together within a
limited space.' This is the world that Dickens is describing.

Here he makes but one important exception: Mr. Rouncewell, the ironmaster. Mr. Rouncewell is an ambitious son of
the housekeeper at Chesney Wold, Sir Leicester Dedlock's
country house, who has made himself a place in the world
which Sir Leicester regards as beyond his station. One of the
remarkable scenes of the novel is that in which Rouncewell
comes back, quietly compels Sir Leicester to receive him like a
gentleman and asks him to release one of the maids from his
service so that she may marry Rouncewell's son, a young man
whom he has christened Watt. When Lady Dedlock refuses to
release the maid, Rouncewell respectfully abandons the project, but goes away and has the insolence to run against Sir
Leicester's candidate in the next parliamentary election. (This

theme of the intervention of the industrial revolution in the relations between master and servant has already appeared in *Dombey and Son* in the admirable interview between Dombey and Polly Toodles, whom he is employing as a wetnurse for his motherless child. Polly's husband, who is present, is a locomotive stoker and already represents something anomalous in the hierarchy of British society. When the Dombeys, who cannot accept her real name, suggest calling Polly 'Richards,' she replies that if she is to be called out of her name, she ought to be paid extra. Later, when Dombey makes his railway journey, he runs into Polly's husband, who is working on the engine. Toodles speaks to him and engages him in conversation, and Dombey resents this, feeling that Toodles is somehow intruding outside his own class.)

But in general the magnanimous, the simple of heart, the amiable, the loving and the honest are frustrated, subdued, or destroyed. At the bottom of the whole gloomy edifice is the body of Lady Dedlock's lover and Esther Summerson's father, Captain Hawdon, the reckless soldier, adored by his men, beloved by women, the image of the old life-loving England, whose epitaph Dickens is now writing. Captain Hawdon has failed in that world, has perished as a friendless and penniless man, and has been buried in the pauper's graveyard in one of the foulest quarters of London, but the loyalties felt for him by the living will endure and prove so strong after his death that they will pull that world apart. Esther Summerson has been frightened and made submissive by being treated as the respectable middle class thought it proper to treat an illegitimate child, by one of those Puritanical females whom Dickens so roundly detests. Richard Carstone has been demoralized and ruined; Miss Flite has been driven insane. George Rouncewell, the brother of the ironmaster, who has escaped from Sir Leicester's service to become a soldier instead of a manufacturer and who is treated by Dickens with the sympathy which he usually feels for his military and nautical characters, the men who are doing the hard work of the Empire, is helpless in the hands of moneylenders and lawyers. Caddy Jellyby and her husband, young Turveydrop, who have struggled for a decent life in a poverty partly imposed by the necessity of keeping up old Turveydrop's pretenses, can only produce, in that society where nature is so mutilated and thwarted, a sickly defective child. Mr. Jarndyce himself, the wise and generous, who plays in *Bleak House* a rôle very similar to that of Captain Shotover in Bernard Shaw's *Heartbreak House* (which evidently owes a good deal to *Bleak House*), is an eccentric at odds with his environment, who, in his efforts to help the unfortunate, falls a prey to the harpies of philanthropy.

With this indifference and egoism of the middle class, the social structure must buckle in the end. The infection from the poverty of Tom-all-Alone's will ravage the mansions of country gentlemen. Lady Dedlock will inevitably be dragged down from her niche of aristocratic idleness to the graveyard in the slum where her lover lies. The idea that the highest and the lowest in that English society of shocking contrasts are inextricably tied together has already appeared in the early Dickens—in Ralph Nickleby and Smike, for example, and in Sir John Chester and Hugh—as a sort of submerged motif which is never given its full expression. Here it has been chosen deliberately and is handled with immense skill so as to provide the main moral of the fable. And bound up with it is another motif which has already emerged sharply in Dickens. Dickens had evidently in the course of his astonishing rise, found himself up against the blank and chilling loftiness—what the French call *la morgue anglaise*—of the English upper classes: as we shall see, he developed a pride of his own, with which he fought it to his dying day. Pride was to have been the theme of *Dombey*: the pride of Edith Dombey outdoes the pride of Dombey and levels him to the ground. But in *Bleak House*, the pride of Lady Dedlock, who has married Sir Leicester Dedlock for position, ultimately rebounds on herself. Her behavior toward the French maid Hortense is the cause of her own debasement. For where it is a question of pride, a high-tempered girl from the South of France can outplay Lady Dedlock: Hortense will not stop at the murder which is the logical upshot of the course of action dictated by her wounded feelings. Dickens is criticizing here one of the most unassailable moral props of the English hierarchical system.

Between *Dombey and Son* and *Bleak House*, Dickens published *David Copperfield*. It is a departure from the series of his

social novels. Setting out to write the autobiography of which
the fragments appear in Forster's *Life*, Dickens soon changed
his mind and transposed this material into fiction. In the first
half of *David Copperfield*, at any rate, Dickens strikes an enchanting vein which he had never quite found before and
which he was never to find again. It is the poem of an idealized
version of the loves and fears and wonders of childhood; and
the confrontation of Betsey Trotwood with the Murdstones
is one of Dickens' most successful stagings of the struggle
between the human and the anti-human, because it takes place
on the plane of comedy rather than on that of melodrama. But
Copperfield is not one of Dickens' deepest books: it is something in the nature of a holiday. David is too candid and simple
to represent Dickens himself; and though the blacking warehouse episode is utilized, all the other bitter circumstances of
Dickens' youth were dropped out when he abandoned the
autobiography.

V

With *Little Dorrit* (1855–57), Dickens' next novel after *Bleak
House* and *Hard Times*, we enter a new phase of his work. To
understand it, we must go back to his life.

Dickens at forty had won everything that a writer could expect to obtain through his writings: his genius was universally
recognized; he was fêted wherever he went; his books were
immensely popular; and they had made him sufficiently rich to
have anything that money can procure. He had partly made up
for the education he had missed by traveling and living on the
Continent and by learning to speak Italian and French. (Dickens' commentary on the continental countries is usually not
remarkably penetrating; but he did profit very much from his
travels abroad in his criticism of things in England. Perhaps no
other of the great Victorian writers had so much the consciousness that the phenomena he was describing were of a character
distinctively English.) Yet from the time of his first summer at
Boulogne in 1853, he had shown signs of profound discontent
and unappeasable restlessness; he suffered severely from
insomnia and, for the first time in his life, apparently, worried
seriously about his work. He began to fear that his vein was
drying up.

I believe that Forster's diagnosis—though it may not go to the root of the trouble—must here be accepted as correct. There were, he intimates, two things wrong with Dickens: a marriage which exasperated and cramped him and from which he had not been able to find relief, and a social maladjustment which his success had never straightened out.

The opportunities of the young Dickens to meet eligible young women had evidently been rather limited. That he was impatient to get married, nevertheless, is proved by his announcing his serious intentions to three girls in close succession. The second of these was Maria Beadnell, the original of Dora in *David Copperfield* and, one supposes, of Dolly Varden, too, with whom he fell furiously in love, when he was eighteen and she nineteen. Her father worked in a bank and regarded Charles Dickens, the stenographer, as a young man of shabby background and doubtful prospects; Maria, who seems to have been rather frivolous and silly, was persuaded to drop her suitor—with the result for him which may be read in the letters, painful in their wounded pride and their backfiring of a thwarted will, which he wrote her after the break. This was one of the great humiliations of Dickens' early life (he was at that time twenty-one) and, even after he had liquidated it in a sense by depicting the futilities of David's marriage with Dora, the disappointment still seems to have troubled him and Maria to have remained at the back of his mind as the Ideal of which he had been cheated.

He lost very little time, however, in getting himself a wife. Two years after his rejection by Maria Beadnell, he was engaged to the daughter of George Hogarth, a Scotchman, who, as the law agent of Walter Scott and from having been mentioned in the *Noctes Ambrosianae*, was invested with the prestige of having figured on the fringes of the Edinburgh literary world. He asked Dickens to write for the newspaper which he was editing at that time in London, and invited the young man to his house. There Dickens found two attractive daughters, and he married the elder, Catherine, who was twenty. But the other daughter, Mary, though too young for him to marry—she was only fifteen when he met her—had a strange hold on Dickens' emotions. When, after living with the Dickenses for a year after their marriage, she suddenly died in Dickens' arms, he was so overcome by grief that he stopped writing *Pickwick* for two months and insisted in an obsessed and morbid way on his desire to be buried beside her: 'I can't think there ever was love like I bear her. . . . I have never had her ring off my finger day or night, except for an instant at a time, to wash my hands, since she died. I have never had her sweetness and excellence absent from my mind so long.' In *The Old Curiosity Shop*, he apotheosized her as Little Nell. What basis this emotion may have had in the fashionable romanticism of the period or in some peculiar psychological pattern of Dickens', it is impossible on the evidence to say. But this passion for an innocent young girl is to recur in Dickens' life; and in the meantime his feeling for Mary Hogarth seems to indicate pretty clearly that even during the early years of his marriage he did not identify the Ideal with Catherine.

Catherine had big blue eyes, a rather receding chin and a sleepy and languorous look. Beyond this, it is rather difficult to get a definite impression of her. Dickens' terrible gallery of shrews who browbeat their amiable husbands suggests that she may have been a scold; but surely Dickens himself was no Joe Gargery or Gabriel Varden. We do not know much about Dickens' marriage. We know that, with the exception of his sister-in-law Georgina, Dickens grew to loathe the Hogarths, who evidently lived on him to a considerable extent; and we must assume that poor Catherine, in both intellect and energy, was a good deal inferior to her husband. He lived with her, however, twenty years, and, although it becomes clear toward the end that they were no longer particularly welcome, he gave her during that time ten children.

And if Dickens was lonely in his household, he was lonely in society, also. He had, as Forster indicates, attained a pinnacle of affluence and fame which made him one of the most admired and most sought-after persons in Europe without his really ever having created for himself a social position in England, that society *par excellence* where everybody had to have a definite one and where there was no rank reserved for the artist. He had gone straight, at the very first throw, from the poor tenement, the prison, the press table, to a position of imperial supremacy over the imaginations of practically the whole literate world; but in his personal associations, he cultivated the companionship of inferiors rather than—save, perhaps, for Carlyle—of intellectual equals. His behavior toward Society, in the capitalized sense, was rebarbative to the verge of truculence; he refused to learn its patter and its manners; and his satire on the fashionable world comes to figure more and more prominently in his novels. Dickens is one of the very small group of British intellectuals to whom the opportunity has been offered to be taken up by the governing class and who have actually declined that honor.

His attitude—which in the period we have been discussing was still that of the middle-class 'Radical' opposing feudal precedent and privilege: Mr. Rouncewell, the ironmaster, backed against Sir Leicester Dedlock—is illustrated by the curious story of his relations with Queen Victoria. In 1857, Dickens got up a benefit for the family of Douglas Jerrold, in which he and his daughters acted. The Queen was asked to be one of the sponsors; and, since she was obliged to refuse any such request for fear of being obliged to grant them all, she invited Dickens to put on the play at the palace. He replied that he 'did not feel easy as to the social position of my daughters, etc., at a Court under those circumstances,' and suggested that the Queen might attend a performance which should be given for her alone. She accepted, and sent backstage between the acts asking Dickens to come and speak to her. 'I replied that I was in my Farce dress, and must beg to be excused. Whereupon she sent again, saying that the dress "could not be so ridiculous as that," and repeating the request. I sent my duty in reply, but again hoped Her Majesty would have the kindness to excuse my presenting myself in a costume and appearance that were not my own. I was mighty glad to think, when I woke this morning, that I had carried the point.' The next year he was approached on behalf of the Queen, who wanted to hear him read the *Christmas Carol*; but he expressed his 'hope that she would indulge me by making one of some audience or other—for I thought an audience necessary to the effect.' It was only in the last year of his life—and then only on what seems to have been the pretext on the Queen's part that she wanted to look at some photographs of the battlefields of the Civil War which Dickens had brought back from America—that an interview was finally arranged. Here the record of Dickens' lecture manager, George Dolby, supplements the account given by Forster. Dickens told Dolby that 'Her Majesty had received him most graciously, and that, as Court etiquette requires that no one, in an ordinary interview with the sovereign, should be seated, Her Majesty had remained the whole time leaning over the head of a sofa. There was a little shyness on both sides at the commencement, but this wore away as the conversation proceeded.' When Victoria regretted that it had not been possible for her ever to hear Dickens read, he replied that he had made his farewell to the platform; when she said that she understood this, but intimated that it would be gracious on Dickens' part so far to forget his resolve as to give her the pleasure of hearing him, he insisted that this would be impossible. Not impossible, perhaps, said the Queen, but inconsistent, no doubt —and she knew that he was the most consistent of men. Yet they parted on very good terms: she invited him to her next levee and his daughter to the drawing-room that followed. If there is some stickling for his dignity on Dickens' part here, there is evidently also some scruple on the Queen's.

To be caught between two social classes in a society of strict stratifications—like being caught between two civilizations, as James was, or between two racial groups, like Proust—is an excellent thing for a novelist from the point of view of his art, because it enables him to dramatize contrasts and to study interrelations which the dweller in one world cannot know. Perhaps something of the sort was true even of Shakespeare, between the provincial bourgeoisie and the Court. Dostoevsky, who had a good deal in common with Dickens and whose career somewhat parallels his, is a conspicuous example of a writer who owes his dramatic scope at least partly to a social maladjustment. The elder Dostoevsky was a doctor and his family origins were obscure, so that his social position was poor in a Russia still predominantly feudal; yet he bought a country estate and sent his sons to a school for the children of the nobility. But the family went to pieces after the mother's death: the father took to drink and was murdered by his serfs for his cruelty. Dostoevsky was left with almost nothing, and he slipped down into that foul and stagnant underworld of the Raskólnikovs and Stavrógins of his novels. Dickens' case had been equally anomalous: he had grown up in an uncomfortable position between the upper and the lower middle classes, with a dip into the proletariat and a glimpse of the aristocracy through their trusted upper servants. But this position, which had been useful to him as a writer, was to leave him rather isolated in English society. In a sense, there was no place for him to go and belong; he had to have people come to him.

And in the long run all that he had achieved could not make up for what he lacked. *Little Dorrit* and *Great Expectations* (1860–61), which follows it after *A Tale of Two Cities*, are full of the disillusion and discomfort of this period of Dickens' life. The treatment of social situations and the treatment of individual psychology have both taken turns distinctly new.

Dickens now tackles the Marshalsea again, but on a larger scale and in a more serious way. It is as if he were determined once for all to get the prison out of his system. The figure of his father hitherto has always haunted Dickens' novels, but he has never known quite how to handle it. In Micawber, he made him comic and lovable; in Skimpole, he made him comic and unpleasant—for, after all, the vagaries of Micawber always left somebody out of pocket, and there is another aspect of Micawber—the Skimpole aspect he presented to his creditors. But what kind of person, really, had John Dickens been in himself? How had the father of Charles Dickens come to be what he was? Even after it had become possible for Charles to provide for his father, the old man continued to be a problem up to his death in 1851. He got himself arrested again, as the result of running up a wine bill; and he would try to get money out of his son's publishers without the knowledge of Charles. Yet Dickens said to Forster, after his father's death: 'The longer I live, the better man I think him'; and *Little Dorrit* is something in the nature of a justification of John.

Mr. Dorrit is 'a very amiable and very helpless middle-aged gentleman . . . a shy, retiring man, well-looking, though in an effeminate style, with a mild voice, curling hair, and irresolute hands—rings upon the fingers in those days—which nervously wandered to his trembling lip a hundred times in the first half-hour of his acquaintance with the jail.' The arrival of the Dorrit family in prison and their gradual habituation to it are done with a restraint and sobriety never displayed by Dickens up to now. The incident in which Mr. Dorrit, after getting

used to accepting tips in his rôle of the Father of the Marshalsea, suddenly becomes insulted when he is offered copper
half-pence by a workman, has a delicacy which makes up in
these later books for the ebb of Dickens' bursting exuberance.
If it is complained that the comic characters in these novels,
the specifically 'Dickens characters,' are sometimes mechanical
and boring, this is partly, perhaps, for the reason that they stick
out in an unnatural relief from a surface that is more quietly
realistic. And there are moments when one feels that Dickens
might be willing to abandon the 'Dickens character' altogether if it were not what the public expected of him. In any
case, the story of Dorrit is a closer and more thoughtful study
than any that has gone before of what bad institutions make of
men.

But there is also in *Little Dorrit* something different from
social criticism. Dickens is no longer satisfied to anatomize the
organism of society. The main symbol here is the prison (in
this connection, Mr. Jackson's chapter is the best thing that
has been written on *Little Dorrit*); but this symbol is developed in a way that takes it beyond the satirical application of
the symbol of the fog in *Bleak House* and gives it a significance
more subjective. In the opening chapter, we are introduced,
not to the debtors' prison, but to an ordinary jail for criminals,
which, in the case of Rigaud and Cavalletto, will not make the
bad man any better or the good man any worse. A little later,
we are shown an English business man who has come back
from many years in China and who finds himself in a London
—the shut-up London of Sunday evening—more frightening,
because more oppressive, than the thieves' London of *Oliver
Twist*. '"Heaven forgive me," said he, "and those who trained
me. How I have hated this day!" There was the dreary Sunday
of his childhood, when he sat with his hands before him,
scared out of his senses by a horrible tract which commenced
business with the poor child by asking him, in its title, why he
was going to Perdition?' At last he gets himself to the point of
going to see his mother, whom he finds as lacking in affection
and as gloomy as he could have expected. She lives in a dark
and funereal house with the old offices on the bottom floor,
one of the strongholds of that harsh Calvinism plus hard business which made one of the mainstays of the Victorian Age;

she lies paralyzed on 'a black bier-like sofa,' punishing herself and everyone else for some guilt of which he cannot discover the nature. The Clennam house is a jail, and they are in prison, too. So are the people in Bleeding Heart Yard, small tenement-dwelling shopkeepers and artisans, rack-rented by the patriarchal Casby; so is Merdle, the great swindler-financier, imprisoned, like Kreuger or Insull, in the vast scaffolding of fraud he has contrived, who wanders about in his expensive house—itself, for all its crimson and gold, as suffocating and dark as the Clennams'—afraid of his servants, unloved by his wife, almost unknown by his guests, till on the eve of the collapse of the edifice he quietly opens his veins in his bath.

At last, after twenty-five years of jail, Mr. Dorrit inherits a fortune and is able to get out of the Marshalsea. He is rich enough to go into Society; but all the Dorrits, with the exception of the youngest, known as 'Little Dorrit,' who has been born in the Marshalsea itself and has never made any pretensions, have been demoralized or distorted by the effort to remain genteel while tied to the ignominy of the prison. They cannot behave like the people outside. And yet that outside world is itself insecure. It is dominated by Mr. Merdle, who comes, as the story goes on, to be universally believed and admired—is taken up by the governing class, sent to Parliament, courted by lords. The Dorrits, accepted by Society, still find themselves in prison. The moral is driven home when old Dorrit, at a fashionable dinner, loses control of his wits and slips back into his character at the Marshalsea: '"Born here," he repeated, shedding tears. "Bred here. Ladies and gentlemen, my daughter. Child of an unfortunate father, but—ha—always a gentleman. Poor, no doubt, but—hum—proud."' He asks the company for 'Testimonials,' which had been what he had used to call his tips. (Dr. Manette, in *A Tale of Two Cities*, repeats this pattern with his amnesic relapses into the shoe-making he has learned in prison.) Arthur Clennam, ruined by the failure of Merdle, finally goes to the Marshalsea himself; and there at last he and Little Dorrit arrive at an understanding. The implication is that, prison for prison, a simple incarceration is an excellent school of character compared to the dungeons of Puritan theology, of modern business, of money-ruled Society, or of the poor people of Bleeding Heart Yard who are swindled and bled by all of these.

The whole book is much gloomier than *Bleak House*, where the fog is external to the characters and represents something removable, the obfuscatory elements of the past. The murk of *Little Dorrit* permeates the souls of the people, and we see more of their souls than in *Bleak House*. Arthur Clennam, with his broodings on his unloving mother, who turns out not to be his real mother (a poor doomed child of natural impulse, like Lady Dedlock's lover), is both more real and more depressing than Lady Dedlock. Old Dorrit has been spoiled beyond repair: he can never be rehabilitated like Micawber. There is not even a villain like Tulkinghorn to throw the odium on a predatory class: the official villain Blandois has no organic connection with the story save as a caricature of social pretense. (Though the illustrations suggest that he may have been intended as a sort of cartoon of Napoleon III, whose régime Dickens loathed—in which case the tie-up between Blandois and the Clennams may figure a close relationship between the shady financial interests disguised by the flashy façade of the Second Empire and the respectable business interests of British merchants, so inhuman behind their mask of morality. Blandois is crushed in the end by the collapse of the Clennams' house, as people were already predicting that Napoleon would be by that of his own.) The rôle of the Court of Chancery is more or less played by the Circumlocution Office and the governing-class family of Barnacles—perhaps the most brilliant thing of its kind in Dickens: that great satire on all aristocratic bureaucracies, and indeed on all bureaucracies, with its repertoire of the variations possible within the bureaucratic type and its desolating picture of the emotions of a man being passed on from one door to another. But the Circumlocution Office, after all, only influences the action in a negative way.

The important thing to note in *Little Dorrit*—which was originally to have been called *Nobody's Fault*—is that the fable is here presented from the point of view of imprisoning states of mind as much as from that of oppressive institutions. This is illustrated in a startling way by *The History of a Self-Tormentor*, which we find toward the end of the book. Here Dickens, with a remarkable pre-Freudian insight, gives a sort of case history of a woman imprisoned in a neurosis which has condemned her to the delusion that she can never be loved. There is still, to be sure, the social implication that her orphaned childhood and her sense of being slighted have been imposed on her by the Victorian attitude toward her illegitimate birth. But her handicap is now simply a thought-pattern, and from that thought-pattern she is never to be liberated.

Dickens' personal difficulties make themselves felt like an ache at the back of *Little Dorrit*—in which he represents his hero as reflecting: 'Who has not thought for a moment, sometimes?—that it might be better to flow away monotonously, like the river, and to compound for its insensibility to happiness with its insensibility to pain.' The strain of his situation with his wife had become particularly acute the year that the book was begun. Dickens had been very much excited that February to get a letter from Maria Beadnell, now married. The readiness and warmth of his response shows how the old Ideal had lighted up again. He was on the point of leaving for Paris, and during his absence he looked forward eagerly to seeing her: he arranged to meet her alone. The drop in the tone of his letters after this meeting has taken place is blighting to poor Mrs. Winter. He had found her banal and silly, with the good looks of her girlhood gone. He put her into his new novel as Flora Finching, a sort of Dora Spenlow vulgarized and transmogrified into a kind of Mrs. Nickleby—that is, into another version of Dickens' unforgiven mother. It seems clear that the type of woman that Dickens is chiefly glorifying during the years from *Martin Chuzzlewit* through *Little Dorrit*: the devoted and self-effacing little mouse, who hardly aspires to be loved, derives from Georgina Hogarth, his sister-in-law. Georgina, who had been eight when Dickens was married, had come to womanhood in the Dickens household. Dickens grew fond of her, explaining that his affection was due partly to her resemblance to her dead sister. She gradually took over the care of the children, whom Dickens complained of their mother's neglecting; and became the real head of the household— creating a situation which is reflected in these heroines of the novels. The virtues of Ruth Pinch are brought out mainly through her relation to her brother Tom; Esther Summerson, who keeps house for Mr. Jarndyce but does not suspect that he wants to marry her, is suspended through most of *Bleak House* in a relation to him that is semi-filial; Little Dorrit is shown throughout in a sisterly and filial relation, and Arthur Clennam, before he figures as a lover, plays simply, like Mr. Jarndyce, the rôle of a protective and elderly friend. In the love of Little Dorrit and Clennam, there seems to be little passion, but a sobriety of resignation, almost a note of sadness: they 'went down,' Dickens says at the end, 'into a modest life of usefulness and happiness,' one of the objects of which was to be 'to give a mother's care . . . to Fanny's [her sister's] neglected children no less than to their own.'

These children of Dickens'—he now had nine—were evidently giving him anxiety. He used to grumble about their lack of enterprise; and it would appear from Mrs. Perugini's story, which trails off in a depressing record of their failures and follies and untimely deaths, that in general they did not turn out well. The ill-bred daughter and worthless son of Dorrit probably caricature Dickens' fears. Surely the Dorrits' travels on the Continent caricature the progress of the Dickenses. Old Dorrit's rise in the world is no rescue at the end of a fairy tale, as it would have been in one of the early novels. The point of the story is that this rise can be only a mockery: the Dorrits will always be what the Marshalsea has made them.

The theme of *Little Dorrit* is repeated in *Great Expectations* (1860–61). This second of Dickens' novels in which the hero tells his own story is like an attempt to fill in some of the things that have been left out of *David Copperfield*. The story is the reverse of the earlier one. David was a gentleman by birth, who by accident became a wage slave. Pip is a boy out of the blacksmith's shop, who by accident gets a chance to become a gentleman. He straightway turns into a mean little snob.

The formula of *Bleak House* is repeated, too. The solution of the puzzle is again Dickens' moral, here more bitterly, even hatefully, delivered. Pip owes his mysterious income to the convict whom in his childhood, he befriended on the marshes. Abel Magwitch himself had been a wretched tinker's boy, who had 'first become aware of [himself] a-thieving turnips for a living.' Later he had been exploited by a gentlemanly rotter turned crook, who had left Magwitch to take the rap when they had both fallen into the hands of the law. The poor rascal had been impressed by the advantage that his companion's social status—he had been to the public school—had given him in the eyes of the court; and when Magwitch later prospered in New South Wales, he decided to make a gentleman of Pip. Thus Pip finds himself in a position very similar to Lady Dedlock's: the money that chains him to Magwitch will not merely associate him with a poverty and ignorance more abject than that from which he has escaped, but will put him under obligations to an individual who represents to him the dregs of the underworld, a man with a price on his head. Not only this; but the proud lady here—who has known Pip in his first phase and scorns him because she thinks him a common village boy—turns out to be the daughter of Magwitch and of a woman who has been tried for murder and who is now employed in the humble capacity of housekeeper by the lawyer who got her off.

The symbol here is the 'great expectations' which both Pip and Estella entertain: they figure (Mr. T. A. Jackson has here again put his finger on the point) the Victorian mid-century optimism. Estella and Pip have both believed that they could count upon a wealthy patroness, the heiress of a now disused brewery, to make them secure against vulgarity and hardship. But the patroness vanishes like a phantom, and they are left with their leisure-class habits and no incomes to keep them up. They were originally to lose one another, too: the tragedies in Dickens' novels are coming more and more to seem irremediable. Estella was to marry for his money a brutal country squire, and Pip was never to see her again except for one brief meeting in London. Here is the last sentence of the ending that Dickens first wrote: 'I was very glad afterwards to have had the interview; for, in her face, and in her voice, and in her touch, she gave me the assurance that suffering had been stronger than Miss Havisham's teaching, and had given her a heart to understand what my heart used to be.'

This was to have been all, and it was perfect in tone and touch. But Bulwer Lytton made Dickens change it to the ending we now have, in which Estella's husband gets killed and Pip and she are united. Dickens was still a public entertainer who felt that he couldn't too far disappoint his audience.

In *Little Dorrit* and *Great Expectations*, there is, therefore, a great deal more psychological interest than in Dickens' previous books. We are told what the characters think and feel, and even something about how they change. And here we must enter into the central question of the psychology of Dickens' characters.

The world of the early Dickens is organized according to a dualism which is based—in its artistic derivation—on the values of melodrama: there are bad people and there are good people, there are comics and there are characters played straight. The only complexity of which Dickens is capable is to make one of his noxious characters become wholesome, one of his clowns turn into a serious person. The most conspicuous example of this process is the reform of Mr. Dombey, who, as Taine says, 'turns into the best of fathers and spoils a fine novel.' But the reform of Scrooge in *A Christmas Carol* shows the phenomenon in its purest form.

We have come to take Scrooge so much for granted that he seems practically a piece of Christmas folklore; we no more inquire seriously into the mechanics of his transformation than we do into the transformation of the Beast in the fairy tale into the young prince that marries Beauty. Yet Scrooge represents a principle fundamental to the dynamics of Dickens' world and derived from his own emotional constitution. It was not merely that his passion for the theater had given him a taste for melodramatic contrasts; it was rather that the lack of balance between the opposite impulses of his nature had stimulated an appetite for melodrama. For emotionally Dickens *was* unstable. Allowing for the English restraint, which masks what the Russian expressiveness indulges and perhaps over-expresses, and for the pretenses of English biographers, he seems almost as unstable as Dostoevsky. He was capable of great hardness and cruelty, and not merely toward those whom he had cause to resent: people who patronized or intruded on him. On one occasion, in the presence of other guests, he ordered Forster out of his house over some discussion that had arisen at dinner;

he was certainly not gentle with Maria Winter; and his treatment of Catherine suggests, as we shall see, the behavior of a Renaissance monarch summarily consigning to a convent the wife who has served her turn. There is more of emotional reality behind Quilp in *The Old Curiosity Shop* than there is behind Little Nell. If Little Nell sounds bathetic today, Quilp has lost none of his fascination. He is ugly, malevolent, perverse; he delights in making mischief for its own sake; yet he exercises over the members of his household a power which is almost an attraction and which resembles what was known in Dickens' day as 'malicious animal magnetism.' Though Quilp is ceaselessly tormenting his wife and browbeating the boy who works for him, they never attempt to escape: they admire him; in a sense they love him.

So Dickens' daughter, Kate Perugini, who had destroyed a memoir of her father that she had written, because it gave 'only half the truth,' told Miss Gladys Storey, the author of *Dickens and Daughter*, that the spell which Dickens had been able to cast on his daughters was so strong that, after he and their mother had separated, they had refrained from going to see her, though he never spoke to them about it, because they knew that he did not like it, and would even take music lessons in a house just opposite the one where she was living without daring to pay her a call. 'I loved my father,' said Mrs. Perugini, 'better than any man in the world—in a different way of course. . . . I loved him for his faults.' And she added, as she rose and walked to the door: 'my father was a wicked man—a very wicked man.' But from the memoirs of his other daughter Mamie, who also adored her father and seems to have viewed him uncritically, we hear of his colossal Christmas parties, of the vitality, the imaginative exhilaration, which swept all the guests along. It is Scrooge bursting in on the Cratchits. Shall we ask what Scrooge would actually be like if we were to follow him beyond the frame of the story? Unquestionably he would relapse when the merriment was over—if not while it was still going on—into moroseness, vindictiveness, suspicion. He would, that is to say, reveal himself as the victim of a manic-depressive cycle, and a very uncomfortable person.

This dualism runs all through Dickens. There has always to be a good and a bad of everything: each of the books has its counterbalancing values, and pairs of characters sometimes counterbalance each other from the casts of different books. There has to be a good manufacturer, Mr. Rouncewell, and a bad manufacturer, Mr. Bounderby; a bad old Jew, Fagin, and a good old Jew, Riah; an affable lawyer who is really unscrupulous, Vholes, and a kindly lawyer who pretends to be unfeeling, Jaggers; a malicious dwarf, Quilp, and a beneficent dwarf, Miss Mowcher (though Dickens had originally intended her to be bad); an embittered and perverse illegitimate daughter, Miss Wade, the Self-Tormentor, and a sweet and submissive illegitimate daughter, Esther Summerson. Another example of this tendency is Dickens' habit, noted by Mr. Kingsmill, of making the comic side of his novels a kind of parody on the sentimental side. Pecksniff is a satire on that domestic sentiment which wells up so profusely in Dickens himself when it is a question of a story for the Christmas trade; the performances of the Vincent Crummleses provide a burlesque of the stagy plot upon which *Nicholas Nickleby* is based.

Dickens' difficulty in his middle period, and indeed more or less to the end, is to get good and bad together in one character. He had intended in *Dombey and Son* to make Walter Gay turn out badly, but hadn't been able to bring himself to put it through. In *Bleak House*, however, he had had Richard Carstone undergo a progressive demoralization. But the real beginnings of a psychological interest may be said to appear in *Hard Times*, which, though parts of it have the crudity of a cartoon, is the first novel in which Dickens tries to trace with any degree of plausibility the processes by which people become what they are. We are given a certain sympathetic insight into what has happened to the Gradgrind children; and the conversion of Mr. Gradgrind is very much better prepared for than that of Mr. Dombey. In *Great Expectations* we see Pip pass through a whole psychological cycle. At first, he is sympathetic, then by a more or less natural process he turns into something unsympathetic, then he becomes sympathetic again. Here the effects of both poverty and riches are seen from the inside in one person. This is for Dickens a great advance; and it is a development which, if carried far enough, would end by eliminating the familiar Dickens of the lively but limited stage characters, with their tag lines and their unvarying make-ups.

The crisis of Dickens' later life had already come before *Great Expectations.* That 'old unhappy loss or want of something' which he makes David Copperfield feel after his marriage to Dora had driven him into a dream of retreating to the monastery of the Great St. Bernard, where it had been his original idea to have the whole of *Little Dorrit* take place. But he had ended by resorting to another order which, in mimicking the life of men, may remain almost as impenetrably cut off from it as the monks of the St. Bernard themselves. Dickens embarked upon a series of theatricals, which, though undertaken originally as benefits, took on a semi-professional character and came to look more and more like pretexts for Dickens to indulge his appetite for acting.

He had written Forster of 'the so happy and yet so unhappy existence which seeks its realities in unrealities, and finds its dangerous comfort in a perpetual escape from the disappointment of heart around it.' But now the pressure of this disappointment was to drive him into a deeper addiction to that dangerous comfort of unrealities. It was as if he had actually to embody, to act out in his own person, the life of his imagination. He had always loved acting: as a child, he had projected himself with intensity into the characters of the plays he had seen. He had always loved amateur theatricals and charades. He used to say that it relieved him, if only in a game, to throw himself into the personality of someone else. His whole art had been a kind of impersonation, in which he had exploited this or that of his impulses by incorporating it in an imaginary person rather than—up to this point, at any rate—exploring his own personality. The endings of his early novels, in which the villain was smashingly confounded and the young juvenile got the leading woman, had been the conventional dénouements of Drury Lane. Whole scenes of *Barnaby Rudge* had been highflown declamations in a blank verse which connects Dickens almost as closely with the dramatic tradition of Shakespeare as with the fictional tradition of Fielding. Dickens admitted that he found it difficult, whenever he became particularly serious, to refrain from falling into blank verse; and though his prose, like everything else in his art, underwent a remarkable development, tightening up and becoming cleaner, he never quite got rid of this tendency. The scene in which Edith Dombey turns upon and unmasks Mr. Carker, with its doors arranged for exits and entrances, its suspense engineered through the presence of the servants, its set speeches, its highfalutin language, its hair-raising reversal of rôles, its interruption at the climactic moment by the sudden sound of the bell that announces the outraged husband—this scene, which is one of the worst in Dickens, must be one of the passages in fiction most completely conceived in terms of the stage. In *Bleak House*, he is still theatrical, but he has found out how to make this instinct contribute to the effectiveness of a novel: the theatrical present tense of the episodes which alternate with Esther Summerson's diary does heighten the excitement of the narrative, and the theatrical Lady Dedlock is an improvement on Edith Dombey. Yet in the novels that follow *Bleak House*, this theatricalism recurs as something never either quite eliminated from or quite assimilated by Dickens' more serious art, an element which remains unreal if it is not precisely insincere and on which his stories sometimes run aground. Later, when he was giving his public readings, he wrote a whole series of stories—*Somebody's Luggage, Mrs. Lirriper, Doctor Marigold*— which were primarily designed for public performance and in which excellent character monologues lead up to silly little episodes in the bad sentimental taste of the period which Dickens had done so much to popularize. Dickens had a strain of the ham in him, and, in the desperation of his later life, he gave in to the old ham and let him rip.

That this satisfied the deeper needs of Dickens as little as it does those of his readers seems to be proved by what followed. He met behind the scenes of the theater sometime in '57 or '58 a young girl named Ellen Ternan, the daughter of a well-known actress. When Dickens first saw her, she was hiding behind one of the properties and crying because she had to go on in a costume that offended her sense of modesty. Dickens reassured her. She was eighteen, and she evidently appealed to that compassionate interest in young women which had made him apotheosize Mary Hogarth. He saw her again and became infatuated. He had been complaining to Forster that 'a sense comes always crashing on me now, when I fall into low spirits, as of one happiness I have missed in life, and one friend and companion I have never made'; and it must have seemed to him that now he had found her.

He had made an agreement with Catherine in the early days of their marriage that if either should fall in love with anyone else, he should frankly explain to the other. He now told her that he was in love with Miss Ternan and compelled her to call on the girl. Dickens conducted the whole affair with what appears to us the worst possible taste, though I shall show in a moment that there were special reasons why his behavior seemed natural to him. He arranged to have Ellen Ternan take part in his benefit performances, and, whether by design or not, gave her rôles which ran close enough to the real situation to offend Mrs. Dickens. Mr. Wright, who first made this whole episode public in 1934, believes, probably rightly, that Sydney Carton is Dickens' dramatization of the first hopeless phase of his love. In the spring of '58, however, Dickens arranged a separation from Catherine and left her with one of their sons in London while he removed with the rest of the children and Georgina to the new place he had bought at Gadshill. He published a statement in *Household Words* and circulated a singular letter which was not long in getting into print, in which he explained that he and Catherine had nothing whatever in common and should never have got married; defended, without naming her, Ellen Ternan; and denounced, without naming them, as 'two wicked persons' his mother-in-law and his sister-in-law Helen for having intimated that there could be 'on this earth a more virtuous and spotless creature' than Ellen. It was true that he and Ellen had not been lovers; but he now induced Ellen to be his mistress and set her up in an establishment of her own. He wrote her name into his last three novels as Estella Provis, Bella Wilfer, and finally Helena Landless— her full name was Ellen Lawless Ternan.

In order to understand what is likely to seem to us on Dickens' part a strange and disagreeable exhibitionism, we must remember his relation to his public. Perhaps no other kind of writer depends so much on his audience as the novelist. If the novelist is extremely popular, he may even substitute his relation to his public for the ordinary human relations. And for this reason he responds to his sales in a way which may seem ridiculous to a writer in a different field; yet to the novelist the rise or the drop in the number of the people who buy his books may be felt in very much the same way as the coolness or the passion of a loved one. In Dickens' case, a falling-off in the popularity of his monthly instalments would plunge him into anxiety and depression. He had played up Sam Weller in *Pickwick* because he saw that the character was going well, and he sent Martin Chuzzlewit to America because he found that interest in the story was flagging. And now it had come to be true in a sense that his only companion in his fictional world was the public who saw him act and read his novels. When he began, as he did that same spring, to give regular public readings—which enabled him to live these novels, as it were, in his own person, and to feel the direct impact on his audience—the relation became more intimate still. For Dickens, the public he addressed in this statement about his marriage was probably closer than the wife by whom he had had ten children; and now that he had fallen in love with Ellen, instead of finding in her a real escape from the eternal masquerade of his fiction, his first impulse was to transport her to dwell with him in that imaginary world itself, to make her a character in a novel or play, and to pay court to her in the presence of his public.

But the old sense of 'loss or want' does not seem to have been cured by all this. 'My father was like a madman,' says Mrs. Perugini, 'when my mother left home. This affair brought out all that was worst—all that was weakest in him. He did not care a damn what happened to any of us. Nothing could surpass the misery and unhappiness of our home.' And this misery still hung over the household, in spite of Dickens' festive hospitality, even after the separation had been arranged. Poor Mrs. Dickens in her exile was wretched—'Do you think he is sorry for me?' she asked Kate on one of the only two occasions when she ever heard her mother mention her father—and there was always at the back of their consciousness this sense of something deeply wrong. Kate Dickens, with more independence than Mamie, does not seem much to have liked having Miss Ternan come to Gadshill; and she finally married a brother of Wilkie Collins, without really caring about him, in order to get away from home. After the wedding, which Mrs. Dickens had not attended, Mamie found her father weeping in

Kate's bedroom, with his face in her wedding dress: 'But for me,' he said to her, 'Katy would not have left home.'

This episode of Ellen Ternan has been hushed up so systematically, and the information about it is still so meager, that it is difficult to get an impression of Ellen. We do, how-ever, know something about what Dickens thought of her from the heroines in his last books who are derived from her. Estella is frigid and indifferent: it amuses her to torture Pip, who loves her 'against reason, against promise, against peace, against hope, against happiness, against all discouragement that could be'; she marries a man she does not love for his money. Bella Wilfer up to her conversion by Mr. Boffin is equally intent upon money—which was certainly one of the things that Ellen got out of her liaison with Dickens. Both Estella and Bella are petulant, spoiled and proud. They represent, as it were, the qualities of the Edith Dombey-Lady Dedlock great lady com-bined with the capriciousness of Dora Spenlow—the old ele-ments of Dickens' women simply mixed in a new way. And these novels of Dickens in which Ellen figures show perhaps more real desperation than *Little Dorrit* itself, with its closing note of modest resignation. It seems to be the general opinion that Ellen was neither so fascinating nor so gifted as Dickens thought her. After his death, she married a clergyman, and she confided to Canon Benham that she had loathed her relation-ship with Dickens and deeply regretted the whole affair. She had borne Dickens a child, which did not live. It may be—though we have no date—that Dickens' short story, *Doctor Marigold* (1865), which became one of his favorite readings, the monologue of a traveling 'cheap jack,' who keeps an audi-ence entertained with his patter while his child is dying in his arms, is a reflection of this event.

In spite of the energy of a *diable au corps* which enabled him to put on his plays and to perform prodigies of walking and mountain-climbing at the same time that he was composing his complicated novels, the creative strain of a lifetime was beginning to tell heavily on Dickens. He had always felt under an obligation to maintain a standard of living conspicuously lavish for a literary man: in his statement about his separation from his wife, he boasts that he has provided for her as gener-ously 'as if Mrs. Dickens were a lady of distinction and I a man of fortune.' And now he was compelled both by the demon that drove him and by the necessity of earning money in order to keep up the three establishments for which he had made himself responsible and to launch his sons and daughters on the world, to work frantically at his public readings. His nervous disorders persisted: he was troubled while he was writing *Great Expectations* with acute pains in the face; and he developed a lameness in his left foot, which, though he blamed it on taking walks in heavy snowstorms, was also evidently due to the burning-out of his nerves. He was maimed by it all the rest of his life. 'Twice last week,' he writes in '66, 'I was seized in a most distressing manner apparently in the heart; but, I am persuaded, only in the nervous system.'

Three years had passed since *Great Expectations* before Dickens began another novel; he worked at it with what was for him extreme slowness, hesitation and difficulty; and the book shows the weariness, the fears and the definitive disappointments of this period.

This story, *Our Mutual Friend* (1864–65), like all these later books of Dickens, is more interesting to us today than it was to Dickens' public. It is a next number in the Dickens sequence quite worthy of its predecessors, a development out of what has gone before that is in certain ways quite different from the others. It may be said Dickens never really repeats himself: his thought makes a consistent progress, and his art, through the whole thirty-five years of his career, keeps going on to new materials and effects; so that his work has an interest and a meaning as a whole. The difficulty that Dickens found in writing *Our Mutual Friend* does not make itself felt as anything in the nature of an intellectual disintegration. On the contrary, the book compensates for its shortcomings by the display of an intellectual force which, though present in Dickens' work from the first, here appears in a phase of high tension and a condition of fine muscular training. The Dickens of the old eccentric 'Dickens characters' has here, as has often been noted, become pretty mechanical and sterile. It is a pity that the creator of Quilp and of Mrs. Jarley's waxworks should have felt himself under the necessity of fabricating Silas Wegg and the stuffed animals of Mr. Venus. Also, the complex Dickens plot has come to seem rather tiresome and childish. But Dickens has here distilled the mood of his later years, dramatized the tragic discrepancies of his character, delivered his final judgment on the whole Victorian exploit, in a fashion so impressive that we realize how little the distractions of this period had the power to direct him from the prime purpose of his life: the serious exercise of his art.

As the fog is the symbol for *Bleak House* and the prison for *Little Dorrit*, so the dust-pile is the symbol for *Our Mutual Friend*. It dominates even the landscape of London, which has already been presented by Dickens under such a variety of aspects, but which now appears—though with Newgate looming over it as it did in *Barnaby Rudge*—under an aspect that is new: 'A gray dusty withered evening in London city has not a hopeful aspect,' he writes of the day when Bradley Headstone goes to pay his hopeless court to Lizzie Hexam. 'The closed warehouses and offices have an air of death about them, and the national dread of color has an air of mourning. The towers and steeples of the many house-encompassed churches, dark and dingy as the sky that seems descending on them, are no relief to the general gloom; a sun-dial on a church-wall has the look, in its useless black shade, of having failed in its business enterprise and stopped payment for ever; melancholy waifs and strays of housekeepers and porters sweep melancholy waifs and strays of papers and pins into the kennels, and other more melancholy waifs and strays explore them, searching and stooping and poking for everything to sell. The set of humanity outward from the City is as a set of prisoners departing from gaol, and dismal Newgate seems quite as fit a stronghold for the mighty Lord Mayor as his own state-dwelling.'

The actual dust-pile in question has been amassed by a dust-removal contractor, who has made out of it a considerable fortune. The collection of refuse at that time was still in private hands, and was profitable because the bones, rags and cinders, and even the dust itself, were valuable for various kinds of manufacture. The plot of *Our Mutual Friend* has to do with the struggle of a number of persons to get possession of or some share in this money. (The other principal industry which figures in *Our Mutual Friend* is the robbing of the dead bodies in the Thames.) But the real meaning of the dust-pile is not in doubt: 'My lords and gentlemen and honorable lords,' writes Dickens, when the heap is being carted away, 'when you in the course of your dust-shoveling and cinder-raking have piled up a mountain of pretentious failure, you must off with your honorable coats for the removal of it, and fall to the work with the power of all the queen's horses and all the queen's men, or it will come rushing down and bury us alive.'

Dickens' line in his criticism of society is very clear in *Our Mutual Friend*, and it marks a new position on Dickens' part, as it results from a later phase of the century. Dickens has come at last to despair utterly of the prospering middle class. We have seen how he judged the morality of the merchants. In *Bleak House*, the ironmaster is a progressive and self-sustaining figure who is played off against parasites of various sorts; but in *Hard Times*, written immediately afterward, the later development of Rouncewell is dramatized in the exploiter Bounderby, a new kind of Victorian hypocrite, who pretends to be a self-made man. In *Little Dorrit*, the one set of characters who are comparatively healthy and cheerful still represent that middle-class home which has remained Dickens' touchstone of virtue; but even here there is a distinct change in Dickens' attitude. Mr. Meagles, the retired banker, with his wife and his beloved only daughter, become the prey of Henry Gowan, a well-connected young man of no fortune who manages to lead a futile life (the type has been well observed) between the social and artistic worlds without ever making anything of either. But the smugness and insularity, even the vulgarity, of the Meagleses is felt by Dickens as he has never felt it in connection with such people before. After all, in taking in Tattycoram, the foundling, the Meagleses could not help making her feel her position of inferiority. A little more emphasis in this direction by Dickens and the Meagleses might seem to the reader as odious as they recurrently do to her. Tattycoram herself, with her painful alternations between the extremes of affection and resentment, probably reflects the oscillations of Dickens himself at this period.

But the resentment is to get the upper hand. The Meagleses turn up now as the Podsnaps, that horrendous middle-class family, exponents of all the soundest British virtues, who, however, are quite at home in a social circle of sordid adventurers

and phony *nouveaux riches*, and on whom Dickens visits a
satire as brutal as themselves. Gone are the high spirits that
made of Pecksniff an exhilarating figure of fun—gone with the
Yoho! of the stagecoach on which Tom Pinch traveled to London. The Podsnaps, the Lammles, the Veneerings, the Fledge-
bys, are unpleasant as are no other characters in Dickens. It
comes to us as a disturbing realization that Dickens is now
afraid of Podsnap (who, with his talk about the paramount
importance of not bringing the blush to the young person's
cheek, would of course have been the loudest among those
who disapproved of Dickens' affair with Miss Ternan). And
Fledgeby, the young moneylender of the second generation,
with his peachy cheeks and slender figure, who lives in the Albany and dines out—Grandfather Smallweed is a man beside
him! It is startling to find that Dickens has here even hit upon
a principle which another group of commercial-patriotic rotters
were later to exploit on a large scale. One of the ugliest scenes
in Dickens is that in which Fledgeby ascribes his own characteristics to the gentle old Jew Riah and makes him the agent of
his meanness and sharp-dealing. And not content with making
Fledgeby a cur, Dickens himself shows a certain cruelty in
having him ultimately thrashed by Lammle under circumstances of peculiar ignominy and then having the little dolls'
dressmaker apply plasters with pepper on them to his wounds.
This incident betrays a kind of sadism which we never felt in
Dickens' early work—when Nicholas Nickleby beat Squeers,
for example—but which breaks out now and then in these
later books in a disagreeable fashion.

If the middle class has here become a monster, the gentry
have taken on an aspect more attractive than we have ever
known them to wear as a class in any previous novel of Dickens. If an increase of satiric emphasis turns the Meagleses into
the Podsnaps, so a shift from the satirical to the straight turns
the frivolous and idle young man of good family, who has hitherto always been exhibited as more or less of a scoundrel—
James Harthouse or Henry Gowan—into the sympathetic Eugene Wrayburn. Eugene and his friend Mortimer Lightwood,
the little old diner-out named Twemlow, the only gentleman
in the Veneerings' circle, and the Reverend Frank Milvey, 'expensively educated and wretchedly paid,' the Christian turned

social worker, are the only representatives of the upper strata who are shown as having decent values; and they are all the remnants of an impoverished gentry. Outside these, you find the decent values—or what Dickens intends to be such—in an impoverished proletariat and lower middle class: the modest clerk, the old Jew, the dolls' dressmaker, the dust-contractor's foreman, the old woman who minds children for a living. And the chief heroine is not Bella Wilfer, who has to be cured of her middle-class ideals, but Lizzie Hexam, the illiterate daughter of a Thames-side water-rat. Dickens has here, for the first time in his novels, taken his leading woman from the lowest class; and it will be the principal moral of *Our Mutual Friend* that Wrayburn will have the courage to marry Lizzie. The inevitable conjunction of the high with the low is not here to result in a tragedy but to figure as a fortunate affair. Nor does it involve the whole structure of society in the same way as in the earlier novels: the mechanics are somewhat different. The point is made that the Podsnap-Veneering upper scum of the successful middle class remain unaffected by what has happened and do not seriously affect anyone else. Such people, in Dickens' view, have by this time become completely dissociated from anything that is admirable in English life. Simply, Eugene Wrayburn no longer appears at the Veneerings' parties. When they sneer at the unseemliness of his marriage, Mr. Twemlow suddenly flares up and declares with an authority which makes everyone uncomfortable that Eugene has behaved like a gentleman; and that is the end of the book.

Dickens has aligned himself in *Our Mutual Friend* with a new combination of forces. Shrinking from Podsnap and Veneering, he falls back on that aristocracy he had so savagely attacked in his youth, but to which, through his origins, he had always been closer than he had to the commercial classes. After all, Sir John Chester had had qualities of coolness, grace and ease which, when they appear in an excellent fellow like Eugene, are infinitely preferable to Podsnap. The Chartist movement in England had run into the sands in the fifties; but during the sixties the trade union movement had been making remarkable progress. Dickens had begun *Our Mutual Friend* in the autumn of 1863, and the first number appeared the following May. In July definite steps were taken at a meeting of

French and English workers for an 'international working men's alliance,' and the Workers' International, under the guidance of Karl Marx, was founded at the end of September. This trend may have influenced Dickens, for the final implication of his story is—to state it in the Marxist language—that the declassed representatives of the old professional upper classes may unite with the proletariat against the commercial middle class.

There is, however, another element that plays an important rôle in the story: the proletarian who has educated himself to be a member of this middle class. Lizzie Hexam has a brother, whom she has induced to get an education and who, as soon as he has qualified himself to teach, drops his family even more callously than Pip did his; and the schoolmaster of Charley Hexam's school, another poor man who has advanced himself, is the villain of *Our Mutual Friend*. We are a long way here from the days when the villains and bad characters in Dickens, the Quilps and the Mrs. Gamps, could be so fascinating through their resourcefulness and vitality that, as G. K. Chesterton says, the reader is sorry at the end when they are finally banished from the scene and hopes that the discredited scoundrel will still open the door and stick his head in and make one more atrocious remark. Such figures are so much all of a piece of evil that they have almost a kind of innocence. But here Bradley Headstone has no innocence: he is perverted, tormented, confused. He represents a type which begins to appear in these latest novels of Dickens and which originally derives perhaps from those early theatrical villains, of the type of the elder Rudge or Monks in *Oliver Twist*, skulking figures with black looks and ravaged faces: a literary convention of which one would suppose it would be impossible to make anything plausible. Yet Dickens does finally succeed in giving these dark figures reality.

In Bradley Headstone's case, it is his very aspirations which have gone bad and turned the stiff and anxious schoolmaster into a murderer. He wants to marry Lizzie Hexam and he is wounded by her preference for Eugene, whose nonchalance and grace infuriate him because he knows he can never achieve them. In order to make himself a place in society, he has had rigorously to repress his passions; and now that they finally break out, it is more horrible than Bill Sikes or Jonas Chuzzle-wit, because we understand Bradley as a human being. Bradley is the first murderer in Dickens who exhibits any complexity of character. And he is the first to present himself as a member of respectable Victorian society. There is a dreadful and convincing picture of the double life led by Headstone as he goes about his duties as a schoolmaster after he has decided to murder Eugene. In *Great Expectations*, the Ellen Ternan character, Estella, rejects the love of the hero. In *Our Mutual Friend*, Bella Wilfer rejects Rokesmith in much the same way—though less cruelly, and though she later marries him. But Rokesmith is a colorless character, and the real agonies of frustrated passion appear in *Our Mutual Friend* in the scene between Bradley and Lizzie. This is the kind of thing—the Carker and Edith Dombey kind of thing—that is likely to be bad in Dickens; but here it has a certain reality and a certain unpleasant power. Who can forget the tophatted schoolmaster striking his fist against the stone wall of the church?

The inference is, of course, that Bradley, if he had not been shipwrecked in this way, would have approximated as closely as possible to some sort of Murdstone or Gradgrind. But his death has a tragic symbolism which suggests a different kind of moral. In order to escape detection, he has disguised himself at the time of the murder as a disreputable waterside character who is known to have a grievance against Eugene. When the man finds out what has happened, he makes capital of it by blackmailing Bradley. Headstone finally tackles him on the edge of the deep lock of a canal, drags him into the water, and holds him under until he is drowned; but in doing so, he drowns himself. It is as if the illiterate ruffian whom he would now never be able to shake off has come to represent the brutish part of Bradley's own nature. Having failed to destroy Eugene, he destroys himself with the brute.

VI

In *The Mystery of Edwin Drood*, the motif of Bradley Headstone is, with certain variations, repeated.

This novel, written five years later, Dickens never lived to finish, and it is supposed to have been left an enigma. We must first try to solve this enigma; and to do so we must proceed with a consciousness of the real meaning of Dickens' work. For though it is true that *Edwin Drood* has been enormously written about, it has been always from the point of view of trying to find out what Dickens intended to do with the plot. None of the more serious critics of Dickens has ever been able to take the novel very seriously. They persist in dismissing it as a detective story with good touches and promising characters, but of no interest in the development of Dickens' genius. Bernard Shaw, who is interested in the social side of Dickens, declares that it is 'only a gesture by a man three quarters dead'; and it is true, as Forster remarked, that *The Mystery of Edwin Drood* seems quite free from the social criticism which had grown more biting as Dickens grew older; but what Forster and Shaw do not see is that the psychological interest which had been a feature of Dickens' later period is carried farther in *Edwin Drood*. Like all the books that Dickens wrote under the strain of his later years, it has behind it bitter judgments and desperate emotions. Here as elsewhere the solution of the mystery was to have said something that Dickens wanted to say.

It did not, it is true, become possible to gauge the full significance of the novel until certain key discoveries had been made in regard to the plot itself; but the creation of such a character as John Jasper at this point in Dickens' development should have had its significance for any student of Dickens and should have led to a more careful consideration, in the light of certain hints supplied by Forster, of the psychological possibilities of the character. It has remained for two American scholars to hit upon the cardinal secrets that explain the personality of Jasper. As both these discoveries have been made since the publication in 1912 of W. Robertson Nicoll's otherwise comprehensive book, *The Problem of Edwin Drood*, they have not received attention there; they are not included by Thomas Wright in the bibliography of *Edwin Drood* in his *Life of Charles Dickens*, published in 1936; and so far as I know, up to the present time, nobody who has written about Dickens has been in a position to combine these ideas. Yet what happens when one puts them together is startling: the old novel acquires a sudden new value. As one can revive invisible ink by holding it over a lamp or bring out three dimensions in a photograph by looking at it through certain lenses, so it is possible to recall to life the character of John Jasper as he must have been conceived by Dickens.

The most important revelation about *Edwin Drood* has been made by Mr. Howard Duffield, who published an article called *John Jasper—Strangler* in *The American Bookman* of February, 1930. Mr. Duffield has here shown conclusively that Jasper is supposed to be a member of the Indian sect of Thugs, who made a profession of ingratiating themselves with travelers and then strangling them with a handkerchief and robbing them. This brotherhood, which had been operating for centuries pretty much all over India and which had given the British government a great deal of trouble before it succeeded in putting them down during the thirties, had already attracted attention in the West. Two of the British officers who had been engaged in the suppression of the Thugs had written books about them—one of them in the form of a story, Meadows Taylor's *Confessions of a Thug*, supposed to be narrated by the Thug himself. Eugène Sue had introduced into *The Wandering Jew* a Thug strangler practicing in Europe; and an American novelist, James de Mille, was publishing a novel called *Cord and Creese*, which dealt with an Englishman affiliated with the Thugs, the same year, 1869, that Dickens began *Edwin Drood*. Dickens' friend, Edward Bulwer Lytton, had already considered using this theme. Dickens himself had mentioned the Thugs in 1857 in connection with a garrotting epidemic in London. The publication in 1868 of Wilkie Collins' detective story, *The Moonstone*, in which a band of Hindu devotees commit a secret murder in England, seems to have inspired Dickens with the idea of outdoing his friend the next year with a story of a similar kind.

Now we know from the statement of Sir Luke Fildes, Dickens' illustrator in *Edwin Drood*, that Dickens intended to have Jasper strangle Drood with the long scarf which he (Jasper) wears around his neck; and we know from many circumstances and certain hints that the story is to have its roots in the East. Neville and Helena Landless are supposed to come from Ceylon; and Mr. Jasper, who smokes opium and sees elephants in his trances, is described as having 'thick, lustrous, well-arranged black hair and whiskers' and a voice that sometimes sounds 'womanish'—in short, as something very much like a Hindu.

Furthermore, as Mr. Duffield has established, John Jasper—
and this explains a good deal that has never been understood
—has been trying to fulfill the ritualistic requirements for a
sanctified and successful Thug murder. The Thugs were wor-
shipers of Kali, the Hindu goddess of destruction, and their
methods had been prescribed by the goddess. They had to
commit their crimes with the fold of cloth which was a fragment of the gown of Kali. Kali's gown was supposed to be
black, and Jasper's scarf is black. This cloth had to be worn, as
Jasper's scarf is. A secret burial place had to be selected, as
Jasper selects Mrs. Sapsea's tomb, before the murder took
place. The omens had to be observed, as is done by Mr. Jasper
when he makes his nocturnal trip to the top of the cathedral
tower; the call of a rook in sight of a river was regarded as a favorable sign, the approving word of the goddess, and that, one
finds, is precisely what Jasper hears. The significance of the
birds is planted plainly at the beginning of Chapter II, when
the Cloisterham rooks are first mentioned: 'Whosoever has observed that sedate and clerical bird, the rook, may perhaps
have noticed that when he wings his way homeward toward
nightfall, in a sedate and clerical company, two rooks will suddenly detach themselves from the rest, will retrace their flight
for some distance, and will there poise and linger; conveying
to mere men the fancy that it is of some occult importance to
the body politic, that this artful couple should pretend to have
renounced connection with it.' The Thug preys exclusively on
travelers: Edwin Drood is going on a journey; and when
Jasper, in his second opium dream, is heard talking to himself
about the murder, it is all in terms of a journey and a fellow
traveler. The Thug is to use exaggerated words of endearment,
as Jasper does with Drood. He is to persuade his victim to
leave his lodging a little after midnight, as Jasper has done with
Drood, and to stupefy him with a drug in his food or drink, as
Jasper has obviously done, first with Edwin and Neville, and
afterwards with Durdles.

Since Jasper is eventually to be caught, he is evidently to
have slipped up in the ritual. Mr. Duffield suggests that his
mistake has been to commit the murder without an assistant;
but he has overlooked the Thug superstition (recorded by Edward Thornton in *Illustrations of the History and Practices of*

the Thugs, published in 1837) that nothing but evil could come of murdering a man with any gold in his possession. Now Drood, unknown to Jasper, is carrying the gold ring which Grewgious has given him for Rosa; and we have it on Dickens' own testimony to Forster that the body is to be identified by this ring, which has survived the effects of the quicklime. True, Edwin had also been wearing the stickpin and the gold watch; but as Jasper knew about these and took care to leave them in the weir, he may have removed them before the murder when Edwin was drugged.

Supplementing this interesting discovery we find a paper by Mr. Aubrey Boyd in the series of *Humanistic Studies* (Volume IX) published by Washington University, in which he shows that Jasper is also a hypnotist. Dickens had always been interested in hypnotism. Forster speaks of his first seriously studying it in 1841. He even found that he himself, with that extraordinarily magnetic personality which made it possible for him so to fascinate his audiences and which exerted, as Mrs. Perugini testifies, so irresistible a power over his family, was able to hypnotize people. His first experiment was performed on his wife in the course of his earlier trip to America. He had, he wrote Forster, been 'holding forth upon the subject rather luminously, and asserting that I thought I could exercise the influence, but had never tried.' 'Kate sat down, laughing, for me to try my hand upon her. . . . In six minutes, I magnetized her into hysterics, and then into the magnetic sleep. I tried again next night, and she fell into the slumber in little more than two minutes. . . . I can wake her with perfect ease; but I confess (not being prepared for anything so sudden and complete) I was on the first occasion rather alarmed.' Later, we hear of his hypnotizing John Leech in order to relieve his pain during an illness.

In the meantime, he had a strange experience, reported by Mrs. Perugini, with an Englishwoman he had met in Genoa in 1844. This lady, who was married to a Swiss printer, was afflicted with delusions that 'took the form of a phantom which spoke to her, and other illusionary figures of the most hideous shapes and gory appearance, which came in a crowd, chattering one to the other as they pursued her, and after a time faded, veiling their loathsome faces as they disappeared into space.' Dickens, who at the time was suffering from a recurrence of the spasms of pain in his side which had afflicted him as a child in the blacking warehouse, hypnotized her once or twice every day and found that he could control the delusions. He seems to have become obsessed with the case: the treatment went on for months. On one occasion, 'he was in such a fever of anxiety to receive a letter from his friend concerning the state of his wife that he watched through a telescope the arrival of the mailbags into port.' He mesmerized her 'in the open country and at wayside inns where . . . they would halt for refreshment or stay the night. He mesmerized her in railway carriages—anywhere, if the moment was opportune. By degrees she became better and more serene in her mind and body.' The delusions were apparently dispelled.

It was obviously on the cards that Dickens would do something with this subject in his novels; and it should have given the Drood experts a lead when they encountered a reference to it in the third chapter of *Edwin Drood*. Robertson Nicoll, disregarding this key passage, mentions the matter in another connection: he sees that Jasper has 'willed' Crisparkle to go to the weir, where he will find the watch and stickpin of Edwin; but he does not inquire farther. It remained for Mr. Boyd, who has some special knowledge of Mesmer and his writings, to recognize that Dickens has introduced the whole repertory of the supposed feats of mesmerism—called also 'animal magnetism' at the time—just as he has reproduced the practices of the Thugs. Mr. Jasper is clearly exercising 'animal magnetism,' in this case the kind known as 'malicious,' on Rosa Budd in the scene where he accompanies her at the piano; he is exercising it on Edwin and Neville when he causes them to quarrel in his rooms. It was supposed in Dickens' time that this influence could be projected through the agency of mere sound: hence the insistent keynote in the piano scene and the swelling note of the organ that frightens Rosa in the garden. And it was also supposed to penetrate matter: hence Rosa's remark to Helena that she feels as if Jasper could reach her through a wall. It could be made to impregnate objects in such a way as to remain effective after the master of the magnetic fluid was no longer himself on the scene: Jasper has put a spell on the water where Edwin's watch and stickpin are to be found. And it is possible, though Mr. Boyd does not suggest it, that the transmission of Jasper's influence from a distance may also explain the behavior, of which the implausible character has been noted, of the men who pursue and waylay Landless.

The revealing hint here, however, is the passage in the third chapter, of which Boyd has understood the significance and which has led him to a brilliant conjecture: 'As, in some cases of drunkenness,' writes Dickens, 'and in others of animal magnetism, there are two states of consciousness that never clash, but each of which pursues its separate course as though it were continuous instead of broken (thus, if I hide my watch when I am drunk, I must be drunk again before I can remember where), so Miss Twinkleton has two distinct and separate phases of being.' Dickens had told Forster that the originality of his idea for *Drood*, 'a very strong one, though difficult to work' (Dickens' words in a letter), was to consist (Forster's words in recounting a conversation with Dickens) 'in the review of the murderer's career by himself at the close, when its temptations were to be dwelt upon as if, not he the culprit, but some other man, were the tempted. The last chapters were to be written in the condemned cell, to which his wickedness, all elaborately elicited from him as if told of another, had brought him.'

John Jasper has then 'two states of consciousness'; he is, in short, what we have come to call a dual personality. On the principle that 'if I hide my watch when I am drunk, I must be drunk again before I can remember where,' it will be necessary, in order to extort his confession, to find access to that state of consciousness, evidently not the one with which he meets the cathedral world, in which he has committed the murder. The possibility of opium, suggested by Robertson Nicoll, is excluded. Wilkie Collins had just made use of precisely this device in *The Moonstone*: the man who has taken the Moonstone under the influence of laudanum, which has been given him without his being aware of it, is made to repeat his action under the influence of a second dose. The drunkenness in which Jasper will betray himself will not, then, be produced by a drug. Dickens must go Collins one better. Mr. Boyd has evidently solved the puzzle in guessing that Helena Landless is eventually to hypnotize Jasper. In the scene at the piano, where he is working on Rosa with the effect of making her hysterical, Helena maintains an attitude of defiance and announces that she is not afraid of him. It had already been established by Cuming Walters—it was the first of the important discoveries about *Drood*—that Datchery, the mysterious character who comes to Cloisterham to spy on Jasper, is Helena in disguise. We have been told that Helena used to masquerade and pass herself off as a boy; and Dickens' alterations in his text, both the amplifications of the written copy and the later excisions from the proofs, indicate very clearly that he was aiming—in dealing with such details as Helena's wig and her attempts to conceal her feminine hands—to insinuate evidences of her real identity without allowing the reader to find it out too soon. Helena is to get the goods on Jasper, and in the end, having no doubt acquired in India the same secret which he has been exploiting (there may be also, as so often in Dickens, some question of a family relationship), she will put him in a trance and make him speak.

What Mr. Boyd, however, was not in a position to do was combine this idea with the Thug theme. The Thugs were all in a sense divided personalities. Colonel James L. Sleeman, in his book on the subject, emphasizes what he calls this 'Jekyll-and-Hyde' aspect of their activities. The Thugs were devoted husbands and loving fathers; they made a point—again like Mr. Jasper—of holding positions of honor in the community. And in their own eyes they were virtuous persons: they were serving the cult of the goddess. In their case, the Jekyll-and-Hyde aspect of their careers existed only for profane outsiders. They would proudly confess, when they were caught, to the number of lives they had taken. But in the case of Mr. Jasper, there is a respectable and cultivated Christian gentleman living in the same soul and body with a worshiper of the goddess Kali. The murder has been rehearsed in his opium dreams: he has evidently gone to the opium den for that purpose. He has kept himself under the influence of opium all the time he has been plotting the murder. But those who are to put him in prison will not be able to make him take opium. Helena, with her will stronger than his, will have to come to the rescue and hypnotize him.

*

And now what has all this to do with the Dickens we already know? Why should he have occupied the last years of his life in concocting this sinister detective story?

Let us return to his situation at this period. He is still living between Gadshill and the house of Ellen Lawless Ternan, who appears now in *Edwin Drood* with the even closer identification of the name of Helena Landless. The motif of the disagreeable scene between Bradley Headstone and Lizzie Hexam is repeated in the even more unpleasant, though theatrical and unconvincing, interview between Jasper and Rosa Budd— Jasper presenting, like Headstone, a gruesome travesty of the respectable Victorian. The Ellen Ternan heroine is here frankly made an actress: Helena Landless is an impersonator so accomplished that she can successfully play a male character in real life; and she is even more formidable than Estella because she is to stand up to and unmask Jasper. Her strength is to be contrasted not only with the fatal duplicity of Jasper, but with the weakness of Drood and Neville. All of these three men are to perish, and Helena is to marry Mr. Tartar, the foursquare young ex-Navy man, bursting with good spirits, agility and a perhaps rather overdone good health.

Dickens had just finished his public appearances and had said his farewell to the platform. The great feature of his last series of readings had been the murder of Nancy by Sikes, a performance which he had previously tried on his friends and from which Forster and others had tried to dissuade him. He was warned by a woman's doctor of his acquaintance that 'if only one woman cries out when you murder the girl, there will be a contagion of hysteria all over the place.' But Dickens obviously derived from thus horrifying his hearers some sort of satisfaction. The scene was perhaps a symbolical representation of his behavior in banishing his wife. Certainly the murder of Nancy had taken on something of the nature of an obsessive hallucination. Dickens' imagination had always been subject to a tendency of this kind. It had been pointed out by Taine that the fantasies and monomanias of his lunatics only exaggerate characteristics which are apparent in Dickens' whole work— the concentration on and reiteration of some isolated aspect or detail of a person or a place, as Mr. Dick in *David Copperfield* was haunted by King Charles's head. In one of the sketches of

The Uncommercial Traveller, written during these later years, Dickens tells of being obsessed by the image of a drowned and bloated corpse that he had seen in the Paris morgue, which for days kept popping up among the people and things he encountered and sometimes compelled him to leave public places, though it eventually drove him back to the morgue. In the case of the woman in Italy whose delusions he attempted to dispel, one gets the impression that these bloody visions were almost as real to him as they were to her. And now, at the time of these readings, he jokes about his 'murderous instincts' and says that he goes about the street feeling as if he were 'wanted' by the police.

He threw himself at any rate into the murder scene with a passion that became quite hysterical, as if reading it had become at this point in his life a real means of self-expression. At Clifton, he wrote Forster, 'we had a contagion of fainting; and yet the place was not hot. I should think we had from a dozen to twenty ladies taken out stiff and rigid, at various times!' At Leeds, whether to intensify the effect or to avert the possible objections of the audience, he hired a man to rise from the stalls and protest in the middle of the murder scene against daring to read such a thing before ladies—with the result that the people hissed him and put him out. It was the opinion of Dickens' doctor that the excitement and strain of acting this episode were the immediate cause of Dickens' death. It took a long time for him to calm himself after he had performed it, and the doctor, who noted his pulse at the end of each selection, saw that it invariably ran higher after Nancy and Sikes than after any of the other scenes. When Dolby, the manager of Dickens' tours, tried to persuade him to cut down on the murder, reserving it for the larger towns, Dickens had a paroxysm of rage: 'Bounding up from his chair, and throwing his knife and fork on his plate (which he smashed to atoms), he exclaimed: "Dolby! your infernal caution will be your ruin one of these days!"' Immediately afterwards, he began to weep and told Dolby that he knew he was right. The doctors eventually compelled him to interrupt his tour and take a rest.

His son, Sir Henry Dickens, who speaks in his memoir of his father of the latter's 'heavy moods of deep depression, of in-

tense nervous irritability, when he was silent and oppressed,'
tells of an incident that occurred at a Christmas party the winter before Dickens died: 'He had been ailing very much and
greatly troubled with his leg, which had been giving him much
pain; so he was lying on a sofa one evening after dinner, while
the rest of the family were playing games.' Dickens partici-
pated in one of these games, in which you had to remember
long strings of words, contributed by the players in rotation.
When it came around to Dickens, he gave a name which meant
nothing to anybody: 'Warren's Blacking, 30, Strand.' He did
this, says his son, who knew nothing at that time of this
episode in his father's childhood, 'with an odd twinkle and
strange inflection in his voice which at once forcibly arrested
my attention and left a vivid impression on my mind for some
time afterwards. Why, I could not, for the life of me, understand. . . . At that time, when the stroke that killed him was
gradually overpowering him, his mind reverted to the struggles and degradation of his childhood, which had caused him
such intense agony of mind, and which he had never been able
entirely to cast from him.'

Two weeks before his death, he went to a dinner arranged
by Lord and Lady Houghton in order that the Prince of Wales
and the King of Belgium might meet him. Lady Houghton
was a granddaughter of that Lord Crewe in whose house Dickens' grandfather had been butler. She well remembered going
as a child to the housekeeper's room to hear his grandmother
tell wonderful stories. Dickens' neuritic foot was giving him
such trouble at this time that up till almost an hour before dinner he could not be sure of going. He did finally decide to go;
but when he got to the Houghton house, he found that he
could not mount the stairs, and the Prince and the Belgian
king had to come down to meet him.

But now the Dickens who has been cut off from society has
discarded the theme of the rebel and is carrying the theme of
the criminal, which has haunted him all his life, to its logical
development in his fiction. He is to explore the deep entangle-
ment and conflict of the bad and the good in one man. The
subject of *Edwin Drood* is the subject of Poe's *William Wilson*,
the subject of *Dr. Jekyll and Mr. Hyde*, the subject of *Dorian*

Gray. It is also the subject of that greater work than any of these, Dostoevsky's *Crime and Punishment*. Dostoevsky, who owed so much to Dickens and who was probably influenced by the murder in *Chuzzlewit*, had produced in 1866 a masterpiece on the theme at which Dickens is only just arriving in 1869. Raskólnikov—*raskólnik* means dissenter—combines in his single person the two antisocial types of the deliberate criminal and the rebel, which since Hugh in *Barnaby Rudge* have always been kept distinct by Dickens. Dostoevsky, with the courage of his insight, has studied the states of mind which are the results of a secession from society: the contemptuous will to spurn and to crush confused with the impulse toward human brotherhood, the desire to be loved twisted tragically with the desire to destroy and to kill. But the English Dickens with his middle-class audience would not be able to tell such a story even if he dared to imagine it. In order to stage the 'war in the members,' he must contrive a whole machinery of mystification: of drugs, of telepathic powers, of remote oriental cults.

How far he has come and to how strange a goal we recognize when we note that he has returned to that Rochester he had so loved in his boyhood—the Rochester where he had made Mr. Pickwick put up at the Bull Inn and picnic on good wine and cold fowl out of the hampers of the Wardles' barouche. Gadshill was next door to Rochester, and the Cloisterham of the novel is Rochester; but what Dickens finds in Rochester today is the nightmare of John Jasper. There is plenty of brightness in *Edwin Drood* and something of the good things of life: Mrs. Crisparkle's spices, jams and jellies, Mr. Tartar's shipshape rooms; but this brightness has a quality new and queer. The vivid colors of *Edwin Drood* make an impression more disturbing than the dustiness, the weariness, the dreariness, which set the tone for *Our Mutual Friend*. In this new novel, which is to be his last, Dickens has found a new intensity. The descriptions of Cloisterham are among the best written in all his fiction: they have a nervous (in the old sense) concentration and economy rather different from anything one remembers in the work of his previous phases. We are far from the lavish improvisation of the poetical early Dickens: here every descriptive phrase is loaded with implication. It is as if his art, which in *Our Mutual Friend* had seemed to him so sorely fatigued, had rested and found a revival. Dickens has dropped away here all the burden of analyzing society—British imperialism in the East is evidently to play some part in the story, but it is impossible to tell whether or not this is to have any moral implications (though a writer in *The Nassau Literary Magazine* of May, 1882, who complains of the little interest that has been shown in *Edwin Drood*, suggests that the opium traffic may be the social issue here). Dickens, so far as we can see, is exclusively concerned with a psychological problem. The dualism of high and low, rich and poor, has here completely given place to the dualism of good and evil. The remarkable opening pages in which the Victorian choirmaster, with his side whiskers and tall hat, mixes in his opium-vision the picture of the English cathedral with memories of the East and comes to in the squalid den to stagger out, short of breath, to his services, is perhaps the most complex piece of writing from the psychological point of view to be found in the whole of Dickens. But the characters that are healthy, bright and good —Rosa Budd, with her baby name, for example—seem almost as two-dimensional as colored paper dolls. We have got back to the fairy tale again. But this fairy tale contains no Pickwick: its realest figure is Mr. Jasper; and its most powerful artistic effect is procured by an instillation into the greenery, the cathedral, the winter sun, the sober and tranquil old town, of the suggestion of moral uncertainty, of evil. Even the English rooks, which in *The Old Curiosity Shop* had figured simply as a familiar feature of the pleasant old English countryside in which Nell and her grandfather wandered, are here the omens of an invisible terror that comes from outside that English world. The Christmas season itself, of which Dickens has been the laureate, which he has celebrated so often with warm charity, candid hopes and hearty cheer, is now the appointed moment for the murder by an uncle of his nephew.

Mr. Jasper is, like Dickens, an artist: he is a musician, he has a beautiful voice. He smokes opium, and so, like Dickens, leads a life of the imagination apart from the life of men. Like Dickens, he is a skilful magician, whose power over his fellows may be dangerous. Like Dickens, he is an alien from another world; yet, like Dickens, he has made himself respected in the conventional English community. Is he a villain? From the point of view of the cathedral congregation of Cloisterham, who have admired his ability as an artist, he will have been playing a diabolic rôle. All that sentiment, all those edifying high spirits, which Dickens has been dispensing so long, which he is still making the effort to dispense—has all this now grown as false as those hymns to the glory of the Christian God which are performed by the worshiper of Kali? And yet in another land there is another point of view from which Jasper is a good and faithful servant. It is at the command of his imaginative *alter ego* and acting in the name of his goddess that Jasper has committed his crime.

None the less, he is a damned soul here and now. All this bright and pious foreground of England is to open or fade away, and to show a man condemned to death. But it will not be the innocent Pickwick, the innocent Micawber, the innocent Dorrit, whom we are now to meet in jail: nor yet the wicked Fagin, the wicked Dennis, the wicked elder Rudge. It will be a man who is both innocent and wicked. The protest against the age has turned into a protest against self. In this last moment, the old hierarchy of England does enjoy a sort of triumph over the weary and debilitated Dickens, because it has made him accept its ruling that he is a creature irretrievably tainted; and the mercantile middle-class England has had its triumph, too. For the Victorian hypocrite has developed—from Pecksniff, through Murdstone, through Headstone, to his final transformation in Jasper—into an insoluble moral problem which is identified with Dickens' own. As Headstone makes his own knuckles bleed in striking them against the church and drowns himself in order to drown Riderhood, so Jasper is eventually to destroy himself. When he announces in the language of the Thugs that he 'devotes' himself to the 'destruction' of the murderer, he is preparing his own execution. (He is evidently quite sincere in making this entry in his diary, because he has now sobered up from the opium and resumed his ecclesiastical personality. It is exclusively of this personality that the diary is a record.) So Dickens, in putting his nerves to the torture by enacting the murder of Nancy, has been invoking his own death.

In this last condemned cell of Dickens, one of the halves of the divided John Jasper was to have confronted the other half.

But this confrontation—'difficult to work,' as Dickens told Forster—was never, as it turned out, to take place. Dickens in his moral confusion was never to dramatize himself completely, was never in this last phase of his art to succeed in coming quite clear. He was to leave *Edwin Drood* half-finished, with Jasper's confession just around the corner—just about to come to life in those final instalments which he was never to live to write.

He had put in a long day on *Drood* when (June 9, 1870) he had a stroke while he was eating dinner. He got up from the table in his stunned condition and said he must go to London; then he fell to the floor and never recovered consciousness. He died the next afternoon.

2

The Kipling That Nobody Read

THE eclipse of the reputation of Kipling, which began about 1910, twenty-five years before Kipling's death and when he was still only forty-five, has been of a peculiar kind. Through this period he has remained, from the point of view of sales, an immensely popular writer. The children still read his children's books; the college students still read his poetry; the men and women of his own generation still reread his early work. But he has in a sense been dropped out of modern literature. The more serious-minded young people do *not* read him; the critics do not take him into account. During the later years of his life and even at the time of his death, the logic of his artistic development attracted no intelligent attention. At a time when W. B. Yeats had outgrown his romantic youth and was receiving the reward of an augmented glory for his severer and more concentrated work, Rudyard Kipling, Yeats's coeval, who had also achieved a new concentration through the efforts of a more exacting discipline, saw the glory of his young-manhood fade away. And during the period when the late work of Henry James, who had passed into a similar eclipse, was being retrieved and appreciated, when the integrity and interest of his total achievement was finally being understood, no attempt was made, so far as I know, to take stock of Kipling's work as a whole.* The ordinary person said simply that Kipling was 'written out'; the reviewer rarely made any effort to trace the journey from the breeziness of the early short stories to the bitterness of the later ones. The thick, dark and surly little man who had dug himself into Bateman's, Burwash, Sussex, was left to his bristling privacy, and only occasionally evoked a rebuke for the intolerant and vindictive views which, emerging with the suddenness of a snapping turtle, he sometimes gave vent to in public.

*Since this was written, Mr. Edward Shanks has published a book on Kipling. Mr. Shanks addresses himself to the task, but does not make very much progress with it.

But who *was* Kipling? What did he express? What was the history of that remarkable talent which gave him a place, as a craftsman of English prose, among the few genuine masters of his day? How was it that the art of his short stories became continually more skilful and intense, and yet that his career appears broken?

I

The publication of Kipling's posthumous memoirs—*Something of Myself for My Friends Known and Unknown*—has enabled us to see more clearly the causes for the anomalies of Kipling's career.

First of all, he was born in India, the son of an English artist and scholar, who had gone out to teach architectural sculpture at the Fine Arts School in Bombay and who afterwards became curator of the museum at Lahore. This fact is, of course, well known; but its importance must be specially emphasized. It appears that up to the age of six Kipling talked, thought and dreamed, as he says, in Hindustani, and could hardly speak English correctly. A drawing of him made by a schoolmate shows a swarthy boy with lank straight hair, who might almost pass for a Hindu.

The second important influence in Kipling's early life has not hitherto been generally known, though it figures in the first chapter of *The Light That Failed* and furnished the subject of *Baa, Baa, Black Sheep*, one of the most powerful things he ever wrote. This story had always seemed rather unaccountably to stand apart from the rest of Kipling's work by reason of its sympathy with the victims rather than with the inflictors of a severely repressive discipline; and its animus is now explained by a chapter in Kipling's autobiography and by a memoir recently published by his sister. When Rudyard Kipling was six and his sister three and a half, they were farmed out for six years in England with a relative of Kipling's father. John Lockwood Kipling was the son of a Methodist minister, and this woman was a religious domestic tyrant in the worst English tradition of Dickens and Samuel Butler. The boy, who had been petted and deferred to by the native servants in India, was now beaten, bullied with the Bible, pursued with constant suspicions and broken down by cross-examinations. If one of the children spilled a drop of gravy or wept over a letter from their parents in Bombay, they were forbidden to speak to one another for twenty-four hours. Their guardian had a violent temper and enjoyed making terrible scenes, and they had to learn to propitiate her by fawning on her when they saw that an outburst was imminent.

'Looking back,' says Mrs. Fleming, Kipling's sister, 'I think the real tragedy of our early days, apart from Aunty's bad temper and unkindness to my brother, sprang from our inability to understand why our parents had deserted us. We had had no preparation or explanation; it was like a double death, or rather, like an avalanche that had swept away everything happy and familiar. . . . We felt that we had been deserted, "almost as much as on a doorstep," and what was the reason? Of course, Aunty used to say it was because we were so tiresome, and she had taken us out of pity, but in a desperate moment Ruddy appealed to Uncle Harrison, and he said it was only Aunty's fun, and Papa had left us to be taken care of, because India was too hot for little people. But we knew better than that, because we had been to Nassick, so what was the real reason? Mamma was not ill, like the seepy-weepy Ellen Montgomery's mamma in *The Wide, Wide World*. Papa had not had to go to a war. They had not even lost their money; if they had, we could have swept crossings or sold flowers, and it would have been rather fun. But there was no excuse; they had gone happily back to our own lovely home, and had not taken us with them. There was no getting out of that, as we often said.

'Harry (Aunty's son), who had all a crow's quickness in finding a wound to pick at, discovered our trouble and teased us unmercifully. He assured us we had been taken in out of charity, and must do exactly as he told us. . . . We were just like workhouse brats, and none of our toys really belonged to us.'

Rudyard had bad eyes, which began to give out altogether, so that he was unable to do his work at school. One month he destroyed his report so that his guardians at home shouldn't see it; and for punishment was made to walk to school with a placard between his shoulders reading 'Liar.' He had finally a severe nervous breakdown, accompanied by partial blindness, and was punished by isolation from his sister. This breakdown, it is important to note, was made horrible by hallucinations. As a mist, which seemed to grow steadily thicker, shut him in from the rest of the world, he would imagine that blowing curtains were specters or that a coat on a nail was an enormous black bird ready to swoop down upon him.

His mother came back at last, saw how bad things were—when she went up to kiss him good-night, he instinctively put up his hand to ward off the expected blow—and took the children away. But the effects of those years were lasting. Mrs. Fleming tells us that her revulsion against Aunty's son Harry conditioned her reactions toward people who resembled him through all the rest of her life, and says that when, thirty years later, she set out in Southsea one day to see if the 'House of Desolation' were still standing, her heart failed her, and she hurried back: 'I dared not face it.' Rudyard himself told her that he had had a similar experience: 'I think we both dreaded a kind of spiritual imprisonment that would affect our dreams. Less than four years ago [she is writing in 1939], I asked him whether he knew if the house still stood. "I don't know, but if so, I should like to burn it down and plough the place with salt."'

Kipling asserts that this ordeal had 'drained me of any capacity for real, personal hate for the rest of my days'; and his sister denies that it produced in him any permanent injurious effects: 'According to their gloomy theories [the theories of the psychoanalysts], my brother should have grown up morbid and misanthropic, narrow-minded, self-centered, shunning the world, and bearing it, and all men, a burning grudge; for certainly between the ages of six and eleven he was thwarted at every turn by Aunty and the odious Harry, and inhibitions were his daily bread.' Yet here is the conclusion of the story which Kipling made out of this experience: 'There! "Told you so,"' says the boy to his sister. 'It's all different now, and we see just as much of mother as if she had never gone.' But, Kipling adds: 'Not altogether, O Punch, for when young lips have drunk deep of the bitter waters of Hate, Suspicion, and Despair, all the Love in the world will not wholly take away that knowledge; though it may turn darkened eyes for a while to the light, and teach Faith where no Faith was.'

And actually the whole work of Kipling's life is to be shot through with hatred.

He was next sent to a public school in England. This school, the United Services College, at a place called Westward Ho!, had been founded by Army and Navy officers who could not afford to send their sons to the more expensive schools. The four and a half years that Kipling spent there gave him *Stalky & Co.*; and the relation of the experience to the book provides an interesting psychological study. The book itself, of course, presents a hair-raising picture of the sadism of the English public-school system. The older boys have fags to wait on them, and they sometimes torment these younger boys till they have reduced them almost to imbecility; the masters are constantly caning the boys in scenes that seem almost as bloody as the floggings in old English sea stories; and the boys revenge themselves on the masters with practical jokes as catastrophic as the Whams and Zows of the comic strip.

The originals of two of Kipling's characters—Major-General L. C. Dunsterville and Mr. G. C. Beresford—have published in their later years (*Stalky's Reminiscences* and *Schooldays with Kipling*) accounts rather discrepant with one another of life at the United Services College. Mr. Beresford, who is a highbrow in *Stalky & Co.* and reads Ruskin in the midst of the mêlée, turns out to be a Nationalist Irishman, who is disgusted with his old friend's later imperialism. He insists that the fagging system did not exist at Westward Ho!; that the boys were never caned on their bare shoulders; and that Kipling, so far as he remembers, was never caned at all except by a single exceptional master. Dunsterville, on the other hand, reports that the younger boys were barbarously bullied by the older: held out of high windows by their ankles and dropped down a stair-well in 'hangings' which in one case broke the victim's leg; and that 'in addition to the blows and the kicks that inevitably accompanied the bullying,' he 'suffered a good deal from the canes of the masters, or the ground-ash sticks of the prefects. I must have been perpetually black and blue. That always sounds so dreadful. . . . But the truth of the matter is, any slight blow produces a bruise. . . . And with one or two savage exceptions, I am sure that the blows I received as a result of bullying or legitimate punishment were harmless enough. . . .' 'Kicks and blows,' he goes on, 'I minded little, but the moral effect was depressing. Like a hunted animal I had to keep all my senses perpetually on the alert to escape from the toils of the hunter—good training in a way, but likely to injure permanently a not very robust temperament. I was robust enough, I am glad to say, and possibly benefited by the treatment.'

Kipling was, of course, not robust; and the school evidently aggravated the injury which had been done him during his captivity at Southsea. He admits, in *Something of Myself*, that the fagging system was not compulsory; but he asserts that the discipline was brutal, that the students were wretchedly fed, and that he himself, addicted to books and too blind to participate in games, endured a good deal of baiting. The important thing is that he suffered. If we compare the three accounts of Westward Ho!—*Stalky & Co.* with the reminiscences of the two others—the emphasis of Kipling's becomes plain. It is significant that the single master whom Beresford mentions as persecuting the boys should have been inquisitorial and morbidly suspicious—that is, that he should have treated Kipling in the same way that he had already been treated by the *Baa, Baa, Black Sheep* people. And it is also significant that this master does not figure in *Stalky & Co.*, but only appears later in one of the more scrupulous stories which Kipling afterward wrote about the school. The stimulus of unjust suspicion, which did not leave any lasting bitterness with Beresford, had evidently the effect upon Kipling of throwing him back into the state of mind which had been created by the earlier relationship—just as the kickings and canings that Dunsterville nonchalantly shook off sunk deep into the spirit of Kipling. For a boy who has been habitually beaten during the second six years of his life, any subsequent physical punishment, however occasional or light, may result in the reawakening of the terror and hatred of childhood. It thrust him back into the nightmare again, and eventually made a delirium of the memory of Westward Ho!. *Stalky & Co.*—from the artistic point of view, certainly the worst of Kipling's books: crude in writing, trashy in feeling, implausible in a series of contrivances which resemble moving-picture 'gags'—is in the nature of an hysterical outpouring of emotions kept over from school-days, and it

probably owes a part of its popularity to the fact that it provides the young with hilarious and violent fantasies on the
theme of what they would do to the school bully and their
masters if the laws of probability were suspended.

We shall deal presently with the social significance which
Kipling, at a later period, was to read back into Westward Ho!.
In the meantime, we must follow his adventures when he
leaves it in July, 1882, not yet quite seventeen, but remarkably
mature for his age and with a set of grown-up whiskers. He
went back to his family in India, and there he remained for
seven years. The Hindu child, who had lain dormant in England, came to life when he reached Bombay, and he found
himself reacting to the old stimuli by beginning to talk Hindustani without understanding what he was saying. *Seven
Years Hard* is his heading for his chapter on this phase of his
life. His family—as we gather from his address on *Independence*
—were by no means well-to-do; and he started right in on a
newspaper in Lahore as sole assistant to the editor, and worked
his head off for a chief he detested. It was one of the duties of
the English journalist in India to play down the periodical epi-
demics. Kipling himself survived dysentery and fever, and kept
on working through his severest illnesses. One hot night in
1886, when he felt, as he says, that he 'had come to the edge of
all endurance' and had gone home to his empty house with the
sensation that there was nothing left in him but 'the horror of
a great darkness, that I must have been fighting for some days,'
he read a novel by Walter Besant about a young man who had
wanted to be a writer and who had eventually succeeded in his
aim. Kipling decided he would save some money and get away
to London. He wrote short stories called *Plain Tales from the
Hills*, which were run to fill up space in the paper, and he
brought out a book of verse. His superiors disapproved of his
flippancy, and when he finally succeeded in leaving India, the
managing director of the paper, who had considered him overpaid, told the young man that he could take it from him that
he would never be worth anything more than four hundred
rupees a month.

The Kipling of these early years is a lively and sympathetic
figure. A newspaper man who has access to everything, the son
of a scholar who has studied the natives, he sees the commu-

nity, like Asmodeus, with all the roofs removed. He is interested in the British of all classes and ranks—the bored English ladies, the vagabond adventurers, the officers and the soldiers both. 'Having no position to consider,' he writes, 'and my trade enforcing it, I could move at will in the fourth dimension. I came to realize the bare horrors of the private's life, and the unnecessary torments he endured. . . . Lord Roberts, at that time Commander-in-chief of India, who knew my people, was interested in the men, and—I had by then written one or two stories about soldiers—the proudest moment of my young life was when I rode up Simla Mall beside him on his usual explosive red Arab, while he asked me what the men thought about their accommodations, entertainment-rooms, and the like. I told him, and he thanked me as gravely as though I had been a full Colonel.' He is already tending to think about people in terms of social and racial categories; but his interest in them at this time is also personal: 'All the queer outside world would drop into our workshop sooner or later— say a Captain just cashiered for horrible drunkenness, who reported his fall with a wry, appealing face, and then—disappeared. Or a man old enough to be my father, on the edge of tears because he had been overpassed for Honors in the Gazette. . . . One met men going up and down the ladder in every shape of misery and success.' And he gives us in his soldier stories, along with the triumphs of discipline and the exploits of the native wars, the hunger of Private Ortheris for London when the horror of exile seizes him; the vanities and vices of Mulvaney which prevent him from rising in the service (*The Courting of Dinah Shadd*, admired by Henry James, is one of the stories of Kipling which sticks closest to unregenerate humanity); even the lunatic obsessions and the crack-up of the rotter gentleman ranker in *Love-o'-Women*.

The natives Kipling probably understood as few Englishmen did in his time; certainly he presented them in literature as nobody had ever done. That Hindu other self of his childhood takes us through into its other world. The voices of alien traditions—in the monologues of *In Black and White*—talk an English which translates their own idiom; and we hear of great lovers and revengers who live by an alien code; young men who have been educated in England and, half-dissociated from native life, find themselves impotent between two civilizations; fierce Afghan tribesmen of the mountains, humble people who have been broken to the mines; loyal Sikhs and untamed mutineers. It is true that there is always the implication that the British are bringing to India modern improvements and sounder standards of behavior. But Kipling is obviously enjoying for its own sake the presentation of the native point of view, and the whole Anglo-Indian situation is studied with a certain objectivity.

He is even able to handle without horror the mixture of the black and the white. 'The "railway folk,"' says Mr. E. Kay Robinson, who worked with him on the paper in Lahore, 'that queer colony of white, half white and three-quarters black, which remains an uncared-for and discreditable excrescence upon British rule in India, seemed to have unburdened their souls to Kipling of all their grievances, their poor pride, and their hopes. Some of the best of Kipling's work is drawn from the lives of these people; although to the ordinary Anglo-Indian, whose social caste restrictions are almost more inexorable than those of the Hindu whom he affects to despise on that account, they are as a sealed book.' And one of the most sympathetic of these early stories—the once famous *Without Benefit of Clergy*—is a picture of an Anglo-Indian union: an English official who lives with a Mahomedan girl. Though Kipling deals rarely in fortunate lovers, these lovers enjoy their happiness for a time. To their joy, the mother gives birth to a son, who turns into 'a small gold-colored little god,' and they like to sit on the roof and eat almonds and watch the kites. But then the baby dies of the fever, and the young wife dies of the cholera; and the husband is called away to fight the famine and the epidemic. Even the house where they have lived is destroyed, and the husband is glad that no one else will ever be able to live there. This idyl, unhallowed and fleeting, is something that the artist in Kipling has felt, and put down for its sweetness and pathos.

Through all these years of school and of newspaper work, with their warping and thwarting influences, Kipling worked staunchly at mastering his craft. For he had been subjected to yet another influence which has not been mentioned yet. His father was a painter and sculptor, and two of his mother's sisters were married to artists—one to Edward Poynter, the Academician, and the other to the pre-Raphaelite, Burne-Jones. Besides India and the United Services College, there had been the pre-Raphaelite movement. In England, Kipling's vacation had always been spent in London with the Burne-Joneses. Mr. Beresford says that Kipling's attitude at school had been that of the aesthete who disdains athletics and has no aptitude for mechanical matters, that he was already preoccupied with writing, and that his literary proficiency and cultivation were amazingly developed for his age. He had had from his childhood the example of men who loved the arts for their own sake and who were particularly concerned about craftsmanship (it is also of interest that his father's family had distinguished themselves in the eighteenth century as founders of bronze bells). Kipling evidently owes his superiority as a craftsman to most of even the ablest English writers of fiction of the end of the century and the early nineteen hundreds, to this inspiration and training. Just as the ballad of *Danny Deever* derives directly from the ballad of *Sister Helen*, so the ideal of an artistic workmanship which shall revert to earlier standards of soundness has the stamp of William Morris and his circle. In 1878, when Rudyard was twelve years old, his father had taken him to the Paris Exhibition and insisted that he learn to read French. The boy had then conceived an admiration for the civilization of the French which evidently contributed later to his interest in perfecting the short story in English.

With all this, his earlier experience in the 'House of Desolation' had equipped him, he says, with a training not unsuitable for a writer of fiction, in that it had 'demanded constant wariness, the habit of observation, and attendance on moods and tempers; the noting of discrepancies between speech and action; a certain reserve of demeanor; and automatic suspicion of sudden favors.'

With such a combination of elements, what might one not expect? It is not surprising to learn that the young Kipling contemplated, after his return to England, writing a colonial *Comédie Humaine*. 'Bit by bit, my original notion,' he writes, 'grew into a vast, vague conspectus—Army and Navy List, if you like—of the whole sweep and meaning of things and efforts and origins throughout the Empire.' Henry James, who wrote an appreciative preface for a collection of Kipling's early stories, said afterwards that he had thought at that time that it might perhaps be true that Kipling 'contained the seeds of an English Balzac.'

II

What became of this English Balzac? Why did the author of the brilliant short stories never develop into an important novelist?

Let us return to *Baa, Baa, Black Sheep* and the situation with which it deals. Kipling says that his Burne-Jones aunt was never able to understand why he had never told anyone in the family about how badly he and his sister were being treated, and he tries to explain this on the principle that 'children tell little more than animals, for what comes to them they accept as eternally established,' and says that 'badly-treated children have a clear notion of what they are likely to get if they betray the secrets of a prison-house before they are clear of it.' But *is* this inevitably true? Even young children do sometimes run away. And, in any case, Kipling's reaction to this experience seems an abnormally docile one. After all, Dickens made David Copperfield bite Mr. Murdstone's hand and escape; and he makes war on Mr. Murdstone through the whole of his literary career. But though the anguish of these years had given Kipling a certain sympathy with the neglected and persecuted, and caused him to write this one moving short story, it left him—whether as the result of the experience itself or because he was already so conditioned—with a fundamental sub-missiveness to authority.

Let us examine the two books in which Kipling deals, respectively, with his schooldays and with his youth in India: *Stalky & Co.* and *Kim*. These works are the products of the author's thirties, and *Kim*, at any rate, represents Kipling's most serious attempt to allow himself to grow to the stature of a first-rate creative artist. Each of these books begins with an antagonism which in the work of a greater writer would have developed into a fundamental conflict; but in neither *Stalky* nor *Kim* is the conflict ever permitted to mount to a real crisis. Nor can it even be said to be resolved: it simply ceases to figure as a conflict. In *Stalky*, we are at first made to sympathize with the baiting of the masters by the schoolboys as their rebellion against a system which is an offense against human dignity; but then we are immediately shown that all the ragging and flogging are justified by their usefulness as a training for the military caste which is to govern the British Empire. The boys are finally made to recognize that their headmaster not only knows how to dish it out but is also able to take it, and the book culminates in the ridiculous scene—which may perhaps have its foundation in fact but is certainly flushed by a hectic imagination—in which the Head, in his inflexible justice, undertakes personally to cane the whole school while the boys stand by cheering him wildly.

There is a real subject in *Stalky & Co.*, but Kipling has not had the intelligence to deal with it. He cannot see around his characters and criticize them, he is not even able properly to dramatize; he simply allows the emotions of the weaker side, the side that is getting the worst of it, to go over to the side of the stronger. You can watch the process all too clearly in the episode in which Stalky and his companions turn the tables on the cads from the crammers' school. These cads have been maltreating a fag, and a clergyman who is represented by Kipling as one of the more sensible and decent of the masters suggests to Stalky & Co. that they teach the bullies a lesson. The former proceed to clean up on the latter in a scene which goes on for pages, to the reckless violation of proportion and taste. The oppressors, true enough, are taught a lesson, but the cruelty with which we have already been made disgusted has now passed over to the castigators' side, and there is a disagreeable implication that, though it is caddish for the cads to be cruel, it is all right for the sons of English gentlemen to be cruel to the cads.

Kim is more ambitious and much better. It is Kipling's only successful long story: an enchanting, almost a first-rate book, the work in which more perhaps than in any other he gave the sympathies of the imagination free rein to remember and to explore, and which has in consequence more complexity and density than any of his other works. Yet the conflict from which the interest arises, though it is very much better presented, here also comes to nothing: the two forces never really engage. Kim is the son of an Irish soldier and an Irish nursemaid, who has grown up as an orphan in India, immersed in and assimilated to the native life, so that he thinks, like the young Kipling, in Hindustani. The story deals with the gradual dawning of his consciousness that he is really a Sahib. As a child he has been in the habit of making a little money by carrying messages for a native agent of the British secret service, and the boy turns out to be so bright and so adept at acting the rôle of a native that the authorities decide to train him. He is sent to an English school but does not willingly submit to the English system. Every vacation he dresses as a native and disappears into the sea of native life. The Ideal of this side of his existence is represented by a Thibetan lama, a wandering Buddhist pilgrim, whom he accompanies in the character of a disciple.

Now what the reader tends to expect is that Kim will come eventually to realize that he is delivering into bondage to the British invaders those whom he has always considered his own people, and that a struggle between allegiances will result. Kipling has established for the reader—and established with considerable dramatic effect—the contrast between the East, with its mysticism and its sensuality, its extremes of saintliness and roguery, and the English, with their superior organization, their confidence in modern method, their instinct to brush away like cobwebs the native myths and beliefs. We have been shown two entirely different worlds existing side by side, with neither really understanding the other, and we have watched the oscillations of Kim, as he passes to and fro between them. But the parallel lines never meet; the alternating attractions felt by Kim never give rise to a genuine struggle. And the climax itself is double: the adventures of the Lama and of Kim simply arrive at different consummations, without any final victory or synthesis ever being allowed to take place. Instead, there are a pair of victories, which occur on separate planes and do not influence one another: the Lama attains to a condition of trance which releases him from what the Buddhists call the Wheel of Things at the same moment that the young Anglo-Indian achieves promotion in the British secret service.

The salvation of the Lama has been earned by penitence for a moment of passion: he had been tempted to kill a man who had torn his sacred chart and struck him, a Russian agent working against the British. But the pretenses of Kim to a spiritual vocation, whatever spell has been exerted over him by the Lama, are dispelled when the moment for action comes, when the Irishman is challenged to a fight: Kim knocks the Russian down and bangs his head against a boulder. 'I am Kim. I am Kim. And what is Kim?' his soul repeats again and again, in his exhaustion and collapse after this episode. He feels that his soul is 'out of gear with its surroundings—a cog-wheel unconnected with any machinery, just like the idle cog-wheel of a cheap Beheea sugar-crusher laid by in a corner.' But he now gets this unattached soul to find a function in the working of the crusher—note the mechanical metaphor: dissociating himself from the hierarchy represented by the Abbot-Lama, he commits himself to a rôle in the hierarchy of a practical organization. (So the wolf-reared Mowgli of the *Jungle Books*, the prototype of Kim, ends up rather flatly as a ranger in the British Forestry Service.) Nor does Kipling allow himself to doubt that his hero has chosen the better part. Kim must now exploit his knowledge of native life for the purpose of preventing and putting down any native resistance to the British; but it never seems to occur to his creator that this constitutes a betrayal of the Lama. A sympathy with the weaker party in a relationship based on force has again given way without a qualm to a glorification of the stronger. As the bullying masters of *Stalky & Co.* turn into beneficent Chirons, so even the overbearing officer who figures on his first appearance in *Kim* as a symbol of British stupidity turns out to be none other than Strickland, the wily police superintendent, who has here been acting a part. (It should also be noted that the question of whether or not Kim shall allow himself to sleep with a native woman has here become very important, and that his final emergence as a Sahib is partly determined by his decision in the negative. This is no longer the Kipling of *Without Benefit of Clergy*.)

The Lama's victory is not of this world: the sacred river for which he has been seeking, and which he identifies in his final revelation with a brook near which his trance has occurred, has no objective existence, it is not on the British maps. Yet the anguish of the Lama's repentance—a scene, so far as I remember, elsewhere unmatched in Kipling—is one of the most effective things in the book; and we are to meet this Lama again in strange and unexpected forms still haunting that practical world which Kipling, like Kim, has chosen. The great eulogist of the builder and the man of action was no more able to leave the Lama behind than Kim had been able to reconcile himself to playing the game of English life without him.

III

The fiction of Kipling, then, does not dramatize any fundamental conflict because Kipling would never face one. This is probably one of the causes of his lack of success with long novels. You can make an effective short story, as Kipling so often does, about somebody's scoring off somebody else; but this is not enough for a great novelist, who must show us large social forces, or uncontrollable lines of destiny, or antagonistic impulses of the human spirit, struggling with one another. With Kipling, the right and the wrong of any opposition of forces is usually quite plain at the start; and there is not even the suspense which makes possible the excitement of melodrama. There is never any doubt as to the outcome. The Wrong is made a guy from the beginning, and the high point of the story comes when the Right gives it a kick in the pants. Where both sides are sympathetically presented, the battle is not allowed to occur.

But this only drives us back on another question: how was it that the early Kipling, with his sensitive understanding of the mixed population of India, became transformed into the later Kipling, who consolidated and codified his snobberies instead of progressively eliminating them as most good artists do, and who, like Kim, elected as his lifework the defense of the British Empire? The two books we have been discussing indicate the end of a period in the course of which Kipling had arrived at a decision. *Stalky* came out in 1899, and *Kim* in 1901. The decade of the nineties had been critical for Kipling; and in order to understand the new phase of his work which had begun by the beginning of the century, we must follow his adventures in the United States, which he visited in 1889, where he lived from 1892 to 1896, and to which he tried to return in 1899. Kipling's relations with America are certainly the most important factor in his experience during these years of his later twenties and early thirties; yet they are the link which has been dropped out of his story in most of the accounts of his life and which even his posthumous memoirs, revelatory in respect to his earlier years, markedly fail to supply.

The young man who arrived in London in the fall of 1889 was very far from being the truculent British patriot whom we knew in the nineteen hundreds. He had not even gone straight back to England, but had first taken a trip around the world, visiting Canada and the United States. Nor did he remain long in the mother-country when he got there. His whole attitude was that of the colonial who has sweated and suffered at the outposts of Empire, making the acquaintance of more creeds and customs than the philosophy of London dreamt of, and who feels a slight touch of scorn toward the smugness of the people at home, unaware of how big, varied and active the world around them is. His 'original notion,' he says, had been to try 'to tell the Empire something of the world outside England—not directly but by implication': 'What can they know of England who only England know?' He rounded out his knowledge of the colonies by traveling in New Zealand, Australia, South Africa and Southern India. In the January of 1892, he married an American wife.

Kipling's experience of the United States was in certain ways like that of Dickens. Neither of them fitted very well into the English system at home, and both seem to have been seeking in the new English-speaking nation a place where they could be more at ease. Both winced at the crudeness of the West; both were contemptuously shocked by the boasting—the Pacific Coast in Kipling's day was what the Mississippi had been in Dickens'. Both, escaping from the chilliness of England, resented the familiarity of the States. Yet Kipling, on the occasion of his first visit, which he records in *From Sea to Sea*, is obviously rejoiced by the naturalness of social relations in America. He tells of 'a very trim maiden' from New Hampshire, with 'a delightful mother and an equally delightful father, a heavy-eyed, slow-voiced man of finance,' whom he met in the Yellowstone. 'Now an English maiden who had stumbled on a dust-grimed, lime-washed, sun-peeled collarless wanderer come from and going to goodness knows where, would, her mother inciting her and her father brandishing his umbrella, have regarded him as a dissolute adventurer. Not so those delightful people from New Hampshire. They were good enough to treat me—it sounds almost incredible—as a human being, possibly respectable, probably not in immediate need of financial assistance. Papa talked pleasantly and to the point. The little maiden strove valiantly with the accent of her birth and that of her reading, and mamma smiled benignly in the background. Balance this with a story of a young English idiot I met knocking about inside his high collars, attended by a valet. He condescended to tell me that "you can't be too careful who you talk to in these parts," and stalked on, fearing, I suppose, every minute for his social chastity. Now that man was a barbarian (I took occasion to tell him so), for he comported himself after the manner of the headhunters of Assam, who are at perpetual feud one with another.'

He declares his faith in the Americans in a conversation with an Englishman 'who laughed at them.' '"I admit everything," said I. "Their Government's provisional; their law's the notion of the moment; their railways are made of hairpins and matchsticks, and most of their good luck lives in their woods and mines and rivers and not in their brains; but, for all that, they be the biggest, finest, and best people on the surface of the globe! Just you wait a hundred years and see how they'll behave when they've had the screw put on them and have forgotten a few of the patriarchal teachings of the late Mr. George Washington. Wait till the Anglo-American-German-Jew—the Man of the Future—is properly equipped. He'll have just the least little kink in his hair now and again; he'll carry the English lungs above the Teuton feet that can walk forever; and he will wave long, thin, bony Yankee hands with the big blue veins on the wrist, from one end of the earth to the other. He'll be the finest writer, poet, and dramatist, 'specially dramatist, that the world as it recollects itself has ever seen. By virtue of his Jew blood—just a little, little drop—he'll be a musician and a painter, too. At present there is too much balcony and too little Romeo in the life-plays of his fellow-citizens. Later on, when the proportion is adjusted and he sees the possibilities of his land, he will produce things that will make the effete East stare. He will also be a complex and highly composite administrator. There is nothing known to man that he will not be, and his country will sway the world with one foot as a man tilts a see-saw plank!"

"'But this is worse than the Eagle at its worst. Do you seriously believe all that?" said the Englishman.

"'If I believe anything seriously, all this I most firmly believe. You wait and see. Sixty million people, chiefly of English instincts, who are trained from youth to believe that nothing is impossible, don't slink through the centuries like Russian peasantry. They are bound to leave their mark somewhere, and don't you forget it.'"

'I love this People . . .' he wrote. 'My heart has gone out to them beyond all other peoples.' And he reiterated his faith, in the poem called *An American*, in which 'The American spirit speaks':

> Enslaved, illogical, elate,
>   He greets th' embarrassed Gods, nor fears
> To shake the iron hand of Fate
>   Or match with Destiny for beers.
>
> So, imperturbable he rules,
>   Unkempt, disreputable, vast—
> And, in the teeth of all the schools,
>   I—I shall save him at the last!

Kipling took his wife to America, and they lived for a time on the estate of her family in Brattleboro, Vermont; then Kipling built a large house: his books were already making him rich. They lived in the United States four years; two daughters were born to them there. Kipling was ready to embrace America, or those aspects of America which excited him; he began using American subjects for his stories: the railroads in *.007*, the Gloucester fishermen in *Captains Courageous*. He enormously admired Mark Twain, whose acquaintance he had made on his first visit. Yet the effect of contact with the United States was eventually to drive Kipling, as it had Dickens, back behind his British defenses. A disagreeable episode occurred which, undignified and even comic though it seems, is worth studying because it provided the real test of Kipling's fitness to flourish

in America, and not merely the test of this, but, at a critical
time in his life, of the basic courage and humanity of his
character.

The story has been told since Kipling's death in a book
called *Rudyard Kipling's Vermont Feud* by Mr. Frederick F. Van
de Water. A brother of Mrs. Kipling's, Kipling's friend Wolcott
Balestier, had been in the publishing business with Heinemann
in London, and Mrs. Kipling had lived much in England and
was by way of being an Anglophile. Thus the impulse on
Kipling's part to assimilate himself to the Americans was neu-
tralized in some degree by Mrs. Kipling's desire to be English.
Kipling, who was accustomed to India, had his own instinctive
rudeness. In Vermont, he and Mrs. Kipling tended to stick to
the attitudes of the traditional governing-class English maintaining their caste in the colonies: they drove a tandem with a
tophatted English coachman, dressed every night for dinner,
kept their New England neighbors at a distance.

But Mrs. Kipling had a farmer brother who—the family
were partly French—was as Americanized as possible. He was
a drinker, a spendthrift and a great local card, famous alike for
his ribaldry, his sleigh-racing and his gestures of generosity of
a magnificence almost feudal. Mr. Van de Water tells us that,
at the time he knew Beatty Balestier, he had the swagger of
Cyrano de Bergerac and a leathery face like 'an ailing eagle.'
His farm and family suffered. The Kiplings lent him money,
and he is said to have paid it back; but they disapproved of his
disorderly existence. They seem to have persisted in treating
him with some lack of consideration or tact. Beatty was, in any
case, the kind of man—unbalanced in character but independent in spirit—who is embittered by obligations and furiously
resents interference. Kipling went to Beatty one day and
offered to support his wife and child for a year if Beatty would
leave town and get a job. He was surprised at the explosion he
provoked. This was followed by a dispute about some land
across the road from the Kiplings' house. The land belonged
to Beatty and he sold it for a dollar to the Kiplings, who were
afraid that someone would some day build on it—on the
friendly understanding, as he claimed, that he could continue
to use it for mowing. When the transfer had been effected,
Mrs. Kipling set out to landscape-garden it. The result was

that Beatty stopped speaking to them and refused to receive Kipling when he came to call.

This went on for about a year, at the end of which a crisis occurred. Kipling was indiscreet enough to remark to one of the neighbors that he had had 'to carry Beatty for the last year—to hold him up by the seat of his breeches.' This soon reached his brother-in-law's ears. One day Beatty, driving his team and drunk, met Kipling riding his bicycle. He blocked the road, making Kipling fall off, and shouted angrily: 'See here! I want to talk to you!' Kipling answered, 'If you have anything to say, say it to my lawyers.' 'By Jesus, this is no case for lawyers!' retorted Beatty, loosing a tirade of profanity and abuse. He threatened Kipling, according to Kipling, to kill him; according to Beatty, merely to beat him up if he did not make a public retraction.

Kipling had always deplored the lawlessness of America; in his account of his first trip through the West, his disgust and trepidation over the shootings of the frontier are expressed in almost every chapter. And he now became seriously alarmed. He proceeded to have Beatty arrested on charges of 'assault with indecent and opprobrious names and epithets and threatening to kill.' He did not realize that that kind of thing was not done in the United States, where such quarrels were settled man to man, and he could not foresee the consequences. Beatty, who loved scandal, was delighted. He allowed the case to come into court and watched Kipling, who hated publicity, make himself ridiculous in public. The Kiplings at last fled abroad—it was August, 1896—before the case could come before the Grand Jury.

'So far as I was concerned,' says Kipling of his relations with Americans in general, 'I felt the atmosphere was to some extent hostile.' It was a moment of antagonism toward England. In the summer of 1895, Venezuela had appealed to the United States for protection against the English in a dispute over the boundaries of British Guiana, and President Cleveland had invoked the Monroe Doctrine and demanded in strong language that England submit the question to arbitration. The Jameson raid on the Transvaal Republic early in 1896, an unauthorized and defeated attempt by an agent of the British South Africa Company to provoke a rising against the Boers, had

intensified the feeling against England. Kipling was brought
face to face with the issue by an encounter with another American who seemed almost as unrestrained as Beatty Balestier.
When Kipling met Theodore Roosevelt, then Assistant Secretary of the Navy, the latter 'thanked God in a loud voice that
he had not one drop of British blood in him,' that his ancestry
was pure Dutch, and declared that American fear of the British
would provide him with funds for a new navy. John Hay had
told Kipling that it was hatred of the English that held the
United States together.

But during the years that immediately followed the
Kiplings' return to England, American relations with England
improved. The United States took over the Philippines in 1898
as a result of the Spanish War, and annexed the Hawaiian
Islands; and the imperialistic England of Joseph Chamberlain,
in fear of Germany, which had favored the Spanish, became extremely sympathetic with the policy of the United States. At
the beginning of 1899, then, Rudyard Kipling set forth on an
attempt to retrieve his position in America, where he had
abandoned the big Brattleboro house. He first composed the
celebrated set of verses in which he exhorted the United States
to collaborate with the British Empire in 'taking up the White
Man's burden' of 'your new-caught, sullen peoples, half-devil
and half-child,' who were to be benefited and disciplined in
spite of themselves, though at a bitter expense to their captors;
and had the poem published on both sides of the Atlantic early
in February, at the moment of his sailing for America. But
what confronted him on his landing was an announcement in
the New York papers that Beatty Balestier was bringing a
$50,000 countersuit against him for 'malicious persecution,
false arrest and defamation of character'; and the report that
Beatty himself either had arrived in New York or was just
about to arrive. It was simply another of Beatty's gestures: no
suit was ever brought; but it prevented the Kiplings from returning to Vermont. Rudyard had caught cold on the boat,
and he now came down with double pneumonia and seemed
in danger of not pulling through. His two little girls had pneumonia, too, and one of them died while he was ill. When he recovered, he had to hear of her death. He went back to

England in June, as soon as he was able to travel, and never tried to live in the United States again.

'It will be long and long,' he wrote in a letter supposed to date from 1900, 'before I could bring myself to look at the land of which she [his daughter] was so much a part.' And his cousin Angela Thirkell writes that, 'Much of the beloved Cousin Ruddy of our childhood died with Josephine and I feel that I have never seen him as a real person since that year.'

The fear and hatred awakened in Kipling by those fatal six years of his childhood had been revived by the discipline of Westward Ho! The menaces of Beatty Balestier, behind which must have loomed for Kipling all that was wild, uncontrollable, brutal in the life of the United States, seem to have prodded again the old inflammation. The schoolboy, rendered helpless in a fight by his bad eyes and his small stature, was up against the bully again, and fear drove him to appeal to the authorities. How else can we account for the fact that the relations of Kipling with Beatty were ever allowed to get to this point? The truth was, as Beatty himself later confessed to Mr. Van de Water, that Rudyard had become involved in a family quarrel between himself and his sister; and one's impulse is to say that Kipling ought to have been able to find some way of extricating himself and making contact with the rather childlike friendliness that seems to have lurked behind the rodomontade of Beatty. But the terrible seriousness of the issue which the incident had raised for Kipling is shown by his statement at the hearing that he 'would not retract a word under threat of death from any living man.'

IV

It was the fight he had fought at school, and he would not capitulate to Beatty Balestier. But he surrendered at last to the 'Proosian Bates.' He invoked the protection of the British system and at the same time prostrated himself before the power of British conquest, which was feared in the United States and which even at that moment in South Africa—the Transvaal Republic declared war on Great Britain in the October of the year of his return—was chastising truculent farmers.

It is at the time of his first flight from America and during the years before his attempt to return—1897–99—that Kipling goes back to his school-days and depicts them in the peculiar colors that we find in *Stalky & Co.* How little inevitable these colors were we learn from Mr. Beresford's memoir. The head master of Westward Ho!, it appears, though really known as the 'Proosian Bates,' was by no means the intent Spartan trainer for the bloody and risky work of the Empire into which Kipling thought it proper to transform him. The fact was that Mr. Cormell Price had been literary rather than military, a friend of Edward Burne-Jones and an earnest anti-Imperialist. He and Burne-Jones had actually organized, at the time of the Russo-Turkish War, a Workers' Neutrality Demonstration against British intervention. But Kipling must now have a head master who will symbolize all the authority of the British educational system, and a school that will represent all that he has heard or imagined—see his highlighting of the fagging system —about the older and more official public schools. The colonial who has criticized the motherland now sets out systematically to glorify her; and it is the proof of his timidity and weakness that he should loudly overdo this glorification.

And now, having declared his allegiance, he is free to hate the enemies of England. His whole point of view has shifted. The bitter animus so deeply implanted by those six years of oppression of his childhood has now become almost entirely dissociated from the objects by which it was originally aroused. It has turned into a generalized hatred of those nations, groups and tendencies, precisely, which stand toward the dominating authority in the relationship of challengers or victims.

The ideal of the 'Anglo-American-German Jew,' which at the time of Kipling's first trip to America represented for him the future of civilization, now immediately goes by the board. His whole tone toward the Americans changes. In *An Error in the Fourth Dimension*—in *The Day's Work*, published in 1898— he makes a rich Anglicized American, the son of a railroad king, deciding for no very good reason that he must immediately go to London, flag and stop an English express train. The railroad first brings charges against him, then decides that he must be insane. They cannot understand his temerity, and he cannot understand their consternation at having the British routine interrupted. Kipling no longer admires the boldness of

Americans: this story is a hateful caricature, so one-sided that the real comedy is sacrificed. *The Captive* followed in 1902. Here a man from Ohio named Laughton O. Zigler sells to the Boers, during their war with the British, a new explosive and a new machine-gun he has invented. He is captured by the English, who grin at him and ask him why he 'wasn't in the Filipeens suppressing our war!' Later he runs into a man from Kentucky, who refuses to shake his hand and tells him that 'he's gone back on the White Man in six places at once—two hemispheres and four continents—America, England, Canada, Australia, New Zealand, and South Africa. . . . Go on and prosper . . . and you'll fetch up by fighting for niggers, as the North did.' As a result of these taunts, and of the respect which has been inspired in him by the spectacle of the splendid behavior of the British, Mr. Zigler gives them the formula for his explosive, insists upon remaining their prisoner, and resolves to settle permanently in South Africa. A still later story, *An Habitation Enforced*, in a collection published in 1909, tells of the victory of the English countryside over an American business man and his wife, who have been aimlessly traveling about Europe. The American wife discovers that her own ancestors came originally from the very locality where they have settled, and they are finally—it is the climax of the story—accepted by the English: 'That wretched Sangres man has twice our money. Can you see Marm Conant slapping him between the shoulders? Not by a jugful! The poor beast doesn't exist!' The Americans succumb, deeply gratified. The husband had had a breakdown from overwork, but his equanimity is quite re-established. In short, Kipling's attitude toward Americans has now been almost reversed since the day of his first visit to the States when he had written, 'I love this People.' He now approves of them only when they are prepared to pay their tribute to Mother England and to identify her interests with theirs.

Later still, during the first years of the World War when Americans were figuring as neutrals, his bitterness became absolutely murderous—as in *Sea Constables: A Tale of '15*. And so had his feeling against the Germans even before the war had begun. In *The Edge of the Evening* (1913), Laughton O. Zigler of Ohio turns up again, this time in England, as occupant of a Georgian mansion inherited by one of the British officers who captured him in South Africa. 'Bein' rich suits me. So does your country, sir. My own country? You heard what that Detroit man said at dinner. "A government of the alien, by the alien, for the alien." Mother's right, too. Lincoln killed us. From the highest motives—but he killed us.' What his mother had said was that Lincoln had 'wasted the heritage of his land by blood and fire, and had surrendered the remnant to aliens': '"My brother, suh," she said, "fell at Gettysburg in order that Armenians should colonize New England today."' (*Something of Myself* confirms the assumption that these were Kipling's own views.) One night a foreign plane makes a forced landing on the estate. Two men get out of the plane, and one of them shoots at his lordship. Zigler lays him out with a golf-club while another of the Englishmen present collars the other man and breaks his neck (it is all right for an American to be lawless, or even for the right sort of Englishman, if he is merely laying low the alien who is the natural enemy of both). They put the dead German spies in the plane and send it up and out over the Channel.

Kipling is now, in fact, implacably opposed to every race and nation which has rebelled against or competed with the Empire, and to every movement and individual—such as the liberals and Fabians—in England who has criticized the imperial policies. His attitude toward the Irish, for example, illustrates the same simple-minded principle as his attitude toward the Americans. So long as the Irish are loyal to England, Kipling shows the liveliest appreciation of Irish recklessness and the Irish sense of mischief: Mulvaney is Irish, McTurk is Irish, Kim is Irish. But the moment they display these same qualities in agitation against the English, they become infamous assassins and traitors. Those peoples who have never given trouble—the Canadians, the New Zealanders, the Australians—though Kipling has never found them interesting enough to write about on any considerable scale, he credits with the most admirable virtues.

And as a basis for all these exclusions, he has laid down a more fundamental principle for the hatred and fear of his fellows: the anti-democratic principle. We are familiar with the case of the gifted man who has found himself at a disadvantage in relation to his social superiors and who makes himself the champion of all who have suffered in a similar way. What is not so familiar is the inverse of this: the case of the individual who at the period when he has most needed freedom to develop superior abilities has found himself cramped and tormented by the stupidity of social inferiors, and who has in consequence acquired a distrust of the whole idea of popular government. Rudyard Kipling was probably an example of this. The ferocious antagonism to democracy which finally overtakes him must have been fed by the fear of that household at Southsea which tried to choke his genius at its birth. His sister says that through all this period he was in the habit of keeping up their spirit by reminding himself and her that their guardian was 'of such low caste as not to matter . . . She was a *Kuch-nay*, a Nothing-at-all, and that secret name was a great comfort to us, and useful, too, when Harry practised his talent for eavesdropping.' Some very unyielding resistance was evidently built up at this time against the standards and opinions of people whom he regarded as lower-class.

The volume called *Traffics and Discoveries*, published in 1904, marks the complete metamorphosis of Kipling. The collection that preceded, *The Day's Work*, though these tendencies had already begun to appear in it, still preserves certain human values: the English officials in the Indian stories—*The Tomb of His Ancestors* and *William the Conqueror*—still display some sympathetic interest in the natives. But the Kipling of the South African stories is venomous, morbid, distorted.

When the Boer War finally breaks, Kipling is at once on the spot, with almost all the correct reactions. He is now at the zenith of his reputation, and he receives every official courtesy. And though he may criticize the handling of a campaign, he never questions the rightness of its object. He has the impulse to get close to the troops, edits a paper for the soldiers; but his attitude toward the Tommy has changed. He had already been entertained and enlightened by Lord Dufferin, the British Viceroy in India. Hitherto, he tells us in his memoirs, he 'had seen the administrative machinery from beneath, all stripped and overheated. This was the first time I had listened to one who had handled it from above.' Another passage from *Something of Myself* shows how his emphasis has altered: 'I happened to fall unreservedly, in darkness, over a man near the train, and filled my palms with gravel. He explained in an even voice that he was "fractured 'ip, sir. 'Ope you ain't 'urt your-self, sir?" I never got at this unknown Philip Sidney's name. They were wonderful even in the hour of death—these men and boys—lodgekeepers and ex-butlers of the Reserve and raw town-lads of twenty.' Here he is trying to pay a tribute; yet it is obvious that the Kipling who was proud to be questioned in India by Lord Roberts as if he were a colonel has triumphed over the Kipling who answered him as a spokesman for the un-fortunate soldiers. Today he is becoming primarily a man whom a soldier addresses as 'sir,' as a soldier is becoming for Kipling a man whose capacity for heroism is indicated by re-maining respectful with a fractured hip. The cockney Ortheris of *Soldiers Three* and the officer who had insulted him at drill had waived the Courts Martial manual and fought it out man to man; but by the time of the Boer War the virtue of Kipling's officers and soldiers consists primarily in knowing their stations.

Kipling had written at the beginning of the war, a poem called *The Absent-Minded Beggar*, which was an appeal for contributions to a fund for the families of the troops in South Africa; but this poem is essentially a money-raising poem: it had nothing like the spontaneous feeling of,

> I went into a public-'ouse to get a pint o' beer;
> The publican 'e up an' sez, 'We serve no red-coats here.'

The Barrack-Room Ballads were good in their kind: they gave the Tommy a voice, to which people stopped and listened. Kipling was interested in the soldier for his own sake, and made some effort to present his life as it seemed to the soldier himself. The poem called *Loot*, for example, which worries Mr. Edward Shanks because it appears to celebrate a reprehensible practice, is in reality perfectly legitimate because it simply de-scribes one of the features of the soldier's experience in India. There is no moral one way or the other. The ballads of *The Five Nations*, on the other hand, the fruits of Kipling's experi-ence in South Africa, are about ninety per cent mere rhymed journalism, decorating the readymade morality of a patriotic partisan. Compare one of the most successful of the earlier se-ries with one of the most ambitious of the later.

The Injian Ocean sets an' smiles
　　So sof', so bright, so bloomin' blue;
There aren't a wave for miles an' miles
　　Excep' the jiggle from the screw:
The ship is swep', the day is done,
　　The bugle's gone for smoke and play;
An' black agin' the settin' sun
　　The Lascar sings, '*Hum deckty hai!*'

For to admire an' for to see,
　　For to be'old this world so wide—
It never done no good to me,
　　But I can't drop it if I tried!

Contrast this with *The Return* (from South Africa).

Peace is declared, an' I return
　　To 'Ackneystadt, but not the same;
Things 'ave transpired which made me learn
　　The size and meanin' of the game.
I did no more than others did,
　　I don't know where the change began;
I started as an average kid,
　　I finished as a thinkin' man.

If England was what England seems
　　An' not the England of our dreams,
But only putty, brass an' paint,
　　'Ow quick we'd drop 'er! But she ain't!

Before my gappin' mouth could speak
　　I 'eard it in my comrade's tone;
I saw it on my neighbor's cheek
　　Before I felt it flush my own.
An' last it come to me—not pride,
　　Nor yet conceit, but on the 'ole
(If such a term may be applied),
　　The makin's of a bloomin' soul.

This is hollow, synthetic, sickening. '*Having no position to consider and my trade enforcing it, I could move at will in the fourth dimension.*' He *has* a position to consider today, he eats at the captain's table, travels in special trains; and he is losing the freedom of that fourth dimension. There is a significant glimpse of the Kipling of the South African imperialist period in the diary of Arnold Bennett: 'I was responding to Pauline Smith's curiosity about the personalities of authors when Mrs. Smith began to talk about Kipling. She said he was greatly disliked in South Africa. Regarded as conceited and unapproachable. The officers of the Union Castle ships dreaded him, and prayed not to find themselves on the same ship as him. It seems that on one ship he had got all the information possible out of the officers, and had then, at the end of the voyage, reported them at headquarters for flirting with passengers—all except the chief engineer, an old Scotchman with whom he had been friendly. With this exception they were all called up to headquarters and reprimanded, and now they would have nothing to do with passengers.'

As for the Indians, they are now to be judged rigorously on the basis of their loyalty to the English in Africa. There are included in *Traffics and Discoveries* two jingoistic Sunday School stories which are certainly among the falsest and most foolish of Kipling's mature productions. In *The Comprehension of Private Copper*, he vents his contempt on an Anglicized Indian, the son of a settler in the Transvaal, who has sided with the Boers against the English; *A Sahibs' War*, on the other hand, presents an exemplary Sikh, who accompanies a British officer to South Africa, serves him with the devotion of a dog, and continues to practice after his leader's death the public-school principles of sportsmanship he has learned from him, in the face of the temptation to a cruel revenge against the treachery of the Boers. As for the Boers themselves, Kipling adopts toward them a systematic sneer. The assumption appears to be that to ambush the British is not cricket. Though the Dutch are unquestionably white men, Kipling manages somehow to imply that they have proved renegades to white solidarity by allying themselves with the black natives.

One is surprised to learn from *Something of Myself* that over a period of seven years after the war (1900–07), Kipling spent almost half his time in South Africa, going there for five or six months of every year. He seems to have so little to show for it: a few short stories, and most of these far from his best. He had made the acquaintance of Cecil Rhodes, and must simply have sat at his feet. The Kiplings lived in a house just off the Rhodes estate; and Kipling devotes long pages to the animals in Rhodes's private zoo and to architectural details of Rhodes's houses. Even writing in 1935, he sounds like nothing so much as a high-paid publicity agent. It turns out that the Polonius-precepts in the celebrated verses called *If——* were inspired by Kipling's conception of the character of Dr. Jameson, the leader of the Jameson raid.

It may be worth mentioning here in connection with Kipling's submission to official authority that he has been described by a close friend, Viscount Castlerosse, as having abdicated his authority also in other important relations. 'They [the Kiplings],' he says, 'were among the few happy pairs I have ever met; but as far as Kipling was concerned, his married life was one of complete surrender. To him Carrie, as he called her, was more than a wife. She was a mistress in the literal sense, a governess and a matron. In a lesser woman I should have used the term "nurse." Kipling handed himself over bodily, financially and spiritually to his spouse. He had no banking account. All the money which he earned was handed over to her, and she, in turn, would dole him out so much pocket money. He could not call his time or even his stomach his own. . . .

'Sometimes in the evening, enlivened by wine and company, he would take a glass more than he was accustomed to, and then those great big eyes of his would shine brightly behind his strong spectacles, and Rud would take to talking faster and his views would become even more emphatic. If Mrs. Kipling was with him, she would quickly note the change and, sure enough, in a decisive voice she would issue the word of command: "Rud, it is time you went to bed," and Rud always discovered that it was about time he went to bed.

'I myself during the long years never once saw any signs of murmuring or of even incipient mutiny.'

In any case, Kipling has committed one of the most serious sins against his calling which are possible for an imaginative writer. He has resisted his own sense of life and discarded his own moral intelligence in favor of the point of view of a dominant political party. To Lord Roberts and Joseph Chamberlain he has sacrificed the living world of his own earlier artistic creations and of the heterogeneous human beings for whom they were offered as symbols. Here the constraint of making the correct pro-imperialist point is squeezing out all the kind of interest which is proper to a work of fiction. Compare a story of the middle Kipling with a story by Stephen Crane or Joseph Conrad, who were dealing with somewhat similar subjects. Both Conrad and Crane are pursuing their independent researches into the moral life of man. Where the spy who is the hero of *Under Western Eyes* is a tormented and touching figure, confused in his allegiances by the circumstances of his birth, a secret agent in Kipling must invariably be either a stout fellow, because his ruses are to the advantage of the British, or a sinister lying dog, because he is serving the enemy. Where the killing of *The Blue Hotel* is made to implicate everybody connected with it in a common human guilt, a killing in a story by Kipling must absolutely be shown to be either a dastardly or a virtuous act.

To contrast Kipling with Conrad or Crane is to enable us to get down at last to what is probably the basic explanation of the failure of Kipling's nerve. He lacked faith in the artist's vocation. We have heard a good deal in modern literature about the artist in conflict with the bourgeois world. Flaubert made war on the bourgeois; Rimbaud abandoned poetry as piffling in order to realize the adventure of commerce; Thomas Mann took as his theme the emotions of weakness and defeat of the artist overshadowed by the business man. But Kipling neither faced the fight like Flaubert, nor faced the problem in his life like Rimbaud, nor faced the problem in his art like Mann. Something in him, something vulgar in the middle-class British way, something perhaps connected with the Methodist ministers who were his grandfathers on both sides, a tradition which understood preaching and could understand craftsmanship, but had a good deal of respect for the powers that governed the material world and never thought of putting the artist on a par with them—something of this sort at a given point prevented Kipling from playing through his part, and betrayed him into dedicating his talents to the praise of the practical man. Instead of *becoming* a man of action like Rimbaud, a course which shows a boldness of logic, he fell into the ignominious rôle of the artist who prostrates his art before the achievements of soldiers and merchants, and who is always declaring the supremacy of the 'doer' over the man of ideas.

The results of this are very curious and well worth studying from the artistic point of view—because Kipling, it must always be remembered, was a man of really remarkable abilities. Certain of the symptoms of his case have been indicated by George Moore and Dixon Scott, whose discussions of him in *Avowals* and *Men of Letters* are among the few first-rate pieces of criticism that I remember to have seen on the subject. George Moore quotes a passage from *Kim*, a description of evening in India, and praises it for 'the perfection of the writing, of the strong masculine rhythm of every sentence, and of the accuracy of every observation'; but then goes on to point out that 'Mr. Kipling has seen much more than he has felt,' that 'when we come to analyze the lines we find a touch of local color not only in every sentence, but in each part between each semicolon.' So Scott diagnoses admirably the mechanical ingenuity of plot that distinguishes the middle Kipling. 'Switch,' he says, 'this imperatively map-making, pattern-making method upon . . . the element of human nature, and what is the inevitable result? Inevitably, there is the same sudden stiffening and formulation. The characters spring to attention like soldiers on parade; they respond briskly to a sudden description; they wear a fixed set of idiosyncrasies like a uniform. A mind like this *must* use types and set counters; it feels dissatisfied, ineffective, unsafe, unless it can reduce the fluid waverings of character, its flitting caprices and twilit desires, to some tangible system. The characters of such a man will not only be definite; they will be definitions.' And he goes on to show how Kipling's use of dialect makes a screen for his relinquishment of his grip on the real organism of human personality: 'For dialect, in spite of all its air of ragged lawlessness, is wholly impersonal, typical, fixed, the code of a caste, not the voice of an individual. It is when the novelist sets his characters talking the King's English that he really puts his capacity for reproducing the unconventional and capricious on its trial. Mr. Kipling's plain conversations are markedly unreal. But honest craftsmanship and an ear for strong rhythms have provided him with many suits of dialects. And with these he dresses the talk till it seems to surge with character.'

The packed detail, the automatic plot, the surfaces lacquered with dialect, the ever-tightening tension of form, are all a part of Kipling's effort to impose his scheme by main force. The strangest result of this effort is to be seen in a change in the subject matter itself. Kipling actually tends at this time to abandon human beings altogether. In that letter of Henry James in which he speaks of his former hope that Kipling might grow into an English Balzac, he goes on: 'But I have given that up in proportion as he has come steadily from the less simple in subject to the more simple—from the Anglo-Indians to the natives, from the natives to the Tommies, from the Tommies to the quadrupeds, from the quadrupeds to the fish, and from the fish to the engines and screws.' This increasing addiction of Kipling to animals, insects and machines is evidently to be explained by his need to find characters which will yield themselves unresistingly to being presented as parts of a system. In the *Jungle Books*, the animal characters are each one all of a piece, though in their ensemble they still provide a variety, and they are dominated by a 'Law of the Jungle,' which lays down their duties and rights. The animals have organized the Jungle, and the Jungle is presided over by Mowgli in his function of forest ranger, so that it falls into its subsidiary place in the larger organization of the Empire.

Yet the *Jungle Books* (written in Vermont) are not artistically off the track; the element of obvious allegory is not out of place in such fairy tales. It is when Kipling takes to contriving these animal allegories for grown-ups that he brings up the reader's gorge. What is proved in regard to human beings by the fable called *A Walking Delegate*, in which a pastureful of self-respecting horses turn and rend a yellow loafer from Kansas, who is attempting to incite them to rebellion against their master, Man? A labor leader and the men he is trying to organize are, after all, not horses but men. Does Kipling mean to imply that the ordinary workingman stands in the same relation to the employing and governing classes as that in which the horse stands to its owner? And what is proved by *The Mother Hive*, in which an invasion of wax-moths that ruin the stock of the swarm represents the infiltration of socialism? (Compare these with that more humane fable of 1893, *The Children of the Zodiac*, which deals with gods become men.) And, though the discipline of a military unit or of the crew of a ship or a plane may provide a certain human interest, it makes us a little uncomfortable to find Kipling taking up locomotives and representing '.007' instead of the engineer who drives it as the hero of the American railroad; and descending even to the mechanical parts, the rivets and planks of a ship, whose drama consists solely of being knocked into place by the elements so that it may function as a co-ordinated whole.

We may lose interest, like Henry James, in the animal or mechanical characters of Kipling's middle period; but we must admit that these novel productions have their own peculiar merit. It is the paradox of Kipling's career that he should have extended the conquests of his craftsmanship in proportion to the shrinking of the range of his dramatic imagination. As his responses to human beings became duller, his sensitivity to his medium increased.

In both tendencies he was, of course, quite faithful to certain aspects of the life of his age. It was a period, those early nineteen hundreds, of brilliant technological improvement and of generally stunted intelligence. And Kipling now appeared as the poet both of the new mechanical methods and of the ideals of the people who spread them. To re-read these stories today is to feel again a little of the thrill of the plushy transcontinental Pullmans and the spic-and-span transatlantic liners that carried us around in our youth, and to meet again the bright and bustling people, talking about the polo field and the stock market, smart Paris and lovely California, the latest musical comedy and Kipling, in the smoking-rooms or among the steamer-chairs.

Kipling reflected this mechanical progress by evolving a new prose technique. We have often since Kipling's day been harangued by the Futurists and others about the need for artistic innovations appropriate to the life of the machine age; but it is doubtful whether any rhapsodist of motor-cars or photographer of dynamos and valves has been so successful at this as Kipling was at the time he wrote *The Day's Work*. These stories of his get their effects with the energy and accuracy of engines, by means of words that, hard, short and close-fitting, give the impression of ball-bearings and cogs. Beside them, the spoutings of the machine fans look like the old-fashioned rhetoric they are. For these latter could merely whoop and roar in a manner essentially romantic over the bigness, the power, the speed of the machines, whereas Kipling exemplified in his form itself the mechanical efficiency and discipline, and he managed to convey with precision both the grimness and the exhilaration which characterized the triumph of the machine.

He also brought to perfection the literary use of the language of the specialized industrial world. He must have been the principal artisan in the creation of that peculiar modern *genre* in which we are made to see some comedy or tragedy through the cheapening or obscuring medium of technical vocabulary or professional slang. He did not, of course, invent the dialect monologue; but it is improbable that we should have had, for example, either the baseball stories of Ring Lardner or the Cyclops episode in *Ulysses* if Kipling had never written.

This is partly no doubt pure virtuosity. Mr. Beresford says that Kipling was by nature as unmechanical as possible, could do nothing with his hands except write; and I have heard an amusing story of his astonishment and admiration at the mechanical proficiency of an American friend who had simply put a castor back on a chair. He had never worked at any of the processes he described, had had to get them all up through the methods of the attentive reporter. But it is virtuosity on a much higher level than that of the imitation literature so often admired in that era. Where Stevenson turns out paler *pastiches* of veins which have already been exploited, Kipling really finds new rhythms, new colors and textures of words, for things that have not yet been brought into literature. For the most part a second-rate writer of verse, because though he can imitate the language of poetry as he can imitate all the other languages, he cannot compensate for the falsity of his feeling by his sharp observation and his expert technique, he is extraordinary as a worker in prose. It is impossible still for a prose writer to read, for example, the first part of *The Bridge-Builders* without marveling at the author's mastery. How he has caught the very look and feel of the materials that go to make bridges and of the various aspects of the waters they have to dominate! And the maneuvers of modern armies against the dusty South African landscapes, and the tempo of American trains, and the relation of the Scotch engineer to the patched-up machines of his ship. The Kipling who put on record all these things was an original and accomplished artist.

For the rest, he writes stories for children. One is surprised in going back over Kipling's work to find that, dating from the time of his settling with his family in Vermont, he published no less than nine children's books: the two *Jungle Books, Captains Courageous, Just So Stories, Stalky & Co., Puck of Pook's Hill, Rewards and Fairies, A History of England, Land and Sea Tales for Scouts and Scouts Masters.* It is as if the natural human feelings progressively forced out of his work by the rigors of organization for its own sake were seeking relief in a reversion to childhood, when one has not yet become responsible for the way that the world is run, where it is enough to enjoy and to wonder at what we do not yet understand. And, on the other hand, the simplified morality to which Kipling has now committed himself is easier to make acceptable to one's readers and oneself if one approaches it from the point of view of the child. (The truth is that much of his work of this period which aims at the intelligence of grown people might almost equally well be subtitled *For Scouts and Scouts Masters.*) These stories, excellent at their best, are most successful when they are *most* irresponsible—as in the *Just So Stories;* least so, as in *Captains Courageous,* when they lean most heavily on the schoolboy morality.

The most ambitious of them—the two series about Puck of Pook's Hill (1906 and 1910)—have, I know, been much admired by certain critics, including the sensitive Dixon Scott; but my own taste rejects them on re-reading them as it did when I read them first at the age for which they were presumably intended. Kipling tells us that the stories in *Rewards and Fairies* were designed to carry a meaning for adults as well as to interest children. But their technical sophistication puts them slightly above the heads of children at the same time that their sugared exploitation of Kipling's Anglo-Spartan code of conduct makes them slightly repugnant to grown-ups.

They are, to be sure, the most embroidered productions of Kipling's most elaborate period. The recovery of obsolete arts and crafts, the re-creation of obsolete idioms, are new pretexts for virtuosity. Kipling's genius for words has been stimulated by the discovery of the English earth and sea; he spreads on the rich grassiness of the English country, the dense fogginess of the English coast, the layers upon layers of tradition that cause the English character to seem to him deep-rooted, deep-colored, deep-meaning. He has applied all his delicacy and strength to this effort to get the mother-country into prose; but his England is never so real as was his India; and the effect, for all the sinewy writing, is somehow fundamentally decadent. The Normans and the Saxons and the Elizabethans, the great cathedral-builders and sailors and divines, perpetrating impossible 'gags,' striking postures that verge on the 'ham,' seem almost to anticipate Hollywood. The theme of the rôle and the ordeal of the artist which figures in *Rewards and Fairies* suffers from being treated in the vein of *Stalky & Co*. In the story called *The Wrong Thing*, he embarks on a promising subject: the discrepancy between the aim of the artist who is straining to top the standards of his craft, and the quite irrelevant kinds of interest that the powers that employ him may take in him; but he turns it into a farce and ruins it.

Kipling's England is perhaps the most synthetic of all his creations of this period, when he depends so much on tools and materials as distinguished from sympathy and insight. Scott says that these stories are opalescent; and this is true, but they show the defects of opals that have been artificially made and whose variegated glimmerings and shiftings do not seem to convey anything mysterious.

v

Yet, in locating the Ideal in the Empire, Kipling was not without his moments of uneasiness. *If* the Empire is really founded on self-discipline, the fear of God, the code of *noblesse oblige,* if it really involves a moral system, then we are justified in identifying it with 'the Law'; but suppose that it is not really so dedicated.

> If England was what England seems,
> An' not the England of our dreams,
> But only putty, brass an' paint,
> 'Ow quick we'd drop 'er! *But she ain't!*

Yet *Recessional*, perhaps the best set of verses that Kipling ever wrote, is a warning that springs from a doubt; and the story called *The Man Who Would Be King* is surely a parable of what might happen to the English if they should forfeit their moral authority. Two low-class English adventurers put themselves over on the natives of a remote region beyond Afghanistan, organize under a single rule a whole set of mountain tribes; but the man who has made himself king is destroyed by the natives that have adored him the instant they come to realize that he is not a god, as they had supposed, but a man. The Wesleyan preacher in Kipling knows that the valiant dust of man can build only on dust if it builds not in the name of God; and he is prepared to pound the pulpit and call down the Almighty's anger when parliamentarians or ministers or generals debauch their office or hold it light. Kipling always refused official honors in order to keep himself free; and his truculence had its valuable aspect in that it aided him to resist the briberies of his period of glory and fortune. In the volume of his collected addresses, which he calls *A Book of Words*, there are some sincere and inspiriting sermons. 'Now I do not ask you not to be carried away by the first rush of the great game of life. That is expecting you to be more than human,' he told the students at McGill University in the fall of 1907, when the height of his popularity was past. 'But I *do* ask you, after the first heat of the game, that you draw breath and watch your fellows for a while. Sooner or later, you will see some man to whom the idea of wealth as mere wealth does not appeal, whom the methods of amassing that wealth do not interest, and who will not accept money if you offer it to him at a certain price. At first you will be inclined to laugh at this man and to think that he is not "smart" in his ideas. I suggest that you watch him closely, for he will presently demonstrate to you that money dominates everybody except the man who does not want money. You may meet that man on your farm, in your village, or in your legislature. But be sure that, whenever or wherever you meet him, as soon as it comes to a direct issue between you, his little finger will be thicker than your loins. You will go in fear of him: he will not go in fear of you. You will do what he wants: he will not do what you want. You will find that you have no weapon in your armoury with which you can attack him; no argument with which you can appeal to him. Whatever you gain, he will gain more.'

If Kipling *had* taken a bribe, it was not that of reputation or cash; it was rather the big moral bribe that a political system can offer: the promise of mental security. And even here a peculiar integrity—as it were, an integrity of *temperament* that came to exist in dissociation from the intellect—survived the collapse of the system and saved Kipling in the end from his pretenses. How this happened is the last chapter of his story.

There was, as I say, a Wesleyan preacher in Kipling. The Old Testament served him as an armory of grim instances and menacing visions to drive home the imperial code; or, on occasions when the imperial masters failed to live up to this code, of scorching rhetorical language (though with more of malignancy than of grandeur) for the chastisement of a generation of vipers. But Kipling had no real religion. He exploited, in his poems and his fiction, the mythology of a number of religions. We may be inclined to feel, in reading Kipling—and to some extent we shall be right—that the various symbols and gods which figure in his stories and poems are mere properties which the writer finds useful for his purposes of rhetoric or romance. Yet we cannot but suspect in *Kim* and in the stories of metempsychosis that Kipling has been seriously influenced by the Buddhism which he had imbibed with his first language in his boyhood. Mr. Beresford corroborates this: he says that the Kipling of Westward Ho! talked Buddhism and reincarnation. And it is certainly with Buddhism that we first find associated a mystical side of Kipling's mind which, in this last phase, is to emerge into the foreground.

We left the Lama of *Kim* attaining the Buddhist ecstasy and escaping from the Wheel of Things at the same moment that

Kim gets promotion and finally becomes a spoke in the wheel of British administration. But the world-beyond of the Lama is to seep back into Kipling's work in queer and incongruous forms. Among the strained political fables of the collection called *Traffics and Discoveries*, which is the beginning of the more somber later Kipling, there is a story of a wireless operator who is possessed by the soul of Keats. It may be that Kipling's Southsea experience, in driving him back into his imagination for defense against the horror of reality, had had the effect both of intensifying his fancies and of dissociating them from ordinary life—so that the ascent out of the Wheel of Things and the visitations of an alien soul became ways of representing this. The effort of the grown-up Kipling to embrace by the imagination, to master by a disciplined art, what he regarded as the practical realities is to be subject to sudden recoils. In the Kipling of the middle period, there is a suppressed but vital element which thrusts periodically a lunatic head out of a window of the well-bricked façade.

This element is connected with the Lama, but it is also connected with something else more familiar to the Western world: the visitations and alienations of what is now known as neurotic personality. Here again Kipling was true to his age. While the locomotives and airplanes and steamers were beating records and binding continents, the human engine was going wrong. The age of mechanical technique was also the age of the nerve sanitarium. In the stories of the early Kipling, the intervention of the supernatural has, as a rule, within the frame of the story itself, very little psychological interest; but already in '*They*' and *The Brushwood Boy* the dream and the hallucination are taking on a more emphatic significance. With *The House Surgeon* and *In the Same Boat*, they are in process of emerging from the fairy tale: they become recognizable as psychiatric symptoms. The depression described in *The House Surgeon* has been transferred, by the artifice of the story, to persons unconcerned in the tragedy through the influence from a distance of someone else; but the woman with whom the terror originates is suffering morbidly from feelings of guilt, and the sensations are evidently based on the first-hand experience of the author.

'And it was just then that I was aware of a little gray shadow, as it might have been a snowflake seen against the light, floating at an immense distance in the background of my brain. It annoyed me, and I shook my head to get rid of it. Then my brain telegraphed that it was the forerunner of a swift-striding gloom which there was yet time to escape if I would force my thoughts away from it, as a man leaping for life forces his body forward and away from the fall of a wall. But the gloom overtook me before I could take in the meaning of the message. I moved toward the bed, every nerve already aching with the foreknowledge of the pain that was to be dealt it, and sat down, while my amazed and angry soul dropped, gulf by gulf, into that horror of great darkness which is spoken of in the Bible, and which, as the auctioneers say, must be experienced to be appreciated.

'Despair upon despair, misery upon misery, fear after fear, each causing their distinct and separate woe, packed in upon me for an unrecorded length of time, until at last they blurred together, and I heard a click in my brain like the click in the ear when one descends in a diving bell, and I knew that the pressures were equalized within and without, and that, for the moment, the worst was at an end. But I knew also that at any moment the darkness might come down anew; and while I dwelt on this speculation precisely as a man torments a raging tooth with his tongue, it ebbed away into the little gray shadow on the brain of its first coming, and once more I heard my brain, which knew what would recur, telegraph to every quarter for help, release or diversion.'

And although the periodical irrational panics of the couple of *In the Same Boat* are explained as the result of pre-natal shocks, the description of the man and woman themselves, with their 'nerve doctors,' their desperate drug-taking, their shaky and futile journeys in flight from their neurotic fears, their peculiar neurotic relationship, constitutes an accurate account of a phenomenon of contemporary life which, at the time that Kipling was writing, had hardly been described in fiction.

Observe that in both these stories, as in the stories of war neurosis that will follow, the people who suffer thus are quite innocent, their agony is entirely unearned. I believe that the only cases in which the obsessive horror is connected with any kind of guilt are those in which a man is hounded to death by

the vision of a woman he has wronged. This theme recurs reg-
ularly with Kipling from the time of *The Phantom Rickshaw*,
one of the very first of his short stories, through the remarkable *Mrs. Bathurst* of his middle period, and up to the strange
and poisoned *Dayspring Mishandled*, which was one of the last
things he wrote. We cannot speculate with very much assurance on the relation of this theme of betrayal to the other recurring themes of Kipling's work. We do not know enough
about his life to be able to assign it to an assumption on the
part of the six-year-old Kipling that he must somehow have
sinned against the mother who had abandoned him so inexplicably at Southsea; or to relate it to the strange situation of
Dick Heldar in *The Light That Failed*, who vainly adores, and
goes blind in adoring, the inexplicably obdurate Maisie. All we
can say is that the theme of the anguish which is suffered with
out being deserved has the appearance of having been derived
from a morbid permanent feeling of injury inflicted by his experience at Southsea.

Certainly the fear of darkness passing into the fear of blindness which runs all through his work from *The Light That
Failed* to '*They*' is traceable directly to his breakdown and to
the frightening failure of his eyes. This was a pattern he seems
to have repeated. Illnesses were critical for Kipling. It was after
his illness in India that he set out to contend with a society
which must have seemed to him indifferent and brutal by
making himself a writer; and it was after his illness in New York
that he decided to turn his back on America and to accept all
the values that that retreat implied. It was after the breakdown
in which Kim had brooded on his true identity that he
emerged as a fullblown British agent. From the darkness and
the physical weakness, the Kipling of the middle period has
come forth with tightened nerves, resolved to meet a state of
things in which horses are always being whipped or having
their heads blown off, in which schoolboys are bullied and
flogged, in which soldiers are imprisoned in barracks and fed
to the bayonets and guns, by identifying himself with horses—
as in the story called *A Walking Delegate*—that gang together
to kick and maul another horse, with schoolboys—as in *The
Moral Reformers* of *Stalky*—that gloat in torturing other
schoolboys, with soldiers that get the sharpest satisfaction from

stabbing and pot-shotting other soldiers. He has set himself with all the stiff ribs of a metal-armatured art to stand up to this world outside that gets its authority from its power to crush and kill: the world of the Southsea house that has turned into the world of the Empire; to compete with it on its own terms. And yet the darkness and the illness return. It is a key to the whole work of Kipling that the great celebrant of physical courage should prove in the long run to convey his most moving and convincing effects in describing moral panic. Kipling's bullyings and killings are contemptible: they are the fantasies of the physically helpless. The only authentic heroism to be found in the fiction of Kipling is the heroism of moral fortitude on the edge of a nervous collapse.

And in the later decades of Kipling's life the blackness and the panic close down; the abyss becomes more menacing. It is the Crab, both devil and destiny, which in the story called *The Children of the Zodiac* lies always in wait for the poet and finally comes to devour him. The nurse-like watchfulness of Mrs. Kipling and Kipling's fear of stepping out of her régime, which appeared to his friend an impediment to the development of his genius, were no doubt, on the contrary, in his extreme instability, a condition of his being able to function at all—just as the violence of his determination to find the answer to the problems of society and a defense against the forces that plagued him in the program of an imperialist government was evidently directly related to the violence of desperation of his need.

But now both of these shelters he had built himself—the roof of his family life, the confidence of his political idealism—were suddenly to be broken down.

In 1914–18, the British Empire collided with a competitor. All England went to war, including Kipling's only son. The boy, not yet out of his teens, was killed in an attack before Loos in September 1915, and his body was never found. John Kipling had at first been reported missing, and his father waited for months in the hope of getting a letter from Germany announcing that he had been taken prisoner.

These war years left Kipling defenseless. It had been easy to be grimly romantic on the subject of the warfare in India when

Kipling had never seen fighting; it had even been possible, as a reporter at the front, to Meissonier the campaign in South Africa in the bright colors of the new nineteenth century. But the long systematic waste of the trench warfare of the struggle against Germany discouraged the artistic exploitation of the cruelties and gallantries of battle. The strain of the suspense and the horror taxed intolerably those attitudes of Kipling's which had been in the first instance provoked by a strain and which had only at the cost of a strain been kept up.

From even before the war, the conduct of British policy had been far from pleasing to Kipling. He saw clearly the careerism and the venality of the modern politician; and he was bitterly opposed on principle to the proposals of the radicals and liberals. In May, 1914, when civil war with Ulster was threatening, he delivered at Tunbridge Wells and allowed to be circulated as a penny leaflet a speech against the Home Rule Bill of a virulence almost hysterical. The attempt to free Ireland he excoriates as on a level with the Marconi scandals. 'The Home Rule Bill,' he declares, 'broke the pledged faith of generations; it officially recognized sedition, privy conspiracy and rebellion; it subsidized the secret forces of boycott, intimidation and murder; and it created an independent stronghold in which all these forces could work together, as they have always and openly boasted that they would, for the destruction of Great Britain.'

This was to remain Kipling's temper in public questions. The victory of the Bolsheviks in Russia of course made the picture blacker: one sixth of the area of the globe, he said, had 'passed bodily out of civilization.'

> Our world has passed away,
> In wantonness o'erthrown.
> There is nothing left to-day
> But steel and fire and stone!

he wrote when the war began. And when Kipling was sickened and broken with steel and fire and stone, there was little for his spirit to lean on.

Little but the practice of his craft, which now reflects only the twisted fragments of Kipling's exploded cosmos.

These latest stories of Kipling's have attracted meager attention for reasons that are easily comprehensible. The disappearance in the middle Kipling of the interest in human beings for
their own sake and the deliberate cultivation of the excommu-
nicatory imperialist hatreds had already had the effect of discouraging the appetite of the general public; and when the
human element reappeared in a new tormented form in
Kipling's later stories, the elliptical and complex technique
which the writer had by that time developed put the general
reader off. On the other hand, the highbrows ignored him,
because, in the era of Lawrence and Joyce, when the world was
disgusted with soldiering and when the imperialisms were apparently deflated, they could take no interest in the point of
view. In their conviction that Kipling could never hold water,
they had not even enough curiosity to wonder what had happened to an author who must have enchanted them in their
childhood. And in a sense they were, of course, correct.
Kipling *had* terribly shrunk; he seemed a man who had had a
stroke and was only half himself—whereas Yeats was playing
out superbly the last act of a personal drama which he had sustained unembarrassed by public events, and Henry James was
now seen in retrospect to have accomplished, in his long career, a prodigy of disinterested devotion to an art and a criticism of life. Where there was so much wreckage around,
political, social and moral, the figure of the disinterested artist
commanded especial respect.

Yet the Kipling who limped out of the wreckage, shrunken
and wry though he looks, has in a sense had his development
as an artist. Some of these stories are the most intense in feeling
as they are among the most concentrated in form that Kipling
ever wrote; to a writer, they are perhaps the most interesting.
The subjects are sometimes hard to swallow, and the stories
themselves—through a tasteless device which unfortunately
grew on Kipling as he got older—are each preceded and followed by poems which elaborate or elucidate their themes in
the author's synthetic verse and which dull the effect of the excellent prose. But here Kipling's peculiar method, trained with
deadly intention, scores some of its cleanest hits.

Let us, however, first consider the subjects of these final collections of stories (*A Diversity of Creatures, Debits and Credits,*

and *Limits and Renewals*). The fragments of the disintegrated Kipling fall roughly into five classes: tales of hatred, farces based on practical jokes, studies of neurotic cases, tales of fellowship in religion, and tales of personal bereavement.

The tales of hatred—hatred of Americans and the Germans: *Sea Constables* and *Mary Postgate*—become murderous at the time of the war (though they give place to other kinds of themes later). The hatred of democracy—in the satire called *As Easy as A.B.C.* (which appeared in 1912)—is carried to lengths that would be Swiftian if Kipling had subjected the whole human race to the death ray of his abstract contempt, but which—as Edward Shanks points out—is rendered rather suspect by the exemption from the annihilating irony of a group of disciplined officials. The morals of these stories are odious and the plots mostly contrived and preposterous; yet they acquire a certain dignity from the desperation of bitterness that animates them.

Then there are the practical jokes—a category which includes the comic accidents: practical jokes engineered by the author. These have always been a feature of Kipling. His addiction to this form of humor seems to have derived originally from the boobytraps and baitings of Westward Ho!; later, changing sides, he identified them rather with the lickings-into-shape inflicted by regimental raggings. The victims of these pulverizing hoaxes fall into two classes: petty tyrants, who humiliate and bully, and who always have to be cads; and political idealists and godless intellectuals, who have to be nincompoops. Kipling likes nothing better than to hurl one of these latter into a hive of bees or, as in one of his early stories, to silence his opinions by a sunstroke. A first principle of Kipling's world is revenge: the humiliated must become the humiliator. One might expect this kind of thing to disappear in the work of the latest Kipling; but the formula becomes instead much more frequent, and it comes to play a special rôle. The practical joke with its extravagant laughter is a violent if hollow explosion for the relief of nervous strain; and the severity of this strain may be gauged by the prodigious dimensions of the hoaxes in which Kipling now labors to concentrate the complex calculation of an Ibsen and the methodical ferocity of a Chinese executioner.

In some of these stories, the comic disaster is exploited as a therapeutic device. There are six stories of war neurosis in Kipling's last two collections. The situation of the shattered veteran provided him with an opportunity for studying further a subject which had haunted him all his life: the condition of people who seem to themselves on the borderline of madness. Here the sufferers are still perfectly guiltless. In one case, an appearance of guilt, in another, a conviction of guilt, turn out to be actually unjustified. But the picture is now more realistically filled out than it was by the pre-natal occurrences which were the best Kipling could do for motivation for the neurotics of *In the Same Boat*. The war supplies real causes for derangement; and Kipling sees that such short-circuits may be mended by going back to the occasion that gave rise to the obsession and disentangling the crossed wires. But his principal prescriptions for saving people from the effects of the horror and the strain of the war are such apropos comic accidents and well-aimed benevolent frauds as, in reality, are rarely possible and which would be of doubtful efficacy if they were. In one story, the fantasy of the sick man turns out to be based on a reading in hospital of a novel by Mrs. Ewing (as the soldiers in *The Janeites* find solace in the novels of Jane Austen)—which also gives the veteran, when he recovers, a beneficent interest in life: that of planting wayside gardens. Another ex-soldier is saved by a dog.

Kipling's homeless religious sense resorts to strange fellowships and faiths to bolster up his broken men. He had been made a Freemason in India, and Freemasonry had figured in *Kim* and had seemed to crop up in the guise of Mithraism in the Roman stories of *Puck of Pook's Hill*. Now he invents, for a new series of stories, a circle of philanthropic Masons who meet in the back room of a tobacconist's and who try to help men that have been wrecked by the war. A new ideal—but a new ideal conceived by a tired and humbled man—of a brotherhood which shall not be delimited by the exclusions of a fighting unit or caste begins to appear in these stories. Mithraism figures again in *The Church That Was at Antioch*: the young Roman officer turned Mithraist says of his mother, 'She follows the old school, of course—the home-worships and the strict Latin Trinity. . . . But one wants more than that'; and he ends by getting murdered by the Jews in revenge for his protection of the Apostle Paul. In another story, *The Manner of Men*, Saint Paul appears again and rescues a neurotic sea-captain: 'Serve Caesar,' says Paul. 'You are not canvas I can cut to advantage at present. But if you serve Caesar you will be obeying at least some sort of law. . . . If you take refuge under Caesar at sea, you may have time to think. Then I may meet you again, and we can go on with our talks. But that is as the God wills. What concerns you *now*,' he concludes, in a tone that recalls at the same time the Buchmanite and the psychoanalyst, 'is that, by taking service, you will be free from the fear that has ridden you all your life.'

The Paul of these final stories, so different from his early heroes, may evidently tell us something about Kipling's changed conception of himself. Paul had preached the Word to the Gentiles as Kipling had preached the Law to the colonials and the Americans; Paul, like Kipling, is ill-favored and undersized, 'a little shrimp of a man,' who has 'the woman's trick of taking the tone and color of whoever he talked to' and who is scarred from old floggings and from his encounters with the beasts of the arena. Paul, like Kipling, is brash and tense; he is dedicated to a mission which has saved him from fear. But observe that, though he advises the shaky captain to take service with Caesar for a time, he has himself gone on to something higher.

This, then, is quite another Kipling. His prophets have an altered message: Kipling is losing his hatred. His captains have been afraid all their lives. His soldiers are no longer so cocky, so keen to kill inferior peoples, so intent on the purposes of the Empire. And officers and soldiers are now closer, as they were in the earliest stories: they are now simply civilians back in mufti, between whom the bond of having been in the war is stronger than the class differences of peace-time. And they are the remnants of a colossal disaster. I shall quote one of the pieces in verse with which Kipling supplements these stories, because, indifferent though it is as poetry, it strikingly illustrates this change:

> I have a dream—a dreadful dream—
>   A dream that is never done,

I watch a man go out of his mind,
　　And he is My Mother's Son.

They pushed him into a Mental Home,
　　And that is like the grave:
For they do not let you sleep upstairs,
　　And you're not allowed to shave.

And it was *not* disease or crime
　　Which got him landed there,
But because they laid on My Mother's Son
　　More than a man could bear.

What with noise, and fear of death,
　　Waking, and wounds and cold,
They filled the Cup for My Mother's Son
　　Fuller than it could hold.

They broke his body and his mind
　　And yet they made him live,
And they asked more of My Mother's Son
　　Than any man could give.

For, just because he had not died
　　Nor been discharged nor sick:
They dragged it out with My Mother's Son
　　Longer than he could stick. . . .

And no one knows when he'll get well—
　　So, there he'll have to be:
And, 'spite of the beard in the looking-glass,
　　I know that man is me!

The theme of inescapable illness dominates the whole later
Kipling. In some cases, the diseases are physical, but there is
always the implication of a psychological aspect. In *A Madonna
of the Trenches* and *The Wish House*—gruesome ghost stories of
love and death that make *The End of the Passage* and *The Mark
of the Beast* look like harmless bogey tales for children—cancer
serves as a symbol for rejected or frustrated love. And it is not
clear in *Dayspring Mishandled* whether the detestable literary
man Castorley is being poisoned by his wife and the doctor or
by the consciousness of the wrong he has committed. The

strangest of all these stories is *Unprofessional*, in which cancer, spasms of insanity, the aftermath of the war, and the influence of the something beyond human life combine in a clinical fantasy on the beneficent possibilities of science. Here the white mice and the London woman convulsed with suicidal seizures, sets toward death periodically imparted by mysterious cosmic tides, are Kipling's uncanniest image for the workings of nervous disorders.

The old great man is back again in the 'House of Desolation' at Southsea, tormented unjustly, ill, deserted by those he loves, and with the haunted darkness descending on that world which his determined effort had once enabled him to see so distinctly. In one of the latest of his stories, *Proofs of Holy Writ*, he makes Shakespeare speak to Ben Jonson of a man whom Shakespeare describes as 'going down darkling to his tomb 'twixt cliffs of ice and iron'—phrases hardly characteristic of Shakespeare but extremely appropriate to Kipling.

It is striking that some of the most authentic of Kipling's early stories should deal with children forsaken by their parents and the most poignant of his later ones with parents bereaved of their children. The theme of the abandoned parent seems to reflect in reversal the theme of the abandoned child. The former theme has already appeared in '*They*' (written after the death of Kipling's daughter), associated with the themes of blindness and the deprivation of love; and even before that, in *Without Benefit of Clergy*.

Certainly two of these last stories of Kipling's are among the most moving he wrote. There is a passage in *Mary Postgate* like the plucking of a tightened string that is just about to break. The plain and dull English female 'companion' is to burn up the belongings of a young soldier—like most of Kipling's children, an orphan—to whom she has stood in a maternal rôle and who has just been killed in a plane. Kipling tells in one of his typical inventories of the items, mainly relics of boyhood sports, that Mary has to destroy; and then: 'The shrubbery was filling with twilight by the time she had completed her arrangements and sprinkled the sacrificial oil. As she lit the match that would burn her heart to ashes, she heard a groan or a grunt behind the dense Portugal laurels.' *The match that would burn her heart to ashes*: they are the first words that we

have yet encountered, the only words that we shall have encountered, that are not matter-of-fact; and here the observation of Kipling, of which George Moore complained that it
was too systematic and too technical, making it *Portugal laurels* where another writer would have simply written *shrubbery*
—here this hardness of concrete detail is suddenly given new
value by a phrase on another plane.

So in that other remarkable story, *The Gardener*, Kipling's
method of preparing a finale by concealing essential information in an apparently casual narrative produces an effect of
tremendous power. This method, which Kipling has developed
with so much ingenuity and precision, serves in some of his
stories to spring surprises that are merely mechanical; but it
has always had its special appropriateness to those aspects of
the English character with which Kipling has been particularly
concerned in that it masks emotion and purpose under a pretense of coldness and indifference; and here it is handled in a
masterly fashion to dramatize another example of the impassive Englishwoman. The implications of *Mary Postgate* prevent
us from accepting it fully: we know too well that the revenge-
ful cruelty which impels the heroine of the story to let the
shattered German aviator die is shared by the author himself.
But *The Gardener* may conquer us completely. I am not sure
that it is not really the best story that Kipling ever wrote. Like
the rest of even the best of Kipling, it is not quite on the highest level. He must still have his fairy-tale properties; and we
may be disposed to protest at his taste when we find that the
Puck of Pook's Hill element is supplied by the apparition of
Jesus. But if we have been following Kipling's development, we
recognize that this fact is significant. The rôle that Christ has
formerly played in Kipling—as in the poem called *Cold Iron*—
has been that of a *pukka Sahib* who knows how to take his
punishment. This is the first time, so far as I remember, that
Kipling's Christ has shown pity—as Kipling pities now rather
than boasts about the self-disciplined and much-enduring
British. And the symbol at once bares the secret and liberates
the locked-up emotion with a sudden and shocking force. The
self-repression and the hopeless grief of the unmarried mother
in *The Gardener* speak for the real Kipling. Here he has found

for them intense expression in the concentrated forms of his art.

The big talk of the work of the world, of the mission to command of the British, even the hatefulness of fear and disappointment, have largely faded away for Kipling. He composes as a memorial to his son and to the system in devotion to which the half-American boy has died a history of the Irish Guards in the war, in which Lieutenant John Kipling is hardly mentioned. But, meticulously assembling, by the method by which he once seemed to build so solidly, the scattered memories of his son's battalion, he seems merely to be striving, by wisps and scraps, to re-create the terrible days that preceded the death of his child. Even the victory over the Germans can never make that right.

3

Uncomfortable Casanova

WHY has Jacques Casanova attracted so little attention in English? So far as I know there is nothing very serious except Havelock Ellis's essay, and that does not go far into the subject. Mr. S. Guy Endore's book, though a good piece of work in its way, is only a popular biography. Yet the Chevalier de Seingalt was a most remarkable man, who had some of the qualities of greatness. The Prince de Ligne listed his name with those of Louis XV, Frederick the Great, Beaumarchais, d'Alembert and Hume as among the most interesting men he had known, and the great sharper really belongs in that company.

When we begin reading Casanova's *Memoirs*, we think him amusing but cheap. Yet we end by being genuinely impressed by him.

He was a type who was very familiar in the America of the boom of the twenties. In our time he might have had the career of a Rothstein or a Nicky Arnstein or a Dapper Don Tourbillon, but he would have far transcended the sphere of such men and he would have felt for them the uneasy scorn that he felt for St. Germain and Cagliostro. For Casanova was only half of the underworld—he lived half in darkness, half in light. But the sound and superior part of him was always insecure because it was based on knavery: hence his succession of misadventures and the final unsatisfactoriness of his life. Casanova was an uncomfortable man—he could never make his life come right. And it makes us uncomfortable to read about him.

There is a sound kind of coarseness, which is not incompatible with the finest work or the most scrupulously ordered life: the coarseness of animality or of the hand-to-hand struggle with existence, which may nourish such work and such a life. And there is a bad kind of coarseness which spoils everything, even where a man is equipped with genuinely superior gifts. The coarseness of Casanova was the bad kind. He came out of the Venetian actors' world, and was never sure whether his mother, a shoemaker's daughter, had had him by a down-at-heels nobleman who had gone on the stage and married her or by the manager of the theater where she acted. From some heritage of moral squalor Casanova could never emerge, and he was ravaged by it all his life more vitally than by any of the diseases that were his mere superficial exasperations.

But the superior qualities of such a man have continually to keep themselves sharp against the dangers that always confront him, the dangers that he can never get away from because they are part of himself. The drama of Casanova's career creates a tension which is both exciting and trying because his highly developed intelligence, his genius as an actor on the stage of life, are always poised on the brink of a pit where taste, morals, the social order, the order of the world of the intellect, may all be lost in the slime. Yet even when he has slipped to the bottom, he keeps his faculties clear; and so he commands our respect.

We have had an immense amount of controversy as to whether Casanova told the truth in connection with this or that incident, and a good many inaccuracies have been proved on him. But whether he falsified the facts unconsciously or deliberately makes very little difference. In his own way Casanova was truthful; it may even be said that one of his most admirable traits—not as a man but as a writer—was precisely a fidelity to truth. He may have invented some of the adventures in the *Memoirs*, but his story follows reality for all that. Someone has said that if the *Memoirs* is a novel, Casanova is the greatest novelist who ever lived. Though he was personally extremely vain, he certainly spares himself as little as any autobiographer on record. It is not true, as the popular legend seems to have it, that he represents himself as triumphing easily over innumerable complacent women. On the contrary, he will sometimes devote the better part of a volume to a detailed description of some siege in which he ignominiously failed. The ultimate aim of Casanova is not so much to glorify himself as to tell us an astonishing story that illustrates how people behave, the way in which life works out.

When other writers borrow from Casanova, they are likely to sentimentalize or romanticize him where Casanova's great virtue is his mercilessness with romantic and sentimental conventions. I remember an attempt at a popular play based on the Henriette episode. Henriette in the *Memoirs* is a young French girl who has run away from home in men's clothes and whom the youthful Casanova meets in his travels. She is the first French girl he has known, the first *jeune fille spirituelle*; and his love affair with her has a freshness and seriousness, almost a kind of ecstasy, that none has ever had for him before and that none is ever to have again. He happens to have money at the time and is able to buy her a whole wardrobe of pretty clothes. They go to Parma together, and there they live in style. Casanova gets a box at the opera; they take the air in the public gardens with the royalties—till she is recognized by one of the courtiers and is compelled to go back to her family. Casanova's account of this episode is one of the most attractive love affairs in literature. When he and Henriette have finally had to part, at Geneva, he finds that she has written with her diamond on the window of their room at the inn: 'You will forget Henriette, too.' Now the contemporary play I speak of exploited this charming story and then followed it with a conventional sequel made up out of the whole cloth, in which Casanova many years later was made to come back to the inn to find Henriette grown old and with a son who turns out to be his.

But what happens in the *Memoirs* is quite different. Casanova does come back to the inn, middle-aged, down on his luck and with a depressing venereal disease. He *has* forgotten about staying there with Henriette, and he does not even recognize their room till he notices the writing on the window: 'Remembering in a flash the moment when Henriette had written those words thirteen years before, I felt the hair stand up on my head. . . . Overcome, I dropped into a chair. . . . Comparing the self I was now with the self I had been then, I had to recognize that I was less worthy to possess her. I still knew how to love, but I realized I had no longer the delicacy that I had had in those earlier days, nor the feelings which really justify the transports of the senses, nor the same tender ways, nor finally a certain probity which extends itself even to one's weaknesses; but what frightened me was to have to acknowledge that I no longer possessed the same vigor.'

Years afterwards, while he is traveling in Provence, his coach breaks down in the middle of the night and some people who live near the road take him in. The mistress of the house hides her face in the hood she has worn out-of-doors—then as soon as they have got into the house, she announces that she has sprained her ankle and is obliged to take to her bed, so that Casanova is only permitted to wait upon her in her room and talk to her through the bed-curtains. He does not find out till after he has left that the countess is Henriette, who has by this time grown so fat that she cannot bear to have him see her. But he has been traveling with a tough little Venetian girl of bisexual capabilities, and the countess carries on a flirtation with her and finally makes her sleep with her. This is all life has left of their romance.

The real theme of Casanova is the many things a life may hold—the many rôles a man may play and the changes brought by time. I have never read a book—either autobiography or fiction—which seems to give you a life so completely. I know of no book which shows so strikingly the rhythmic recurrences which character produces in personal destiny. Casanova's adventures are always different but always the same thing. He arrives in some new place, he puts himself over, he achieves brilliant social successes or performs dashing deeds, his best qualities and gifts have full scope, then he overplays his hand or misses his step or something discreditable is discovered about him, and he has to make his getaway. There was something about him, one supposes, that in the long run made people find him intolerable. And his love affairs have their pattern, too: when the responsibilities involved in them become onerous, he marries the ladies off if he can; if not, he gently lets the affair lapse.

The first part of the story is funny and gay—it has a Venetian carnival liveliness; the last part, although it is told with the eighteenth-century rapidity and dryness, is almost unbearably sad. It is probable that Casanova was never able to bring himself to finish it. The manuscript as we have it does not cover the whole of the period indicated by Casanova in his title: it stops just as he is returning to Venice, but gets him no farther than Trieste. He had been banished by the Inquisition and was allowed to return to his native city only at the price of acting as a spy for them. It was the most humiliating episode in his life;

and he has remarked by the way several times that he is not sure he will have the courage to go through with his original project of writing his life up to the year 1797. He may also have been guilty of a Freudian oversight in dropping out two chapters near the end. They were missing in the Brockhaus manuscript, but were found later by Arthur Symons at Dux; and they turn out to contain the dismal climax of Casanova's adventure with two girls upon whom he had been trying to work by an old and well-tried technique of his. He had discovered that you could go a long way with girls if you took them to masquerades in pairs; but on this occasion the girls did not fall, and Casanova before the evening was over got mercilessly razzed by the masqueraders.

Yet in his final asylum at Dux, where his patron left him alone for long periods and where he was constantly bedeviled by the servants, where he sometimes contemplated suicide, he did get down most of the story; and it is one of the most remarkable presentations in literature of a man's individual life as it seems to him in the living. All the appetites are there—fine dinners, attractive women, amusements; and the exhilaration of travel, of fighting for one's personal pride, of the winning of wealth and consideration, of winning one's personal liberty. There is in Casanova's account of his escape from the Leads prison in Venice, whether he fabricated the story or not, something more than a mere tale of adventure: he has made of it a thrilling expression of the hatred of the human spirit for jails, of the will to be free that breaks away in contempt of the remonstrances of reason (in the person of the appalled old count who refuses to join the others and keeps telling them why they cannot succeed).

There is even the appetite of the intellect: the great raconteur loved the conversation of men like d'Alembert and Voltaire; and the master gambler was an amateur mathematician. And when one can have no more brilliant dinners and make love to no more women, when one has no longer appreciative companions to listen to one's stories and can no longer travel and try one's luck—one can at least summon one's intellectual resources, work at problems, write one's memoirs; one can still test one's nerve and strength by setting down an account of life as one has found it, with all its anticlimax and scandal, one's own impossible character and all. The writing of the *Memoirs* represented a real victory of the mind and the spirit. Scoundrels like Casanova do not usually put themselves on record, and when they do they are usually at pains to profess the morality of respectable people. There is a certain amount of this, as we shall see in a moment, in Casanova's autobiography, too; but when all Casanova's obeisances to the established authorities have been made, life itself in his story turns out to be an outlaw like him. He confesses in his preface that he considers it a creditable deed to fleece a fool; and in reading him, we get to a point where we ourselves almost feel impatience when Casanova's prospective victims fail to succumb to his confidence games. He said that he feared the *Memoirs* were '*par trop cynique*' ever to be published. And he was apparently right: the original manuscript still lies locked up in Brockhaus's vaults in Leipzig, and no one knows what the editors may have omitted.

The *Memoirs*, then, required the courage of an individual point of view—and they required a capacity for feeling. Has any novelist or poet ever rendered better than Casanova the passing glory of the personal life?—the gaiety, the spontaneity, the generosity of youth: the ups and downs of middle age when our character begins to get us and we are forced to come to terms with it; the dreadful blanks of later years, when what is gone is gone. All that a life of this kind can contain Casanova put into his story. And how much of the world!—the eighteenth century as you get it in no other book; society from top to bottom; Europe from England to Russia; a more brilliant variety of characters than you can find in any eighteenth-century novel.

But the interests of such a man are limited. Casanova knew better than anyone how the world and how one's personal vicissitudes went. But he had very little imagination for the larger life of society. He saw the corruption of the old régime in France and commented on it after the Revolution, but he had never been among those who wanted to see the old régime go. On the contrary—like a Rothstein—he was content with the world as he found it. Though the Inquisition had nearly done for him, he never ceased to treat it with respect and was willing in his last bad days to turn informer and report to these censors—though rather inefficiently, it appears—on naked models in the Venetian art-schools and indecent and ungodly books in the libraries. Though he had at other times called himself a 'philosopher' and in his speculative writings had vaguely foreshadowed Darwinism, he had never criticized Church or State. He accepted all the current worldly values— the hierarchies, institutions, dominations. He never questioned, never protested, defended his honor according to the code, but never brought up in connection with anything the principle of a larger issue. Casanova's originality was largely confined to a sort of personal effrontery which, having persisted all through his life in spite of his repeated attempts to reform it, had ended by acquiring in his *Memoirs* a certain intellectual dignity when he had found finally that all his struggles to make himself a place in society were vain and that this was the only companion that was left him in his solitude at Dux.

A man of superior intelligence as he knew himself to be, he had always aimed at the good things of the world as the rich and powerful judged good things. What he really wanted, to be sure, was something different from what they wanted. He does not seem to have cared about social position or financial security for their own sakes: what he enjoyed was the adventure of playing a rôle, creating a situation; whereas the powerful and the rich only wanted to follow their routine. But his drama was usually conceived in terms of their values. It was the cheap side of him, the lackey in him, which did not look beyond the habits of his masters.

And this is a part of the explanation of the fact that Casanova has attracted comparatively so little serious attention. In English of course it is his scandalous reputation which has made him practically taboo—so that he has remained largely unknown to the English-reading public save for volumes of erotic excerpts in libraries of classic pornography. But in general it may be said that what is good in Casanova makes serious readers too uneasy and what is inferior disgusts them too much for him to become an accepted classic. There are a whole host of people on the Continent studying Casanova; but Casanovists seem almost in the category of stamp and coin collectors and people who devote their lives to looking for buried

Spanish treasure. They are mostly preoccupied with verifying dates and tracking down identities. Casanova, fascinating though he is, does not lead to anything bigger than himself.

Compare him with Rousseau, for example. Rousseau was a much less attractive man, and his *Confessions* are infinitely less readable than Casanova's *Memoirs*. At his best, to my taste at any rate, he is still pretty flavorless and Swiss. Yet the Geneva clockmaker's son in a situation not unlike Casanova's—he, too, had been a vagabond, a thief, a hanger-on of the great, had suffered as a battered-about apprentice and a servant in rich men's houses—made an issue of his maladjustment. Casanova could show considerable strength of character in compelling the great to treat him as an equal—as when he forced Count Branicki to fight a duel and afterwards became his friend; but it never seems to have occurred to the actor's son to say, after he had come one of his croppers masquerading as a man of quality: 'I am better at being a great lord than you people are yourselves—for I have the personality and the imagination and the brains to create such a gorgeous great lord as your silly conventional society never dreamed of—hence I am superior to you and hence do not need to compete with you!' Whereas Rousseau finally came to the conclusion that the times must be out of joint when Rousseau found himself out of place. From the moment of his sudden revelation, on the way to see Diderot at Vincennes, that man was by nature good and that it was institutions alone which had corrupted him, that all his own miseries had been due, not to his aberrations and short-comings, but to the sins of the society that had bred him—from this moment he stuck to his point at the price of re-signing from society, of exiling himself even from those circles in which the other eighteenth-century philosophers had found so agreeable a welcome and so sympathetic a hearing.

You may say that it was Rousseau's neurotic character which prevented him from getting on with people and that he took it out in scolding society; and you may say that Casanova was at least as near to an accurate account of the situation when he attributed his own misfortunes to his faults. But the fact was that Rousseau had been led to a general truth by his individual case and, in spite of his ignominious adventures, had the courage and dignity of one who knew it. He belonged to the class of thinkers who, in opposing the prevalent philosophy of their time, find that they have behind them a great pressure of unformulated general feeling and who themselves prevail as the spokesmen of the age that follows theirs.

Casanova once came with a lady of quality to pay a visit to Rousseau in his retirement. The callers found him lacking in affability and failed to get very much out of him, though Casanova admitted that Rousseau had talked intelligently. Madame d'Urfé thought him boorish, and they laughed about him after they had left.

Casanova, ignoring his many humiliations, was still trying to crash the gate at a time when Rousseau, for all his clumsiness, had got hold of the lever of the Revolution.

4

Justice to Edith Wharton

BEFORE Edith Wharton died, the more commonplace work of her later years had had the effect of dulling the reputation of her earlier and more serious work. It seemed to me that the notices elicited by her death did her, in general, something less than justice; and I want to try to throw into relief the achievements which did make her important during a period— say, 1905–1917—when there were few American writers worth reading. This essay is therefore no very complete study, but rather in the nature of an impression by a reader who was growing up at that time.

Mrs. Wharton's earliest fiction I never found particularly attractive. The influences of Paul Bourget and Henry James seem to have presided at the birth of her talent; and I remember these books as dealing with the artificial moral problems of Bourget and developing them with the tenuity of analysis which is what is least satisfactory in James. The stories tended to take place either in a social void or against a background of Italy or France which had somewhat the character of expensive upholstery. It was only with *The House of Mirth*, published in 1905, that Edith Wharton emerged as an historian of the American society of her time. For a period of fifteen years or more, she produced work of considerable interest both for its realism and its intensity.

One has heard various accounts of her literary beginnings. She tells us in her autobiography that a novel which she had composed at eleven and which began, 'Oh, how do you do, Mrs. Brown? . . . If only I had known you were going to call, I should have tidied up the drawing room'—had been returned by her mother with the chilling comment, 'Drawing-rooms are always tidy.' And it is said that a book of verse which she had written and had had secretly printed was discovered and destroyed by her parents, well-to-do New Yorkers of merchant stock, who thought it unladylike for a young woman to write. It seems to be an authentic fact, though Mrs. Wharton does not mention it in her memoirs, that she first seriously began to write fiction after her marriage during the period of a nervous breakdown, at the suggestion of Dr. S. Weir Mitchell, who himself combined the practice of literature with his pioneer work in the field of female neuroses. Thereafter she seems to have depended on her writing to get her through some difficult years, a situation that became more and more painful. Her husband, as she tells us, had some mental disease which was steadily growing worse from the very first years of their marriage, and he inhabited a social world of the rich which was sealed tight to intellectual interests. Through her writing, she came gradually into relation with the international literary world and made herself a partially independent career.

Her work was, then, the desperate product of a pressure of maladjustments; and it very soon took a direction totally different from that of Henry James, as a lesser disciple of whom she is sometimes pointlessly listed. James's interests were predominantly esthetic: he is never a passionate social prophet; and only rarely—as in *The Ivory Tower*, which seems in turn to have derived from Mrs. Wharton—does he satirize plutocratic America. But a passionate social prophet is precisely what Edith Wharton became. At her strongest and most characteristic, she is a brilliant example of the writer who relieves an emotional strain by denouncing his generation.

It is true that she combines with indignation against a specific phase of American society a general sense of inexorable doom for human beings. She was much haunted by the myth of the Eumenides; and she had developed her own deadly version of the working of the Aeschylean necessity—a version as automatic and rapid, as decisive and as undimmed by sentiment, as the mechanical and financial processes which during her lifetime were transforming New York. In these books, she was as pessimistic as Hardy or Maupassant. You find the pure expression of her hopelessness in her volume of poems, *Artemis to Actaeon*, published in 1909, which, for all its hard accent and its ponderous tone, its 'impenetrables' and 'incommunicables' and 'incommensurables,' its 'immemorial altitudes august,' was not entirely without interest or merit. 'Death, can it be the years shall naught avail?' she asks in one of the sonnets called

Experience: "'Not so," Death answered. "They shall purchase sleep."' But in the poem called *Moonrise over Tyringham*, she seems to be emerging from a period of strain into a relatively tranquil stoicism. She is apostrophizing the first hour of night:

> Be thou the image of a thought that fares
> Forth from itself, and flings its ray ahead,
> Leaping the barriers of ephemeral cares,
> To where our lives are but the ages' tread,
>
> And let this year be, not the last of youth,
> But first—like thee!—of some new train of hours,
> If more remote from hope, yet nearer truth,
> And kin to the unpetitionable powers.

But the catastrophe in Edith Wharton's novels is almost invariably the upshot of a conflict between the individual and the social group. Her tragic heroines and heroes are the victims of the group pressure of convention; they are passionate or imaginative spirits, hungry for emotional and intellectual experience, who find themselves locked into a small closed system, and either destroy themselves by beating their heads against their prison or suffer a living death in resigning themselves to it. Out of these themes she got a sharp pathos all her own. The language and some of the machinery of *The House of Mirth* seem old-fashioned and rather melodramatic today; but the book had some originality and power, with its chronicle of a social parasite on the fringes of the very rich, dragging out a stupefying routine of week-ends, yachting trips and dinners, and finding a window open only twice, at the beginning and at the end of the book, on a world where all the values are not money values.

The Fruit of the Tree, which followed it in 1907, although its characters are concerned with larger issues, is less successful than *The House of Mirth*, because it is confused between two different kinds of themes. There is a more or less trumped-up moral problem *à la* Bourget about a 'mercy killing' by a high-minded trained nurse, who happened to have an 'affinity,' as they used to say at that period, with the husband of the patient. But there is also the story of an industrial reformer, which is on the whole quite ably handled—especially in the opening

scenes, in which the hero, assistant manager of a textile mill, is
aroused by an industrial accident to try to remove the conditions which have caused it and finds himself up against one of
those tight family groups that often dominate American factory towns, sitting ensconced in their red-satin drawing-rooms
on massively upholstered sofas, amid heavy bronze chandeliers
and mantels surmounted by obelisk clocks; and in its picture of
his marriage with the mill-owning widow and the gradual
drugging of his purpose under the influence of a house on
Long Island of a quality more gracious and engaging but on
an equally overpowering scale.

Edith Wharton had come to have a great hand with all
kinds of American furnishings and with their concomitant
landscape-gardening. Her first book had been a work on interior decorating; and now in her novels she adopts the practice of
inventorying the contents of her characters' homes. Only Clyde
Fitch, I think, in those early nineteen-hundreds made play to
the same degree with the miscellaneous material objects with
which Americans were surrounding themselves, articles which
had just been manufactured and which people were being induced to buy. I suppose that no other writer of comedies of
any other place or time has depended so much on stage sets
and, especially, on stage properties: the radiators that bang in
Girls, the artificial orange in *The Truth*, the things that are
dropped under the table by the ladies in the second act of *The
Climbers*. But in the case of Edith Wharton, the *décors* become
the agents of tragedy. The characters of Clyde Fitch are embarrassed or tripped up by these articles; but the people of
Edith Wharton are pursued by them as by spirits of doom and
ultimately crushed by their accumulation. These pieces have
not been always made newly: sometimes they are *objets d'art*,
which have been expensively imported from Europe. But the
effect is very much the same: they are something extraneous to
the people and, no matter how old they may be, they seem to
glitter and clank with the coin that has gone to buy them. A
great many of Mrs. Wharton's descriptions are, of course, satiric
or caustic; but when she wants to produce an impression of
real magnificence, and even when she is writing about Europe,
the thing still seems rather inorganic. She was not only one of
the great pioneers, but also the poet, of interior decoration.

In *The Custom of the Country* (1913), Mrs. Wharton's next novel about the rich—*The Reef* is a relapse into 'psychological problems'—she piles up the new luxury of the era to an altitude of ironic grandeur, like the glass mountain in the *Arabian Nights*, which the current of her imagination manages to make incandescent. The first scene sets the key for the whole book: 'Mrs. Spragg and her visitor were enthroned in two heavy gilt armchairs in one of the private drawing-rooms of the Hotel Stentorian. The Spragg rooms were known as one of the Looey suites, and the drawing-room walls, above their wainscoting of highly varnished mahogany, were hung with salmon-pink damask and adorned with oval portraits of Marie Antoinette and the Princess de Lamballe. In the center of the florid carpet a gilt table with a top of Mexican onyx sustained a palm in a gilt basket tied with a pink bow. But for this ornament, and a copy of *The Hound of the Baskervilles* which lay beside it, the room showed no traces of human use, and Mrs. Spragg herself wore as complete an air of detachment as if she had been a wax figure in a show-window.' In the last pages—it is an admirable passage—Undine Spragg's little boy is seen wandering alone amid the splendors of the Paris *hôtel* which has crowned his mother's progress from the Stentorian: 'the white fur rugs and brocade chairs' which 'seemed maliciously on the watch for smears and ink-spots,' 'his mother's wonderful lacy bedroom, all pale silks and velvets, artful mirrors and veiled lamps, and the boudoir as big as a drawing-room, with pictures he would have liked to know about, and tables and cabinets holding things he was afraid to touch,' the library, with its 'rows and rows of books, bound in dim browns and golds, and old faded reds as rich as velvet: they all looked as if they might have had stories in them as splendid as their bindings. But the bookcases were closed with gilt trellising, and when Paul reached up to open one, a servant told him that Mr. Moffatt's secretary kept them locked because the books were too valuable to be taken down.'

It is a vein which Sinclair Lewis has worked since—as in the opening pages of *Babbitt*, where Babbitt is shown entangled with his gadgets; and in other respects *The Custom of the Country* opens up the way for Lewis, who dedicated *Main Street* to Edith Wharton. Mrs. Wharton has already arrived at a method

of doing crude and harsh people with a draftsmanship crude
and harsh. Undine Spragg, the social-climbing divorcée,
though a good deal less humanly credible than Lily Bart of *The
House of Mirth*, is quite a successful caricature of a type who
was to go even farther. She is the prototype in fiction of the
'gold-digger,' of the international cocktail bitch. Here the
pathos has been largely subordinated to an implacable animos-
ity toward the heroine; but there is one episode both bitter
and poignant, in which a discarded husband of Undine's, who
has been driven by her demands to work in Wall Street and left
by her up to his neck in debt, goes home to Washington
Square through 'the heat, the noise, the smells of disheveled
midsummer' New York, climbs to the room at the top of the
house where he has kept his books and other things from college, and shoots himself there.

The other side of this world of wealth, which annihilates
every impulse toward excellence, is a poverty which also annihilates. The writer of one of the notices on Mrs. Wharton's
death was mistaken in assuming that *Ethan Frome* was a single
uncharacteristic excursion outside the top social strata. It is
true that she knew the top strata better than she knew anything else; but both in *The House of Mirth* and *The Fruit of the
Tree*, she is always aware of the pit of misery which is implied
by the wastefulness of the plutocracy, and the horror or the
fear of this pit is one of the forces that determine the action.
There is a Puritan in Edith Wharton, and this Puritan is always
insisting that we must face the unpleasant and the ugly. Not to
do so is one of the worst sins in her morality; sybarites like Mr.
Langhope in *The Fruit of the Tree*, amusing himself with a dilettante archaeology on his income from a badly-managed factory, like the fatuous mother of *Twilight Sleep*, who feels so
safe with her facial massage and her Yogi, while her family goes
to pieces under her nose, are among the characters whom she
treats with most scorn. And the three novels I have touched
on above were paralleled by another series—*Ethan Frome*,
Bunner Sisters and *Summer*—which dealt with *milieux* of a different kind.

Ethan Frome is still much read and well-known; but *Bunner
Sisters* has been undeservedly neglected. It is the last piece in

the volume called *Xingu* (1916), a short novel about the length of *Ethan Frome*. This story of two small shopkeepers on Stuyvesant Square and a drug-addict clockmaker from Hoboken, involved in a relationship like a triple noose which will gradually choke them all, is one of the most terrible things that Edith Wharton ever wrote; and the last page, in which the surviving sister, her lifelong companion gone and her poor little business lost, sets out to look for a job, seems to mark the grimmest moment of Edith Wharton's darkest years. Here is not even the grandeur of the heroic New England hills: '"Ain't you going to leave the *ad*-dress?" the young woman called out after her. Ann Eliza went out into the thronged street. The great city, under the fair spring sky, seemed to throb with the stir of innumerable beginnings. She walked on, looking for another shop window with a sign in it.'

Summer (1917), however, returns to the Massachusetts of *Ethan Frome*, and, though neither so harrowing nor so vivid, is by no means an inferior work. Making hats in a millinery shop was the abyss from which Lily Bart recoiled; the heroine of *Summer* recoils from the nethermost American social stratum, the degenerate 'mountain people.' Let down by the refined young man who works in the public library and wants to become an architect, in a way that anticipates the situation in Dreiser's *American Tragedy*, she finds that she cannot go back to her own people and allows herself to be made an honest woman by the rather admirable old failure of a lawyer who had brought her down from the mountain in her childhood. It is the first sign on Mrs. Wharton's part of a relenting in the cruelty of her endings. 'Come to my age,' says Charity Royall's protector, 'a man knows the things that matter and the things that don't; that's about the only good turn life does us.' Her blinding bitterness is already subsiding.

But in the meantime, before *Summer* was written, she had escaped from the hopeless situation created by her husband's insanity. The doctors had told her he was hopeless; but she had had difficulty in inducing his family to allow her to leave him with an attendant. The tragedy of *Bunner Sisters* is probably a transposition of this; and the relief of the tension in *Summer* is evidently the result of her new freedom. She was at last finally detached from her marriage; and she took up her permanent residence in France. The war came, and she threw herself into its activities.

And now the intensity dies from her work as the American background fades. One can see this already in *Summer*, and *The Age of Innocence* (1920) is really Edith Wharton's valedictory. The theme is closely related to those of *The House of Mirth* and *Ethan Frome*: the frustration of a potential pair of lovers by social or domestic obstructions. But setting it back in the generation of her parents, she is able to contemplate it now without quite the same rancor, to soften it with a poetic mist of distance. And yet even here the old impulse of protest still makes itself felt as the main motive. If we compare *The Age of Innocence* with Henry James's *Europeans*, whose central situation it reproduces, the pupil's divergence from the master is seen in the most striking way. In both cases, a Europeanized American woman—Baroness Münster, Countess Olenska—returns to the United States to intrude upon and disturb the existence of a conservative provincial society; in both cases, she attracts and almost captivates an intelligent man of the community who turns out, in the long run, to be unable to muster the courage to take her, and who allows her to go back to Europe. Henry James makes of this a balanced comedy of the conflict between the Bostonian and the cosmopolitan points of view (so he reproached her with not having developed the theme of Undine Spragg's marriage with a French nobleman in terms of French and American manners, as he had done with a similar one in *The Reverberator*); but in Edith Wharton's version one still feels an active resentment against the pusillanimity of the provincial group and also, as in other of her books, a special complaint against the timid American male who has let the lady down.

Up through *The Age of Innocence*, and recurring at all points of her range from *The House of Mirth* to *Ethan Frome*, the typical masculine figure in Edith Wharton's fiction is a man set apart from his neighbors by education, intellect and feeling, but lacking the force or the courage either to impose himself or to get away. She generalizes about this type in the form in which she knew it best in her autobiographical volume: 'They combined a cultivated taste with marked social gifts,' she says;

but 'their weakness was that, save in a few cases, they made so little use of their ability': they were content to 'live in dilettant-ish leisure,' rendering none of 'the public services that a more enlightened social system would have exacted of them.' But she had described a very common phenomenon of the America of after the Civil War. Lawrence Selden, the city lawyer, who sits comfortably in his bachelor apartment with his flowerbox of mignonette and his first edition of La Bruyère and allows Lily Bart to drown, is the same person as Lawyer Royall of *Summer*, with his lofty orations and his drunken lapses. One could have found him during the big-business era in almost any American city or town: the man of superior abil-ities who had the impulse toward self-improvement and inde-pendence, but who had been more or less rendered helpless by the surf of headlong money-making and spending which car-ried him along with its breakers or left him stranded on the New England hills—in either case thwarted and stunted by the mediocre level of the community. In Edith Wharton's novels these men are usually captured and dominated by women of conventional morals and middle-class ideals; when an excep-tional woman comes along who is thirsting for something dif-ferent and better, the man is unable to give it to her. This special situation Mrs. Wharton, with some conscious historical criticism but chiefly impelled by a feminine animus, has dra-matized with much vividness and intelligence. There are no first-rate men in these novels.

The Age of Innocence is already rather faded. But now a sur-prising lapse occurs. (It is true that she is nearly sixty.)

When we look back on Mrs. Wharton's career, it seems that everything that is valuable in her work lies within a quite sharply delimited area—between *The House of Mirth* and *The Age of Innocence*. It is sometimes true of women writers—less often, I believe, of men—that a manifestation of something like genius may be stimulated by some exceptional emotional strain, but will disappear when the stimulus has passed. With a man, his professional, his artisan's life is likely to persist and evolve as a partially independent organism through the vicissi-tudes of his emotional experience. Henry James in a virtual vacuum continued to possess and develop his *métier* up to his very last years. But Mrs. Wharton had no *métier* in this sense. With her emergence from her life in the United States, her settling down in the congenial society of Paris, she seems at last to become comfortably adjusted; and with her adjustment, the real intellectual force which she has exerted through a decade and a half evaporates almost completely. She no longer maims or massacres her characters. Her grimness melts rapidly into benignity. She takes an interest in young people's problems, in the solicitude of parents for children; she smooths over the misunderstandings of lovers; she sees how things may work out very well. She even loses the style she has mastered. Beginning with a language rather ponderous and stiff, the worst features of the style of Henry James and a stream of clichés from old novels and plays, she finally—about the time of *Ethan Frome*—worked out a prose of flexible steel, bright as electric light and striking out sparks of wit and color, which has the quality and pace of New York and is one of its distinctive artistic products. But now not merely does she cease to be brilliant, she becomes almost commonplace.

The Glimpses of the Moon, which followed *The Age of Innocence*, is, as someone has said, scarcely distinguishable from the ordinary serial in a women's magazine; and indeed it is in the women's magazines that Mrs. Wharton's novels now begin first to appear. *A Son at the Front* is a little better, because it had been begun in 1918 and had her war experience in it, with some of her characteristic cutting satire at the expense of the belligerents behind the lines. It is not bad as a picture of the emotions of a middle-aged civilian during the war—though not so good as Arnold Bennett's *The Pretty Lady*.

Old New York was a much feebler second boiling from the tea-leaves of *The Age of Innocence*. I have read only one of Mrs. Wharton's novels written since *Old New York*: *Twilight Sleep* is not so bad as her worst, but suffers seriously as a picture of New York during the middle nineteen-twenties from the author's long absence abroad. Mrs. Wharton is no longer up on her American interior-decorating—though there are some characteristic passages of landscape-gardening: "'Seventy-five thousand bulbs this year!" she thought as the motor swept by the sculptured gateway, just giving and withdrawing a flash of turf sheeted with amber and lilac, in a setting of twisted and scalloped evergreens.'

The two other books that I have read since then—*The Writing of Fiction* (which does, however, contain an excellent essay on Proust) and the volume of memoirs called *A Backward Glance*—I found rather disappointing. The backward glance is an exceedingly fleeting one which dwells very little on anything except the figure of Henry James, of whom Mrs. Wharton has left a portrait entertaining but slightly catty and curiously superficial. About herself she tells us nothing much of interest; and she makes amends to her New York antecedents for her satire of *The Age of Innocence* by presenting them in tinted miniatures, prettily remote and unreal. It is the last irony of *The Age of Innocence* that Newland Archer should become reconciled to 'old New York.' 'After all,' he eventually came to tell himself, 'there was good in the old ways.' Something like this seems to have happened to Edith Wharton. Even in *A Backward Glance*, she confesses that 'the weakness of the social structure' of her parents' generation had been 'a blind dread of innovation'; but her later works show a dismay and a shrinking before what seemed to her the social and moral chaos of an age which was battering down the old edifice that she herself had once depicted as a prison. Perhaps, after all, the old mismated couples who had stayed married in deference to the decencies were better than the new divorced who were not aware of any duties at all.

The only thing that does survive in *A Backward Glance* is some trace of the tremendous blue-stocking that Mrs. Wharton was in her prime. The deep reverence for the heroes of art and thought—though she always believed that Paul Bourget was one of them—of the woman who in earlier days had written a long blank-verse poem about Vesalius, still makes itself felt in these memoirs. Her culture was rather heavy and grand —a preponderance of Goethe and Schiller, Racine and La Bruyère—but it was remarkably solid for an American woman and intimately related to her life. And she was one of the few Americans of her day who cared enough about serious literature to take the risks of trying to make some contribution to it. Professor Charles Eliot Norton—who had, as she dryly remarks, so admirably translated Dante—once warned her that 'no great work of the imagination' had 'ever been based on illicit passion.' Though she herself in her later years was reduced to contemptuous complaints that the writers of the new generations had 'abandoned creative art for pathology,' she did have the right to insist that she had 'fought hard' in her earlier days 'to turn the wooden dolls' of conventional fiction 'into struggling, suffering human beings.' She had been one of the few such human beings in the America of the early nineteen hundreds who found an articulate voice and set down a durable record.

———

The above was written in 1937. An unfinished novel by Edith Wharton was published in 1938. This story, *The Buccaneers*, deserves a word of postscript. The latter part of it, even allowing for the fact that it was never carried beyond a first draft, seems banal and a little trashy. Here as elsewhere the mellowness of Mrs. Wharton's last years has dulled the sharp outlines of her fiction: there are passages in *The Buccaneers* which read like an old-fashioned story for girls. But the first section has a certain brilliance. The figures of the children of the *nouveaux riches* at Saratoga during the seventies, when the post-Civil-War fortunes were rolling up, come back rather diminished in memory but in lively and charming colors, like the slides of those old magic lanterns that are mentioned as one of their forms of entertainment. And we learn from Mrs. Wharton's scenario for the unfinished part of the tale that it was to have had rather an interesting development. She has here more or less reversed the values of the embittered *Custom of the Country*: instead of playing off the culture and tradition of Europe against the vulgar Americans who are insensible to them, she dramatizes the climbing young ladies as an air-clearing and revivifying force. In the last pages she lived to write she made it plain that the hard-boiled commercial elements on the rise in both civilizations were to come to understand one another perfectly. But there is also an Anglo-Italian woman, the child of Italian revolutionaries and a cousin of Dante Gabriel Rossetti, who has been reduced to working as a governess and who has helped to engineer the success of the American girls in London. The best of these girls has been married to a dreary English duke, who represents everything least human in the English aristocratic system. Laura Testvalley was to forfeit her own hopes of capturing an amateur esthete of the older generation of the nobility in order to allow the young American to elope with an enterprising young Englishman; and thus to have let herself in for the fate of spending the rest of her days in the poverty and dulness of her home, where the old revolution had died. As the light of Edith Wharton's art grows dim and at last goes out, she leaves us, to linger on our retina, the large dark eyes of the clever spinster, the serious and attentive governess, who trades in worldly values but manages to rebuff these values; who, in following a destiny of solitude and discipline, contends for the rights of the heart; and who, child of a political movement played out, yet passes on something of its impetus to the emergence of the society of the future.

5

Hemingway: Gauge of Morale

ERNEST HEMINGWAY'S *In Our Time* was an odd and original book. It had the appearance of a miscellany of stories and fragments; but actually the parts hung together and produced a definite effect. There were two distinct series of pieces which alternated with one another: one a set of brief and brutal sketches of police shootings, bullfight crises, hangings of criminals, and incidents of the war; and the other a set of short stories dealing in its principal sequence with the growing-up of an American boy against a landscape of idyllic Michigan, but interspersed also with glimpses of American soldiers returning home. It seems to have been Hemingway's intention—'*In Our Time*'—that the war should set the key for the whole. The cold-bloodedness of the battles and executions strikes a discord with the sensitiveness and candor of the boy at home in the States; and presently the boy turns up in Europe in one of the intermediate vignettes as a soldier in the Italian army, hit in the spine by machine-gun fire and trying to talk to a dying Italian: '*Senta*, Rinaldi. *Senta*,' he says, 'you and me, we've made a separate peace.'

But there is a more fundamental relationship between the pieces of the two series. The shooting of Nick in the war does not really connect two different worlds: has he not found in the butchery abroad the same world that he knew back in Michigan? Was not life in the Michigan woods equally destructive and cruel? He had gone once with his father, the doctor, when he had performed a Caesarean operation on an Indian squaw with a jackknife and no anaesthetic and had sewed her up with fishing leaders, while the Indian hadn't been able to bear it and had cut his throat in his bunk. Another time, when the doctor had saved the life of a squaw, her Indian had picked a quarrel with him rather than pay him in work. And Nick himself had sent his girl about her business when he had found out how terrible her mother was. Even fishing in Big Two-Hearted River—away and free in the woods—he had been con-

418

scious in a curious way of the cruelty inflicted on the fish, even of the silent agonies endured by the live bait, the grasshoppers kicking on the hook.

Not that life isn't enjoyable. Talking and drinking with one's friends is great fun; fishing in Big Two-Hearted River is a tranquil exhilaration. But the brutality of life is always there, and it is somehow bound up with the enjoyment. Bullfights are especially enjoyable. It is even exhilarating to build a simply priceless barricade and pot the enemy as they are trying to get over it. The condition of life is pain; and the joys of the most innocent surface are somehow tied to its stifled pangs.

The resolution of this dissonance in art made the beauty of Hemingway's stories. He had in the process tuned a marvelous prose. Out of the colloquial American speech, with its simple declarative sentences and its strings of Nordic monosyllables, he got effects of the utmost subtlety. F. M. Ford has found the perfect simile for the impression produced by this writing: 'Hemingway's words strike you, each one, as if they were pebbles fetched fresh from a brook. They live and shine, each in its place. So one of his pages has the effect of a brook-bottom into which you look down through the flowing water. The words form a tesellation, each in order beside the other.'

Looking back, we can see how this style was already being refined and developed at a time—fifty years before—when it was regarded in most literary quarters as hopelessly non-literary and vulgar. Had there not been the nineteenth chapter of *Huckleberry Finn*?—'Two or three nights went by; I reckon I might say they swum by; they slid along so quick and smooth and lovely. Here is the way we put in the time. It was a monstrous big river down there—sometimes a mile and a half wide,' and so forth. These pages, when we happen to meet them in Carl Van Doren's anthology of world literature, stand up in a striking way beside a passage of description from Turgenev; and the pages which Hemingway was later to write about American wood and water are equivalents to the transcriptions by Turgenev—the *Sportsman's Notebook* is much admired by Hemingway—of Russian forests and fields. Each has brought to an immense and wild country the freshness of a new speech and a sensibility not yet conventionalized by literary associations. Yet it *is* the European sensibility which has come to Big Two-Hearted River, where the Indians are now obsolescent; in those solitudes it feels for the first time the cold current, the hot morning sun, sees the pine stumps, smells the sweet fern. And along with the mottled trout, with its 'clear water-over-gravel color,' the boy from the American Middle West fishes up a nice little masterpiece.

In the meantime there had been also Ring Lardner, Sherwood Anderson, Gertrude Stein, using this American language for irony, lyric poetry or psychological insight. Hemingway seems to have learned from them all. But he is now able to charge this naïve accent with a new complexity of emotion, a new shade of emotion: a malaise. The wholesale shattering of human beings in which he has taken part has given the boy a touch of panic.

II

The next fishing trip is strikingly different. Perhaps the first had been an idealization. Is it possible to attain to such sensuous bliss merely through going alone into the woods: smoking, fishing, and eating, with no thought about anyone else or about anything one has ever done or will ever be obliged to do? At any rate, today, in *The Sun Also Rises*, all the things that are wrong with human life are there on the holiday, too—though one tries to keep them back out of the foreground and to occupy one's mind with the trout, caught now in a stream of the Pyrenees, and with the kidding of the friend from the States. The feeling of insecurity has deepened. The young American now appears in a seriously damaged condition: he has somehow been incapacitated sexually through wounds received in the war. He is in love with one of those international sirens who flourished in the cafés of the post-war period and whose ruthless and uncontrollable infidelities, in such a circle as that depicted by Hemingway, have made any sort of security impossible for the relations between women and men. The lovers of such a woman turn upon and rend one another because they are powerless to make themselves felt by *her*.

The casualties of the bullfight at Pamplona, to which these young people have gone for the *fiesta*, only reflect the blows and betrayals of demoralized human beings out of hand. What is the tiresome lover with whom the lady has just been off on a casual escapade, and who is unable to understand that he has been discarded, but the man who, on his way to the bull ring, has been accidentally gored by the bull? The young American who tells the story is the only character who keeps up standards of conduct, and he is prevented by his disability from dominating and directing the woman, who otherwise, it is intimated, might love him. Here the membrane of the style has been stretched taut to convey the vibrations of these qualms. The dry sunlight and the green summer landscapes have been invested with a sinister quality which must be new in literature. One enjoys the sun and the green as one enjoys suckling pigs and Spanish wine, but the uneasiness and apprehension are undruggable.

Yet one can catch hold of a code in all the drunkenness and the social chaos. 'Perhaps as you went along you did learn something,' Jake, the hero, reflects at one point. 'I did not care what it was all about. All I wanted to know was how to live in it. Maybe if you found out how to live in it you learned from that what it was all about.' 'Everybody behaves badly. Give them the proper chance,' he says later to Lady Brett. '"You wouldn't behave badly." Brett looked at me.' In the end, she sends for Jake, who finds her alone in a hotel. She has left her regular lover for a young bullfighter, and this boy has for the first time inspired her with a respect which has restrained her from 'ruining' him: 'You know it makes one feel rather good deciding not to be a bitch.' We suffer and we make suffer, and everybody loses out in the long run; but in the meantime we can lose with honor.

This code still markedly figures, still supplies a dependable moral backbone, in Hemingway's next book of short stories, *Men Without Women*. Here Hemingway has mastered his method of economy in apparent casualness and relevance in apparent indirection, and has turned his sense of what happens and the way in which it happens into something as hard and clear as a crystal but as disturbing as a great lyric. Yet it is usually some principle of courage, of honor, of pity—that is, some principle of sportsmanship in its largest human sense—upon which the drama hinges. The old bullfighter in *The Undefeated* is defeated in everything except the spirit which will not accept defeat. You get the bull or he gets you: if you die, you can die game; there are certain things you cannot do. The burlesque show manager in *A Pursuit Race* refrains from waking his advance publicity agent when he overtakes him and realizes that the man has just lost a long struggle against whatever anguish it is that has driven him to drink and dope. 'They got a cure for that,' the manager had said to him before he went to sleep; '"No," William Campbell said, "they haven't got a cure for anything."' The burned major in *A Simple Enquiry*—that strange picture of the bedrock stoicism compatible with the abasement of war—has the decency not to dismiss the orderly who has rejected his proposition. The brutalized Alpine peasant who has been in the habit of hanging a lantern in the jaws of the stiffened corpse of his wife, stood in the corner of the woodshed till the spring will make it possible to bury her, is ashamed to drink with the sexton after the latter has found out what he has done. And there is a little sketch of Roman soldiers just after the Crucifixion: 'You see me slip the old spear into him?—You'll get into trouble doing that some day.—It was the least I could do for him. I'll tell you he looked pretty good to me in there today.'

This Hemingway of the middle twenties—*The Sun Also Rises* came out in '26—expressed the romantic disillusion and set the favorite pose for the period. It was the moment of gallantry in heartbreak, grim and nonchalant banter, and heroic dissipation. The great watchword was 'Have a drink,' and in the bars of New York and Paris the young people were getting to talk like Hemingway.

III

The novel, *A Farewell to Arms*, which followed *Men Without Women*, is in a sense not so serious an affair. Beautifully written and quite moving of course it is. Probably no other book has caught so well the strangeness of life in the army for an American in Europe during the war. The new places to which one was sent of which one had never heard, and the things that turned out to be in them; the ordinary people of foreign countries as one saw them when one was quartered among them or obliged to perform some common work with them; the pleasures of which one managed to cheat the war, intensified by the uncertainty and horror—and the uncertainty, nevertheless, almost become a constant, the horror almost taken for granted; the love affairs, always subject to being suddenly broken up and yet carried on while they lasted in a spirit of irresponsible freedom which derived from one's having forfeited control of all one's other actions—this Hemingway got into his book, written long enough after the events for them to present themselves under an aspect fully idyllic.

But *A Farewell to Arms* is a tragedy, and the lovers are shown as innocent victims with no relation to the forces that torment them. They themselves are not tormented within by that dissonance between personal satisfaction and the suffering one shares with others which it has been Hemingway's triumph to handle. *A Farewell to Arms*, as the author once said, is a *Romeo and Juliet*. And when Catherine and her lover emerge from the stream of action—the account of the Caporetto retreat is Hemingway's best sustained piece of narrative —when they escape from the alien necessities of which their romance has been merely an accident, which have been writing their story for them, then we see that they are not in themselves convincing as human personalities. And we are confronted with the paradox that Hemingway, who possesses so remarkable a mimetic gift in getting the tone of social and national types and in making his people talk appropriately, has not shown any very solid sense of character, or, indeed, any real interest in it. The people in his short stories are satisfactory because he has only to hit them off: the point of the story does not lie in personalities, but in the emotion to which a situation gives rise. This is true even in *The Sun Also Rises*, where the characters are sketched with wonderful cleverness. But in *A Farewell to Arms*, as soon as we are brought into real intimacy with the lovers, as soon as the author is obliged to see them through a searching personal experience, we find merely an idealized relationship, the abstractions of a lyric emotion.

With *Death in the Afternoon*, three years later, a new development for Hemingway commences. He writes a book not merely in the first person, but in the first person in his own character as Hemingway, and the results are unexpected and disconcerting. *Death in the Afternoon* has its value as an exposition of bullfighting; and Hemingway is able to use the subject as a text for an explicit statement of his conception of man

eternally pitting himself—he thinks the bullfight a ritual of this
—against animal force and the odds of death. But the book is
partly infected by a queer kind of maudlin emotion, which
sounds at once neurotic and drunken. He overdoes his glorification of the bravery and martyrdom of the bullfighter. No
doubt the professional expert at risking his life single-handed
is impressive in contrast to the flatness and unreality of much
of the business of the modern world; but this admirable minia-
turist in prose has already made the point perhaps more
tellingly in the little prose poem called *Banal Story*. Now he off-
sets the virility of the bullfighters by anecdotes of the male ho-
mosexuals that frequent the Paris cafés, at the same time that
he puts his chief celebration of the voluptuous excitement of
the spectacle into the mouth of an imaginary old lady. The
whole thing becomes a little hysterical.

The master of that precise and clean style now indulges in
purple patches which go on spreading for pages. I am not one
of those who admire the last chapter of *Death in the Afternoon*,
with its rich, all too rich, unrollings of memories of good times
in Spain, and with its what seem to me irrelevant reminiscences
of the soliloquy of Mrs. Bloom in *Ulysses*. Also, there are interludes of kidding of a kind which Hemingway handles with skill
when he assigns them to characters in his stories, but in connection with which he seems to become incapable of exercising good sense or good taste as soon as he undertakes them
in his own person (the burlesque *Torrents of Spring* was an
early omen of this). In short, we are compelled to recognize
that, as soon as Hemingway drops the burning-glass of the disciplined and objective art with which he has learned to concentrate in a story the light of the emotions that flood in on
him, he straightway becomes befuddled, slops over.

This befuddlement is later to go further, but in the meantime he publishes another volume of stories—*Winner Take
Nothing*—which is almost up to its predecessor. In this collection he deals much more effectively than in *Death in the
Afternoon* with that theme of contemporary decadence which
is implied in his panegyric of the bullfighter. The first of these
stories, *After the Storm*, is another of his variations—and one
of the finest—on the theme of keeping up a code of decency
among the hazards and pains of life. A fisherman goes out to

plunder a wreck: he dives down to break in through a port-hole, but inside he sees a woman with rings on her hands and her hair floating loose in the water, and he thinks about the passengers and crew being suddenly plunged to their deaths (he has almost been killed himself in a drunken fight the night before). He sees the cloud of sea birds screaming around, and he finds that he is unable to break the glass with his wrench and that he loses the anchor grapple with which he next tries to attack it. So he finally goes away and leaves the job to the Greeks, who blow the boat open and clean her out.

But in general the emotions of insecurity here obtrude themselves and dominate the book. Two of the stories deal with the hysteria of soldiers falling off the brink of their nerves under the strain of the experiences of the war, which here no longer presents an idyllic aspect; another deals with a group of patients in a hospital, at the same time crippled and hopeless; still another (a five-page masterpiece) with a waiter, who, both on his own and on his customers' account, is reluctant to go home at night, because he feels the importance of a 'clean well-lighted cafe' as a refuge from the 'nothing' that people fear. *God Rest You Merry, Gentlemen* repeats the theme of cas-tration of *The Sun Also Rises*; and four of the stories are con cerned more or less with male or female homosexuality. In the last story, *Fathers and Sons*, Hemingway reverts to the Michi-gan woods, as if to take the curse off the rest: young Nick had once enjoyed a nice Indian girl with plump legs and hard little breasts on the needles of the hemlock woods.

These stories and the interludes in *Death in the Afternoon* must have been written during the years that followed the stock-market crash. They are full of the apprehension of losing control of oneself which is aroused by the getting out of hand of a social-economic system, as well as of the fear of impotence which seems to accompany the loss of social mastery. And there is in such a story as *A Clean Well-Lighted Place* the feeling of having got to the end of everything, of having given up heroic attitudes and wanting only the illusion of peace.

IV

And now, in proportion as the characters in his stories run out of fortitude and bravado, he passes into a phase where he is occupied with building up his public personality. He has already now become a legend, as Mencken was in the twenties; he is the Hemingway of the handsome photographs with the sportsmen's tan and the outdoor grin, with the ominous resemblance to Clark Gable, who poses with giant marlin which he has just hauled in off Key West. And unluckily—but for an American inevitably—the opportunity soon presents itself to exploit this personality for profit: he turns up delivering Hemingway monologues in well-paying and trashy magazines; and the Hemingway of these loose disquisitions, arrogant, belligerent and boastful, is certainly the worst-invented character to be found in the author's work. If he is obnoxious, the effect is somewhat mitigated by the fact that he is intrinsically incredible.

There would be no point in mentioning this journalism at all, if it did not seem somewhat to have contributed to the writing of certain unsatisfactory books. *Green Hills of Africa* (1935) owes its failure to falling between the two *genres* of personal exhibitionism and fiction. 'The writer has attempted,' says Hemingway, 'to write an absolutely true book to see whether the shape of a country and the pattern of a month's action can, if truly presented, compete with a work of the imagination.' He does try to present his own rôle objectively, and there is a genuine Hemingway theme—the connection between success at big-game hunting and sexual self-respect—involved in his adventures as he presents them. But the sophisticated technique of the fiction writer comes to look artificial when it is applied to a series of real happenings; and the necessity of sticking to what really happened makes impossible the typical characters and incidents which give point to a work of fiction. The monologues by the false, the publicity, Hemingway with which the narrative is interspersed are almost as bad as the ones that he has been writing for the magazines. He inveighs with much scorn against the literary life and against the professional literary man of the cities; and then manages to give the impression that he himself is a professional literary man of the touchiest and most self-conscious kind. He delivers a self-confident lecture on the high possibilities of prose writing; and then produces such a sentence as the following: 'Going downhill steeply made these Spanish shooting boots too short in the toe and there was an old argument, about this length of boot and whether the bootmaker, whose part I had taken, unwittingly first, only as interpreter, and finally embraced his theory patriotically as a whole and, I believed, by logic, had overcome it by adding onto the heel.' As soon as Hemingway begins speaking in the first person, he seems to lose his bearings, not merely as a critic of life, but even as a craftsman.

In another and significant way, *Green Hills of Africa* is disappointing. *Death in the Afternoon* did provide a lot of data on bullfighting and build up for us the bullfighting world; but its successor tells us little about Africa. Hemingway keeps affirming—as if in accents of defiance against those who would engage his attention for social problems—his passionate enthusiasm for the African country and his perfect satisfaction with the hunter's life; but he has produced what must be one of the only books ever written which make Africa and its animals seem dull. Almost the only thing we learn about the animals is that Hemingway wants to kill them. And as for the natives, though there is one fine description of a tribe of marvelous trained runners, the principal impression we get of them is that they were simple and inferior people who enormously admired Hemingway.

It is not only that, as his critics of the Left had been complaining, he shows no interest in political issues, but that his interest in his fellow beings seems actually to be drying up. It is as if he were throwing himself on African hunting as something to live for and believe in, as something through which to realize himself; and as if, expecting of it too much, he had got out of it abnormally little, less than he is willing to admit. The disquiet of the Hemingway of the twenties had been, as I have said, undruggable—that is, in his books themselves, he had tried to express it, not drug it, had given it an appeasement in art; but now there sets in, in the Hemingway of the thirties, what seems to be a deliberate self-drugging. The situation is indicated objectively in *The Gambler, the Nun and the Radio*, one of the short stories of 1933, in which everything from daily bread to 'a belief in any new form of government' is characterized as 'the opium of the people' by an empty-hearted patient in a hospital.

*

But at last there did rush into this vacuum the blast of the social issue, which had been roaring in the wind like a forest fire.

Out of a series of short stories that Hemingway had written about a Florida waterside character he decided to make a little epic. The result was *To Have and Have Not*, which seems to me the poorest of all his stories. Certainly some deep agitation is working upon Hemingway the artist. Craftsmanship and style, taste and sense, have all alike gone by the board. The negative attitude toward human beings has here become definitely malignant: the hero is like a wooden-headed Punch, always knocking people on the head (inferiors—Chinamen or Cubans); or, rather, he combines the characteristics of Punch with those of Popeye the Sailor in the animated cartoon in the movies. As the climax to a series of prodigies, this stupendous pirate-smuggler named Harry Morgan succeeds, alone, unarmed, and with only a hook for one hand—though at the cost of a mortal wound—in outwitting and destroying with their own weapons four men carrying revolvers and a machine gun, by whom he has been shanghaied in a launch. The only way in which Hemingway's outlaw suffers by comparison with Popeye is that his creator has not tried to make him plausible by explaining that he does it all on spinach.

The impotence of a decadent society has here been exploited deliberately, but less successfully than in the earlier short stories. Against a background of homosexuality, impotence and masturbation among the wealthy holiday-makers in Florida, Popeye-Morgan is shown gratifying his wife with the same indefatigable dexterity which he has displayed in his other feats; and there is a choral refrain of praise of his *cojones*, which wells up in the last pages of the book when the abandoned Mrs. Popeye regurgitates Molly Bloom's soliloquy.

To be a man in such a world of maggots is noble, but it is not enough. Besides the maggots, there are double-crossing rats, who will get you if they are given the slightest chance. What is most valid in *To Have and Have Not* is the idea—conveyed better, perhaps, in the first of the series of episodes than in the final scenes of massacre and agony—that in an atmosphere (here revolutionary Cuba) in which man has been set against man, in which it is always a question whether your companion is not preparing to cut your throat, the most sturdy and straightforward American will turn suspicious and cruel. Harry Morgan is made to realize as he dies that to fight this bad world alone is hopeless. Again Hemingway, with his barometric accuracy, has rendered a moral atmosphere that was prevalent at the moment he was writing—a moment when social relations were subjected to severe tensions, when they seemed sometimes already disintegrating. But the heroic Hemingway legend has at this point invaded his fiction and, inflaming and inflating his symbols, has produced an implausible hybrid, half Hemingway character, half nature myth.

Hemingway had not himself particularly labored this moral of individualism *versus* solidarity, but the critics of the Left labored it for him and received his least creditable piece of fiction as the delivery of a new revelation. The progress of the Communist faith among our writers since the beginning of the depression has followed a peculiar course. That the aims and beliefs of Marx and Lenin should have come through to the minds of intellectuals who had been educated in the bourgeois tradition as great awakeners of conscience, a great light, was quite natural and entirely desirable. But the conception of the dynamic Marxist will, the exaltation of the Marxist religion, seized the members of the professional classes like a capricious contagion or hurricane, which shakes one and leaves his neighbor standing, then returns to lay hold on the second after the first has become quiet again. In the moment of seizure, each one of them saw a scroll unrolled from the heavens, on which Marx and Lenin and Stalin, the Bolsheviks of 1917, the Soviets of the Five-Year Plan, and the GPU of the Moscow trials were all a part of the same great purpose. Later the convert, if he were capable of it, would get over his first phase of snow blindness and learn to see real people and conditions, would study the development of Marxism in terms of nations, periods, personalities, instead of logical deductions from abstract propositions or—as in the case of the more naïve or dishonest—of simple incantatory slogans. But for many there was at least a moment when the key to all the mysteries of human history seemed suddenly to have been placed in their hands, when an infallible guide to thought and behavior seemed to have been given them in a few easy formulas.

Hemingway was hit pretty late. He was still in *Death in the Afternoon* telling the 'world-savers,' sensibly enough, that they should 'get to see' the world 'clear and as a whole. Then any part you make will represent the whole, if it's made truly. The thing to do is work and learn to make it.' Later he jibed at the literary radicals, who talked but couldn't take it; and one finds even in *To Have and Have Not* a crack about a 'highly paid Hollywood director, whose brain is in the process of outlasting his liver so that he will end up calling himself a Communist, to save his soul.' Then the challenge of the fight itself—Hemingway never could resist a physical challenge—the natural impulse to dedicate oneself to something bigger than big-game hunting and bullfighting, and the fact that the class war had broken out in a country to which he was romantically attached, seem to have combined to make him align himself with the Communists as well as the Spanish Loyalists at a time when the Marxist philosophy had been pretty completely shelved by the Kremlin, now reactionary as well as corrupt, and when the Russians were lending the Loyalists only help enough to preserve, as they imagined would be possible, the balance of power against Fascism while they acted at the same time as a police force to beat down the real social revolution.

Hemingway raised money for the Loyalists, reported the battle fronts. He even went so far as to make a speech at a congress of the League of American Writers, an organization rigged by the supporters of the Stalinist régime in Russia and full of precisely the type of literary revolutionists that he had been ridiculing a little while before. Soon the Stalinists had taken him in tow, and he was feverishly denouncing as Fascists other writers who criticized the Kremlin. It has been one of the expedients of the Stalin administration in maintaining its power and covering up its crimes to condemn on trumped-up charges of Fascist conspiracy, and even to kidnap and murder, its political opponents of the Left; and, along with the food and munitions, the Russians had brought to the war in Spain what the Austrian journalist Willi Schlamm called that diversion of doubtful value for the working class: 'Herr Vyshinsky's Grand Guignol.'

The result of this was a play, *The Fifth Column*, which, though it is good reading for the way the characters talk, is an exceedingly silly production. The hero, though an Anglo-American, is an agent of the Communist secret police, engaged in catching Fascist spies in Spain; and his principal exploit in the course of the play is clearing out, with the aid of a single Communist, an artillery post manned by seven Fascists. The scene is like a pushover and getaway from one of the cruder Hollywood Westerns. It is in the nature of a small boy's fantasy, and would probably be considered extravagant by most writers of books for boys.

The tendency on Hemingway's part to indulge himself in these boyish day-dreams seems to begin to get the better of his realism at the end of *A Farewell to Arms*, where the hero, after many adventures of fighting, escaping, love-making and drinking, rows his lady thirty-five kilometers on a cold and rainy night; and we have seen what it could do for Harry Morgan. Now, as if with the conviction that the cause and the efficiency of the GPU have added several cubits to his stature, he has let this tendency loose; and he has also found in the GPU's grim duty a pretext to give rein to the appetite for describing scenes of killing which has always been a feature of his work. He has progressed from grasshoppers and trout through bulls and lions and kudus to Chinamen and Cubans, and now to Fascists. Hitherto the act of destruction has given rise for him to complex emotions: he has identified himself not merely with the injurer but also with the injured; there has been a masochistic complement to the sadism. But now this paradox which splits our natures, and which has instigated some of Hemingway's best stories, need no longer present perplexities to his mind. The Fascists are dirty bastards, and to kill them is a righteous act. He who had made a separate peace, who had said farewell to arms, has found a reason for taking them up again in a spirit of rabietic fury unpleasantly reminiscent of the spy mania and the sacred anti-German rage which took possession of so many civilians and staff officers under the stimulus of the last war.

Not that the compensatory trauma of the typical Hemingway protagonist is totally absent even here. The main episode is the hero's brief love affair and voluntary breaking off with a beautiful and adoring girl whose acquaintance he has made in Spain. As a member of the Junior League and a graduate of

Vassar, she represents for him—it seems a little hard on her—
that leisure-class playworld from which he is trying to get
away. But in view of the fact that from the very first scenes he
treats her with more or less open contempt, the action is rather
lacking in suspense as the sacrifice is rather feeble in moral
value. One takes no stock at all in the intimation that Mr. Philip
may later be sent to mortify himself in a camp for training
Young Pioneers. And in the meantime he has fun killing
Fascists.

In *The Fifth Column*, the drugging process has been carried
further still: the hero, who has become finally indistinguishable from the false or publicity Hemingway, has here dosed
himself not only with whiskey, but with a seductive and de-
sirous woman, for whom he has the most admirable reasons
for not taking any responsibility, with sacred rage, with the excitement of a bombardment, and with indulgence in that
headiest of sports, for which he has now the same excellent
reasons: the bagging of human beings.

v

You may fear, after reading *The Fifth Column*, that Hemingway will never sober up; but as you go on to his short stories of
this period, you find that your apprehensions were unfounded.
Three of these stories have a great deal more body—they are
longer and more complex—than the comparatively meager anecdotes collected in *Winner Take Nothing*. And here are his
real artistic successes with the material of his adventures in
Africa, which make up for the miscarried *Green Hills*: The
Short Happy Life of Francis Macomber and *The Snows of Kilimanjaro*, which disengage, by dramatizing them objectively,
the themes he had attempted in the earlier book but that had
never really got themselves presented. And here is at least a
beginning of a real artistic utilization of Hemingway's experience in Spain: an incident of the war in two pages which out-
weighs the whole of *The Fifth Column* and all his Spanish
dispatches, a glimpse of an old man, 'without politics,' who
has so far occupied his life in taking care of eight pigeons, two
goats and a cat, but who has now been dislodged and separated from his pets by the advance of the Fascist armies. It is a
story which takes its place among the war prints of Callot and

Goya, artists whose union of elegance with sharpness has already been recalled by Hemingway in his earlier battle pieces: a story which might have been written about almost any war.

And here—what is very remarkable—is a story, *The Capital of the World*, which finds an objective symbol for, precisely, what is wrong with *The Fifth Column*. A young boy who has come up from the country and waits on table in a pension in Madrid gets accidentally stabbed with a meat knife while playing at bullfighting with the dishwasher. This is the simple anecdote, but Hemingway has built in behind it all the life of the pension and the city: the priesthood, the working-class movement, the grown-up bullfighters who have broken down or missed out. 'The boy Paco,' Hemingway concludes, 'had never known about any of this nor about what all these people would be doing on the next day and on other days to come. He had no idea how they really lived nor how they ended. He did not realize they ended. He died, as the Spanish phrase has it, full of illusions. He had not had time in his life to lose any of them, or even, at the end, to complete an act of contrition.' So he registers in this very fine piece the discrepancy between the fantasies of boyhood and the realities of the grown-up world. Hemingway the artist, who feels things truly and cannot help recording what he feels, has actually said good-bye to these fantasies at a time when the war correspondent is making himself ridiculous by attempting to hang on to them still.

The emotion which principally comes through in *Francis Macomber* and *The Snows of Kilimanjaro*—as it figures also in *The Fifth Column*—is a growing antagonism to women. Looking back, one can see at this point that the tendency has been there all along. In *The Doctor and the Doctor's Wife*, the boy Nick goes out squirrel-hunting with his father instead of obeying the summons of his mother; in *Cross Country Snow*, he regretfully says farewell to male companionship on a skiing expedition in Switzerland, when he is obliged to go back to the States so that his wife can have her baby. The young man in *Hills Like White Elephants* compels his girl to have an abortion contrary to her wish; another story, *A Canary for One*, bites almost unbearably but exquisitely on the loneliness to be endured by a wife after she and her husband shall have separated; the peasant of *An Alpine Idyll* abuses the corpse of his wife (these last three appear under the general title *Men Without Women*). Brett in *The Sun Also Rises* is an exclusively destructive force: she might be a better woman if she were mated with Jake, the American; but actually he is protected against her and is in a sense revenging his own sex through being unable to do anything for her sexually. Even the hero of *A Farewell to Arms* eventually destroys Catherine—after enjoying her abject devotion—by giving her a baby, itself born dead. The only women with whom Nick Adams' relations are perfectly satisfactory are the little Indian girls of his boyhood who are in a position of hopeless social disadvantage and have no power over the behavior of the white male—so that he can get rid of them the moment he has done with them. Thus in *The Fifth Column* Mr. Philip brutally breaks off with Dorothy—he has been rescued from her demoralizing influence by his enlistment in the Communist crusade, just as the hero of *The Sun Also Rises* has been saved by his physical disability—to revert to a little Moorish whore. Even Harry Morgan, who is represented as satisfying his wife on the scale of a Paul Bunyan, deserts her in the end by dying and leaves her racked by the cruelest desire.*

And now this instinct to get the woman down presents itself frankly as a fear that the woman will get the man down. The men in both these African stories are married to American bitches of the most soul-destroying sort. The hero of *The Snows*

*There would probably be a chapter to write on the relation between Hemingway and Kipling, and certain assumptions about society which they share. They have much the same split attitude toward women. Kipling anticipates Hemingway in his beliefs that 'he travels the fastest that travels alone' and that 'the female of the species is more deadly than the male'; and Hemingway seems to reflect Kipling in the submissive infra-Anglo-Saxon women that make his heroes such perfect mistresses. The most striking example of this is the amoeba-like little Spanish girl, Maria, in *For Whom the Bell Tolls*. Like the docile native 'wives' of English officials in the early stories of Kipling, she lives only to serve her lord and to merge her identity with his; and this love affair with a woman in a sleeping-bag, lacking completely the kind of give and take that goes on between real men and women, has the all-too-perfect felicity of a youthful erotic dream. One suspects that *Without Benefit of Clergy* was read very early by Hemingway and that it made on him a lasting impression. The pathetic conclusion of this story of Kipling's seems unmistakably to be echoed at the end of *A Farewell to Arms*.

of Kilimanjaro loses his soul and dies of futility on a hunting expedition in Africa, out of which he has failed to get what he had hoped. The story is not quite stripped clean of the trashy moral attitudes which have been coming to disfigure the author's work: the hero, a seriously intentioned and apparently promising writer, goes on a little sloppily over the dear early days in Paris when he was earnest, happy and poor, and blames a little hysterically the rich woman whom he has married and who has debased him. Yet it is one of Hemingway's remarkable stories. There is a wonderful piece of writing at the end when the reader is made to realize that what has seemed to be an escape by plane, with the sick man looking down on Africa, is only the dream of a dying man. The other story, *Francis Macomber*, perfectly realizes its purpose. Here the male saves his soul at the last minute, and then is actually shot down by his woman, who does not want him to have a soul. Here Hemingway has at last got what Thurber calls the war between men and women right out into the open and has written a terrific fable of the impossible civilized woman who despises the civilized man for his failure in initiative and nerve and then jealously tries to break him down as soon as he begins to exhibit any. (It ought to be noted, also, that whereas in *Green Hills of Africa* the descriptions tended to weigh down the narrative their excessive circumstantiality, the landscapes and animals of *Francis Macomber* are alive and unfalteringly proportioned.)

Going back over Hemingway's books today, we can see clearly what an error of the politicos it was to accuse him of an indifference to society. His whole work is a criticism of society: he has responded to every pressure of the moral atmosphere of the time, as it is felt at the roots of human relations, with a sensitivity almost unrivaled. Even his preoccupation with licking the gang in the next block and being known as the best basketball player in high school has its meaning in the present epoch. After all, whatever is done in the world, political as well as athletic, depends on personal courage and strength. With Hemingway, courage and strength are always thought of in physical terms, so that he tends to give the impression that the bullfighter who can take it and dish it out is more of a man

than any other kind of man, and that the sole duty of the revolutionary socialist is to get the counter-revolutionary gang
before they get him.

But ideas, however correct, will never prevail by themselves:
there must be people who are prepared to stand or fall with
them, and the ability to act on principle is still subject to the
same competitive laws which operate in sporting contests and
sexual relations. Hemingway has expressed with genius the
terrors of the modern man at the danger of losing control of
his world, and he has also, within his scope, provided his own
kind of antidote. This antidote, paradoxically, is almost entirely
moral. Despite Hemingway's preoccupation with physical contests, his heroes are almost always defeated physically, nervously, practically: their victories are moral ones. He himself,
when he trained himself stubbornly in his unconventional un-
marketable art in a Paris which had other fashions, gave the
prime example of such a victory; and if he has sometimes,
under the menace of the general panic, seemed on the point of
going to pieces as an artist, he has always pulled himself together the next moment. The principle of the Bourdon gauge,
which is used to measure the pressure of liquids, is that a tube
which has been curved into a coil will tend to straighten out in
proportion as the liquid inside it is subjected to an increasing
pressure.

————

The appearance of *For Whom the Bell Tolls* since this essay
was written in 1939 carries the straightening process further.
Here Hemingway has largely sloughed off his Stalinism and
has reverted to seeing events in terms of individuals pitted
against specific odds. His hero, an American teacher of Spanish
who has enlisted on the side of the Loyalists, gives his life to
what he regards as the cause of human liberation; but he is
frustrated in the task that has been assigned him by the confusion of forces at cross-purposes that are throttling the Loyalist
campaign. By the time that he comes to die, he has little to
sustain him but the memory of his grandfather's record as a
soldier in the American Civil War. The psychology of this
young man is presented with a certain sobriety and detachment
in comparison with Hemingway's other full-length heroes; and

the author has here succeeded as in none of his earlier books in externalizing in plausible characters the elements of his own complex personality. With all this, there is an historical point of view which he has learned from his political adventures: he has aimed to reflect in this episode the whole course of the Spanish War and the tangle of tendencies involved in it.

The weaknesses of the book are its diffuseness—a shape that lacks the concision of his short stories, that sometimes sags and sometimes bulges; and a sort of exploitation of the material, an infusion of the operatic, that lends itself all too readily to the movies.

6

The Dream of H. C. Earwicker

JAMES JOYCE'S *Ulysses* was an attempt to present directly the thoughts and feelings of a group of Dubliners through the whole course of a summer day. *Finnegans Wake* is a complementary attempt to render the dream fantasies and the half-unconscious sensations experienced by a single person in the course of a night's sleep.

This presents a more difficult problem to the reader as well as to the writer. In *Ulysses*, the reader was allowed to perceive the real objective world in which the Blooms and Dedalus lived, and their situation and relationships in that world, so that its distortions or liquefactions under the stress of special psychological states still usually remained intelligible. But in *Finnegans Wake* we are not supplied with any objective data until the next to the last chapter, when the hero—and then only rather dimly—wakes up for a short time toward morning; and we are dealing with states of consciousness which, though they sometimes have something in common with the drunken imaginations of the Night Town scene in *Ulysses* or the free associations of Mrs. Bloom's insomniac reveries, are even more confused and fluid than these; so that it becomes on a first reading the reader's prime preoccupation to puzzle out who the dreamer is and what has been happening to him. And since Joyce has spent seventeen years elaborating and complicating this puzzle, it is hardly to be expected that one reading will suffice to unravel it completely.

Let me try to establish, however, some of the most important facts which provide the realistic foundation for this immense poem of sleep. The hero of *Finnegans Wake* is a man of Scandinavian blood, with what is apparently an adapted Scandinavian name: Humphrey Chimpden Earwicker, who keeps a pub called The Bristol in Dublin. He is somewhere between fifty and sixty, blond and ruddy, with a walrus mustache, very strong but of late years pretty fat. When embarrassed, he has a tendency to stutter. He has tried his hand at a number of oc-

cupations; has run for office and has gone through a bankruptcy. He is married to a woman named Ann, a former sales-
girl, who is more or less illiterate and whose maiden name
seems to have begun with Mac. They are both Protestants in a
community of Catholics, he an Episcopalian and she a Presbyterian; and by reason both of his religion and of his queer-
sounding foreign name, he feels himself, like Bloom in *Ulysses*,
something of an alien among his neighbors. The Earwickers
have three children—a girl named Isobel, who has evidently
passed adolescence, and two younger boys, twins: Kevin and
Jerry. There are also a maid-of-all-work called Kate and a man
about the place called Tom.

It is a Saturday night in summer, after a disorderly evening
in the pub. Somebody—probably Earwicker himself—has been
prevailed upon to sing a song: later, when it was closing time,
he had to put a man outside, who abused him and threw
stones at the window. There has also been a thunderstorm.
Earwicker has been drinking off and on all day and has perhaps
gone to bed a little drunk. At any rate, his night is troubled. At
first he dreams about the day before, with a bad conscience
and a sense of humiliation: then, as the night darkens and he
sinks more deeply into sleep, he has to labor through a nightmare oppression.

He and his wife are sleeping together; but he has no longer
any interest in her as a woman. He is preoccupied now with his
children. His wife is apparently much younger than he, was
only a girl when he married her; so that it is easy for him to
confuse his first feelings for her with something like an erotic
emotion which is now being aroused by his daughter. And his
affection for his favorite son is even acquiring homosexual associations. Little Kevin is relatively sedate: named after the
ascetic St. Kevin, he may be destined for the Catholic priesthood. Jerry (Shem) is more volatile and has given evidences of
a taste for writing; and it is Jerry rather than Kevin (Shaun)
with whom the father has tended to identify himself.

To tell the story in this way, however, is to present it the
wrong way around. It depends for its dramatic effect on our
not finding out till almost the end—pages 555–590, in which
Earwicker partially wakes up—that the flights of erotic fantasy
and the horrors of guilt of his dream have been inspired by his

feelings for his children. The pub is on the edge of the Phoenix Park, between it and the River Liffey and not far from the suburb of Chapelizod, which is said to have been the birthplace of Iseult. At the very beginning of the dream, we find Earwicker figuring as Tristram; and through the whole night he is wooing Iseult; he carries her off, he marries her. The Freudian censor has intervened to change *Isobel* into *Iseult la Belle*—as well as to turn the ana (upper)-Liffey, which figures in the dream as a woman, into *Anna Livia Plurabelle*. The idea of incest between father and daughter is developed on page 115; the transition from Isobel to Iseult is indicated in the 'Icy-la-Belle' of page 246; and the sister of the twins is designated by her family nickname 'Izzy' on page 431. But, though the boys have been given their real names and planted pretty clearly—on pages 26–27—it is not until almost the end—on page 556—that a definite identification of Earwicker's daughter with Iseult is made. In the same way, it is not until the passage on pages 564–565 that we are led to connect with Earwicker's son the homosexual motif which has first broken into his dream with the ominous incident of the father's accosting a soldier in the park and subsequently being razzed by the police, and which works free toward morning—page 474—to the idea, not related to actuality, of 'some chubby boy-bold love of an angel.'

In the meantime, the incest taboo and the homosexuality taboo have together—as in the development of Greek tragedy out of the old myths of cannibalism and incest—given rise, during Earwicker's effortful night, to a whole mythology, a whole morality. He is Tristram stealing Iseult, yes; but—at the suggestion of an Adam's mantelpiece in the bedroom where he is sleeping—he is also Adam, who has forfeited by his sin the Paradise of the Phoenix Park; at the suggestion of a copy of Raphael's picture of Michael subduing Satan which hangs on the bedroom wall, he is an archangel wrestling with the Devil. And he has fallen not merely as Adam but also as Humpty Dumpty (he is fat and his first name is Humphrey); as the hero of the ballad of *Finnegan's Wake*, who fell off a scaffold while building a house (but came to life again at the sound of the word 'Whisky'); and as Napoleon (an obelisk dedicated to Wellington is a feature of the Phoenix Park, though there is apparently no Wellington Museum). Since the landmarks of the life of Swift still keep their prestige in Dublin, he is Swift, who loved Stella and Vanessa with the obstructed love of a father and whose mind was finally blotted by madness: Swift's cryptic name for Stella, 'Ppt,' punctuates the whole book.

And Earwicker is also making up in sleep for an habitual feeling of helplessness due to his belonging to a racial and religious minority. He is sometimes the first Danish conqueror of Ireland, who sailed up that very Liffey; sometimes Oliver Cromwell, that other hated heathen invader.

But it is Joyce's further aim to create, through Earwicker's mythopœic dream, a set of symbols even more general and basic. He has had the idea of making Earwicker, resolved into his elemental components, include the whole of humanity. The river, with its feminine personality, Anna Livia Plurabelle, comes to represent the feminine principle itself. At one time or another all the women who figure in Earwicker's fantasy are merged into this stream of life which, always renewed, never pausing, flows through the world built by men. The daughter, still a little girl, is early identified with a cloud, which will come down to earth as rain and turn into the rapid young river; the Anna Livia Plurabelle chapter describes a lively woman's coming-of-age; in the end, the mature river, broader and slower now, will move toward her father, the sea. The corresponding masculine principle is symbolized by the Hill of Howth, which rises at the mouth of the Liffey; and the idea of the hill as a citadel and the idea of the city as a male construction associate themselves with this: the man is a hill that stands firm while the river runs away at his feet; he is a fortress, he is Dublin, he is all the cities of the world.

And if Earwicker is animated in sleep by the principles of both the sexes, he has also a double existence in the rôles of both Youth and Old Age. Canalizing his youthful impulses in a vision of himself as his favorite son, he dreams himself endowed with a resilience to go out and try life again; exalted by a purity of idealism which has not yet been tainted by experience, and yet bubbling with roguish drolleries, blithely beloved by the girls. On the other hand, foreshadowing his own decline, he sees the vision of a chorus of old men, who, drivelingly reminiscent, at the same time gloat and scold at the thought of the vigorous young Tristram kissing Iseult on the other side of the bushes, and exclaim in admiration—an expansion of Earwicker's feelings at the sight of his own sleeping son—over the form of the sleeping Earwicker (Shaun-Jerry). The old men are named Matthew Gregory, Marcus Lyons, Luke Tarpey and Johnny MacDougall; and they are identified variously with the four apostles, the Four Masters (early sages of Irish legend), the Four Waves of Irish mythology, the four courts of Dublin, and the four provinces of Ireland (Johnny MacDougall is evidently Ulster: he always follows at some distance behind the others). These fathers are always associated with a gray ass and sycamore trees, and have perhaps been suggested to Earwicker by four sycamore trees on the Liffey, among which a neighbor's donkey has been grazing. All of these major motifs are woven in and out from beginning to end of the book, and each at a given point receives a complete development: the woman-river in pages 196–216—the well-known Anna Livia Plurabelle chapter; the male city-fortress-hill in pages 531–554 (already published separately as *Haveth Childers Everywhere*); the Young Man in the chapters about Shaun, pages 403–473; and the Old Men, providing a contrast, just before, in 383–399.

There are also a stone and an elm on opposite sides of the Liffey, which represent the death principle and the life principle (Ygdrasil). The tree has several graciously rustling solos (a notable one at the end, beginning on page 619), and in the Anna Livia Plurabelle chapter she has a long conversation with the stone, which blends with the gossip of two old washerwomen drying clothes on the riverbank. This dialogue is only one of many dialogues which are really always the same disputation, and in which one of the parties, like the stone, is always hard-boiled, immobile and prosaic, while the other is sensitive, alive, rather light-mindedly chattering or chirping. The tougher of the two parties in these interchanges is always browbeating or bullying the other. Sometimes they are Satan and Saint Michael; sometimes they are transmogrified antitheses derived from Aesop's fables: the Mookse and the Gripes (the Fox and the Grapes), the Ondt and the Gracehoper (the Ant and the Grasshopper); but all these dualisms are evidently connected with the diverse temperaments of Earwicker's twins (who sometimes appear as Cain and Abel), and represent the diverse elements in the character of Earwicker himself, as these struggle within his own consciousness, the aggressive side sometimes reflecting certain powers in the external world—the force of hostile opinion or the police—which he now fears, now feels he can stand up to. The various pairs, however, shift their balance and melt into one another so readily that it is impossible to give any account of them which will cover all the cases in the book.

Besides all this, just as Joyce in *Ulysses* laid the *Odyssey* under requisition to help provide a structure for his material— material which, once it had begun to gush from the rock of Joyce's sealed personality at the blow of the Aaron's rod of free association, threatened to rise and submerge the artist like the flood which the sorcerer's apprentice let loose by his bedeviled broom; so in the face of an even more formidable danger, he has here brought in the historical theory of the eighteenth-century philosopher, Giambattista Vico, to help him to organize *Finnegans Wake*. It was Vico's idea that civilizations always pass through three definite phases: a phase when people imagine gods, a phase when they make up myths about heroes, and a phase when they see things in terms of real men. It will be noted that the figures mentioned above divide themselves among these three categories of beings. Vico further believed that history moved in cycles and that it was always repeating itself, which—to the frequent exasperation of the reader—*Finnegans Wake* is also made to do. And there is also a good deal more out of Vico, which you can find out about in *Our Examgination** but which seems even more idle and forced than the most forced and idle aspects of the

*Our Examgination Round His Factification for Incamination of Work in Progress, published by New Directions at Norfolk, Connecticut. This is a collection of papers from *Transition*, the Paris magazine in which *Finnegans Wake* first appeared. The writers have taken their cues from Joyce himself, and he seems to have chosen this way of providing the public with a key. It is, in fact, rather doubtful whether without the work done by *Transition* it would be possible to get the hang of the book at all. See also Mr. Max Eastman's account of an interview with Joyce on the subject in Part III, Chapter III, of *The Literary Mind*.

Odysseyan parallel in *Ulysses*. The fact that there is a Vico Road
in the Dublin suburb Dalkey—'The Vico Road goes round
and round to meet where terms begin'—gives Joyce a peg in
actuality on which to hang all this theory.

There is one important respect in which Joyce may seem to
depart from Vico. Vico, so far as is known, did not believe in
progress: his cycles did not spiral toward an earthly goal; his
hope for salvation was in heaven. But the cycles of *Finnegans
Wake* do result in a definite progression. As Earwicker lives
through from darkness to light, he does slough off his feeling
of guilt. By morning the Devil has been vanquished by
Michael; Youth has bounded free of Age; the Phoenix of Vico
and the Phoenix Park has risen from its ashes to new flight;
Tristram has built a castle (Howth Castle) for his bride; and
Iseult, once the object of an outlawed love, now married and
growing older, turns naturally and comfortably at last into the
lawful wife in the bed beside him, whom Earwicker is making
an effort not to jab with his knees; the tumult and turbidity of
Saturday night run clear in the peace of Sunday morning; the
soul, which has been buried in sleep, is resurrected, refreshed,
to life.

Yet if one looks at the book as a whole, one finds that the
larger cycle does return upon itself. This will be seen when I
discuss the last pages. In the meantime, let me merely point
out that we do not find in *Finnegans Wake* any climax of exaltation comparable either to the scene where Stephen Dedalus
realizes his artist's vocation or to Molly Bloom's great affirmative. The later book represents an aging phase in the constant
human subject with which the series of Joyce's books has dealt.
This subject—which must never be lost sight of, though in this
case it is easy to do so—is the nexus of intimate relationships
involved in a family situation. We find it first in the *Portrait of
an Artist* in the attitude of Dedalus toward his family, and in
the delicate but vital displacement in the relations of the young
married couple who figure in the short story called *The Dead*.
In *Exiles*, another young married couple come back from
abroad with a son, and a more serious displacement takes place
when the wife meets an old lover. In *Ulysses*, the relations of
man and wife, by this time almost middle-aged, have been affected by more serious readjustments, and they are related in a

complex way to the relations of the Blooms to their children, of Dedalus to his parents, and of both the Blooms to Dedalus. Now, in *Finnegans Wake*, the husband and wife have reached an age at which, from the emotional point of view, they seem hardly important to one another, and at which the chief source of interest is the attitude of the father toward the children— 'the child we all love to place our hope in,' as Earwicker thinks in the last moments before the rising sun wakes him up. (We have already had intimations of this relationship in the adoptively paternal instincts of Bloom toward the spiritually parentless Dedalus; in Joyce's little lyric poems, poignant to the point of anguish, that deal with his own children; and in the poem called *Ecce Puer*, in which the family cycle appears.)

Here this family situation has been explored more profoundly by Joyce than in any of his previous books. In sleep, the conventions and institutions with which we discipline and give shape to our lives are allowed partly to dissolve and evaporate, so as partly to set free the impulses of the common human plasm out of which human creatures are made; and then the sexual instincts of the man and the woman, the child's instinct and the parent's instinct, the masculine and feminine principles themselves, come into play in confusing ways, shadow forth disturbing relationships, which yet spring from the prime processes of life. *Finnegans Wake* carries even farther the kind of insight into such human relations which was already carried far in *Ulysses*; and it advances with an astounding stride the attempt to find the universally human in ordinary specialized experience which was implied in the earlier book by the Odysseyan parallel. Joyce will now try to build up inductively the whole of human history and myth from the impulses, conscious and dormant, the unrealized potentialities, of a single human being, who is to be a man even more obscure and even less well-endowed, even less civilized and aspiring, than was Leopold Bloom in *Ulysses*.

Finnegans Wake, in conception as well as in execution, is one of the boldest books ever written.

II

In order to get anything out of *Finnegans Wake*, you must grasp a queer literary convention. It has been said by T. S. Eliot that Joyce is the greatest master of language in English since Milton. Eliot has also pointed out that Milton is mainly a writer for the *ear*. Now Joyce through a large part of his adult life has been almost as blind as Milton; and he has ended, just as Milton did, by dealing principally in auditory sensations. There is as little visualization in *Finnegans Wake* as in *Samson Agonistes*. Our first criticism, therefore, is likely to be that nothing is *seen* in Earwicker's dream. It is, after all, not uncommon in dreams to have the illusion of seeing people and places as clearly as when we are awake; and in the dream literature with which we are already familiar—*Alice in Wonderland*, *The Temptation of Saint Anthony*—the dreamers are visited by plain apparitions, not merely by invisible voices. But we must assume with *Finnegans Wake* that Earwicker's imagination, like Joyce's, is almost entirely auditory and verbal. We have been partly prepared by *Ulysses*, in which we listen to the thoughts of the characters but do not see them very distinctly.

But there is another and more serious difficulty to be got over. We are continually being distracted from identifying and following Earwicker, the humble proprietor of a public house, who is to encompass the whole microcosm of the dream, by the intrusion of all sorts of elements—foreign languages, literary allusions, historical information—which could not possibly have been in Earwicker's mind. The principle on which Joyce is operating may evidently be stated as follows. If the artist is to render directly all the feelings and fancies of a sleeper, primitive, inarticulate, infinitely imprecise as they are, he must create a literary medium of unexampled richness and freedom. Now it is also Joyce's purpose in *Finnegans Wake* to bring out in Earwicker's consciousness the processes of universal history: the languages, the cycles of society, the typical relationships of legend, are, he is trying to show us, all implicit in every human being. He has, as I have indicated, been careful to hook up his hero realistically with the main themes of his universal fantasia: the Bible stories, the Battle of Waterloo, Tristram and Iseult, and so forth. But since Earwicker's implications *are* shown to be universal, the author has the right to summon all the resources of his superior knowledge in order to supply a vehicle which will carry this experience of sleep. He has the same sort of justification for making the beings in Earwicker's dream speak Russian in fighting the siege of Sebastopol (which has got in by way of a picture hanging in Earwicker's house) as Thomas Hardy has, for example, to describe in his own literary vocabulary a landscape seen by an ignorant person. If it is objected that in *Finnegans Wake* the author is supposed to be not *describing*, but presenting the hero's consciousness directly, Joyce might reply that his procedure had precedent not only in poetry, but also in pre-naturalistic fiction: even the characters of Dickens were allowed to make speeches in blank verse, even the characters of Meredith were allowed to converse in apothegms. Why shouldn't H. C. Earwicker be allowed to dream in a language which draws flexibility and variety from the author's enormous reservoir of colloquial and literary speech, of technical jargons and foreign tongues?

Yet here is where the reader's trouble begins, because here, in spite of the defense just suggested, a convention that seems indispensable has been disconcertingly violated. What Joyce is trying to do is to break out of the Flaubertian naturalism into something that moves more at ease and that commands a wider horizon, something that is not narrowly tied down to the data about a certain man living in a certain year on a certain street of a certain city; and the reaction is of course quite natural: it was inevitable that the symbol and the myth, the traditional material of poetry, should have asserted themselves again against the formulas of scientific precision which had begun to prove so cramping. But here the act of escaping from them shocks, just as it sometimes did in Proust. Proust argues in an impressive way, in the final section of his novel, the case against nineteenth-century naturalism; yet who has not been made uncomfortable at finding that Proust's personal manias have been allowed to affect the structure of his book: that a story which has been presented as happening to real people should not maintain a consistent chronology, that it should never be clear whether the narrator of the story is the same person as the author of the book, and that the author, who ought to know everything, should in some cases leave us in doubt as to the facts about his hero? One had felt, in reading *Ulysses*, a touch of the same uneasiness when the phantasmagoria imagined by Bloom in the drunken Night Town scene was enriched by learned fancies which would seem to be more

appropriate to Dedalus. And now in *Finnegans Wake* the bal-
loon of this new kind of poetry pulls harder at its naturalistic
anchor. We are in the first place asked to believe that a man like
H. C. Earwicker would seize every possible pretext provided
by his house and its location to include in a single night's
dream a large number of historical and legendary characters.
And is it not pretty farfetched to assume that Earwicker's
awareness of the life of Swift or the Crimean War is really to be
accurately conveyed in terms of the awareness of Joyce, who
has acquired a special knowledge of these subjects? Also, what
about the references to the literary life in Paris and to the book
itself as Work in Progress, which take us right out of the mind
of Earwicker and into the mind of Joyce?

There are not, to be sure, very many such winks and nudges
as this, though the shadow of Joyce at his thankless task seems
sometimes to fall between Earwicker and us. Joyce has evidently set himself limits as to how far he can go in this direction; and he may urge that since Earwicker is universal man, he
must contain the implications of Joyce's destiny as he does
those of Swift's and Napoleon's, though he has never heard of
him as he has of them, and that to give these implications a
personal accent is only to sign his canvas. Yet, even granting all
this and recognizing the difficulty of the task and accepting
without reservation the method Joyce has chosen for his purpose, the result still seems unsatisfactory, the thing has not
quite come out right. Instead of the myths' growing out of
Earwicker, Earwicker seems swamped in the myths. His personality is certainly created: we get to know him and feel sympathy for him. But he is not so convincing as Bloom was: there
has been too much literature poured into him. He has exfoli-
ated into too many arabesques, become hypertrophied by too
many elements. And not merely has he to carry this load of
myths; he has also been all wound round by what seems
Joyce's growing self-indulgence in an impulse to pure verbal
play.

Here another kind of difficulty confronts us. There is actually a special kind of language which people speak in dreams
and in which they sometimes even compose poetry. This language consists of words and sentences which, though they

seem to be gibberish or nonsense from the rational point of view, betray by their telescopings of words, their combinations of incongruous ideas, the involuntary preoccupations of the sleeper. Lewis Carroll exploited this dream language in *Jabberwocky*, and it has been studied by Freud and his followers, from whom Joyce seems to have got the idea of its literary possibilities. At any rate, *Finnegans Wake* is almost entirely written in it.

The idea was brilliant in itself, and Joyce has in many cases carried it out brilliantly. He has created a whole new poetry, a whole new humor and pathos, of sentences and words that go wrong. The special kind of equivocal and prismatic effects aimed at by the symbolist poets have here been achieved by a new method and on psychological principles which give them a new basis in humanity. But the trouble is, it seems to me, that Joyce has somewhat overdone it. His method of giving words multiple meanings allows him to go on indefinitely introducing new ideas; and he has spent no less than seventeen years embroidering *Finnegans Wake* in this way.

What has happened may be shown by the following examples. First, a relatively simple one from a passage about the Tree: 'Amengst menlike trees walking or trees like angels weeping nobirdy aviar soar anywing to eagle it!' It is quite clear in the last seven words how an ornithological turn has been given to 'nobody ever saw anything to equal it.' Here is a more complex one: Earwicker, picturing himself in the chapter in which he partially wakes up, is made to designate his hair with the phrase 'beer wig.' This has as its basis *bar wig*, which has rushed into the breach as *beer wig* under the pressure of Earwicker's profession as a dispenser of drinks in his pub, of the fact that his hair is yellow, and of his tendency to imagine that his queer last name is being caricatured by his neighbors as 'Earwigger' —a tendency which has led to his dream being impishly haunted by earwigs. There are thus four different ideas compressed in these two words. But let us examine—with the aid of the hints provided by the *Exagmination*—an even more complicated passage. Here is Earwicker-Joyce's depiction of the madness and eclipse of Swift: 'Unslow, malswift, pro mean, proh noblesse, Atrahore, melancolores, nears; whose glauque eyes glitt bedimmed to imm; whose fingrings creep o'er skull:

till quench., asterr mist calls estarr and graw, honath Jon raves homes glowcoma.' This passage, besides the more or less obvious ones, contains apparently the following ideas: Laracor, Swift's living in Ireland, combined with the *atra cura, black care,* that rides behind the horseman in the first poem of Book Three of Horace's *Odes*; the Horatian idea that death comes to the mean and the noble alike; *proh,* the Latin interjection of regret, and *pro,* perhaps referring to Swift's championship of the impoverished Irish; *melancolores, melancholy* plus *black-colored*; *glauque,* French *gray-blue,* plus Greek *glaux, owl—* gray evening plus Swift's blue eyes, which also had an owlish appearance; in *glitt bedimmed to imm,* the doubled consonants evidently represent a deadening of the senses; *creep o'er skull,* French *crépuscule, twilight*; *asterr,* Greek *aster, star,* Swift's Stella, whose real name was Esther; Vanessa's real name was Hester—so Stella calls Hester a (q)wench; perhaps German *mist, dung, trash,* plays some part here, too—as well as German *starr, rigid*; *graw* evidently contains German *grau,* gray; *honath Jon* is *honest John* and *Jonathan*; *glowcoma* is *glaucoma,* a kind of blindness, plus the idea of a pale glow of life persisting in a coma. This passage has some beauty and power; but isn't it overingenious? Would anyone naturally think of Horace when he was confronted with 'Atrahore'? And, even admitting that it may be appropriate to associate Latin with Swift, how does the German get in? Swift did not know German nor had he any German associations.*

In some cases, this overlaying of meanings has had the result of rendering quite opaque passages which at an earlier stage— as we can see by comparing the finished text with some of the sections as they first appeared—were no less convincingly dreamlike for being more easily comprehensible. You will find three versions of a passage in *Anna Livia Plurabelle* on page

---

*I chose this passage because a partial exposition of it, which I take to be more or less authoritative, had appeared in the *Exagmination* (in the paper by Mr. Robert McAlmon). I did not remember to have read it in its place in *Finnegans Wake*, and was unable to find it when I looked for it. Since then I have been told by another reader who has been over and over the book that this sentence about Swift is not included. This is interesting because it indicates the operation of a principle of selection. Joyce suffered himself from glaucoma, and it may be that he eliminated the reference because he felt that it was too specifically personal.

164 of the *Exagmination*; and on page 213 of the book you will
see that Joyce has worked up still a fourth. My feeling is that
he ought to have stopped somewhere between the second and
the third. Here is Version 1 of 1925: 'Look, look, the dusk is
growing. What time is it? It must be late. It's ages now since I
or anyone last saw Waterhouse's clock. They took it asunder, I
heard them say. When will they reassemble it?' And here is Version 4 of 1939: 'Look, look, the dusk is growing. My branches
lofty are taking root. And my cold cher's gone ashley. Fieluhr?
Filou! What age is at? It saon is late. 'Tis endless now senne
eye or erewone last saw Waterhouse's clogh. They took it asunder, I hurd thum sigh. When will they reassemble it?' There
is a gain in poetry, certainly; but in the meantime the question
and the answer have almost disappeared. Has it really made
Anna Livia any more riverlike to introduce the names of several hundred rivers (*saon* is *Saône* doing duty as *soon*, and *cher*
is the *Cher* for French *chair*)—as he also introduces in other
sections the names of cities, insects, trees? And why drag in
Erewhon? In the same way, the talk of the Old Men, which,
when it first came out in *Navire d'Argent*, seemed almost
equal in beauty to the Anna Livia Plurabelle chapter, has now
been so crammed with other things that the voices of the actual speakers have in places been nearly obliterated.

Joyce has always been rather deficient in dramatic and narrative sense. *Ulysses* already dragged; one got lost in it. The moments of critical importance were so run in with the rest that
one was likely to miss them on first reading. One had to think
about the book, read chapters of it over, in order to see the
pattern and to realize how deep the insight went. And *Finnegans Wake* is much worse in this respect. The main outlines of
the book are discernible, once we have been tipped off as to
what it is all about. It is a help that, in forming our hypothesis,
the principle of Occam's razor applies; for it is Joyce's whole
design and point that the immense foaming-up of symbols
should be reducible to a few simple facts. And it must also be
conceded by a foreigner that a good deal which may appear
to him mysterious would be plain enough to anyone who
knew Dublin and something about Irish history, and that what
Joyce has done here is as legitimate as it would be for an American writer to lay the scene of a similar fantasy somewhere on

Riverside Drive in New York and to assume that his readers would be able to recognize Grant's Tomb, green buses, Columbia University and the figure of Hendrik Hudson. A foreign reader of *Finnegans Wake* should consult a map of Dublin, and look up the articles on Dublin and Ireland in the *Encyclopedia Britannica*.

Yet it seems to me a serious defect that we do not really understand what is happening till we have almost finished the book. *Then* we can look back and understand the significance of Earwicker's stuttering over the word *father* on page 45; we can see that 'Peder the Greste, altipaltar' on page 344 combines, along with Peter the Great and *agreste*, *pederast* and *pater*; we can conclude that the allusion on page 373 about 'begetting a wife which begame his niece by pouring her young-things into skintighs' refers back to the little story on pages 21–23, and that this whole theme is a device of the 'dream-work' to get over the incest barrier by disguising Earwicker's own children as the children of a niece.

But in the meantime we have had to make our way through five hundred and fifty-four pages; and there is much that is evidently important that we still do not understand. How, for example, is the story of the 'prankquean' just mentioned related to the motif of the letter scratched up by the chicken from the dump heap; and what is the point about this letter? The theme is developed at prodigious length in the chapter beginning on page 104; and it flickers all through the book. It turns up near the end—pages 623–624 with new emotional connotations. The idea of letters and postmen plays a prominent part all through. Little Kevin is represented as giving the postman's knock; and Earwicker—though he here seems to be identifying himself with the other son, Jerry—is caught up into a long flight of fantasy in which he imagines himself a postman. The letter comes from Boston, Massachusetts, and seems to have been written by some female relation, perhaps the niece mentioned above. One feels that there is a third woman in the story, and that something important depends on this. Yet a considerable amount of rereading has failed, in the case of the present writer, to clear the matter up.

Finnegans Wake, in the actual reading, seems to me for two thirds of its length not really to bring off what it attempts. Nor do I think it possible to defend the procedure of Joyce on the basis of an analogy with music. It is true that there is a good deal of the musician in Joyce: his phonograph record of *Anna Livia* is as beautiful as a fine tenor solo. But nobody would listen for half an hour to a composer of operas or symphonic poems who went on and on in one mood as monotonously as Joyce has done in parts of *Finnegans Wake*, who scrambled so many motifs in one passage, or who returned to pick up a theme a couple of hours after it had first been stated, when the listeners would inevitably have forgotten it.*

*This essay was written in the summer of 1939, just after *Finnegans Wake* came out, and I have reprinted it substantially as it first appeared. Since then an article by Mr. John Peale Bishop in *The Southern Review* of summer, 1939, and studies by Mr. Harry Levin in *The Kenyon Review* of Autumn, 1939, and in *New Directions* of 1939, have thrown further light on the subject; and I have also had the advantage of discussions with Mr. Thornton Wilder, who has explored the book more thoroughly than anyone else I have heard of. It is to be hoped that Mr. Wilder will some day publish something about *Finnegans Wake*; and in the meantime those interested in the book should consult the essays mentioned, upon which I have sometimes drawn in revising the present study.

One suggestion of Mr. Bishop's should certainly be noted here. He believes that the riddle of the letter is the riddle of life itself. This letter has been scratched up from a dung-heap and yet it has come from another world; it includes in its very brief length marriage, children and death, and things to eat and drink—all the primary features of life, beyond which the ideas of the illiterate writer evidently do not extend; and Earwicker can never really read it, though the text seems exceedingly simple and though he confronts it again and again.

I ought to amend what is said in this essay on the basis of a first reading by adding that *Finnegans Wake*, like *Ulysses*, gets better the more you go back to it. I do not know of any other books of which it is true as it is of Joyce's that, though parts of them may leave us blank or repel us when we try them the first time, they gradually build themselves up for us as we return to them and think about them. That this should be true is due probably to some special defect of *rapport* between Joyce and the audience he is addressing, to some disease of his architectural faculty; but he compensates us partly for this by giving us more in the long run than we had realized at first was there, and he eventually produces the illusion that his fiction has a reality like life's, because, behind all the antics, the pedantry, the artificial patterns, something organic and independent of these is always revealing itself; and we end by recomposing a world in our mind as we do from the phenomena of experience. Mr. Max Eastman reports that Joyce once said to him, during a conversation on *Finnegans Wake*, when Mr. Eastman had suggested to Joyce that the demands made on the reader were too heavy and that he perhaps ought to provide a key: 'The demand that I make of my reader is that he should devote his whole life to reading my works.' It is in any case probably true that they will last you a whole lifetime.

I believe that the miscarriage of *Finnegans Wake*, in so far as it does miscarry, is due primarily to two tendencies of Joyce's which were already in evidence in *Ulysses*: the impulse, in the absence of dramatic power, to work up an epic impressiveness by multiplying and complicating detail, by filling in abstract diagrams and laying on intellectual conceits, till the organic effort at which he aims has been spoiled by too much that is synthetic; and a curious shrinking solicitude to conceal from the reader his real subjects. These subjects are always awkward and distressing: they have to do with the kind of feelings which people themselves conceal and which it takes courage in the artist to handle. And the more daring Joyce's subjects become, the more he tends to swathe them about with the fancywork of his literary virtuosity. It is as if it were not merely Earwicker who was frightened by the state of his emotions but as if Joyce were embarrassed, too.

Yet, with all this, *Finnegans Wake* has achieved certain amazing successes. Joyce has caught the psychology of sleep as no one else has ever caught it, laying hold on states of mind which it is difficult for the waking intellect to re-create, and distinguishing with marvelous delicacy between the different levels of dormant consciousness. There are the relative vividness of events reflected from the day before; the nightmare viscidity and stammering of the heavy slumbers of midnight; the buoyance and self-assertive vitality which gradually emerge from this; the half-waking of the early morning, which lapses back into the rigmaroles of dreams; the awareness, later, of the light outside, with its effect as of the curtain of the eyelids standing between the mind and the day. Through all this, the falling of twilight, the striking of the hours by the clock, the morning fog and its clearing, the bell for early mass, and the rising sun at the window, make themselves felt by the sleeper. With what brilliance they are rendered by Joyce! And the voices that echo in Earwicker's dream—the beings that seize upon him and speak through him: the Tree and the River, the eloquence of Shaun, the mumbling and running-on of the Old Men; the fluttery girl sweetheart, the resigned elderly wife; the nagging and jeering gibberish—close to madness and recalling the apparition of Virag in the Walpurgisnacht scene of *Ulysses*, but here identified with the Devil—which comes like an incubus with the darkness and through which the thickened voices of the Earwicker household occasionally announce themselves startlingly: 'Mawmaw, luk, your beeftay's fizzin' over' or 'Now a muss wash the little face.' Joyce has only to strike the rhythm and the timbre, and we know which of the spirits is with us.

Some of the episodes seem to me wholly successful: the Anna Livia chapter, for example, and the end of *Haveth Childers Everywhere*, which has a splendor and a high-spirited movement of a kind not matched elsewhere in Joyce. The passage in a minor key which precedes this major *crescendo* and describes Earwicker's real habitations—'most respectable . . . thoroughly respectable . . . partly respectable,' and so forth —is a masterpiece of humorous sordidity (especially 'copious holes emitting mice'); and so is the inventory—on pages 183– 184—of all the useless and rubbishy objects in the house where Shem the Penman lives. The *Ballad of Persse O'Reilly* (*perce- oreille*, earwig)—which blazons the shame of Earwicker—is real dream literature and terribly funny; as is also the revelation —pages 572–573—of the guilty and intricate sex relationships supposed to prevail in the Earwicker family, under the guise of one of those unintelligible summaries of a saint's legend or a Latin play. The waking-up chapter is charming in the passage —page 565—in which the mother comforts the restless boy and in the summing-up—page 579—of the married life of the Earwickers; and it is touchingly and thrillingly effective in throwing back on all that has gone before the shy impover- ished family pathos which it is Joyce's special destiny to ex- press.

Where he is least happy, I think, is in such episodes as the voyage, 311 ff., the football game, 373 ff., and the siege of Sebastopol, 338 ff. (all in the dense nightmarish part of the book, which to me is, in general, the dullest). Joyce is best when he is idyllic, nostalgic, or going insane in an introspective way; he is not good at energetic action. There is never any di- rect aggressive clash between the pairs of opponents in Joyce, and there is consequently no real violence (except Dedalus' smashing the chandelier in self-defense against the reproach of his dead mother). All that Joyce is able to do when he wants to represent a battle is to concoct an uncouth gush of language.

In general one feels, also, in *Finnegans Wake* the narrow limitations of Joyce's interests. He has tried to make it universal by having Earwicker take part in his dream in as many human activities as possible: but Joyce himself has not the key either to politics, to sport or to fighting. The departments of activity that come out best are such quiet ones as teaching and preaching.

The finest thing in the book, and one of the finest things Joyce has done, is the passage at the end where Ann, the wife, is for the first time allowed to speak with her full and mature voice. I have noted that Joyce's fiction usually deals with the tacit readjustment in the relationships between members of a family, the almost imperceptible moment which marks the beginning of a phase. In *Finnegans Wake*, the turning-point fixed is the moment when the husband and wife know definitely —they will wake up knowing it—that their own creative sexual partnership is over. That current no longer holds them polarized—as man and woman—toward one another; a new polarization takes place: the father is pulled back toward the children. 'Illas! I wisht I had better glances,' he thinks he hears Ann-Anna saying (page 626) 'to peer to you through this baylight's growing. But you're changing, acoolsha, you're changing from me, I can feel. Or is it me is? I'm getting mixed. Brightening up and tightening down. Yes, you're changing, sonhusband, and you're turning, I can feel you, for a daughter-wife from the hills again. Imlamaya. And she is coming. Swimming in my hindmoist. Diveltaking on me tail. Just a whisk brisk sly spry spink spank sprint of a thing theresomere, saultering. Saltarella come to her own. I pity your oldself I was used to. Now a younger's there.' It is the 'young thin pale soft shy slim slip of a thing, sauntering by silvamoonlake' (page 202 in the Anna Livia Plurabelle section) that she herself used to be, who now seems to her awkward and pert; and the wife herself is now the lower river running into the sea. The water is wider here; the pace of the stream is calmer: the broad day of experience has opened. 'I thought you were all glittering with the noblest of carriage. You're only a bumpkin. I thought you the great in all things, in guilt and in glory. You're but a puny. Home!' She sees him clearly now: he is neither Sir Tristram nor Lucifer; and he is done with her and she with him. 'I'm

loothing them that's here and all I lothe. Loonely in me lone-
ness. For all their faults. I am passing out. O bitter ending! I'll
slip away before they're up. They'll never see me. Nor know.
Nor miss me. And it's old and old it's sad and old it's sad and
weary I go back to you, my cold father, my cold mad father, my
cold mad feary father.' . . . The helpless and heartbreaking
voices of the Earwicker children recur: 'Carry me along, taddy,
like you done through the toy fair'—for now she is herself the
child entrusting herself to the sea, flowing out into the daylight that is to be her annihilation . . . 'a way a lone a last a
loved a long the' . . .

The Viconian cycle of existence has come full circle again.
The unfinished sentence which ends the book is to find its
continuation in the sentence without a beginning with which
it opens. The river which runs into the sea must commence as
a cloud again; the woman must give up life to the child. The
Earwickers will wake to another day, but the night has made
them older: the very release of the daylight brings a weariness
that looks back to life's source.

In these wonderful closing pages, Joyce has put over all he
means with poetry of an originality, a purity and an emotional
power, such as to raise *Finnegans Wake*, for all its excesses, to
the rank of a great work of literature.

7

Philoctetes:
The Wound and the Bow

THE *Philoctetes* of Sophocles is far from being his most popular play. The myth itself has not been one of those which have excited the modern imagination. The idea of Philoctetes' long illness and his banishment to the bleak island is dreary or distasteful to the young, who like to identify themselves with men of action—with Heracles or Perseus or Achilles; and for adults the story told by Sophocles fails to set off such emotional charges as are liberated by the crimes of the Atreidai and the tragedies of the siege of Troy. Whatever may have been dashing in the legend has been lost with the other plays and poems that dealt with it. Philoctetes is hardly mentioned in Homer; and we have only an incomplete account of the plays by Aeschylus and Euripides, which hinged on a critical moment of the campaign of the Greeks at Troy and which seem to have exploited the emotions of Greek patriotism. We have only a few scattered lines and phrases from that other play by Sophocles on the subject, the *Philoctetes at Troy*, in which the humiliated hero was presumably to be cured of his ulcer and to proceed to his victory over Paris.

There survives only this one curious drama which presents Philoctetes in exile—a drama which does not supply us at all with what we ordinarily expect of Greek tragedy, since it culminates in no catastrophe, and which indeed resembles rather our modern idea of a comedy (though the record of the lost plays of Sophocles show that there must have been others like it). Its interest depends almost as much on the latent interplay of character, on a gradual psychological conflict, as that of *Le Misanthrope*. And it assigns itself, also, to a category even more special and less generally appealing through the fact (though this, again, was a feature not uncommon with Sophocles) that the conflict is not even allowed to take place between a man and a woman. Nor does it even put before us the spectacle—

which may be made exceedingly thrilling—of the individual in conflict with his social group, which we get in such plays devoid of feminine interest as *Coriolanus* and *An Enemy of the People*. Nor is the conflict even a dual one, as most dramatic conflicts are—so that our emotions seesaw up and down between two opposed persons or groups: though Philoctetes and Odysseus struggle for the loyalty of Neoptolemus, he himself emerges more and more distinctly as representing an independent point of view, so that the contrast becomes a triple affair which makes more complicated demands on our sympathies.

A French dramatist of the seventeenth century, Chateaubrun, found the subject so inconceivable that, in trying to concoct an adaptation which would be acceptable to the taste of his time, he provided Philoctetes with a daughter named Sophie with whom Neoptolemus was to fall in love and thus bring the drama back to the reliable and eternal formula of Romeo and Juliet and the organizer who loves the factory-owner's daughter. And if we look for the imprint of the play on literature since the Renaissance, we shall find a very meager record: a chapter of Fénelon's *Télémaque*, a discussion in Lessing's *Laocoön*, a sonnet of Wordsworth's, a little play by André Gide, an adaptation by John Jay Chapman—this is all, so far as I know, that has any claim to interest.

And yet the play itself *is* most interesting, as some of these writers have felt; and it is certainly one of Sophocles' masterpieces. If we come upon it in the course of reading him, without having heard it praised, we are surprised to be so charmed, so moved—to find ourselves in the presence of something that is so much less crude in its subtlety than either a three-cornered modern comedy like *Candida* or *La Parisienne* or an underplayed affair of male loyalty in a story by Ernest Hemingway, to both of which it has some similarity. It is as if having the three men on the lonely island has enabled the highly sophisticated Sophocles to get further away from the framework of the old myths on which he has to depend and whose barbarities, anomalies and absurdities, tactfully and realistically though he handles them, seem sometimes almost as much out of place as they would in a dialogue by Plato. The people of the *Philoctetes* seem to us more familiar than they do in most of the other Greek tragedies;* and they take on for us a more intimate meaning. Philoctetes remains in our mind, and his incurable wound and his invincible bow recur to us with a special insistence. But what is it they mean? How is it possible for Sophocles to make us accept them so naturally? Why do we enter with scarcely a stumble into the situation of people who are preoccupied with a snakebite that lasts forever and a weapon that cannot fail?

Let us first take account of the peculiar twist which Sophocles seems to have given the legend, as it had come to him from the old epics and the dramatists who had used it before him.

The main outline of the story ran as follows: The demigod Heracles had been given by Apollo a bow that never missed its mark. When, poisoned by Deianeira's robe, he had had himself burned on Mount Oeta, he had persuaded Philoctetes to light the pyre and had rewarded him by bequeathing to him this weapon. Philoctetes had thus been formidably equipped when he had later set forth against Troy with Agamemnon and Menelaus. But on the way they had to stop off at the tiny island of Chrysè to sacrifice to the local deity. Philoctetes approached the shrine first, and he was bitten in the foot by a snake. The infection became peculiarly virulent; and the groans of Philoctetes made it impossible to perform the sacrifice, which would be spoiled by ill-omened sounds; the bite began to suppurate with so horrible a smell that his companions could not bear to have him near them. They removed him to Lemnos, a neighboring island which was much larger than Chrysè and inhabited, and sailed away to Troy without him.

Philoctetes remained there ten years. The mysterious wound never healed. In the meantime, the Greeks, hard put to it at Troy after the deaths of Achilles and Ajax and baffled by the confession of their soothsayer that he was unable to advise them further, had kidnaped the soothsayer of the Trojans and had forced him to reveal to them that they could never win till they had sent for Neoptolemus, the son of Achilles, and given

---

*'Apropos of the rare occasions when the ancients seem just like us, it always has seemed to me that a wonderful example was the repentance of the lad in the (*Philoctetes*?) play of Sophocles over his deceit, and the restoration of the bow.'—Mr. Justice Holmes to Sir Frederick Pollock, October 2, 1921.

him his father's armor, and till they had brought Philoctetes and his bow.

Both these things were done. Philoctetes was healed at Troy by the son of the physician Asclepius; and he fought Paris in single combat and killed him. Philoctetes and Neoptolemus became the heroes of the taking of Troy.

Both Aeschylus and Euripides wrote plays on this subject long before Sophocles did; and we know something about them from a comparison of the treatments by the three different dramatists which was written by Dion Chrysostom, a rhetorician of the first century A.D. Both these versions would seem to have been mainly concerned with the relation of Philoctetes to the success of the Greek campaign. All three of the plays dealt with the same episode: the visit of Odysseus to Lemnos for the purpose of getting the bow; and all represented Odysseus as particularly hateful to Philoctetes (because he had been one of those responsible for abandoning him on the island), and obliged to resort to cunning. But the emphasis of Sophocles' treatment appears fundamentally to have differed from that of the other two. In the drama of Aeschylus, we are told, Odysseus was not recognized by Philoctetes, and he seems simply to have stolen the bow. In Euripides, he was disguised by Athena in the likeness of another person, and he pretended that he had been wronged by the Greeks as Philoctetes had been. He had to compete with a delegation of Trojans, who had been sent to get the bow for their side and who arrived at the same time as he; and we do not know precisely what happened. But Dion Chrysostom regarded the play as 'a masterpiece of declamation' and 'a model of ingenious debate,' and Jebb thinks it probable that Odysseus won the contest by an appeal to Philoctetes' patriotism. Since Odysseus was pretending to have been wronged by the Greeks, he could point to his own behavior in suppressing his personal resentments in the interests of saving Greek honor. The moral theme thus established by Aeschylus and Euripides both would have been simply, like the theme of the wrath of Achilles, the conflict between the passions of an individual—in this case, an individual suffering from a genuine wrong—and the demands of duty to a common cause.

This conflict appears also in Sophocles; but it takes on a

peculiar aspect. Sophocles, in the plays of his we have, shows himself particularly successful with people whose natures have been poisoned by narrow fanatical hatreds. Even allowing for the tendency of Greek heroes, in legend and history both, to fly into rather childish rages, we still feel on Sophocles' part some sort of special point of view, some sort of special sympathy, for these cases. Such people—Electra and the embittered old Oedipus—suffer as much as they hate: it is because they suffer they hate. They horrify, but they waken pity. Philoctetes is such another: a man obsessed by a grievance, which in his case he is to be kept from forgetting by an agonizing physical ailment; and for Sophocles his pain and hatred have a dignity and an interest. Just as it is by no means plain to Sophocles that in the affair of Antigone *versus* Creon it is the official point of view of Creon, representing the interests of his victorious faction, which should have the last word against Antigone, infuriated by a personal wrong; so it is by no means plain to him that the morality of Odysseus, who is lying and stealing for the fatherland, necessarily deserves to prevail over the animus of the stricken Philoctetes.

The contribution of Sophocles to the story is a third person who will sympathize with Philoctetes. This new character is Neoptolemus, the young son of Achilles, who, along with Philoctetes, is indispensable to the victory of the Greeks and who has just been summoned to Troy. Odysseus is made to bring him to Lemnos for the purpose of deceiving Philoctetes and shanghai-ing him aboard the ship.

The play opens with a scene between Odysseus and the boy, in which the former explains the purpose of their trip. Odysseus will remain in hiding in order not to be recognized by Philoctetes, and Neoptolemus will go up to the cave in which Philoctetes lives and win his confidence by pretending that the Greeks have robbed him of his father's armor, so that he, too, has a grievance against them. The youth in his innocence and candor objects when he is told what his rôle is to be, but Odysseus persuades him by reminding him that they can only take Troy through his obedience and that once they have taken Troy, he will be glorified for his bravery and wisdom. 'As soon as we have won,' Odysseus assures him, 'we shall conduct ourselves with perfect honesty. But for one short day of dishonesty, allow me to direct you what to do—and then forever after you will be known as the most righteous of men.' The line of argument adopted by Odysseus is one with which the politics of our time have made us very familiar. 'Isn't it base, then, to tell falsehoods?' Neoptolemus asks. 'Not,' Odysseus replies, 'when a falsehood will bring our salvation.'

Neoptolemus goes to talk to Philoctetes. He finds him in the wretched cave—described by Sophocles with characteristic realism: the bed of leaves, the crude wooden bowl, the filthy bandages drying in the sun—where he has been living in rags for ten years, limping out from time to time to shoot wild birds or to get himself wood and water. The boy hears the harrowing story of Philoctetes' desertion by the Greeks and listens to his indignation. The ruined captain begs Neoptolemus to take him back to his native land, and the young man pretends to consent. (Here and elsewhere I am telescoping the scenes and simplifying a more complex development.) But just as they are leaving for the ship, the ulcer on Philoctetes' foot sets up an ominous throbbing in preparation for one of its periodical burstings: 'She returns from time to time,' says the invalid, 'as if she were sated with her wanderings.' In a moment he is stretched on the ground, writhing in abject anguish and begging the young man to cut off his foot. He gives Neoptolemus the bow, telling him to take care of it till the seizure is over. A second spasm, worse than the first, reduces him to imploring the boy to throw him into the crater of the Lemnian volcano: so he himself, he says, had lit the fire which consumed the tormented Heracles and had got in return these arms, which he is now handing on to Neoptolemus. The pain abates a little; 'It comes and goes,' says Philoctetes; and he entreats the young man not to leave him. 'Don't worry about that. We'll stay.' 'I shan't even make you swear it, my son.' 'It would not be right to leave you' (it would not be right, of course, even from the Greeks' point of view). They shake hands on it. A third paroxysm twists the cripple; now he asks Neoptolemus to carry him to the cave, but shrinks from his grasp and struggles. At last the abscess bursts, the dark blood begins to flow. Philoctetes, faint and sweating, falls asleep.

The sailors who have come with Neoptolemus urge him to make off with the bow. 'No,' the young man replies. 'He cannot hear us; but I am sure that it will not be enough for us to recapture the bow without him. It is he who is to have the glory—it was he the god told us to bring.'

While they are arguing, Philoctetes awakes and thanks the young man with emotion: 'Agamemnon and Menelaus were not so patient and loyal.' But now they must get him to the ship, and the boy will have to see him undeceived and endure his bitter reproaches. 'The men will carry you down,' says Neoptolemus. 'Don't trouble them: just help me up,' Philoctetes replies. 'It would be too disagreeable for them to take me all the way to the ship.' The smell of the suppuration has been sickening. The young man begins to hesitate. The other sees that he is in doubt about something: 'You're not so overcome with disgust at my disease that you don't think you can have me on the ship with you?'—

> οὐ δή σε δυσχέρεια τοῦ νοσήματος
> ἔπεισεν ὥστε μή μ' ἄγειν ναύτην ἔτι;

The answer is one of the most effective of those swift and brief speeches of Sophocles which for the first time make a situation explicit (my attempts to render this dialogue colloquially do no justice to the feeling and point of the verse):

> ἅπαντα δυσχέρεια, τὴν αὑσῦ φύοιν
> ὅταν λιπών τις δρᾷ τὰ μὴ προσεικότα.

'Everything becomes disgusting when you are false to your own nature and behave in an unbecoming way.'

He confesses his real intentions; and a painful scene occurs. Philoctetes denounces the boy in terms that would be appropriate for Odysseus; he sees himself robbed of his bow and left to starve on the island. The young man is deeply worried: 'Why did I ever leave Scyros?' he asks himself. 'Comrades, what shall I do?'

At this moment, Odysseus, who has been listening, pops out from his hiding place. With a lash of abuse at Neoptolemus, he orders him to hand over the arms. The young man's spirit flares up: when Odysseus invokes the will of Zeus, he tells him that he is degrading the gods by lending them his own lies. Philoctetes turns on Odysseus with an invective which cannot fail to impress the generous Neoptolemus: Why have they come for him now? he demands. Is he not still just as ill-omened and loathsome as he had been when they made him an outcast? They have only come back to get him because the gods have told them they must.

The young man now defies his mentor and takes his stand with Philoctetes. Odysseus threatens him: if he persists, he will have the whole Greek army against him, and they will see to it that he is punished for his treason. Neoptolemus declares his intention of taking Philoctetes home; he gives him back his bow. Odysseus tries to intervene; but Philoctetes has got the bow and aims an arrow at him. Neoptolemus seizes his hand and restrains him. Odysseus, always prudent, beats a quiet retreat.

Now the boy tries to persuade the angry man that he should, nevertheless, rescue the Greeks. 'I have proved my good faith,' says Neoptolemus; 'you know that I am not going to coerce you. Why be so wrongheaded? When the gods afflict us, we are obliged to bear our misfortunes; but must people pity a man who suffers through his own choice? The snake that bit you was an agent of the gods, it was the guardian of the goddess's shrine, and I swear to you by Zeus that the sons of Asclepius will cure you if you let us take you to Troy.' Philoctetes is incredulous, refuses. 'Since you gave me your word,' he says, 'take me home again.' 'The Greeks will attack me and ruin me.' 'I'll defend you.' 'How can you?' 'With my bow.' Neoptolemus is forced to consent.

But now Heracles suddenly appears from the skies and declares to Philoctetes that what the young man says is true, and that it is right for him to go to Troy. He and the son of Achilles shall stand together like lions and shall gloriously carry the day.—The *deus ex machina* here may of course figure a change of heart which has taken place in Philoctetes as the result of his having found a man who recognizes the wrong that has been done him and who is willing to champion his cause in defiance of all the Greek forces. His patron, the chivalrous Heracles, who had himself performed so many generous exploits, asserts his influence over his heir. The long hatred is finally exorcised.

In a fine lyric utterance which ends the play, Philoctetes says farewell to the cavern, where he has lain through so many nights listening to the deep-voiced waves as they crashed against the headland, and wetted by the rain and the spray blown in by the winter gales. A favorable wind has sprung up; and he sails away to Troy.

It is possible to guess at several motivations behind the writing of the *Philoctetes*. The play was produced in 409, when—if the tradition of his longevity be true—Sophocles would have been eighty-seven; and it is supposed to have been followed by the *Oedipus Coloneus*, which is assigned to 405 or 406. The latter deals directly with old age; but it would appear that the *Philoctetes* anticipates this theme in another form. Philoctetes, like the outlawed Oedipus, is impoverished, humbled, abandoned by his people, exacerbated by hardship and chagrin. He is accursed: Philoctetes' ulcer is an equivalent for the abhorrent sins of Oedipus, parricide and incest together, which have made of the ruler a pariah. And yet somehow both are sacred persons who have acquired superhuman powers, and who are destined to be purged of their guilt. One passage from the earlier play is even strikingly repeated in the later. The conception of the wave-beaten promontory and the sick man lying in his cave assailed by the wind and rain turns up in the *Oedipus Coloneus* (Coloneus was Sophocles' native deme) with a figurative moral value. So the ills of old age assail Oedipus. Here are the lines, in A. E. Housman's translation:

> This man, as me, even so,
> Have the evil days overtaken;
> And like as a cape sea-shaken
> With tempest at earth's last verges
> And shock of all winds that blow,
> His head the seas of woe,
> The thunders of awful surges
> Ruining overflow;
>
> Blown from the fall of even,
>   Blown from the dayspring forth,
> Blown from the noon in heaven,
>   Blown from night and the North.

But Oedipus has endured as Philoctetes has endured in the teeth of all the cold and the darkness, the screaming winds and the bellowing breakers: the blind old man is here in his own person the headland that stands against the storm.

We may remember a widely current story about the creator of these two figures. It is said that one of Sophocles' sons brought him into court in his advanced old age on the complaint that he was no longer competent to manage his property. The old poet is supposed to have recited a passage from the play which he had been writing: the chorus in praise of Coloneus, with its clear song of nightingales, its wine-dark ivy, its crocus glowing golden and its narcissus moist with dew, where the stainless stream of the Cephisus wanders through the broad-swelling plain and where the gray-leaved olive grows of itself beneath the gaze of the gray-eyed Athena—shining Colonus, breeder of horses and of oarsmen whom the Nereids lead. The scene had been represented on the stage and Sophocles had been made to declare: 'If I am Sophocles, I am not mentally incapable; if I am mentally incapable, I am not Sophocles.' In any case, the story was that the tribunal, composed of his fellow clansmen, applauded and acquitted the poet and censored the litigating son. The ruined and humiliated heroes of Sophocles' later plays are still persons of mysterious virtue, whom their fellows are forced to respect.

There is also a possibility, even a strong probability, that Sophocles intended Philoctetes to be identified with Alcibiades. This brilliant and unique individual, one of the great military leaders of the Athenians, had been accused by political opponents of damaging the sacred statues of Hermes and burlesquing the Eleusinian mysteries, and had been summoned to stand trial at Athens while he was away on his campaign against Sicily. He had at once gone over to the Spartans, commencing that insolent career of shifting allegiances which ended with his returning to the Athenian side. At a moment of extreme danger, he had taken over a part of the Athenian fleet and had defeated the Spartans in two sensational battles in 411 and 410, thus sweeping them out of the Eastern Aegean and enabling the Athenians to dominate the Hellespont. The *Philoctetes* was produced in 409, when the Athenians already wanted him back and were ready to cancel the charges against him and to restore him to citizenship. Alcibiades was a startling example of a bad character who was indispensable.

Plutarch says that Aristophanes well describes the Athenian feeling about Alcibiades when he writes: 'They miss him and hate him and long to have him back.' And the malady of Philoctetes may have figured his moral defects: the unruly and unscrupulous nature which, even though he seems to have been innocent of the charges brought against him, had given them a certain plausibility. It must have looked to the Athenians, too, after the victories of Abydos and Cyzicus, as if he possessed an invincible bow. Plutarch says that the men who had served under him at the taking of Cyzicus did actually come to regard themselves as undefeatable and refused to share quarters with other soldiers who had fought in less successful engagements.

Yet behind both the picture of old age and the line in regard to Alcibiades, one feels in the *Philoctetes* a more general and fundamental idea: the conception of superior strength as inseparable from disability.

For the superiority of Philoctetes does not reside merely in the enchanted bow. When Lessing replied to Winckelmann, who had referred to Sophocles' cripple as if he were an example of the conventional idea of impassive classical fortitude, he pointed out that, far from exemplifying impassivity, Philoctetes becomes completely demoralized every time he has one of his seizures, and yet that this only heightens our admiration for the pride which prevents him from escaping at the expense of helping those who have deserted him. 'We despise,' say the objectors, 'any man from whom bodily pain extorts a shriek. Ay, but not always; not for the first time, nor if we see that the sufferer strains every nerve to stifle the expression of his pain; not if we know him otherwise to be a man of firmness; still less if we witness evidences of his firmness in the very midst of his sufferings, and observe that, although pain may have extorted a shriek, it has extorted nothing else from him, but that on the contrary he submits to the prolongation of his pain rather than renounce one iota of his resolutions, even where such a concession would promise him the termination of his misery.'

For André Gide, in his *Philoctète,* the obstinacy of the invalid hermit takes on a character almost mystical. By persisting in his bleak and lonely life, the Philoctetes of Gide wins the love of a more childlike Neoptolemus and even compels the respect of a less hard-boiled Odysseus. He is practicing a kind of virtue superior not only to the virtue of the latter, with his code of obedience to the demands of the group, but also to that of the former, who forgets his patriotic obligations for those of a personal attachment. There is something above the gods, says the Philoctetes of Gide; and it is virtue to devote oneself to this. But what is it? asks Neoptolemus. I do not know, he answers; oneself! The misfortune of his exile on the island has enabled him to perfect himself: 'I have learned to express myself better,' he tells them, 'now that I am no longer with men. Between hunting and sleeping, I occupy myself with thinking. My ideas, since I have been alone so that nothing, not even suffering, disturbs them, have taken a subtle course which sometimes I can hardly follow. I have come to know more of the secrets of life than my masters had ever revealed to me. And I took to telling the story of my sufferings, and if the phrase was very beautiful, I was by so much consoled; I even sometimes forgot my sadness by uttering it. I came to understand that words inevitably become more beautiful from the moment they are no longer put together in response to the demands of others. . . .' The Philoctetes of Gide is, in fact, a literary man: at once a moralist and an artist, whose genius becomes purer and deeper in ratio to his isolation and outlawry. In the end, he lets the intruders steal the bow after satisfying himself that Neoptolemus can handle it, and subsides into a blissful tranquillity, much relieved that there is no longer any reason for people to seek him out.

With Gide we come close to a further implication, which even Gide does not fully develop but which must occur to the modern reader: the idea that genius and disease, like strength and mutilation, may be inextricably bound up together. It is significant that the only two writers of our time who have especially interested themselves in Philoctetes—André Gide and John Jay Chapman—should both be persons who have not only, like the hero of the play, stood at an angle to the morality of society and defended their position with stubbornness, but who have suffered from psychological disorders which have made them, in Gide's case, ill-regarded by his fellows; in Chapman's case, excessively difficult. Nor is it perhaps accidental that Charles Lamb, with his experience of his sister's insanity, should in his essay on *The Convalescent* choose the figure of Philoctetes as a symbol for his own 'nervous fever.'

And we must even, I believe, grant Sophocles some special insight into morbid psychology. The tragic themes of all three of the great dramatists—the madnesses, the murders and the incests—may seem to us sufficiently morbid. The hero with an incurable wound was even a stock subject of myth not confined to the Philoctetes legend: there was also the story of Telephus, also wounded and also indispensable, about which both Sophocles and Euripides wrote plays. But there is a difference between the treatment that Sophocles gives to these conventional epic subjects and the treatments of the other writers. Aeschylus is more religious and philosophical; Euripides more romantic and sentimental. Sophocles by comparison is clinical. Arthur Platt, who had a special interest in the scientific aspect of the classics, says that Sophocles was scrupulously up-to-date in the physical science of his time. He was himself closely associated by tradition with the cult of the healer Asclepius, whose son is to cure Philoctetes: Lucian had read a poem which he had dedicated to the doctor-god; and Plutarch reports that Asclepius was supposed to have visited his hearth. He is said also to have been actually a priest of another of the medical cults. Platt speaks particularly of his medical knowledge —which is illustrated by the naturalism and precision of his description of Philoctetes' infected bite.

But there is also in Sophocles a cool observation of the behavior of psychological derangements. The madness of Ajax is a genuine madness, from which he recovers to be horrified at the realization of what he has done. And it was not without good reason that Freud laid Sophocles under contribution for the naming of the Oedipus complex—since Sophocles had not only dramatized the myth that dwelt with the violation of the incest taboo, but had exhibited the suppressed impulse behind it in the speech in which he makes Jocasta attempt to reassure Oedipus by reminding him that it was not uncommon for men to dream about sleeping with their mothers—'and he who thinks nothing of this gets through his life most easily.' Those who do not get through life so easily are presented by Sophocles with a very firm grasp on the springs of their abnormal conduct. Electra is what we should call nowadays schizophrenic:

the woman who weeps over the urn which is supposed to contain her brother's ashes is not 'integrated,' as we say, with the fury who prepares her mother's murder. And certainly the fanaticism of Antigone—'fixated,' like Electra, on her brother—is intended to be abnormal, too. The banishment by Jebb from Sophocles' text of the passage in which Antigone explains the unique importance of a brother and his juggling of the dialogue in the scene in which she betrays her indifference to the feelings of the man she is supposed to marry are certainly among the curiosities of Victorian scholarship—though he was taking his cue from the complaint of Goethe that Antigone had been shown by Sophocles as acting from trivial motives and Goethe's hope that her speech about her brother might some day be shown to be spurious. Aristotle had cited this speech of Antigone's as an outstanding example of the principle that if anything peculiar occurs in a play the cause must be shown by the dramatist. It was admitted by Jebb that his rewriting of these passages had no real textual justification; and in one case he violates glaringly the convention of the one-line dialogue. To accept his emendation would involve the assumption that Aristotle did not know what the original text had been and was incapable of criticizing the corrupted version. No: Antigone forgets her fiancé and kills herself for her brother. Her timid sister (like Electra's timid sister) represents the normal feminine point of view. Antigone's point of view is peculiar, as Aristotle says. (The real motivation of the Antigone has been retraced with unmistakable accuracy by Professor Walter R. Agard in *Classical Philology* of July, 1937.)

These insane or obsessed people of Sophocles all display a perverse kind of nobility. I have spoken of the authority of expiation which emanates from the blasted Oedipus. Even the virulence of Electra's revenge conditions the intensity of her tenderness for Orestes. And so the maniacal fury which makes Ajax run amok, the frenzy of Heracles in the Nessus robe, terribly though they transform their victims, can never destroy their virtue of heroes. The poor disgraced Ajax will receive his due of honor after his suicide and will come to stand higher in our sympathies than Menelaus and Agamemnon, those obtuse and brutal captains, who here as in the *Philoctetes* are obviously no favorites of Sophocles'. Heracles in his final moments bids his spirit curb his lips with steel to keep him from crying out, and carry him through his self-destructive duty as a thing that is to be desired.

Some of these maladies are physical in origin, others are psychological; but they link themselves with one another. The case of Ajax connects psychological disorder as we get it in Electra, for example, with the access of pain and rage that causes Heracles to kill the herald Lichas; the case of Heracles connects a poisoning that produces a murderous fury with an infection that, though it distorts the personality, does not actually render the victim demented: the wound of Philoctetes, whose agony comes in spasms like that of Heracles. All these cases seem intimately related.

It has been the misfortune of Sophocles to figure in academic tradition as the model of those qualities of coolness and restraint which that tradition regards as classical. Those who have never read him—remembering the familiar statue—are likely to conceive something hollow and marmoreal. Actually, as C. M. Bowra says, Sophocles is 'passionate and profound.' Almost everything that we are told about him by the tradition of the ancient world suggests equanimity and amiability and the enjoyment of unusual good fortune. But there is one important exception: the anecdote in Plato's *Republic* in which Sophocles is represented as saying that the release from amorous desire which had come to him in his old age had been like a liberation from an insane and cruel master. He *has* balance and logic, of course: those qualities that the classicists admire; but these qualities only count because they master so much savagery and madness. Somewhere even in the fortunate Sophocles there had been a sick and raving Philoctetes.

And now let us go back to the *Philoctetes* as a parable of human character. I should interpret the fable as follows. The victim of a malodorous disease which renders him abhorrent to society and periodically degrades him and makes him helpless is also the master of a superhuman art which everybody has to respect and which the normal man finds he needs. A practical man like Odysseus, at the same time coarse-grained and clever, imagines that he can somehow get the bow without having Philoctetes on his hands or that he can kidnap Philoctetes the bowman without regard for Philoctetes the invalid.

But the young son of Achilles knows better. It is at the moment when his sympathy for Philoctetes would naturally inhibit his cheating him—so the supernatural influences in Sophocles are often made with infinite delicacy to shade into subjective motivations—it is at this moment of his natural shrinking that it becomes clear to him that the words of the seer had meant that the bow would be useless without Philoctetes himself. It is in the nature of things—of this world where the divine and the human fuse—that they cannot have the irresistible weapon without its loathsome owner, who upsets the processes of normal life by his curses and his cries, and who in any case refuses to work for men who have exiled him from their fellowship.

It is quite right that Philoctetes should refuse to come to Troy. Yet it is also decreed that he shall be cured when he shall have been able to forget his grievance and to devote his divine gifts to the service of his own people. It is right that he should refuse to submit to the purposes of Odysseus, whose only idea is to exploit him. How then is the gulf to be got over between the ineffective plight of the bowman and his proper use of his bow, between his ignominy and his destined glory? Only by the intervention of one who is guileless enough and human enough to treat him, not as a monster, nor yet as a mere magical property which is wanted for accomplishing some end, but simply as another man, whose sufferings elicit his sympathy and whose courage and pride he admires. When this human relation has been realized, it seems at first that it is to have the consequence of frustrating the purpose of the expedition and ruining the Greek campaign. Instead of winning over the outlaw, Neoptolemus has outlawed himself as well, at a time when both the boy and the cripple are desperately needed by the Greeks. Yet in taking the risk to his cause which is involved in the recognition of his common humanity with the sick man, in refusing to break his word, he dissolves Philoctetes' stubbornness, and thus cures him and sets him free, and saves the campaign as well.

CLASSICS AND COMMERCIALS

A Literary Chronicle of the Forties

CONTENTS

Archibald MacLeish and the Word

M R. ARCHIBALD MACLEISH, in his new role of Librarian of Congress, has suddenly taken a turn which must be astonishing even to those who have followed his previous career.

In a speech before the American Association for Adult Education, which has been prominently reported in the newspapers and printed by the *New Republic* in its issue of June 10, he has declared that the war novels of such writers as John Dos Passos and Ernest Hemingway (to name only the Americans mentioned), in their railing against "the statements of conviction, of purpose and of belief on which the war of 1914–18 was fought," have left the younger generation "defenseless against an enemy whose cynicism, whose brutality and whose stated intention to enslave present the issue of the future in moral terms—in terms of conviction and belief." Without, says Mr. MacLeish, attempting to "judge these writers," and confessing that he himself at one time indulged a similar impulse, he sternly insists that Dos Passos, Hemingway and Company "must face the fact that the books they wrote in the years just after the War have done more to disarm democracy in the face of fascism than any other single influence."

Now, in the first place, it is obviously absurd for Mr. MacLeish to cite, as he does, two passages describing the feelings of characters in novels by Dos Passos and Hemingway as evidence of the authors' own lack of convictions or of a tendency of their books to "disarm democracy." If anything could be plain to a reader of Dos Passos, it is the fact that moral principles play a more serious part in his work than in that of almost any other important American novelist and that his sympathies are passionately democratic. And if anything could be plain to a reader of Hemingway, it is the fact that he is constantly preoccupied with ideals of gallantry and honor, and is pugnacious almost to the point of madness. Neither Dos Passos nor Henri Barbusse, also cited by Mr. MacLeish, has ever asserted or believed as Mr. MacLeish declares they have, "that nothing men can put into words is worth fighting for"; but the conflict in which Dos Passos and Barbusse were interested during the years of World War I was the fight on the labor front. One of the first things that Barbusse did after the war was to publish an intransigent radical tract called *Le Couteau entre les Dents* which was certainly a "statement of conviction, of purpose and of belief," if any has ever existed. Barbusse became a militant Left journalist and remained one up to his death. But Mr. MacLeish, who is now so eager to fight, takes no account of this kind of militancy. He sounds as if he had never heard of the class war, which has certainly, since the Bolshevist revolution, made itself felt in our world as the fundamental, seismic conflict. Nor can the writers mentioned by Mr. MacLeish be accused, in this connection, of having failed to take fighting slogans seriously: Henri Barbusse, for example, erred in the other direction—by not being critical enough.

It is true that the books of these novelists gave voice to a certain disillusionment with the cause of the Allies in the last war as a struggle for "justice and humanity," as an effort to "save democracy." But it would be necessary for Mr. MacLeish, if he wants to discount what they said, to expound his own view of the last war and to deal with such questions as these: Should not the Allies have put an end to it in January, 1916, by concluding a peace with Austria at the time of the Austrian peace offers? Should the United States have ever gone into it? Did we do anything except prolong it unnecessarily and leave the situation worse than it otherwise might have been? Would not the belligerent nations have made an earlier peace, on a basis less dangerous for the world?—for has it not been precisely the situation of Germany, as she was left by the Allies after their victory, humiliated, dismembered, crushed, mortgaged with an indemnity for generations, that has furnished Hitler his fatal opportunity to figure as a national savior? Did not Wilson, with his enthusiasm for the rights of·small nations, derived from the tradition of the Confederacy, simply play into the hands of the Allied statesmen, who wanted to break up Central Europe in order to weaken it and who left it a prey to the first adventurer with the audacity to put it together again? Were there not, in short, very good reasons why anyone who had served in the last war should have considered the Allied slogans an imposture? Mr. MacLeish does concede that the novelists in question were only dramatizing in their fiction "what all of us who were in the war believed." "But," he adds, "they are nevertheless words which have borne bitter and dangerous fruit."

What fruit? Can it really be admitted that the reading of those novels about army life has been the cause of the more general skepticism which seems to be current today as to the value for either Europe or ourselves of the United States' engaging in foreign wars? This skepticism, the skepticism, say, of Charles A. Beard, is surely not the result—save, perhaps, to a very minor degree—of the impression made by disillusioned novelists; it is the result of the same natural causes which also produced their novels and which were as much historical realities at the moment of Mr. MacLeish's writing as the morning after the Versailles Treaty.

But now we come to another point which Mr. MacLeish seems to be trying to make in this extraordinarily confused piece. He evidently has some idea that writers should censor themselves in the interests of—it is not clear what; in the interests of some extremely vague idea of what is necessary to "defend ourselves against fascism." This is the author of that poem on the "Social Muse," which appeared only a few years ago in the pages of the same magazine which has published his recent speech—that poem in which Mr. MacLeish depicted the ignominious end of writers who went in for causes, and declared that the role of the poet was that of the woman who follows the armies and sleeps with the soldiers of both camps. (*It is also strictly forbidden to mix in maneuvers. . . . Is it just to demand of us to bear arms?*) But it will not surprise anyone at this time of day to have it demonstrated that Mr. MacLeish has repudiated an earlier position. He has surely in the course of his career struck a greater variety of attitudes and been ready to repudiate them faster than any other reputable writer of our time; and in the piece under consideration he does not hesitate to tell us that he himself has sinned in the past as Hemingway and Dos Passos have sinned. But today he has been forced to recognize that "perhaps the luxury of the complete confession, the uttermost despair, the farthest doubt, should be denied themselves by writers living in any but the most orderly and settled times." Well, you will not find the farthest doubt or the uttermost despair in the writers whom Mr. MacLeish mentions; they all believe pretty strongly in something. But even if this doubt and despair were there, as they may be in certain other writers, would it really be our duty to dissuade them, as Mr. MacLeish would dissuade them, from uttering their true opinions?

It is hard to see how any person to whom literature was even for a moment real could have written the sentence I have quoted. The farthest doubt and the uttermost despair are, of course, not "luxuries" at all to anyone except a literary "irresponsible," who feels that he can choose his moods, as if they were suits from a well-stocked wardrobe. They are the expressions of the bewilderment or the bitterness imposed on the human spirit by precisely those periods of history which are the reverse of orderly and settled. One would like to ask Mr. MacLeish whether he believes that the dignity of this spirit was lowered by the skepticism of Montaigne or the gloom of the romantic poets, or that any useful end for civilization would have been served by their suppressing what they thought and felt.

But the most remarkable statement in Mr. MacLeish's speech just precedes the one I have quoted. "Perhaps writers," he says, "having so great a responsibility to the future, must not weaken the validity of the Word even when the deceptions of the Word have injured them." That is, if you have ever suffered as a victim to somebody or other's meretricious propaganda, you should not attempt to expose it, but ought to let others go on being duped, for fear of destroying the integrity of "the Word." It is exactly as if a banker were to consider it against his interests to notify the authorities that there was counterfeit money abroad. Mr. MacLeish quotes a statement by John Chamberlain to the effect that the younger generation "distrusts not only slogans and all tags, but even all words —distrusts, that is to say, all statements of principle and conviction, all declarations of moral purpose." Is the logical alternative, then—for fear of impairing "The Word"—to accept all these declarations? Words, for Mr. MacLeish, are apparently ends in themselves—not a technique for understanding, a medium for putting on record, the vicissitudes of human experience, a medium and a technique which must constantly be renewed to meet the requirements of changing experience. The truth is that when the new words come in, the old must be put away; and it is one of the duties of the writer to avoid using outworn words that no longer have any real meaning.

And now let us ask again: in the interests of precisely what has Mr. MacLeish thought it proper to denounce as "disastrous" and "dangerous" the influence of a number of writers whom he characterizes as "honest men," among "the best and most sensitive of my generation"? Mr. MacLeish does not make this clear; but the whole tone of his speech sounds ominously as if he might be trying to prepare us for a new set of political slogans, of "declarations of moral purposes," to be let loose from the same sort of sources as those that launched the publicity of World War I. Mr. MacLeish is today an official, and he strikes us as a little uneasy as to whether the utterances of officials will everywhere be taken quite seriously. He may possibly be haunted by the memory that in the company he sometimes kept before he removed to Washington—*Dos who saw the tyrants in the lime, Ernest that saw the first snow in the fox's feather . . . O living men . . . receive me among you!*—such utterances were not always well received.

Mr. MacLeish is at pains to tell us that he does not want to burn any books or to regiment people's minds; but it is not very reassuring, at this moment of strain and excitement, to find the Librarian of Congress making a fuss about "dangerous" books. He has a good deal to say about liberty in the latter part of his speech, but he makes it perfectly plain that he believes that, as a matter of policy, certain kinds of dissentient writers should be discouraged from expressing their ideas.

There is one passage in this high-principled declaration which plunges it into utter insanity and almost disarms criticism. Mr. MacLeish, in his list of deleterious authors, includes Erich Maria Remarque, the author of *All Quiet on the Western Front*, and Andreas Latzko, the author of *Men in War*. The Librarian has forgotten that Latzko and Remarque, after all, had been soldiering during the war in behalf of "statements of conviction" and "declarations of moral purpose" on the opposite side from those of the Allies—in view of which Mr. MacLeish ought logically to be in favor of there having been more Remarques and Latzkos to demoralize the enemy side. As a matter of fact, the film that was made from *All Quiet on the Western Front* has been violently attacked by the Nazis, who feared its effect on the public. If the books of Remarque and Latzko had really been influential, the Nazis would not now be in France. If this school of writers in general had had the importance which Mr. MacLeish assigns to them, we should have had no second World War at all.

July 1, 1940

Van Wyck Brooks's Second Phase

VAN WYCK BROOKS has now suffered the fate of many a good writer before him. Beginning as an opposition critic, read by a minority of the public, he has lived to become a popular author, read by immense numbers of people and awarded a Pulitzer prize—with the result that the ordinary reviewers are praising him indiscriminately and the highbrows are trying to drop him. One has seen the same sort of thing happen with Eugene O'Neill, with Edna Millay, with Hemingway, with Thornton Wilder—and always to the obscuration of their actual merits and defects.

Let me begin then by stating some of the objections which are being made to Brooks's books on New England by those readers to whom it is most distasteful to see him become the darling of the women's clubs.

1. Brooks's work falls into two distinct divisions, with the break just before his volume on Emerson. The early Brooks was somber and despairing. In the tones of a Jeremiah, he cried out against America for ruining her writers and against the American writers for allowing themselves to be ruined. This period reached its nadir of gloom in the essay on *The Literary Life in America*, contributed to Harold Stearns's symposium *Civilization in the United States*, in which Brooks announced the total extinction of literary genius in America just at the moment when it was again lighting up. But he had already produced work of great importance in *America's Coming-of-Age* and *The Ordeal of Mark Twain*; and the Brooks of this early period was a searching and original critic, probably, for the writers of those years, the principal source of ideas on the cultural life of the United States. People got from him, not only, as they did also from Mencken, a sense of the second-rateness of recent American writing and a conviction of the need for something better, but also an historical perspective and an analysis of the causes of what was wrong. Though one ended by becoming exasperated with the laments of the early

Brooks, one owed him an immense debt, and one associated what one owed him with his sense of the national failure.

It was, then, with something of surprise that we found him, in *The Flowering of New England*, suddenly chortling and crooning in a manner little short of rapturous over those same American household classics—Lowell, Longfellow, Emerson *et al.*—whose deficiencies, in his memorable chapter on *Our Poets* in *America's Coming-of-Age*, he had so unflinchingly forced us to recognize. In the attempt to provide America, as he said, with a "usable" literary past, he seemed to some to have gone too far in the direction of glorification and to have substituted for the bitter insight of *The Ordeal of Mark Twain* the pageant of an historical mural, in which the figures were larger than life and the colors laid on too brightly, and in which the hidden springs of character were not examined at all. One missed the intensity of his early work; he seemed now to be *too much* pleased with everybody; there was no longer any tension of conflict.

2. Moreover, the bold brushwork of these frescoes involved an inordinate development of a feature of Brooks's method which had figured with unhappy results in *The Pilgrimage of Henry James*. Mr. Brooks in an evil hour had read the books of a Frenchman named Léon Bazalgette, who wrote lives of Thoreau and Whitman, and who adopted the practice of describing his subjects in a medium confected of phrases taken without quotes from their own works. Mr. Brooks has imitated this practice: he has attempted to convey the qualities of the literary personalities he deals with by compounding a kind of paste out of their writings. This paste he spreads on the page and expects it to give us the essence of his author. But, though sometimes, as in the case of an inferior figure like Longfellow, he does succeed in extracting thus a tone and a color which we should not easily catch in dipping into Longfellow himself, since it is necessary to boil down a good deal of such a poet in order to distinguish a flavor—on the other hand, with a first-rate writer like Emerson or Hawthorne or Thoreau, you simply get a sort of predigested sample which seems to have had all the vitamins taken out of it and which causes constant irritation to an admirer of these authors, because it gives the impression of a travesty that is always just off-key and off-color.

This is especially a pity, because Brooks is himself an individual and beautiful writer, whose accent has a fine clarity, and what we get in these confected passages is neither the true Brooks nor his subject. It is a method, furthermore, which involves what amounts to an abdication of the critic, who is here neither speaking about his subject nor allowing his subject to speak for himself. What is the value of all the *as one might call it*'s scattered through the pages of Brooks? If it is Brooks who is calling it this or that, the interpolation is totally unnecessary; if, on the other hand, it is someone else, the author ought to tell us who. What is the explanation of the statement, in connection with Charles Eliot Norton, that "his field was of imagination all compact"? If the sentence is Brooks's sentence, he ought not to load it down with this antique cliché; if the opinion is that of some previous critic, the cliché was not worth preserving. Who is it who exclaims of Francis Parkman, "*Eccovi*, this child has been in hell"? Mr. Brooks pointing up his picture with a familiar literary allusion or some Bostonian addicted to Dante? Many phrases which are striking in their contexts lose their significance and seem merely grotesque when they are embedded in the text of someone else. Thus we read in Brooks's account of Louisa M. Alcott that, "She liked to watch the moon. She had good dreams. She had pleasant times with her mind." A footnote explains this last phrase, which turns out to have been taken from a diary written at the age of twelve, in which the words do not sound so grotesque as when sprung on us without preparation. Surely it would have been much more sensible to have quoted the diary in the first place.

3. It has sometimes been said of Mr. Brooks that he is not really a literary critic because he is not interested in literature as an art and lies indeed under serious suspicion of not being able to tell chalk from cheese. There is in this charge this much of truth: Van Wyck Brooks concerns himself with literature mainly from the point of view of its immediate social significance. He is not particularly sensitive to form and style in themselves, and he is not particularly responsive to any other than social morals. Thus, in this latest volume, you find the extraordinary statement that there was "no unity" in Henry Adams' style and that, "except for recurrent conceptions and phrases" his various books "might all have been written by

various hands"—whereas a diligent reader of Adams would, I think, be able to recognize a paragraph from any of his books by its rhythm and tone alone. The bland, ironic, weak-backed sentences of *The Education of Henry Adams* are already in *The History of the United States*. And thus in the charges brought, on page 402, against the later Henry James, we find the strange complaint that James is in the habit of describing his characters "as 'eminent,' as 'wonderful,' 'noble' and 'great'" and then making them perform discreditable actions—an objection which shows a complete incomprehension both of James's all-pervasive irony and of the complexity of his moral vision. And if you look up, among the poems, say, of Lowell, the lyrics recommended by Mr. Brooks, you are likely to be disappointed.

It is perhaps true that Mr. Brooks has to have the status of his authors settled for him before he begins. He seems to accept his subjects as objective facts, as stars of established magnitudes, which he studies in their known relations, their already determined orbits. This assumption is borne out by his extravagant praise of mediocrity among his contemporaries combined with his puzzled indifference to some of the most remarkable writers of his time at the moment of their first emergence. His ineptitude at appraising for himself has become especially conspicuous in connection with this general history. The early Brooks was always comparing our writers with European writers to the disadvantage of the United States. The later Brooks is whooping it up for America's "usable past," but he still leaves in doubt the comparative values of the American writers whose work he describes, in relation to the rest of the world. Doesn't Emerson look meager beside Goethe? Wasn't Thoreau, by any standards, one of the first prose writers of the nineteenth century? Isn't Henry James, for all his shortcomings, a more important novelist than Thackeray? Brooks does not try to answer these questions—of a kind that have been forced on the attention of the expatriate Eliot and James and which they have sometimes discussed acutely. He has been so far, in his history of our literature, almost exclusively occupied with his subjects in relation to the American scene.

When one has said all this, however, one finds that one has

done little more than define the terms themselves on which Van Wyck Brooks has undertaken an immense and difficult task; and what is valid in these objections applies in general less to his new volume than to the one that went before.

Even in *The Flowering of New England* the nature of the task itself partly explains the extravagances. The magnification of the New England poets may be justified on the ground that the author is presenting them as they presented themselves to the audience that thought them great; and it is one of the most striking proofs of Mr. Brooks's possession of the historical imagination that he is able to see the events of the past not merely in retrospect, that he does not merely estimate facts, sum up tendencies, compose obituaries, but that he can show us movements and books as they loomed upon the people to whom they were new. The reader of *The Flowering of New England* beheld the Boston of the first decades of the Republic coming at him, as it were, head-on; and this was what made the book so important. It brought home even to people who had already some acquaintance with the subject as no other book had done what post-revolutionary New England had meant to the America of its day as the cultural spokesman for the new humanity that was to be built in the United States. To get this over to a generation which had known only a shrivelled Boston overlaid with industrial vulgarity and who had probably not very often reopened the New England poets since their schooldays, required some expanse of canvas and some special expenditure of oils.

In his *Indian Summer* of New England, Mr. Brooks is aiming at a different effect: he has here to show us the old virtue passing out of Boston; and it is noticeable that in this second volume the colors are not spread on so thick. Furthermore, he has succeeded in freeing himself, after the first hundred pages or so, from the viscousness produced in *The Flowering* by his stirring into the stream of the story the *ipsissima verba* of his subjects. The presentations of artistic personalities become noticeably more fluent and felicitous with the portraits of the later chapters. This kind of evocation Mr. Brooks has now fully mastered and the Mary E. Wilkins, the Amy Lowell, the E. A. Robinson and the Robert Frost are the best things of the kind he has done.

Indeed, Mr. Brooks has now mastered the whole art of this historical-biographical narrative—an art which has its special difficulties unknown to the teller of invented fables. To reduce this kind of actual material to a story which will carry the reader along, to find a scale and provide a variety which will make it possible to hold his attention, becomes a species of ob-stacle race, in which the writer has made a wager to play a graceful and entertaining role while hampered by the necessity of sticking to texts, of assembling scattered data and of orga-nizing a complicated unity.

What, precisely, *is* Mr. Brooks's story? It is not perhaps quite a history of literature. Nor is it—since he somewhat slights philosophy and theology—quite the history of "the New En-gland mind" which he announced in his first volume. It is rather a history of New England society as reflected in its cul-tural activities. If Mr. Brooks is not always alive to the values of his American subjects in the larger Western setting, he is a master, our only real master since the death of Vernon Par-rington, of the social interpretation of literature inside the na-tional frame. To read his *Indian Summer* of New England is, for an American old enough to have been young in the period described, a constantly fascinating and surprising revelation. You will find out in this new book of Mr. Brooks why people went abroad every spring, and why they sometimes went and never came back. See the chapter called *The Post-War Years*, in which he tells how the commercial development that followed the Civil War extinguished the old enthusiasm for culture along with the republican ideals and made cultivated people in gen-eral ashamed of the United States—a chapter which perhaps provides the most satisfactory analysis that has yet been made of this situation and which may well become the classical ac-count of it. In the same chapter, you will find out why the ladies in your childhood read the English Kipling and Conan Doyle, and why you were told that Mark Twain was "vulgar." You will find out why your aunt studied botany and why some cousin who had to go West for his health taught you to name the birds without a gun. You will find out the real significance of *The Peterkin Papers*, that monstrous, matter-of-fact comic fantasy that haunts you like a dream of childhood. You will

learn who all those people really were whose writings you have
never thought to look into since you were old enough to select
your own reading and who have remained to you familiar but
phantasmal myths, always referred to with their middle names,
inseparable from them as Homeric epithets or Russian patro-
nymics: Helen Hunt Jackson, Thomas Bailey Aldrich, Charles
Dudley Warner, Edward Rowland Sill. You will learn how
Edward Estlin Cummings of Patchin Place, New York, is connected with Ralph Waldo Emerson of Concord.

Mr. Brooks's study of New England is, in short, one of the
three or four prime light-diffusing works on the history of
American society—I should include also the Beards' *Rise of
American Civilization* and Dos Passos' *U.S.A.*—that have appeared in our own time. It is one of the key books of our period, which places us in time and space and which tells us what
to think of ourselves. What Mr. Brooks *used* to tell us to think
was depressing, though up to a point also bracing; and his reversal of feeling in *The Flowering of New England* did seem a
little overwrought. But in this last volume, he has hit an equilibrium. His account of the decline of Boston is not lugubrious
in his early manner: the whole tone is one of pride and confidence. His last pages on the revival of the New England tradition in the writers of the cosmopolitan decade that followed
1914 are among the most eloquent he has written, and among
the most impressive. The medium and field he has chosen are
justified, as every writer's must be, by his success in producing
by means of them an interesting and beautiful book. Mr.
Brooks's love of literature is not to be proved or disproved by
his habit of evaluating authors in terms of their social implications against the immediate local background any more than
the knowledge of humanity of a novelist is to be tested by his
setting or his not setting his characters in relation to the rest of
the world or by his neglect, in his preoccupation with his own
particular scale of values, of someone else's different scale. It is
implicit in the purity of his enthusiasms and in his own splendid abilities as an artist.

September 30, 1940

The Boys in the Back Room

"Set 'em up for the boys in the back room."

1. JAMES M. CAIN

RISING from a long submergence in the politics and literature of the nineteenth century, during which I read almost nothing that people were reading, I have just regaled myself with practically the complete works of James M. Cain, Horace McCoy, Richard Hallas, John O'Hara, William Saroyan, John Steinbeck and Hans Otto Storm. These writers are all of fairly recent arrival; they have most of them been influenced by Hemingway; they all live or have lived in California, and they have all, to a greater or lesser extent, written about that State. They thus constitute a sort of group, and they suggest certain generalizations.

Let us begin with Mr. Cain and his school. *The Postman Always Rings Twice* came out in 1934; and Mr. Cain's second novel, *Serenade*, in 1937. They were followed by other similar novels which apparently derived from Mr. Cain. The whole group stemmed originally from Hemingway, but it was Hemingway turned picaresque; and it had its connections also with the new school of mystery writers of the type of Dashiell Hammett.

Mr. Cain remained the best of these novelists. Horace McCoy, the author of *They Shoot Horses, Don't They?* and *I Should Have Stayed Home*, had a subject with possibilities: the miserable situation of movie-struck young men and women who starve and degrade themselves in Hollywood; and the first of his books is worth reading for its description of one of those dance marathons that were among the more grisly symptoms of the early years of the depression. But the faults of Mr. McCoy's first novel—lack of characterization, lack of motivation—show up much more nakedly in the second. *You Play the Black and the Red Comes Up*, by a writer who calls himself Richard Hallas, is a clever pastiche of Cain which is mainly as two-dimensional as a movie. It is indicative of the degree to which this kind of writing has finally become formularized that it should have been possible for a visiting Englishman—the real author is Eric Knight—to tell a story in the Hemingway-Cain vernacular almost without a slip.

The hero of the typical Cain novel is a good-looking down-and-outer, who leads the life of a vagrant and a rogue. He invariably falls under the domination—usually to his ruin—of a vulgar and determined woman from whom he finds it impossible to escape. In the novels of McCoy and Hallas, he holds our sympathy through his essential innocence; but in the novels of Cain himself, the situation is not so simple. Cain's heroes are capable of extraordinary exploits, but they are always treading the edge of a precipice; and they are doomed, like the heroes of Hemingway, for they will eventually fall off the precipice. But whereas in Hemingway's stories, it is simply that these brave and decent men have had a dirty deal from life, the hero of a novel by Cain is an individual of mixed unstable character, who carries his precipice with him like Pascal.

His fate is thus forecast from the beginning; but in the meantime he has fabulous adventures—samples, as it were, from a *Thousand and One Nights* of the screwy Pacific Coast: you have jungle lust in roadside lunch-rooms, family motor-trips that end in murder, careers catastrophically broken by the vagaries of bisexual personality, the fracas created by a Mexican Indian introduced among the phonies of Hollywood.

All these writers are also preëminently the poets of the tabloid murder. Cain himself is particularly ingenious in tracing from their first beginnings the tangles that gradually tighten around the necks of the people involved in those bizarre and brutal crimes that figure in the American papers; and is capable even of tackling—in *Serenade*, at any rate—the larger tangles of social interest from which these deadly little knots derive. Such a subject might provide a great novel: in *An American Tragedy*, such a subject did. But as we follow, in a novel by Mr. Cain, the development of one of his plots, we find ourselves more and more disconcerted at knocking up—to the destruction of illusion—against the blank and hard planes and angles of something we know all too well: the wooden old conventions of Hollywood. Here is the Hollywood gag: the echo of the murdered man's voice reverberating from the mountains when the man himself is dead, and the party in *Serenade*, in which the heroine stabs the villain under cover of acting out a bullfight; the punctual Hollywood coincidence: the popping-up of the music-loving sea-captain, who is the *deus ex machina* of *Serenade*; the Hollywood reversal of fortune: the singer who loses his voice and then gets it back again, becoming famous and rich in a sequence that lasts about three minutes.

Mr. Cain is actually a writer for the studios (as are also, or have also been, Mr. Hallas and Mr. McCoy). These novels are produced in his off-time; and they are a kind of Devil's parody of the movies. Mr. Cain is the *âme damnée* of Hollywood. All the things that have been excluded by the Catholic censorship: sex, debauchery, unpunished crime, sacrilege against the Church—Mr. Cain has let them loose in these stories with a gusto as of pent-up ferocity that the reader cannot but share. What a pity that it is impossible for such a writer to create and produce his own pictures!

In the meantime, *Serenade* is a definite improvement on *The Postman*. It, too, has its trashy aspect, its movie fore-shortenings and its too-well oiled action; but it establishes a surer illusion. *The Postman* was always in danger of becoming unintentionally funny. Yet even there brilliant moments of insight redeemed the unconscious burlesque; and there is enough of the real poet in Cain—both in writing and in imagination—to make one hope for something better than either.

2. JOHN O'HARA

John O'Hara also derives from Hemingway, and his short stories sound superficially like Hemingway's. His longer stories, like Cain's, have it in common with Hemingway that the heroes and heroines are doomed. But O'Hara's main interest in life is of an entirely different kind from Hemingway's, and his writing really belongs to a different category of fiction.

O'Hara is not a poet like Hemingway, but primarily a social commentator; and in this field of social habits and manners, ways of talking and writing letters and dressing, he has done work that is original and interesting. It is essentially the same kind of thing that Henry James and his followers developed, but the center of attention has shifted. The older novelist dealt almost exclusively with a well-to-do upper stratum, and the chief contrast he had to depict was between the American upper classes and the European upper classes, or between the established and cultivated people and the vulgar *nouveaux riches*. John O'Hara subjects to a Proustian scrutiny the tight-knotted social web of a large Pennsylvania town, the potpourri of New York night-life in the twenties, the nondescript fringes of Hollywood. In all this he has explored for the first time from his peculiar semi-snobbish point of view a good deal of interesting territory: the relations between Catholics and Protestants, the relations between college men and non-college men, the relations between the underworld and "legitimate" business, the ratings of café society; and to read him on a fashionable bar or the Gibbsville country club is to be shown on the screen of a fluoroscope gradations of social prestige of which one had not before been aware. There is no longer any hierarchy here, of either cultivation or wealth: the people are all being shuffled about, hardly knowing what they are or where they are headed, but each is clutching some family tradition, some membership in a select organization, some personal association with the famous, from which he tries to derive distinction. But in the meantime, they mostly go under. They are snubbed, they are humiliated, they fail. The cruel side of social snobbery is really Mr. O'Hara's main theme. Only rarely, as in the excellent story called *Price's Always Open*, do the forces of democracy strike back.

This social surface, then, Mr. O'Hara analyzes with delicacy, and usually with remarkable accuracy. His grasp of what lies underneath it is not, however, so sure. His point of view toward his principal characters tends to be rather clinical; but even where his diagnosis is clear, we do not share the experience of the sufferer. The girl in *Butterfield 8* is a straight case of a Freudian complex, somewhat aggravated by social maladjustment; but we don't really know her well. Julian English of *Appointment in Samarra* is apparently the victim of a bad heredity worked upon by demoralizing influences; yet the emotions that drive him to suicide are never really shown. The whole book is in the nature of an explanation of why Julian threw the highball in the face of the Irish climber; yet the explanation doesn't convince us that the inevitable end for Julian would be the suicide to which his creator brings him. As for Mr. O'Hara's latest novel, *Hope of Heaven*, a story of Hollywood, I have not been able to fathom it at all—though here, too, there seems to be discernible a Freudian behavior-pattern. One wonders whether the personality of the script-writer who is telling the story is intended to play some role of which he himself is unaware, in connection with the conduct of the other characters, or whether the author himself does not quite know what he is doing.

One gets the impression—confirmed by a statement which Mr. O'Hara is reported to have made—that he improvises more or less and never reworks or revises. His longer stories always sound like first drafts which ought to be trimmed and tightened up—which might be turned into very fine little novels, but which, as it is, remain rather diffuse and rather blurred as to their general intention. What is the relevance to the story, for example, of the newspaperwoman in *Appointment in Samarra*, whose career is described on such a scale? The account of her beginnings is amusing, but the part she plays in the drama doesn't seem to warrant this full-length introduction. What is the point of the newspaper reporter who suddenly gets into the picture, and more or less between us and it, at the end of *Butterfield 8*? What on earth is the justification—aside from establishing the atmosphere for a drama of general crookedness—of the long story about the man who stole the traveler's checks at the beginning of *Hope of Heaven*? If Mr. O'Hara has definite ideas about the meaning of these characters in his scheme, I can't see that he has brought it out. He seems merely to be indulging his whims. He happens, however, to be gifted with a clean, quick and sure style, which by itself gives an impression of restraint; and the unfaltering neatness of his writing carries him over a good deal of thin ice. But he appears, in perfecting this style, to have been following, from the point of view of architecture, a line of least resistance. Each of his novels has been less successful, less ambitious and less well-disciplined than the one that went before; but while the long stories have been deteriorating, the short stories have been improving: in the most successful of them he has achieved his characteristic effects as he has hardly been able to do in his novels. The best of his work, in my opinion, consists of *Appointment in Samarra*, the admirable long short story called *The Doctor's Son* in the collection of that name, and the short pieces of *Files on Parade* (though there are also a few memorable ones in the early volume—such as *Ella and the Chinee*).

As for *Pal Joey*, his last-published book, it is funny, well-phrased, well-observed; but, heel for heel, Pal Joey is a comedown after Julian English. *Appointment in Samarra* is a memorable picture both of a provincial snob, a disorganized drinking-man of the twenties, and of the complexities of the social organism in which he flourished and perished. But Pal Joey is merely an amoeba of the night-life of the jitter-bug era; and he is a little amoeba-monster. It is not that one objects to O'Hara's creating a monster—*Pal Joey* is successful as satire precisely because the author is not afraid to go the whole hog; but that he seems to represent a contraction of John O'Hara's interests.

The truth is perhaps that O'Hara has never really had his bearings since he dropped Gibbsville, Pa. He was all awash in *Butterfield 8* in the night life of New York—though he still kept some capacity for judgment; and in *Hope of Heaven* he showed serious signs of suffering from Hollywood light-headedness. He partly retrieved himself by becoming the outstanding master of the *New Yorker* short-story-sketch; but we expected, and still expect, more of him.

3. WILLIAM SAROYAN

The refrain becomes monotonous; but you have to begin by saying that Saroyan, too, derives from Hemingway. The novelists of the older generation—Hemingway himself, Dos Passos, Faulkner, Wilder—have richer and more complex origins, they belong to a bigger cultural world. But if the most you can say of John O'Hara is that he has evidently read Ring Lardner and F. Scott Fitzgerald as well as Hemingway, the most you can say of Saroyan is that he has also read Sherwood Anderson (though he speaks of having looked into a book which he bought for a nickel at a bookstore and which was in Swedish

and had pictures of churches). When you remember that Lardner and Anderson were among the original ingredients in
Hemingway, you see how limited the whole school is.

But what distinguishes Saroyan from his fellow disciples is
the fact that he is not what is called hard-boiled. What was surprising and refreshing about him when he first attracted notice, was that, although he was telling the familiar story about
the wise-guy who went into the bar, and I said and the bar-
tender said and I said, this story with Saroyan was never cruel,
but represented an agreeable mixture of San Francisco bon-
homie and Armenian Christianity. The fiction of the school of
Hemingway had been full of bad drunks; Saroyan was a novelty: a good drunk. The spell exerted in the theater by his play,
The Time of Your Life, consisted in its creating the illusion of
friendliness and muzzy elation and gentle sentimentality which
a certain amount of beer or rye will bring on in a favorite bar.
Saroyan takes you to the bar, and he produces for you there a
world which is the way the world would be if it conformed to
the feelings instilled by drinks. In a word, he achieves the feat
of making and keeping us boozy without the use of alcohol
and purely by the stimulus of art. It seems natural that the cop
and the labor leader should be having a drink together; that
the prostitute should prove to be a wistful child, who eventually gets married by someone that loves her; that the tall tales
of the bar raconteur should turn out to be perfectly true, that
the bar millionaire should be able to make good his munificent
philanthropical offers—that they should be really Jack the
Giant-Killer and Santa Claus; and that the odious vice-
crusader, who is trying to make everybody unhappy, should be
bumped off as harmlessly as the comic villain in an old-
fashioned children's "extravaganza."

These magical feats are accomplished by the enchantment of
Saroyan's temperament, which induces us to take from him a
good many things that we should not accept from other
people. With Saroyan the whole trick is the temperament; he
rarely contrives a machine. The good fairy who was present at
his christening thus endowed him with one of the most precious gifts that a literary artist can have, and Saroyan never
ceases to explain to us how especially fortunate he is: "As I say,
I do not know a great deal about what the words come to, but

the presence says, Now don't get funny; just sit down and say something; it'll be all right. Say it wrong; it'll be all right anyway. Half the time I *do* say it wrong, but somehow or other, just as the presence says, it's right anyhow. I am always pleased about this. My God, it's wrong, but it's all right. It's really all right. How did it happen? Well that's how it is. It's the presence, doing everything for me. It's the presence, doing all the hard work while I, always inclined to take things easy, loaf around, not paying much attention to anything, much, just putting down on paper whatever comes my way."

Well, we don't mind Saroyan's saying this, because he is such an engaging fellow; and we don't mind his putting down on paper whatever happens to come his way. It is true that he has been endowed with a natural felicity of touch which prevents him from being offensive or tiresome in any of the more obvious ways; and at their best his soliloquies and stories recall the spontaneous songs of one of those instinctive composers who, with no technical knowledge of music, manage to finger out lovely melodies. Yet Saroyan is entirely in error in supposing that when he "says it wrong," everything is really all right. What is right in such a case is merely this instinctive sense of form which usually saves him—and even when he is clowning —from making a fool of himself. What *is* wrong, and what his charm cannot conceal, is the use to which he is putting his gifts. It is a shock for one who very much enjoyed *The Daring Young Man on the Flying Trapeze* to go back to reading Saroyan in his latest collection, *The Trouble with Tigers*. There is nothing in the book so good as the best things in *The Flying Trapeze*, and there is a good deal that is not above the level of the facility of a daily columnist. A columnist, in fact, is what William Saroyan seems sometimes in danger of becoming— the kind of columnist who depends entirely on a popular personality, the kind who never reads, who does not know anything in particular about anything, who merely turns on the tap every day and lets it run a column.

It is illuminating to compare this inferior stuff with the contents of a less well-known collection published in California. This volume, *Three Times Three*, consists mainly of miscellaneous pieces which the author seems to regard as not having quite come off. The result is something a great deal more interesting than the slick and rather thin stuff of *Tigers*. One of these pieces, *The Living and the Dead*, of which the author rightly says that it is not so good as it ought to be, seems to me, in spite of the fact that it miscarries to some degree, one of the best things Saroyan has written. The scene with the Armenian grandmother after the departure of the money-collecting Communist is of a startling and compelling beauty. This theme of the foreign-born asserting in modern America the virtues of an older society is one of the principal themes in Saroyan; whenever it appears—as in the short story called *70,000 Assyrians*—it takes his work out of the flat dimensions of the guy watching life in the bar; and here he has brought it into play for one of his most poignant effects. This is followed by an admirable scene, in which the young man walks out on the street and sees a child crying at a window, and reflects that for "the children of the world eternally at the window, weeping at the strangeness of this place," where the Communist must always look forward to a perfected society of the future, where his grandmother must always look backward to a world that has gone with her youth and that could never really have been as she remembers it, it is natural enough to escape into the "even more disorderly universe" of drunkenness, a state sad enough in itself. But the conception, with its three motifs, required a little doing; and Saroyan, as he confesses, did not quite bring it off. He would have had to take the whole thing more seriously and to work it out with more care; and he knows that he can get away with an almost infinite number of less pretentious pieces without having their second-rateness complained of.

Rudyard Kipling said one very good thing about writing: "When you know what you can do, do something else." Saroyan *has* tackled in his plays something larger and more complicated than his stories; but these plays seem now to be yielding to a temptation to turn into columns, too. The three that have been acted and printed have many attractive and promising features in a vein a little like J. M. Barrie's; but George Jean Nathan in the *American Mercury* has given a disquieting account of no less than five new plays by Saroyan that have already been unsuccessfully tried out. There was a rumor that Mr. Nathan had been trying to induce Saroyan to take the trouble to acquaint himself with a few of the classics of the theater, but it sounds as if the attempt had come to naught.

In the meantime, Saroyan goes on with his act, which is that of the unappreciated genius who is not afraid to stand up for his merits. This only obscures the issue. Most good artists begin by getting bad reviews; and Saroyan, in this regard, has been rather remarkably fortunate. So let him set his mind at rest. Everybody who is capable of responding to such things appreciates what is fine in his work. The fact that a number of people who do not know good theatrical writing from bad or whose tastes lie in other directions have failed to recognize Saroyan is no excuse for the artist to neglect his craft. He will be judged not by his personality act or by his ability to get produced and published—which he has proved to the point of absurdity; but by work that functions and lasts.

With his triumph there has crept into Saroyan's work an unwelcome suggestion of smugness. One has always had the feeling with his writing that, for all its amiability and charm, it has had behind it the pressure of a hard and hostile environment, which it has required courage to meet, and that this courage has taken the form of a debonair kidding humor and a continual affirmation of the fundamental kindliness of people —a courage which, in moments when it is driven to its last resources and deepest sincerity, is in the habit of invoking a faith in the loyalties of straight and simple people—Armenians, Czechs, Greeks—surviving untouched by the hatreds of an abstract and complex world. In Saroyan the successful playwright, for whom that pressure has been partially relieved, there seems to be appearing an instinct to exploit this theme of loving-kindness and of the goodness and rightness of things; and there is perhaps a just perceptible philistinism. If Saroyan, in *Love's Old Sweet Song*, has hit upon precisely the right way to make fun of *Time* magazine, he has, on the other hand, here, in what sounds like a skit on *The Grapes of Wrath*, at least grazed the familiar complacency which declares the unemployed are all bums. This is the path that leads to Eddie Guest, Professor William Lyon Phelps and Dr. Frank Crane; and let not Mr. Saroyan deceive himself: no writer has a charmed life.

4. HANS OTTO STORM

With Hans Otto Storm and John Steinbeck, we get into more ambitious writing.

The work of Mr. Storm has been presented to the public in a curious and probably misleading way. His first two books, *Pity the Tyrant* and *Made in U.S.A.* (the latter published only in a limited edition), attracted relatively little attention. They were both novelettes. *Pity the Tyrant*, one of those stories about an "I" who travels and loves and runs risks and reflects with a sardonic detachment on the things that go on around him, seemed to attach itself to the general school of Hemingway. *Made in U.S.A.* had no "I" and was an exercise in objectivity: a story about people on a ship that ran aground, worked out as a social fable. Both stories had a concentration of form and a kind of conscientiousness in their approach to their material that were rare enough to excite interest in the author.

These books were followed in the fall of 1940 by a very long novel, *Count Ten*, which was enormously advertised by the publishers. To the surprise of Mr. Storm's readers, this book turned out, however, to be very much inferior on the whole to the ones that had gone before and to show what seemed internal evidence of having been written earlier than they. *Count Ten* gives distinctly the impression of being one of those autobiographical novels that young men begin in college and carry around for years in old trunks, keeping them at the back of their minds as refractors for their subsequent experience, but returning to work on them after intervals so long that the texture of the book is always changing, and that the story, when it finally appears, fluctuates between callowness and maturity, literal fact and developing invention. The characters encountered by the hero of *Count Ten* have a sort of goofy unreality which lets us down in an embarrassing way after the pretty well-observed social types of Mr. Storm's other novels; and the book is full of violent incidents which occur, as it were, offstage, in the blank lines between one chapter and the next, and which have no real emotional effect on what follows. The hero preserves a certain consistency; but the story of his adventures rambles on with little proportion, composition or climax. The writing, too, is far below the level of the author's earlier published novels. His style has always been hampered by an uncertainty about idiomatic English and a proclivity for German locutions, and, though his instinct for expressing himself has its own kind of sensitive precision, his language is always here a little cockeyed.

Yet *Count Ten* is not uninteresting to read. Implausible though a good deal of it is, it evidently makes use of actual experience; and the experience of Hans Otto Storm has been of a kind rather unusual among our fiction-writers. In the first place, Mr. Storm, though a radical, is not, like so many other novelists, a radical of the depression vintage. He is—one gathers from *Count Ten*—the descendant of German refugees of the Revolution of 1848 settled in Southern California. The hero of his novel, at any rate, begins by going to jail for resisting the draft in the last war and ends by going to jail again as the result of his activities as campaign manager for a movement evidently drawn from Upton Sinclair's EPIC. He has, in the meantime, had a successful career as an agent of the mining interests. Mr. Storm's perspectives from the Left are obviously a good deal longer than those of the ordinary California Communist: he is both practically more sophisticated and historically better informed.

Mr. Storm is unusual in another way. These youthful autobiographical fictions usually tell the stories of young men who want to be writers, and they do not as a rule get far from the literary life itself. But Mr. Storm is neither a journalist nor a script writer, not a man who has made his living by writing at all: he is a trained engineer; and his hero builds and flies planes, works on a construction gang, sails a ship, runs a furniture business in which he manufactures the furniture himself, and becomes a mining prospector in South America. An engineer who thus goes in for literature is such a novelty that Hans Otto Storm is able to carry us with him because we have never listened to precisely his story before. His writing about the sea —in *Made in U.S.A.* and in the episode of the yacht in *Count Ten*—without the parade of technical knowledge which is the betrayal of the layman in Kipling, gives us a much more intimate sense of living the life of the ship than we get from *The Ship That Found Herself* or *The Devil and the Deep Sea*.

Add to this equipment—to this first-hand knowledge of aspects of American life which few American writers know at all—a mentality which is culturally closer to Europe than that of most American writers (there is a suggestion of Conrad about him); and you get something quite unique in our fiction. Mr. Storm has so far, it seems to me, done his best work in *Pity the Tyrant*. Both the earlier published books show an application of engineering aptitude to the technique of constructing novels which is strangely absent in *Count Ten*; but *Pity the Tyrant* has a freshness and vividness which do not appear to the same degree in *Made in U.S.A.*, a more systematic affair. The South American episodes in *Count Ten* sound like mere juvenile sketches for it. Here in this story of an American technician involved in a Peruvian revolution and sorely perplexed between his job, his proletarian political sympathies and a love affair with a South American lady, Mr. Storm does succeed in dramatizing one of those cases of social conscience which do not come off so well in *Count Ten*. Here he really attains intensity; and *Pity the Tyrant*—though not quite in the class with Hemingway and Stephen Crane—belongs among the more distinguished products of this tradition of American storytelling.

5. John Steinbeck

John Steinbeck is also a native Californian, and he has occupied himself more with the life of the State than any of these other writers. His exploration in his novels of the region of the Salinas Valley has been more tenacious and searching than anything else of the kind in our recent fiction, with the exception of Faulkner's exhaustive study of the State of Mississippi.

And what has Mr. Steinbeck found in this country he knows so well? I believe that his virtuosity in a purely technical way has tended to obscure his themes. He has published eight volumes of fiction, which represent a variety of forms and which have thereby produced an illusion of having been written from a variety of points of view. *Tortilla Flat* was a comic idyl, with the simplification almost of a folk tale; *In Dubious Battle* was a strike novel, centering around Communist organizers and following a fairly conventional pattern; *Of Mice and Men* was a compact little drama, contrived with almost too much cleverness, and a parable which criticized humanity from a nonpolitical point of view; *The Long Valley* was a series of short stories, dealing mostly with animals, in which poetic symbols were presented in realistic settings and built up with concrete detail; *The Grapes of Wrath* was a propaganda novel, full of preachments and sociological interludes, and developed on the scale of an epic. Thus attention has been diverted from the content of Mr. Steinbeck's work by the fact that when his curtain goes up, he always puts on a different kind of show.

Yet there is in Mr. Steinbeck's fiction a substratum which remains constant and which gives it a certain weight. What is constant in Mr. Steinbeck is his preoccupation with biology. He is a biologist in the literal sense that he interests himself in biological research. The biological laboratory in the short story called *The Snake* is obviously something which he knows at first hand and for which he has a strong special feeling; and it is one of the peculiarities of his vocabulary that it runs to biological terms. But the laboratory described in *The Snake*, the tight little building above the water, where the scientist feeds white rats to rattlesnakes and fertilizes starfish ova, is also one of the key images of his fiction. It is the symbol of Mr. Steinbeck's tendency to present human life in animal terms.

Mr. Steinbeck almost always in his fiction is dealing either with the lower animals or with humans so rudimentary that they are almost on the animal level; and the relations between animals and people are as intimate as those in the zoöphile fiction of David Garnett and D. H. Lawrence. The idiot in *The Pastures of Heaven*, who is called Little Frog and Coyote, shows his kinship with the animal world by continually making pictures of birds and beasts. In *Tortilla Flat*, there is the Pirate, who lives in a kennel with his dogs and has practically forgotten human companionship. In *In Dubious Battle*, there is another character whose personality is confused with that of his dogs. In *The Grapes of Wrath*, the journey of the Joads is figured at the beginning by the progress of a turtle, and is accompanied and parodied all the way by animals, insects and birds. When the expropriated sharecroppers in Oklahoma are compelled to abandon their farm, we get an extended picture of the invasion of the house by the bats, the weasels, the owls, the mice and the pet cats that have gone back to the wild. Lennie in *Of Mice and Men* likes to carry around pet animals, toward which as well as toward human beings he has murderous animal instincts. The stories in *The Long Valley* are almost entirely about plants and animals; and Mr. Steinbeck does not give the effect, as Lawrence or Kipling does, of romantically raising the animals to the stature of human beings, but rather of assimilating the human beings to animals. *The Chrysanthemums*, *The White Quail* and *The Snake* deal with women who identify themselves with, respectively, chrysanthemums, a white quail and a snake. In *Flight*, a young Mexican boy, who has killed a man and run away into the mountains, is finally reduced to a state so close to that of the beasts that he is apparently mistaken by a mountain lion for another four-footed animal; and in the fantasy *Saint Katy the Virgin*, in which a vicious pig is made to repent and become a saint, the result is not to dignify the animal as the *Little Flowers of Saint Francis* does, for example, with the wolf of Agubbio, but to make human religion ridiculous.

Nor does Steinbeck love his animals as D. H. Lawrence does. The peculiar point of view is well analyzed in connection with Thomas Wayne in *To a God Unknown*: "He was not kind to animals; at least no kinder than they were to each other, but he must have acted with a consistency beasts could understand, for all creatures trusted him. . . . Thomas liked animals and understood them, and he killed them with no more feeling than they had about killing each other. He was too much an animal himself to be sentimental." And Steinbeck does not even dwell much, as Lawrence likes to do, on the perfections of his various beasts each after its own kind. It is the habits and behavior of the animals, not the impression they make, that interests him.

The chief subject of Mr. Steinbeck's fiction has been thus not those aspects of humanity in which it is most thoughtful, imaginative, constructive, nor even those aspects of animals that seem most attractive to humans, but rather the processes of life itself. In the ordinary course of nature, living organisms are continually being destroyed, and among the principal things that destroy them are the predatory appetite and the competitive instinct that are necessary for the very survival of eating and breeding creatures. This impulse of the killer has been preserved in a simpleton like Lennie of *Of Mice and Men* in a form in which it is almost innocent; and yet Lennie has learned from his more highly developed friend that to yield to it is to do something "bad." In his struggle against the instinct, he loses. Is Lennie bad or good? He is betrayed as, the author implies, all our human intentions are, by the uncertainties of our animal nature. And it is only, as a rule, on this primitive level that Mr. Steinbeck deals with moral questions: the virtues like the crimes, for him, are still a part of these planless and almost aimless, of these almost unconscious, processes. The preacher in *The Grapes of Wrath* is disillusioned with the human moralities, and his sermon at the grave of Grampa Joad, so lecherous and mean during his lifetime, evidently gives expression to Mr. Steinbeck's own point of view: "This here ol' man jus' lived a life an' jus' died out of it. I don't know whether he was good or bad, but that don't matter much. He was alive, an' that's what matters. An' now he's dead, an' that don't matter. Heard a fella tell a poem one time, an' he says, 'All that lives is holy.'"

The subject of *The Grapes of Wrath*, which is supposed to deal with human society, is the same as the subject of *The Red Pony*, which is supposed to deal with horses: loyalty to life itself. The men who feel themselves responsible for having let the red pony die must make up for it by sacrificing the mare in order that a new pony may be brought into the world alive. And so Rose of Sharon Joad, with her undernourished baby born dead, must offer her milk, in the desolate barn which is all she has left for a shelter, to another wretched victim of famine and flood, on the point of death from starvation. To what end should ponies and Oakies continue to live on the earth? "And I wouldn' pray for a ol' fella that's dead," the preacher goes on to say. "He's awright. He got a job to do, but it's all laid out for 'im an' there's on'y one way to do it. But us, we got a job to do, an' they's a thousan' ways, an' we don' know which one to take. An' if I was to pray, it'd be for the folks that don't know which way to turn."

This preacher who has lost his religion does find a way to turn: he becomes a labor agitator; and this theme has already been dealt with more fully in the earlier novel, *In Dubious Battle*. But what differentiates Mr. Steinbeck's picture of a labor movement with radical leadership from most treatments of such subjects of its period is again the biological point of view. The strike leaders, here, are Communists, as they are in many labor novels, but *In Dubious Battle* is not really based on the formulas of Communist ideology. The kind of character produced by the Communist movement and the Communist strategy in strikes (of the Communism of the day before yesterday) is *described* by Mr. Steinbeck, and it is described with a certain amount of admiration; yet the party member of *In Dubious Battle* does not talk like a Marxist of even the Stalinist revision. The cruelty of these revolutionists, though they are working for a noble ideal and must immolate themselves in the struggle, is not palliated by the author any more than the cruelty of the half-witted Lennie; and we are made to feel all through the book that, impressive though the characters may be, they are presented primarily as examples of how life in our age behaves. There is developed in the course of the story—especially by a fellow-traveler doctor who seems to come closer than the Communist to expressing Mr. Steinbeck's own ideas—a whole philosophy of "group-man" as an "animal."

"It might be like this, Mac: When group-man wants to move, he makes a standard. 'God wills that we recapture the Holy Land'; or he says 'We fight to make the world safe for democracy'; or he says, 'We will wipe out social injustice with communism.' But the group doesn't care about the Holy Land, or Democracy, or Communism. Maybe the group simply wants to move, to fight, and uses these words simply to reassure the brains of individual men. . . ."

"How," asks Mac, "do you account for people like me, directing things, moving things? That puts your group-man out."

"You might be an effect as well as a cause, Mac. You might be an expression of group-man, a cell endowed with a special function, like an eye cell, drawing your force from group-man, and at the same time directing him, like an eye. Your eye both takes orders from and gives orders to your brain."

"This isn't practical," objects Mac. "What's all this kind of talk got to do with hungry men, with lay-offs and unemployment?"

"It might have a great deal to do with them. It isn't a very long time since tetanus and lockjaw were not connected. There are still primitives in the world who don't know children are the result of intercourse. Yes, it might be worth while to know more about group-man, to know his nature, his ends, his desires. They're not the same as ours. The pleasure we get in scratching an itch causes death to a great number of cells. Maybe group-man gets pleasure when individual men are wiped out in a way."

Later, when the mob of striking fruit-pickers begins to get out of hand, the Communists themselves begin to think of them in these infra-human terms:

"They're down there now. God, Mac, you ought to of seen them. It was like all of them disappeared, and it was just one big animal, going down the road. Just all one animal." . . .
"The *animal* don't want the barricade. I don't know what it wants. Trouble is, guys that study people always think it's men, and it isn't men. It's a different kind of animal. It's as different from men as dogs are. Jim, it's swell when we can use it, but we don't know enough. When it gets started it might do anything."

So the old pioneer of *The Leader of the People* describes a westward migration which he himself once led as "a whole bunch of people made into one big crawling beast. . . . Every man wanted something for himself, but the big beast that was all of them wanted only westering."

This tendency on Steinbeck's part to animalize humanity is evidently one of the causes of his relative unsuccess at creating individual humans. The *paisanos* of *Tortilla Flat* are not really quite human beings: they are cunning little living dolls that amuse us as we might be amused by pet guinea-pigs, squirrels or rabbits. They are presented through a special convention which is calculated to keep them cut off from any kinship with the author or the reader. In *The Grapes of Wrath*, on the other hand, Mr. Steinbeck has summoned all his resources to make the reader feel his human relationship with the family of dispossessed farmers; yet the result of this, too, is not quite real. The characters of *The Grapes of Wrath* are animated and put through their paces rather than brought to life; they are like excellent character actors giving very conscientious performances in a fairly well-written play. Their dialect is well managed, but they always sound a little stagy; and, in spite of Mr. Steinbeck's efforts to make them figure as heroic human symbols, one cannot help feeling that these Okies, too, do not exist for him quite seriously as people. It is as if human sentiments and speeches had been assigned to a flock of lemmings on their way to throw themselves into the sea. One remembers the short story called *Johnny Bear*. Johnny Bear is another of Steinbeck's idiots: he has exactly the physique of a bear and seems in almost every way subhuman; but he is endowed with an uncanny gift for reproducing with perfect mimicry the conversations he overhears, though he understands nothing of their human meaning.

It is illuminating to look back from *The Grapes of Wrath* to one of the earliest of Steinbeck's novels, *To a God Unknown*. In this book he is dealing frankly with the destructive and reproductive forces as the cardinal principles of nature. In one passage, the hero is described by one of the other characters as never having "known a person": "You aren't aware of persons, Joseph; only people. You can't see units, Joseph, only the whole." He finds himself, almost unconsciously and in contravention of Christianity, practicing a primitive nature cult, to which, in time of terrible drought, he sacrifices first his wife, then himself, as blood offerings to bring the rain. This story, though absurd, has a certain interest, and it evidently represents, on the part of Steinbeck just turned thirty, an honorably sincere attempt to find expression for his view of the world and his conception of the powers that move it. When you husk away the mawkish verbiage from the people of his later novels, you get down to a similar conception of a humanity not of "units" but lumped in a "whole," to a vision equally grim in its cycles of extinction and renewal.

Not, however, that John Steinbeck's picture of human beings as lemmings, as grass that is left to die, does not have its striking validity for the period in which we are living. In our time, Shakespeare's angry ape, drest in his little brief authority, seems to make of all the rest of mankind angry apes or cowering rodents. The one thing that was imagined with intensity in Aldous Huxley's novel, *After Many a Summer Dies the Swan*, was the eighteenth-century exploiter of the slave-trade degenerating into a fetal anthropoid. Many parts of the world are today being flooded with migrants like the Joads, deprived of the dignity of a human society, forbidden the dignity of human work, and made to flee from their houses like prairie-dogs driven before a prairie fire. Aldous Huxley has a good deal to say, as our American "Humanists" did, about a fundamental moral difference which he believes he is able to discern between a human and an animal level, and the importance of distinguishing between them; and, like the Humanists, he has been frightened back into one of those synthetic cults which do duty for our evaporated religions. The doctor of *In Dubious Battle* is made, on the contrary, to deprecate even such elements of religion as have entered into the labor cause at the same time that he takes no stock in the utopianism of the Marxists. When he is depressed by the barbarity of the conflict and is reminded by the neophyte Jim that he "ought to think only of the end: out of all this struggle a good thing is going to grow," he answers that in his "little experience the end is never very different in its nature from the means . . . It seems to me that man has engaged in a blind and fearful struggle out of a past he can't remember, into a future he can't foresee nor understand. And man has met and defeated every obstacle, every enemy except one. He cannot win over himself. How mankind hates itself." "We don't hate ourselves," says Jim. "We hate the invested capital that keeps us down." "The other side is made of men, Jim, men like you. Man hates himself. Psychologists say a man's self-love is balanced neatly with self-hate. Mankind must be the same. We fight ourselves and we can only win by killing man."

The philosophy of Mr. Steinbeck is obviously not satisfactory in either its earlier or its later form. He has nothing to oppose to this vision of man's hating and destroying himself except an irreducible faith in life; and the very tracts he writes for the underdog let us see through to the biological realism which is his natural habit of mind. Yet I prefer his approach to the animal-man to the mysticism of Mr. Huxley; and I believe that we shall be more likely to find out something of value for the control and ennoblement of life by studying human behavior in this spirit than through the code of self-contemplation that seems to grow so rootlessly and palely in the decay of scientific tradition which this latest of the Huxleys represents.

For the rest, Mr. Steinbeck is equipped with resources of observation and invention which are exceptional and sometimes astonishing, and with color which is all his own but which does not, for some reason, possess what is called magic. It is hard to feel that any of his books, so far, is really first-rate.

He has provided a panorama of California farm-life and California landscape which is unique in our literature; and there are passages in some ways so brilliant that we are troubled at being forced to recognize that there is something artistically bad about them. Who has ever caught so well such a West Coast scene as that in *To a God Unknown* in which we visit the exalted old man, with the burros, who has built his hut high on the cliff so that he can look down on the straight pillars of the redwoods and off at the sea far below, and know that he is the last man in the western world to see the sun go down? What is wrong here is the animal sacrifice which the old man performs at this moment and which reminds us of the ever-present paradox of the mixture of seriousness and trashiness in the writing of Mr. Steinbeck. I am not sure that *Tortilla Flat*, by reason of the very limitations imposed by its folktale convention, is not artistically his most successful work.

Yet there remains behind the journalism, the theatricalism and the tricks of his other books a mind which does seem first-rate in its unpanicky scrutiny of life.

6. Facing the Pacific

Contemporary California has thus been described by our novelists on a very extensive scale. It has probably had as much attention as any other part of the country. Yet the California writers—and this is true even of Steinbeck, the most gifted of them—do not somehow seem to carry a weight proportionate to the bulk of their work.

Why is this? All visitors from the East know the strange spell of unreality which seems to make human experience on the Coast as hollow as the life of a troll-nest where everything is out in the open instead of being underground. I have heard a highly intelligent Los Angeles lawyer who had come to California from Colorado remark that he had periodically to pinch himself to remind himself of the fact that he was living in an abnormal, a sensational, world which he ought to get down on paper, but that he could never pull out of the trance sufficiently to react and to judge in what he still at the back of his mind considered the normal way. There is in one of these

Hollywood novels, *You Play the Black and the Red Comes Up*, a veracious account of the feelings of a man leaving Southern California. The hero has just crossed the mountains after a great career of love and crime. And yet "it was like all I had done in California was just a dream. And at first it felt good, and then it felt worse, because Sheila was only a dream with everything else. And that was bad. I could remember everything about California, but I couldn't feel it. I tried to get my mind to remember something that it could feel, too, but it was no use. It was all gone. All of it. The pink stucco houses and the palm trees and the stores built like cats and dogs and frogs and ice-cream freezers and the neon lights round everything."

This is partly no doubt a matter of climate: the empty sun and the incessant rains; and of landscape: the dry mountains and the void of the vast Pacific; of the hypnotic rhythms of day and night that revolve with unblurred uniformity, and of the surf that rolls up the beach with a beat that seems expressionless and purposeless after the moody assaults of the Atlantic. Add to this the remoteness from the East and the farther remoteness from Europe. New York has its own insubstantiality that is due to the impermanence of its people, of its buildings, of its business, of its thoughts; but all the wires of our western civilization are buzzing and crossing here. California looks away from Europe, and out upon a wider ocean toward an Orient with which as yet any cultural communication is difficult.

This problem of the native Californian to find a language for the reality of his experience is touched upon in Hans Otto Storm's *Count Ten*. "If things now and then did not look real to you; if you were bothered by that particular question, Eric thought, then you ought certainly to keep off the Gulf of California. It hadn't looked real the time they did or did not bathe their feet in it and eat the clams, and it certainly did not look real now, this deadish place where no ships ever came and where the waves move with such an unutterable weariness." The hero is puzzled but his interest is pricked by an Easterner he meets at Berkeley, who misses the New England seasons and tries to explain to him the dramatic character which they impart to the cycle of the year; and when, gazing over San Francisco bay, he quotes Heine to one of his girls, she objects: " 'That isn't Heine any more. It's a hakku. It makes me think of tea-cakes without salt.' She shivered a little. 'It's getting cold. No, that doesn't click in California. In California you can't sit and meditate on through the sunset.'" The young man applies himself to learning Chinese.

Add to this that the real cultural center, San Francisco, with its cosmopolitanism and its Bohemian clubs, the city of Bret Harte and Ambrose Bierce, was arrested in its natural development by the earthquake of 1906, and that thereafter the great anti-cultural amusement-producing center, Los Angeles, grew up, gigantic and vulgar, like one of those synthetic California flowers, and tended to drain the soil of the imaginative life of the State. (It is a question how much the movies themselves have been affected by the California atmosphere: might they not have been a little more interesting under the stress of affairs in the East?) In this city that swarms with writers, none yet has really mustered the gumption to lay bare the heart and bowels of the moving-picture business. The novels I have mentioned above only trifle with the fringes of Hollywood, as the stage comedies like *Boy Meets Girl* only kid it in a superficial way. A novel on a higher level of writing than any of those I have mentioned—*The Day of the Locust* by Nathanael West—is also mostly occupied with extras and gives mere glimpses into the upper reaches. Aldous Huxley's California novel, *After Many a Summer Dies the Swan*, does not get even so far into the subject as his compatriot Mr. Eric Knight, the author, under a pseudonym, of *You Play the Black etc.* Mr. Huxley here seems well on his way to becoming a second-rate American novelist. Satirizing in more or less conventional fashion the Hearstian millionaire, the vapid Hollywood beauty and the burlesque pomps of a Los Angeles cemetery, he has succumbed to one of the impostures with which the Golden State deludes her victims: the Burbankized West Coast religion; and Mr. Huxley and his ally, Mr. Gerald Heard, will be lucky if they do not wake up some morning to find themselves transformed into Yogis and installed in one of those Wizard-of-Oz temples that puff out their bubble-like domes among the snack bars and the lion ranches.

The novel about Hollywood with most teeth in it is still that intrepid satire by Miss Anita Loos called *The Better Things of Life*, which came out serially in the *Cosmopolitan* and was repeatedly announced by her publishers, but which never appeared between covers. It seems to be true, in general, of Hollywood as a subject for fiction that those who write about it are not authentic insiders and that those who know about it don't write.*

But, as I say, it is not merely in Los Angeles that the purposes and passions of humanity have the appearance of playing their roles in a great open-air amphitheater which lacks not only acoustics to heighten and clarify the speeches but even an attentive audience at whom they may be directed. The paisanos of *Tortilla Flat* also eat, love and die in a golden and boundless sunlight that never becomes charged with their energies; and the rhapsodies of William Saroyan, diffused in this non-vibrant air, pass without repercussions. Even the monstrous, the would-be elemental, the would-be barbaric tragedies which Robinson Jeffers heaps up are a little like amorphous cloud-dramas that eventually fade out to sea, leaving only on our faces a slight moisture and in our ears an echo of hissing. It is probably a good deal too easy to be a nihilist on the coast at Carmel: your very negation is a negation of nothing.

One theme does, however, it must be said, remain serious for the California novelists: the theme of the class war. The men and women of the Cain-O'Hara novels are doomed: they are undone by their own characters or by circumstances. But in time—as in Cain's *Serenade* and O'Hara's *Hope of Heaven*†—the socialist diagnosis and the socialist hope begin

---

*The relation between the movies and prose fiction works in two ways. There are the actual writers for the pictures like Mr. West and Mr. Cain who produce sour novels about Hollywood. And there are the serious novelists who do not write for the films but are influenced by them in their novels. Since the people who control the movies will not go a step of the way to give the script-writer a chance to do a serious script, the novelist seems, consciously or unconsciously, to be going part of the way to meet the producers. John Steinbeck, in *The Grapes of Wrath*, has certainly learned from the films—and not only from such documentary pictures as those of Pare Lorentz, but from the sentimental symbolism of Hollywood. The result is that *The Grapes of Wrath* has poured itself on to the screen as easily as if it had been written in the studios, and that it is probably the sole serious story on record that seems almost equally effective as a book and as a film. Ernest Hemingway's *For Whom the Bell Tolls*, which also has elements of movie romance, was instantly snapped up by Hollywood.

†O'Hara is not yet a Californian either by birth or by adoption. Except in *Hope of Heaven*, he had always had the Eastern edge and tension.

to appear in the picture. This has been true, of course, during the thirties, of our American fiction in general; but the labor cause has been dramatized with more impact by these writers of the Western coast than it has been, on the whole, in the East, where the formulas of Marxist theory have been likely to take the place of experience. I do not mean the Hollywood Stalinism which is satirized by Mr. McCoy in the swimming-pool scene of *I Should Have Stayed Home*: I mean the tradition of radical writing which Californians like Storm and Steinbeck are carrying on from Frank Norris,* Jack London and Upton Sinclair.

This tradition dates from Henry George, who witnessed, in the sixties and seventies, the swallowing-up of the State—in what must have been record time—by capital; and California has since been the scene of some of the most naked and savage of American labor wars. The McNamaras, Mooney and Billings, the Wobblies and Vigilantes, the battles of the longshoremen and the fruit-pickers, the San Francisco general strike—these are names and events that have wrung blood and tears in the easy California climate; and it is this conflict that has kept Mr. Storm afloat in the Pacific vacuum, fixed securely in his orientation toward the east of the social world, and that has communicated to Mr. Steinbeck the impetus that has carried the Joad jalopy into the general consciousness of the nation.

Here the novelists of California know what they are talking about, and they have something arresting to say. In describing their special mentality, I do not, of course, in the least, mean to belittle their interest or value. The writing of the Coast, as I say, may seem difficult to bring into focus with the writing that we know in the East. But California, since we took it from the Mexicans, has always presented itself to Americans as one of

---

*Steinbeck's close relationship with Norris is indicated by what is evidently a borrowing from *McTeague* in *Of Mice and Men*. The conversation that is so often repeated between Norris's Polish junk dealer and the cracked Spanish-American girl, in which he is always begging her to describe for him the gold table service she remembers from her childhood, must have suggested the similar dialogue that recurs between Lennie and George, in which the former is always begging the latter to tell him more about the rabbit farm they are going to have together. Steinbeck's attitude toward his rudimentary characters may, also, owe something to Norris—who, like him, alloys his seriousness with trashiness.

the strangest and most exotic of their exploits; and it is the function of the literary artist to struggle with new phases of experience, and to try to give them beauty and sense.

POSTSCRIPT

These notes were first written during the autumn and early winter of 1940. Since then, several events have occurred which require a few words of postscript.

On December 21, 1940, F. Scott Fitzgerald suddenly died in Hollywood; and, the day after, Nathanael West was killed in a motor accident on the Ventura boulevard. Both men had been living on the West Coast; both had spent several years in the studios; both, at the time of their deaths, had been occupied with novels about Hollywood.

The work of Nathanael West derived from a different tradition than that of these other writers. He had been influenced by those post-war Frenchmen who had specialized, with a certain preciosity, in the delirious and diabolic fantasy that descended from Rimbaud and Lautréamont. Beginning with *The Dream Life of Balso Snell*, a not very successful exercise in this vein of phantasmagoria, he published, after many revisions, a remarkable short novel called *Miss Lonelyhearts*. This story of a newspaper hack who conducts an "advice to the lovelorn" department and eventually destroys himself by allowing himself to take too seriously the sorrows and misfortunes of his clients, had a poetic-philosophical point of view and a sense of phrase as well as of chapter that made it seem rather European than American. It was followed by *A Cool Million*, a less ambitious book, which both parodied Horatio Alger and more or less reproduced *Candide* by reversing the American success story. In his fourth book, *The Day of the Locust*, he applied his fantasy and irony to the embarrassment of rich materials offered by the movie community. I wrote a review of this novel in 1939, and I shall venture to append it here—with apologies for some repetition of ideas expressed above—to make the California story complete:

Nathanael West, the author of *Miss Lonelyhearts*, went to Hollywood a few years ago, and his silence had been causing his readers alarm lest he might have faded out on the Coast as so many of his fellows have done. But Mr. West, as this new book happily proves, is still alive beyond the mountains, and quite able to set down what he feels and sees—has still, in short, remained an artist. His new novel, *The Day of the Locust*, deals with the nondescript characters on the edges of the Hollywood studios: an old comic who sells shoe polish and his film-struck daughter; a quarrelsome dwarf; a cock-fighting Mexican; a Hollywood cowboy and a Hollywood Indian; and an undeveloped hotel clerk from Iowa, who has come to the Coast to enjoy his savings—together with a sophisticated screen-writer, who lives in a big house that is "an exact repro-duction of the old Dupuy mansion near Biloxi, Mississippi." And these people have been painted as distinctly and polished up as brightly as the figures in Persian miniatures. Their speech has been distilled with a sense of the flavorsome and the char-acteristic which makes John O'Hara seem pedestrian. Mr. West has footed a precarious way and has not slipped at any point into relying on the Hollywood values in describing the Hollywood people. The landscapes, the architecture and the interior decoration of Beverly Hills and vicinity have been han-dled with equal distinction. Everyone who has ever been in Los Angeles knows how the mere aspect of things is likely to paralyze the aesthetic faculty by providing no *point d'appui* from which to exercise its discrimination, if it does not actually stun the sensory apparatus itself, so that accurate reporting becomes impossible. But Nathanael West has stalked and caught some fine specimens of these Hollywood lepidoptera and impaled them on fastidious pins. Here are Hollywood restaurants, apartment houses, funeral churches, brothels, evangelical temples and movie sets—in this latter connection, an extremely amusing episode of a man getting nightmarishly lost in the Battle of Waterloo. Mr. West's surrealist beginnings have stood him in good stead on the Coast.

The doings of these people are bizarre, but they are also sor-did and senseless. Mr. West has caught the emptiness of Holly-wood; and he is, as far as I know, the first writer to make this emptiness horrible. The most impressive thing in the book is his picture of the people from the Middle West who, retiring to sunlit leisure, are trying to leave behind them the meagerness of their working lives; who desire something different from what they have had but do not know what they desire, and have no other resources for amusement than gaping at movie stars and listening to Aimee McPherson's sermons. In the last episode, a crowd of these people, who have come out to see the celebrities at an opening, is set off by an insane act of violence on the part of the cretinous hotel clerk, and gives way to an outburst of mob mania. The America of the murders and rapes which fill the Los Angeles papers is only the obverse side of the America of the inanities of the movies. Such people—Mr. West seems to say—dissatisfied, yet with no ideas, no objectives and no interest in anything vital, may in the mass be capable of anything. The daydreams purveyed by Hollywood, the romances that in movie stories can be counted on to have whisked around all obstacles and adroitly knocked out all "menaces" by the time they have run off their reels, romances which their fascinated audiences have never been able to live themselves—only cheat them and embitter their frustration. Of such mobs are the followers of fascism made.

I think that the book itself suffers a little from the lack of a center in the community with which it deals. It has less concentration than *Miss Lonelyhearts*. Mr. West has introduced a young Yale man who, as an educated and healthy human being, is supposed to provide a normal point of view from which the deformities of Hollywood may be criticized; but it is also essential to the story that this young man should find himself swirling around in the same aimless eddies as the others. I am not sure that it is really possible to do anything substantial with Hollywood except by making it, as John Dos Passos did in *The Big Money*, a part of a larger picture which has its center in a larger world. But in the meantime Nathanael West has survived to write another distinguished book—in its peculiar combination of amenity of surface and felicity of form and style with ugly subject matter and somber feeling, quite unlike —as *Miss Lonelyhearts* was—the books of anyone else.

Scott Fitzgerald, who at the time of his death had published only short stories about the movies, had been working for some time on a novel* in which he had tackled the key figure of the industry: the successful Hollywood producer. This subject has also been attempted, with sharp observation and much humor, by Mr. Budd Schulberg, Jr., whose novel *What Makes Sammy Run* has been published since my articles were written. But Mr. Schulberg is still a beginner, and his work in *What Makes Sammy Run* does not rise above the level of a more sincere and sensitive George Kaufman; whereas Scott Fitzgerald, an accomplished artist, had written a considerable part of what promised to be by all odds the best novel ever devoted to Hollywood. Here you are shown the society and the business of the movies, no longer through the eyes of the visitor to whom everything is glamorous or ridiculous, but from the point of view of people who have grown up or lived with the industry and to whom its values and laws are their natural habit of life. These are criticized by higher standards and in the knowledge of wider horizons, but the criticism is implicit in the story; and in the meantime, Scott Fitzgerald, by putting us inside their group and making us take things for granted, is able to excite an interest in the mixed destiny of his Jewish producer of a kind that lifts the novel quite out of the class of this specialized Hollywood fiction and relates it to the story of man in all times and all places.

Both West and Fitzgerald were writers of a conscience and with natural gifts rare enough in America or anywhere; and their failure to get the best out of their best years may certainly be laid partly to Hollywood, with its already appalling record of talent depraved and wasted.

1940–41

*Later published as *The Last Tycoon*.

Max Eastman in 1941

MAX EASTMAN, during the year just past, has published two remarkable books: *Stalin's Russia and The Crisis in Socialism* and *Marxism: Is It Science?* There is perhaps no contemporary figure whose importance is so difficult to estimate.

From 1913 to 1922, as editor of *Masses* and the *Liberator*, Max Eastman was one of the dominant figures of the intellectual life of New York. After 1922, his reputation was in relative eclipse. In that year he went to Europe and remained there for five years. In the course of a sojourn in Russia, he became identified with the Trotskyist side of the Stalin-Trotsky split; and as a result, he was subjected after his return to a systematic vilification and boycott which was continued through the thirties when so many of the intelligentsia fell under the influence of the Stalinists. Today he is emerging again, and it is time some attempt was made to appreciate his real role and stature.

It is not the purpose of this article, however, to attempt a complete account of his career. In order to do that, it would be necessary to write a good deal of history, political and journalistic, and to trace his extensive influence through the channels of his personal relations. For four years an instructor in Philosophy at Columbia, he continued to figure as a teacher even after he became editor of the *Masses*. He is one of those men who have a natural genius for stimulating trains of thinking and suggesting ideas to others, whose thought, instead of having its complete development inside his own head and being completely contained in his own books, interfuses and interchanges in its processes with the minds of those around him, supplying lights and starting impulses for personalities quite different from the teacher's own. This is not to say that there has ever been anything that could be called an Eastman school of thought: on the contrary, it is characteristic of this type of suggestive mind that it does not turn out disciples. This is a quite different kind of teaching from that of an Irving Babbitt, who must either overpower his pupil or goad him into rebellion. Yet of the many kinds of intellectuals who were young enough to learn anything at all during the decade of

1910–20, it is probable that an enormous number owe a special debt to Max Eastman—from the artist who was encouraged to draw pictures, the poet who was encouraged to write poems, for the *Liberator* and the *Masses*, to the journalist whom a conversation with Max first induced to follow out the implications of the emotions aroused by a strike. The writer of this article well remembers his having had his first introduction to psychoanalysis in a magazine article by Max—the quiet and common-sense explanation with the drawl that carried over into print and that exerted so different a persuasive power from that of the ordinary professor. The editors of the *Masses* themselves, whose boss behind the Kremlin walls was recently denouncing Max Eastman as a "notorious gangster" and "crook," would not now have their magazine, with whatever is individual in its format and its tone, if Max had not created it for them.

In 1922, Max Eastman went abroad to study the Russian Revolution, and did not return till 1927. He had, as I have said, during his absence become partially forgotten in New York, and from the time of the banishment of Trotsky in 1925, the partisans of Stalin applied their pressure to make this oblivion as complete as possible. When his presence among us again began to make itself felt, he seemed to wear a different aspect. This aspect was partly the invention of those political enemies of Max, who at that time ruled the radical roost. It was in the days before the Moscow frame-ups had discredited the verdicts of Communists and when it was possible to seem to back with the austere authority of Lenin the condemnation of a revolutionist who was supposed to have gone soft. And this treatment—together perhaps with the difficulties of readjustment to an American scene which had very much changed during the middle twenties—had the result of engendering in Max himself, always excessively sensitive to atmosphere, a less generous and outgoing attitude.

The Max Eastman of the *Masses* and the *Liberator*, who had appreciated and encouraged and aroused, and who had stood at the center of things, had turned into a critic on the sidelines who girded and jeered and complained, and whose preachments seemed mainly negative. *The Enjoyment of Poetry* of 1913 had communicated the exhilaration of a lover of lyric verse, and it naturally went into the hands of every teacher of English in the country who cared enough about literature to know that he had to give his students something more than the right answers to the examination questions. *The Literary Mind* of 1931, obscured by a premature old-fogeyism, made itself disagreeable at the expense of precisely the boldest and most serious of those writers who were working to carry on the great tradition of literature, and it succeeded in irritating everybody who was trying to fight the battle of Joyce and Eliot against the Philistines who were yapping at them. In the same way, the friend of John Reed, the inspirer of Mike Gold, the unsuppressible editor of the *Masses* claimed attention with a critique of Marxism which demonstrated by relentless analysis the Marxist inconsistencies and superstitions without conveying the revolutionary ardor which had animated Marx and Lenin and which had taken Max Eastman himself to Russia. Moreover, this man who had lent to his cause a gift of grace and charm and a power of dealing straight with threatening issues, now developed controversial manners which disquieted his admirers and which weakened the force of certain very sound things that he was trying at this time to say. In arguing with Sidney Hook or in criticizing Ernest Hemingway, he adopted a bitter or a malicious tone which the situation did not seem to warrant, and he went in for a modern variation of the old device of imputing motives by gratuitously psychoanalyzing his subjects and attempting to undermine their philosophical positions or the products of their artistic activity, by showing that they were suffering from adolescent fixations or infantile illusions of inferiority. This whole period of Max Eastman's writings was damaged by a peculiar disgruntled tone. In dealing even with those contemporary figures—Trotsky and Freud, for example—whose ideas he has courageously defended, he sounded as if he were airing a grievance, the nature of which was never made plain.

Now for a fighter, for a worker in ideas, it is dangerous, it may prove fatal to one's effectiveness, to betray that one's feelings have been hurt. The critic must remain invulnerable. When goaded, he should show himself not peevish, but indignant, with a background of scorn. This Max Eastman at his best knows how to do; and he has written a few superb polemics. But up until about the middle of the thirties he was tending to fall into the querulousness of the partisan whose side has had reverses, of the prophet who has lost his public. The isolation in which Max found himself was at this time all the more complete because he did not belong even to a minority. He was as incapable of submitting politically to the imperious dictatorship of Trotsky as of subscribing to the Marxist Dialectic, and he had to forego even the support of the leader whose obloquy and defeat he had shared.

In 1934 the murder of Sergei Kirov announced the doom of those liberalizing elements in Russia which had still made it possible for liberals abroad to give Stalin the benefit of the doubt, and precipitated the wholesale purge of the revolutionary generations which covered up the official rejection of the original Stalinist aims. The American intellectuals who had been depending for their ideas about Russia on the wonderfully dramatized photographs of *USSR in Construction* and who had been kept slightly boozy by the flattery of the League of American Writers now commenced to sober up, and the news of the Hitler-Stalin pact nipped the illusions of all but the dullest. In the scene of devastation that followed, Max Eastman, who had first published the Testament of Lenin and who had been warning people since 1925 against the tendencies that had now triumphed, was seen standing like a stout if slightly twisted lone pine. He began to reacquire credit; people quoted him with respect again. The young no longer shrank from his contact as from a damned soul who had blasphemed the Kremlin. And Max himself seemed to muster new forces. *Stalin's Russia and the Crisis in Socialism* and *Marxism: Is It Science?* have presented what is, so far as I know, the most intelligent and searching as well as the best informed discussion of the implications of the Marxist movement and the development of the Revolution in Russia that has yet appeared in English.

Let us, however, for a moment look back over the whole sequence of Max Eastman's books during this period of his partial eclipse. A glance into *The Literary Mind* today reveals, rather surprisingly to one who was prejudiced against the book when it first appeared, that it was distinguished by a deeper comprehension of the real issues raised by contemporary literature than almost anything else that had been written during the twenties. The end of the twenties was marked by a hullabaloo of aesthetic crankery, philosophical pedantry and academic moralizing; and Max Eastman was almost alone in his attempt to work out as an enlightened modern man the larger relations of art and science to one another, and of both to the society behind them. It is significant of Max's demand for clarity of understanding that, though rather unsympathetic with Joyce, he should have interviewed him in Paris and brought back the only straight story of what he was trying to do in *Finnegans Wake*. The account of this interview in *The Literary Mind* is more valuable to the student of Joyce than much of the stuff that was written by his admirers.

When we go back to Max Eastman's own poetry, published that same year in a collected edition, we decide that he had a much better right than the young people of that era allowed him to talk to them about what poetry ought to be. His verse has perhaps never been brought to the high pitch of craftsmanship and intensity that produces the perfect poem; and it indulges certain deplorable vices. Max has never quite got away from the sentimental and amateurish verse that dominated the field in America during the nineties of the last century and the first decade of this. He still tends to hover around the precincts of the magazine mausoleum of Stedman's *American Anthology*, and he has never really understood the housecleaning, the raising of artistic standards, effected by Eliot and Pound. Moreover, it is true that when Max tries to talk about the emotions directly, he is likely to become rhetorical and turbid. Yet there *is* a lyric poet in Max Eastman, a personal voice, an original imagery, a temperament volatile and fugitive, glistening in delightful sun or vibrating from moments of feeling, that is particularly felicitous in those of his poems that get their images from birds or water—from the tranquil pools of the forest, from the shots of silver spray, from the drops on the window-pane casting a silver shadow, from the ferns, from the wet-petaled lilies, from the delicate-leaved bamboo, from the king-bird with quivering tiny wings, from the slender wild egret, from the breath-taking realization of the beauty of a woman, when the mind flickers electrically with bright perceptions.

As for his writings on the politics of the Left, one who has recently worked in this field and who has been through the whole series of Max Eastman's books inspired by the Russian Revolution will testify that he has found them the most valuable of the commentaries in English on this subject so inflammatory to prejudice. Whoever wants to understand the real (as distinguished from the artificial) exchange during the period after the War between Soviet Russia and the United States will have to read Max Eastman as well as John Reed: *Since Lenin Died, Leon Trotsky, Marx and Lenin, and the Science of Revolution* (now incorporated for the most part in *Marxism: Is it Science?*), *Venture, Artists in Uniform*, and the two newest books which I have mentioned.

John Reed and Max Eastman both observed the Russian Revolution at first hand. John Reed, American adventurer and democratic idealist, gave Lenin to America as an American, and died for what he believed to be the purposes of the Revolution. Max Eastman, with his cooler spirit and his better intellectual equipment, carefully studied its texts, analyzed its fundamental ideas, watched its politics, assessed its personalities; and he lived to see its betrayal and burial. Through all this, he remained as American as Reed. Mark Twain, the friend of his parents, had had his influence on Eastman's youth in Elmira: Max's manner as a public speaker is in the tradition of Mark Twain: the dead-pan drollery and the casual drawl that disguises perfect timing. With a considerable cosmopolitan culture, Max Eastman brought to Moscow the Yankee skepticism and the humane common sense of Mark Twain's *Innocents Abroad*. And no power on earth could prevail upon him to succumb to the Marxist jargon, which has concealed so much confusion, so much intellectual insincerity and so much deliberate fraud. When Max has got the Marxist ideas into English, the historical mythology of Marxism is seen to have disappeared: nothing remains but what is intelligible to American modes of thought and applicable to American actualities.

Max Eastman's great contribution to the study of this subject in English has been to go to the mat with the fundamental

conceptions of Marxism. It has usually been true that the professional philosophers have left Marxism disdainfully alone,
while the political adherents of the Marxist sects have failed to
examine the Marxist philosophy. Max Eastman, a trained
philosopher, showed the inadequacy of the Marxist system,
which Marx, in his preoccupation with politics, had never
found the time to work out; and he dragged out the theological delusions, carried over from the old religion by way of German idealistic philosophy, which were concealed by the
scientific pretensions of Marx. For the pragmatical American
mind, the ideas and literature of Marxism are peculiarly difficult to grapple with; and the American, when converted, tends
to accept them, as he does Methodism or Christian Science, as
a simple divine revelation. The fact that Marx and Engels combined an unexamined idealism with real and great intellectual
genius has made it possible for American intellectuals to
whoop it up for the Marxist religion, under the impression that
they were applying to the contemporary world a relentless intellectual analysis; and, strong in the assurance of standing
right with the irresistible forces of History, the Marxist substitute for the old-fashioned Providence, they have felt confident
that History would see them through without further intellectual effort on their part, and swallowed all the absurd policies and the expedient lies that the Stalinist agents fed them
just as the obedient Catholic swallows the priest's doctrine.

Max Eastman has differed from these thinkers turned gapers
in being an intellectual who really works at it. The thing that
strikes one today in reviewing the work of the last twenty years
by this radical who is supposed to have wilted is not the soft-
ness of his mind but its toughness. He went to study in the Soviet Union the implications and the possibilities of the socialist
doctrine he had been preaching, and he proceeded to formulate his conclusions in a series of writings on which he continued to labor when the fashion had quite turned against
radicalism, which he had in some instances to publish at his
own expense and which received almost no attention. One
cannot see that movements and fashions have affected in any
way—except to make him at times a little irritable—Max's testimony to what he thought true. The child of a mother and
father both ordained Congregational ministers, with a long

ancestry of parsons behind him, he has been upheld perhaps by a vocation neither political nor artistic, a conviction that there is an indispensable part to be played in human society by persons who make it their business to keep clear of the standards of the world and to stick by certain instincts of thinking and feeling whose value is not measured by their wages, and which it is always to the immediate interest of some group to mutilate, imprison or suppress. I know that I have produced in this paragraph a strange blend of the intellectual and the spiritual callings, as they are commonly understood, but it is only in some such special terms that it is possible to describe the role of Max Eastman.

This role has its weaknesses, of course; and in these weaknesses are to be located perhaps the ultimate reasons for Max Eastman's eclipse. There is probably something basic in common between the charges brought against him, respectively, by the politicos and by the poets. Both have felt that he was criticizing them severely, and even on occasion ill-naturedly, without sharing the rigors of their tasks. After all, Max Eastman was a poet who had not accepted the last discipline of his craft; a revolutionist who had stepped out of the battle to explain that the outcome was uncertain; a philosopher who held no chair; a journalist who had allowed his magazine to be captured by an opposition that parodied it in the interests of everything that Eastman most desired to fight. Above all, he was continually going on about something he called "science" —though he himself was no species of scientist and had had, so far as one could discover, no scientific training at all—with which he was always laying about him at philosophers, partisans and poets alike. I do not know how it happened that Max Eastman became so obsessed by the idea of science: he has erected it into a totem, about which it is as if he has talked too much because he has not known what clan he belonged to. So, also, the continual emphasis on what he calls "living" may have compensated his failure to cultivate intensively the several departments in which he has worked. Certainly Max has written with eloquence, as a non-scientific essayist can—for example, in the essay on *What Science Is* in his *Marxism: Is it Science?*— about the spirit and objectives of the scientist; and he has conveyed his conviction that "living," in a world where abstraction and specialization have been resulting in wholesale destruction, has an importance and rights of its own. But it is true that one has sometimes felt that these words were being waved in one's face at moments when Max himself might well have been more scientific about, as well as more alive to, certain things that were happening in the world about him.

This said, and it has already been said often, we must recognize that Max Eastman, after all, has justified his anomalous role of preacher-teacher-critic-poet. He has justified it in a way quite distinct from the way in which he first attracted attention —that is, as a public figure; he presents himself to his contemporaries today *as primarily a writer to be read*. The public figure in Max—by a process probably not very congenial to him—has, in his lecturing and popularizing, become to some extent disassociated from the independent student and thinker who sometimes had to publish at his own expense and could rarely hope to sell. This is the Eastman of *The Enjoyment of Laughter* and of the *Anthology for the Enjoyment of Poetry*— entertaining and readable books appropriate for bringing in money.

But, on the other hand, his serious writing has been growing a good deal more interesting. One remembers his *Liberator* articles as having seemed a little diffuse and lacking in bony structure. But the prose of these recent books has a clarity and terseness of form, an intellectual edge, which would be hard to match elsewhere today in the American literature of ideas. This prose is not primarily an instrument for polemics but the medium for a point of view. The writings of Max Eastman make a commentary, imaginative, witty, sharp, uncompromising in its adherence to the line of its own conscience, not unlike that of André Gide; and the audience of intellectuals which has surely overrated Gide has underrated Max Eastman. His novel *Venture*, for example, which passed almost unnoticed in 1927, before the torrent of strike novels had started, is an idea-novel of the type of Gide's, which deals with the problems of industry in a most unconventional way. The Platonic-Nietzschean capitalist, who talks his young disciple into Bolshevism by expounding his ideals of a superior caste without perceiving that a superior caste may pursue anti-capitalist aims, is one of Eastman's best inspirations; and the book is full of his characteristic aphorisms, finely phrased and often acute, on the various aspects of experience.

Max Eastman's comprehension of the modern world is limited in certain respects, and this is probably another reason for the recent neglect of his work. As his novel is quite non-naturalistic, so his discussion of the Soviet Union and of the general situation of the West does not include an adequate picture of economic and social conditions. It is strange that this student of Marxism should never have learned from Marx what is certainly most valid in his system: the class analysis of historical happenings. Max Eastman, as Philip Rahv has pointed out, tends to talk as if the fallacies of Marxism had by themselves wrecked the Leninist revolution, and is not interested in finding out how the development of social forces has affected the application of ideas. But though it is true that he thinks mainly in terms of psychological motivations, of philosophical and moral positions, his criticism along these lines has, nevertheless, proved extremely salutary at a time when people were trusting to arrangements of statistical figures to demonstrate the rights and wrongs of History without being able to smell the corpses in the Lubyanka or to take stock of what was healthy at home. Max Eastman has continued to perform for us the same function that he did in the first World War: that of the winter log that floats in the swimming-pool and prevents the concrete from cracking by itself taking the pressure of the ice.

He is also the unpopular foreigner who opens the window on the Russian train; the indiscreet guest who saves the banquet by making fun of the guest of honor; the rude and ill-regarded professor whose courses the brighter students all find out they have to take. And these courses are now available in their definitive and polished form in *Stalin's Russia* and *Marxism: Is It Science?*

February 10, 1941

T. K. Whipple

I FIRST KNEW T. K. Whipple in the winter of 1912–13. He was
a senior at Princeton then and editor of the *Nassau Literary
Magazine*, and I was a freshman contributor. The *Lit* had been
rather in eclipse up to the time that T. K. (whom the campus
called "Teek") had taken command of it the year before.
Robert Shafer, since known as a critic and a follower of Paul
Elmer More, was, I believe, the first editor in a series that rep-
resented a new period of literary activity at Princeton—the first
since the early nineties, the days of Booth Tarkington and
Jesse Lynch Williams. Whipple took over from Shafer, and
the succeeding boards included John Peale Bishop, Hamilton
Fish Armstrong, Isador Kaufman, W. Stanley Dell, Raymond
Holden, F. Scott Fitzgerald, John Biggs, Jr., and myself.
Among the contributors were Keene Wallis and A. O'Brien-
Moore. Up to the time of Whipple's editorship the *Lit* had
had the existence of a mouse that lurked timidly in a crevice of
the college life. I remember Teek telling me of the hopelessness with which he and the other editors had canvassed the
college rooms for subscriptions. The freshmen would buy tiger
pictures, but they knew from the lack of confidence with
which the salesmen for the *Lit* approached them that the magazine was not taken seriously.

In the new era the *Lit* came to life. It made connections
with the other college activities: the *Princetonian* and the Triangle Club; and at the same time it defended with boldness
positions that were antagonistic to both official and undergraduate opinion. We engaged in sharp controversies with the
Princetonian over the problems of the curriculum and academic freedom, and there was a moment, under the editorship
of John Bishop, when Bishop's poetry—which seemed very
"modern" —created an issue on the campus almost comparable to the fight over the eating-club system. We had an awfully
good time out of the *Lit* and got some excellent practice in
writing and being read—for which courses in "creative writing"
had not yet at that date become necessary; and we were usually
able to cut, at the end of the year, a melon which yielded each

of us a slice of about fifty dollars. Teek Whipple, who had stayed on at the Graduate School after his graduation in 1913, had been with us through all this period. He had helped and advised, and he had written for the *Lit* in his limpid and witty prose; and he had thus given the whole evolution a continuity it would not otherwise have had. He had somehow established the atmosphere in which the *Lit* was flourishing, and he continued to water its roots.

Not that he was in the least a promoter or the kind of man who likes to pull strings. He was a long-legged, loose-jointed fellow, with pale blond hair and a Missouri drawl, whose expression, with its wide grin, seemed at once sad and droll. His movements and manner were languid when he was lounging on a window seat or Morris chair; but when one saw him striding the campus, hump-shouldered and hands in pockets, one felt in him a purposive independence. All that he did he did unobtrusively, but definitely and with conviction. In some ways he was remarkably mature for an American undergraduate. His enthusiasm for our Princeton humanism—by which I mean the tradition of, say, Lionel Johnson, a great favorite of T. K.'s at this time, not the Humanism of Babbitt and More—burned in an air that was dryer than the rather humid and dreamy atmosphere that tended to beglamor our minds: an air of disillusioned common sense; and he seemed sure in the decisions of his judgment and taste as few men at college do. I remember it as characteristic of him that when I told him I was reading *Marius the Epicurean* and began to grope for phrases to express my mixed feelings about it, he said at once that it "would be a good book if it were not so badly written." And his devotion to literature was never dilettante-ish, as it is likely to be with undergraduates, nor did it ever become a matter of routine, as it is likely to do with professors: it was something fundamental to his life. He presented an unusual combination of Princetonian and Middle Westerner—of pleasantry, casualness and elegance with homeliness, simplicity and directness. Though he was not intellectually the most energetic or imaginatively the most brilliant of the group, he had something that is very rare and a little hard to define. He diffused a quiet kind of light that accompanied him like a nimbus.

You were always glad to see him; you always knew the glow was there; and in that medium the *Lit* revived.

T. K. and I, when I got to be editor for the year 1915–16, worked together in renovating the magazine and laying for it a firmer base. We changed the type and format, as new editors are likely to do, and we gave it a permanent cover, with an owl and the motto from Horace so often invoked by Poe: *Omne tulit punctum, qui miscuit utile dulci*; we reorganized the magazine and established an editorial procedure; and we refurnished and redecorated the *Lit* offices. One of the features of this latter transformation was a large wooden settle, painted black, in the back of which we sawed diamond-shaped holes and which we set against the long front windows in such a way that, though we were screened from the campus, we were able to watch all that went on there—a device that we regarded as at once a symbol and a facilitation of the semi-godlike role of the critic. These activities of ours, of course—though at that time we did not know it—were a reflection, perhaps, rather, a part, of the general revival of literary activity that was going on all through the United States, and they were paralleled in the other colleges. We amused ourselves by sending one day for two little volumes of verse which had been printed by the author himself in Rutherford, New Jersey, and which had been advertised in the local paper. We had a library of bad poetry in the *Lit* office, and we hoped they would turn out to be funny; but we were puzzled by what we got. The poems *were* some of them quite funny, regarded from the conventional point of view; but they had also a kind of spare dignity, and were they wholly without merit? The poet was William Carlos Williams. A volume of plays called *Thirst* which reached us in 1914 was reviewed in the *Lit* as follows: "This volume, by Eugene G. O'Neill, contains five one-act plays which, if it were not for the author's manifest intention of making them something else, we should call very trashy."

I had begun to have hopes of America's producing some first-rate writers. It was true that the only contemporaries (Henry James was already a classic) that I could read with any genuine enthusiasm were Edith Wharton and E. A. Robinson; but the year before I came to college I had discovered H. L.

Mencken, and I could see that there were possibilities for a kind of American literature which would not necessarily be published, as Mrs. Wharton and Robinson were, under the auspices of W. C. Brownell, at that time chief editor at Scribner's. Mr. Brownell, as I was afterwards to learn, was rejecting at that very moment—admitting that the book was able but declaring that such a packet of blasphemies could never be published by Scribner's—Van Wyck Brooks's important essay, *America's Coming-of-Age*, which complained rather impatiently of our national classics and demanded something better. But between our generation and the Civil War there had extended a kind of weedy or arid waste where people with an appreciation of literature had hardly hoped to find anything of value growing and where they had tended to be suspicious of anything that did manage to bloom; and T. K., a few years older than I, had grown up with the outlook of this period. Not only was there no interest at that time on the part of the conventional academic world in anything that American writers were doing or might do; there was not even any real interest in our classics. I remember my surprise at hearing that Professor T. R. Lounsbury of Yale was occupying himself with American subjects. At Princeton, Duncan Spaeth was a permanent scandal by reason of his admiration for Whitman: "Born on Long Island, died in Camden—found life beautiful!" Dr. Spaeth used to roar in defiance of people who, living close to Camden, assumed that it was too far away from the localities mentioned in *The Scholar Gypsy* to inspire the right kind of poetry. Thus, though T. K. read Mencken, too, with evident appetite, he used to confront me with incomprehension when I talked to him about working our own field. "You mean," I remember his saying to me one day at the Graduate School, when I was telling him that I'd rather stay at home than do as James and the rest had done, "that you'd rather be a big toad in a small puddle?"

I believe that those years at the Graduate School were, apart from his interest in the *Lit*, rather a barren time for T. K. I think of him always as enmeshed in two interminable Ph.D. theses: one on the influence of the Greek orator Isocrates on Milton's prose style, the other on the seventeenth-century epigram. There was something rather nightmarish about it: at first there had been only one thesis, which he was never able to finish, and then presently there were two, and I felt that the whole thing was hopeless. I used to go over to see him in the Graduate School, a sumptuous Gothic creation which had just been erected by Ralph Adams Cram in the middle of the Princeton golf links and which was then being broken in. T. K. would invite me to a dreary enough dinner in the immense medieval dining hall, where the faculty sat on a dais and the students filed in in black gowns to the boom of a fugue of Bach from a hand-carved organ loft. The Graduate School was a luxurious affair, and there was something about that life he liked. But, as a man from Kansas City, he couldn't help being funny about the suits of armor in the halls; and I never went over to see him without a feeling of desolation. I would traverse the enclosed court, where the new gray stone in its rawness did not in the least remind you of the stone of Oxford or Cambridge. I would ascend the monastic stair, knock at the oaken door, and find T. K. inert in his Morris chair, imprisoned amid the leaded windows, unable to bring himself to get through any more volumes of seventeenth-century epigrams and unwilling or without any appetite to read anything more stimulating. It was as if he had succumbed to some terrible doom from which he was powerless to save himself and from which nobody else could save him. The whole spectacle gave me a horror of Ph.D. theses from which I have never recovered.

Then the United States entered the War, and the board of the *Lit* were dispersed. T. K. somehow managed to finish his thesis and get his Ph.D. degree, and he enlisted in the Marines and went to France. There he came down with sarcoma of the bladder and spent many miserable months in hospital. After the war, he taught English for a time at Union College, Schenectady—a town of which he wrote me that the inhabitants were "devoid of the attractive qualities alike of men and of animals."

I felt even more depressed about him than I had when he was studying at the Graduate School, so I was very much surprised and cheered when I suddenly found him emerging in an entirely new role. I began to come upon articles by him on contemporary American subjects—articles of a quality which set them apart from anything else of the kind being done; and when I would see him on his rare trips to New York I would find him full of something more than even his old enthusiasm of the *Lit* days about what was being written in America. In 1928 he published a volume called *Spokesmen*, which contained essays on Henry Adams, E. A. Robinson, Dreiser, Frost, Anderson, Cather, Sandburg, Lindsay, Lewis and O'Neill—the whole literary world of the twenties, in which I did not know he had been interested. He said in his foreword that Van Wyck Brooks had "first awakened" in him "the desire to try to understand the United States." There was no ballyhoo in *Spokesmen*; there was not even the patriotic leniency that lets its subjects off from damaging questions and comparisons; but there was the definite recognition that a new cultural era had opened. "Americans," he wrote, "for the first time in their history are seeking honest self-knowledge instead of self-glorification. The nation is self-conscious, with an eager curiosity as to all that concerns itself past or present, with a genuine desire to get acquainted with itself. It is willing to be told bitter truth, so long as it is told something about itself. If anyone is skeptical as to the awakening in the United States, I invite him to revert in his mind to the year 1910 or thereabouts, and ask himself whether the United States is not more alive now than then. . . . All over the United States there is a stirring and a striving—after no one knows what. But the new life has already by its achievements established a claim to respect. It has produced buildings and books and plays and pictures which entitle it to admiration."

In the meantime he had gone to teach at Berkeley, where his courses became extremely popular. He had sometimes a nostalgia for Princeton, and he used to complain of the vacuity of California; but he found there an eager audience and security in his academic position, and he seems to have felt behind him the life of the whole country as I had never known him to do in the East. His field was lying right there before him, though he hadn't been able to see it from the Princeton Graduate School, and as soon as he began to work it, it was plain that this was the thing he should do. The Middle Westerner in T. K. came forward to meet the Middle Western writers who were playing such a conspicuous part in the American literature of the period; but he met them with the cultivated intelligence which was supposed to be characteristic of the East. He was, I think, the first of our critics to study the new novelists and dramatists and poets at the same time appreciatively and calmly, to try to see the work of each as a whole and to make some sort of summary of it. Mencken and Rascoe and the rest had induced people to read the new writers; and now the process of understanding them and appraising them was beginning with T. K. Whipple.

These essays of T. K.'s, to one who had known him, were a special cause of satisfaction. When one is ten years out of college, one has already seen so many gifted friends fail to do any of the things one had hoped of them, and it was stimulating to find a man who had never made pretensions or been petted accomplishing something excellent. His writing had certain characteristics excessively rare in the twenties: he knew precisely what he wanted to say, and he said it with equanimity. He somehow—what seems to me unique among the men of my acquaintance of our generation—got through not only the twenties but even the thirties without being thrown off his base. The good sense and good taste which had distinguished him at college in the placid days before the war somehow survived all those years when other people were going to pieces and finding themselves bent into unexpected shapes. I had felt in him already at college a stoicism, a kind of resignation, which was not at all characteristic of the American undergraduate. I had been struck by his quoting to me from *Rasselas*, seriously and not merely for the phrase, the characterization of human life as a state (I may not have it quite right) "where much is to be suffered and little known." Now the malady which had disabled him in the army was menacing him with painful recurrences, which continued through the whole last twenty years of his life; and it may be that a conscious or unconscious awareness of the fate that was always following him contributed to make him indifferent to many things through which others became demoralized.

It was all the more remarkable, then, that a new social-political interest should have begun to show itself in his work. I was surprised again in the thirties at the force of the democratic instincts which were aroused in him by the literature of the Left and which caused him to declare himself a socialist.

This was a common enough phenomenon at that period, but it was not common to find criticism from the Left so unhysterical and unstampeded as Whipple's. One sees in his later essays how the fine discriminations and pressures of his mind had managed to digest even a considerable dose of Marxism without absorbing from it anything but nourishment; and, looking back on his career at college, with its emphases that were so quiet yet so definite, his attitude toward the eating-club system and his policy with contributors to the *Lit*, I could see now that these equalitarian instincts were not getting out of hand because they had always been there and had always been reckoned with. I imagine that his experience of the War, in which he had served without a commission, had wakened, as it did in most such cases, a sympathy with the common man that remained with him ever after. He had shared the solidarity of the Marine Corps, and he always felt the special pride in it which is characteristic of that branch of the service.

He responded at any rate to the times with a liveliness and youthfulness that seemed amazing—though I have found that those men and women who really live in close contact with the arts remain young when the people who live with the ups and downs of business, of the stock market or of current politics, become stale with middle age. I last saw him in 1938 when he had got a sabbatical year from Berkeley and come East to write a new book. He could hardly have been fuller of projects if he had just graduated from college. He had come out to see me in the country, and it was quite like the old *Nassau Lit* days when he had used to drop over from the Graduate School. But now he was no longer blocked by the style of Isocrates. He was going to write about things that excited him and about which he had something to say, and he knew that there were people who would read him.

He died suddenly of an attack of his malady in the spring of the following year, June 3, 1939. The pieces he had left completed were published after his death by the University of California Press, under the title *Study Out the Land*, a phrase from a poem of Whitman's; and they show how the glow of that light which had survived days of dullness and days of pain was intensified to a special brightness just before it went out.

December, 1942

The Antrobuses and the Earwickers

THE *Saturday Review of Literature* of December 19, 1942, published an article by Joseph Campbell and Henry Morton Robinson asserting that Thornton Wilder's play *The Skin of Our Teeth* derives from James Joyce's *Finnegans Wake*. At the time this article appeared I had been concocting the following little parody, based on Book I, Chapter 6, of Joyce's book. I had had some correspondence with Wilder on the subject of *Finnegans Wake*, and I had intended to send him this as a joke. I did not, however, send it because I was afraid it might look as if it had been inspired by the invidious *Saturday Review* article. I did not approve of the tone of that article, but its principal contentions were true, and since they have generally been received with incredulity, I may as well produce my burlesque:

What pyorrheotechnical edent and end of the whirled in comet stirp (a) brings dionysaurus to Boredway yet manages to remain good bronx orpheus; (b) gave Jed harrors but made Mike meyerbold; (c) was voted a tallulahpalooza and triumpet allakazan by the waitups of the dramatical dimout; (d) stamps them bump, backs them bim, oils them in the bowels and rowels them in the aisles, causes them to beep buckups and sends them hope sobhappy; (e) adds a dash of the commedia deadhearty and a flicker of Fleerandello to the whoopfs of *Hellzapiaffin*; (f) sidesteps coprofoolya but seminates heimatophilia; (G!) translimitates polyglint prosematics into plain symbol words of one syrupull; (H———!!!) disinfects Anna Livia and amenicanizes H. C. Earwicker?

Answer: Skinnegone Sleek.

The Messrs. Campbell and Robinson are, then, quite correct in their assertion that Wilder owes something to Joyce. *The Skin of Our Teeth* is based on *Finnegans Wake*—as Mr. Carl Ballett, Jr., another writer in the *Saturday Review*, has pointed out—in very much the same way *The Woman of Andros* was based on Terence's *Andria*. It would certainly have amused

Joyce to know that a Broadway play inspired by *Finnegans Wake* had been praised by critics who were under the impression that his book was unintelligible gibberish. People like Mr. Wolcott Gibbs, who has ridiculed, in a skit in the *New Yorker*, the discoveries of the Campbell-Robinson article, make a very naïve mistake when they assume that situations presented in the straight English of Thornton Wilder's play can have nothing to do with situations presented in the "kinks english" of sleep in which *Finnegans Wake* is written. It is precisely the same mistake that they would make if they insisted that *The Woman of Andros* could have nothing to do with Terence because Terence wrote in Latin. In Mr. Gibbs's case, it is clear that he has looked at the first page of *Finnegans Wake*, one of the relatively few passages in the book which present a real appearance of opacity, and emitted a hoot of derision. That he has not explored Joyce for himself is proved by his invoking a passage which is not in *Finnegans Wake* at all but which was printed in an article by Robert McAlmon before Joyce had removed it from his manuscript.

Mr. Gibbs's readiness to scoff at the borrowings indicated by Campbell and Robinson is due to his not understanding the peculiar kind of close attention to phrases, words and rhythms which the reader of *Finnegans Wake* must cultivate. Words and rhythms here have been given a different value from their value in ordinary books: they do not merely describe, they *represent*, the characters and the elements of the plot; and any real addict of *Finnegans Wake* recognizes in Wilder's play—though these may sometimes have been brought into it unconsciously—cadences and words to which Joyce has given a life of their own. The general indebtedness to Joyce in the conception and plan of the play is as plain as anything of the kind can be; it must have been conscious on Wilder's part. He has written and lectured on *Finnegans Wake*; is evidently one of the persons who has most felt its fascination and most patiently explored its text.

This derivation would not necessarily affect one way or the other the merits of Wilder's play. Joyce is a great quarry, like Flaubert, out of which a variety of writers have been getting and will continue to get a variety of different things; and Wilder is a genuine poet with a form and imagination of his own who may find his themes where he pleases without incurring the charge of imitation. I do not think that *The Skin of Our Teeth* is one of Wilder's very best things, but it is certainly an adroit and amusing play on a plane to which we have not been accustomed in the American theater lately, with some passages of Wilder's best. It deserves a good deal of the praise it has had, and all of the success.

It is probably true, however—though what Wilder is trying to do is quite distinct from what Joyce is doing—that the state of saturation with Joyce in which the play was written has harmed it in certain ways: precisely, in distracting Wilder from his own ideas and effects; and that it suffers, as a serious work, from the comparison suggested with Joyce.

In the first act, you get, for example, the following line spoken by Sabina in her description of Mr. Antrobus: "Of course, every muscle goes tight every time he passes a policeman; but what I think is that there are certain charges that ought not to be made, and I think I may add, ought not to be allowed to be made; we're all human; who isn't?" This has obviously been caught over from the first book of *Finnegans Wake*, in which Earwicker, in his fallen role of Lucifer-Napoleon-Finnegan-Humpty Dumpty-Adam, is arrested for obscure offenses. But this theme of apprehensive guilt, developed by Joyce at length, gets no further attention from Wilder. Antrobus, in the second act, becomes self-important and careless, falls for the hussy Sabina and is ready to divorce his wife; but we do not hear anything about him which makes us see why he should fear the police. The scene in the third act between Antrobus and Cain, which seems to have great possibilities, falls flat for the reason that the father is not made to share the son's guilt. It is as if *The Skin of Our Teeth* needed something which can only be found in *Finnegans Wake*. Again, the letter which, in the second act, Mrs. Antrobus throws into the sea is Wilder's echo of the letter which plays such a conspicuous part in Joyce. But this scene is rather pointless in the play because it is simply something caught over and has no connection with anything else; and rather irritating to readers of Joyce because the letter (pp. 623–624) is one of the main themes of *Finnegans Wake*, in which it represents the mystery of life itself, whereas Wilder has merely exploited—and in a rather sentimental way—Mrs. Earwicker's feminine version of it.

Again, the character of Sabina-Lilith seems conventional and even a little philistine in comparison with the corresponding characters both in *Finnegans Wake* and in Bernard Shaw's *Back to Methuselah*, another work of which *The Skin of Our Teeth*, in certain of its aspects, reminds us. The Lilith of Joyce is Lily Kinsella, who plays the remote and minor role of a woman who is odious to Mrs. Earwicker for having once had designs on Earwicker; but the conception of the Woman as Seductress is impossible to identify with any of the individual women of either the Earwicker family or the dream-myth. You cannot put your finger on her or isolate her, because she may under appropriate circumstances be incorporated in any one of them: by the wife in her younger phase, by the daughter in her adolescence, by the niece who figures as the "prankquean." She is something that any woman may be, at some period or moment in her life. The Lilith of Shaw is the principle of change that always breaks up the pattern and leads on to something different and higher. But the Lilith of Wilder is a hussy: parlor-maid, gold-digger, camp-follower—a familiar enough comic type, perhaps a little bit too close to Mrs. Antrobus' disapproving notion of her.

Finally, I believe that Wilder has been somewhat embarrassed and impeded by the model of the Earwicker family. He has taken over the Earwicker daughter—in *The Skin of Our Teeth*, Gladys—and done with her practically nothing; and he seems to have tried to avoid taking over the twin Earwicker brothers, who give Joyce a Shaun as well as a Shem, an Abel as well as a Cain, and who figure in their duality the conflict inside the personality of their father. Wilder has got rid of Abel by having him killed by Cain in the Ice Age phase of the Antrobuses before the play begins; and in the subsequent phases he does not show us or hardly shows us the people whom Cain attacks. Thus we never see Cain confronted, as Joyce's Shem always is, by his inevitable complementary opponent—with the result that there is no real dramatization of the "war in the members" in humanity. Even the scene between Cain and Antrobus fails, as I have noted above, to get this conflict into the play. The pages of *Finnegans Wake*, with their words that take on malign meanings, produce a queer effect of uncertainty. The Antrobuses are a little too cozy, even when ruined by war.

January 30, 1943

Alexander Woollcott of the Phalanx

ALEXANDER WOOLLCOTT is dead; and a hostile obituary in the New York *Herald Tribune*, which dwelt on his disagreeable traits, has prompted me to try to pay some tribute to his more attractive ones.

I knew Woollcott only slightly, but my relations with him were based on an aspect of him which may not have been very well known. He was born at the North American Phalanx near Red Bank, New Jersey, and I was born at Red Bank. The North American Phalanx was one of the longest-lived of the socialist communities that flourished in the middle of the last century, and Woollcott's grandfather was for many years the head of it. My family knew all his family, and my grandfather, who was a doctor at Eatontown, brought Woollcott into the world.

When I first came to New York and met Woollcott, I did not connect him with the Woollcotts of Red Bank or the curious old Fourierist building, half barracks and half hotel, to which I had been taken, as a child, to call. At that time, when I had just started working in the office of *Vanity Fair*, to which he was a distinguished contributor, I saw his more erinaceous side. I provoked him to ferocity one day by asking him who the Father Duffy was to whom he was in the habit of referring as if he were the Apostle Paul. I had spent a year and a half in France during the war but had not been aware of Father Duffy; and I had not grasped the fact that Woollcott had created for himself a calendar of saints whose glory must not be questioned. But one day at the Algonquin he asked me whether I was the son of Lawyer Wilson of Red Bank, and we talked about the Phalanx. He told me about a Fourierist uncle who had devoted himself to painting with so much single-mindedness and so little material success that he had finally had to go into bankruptcy. My father had extricated him from his troubles; and I presently discovered that a picture that hung in my mother's house—the old phalanstery building itself dimly looming behind the fresh green of the straight-stemmed New Jersey forest—was one of this uncle's productions, which at that time he had given my father. I had been struck, when Woollcott told me of this incident, by the evident admiration he felt for the completeness of his uncle's unworldliness: not only for the immense number of pictures he had painted but for the enormous sum of money he had failed for.

From then on our relations were cordial. When a play of mine was done at the Provincetown Playhouse in the early nineteen twenties, Alec, then the dramatic critic of the *Times*, wrote a rather sympathetic review of it, but ended by explaining that his judgment might possibly have been somewhat softened by the fact that thirty-odd years before a certain kindly old country doctor had been called on a snowy night to attend Mrs. Woollcott of the Phalanx, etc. When he found out later on that the kindly old doctor had gone to Hamilton College, of which Alec was one of the most loyal alumni, my grandfather came to figure, from his connection with Alec's birth, as a species of Angel of the Annunciation; and I was surprised to find myself involved in one of those sentimental myths on which he fed the unsatisfied affections that had for objects only his heroes, his friends and the memories of his family.

This myth would occasionally crop up in his writings, and even after I ceased to see him, I would hear from him from time to time. One day I ran into him in New York in the street somewhere in the West Forties. He was going very fast, but stopped a second and said brusquely, "I'm having a play produced!" I asked him what it was called. "*The Crime in the Whistler Room*," he snapped and passed on. *The Crime in the Whistler Room* had been the title of my play at the Provincetown. Later on, when I published a study of Kipling, he wrote me several long letters on the subject, about which he had some sober and shrewd ideas. I had also, however, been writing about Dickens and praising his gloomy later novels; and this elicited from Alec a sulky "I do not care to discuss Dickens with you." He did, nevertheless, indicate his preferences; and I could see him as a child in the phalanstery lying in the hammock on a summer day with *Pickwick* or *David Copperfield*. His point of view was perfectly infantile. It turned out that he did not like *Bleak House* simply because it was the only one of the novels which he had not read as a child.

In the meantime, however, in the years of the depression, I had had with him a curious interview. I had been travelling

around the country doing articles on labor and economic conditions, and he wrote me that he had been reading these articles and said he would like to talk to me. I invited him to
dinner, but he answered that he was a much older man than I
and that I ought to come to him. So I called on him at Sutton
Place, where he occupied a splendid apartment looking out on
the East River. As soon as I entered the room, he cried out,
without any other greeting: "You've gotten very fat!" It was
his way of disarming, I thought, any horror I might have felt at
his own pudding-like rotundity, which had trebled since I had
seen him last. He did not rise and was wearing a dressing-
gown, so I asked whether he had been ill. He shortly replied
that he hadn't; and wanted to know whether I thought he was
ill because he was wearing a dressing-gown. There were other
guests, and they kept coming and going. Drinks were brought
by a butler: Woollcott never stirred from his chair; and there
was a backgammon board, at which people were playing. A
secretary in a room beyond was typing an article for him; and
he would rap out from time to time peremptory orders to the
butler, who was feeding a phonograph in a neighboring room
with Gilbert and Sullivan records.

He made no attempt to talk to me, and I wondered why he
had wanted to see me. At last there came a moment, however,
when all the guests had gone and there was nobody but him
and me. His demeanor changed entirely. He began to speak
naturally and frankly: a note of uncertainty came into his voice,
and a look of distressful anxiety tightened his brows above his
spectacles. He asked me about the Communist movement in
America. I told him a little, and he went on to talk about the
North American Phalanx—on which he had been collecting
material and about which he meant some day to write. He said
that he had always known that labor was going to be the great
force in the modern world; and he told me about the Labor
Day rites at the Phalanx, over which his grandfather had
presided. He said that the kind of reporting that I had been
doing for the *New Republic* was the kind of thing he should
like to do himself: he should like to go around the country and
see what was going on—he had friends in the West and the
South whom it would be easy for him to visit; and the only consideration that had prevented him from carrying out this proj-

ect was the fact that, reduced as his income was, he had difficulty in finding a chauffeur who could also do dictation and
typing.

Then another batch of guests came in, and Woollcott resumed his role in that theatrical-journalistic world in which he
was both a "personality" of print and a "star" in an eccentric
part. I wasn't sure that anybody but me could recognize in his
anagrams and croquet, his Dickens and Gilbert and Sullivan,
his idealization of the stars of the early nineteen hundreds such
as the Barrymores and Mrs. Fiske, and his general wide-eyed
excitement of the semi-suburban Jerseyman over all that was
going on in New York—could recognize in this the persistence
of the atmosphere and the habits of an old-fashioned childhood, but seemed quite exotic, a pose, in the modern New
York of the thirties.

When *The Man Who Came to Dinner* was done on the stage,
I was rather depressed to hear that Alec was acting in the West
the character drawn from himself. But when I saw the play in
New York, I ceased to be troubled by this. Kaufman's comedy
was stupid enough; and it was slightly offensive, like most of
his things, because it was an exploitation by an expert contriver
of curtains and exploder of firecracker laughs of an idea that
had better possibilities. But its very comic-supplement mechanics made Woollcott's participation in it a relatively innocent
matter. Kaufman had put on the stage some of Woollcott's
superficial idiosyncrasies without ever even attempting to do
anything with his real personality. The bad side of the Kaufman character was simply a combination of fiendishness and
childishness, while the better side was simply a stage Santa
Claus, straight out of the last act of a George Arliss play. A por-
trayer of the actual Woollcott would have had to show how his
arrogance and venom arose from the vulnerability of an excessively sensitive man rather badly favored by nature and afflicted
by glandular disorders. When Woollcott addressed his friends
as "Repulsive," it was like his receiving me with a hoot at my
increasing weight: he was afraid you were going to find him so.
And a serious portrait of Woollcott would have had to show
the lifelong inspiration for him of the Fourierist background of
the Phalanx.

His interest in communism, so far as I know, did not have

any practical upshot; but a certain queer moral authority which he exerted throughout his career was derived from the idealism that had bankrupted the Phalanx; and what made him seem impossible to editors, to producers whose plays he reviewed and to the arrangers of radio programs, were not entirely his fits of bad temper but also a boldness and an independence, learned in the same school, that made him intolerant of other people's policies when they conflicted with his own judgment, and prevented him from hesitating a moment about throwing up any job, no matter how fraught with prestige, when principle demanded a choice between submission and resignation. The idea that "social betterment" and the "elevating" effects of the arts were the most important things in the world and causes to be served gratuitously was always alive in his mind; and one might be very far from sharing a good many of his enthusiasms and very much dislike his way of expressing them, and yet feel that his lights were not vulgar ones and that Alec had not betrayed them.

He had it, moreover, in common with the older American radicalism that, in the days of totalitarian states and commercial standardization, he did not hesitate to assert himself as a single unique human being: he was not afraid to be Alexander Woollcott; and even when Alexander Woollcott was horrid, this somehow commanded respect. In *The Man Who Came to Dinner*, it made him a kind of folk-hero.

February 6, 1943

The Poetry of Angelica Balabanoff

ANGELICA BALABANOFF is a once well-known Russian Socialist, who has been living of recent years in this country.
The career of Comrade Balabanoff has involved her in political
defeats which have brought her, also, much disillusion in regard to personalities and movements. She played an energetic
and a high-hearted role in the campaigns of the Italian Socialists of the period before the first world war, and was a friend
and confidante of Mussolini in his early pseudo-Socialist phase;
she was a member of the Socialist minority who kept alive the
Zimmerwald peace movement in Europe in the teeth of the
belligerent nations; she joined the Bolsheviks in 1917, returned
to Russia after the Revolution and became the first secretary of
the Comintern. In those early days of the Soviet Union, she
remained on good terms with Lenin, but was unable to reconcile herself to the splintering tactics of the Comintern leaders
and the provocative methods of the Cheka, and was eventually
eliminated in a way that today seems gentle, at the end of 1921,
in the days before critics of the official line were forced to appear at public trials and confess themselves guilty of treason.

On her departure from the Soviet Union, as she was crossing
the sea to Sweden, she found herself ill and depressed; and to
fortify herself against seasickness, in the midst of a storm that
came up, she resorted to reciting to herself and to translating
into other languages some poems that she had learned in her
girlhood. Later, as she tells us in her autobiography *My Life as
a Rebel*, too ill for political activity and "so weakened by work
and undernourishment that I had felt like an old woman at
forty-three," she began to compose poetry of her own "in various languages with the greatest facility. I seemed to be overwhelmed, carried away by a flood of rhythm." She wrote
poems in all the languages she knew: Russian, German, French,
Italian and English. It was her method of recovering from collapse, and it has proved one of the consolations of her years of
disappointment and retirement.

These poems have now been published in a volume which,
though hardly a first-rate work of literature, must be unique as

a literary curiosity and has its place in the revolutionary record. It is also a symptom of the pressure, in our time, of the need for an international language. We have lost medieval Latin and eighteenth-century French, and have not yet arrived at Basic English; and in the meantime we have to do the best we can talking all the languages at once, like Marx and Engels in their correspondence, like Joyce in *Finnegans Wake*, like Eugene Jolas in his polyglot poetry, and like Angelica Balabanoff in these poems. She developed a habit of writing the same poem in each of her five languages, and these pieces are not translations because there is no original: they are quite distinct treatments of the same theme. They are all written in the same kind of meter, very irregular, a little vague. The author is so completely internationalized that the versions in her native Russian do not even seem much different from or better than the others. She has relatively little sense of the metrical differences of the various languages, and it is hard to tell whether or not she even allows for the metrical value of the silent final *e* in French.

Such pieces are better adapted for platform than for private reading. They become unexpectedly impressive when the author herself recites them; and their usefulness as perorations before audiences of different nationalities seems to have given her a special inducement to multiply her polyglot versions. In any case, they constitute a document that has at the moment a peculiar pathos. If anybody has been wondering, in this era of spy-infested police-states, of hideous mechanical warfare and of streamlined political pressure groups—if anybody has been wondering what has become of humanitarianism, of socialist internationalism and of militant intellectual courage—well, here they all are in this book. Defeated and driven underground, in the case of Angelica Balabanoff, by fascism, by Communist chicanery, by nationalistic wars, they have burst out through another channel. It is a relief as well as a surprise to find someone, at the present time, who has never doubted the dignity of the working "masses" and who still wants to educate and lead them rather than to manipulate and drive them, who feels sympathy with their human sufferings instead of contempt for their animal helplessness. And here you have, also, the recent emotions of one who has given her life to the more generous socialist ideals and has not been discouraged in her loyalty. In one of the most touching of her poems Comrade Balabanoff writes:

> *J'ai cherché la vérité*
> *Et je l'ai adorée,*
> *C'est à elle que j'ai immolé*
> *Ce que je suis et ce que j'ai été*
> *Et je meurs oubliée . . .*
> *Courbés sous le joug invisible*
> *De leur misère,*
> *Je les vois tous les jours résignés et paisibles*
> *Gravir leur calvaire . . .*
> *Tandis que mon coeur embrasse*
> *Leur souffrance infinie*
> *Il se serre avec une atroce angoisse*
> *Et ne bat plus . . .*
> *Je meurs saluant la mort,*
> *Comme un voyageur arrivé au port*
> *Après une longue traversée*
> *Qu'il n'a ni voulue, ni aimée . . .*

November 27, 1943

Mr. Joseph E. Davies as a Stylist

I HAVE just been reading *Mission to Moscow*, Mr. Joseph E. Davies' book, after seeing the film of the same title. The picture, I find, coincides with the book in almost no respect. The real Mr. Joseph Davies, for example, is a shrewd corporation lawyer who contributed to the Roosevelt campaign fund and was appropriately rewarded with an ambassadorship. The Davies of the Warner Brothers picture is a plain rugged American business man, played by Mr. Walter Huston rather like a more elderly version of Sinclair Lewis's Dodsworth, who demurs with a touching humility when the President asks him to go to Russia, and protests that he is really not qualified because he has had no diplomatic training. The real Mr. Davies was sent for the perfectly specific purpose of discussing a trade agreement and arranging for the settlement of debts contracted by the Kerensky government. But these objectives do not figure in the film. The Hollywood Mr. Davies is simply entrusted with a mission of reporting on the Soviet Union. The real Mr. Davies was troubled by the tyrannies of the Stalinist police state. "No physical betterment of living standards," he wrote in *Mission to Moscow*, "could possibly compensate for the utter destruction of liberty of thought or speech and the sanctity of the individual . . . The government is a dictatorship not 'of the proletariat,' as professed, but 'over the proletariat.' It is completely dominated by one man." One could quote him in this sense at length.

There is one point, however, in which the film is quite faithful to the real Mr. Davies. When the Davies of Walter Huston is made to attend the Moscow trials, he enunciates the following statement: "Based on twenty years of trial practice, I'd be inclined to believe these men's testimony." The trials themselves, it is true, are represented falsely, and this is not precisely the kind of thing that Mr. Davies was saying about them at the time; but the undependable syntax of the Warner Brothers' Davies is absolutely true to life. I should say, indeed, from reading the book, that the author of *Mission to Moscow* is, so far as my knowledge extends, the greatest master of bad official English since the late President Harding.

The prose style of President Harding has been analyzed by H. L. Mencken in his admirable little paper, *A Short View of Gamalielese*; and this piece, which I have lately been rereading, has stimulated me to try to do some justice to the beauties of Mr. Davies' writing.

Let me begin with one of the cultural notes with which Davies the connoisseur and man of taste diversifies his record of affairs of state, a passage which illustrates brilliantly his skill in producing the effect of surprise:

"For weeks there have been celebrations of the centenary of Pushkin's death all over the country. He is a combination of Byron and Shakespeare for the Russian people. He was a liberal in thought and married to a noblewoman who, it is alleged, was a mistress of the tsar. He was killed in a duel, which, as the story goes, was a frame-up. Both the opera and the ballet were based on Pushkin's works and the music was by the great Tchaikovsky. The opera was *Eugen Onegin*, a romantic story of two young men of position whose friendship was broken up over a misunderstanding and lovers' quarrel which resulted in a duel in which the poet was killed. It was significant of Pushkin's own end and oddly enough was written by him."

The sequence of relative pronouns here in the sentence before the last, each one depending on the one before, is a very fine bit of writing, but it only prepares for the climax. It drags us, by a series of hitches, up an incline like the hump on a roller-coaster, from the top of which we suddenly dip into a dizzying and breath-depriving excitement. What is it that makes the next sentence so startling? Not syntax, for the syntax is normal. Not logic: no mere fallacy is involved. We cannot assign this sleight to any of the familiar categories of rhetorical or logical error. The device is original and daring; it takes us a moment to grasp it; but then we become aware that the trick consists of first explaining that the opera which Mr. Davies calls *Eugen Onegin* (though this is neither the Russian nor the English form of the title) is based on Pushkin's poem; then of indicating a striking parallel between the circumstances of Pushkin's death and the poem; and then of suddenly making the point that, by some

scarcely believable coincidence, the poem was written by Pushkin. But to paraphrase the passage thus is to rob it of all its
thrill. The whole effect depends on the quickness of the shift
in the sense and on the simple phrase *oddly enough*, at once arresting and casual. Only a bad writer of special gifts could have
hit upon and placed this phrase. It is as if a long red carpet
upon which we had been walking, on our way to some ceremony of state, had suddenly been pulled out from under us.

There is, however, one example even bolder of Mr. Davies'
ability to baffle and to dazzle:

> "The peace of Europe, if maintained, is in imminent danger of
> being a peace imposed by the dictators, under conditions where all
> of the smaller countries will speedily rush in to get under the shield of
> the German aegis, and under conditions where, even though there be
> a concert of power, as I have predicted to you two years ago, with
> 'Hitler leading the band.'"

Here the opening is weighty and portentous: a veteran man
of affairs with a large experience of Europe is about to deliver
a considered opinion. The first indication of anything queer
comes with *the shield of the German aegis*; but although this
gives us pause for a moment, we immediately reassure ourselves by concluding that Mr. Davies surely knows that a shield
is an aegis, and has allowed himself the little tautology, in the
exuberance of his enjoyment of his official position, as a mere
rhetorical flourish. But then we come to the *as I have predicted
to you two years ago*. The tense here is incorrect: it should be *as
I predicted to you two years ago*. We conclude that Mr. Davies
does not know this, but that, even though he does not know
it, the instinct of his genius has guided him to hit upon the
perfect deviation which, by adding to the solemnity of the tone
at the same time as to the absurdity of the writing, will lead
the way to the final effect. And what an effect it is! The sentence
never comes to a conclusion. It is a new sort of aposiopesis—
an aposiopesis with a full-stop at the end. Yet the grammatical
impossibility has with wonderful art been half-concealed. The
writer has first given us an adverbial clause beginning with
under conditions where, which completes itself in the logical
way, but then he has gone on to another clause, which begins
in the same way: *and under conditions where*. Since we have

just seen the first one brought off, we are prepared for the fulfilment of the second. But this second clause is never completed. Mr. Davies, by a rare stroke of art, starts another subordinate clause, *even though there be*, etc., and at the end of this clause he stops. On first reading, we fail to grasp it; we go back and read the sentence again. The use of the subjunctive here, *even though there be*, is another of his fine manipulations to give us confidence in the structure of his thought. We find it very hard to believe that a man who can use the subjunctive in this noble traditional way would be capable of leaving his sentence with one end sticking out in the air, like the rope in the Indian rope trick. And yet Mr. Davies *has* left it so, and we can only accept and wonder, just as we can only accept and wonder at his giving the public his word for the authenticity of all the testimony that is supposed to be quoted, in his film, from the records of the Moscow trials and that includes a confession by Tukhachevsky imagined and written by Hollywood; at his flying back from Moscow on his second mission with the advertisement *Mission to Moscow* painted, in English and Russian, in large yellow letters on his plane; and at his watching with gratification, in the company of Stalin and his retinue, while this film was shown in the Kremlin.

Let me finally quote a passage less distinguished by brilliance of language than by the felicity with which it mirrors the qualities of the man himself. Mr. Davies is reporting an interview with a representative of the Soviet Foreign Office, at which the trade agreement and the debts were discussed:

"He stated that they were having difficulty, in connection with guaranteeing $4,000,000 of purchases in the United States. . . . I stated quite frankly, however, that while, personally, I made these admissions to him 'and against interest,' that [*sic*] quite frankly I had absolutely no tolerance for a position that would haggle over an increase of $10,000,000 in purchases (from $30,000,000 to $40,000,000) in view of both the equities and the practicalities of this situation; that in my opinion it was not an evidence of approaching the matter in a broad-minded and appreciative attitude of the position which Secretary Hull had taken so fairly and in such a large-minded way on this particular problem."

The style here, of course, is remarkable, as Mr. Davies' style always is. The superfluous *that* is good. The *broad-minded* and *large-minded* are like the flourish of persuasive hands brushing doubts and inhibitions aside; and in the next sentence but one we already see the spell that is cast by the verbal incantation, taking effect on the Soviet department head:

"Mr. Neymann manifested a very fair-minded attitude in reply and stated in conclusion that he would not be disposed to quarrel with that point of view . . ."

But there glints through in this passage, when the figures are named, the relentless *fortiter in re*—to resort to a kind of ornament much relished by Mr. Davies—which always lurks behind his *suaviter in modo*. Mr. Davies is of Welsh blood, he tells us, and, like a Welshman, he knows how to combine an elevated and shimmering eloquence with a certain subtlety of practical shrewdness. The glint is half lost in the mist; the purpose is half obscured by the shower of flattering words that, meaningless though most of them are, rather soothe us and please us as we read. These words may perhaps have made it easier for Mr. Davies, at the time of his embassy, to further the interests of the United States; but there are moments when the metallic gleam that pierces from time to time the shifting lights of Mr. Davies' language, has the look of an eye fixed intently on opportunities for conspicuous self-dramatization.

Winter, 1944

Thoughts on Being Bibliographed*

THERE has come a sort of break in the literary movement that was beginning to feel its first strength in the years 1912–16, at the time I was in college at Princeton: the movement on which I grew up and with which I afterwards worked. The first prophets of that movement are patriarchs now—classics or pseudo-classics. Of the writers in their late forties or their fifties, some go on rather somniferously bringing out just the same kind of books that they were writing with more energy twenty years ago; and others, who have practised an intenser art and seemed to promise self-renewal, are in a state of suspended animation. Two of the best of our poets of fiction, Sherwood Anderson and F. Scott Fitzgerald, have died prematurely, depriving us of a freshening and an exhilarating influence that had been felt by us as principles of life, and leaving a sad sense of work uncompleted (though Anderson was in his sixties, it was impossible to think of him as aging, and though he had published a score of books, he seemed always still making his way toward some further self-realization). Certain others of our top rank of writers have disconcertingly abandoned their own standards and published work so outrageously awful that it suggests premature senility. Others yet, whom we might have been regarding as men of still-maturing abilities, on the verge of more important things, have turned up suddenly in the role of old masters with the best of their achievement behind them, and are attempting to pass on the torch, with paternal and hieratic gestures, to a war-driven younger generation which has obviously no idea what to do with it.

These "classes" who have come on since the depression—it is a better word here than the vague "generations"—have found themselves involved in very different conditions from the ones into which we emerged at the end of the last war. For us, a variety of elements seemed to contribute to produce an atmosphere that was liberating and stimulating. The shadow of Big Business that had oppressed American culture in our

*Written for the *Princeton University Library Chronicle* of February, 1944, in which a bibliography of my work appeared.

childhood seemed finally to be passing away. Woodrow Wilson, for all his shortcomings, had something of the qualities of the presidents of the earlier years of the Republic: he was a writer and thinker of a kind, and, though most of his reforms were aborted, he did succeed, on the plane of ideas at least, in dissociating the government of the United States from financial and industrial interests, and presided with some moral dignity over the entry of the United States out of its complacent provinciality on to the larger stage of the world. Later, a livid spark seemed to flash from the American labor movement in the direction of the Russian Revolution. And then the period of "prosperity" began, and there was no end of money around, which publishers and editors and foundations could dispose of as well as brokers. The American writer at this moment seemed at last to be getting all the breaks, and it was not always obvious to him that he was in danger of becoming debauched by an atmosphere of fantastic speculation. In the last years of the century before, a "straight" writer like Stephen Crane or Dreiser had found that it demanded all his stubbornness and courage even to get his novels published, and that he then had to be prepared to face public suppression and private slander, while the quieter kind of artist was left simply to die of chill. In that era, it was possible for Theodore Roosevelt to acquire a reputation as a great patron of the national letters by procuring for E. A. Robinson a job in the custom-house. But now in our day it was altogether different. The young man or young woman was scarcely out of college when his first novel was seized on by a publisher who exploited instead of censoring whatever in it was improper or disturbing, and he soon found himself a figure of glamor in the world between the Algonquin and Greenwich Village, at a kind of fancy-dress party of frantic self-advertisement. Even the older and more sober writers who had survived the inhospitable period suffered sometimes from the dazzling Klieg lights and the forcing of immediate profits —as Anderson was persuaded, I feel, to write a spurious best-seller in *Dark Laughter* before his always reliable instincts led him back to his small towns and obscurity. The less mature writers, in that period, often gambled, without quite being aware of it, on values that had been overinflated, like those of the Boom days of the stock market.

In any case, at the end of the twenties, a kind of demoralization set in, and this was followed by a shrinkage of those values, and for the writer the conditions became different again.
There was suddenly very little money around, and the literary
delirium seemed clearing. The sexual taboos of the age before
had been dismissed both from books and from life, and there
was no need to be feverish about them; liquor was legal again,
and the stock market lay gasping its last. The new "classes" of
intellectuals—it was a feature of the post-Boom period that
they tended to think of themselves as "intellectuals" rather than
as "writers"—were in general sober and poor, and they applied
the analysis of Marxism to the scene of wreckage they faced.
This at least offered a discipline for the mind, gave a coherent
picture of history and promised not only employment but
the triumph of the constructive intellect. But then, within the
decade that followed, the young journalists and novelists and
poets who had tried to base their dreams on bedrock, had the
spectacle, not of the advent of "the first truly human culture,"
the ideal of Lenin and Trotsky, but of the rapid domination of
Europe by the state socialism of Hitler and Stalin, with its
strangling of political discussion and its contemptuous exter-
mination of art; and they no longer knew what to think. In
some cases, under the illusion that the bureaucracy that ran
Russia was still Lenin and that they were serving the cause of a
better world by calling themselves Communists in secret, they
fell a pathetically easy prey to the two great enemies of literary
talent in our time: Hollywood and Henry Luce, who reduced
them to a condition where they appeared to have been subjected to druggings and secret operations and converted into
creatures so radically deprived of any kind of personal self-
confidence that they had hardly the moral conviction that
gives a dignity to genuine unhappiness. Those who have not
lent themselves to this fate have for the most part fallen back
on teaching, a profession where they are at least in a position
to keep in touch with the great work of the past instead of degrading the taste of the present. Though we are left now with
very little journalism of the literary and liberal kind that flourished just after the last war, we are witnessing the curious
phenomenon—which would have been quite inconceivable in
my college days—of young men teaching English or French

in the most venerable schools and universities at the same time that they hold radical political opinions and contribute to "advanced" magazines. The youngest classes of all, the ones not yet out of or just out of school, emerge into manhood on the contemporary stage at the moment when the curtain is down and the scenery is being shifted, and find themselves dispatched into the services with no chance to think seriously of literary careers.

It is thus, as I have said, rather difficult for the veteran of letters of the earlier crop who is retiring a little before his time, to find an appropriate young master on whom to bestow the accolade. On their side, the younger people want precisely to thrust him into a throne and have him available as an object of veneration. The literary worker of the twenties who had recently thought of himself as merely—to change the figure—attempting to keep alive a small fire while the cold night was closing down, is surprised and even further disquieted to find himself surrounded by animals, attracted or amazed by the light, some of which want to get into the warmth but others of which are afraid of him and would feel safer if they could eat him. What is wonderful to both these groups is that the man should have fire at all. What is strange is that he should seem to belong to a kind of professional group, now becoming extinct and a legend, in which the practice of letters was a common craft and the belief in its value a common motivation. The journalist of the later era is troubled at the thought of a writer who works up his own notions and signs his own name; and for the literary man in a college, incorporated in that quite different organism, the academic profession, with its quite other hierarchies of value and competitions for status, the literary man of the twenties presents himself as the distant inhabitant of another intellectual world; and he figures as the final installment of the body of material to be studied. The young men of our earlier classes saw in literature a sphere of activity in which they hoped themselves to play a part. You read Shakespeare, Shelley, George Meredith, Dostoevsky, Ibsen, and you wanted, however imperfectly and on however infinitesimal a scale, to learn their trade and have the freedom of their company. I remember Scott Fitzgerald's saying to me, not long after we had got out of college: "I want to be one of the greatest writers who have ever lived, don't you?" I had not myself quite entertained this fantasy because I had been reading Plato and Dante. Scott had been reading Booth Tarkington, Compton Mackenzie, H. G. Wells and Swinburne; but when he later got to better writers, his standards and his achievement went sharply up, and he would always have pitted himself against the best in his own line that he knew. I thought his remark rather foolish at the time, yet it was one of the things that made me respect him; and I am sure that his intoxicated ardor represented a healthy way for a young man of talent to feel. The young men of the later classes have too often seemed inhibited from these impulses. The good fortune of the college faculties in acquiring some of the ablest of them has, I fear, been offset by the curbs thus imposed on the writers themselves. But it had been true from the beginning of many of these men that they were resigned to classify and to analyze: it was the case with the Marxist critics as well as with the teachers who read Eliot. Marxism, as Trotsky said, had produced a new political culture but no distinctive artistic culture. The young intellectuals of the thirties *did* want to join Marx and Lenin in their great field of intellectual historical action; but when the problems of historical action seemed to have been removed in Europe to a less intellectual plane, they could only take sanctuary in learned research. The scholarship of Marxism in some cases shaded easily into the scholarship of the English Department; and the inquest on literary culture from the social-economic point of view was contracted to a simple ambition to get the whole thing under glass. And this is where this bibliography comes in.

I visited Princeton last spring, and one evening, at the house of a professor, I uneasily became aware that this all-absorbing scholarship was after me. I had already been slightly troubled by the efforts of the Princeton Librarian to collect the letters of Mencken and by his project of bringing out a volume of them while the writer was still alive. I still thought of Mencken as a contemporary, whose faculties showed no signs of failing; I still looked forward to reading what he should write. That the librarian should have been able to induce him to accept this semi-posthumous status seemed to me an ominous sign that

the movement was folding back on itself before having finished its work. And now they were creeping up on me, who
was fifteen years younger than Mencken and had arrived at
middle age under the illusion that I had not yet really begun to
write. I had even a chilling impression that the forces of bibliography would prefer me already to be dead, since the record
could then be completed.

I have lent myself, however, to their dubious design under
the persuasion of Arthur Mizener (who of course ought to be
writing his own essays and poems instead of cataloguing
Archibald MacLeish's and mine). My scholarly instincts were
tempted as well as my literary vanity, and I have ended by
scraping up items of nauseating puerilia and insignificant reviews and paragraphs which the Library might never have
found for itself and which might better perhaps have been left
unidentified. Having thus, to this extent, fallen a victim to the
folding-back process myself, I may as well complete my lapse
by playing the patriarch, too, and performing a brief obituary
on my work as it is bibliographed here—a process which will
lead me again to the general questions with which I began.

This list, then, is the record of a journalist, and the only real
interest it can have is that of showing how a journalist works.
When I speak of myself as a journalist, I do not of course mean
that I have always dealt with current events or that I have not
put into my books something more than can be found in my
articles; I mean that I have made my living mainly by writing
in periodicals. There is a serious profession of journalism, and
it involves its own special problems. To write what you are interested in writing and to succeed in getting editors to pay for
it, is a feat that may require pretty close calculation and a good
deal of ingenuity. You have to learn to load solid matter into
notices of ephemeral happenings; you have to develop a resourcefulness at pursuing a line of thought through pieces on
miscellaneous and more or less fortuitous subjects; and you
have to acquire a technique of slipping over on the routine of
editors the deeper independent work which their over-anxious
intentness on the fashions of the month or the week have conditioned them automatically to reject, as the machines that
make motor parts automatically reject outsizes. My principal
heroes among journalists in English have been DeQuincey,

Poe and Shaw, and they have all, in their various manners, shown themselves masters of these arts. Poe in particular—though at the cost of an effort which was one of the pressures that shattered him—succeeded in selling almost all he wrote to the insipid periodicals of his day, studying the forms that were effective with the public, passing off his most anguished visions in the guise of mystery stories, and, by getting the editors, in some cases, to print pieces that had been published before but of which he had prepared new versions, scoring the triumph of thus making them pay him for the gratuitous labor of rewriting demanded by his artistic conscience. The masterpieces excreted like precious stones by the subterranean chemistry of his mind were sprinkled into a rapid stream of news letters and daily reviewing that was itself made to feed his interests and contribute to his higher aims. And Bernard Shaw, when he was doing for the *Saturday Review* the weekly chronicle of the London theaters, succeeded, without ever being dull, in gradually impressing on his readers his artistic and moral principles. My own strategy—to make an anti-climax—has usually been, first to get books for review or reporting assignments to cover on subjects in which I happened to be interested; then, later, to use the scattered articles for writing general studies of these subjects; then, finally, to bring out a book in which groups of these essays were revised and combined. There are usually to be distinguished in the writings listed here at least two or three stages; and it is of course by the books that I want to stand, since the preliminary sketches quite often show my subjects in a different light and in some cases, perhaps, are contradicted by my final conclusions about them. This method of working out in print one's treatment of something one is studying involves a certain amount of extra writing and consequently of energy wasted; but it does have the advantage of allowing one's ideas first to appear in a tentative form, so that they are exposed to correction and criticism. My non-critical and non-reportorial productions I have also to some extent smuggled in, and their forms may have been sometimes affected by the importunate consideration of the usefulness of detachable units of the right size for magazines.

As for the content of all these articles, I see that I was more or less consciously trying to follow a definite tradition. I had

been stimulated at boarding-school and college by the examples of Shaw and Mencken, and, to a lesser extent, by that of
James Huneker. All these men were exciting in their day
because they had news to bring and unconventional causes to
serve. In Huneker's case, it was simply a matter of communi-
cating to the United States, then backward to what seems an
incredible degree in its assimilation of cultural movements
abroad, the musical and literary happenings of the preceding
half-century in Europe. But Mencken and Shaw were the
prophets of new eras in their national cultures to which they
were also important contributors; and, though their conceptions of their social aims differed, both were carrying on that
work of "Enlightenment" of which the flame had been so
fanned by Voltaire. I suppose that I, too, wanted to prove myself a "soldier in the Liberation War of humanity" and to speak
for the "younger generation" who were "knocking at the
door": such phrases were often in my head. But for American
writing, when I came upon the scene, the battle had mostly
been won: I was myself a beneficiary of the work that had been
done by Mencken and others. There remained for the young
journalist, however, two roads that had still to be broken: the
road to the understanding of the most recent literary events in
the larger international world—Joyce, Eliot, Proust, etc.—
which were already out of the range of readers the limits of
whose taste had been fixed by *Egoists* and *The Quintessence of
Ibsenism*; and to bring home to the "bourgeois" intellectual
world the most recent developments of Marxism in connection with the Russian Revolution. I was of course far from
being either alone or first in popularizing either of these subjects; but they were the matters with which I was mostly concerned, and I felt that what I was doing had some logical
connection with the work of the older men I admired.

And now what is the next logical step? I am today past the
age for this kind of activity; but I have been wondering in the
last few years, and especially going back over my work in this
list, what the next phase of literature will be and what is to
become of the "Enlightenment." Well, in the literary field, it
does look as if the movements for which people have been
fighting had, if not actually run their courses, at least com-

pleted certain phases of their development. Two of the tendencies that have stimulated most controversy, both *vis-à-vis*
traditional methods and in conflict with one another: naturalism and symbolism—culminated and fused in the work of
Joyce at the time that he wrote *Ulysses*. And there was also embodied in *Ulysses* an exploitation or a parallel exploration of the
Freudian tendencies in psychology which had themselves had
to fight for their lives and which could still seem sensational in
fiction. *The Waste Land* came out the same year as *Ulysses*:
1922; and the result was one of those blood-heating crises that
have been occurring periodically in literature since the first
night of *Hernani* in 1830: howls of denunciation, defiant ap-
plause and defense, final vindication and triumph. But when
the successor to *Ulysses* arrived, even more daring and equally
great though it was, its reception was completely different; and
the difference is significant and perhaps marks the drop of a
trajectory in modern literature. Such occasions had never been
deprived in the past either of evening clothes to hiss from the
boxes or of young men to wear the red vest of Gautier; but the
appearance of *Finnegans Wake*, instead of detonating a battle,
was received with incurious calm. No exalted young journalists
defended it; no old fogeys attacked it with fury. The reviewers
spoke respectfully of Joyce while deprecating an aberration,
and detoured around the book without giving it the smallest
attention; and among the older writers who had been interested in *Ulysses*, now comfortably ensconced in their niches, a
few read it, but most ignored. The only group of intellectuals
that gave a serious hearing to this work turned out, by a curious reversal of the traditional situation, to be made up, precisely, of members of the profession which had become
proverbial as the enemies of anything new. *Finnegans Wake*
went straight from the hands of Joyce into the hands of the
college professors, and is today not a literary issue but a subject of academic research. Nor is this, in my opinion, entirely
due to the complex erudition of the book itself or to the ab-
struseness of some of its meanings: *Finnegans Wake* gives a
scope to Joyce's *lyric* gift in a way that *Ulysses* did not, and it
makes a new departure in the merging of the techniques of the
novel and verse that ought to be of special interest to poets
and fiction-writers both. The fate of *Finnegans Wake* is partly,

I believe, the result of the process which I have mentioned above: the inevitable gravitation toward teaching jobs of able young literary men who can find no decent work outside them. In the twenties, Mr. Harry Levin, who has written so brilliantly on Joyce, would undoubtedly have been editing the *Dial* and going to bat for *Ulysses* in its pages: today he teaches English at Harvard, while an old-red-waistcoat-wearer like me who made a move to get the garment out of moth-balls at the time *Finnegans Wake* was published, is being treated to a quiet bibliography under the auspices of the Princeton Library, where, as I remember, in 1912, Ernest Dowson and Oscar Wilde were the latest sensational writers who had got in past the stained-glass windows.

As for the Marxist or social-economic branch of the naturalistic school—John Dos Passos and André Malraux—it has definitely passed into eclipse, either perplexed or suppressed by the war. The reaction against all forms of naturalism in the direction of universalizing mythologies which had already been a vital element in Yeats and Eliot and Joyce and Mann, and which has lately taken the form of a cult for the psychological fantasies of Kafka, natural and useful though this shift may be, hardly constitutes, as some of its partisans insist, a great renovating subversive movement for which its champions must still contend. An attempt to get back to the pure fairy-tale would certainly be retrograde if it ever became formidable; and in the meantime, what, from the artistic point of view, have Kafka and his emulators done—though they reflect a different moral atmosphere—that had not already been done in the nightmares of Gogol and Melville and Poe?

In the case of political journalism, something similar has taken place. The exponents of the various traditions of radical and liberal writing have mostly been stunned or flattened out by Hitler's bombs and tanks. The socialists are now for the most part simply patriots, as they inevitably become in time of war; the Communists are Russian nationalists who would not recognize a thought of Lenin's if they happened by some mistake to see one; the liberal weeklies are not merely dull shades of the luminous spirits they once were, but false phantoms whose non-incandescence is partly due to an alien mixture of the gases of propaganda injected by the Stalinists and the

British. All this press of the Left had been losing its best talent, through its own mediocrity and timidity, to the Curtis and Luce organizations. But the *Saturday Evening Post*, our old enemy, seems itself to have passed into a decline, and to have abandoned the talent-wrecking field to *Fortune* and *Time* and *Life*, whose success during the last fifteen years has been one of the main events of our journalism. The method of summarizing the news which has been characteristic of these magazines has had of course its considerable value. It is a logical result of the need to survey and to articulate the happenings which wireless and airplane can bring us so much quicker and in so much greater abundance than was possible in the past. The kind of reports that you find in *Time*, factual, lucid and terse, give you something that you cannot get from the newspapers or the liberal weeklies; and they compensate by compactness and relative perspective for the shredding and dilution of the radio. But the competence of presentation tends to mask the ineptitude and the cynicism of the mentality behind the report; and the effect on the public consciousness may be almost as demoralizing in its more noncommittal way as the tirades of the old Yellow Press. For you cannot have a presentation of facts without implying also an attitude; and the attitude of the Luce publications has been infectious though it is mainly negative. The occasional statements of policy signed by Mr. Luce and others which appear in these magazines are on the level of Sixth Form orations or themes: they confirm the impression one gets from the rest of a complete absence of serious interpretation on the part of the editorial director; and the various points of view of the men who put *Time* together, appear to have been mashed down and to figure in what they print only as blurred streaks of coloration that blot the machine-finished surface. Their picture of the world gives us sometimes simply the effect of schoolboy mentalities in a position to avail themselves of a gigantic research equipment; but it is almost always tinged with a peculiar kind of jeering rancor. There is a tendency to exhibit the persons whose activities are chronicled, not as more or less able or noble or amusing or intelligent human beings, who have various ways of being right or wrong, but—because they are presented by writers who are allowed no points of view themselves—as manikins, sometimes cocky, sometimes busy, sometimes zealous, sometimes silly, sometimes gruesome, but in most cases quite infra-human, who make speeches before guinea-pig parliaments, issue commands and move armies of beetles back and forth on bas-relief battle-maps, indulge themselves maniacally in queer little games of sport, science, art, beer-bottle-top collecting or what-not, squeak absurd little boasts and complaints, and pop up their absurd little faces in front of the lenses of the Luce photographers—adding up to a general impression that the pursuits, past and present, of the human race are rather an absurd little scandal about which you might find out some even nastier details if you met the editors of *Time* over cocktails. This habit of mind must have been prompted in the beginning by a natural reaction from the habit of the period just before, when Charley Schwab, Charley Mitchell and Herbert Hoover had all been celebrated as great public figures; but it has turned into purely gratuitous caricature—that is, caricature without a purpose. The journalism of the age of Voltaire was a journalism that was mainly purpose with a selection of relevant facts, and its inadequacies have often been noted; but a journalism which aims merely at facts, with no political or moral intent, ends by dispensing with even the conviction that the human race ought to go on, and so cannot help making it hateful. Who would drive a plane or man a ship or write a sentence or perform an experiment, or even build a factory or organize a business, to perpetuate the race shown in *Time*? It is the part of an educated man—and the employees of Henry Luce are far from the old-fashioned illiterate reporters—to try to give life some value and point; but these papers which were started on the assumption, to quote an early statement of Luce's "that most people are not well-informed, and that something ought to be done," have ended by having nothing to tell them that appears to be worth the telling.

In all this, it is very hard to know whether tendencies are coming or going, whether movements are running down or merely being interrupted. But certainly, as I said at the beginning, a definite break has occurred. It is the moment, perhaps, failing anything better, for an innocent bibliography. Tomorrow the cessation of the war will be turning loose again those forces that are in conflict within all our nations, and setting free, with the end of the slaughter, the creative instincts again. We must hope that the men who will come out of the services will do again as they did in 1919: both demand and provide better work. But, in the meantime, in spite of bibliographies and their effect of well-ordered finality, we must apply ourselves to bridging a gap; and the risks of the civilian writer which he is bound to accept in war-time are poor remuneration or complete lack of market, public disapproval, self-doubt.

1943

Through the Embassy Window:
Harold Nicolson

The Desire to Please is the second installment of Harold Nicolson's memoirs of his family and his childhood, of which the first installment was the volume called *Helen's Tower.* The general title *In Search of the Past* evidently echoes Proust; but the purpose of Mr. Nicolson's own chronicle seems a little vague.

Mr. Nicolson's ancestry is varied and distinguished: it has included a viceroy of India, a celebrated Irish patriot and a veteran diplomat, his father. His childhood, as he tells us in this book, was spent mostly out of England in the embassies. From Persia, where he was born, his father, he says, "went to Constantinople; from Constantinople to Budapest; from Hungary to Sofia; from Bulgaria to Morocco; from Morocco to Madrid and from Madrid to Russia"; and the son in his earlier years continued the diplomatic tradition: he was present at the Peace Conference, in the British delegation, and he accompanied Lord Curzon to Locarno. His experience has thus been unusual, and one would expect of him a story more interesting than these volumes and his studies in diplomacy have yet turned out to be. He is often engaging and sometimes brilliant—he has a genuine literary gift; and it is only after we have been reading him a little that we begin to feel his limitations.

There is a passage in the present volume which is significant in this connection. Harold Nicolson tells us how wistfully he longed in his childhood for a permanent home; how much he "wanted to be localized and concentrated." But he had never any home except the Embassy, always in a new country, but always the same official world. And this is a part of the explanation both of the unsatisfactoriness of his writing and of the fact that we should find this unsatisfactoriness surprising. We were expecting from so cosmopolitan a figure, who has read such a variety of books and met so many famous people, something a little more exciting. We did not realize that throughout his travels he has only resided in one country: the British Foreign Office; and that he has approached the prime ministers and kings as members of the special caste to which he himself belongs: the caste of professional officials. If he is not able to make their activity ever seem quite real, it is partly because he has never been in contact with any other kind of life, and so has no real means of judging them. When you set out to read, say, his account of the Peace Conference or his recent article on Boris of Bulgaria, you may be prepared to be taken behind the scenes; but what you find are merely pictures of persons and places which, neat and bright though they are, leave you with the conviction that, whatever was happening, Harold Nicolson did not know much about it. The great social groups and movements of which the pressures are felt and reflected in the embassies, the parliaments, the palaces, seem to exist for him only remotely: they are merely the armies and mobs—"mob" is a favorite word of his for any kind of popular demonstration —that make the background of dim figures in his picture book. And this picture book, for all the cleverness which the author has brought to his drawings, tells in general a school-boy story in which England is always St. George. Mr. Nicolson has been quite uncontaminated by the more cynical aspects of foreign policy. He is still the good little governing-class boy who accepts the version of things supplied by his English governess. This governess is a feature of all the books in which he writes of his childhood experience, and though she is treated with affectionate humor, her influence seems to pervade them. Harold Nicolson gives us the impression of standing, well-brushed and well-bred, a credit to this admirable woman's care, looking out through the Embassy window at the streets of strange non-English cities which he knows that he mustn't explore.

Not that the life beyond the window doesn't interest him. He has a lively enthusiasm for poetry, and he used in his younger days to like to write on literary subjects. Some of his books about poets were excellent—but here, too, the glass intervened. He could never really drop the idea that literary people were freaks and essentially disreputable characters. There was some merit in his opinion that the failure of Verlaine —Nicolson is a real connoisseur of verse—to achieve the highest intensity of poetry was due to the moral instability of the poet; but it was priggish to be shocked by Verlaine, as Nicolson obviously was, and to dismiss him with a sharp tone of reprimand; and it was priggish to be so prim about the harmless enough vices of Swinburne. As for his book on the last phase of Byron, readable and vivid though it is, admirable though it is in its circumstantial tracing of the events of the expedition to Greece, it is made irritating by a tone of irony, evidently caught over from Strachey—a tone which implies with Strachey a definite line of criticism but in the prissy and invidious form in which it is applied by Nicolson seems rarely to have any point. The biographer must have had some real sympathy with Byron to write this book on his last desperate days; he seems in fact to feel a kind of fascination with the more scandalous type of poets; but when he comes to look into their histories, he is forced in a reflex action to detach himself socially from their company by a quiet but well-placed accent of amusement, disapproval, disdain.

This new book, which deals with the adventures of Nicolson's ancestor Hamilton Rowan, has the same kind of faults as the Byron, but is a great deal worse in this way. It is as if the anxieties of the war and perhaps his recent term in Parliament had stimulated Nicolson's sense of his official responsibility at the expense of his literary intelligence. It may be noted in passing as a characteristic touch that, in explaining his interest in Rowan and asserting that he himself, if he had happened to grow up in Ireland, might have found himself "at variance with kith and class and creed," he should remark that he might "have been lost in the mists of the Abbey Theatre"—an easy and inaccurate banality of which I believe he would have been ashamed in the days when he was writing about Verlaine. But the whole book shows a worried solicitude to maintain a correct official attitude which, given the character of the hero and the fact that he was the biographer's great-great-grandfather, becomes comic and seems almost perverse.

Hamilton Rowan was an eighteenth-century gentleman of property of the "Protestant Ascendancy" in Ireland, who, stimulated by the French and the American Revolutions, took the side of the Irish against the English, got sent to jail for circulating a pamphlet that advocated suffrage for Catholics, incurred a more serious penalty by associating himself with a project of Wolfe Tone's for a French invasion of Ireland, succeeded in escaping to France, was in Paris at the fall of Robespierre and became disgusted with the Terror, came to America and earned a poor living as hired man, printmaker and brewer, and ultimately asked for a pardon, obtained it and returned to his property amidst a tumultuous welcome by the Irish. Hamilton Rowan, on his descendant's own showing, seems rather a noble fellow. Certainly he behaved with imprudence in allowing Wolfe Tone's proposal to be circulated in his own handwriting; but such mistakes seem easily attributable to a certain natural recklessness and arrogance often displayed by eighteenth-century gentlemen. It would not seem to deserve the wringing of hands, the anguished cry of "Why? Why? Why?" with which the great-great-grandson of Rowan is continually interrupting his story in perplexity over his ancestor's wrongheadedness. Mr. Nicolson is even unable to tell of one of those eighteenth-century carouses at which Liberty and Equality were toasted, without shrugging his shoulders to indicate that that is not the sort of thing that is countenanced by the Foreign Office; and he dwells with what sounds like an unpleasant satisfaction on the poverty and humiliation into which his ancestor's mad courses brought him. He apologizes for his story in advance by speaking of Hamilton Rowan's "really deplorable career"; but when we have read this story, we see that it can be described as deplorable only on the assumption— which Hamilton Rowan certainly did not share—that the most praiseworthy object in life is always to remain clean and correct, and never to get into trouble. There is an element of coy and sly humor in this attitude of Mr. Nicolson's; but it is a humor that almost always works in the conventional direction, and it is plain that the heroic romanticism and the humanitarian enthusiasm of that age simply make Mr. Nicolson nervous.

On the subject of the Irish he surpasses himself: "It seems strange to me that more than a century after his death Hamilton Rowan should still be classed among the heroes. I quite see that the Irish memory is different in quality from the English memory. . . . Much as I like the Irish, deeply though I wish them well, I regret that the proportions between their memory and their forgetfulness, between their forgiveness and their rancor, should be so disarranged." These are phrases appropriate for a public speech; in their context here they only suggest that Mr. Nicolson is rather frightened by his whole Irish family connection.

I don't, however, want to leave the subject without offsetting my account of this biography by mentioning what seems to me the one very good book that Harold Nicolson has written. *Some People* is a series of stories about types that Mr. Nicolson has known: a French snob, a Ronald Firbank aesthete, a phony expert on foreign affairs, an English lord and his valet. It is at once his most candidly personal and his most irresponsible production, and it succeeds in touching off as none of his other books does the memories of his diplomatic experience into something like artistic ignition—because he has here turned *in* on this experience instead of trying to see the rest of the world *through* it. The fantastic characters of *Some People* are as funny and as well observed as anything in Max Beerbohm or Evelyn Waugh, and Mr. Nicolson has managed to present himself as a kind of comic character, too, in a way that illustrates much more delicately than I have been able to do his relationship both to politics and to literature. I am not much of a rereader of fiction, but I can never look into *Some People* without reading several of the stories through, and I have been opening every new book of Nicolson's with an eagerness which, though gradually diminished, is still always stirred by the hope of finding something else as good.

January 1, 1944

Kay Boyle and
The Saturday Evening Post

I PICKED UP Kay Boyle's *Avalanche* in the hope of finding a novel worth reading, and have been somewhat taken aback to get nothing but a piece of pure rubbish.

Aside from a few literary devices such as italicized "interior monologues," *Avalanche* is simply the usual kind of thing that is turned out by women writers for the popular magazines. A blond heroine, half French, half American, who fled France when the Germans came, returns to work with a relief committee and becomes involved in the underground movement in the mountains of the Haute-Savoie. The villain is a Gestapo agent masquerading as a Swiss clock manufacturer, who sneers at the French so openly and makes himself in general so provocatively unpleasant that the reader is at first led to think that this character must himself be a French patriot masquerading as a German spy, and is later impelled to wonder how he has ever held down his job. The hero, Bastineau, leader of the mountain resistance, combines the glamor of Charles Boyer with the locomotive proficiency of Superman. Adored by his followers almost as a god, he constantly outwits the Germans, performs prodigies of fidelity to the Girl and, like the Frankenstein monster of the movies, is always pretending to be killed and then sensationally coming to life. The Girl herself keeps the story going only by exercising so stubborn a stupidity that it becomes difficult to understand how any underground movement could have trusted her: she is thoroughly mystified by the snarling Gestapo agent and is puzzled at finding that her old friends of the village avoid her when they see her in his company; and it takes her the greater part of the book to grasp the facts of the secret opposition, which one would think must have been perfectly plain to her from the things she has seen and heard even if she had not just come from America and so shared with the reader the advantage of having read the American papers.

The climax is terrific: just at the instant when the Gestapo man is about to shoot the Girl, the hero leaps down through a large open chimney "easily, gracefully as a jumper on skis . . . his arms spread like a diver's, his eyes and teeth pure white and savage in his face," singing "*L'Infant'rie Alpin-e, voilà mes amours!*" "And then he was on de Vaudois' head and shoulders, his knees locked around him, the heel of one boot cracking the right wrist so that the shot went wild across the kitchen." It is the work of a moment to dispatch the Nazi and to ask the Girl to be his wife. " 'Yes,' said Fenton, 'yes,' and her eyes moved on his face before her, touching the silky brows, and the hair springing back from his forehead; seeing the clear white teeth, and the deep sweet lines of the sun and the weather at his eyes and mouth. 'Yes, Bastineau. Yes, Bastineau,' she said." "*Monsieur le curé*" has just popped in, and he marries them that very night.

I have heard Miss Boyle praised as a stylist, but, though there are in *Avalanche* a few fine images and gray and white mountain landscapes, I cannot see how a writer with a really sound sense of style could have produced this book even as a potboiler. One recognizes the idiom of a feminized Hemingway: "There was one winter when the blizzard got us part way up . . . If you looked in the direction the wind was coming from, your breath stopped suddenly as if someone took you by the throat"; and a sobbing Irish lilt: "He touches my hand as if it were a child's hand, and his promise of love is given to a woman. To him it is nothing to walk into a mountain refuge and find me, and to me it's the three years without him that have stopped crying their hearts out at last." And, for the rest, there are several tricks that Miss Boyle overworks with exasperating effect. She is always giving possessives to inanimate objects, so that you have "the weather's break," "the balcony's rail," and "the mitten's pattern" all within a space of sixteen lines; and there is a formula that recurs so often in the passages of conversation that one can almost say the whole book is built of it: " 'They're fiercer, more relentless,' he said, and the sound of threat was there:" " 'And there is de Vaudois,' he said, and he put the mittens on;" " 'You're French, partly French,' he said, and his eyes were asking the promise of her"—these are quoted from a space of less than two pages. Sometimes you get both these devices together: "'What is the story of that?' said de Vaudois, and his eye went suddenly shrewd beneath his hat's crisp brim."

Miss Boyle has indulged herself, also, in the bad romantic habit of making foreign conversation sound translated. It is perhaps a part of her Hemingway heritage. A Spaniard, Arturo Barea, has demonstrated in an essay in *Horizon*, that the dialogue of *For Whom the Bell Tolls* is not really a translation of Spanish but a language of Hemingway's own. So Miss Boyle— to take her at her simplest, where there is no question of special eloquence involved—will have her characters make speeches like the following:

> "And Bastineau? What of Bastineau?"
> "One by one they've gone from us."
> "A friend come back from America is here."

Now this is certainly not colloquial English; but when you try putting it into French, you have:

> "*Et Bastineau? Quoi de Bastineau?*"
> "*L'un après l'autre, ils s'en sont allés de nous.*"
> "*Une amie revenue de l'Amérique est ici.*"

—which is even more impossible as French. My best guess at the kind of thing you would get if the last of these thoughts, for example, were naturally expressed in French would be "*Voici une amie revenue de l'Amérique*"—of which the natural English would be "Here's a friend of ours who's come back from America." But Miss Boyle needs the false solemnity, the slow-motion portentousness, that this Never Never language gives in order to carry off her story.

It is easy to be funny about *Avalanche* but it has its depressing aspect. I have not read much else by Kay Boyle since her very early work, so that I do not have a definite opinion about the value of her writing as a whole; but I know from those early stories, written when she lived abroad and printed in the "little" magazines of the American *émigrés*, that she was at least making an effort at that time to produce something of serious interest. Today she is back at home, and *Avalanche* was written for the *Saturday Evening Post*. I did not see it there, but I have been haunted since I read it by a vision of *Saturday Evening Post* illustrations, in which the ideal physical types of the skin-lotion and shaving-soap ads are seen posing on snowy slopes. Nor do I doubt that this novel was constructed with an eye to the demands of Hollywood, that intractable magnetic mountain which has been twisting our fiction askew and on which so many writers have been flattened. I have been thinking, since I finished this book, about the alloy of dubious metal that already existed in *For Whom the Bell Tolls* and was naturally drawn to the Hollywood magnet, and of how Hemingway's novel of the Spanish war came back in its pancake form as one of the stupidest films on record. I have been thinking, also, of *The Moon Is Down*, and of Steinbeck's remarkable innovation: a novel contrived in such a way that it was convertible almost without change into a play for the stage or a movie—perhaps into a comic strip. And I think about the days of *This Quarter* and *Transition*, full of nonsense though those magazines were, with a wistfulness it would have surprised me in that period to be told I should ever feel.

January 15, 1944

The Life and Times of
John Barrymore

I F you merely take a glance at *Good Night, Sweet Prince*, Gene
Fowler's biography of John Barrymore, you may suppose
that it is a cheap journalistic job.

Certainly the style couldn't be more journalistic in a flowery
old-fashioned way, which has sometimes a tinge of O. Henry,
sometimes a tinge of Woollcott ("A block to the east of the
Arch Street Theatre lay the wise bones of Benjamin Franklin").
For Mr. Fowler, Broadway is inevitably "this street of fickle
lustre," a distiller a "maker of spirituous delicacies," and Shakespeare "Stratford's first gentleman"; cigarette-smoking is
"bronchial debauchery," hair on the chest "torsorial upholstery" and the men's washroom "ammoniac grottos" equipped
with "cracked and homely porcelains." When he wants to convey the idea that some white mice were multiplying rapidly, he
says that the "snowy rodents were fruitful"; and when Barrymore sets out to play Hamlet, or take on "the Danish assignment," Mr. Fowler says that he "announced . . . his decision
to draw on the black tights of the classic Scandinavian." His
notion of syntax and the meaning of words is also of the
vaguest. When it is a question of anybody's conduct, the word
"behaviorism" is always summoned: "After the passing of his
grandmother he entered upon a bouncing behaviorism"; and
when, in reporting an interview with Alexander Woollcott, he
seems to feel that he should make an effort to have this cele-
brator of Hamilton College talk like an educated man, he produces the following tribute to grammar: "'And when you
write of him, as I fear you shall, for heaven's sake remember
one thing.'"

The language of Mr. Fowler has no structure and no har-
monics. It is something that is exhaled like breath or exuded
like perspiration. And yet the fuzzy raffish style of this book
has its special appropriateness to the subject: it is a literary
equivalent for the atmosphere in which the events take place.
What we get here is the folklore of the Barrymores; and, as

you read, you can smell the aroma of the Manhattans and highballs and cigars of the old Hoffman House and the Knickerbocker bar, you seem to drift on the long late conversations at the Players club and the Lambs on which the Barrymore mythology was nourished. John Barrymore did in a sense live his legend; but you cannot really feel its validity unless you see it presented in terms of the smoking room, the city room, the green room, of the mirrors behind the bar and the shaded lamps at the club, all elements of urban life themselves rather remotely associated with the realities of common day. In this world of nocturnal fancy, Jack Barrymore was a fabulous character: a great drinker, a great man with women, a great comedian of public and private life, and finally a great maker of money. Gene Fowler, with his word-slinging jargon and his husky-throated sports-writer humor, is the right person to tell this story which might otherwise never have been told; and his book contains a most entertaining collection of funny theatrical anecdotes, phantasmagoric binges and what would in the days of the Knickerbocker bar have been described as "gorgeous yarns."

Yet this *Life and Times of John Barrymore* is absorbing for another reason, too; and the author has put into it something more than the favorite tales of a raconteur. The truth is that you get from this chronicle a much more convincing picture of its subject than you usually expect to find in either a fan or an official biography. Gene Fowler shows both insight into Barrymore and delicacy in handling his difficult case; and the piecing together of the record becomes fascinating because it is directed by a definite conception, always sympathetic but also quite realistic, of the man inside the reputation.

To begin with: the evidence of this book establishes indubitably a fact which the more fanatical admirers of the Barrymores are sometimes rather loath to admit. The generation of the Barrymore family that included John, Lionel and Ethel never really wanted to be on the stage. Their father, an Englishman named Blythe, who had assumed the stage name of Barrymore, was the son of an officer in India and had been educated at Harrow and Oxford. It was expected that he would read for the law, and his taking to the stage was a kind of a lapse, which, in spite of the long theater tradition on the mother's side of the family, the children seemed anxious to retrieve. "We became actors," says Ethel Barrymore, as reported by Mr. Fowler, "not because we wanted to go on the stage but because it was the thing we could do best." And Lionel corroborates this: "Neither Jack nor myself preferred the stage. We both wanted to become painters. Yet it seemed that we had to be actors. It was as if our father had been a street-cleaner and had dropped dead near a fire hydrant, and we went to pick up his shovel and broom to continue his work. Perhaps we didn't clean the corners well, but we did a better job at it than someone who never had been in the environment. What other thing could we have done better?"

This covers the case precisely. The Barrymores have occupied a position which has been at least as much social as theatrical. Seeing them on the stage was not always so very much different from meeting them in private life; and there was a tendency on the part of the public to imagine that the events of the play were happening to John or Ethel. They were none of them, even John, great actors, because they never had the actor's vocation. You see it very clearly if you compare them with their uncle John Drew, who, glass of fashion and mold of form though he was, took the theater with professional seriousness, and even in his later years, at his blindest and most arthritic, kept his cast and himself up to scratch with the rigor of an old general at maneuvers; whereas, as Gene Fowler tells us, the father of the three, Maurice Barrymore, used to neglect to memorize his lines and "contrive amazing excursions from the text," and John carried this cavalier treatment of the conventions and discipline of the stage to what must have been unprecedented lengths—breaking up his fellow-actors with elaborate and cruel jokes, stepping out of his character to denounce the audience and, in general, doing everything possible to sabotage an occupation he scorned.

The artistic deficiencies of the Barrymores were thrown into striking relief at the time—the season of 1922–23—when the Moscow Art Theater first visited America. That was also the season when the Barrymores were attempting their most ambitious roles: that fall John had opened in *Hamlet* and Ethel in Hauptmann's *Rose Bernd*; but when one compared these productions with the Russian ones, they had almost the aspect of private theatricals. Kachalov, of the Moscow Art Theater, was by way of being the Russian John Barrymore—that is, he was a good-looking and popular actor with a romantic reputation, who was supposed to do a good deal of drinking. But, if you went to see Kachalov in a play, you would find the dilapidated baron of Gorky's *The Lower Depths* or the elderly and bourgeois Stockmann of Ibsen's *An Enemy of the People*. If you had failed to look at the program, you might sit through a couple of acts before you recognized Kachalov at all: you had absolutely had the illusion that you were watching the creation of the dramatist. When you went to see John Barrymore in *Hamlet*, however, what you found was John Barrymore in *Hamlet*. His voice was better-trained than it had been and he had cultivated a new kind of vehemence; but he was obviously the same engaging fellow who had been playing around with the stage for years; and as the run of the show continued—one story Mr. Fowler does not tell—he would kid with the audiences at Shakespeare's expense by substituting, in the play scene, "Hollywood, Hollywood!" for "Wormwood, wormwood!" So Ethel, as Rose Bernd, a part in which a Russian actress would completely have incorporated herself, made a conscientious effort for a scene or two to impersonate a country girl who had been gotten with child by her master, then would drop the whole thing and smile graciously and become her delightful self.

Yet John Barrymore was a gifted person, and he counted for something in the life of his time. The extracts from his letters and diaries which Mr. Fowler has included in this book show his wit and his sensibility, and a refractory integrity of character which has nothing in common with the temperament of the ordinary popular actor. He belonged to an American tradition of the high-strung man of talent who makes hay of the American standards—runs amuck, takes to dissipation and is broken down young. But poor Barrymore never realized himself in either his painting or his acting as, say, Poe or Stephen Crane did in his writing, and he never found the right thing to do or be. It was only when some aspect of a character he was playing coincided with some aspect of his own personality that he was really creative on the stage: the scenes in which Hamlet takes his bitterness out in baiting the various figures of the Court, the opening of *Richard III*—one of the moments he came closest to greatness—in which the young Richard, full of envy as he sees how his deformities must cripple his life, vows himself, with a young man's spirit that moves us for the moment with its passion, to revenge upon normal humanity. Though I saw John Barrymore, through the years, in most of his important parts, from *The Fortune Hunter* to *Hamlet*, I can remember, leaving aside the light comedies, only one in which he seemed indistinguishable from the character he was impersonating: the bank clerk in Galsworthy's *Justice*, who commits a forgery out of love for a woman and is sentenced to solitary confinement. This came at the beginning of the period when Barrymore's friends were trying to persuade him to take his dramatic abilities more seriously, and it gave him a chance, I suppose, to identify with the character he was playing all that shrinking and uncertainty of his nature which, according to Mr. Fowler, made a lady who knew him well call him "a confused child."

He tried hard to find some role in life itself that he could count on and that would express him; and this biography is the story of his successive attempts. A disturbing and saddening story; for whenever, through exercise of will, he had achieved a high point of intensity by imposing on life his personal dream, the role always failed and let him down with a crash. First there was the effort of hard training that raised him to his Shakespearean roles, which he tired of and discarded so soon; then there was the quite different effort, inspired, when he was forty-three, by his idealization of Dolores Costello, to find at last some high and enduring ground as lover, husband, father. John Barrymore's solitary voyage on his yacht, as recorded by himself in his diary, when he is exalted by his vision of his love, yet living with his own thoughts and obviously happier alone with them than he is ever likely to be in his relations with other people, makes an attractive episode in his story but contains its tragic implications. The dream went to pieces when he tried to embrace it, as he had evidently the premonition it would do, and he had lost forever now the fine dignity of his independence, which had been partly sustained by the dream. It is quite plain from Mr. Fowler's account that the débâcle of John

Barrymore's final years was almost as much the result of an actual loss of his faculties as the complete mental breakdown which his father had had at about the same age; yet in this hideous self-parody and self-ruination there was also perhaps a kind of arrogance, a paroxysm of contempt for the stage, and a last desperate effort in an inverted form to achieve that extreme intensity that enables one to realize oneself.

January 22, 1944

"Never Apologize, Never Explain":
The Art of Evelyn Waugh

I DID NOT read Evelyn Waugh at the time when he was first attracting attention. I never got started on him till a year ago, when I picked up a reprint of *Decline and Fall* and was so much exhilarated by it that I went on to *Vile Bodies*, and then read his four other novels in the order in which they were written. I may thus lay claim to a fresh impression of Evelyn Waugh's work—an impression, I believe, not much influenced by any journalistic interest that work may have had, appearing at the end of the twenties, as a picture of the delirium of that period. Nothing can taste staler today than some of the stuff that seemed to mean something then, that gave us twinges of bitter romance and thrills of vertiginous drinking. But *The Great Gatsby* and *The Sun Also Rises* hold up; and my feeling is that these novels of Waugh's are the only things written in England that are comparable to Fitzgerald and Hemingway. They are not so poetic; they are perhaps less intense; they belong to a more classical tradition. But I think that they are likely to last and that Waugh, in fact, is likely to figure as the only first-rate comic genius that has appeared in English since Bernard Shaw.

The great thing about *Decline and Fall*, written when the author was twenty-five, was its breath-taking spontaneity. The latter part of the book leans a little too heavily on Voltaire's *Candide*, but the early part, that hair-raising harlequinade in a brazenly bad boys' school, has an audacity that is altogether Waugh's and that was to prove the great principle of his art. This audacity is personified here by an hilarious character called Grimes. Though a schoolmaster and a "public-school man," Grimes is frankly and even exultantly everything that is most contrary to the British code of good behavior: he is a bounder, a rotter, a scoundrel, but he never has a moment of compunction. He is supplemented by Philbrick, the butler, a graduate of the underworld, who likes to tell about revolting crimes. This audacity in Waugh's next book, *Vile Bodies*, is the property of the infantile young people who, at a time "in the near future, when existing social tendencies have become more marked," are shown drinking themselves into beggary, entangling themselves in absurd sexual relationships, and getting their heads cracked in motor accidents. The story has the same wild effect of reckless improvisation, which perfectly suits the spirit of the characters; but it is better sustained than *Decline and Fall*, and in one passage it sounds a motif which for the first time suggests a standard by which the behavior of these characters is judged: the picture of Anchorage House with its "grace and dignity and other-worldliness," and its memories of "people who had represented their country in foreign places and sent their sons to die for her in battle, people of decent and temperate life, uncultured, unaffected, unembarrassed, unassuming, unambitious people, of independent judgment and marked eccentricities."

In *Black Mischief* there is a more coherent story and a good deal of careful planning to bring off the surprises and shocks. There are descriptions of the imaginary black kingdom of Azania, which is the principal scene of the action, that are based on the author's own travels and would not be out of place in a straight novel. We note that with each successive book Evelyn Waugh is approaching closer to the conventions of ordinary fiction: with each one—and the process will continue—we are made to take the characters more seriously as recognizable human beings living in the world we know. Yet the author never reaches this norm: he keeps his grasp on the comic convention of which he is becoming a master—the convention which makes it possible for him to combine the outrageous with the plausible without offending our sense of truth. It is a triumph for him to carry from book to book the monsters of *Decline and Fall* and to make us continue to accept them as elements in later novels that touch us or stir us with values quite different from those of the earlier ones. There are two important points to be noted in connection with *Black Mischief*. The theme of the decline of society is here not presented merely in terms of night-club London: it is symbolized by the submergence of the white man in the black savagery he is trying to exploit. The theme of audacity is incarnated here, not in a Philbrick or a Grimes, but in a bad-egg aristocrat, who steals his mother's emeralds to run away from England, manipulates the politics of Azania by talking modern ideas to the native king and, forced at last to flee the jungle, eats his sweetheart unawares at a cannibal feast.

A Handful of Dust, which followed, is, it seems to me, the author's masterpiece. Here he has perfected his method to a point which must command the admiration of another writer even more perhaps than that of the ordinary non-literary reader—for the latter may be carried from scene to scene of the swift and smooth-running story without being aware of the skill with which the author creates by implication an atmosphere and a set of relations upon which almost any other novelist would spend pages of description and analysis. The title comes from T. S. Eliot's line, "I will show you fear in a handful of dust," but, except on the title page, the author nowhere mentions this fear. Yet he manages to convey from beginning to end, from the comfortable country house to the clearing in the Brazilian jungle, the impression of a terror, of a feeling that the bottom is just about to drop out of things, which is the whole motivation of the book but of which the characters are not shown to be conscious and upon which one cannot put one's finger in any specific passage. A charming woman of the aristocracy deserts a solid county husband and a high-spirited little boy to have a love affair with the underbred and uninteresting son of a lady interior decorator; the child is killed at a hunt; the husband runs away to Brazil and ends as the captive of an illiterate halfbreed, who keeps him for years in the jungle reading the novels of Dickens aloud. The audacity here is the wife's: her behavior has no justification from any accepted point of view, whether conventional or romantic. Nor does the author help out with a word of explicit illumination. He has himself made of audacity a literary technique. He exemplifies, like so many of his characters, the great precept of Benjamin Jowett to young Englishmen just starting their careers: "Never apologize, never explain."

The next novel *Scoop* is not quite so good as the ones just before and just after it, but it has in it some wonderful things. A quiet country gentleman, who writes nature notes for a big London paper called the *Daily Beast*, gets railroaded, through a confusion of identities, to another of Waugh's Negro countries, where he is supposed to act as war correspondent. The story is simpler than usual, and it brings very clearly to light a lineup of opposing forces which has always lurked in Evelyn Waugh's fiction and which is now even beginning to give it a certain melodramatic force. He has come to see English life as a conflict between, on the one hand, the qualities of the English upper classes, whether arrogant, bold and outrageous or stubborn, unassuming and eccentric, and, on the other, the qualities of the climbers, the careerists and the commercial millionaires who dominate contemporary society. The story of William Boot comes to its climax when the grown-up public-school boy faces down the Communist boss of Ishmaelia, who is trying to get him off the scene while a revolution takes place: " 'Look here, Dr. Benito,' said William. 'You're being a bore. I'm not going.' " And the book has a more cheerful moral than any of its predecessors: William succeeds in holding his own against the barbarisms both of Africa and of London, and in the end he returns to the country, where they cannot get him again and where he continues to write his notes about the habits of the local fauna—though "outside the owls hunted maternal rodents and their furry broods." If this book is less exciting than the others, it is perhaps because the theme of audacity appears mainly in connection with the *Daily Beast*, with which the author cannot feel any sympathy.

Waugh's most recent novel, *Put Out More Flags*, written during and about the war, has an even more positive moral. Basil Seal, the aristocratic scoundrel who has already figured in *Black Mischief*, exploits the war to his own advantage by informing against his friends and shaking down his sister's county neighbors with threats of making them take in objectionable refugees, but finally he enlists in the Commandos, who give him for the first time a legitimate field for the exercise of his resourcefulness and nerve. Evelyn Waugh's other well-born wastrels are already in the "corps d'élite," somewhat sobered after years of "having fun." "There's a new spirit abroad. I see it on every side," says stupid old Sir Joseph Mainwaring. "And, poor booby," says the author, "he was bang right." We see now that not only has the spirit of audacity migrated from the lower to the upper classes, but that the whole local emphasis has shifted. The hero of *Decline and Fall* was a poor student reading for the church, whose career at Oxford was wrecked by the brutality of a party of aristocratic drunks: "A shriller note could now be heard rising from Sir Alastair's rooms; any who have heard that sound will shrink at the recollection of it; it is the sound of the English county families baying for broken glass." And at the end he is addressed as follows by another and more considerate young nobleman: "You know, Paul, I think it was a mistake you ever got mixed up with us; don't you? We're different somehow. Don't quite know how. Don't think that's rude, do you, Paul?" But it is now this young man, Percy Pastmaster, and Sir Alastair Digby-Vaine-Trumpington and the English county families generally who are the heroes of *Put Out More Flags*. Evelyn Waugh has completely come over to them, and the curious thing is that his snobbery carries us with it. In writing about Harold Nicolson, I remarked on his fatal inability to escape from the psychology of the governing class, which was imposed on him by birth and office. The case of Waugh is the opposite of this: he has evidently approached this class, like his first hero, from somewhere outside, and he has had to invent it for himself. The result is that everything is created in his work, nothing is taken for granted. The art of this last novel is marvellous. See the episode in which Basil Seal blackmails the young married woman: the attractiveness of the girl, which is to prompt him to try a conquest, and her soft-ness, which will permit his success (Evelyn Waugh is perhaps the only male writer of his generation in England who is able to make his women attractive), are sketched in with a few physical details and a few brief passages of dialogue that pro-duce an impression as clear and fresh as an eighteenth-century painting.

Evelyn Waugh is today a declared Tory and a Roman Catholic convert; he believes in the permanence of the social classes and, presumably, in the permanence of evil. It has been pointed out by Mr. Nigel Dennis in an article in the *Partisan Review* that this would make him rather a dubious guide for England after the war. But, after all, he does not set up as a guide; and his opinions do not damage his fiction. About this fiction there is nothing schematic and nothing doctrinaire; and, though the characters are often stock types—the silly ass, the vulgar parvenu, the old clubman, etc.—everything in it has grown out of experience and everything has emotional value.

Put Out More Flags leaves you glowing over the products of public schools and country houses as examples of the English character; but it is not a piece of propaganda: it is the satisfying expression of an artist, whose personal pattern of feeling no formula will ever fit, whether political, social or moral. For the savagery he is afraid of is somehow the same thing as the audacity that so delights him.

March 4, 1944

John Mulholland and the Art of Illusion

JOHN MULHOLLAND is a top-notch magician, the editor of the magicians' magazine, the *Sphinx*, and one of the world's leading authorities on professional magic. He is also probably the best writer in the field since the Englishman who called himself Louis Hoffmann. "Hoffmann" was a barrister named Lewis, who led a kind of second life as a conjuror and produced, in his *Modern Magic, More Magic, Later Magic* and *Latest Magic*, which began coming out in the seventies, a series of treatises in the soundest tradition of British expository writing: dense, comprehensive, exact and ornamented with Latin quotations. These books became classics and some of them are still in print. Though in certain respects out of date, they are, I believe, the only works on their subject which have long remained in circulation.

The literature of magic is now immense, but it mostly consists of technical writings intended for professional magicians. The articles on conjuring in the *Encyclopaedia Britannica* have always been unsatisfactory. The best-known one was written by Maskelyne, the proprietor of the Egyptian Hall, a famous theater of magic in London, and it is mainly in the nature of an encomium on the wonders of the Egyptian Hall. The late Harry Houdini, a great student of the subject, succeeded in getting this article cut down—it had, besides, been rather snooty about American magicians—when the new edition of the *Britannica* was prepared under American auspices, and had a paragraph on himself added, but it is still incomplete and out of date. Houdini had a voracious curiosity about everything connected with the miraculous and a desire to master all its arts. He read enormously and wrote several books, and he marks the emergence in his field of a spirit of scientific inquiry. But it was not till Mr. Mulholland appeared that this department of human activity was explored in all its aspects and branches by a scholarly and critical intelligence which knew how to express itself. When further encyclopedia articles have to be written, Mr. Mulholland ought to write them.

Mr. Mulholland's new book—*The Art of Illusion: Magic for*

Men to Do—is not one of his most important works, but it is perfect for its limited purpose: to teach the beginner a few primary principles and to provide him with an effective repertoire which requires neither sleight of hand nor difficult apparatus. Mr. Mulholland makes some very shrewd remarks on the general psychology of magic, and he has selected his tricks with care. If he has not given us an up-to-date Hoffmann, this is partly the fault of the times. From the directions and diagrams of Hoffmann it was possible to learn the rudiments of sleight of hand and how to build your own apparatus; but magic has, it seems, fallen a victim to the same pressures that produce outlines of philosophy and digests of famous novels. A growth in interest in non-professional conjuring has been accompanied by an increasing reluctance to take any trouble about it, so that the amateur is likely to satisfy himself with devices that require no more skill to operate than the jokes on sale at novelty shops. Mr. Mulholland has at least tried to show him that the chief pride of the magician is derived not from exploiting mechanical toys but from putting something over on his audience, and that you can be far more amazing with an ordinary coin, a piece of string or a pack of cards than with a pocketful of gadgets.

This whole matter of mystifying people is more interesting than may be supposed. A little acquaintance with the subject will afford a startling revelation of the common human incapacity to observe or report correctly; and anyone who has deluded an audience into believing that he was doing something which he had merely suggested to their minds, while he was actually doing something else that they were perfectly in a position to notice, will always have a more skeptical opinion of the value of ordinary evidence. Mr. Mulholland has written three fascinating books, from which a great deal may be learned: two on the history of professional conjuring, *The Story of Magic* and *Quicker than the Eye*, and one, perhaps the best that has been done, on the history of spiritualism, *Beware Familiar Spirits*. With the advance of the scientific method, the field of thaumaturgy has come to be split between two groups of miracle-workers who grow more and more antagonistic. On the one hand, you have the magicians, who want to be admired for their skill; on the other, the mind-readers and the mediums, who claim to possess supernatural powers. When magicians like Houdini and Mulholland try to show people, in the interests of truth, that there is not a single feat on record as having been performed by a mind-reader or a medium that a magician would accept as genuine, they find themselves confronted with a will to believe against which they are utterly helpless. Mr. Mulholland points out that, though the Fox sisters confessed to the fraudulence of their manifestations, and though one of them actually went on tour exposing her own tricks, they are still venerated as authentic by spiritualists; that the late Sir Arthur Conan Doyle gave a gratuitous endorsement to a mind-reader named Zancig who had never pretended to be genuine and was a member of the Society of American Magicians; and that the faithful of the spiritualist cult even insisted that Houdini himself, though for some reason he chose to deny it, performed his feats through supernatural agency.

One aspect of the subject on which, so far as I know, Mr. Mulholland has not written but on which one would like to hear him is the special psychology of magicians and of the people who like to see them perform. That the attraction of magic may be felt as irresistible by certain kinds of people seems indicated by Lewis-Hoffmann and by the late Dr. Samuel C. Hooker, who had one of the strangest of American careers. Dr. Hooker was an able chemist, who made a fortune in sugar refining and was known as "the father of the beet-sugar industry," but he retired from business in his forties and occupied the rest of his life with magic. His aim was to astonish the magicians themselves, and the great triumph of his later years was to baffle Houdini and Thurston with a Teddy-bear's head that floated in the air and playing cards that stood on end and answered questions. The function of the magician has characteristics in common with those of the criminal, of the actor and of the priest (it was quite natural that Charles Dickens, who had affinities with all three, should become an enthusiastic magician); and he enjoys certain special advantages impossible for these professions. Unlike the criminal, he has nothing to fear from the police; unlike the actor, he can always have the stage to himself; unlike the priest, he need not trouble about questions of faith in connection with the mysteries at which he presides. This is perhaps one of the reasons that magicians, though sometimes rather egoistic, usually appear to be happy in their work. I have never met or heard of an accomplished magician who did not seem to be delighted with himself and to enjoy amazing people with tricks off the stage as well as on.

There is, besides, more to these feats and to our pleasure in them than we are likely to be conscious of. Some of the tricks that have lasted longest and become fixed in the popular imagination must be the remnants of fertility rites. The wand is an obvious symbol, and has its kinship with Aaron's rod and the Pope's staff that puts forth leaves in *Tannhäuser*. Its production of rabbits and flowers from a hat has become the accepted type-trick of conjuring. And the magician who escapes from the box: what is he but Adonis and Attis and all the rest of the corn gods that are buried and rise? This was quite plain in the case of Houdini, who was continually inventing new ways, each more challenging than the last, to get himself buried and bound, and who seemed to experience, in breaking away, an actual exaltation. The ordeals to which he subjected himself were dangerous and sometimes nearly cost him his life: he had himself sunk in a river, immersed in a can of milk, frozen in a cake of ice, hung upside down to a bridge and confined by every possible kind of shackle and rope in every possible kind of trunk and sack; and he was evidently not driven merely by motives of fame and money, but gave the impression of obeying some private compulsion to enact again and again a drama of death and resurrection. These old type-tricks can still create excitement and give both audience and magician satisfaction; and it is significant both that conjuring should never have died out, though people no longer take it for real, and that, recovering today from a period when it followed the tendency of the age by going in very heavily for machinery, it should have reverted—like painting after its photographic phase—to something both more primitive and more impressive; so that the conjuror's public today asks for nothing better than to watch the incomparable Cardini stand silent in an opera cloak and impassively produce from bare hands an endless quantity of cards and cigarettes.

March 11, 1944

What Became of Louis Bromfield

$\mathbf{I}$N THE DAYS of *The Green Bay Tree* and *The Strange Case of Miss Annie Spragg*, Mr. Louis Bromfield used to be spoken of as one of the younger writers of promise. By the time he had brought out *Twenty-four Hours*, it was more or less generally said of him that he was definitely second-rate. Since then, by unremitting industry and a kind of stubborn integrity that seems to make it impossible for him to turn out his rubbish without thoroughly believing in it, he has gradually made his way into the fourth rank, where his place is now secure.

His new novel, *What Became of Anna Bolton*, is one of his most remarkable achievements. The story begins in the London season of 1937, and in a succession of brilliant scenes which, for the density of the social picture, recall the opening of *War and Peace*, Mr. Bromfield makes us acquainted with a vivid and varied company from that international haut monde about which he writes with authority. As we pass among these glittering worldlings, Mr. Bromfield characterizes each one with a magically evocative phrase. There are fading Lady Kernogan, "quite simply a tart, with certain superior qualities"; Major von Kleist from the German Embassy, "with the peculiar erect stiff carriage of Prussian military men"; Lady Haddonfield, "whom the years had turned into a rather handsome bony mare" and who at fifty "loved politics and intrigue and was considered the greatest hostess of the Tory Party." But cynosure of all smart London is the American Anna Bolton, of unknown origins but immense wealth, who stands at the top of the staircase of the great Georgian house she has rented, "triumphant and handsome and hard," welcoming "a gaudy, dying world." "There, side by side," thinks a young American guest, as he sees Lady Haddonfield and Mrs. Bolton, "receiving half of Europe, stand the two hardest, most ambitious bitches in the world!" And yet, he notes, Anna Bolton looks "like a fine race horse in training."

This young American, a foreign correspondent—it is he who tells Anna's story—is the only person present who knows who Anna Bolton is, for he comes from her home town of

Lewisburg, Ohio, and went to school with her years ago. Mr. Bromfield, at this point, by a deft device, takes us back to Anna Bolton's childhood; and, brilliant social observer that he is, as much at home among the stratifications of a small American town as among the nuances of rank in a London drawing-room, he shows us the unbridgeable difference between the well-to-do classes of Lewisburg and those who, in a racy collo-quial phrase which becomes one of the leit-motifs of the story, live "on the wrong side of the tracks." Anna Bolton, we are startled to hear, was once simply Annie Scanlon, the daughter of an Irish cleaning woman and a drunken Irish brakeman, who lived just beyond the railroad crossing. When little Annie first went to high school, the other children couldn't help noticing her "because of her bold looks and coloring—her red hair and blue eyes and a figure developed beyond her years. It was a figure like that of a young Venus Genetrix, made for love, made for bearing children." "Even the high-school boys who didn't understand such things felt them by instinct," Mr. Bromfield tells us shrewdly, with one of his revealing insights into the psychology of adolescence.

Annie fell in love with Tom Harrigan, "the very core" of whose attraction "was a kind of healthy animal magnetism," "as good-looking a boy as I have ever seen—the Irish kind with black curly hair and blue eyes and high color, with big heavy shoulders and long straight legs. . . . I suppose he fell in love the same way he did everything else. He knew what it was all about without being told. He knew with the sure in-stinct of a young male animal what it was he wanted and went for it." He seduced Annie and made her pregnant, but when she told him, "he was not puzzled at all. He said quite simply, with a curious mature wisdom, 'We'll get married. After all that's why we love each other. That's the way things are. That's why people fall in love—to have babies. That's the way it was meant to be.'" But Annie is "shanty Irish" and Tom "lace-curtain Irish," a further shade of social distinction of which Mr. Bromfield makes us aware. Tom's rich parents object, but he marries her, and Tom gets himself a job as an automobile salesman in Pittsburgh, and there their baby is born. They are ideally happy together till one day Tom is killed in a motor ac-cident, and that same year the baby catches measles, develops pneumonia and dies. In the hands of a less skillful artist, the death of Annie's husband and her baby might seem rather impromptu and meaningless, a gratuitous visitation of tragedy, but Mr. Bromfield has taken care to make Tom Harrigan so completely unconvincing a character that we do not complain of or notice any lack of plausibility in his death. Since we have never for a moment believed in him, we are not touched by what happens to him. The important thing is the effect on Anna. "I met her on the street," the narrator says, "the day she came back from the funeral of the baby. Something had happened to her eyes. They were like stone, as if there were no more tears in them." There seems to be an assumption in all this and through the whole of Anna's story that she is the victim of the "intricate, senseless pettiness and wornout traditions" of the town where she was born; yet she had obviously done pretty well for herself, and, though Tom had had his fatal accident while hurrying in answer to a telegram, apparently a pretext to lure him home, announcing that his father was dangerously ill, the disastrous end of her marriage can hardly be charged to small-town snobbery. That Mr. Bromfield should have arranged this accident and have made Anna feel this grievance is of the essence of his tragic conviction, somewhat akin to Thomas Hardy's, of the unpredictability of human events.

And then Anna turns up in Europe with a fortune that a rich second husband has left her, riding the high tide of social success and as if "sitting perpetually in a theater box watching a corrupt but breathless play." For Mr. Bromfield, with his epic sense of social forces, paints around her the larger background of the disintegration of Europe. "It was a world dominated by too many intriguers, by too many small people, a world lost for lack of decency and leadership, with scarcely a statesman in it . . . Vienna was like an old whore who had once been very pretty. . . . In France the people were on the brink of revolt against the corruption and intrigue of their own government. But Rome was worst of all. . . . Rome was the mad carnival of Europe at its worst. . . . And strangest of all there was a mad, sinister, vagrant who took the name of Hitler."

But Anna is too vital a creature to fall a victim to this decadence of the Old World, and how she fares when war comes to France makes the chief drama of Mr. Bromfield's story. Leaving

the Ritz, which has become her home, she flees Paris before
the Nazi invasion, but her escape is held up by an air raid, in
which she sees a woman killed. The husband of this woman,
though Anna protests, makes her drive him to the nearest
town. "He said, in a very quiet voice, 'You're going where I
tell you. I know your kind. You're the cause of everything.'
And suddenly he slapped her hard on the side of the face."
This is the beginning of awakening for Anna. She has recognized already in this arrogant young fellow a resemblance to
the man she once loved: "She felt suddenly faint and leaned
against the car, letting the torch fall to the ground at her side.
For what she had seen was Tom Harrigan—a big man with blue
eyes and dark, curly hair." Here again we might be tempted to
feel, in the case of a less adroit novelist, that the appearance in
Anna's life of a second man who is virtually a replica of the
first, with a child who closely resembles her own child, strains
a little the legitimate license which we are accustomed to ac-
cord to fiction; but since the character of the first Tom Harrigan has the two-dimensional quality of a paper doll, it is not
difficult to accept an exact duplicate cut out of the same piece
of paper.

This second Tom Harrigan is a Russian, perhaps a better
man than the first Tom, for he possesses the simple courage,
perfect honesty and vast humanity characteristic of his race. In
the love between him and Anna, Mr. Bromfield seems to give
us a symbol of the union between Russia and the United States
which was cemented at Teheran. Not that the author necessarily accepts the Soviet experiment in toto; for, in spite of Tom
II's rude behavior on the occasion of his first meeting with
Anna, he turns out to be very well-born, the son of a White
Russian émigré, and thus keeps up the high social tone which
Mr. Bromfield has taught us to expect in his fiction.

Anna takes in his motherless child and she sets up a canteen
for refugees in a town just over the line in then still unoccu-
pied France. She works her high connections in Paris and her
acquaintance with the Prussian von Kleist, to get supplies for
the despoiled population, but she refuses to marry von Kleist,
who wants her, as he tells her, "because I am tired and sick and
corrupt and you are strong and healthy and young"—a decision from which, also, it is possible for the politically minded

reader to draw a significant moral. She finds that she loves this young Russian, who is active in the underground movement, and for the first time, after many arid years of pleasure-seeking and worldly notoriety, Anna Bolton at last finds herself. Her companion, Harriet Godwin, puts it eloquently in the memorable scene in which Harriet is dying: "I've seen something happen to you, my dear, something miraculous. . . . I think I've seen you grow a soul." "That is really what this story is about," Mr. Bromfield has already told us, "how Anna changed and came to be born at last as a whole person, without deformity, how Anna learned understanding and humanity, and the value of things of life."

When the United States declares war, Anna's position in France becomes impossible, and she escapes to Algiers with the second Tom. There the narrator meets her again. "She turned toward me and I knew at once the woman was Anna Bolton, yet as I saw her in full face there was something about her that was not Annie Scanlon, at least not the Annie I had known. The hard look was no longer in the eyes. There was no hardness about the mouth. The experience was an extraordinary one." She is married and thoroughly happy. When this old friend sees her Russian husband, "it seemed to me that Tom Harrigan was looking at me. . . . I heard Anna saying, 'You see?' And then softly in English in that warm new voice of hers, she said, 'I am very grateful. God gave me another chance.'"

Mr. Bromfield, in *What Became of Anna Bolton*, has accomplished something in the nature of a miracle. In hardly more than sixty thousand words—a story that recalls, by its length, *A Lost Lady* and *Ethan Frome*—he has produced, by severe compression, a small masterpiece of pointlessness and banality. Most novelists of Mr. Bromfield's rank have some hobby about which they become interesting, some corner of life which they know and about which they have something to tell, some humor or infectious sentimentality or capacity for creating suspense; and it must have cost Louis Bromfield a rigorous labor of exclusion to achieve this smooth and limpid little novel in which there is not a single stroke of wit, not a scene of effective drama, not a phrase of clean-minted expression, and hardly a moment of credible human behavior.

*

I have been trying to describe this production in the manner appropriate to it—that is, as far as possible, in the language of the ladies who admire Louis Bromfield and who write enthusiastic reviews in the *Times* and the *Herald Tribune*. But the truth is that the book reviewer is baffled when he attempts to give an account of a work which has already turned its back on literature and embarrasses him on every page by stretching out its arms to Hollywood. He comes to feel that what he ought to have done was simply to pass it along to the movie department. For the characters of Louis Bromfield are hardly even precisely stock fiction characters: they are blank spaces like the figures on billboards before the faces have been painted in. When their features are finally supplied, they will be the features of popular actors. Mr. Bromfield seems to have made it easy, by giving Anna a similar name, for his heroine to wear the face of Ann Sheridan, who, not so very far back, in *Kings Row*, was playing just such an Irish girl from the other side of the tracks, in love with a rich young man; and in the same way Eric von Kleist can merge readily into Erich von Stroheim. No doubt the public will see them soon and will not mind if what they are and do has no logic and no motivation, no likeness of any kind to life. But the book reviewer is rather up against it, since he has to have something to take hold of, even to say that a book ought to be better, and *Anna Bolton* completely eludes him because it is really sub-literary and proto-film.

April 8, 1944

A review by Mary Ross published in the *New York Herald Tribune* after the above article was written, closed with the following paragraph:

"This is a simply told and unassuming story, centered in the figure of a proud Irish girl from an American town, rather than the decadent glitter of pre-war Europe or the contrast of gluttony and misery which followed the fall of France. Mr. Bromfield brings the war close, as the story is told in the first person by David Sorrell, but it will be Anna herself that you will remember. This is an appealing novel which it is hard to lay down, and I think it will be hard to forget."

J. Dover Wilson on Falstaff

I DARE SAY that no other national poet presents quite the same problem as Shakespeare to the academic critics who study him. Goethe and Dante were great writers by vocation: they were responsible and always serious; they were conscious of everything they did, and everything they did was done with intention; they were great students and scholars themselves, and so always had something in common with the professional scholars who were to work over them. And this was hardly less true of Pushkin. But Shakespeare was not a scholar or self-consciously a spokesman for his age as Dante and Goethe were; he was not even an "intellectual." He was what the sports-writers call a "natural," and his career was the career of a playwright who had to appeal to the popular taste. He began by feeding the market with potboilers and patching up other people's plays, and he returned to these trades at the end. In the meantime, he had followed his personal bent by producing some extraordinary tragedies which seem to have got rather beyond the range of the Elizabethan theater and by allowing even his potboiling comedies to turn sour to such a degree as apparently to become unpalatable to his public. But he displayed all along toward his craft a rather superior and cavalier attitude which at moments even verged on the cynical—a kind of attitude which a Dante, or a Dostoevsky, could hardly have understood. He retires as a serious artist—in *Cymbeline* and *The Winter's Tale*—before he has stopped writing and says farewell to his audience, in *The Tempest*, through a delightful and rather thoughtful masque.

It would perhaps be an exaggeration to say, as John Jay Chapman did, that Shakespeare regarded the writing of plays as a harmless kind of nonsense. He had certainly, by the end of his life, come to see himself in the role of Prospero: a powerful and splendid enchanter. But it is difficult for the professional scholar to understand the professional playwright; and there is always the danger that a pedant who does come to direct his attention upon the theatrical tradition behind Shakespeare may end by attempting to resolve him into terms of mere stage conventions. It is equally difficult for the scholarly critic who has been nourished on the moralistic literature of the English or American nineteenth century to understand a pure enchanter for whom life is not real and earnest but a dream that must finally fade like the dramas in which he reflects it. Mr. J. Dover Wilson, the English scholar, whose books on *Hamlet* are well known and who has just published a study of *Henry IV* called *The Fortunes of Falstaff*, is an exception to both these limitations, and he has criticized them with much common sense. A good deal of his recent book is occupied, in fact, with exposing various errors that derive from these sources; and, though always pleasant to read, it is thus not always of especial interest to the ordinary reader or playgoer who is accustomed to getting Shakespeare at first hand and has never been bemused by the atmosphere, so curiously un-Shakespearean, engendered by the dramatist's commentators. It does not occur to us today to try, as was at one time a critical fashion, to examine the creations of Shakespeare as if they were actual persons about whom it would be possible to assemble complete and consistent biographies. Mr. Wilson shows how very different the development of Falstaff is from even the kind of presentation of character that one gets in a modern novelist who has worked out a dossier in advance. He makes us see how the personality of Falstaff is created as the long play progresses, and how it exists only in terms of this play. Nor is the ordinary admirer of Shakespeare very likely to have been misled by the theory of certain critics who cannot bear to admit that Falstaff is a rascal and who have attempted to prove, for example, that he never behaved like a coward: a school of opinion not hard to confute.

Mr. Wilson does occasionally himself fall into another kind of error. He belongs to the rarer group of critics—of whom A. W. Verrall, the Greek scholar, is one of the most conspicuous examples—who have themselves a touch of the creative artist, whose virtue is that they seem to wake the text to a new dynamic life by force of their own imaginations and whose fault is that they sometimes read into it new dramas of their own invention. This last is what has happened, I think, in the case of Mr. Wilson's version of the scene after the Gad's Hill robbery, in which Falstaff boasts of having put to rout a group of assailants whose number increases in the course of the conversation as the boastful mood carries him away. Mr. Wilson has convinced himself that this passage is not merely a comic "gag" of Shakespeare's not quite top vintage—in spite of the fact that these plays, especially *Henry V*, are full of crude and implausible jokes—but a particularly subtle bit of comedy only to be grasped by the most intelligent spectators: Falstaff has been aware all the time, according to Mr. Wilson, that the two men who chased him were the Prince and Poins, and, in boasting to them now of his boldness, he is merely playing up to their joke for reasons which Mr. Wilson leaves rather unclear. If Falstaff really knew all the time that his antagonists were the Prince and Poins, then he must also have been merely pretending when at Gad's Hill he ran away from them roaring —a supposition which is surely absurd and which it seems to me that Mr. Wilson rather slips out of facing. And, as it proceeds, Mr. Wilson's story of the affair of Prince Henry and Falstaff gets slightly at a tangent to Shakespeare's. He is excellent in tracing the phases through which Prince Hal and his companion pass in the two parts of *Henry IV* (the growing sense of responsibility of Hal under pressure of his father's impending death and the simultaneously increasing impudence of Falstaff, what Mr. Wilson calls his "comic *hubris*," which has been stimulated by the undeserved glory that he has acquired at the Battle of Shrewsbury); and in pointing out that the dramatist has been plotting these curves all along for the moment when they shall intersect, with the inevitable disastrous result. He is contending against the disposition to become sentimental over Falstaff and to denounce the crowned Hal as mean-spirited and harsh when he turns him off at the end so firmly. But I think that Mr. Wilson overdoes his case in trying to reduce the pathos when he talks about the "wicked smile" of Falstaff just after the repudiation, as he says, "Master Shallow, I owe you a thousand pound." The old man has been completely discredited; he must accept his humiliation, and he is sportsmanlike and hence pathetic. It is perhaps Falstaff's greatest line, the first stroke that makes us sympathize with him completely. It prepares the way in turn for the report of Falstaff's death in *Henry V*. And I think that Mr. Wilson goes entirely off the track—since he has already shown the close continuity between the two parts of *Henry IV*—in trying to rule out this deathbed as irrelevant. It is true that in the epilogue to *Henry IV* Shakespeare had announced to his audience an intention of making Falstaff play in *Henry V* a more considerable and more comic role than he does in the play which he actually wrote. But we do not know what Shakespeare may have then thought of writing; we only know what he did write; and he certainly shows Falstaff crushed. This is not a made-to-order sequel like *The Merry Wives of Windsor*: it is the true end of Falstaff's story.

I want to suggest another kind of view of the relation between Falstaff and Hal which has not occurred to Mr. Wilson and which—though my reading in this field is not great— I have never seen expressed. Certainly it is true, as Mr. Wilson insists, that *Henry IV* is not open to criticism on the ground that Prince Hal is the hero and that he is made to behave like a prig. As is usual with Shakespeare, the two main personalities are played off against one another with the full dramatic effectiveness that results from his making us feel that each is fulfilling the laws of his nature and that there is no easy escape from a conflict in which one of them has to break. Mr. Wilson has shown us, furthermore, that the adventures of Prince Hal with Falstaff run true to a traditional formula derived from the "morality" of Everyman or Youth and his temptation by Vanity and Riot, at the end of which the Elizabethan audience would expect to see virtue triumphant. But there is surely something more to this problem. Mr. Wilson, who much invokes Dr. Johnson as a witness to the worthiness of Henry, fails to take account of his remark to the effect that the reader's interest suffers a fatal slump from the moment when Falstaff and his friends fall victims to the new Henry's reforms. Most people probably do feel this. Most people probably feel that *Henry V* is, for Shakespeare, relatively thin and relatively journalistic. But if the dramatist really meant Henry V to be taken as a model of a prince, why should this be the case?

I believe that in Shakespeare's more conventional plays, we must always, in order to understand them, look for a personal pattern behind the ostensible plot. In saying, as I did above, that Shakespeare was a fabricator of potboilers both at the beginning and at the end of his life, I did not of course mean to imply that these pieces, even aside from their magnificent poetry, had nothing in them of serious interest. On the contrary, he could hardly write anything without projecting real emotional conflicts in the form of imagined personalities. Now, these Henry plays just precede *Julius Caesar*, and *Julius Caesar* just precedes *Hamlet*. The great salient patterns of Shakespeare that give us symbols for what is most personal and most profound are beginning to take shape in these chronicles. The reader finds his sympathy weighted (as no doubt the Elizabethans did, since Falstaff became so tremendously popular) for Falstaff as against Hal, because Shakespeare, though he can give us both sides and holds the dramatic balance, is identifying himself with Falstaff in a way he cannot do with the Prince. He has already made us sympathize queerly with those of his characters who have been bent out of line by deformities or social pressures, whose morality is twisted, whose motives are mixed. Faulconbridge runs away with *King John*, and Shylock, the villain of *The Merchant of Venice*, becomes by a single speech a great deal more interesting than Antonio. Has not even Richard III in his horrid way a fascination—as of a Quilp or a Punch whose motives we have been made to understand —which the author could not possibly give Richmond? Falstaff is not deformed in quite the same obvious way as these others, but he is both physically and morally monstrous, and his nature is also mixed. And from Falstaff through Brutus to Hamlet is not such a great step. Hamlet is also complex and also out of tune, though what is wrong with him is less obvious still; like Falstaff, he is at once quick-witted and extremely inept at action, a brilliant and constant talker and a man always at odds with his social group. The opposition between Falstaff and Henry unmistakably reappears in the contrast between Hamlet and Fortinbras; and "Master Shallow, I owe you a thousand pound," with the deathbed scene that follows, is to flower into the tragic eloquence of that series of final scenes in which Shakespeare is to make us feel that Hamlet and Othello and Lear and Antony and Coriolanus, for all their confusion and failure, have been rarer and nobler souls than the opponents, unworthy or worthy, who have brought their destruction about. In *Hamlet*, the Falstaff figure, with changed mask but a similar voice, holds the undisputed center of the stage;

Prince Henry has dwindled to Fortinbras, who is felt mainly as an offstage force, but still represents the straight man of action who is destined to take over in the end. But later we shall have Antony and Octavius, Coriolanus and Aufidius. Here, too, the balance will be evenly held, and we shall never get melodrama. We are not allowed to sentimentalize over Antony any more than we are over Falstaff. Octavius is perfectly right: he does his duty as Henry does; but we shall always like Antony better, just as we did poor old Falstaff. Falstaff and Richard II are the two most conspicuous prototypes of Shakespeare's tragic heroes.

April 29, 1944

A Toast and a Tear for Dorothy Parker

REREADING Dorothy Parker—in the Viking Portable Library—has affected me, rather unexpectedly, with a distinct attack of nostalgia. Her poems do seem a little dated. At their best, they are witty light verse, but when they try to be something more serious, they tend to become a kind of dilution of A. E. Housman and Edna Millay. Her prose, however, is still alive. It seems to me as sharp and as funny as in the years when it was first coming out. If Ring Lardner outlasts our day, as I do not doubt that he will, it is possible that Dorothy Parker will, too.

But the thing that I have particularly felt is the difference between the general tone, the psychological and literary atmosphere, of the period—the twenties and the earlier thirties—when most of these pieces of Mrs. Parker's were written, and the atmosphere of the present time. It was suddenly brought home to me how much freer people were—in their emotions, in their ideas and in expressing themselves. In the twenties they could love, they could travel, they could stay up late at night as extravagantly as they pleased; they could think or say or write whatever seemed to them amusing or interesting. There was a good deal of irresponsibility, and a lot of money and energy wasted, and the artistic activities of the time suffered somewhat from its general vices, but it was a much more favorable climate for writing than the period we are in now.

The depression put a crimp in incomes, and people began to have to watch their pockets. Then they began to watch their politics. The whole artistic and intellectual world became anxiously preoccupied with making sure that their positions were correct in relation to the capitalist system and the imminence or the non-imminence of a social revolution; they spent a good deal of time and print arguing with one another about it. Some writers who had been basing their work on the uproar and glamor of the boom grew discouraged and more or less stopped. The young writers who came out of college were likely to be short of cash and have no prospect of easy jobs; they were obliged to be circumspect. The tougher ones tried to work with the Communists or other radical groups; the more conventional became professors. Some tried to do both at the same time, with uncomfortable and unsatisfactory results, for they found themselves in the situation of being obliged to worry about both their standing with the academic authorities and the purity of their political line.

With the writings of Dorothy Parker you are still as far away from all this as you are with those of Scott Fitzgerald. It is a relief and a reassurance, in reading her soliloquies and dialogues —her straight short stories, which are sometimes sentimental, do not always wear quite so well—to realize how recklessly clever it used to be possible for people to be, and how personal and how direct. All her books had funereal titles, but the eye was always wide open and the tongue always quick to retort. Even those titles were sardonic exclamations on the part of an individual at the idea of her own demise. The idea of the death of a society had not yet begun working on people to paralyze their response to experience.

But the literary movement of the twenties showed a tendency to break down and peter out which we never should have expected at that time, when it seemed to us that American writing had just had a brilliant rebirth. It was a shock to know that Scott Fitzgerald, who had seemed to be still on his way to fulfilling the promise of imperfect books, was suddenly and prematurely dead; and we soon found that this imperfect work had almost the look of a classic: its value had been heightened by its rarity, since there was not going to be any more of it either by him or by anyone else. And we find when we take up this new volume, which contains Dorothy Parker's complete published works, that a similar shift of feeling occurs. Mrs. Parker is not yet dead nor has she altogether ceased writing: there are several new stories in this volume, and they hold up with the earlier ones. But she nowadays produces little, and she has suffered, to our disappointment, one of the dooms of her generation. A decade or more ago she went out to Hollywood and more or less steadily stayed there, and, once away from her natural habitat, New York, she succumbed to the expiatory mania that has become epidemic with film-writers and was presently making earnest appeals on behalf of those organizations which talked about being "progressive" and succeeded in convincing their followers that they were working for the social revolution, though they had really no other purpose than to promote the foreign policy of the Soviet Union. She ought, of course, to have been satirizing Hollywood and sticking pins into fellow-travellers; but she has not, so far as I know, ever written a word about either. There are among the new pieces here a couple that deal with the war—*The Lovely Leave* and *Song of the Shirt, 1941*—but this collection mostly makes you feel that you are reliving a vanished era. Except for one sketch of the Spanish War, the record seems to break off abruptly sometime in the early thirties.

Yet it, too, this collected volume, has a value derived from rarity—a rarity like that of steel penknives, good erasers and real canned sardines, articles of which the supply has almost given out and of which one is only now beginning to be aware of how excellent the quality was. It seems to me, though I shall name no names, that it has been one of the features of this later time that it produces imitation books. There are things of which one cannot really say that they are either good books or bad books; they are really not books at all. When one has bought them, one has only got paper and print. When one has bought Dorothy Parker, however, one has really got a book. She is not Emily Brontë or Jane Austen, but she has been at some pains to write well, and she has put into what she has written a voice, a state of mind, an era, a few moments of human experience that nobody else has conveyed. And the format of this volume, as is not always the case, is appropriate to and worthy of the contents. It is compact, well printed, and small, easy to carry and handle: the kind of thing that ought to be encouraged, as distinguished from the more ponderous type of omnibus. The title is simply *Dorothy Parker.*

May 20, 1944

A Treatise on Tales of Horror

THERE has lately been a sudden revival of the appetite for tales of horror. First, Pocket Books published *The Pocket Mystery Reader* and *The Pocket Book of Mystery Stories*. Then came *Tales of Terror*, with an introduction by Boris Karloff; *Creeps by Night*, with an introduction by Dashiell Hammett; and *Best Ghost Stories of M. R. James* (all three brought out by World). Finally, Random House has produced a prodigious anthology called *Great Tales of Terror and the Supernatural*, edited by Herbert A. Wise and Phyllis Fraser.

One had supposed that the ghost story itself was already an obsolete form; that it had been killed by the electric light. It was only during the ages of candlelight that the race of ghosts really flourished, though they survived through the era of gas. A candle can always burn low and be blown out by a gust of air, and it is a certain amount of trouble to relight it, as is also the case with a gas-jet. But if you can reach out and press a button and flood every corner of the room, leaving the specter quite naked in his vapor, or if you can transfix him out of doors with a flashlight, his opportunities for haunting are limited. It is true that one of the most famous of ghost stories, Defoe's *Apparition of Mrs. Veal*, takes place in the afternoon; that it is a part of the effectiveness of *The Turn of the Screw* that its phantoms appear outdoors in broad daylight as well as indoors at night; and that that eeriest of all ghost stories supposed to be true, the anonymous book called *An Adventure*, purports to give the experiences of two English ladies visiting Versailles in the afternoon; but these are all in the nature of tours de force on the part of the apparitions or the authors. The common run of ghost needed darkness. It will be noticed in all these anthologies that most of the writers belong by training to the last decades of the nineteenth century, even though a few of their stories have been written in the first years of this.

What is the reason, then—in these days when a lonely country house is likely to be equipped with electric light, radio and telephone—for our returning to these antiquated tales? There are, I believe, two reasons: first, the longing for mystic experience which seems always to manifest itself in periods of social confusion, when political progress is blocked: as soon as we feel that our own world has failed us, we try to find evidence for another world; second, the instinct to inoculate ourselves against panic at the real horrors loose on the earth—Gestapo and G.P.U., tank attacks and airplane bombings, houses rigged with booby-traps—by injections of imaginary horror, which soothe us with the momentary illusion that the forces of madness and murder may be tamed and compelled to provide us with a mere dramatic entertainment. We even try to make them cozy and droll, as in *Arsenic and Old Lace*, which could hardly have become popular or even been produced on the stage at any other period of our history. This craving for homeopathic horror first began to appear some years ago in the movies—with the Frankenstein monsters, the werewolves, the vampires and the insane sadistic scientists, of whom such a varied assortment are now to be seen along West Forty-second Street; and recently, in such films as *The Uninvited*, the pictures, too, have been reaching back to pull toward us the phantom fringe which has been exploited by these anthologies.

The best of these volumes is the new Random House one, because it is the most comprehensive (though the book itself has the fault of so many American omnibuses and anthologies of being too cumbersome to handle comfortably in bed, the only place where one is likely to read ghost stories), and not unintelligently edited. The two collections in the Pocket Book series, both edited by Miss Lee Wright, are, however, quite well selected, and have the merit of costing only a quarter each. And yet one cannot read a large number of pieces in any of these compilations without feeling rather let down. The editors are always building up their authors: "Certain of these stories, like *Lost Hearts* and *The Ash-Tree*," says the foreword to the *Best Ghost Stories of M. R. James*, ". . . should, we think, be skipped altogether by the squeamish and faint of heart"; a story by Robert Hichens is "unsurpassed for its subtle unfolding of a particularly loathsome horror"; and *Caterpillars*, by E. F. Benson, is "brilliantly told, and without doubt . . . one of the most horrifying stories in this collection." Now, I find it very hard to imagine that any of these particular tales could scare anybody over ten. Two of them simply play on the gooseflesh that is stimulated in certain people by the idea of caterpillars or spiders, and demon caterpillars and demon spiders very easily seem absurd. Other stories much esteemed by these anthologists, such as the one mentioned above, by Robert Hichens—*How Love Came to Professor Guildea*—or Helen R. Hull's *Clay-Shuttered Doors*, have promising macabre ideas—a great scientist who has cut himself off from all human relationships but is driven to desperation by an invisible imbecile who loves him; the wife of an ambitious New Yorker, who regalvanizes her decaying body and goes on playing her social role several months after she has been killed in a motor accident—but they are trashily or weakly done and do not realize their full possibilities. In either case, the authors content themselves with suggesting unpleasant sensations. They fail to lay hold on the terrors that lie deep in the human psyche and that cause man to fear himself.

These collections, of course, aim primarily at popular entertainment; they do not pretend to a literary standard. But I should like to suggest that an anthology of considerable interest and power could be compiled by assembling horror stories by really first-rate modern writers, in which they have achieved their effects not merely by attempting to transpose into terms of contemporary life the old fairy-tales of goblins and phantoms but by probing psychological caverns where the constraints of that life itself have engendered disquieting obsessions.

I should start off with Hawthorne and Poe, who are represented in these collections, but I should include, also, Melville and Gogol, who are not. The first really great short stories of horror came in the early or middle nineteenth century, when the school of Gothic romance had achieved some sophistication and was adopting the methods of realism. All four of these authors wrote stories that were at the same time tales of horror and psychological or moral fables. They were not interested in spooks for their own sake; they knew that their demons were symbols, and they knew what they were doing with these symbols. We read the tales of Poe in our childhood, when all that we are likely to get out of them is shudders, yet these stories are also poems that express the most intense emotions. *The Fall of the House of Usher* is not merely an ordinary ghost story:

the house—see the opening paragraph—is an image for a human personality, and its fate—see the fissure that runs through the wall—is the fate of a disrupted mind. And as for Gogol, he probably remains the very greatest master in this genre. I should put in at least *Viy* and *The Nose*—the former, a vampire story, one of the most terrific things of its kind ever written, and the latter, though it purports to be comic, almost equally a tale of horror, for it is charged with the disguised lurking meaning of a fear that has taken shape as a nightmare. I should include, also, *Bartleby the Scrivener* of Melville, which oddly resembles Gogol in this vein of the somber-grotesque, as well as *Benito Cereno*, a more plausible yet still nightmarish affair, which ought to be matched farther on by Conrad's *Heart of Darkness*.

In the latter part of the century, however, the period to which Conrad belongs, these fables tend to become impure. There was by that time much more pressure on the artist to report the material and social facts of the nineteenth-century world, and it seems difficult to combine symbolism with the inventories of naturalistic fiction or the discussion of public affairs. You have Stevenson, Kipling, Henry James. In Stevenson's case alone, this pressure did not inhibit his fancy, for he rarely wrote anything but fairy-tales, but he has much less intensity and substance than Conrad or Kipling or James. Nevertheless, though I might do without Jekyll and Hyde, I think I should have to have *Olalla* and *Thrawn Janet* (it is queer that a writer so popular in his time should be represented in none of these collections). But with Kipling you run into the cramping effects of a technical and practical period. I should include a couple of stories of Kipling's—say, *At the End of the Passage* and *Mrs. Bathurst*—as examples of borderline cases of the genuinely imaginative story which is nevertheless not first-rate. In such an early tale of Kipling's as *At the End of the Passage* or *The Phantom Rickshaw*, he is trying to write a mere vulgar ghost story, but something else that is authentic gets in. If we have carefully studied Kipling, we can recognize in the horrors of these tales—the blinded phantom, the wronged woman—obsessions that recur in his work and to which we can find the key in his life. But a story of this kind should convey its effect without our having to track down its symbols. We need nothing but the story itself to tell us that the author of *Viy* has put all the combined fascination and fear with which he was inspired by women into the vigil of the young student in the little wooden church beside the coffin of the farmer's daughter. When Kipling sets out later on to work up a more complex technique and attempts several layers of meaning, he gives us a piece like *Mrs. Bathurst*—the pursuit by a wronged woman, again—in which, however, the main character's sense of guilt is tied up through the symbol of the woman with his duty to the British Empire in connection with the Boer War, and he introduces a political element which seems clumsy and out of place in a ghost story and somehow gives Mrs. Bathurst a slight tinge of the newspaper cartoon. Henry James, a more serious writer, produced a strange special case in *The Turn of the Screw*. He asserted that he, too, had aimed merely at a conventional ghost story intended for a more knowing audience than that susceptible to the ordinary kind; but readers familiar with his work and conscious of his preoccupations have tended to see in the tale something more: the governess is not really, as she tells us, defending the children in her charge against the influence of malevolent spirits, she is frightening them herself with the projections of her own repressed emotions. There are, however, points in the story which are difficult to explain on this theory, and it is probable that James, like Kipling, was unconscious of having raised something more frightening than the ghosts he had contemplated. At any rate, I should put in *The Turn of the Screw*, and also *The Jolly Corner*, which seems to me James's other best ghost story. In this latter case, the author is of course quite conscious of what he is doing, but there is here, as in *Mrs. Bathurst*, an element rather difficult to assimilate (though Henry James does make us accept it) in the issue between England and the United States, a social and historical problem, which provides the moral of the fable.

During this period there were some very good ghost stories done by popular writers of distinction like Conan Doyle and W. W. Jacobs, but, capital fairy-tales though *The Monkey's Paw* and *Playing With Fire* are, I should not admit them to my ideal collection. Nor should I—on the basis of the specimens I have read—include anything from a different school, which grew up in the late years of the century and which was stimulated perhaps by the encroachments of the spread of the new methods of lighting on the old-fashioned kind of ghost. This school, which is represented abundantly in the Random House collection, derives, I take it, from Arthur Machen, and features, instead of resurrected bodies and insubstantial phantoms, a demonology of ancient cults driven underground by Christianity but persisting into our own day, and exploits the identification of the Devil with the pagan god Pan. Machen's story on this theme called *The Great God Pan* (in the Random House collection) seems to me to sum up in a fatal way everything that was most "ham" in the aesthetic satanism of the *fin de siècle*. M. R. James, a great favorite of these anthologists, played countless variations on this theme and had some really fiendish flashes of fancy, but he never took any trouble to make his stories seem even halfway plausible, so his hobgoblins are always verging on parody.

A better writer is Algernon Blackwood, who belongs to this same general group and has an even greater reputation than M. R. James. He, too, tends to lean on anti-human creatures that embody the forces of nature, but he is interesting for another reason: you can see in him very clearly the shift from a belief in evil spirits as things that come to plague us from outside to a consciousness of terrors inside us that merely take possession of our minds. But where Kipling or Henry James knew how to dramatize these terrors in solid images that command our credence, Blackwood, beginning as a rule with a locale which he has actually observed and which he more or less convincingly describes, invariably transposes the story, from the moment when the supernatural element appears, onto a plane of melting, gliding nightmare where nothing seems really to be taking place. Now, a story of this kind, to impress us, must *never* seem to be a dream. The tales of Poe, for all the wildness of their fantasy, are as circumstantial as Swift or Defoe; when Gogol retells a Ukrainian legend, he so stiffens its texture with authentic detail that we seem to hear the voices of the peasants and smell the countryside.

I should, therefore, decline to pass Algernon Blackwood, but I should certainly admit Walter de la Mare, who sometimes errs in the direction of the too dreamlike but makes up for it through poetic imagination. His story called *Seaton's*

Aunt comes close to being a masterpiece in this genre, and I should include also *Out of the Deep*, which is equally good in conception though not quite so good in execution. (The first of these has been included in *The Pocket Book of Mystery Stories* and the second in the Random House anthology.) De la Mare, a great admirer of Poe, has done work that is quite his own in this field of supernatural fiction; it is in my opinion superior to his verse. His stories at their best are poetic, psychologically subtle and creepy to a high degree.

And, finally, I should include Franz Kafka, also absent from any of these collections. Stories like *The Metamorphosis* and *Blumfeld, an Elderly Bachelor* are among the best things of their kind. The first of these unpleasant pieces deals with a young travelling salesman who suddenly wakes up one morning to find that he has turned into an enormous roach, to the horror of his parents, with whom he lives and who have been counting on him to pay off their debts; the second tells of an office worker, a selfish and bureaucratic upper clerk, who is haunted by two little bouncing balls that represent his niggardly consciousness of two children that help him in his office. The stories that Kafka has written on these two unconventional subjects are at the same time satires on the bourgeoisie and visions of moral horror; narratives that are logical and compel our attention, and fantasies that generate more shudders than the whole of Algernon Blackwood and M. R. James combined. A master can make it seem more horrible to be pursued by two little balls than by the spirit of a malignant Knight Templar, and more natural to turn into a cockroach than to be bitten by a diabolic spider. Kafka, who was writing these stories at the time of the last World War, had brought back the tale of terror to the true vein of Gogol and Poe. In his realm of imagination no social or political problems intrude in such a way as to spoil the show. The modern bourgeoisie and the Central European bureaucracy have turned into the enchanted denizens of a world in which, prosaic though it is, we can find no firm foothold in reality and in which we can never even be certain whether souls are being saved or damned. As an artist in this field of horror, Kafka is among the greatest. Living in the era of Freud, he went straight for the morbidities of the psyche with none of the puppetry of specters and devils that

earlier writers still carried with them. Whether his making out
of these subjects at that time of day the Hoffmannesque fantasies that he did make, and whether the rapt admiration for
them in *our* time represents a retrogression or a progress in the
development of modern literature in general, I shall not attempt to decide.

May 27, 1944

A Guide to Finnegans Wake

A *Skeleton Key to Finnegans Wake*, by Joseph Campbell and Henry Morton Robinson, is an indispensable book for anyone interested in Joyce and should make many new readers for *Finnegans Wake*.

This last book of James Joyce is a very great poem, one of the top works of literature of our time. It is in some ways, in fact, a more extraordinary production than *Ulysses*—digging deeper into human psychology, breaking new intellectual ground and exhibiting Joyce's musical genius as perhaps none of his other books does. Yet *Finnegans Wake* has acquired the reputation of being inordinately difficult to read, and Joyce has even been accused in some quarters of having perpetrated an insolent hoax or excreted an insane mess of gibberish. Even readers who have admired *Ulysses* have been reluctant to tackle its successor. But the book has now been out five years, and it is time that these doubts and inhibitions were dispelled. The appearance of the Campbell-Robinson key should open a new era in the acceptance and currency of *Finnegans Wake*. In recommending this guide, however, I want to make a few suggestions of my own which are, it seems to me, needed to supplement this introduction.

In the first place, it is an excellent thing, though perhaps not absolutely required, for the reader to be fairly familiar with the other writings of Joyce. Then, it will help this reader immensely if he comes to *Finnegans Wake* with some acquaintance with Virgil, Dante and Milton. It is a better equipment for Joyce to know something of the most accomplished masters of the writing of fiction in verse than to have formed one's ideas of literary art from the reading of modern novels. The art of narrative literature was brought by the great epic poets of the past to a point from which it later declined with the rise of the prose novel. A man like Dante has a command of language, a power to make it render the nuances of atmosphere, color, sound, phases of feeling and traits of personality, in comparison with which the writing of even a respectable novelist of the infancy of the novel, like Fielding, seems quite wooden, hardly writing at all. It was only with the Romantics that the language of prose fiction began to be flexible and sensitive enough to represent directly—by the sound and the look and the connotations of words—the things that it was describing. Flaubert was the first writer of prose fiction to challenge the ancients on this ground, and Flaubert had his limitations: his effects, like his mood, are monotonous. But he was studied and emulated by Joyce, whose range was enormously wider and who turned out to be, in fact, as T. S. Eliot said, the greatest master of language in English since Milton. *Ulysses* and *Finnegans Wake* are epics which not only perform feats of style hitherto unknown in the novel but also, like the *Æneid* and *The Divine Comedy*, deal with national myths and the destiny of man in a way that is unexpected for the ordinary novel reader. *Ulysses* had still enough of the framework of conventional fiction so that this ordinary reader could navigate it at the cost of a little effort. *Finnegans Wake*, however, though it was more "realistic" than it looked at first sight, seemed completely to have cast off the conventions.

The epic of *Ulysses* consisted of a day in the lives of certain characters; that of *Finnegans Wake* covers the sleeping life of a man during a single night. The next difficulty is to grasp this design. We may understand the purpose of Dante to construct an all-comprehensive poem out of a vision of Hell, Purgatory and Heaven; and we may not be baffled in the least by such literary renderings of dream or trance as De Quincey's opium rhapsodies, Flaubert's *Tentation de Saint Antoine*, Lewis Carroll's Alice books or the dreams in Dostoevsky's novels. Yet we may not be prepared for a book of more than six hundred pages which plunges us into a man's sleeping mind and keeps us there till he is about to wake up. Nor is it easy at first to realize that Joyce is using the resources of a poet not only to present the billowing emotions and the kaleidoscopic imagery of a dream but also to render with accuracy all the physical states of sleep. I may give a simple example, since the authors of the *Skeleton Key* have not emphasized this aspect of *Finnegans Wake*. The heavy breathing and the snoring of the hero run all through the book and are exploited for poetic effects which it might well be thought that no great poet would be so bold or so absurd as to attempt and which yet are made to contribute triumphantly to some of Joyce's most lyrical writing. The heaving of the four deep breaths which always marks the hero's subsidence into a deeper stratum of sleep provides much grotesque humor, such as the "What a hauhauhauhaudibble thing, to be cause! How, Mutt?" of the inarticulate conversation between the loutish prehistoric men; but it also gives the fall of darkness and the widening of the river at the close of the "Anna Livia Plurabelle" chapter, one of the incomparably beautiful things in the book: "Dark hawks hear us. Night! Night! My ho head halls. I feel as heavy as yonder stone," etc.

The sleeper in *Finnegans Wake* is a man named H. C. Earwicker, who keeps a pub on the Liffey and has a family consisting of a wife, one daughter and twin sons. The nexus of his family relations and Earwicker's career in Dublin are the immediate materials of his dream, but Joyce, with his epic intentions and a kind of modern Jungian conception of a myth-creating mind of the race, has contrived to make his dream universal. How he has done this I need not explain in detail because Campbell and Robinson have explained it better than anybody else has yet done. The dream itself is a myth, with characters and a plot of its own, and though its main elements multiply their aspects with all the shifting metamorphosis of a dream, they are constant and perfectly plain. Do not be put off by the opening pages, which have mysteries for even the adept at Joyce. Earwicker has fallen asleep: he has lost consciousness, but he is not yet dreaming. The moment seems dark and blank, but it is a blur of all his being holds. Joyce has resorted to the device, in *Finnegans Wake*, of conveying the ambiguities and vagueness of the visions and sensations of sleep by the invention of punning portmanteau words like the language of *Jabberwocky*, and these words have here been crammed with meanings to a point where all the many symbols appear hopelessly jumbled and mashed. Messrs. Campbell and Robinson, however, have unpacked a good many of these meanings, so that we can see what was in the portmanteaux of the first paragraphs of *Finnegans Wake*, and thus have eliminated one of the obstacles which have been baffling the willing reader. When you get through this choked defile and the action of the dream begins, you will find yourself among recognizable presences that flicker but speak and move, and the powerful current of language will continue to carry you along even through queer interruptions and eclipses. If you will read the Campbell-Robinson synopsis at the beginning of their *Skeleton Key*, you will see that the large architecture of *Finnegans Wake*, in spite of the complication of detail, is solid, precise and simple, as the principal themes of the book are matters of obvious universal experience, so utterly commonplace that the difficulty in grasping them comes sometimes from the sophisticated reader's unreadiness to accept anything so little esoteric as the basic facts of family life, the mixed moral nature of man and the phenomena of birth, growth and death rather than from the dense psychological web which Joyce has spun among them or the variegated legendry and language with which they have been embroidered.

The great thing is to get the hang and to follow the line of the myth, and this Campbell and Robinson will help you to do. They have provided a paraphrase of Joyce which disentangles and tightens this line. One may not approve every step of their trail, every abridgment, selection or reading, and they have sometimes made actual errors, but they have opened up the book to the public at the cost of much patience and care, and they deserve a citation from the Republic of Letters for having succeeded in bringing it out at this time. Mr. Campbell is a folklore scholar, with considerable knowledge of Ireland, who is particularly qualified to interpret Joyce on his mythological and historical sides; Mr. Robinson, who is an editor of *Reader's Digest*, here applies a special skill acquired in whittling down magazine articles to condensing a masterpiece.

This condensation, of course, is compelled to leave a great deal out. The authors' paraphrase of Joyce necessarily strips away most of the master's magnificent poetry, and thus transmits no idea at all of the *emotional* power of the original, since, where everything is not merely described but represented directly, the style is involved with the content to a degree which is not common with contemporary writers. In the Campbell-Robinson key, you will find almost no indication of the infinite variation in the texture and tone of the writing which reflects the various phases of the night.

Another matter which the authors neglect, in holding on to

the sequence of the myth, is the family situation, which has its grip on the whole fantasia. The real story behind the dream story is something that we have to guess at and which it becomes one of the fascinations of reading *Finnegans Wake* to work out. There are moments when it breaks through the myth with its insistent and naked facts, and it is at all times the hidden director which determines the shape of the dream by its alternate impulsions and checks, its quick blendings and its sudden reversals. The sleeper, who passes from fatigue to refreshment, from death to resurrection, is enacting a universal drama which is enacted every night by every man in the world; but every man is a particular man, and this man is a particular Dubliner, asleep on a certain night in a room above a certain pub in the bosom of a certain family. The authors of the *Skeleton Key* have pretty nearly combed the real family away in presenting their simplification of the myth; they tend to disregard the indications which Joyce is very careful to plant about Earwicker's real situation; and they do not always seem quite clear about the author's technique in dealing with the connection between the dream and these realities. They, for example, simply follow the language of the dream in the question-and-answer chapter, which is intended, though the real questions and answers are always just around the corner from the dreamed ones, to give the reader a very definite statement of the location and personnel of the household; and they seem to think that Earwicker, through part of the book, has been lying drunk on the floor of the pub and that he goes upstairs to bed at some point, and, later, in the scene before dawn, when one of the twins wakes the mother and she goes into his room to calm him, that the husband gets up and goes in with her and afterwards has intercourse with her; whereas it is plain that, in the first case, the falling on the floor and the going upstairs themselves take place in the dream, and that, in the second, he has hardly awakened but, half aware of what his wife is doing, has sunk back into fitful slumber. It is an essential feature of the plan of the book, it makes its artistic unity, that Earwicker shall be always in bed and that he shall never wake up till morning—just the moment after the book ends. The later chapters of the *Skeleton Key* are thus definitely unsatisfactory. The authors prove themselves heroically strong in the cracking of such formidable nuts as the colloquy between St. Patrick and the Archdruid, but they are weak and even misleading on the more obvious human elements which make the end of *Finnegans Wake* one of the greatest things Joyce ever wrote.

In any case, if you have not tried *Finnegans Wake*, you cannot do better than get it and get the Campbell-Robinson key and prepare to have them around for years. A few more last words of guidance. The conditions for reading this book are different, so far as I know, from those for reading any other ever written. You have to take it rather slowly, a section at a time, and you have to keep on rereading it. Joyce worked on it through seventeen years, and it is equivalent to about seventeen books by the ordinary gifted writer. You may think it too much that Joyce should ask you to strain your wits over solving his elaborate puzzles, but the fact is that a good deal of the book, once you see the general pattern, is readable and comprehensible even when the language is queer. Joyce counts on a certain dimness to give the effect of a dream; and for people who do like to solve puzzles, the puzzles are fun to solve. Today, when we are getting so many books in which the style is perfectly clear but the meaning nonexistent or equivocal, it affords a certain satisfaction to read something that looks like nonsense on the surface but underneath makes perfect sense. Admirers of Balzac and Trollope think nothing of devoting years to reading their favorites through, and why should we grudge time to Joyce? The demands that he makes are considerable, but the rewards he provides are astounding. I do not deny that he is tedious at times: I am bored by the relentless *longueurs* of some of the middle chapters of *Finnegans Wake* just as I am bored by those of the latter part of *Ulysses*, and I have found it puts me straight to sleep to try to follow the charting of these wastes which has intrepidly been carried out by the authors of the *Skeleton Key*, just as it did to read Joyce's original. But it is an exciting, a unique experience to find pages that have seemed to us meaningless start into vivid life, full of energy, brilliance, passion. The chance to be among the first to explore the wonders of *Finnegans Wake* is one of the few great intellectual and aesthetic treats that these last bad years have yielded.

August 5, 1944

A Novel by Salvador Dali

SALVADOR DALI has published a novel, and it is startling, but not at all in the same way as his famous deliquescent pianos and ladies full of bureau drawers. It is one of the most old-fashioned novels that anybody has written in years, for it consists almost exclusively of a potpourri of the properties, the figures and the attitudes of the later and gamier phases of French romantic writing. The preposterous Lesbian boudoir of Balzac's *Fille aux Yeux d'Or*; the proud and perverse aristocrats of Barbey d'Aurevilly's *Diaboliques*, with their grandiose duels of sex; the exalted erotic mysticism of Villiers de l'Isle-Adam's *Axel*; the cultivation of artificial sensations of Huysmans' Des Esseintes and the demonological researches of his Durtal—all these have been disinterred by Mr. Dali in *Hidden Faces* and put through their old routines to the tune of an improvised style which makes the whole thing seem to verge on parody. The only relatively up-to-date elements are a superficial injection of Freudianism and an overlay of surrealist rhetoric—when, if you follow me, Mr. Dali allows the milliped and Boschesque crustaceans of his hermetic imagination to caress the tentacular algae of his subaqueous and electrified impudicity or the nacreous and colubrine doves of a psychosomatic idealism to circle in shimmering syndromes the façades of a palladian narcissism. But this modernism is more than offset by the uncontrollable tendency of his characters to write one another long letters that sound like a burlesque of *Werther* or *La Nouvelle Héloïse:* "Dear Hervé—my beloved—is it a dream to be able to call you thus? Know, my beloved, that of your letter I have retained only your first words of love, which will remain engraved in my heart till after I am dead. Even when the worms shall have gnawed this heart away they will have to perish and be consumed in turn at the bottom of my coffin, curled up in the form of the letters of the inscription they have devoured, so true it is that this inscription must be and shall be the last reality that can be effaced from my existence!"

In an atmosphere of ringing aristocratic names, men and

women of resplendent beauty, and balls and banquets of incredible luxury, which will take the English-speaking reader
back to Disraeli, Bulwer-Lytton and Ouida, it is a surprise to
hear suddenly about Hitler, the Communists or the Maginot
Line. But the war does descend on Mr. Dali's world (though
the truth is that, for all the grasp that Mr. Dali displays of his
time, it might almost as well be the Crimean War or the fall of
the Second Empire). And what do they all do then—these iridescent Comtes de Grandsailles and Vicomtes d'Angerville and
Princes d'Orminy and Solanges de Cléda, with their Byzantine
bouquets made of jewels, their elegant and daring toilettes,
their opium-smoking and their cold, depraved passions? Why,
their versatile creator drops at once the preciosity in which he
has been clothing them and makes them behave almost exactly
like so many characters by Louis Bromfield—with whom, I
fear, Salvador Dali has something fundamentally in common.
When they realize the plight of France, they gallantly pull themselves together and begin performing prodigies of heroism—
proving, by their readiness to sacrifice themselves, the stuff of
which the French nobility, even in its decadence, is made. The
truth is, in fact, that the point of view of the Catalonian Dali is,
to all intents and purposes, that of some trashy old French roy-
alist snob such as Barbey d'Aurevilly, who, as I say, seems to
haunt *Hidden Faces*. It is touching to find Mr. Haakon M.
Chevalier, who has translated Dali's novel, attempting to reassure us in a foreword by implying that the author has been fa-
vorably impressed by the Russian Revolution and pointing out
his sympathy with the peasant. Mr. Dali's attitude toward the
peasant is that of a romantic *grand seigneur*, or, rather, of one
who has read a good deal about the attitudes of *grand
seigneurs*, and his attitude toward Communists and Anarchists
and all that they try to do is one of perkily-mustachioed
disdain.

One element appears in his novel which had not entered the
cosmos of Barbey: the role of the United States as a power to
be reckoned with by Europe. But this power is represented for
Dali by a *richissime* American girl distinguished by the selfishness, arrogance, frigidity and long-limbed blond beauty which
had already become the standard attributes for such characters

in French fiction, and a dashing and indomitable young aviator bearing the fine Virginian name of John Randolph, who repudiates the "revolutionary illusions" that had led him to aid the Loyalists in the Spanish Civil War, and declares, "I, too, believe once more in the ineradicable forces of tradition and aristocracy." When he and the Comte de Grandsailles (great noble and upholder of the feudal ideal) come to confront one another through their oxygen masks, just before taking off on a perilous flight, "their eyes appeared alike, equally pure, and in neither case could one tell whether it was exaltation or coldness that gave them their greater luster. With a single impulse the two men removed their gloves, and their hands clasped for a moment, like those of wrestlers." Yet the moment will later arrive when they must come to blows in America over the *richissime* Veronica, and here there is something flattering for the land in which Mr. Dali is sojourning, if not something for its great moving-picture industry: "'A curious country, America, don't you think, Randolph?' said the Count of Grandsailles, making a face after biting into a piece of pear impaled on his fork, and putting down his implement on the edge of the plate. 'Its fruit has no flavor, its women have no shame, and its men are without honor!' . . . 'The fruit of our country,' said Randolph, measuring each syllable, 'have the flavor of liberty and hospitality, which you have basely taken advantage of to feed yourself and your secrets; our women are those whom you try unsuccessfully to corrupt, to pervert and make sterile, and our men are those who have the honor of sacrificing their lives in that Europe of yours to redeem the honor which you weren't men enough to defend and shamefully lost to the enemy.'"

Yet, in spite of this concession to current events, it is always the Comte de Grandsailles, with his eccentric and faultless taste and his satanic and devious temperament, who enchants his creator, Dali. The war, from the author's point of view, is being fought to save the honor of old France—betrayed by ignoble politicians—against the upstart and ill-bred Nazis.

All this is not, of course, to say that the painter of *Debris of an Automobile Giving Birth to a Blind Horse Biting a Telephone* is not a very clever fellow, or that his novel may not afford entertainment. I have been quoting from the later part, which is more or less unadorned balderdash; but the earlier chapters, which the author has been at more pains to embroider and dramatize, have passages, images, ideas that lend them at moments an illusion of brilliance. There is the theory, not entirely implausible, put forward by one of the characters about Hitler: that he is really an heroic masochist, whose true hope and goal is defeat, though he has pledged himself to play the game according to all the rules and make every effort to win, before he will be able to fulfill himself by provoking his own annihilation. There is the satire on pre-war French culture implicit in the relation between the Comte de Grandsailles and his factotum, the local notary. The notary is rude and provincial but has a gift of pungent wit; the Count, who lacks originality, is always stopping the conversation to write down the other's good things, and he then sorts them into various categories, reduces them to polished form, and passes in Paris for a witty talker. And there is also a long gruesome account of an opium and heroin jag which has something of the same kind of fascination as Charles Jackson's *The Lost Weekend* (it may be that the epic of drugging is a genre which has arrived in our era).

But, on the evidence of *Hidden Faces*, I should say that Mr. Dali was no writer. I cannot believe that the translator has betrayed him. Mr. Haakon M. Chevalier certainly knows French perfectly, and when he is doing his own work, he can command a very sound English prose. He complains in his foreword here of the redundancies and mixed metaphors of Dali, and explains that he has done what he could to trim his language and straighten out his style. I think he might still have spared the reader a certain amount of stumbling by the exercise of a little more care about not carrying over French tenses; and not inflicted on him such sentences as "His face . . . gave witness that the emotions of his heart with their weakness had no right to cloud the clean limpidness of his diction" (where the more correct word "limpidity" would have saved him at least from one of the endings in "ness"); or such English as "she saw a figure approaching her . . . without scarcely noticing it" and "Cécile and I will arrive only in the last moment." He might even, one might think, have told Dali that "*nemo*" does not mean "nothing," and that the man who made the clock with glass works was not "Oudin" but Robert-Houdin. Yet I definitely get the impression that Mr. Chevalier has been somewhat demoralized by his original's Hispanic French and orgies of loose-squandered verbiage, and that he has here not been quite himself.

On Dali's side, one finds in this novel none of the qualities that are good in his pictures, which are certainly not deficient in craftsmanship: there is no clarity, no sharp-focussed vividness, no delicacy or firmness of line. We are far from the beneficent influences that have presided over his development as a painter: Picasso and Chirico, Velásquez and Vermeer. Dali's literary models have been bad ones, and, from the moment that he abandoned his real métier, they have swept him into a retrogression that affords one of the most curious examples of the contemporary stoppage and lapse of the arts in collision with the political crisis.

July 1, 1944

A Long Talk About Jane Austen

THERE have been several revolutions of taste during the last century and a quarter of English literature, and through them all perhaps only two reputations have never been affected by the shifts of fashion: Shakespeare's and Jane Austen's. We still agree with Scott about Jane Austen, just as we agree with Ben Jonson about Shakespeare. From Scott, Southey, Coleridge and Macaulay (to say nothing of the Prince Regent, who kept a set of her works "in every one of his residences") to Kipling and George Moore, Virginia Woolf and E. M. Forster, she has compelled the amazed admiration of writers of the most diverse kinds, and I should say that Jane Austen and Dickens rather queerly present themselves today as the only two English novelists (though not quite the only novelists in English) who belong in the very top rank with the great fiction writers of Russia and France. Jane Austen, as Mr. Stark Young once said, is perhaps the only English example of that spirit of classical comedy that is more natural to the Latin people than to ours and that Molière represents for the French. That this spirit should have embodied itself in England in the mind of a well-bred spinster, the daughter of a country clergyman, who never saw any more of the world than was made possible by short visits to London and a residence of a few years in Bath and who found her subjects mainly in the problems of young provincial girls looking for husbands, seems one of the most freakish of the many anomalies of English literary history.

In *Speaking of Jane Austen*, by G. B. Stern and Sheila Kaye-Smith, two of Jane Austen's sister novelists have collaborated to pay her homage. Both Miss Stern and Miss Kaye-Smith have read the six novels again and again, and they have at their fingers' ends every trait, every speech, every gesture of every one of Jane Austen's people. Here they discuss, in alternate chapters, which give the effect of a conversation, a variety of aspects of their subject. Miss Kaye-Smith is especially concerned with the historical background of the novels: she turns up a good deal that is interesting about the costume and food of the period and the social position of clergymen, and she traces the reflection, so meager and dim, of the cataclysmic political events that took place during Miss Austen's lifetime. Miss Stern is more preoccupied with the characters, whom she sometimes treats as actual people, classifying them on principles of her own and speculating about their lives beyond the story; sometimes criticizes from the point of view of a novelist who would see the situation in some cases a little differently, modifying or filling out a character or assigning a heroine to a different mate. The two ladies debate together the relative merits of the novels, agreeing that *Pride and Prejudice* belongs not at the top but toward the bottom of the list, and partly agreeing and partly not as to which of the characters are least successful. They have notes on Miss Austen's language and they underline some of her fine inconspicuous strokes. They make an effort to evoke the personalities of characters who are mentioned but never appear, and they have concocted a terrific quiz, which few readers, I imagine, could pass.

The book thus contains a good deal that will be interesting to those interested in Jane Austen, though neither Miss Stern nor Miss Kaye-Smith, it seems to me, really goes into the subject so deeply as might be done. My impression is that the long study of Jane Austen which has lately been published by Queenie Leavis in the English magazine called *Scrutiny* gets to grips with her artistic development in a way that the present authors, who do not mention Mrs. Leavis' essay, have scarcely even attempted to do. Yet *Speaking of Jane Austen*, as an informal symposium, revives the enthusiasm of the reader and stimulates him to think about the questions suggested by Miss Kaye-Smith and Miss Stern. Let me contribute a few comments of my own which will bring certain of these matters to attention:

1. The half-dozen novels of Jane Austen were written in two sets of three each, with an interval of about ten years between the two: *Pride and Prejudice*, *Sense and Sensibility* and *Northanger Abbey*; *Mansfield Park*, *Emma* and *Persuasion*. The first of these lots, both in its satiric comedy and in the pathos of *Sense and Sensibility*, is quite close to the eighteenth century, whereas the second, with its psychological subtlety and

such realism as the episode in *Mansfield Park* in which Fanny goes back to her vulgar home, is much closer to what we call "modern." In the second lot, the set comic character of the type of Lady Catherine de Bourgh, who at moments, as Miss Stern points out, falls into the tone of an old-fashioned play, tends to give way to another kind of portraiture—as in the small country community of *Emma*—which is farther from caricature and more recognizable as a picture of everyday life, and in *Persuasion*, a sensitivity to landscape and a tenderness of feeling appear that have definitely a tinge of the romantic. It is not true, as has been sometimes complained, that Miss Austen took no interest in nature, though this last novel is the only one of her books of which one clearly remembers the setting. Miss Kaye-Smith does note of *Persuasion* that "the weather and scenery have taken on some of the emotional force that permeates the whole book." But both authors seem to treat the novels as if they have always coëxisted in time, instead of forming a sequence. What I miss in *Speaking of Jane Austen* is any account of the successive gradations, literary and psychological, which lead from *Pride and Prejudice* to *Persuasion*.

2. The authors of this book both believe that there is something wrong with *Mansfield Park*, and they have a great deal to say about it. They feel that the chief figure, Fanny Price, a poor relation who immolates herself to the family of a great country house, is too meaching—too "creep-mouse," Miss Kaye-Smith says—to be an altogether sympathetic heroine, and that in this case the author herself, in a way that is not characteristic, adopts a rather pharisaical attitude toward the more fun-loving and sophisticated characters. Miss Kaye-Smith tries to explain this attitude by suggesting that Jane Austen at this period may have come under the influence of the Evangelical Movement, to which two references are to be found in the book.

To the reviewer, this line of criticism in regard to *Mansfield Park* is already very familiar—it seems to represent a reaction which is invariable with feminine readers; yet I have never felt particularly the importance of the objections that are made on these grounds nor been shaken in my conviction that *Mansfield Park* is artistically the most nearly perfect of the novels. It is true that I have not read it for thirty years, so that I have had time to forget the moralizings that bother Miss Kaye-Smith and Miss Stern, but the sensations I remember to have had were purely aesthetic ones: a delight in the focussing of the complex group through the ingenuous eyes of Fanny, the balance and harmony of the handling of the contrasting timbres of the characters, which are now heard in combination, now set off against one another. I believe that, in respect to Jane Austen's heroines, the point of view of men readers is somewhat different from that of women ones. The woman reader wants to identify herself with the heroine, and she rebels at the idea of being Fanny. The male reader neither puts himself in Fanny's place nor imagines himself marrying Fanny any more than he does the nice little girl in Henry James's *What Maisie Knew*, a novel which *Mansfield Park* in some ways quite closely resembles. What interests him in Miss Austen's heroines is the marvellous portraiture of a gallery of different types of women, and Fanny, with her humility, her priggishness and her innocent and touching good faith, is a perfect picture of one kind of woman.

Whatever tone Jane Austen may sometimes take, what emerge and give the book its value are characters objectively seen, form and movement conceived aesthetically. It is this that sets Jane Austen apart from so many other women novelists— whether, like the author of *Wuthering Heights* or the author of *Gone With the Wind*, of the kind that make their power felt by a projection of their feminine day-dreams, or of the kind, from *Evelina* to *Gentlemen Prefer Blondes*, that amuse us by mimicking people. Miss Austen is almost unique among the novelists of her sex in being deeply and steadily concerned, not with the vicarious satisfaction of emotion (though the Cinderella theme, of course, does figure in several of her novels) nor with the skillful exploitation of gossip, but, as the great masculine novelists are, with the novel as a work of art.

3. *Emma*, which both these critics adore, is with Jane Austen what *Hamlet* is with Shakespeare. It is the book of hers about which her readers are likely to disagree most; they tend either to praise it extravagantly or to find it dull, formless and puz-

zling. The reason for this, I believe, is that, just as in the case of *Hamlet*, there is something outside the picture which is never made explicit in the story but which has to be recognized by the reader before it is possible for him to appreciate the book. Many women readers feel instinctively the psychological rightness of the behavior attributed to Emma, and they are the ones who admire the novel. Some male readers, like Justice Holmes, who was certainly a connoisseur of fiction yet who wrote to Sir Frederick Pollock that, "bar Miss Bates," he was "bored by *Emma*," never succeed in getting into the story because they cannot see what it is all about. Why does Emma take up her two protégées? Why does she become so much obsessed by her plans for them? Why does she mistake the realities so and go so ludicrously wrong about them? Why does it take her so unconscionably long to reach the obvious rapprochement with Knightley?

The answer is that Emma is not interested in men except in the paternal relation. Her actual father is a silly old woman: in their household it is Emma herself who, motherless as she is, assumes the functions of head of the family; it is she who takes the place of the parent and Mr. Woodhouse who becomes the child. It is Knightley who has checked and rebuked her, who has presided over her social development, and she accepts him as a substitute father; she finally marries him and brings him into her own household, where his role is to reinforce Mr. Woodhouse. Miss Stern sees the difficulties of this odd situation. "Oh, Miss Austen," she cries, "it was *not* a good solution; it was a bad solution, an unhappy ending, could we see beyond the last pages of the book." But among the contretemps she foresees she does not mention what would surely have been the worst. Emma, who was relatively indifferent to men, was inclined to infatuations with women; and what reason is there to believe that her marriage with Knightley would prevent her from going on as she had done before: from discovering a new young lady as appealing as Harriet Smith, dominating her personality and situating her in a dream-world of Emma's own in which Emma would be able to confer on her all kinds of imaginary benefits but which would have no connection whatever with her condition or her real possibilities?

This would worry and exasperate Knightley and be hard for him to do anything about. He would be lucky if he did not presently find himself saddled, along with the other awkward features of the arrangement, with one of Emma's young protégées as an actual member of the household.

I do not mean to suggest for *Emma* any specific Freudian formula, but I feel sure that it is the one of her novels in which the author's own peculiar "conditioning" is most curiously and clearly seen. Jane Austen spent all her life with persons related to her by blood—her parents, her five brothers, her single unmarried sister—and the experience behind the relationships imagined by her in her novels is always an experience of relationships of blood, of which that between sisters is certainly the most deeply felt. Miss Stern and Miss Kaye-Smith are agreed with George Moore that Marianne's love for Willoughby in *Sense and Sensibility* is the most passionate thing in Jane Austen; but isn't it rather the emotion of Elinor as she witnesses her sister's disaster than Marianne's emotion over Willoughby of which the poignancy is communicated to the reader? The involvement with one another of the sisters is the real central theme of the book, just as the relation of Elizabeth to her sisters is so vital a part of *Pride and Prejudice*. For, though Miss Austen's intelligence was free to follow and understand other women when they were flirting or comfortably married, hunting husbands or breaking their hearts, she seems always to have been held suspended by the web of her original family ties. To some special equilibrium of the kind, which she never felt the necessity of upsetting, she must partly have owed the coolness, the patience, the poise, the leisure of mind to work at writing for its own sake, that made it possible for her to become a great artist. The solicitude of the sober Elinor Dashwood watching her giddy sister Marianne becomes in time the detached interest of the author looking on at the adventures of her heroines. In the last of her novels, *Persuasion*, one does find a different element and feel a personal emotion of the author's—a tinge of sadness at a woman's self-fulfilment missed—but the pattern is still much the same. Anne Elliot is herself a young sister: she, too, has a big sister, Lady Russell, who, like Emma, has misled her protégée—in this case, by discouraging her from marrying and nearly spoiling her life. Miss Stern and Miss Kaye-Smith do not care much for Lady Russell as a character; but she is worth thinking seriously about as a very important motif in Jane Austen. The comedy of the false sister-relationship of *Emma* has turned into something almost tragic.

June 24, 1944

"You Can't Do This to Me!" Shrilled Celia

*T*he Robe, by Lloyd C. Douglas, has become, from the point of view of sales, one of the greatest successes of publishing history. Published in October, 1942, it stood at one time at the head of the best-seller list for fiction for eleven consecutive months, and is still well up toward the top. It has sold, in less than two years, one million, four hundred and fifty thousand copies, and the publishers estimate that it has been read by five times that number of people. Houghton Mifflin, with their restricted supply of paper, have twice had the book reset in order to reduce the number of pages, and have had to resort to other special economies to meet the demand at all. They have announced, in the *Publishers' Weekly*, a vast new advertising campaign for August, and one sometimes gets the impression that they have ceased to bring out any other books. One of their publicity releases reports that a copy of *The Robe*, auctioned off at the opening of the Fifth War Loan Drive, brought $525,000 in War Bonds.

Never having looked into this book, I lately decided that it was time for me to take cognizance of it. I have procured a copy of *The Robe*, and what I have found in it has been rather surprising. Instead of the usual trash aimed at Hollywood and streamlined for the popular magazines, one is confronted with something that resembles an old-fashioned historical novel for young people. Here is the tone of the opening page: "Because she was only fifteen and busy with her growing up, Lucia's periods of reflection were brief and infrequent, but this morning she felt weighted with responsibility. Last night her mother, who rarely talked to her about anything more perplexing than the advantages of clean hands and a pure heart, had privately discussed the possible outcome of Father's reckless remarks yesterday in the Senate, and Lucia, flattered by this confidence, had declared maturely that Prince Gaius wasn't in a position to do anything about it. But after she had gone to bed, Lucia began to fret. . . . They would all have to be careful now or they might get into serious trouble. The birds had awakened her early. She was not yet used to their flutterings and twitterings; for they had returned much sooner than usual, Spring having arrived and unpacked before February's lease was up. Lucia roused to a consciousness of the fret that she had taken to bed with her. It was still there, like a toothache. . . . For the past year or more, Lucia had been acutely conscious of her increasing height and rapid development into womanhood, but here on this expanse of tessellated tiling she always felt very insignificant. . . . No matter how old she became, she would be ever a child here."

There are five hundred and fifty-six pages of this. It is a story of the Roman Empire in the days of early Christianity, and its appeal is exactly the same as that of *The Last Days of Pompeii*, *Quo Vadis?* and *Ben-Hur*. The surface has been brought up to date by diluting the old grandiose language of the novel of ancient Rome with a jargon which sounds as if Dr. Douglas had picked it up during the years when, as the publishers' leaflet tells us, he was a counsellor of college students at the Universities of Michigan and Illinois. The aristocratic Romans are always saying things like "You're definitely drunk," "But what's the matter with idols? They're usually quite artistic!," "Indeed! Well—she'd better be good!," "I wouldn't know," "What do you mean—'a Christian'?" At one point a lady of Tiberius' court addresses her noble lover as follows: "You liked me well enough until you came here and noticed this Gallus girl's curves! And it's plain to see she despises you! . . You can't do this to me! Where will *you* stand with Sejanus when I tell him you have treated me like an ordinary trollop?" But, for the rest, it is as leisurely, as formless and as careful of all the maidenly proprieties as any novel of the nineteenth century. It differs from Bulwer-Lytton only in being written worse. Dr. Douglas has woven, in *The Robe*, an almost unrivalled fabric of old clichés, in which one of the only attempts at a literary heightening of effect is the substitution for the simple "said" of other more pretentious verbs—so that the characters are always shrilling, barking, speculating, parrying, wailing, wheedling or grunting whatever they have to say.

It is so difficult, when one first glances into *The Robe*, to imagine that any literate person with even the faintest trace of literary taste could ever get through more than two pages of it for pleasure that one is astounded and terrified at the thought that seven million Americans have found something in it to hold their attention. What is the explanation of this? Dr. Douglas himself, in an article distinguished by both modesty and good sense (*Why I Wrote "The Robe,"* in the June *Cosmopolitan*), has indicated a part of the answer. In the first place, he says, you can always score a success by writing a novel about Jesus, if you take care to avoid the controversies which have split the later Christians into sects. He cites *Ben-Hur*, which "sold more than a million copies during one of the most placid decades in American history," and a novel called *In His Steps*, by a clergyman in Kansas. But there is also, perhaps, he adds, a special reason why a novel about Jesus should be widely read at this time. It is quite natural that people should find it a relief to hear about somebody who was interested in healing the blind and the crippled rather than in blinding and crippling people, and in comforting the persecuted rather than in outlawing large groups of human beings. This must certainly be true, and there are also special reasons why Dr. Douglas' picture of Jesus should particularly command attention. Dr. Douglas, who is a Congregational minister and the son of a country parson, has an asset which can only be described as old-time Christian feeling. He is a genuine man of God of the type that used to do his best in the American small-town pulpit and that the community felt it could rely on. He is an anachronism, but he represents something that a good many Americans must feel to be reassuring. And, besides this, he has given to *The Robe* one virtue which can make a good bad novel, just as it constitutes a *sine qua non* for every really excellent one: he has imagined the whole thing for himself. *The Robe* has not been made out of other books: Dr. Douglas has lived the story—he has attempted to see for himself how the Christians would look to the Romans and how the Romans would look to the Jews. The fact that this has been done many times before does not deter Dr. Douglas or prevent him from creating in his story a certain atmosphere of suspense and adventure. He has set out to track down a conceivable Jesus in an alien but conceivable world; and his book, on its lower level, has the same kind of dramatic effectiveness as Bernard Shaw's *Saint Joan*. Finally, we must count it to him for righteousness that Dr. Douglas has had the courage to let his hero and heroine, at the end of the story, be executed as martyrs to the new religion instead of leaving them on the threshold of a comfortable marriage with a starry-eyed kiss and a fadeout.

When, therefore, one compares *The Robe* with the frankly faked publishers' goods with which the public are usually fed, one sees that Dr. Douglas' novel is a work of a certain purity and that the author deserves a certain respect. It is rather to the credit of the millions who have been buying or borrowing *The Robe* that they should prefer a long and tedious novel about the influence of the power of Jesus on the Roman who carried out the crucifixion to the livelier and easier productions which have been specially flavored to please them. It demonstrates that the ordinary reader, even in our ghastly time, does long for moral light, that he cannot live by bilge alone. But that seven and a half million Americans should not find it in the least distasteful to devour five hundred and fifty pages of Dr. Douglas' five-and-ten-cent-store writing is something to give pause to anyone who may have supposed that the generation of Mencken had lifted American taste a little above the level of Gene Stratton-Porter and Harold Bell Wright.

August 26, 1944

Aldous Huxley in the World Beyond Time

ALDOUS HUXLEY'S new novel, *Time Must Have a Stop*, is a good deal better than his last one, *After Many a Summer Dies the Swan*. For one thing, he has returned to Europe for his characters and his settings, and he is much more successful with the English intellectuals in the London and Florence of the twenties than he was, in the earlier book, with an American millionaire and his hangers-on. His people, in many cases, are still conventional figures of satire: the disgusting voluptuary who lives in Italy and talks about the art of life, the rude rich old lady who has a pet Pomeranian and raps out imperious orders, and an up-to-date version of the hard Gradgrind parent, who is a socialist instead of a utilitarian; but Huxley does not run here the same risk of an obvious and purely external caricature that he did in his California fantasia. Here there is much more that is piquant in the social observation, much more wit in the talk and the unspoken thoughts of the characters, much more novelty of invention in the action. And along with this there goes an improvement in his handling of the religious element which has lately come to figure in his fiction. Huxley's peculiar version of the life of contemplation and revelation was expounded in *After Many a Summer* by a boring non-satirical character who read homilies to the other characters with an insufferable air of quiet authority and who constantly made the reader feel that it would have been better if he, too, had been satirically treated as a typical California crank. But in this new novel these matters have been dramatized and incorporated in the story on the same level as the other material. The voluptuary dies of a stroke, and we follow him into the non-sensual world. We see him drift about the fringes of the Divine within its gravitational field; return at moments to communicate with his friends through the agency of an extremely stupid medium, who garbles what he is trying to say; and finally, shrinking from absorption in God, get himself born back into humanity in the body of a baby expected by the wife of one of the other characters. Now, one may not be prepared to accept Huxley's views about spiritualistic phenomena and the

Platonic rebirth of souls, but the whole thing has been given plausibility—though queer, it is never creepy—by treating the disembodied vicissitudes of Eustace Barnack's soul in the same dry or droll way as the adventures of his consciousness while still in the flesh. The result of threading this in with the doings of the characters who are still alive is an effect which must be new in fiction. In its essentially rather dismal and dark-brown way, *Time Must Have a Stop* is quite a brilliant performance.

It is difficult, however, for Huxley to celebrate convincingly in a novel his present ideals of abnegation and withdrawal from the things of the world, just as it was for T. S. Eliot, in *Murder in the Cathedral*, to celebrate the ideal of humility. These are virtues which—unlike some others: courage and brotherly love, for example—do not lend themselves to being illustrated in public by clever and accomplished writers, long admired and much in view. Just as Eliot's Thomas Becket becomes superior to the verge of snobbery in his perfect achievement of meekness, so Bruno Rontini, the contemporary saint of Huxley's latest novel, seems sometimes attainted by the smart virtuosity of so many of Huxley's other characters in his insight into other people's states of mind, his power to forecast what they are going to do and an ability to outmaneuver them morally which gives almost the impression of scoring off them—all talents that have something in common with those of the infallible detective that figures in so much mystery fiction. Aldous Huxley sharply criticizes Dante for carrying up into Heaven his partisan antagonisms and his pride, but the danger with Huxley himself is that he will turn Buddha, Pascal and St. John of the Cross into another neat performance for the salon. It must, however, be said that his descriptions of the dissociated trancelike states in which his characters sometimes feel or seem about to feel a super-corporeal union with God have a certain sound of authenticity and convince one that they are based on experience.

One's objection to what, at this point in his career, can only be called the moral teaching of Huxley is not that it is not de-rived from real states of exaltation, but that these states of ex-altation themselves imply an incomplete experience of the earthly possibilities of human life. Huxley's satire has always been founded not only upon a distaste for humanity but also upon a real incapacity for understanding most of the things that seemed to other people important and exciting. It used to be fashionable to call him "intelligent," but he was never particularly intelligent. His habit of reading the *Encyclopaedia Britannica* gives the quality of his appetite for facts and ideas; his interest in the great intellectual movements that were bringing most light in his own time was on exactly the same level as his interest in a twelfth-century heresy, a queer species of carnivorous plant, a special variety of Romanesque architecture or a Greek poet surviving in fragments. Freud, Lenin, Einstein, Joyce—he sometimes expressed about them, in his casual essays, opinions as obtuse and philistine as those of the ordinary Fleet Street journalist. The new paths that they opened, the new hopes that they woke, were not opened or awakened for Huxley. For Huxley, in his satirical novels, the man whose imagination was aroused by, say, the quantum theory did not appear any more interesting than the old-fashioned pre-quantum mechanist, or the connoisseur of abstract painting than the fancier of Victorian bric-a-brac.

For the satirist, of course, this attitude may provide a basis for valid work. The Lilliputians of Swift seem too little, no matter what they do; the Bouvard and Pécuchet of Flaubert (invoked by one of the characters of *Time Must Have a Stop*) remain numskulls no matter what sciences or arts they think they are experimenting with. But Huxley is not, like Swift or Flaubert, complete and self-sufficient as a satirist. He has not even had the real love of writing, the power to express himself through art, of Evelyn Waugh or Ronald Firbank, the novels of both of whom may very well last longer than Huxley's. Merely a manipulator of Punch-and-Judy figures, he has inevitably to shake them off his hands and to use these hands in pulpit gestures as he comes forward to preach his way of life; and in this role his defects of intelligence again become fatally clear. We realize that his readiness to reject the world is due to his not knowing what is in it. That mixed and immature humanity which has been handled by the great artists and the great thinkers of his time—Huxley was not impressed by what they had been able to create from it because he had never had the full sense of what that humanity was like and, hence, of what it might become. His whole ascetic system, for example, is arrived at by way of the conclusion that "the flesh," though theoretically to be tolerated as a device for perpetuating the species, can never, through sexual selection or through the idealizations of love, become a part of our higher activities. In this novel, sex is never represented as anything but cold or perverse. There is nothing beyond momentary pleasure in any of the amorous relations of *Time Must Have a Stop*. Of the fact that the relations between men and women are involved in everything humanity builds—in the forms of art, in the structure of thought, in the incitement to achievement and leadership— you will get no inkling from Huxley. This would be perfectly all right in a satire which did not purport to be anything else— the satirist has always the license to turn down the flame of life in order to let us take account more grimly of the mechanical aspect of the fixtures and the sordidness of the surrounding room; but it is very misleading in a fable which pretends to bring us solemnly to consider the fundamental problems of human behavior and destiny.

Aldous Huxley would probably say, in reply to the objection above, that it does not really matter what we build on this earth. Our retort would be: How does he know?, since he has taken little part in the building. His inability to build solidly in his novels is itself an evidence of this. You cannot live in them; the author himself has not lived in them. He has always found it easy to drop them in order to report on his spiritual progress. The epilogue to *Time Must Have a Stop* consists mostly of a series of *pensées*, the journal of the central character, a poet who is schooling himself in the discipline of self-renunciation. These last pages have a terseness of writing and an accent of moral sincerity that one has hardly found before in Huxley. But what sort of general validity can be expected of a set of principles derived from the diminished and distorted world invented by the author of this novel? Since the story is admittedly a satire, it should follow that a religious system deduced from the conduct of its characters is either not wholly serious or not susceptible of wide application.

September 2, 1944

Vladimir Nabokov on Gogol

IF YOU READ E.-M. de Vogüé's *Le Roman Russe*, you will learn that Nikolai Gogol was a pioneer of Russian realism; if you read Mérimée's essay on him, you will be told that he was first of all a satirist, who, if he had written in a more widely read language, might well have "acquired a reputation equal to that of the best English humorists"; and these two notions have remained the chief elements in the Western conception of Gogol. If we set out to read Gogol himself, we may be puzzled to find he does not fit them. We soon recognize that we are a long way here from the familiar Russian realism, of which the purest example is Tolstoy. Gogol's characters are social types, but they are also mythical monsters; his backgrounds are vulgar in a way that was new in Russian fiction, but the sordid detail is intensified, thrown into a dramatic relief which does not allow any illusion that we are watching the lives of ordinary people; and both characters and backgrounds, by a strange Homeric growth, are continually putting forth gigantic similes involving characters and scenes of their own, which give the whole thing a queer other dimension. And though we may laugh at *The Inspector General*, we shall find that Gogol's stories inspire more horror than mirth, and a horror rather tragic than satiric. We shall also find long passages of prose lyricism that probably—for richness of texture combined with emotional power—beat anything else of the kind written by anyone in the nineteenth century.

The truth is, in fact, that Gogol, who called his *Dead Souls* a poem, is primarily a great *poet*, in a sense that sets him rather apart from the other most-read Russian novelists, though there is a side of Dostoevsky which has something in common with him. Gogol's characters and his grotesque details are symbols for states of the soul; his meanings and his moods are complex. Writing in the same period as Melville and Poe, he is much closer to them than to the later realists. He worked on a far bigger scale than Poe and he realized himself as an artist more completely than Melville did, but the St. Petersburg petty officials of Gogol's short stories of the supernatural belong to the same world as the damned Virginia gentlemen of Poe's, and one of the books that *Dead Souls* most resembles, for all the differences between the ostensible subjects, is certainly *Moby Dick*, in which Ahab's pursuit of the white whale is no more merely a fishing expedition than Chichikov's journey through Russia to buy up titles to deceased serfs is merely a swindling trip.

This is the great point that Vladimir Nabokov makes in his new book on Gogol—*Nikolai Gogol*—one of the best volumes so far in the interesting series called *Makers of Modern Literature*. Mr. Nabokov is himself a poet who has developed a complicated imagery and a novelist of the non-realistic sort, and he has written the kind of book which can only be written by one artist about another—an essay which takes its place with the very small body of first-rate criticism of Russian literature in English. Nabokov's *Gogol* must be henceforth read by anybody who has any serious interest in finding out about Russian culture. Not only has he shifted the lighting on the conventional picture of Gogol in such a way as to bring out his real genius as no other writer in English has done, but he has labored to give the reader some accurate impression of Gogol's style—a feature of his art which has come off badly in most of the English translations. The author of *Dead Souls*, a Ukrainian who wrote in Russian, had a peculiar interest in language of a kind that was somewhat akin to Joyce's. All the main characters in *Dead Souls* are collectors, and Gogol collected words. He liked the jargons of special occupations and special social strata; he liked to use unexpected verbs; he liked to invent words of his own; and he worked at making elaborate set-pieces as tangled and full of hidden implications as the jungle of the cracked landowner Plushkin's estate, as compelling in their rhythm and their cumulative power as Chichikov's departure in his carriage, that takes him through the little country towns and finally out into the steppe—"crows like flies, a limitless horizon"—and culminates later in the vision of Russia hurtling through the world like a troika while the other nations look on amazed. Mr. Nabokov has here described some of the devices of Gogol's style, and he has translated some famous passages into an English that attempts to reproduce their effects and that will give the reader some idea of why Russians sometimes know them by heart.

The chief faults of Mr. Nabokov's book are due to the fact that he is fundamentally a fiction writer and that Gogol, having been a real man, does not lend himself to the author's accomplished technique of sudden sidelights and juxtaposed glimpses quite so readily as if he had been a character invented by Nabokov himself. The effort to apply to Gogol the usual methods of the Nabokov portraiture has resulted in a certain amount of violence to the subject's career and work: large areas of both are skipped over, and the aspects that have been treated at length seem sometimes rather capriciously chosen. The reader is also annoyed by the frequent self-indulgence of the author in poses, perversities and vanities that sound as if he had brought them away from the St. Petersburg of the early nineteen-hundreds and piously preserved them in exile; and, along with them, a kind of snapping and snarling on principle at everything connected with the Russian Revolution that sometimes throws the baby out with the blood bath—to be guilty of a species of witticism to which Mr. Nabokov is much addicted and which tends, also, a little to disfigure his book. His puns are particularly awful. In writing English, he has not yet acquired the sense of how horribly "the government specter" and "Gogol's spas were not really spatial" are calculated to grate on English-speaking readers. Aside from this, in spite of some errors, Mr. Nabokov's mastery of English almost rivals Joseph Conrad's.

September 9, 1944

Katherine Anne Porter

MISS KATHERINE ANNE PORTER has published a new
book of stories, her third: *The Leaning Tower and Other
Stories.* To the reviewer, Miss Porter is baffling because one cannot take hold of her work in any of the obvious ways. She makes
none of the melodramatic or ironic points that are the stock in
trade of ordinary short story writers; she falls into none of the
usual patterns and she does not show anyone's influence. She
does not exploit her personality either inside or outside her
work, and her writing itself makes a surface so smooth that the
critic has little opportunity to point out peculiarities of color
or weave. If he is tempted to say that the effect is pale, he is
prevented by the realization that Miss Porter writes English of
a purity and precision almost unique in contemporary American fiction. If he tries to demur that some given piece fails to
mount with the accelerating pace or arrive at the final intensity
that he is in the habit of expecting in short stories, he is de-
terred by a nibbling suspicion that he may not have grasped its
meaning and have it hit him with a sudden impact some minutes after he has closed the book.

Not that this meaning is simple to formulate even after one
has felt its emotional force. The limpidity of the sentence, the
exactitude of the phrase, are deceptive in that the thing they
convey continues to seem elusive even after it has been communicated. These stories are not illustrations of anything that
is reducible to a moral law or a political or social analysis or
even a principle of human behavior. What they show us are human relations in their constantly shifting phases and in the moments of which their existence is made. There is no place for
general reflections; you are to live through the experience as
the characters do. And yet the writer has managed to say something about the values involved in the experience. But what is
it? I shall try to suggest, though I am afraid I shall land in
ineptitude.

Miss Porter's short stories lend themselves to being sorted
into three fairly distinct groups. There are the studies of family
life in working-class or middle-class households (there are two

of these in *The Leaning Tower*), which, in spite of the fact that the author is technically sympathetic with her people, tend to be rather bitter and bleak, and, remarkable though they are, seem to me less satisfactory than the best of her other stories. The impression we get from these pieces is that the qualities that are most amiable in human life are being gradually done to death in the milieux she is presenting, but Miss Porter does not really much like these people or feel comfortable in their dismal homes, and so we, in turn, don't really much care. Another section of her work, however, contains what may be called pictures of foreign parts, and here Miss Porter is much more successful. The story which gives its name to her new collection and which takes up two-fifths of the volume belongs to this category. It is a study of Germany between the two wars in terms of a travelling American and his landlady and fellow-lodgers in a Berlin rooming house. By its material and its point of view, it rather recalls Christopher Isherwood's *Goodbye to Berlin*, but it is more poetic in treatment and more general in implication. The little plaster leaning tower of Pisa which has been cherished by the Viennese landlady but gets broken by her American tenant stands for something in the destruction of which not merely the Germans but also the Americans have somehow taken a criminal part (though the American is himself an artist, he finds that he can mean nothing to the Germans but the power of American money). So, in a fine earlier story, *Hacienda*, a Mexican peon is somehow destroyed—with no direct responsibility on the part of any of the elements concerned—by a combination of Soviet Russians intent on making a Communist movie, their American business manager and a family of Mexican landowners.

In both cases, we are left with the feeling that, caught in the meshes of interwoven forces, some important human value has been crushed. These stories especially, one gathers, are examples of what Miss Porter means when she says, in her foreword to *Flowering Judas* in the Modern Library edition, that most of her "energies of mind and spirit have been spent in the effort to grasp the meaning" of the threats of world catastrophe in her time, "to trace them to their sources and to understand the logic of this majestic and terrible failure of the life of man in the Western world."

But perhaps the most interesting section of Katherine Anne Porter's work is composed of her stories about women—particularly her heroine Miranda, who figured in two of the three novelettes that made up her previous volume, *Pale Horse, Pale Rider*. The first six pieces of *The Leaning Tower* deal with Miranda's childhood and her family background of Louisianians living in southern Texas. This is the setting in which Miss Porter is most at home, and one finds in it the origins of that spirit of which the starvation and violation elsewhere make the subjects of her other stories. One recognizes it in the firm little sketches that show the relations between Miranda's grandmother and her lifelong colored companion, the relations between the members of the family and the relations between the family and the Negro servants in general. Somewhere behind Miss Porter's stories there is a conception of a natural human spirit in terms of their bearing on which all the other forces of society are appraised. This spirit is never really idealized, it is not even sentimentalized; it can be generous and loving and charming, but it can also be indifferent and careless, inconsequent, irresponsible and silly. If the meaning of these stories is elusive, it is because this essential spirit is so hard to isolate or pin down. It is peculiar to Louisianians in Texas, yet one misses it in a boarding house in Berlin. It is the special personality of a woman, yet it is involved with international issues. It evades all the most admirable moralities, it escapes through the social net, and it resists the tremendous oppressions of national bankruptcies and national wars. It is outlawed, driven underground, exiled; it becomes rather unsure of itself and may be able, as in *Pale Horse, Pale Rider*, to assert itself only in the delirium that lights up at the edge of death to save Miranda from extinction by war flu. It suffers often from a guilty conscience, knowing too well its moral weakness; but it can also rally bravely if vaguely in vindication of some instinct of its being which seems to point toward justice and truth.

But I said that this review would be clumsy. I am spoiling Miss Porter's stories by attempting to find a formula for them when I ought simply to be telling you to read them (and not merely the last volume but also its two predecessors). She is absolutely a first-rate artist, and what she wants other people to know she imparts to them by creating an object, the self-developing organism of a work of prose. The only general opinion on anything which, in her books, she has put on record has been a statement about her craft of prose fiction, and I may quote it—from the foreword to which I have referred—as more to the purpose than anything that the present critic could say. Here is the manifesto of the builder of this solid little sanctuary, so beautifully proportioned and finished, for the queer uncontrollable spirit that it seems to her important to save:

"In the face of such shape and weight of present misfortune, the voice of the individual artist may seem perhaps of no more consequence than the whirring of a cricket in the grass, but the arts do live continuously, and they live literally by faith; their names and their shapes and their uses and their basic meanings survive unchanged in all that matters through times of interruption, diminishment, neglect; they outlive governments and creeds and the societies, even the very civilizations that produced them. They cannot be destroyed altogether because they represent the substance of faith and the only reality. They are what we find again when the ruins are cleared away. And even the smallest and most incomplete offering at this time can be a proud act in defense of that faith."

September 30, 1944

A Picture to Hang in the Library:
Brooks's Age of Irving

T HE NEW volume of Van Wyck Brooks's literary history of the United States, *The World of Washington Irving*, though the third in order of publication, is the first in chronological order. It covers the ground from 1800 to the early years of the forties, and treats at length Jefferson, Audubon, Cooper, Irving, Simms, Poe, Bryant and Willis. It treats also dozens of minor figures and deals not only with literature proper but with political oratory, the reports of explorers and naturalists, the folklore of Davy Crockett and Mike Fink, and ethnological and archeological study; and it contains so much information about painting, music, landscape-gardening, architecture, mechanical invention and social manners that it might almost be more appropriately described as a history of American culture.

These decades were enormously lively: the country was still uncommercialized; the Americans were still exhilarated by the success of the Revolution and the adventure of the new country; the great intellectual figures were many-sided in their interests and talents, and men of the great worlds of society, geography and nature. There was a splendor of the Renaissance about figures like Jefferson and Audubon; Joel Barlow, diplomat, promoter and poet; Samuel F. B. Morse, who was a painter as well as a mechanical genius; William Dunlap, who was a painter, a historian of painting, a dramatist and a theatrical producer; and even Cooper, sailor, landowner, novelist, historian and critic of society—though we remember only his Indian tales. Poe—whom we greatly slight by reading him mainly for his tales of horror—was also typical of the period in the variety of his curiosities and his virtuosity in literary form. It is a wonderful period to go back to, and Mr. Brooks has written about it what seems to me so far the most attractive volume of the series that began with *The Flowering of New England*. The book is quite free from the cloggedness and overpainting that sometimes appeared in the earlier volumes. He has mastered his method so completely that we never get the effect of labor: style, narrative and organization have been brought to a point of perfection seldom reached in our historical and critical writing. Yet he has had to assimilate vast masses of print, surveying the whole field afresh and reading all the books for himself, and he has accepted none of the conventional limits by which scholars simplify their tasks: his light overflows these limits and seems to penetrate every crevice, reveal every in-between phase, of the observing and imagining American mind of the early years of the Republic. For the reader who is curious about cultural phenomena, there is not a dull page or dull footnote in the book. Mr. Brooks has the answers to all the questions with which the academic historians of literature will not usually help you much. Why did the South—apart from the political writing that accompanied the Revolution—produce so little in the way of literature? Why did people set so much store by Bryant? Why did they devour Washington Irving? How and when did the piety and prudery which have so tended to stunt the national art and thought close down on the free-thinking plain-speaking tradition of the realistic and cosmopolitan minds that presided at the birth of the Republic? What was the effect of the actual experience of the putting into practice of social equality and of the career open to the talents on the classically educated men of property who had defended the democratic ideal against the political tradition of Europe? How did they meet the age of Andrew Jackson?

To explain and dramatize all these matters is what Mr. Brooks can do as no one else in the United States has done it. Rarely, in fact, outside France has the appetite for learning been united with intelligence and literary ability to the degree that we find it here. He has put on the whole picture a color, a finish, a glaze like those of the best paintings of the period: the portraits of the pupils of Benjamin West, the genre studies of Mount and Bingham, the landscapes of the Hudson River school. You can hang this new volume in your library uninhibited by any embarrassment such as you may have felt in connection with his New England portraits, over a sometimes too fulsome treatment and a sometimes too pink-and-blue palette. You may occasionally pull yourself up with the reflection that the ripe and harmonious picture must still, to some extent, represent an idealization; but, after all, what Mr. Brooks is engaged on is not a sociological report but a presentation of the early eighteen-hundreds through the eyes of imaginative writers who brought to it their own color and excitement, and an account of these writers from the point of view of how they looked and what they meant to their contemporaries. (It is curious to contrast this volume with the bleak surveys of American civilization in 1800 and 1817 of Henry Adams' history. Though Adams is telling the same story of the birth of a national character and culture, an American intellectual, in the trust-ridden eighties and nineties, was not able to believe in these with such certainty as a man of Mr. Brooks's generation, and could not, therefore, find in our past so much to be cheerful about.)

In this reliving of the visions of our fathers, the question of absolute values becomes, for Mr. Brooks's purpose, unimportant and almost irrelevant. But there is a common complaint against this series that, in neglecting to deal with such values, in failing to measure the American writers by the best that has been done in the world, Mr. Brooks has been shirking the true business of the critic. This complaint has less force in the present case than it had in connection with the previous volumes, because the author does not here overinflate the men of mediocre ability as he did in the earlier books. He does not mislead us by creating the impression that Cooper and Washington Irving, the two dominant writers of the era, were men of greater talent than they were. Yet the question has still to be dealt with. Between *The World of Washington Irving* and its immediate predecessor in the series, *New England: Indian Summer*, Mr. Brooks has published a more personal book, *Opinions of Oliver Allston*, in which he has stigmatized as "coterie-literature" the work of some of the greatest of his contemporaries, and revealed that his own standards of excellence are still more or less those of an enthusiastic young man in his twenties in the heyday of H. G. Wells, a young man for whom Tolstoy and Ibsen, on the one hand, and Victor Hugo and Browning, on the other, all inhabit the same empyrean of greatness. But the paradox of Brooks's career is that he has himself been able to develop into one of the first-rate American writers of his time without achieving any commensurate development of his appreciation of other writers save as material for cultural history. He has, in the present volume, one case of an artist—Poe—who takes his place in a company far higher than that of his literary companions in the book. One looked forward with interest to his handling of Poe as a test case of his literary judgment, and since Poe is a great favorite of mine, I watched Mr. Brooks like a hawk during the chapters in which he deals with this subject, so peculiarly fraught with pitfalls—moral, social, aesthetic and regional—which has probably given rise to more rubbishy and vulgar writing, both romantic and denunciatory, than any other American career with the exception of Abraham Lincoln's. Now Mr. Brooks has walked right through all these pitfalls with perfect delicacy, coolness and sense, and he has brought to his presentation of Poe's pathological personality a touch of that psychological insight which, I believe, has not appeared in his work since *The Ordeal of Mark Twain*. Van Wyck Brooks's interest in Poe is not the interest of Baudelaire or of Walter de la Mare, but from his own entirely different point of view he can indicate correctly Poe's importance: "With Poe another age had opened," he says, "intenser, profounder than [Washington Irving's]"; and this makes us see Poe in his historical perspective as we may not have done before.

In his attempts to evaluate literature, Mr. Brooks is still likely to fall back on rather vague and conventional phrases. He says of Bryant's poem *To a Waterfowl* that it is "the most intense of all his poems, in which for a moment he entered the realm of magic." Well, I know that Mr. Yvor Winters admires this poem of Bryant's, but I doubt whether it would be possible to find many modern poets who would agree with Mr. Brooks. If the magic he means is the magic that Matthew Arnold introduced into literary criticism with a famous discussion of such passages as Shakespeare's "daffodils, That come before the swallow dares, and take The winds of March with beauty," then Bryant's poor old waterfowl that guides through the boundless air his certain flight and brings to the poet the conviction that God will lead his steps aright can scarcely deserve that description.

And here is a passage on the prose of Cooper: "With his marked feeling for the sublime, he rose moreover now and then to moments of the noblest and most eloquent prose. Such were the descriptions of the icefields in *The Sea Lions*—a tale of American sealers in antarctic waters—the vast mass of floating mountains, generally of a spectral white, through which the mariners moved in an unknown sea. The walls, like ridges of the Alps, bowed and rocked and ground one another, stirred by the restless ocean, with a rushing sound, and sometimes a prodigious plunge as of a planet falling tossed the water over the heaving ramparts. The cliffs, half a league in length, with their arches and pinnacles and towers and columns, suggested the streets of some fantastic city that was floating in the sunlight in the sea, black here and there in certain lights and orange on the summits, throwing out gleams and hues of emerald and gold." Now if someone were to speak to you suddenly of "the noblest and most eloquent prose," in connection with a work of fiction, you might think of Melville, you might think of Flaubert, you might think of D. H. Lawrence; but you would not be at all likely to think of anything you had ever read in Cooper, where an occasional poetry of atmosphere seems barely to manage to seep through the verbose and clumsy writing. If there is something in Cooper as good as Mr. Brooks seems here to suggest, then you feel that you ought to know about it. But when you look up the icebergs in *The Sea Lions*, you find that Van Wyck Brooks has not merely been reflecting the glory of something that is much better in the original: he has put together his very pretty passage out of more or less undistinguished bits scattered through a great number of pages: "Each time, however, the sun's rays soon came to undeceive him; and that which had so lately been black and frowning, was, as by the touch of magic, suddenly illuminated, and became bright and gorgeous, throwing out its emerald hues, or perhaps a virgin white, that filled the beholder with delight, even amid the terrors and dangers by which, in very truth, he was surrounded. The glorious Alps themselves, those wonders of the earth, could scarcely compete in scenery with the views that nature lavished, in that remote sea, on a seeming void. . . . The passages between the bergs, or what might be termed the streets and lanes of this mysterious-looking, fantastical, yet sublime city of the ocean, were numerous, and of every variety," etc., etc.

The creation is not Cooper's but Brooks's: he has sifted out the images from *The Sea Lions* and made out of them something quite new. With the work of a Thoreau or a Hawthorne, this method does not succeed, because you cannot rewrite a good writer: you can only discolor and weaken. But with somebody like Cooper, Mr. Brooks has a field almost like that of the artist who deals directly with crude experience. And how many inferior or tedious writers he must have transmuted in this book! We cannot compare the art with the phenomena themselves so readily as we can in the novelist's case; but when we go to the trouble of doing so, we are amazed at the skill with which Brooks has been turning the old carriage springs, spectacle frames and pickaxes of 1800–1840 into a fine-beaten kind of white gold.

October 7, 1944

Why Do People Read Detective Stories?

F OR YEARS I have been hearing about detective stories. Almost everybody I know seems to read them, and they have long conversations about them in which I am unable to take part. I am always being reminded that the most serious public figures of our time, from Woodrow Wilson to W. B. Yeats, have been addicts of this form of fiction. Now, except for a few stories by Chesterton, for which I did not much care, I have not read any detective stories since one of the earliest, if not the earliest, of the imitators of Sherlock Holmes—a writer named Jacques Futrelle, now dead, who invented a character called the Thinking Machine and published his first volume of stories about him in 1907. Enchanted though I had been with Sherlock Holmes, I got bored with the Thinking Machine and dropped him, beginning to feel, at the age of twelve, that I was outgrowing that form of literature.

Since, however, I have recently been sampling the various types of popular merchandise, I have decided that I ought to take a look at some specimens of this kind of fiction, which has grown so tremendously popular and which is now being produced on such a scale that the book departments of magazines have had to employ special editors to cope with it. To be sure of getting something above the average, I waited for new novels by writers who are particularly esteemed by connoisseurs. I started in with the latest volume of Rex Stout's Nero Wolfe stories: *Not Quite Dead Enough.*

What I found rather surprised me and discouraged my curiosity. Here was simply the old Sherlock Holmes formula reproduced with a fidelity even more complete than it had been by Jacques Futrelle almost forty years ago. Here was the incomparable private detective, ironic and ceremonious, with a superior mind and eccentric habits, addicted to overeating and orchid-raising, as Holmes had his enervated indulgence in his cocaine and his violin, yet always prepared to revive for prodigies of intellectual alertness; and here were the admiring stooge, adoring and slightly dense, and Inspector Lestrade of Scotland Yard, energetic but entirely at sea, under the new name of Inspector Cramer of Police Headquarters. Almost the only difference was that Nero Wolfe was fat and lethargic instead of lean and active like Holmes, and that he liked to make the villains commit suicide instead of handing them over to justice. But I rather enjoyed Wolfe himself, with his rich dinners and quiet evenings in his house in farthest West Thirty-fifth Street, where he savors an armchair sadism that is always accompanied by beer. The two stories that made up this new book—*Not Quite Dead Enough* and *Booby Trap*—I found rather disappointing; but, as they were both under the usual length and presented the great detective partly distracted from his regular profession by a rigorous course of training for the Army, I concluded that they might not be first-rate examples of what the author could do in this line and read also *The Nero Wolfe Omnibus*, which contains two earlier book-length stories: *The Red Box* and *The League of Frightened Men*. But neither did these supply the excitement I was hoping for. If the later stories were sketchy and skimpy, these seemed to have been somewhat padded, for they were full of long episodes that led nowhere and had no real business in the story. It was only when I looked up Sherlock Holmes that I realized how much Nero Wolfe was a dim and distant copy of an original. The old stories of Conan Doyle had a wit and a fairy-tale poetry of hansom cabs, gloomy London lodgings and lonely country estates that Rex Stout could hardly duplicate with his backgrounds of modern New York; and the surprises were much more entertaining: you at least got a room with a descending ceiling or a snake trained to climb down the bellrope, whereas with Nero Wolfe—though *The League of Frightened Men* makes use of a clever psychological idea—the solution of the mystery was not usually either fanciful or unexpected. I finally got to feel that I had to unpack large crates by swallowing the excelsior in order to find at the bottom a few bent and rusty nails, and I began to nurse a rankling conviction that detective stories in general are able to profit by an unfair advantage in the code which forbids the reviewer to give away the secret to the public—a custom which results in the concealment of the pointlessness of a good deal of this fiction and affords a protection to the authors which no other department of writing enjoys. It is not difficult to create suspense by making people await a revelation, but it does demand a certain talent to come through with a criminal device which is ingenious or picturesque or amusing enough to make the reader feel that the waiting has been worth while. I even began to mutter that the real secret that Author Rex Stout had been screening by his false scents and interminable divagations was a meagerness of imagination of which one only came to realize the full ghastliness when the last chapter had left one blank.

I have been told by the experts, however, that this endless carrying on of the Doyle tradition does not represent all or the best that has been done with the detective story during the decades of its proliferation. There has been also the puzzle mystery, and this, I was assured, had been brought to a high pitch of ingenuity in the stories of Agatha Christie. So I have read also the new Agatha Christie, *Death Comes as the End*, and I confess that I have been had by Mrs. Christie. I did not guess who the murderer was, I was incited to keep on and find out, and when I did finally find out, I was surprised. Yet I did not care for Agatha Christie and I hope never to read another of her books. I ought, perhaps, to discount the fact that *Death Comes as the End* is supposed to take place in Egypt two thousand years before Christ, so that the book has a flavor of Lloyd C. Douglas not, I understand, quite typical of the author. ("No more Khay in this world to sail on the Nile and catch fish and laugh up into the sun whilst she, stretched out in the boat with little Teti on her lap, laughed back at him"); but her writing is of a mawkishness and banality which seem to me literally impossible to read. You cannot *read* such a book, you run through it to see the problem worked out; and you cannot become interested in the characters, because they never can be allowed an existence of their own even in a flat two dimensions but have always to be contrived so that they can seem either reliable or sinister, depending on which quarter, at the moment, is to be baited for the reader's suspicion. This I had found also a source of annoyance in the case of Mr. Stout, who, however, has created, after a fashion, Nero Wolfe and Archie Goodwin and has made some attempt at characterization of the people that figure in the crimes; but Mrs. Christie, in proportion as she is more expert and concentrates more narrowly on the puzzle, has to eliminate human interest completely, or, rather, fill in the picture with what seems to me a distasteful parody of it. In this new novel, she has to provide herself with puppets who will be good for three stages of suspense: you must first wonder who is going to be murdered, you must then wonder who is committing the murders, and you must finally be unable to foresee which of two men the heroine will marry. It is all like a sleight-of-hand trick, in which the magician diverts your attention from the awkward or irrelevant movements that conceal the manipulation of the cards, and it may mildly entertain and astonish you, as such a sleight-of-hand performance may. But in a performance like *Death Comes as the End*, the patter is a constant bore and the properties lack the elegance of playing cards.

Still fearing that I might be unjust to a department of literature that seemed to be found so absorbing by many, I went back and read *The Maltese Falcon*, which I assumed to be a classic in the field, since it had been called by Alexander Woollcott "the best detective story America has yet produced" and since, at the time of its publication, it had immediately caused Dashiell Hammett to become—in Jimmy Durante's phrase, referring to himself—"duh toast of duh intellectuals." But it was difficult for me to understand what they had thought—in 1930—they were toasting. Mr. Hammett did have the advantage of real experience as a Pinkerton detective, and he infused the old formula of Sherlock Holmes with a certain cold underworld brutality which gave readers a new shudder in the days when it was fashionable to be interested in gangsters; but, beyond this, he lacked the ability to bring the story to imaginative life. As a writer, he is surely almost as far below the rank of Rex Stout as Rex Stout is below that of James Cain. *The Maltese Falcon* today seems not much above those newspaper picture-strips in which you follow from day to day the ups and downs of a strong-jawed hero and a hardboiled but beautiful adventuress.

What, then, is the spell of the detective story that has been felt by T. S. Eliot and Paul Elmer More but which I seem incapable of feeling? As a department of imaginative writing, it looks to me completely dead. The spy story may perhaps only now be realizing its poetic possibilities, as the admirers of

Graham Greene contend; and the murder story that exploits psychological horror is an entirely different matter. But the detective story proper had borne all its finest fruits by the end of the nineteenth century, having only declined from the point where Edgar Allan Poe had been able to communicate to M. Dupin something of his own ratiocinative intensity and where Dickens had invested his plots with a social and moral significance that made the final solution of the mystery a revelatory symbol of something that the author wanted seriously to say. Yet the detective story has kept its hold; had even, in the two decades between the great wars, become more popular than ever before; and there is, I believe, a deep reason for this. The world during those years was ridden by an all-pervasive feeling of guilt and by a fear of impending disaster which it seemed hopeless to try to avert because it never seemed conclusively possible to pin down the responsibility. Who had committed the original crime and who was going to commit the next one?—that second murder which always, in the novels, occurs at an unexpected moment when the investigation is well under way; which, as in one of the Nero Wolfe stories, may take place right in the great detective's office. Everybody is suspected in turn, and the streets are full of lurking agents whose allegiances we cannot know. Nobody seems guiltless, nobody seems safe; and then, suddenly, the murderer is spotted, and—relief!—he is not, after all, a person like you or me. He is a villain—known to the trade as George Gruesome—and he has been caught by an infallible Power, the supercilious and omniscient detective, who knows exactly where to fix the guilt.

October 14, 1944

Bernard Shaw on the Training
of a Statesman

Everybody's Political What's What?, by Bernard Shaw, is a supplement rather than a companion piece to *The Intelligent Woman's Guide to Socialism and Capitalism*. The *Guide* came out in 1928 when the author was seventy-two and his mind was still in perfectly good working order; the *What's What?* appears sixteen years later, when Bernard Shaw is eighty-eight and his powers show signs of failing. There is nothing in this new book like the clear line of thought that made the *Guide* a great piece of exposition, and nothing so eloquent as its magnificent peroration on the evils of capitalism. The *What's What?* is not, in fact, an expository work at all in the same sense that the earlier book was. It is a treatise on a classical model that was popular in the Renaissance, when Castiglione wrote his *Courtier* and Machiavelli his *Prince*. Shaw might have called his book *The Statesman*, because its subject is the education of the ideal statesman of the future.

The old-fashioned ideal of democracy—one man, one vote —says Shaw, must today be regarded as discredited. It was inevitable that the modern dictators, who wanted to get something done, should sweep aside the impotent parliaments. But what we need—i.e., what England needs—are a new class of public servants, specially trained and tested as lawyers and doctors are, and registered as "mentally capable of functioning efficiently" in municipal or national office. (There should be not merely one Cabinet but several—"for cultural questions, industrial questions, agricultural questions," etc.) There would be plenty of such candidates available, since the opportunity for higher education would be thrown open to the whole population by a system of state-endowed schools, and it would be possible for able individuals from all classes of society to qualify; and these candidates would represent conflicting opinions and interests. The larger questions of public policy could thus still be determined by a popular vote that would select among these qualified candidates (though the voters themselves, one gathers, would have to be qualified for the franchise by some-thing more than a literacy test). Now, given this state of things, how much should such an official have to learn of the various departments of knowledge and precisely how far should he allow himself to go in controlling the activities of society? The whole book is hung on this imaginary statesman and a variety of subjects are discussed—political, economic, so-cial, religious, aesthetic, hygienic—in relation to his probable point of view. This discussion is rather informal and not partic-ularly systematic; as Shaw says, he has "omitted much that has been dealt with by other writers" and aimed "rather at re-minders of the overlooked, and views from new or neglected angles." The result is something unexpectedly close, for Shaw, to such ancient and garrulous works as Montaigne's *Essays* and Burton's *Anatomy*. The book runs much to personal anec-dotes and curious historical examples, and contains many rem-iniscences of the author's long and full career, as well as stories about his father, his uncles, his grandfather and even his great-grandfather.

In comparison with Shaw's other productions—even with the work of his seventies—the *What's What?* is, thus, rather re-laxed. Bernard Shaw is still earnest and still self-assertive, but he can ruminate now on the years he has known, the many subjects in which he has been interested, and can even gossip about them. He is sometimes betrayed by the lapses of a longevity that is rivalling Voltaire's. He frequently repeats his examples and makes the same point several times, and in his chapter on *Law and Tyranny* he reiterates almost unaltered, from fifty pages before, a whole mass of material on the history of medicine—anecdotes, instances and all. There are passages where he seems to be losing the thread and led astray by ob-sessive associations, so that they make on us a little the impres-sion of the dream explanations in *Finnegans Wake* that are always changing the subject, and we feel that these pages are hardly real, that we are reading Bernard Shaw in our sleep. He has always had the habit—rather confusing in his prefaces, though essential to his genius as a dramatist—of presenting the different aspects of a subject all with a kind of biting over-emphasis, as if they were not parts of a general survey, but ac-tually contradictory attitudes; and this habit gives sometimes here a certain effect of disintegration. You may find, for example, on the same page, two apparently irreconcilable statements: "I, an artist-philosopher, mistrust laboratory methods because what happens in a laboratory is contrived and dictated . . . but the artist's workshop is the whole universe as far as he can comprehend it; and he can neither contrive nor dictate what happens there: he can only observe and interpret events that are beyond his control"; "But let no statesman or elector imagine that an artist cannot be as dangerous a fool as a laboratory researcher. The painting, the statue, the symphony, the fable, whether narrative or dramatic, is as completely contrived, selected, dictated and controlled by the artist as the laboratory experiment by the scientist." And his egoism seems to have increased instead of fading out with age. Once the panache of the young critic and dramatist, which he carried with defiance and dash, it now droops and looks out of place: today it makes you rather uncomfortable to find on every fourth or fifth page the recurrent "Take my case" or its equivalent, and you eventually learn to wince at his familiar enumerations of the names of great men of genius as you wait for the inevitable inclusion of his own.

And yet, for all this, the *Political What's What?* is one of the new books that are worth reading this year. Shaw's faculties still remain active to a perfectly amazing degree. There are stretches—such as the chapter on Pavlov and the sections that immediately follow—in which he writes with an incisive directness that seems hardly to have been dulled by age. And it is fascinating to see into the mind of a man who can look back over so long a life and who retains his capacity to compare and judge. We have glimpses into his school days in Dublin, his activity as a clerk for an estate agent, his experience in London as a municipal councillor, as a speaker for the Fabian Society, as a critic of painting, music and the theater; and there are expert observations on politics and society by one who has been scrutinizing public affairs since his conversion to socialism in the eighties. Here are all the main principles of his thought—creative evolution, hero worship, the inevitability of state control, equality of income, the need for religion and the religious character of works of art; and here is, also, a certain amount of old furniture—favorite authorities and fashionable attitudes—

that, if we remember the early nineteen hundreds, the days when *Man and Superman* was shocking, we may associate with golfing pictures and Gibson girls. But Shaw's mind has never really stopped functioning; he has been able, as few old men are, to adapt his fundamental ideas to the demands of the changing reality and to criticize acutely the most recent events. It is an advantage to a social historian to begin with a long view of history, as Shaw did by studying Marx; the great displacements of prestige and power that are the results of revolution and war have thrown many excellent writers off their bases and caused them to die disillusioned, but these do not dismay Bernard Shaw. Here is his diagnosis of World War II: "This is the great corruption of Socialism which threatens us at present. It calls itself Fascism in Italy, National Socialism (Nazi for short) in Germany, New Deal in the United States, and is clever enough to remain nameless in England; but everywhere it means the same thing: Socialist production and Unsocialist distribution. So far, out of the frying pan into the fire. For though Fascism (to call State Capitalism by its shortest name) has doled out some substantial benefits to the proletariat and given bureaucratic status to functionaries who were formerly only casual employees, besides tightening up the public services and preaching a worship of the State (called Totalitarianism) which will lead logically to genuine Socialism, it has produced a world war in which Anglo-American Fascism fights German and Italian Fascism because Fascism is international whilst the capitalists are still intensely national; for when Germany proposes to fashify the whole earth under the Führership of Adolf Hitler, and Italy the same under Benito Mussolini, the Anglo-American Fascists will see Germany damned before they will accept any Fascism that is not of their own making under their own Führers."

He, however, makes an exception for the Soviet Union, where, he says, they have "Democratic Communism." He talks as if the new Russian Constitution had actually been put into practice and he seems to express approval of Stalin's political purges, with a kind of vague fee-faw-fum about the need, in the society of the future, for "liquidating" the socially noxious. (It is a characteristic inconsistency that he should tell us we must concede to the state the right to decree the execution of people who fall into this category at the same time that he indignantly declines to submit to compulsory vaccination and inoculation.)

But even at the points where Shaw's thinking conspicuously fails in coherence, there is still a kind of general wisdom that soaks through the cracks of his argument. It is as if the effect of old age had been at last to break up his rigidities and allow him to arrive at a state of mind where he sees men and institutions a little more under the aspect of eternity: all appropriate developments from their milieux, each performing some natural function. I do not know whether this is what he means when he speaks of having now lived so long that he is beginning to see the dawn of a new way of looking at things; but even this, his latest phase, at an age when most men would be helplessly senile, is full of interest and not without surprises for those who have admired him and followed his work.

October 28, 1944

Reëxamining Dr. Johnson

IT IS a pity that Boswell's *Life of Johnson* should so largely have supplanted for the general reader the writings of Johnson himself. If we know nothing but Boswell and Macaulay's essay, which is read in so many schools, we are likely to have a picture of a great eccentric who was even a bit of a clown. Boswell, in spite of his great respect and of the filial role he assumed, could not help making Johnson a character in an eighteenth-century comedy of manners; Macaulay pointed him up as a monster, at once grotesque and banal, in a bright-colored Victorian novel. And lately the figure of Boswell has become even more prominent at Johnson's expense through the discovery of the Boswell papers and the work of Mr. Chauncey Tinker. That Johnson himself was really one of the best English writers of his time, that he deserved his great reputation, is a fact that we are likely to lose sight of.

Mr. Joseph Wood Krutch, in a new biography called *Samuel Johnson*, has at last provided a study that is designed to restore to Johnson his real literary interest and importance. With all the work that has been done on Johnson and his friends, there has, as he says, been no such biography. "The very intensity of this specialization," he explains in his introduction, "(as well, of course, as the tremendous reputation of Boswell's *Life*) has tended to discourage any attempt in recent times to produce a large inclusive book which would serve to give the general reader a running account of Johnson's life, character and work as they appear in the light of contemporary knowledge and contemporary judgment." Mr. Krutch follows this announcement with some entirely unnecessary apologies for having played down the figure of Boswell. The truth is that he has devoted quite enough attention and given a quite favorable enough account of Boswell, and his nervously apprehensive glances in the direction of the Boswell fans are simply a part of that continued tribute which one dislikes to see exacted to that point by the vain and pushing diarist.

Mr. Krutch, then, has taken on a job which very much needed to be done, and has acquitted himself with honor. This biography is by far the best book that I have ever read by Joseph Wood Krutch. His *Poe*, written back in the twenties, was a rather half-baked performance: incomplete, depending too much on a Freudian oversimplification, insufficiently sympathetic with its subject and somewhat distracted in its judgments by what one might call the despair-hysteria of the period. The *Johnson* is quite another affair. It is scrupulous and comprehensive, and it makes use of the insights of modern psychology in a careful and moderate way—in fact, perhaps leans a little too much over backward in the attempt not to press them too far (since Mr. Krutch has been through Boswell's diary, which is scandalous and has been printed only privately, and since he tells us that Boswell was "neurotic" and has evidently a theory about him, we regret that he has not let us know what this theory is). This new book also shows a capacity for steady and independent judgment, as well as a flexible intelligence, in the discussion both of Johnson's work and of the problems of his personality, that constitute a striking advance in Mr. Krutch's development as a critic.

The only serious general objection that can be brought against Mr. Krutch's treatment is that, in one sense, he does not seem especially close to his subject. Johnson was so solid a man, who saw the world in such concrete terms, and the give-and-take of his age was so lively, direct and brusque, that Mr. Krutch's presentation of them seems, by comparison, attenuated and pallid. His book a little bit lacks *impact*. But he compensates us for this and more or less leads us to forget it by the subtlety, lucidity and sureness of the analysis which he has made his method. And his style—though it has nothing in common with the stout-knotted texture of Johnson, the phrases, the sentences, the paragraphs, that one can feel between one's teeth, though it does sometimes run a little to repetition, to an old-fashioned Southern verbosity and the old-fashioned Southern eloquence of such phrases as "a devotee of Bacchus"—his style has become, on the whole, an admirable instrument for this kind of analysis. Except for an occasional balled-up sentence, the book reads easily and carries you rapidly; and, though it isolates to some extent from the immediate background of their period the principal actors of the Johnson legend, it surrounds them with an even luminosity which, though gentle, is always revealing.

The chapters on Johnson's chief works are not, as so often happens with the products of academic research, merely studies of their historical significance, though Mr. Krutch covers this, too, but—except in the case of Johnson's poems, which Mr. Krutch rather underrates—sound critical appreciations. One hopes that they will stimulate the reading of Johnson. The romantics and their successors have created, by exaggerating Johnson's limitations, an unfair prejudice against him as a critic. Actually, *The Lives of the Poets* and the preface and commentary on Shakespeare are among the most brilliant and the most acute documents in the whole range of English criticism, and the products of a mind which, so far from being parochially local and hopelessly cramped by the taste of its age, saw literature in a long perspective and could respond to the humanity of Shakespeare as well as to the wit of Pope.

One feature of Mr. Krutch's biography I feel moved to dwell upon here a little more than it perhaps deserves from its importance in the whole scale of his book.

There is a tendency in the scholarly writing done by professors and composers of theses that sometimes becomes rather exasperating to the reader outside the college world. This tendency may be briefly described as an impulse on the part of the professors to undermine their subjects or explain them away. An expert on Byron, say, will prove, on purely documentary grounds, that there is no reason to believe that Byron ever had anything to do with women; an authority on Whitman will attempt to show that Whitman had no originality, since everything to be found in his work was already to be found in someone else, and will thereby seem to try to create the impression that there is no real merit in Whitman's poetry. To the outsider, this sounds perverse; but, since these scholars are apparently not the men for perversity, he may be baffled for an explanation. In order to understand this peculiar phenomenon, which it seems to me has been growing more formidable, one must understand, first of all, the relation of the professor to his subjects. This relation is, nine times out of ten, a strained and embarrassing one. The professor would be made most un-comfortable if he had to meet Whitman or Byron; he would not like him—he does not, in fact, like him. But he has gone in for studying literature and he must try to do something to ad-vance himself in that field. His demonstration of Byron's chastity or of the nullity of Whitman's achievement may have no relevance whatever to his author, may indeed amount to an effort to annihilate him, but it *does* constitute a tangible evi-dence of the scholar's assiduous reading, his checking of dates and texts, and his long hours getting something written out. It is also an act of self-assertion which may produce the illusion that a dent has been left in the author, though it may not add anything to our knowledge of him; and it does raise the status of the scholar in the hierarchy of the academic world.

But to the non-academic reader, this, as I say, can only seem rather stupid. Now, there are just a moment or two when Mr. Krutch, who has been teaching at Columbia, gives some evi-dence of being attainted with this tendency. He creates the impression that he is trying to show, in his discussion of John-son's early years in London, that since there is no real docu-mentary proof that Johnson ever missed many dinners, there is no genuine reason for believing that he was as poor as he has been thought to have been; and later, in appraising Johnson's two long poems, Mr. Krutch takes the disheartening line of ar-guing that the first of these fine pieces, *London*, is merely a monument to the bad old habit of stupidly imitating classical models, and the second, *The Vanity of Human Wishes*, mostly a conventional exercise which hardly rises above the level of commonplace eighteenth-century verse. Yet if anything is plain in Johnson's writings and in his attitude toward the destitute and helpless—as Mr. Krutch's own account clearly shows—it is some intimate and scarifying experience of hardship in these undocumented early years. This is one of the elements in the ground-tone, dolorous, steadfast and somber, that gives emo-tional depth to his work; and one feels it especially in these poems, which owe certain of their most effective passages to Johnson's first-hand acquaintance with all but the last of his melancholy catalogue of the miseries of a writer's life: "Toil, envy, want, the patron and the jail."

Mr. Krutch does not often depress us thus, but it is regrettable that he should do so at all. He has not been a professor for long and he should be wary of the dangers of the academic air. As a critic, he has been trained in the best tradition of contemporary literary journalism; but it may be that not only the symptoms just noted, but also a feeling one gets that Johnson has been presented in a vacuum, with no general implications, should be charged to the habitual blankness of the outlook of academic scholarship. When Mr. Krutch wrote *The Modern Temper*, he had a much more definite point of view as a critic of literature in relation to life and of life in relation to history.

November 18, 1944

Leonid Leonov:
The Sophistication of a Formula

Road to the Ocean is a long novel about Soviet Russia by a prominent Soviet novelist. It centers around "socialist construction": the operation of a Russian railroad; but the author, Leonid Leonov, has genuine literary gifts which do not lend themselves readily to propaganda, and he has tried to do something subtler, more complex and more humanly plausible than the ordinary Communist Sunday-school story. Leonov has a novelist's interest in the crude mixed materials of life and a literary sophistication very rare in Soviet fiction. His novel, which is extremely intricate, with a great multiplication of characters, involves elements of the land-owning class dispossessed by the Revolution, of the bourgeois professional class trying to function in the new socialist economy, of the original generation of devoted and intrepid revolutionists who established the Soviet society and of the younger generation of the Komsomol who are helping to get it running in the spirit of Boy and Girl Scouts.

The presentation of all this is quite skillful: the interdependence of the various individuals is gradually brought out in a dramatic but usually not obvious way. Episode leads to episode by transitions apparently meaningless: a character who seems unimportant in one chapter will be shown at full length in the next; till, later a new nexus of relationships which gives the whole picture a new significance is unexpectedly established either by continuing the story in the present or by exploring its earlier phases in the past. For example, the discovery by a Communist historian of a set of old papers in a country house makes a number of the characters fall together into a Chekhovian drama of the old regime and connects them with the original flotation, seen as a typical capitalist swindle, of that railroad which is now the arena of the entirely different exploits of Soviet industrial effort; then the same house, now turned into a "rest home" for vacationing Soviet workers, is made to produce a new grouping of characters and exert a new kind of influence, when the railroad's Politbureau chief goes for a sojourn there. And there are even long-distance projections into the future of the Soviet world which, though sometimes a little tedious, are also handled in a novel way. Through old documents, through the memories of the characters, we have been shown the Russian past; what is the world that they are working for to be? Leonov is much too clever to bore us with a socialist utopia. He gives us the visions of Kurilov, the veteran Politbureau chief who is the central figure of the story, and these visions are conditioned by Kurilov's mood, and thus by his personal situation at the moment, just as the visions of Tsarist Russia are conditioned by the outlook of the Communist historian who has found the old papers and is making out a case against capitalist enterprise, or by the failing and romantic memories of the survivors of the gentry and the merchant class. Moreover, the efforts of Kurilov to imagine the world that is coming—the great wars, the displacements of civilization, the navigation of interplanetary space—are not in the nature of blueprints but merely imperfect, sometimes comic dreams which provide not so much a prophecy as a picture of our own state of mind when we try to prefigure the future.

What Leonov is attempting to do is, therefore, ambitious and interesting, and he has been able to fill in his project with so much lively observation of life, so much entertaining invention of incident, that he carries us quite through his elaborate book. We are conscious from the beginning that the characters are types, but we do not at first sight take them for the conventional types of Soviet fiction. They do not seem to be doing the regulation things or striking the regulation attitudes: the bourgeois who has buried his past is evidently working in all good faith at his Soviet railroad job; the Komsomol engine crew make a mess of their first difficult run. And the internal life of these people is presented with as much circumstantiality as the external detail of their homes and work, so that the author half creates the illusion that he is on intimate terms with his characters. We give him the benefit of the doubt: we assume that he knows what he is doing and that he has something astonishing and revealing in store. It is not till we come to the end that we are definitely let down by Leonov, but then we are badly let down. The *ci-devant* bourgeois yardmaster, with whom we have been led rather to sympathize, is shown as, after all, incapable of going along with the new society: incurably egoistic and cold, he is doomed to plot a dastardly crime against the noble Communist Kurilov, and he must be publicly denounced by his brother, an upright and hardworking surgeon. The bad actress and bitchy little wife is transfigured by her contact with Kurilov and becomes not merely a worker for socialist construction but also, apparently, an excellent artist. Looking back, we become aware that these people have never been real in the first place and that we have simply been distracted from minding it by the technical agility of the author, his succession of diverting anecdotes and his air of being up to something intelligent.

Leonov himself, we conclude, must be somewhat more intelligent than his book. He is extraordinarily resourceful and adroit in evading dangerous issues—either by simply omitting things from his picture or by treating them in an objective way which enables him to remain noncommittal. *Road to the Ocean* was published in 1936, and the story is supposed to take place somewhere around 1932. The class stratification of the Soviet society and the tyranny of Moscow officialdom through the agencies of the propaganda press and the terror of the G.P.U. were well under way by that time. But Leonov has contrived a story all in terms of old revolutionists, struggling intelligentsia and earnest young Komsomols. And, by unobtrusively causing his characters to say or think certain things, he manages to indicate an attitude which is distinctly humane and liberal. He says, for example, of Kurilov's sister, an austere saint of the heroic generation, that "it did not occur to her to take revenge on an enemy's offspring for the crimes of a whole political system." It is true that a few years in the middle thirties, the period when this book must have been written, saw a relative relaxation, in cultural and political matters, of the rigors of the Kremlin dictatorship. But after the murder of the liberal Kirov, in December, 1934, the aspiration behind this was rapidly stifled. The political terror began, and millions of men and women were shot or sent to prison. People who knew one another well were afraid to comment aloud on anything they read in the paper, because denunciations to the authorities like that of Leonov's villain by his brother had now become the order of the day; and tried party workers like Kurilov and his sister were vanishing overnight into the dungeons of the G.P.U., till there was hardly an old Bolshevik left. It was so far from occurring to the rulers of Russia that one ought not to revenge oneself on the children for the political crimes of the fathers that the children of liquidated officials were left orphaned and without support, to be ostracized at school, avoided by their neighbors and sometimes driven to suicide. The forces that Leonov seems to deprecate, that have produced the distortions of his story itself, were the forces that were to dominate in Russia.

The net effect, therefore, of Leonov's book is a peculiarly depressing one. In reading a book by a Frenchman written under the Nazi oppression—such as the *Imaginary Interviews* of André Gide—we share his humiliation in being reduced to guarded statements and riddles. A Russian novel like *Road to the Ocean* embarrasses us in a similar way. I should not say, on the evidence of this book—though Gorky highly praised Leonov—that the author was a first-rate novelist; but, among Soviet writers, he is talented, he does have some serious idea of what literature ought to be, and it is painful to see him working to produce a real social novel that would stand up with Malraux or Dos Passos, only to have to surrender his project to the requirements of the Soviet formula.

It is curious to compare Leonov, almost an official Soviet writer, with another Russian novelist, Mark Aldanov, a non-fellow-travelling émigré. I do not know whether they have influenced one another or whether they have been influenced separately by some general literary tendency, but they are in some respects surprisingly similar. Both like to make their stories out of episodes in the careers of assorted characters whose orbits compose a larger pattern but who may barely intersect one another's; and both have taken for their principal figures old men bred in Tsarist Russia who have survived into the new society but who are now very close to death. Leonov has the great advantage over the author of *The Fifth Seal* that he himself has lived the new society: his material is all first-hand; whereas a weakness of Aldanov's novel is the vagueness, if not sometimes the blankness, of the Soviet backgrounds of the characters whom he sees so clearly in their context as visitors to Western Europe. Yet Aldanov has the advantage of freedom: he can write what he observes and feels; and if we want to see how important that advantage is, we may consider the two books side by side. To do so is to put to ourselves problems about which it is rather difficult to arrive at any definite conclusions. Is Aldanov "better" than Leonov because he is so much more satisfactory from this point of view—because he can choose his effect and achieve it? Would Leonov have been more like Aldanov, more impartial and independent, if he had written his book abroad? Or is Leonov "better" than Aldanov, both because of his more abundant material and because he has been able to associate himself with a great creative social purpose? Assuming that abilities are equal—something of which one can by no means be sure—I am afraid that it is Aldanov, the exile, who enjoys the more important advantage. The Leninist idealism which was stimulating in the Soviet literature of the twenties, which struck a kind of moral vitality into some even of the relatively crude melodramas of the earlier Soviet stage, is perceptibly flagging in *Road to the Ocean*. We are continually being shown the miracles wrought upon human nature by the magic of the revolutionary morality, but we no longer really feel its virtue. Instead, we feel the Soviet state, present not in its habit as it lives, as the old Tsarist officialdom was in Gogol, but in a much more powerful and damaging way: by the mold into which it has crushed the book.

December 9, 1944

Who Cares Who Killed Roger Ackroyd?

THREE MONTHS AGO I wrote an article on some recent detective stories. I had not read any fiction of this kind since the days of Sherlock Holmes, and, since I constantly heard animated discussions of the merits of the mystery writers, I was curious to see what they were like today. The specimens I tried I found disappointing, and I made some rather derogatory remarks in connection with my impressions of the genre in general. To my surprise, this brought me letters of protest in a volume and of a passionate earnestness which had hardly been elicited even by my occasional criticisms of the Soviet Union. Of the thirty-nine letters that have reached me, only seven approve my strictures. The writers of almost all the others seem deeply offended and shocked, and they all say almost exactly the same thing: that I had simply not read the right novels and that I would surely have a different opinion if I would only try this or that author recommended by the correspondent. In many of these letters there was a note of asperity, and one lady went so far as to declare that she would never read my articles again unless I were prepared to reconsider my position. In the meantime, furthermore, a number of other writers have published articles defending the detective story: Jacques Barzun, Joseph Wood Krutch, Raymond Chandler and Somerset Maugham have all had something to say on the subject—nor has the umbrageous Bernard De Voto failed to raise his voice.

Overwhelmed by so much insistence, I at last wrote my correspondents that I would try to correct any injustice by undertaking to read some of the authors that had received the most recommendations and taking the whole matter up again. The preferences of these readers, however, when I had a tabulation of them made, turned out to be extremely divergent. They ranged over fifty-two writers and sixty-seven books, most of which got only one or two votes each. The only writers who got as many as five or over were Dorothy L. Sayers, Margery Allingham, Ngaio Marsh, Michael Innes, Raymond Chandler and the author who writes under the names of Carter Dickson and John Dickson Carr.

The writer that my correspondents were most nearly unanimous in putting at the top was Miss Dorothy L. Sayers, who was pressed upon me by eighteen people, and the book of hers that eight of them were sure I could not fail to enjoy was a story called *The Nine Tailors*. Well, I set out to read *The Nine Tailors* in the hope of tasting some novel excitement, and I declare that it seems to me one of the dullest books I have ever encountered in any field. The first part of it is all about bell-ringing as it is practised in English churches and contains a lot of information of the kind that you might expect to find in an encyclopedia article on campanology. I skipped a good deal of this, and found myself skipping, also, a large section of the conversations between conventional English village characters: "Oh, here's Hinkins with the aspidistras. People may say what they like about aspidistras, but they do go on all the year round and make a background," etc. There was also a dreadful stock English nobleman of the casual and debonair kind, with the embarrassing name of Lord Peter Wimsey, and, although he was the focal character in the novel, being Miss Dorothy Sayers's version of the inevitable Sherlock Holmes detective, I had to skip a good deal of him, too. In the meantime, I was losing the story, which had not got a firm grip on my attention, but I went back and picked it up and steadfastly pushed through to the end, and there I discovered that the whole point was that if a man was shut up in a belfry while a heavy peal of chimes was being rung, the vibrations of the bells might kill him. Not a bad idea for a murder, and Conan Doyle would have known how to dramatize it in an entertaining tale of thirty pages, but Miss Sayers had not hesitated to pad it out to a book of three hundred and thirty, contriving one of those hackneyed cock-and-bull stories about a woman who commits bigamy without knowing it, and larding the whole thing with details of church architecture, bits of quaint lore from books about bell-ringing and the awful whimsical patter of Lord Peter.

I had often heard people say that Dorothy Sayers wrote well, and I felt that my correspondents had been playing her as their literary ace. But, really, she does not write very well: it is simply that she is more consciously literary than most of the other detective-story writers and that she thus attracts attention in a field which is mostly on a sub-literary level. In any serious department of fiction, her writing would not appear to have any distinction at all. Yet, commonplace in this respect though she is, she gives an impression of brilliant talent if we put her beside Miss Ngaio Marsh, whose *Overture to Death* was also suggested by several correspondents. Mr. De Voto has put himself on record as believing that Miss Marsh, as well as Miss Sayers and Miss Allingham, writes her novels in "excellent prose," and this throws for me a good deal of light on Mr. De Voto's opinions as a critic. I hadn't quite realized before, though I had noted his own rather messy style, to what degree he was insensitive to writing. I do not see how it is possible for anyone with a feeling for words to describe the unappetizing sawdust which Miss Marsh has poured into her pages as "excellent prose" or as prose at all except in the sense that distinguishes prose from verse. And here again the book is mostly padding. There is the notion that you could commit a murder by rigging up a gun in a piano in such a way that the victim will shoot himself when he presses down the pedal, but this is embedded in the dialogue and doings of a lot of faked-up English county people who are even more tedious than those of *The Nine Tailors*.

The enthusiastic reader of detective stories will indignantly object at this point that I am reading for the wrong things: that I ought not to be expecting good writing, characterization, human interest or even atmosphere. He is right, of course, though I was not fully aware of it till I attempted *Flowers for the Judge*, considered by connoisseurs one of the best books of one of the masters of this school, Miss Margery Allingham. This tale I found completely unreadable. The story and the writing both showed a surface so wooden and dead that I could not keep my mind on the page. How can you care who committed a murder which has never really been made to take place, because the writer hasn't any ability of even the most ordinary kind to persuade you to see it or feel it? How can you probe the possibilities of guilt among characters who all seem alike, because they are all simply names on the page? It was then that I understood that a true connoisseur of this fiction must be able to suspend the demands of his imagination and literary taste and take the thing as an intellectual problem.

But how you arrive at that state of mind is what I do not understand.

In the light of this revelation, I feel that it is probably irrelevant to mention that I enjoyed *The Burning Court*, by John Dickson Carr, more than the novels of any of these ladies. There is a tinge of black magic that gives it a little of the interest of a horror story, and the author has a virtuosity at playing with alternative hypotheses that makes this trick of detective fiction more amusing than it usually is.

I want, however, to take up certain points made by the writers of the above-mentioned articles.

Mr. Barzun informs the non-expert that the detective novel is a kind of game in which the reader of a given story, in order to play properly his hand, should be familiar with all the devices that have already been used in other stories. These devices, it seems, are now barred: the reader must challenge the writer to solve his problem in some novel way, and the writer puts it up to the reader to guess the new solution. This may be true, but I shall never qualify. I would rather play Twenty Questions, which at least does not involve the consumption of hundreds of ill-written books.

A point made by three of these writers, Mr. Maugham, Mr. De Voto and Mr. Krutch, is that the novel has become so philosophical, so psychological and so symbolic that the public have had to take to the detective story as the only department of fiction where pure story-telling survives.

This seems to me to involve two fallacies. On the one hand, it is surely not true that "the serious novelists of today"—to quote Mr. Maugham's assertion—"have often," in contrast to the novelists of the past, "little or no story to tell," that "they have allowed themselves to be persuaded that to tell a story is a negligible form of art." It is true, of course, that Joyce and Proust—who, I suppose, must be accounted the heaviest going—have their various modern ways of boring and playing tricks on the reader. But how about the dreadful bogs and obstacles that one has to get over in Scott? the interpolated essays in Hugo? the leaking tap of Thackeray's reflections on life, in which the story is always trickling away? Is there anything in first-rate modern fiction quite so gratuitous as these *longueurs*?

Even Proust and Joyce and Virginia Woolf do certainly have stories to tell, and they have organized their books with an intensity which has been relatively rare in the novel and which, to my mind, more than makes up for the occasional viscosity of their narrative.

On the other hand, it seems to me—for reasons suggested above—a fantastic misrepresentation to say that the average detective novel is an example of good story-telling. The gift for telling stories is uncommon, like other artistic gifts, and the only one of this group of writers—the writers my correspondents have praised—who seems to me to possess it to any degree is Mr. Raymond Chandler. His *Farewell, My Lovely* is the only one of these books that I have read all of and read with enjoyment. But Chandler, though in his recent article he seems to claim Hammett as his master, does not really belong to this school of the old-fashioned detective novel. What he writes is a novel of adventure which has less in common with Hammett than with Alfred Hitchcock and Graham Greene— the modern spy story which has substituted the jitters of the Gestapo and the G.P.U. for the luxury world of E. Phillips Oppenheim. It is not simply a question here of a puzzle which has been put together but of a malaise conveyed to the reader, the horror of a hidden conspiracy that is continually turning up in the most varied and unlikely forms. To write such a novel successfully you must be able to invent character and incident and to generate atmosphere, and all this Mr. Chandler can do, though he is a long way below Graham Greene. It was only when I got to the end that I felt my old crime-story depression descending upon me again—because here again, as is so often the case, the explanation of the mysteries, when it comes, is neither interesting nor plausible enough. It fails to justify the excitement produced by the elaborate build-up of picturesque and sinister happenings, and one cannot help feeling cheated.

My experience with this second batch of novels has, therefore, been even more disillusioning than my experience with the first, and my final conclusion is that the reading of detective stories is simply a kind of vice that, for silliness and minor harmfulness, ranks somewhere between smoking and crossword puzzles. This conclusion seems borne out by the violence of the letters I have been receiving. Detective-story readers feel guilty, they are habitually on the defensive, and all their talk about "well-written" mysteries is simply an excuse for their vice, like the reasons that the alcoholic can always produce for a drink. One of the letters I have had shows the addict in his frankest and most shameless phase. This lady begins by pretending, like the others, to guide me in my choice, but she breaks down and tells the whole dreadful truth. Though she has read, she says, hundreds of detective stories, "it is surprising," she finally confesses, "how few I would recommend to another. However, a poor detective story is better than none at all. Try again. With a little better luck, you'll find one you admire and enjoy. Then you, too, may be

A MYSTERY FIEND."

This letter has made my blood run cold: so the opium smoker tells the novice not to mind if the first pipe makes him sick; and I fall back for reassurance on the valiant little band of my readers who sympathize with my views on the subject. One of these tells me that I have underestimated both the badness of detective stories themselves and the lax mental habits of those who enjoy them. The worst of it is, he says, that the true addict, half the time, never even finds out who has committed the murder. The addict reads not to find anything out but merely to get the mild stimulation of the succession of unexpected incidents and of the suspense itself of *looking forward* to learning a sensational secret. That this secret is nothing at all and does not really account for the incidents does not matter to such a reader. He has learned from his long indulgence how to connive with the author in the swindle: he does not pay any real attention when the disappointing dénouement occurs, he does not think back and check the events, he simply shuts the book and starts another.

To detective-story addicts, then, I say: Please do not write me any more letters telling me that I have not read the right books. And to the seven correspondents who are with me and who in some cases have thanked me for helping them to liberate themselves from a habit which they recognized as wasteful of time and degrading to the intellect but into which they had been bullied by convention and the portentously invoked examples of Woodrow Wilson and André Gide—to these staunch and pure spirits I say: Friends, we represent a minority, but Literature is on our side. With so many fine books to be read, so much to be studied and known, there is no need to bore ourselves with this rubbish. And with the paper shortage pressing on all publication and many first-rate writers forced out of print, we shall do well to discourage the squandering of this paper that might be put to better use.

January 20, 1945

"Mr. Holmes, They Were the Footprints of a Gigantic Hound!"

M Y ARTICLE of four weeks ago on detective stories has called forth a burst of correspondence even more overwhelming than that provoked by my earlier piece—well over a hundred letters. But in this case the people who write me mostly agree with my adverse attitude. Among the few letters from those who do not, some, however, are excessively bitter. One lady adds a postscript in which she declares that she has never liked men named Edmund, and another asks me jeeringly how much I have been paid by "the non-detective fiction publishers." The furious reaction of these readers confirms me in my conclusion that detective stories are actually a habit-forming drug for which its addicts will fight like tigers— an opinion that is explicitly corroborated by many of the approving letters. The evangelical note at the end of my piece was intended to have a burlesque flavor, but some of my correspondents seem to have taken it more seriously than it was meant, and write to tell me that, though they have long been addicts, they have made a vow, since reading my article, never to touch another detective story. An old friend, a classical scholar and archeologist, has rather horrified me by writing to confess that he, too, has been a victim of this form of narcotic and that he had already had the intention of doing for it in literature what De Quincey has done for opium-eating.

I will now confess, in my turn, that, since my first looking into this subject last fall, I have myself become addicted, in spells, to reading myself to sleep with Sherlock Holmes, which I had gone back to, not having looked at it since childhood, in order to see how it compared with Conan Doyle's latest imitators. I propose, however, to justify my pleasure in rereading Sherlock Holmes on grounds entirely different from those on which the consumers of the current product ordinarily defend their taste. My contention is that Sherlock Holmes *is* literature on a humble but not ignoble level, whereas the mystery writers most in vogue now are not. The old stories are literature, not because of the conjuring tricks and the puzzles, not because of the lively melodrama, which they have in common with many other detective stories, but by virtue of imagination and style. These are fairy-tales, as Conan Doyle intimated in his preface to his last collection, and they are among the most amusing of fairy-tales and not among the least distinguished.

The Sherlock Holmes stories, almost as much as the Alice books or as Edward Lear's nonsense, were the casual products of a life the main purpose of which was something else, but creations that in some sense got detached from their author and flew away and had a life of their own. Conan Doyle, it seems, worked conscientiously to document his historical romances, which he considered his serious work, but he regarded Holmes and Watson as the paper dolls of rather ridiculous and undignified potboilers, and he paid so little attention to what he wrote about them that the stories are full of inconsistencies, which Doyle never bothered to correct. He forgot Watson's Christian name and later on gave him a new one; he shifted the location of his wound; he began by making an ignorance of literature an essential trait of Holmes's personality and then had him talk about Petrarch and Meredith; and he even, on one occasion, changed the season abruptly from July to September. (It is an odd evidence of Holmes's vitality that some of his admirers should have gone to the trouble of attempting to account for these discrepancies, as if Watson and Holmes had been real men, and that they should actually have published their conjectures in a volume called *Profile by Gaslight*.) Doyle had become so impatient with his hero by the end of the second series in the *Strand Magazine* that he got rid of him by killing him off, totally without preparation, in a manner that was little short of frivolous. But Sherlock Holmes was like a genie let out of a bottle; there was no way of getting him back and, once at large, he was always available to minister to his master's wants. Doyle eventually brought Holmes back to life and wrote five more volumes about him. For perhaps the only time in his life, he had hit upon a genuine spell.

Whence had he mustered this spell and what elements had been mixed to make it? Well, there was Poe, of course, and there was also unquestionably R. L. Stevenson's *New Arabian Nights*. *The Adventure of the Hansom Cab* and *The Adventure of the Superfluous Mansion* must have suggested both the Sherlock Holmes titles and the formula of taking people to unexpected places and having them witness mysterious happenings. But Doyle, though much less "literary" than Stevenson, somehow got solider results, which depended on quite different qualities from Stevenson's suave Oriental tone and the limpid iridescence of his fantasy. For one thing, Stevenson was weak on character, whereas Doyle had produced two real personalities. And, for another, Conan Doyle had created his own vein of fantasy, which was vivider, if rather less fine, than Stevenson's. You see the force of his imagination exemplified in a curious way in some of those stories in which the dénouement is inadequate or disappointing. A young woman goes to work in a country house where she will be extravagantly overpaid if she will consent to have her hair cut short, to wear a dress of electric blue, to sit in certain places at certain times and to allow herself to be made to laugh uproariously at a succession of funny stories told by the master of the house; a professional interpreter of Greek finds himself suddenly shanghaied in a cab and taken to a stuffy London house with velvet furniture, a high white marble mantelpiece and a suit of Japanese armor, where a man who wears glasses and has a giggling laugh compels him to put questions in Greek to a pale and emaciated captive, whose face is all crisscrossed with sticking plaster. Neither of these stories—*The Copper Beeches* or *The Greek Interpreter*—quite lives up to its opening evocation. The way of accounting for the sticking plaster seems, indeed, entirely unsatisfactory, and since Watson tells us that this "singular case" is "still involved in some mystery," we are almost inclined to suspect that the affair concealed something else which the detective had failed to penetrate; but the images have exercised their power—a power that is partly due to their contrast with, their startling emergence from, the dull surface of Victorian London.

Here Doyle is exploiting a device quite remote from the suave story-spinning of Stevenson: he is working in the familiar tradition—in which the English art of fiction has excelled since the days of *Robinson Crusoe*—of the commonplace and common-sense narrative which arouses excitement and wonder. He can make us feel the presence of the "sinister"—to use one of his favorite words—even in a situation which does not include any fantastic ingredient. Take the story of *The Naval Treaty*, which follows *The Greek Interpreter* in Doyle's carefully varied program. A young man in the Foreign Office has been entrusted with an important document, which he has been copying at night in his office. He is alone and there is no entrance to the room save by a corridor that leads to the street. No one except the Foreign Minister knows that he has the treaty. At last he rings for the doorman to bring him some coffee, but an unknown woman answers the bell, large and coarse-faced and wearing an apron. She says that she is the doorman's wife and promises to send the coffee, but some time passes and the coffee does not come, and he goes downstairs to see what is the matter. He finds the doorman asleep, but the man is immediately awakened by a bell that rings loudly overhead.

"'I was boiling the kettle when I fell asleep, sir.' He looked at me and then up at the still quivering bell with an ever-growing astonishment upon his face.
"'If you was here, sir, then who rang the bell?' he asked.
"'The bell!' I cried. 'What bell is it?'
"'It's the bell of the room you were working in.'"

Both these incidents, so soberly told, the appearance of the woman and the ringing of the bell, give us shocks that reverberate. Of course there is no one upstairs in the room and the naval treaty has been taken.

The stories have also both form and style of a kind very much superior to what one finds in our padded novels, though sometimes, it seems to me, the requirements of length for short stories in the *Strand Magazine* compelled Doyle somewhat to skimp his endings. There is wit, not mere tricks, in the "deductions" of Holmes and wit in the dialogue, and not only in the interchanges between Watson and Holmes but even in some of the stagy lines which Doyle's very sure sense of point save from being merely absurd. Take for example, the conclusion of *The Second Stain*:

"'Come, sir,' said he. 'There is more in this than meets the eye. How came the letter back in the box?'

"Holmes turned away smiling from the keen scrutiny of those wonderful eyes.

" 'We also have our diplomatic secrets,' said he and, picking up his hat, he turned to the door."

The writing, of course, is full of clichés, but these clichés are dealt out with a ring which gives them a kind of value, while the author makes speed and saves space so effectively that we are rarely in danger of getting bogged down in anything boring. And the clichés of situation and character are somehow made to function, too, for the success of the general effect. This effect owes its real originality not only to the queer collocations of elements, such as those I have mentioned above, but also to the admirable settings: the somber overcarpeted interiors or the musty empty houses of London, the remote old or new country places, always with shrubbery along the drives; and the characters—the choleric big-game hunters and the high-spirited noble ladies—have been imbued with the atmosphere of the settings and charged with an energy sufficient— like the fierce puppets of a Punch-and-Judy show—to make an impression in their simple roles.

But over the whole epic there hangs an air of irresponsible comedy, like that of some father's rigmarole for children, like that of, say, Albert Bigelow Paine in his stories about the Coon, the Possum and the Old Black Crow who all lived together in a Hollow Tree. The story-teller can make anything happen that will entertain his nightly audience and that will admit some kind of break at bedtime. The invention of Professor Moriarty, that scientific master-mind of crime who was to checkmate the great scientific detective, is simply an improvisation to bring to an end an overlong story, and the duel in which each is straining to outthink and outtrick the other is exhilarating because totally impossible. I do not share the prejudice of some Holmes experts against the two latest series of stories. Inferior though these often are in plot, Doyle amuses himself here in a way which makes them extremely funny. I am delighted by *The Adventure of the Dying Detective*, in which Holmes feigns a tropical disease and refuses to let Watson treat him: "Facts are facts, Watson, and after all, you are only a general practitioner with very limited experience and mediocre qualifications. It is painful to have to say these things, but you leave me no choice." "I was bitterly hurt," says Watson. And it was a capital idea to have Watson himself sometimes undertake the inquiry and bungle it, or, conversely, in other cases, to have Holmes tell the stories instead of Watson, in an attempt to divest them of the fortuitous glamor which he insists that his friend has added. (I have discovered, by the way—though I see that it had already been hinted by Christopher Morley— that Rex Stout's great detective, Nero Wolfe, has the look of having been inspired by one of the most diverting of Doyle's variations: Sherlock's brother Mycroft, who is also a mastermind but who has grown so stout and inert that he is unable to work on a problem till all the data have been dug out and brought him.)

And it all takes place in the Hollow Tree—in that atmosphere of "cozy peril," to quote a phrase from, I think, Mr. Morley, who, in his prefaces to the Sherlock Holmes omnibus and an anthology called *Sherlock Holmes and Dr. Watson*, has written so well on this subject. They will, of course, get safely back to Baker Street, after their vigils and raids and arrests, to discuss the case comfortably in their rooms and have their landlady bring them breakfast the next morning. Law and Order have not tottered a moment; the British police are well in control: they are the stoutest, most faithful fellows in the world if they can only be properly directed by Intellect in the form of a romantic personality possessed by the scientific spirit. All the loose ends of every episode are tidily picked up and tucked in, and even Holmes, though once addicted to cocaine, has been reformed by the excellent Watson. In this world, one can count on the client to arrive at the very moment when his case has just been explained, and Holmes and Watson always find it possible to get anywhere they want to go without a moment's delay or confusion. Here is an incident from *The Greek Interpreter* which illustrates this unfailing punctuality. The interpreter, after his visit to the mysterious house, has been driven away and dropped.

"The carriage which had brought me was already out of sight. I stood gazing round and wondering where on earth I might be, when I saw someone coming towards me in the darkness. As he came up to me I made out that he was a railway porter.

"'Can you tell me what place this is?' I asked.

" 'Wandsworth Common,' said he.

" 'Can I get a train into town?'

" 'If you walk on a mile or so to Clapham Junction,' said he, 'you'll just be in time for the last to Victoria.' "

So, no matter what those queer Greeks do in London, there will always be a British porter and he will always help you to get your train. In the newer kind of mystery novel, this porter would not have been a real porter; he would have had some unintelligible connection with the men in the upholstered house, and, far from helping the poor interpreter to catch the train, he would have involved him in endless further trouble—just as the man who wanted a young woman in an electric blue dress to cut her hair and laugh at his jokes would have turned out to be suffering from some form of derangement suggested by Krafft-Ebing or Freud. One rarely finds the word "sinister" even in mystery fiction today; it implies that a spy or a murder, a piece of treachery or an insane neurosis, is something of exceptional occurrence.

February 17, 1945

Glenway Wescott's War Work

T HE HANDWRITING of Glenway Wescott is unusual and rather arresting. It looks somewhat like the elegant and rigorous script that one finds cut on the copper of sun-dials of the seventeenth and eighteenth centuries: the same clarity, the same heavy shadings, the same inflexibly maintained slant. It always seems to have been engraved in metal rather than merely written on paper. There is in it a certain element of boyishness—big round capitals and rounded "m"s and "n"s— but it is always a copybook boyishness, inseparable from a self-imposed discipline.

Mr. Wescott's style makes a similar impression. One is struck by the firm vigor and the craftman's precision with which the short phrases are cut. Here is a personal and handmade product, the achievement of an individual skill. It, too, may have begun with a copybook, with exercises on classical models, but it is hard to put one's finger on these models. Terse and sharp though the language is as English, the form may be based on French. In any case, this style is as far from the colloquialism of Hemingway as from the literary clichés of Louis Bromfield. When one starts reading anything by Wescott, one always feels a satisfaction which comes as something unexpected.

His new novel, *Apartment in Athens*, has these qualities of style at their best, and, as a work of imagination, it is a longer and better sustained performance than the book just before it, *The Pilgrim Hawk*. It is the story of a Greek middle-class family upon whom a German officer is quartered, and it suggests an obvious comparison with that widely known and overrated story *Le Silence de la Mer* by Vercors, which deals with a similar situation in France. But it constitutes a curious proof of the superior advantage of possessing imagination to that of being on the spot that Wescott, who has never been in Greece and has seen nothing of occupied Europe, should give us an effect of reality so much more convincing than that produced by a patriotic Frenchman who knows the German occupation at first hand. Two-thirds, at least, of Mr. Wescott's novel compels us to share, in a way that is at once fascinating and painful, the constrained and suffocated life of a little city apartment in the first months after the Greek defeat. The cramped physical and moral conditions, the readjustments in the relationships of the family, the whole distortion of the social organism by the unassimilable presence of the foreigner—all this is most successfully created. I did have the impression—though without knowing much about either Germans or Greeks—that the Greeks have been allowed to become perhaps a little too servile toward the Germans and that the German, in view of what has gone before, has been made to behave, at the end, a little too basely toward the Greeks. Yet the author—up, at least, to this final turn—makes us accept what he tells us as true, and I have not read any other book—either of fiction or of direct documentation—that has given me the feeling of starving and stifling, of falling back on interior positions, constructing interior defenses, reorganizing and redirecting, behind a mask of submission, the whole structure and aim of one's life, as *Apartment in Athens* does.

It is only at the end of the book that we find the illusion failing. This is a common fault in Wescott's fiction. The incisive beginnings are sometimes betrayed by a tendency to blur at the close; the sure hand, with its deliberate strokes, seems to falter when it comes to the point of drawing the action to a head and driving the meaning home. In the case of *Apartment in Athens*, the line for the story to follow would seem to be clear enough, yet the incidents cease to be vivid, and the psychological atmosphere is violated by the intrusion of a passage of propaganda which throws the whole story out. The Greek father, sent to jail by the Nazi, smuggles out to his wife a long letter, in which he not only preaches resistance to Germany but also urges that his brother-in-law in the underground shall immediately betake himself to the United States and devote himself to a rather vague project of soliciting support for the Greeks—and this in spite of the fact that the prisoner knows little about America and little about what his brother-in-law is doing at home. He states his message to the Americans as follows: "It is important for them to be told what we have learned from the German rule and misrule. I want Petros to tell them. For if we all continue to take our cue in world politics from the Germans as we have done—in reckless appreciation of them when they are on their good behavior, only fighting when they choose to fight, and pitying them whenever they ask for pity—sooner or later they will get what they want: a world at their mercy."

Glenway Wescott has called this book his "war work," but I don't think that ought to let him out of a strict accountability to ideals which he himself has certainly tried to serve. After all, *Apartment in Athens* is the most ambitious piece of fiction that he has published in many years, and we expect of it some revelation of deeper insight and longer range than the mere admonition that the Germans should be restrained from making any more wars. Opposition to the encroachments of the Nazis is now part of the daily business of life, like keeping the house warm and wearing a coat, in order to escape pneumonia; we do not need Glenway Wescott to remind us. But we do need the Glenway Wescotts to tell us what is going on inside ourselves and the Nazis. Through the greater part of this book, Mr. Wescott *is* trying to tell us, and though the story itself carries us on with a skillfully created suspense, it is the explanation of human relations that holds our serious interest. Yet the author does seem rather to drop, or at least to relax, this effort when he consigns his Greek citizen to jail, where we no longer share his intimate life, and sets him to editorializing.

In general, it has been disappointing to find so many writers of serious talent turning away from the study of human behavior to reassure themselves and their readers by invoking some immediate political program or reviving some obsolete religion. Glenway Wescott, like Kay Boyle in *Avalanche*—though the two books have nothing else in common—has, as it were, passed on to characters who disappear in the European underground, problems which he ought to be tackling right out in the open of the United States. The result of this propagandizing is simply to land the writer in melodrama: Wescott not so abjectly as Miss Boyle, but still with some slight loss of caste. It is too easy an evasion of the difficulties of the present situation of man to try to meet them with the symbols of a mythology—whether religious or patriotic. For a writer to pretend today that it is enough for the reader to know that the Germans must be defeated is as much to stake one's art on a childish faith—in a sense, in the very myth which the Nazis themselves have created—as to pretend, as other writers are doing, that it is enough for a writer to believe in the civilizing role of the United States or in the triumph—or, for that matter, in the curbing, if that is regarded as an ultimate goal—of the power of Soviet Russia.

March 3, 1945

A Cry from the Unquiet Grave

CYRIL CONNOLLY founded in 1939 the English literary monthly *Horizon*, and has been publishing it ever since. *Horizon* has been a fine magazine and Mr. Connolly an exceptional editor. It seemed to me a proof of his merit, when I was in London at the end of the war, that, in the literary and Left political worlds, almost everybody complained about him and it, but that everybody, at the same time, seemed in some degree dependent on them. The danger of such magazines is that they are likely to fall into the hands of a group and reflect its limitations and smugness, or that they try, without exercising taste, systematically to proceed on some policy in the interests of which they feel obliged to print mediocre or boring stuff. Mr. Connolly appears to have published only things that he himself has found interesting, and to have been constrained as little as possible by preconceptions—the worst handicaps for a magazine—of what *Horizon*'s clientele would like to read. He would print papers on Benjamin Constant or the minor French romantics which irritated both the Left and the people who thought that it was immoral to disregard the war, and he brought out, in several installments, an orthodox Communist tract which annoyed both the littérateurs and the more emancipated Leftists. He published some of the best reporting—of an unofficial and personal kind—that was written about the war, and he elicited from Augustus John his delightful discursive memoirs, in which history is unimportant and chronology does not exist. One feature, I imagine, pleased nobody: a goose-flesh-producing document called *Naughty Mans*, in which a father reported in baby-talk the reactions of his son to the war, between the ages of three and five.

Mr. Connolly also showed his special gifts in thinking up some really happy ideas for series to be written to order. There is in general, for a literary man, nothing more disheartening in the world than an editor's idea for a series, but Mr. Connolly has got up some good ones, such as the articles on *Where Shall John Go?*, in which people who know various countries intimately have been sending in informal reports on what it is like to live in them. It is characteristic of Mr. Connolly that he will not admit to this series any article that praises a country too lavishly. *Horizon*, in its political outlook, has stood against the current in Europe by being quietly anti-nationalistic, and it has tried, in the cultural field, to reestablish the wrecked communications between different parts of the world.

Though *Horizon*, to the occasional reader, may have appeared rather relaxed and casual, you came to feel, if you followed it month by month, that the magazine must have behind it a personality of some courage and distinction. In Mr. Connolly's new book, *The Unquiet Grave*, that personality reveals itself. This book is a sort of journal, kept through the years of the war—a collection of what the French call *pensées*, that invokes and to some extent imitates Pascal, La Rochefoucauld and Chamfort. But the writer has made a form of his own. There are themes that weave in and out in a fashion rather symphonic than aphoristic: the memories of a love affair, alternately nostalgic and aggrieved; the fluctuation between a physical well-being that seems always to involve self-indulgence and a reviving moral sense that tends to stick in emotions of remorse; a yearning for the oblivion of drugs that is corrected by a seeking for strength in the work of the great artists and moralists; a disaffected attitude toward the war which lets him in for a feeling of guilt, and a sympathy with revolutionary forces which does not prevent him from dreading the advent of the coöperative state; a disgust with the contemporary world and a searching for the causes of its destructiveness. All this is attached, more or less, to the figure of Palinurus, the helmsman of the *Æneid*, who, succumbing to sleep and soft dreams, falls overboard holding the tiller, and who sustains himself for three days on a fragment of floating timber, but, reaching shore, is done to death by the natives. Mr. Connolly has his own version of the Palinurus story. The helmsman of the Trojans, he suggests, may have gone overboard on purpose, in disgust with the callousness of Æneas, for whom Dido has just killed herself, and discouragement with the expedition, which he has come to believe is doomed. It requires, he thinks, some explaining that Palinurus should have carried away, with the tiller, a part of the stern of the ship, which he was able to use as a raft. Virgil's helmsman, Mr. Connolly concludes, is "surely . . . a typical example of antisocial hysteroid resentment!" He signs his book "Palinurus."

This small volume—a scant hundred and fifty pages—is one of the books that has interested me most, as it is certainly one of the best written, that have come out of wartime England. They make no attempt, these pages, to impress by drama or message, and they are the better for being unpretentious. They keep free of all the wartime falsities, and, in rendering a candid account of the experience of one worried and dissatisfied man, they touch ailing layers of consciousness that are common to us all but which we have usually avoided discussing. In form, the little essays and epigrams by which the insights of the aphorist are conveyed are concentrated, exact and lucid (it is only when he is groping among general ideas that the thinking, not the style, becomes sometimes unclear). The passages that deal with memories of Paris and the Riviera are delicious and crisp, like good food to the taste, fresh and bright, like new sights to the eye; and there are descriptions of ferrets and lemurs, quinces and cantaloupes, that express in a novel way the affinities between human beings and the animal and vegetable kingdoms. The truth is, perhaps, that the unquiet grave has been but a kind of bomb-shelter which is giving up a still-living man.

One used to hear it said in London that Cyril Connolly was out of key with the wartime state of mind, but I think that we ought to be grateful that one editor has resisted all pressures and followed his own tastes, and that one good writer has persisted in producing, not what patriotism demanded, but a true natural history of his wartime morale.

October 27, 1945

Cyril Connolly's *The Condemned Playground* is a collection of essays, commentaries, burlesques and travel sketches. It is not so remarkable as *The Unquiet Grave*, but it makes extremely good reading. In matters of literature, Mr. Connolly is not quite a first-rate critic—his disparagement, for example, of A. E. Housman seems to me mistaken from beginning to end —but he is often more to the point than the heavier writers on literary subjects, who set out, with a vocabulary of jargon, to analyze them sociologically, aesthetically or philosophically. He has a genuine classical taste, he is not often influenced by fads, and he reads, and writes about what he reads, because he finds it an agreeable pastime. Literature is for him not a pretext for an impressive article but a strong appetite which he cannot help indulging and which he likes to discuss with others.

This one already knew if one had been reading Mr. Connolly in *Horizon*, but the burlesques in *The Condemned Playground* have come to me as a surprise. These imaginary memoirs and parodies are in a vein distinct from anyone else's, and some of them are really terrific. Mr. Connolly will invent a character—a Communist pansy, an arch young girl, the hero of an Aldous Huxley novel or a self-immolating member of a future totalitarian state—and allow it to possess him like a demon, carrying him away to lengths that are hilarious and a little hysterical. It reminds one of a passage in his early book of memoirs, *Enemies of Promise*, in which he tells of amusing his school-friends with feats of impersonation that would become more and more madly funny but end with his bursting into tears.

I was so much pleased by these burlesques, which seemed to show something like comic genius, that I looked up Mr. Connolly's one novel, *The Rock Pool*, which was published by Scribner's in 1936. Here one finds much the same sort of thing. A mediocre and snobbish young man from Oxford, with a comfortable regular income, spends a summer on the Riviera in an artists' and writers' colony. His first attitude is curious but patronizing: he tells himself that he has come as an observer and will study the community like a rock pool. But the denizens of the pool drag him down into it, demoralize him, plunder him and swindle him, until he finds himself, at last, with no money, left behind with the more abject derelicts who remain in the place through the winter, and in process of becoming one himself. This story, which owes something to *South Wind* and to Compton Mackenzie's novels of Capri, differs from them through its acceleration, which, as in the wildly speeded-up burlesques, has something demoniacal about it. *The Rock Pool* is not quite a success. It starts out as if it were meant for a straight novel and then sacrifices our sympathy for the hero by making his downfall so rapid and so complete that it can move us only to horrified laughter. Yet it convinces us that Cyril Connolly has a talent for the tragi-comic that ought to be given some fuller expression.

July 13, 1946

Both *Enemies of Promise* and *The Rock Pool* have been reprinted since this was written; but people still complain about Connolly. He is one of those writers who, though not aggressive, inspire moral indignation. Some feel that he has done too little and done that little too easily to deserve the prestige he enjoys—that one oughtn't to take seriously nowadays any writer so sybaritic as Connolly has confessed himself to be. It is no use being angry with Connolly. Whatever his faults may be—he has himself described them more brilliantly than anyone else is likely to do—he is one of those fortunate Irishmen, like Goldsmith and Sterne and Wilde, who are born with a gift of style, a natural grace and wit, so that their jokes have the freshness of *jeux d'esprit*, and sometimes their *jeux d'esprit* turn out to stick as classics.

Tales of the Marvellous and the Ridiculous

W HEN, a year and a half ago, I wrote a general article about horror stories, I was reproached by several correspondents for not having mentioned the work of H. P. Lovecraft. I had read some of Lovecraft's stories and had not cared much for them; but the books by and about him have been multiplying so and the enthusiasm of his admirers has been becoming so insistent that I have felt I ought to look into the subject more seriously. There have appeared, mostly in 1945, a collection of his *Best Supernatural Stories*; an unfinished novel, *The Lurker at the Threshold*, completed by August Derleth; a volume of his miscellaneous writings, with appreciations by various writers: *Marginalia*; an essay by him on *Supernatural Horror in Literature*; and *H.P.L.: A Memoir*, by August Derleth. Lovecraft, since his death in 1937, has rapidly been becoming a cult. He had already his circle of disciples who collaborated with him and imitated him, and the Arkham House (in Sauk Center, Wisconsin), which has published *Marginalia* and *The Lurker at the Threshold*, is named from the imaginary New England town that makes the scene of many of his stories. It seems to be exclusively devoted to the productions of Lovecraft and the Lovecraftians. A volume of his letters has been announced.

I regret that, after examining these books, I am no more enthusiastic than before. The principal feature of Lovecraft's work is an elaborate concocted myth which provides the supernatural element for his most admired stories. This myth assumes a race of outlandish gods and grotesque prehistoric peoples who are always playing tricks with time and space and breaking through into the contemporary world, usually somewhere in Massachusetts. One of these astonishing peoples, which flourished in the Triassic Age, a hundred and fifty million years ago, consisted of beings ten feet tall and shaped like giant cones. They were scaly and iridescent, and their blood was a deep green in color. The base of the cone was a viscous foot on which the creatures slid along like snails (they had no stairs in their cities and houses but only inclined planes), and at the apex grew four flexible members, one provided with a head that had three eyes and eight greenish antennae, one with four trumpetlike proboscises, through which they sucked up liquid nourishment, and two with enormous nippers. They were prodigiously inventive and learned, the most accomplished race that the earth has bred. They propagated, like mushrooms, by spores, which they developed in large shallow tanks. Their life-span was four or five thousand years. Now, when the horror to the shuddering revelation of which a long and prolix story has been building up turns out to be something like this, you may laugh or you may be disgusted, but you are not likely to be terrified—though I confess, as a tribute to such power as H. P. Lovecraft possesses, that he at least, at this point in his series, in regard to the omniscient conical snails, induced me to suspend disbelief. It was the race from another planet which finally took their place, and which Lovecraft evidently relied on as creations of irresistible frightfulness, that I found myself unable to swallow: semi-invisible polypous monsters that uttered a shrill whistling sound and blasted their enemies with terrific winds. Such creatures would look very well on the covers of the pulp magazines, but they do not make good adult reading. And the truth is that these stories were hackwork contributed to such publications as *Weird Tales* and *Amazing Stories*, where, in my opinion, they ought to have been left.

The only real horror in most of these fictions is the horror of bad taste and bad art. Lovecraft was not a good writer. The fact that his verbose and undistinguished style has been compared to Poe's is only one of the many sad signs that almost nobody any more pays any real attention to writing. I have never yet found in Lovecraft a single sentence that Poe could have written, though there are some—not at all the same thing —that have evidently been influenced by Poe. (It is to me more terrifying than anything in Lovecraft that Professor T. O. Mabbott of Hunter College, who has been promising a definitive edition of Poe, should contribute to the Lovecraft *Marginalia* a tribute in which he asserts that "Lovecraft is one of the few authors of whom I can honestly say that I have enjoyed every word of his stories," and goes on to make a solemn comparison of Lovecraft's work with Poe's.) One of Lovecraft's worst faults is his incessant effort to work up the expectations of the reader by sprinkling his stories with such adjectives as "horrible," "terrible," "frightful," "awesome," "eerie," "weird," "forbidden," "unhallowed," "unholy," "blasphemous," "hellish" and "infernal." Surely one of the primary rules for writing an effective tale of horror is never to use any of these words —especially if you are going, at the end, to produce an invisible whistling octopus. I happened to read a horror story by Mérimée, *La Vénus d'Ille*, just after I had been investigating Lovecraft, and was relieved to find it narrated—though it was almost as fantastic as Lovecraft—with the prosaic objectivity of an anecdote of travel.

Lovecraft himself, however, is a little more interesting than his stories. He was a Rhode Islander, who hardly left Providence and who led the life of a recluse. He knew a lot about the natural sciences, anthropology, the history of New England, American architecture, eighteenth-century literature and a number of other things. He was a literary man *manqué*, and the impression he made on his friends must partly have been due to abilities that hardly appear in his fiction. He wrote also a certain amount of poetry that echoes Edwin Arlington Robinson—like his fiction, quite second-rate; but his long essay on the literature of supernatural horror is a really able piece of work. He shows his lack of sound literary taste in his enthusiasm for Machen and Dunsany, whom he more or less acknowledged as models, but he had read comprehensively in this special field—he was strong on the Gothic novelists—and writes about it with much intelligence.

As a practitioner in this line of fiction, he regarded himself rightly as an amateur, and did not, therefore, collect his stories in book-form. This was done after his death by his friends. The "Cthulhu Mythos" and its fabricated authorities seem to have been for him a sort of boy's game which he diverted his solitary life by playing with other horror-story fanciers, who added details to the myth and figured in it under distorted names. It is all more amusing in his letters than it is in the stories themselves. His illustrator, Virgil Finlay, he would address as "Dear Monstro Ligriv," and he was in the habit of dating his letters not "66 College Street, Providence" but "Kadath in the Cold Waste: Hour of the Night-Gaunts," "Brink of the Bottomless Gulf: Hour That the Stars Appear Below," "Burrow of the Dholes: Hour of the Charnal Feasting," "Bottomless Well of Yoguggon: Hour That the Snout Appears," etc. He cultivated a spectral pallor. "He never liked to tan," writes a friend, "and a trace of color in his cheeks seemed somehow to be a source of annoyance." The photograph which appears as a frontispiece in *H.P.L.: A Memoir* has been printed—with design, one supposes—in a pinkish transparent red that makes him look both insubstantial and sulphurous.

But Lovecraft's stories do show at times some traces of his more serious emotions and interests. He has a scientific imagination rather similar, though much inferior, to that of the early Wells. The story called *The Color Out of Space* more or less predicts the effects of the atomic bomb, and *The Shadow Out of Time* deals not altogether ineffectively with the perspectives of geological aeons and the idea of controlling the time-sequence. The notion of escaping from time seems the motif most valid in his fiction, stimulated as it was by an impulse toward evasion which had pressed upon him all his life: "Time, space, and natural law," he wrote, "hold for me suggestions of intolerable bondage, and I can form no picture of emotional satisfaction which does not involve their defeat—especially the defeat of time, so that one may merge oneself with the whole historic stream and be wholly emancipated from the transient and ephemeral."

But the Lovecraft cult, I fear, is on even a more infantile level than the Baker Street Irregulars and the cult of Sherlock Holmes.

November 24, 1945

Thackeray's Letters:
A Victorian Document

THERE is no official biography of Thackeray, because he left instructions that none should be written, and, though groups of his letters have been printed, no comprehensive collection was published in the decades that followed his death. A large collection had, however, been made by one of the novelist's granddaughters, Mrs. Richard Thackeray Fuller. In the summer of 1939, a young man from the Harvard Graduate School, Mr. Gordon N. Ray, who had just written a thesis on Thackeray, went to see Mrs. Fuller in England. She asked him to edit these papers, and, since large-scale scholarly publishing seemed impossible in England in wartime, suggested his bringing them out in the United States. Mr. Ray has added to Mrs. Fuller's collection whatever other letters of Thackeray's it was possible to find in America and has published, through the Harvard University Press, the first two immense volumes of *The Letters and Private Papers of William Makepeace Thackeray.* Two more are to be brought out next year. The collection includes "some sixteen hundred of Thackeray's letters, more than a hundred letters to and about him (some of great biographical interest), and nineteen of his diaries and account books." Three-fifths of these letters of Thackeray's had never been published at all, and less than a fourth had been published complete. The editor hopes to add later a fifth installment of letters from English collections, which the war made it impossible to assemble.

The appearance of these volumes is, of course, an event of the first importance. However tepidly one may admire Thackeray, it is impossible not to be fascinated by the extraordinary document they constitute on the London literary world, nineteenth-century society in both London and Paris (one had not realized before how much Thackeray and his family lived in France) and Victorian family life. Thackeray's stipulation that no biography of him should be written was prompted, no doubt, by reluctance to have the circumstances of his wife's insanity and of his attachment to Mrs. Brookfield made public; but we are profiting at last by the long delay, for never perhaps till our era would the descendants of a Victorian great man have consented to such a revelation of the celebrity's private life as these diaries and letters afford. I am not sure that a comparable record exists for any Victorian Englishman. Thackeray kept a diary at intervals, and, during the years that these volumes cover (1817–1851), he was always reporting himself at length to his mother or Mrs. Brookfield with a frankness we should hardly expect; and all the evidence thus provided has here been printed without excisions by the editor, though some had been made by Mrs. Brookfield in the letters written to her. (Certain letters, to Mrs. Brookfield and others, in the possession of Dr. Rosenbach have for some reason been withheld.)

These papers have been presented remarkably well. The edition is both a work of sound scholarship and a book for the ordinary reader. The editor has made it easy to identify Thackeray's friends and get the hang of his rather complicated family by compiling, in Volume I, a small encyclopedic guide to the principal personalities involved, and he has explained in indefatigable footnotes everything that can be explained, and included under the proper dates many anecdotes and descriptions of Thackeray from the memoirs of a variety of persons. The clarity and explicitness and fullness, as well as the good printing, of this Harvard job are unusual in such academic editing. These volumes, in spite of the scale of the material and the elaborateness of the apparatus, are remarkably agreeable to read and easy to find one's way in. (It is curious to note which literary and historical allusions Mr. Ray thinks it worth while to elucidate. When pre-revolutionary classics used to be reprinted in the Soviet Union, the editor always had to explain who such figures as Socrates and Napoleon were. The culture of the United States is not quite so meager as that, but its range of reference is different enough from that of the educated public of Thackeray's day so that we find Mr. Ray writing footnotes for allusions to the *Arabian Nights* and for once well-known names of Greek history. He must have had some nice problems in deciding what the reader would or would not be likely to know, for though he identifies Harmodius and Aristogeiton, he leaves Anaxagoras unexplained.)

The little drawings in Thackeray's letters, as well as a number of other sketches, have been carefully reproduced, and one finds that he had a delicacy as a draftsman that one would scarcely have suspected from the pictures with which he illustrated his books, since, as Mr. Ray points out and as Thackeray complains, the effect of his line was spoilt in transferring the drawings to steel or wood.

These documents offer an opportunity for a complete reconsideration of Thackeray (Mr. Ray promises an eventual biography), and they ought to be made the occasion of critical "reappraisals" of a writer to whom of late not much attention has been paid. I hope to return to the subject when the two remaining volumes come out. In the meantime, on the basis of these first two, one can only indicate disagreement with the opinion, expressed by Mr. Howard Mumford Jones in a leaflet describing the edition, that "the reason why Thackeray temporarily lacks readers is that we have not hitherto known him as a person. . . . There is no Thackeray legend as there is a Brontë legend and a Browning legend." If Thackeray today lacks readers, I believe that it is due to his defects as a novelist, and that, though *Vanity Fair* will remain, the rest of his work is not likely ever much to be read again. Nor can I imagine that this record of his life will create a "Thackeray legend." Interesting though the record is and good though some of his letters are (he is to be seen at his most entertaining in his correspondence with Mrs. Brookfield), we find in them the same weaknesses that prevented him from ever becoming a really top-flight novelist. His lack of intellectual interests appears strikingly in his youthful diary of his travels in Germany and France, where he visited the Weimar of Goethe (who received him for a half-hour's interview, of which Thackeray does not report a word) and the Paris of the early romantics and the early socialists without (though later he praised Victor Hugo and was on good terms with Louis Blanc) showing the faintest interest in either. Beside the great Englishmen of the Victorian era, Thackeray reveals himself here, even more clearly than in his published writings, rather a shallow commentator on life, and wherever we run into a letter by Dickens or by Edward FitzGerald, we get the impression of a soundness and dignity that contrasts with Thackeray's chatter. Snobbery, in the years of his success, became for him as much of a vice as gambling had been in his youth, and these letters show him alternately exulting in his connections with the titled world and trying to chasten or check this proclivity. In the earlier stages, he is as coy as a girl about his acquaintance with the Duke of Devonshire and boasts of having brought him to his (Thackeray's) door; in the later, he announces to someone that he has just destroyed a letter he has written because it is too full of off-hand references to "the great," and, though he has sometimes to refuse invitations in order to be with his children or his relatives, he never fails, in writing about it, to mention just whom he has had to refuse.

Here, also, the falsity that one feels in his novels appears to much worse advantage, because here the human relations are real. Edmund Yates infuriated Thackeray in his later years by calling him a "*faux bonhomme*," but the derogatory descriptions of Thackeray always tend to strike that note, and one is made rather uneasy, in these letters, by his professions of geniality and affection. He is always saying of people that "nothing . . . can be more kind, honest and good-natured," and of writers of his own kind, whom he calls "Satirical-Moralists," he writes to Mark Lemon, "Our profession seems to me as serious as the Parson's own. Please God we'll be honest and kind." Did Thackeray admire those qualities quite so much as he thought? One decides that, though a very demonstrative, he was rather a cold man. The result of his invariable habit of referring to his wife as "the dear little woman," even long after her mental condition has compelled him to put her away, is somehow to make us feel that he has never really cared much about her; and we are revolted, knowing the messy end of his relations with the Brookfield household, when on one occasion he writes to Brookfield invoking his own infant daughter in connection with Brookfield's wife: "By my soul I think my love for the one is as pure as my love for the other—and believe I never had a bad thought for either. If I had, could I shake you by the hand, or have for you a sincere and generous regard? My dear old fellow, you and God Almighty may know all my thoughts about your wife; I'm not ashamed of one of them." I do not mean to imply that Thackeray was anything but attentive in his care of the insane Isabella or anything but formally correct in his attitude toward Mrs. Brookfield, but he is always protesting too much. The sentimentality that mars his novels was an element of his daily life. In the very act of recognizing it and castigating it, he is unable to shake it off: "It was pleasant walking about here in the fields on Thursday and thinking of Annie"—he is writing to his mother about his daughter—"my dear little girl, I hear her voice a dozen times a day, and when I write to her, it's a day's work—blubbering just as I used to do when I left you to go to school—not from any excess of affection filial or paternal as I very well know; but from sentiment as they call it—the situation is pathetic. Look what a sentimental man Sterne was, ditto Coleridge who would have sent his children to the poor house—by Jove, they are a contemptible, impracticable selfish race, Titmarsh [Thackeray] included and without any affectation: Depend upon it, a good honest kindly man not cursed by a genius, that doesn't prate about his affections, and cries very little, & loves his home—he is the real man to go through the world with." But his vision of the "good honest kindly man" is as sentimental as what went before. He is strongest when he is seeing through people and giving a shabby account of the world, but the bitter view he takes of human motives itself implies the sentimental vision, because what he is being bitter about is the fact that human behavior does not live up to this. He can never study motives coolly, as Stendhal or Tolstoy could, and, beside their journals and memoirs, these self-revelations of Thackeray's seem hopelessly second-rate.

December 22, 1945

Splendors and Miseries of
Evelyn Waugh

THE NEW NOVEL by Evelyn Waugh—*Brideshead Revisited* —has been a bitter blow to this critic. I have admired and praised Mr. Waugh, and when I began reading *Brideshead Revisited*, I was excited at finding that he had broken away from the comic vein for which he is famous and expanded into a new dimension. The new story—with its subtitle, *The Sacred and Profane Memories of Captain Charles Ryder*—is a "serious" novel, in the conventional sense, and the opening is invested with a poetry and staged with a dramatic effectiveness which seem to promise much. An English officer, bored with the Army, finds himself stationed near a great country house which has been turned into soldiers' quarters. It is a place that he once used to visit—his life, indeed, has been deeply involved with the Catholic family who lived there. The story reverts to 1923, at the time when Charles Ryder was at Oxford and first met the younger son of the Marchmains, who became his most intimate friend. This early section is all quite brilliant, partly in the manner of the Waugh we know, partly with a new kind of glamor that is closer to Scott Fitzgerald and Compton Mackenzie. It is the period that these older writers celebrated, but seen now from the bleak shrivelled forties, so that everything—the freedom, the fun, the varied intoxications of youth—has taken on a remoteness and pathos. The introduction of the hero to the Catholic family and the gradual revelation of their queerness, their differences from Protestant England, is brought off with accomplished art, and through almost the whole of the first half of the book, the habitual reader of Waugh is likely to tell himself that his favorite has been fledged as a first-rank straight novelist.

But this enthusiasm is to be cruelly disappointed. What happens when Evelyn Waugh abandons his comic convention—as fundamental to his previous work as that of any Restoration dramatist—turns out to be more or less disastrous. The writer, in this more normal world, no longer knows his way: his deficiency in common sense here ceases to be an asset and gets him into some embarrassing situations, and his creative imagination, accustomed in his satirical fiction to work partly in two-dimensional caricature but now called upon for passions and motives, produces mere romantic fantasy. The hero is to have an affair with the married elder daughter of the house, and this is conducted on a plane of banality—the woman is quite unreal—reminiscent of the full-dress adulteries of the period in the early nineteen-hundreds when Galsworthy and other writers were making people throb and weep over such fiction as *The Dark Flower*. And as the author's taste thus fails him, his excellent style goes to seed. The writing—which, in the early chapters, is of Evelyn Waugh's best: felicitous, unobtrusive, exact—here runs to such dispiriting clichés as "Still the clouds gathered and did not break" and "So the year wore on and the secret of the engagement spread from Julia's confidantes and so, like ripples on the water, in ever widening circles." The stock characters—the worldly nobleman, the good old nurse—which have always been a feature of Waugh's fiction and which are all right in a harlequinade, here simply become implausible and tiresome. The last scenes are extravagantly absurd, with an absurdity that would be worthy of Waugh at his best if it were not—painful to say—meant quite seriously. The worldly Lord Marchmain, when he left his wife, repudiated his Catholic faith, and on his deathbed he sends the priest packing, but when the old man has sunk lower, the priest is recalled. The family all kneel, and Charles, who is present, kneels, too. Stoutly though he has defended his Protestantism, his resistance breaks down today. He prays that this time the dying man will not reject the final sacrament, and lo, Lord Marchmain makes the sign of the cross! The peer, as he has drifted toward death, has been soliloquizing at eloquent length: "We were knights then, barons since Agincourt, the larger honors came with the Georges," etc., etc., and the reader has an uncomfortable feeling that what has caused Mr. Waugh's hero to plump on his knees is not, perhaps, the sign of the cross but the prestige, in the person of Lord Marchmain, of one of the oldest families in England.

For Waugh's snobbery, hitherto held in check by his satirical point of view, has here emerged shameless and rampant. His admiration for the qualities of the older British families, as contrasted with modern upstarts, had its value in his earlier novels, where the standards of morals and taste are kept in the background and merely implied. But here the upstarts are rather crudely overdone and the aristocrats become terribly trashy, and his cult of the high nobility is allowed to become so rapturous and solemn that it finally gives the impression of being the only real religion in the book.

Yet the novel is a Catholic tract. The Marchmain family, in their various fashions, all yield, ultimately, to the promptings of their faith and bear witness to its enduring virtue; the skeptical hero, long hostile and mocking, eventually becomes converted; the old chapel is opened up and put at the disposition of the troops, and a "surprising lot use it, too." Now, this critic may perhaps be insensible to some value the book will have for other readers, since he is unsympathetic by conviction with the point of view of the Catholic convert, but he finds it impossible to feel that the author has conveyed in all this any actual religious experience. In the earlier novels of Waugh there was always a very important element of perverse, unregenerate self-will that, giving rise to confusion and impudence, was a great asset for a comic writer. In his new book, this theme is sounded explicitly, with an unaccustomed portentousness and rhetoric, at an early point in the story, when he speaks of "the hot spring of anarchy" that "rose from deep furnaces where was no solid earth, and burst into the sunlight—a rainbow in its cooling vapors with a power the rocks could not repress," and of course it is this hot spring of anarchy, this reckless, unredeemed humanity, that is supposed to be cooled and controlled by the discipline of the Catholic faith. But, once he has come to see this force as sin, Evelyn Waugh seems to be rather afraid of it: he does not allow it really to raise its head—boldly, outrageously, hilariously or horribly—as he has in his other books, and the result is that we feel something lacking. We have come to count on this Serpent; we are not used to seeing it handled so gingerly; and, at the same time, the religion that is invoked to subdue it seems more like an exorcistic rite than a force of regeneration.

There is, however, another subject in *Brideshead Revisited*— a subject which is incompletely developed but which has far more reality than the religious one: the situation of Charles Ryder between the Brideshead family on the one hand and his own family background on the other. This young man has no mother and his only home is with a scholarly and self-centered father, who reduces life to something so dry, so withdrawn, so devoid of affection or color that the boy is driven to look for a home in the family of his Oxford friend and to idealize their charm and grace. What are interesting to a non-Catholic reader are the origins and the evolution of the hero's beglamored snobbery, and the amusing and chilling picture of Charles's holidays at home with his father is one of the very good things in the book.

The comic parts of *Brideshead Revisited* are as funny as anything that the author has done, and the Catholic characters are sometimes good, when they are being observed as social types and get the same kind of relentless treatment as the characters in his satirical books. I do not mean to suggest, however, that Mr. Waugh should revert to his earlier vein. He has been steadily broadening his art, and when he next tries a serious novel, he may have learned how to avoid bathos.

In the meantime, I predict that *Brideshead Revisited* will prove to be the most successful, the only extremely successful, book that Evelyn Waugh has written, and that it will soon be up in the best-seller list somewhere between *The Black Rose* and *The Manatee*.

January 5, 1946

When Evelyn Waugh was converted to Catholicism by the Jesuit Father d'Arcy, he wrote, as a tribute to d'Arcy and in celebration of the rebuilding of Campion Hall, the Jesuit college at Oxford, a short biography of Edmund Campion, the Elizabethan Jesuit martyr. This book, which first appeared in 1935, has now been republished and given a new edition. The story is quite soberly and simply told—with no attempt to create historical atmosphere—and it is not uninteresting to read. Campion is very impressive in the utterances which Mr. Waugh quotes. A man of intellectual distinction, exalted religious vocation and great moral and physical courage, he was the victim, after the suppression of Catholicism in England, of one of those political frame-ups which, though not carried out on the same enormous scale or engineered with the same efficiency as those of our own day, were already a feature of the struggle between Catholicism and Protestantism.

Mr. Waugh's version of history, however, turns out, in its larger perspectives, to be more or less in the vein of *1066 and All That*. Catholicism was a Good Thing and Protestantism was a Bad Thing, and that is all that needs to be said about it. The book is valuable mainly for providing a curious glimpse of the author's conception of modern England. The triumph of Protestantism under Elizabeth meant, he writes, that the country was "secure, independent, insular; the course of her history lay plain ahead: competitive nationalism, competitive industrialism, the looms and coal mines and counting houses, the joint stock companies and the cantonments; the power and the weakness of great possessions." For him, Protestantism is not merely one of the phases of the rise of the middle class; it is the cause of all the phenomena mentioned above. And, in recounting this incident of a period of general religious intolerance, he continually insists on the cruelties of the Protestant persecution of the Catholics but passes lightly over any instance—such as the St. Bartholomew Day's massacre—of the crimes committed by Catholics against Protestants. If we had no source but Mr. Waugh, we might assume that the Society of Jesus had always consisted solely of mild-spirited servants of God, who had never had anything to do with rigging racks or lighting fagots for their enemies.

July 13, 1946

Mr. Waugh has since published two books: *Scott-King's Modern Europe* and *The Loved One*, in which he returns to his earlier manner. Both are short stories rather than novels and both, in comparison with his other work, seem sketchy and incomplete. The first of these, rather like *Scoop*, deals with the misadventures of a teacher from an English public school in Communist-ridden post-war Europe; the second, much the better of the two, with a less ingenuous Englishman in Hollywood. *The Loved One* is extremely funny, but it suffers a little, for an American, from being full of familiar American jokes which Evelyn Waugh has just discovered. It recalls the Nathanael West of *Miss Lonelyhearts* as well as of *The Day of the*

Locust. In connection with Mr. Waugh's Catholicism, it suggests one obvious criticism that nobody, I think, has made. *The Loved One* is a farcical satire on those de luxe California cemeteries that attempt to render death less unpleasant by exploiting all the resources of landscape-gardening and Hollywood mummery. To the non-religious reader, however, the patrons and proprietors of Whispering Glades seem more sensible and less absurd than the priest-guided Evelyn Waugh. What the former are trying to do is, after all, merely to gloss over physical death with smooth lawns and soothing rites; but, for the Catholic, the fact of death is not to be faced at all: he is solaced with the fantasy of another world in which everyone who has died in the flesh is somehow supposed to be still alive and in which it is supposed to be possible to help souls to advance themselves by buying candles to burn in churches. The trappings invented for this other world by imaginative believers in the Christian myth—since they need not meet the requirements of reality—beat anything concocted by Whispering Glades.

George Saintsbury's Centenary

THE CENTENARY of George Saintsbury's birth has been celebrated in England by a memorial volume of his uncollected essays. In this country, Mr. Huntington Cairns has edited a volume of Saintsbury's articles on French literature from the *Encyclopaedia Britannica: French Literature and Its Masters*. These essays are not of Saintsbury's best. He needed more room to do himself justice. The article on *French Literature from the Beginning to 1900* has to account for too many names to have a chance to say anything very interesting about them, but the pieces on single figures—especially the Voltaire —are wonderful feats of condensation that manage, in summarizing a lifetime, to include a maximum of detail and, in their briefly expressed comments, to hit all the nails on the head.

It is a good thing to have these essays in book-form, but what are really most needed now are reprints of Saintsbury's important works, which are out of print and very hard to get. Saintsbury, since his death, has come more and more to stand out as the sole English literary critic of the late-nineteenth early-twentieth centuries, the sole full-length professional critic, who is really of first-rate stature. He is perhaps the only English critic, with the possible exception of Leslie Stephen, whose work is comparable, for comprehensiveness and brilliance, to the great French critics of the nineteenth century. Unlike them, he has no interest in ideas. In religion he was Church of England and in politics an extreme Tory, but his prejudices were rarely allowed to interfere with his appetite for good literature, wherever and by whomever written. He was probably the greatest connoisseur of literature—in the same sense that he was a connoisseur of wines, about which he also wrote—that we have ever had in English. In this, he stood quite outside the academic tradition. Though he contributed to the *Encyclopaedia* and to *The Cambridge History of English Literature*, he has always more or less the air of a man who is showing a friend the sights of some well-studied and loved locality.

In his *History of English Prose Rhythm*, Saintsbury apologizes for his own prose style; but the truth is that his prose is excellent: the rhythm of his own writing never falters. He had, in fact, invented a style of much charm and a certain significance: a modern, conversational prose that carries off asides, jokes and gossip as well as all the essential data by a very strong personal rhythm, that drops its voice to interpolate footnotes without seriously retarding the current, and that, however facetious or garrulous, never fails to cover the ground and make the points. The extreme development of this style is to be seen in the *History of the French Novel* written in Saintsbury's later years and one of the most entertaining of books on literature. It is all a gigantic after-dinner talk with an old gentleman who, to his immense entertainment, has read through the whole of French fiction. The only other writer I know who has created a style similar to Saintsbury's is the late Ford Madox Ford. Both these men are worth attention as writers because they found out how to manage a fine and flexible English prose on the rhythms of informal speech rather than on those of literary convention.

The *History of the French Novel* could never have been written by a Frenchman, because the books and the writers it deals with have not been organized and grouped as would have been done by a French professor. The literature of France itself has always been so much guided and rationalized by a criticism that was an integral part of it that it falls naturally into a well-ordered historical picture. Saintsbury's critical method had been evolved in connection with English literature, which, with its relative indifference to movements and schools and its miscellany of remarkable individuals, does not lend itself to this sort of treatment. In consequence, he stops a good deal longer over somebody like Pigault-Lebrun or Restif de La Bretonne than the ordinary French historian would. He does not need to make them fit into a scheme; he simply likes to tell you about them; and, since you will probably never read them, you do not mind getting them thus at second hand. Now, with English writing, this leisurely method of merely showing a guest the sights succeeds where other methods are inadequate. It is inevitable for academic surveys, English as well as French, to attempt to systematize, and since the material with which the English ones deal has been produced with a minimum of system, a great deal that is important and valuable is invariably left out or slighted. English surveys are likely to be dull, where French surveys may be stimulating, and are nearly always readable. But Saintsbury is never dull, because he misses no point of interest. He is to be seen at his very best in his studies of the minor nineteenth-century writers in his *Collected Essays and Papers*: such people as Peacock, Crabbe, George Borrow, Hogg, Praed and Barham of *The Ingoldsby Legends*. It is impossible to take care of these writers by subsuming them under some bigger name. Each is unlike anyone else, unique and fully developed; each has to be explored for his own sake. And Saintsbury explored and appraised them as nobody else has done. Though more searching essays than Saintsbury's have been written on some of the greater nineteenth-century writers, it would be true in a sense to say that the full history of English nineteenth-century literature has never been written except by Saintsbury.

Nor did his relish for such lesser figures confuse his view of the greater. He made a few rather queer evaluations, as every good critic does—his almost unqualified enthusiasm for Thackeray and his contempt for *Liaisons Dangereuses*; and it is true, as has sometimes been said of him, that he does not plumb the deepest literature deeply. But at least he has arrived by himself at his reasons for the greatness of the greatest. He never takes merits for granted. If the relative amount of space assigned to the various subjects may not always, in a given book of Saintsbury's, seem proportionate to their importance, it is likely to be due to the fact that he had, in his career as a journalist, to treat some of the great figures so many times. If you feel, say, that Shakespeare seems slighted in his *History of Elizabethan Literature*, you will find that he has done him magnificently in *The Cambridge History of English Literature*; if Bulwer-Lytton, in some other work, seems to command as much attention as Dickens, you will find Dickens studied on a larger scale and in a more serious way somewhere else.

He had for a long time had some prejudice against Dante and did not read him till rather late in life, when the tastes of many critics would have already formed a closed cosmos; but when he did sit down at last to *La Commedia Divina*, he conceded its greatness at once. It is curious to find this confession cropping up in the history of the French novel, and it is somehow characteristic of Saintsbury that he should be comparing Dante with some novelist of the nineteenth century, and mention incidentally that he puts him at the top of imaginative fiction. For, except in treating books chronologically, as he might arrange wines in his cellar, he has little real interest in history, and social changes tend merely to annoy him because they distract from the enjoyment of literature. The books are on his shelves like bottles, and it is the most natural thing in the world for him to take down a good medieval vintage made from astringent Italian grapes along with a good dry vintage of French nineteenth-century realism.

February 2, 1946

Ambushing a Best-Seller

THIS MAGAZINE has not always shown foresight in recognizing future successes, and it has sometimes ignored or dismissed in a note novels that were destined to sell hundreds of thousands and to go on selling for years. I have, therefore, lately been watching the publishers' lists in the hope of catching one of these books before it started on its triumphant progress; and, difficult though it seems to be to distinguish the coming best seller from other specimens of inferior fiction, I have decided—from the amount and kind of advertising that the book is being given by the publisher and from the appearance of a picture of the heroine on the cover of *Publisher's Weekly*—that *The Turquoise*, by Anya Seton, has a good chance of landing in the upper brackets. I may be wrong, but I am going to report on it on the assumption that it will be widely read.

The heroine of *The Turquoise*, then, is, as I hardly need to say, a Cinderella. The child of the younger son of a Scottish baronet and of the daughter of a Spanish hidalgo resident in the American Southwest, she is early left a penniless orphan and grows up among the illiterate natives, part Indian, part Spanish, of New Mexico. "Her mouth, always wide, lost its childish innocence, and the lips revealed a passionate curve. Her skin grew moister and more glowing; beneath the dirt and tan shone the velvety whiteness of her Castilian heritage. She was still a thin, ugly child, her gray eyes were still too big for the small face and gave her a goblin look, but she now sometimes showed the first indications of the sex magnetism which was later to give her an illusion of beauty more seductive than actual symmetry." Her natural high breeding and dignity also asserted themselves in the sordid milieux of her early years, so that people instinctively deferred to her quality.

She had been named Santa Fe, after the place where she was born, but her father had been shy of the name for its association with her mother's death. " 'Santa Fe—' said Andrew bitterly, and at the sound of his voice the baby suddenly smiled. 'Aye, 'tis a daft name for ye, small wonder ye smile.' He repeated the name, and this time the last syllable echoed in his mind with a peculiar relevance. 'Fey! There's a true Scottish word will fit you, for ye're fated—doomed to die as we all are, poor bairnie.'" She was doomed, yet she was also chosen, for she had inherited from a Scottish grandmother a gift of mind-reading and second sight, which enabled her not only, by a little concentration, accurately to predict the future but also to know what other people were thinking and to tell them what they had in their pockets. "You are born to great vision, little one," said an old Indian shaman in a "deep, singing tone." "For you they have made thin the curtain which hides the real. But there is danger. You must listen to the voice of the spirit, or your body and its passions will betray you." And he gave her a turquoise pendant, "the color of the Great Spirit's dwelling," in order that she should always remember that her power derives from the Spirit.

She ran away, at the age of seventeen, with a travelling Irish adventurer who had a one-man medicine show. She amazed him by divining at once the ingredients of the "Elixir" he was selling. "There came the sensation of light and a swift impression which she translated into words. 'In this bottle, there is river water—' She paused, then amplified, 'Water from the Rio Grande where you filled it.' Terry made an exclamation and uncrossed his legs. Fey continued calmly, 'There is also whiskey, a little sugar and—chile powder. No more.' She put the bottle on the floor beside her stool, and raised her eyes." He was impressed by her possible usefulness as a feature for his medicine show, a dependable mind-reading act which required no confederate or code; and she, on her side, was attracted to him strongly. "He was twenty-three and of that dashing Irish type which rouses many a woman's imagination. . . . The chin was pugnacious, the mouth, warmly sensual, also showed humor, while the greenish eyes, ill-tempered now, as they often were, seldom produced that impression on women because of their romantic setting of thick dark lashes. He was vivid and very male. Fey, unaccustomed to height and breadth of shoulder, gazed at the ripple of muscles beneath his white silk shirt, and thought him miraculous."

They took to the road together, got married. But her gift, when she debased it, failed her: she could no longer tell prostitutes their original names or inventory the contents of pocketbooks. Dashing Terry—who sincerely admires her but who has to be got out of the way—is rather implausibly made to desert her in a cheap lodging-house in New York. She had been pregnant, though he had not known it, but for a time she was able to earn a living at the Arcadia Concert Saloon. "While she sang, wandering from table to table strumming her guitar and smiling, she diffused sex magnetism, and she titivated the goggling out-of-towners who comprised three-quarters of the Arcadia's patronage." (The proper meaning of "titivate"— here, as often, used for titillate—seems hopelessly to have suffered the fate of "jejune" and "disinterested.") Then she goes to have her baby in a hospital, where a Quaker woman doctor befriends her and tries to persuade her to study medicine. Here she is nursing her baby: "The girl was beautiful; she [the woman doctor] had never realized it before. Or if not exactly beautiful, something far more disturbing. She was alluring, every line of her body, partly unclothed as it now was, pointed to seductive allure."

But the hospital is repellent to Fey: "I loathe sick people and poor people," she tells herself. "I want nothing now of life but luxury and refinement." She has conceived an audacious design on a certain Simeon Tower, the son of a Jewish peddler, who has become one of New York's richest men by dint of his native shrewdness and by "throwing plums to Big Bill Tweed as he rose to power by means of the most corrupt politics ever known in New York." She goes straight to his office in Wall Street and forces her way into his presence. "I think we would like each other," she says. " 'That is a trifle crude,' he said coldly. 'Will you kindly state your business?' His blunt, well-manicured hand made a slight gesture, the prelude to dismissal." But he looks "at the full high outline of her breasts under the leaf-brown silk, at the wide coral-tinted mouth," and succumbs to her seductive allure. He soon gets her a divorce and marries her, and there begins one of those period pageants which, with the recent patriotic exploitation of the American historical legend, have become a cheap and routine feature of so many of our books, plays and films. There is an "at home" at Phoebe and Alice Cary's, at which the visitor is "drawn over to a red settee where Susan B. Anthony and Elizabeth Cady Stanton are discussing . . . the advent of the bustle." (Fey has of course recognized early the greatness of Walt Whitman. Opening *Leaves of Grass* in a book store, " 'This is for me,' she said" at once, "her eyes shining. 'This man understands.' Mr. Tibbins had flushed a dull red. 'That's not a proper book for a young woman to read!' 'Oh, but it is!' said Fey, hardly conscious of him. 'It's true and good. It makes me strong.' And her rapt eyes reread a page.") Simeon is shocked and alarmed by the fact that "on January sixth, Jim Fisk had been shot and killed by Josie Mansfield's paramour, Edward Stokes," and he has a life-or-death struggle with Jay Gould, as "the Mephisto of Wall Street sits like a small black spider silently enmeshing enterprise after enterprise." Simeon Tower has hitherto been excluded from the social Four Hundred, the custodian of which is Ward McAllister; but Fey, with her usual directness— which Simeon "dimly recognized as the product of generations of breeding"—goes to McAllister and asks to be taken in. "It is," he tells her, "my privilege to help guard the—may I say—inner sanctum from pollution"; but "I'll see what I can do," he ends, bowing.

At the first great ball that the Towers give, with Mrs. Astor present, Fey's rascally ex-husband turns up, having impudently crashed the gate. Fey yields again to his Irish charm and spends a night in a raffish hotel with him. But Terry has conceived the idea of blackmailing Simeon Tower and, "sunk in an amorous drowsiness," he murmurs, " 'The old boy's an easy mark.' 'Why do you say that?' She pulled the light chain and the gas flared up, while she contemplated Terry with steady narrowed eyes." "Listen then, Terry," she announces, when she has grasped the situation. "It is finished at last, and I feel for myself a loathing. I was always a—an incident to you, as I have been now. I knew this. I even told myself this over and over, but I— Oh, what's the use! Perhaps it was necessary that by yielding to my body I might become free of it and you."

Unfortunately, Fey's second sight was still in abeyance at this time, so she could not prepare herself for what was about to happen. With the connivance of a villainous secretary, Terry launches his campaign of blackmail, and one day, when he has thrown it in Simeon's teeth that Fey has been unfaithful to him, Simeon takes out a revolver and shoots him. Simeon is sent to the Tombs, and we are led to believe that Fey is going to marry a Scottish relation who has been sent over by her grandfather to find her. But, on a visit to her husband in prison, her power of clairvoyance dramatically comes back (though it is now, it seems, moral insight rather than mind-reading or knowledge of the future). The words of the old Indian return; the past reveals itself to her in a series of blinding flashbacks. She knows she has been to blame. Her consciousness is penetrated "with annihilating truth": "*You are responsible, you!*" She tells her suitor that she can never be his and makes him return to Scotland; she trains herself in hospital work; she goes on the stand at her husband's trial and, by confessing her infidelity, obtains the acquittal of Simeon. Then she takes him away to New Mexico, where they live for the rest of their years in a four-room adobe house, while she ministers to the natives, who "regard her with semi-superstitious reverence." "She had much medical knowledge and she had an almost miraculous intuition as to what ailed the sick bodies or souls which came to her." After her death, she was known as "La Santa."

The Turquoise thus follows a familiar line. It is a typical American novel written by a woman for women. The great thing about this kind of fiction is that the heroine must combine, in one lifetime, as many enjoyable kinds of role as possible: she must be sexually desirable and successful, yet a competent professional woman; she must pass through picaresque adventures, yet attain the highest social position; she must be able to break men's hearts, yet be capable of prodigies of fidelity; she must have every kind of worldly success, yet rise at moments to the self-sacrifice of the saint. She must, in fact, have every possible kind of cake and manage to eat it, too. A bait is laid for masculine readers, also, by periodically disrobing the heroine and writing emphatically of her sexual appetite. And the whole book is written in that tone and prose of the women's magazines which is now so much a standard commodity that it is probably possible for the novelist to pick it up at the corner drugstore with her deodorant and her cold cream.

Yet *The Turquoise* sticks below the level of the more compelling specimens of this fiction by reason of the lack in it of any real feeling of even the feminine day-dreaming kind that does sometimes enliven these books. There is not even a crude human motivation of either the woman or the men. The heroine, who is supposed to be intuitive, full of warm emotions and eager desires, is as incredible in her relations with her husbands as they are in their relations with her. She is made, for example, to lay siege to Simeon simply because she craves money and position, but the stigma of calculation is eliminated by showing her later as passionately in love with her husband—yet not so passionately, it appears still later, that she will not be tempted to slip with Terry. The whole thing is as synthetic, as arbitrary, as basically cold and dead, as a scenario for a film. And now the question presents itself: Will real men and women, in large numbers, as the publishers obviously hope, really buy and read this arid rubbish, which has not even the rankness of the juicier trash? Or have I been using up all this space merely to warn you against a dud? Watch the best-seller lists for the answer.

February 16, 1946

Several people who read this article imagined that it was a burlesque; they assumed, from the absurdity of the story, that I must have made the whole thing up. But *The Turquoise* was perfectly real, and it has justified my worst apprehensions by selling more than nine hundred thousand copies.

The Apotheosis of Somerset Maugham

IT HAS happened to me from time to time to run into some person of taste who tells me that I ought to take Somerset Maugham seriously, yet I have never been able to convince myself that he was anything but second-rate. His swelling reputation in America, which culminated the other day in his solemn presentation to the Library of Congress of the manuscript of *Of Human Bondage*, seems to me a conspicuous sign of the general decline of our standards. Thirty or thirty-five years ago the English novelists that were read in America were at least men like Wells and Bennett, who, though not quite of top rank, were at least by vocation real writers. Mr. Maugham, I cannot help feeling, is not, in the sense of "having the métier," really a writer at all. There are real writers, like Balzac and Dreiser, who may be said to write badly. Dreiser handles words abominably, but his prose has a compelling rhythm, which is his style and which induces the emotions that give his story its poetic meaning. But Mr. Maugham, whose language is always banal, has not even an interesting rhythm.

Now, unless I am looking for facts, I find it extremely difficult to get through books that are not "written." I can read Compton Mackenzie, for example, of the second rank though he is, because he has a gift of style of a not too common kind. But my experience has always been with Maugham that he disappoints my literary appetite and so discourages me from going on. His new novel, *Then and Now*—which I had sworn to explore to the end, if only in order to be able to say that I had read a book of Maugham's through—opposed to my progress, through all the first half, such thickets of unreadableness, that there were moments when I thought I should never succeed.

Then and Now is an historical novel: it deals with Niccolò Machiavelli and tells the story of his mission, as envoy from Florence, to the headquarters of Caesar Borgia, when the latter, in his campaign of domination, appeared at his most effective and most menacing. The way in which this promising subject is handled suggested, I was shocked to discover, one of the less brilliant contributions to a prep-school magazine. Here are Machiavelli and Borgia confronting one another: "Although he had but briefly seen him at Urbino, Machiavelli had been deeply impressed by him. He had heard there how the Duke Guidobaldo da Montefeltro, confiding in Caesar Borgia's friendship, had lost his state and barely escaped with his life; and though he recognized that Il Valentino had acted with shocking perfidy he could not but admire the energy and adroit planning with which he had conducted the enterprise. This was a man of parts, fearless, unscrupulous, ruthless and intelligent, not only a brilliant general but a capable organizer and an astute politician. A sarcastic smile played upon Machiavelli's thin lips and his eyes gleamed, for the prospect of matching his wits with such an antagonist excited him." This narrative from time to time is obstructed by the introduction of thick chunks of historical background that sound as if they had been copied out—so compressed and indigestible are they, so untouched by imagination—from some textbook in the history classroom: "In June of the year with which this narrative is concerned, Arezzo, a city subject to Florence, revolted and declared itself independent. Vitellozzo Vitelli, the ablest of Il Valentino's commanders and bitter enemy of the Florentines because they had executed his brother Paolo, and Baglioni, Lord of Perugia, went to the support of the rebellious citizens and defeated the forces of the Republic," etc., etc. As will be seen from the above sentence, in which, if we glide over the comma, we are at first misled into supposing that Baglioni was executed, before we find that he went with Vitelli, the writing is amateurish. The book is full of ill-composed sentences, bulging with disproportionate clauses that prevent them from coming out right, or confused by "he"s, "him"s and "his"s that apply to different antecedents: a kind of thing that an English master would have been sure to bluepencil in the young student's themes. The language is such a tissue of clichés that one's wonder is finally aroused at the writer's ability to assemble so many and at his unfailing inability to put anything in an individual way: "But Il Valentino appeared to be well pleased. It looked as though he were prepared to let bygones be bygones and restore the repentant rebels to his confidence. . . . But whatever sinister plans he turned round in that handsome head of his, the Duke was evidently not ready to resort to more than veiled threats to induce the Florentines to accede to his demands. . . . The Duke gazed at him thoughtfully. You might have imagined that he was asking himself what kind of a man this was, but with no ulterior motive, from idle curiosity rather. . . . The truth, the unpalatable truth, stared him in the face. . . . He had taken him on this trip from sheer good nature, he had introduced him to persons worth knowing, he had done his best to form him, to show him how to behave, to civilize him, in short; he had not spared his wit and wisdom to teach him the ways of the world, how to make friends and influence people. And this was his reward, to have his girl snatched away from under his very nose." This dullness is only relieved by an occasional dim sparkle of the Wildean wit that made comedies like *Our Betters* amusing without investing them with that distinction which, in Wilde, is the product of style: "If only she knew as much about life as he did she would know that it is not the temptations you have succumbed to that you regret, but those you resisted." But even this kind of thing would not be beyond the competence of a schoolboy.

About halfway through the book, however, we find that what the author has been doing, in his tiresome piling up of dead incident, is introducing the elements of a plot. This plot is pretty well contrived; it could hardly have been worked out by a schoolboy, for it shows a practiced hand, and it carries us through the rest of the book. We find here, furthermore, that the scheming of Caesar to accomplish his political ends is connected, not merely through ingenuities of plot but also by moral implication, with Machiavelli's scheming to make a conquest of the wife of a friend. Machiavelli as well as Borgia is cynical about human motives; Machiavelli (though politically a patriot working for republican Florence) is aiming in his personal relations at power for the sake of power, just as Borgia is. And the victims of both are equally cynics, equally double-dealers. The upshot of the whole affair is that Machiavelli, returning home with a certain admiration for Borgia but in a rage over the duplicity practiced on him by the young wife and her allies, meditates upon his experience and finds in it the material for *Il Principe*, his treatise on Realpolitik, and for his comedy, *La Mandragola*. This, too, shows more knowledge of the world than a schoolboy would have been likely to acquire, but that schoolboy, grown-up and much travelled, having somehow been diverted from his normal career of law, medicine, diplomacy or parliament, might have produced such a novel as *Then and Now*; did, in fact, produce it.

The defenders of Somerset Maugham will tell me that he is "old and tired" now, and that historical novels are not his forte —that it is quite unfair to judge him by *Then and Now*, which is one of the least of his books. I know that he has done better stories, but I am not sure that it *is* quite unfair to judge his quality by *Then and Now*. This quality is never, it seems to me, that either of a literary artist or of a first-rate critic of morals; and it may be worth while to say this at a moment when there seems to be a tendency to step up Mr. Maugham's standing to the higher ranks of English fiction, and when Mr. Maugham himself has been using his position of prestige for a nagging disparagement of his betters. Though Mr. Maugham's claims for himself are always carefully and correctly modest, he usually manages to sound invidious when he is speaking of his top-drawer contemporaries. In an anthology which he edited a few years ago, *Introduction to Modern English and American Literature*—a mixture of good writing and tripe that sets the teeth on edge—we find him patronizing, in what seems to me an insufferable way (and with his customary buzz of clichés), such writers as Henry James, James Joyce and W. B. Yeats. "His influence on fiction," he writes of James, "especially in England, has been great, and though I happen to think it has been a bad influence, its enduring power makes him an important figure. . . . He never succeeded in coming to grips with life. . . . This story (*The Beast in the Jungle*) reads to me like a lamentable admission of his own failure." Of *Ulysses*: "I have read it twice, so I cannot say that I find it unreadable, but . . . like many of his countrymen, Joyce never discovered that enough is as good as a feast, and his prolixity is exhausting." Of Yeats: "Though he could at times be very good company, he was a pompous vain man; to hear him read his own verses was as excruciating a torture as anyone could be exposed to." Well, it is quite true of Henry James that his experience was incomplete and that he wrote about his own deficiencies, and that Joyce is sometimes too prolix, and it may be true that Yeats was sometimes pompous. It is also true that Mr. Maugham partly sweetens his detraction with praise. Yet, from reading this *Introduction*, you would never be able to discover that all these writers belong to a different plane from that of Michael Arlen and Katharine Brush, whose work is also included—to a plane on which Somerset Maugham does not exist at all. Mr. Maugham would apparently suggest to us that all novelists are entertainers who differ only in being more or less boring (though he grants, with a marked lack of enthusiasm, that Henry James supplied, "if not an incentive, at least an encouragement to those who came after him . . . to aim consciously at giving fiction the form and significance that may sometimes make it more than the pastime of an idle hour"). We get the impression of a malcontent eye cocked up from the brackish waters of the *Cosmopolitan* magazine, and a peevish and insistent grumbling. There is something going on, on the higher ground, that halfway compels his respect, but he does not quite understand what it is, and in any case he can never get up there.

There are cases in which Mr. Maugham is able to admire more cordially the work that is done on this higher plane, but even here his way of praising betrays his lack of real appreciation and almost always has a sound of impertinence. So, in his speech at the Library of Congress, we find the following remarks about Proust: "Proust, as we know, was enormously influenced by the now largely discredited philosophy of Henri Bergson and great stretches of his work turn upon it. I suppose we all read with a thrill of excitement Proust's volumes as they came out, but now when we reread them in a calmer mood I think what we find to admire in them is his wonderful humor and extraordinarily vivid and interesting characters that he created in profusion. We skip his philosophical disquisitions and we skip them without loss." Now, it is perfectly obvious here that Mr. Maugham does not know what he is talking about. Some aspects of Bergson's philosophy are still taken very seriously by first-rate philosophers of certain schools; and even if Bergson's whole system were regarded with universal disapproval, that might not affect the validity of the artistic use that Proust has made of one of its features. This feature—the

difference between "time" and "duration": how long something takes by the clock and how long it seems while it is going
on—is itself only one of the features of Proust's metaphysical
picture, which in general has more in common with the implications of relativistic physics than with the Creative Evolution
of Bergson. It is this play on the relativistic principle in the
social and personal fields that gives Proust his philosophical interest and that makes his book, I suppose, the greatest philosophical novel ever written. In *A la Recherche du Temps Perdu*,
the philosophy so pervades the narrative that it is difficult to
see how you could skip it: if you jumped over the "disquisitions," you could still not escape from Proust, in a thousand
intimations and asides, expounding his relativistic theory; and
since the unexpected development of the characters, the astonishing reversals of relationships, all the contrasts and paradoxes
that provide the main interest of the story, are dramatizations
of this theory, it is difficult to understand how a reader can
"admire" the former and yet disregard the latter. The inability
of Mr. Maugham to grasp what there is in Proust helps to explain why he has not been able to make his own work more
interesting.

June 8, 1946

Admirers of Somerset Maugham have protested that this article was unfair to him and have begged me to read his short
stories. I have therefore procured *East Is West*, the collected
volume of these, and made shift to dine on a dozen. They *are*
readable—quite entertaining. The style is much tighter and
neater than it is in *Then and Now*—Mr. Maugham writes best
when his language is plainest. But when he wants to use a
richer idiom, this is the kind of thing you get: "Be this as it
may, Ashenden in the last twenty years had felt his heart go
pit-a-pat because of one charming person after another. He
had had a good deal of fun and had paid for it with a great deal
of misery, but even when suffering most acutely from the
pangs of unrequited love he had been able to say to himself,
albeit with a wry face, after all, it's grist to the mill." These
stories are magazine commodities—all but two of them came
out in the *Cosmopolitan*—on about the same level as Sherlock
Holmes; but Sherlock Holmes has more literary dignity pre-

cisely because it is less pretentious. Mr. Maugham makes play with more serious themes, but his work is full of bogus motivations that are needed to turn the monthly trick. He is for our day, I suppose, what Bulwer-Lytton was for Dickens's: a half-trashy novelist, who writes badly, but is patronized by half-serious readers, who do not care much about writing.

William Saroyan and
His Darling Old Providence

WILLIAM SAROYAN has written a novel evidently based on his experience in the Army. *The Adventures of Wesley Jackson* seems to be flavored with *Huckleberry Finn*, but, as a story of picaresque adventure, it has the novelty of exploiting the idea that Army life may be picaresque. The best things in it are such episodes as that in which the Colonel brings a newspaperman to interview "the ordinary soldier" on how he likes being in the Army, and the picture of the Hollywood directors and writers mobilized to do training documentaries. Mr. Saroyan is here at his strongest in showing the bewildered civilian inducted into his military role and drawing blank after blank as he submits to pointless indignities and finds himself shunted about from one post to another, at first disgruntled, then apathetic, learning how to play tricks on the system and only at moments prodded into spasms of mild rebellion, but uncontrollably shrinking and skulking whenever the realization is thrust on him that he is caught in a giant enterprise for the slaughter of other human beings.

It is a relief, after *The Human Comedy*, Saroyan's previous novel, to read the first part of *Wesley Jackson*. In that earlier book (and film), which was written at a time when the author had no first-hand knowledge of the Army, nobody was ever cross or mean even when you might for a second have thought they were going to be; everybody was perfectly lovely; the whole thing was just a big chummy junket, and even when a good fellow got killed, he wasn't really and truly dead, because his spirit was still able to return (in the movie you could see him right there) and stay on with the people he loved. But there are spots in *Wesley Jackson* where a sharpness of tone and a satirical treatment indicate that Mr. Saroyan has run at last into a few human beings who have rubbed him the wrong way, and he is forced at least to admit that the destiny of man on this earth involves, among other things, deprivation, oppression and death. This new element of relative realism will help you through the sentimentality of the lovable old drunken father (so different from Huckleberry Finn's disreputable drunken father) who for a time follows his boy from post to post but finally goes home, like a dear old chap, to the family he has abandoned, and the erotic insipidity of the women who —ugly and awkward though Wesley is represented as being— are so wonderfully kind to the hero. But when you get to the part where the madam of a just-raided Ohio brothel fixes him up with a girl for nothing and is able, through pull, with no trouble at all, to have him and his friends sent back to New York, which, as a billet, they prefer to Ohio, your confidence begins to be shaken and your stomach gives an ominous quake. And the last part of *Wesley Jackson*, in which the hero finally gets to England and eventually takes part in the invasion of France, is the record of an appalling victory over Saroyan's realistic instincts of the impulse toward self-befuddling and self-protective fantasy. Wesley Jackson, who talks constantly of his trust in God, is specially exempted from misfortune by a darling old Providence who adores him. When he picks up what appears to be a tart in Piccadilly Circus, she turns out to be a sweet little golden-haired seventeen-year-old girl who has run away from home and who, never having slept with a man, is trying pathetically to qualify as a prostitute. Wesley takes her home to his rooms (God quickly got him out of barracks), gives her a bath and makes her his wife, and they are soon going to have a baby, to which Wesley looks forward with tears in his eyes. At last he is sent to France. But don't be alarmed for a minute. Two of his best friends are killed, to be sure, but this becomes a very beautiful thing; and when he is captured by the Germans, they prove charming and presently run away, leaving their prisoners in the camp, from which Wesley escapes back to England. He is pretty well scared for a moment when he discovers that his house has been bombed, but of course his little blue-eyed bride had luckily gone away to the country the night just before this happened, and he finds her safe and sound with her people. Even when Wesley buys tips on the races, both the horses he bets on wins, and the good old tipster is *so* delighted!

It is curious that this part of the novel should sound like an anachronistic regression to the literature of sensibility of the late eighteenth and early nineteenth centuries. There are some passages which seem to indicate that Saroyan has just been reading Dickens—and make us long for one of Dickens' hooting hobgoblins to offset such stuff as this: "I winked back at the flowers and thanked them as if they were God for having me around that way—out in England, out where the Kings and Queens had strolled, out by the lazy old Thames, out with my lovely English girl. After we had slept in the green of Windsor and wakened and kissed and played games involving clouds and their shapes and what they'd changed to, we ate our lunch. Then Jill took off her shoes and stockings to run bare-footed in the grass and dance for me, and oh Jill, I love thy blessed little feet. I chased her and caught her and lifted her off her feet and set her down in the green grass of England and kissed her feet because they were so twinkling and funny and serious. I kissed every toe of each foot, each sole, each arch and each ankle, so Jill kissed my Army shoes to make me laugh, and I laughed, and the flowers winked and laughed and didn't care about the lousy War." But the ready and fluent weeping that Wesley Jackson turns on whenever his finer feelings are touched, as they more and more often are, suggests, though it would probably embarrass, Henry Mackenzie's Man of Feeling or the Sterne of the *Sentimental Journey*. I forbear to quote further. There is a chapter in which Wesley recapitulates practically every thing that has happened in the book and cries over every item, including every individual who has at any time affected him unpleasantly. This is surely some of the silliest nonsense ever published by a talented writer.

June 15, 1946

Oscar Wilde: "One Must Always
Seek What Is Most Tragic"

THE VIKING PRESS has brought out in its Portable Library series a selection from the writings of Oscar Wilde, with a dozen unpublished letters and an introduction by Richard Aldington, and Harper is about to publish a new biography of Wilde by Hesketh Pearson: *Oscar Wilde: His Life and Wit*. This last book is a journalistic job. Mr. Pearson is an actor turned writer, who has also done biographies of Erasmus Darwin, Sydney Smith, Hazlitt, Gilbert and Sullivan, Labouchère, Anna Seward, Tom Paine, Shakespeare, Bernard Shaw and Conan Doyle. His book makes interesting reading, for he has assembled from various sources an immense number of anecdotes and sayings, and he has managed to tell a straighter story than we usually get where Wilde is concerned. Oscar Wilde has hitherto been written about mostly by his personal friends, among whom the vituperative controversies seem with time to become more embittered. Mr. Pearson stands quite clear of all these disputes, and he writes with good sense and good temper. But his book is only another example of the current kind of popular biography that adds little to our knowledge of its subject: non-critical, non-analytic and, though dealing with literary matters, essentially non-literary.

Mr. Pearson does, however, tell Wilde's story with a new emphasis which is all to the good. The public disgrace of Wilde's trial has been allowed so much to blur the outline of the whole of his preceding career and to tarnish the brilliance of his abilities that it is a good thing to have him presented by someone, not afraid to admire him, who restores to him the pride and prestige of the days before his disaster. From Frank Harris's biography, for example, you get an almost completely grotesque picture of Oscar's parents, Sir William and Lady Wilde. Frank Harris, with gusto, makes the most of Sir William's bad reputation as an insatiable seducer of women, and there is little in his chapter on the Wilde family save an account of the scandalous lawsuit in which the elder Wilde became involved, when a more or less deranged young lady, who had come to him as a patient, accused him of having raped her while she was under an anesthetic. Nor does he tell us much more about Lady Wilde than that R. Y. Tyrrell considers her "a hifalutin, pretentious creature" with a "reputation founded on second-rate verse-making." Lord Alfred Douglas, in his ghost-written book *Oscar Wilde and Myself*, permitted his name to be signed to sneers that were quite unwarranted about the origins and standing of the Wildes. Mr. Pearson is, so far as I know, the first of Oscar Wilde's biographers to do his remarkable parents justice, and a new biography of the elder Wilde—*Victorian Doctor*, by T. G. Wilson—gives an even more complete account of the family background of Oscar. This latter book, the work of a Dublin doctor, is a variedly interesting chronicle of political and medical events and of antiquarian research in Ireland, and it confirms Mr. Pearson in establishing the importance of Lady Wilde in the first of these fields and the distinction of her husband in the others. William Wilde, who was knighted for his achievements, was, it seems, one of the greatest aurists and oculists of the English-speaking world of his time; Jane Francesca Elgee (the Elgees were Algiati of Florence, and Oscar's Italian blood should be taken into account in considering his theatrical instincts and his appetite for the ornate), though a somewhat worse than mediocre poet, had played in youth a conspicuous role as a champion of Irish nationalism and later translated from German and French and wrote books on social problems. Both were persons of wide cultivation and remarkable intellectual ability, and they shared also an independence of character and a personal eccentricity that sometimes got them disliked in Dublin.

Oscar was brought up in this tradition, and he followed it from his earliest years. Though he liked to appear offhand and lazy, his assimilative powers were prodigious, and he seems to have been at Oxford the best Greek scholar of his day. Nor was he lacking in strength or courage. The notion of him as soft and wilting has been partly the result of his "aesthetic pose," parodied by Gilbert in *Patience*, partly an unjustified inference from his homosexual habits. On a trip through one of the wilder parts of Greece in his undergraduate days, he carried a gun, Mr. Pearson tells us, and seems to have stood up to the natives as boldly as Byron did, just as later, on his visit to the United States, he won the respect of the cowboys, the Colorado miners and the San Francisco Bohemian Club by the intrepid good humor with which he accepted the crudeness and the outlandishness of pioneer life and by his indomitable head for liquor (a virtue which Lord Alfred Douglas, even at his most vindictive, admits that Wilde retained till a short time before his death). Mr. Pearson, on the testimony of an Oxford Blue of Oscar Wilde's time at Magdalen, is able to explode the story of his having been held under the pump by a group of jeering students, who had also smashed his china. "So far from being a flabby aesthete," says this contemporary, Sir Frank Benson, "there was only one man in the college, and he rowed seven in the Varsity Eight, who had the ghost of a chance in a tussle with Wilde." When a mob that had set out to maul him sent four boys in their cups to his rooms, Wilde succeeded in throwing them out and, picking the last of them up like a baby, "carried him to his rooms, and, having ceremoniously buried him beneath a pile of his own luxurious furniture, invited the spectators, now pro-Oscar to a man, to sample the fellow's wines and spirits, an invitation that was accepted with peculiar pleasure on account of the owner's present plight and past stinginess." It was precisely this self-confidence and audacity that misled him into bringing his libel suit against the Marquess of Queensberry and that sustained him to face trial when the Crown brought its action against him. Mr. Pearson gives an exhilarating version—for which, of course, we can have only Wilde's word—of his reception of the Marquess and a pugilist bodyguard when Queensberry came to his house to insult him: "This is the Marquess of Queensberry," he told his seventeen-year-old footman, "the most infamous brute in London. You are never to allow him to enter my house again." There is thus much in Mr. Pearson's book to confirm W. B. Yeats's view, expressed in his autobiography, that Wilde was "essentially a man of action, that he was a writer by perversity and accident, and would have been more important as soldier or politician."

After the decades of bickering among Wilde's friends as to

who was the cause of his downfall and as to who, in his years of
exile, did or did not give him money, it is a relief to read an account that brings out the stronger side of Wilde's personality,
as well as his natural generosity and kindness, of which Mr.
Pearson gives many instances. But it is a weakness of Mr. Pearson as a biographer of Wilde that he tends to ignore, though
he cannot exclude, his subject's fundamental perversity. Mr.
Pearson's sole attempt to throw light on the complexities and
conflicts of Wilde's nature is a theory that his intellect had developed while his emotions remained immature. But the perversity of Oscar Wilde—by which I do not mean merely his
sexual inversion—was as much a part of his thought as it was
of his emotional life. The whole force of his wit is derived from
it. He regarded himself, as he wrote in *De Profundis*, as "one
of those who are made for exceptions, not for laws." It was
Wilde's special gift, in his writings, to find expression for this
impulse in a form that charms at the same time that it startles,
but this perversity was also the mainspring of the tragedy of
Wilde's career which is somehow so much more impressive
than anything he ever wrote, or, rather, which gives to his
writings an impressiveness they might not otherwise have.

This drama has never as yet really been dealt with by any of
his biographers. The homosexuality that grew on Wilde was
merely among its elements. There was nothing inevitable,
from the moral point of view, in his having been punished for
this. It is absurd for Bernard Shaw to say, as he does in his preface to the new edition of Frank Harris's book on Wilde, that
"Oscar's ruin was caused by his breach of the Criminal Law
Amendment Act and by nothing else." His suit against the
Marquess of Queensberry was a disinterested though an ill-
advised action, prompted by his infatuation with Lord Alfred
Douglas, who, childish and hysterical himself, wanted revenge
against his rabid father, and who never for a second hesitated,
in gratifying his selfish spite, to let Oscar run terrible risks.
Lord Alfred, as he appears in the descriptions of him written
by other people and in his own self-justificatory polemics,
makes such an unpleasant impression that it is only by reading
Dorian Gray and *The Portrait of Mr. W. H.*, in which Wilde,
writing before he met Douglas, describes his romantic ideal,
that we can see how Lord Alfred represented it, and it is only

by reading Douglas' sonnet on Wilde, written after the latter's death, that we can see that Wilde's admiration was not entirely misplaced. But it was certainly, on Wilde's side, this idealization of Douglas, and, on Douglas' side, his adoption of Wilde as a kind of substitute father, who, as he thought, could stand up to his real father, that set the machinery of disaster in motion.

The next question, however, is why Oscar, after losing his suit against Queensberry, insisted on remaining in England to face the second of the criminal trials—the jury having disagreed in the first—in which he was prosecuted by the public authorities on charges arising from the evidence presented by Queensberry in the original suit, when he could perfectly well have escaped to the Continent. The explanations usually given are Wilde's pugnacious Irish pride, stimulated by that of his mother, who had told him that if he ran away she would never speak to him again, and his desire to vindicate his character in the interests of his wife and children. But by that time he already knew what the evidence against him was and he should have foreseen his defeat, as, in fact, he should have had the foresight not to take the legal offensive against Queensberry (Bernard Shaw says he was drunk when he did this). I want to point out that a sense of damnation, a foreboding of tragic failure, is to be found in the writing of Wilde from a time long before he was caught in the particular noose that landed him in Reading Jail. It is the theme of the sonnet *Hélas!* as it is of *Dorian Gray*: it is sounded, as Mr. Pearson notes, even in *An Ideal Husband*. And the conflict that is to end in collapse is reflected by his continual antithesis of what he regarded as his "pagan" side to what he regarded as his "Christian" instincts, by which literary phrases he really referred to his appetites and his moral sense. For an "aesthete" like Wilde's master, Pater, it was possible to savor both points of view in a state of serene contemplation; but, though Wilde could see "beauty" alike in the sensuous pleasures of the one and in the suffering implied by the other, he could not help, behind his smiling boldness, being troubled and torn between them. The impulse of perversity in him was constantly working both ways: it impelled him not only to disconcert the expectations of the conventional world by shocking paradoxes and scandalous behavior, it

caused him also to betray his pagan creed by indulgence in
Christian compunction. There are moments when we get the
impression not merely that he apprehended catastrophe but
that he even in some sense invited it; when we feel that, having
flouted the respectable world by making an immense amount
of money and a conspicuous social success through mockery of
its codes and standards, he turned against his own arrogance
and kicked wealth and success downstairs.

It throws some light on this psychological procedure of
Wilde's to refer to Yeats's portrait of him in *The Trembling of
the Veil*. Yeats describes the Wilde family in Ireland as "very
imaginative and learned," "dirty, untidy" and "daring," and
speaks of Wilde's "half-civilized blood," which did not allow
him to "endure the sedentary toil of creative art." It is certainly true of Wilde that, with much sensitivity and nobility, he
had also a certain coarseness, and his pursuit of the "pagan"
ideal always had a tendency to lead him into vulgar ostentation
and self-indulgence. The trouble is that, when, fed up with
luxury, he turns away in disgust, it is usually not in the direction of the "sedentary toil of creative art" but in the direction
of a version of the Christian ideal of humility and abnegation
—some of his fairy-stories illustrate this appallingly—that is itself ostentatious and vulgar. Yet one finds in him, also, at moments, a sense of guilt and a bitter chagrin at having fallen very
far short of the best that he could imagine. There is, of course,
in *De Profundis*, a certain amount of maudlin Christian emotion, but there is also the other thing. "While I see," he says
soberly enough, "that there is nothing wrong in what one does,
I see that there is something wrong in what one becomes."
One of his principal reproaches against Lord Alfred Douglas,
whether the latter deserved it or not, is that Douglas interfered
with his work, and it is his consciousness of sin for the neglect
of this work rather than grief at having injured his family which
seems to make him feel, in prison, that it is just for him to expiate his debaucheries. Even here, to be sure, he is acting, and
there is testimony, as Mr. Pearson indicates (he might have
added that of Ford Madox Ford), that Oscar sometimes over-
acted the poverty and misery of his final years. But the fact that
he is always acting does not deprive his performance of value.
This performance is not merely literary. In his writing, his

imagination often dresses itself floridly and trashily; it is only at his most intellectual—that is, when we get his wit at its purest and its least arty—that he arrives at an excellent style. One has to combine his writing, the records of his conversation and the sequence of events in his life in order to appreciate Wilde and to see that, though one cannot describe him as precisely a first-rate writer, he did somehow put on a first-rate show.

There is as yet no biography of Wilde which goes at all behind the scenes of this drama, and the only descriptions of him which show any real psychological insight are those of Yeats and Gide. It seems to have been to Gide, always conscious of moral problems, that Wilde, always sensitive to his audience, made the most vivid revelation of his own conception of his role in the successive scenes of the play. "My duty to myself," he told Gide when he saw him in Algeria in January, 1895, at the time when the Marquess of Queensberry had already begun to bait him, "is to amuse myself terrifically . . . no happiness—only pleasure. One must always seek what is most tragic.* . . . My friends are extraordinary; they advise me to be prudent. But prudence!—is that possible for me? It would be to return on my tracks. I must push things as far as possible. I cannot go any further, and something will have to happen—something different." And later, when he had come out of prison and Gide had gone to see him in France: "One must never take up again the same existence one has had before. My life is like a work of art: an artist never repeats the same work—or if he does, it is only for the reason that he did not succeed the first time. My life before I went to prison was the greatest success possible. Now it is a completed thing."

As for the clinical aspect of Oscar Wilde's case, there has been no careful study of it—though he deserves the same kind of attention that has been given to Maupassant and Swift. Mr. Pearson, Dr. Wilson and Frank Harris have pointed out the striking parallel between the last years of Oscar's life and the last years of Sir William Wilde's. Both were dragged down, at the

---

*"*Pas le bonheur! Surtout pas le bonheur. Le plaisir! Il faut vouloir toujours le plus tragique.*" These quotations are from Gide's little book on Wilde. He adds: "*Je n'ai rien inventé, rien arrangé, dans les derniers propos que je cite. Les paroles de Wilde sont présentes à mon esprit, et j'allais dire à mon oreille.*"

height of their fame, by sexual scandals that brought them into court, and the father withdrew afterward from Dublin and almost completely abandoned his profession, just as the son fled to France and ceased to write. Did the father's example here exert a compulsive influence or was some pathological principle operating in both cases? Bernard Shaw suggested, in his memoir in the first edition of Harris's life, that both Oscar and his mother had the physical signs of a derangement of the pituitary gland, and Dr. Wilson has discussed this idea on the basis of more recent researches into the various glandular types. But there is apparently another factor in the pathology of Oscar Wilde—a factor which, so far as I know, has never been emphasized save in the writings of Wilde's quixotic and non-homosexual friend, Robert Harborough Sherard. We are usually told in the books about Wilde, as if it were something of merely casual interest, that he probably died of syphilis. But if he was really a victim of syphilis, it is surely important to know how this malady had been acquired and how long and how severely he had been suffering from it. We learn now from Dr. Wilson's book that he is supposed to have contracted it at Oxford, but he does not pursue the subject. It would help to explain Wilde if it were proved that he was haunted through his adult life by an uncured syphilitic infection, and his illness —made rapidly worse, it is said, by the drinking of his last years—should certainly be taken into account in considering the demoralization into which he finally sank. In the cases of Baudelaire and Maupassant, it seems obvious that the morose disaffection of the one and the desperate pessimism of the other were the shadows of the syphilitic's doom in the days when the disease was incurable. In Wilde's case, the man is so bland, the work so bright-hued and amusing, that his biographers—having already to deal with the problem of his homosexuality—seem reluctant to come to grips with another distasteful factor; but, in shirking it, I believe, they slight also both the interest of Oscar Wilde's work and the tragedy of his life. Read *The Picture of Dorian Gray*, or even the best of his fairy tales, *The Birthday of the Infanta*, with the *Spirochaeta pallida* in mind. In such stories, the tragic heroes are shown in the peculiar position of suffering from organic maladies—in the one case, a moral corruption which grows; in the other, a

permanent repulsiveness—without, up to a point, being forced
to experience the evils entailed by them. Dorian Gray conceals
his vices and is able to evade their consequences; the Dwarf in
The Birthday of the Infanta is not saddened or embittered by
his ugliness because he does not know how he looks. But in the
end, in both cases, the horror breaks out: the afflicted one
must recognize himself and be recognized by other people as
the odious creature he is, and his disease or disability will kill
him. This theme of impending collapse is a recurrent one with
Oscar Wilde, and it must have some very close connection
with his conception of his own nature and its destiny. One can
account for it purely in terms of Wilde's sexual and moral life,
without supposing him to have been doomed by syphilis; yet it
is hard to believe that a nature so elastic and so insouciant
could have been broken so completely and so quickly without
some shattering physical cause.

June 29, 1946

Since the above was written, a volume called *The Trials of
Oscar Wilde* in the *Notable British Trials* series has supplied the
clinical facts that the biographies of Wilde lack. I quote from
Appendix E by the editor, H. Montgomery Hyde: "Certain it
is that Wilde betrayed no signs of abnormality in adolescence
and early manhood. On the contrary, his inclinations seem to
have been decidedly heterosexual. While an undergraduate at
Oxford, he contracted syphilis as the result of a casual connex-
ion, probably with a prostitute. In those days the recognized
treatment for this disease was with mercury. In Wilde's case
this treatment undoubtedly produced the discolouration and
decay of his teeth, which remained a permanent feature of his
appearance for the remainder of his life and added to the general impression of physical overgrowth and ugliness which his
person presented on acquaintance. Nor, it may be added, was
there the slightest suggestion of effeminacy about him, either
at Oxford or at any subsequent period. . . . We know, too,
that he was deeply in love with his wife at the time of their
marriage, and that they experienced normal sexual intercourse.
Indeed, two sons were born of the union before the rift
between them took place. . . . Before proposing to his wife,
Wilde had been to consult a doctor in London, who had

assured him that he was completely cured of his youthful malady. On the strength of his assurance he got married. About two years later he discovered to his dismay that all traces of syphilis had not been eradicated from his system, and it was this unpleasant discovery which obliged him to discontinue physical relations with his wife. In the result, *inter alia*, he turned toward homosexuality." The doctor who attended him in prison reported that Wilde's disease was then in an advanced stage. No wonder he soon ceased to function when he finally got away to the Continent.

George Grosz in the United States

THE AUTOBIOGRAPHY OF GEORGE GROSZ—*A Little Yes and a Big No*—is a most entertaining book and an important document on Germany. Here is the record of a German artist who was disgusted by German war-making and who attacked the makers of war; who spent his youth as a Dadaist rebel in the years of bad food and inflation between the two wars in Germany; who felt the pressure of impending tyranny and, warned, he says, by a Kafka-esque nightmare of blind alleys, covert persecution and a plague of stinking fish, decided to decamp to America at the beginning of 1933. "Yes, it was indeed strange," he writes, "that the deeper significance of my dream remained hidden from me at that time. I know today that a definite Power wanted to save me from annihilation. Why I was to be spared, I do not know. Perhaps it was to serve as a witness." I have not read anything else which has made me feel to what degree life in Germany became intolerable during the years after the Treaty of Versailles. From George Grosz you get the impression that there were only two real courses possible: Hitlerism or flight. Though for a time, after the first of the wars, he allied himself with the political Left, he has a Nietzschean scorn of the masses, and seems never to have believed very strongly in the ability of the working class to recreate contemporary society. He says that he shocked Thomas Mann, when he met him in America in 1933, by predicting that Hitler would last.

Mr. Grosz is also a valuable witness, in his account of his experience in this country, on the subject of the foreign artist who comes to live in the United States. It more or less happened in Grosz's case, as it did with Stravinsky and Auden, that, in obedience to some curious law, his prestige for Americans dwindled from the moment that we had him among us. George Grosz, unlike these other two artists, wanted very much at first to make money in the American way; he admired the American illustrators who drew for our magazines and thought, apparently, that he would like nothing better than to do this sort of work himself, but somehow he was not acceptable. He had hoped to drop the vein of satire which had made him so famous abroad, along with the society it caricatured; but, in spite of his determined efforts to deal with American life in a forward-looking and clean-cut way, the colors that he applied to his street scenes were always overflowing their outlines and the Americans he would have liked to idealize turned out to be "mostly middle-aged and uglier than I had intended." He could only remain himself: an artist with a vision of the world which he could no more prevent his faculties from concentrating their forces to realize than a wild pig in labor with a litter of boars can give birth to china-pig savings-banks.

Eventually, left free in America by the lapse of his reputation and obliged to dig himself in, as is necessary for artistic survival in a country that has no artists' cafés, he worked on into a new phase of development which was for a long time completely "straight"—doing landscapes, lay figures, portraits and nudes that sometimes seemed strangely inexpressive after the extraordinary variety and humanity of his earlier satirical period. (The satirical side of his art is admirably represented by the dozens of drawings included in *A Little Yes and a Big No.*) And at last we found him turning out studies of the grass-fringed contours of sand-dunes, the broken stumps of Adirondack lakes and the filigree of Cape Cod scrub-pine that—quite different in everything save mastery of line from the deliberately ragged caricatures of the pre-Hitler bourgeoisie—had a firmness, a steel-shaving delicacy, only a little softened in its descent from the leaf-drawings of Dürer. The album of George Grosz's work published by Bittner in 1944 gave a retrospective view of this work; and the exhibition of last autumn, at the Associated American Artists, added to it the remarkable water colors of the atrocities of the Nazi movement which represent a further development, more bitter and more brilliant, of his original satirical vein, and a series of apocalyptic paintings, not always perhaps successful but at their best of a frightening tragic force, in which the remnants of a decrepit civilization are seen wallowing on their bellies or frying in an inferno of fire and mud. In the field of the arts, it seems to me that these pictures, with André Malraux's last novel, *La Lutte avec l'Ange*, and Benjamin Britten's opera *Peter Grimes*, are the only productions I know that have expressed the despair and anguish of the years we have been living through and that yet do not discourage but fortify, since they make us feel the vigor of the craftsman who, in grappling with a terrible subject, scores a victory over its terrors. And just as Stravinsky has emerged as a popular national figure whose new music, that was at first ignored, is now played to crowded houses and whose albums of phonograph records are sold out as soon as issued; as the collected poems of Auden have recently caused him to shine far beyond the academic penumbra of the colleges in which he has been teaching, and won him almost the circulation of an American family poet—so the reception of this recent exhibition seemed to indicate that at last George Grosz was coming to play a role in America which, if not quite the one he imagined—since it does not bring him the biggest income—does confer upon him the highest rank.

This exceptionally honest and amusing and revelatory autobiography should effect his complete emergence. What is most striking, as in the artist's pictures, is his freedom from the inveterate myth-mindedness which leads the Germans, so often disastrously, to substitute heroic abstractions for realistic observation and ordinary common sense. There are striking examples of this habit of mind in Stephen Spender's recent book, *European Witness*—not only the excerpts he gives us from a youthful novel of Goebbels', but the blood-chilling battle scene that he translates from a novel by Ernest Jünger, in which the excitement of war is raised to a pitch of barbaric ecstasy that disconcertingly recalls the old sagas. It can be seen also in a most curious form, in the last issue of *Partisan Review*, in the memoirs of a German soldier who was assigned to guard a prison-camp in Poland. This man, whose duty it was to beat, torture and kill other men, writes of the happenings of the life of this prison-camp in terms of a mythology of stalking Deaths, white watching Ghosts, Hills of Calvary and Angels of Vengeance. But this element of grandiose allegory is quite absent from George Grosz's story: he is homely, concrete and human. There is no touch of the mystical imagination, unless his prophetic dream be one—but that is concrete and homely, too. One remembers that the German tradition is not necessarily Hegelian, not necessarily Wagnerian: there are Dürer, Beethoven and Hauptmann. And one realizes today that

George Grosz, in these dark days for the German intellect, has represented what is stoutest and noblest in this other German tradition. The hand that sketched the moral tatters, the deliquescence, of the bourgeoisie could trace the distinct stems and twigs, and fill in the big sweep, of the dunes; and the man who directed the hand may be met in this autobiography: a great German artist, we recognize, who, in becoming an American citizen, has acquired an international passport.

January 4, 1947

An Old Friend of the Family: Thackeray

THE two new volumes of the Thackeray papers edited by Gordon N. Ray—*The Letters and Private Papers of William Makepeace Thackeray*—cover the years from the beginning of 1852 to Thackeray's death at the end of 1863, and they include his two trips to America, where he lectured and made a great deal of money; his row with Dickens and Edmund Yates over the publication of the latter's description of him and the expulsion of Yates from the Garrick Club; Thackeray's campaign and defeat as a parliamentary candidate for Oxford; his editorship of the *Cornhill Magazine*, which gave rise to some curious correspondence between him and his fellow-writers; and his attempts to bring up his two daughters, who had been motherless since his wife went insane and whom he had sometimes, when away on tours, to leave with his own mother—thus precipitating long arguments by letter about the little girls' religious education, in which the strongly anti-fundamentalist Thackeray had to stand up to the formidably pious lady who had sat for Helen Pendennis. There are also some hitherto unpublished comments on the personality and work of Charlotte Brontë, whom Thackeray publicly praised but who seems rather to have nagged him and got under his skin by the challenging and birdlike attacks which she made on him whenever they met; and a long letter to George Henry Lewes, giving an account, at the latter's request, of Thackeray's visit to Weimar in his youth and a conversation he had with Goethe, incidents which he had then recorded in a casual and captious tone but now suffuses with a mellow light of memory. An appendix contains passages from the letters, written by Thackeray to Mrs. Brookfield or to common friends of theirs, which Mr. Ray has been unable to obtain and for which he has been obliged to rely on the fragmentary extracts in auction catalogues. These sometimes give more intimate glimpses into the passions and unpleasantness of the period when Thackeray was in love with Mrs. Brookfield than do the more complete texts in Volume II.

The Thackeray of this final decade makes, in general, a more amiable impression than the Thackeray of the first forty years. A Victorian paterfamilias tied to an insane wife, his flirtations are always painful, but his relations with Sally Baxter, the young American girl he met in New York, are very much lighter and straighter than the depressing affair of Mrs. Brookfield. And, though he seems to have been made rather intolerable by his first social success in London, he cools off later and becomes more civil. At the beginning of Volume III, we still find him boasting rather embarrassingly to a humble woman friend in the country who is coming to teach his daughters music: "Thursday will be the best day to come, that's the soonest. I dine out with the Dean of St. Paul's (you have heard of a large meeting house we have between Ludgate Hill & Cheapside with a round roof?) but by the time I come home, you will have made friends of Miss Trulock & Miss Anny & Miss Harriet." And he still likes to let people know it even when he has to decline an invitation: "Some of the immensest bigwigs have asked me to dinner: but I refuse all to go to the children. My dears. . . . I would rather sit in the brown house [of the American friends to whom he is writing] than at the bigwiggest table." He had evidently had a chip on his shoulder in regard to the aristocracy, for he now bubbles over to his mother: "How much kindness haven't I had from people eager to serve me? It's we who make the haughtiness of the grandees—not they. They're never thinking of it . . . and coming to know people whom I have thought insolent & airgiving, such as Lord & Lady John for instance, I find 2 as simple folks as you & G P—and no more *gêne* at their tea-table than yours"; and, "Did they [his daughters] write to you about Blanche Stanley, who is Lady Airlie now, asking me for a dinner, and walking away to the front drawing room from the other ladies, and only talking to the children till the gentlemen came in? I called her Lady Give-yourself Airlie and that's the only Air giving I've seen amongst the great ladies. The small ones are just as vulgar sometimes: and quite as overbearing."

But he got over this intoxication. His earnings made him independent; and his visit to the United States in 1852–53 gave him for the first time the vision of a completely non-feudal world where one's social position did not depend on the good nature and the good taste of the titled. "There's nothing to

sneer at," he writes friends in England, "—some usages different to ours, but a manliness and fairness that puts our society
to shame often. I like to see the equality, I wince a little at first
when a shopman doesn't say 'Sir' or a coachman says 'Help
that man with his luggage'—but y not? I'm sure that Society
sh^d be as it here is, that no harm should attach to a man for
any honest way of working for his bread, and that a man
should be allowed to be poor. We allow *certain* men to be
poor at home, but not every one." America even goes to his
head, as his first taste of the nobility had: "In travelling in Europe our confounded English pride only fortifies itself, and we
feel that we are better than 'those foreigners,' but it's worth
while coming here that we may think small beer of ourselves
afterwards. Greater nations than ours ever have been are born
in America and Australia—and Truth will be spoken and Freedom will be practiced, and God will be worshipped among
them, as they never have been with the antiquarian trammels
that bind us in the Old World. I look at this, and speculate
on this bright Future, as an Astronomer of a Star; and admire
and worship the beautiful goodness of God." In the South,
though he disapproved of slavery, he thought that the Negroes
were an inferior race and that they were very well off as they
were: "The negroes are happy whatever is said of them, at least
all we see, and the country Planters beg and implore any
Englishman to go to their estates and see for themselves."

But later, again, he somewhat cools off. Returning to Europe, he is disgusted, in Switzerland, to find Americans eating
with their knives and talking bad French or no French, and he
makes a point of writing repeatedly to his friends in the States
about it. And, visiting America a second time, in 1855–56, when
he is older and suffering from two complaints, malaria and
urethral stricture, he finds he does not like it so well. Sally
Baxter is getting married; an antagonism toward England is
mounting; and he sees more of barbarity and squalor when he
explores, with his new series of lectures, the Deep South and
the Mississippi—having, on one occasion, as competitors and
fellow-travellers, a freak show with Wild Men and a Giantess.
"It seems to me," he writes to his daughters, "I am not near so
much in love with the country this time as before—doesn't it
seem so to you?" He still finds "slavery nowhere repulsive—the

black faces invariably happy and plump, the white ones eager
and hard . . . but you read that the other day a woman killed
one child, and tried to kill another and herself rather than go
back to slavery—that a party of fugitives were discovered in a
leaky river boat rather than return."

Yet—his celibate life and his worsening ailments have evidently affected his views of the New and the Old World
both—he does not like England any the better. He becomes,
on the contrary, in his final years, even more bitter against the
life of society and more critical of the aristocracy. "B—— is
spoiled by the heartlessness of London," he had written
already in 1853, "which is awful to think of—the most godless
respectable thing—thing's not the word but I can't get it—I
mean that world is base and prosperous and content, not
unkind—very well bred—very unaffected in manner, not
dissolute—clean in person and raiment and going to church
every Sunday—but in the eyes of the Great Judge of right &
wrong what rank will those people have with all their fine characters and linen? They never feel love, but directly it's born,
they throttle it and fling it under the sewer as poor girls do
their unlawful children—they make up money-marriages and
are content—then the father goes to the House of Commons
or the Counting House, the mother to her balls and visits—
the children lurk upstairs with their governess, and when their
turn comes are bought and sold, and respectable and heartless
as their parents before them." And when, in 1857, he ran for
Parliament as an independent candidate, he declared that he
had incurred "a good deal of ill-will in certain very genteel
quarters in London" for having said "that those gentlemen
with handles to their names, that the members of great aristocratic families had a very great share of public patronage and
government, and that for my part I heartily desired that men
of the people—the working men and educated men of the
people—should have a share in the government." "We hope to
meet in April or May," he writes, in connection with Bayard
Taylor, to an American correspondent, "when I bragged about
taking him into the fashionable world. But I hear that I am in
disgrace with the fashionable world for speaking disrespect-
fully of the Georgy-porgies—and am not to be invited myself,
much more to be allowed to take others into polight Society. I

writhe at the exclusion. . . . I MUST come back & see you all. I praise Mr. Washington five times more here than I did in the States— Our people cheer—the fine folks look a little glum but the celebrated Thacker does not care for their natural ill-temper." And elsewhere, to his mother: "The bigwigs and great folks are furious. The halls of splendor are to be shut to me—and having had pretty nearly enough of the halls of splendor I shall be quite resigned to a quiet life outside them." That phrase "our people" above is significant of the later Thackeray. He had always been, even for an Englishman, excessively and uncomfortably class-conscious; but he had never identified himself so frankly, taking this tone of outspoken defiance, with an educated upper middle class which has interests in conflict with the nobility.

It is particularly, thus, in these later years that what Chesterton called somewhere, I think, Thackeray's "strong but sleepy virility" most resoundingly comes to life. And, as he grows older, the inextinguishable boyishness, which somehow continued to exist in the face of disillusion and illness, becomes more of a saving grace as his age throws it into relief. Thackeray, even for an Englishman, talks a great deal too much about money and, even for a respectable Victorian, too much about his duty to his family and the sacrifices and efforts he is making for them. But he did so love having the dollars and the pounds roll in that he communicates his exhilaration. He never seems to perform a benefaction without publishing it to some correspondent, and he was too eager on one occasion to make himself disagreeable at the expense of a member of his club who had failed to chip in for a fund to help a friend out of serious straits—passing around a malicious cartoon of the Pharisee and the Good Samaritan—till he discovered that the supposed Pharisee had already done his best for the man in a less conspicuous fashion. But he was spontaneously and lavishly generous, and such an incident is counterbalanced by the story told by Mr. Lionel Stevenson, in his recent biography of Thackeray, of his climbing to the garret of another old friend, scolding him for his evil courses, and hiding a hundred-pound note to be discovered after he left. His humor, which in earlier days he had often used to solace his envy or to revenge himself for slights, now becomes more like Edward Lear's, in Lear's familiar letters: an impulsive spilling-over of fun, that has the merit of making hay of formalities. And, though he ate and drank himself to death at the age of fifty-two, just at the moment when he was on the threshold of what he had planned as his most important work, a history of the reign of Queen Anne, he did love a party so, he enjoyed it so much more than research, that we can't be entirely sorry to miss seeing him bore himself. Yet the amiable qualities of Thackeray have at last been so liberally released in proportion as he has found himself freed from the anxieties and constraints of his earlier years that, fatigued with him though we may have come to be in going through these four long volumes, we regret it when we get to the letters in which his daughter writes to the Baxters to tell them about his death—from apoplexy, after dining out, just a day or two before Christmas.

One of the things that have made us impatient with Thackeray is his reluctance to take literature seriously and that carelessness about his novels of which Trollope and Henry James complained. These letters are full of the evidences of his boredom with his later books. On one occasion, when travelling on the Continent, he had to write back to England to find out the Christian names of some of the characters in *The Newcomes*, which he was then still engaged in writing. He *did* take a lot of trouble over *Henry Esmond*, but when it failed to have the success he had hoped for—the result, as he thought, of a bad review—he seems quite to have dropped any idea of classical form or artistic intensity. When Trollope told him that *Esmond* was "not only his best work, but so much the best that there was none second to it," Thackeray answered, "That was what I intended, but I have failed. Nobody reads it. After all, what does it matter?"

Nor, so negligent about literary form, was he remarkably courageous about subject. In spite of his prayers, after *Vanity Fair*, to be given the strength to tell "the Truth," he was easily discouraged by the conventions of the day. He violated the probabilities in *The Newcomes* by allowing Clive to marry Ethel, and, when James Russell Lowell remonstrated with him, begged, "What could a fellow do? So many people wanted 'em married. [The novel had been appearing in monthly parts.] To be sure, I had to kill off poor little Rosey rather suddenly, but shall not a man do what he will with his own?" There was a moment, after the Brookfield affair, when he wanted to write a novel about a man who fell in love with a married woman— she and her husband to be reunited by their affection for their children—but he seems to have been dissuaded by a horrified friend; at any rate, he gave up the idea. When *Madame Bovary* came out, he loathed it. "The book is bad," he declared. "It is a heartless cold-blooded study of the downfall and degradation of a woman." As editor of the *Cornhill Magazine*, he sent back a story of Trollope's on the ground, Trollope says, that it "alluded to a man with illegitimate children, and to the existence of a woman not as pure as she should be"; and a poem of Mrs. Browning's on the ground that it was "an account," as Thackeray wrote her, "of unlawful passion felt by a man for a woman." Trollope retorted: How about *Adam Bede*, *Jane Eyre* and *The Heart of Midlothian*, and, for that matter, how about *The Four Georges*? And Mrs. Browning replied with some spirit: "I am not a 'fast woman'— I don't like coarse subjects, or the coarse treatment of any subject— But I am deeply convinced that the corruption of our society requires, not shut doors and windows, but light and air." He started running the essays of Ruskin later published as *Unto This Last*, but was so frightened by the protests aroused when their socialistic tendencies became apparent that he wrote Ruskin with "many apologies" and "great discomfort to himself," explaining that he must stop them short. (It should be said, in justice to Thackeray, that he liked his job of editor so little that he resigned before the end of the three years that he had originally engaged to serve.)

My own experience in rereading Thackeray has been rather disappointing. In going back to Jane Austen and Dickens, I have found more than I had known was there, and have been even more impressed by them than I had been before. But to go back to Thackeray, in one's later years, when one no longer takes great writers on faith, is to be made more aware of his weaknesses without discovering much that is new. Of course, his vein at its best was excellent; but it is so much merely a vein that is always running thin or insipid. One cannot count on him to do anything solid, and even *Henry Esmond*, though carefully built, has always seemed to me rather flimsy. One falls back on the conclusion, borne out by these letters, that Thackeray had in his day and for a certain length of time thereafter a kind of social value that made him seem a greater writer than he was. He was the chronicler of a middle-class world which, though sometimes humiliated by poverty, always pretended to education and gentility. Dissociating itself from its background of trade, which it had now begun to ridicule, or assimilating itself to the nobility, whose standards it partly adopted, it sought exclusively to identify itself with the professions, with literature and painting, and with the Army and Navy and the Civil Service. The ups and downs of this world and the assertion of its fundamental dignity, as well as a certain dissatisfaction with its methods, aims and rewards, really constitutes Thackeray's whole subject, and he never gets outside that subject. He cannot see society as a whole as Dickens was able to do, with all the paradoxes involved in its structure and the dislocations caused by its growth. He is unable to interest himself in personalities or relations for their own sake, as Henry James or Jane Austen did—in such a way as to use them for materials in composing a work of art. His situations and characters are sketches on a somewhat higher plane, to be sure, than the drawings he dashed off in his letters, but more or less the same sort of thing.

To readers of the group that he wrote for, the monthly installments of his novels were all like a series of letters—full of personal appeals and confidings and whatever reflections on life the event or the mood might suggest—in which Thackeray talked about people that he and they both knew. This explains his popularity in the United States, where he felt so much more at home than Dickens did. Realizing how pleasant and how profitable it would be to enlarge his circle of correspondents, he more or less directly addressed to the American upper classes, with their republican point of view, *The Four Georges* and *The Virginians*, and he cemented this *entente cordiale* by embodying Miss Sally Baxter in the English Ethel Newcome. To such "nice people" on both sides of the water, he became a kind of friend of the family: a gossip who was mostly entertaining, a moralist who was not too severe, a man of the world who had met everyone worth meeting yet did not make his hosts feel provincial, a man of breeding who was always avuncular in correcting the bad manners of the children and a dinner guest who always did justice to the company, the wine and the food. And this role that Thackeray played for his own and the next generation accounts partly, I think, for the high esteem in which his books have been held by such Old World "bourgeois" critics as George Saintsbury and H. L. Mencken. The extravagant praise which has been given by the latter of these to *The Newcomes* and by the former to Thackeray's work as a whole may be due to very early impressions, to their identifying themselves in boyhood with Pendennis and Clive Newcome and Esmond. Up through 1910, I suppose, boys and girls still continued to read Thackeray; but by that time he was no longer so close to the life that they actually knew. I do not believe that his novels will ever mean so much again to either younger or older readers.

February 8, 1947

Gilbert Without Sullivan

Random House has reprinted its collected volume of the *Plays and Poems of W. S. Gilbert*, first published in 1932. It is, in the main, a satisfactory job: it contains all the librettos of the Gilbert and Sullivan operas, two operas written with other composers, and the whole of the *Bab Ballads*. Operas and ballads are illustrated with Gilbert's droll little drawings; and there is a fifty-page preface by Deems Taylor which admirably covers Gilbert's career and the history of the operas. The book is well printed and not too heavy.

One's only complaint would be that the editor has taken space to include an inferior set of *Bab Ballads*, which Gilbert rightly discarded, and a blank-verse play, *The Palace of Truth*, which is certainly not one of his most brilliant things, while he has left out *Haste to the Wedding*, Gilbert's very amusing version of *Le Chapeau de Paille d'Italie*, and has failed to give any examples of his non-operatic farces. Surely it would have been worth while to preserve the burlesque *Hamlet*, called *Rosencrantz and Guildenstern*, and the once popular comedy *Engaged*, which was revived in New York so recently as the twenties. Even aside from the operas, Gilbert had some importance as a dramatist. His serious plays were dreadful. When he tried to drop his characteristic mixture of satire and pure nonsense, he lapsed immediately into sentimental melodrama of the kind that, as Mr. Taylor remarks, he frequently parodied in his comic writings. But he had also another vein, which was anti-sentimental and somewhat tougher than anything in the operas. Such comedies as *Tom Cobb* and *Sweethearts*, which had considerable success in the seventies, must have struck a new note in the theater. What Gilbert seems to have invented was a curious comic convention, derived from a mercantile society, according to which the characters, full of tender and noble sentiments, were shown never to act from any other motives than those of the grimmest self-interest. Their amorous affairs are conducted on a basis of hard cash and advantage, without an atom of human feeling; and they are thus not merely fairy-tale creatures, like the characters in the operas,

758

who make British officials delightful at the same time that they make them absurd and have fun with the British caste system by turning it upside down, but caricatures of a harsher kind. And this abstraction of the motive of cupidity from all the other impulses and passions had its influence on the dramatists who came after Gilbert. If the earlier comedies of Wilde went back to the tradition of Congreve, *The Importance of Being Earnest* unquestionably derived from Gilbert; and though Shaw, in his youthful days as a reviewer of theater and opera, was in general rather snooty about Gilbert, the latter evidently counted for something in the readiness with which it was possible for Shaw to substitute, in such of his early plays as *Arms and the Man* and *You Never Can Tell*, the common-sense motivations, in situations of love and war, for the expected romantic ones.

With Barrie, too, the reversal of social roles that makes the interest of *The Admirable Crichton* probably dates back to *Pinafore*; and the pirates of *Peter Pan* must owe something to those of Penzance. As a figure in this whole development of the modern school of British comedy, Gilbert has, I think, been rather slighted. He has become, in the popular mind, so closely and exclusively associated with Sullivan that he is rarely given serious attention as a dramatist with an independent existence. Yet, as one reads these librettos, one realizes how sharp and how permanent the differences were between the two collaborators, and to what degree these must have been responsible for their finally falling out. They were differences of a kind which made it almost impossible for Gilbert to adapt himself to Sullivan, so that Sullivan was always in the position of trying to assimilate Gilbert. For the latter, though metrically adroit, a marvellous wit in verse, was quite devoid of real lyric talent. Gilbert had no ear for music, and of the magical music of words that distinguishes the meanest lyric of the Elizabethan song-writer Campion, the most ambitious aria of Gilbert is not able to muster a trace; nor could he manage the more commonplace sweetness which, in so many of the poems of Moore, married itself to Irish melodies. Bernard Shaw put his finger on the deficiencies of Gilbert when he called his lyrics "aridly fanciful," and, contrasting his librettos with those that Meilhac and Halévy had written for Offenbach, described them as "a curiously brutalized, embittered, stolidified, middle-classical, mechanical equivalent" for these.

One cannot help sympathizing with Sullivan when he complained that he had to fit his music into a rigid and inhuman mold (one sympathizes particularly with his protest against "the middle-aged woman with fading charms," the inevitable appearance of whom became such a tiresome betrayal of all that was worst in Gilbert: a streak of vulgar cruelty and a tendency to rely on formula). Sullivan's own talent was Irish and Italian: he loved to write pretty music. And Gilbert could never really write prettily—that is, he could never write without a certain hard facetious touch that was then and has remained characteristic of the kind of humorous verse that one finds in English comic weeklies. Sullivan was graceful and romantic; Gilbert, though fantastic, flat-footed. They soon learned how to work together in a well-oiled coördination, but their talents never really blended. Sullivan first expressed his dissatisfaction after the run of *Princess Ida*, requesting from Gilbert "a story of human interest and probability, where the humorous words would come in a humorous (not serious) situation." Gilbert was angry at first, but presently told Sullivan that he had for him just the kind of thing he wanted, and presented him with the libretto of *The Mikado*, which, if it did not precisely meet the requirements, proved such a stupendous success that Sullivan, for the moment, evidently ceased to worry. They went on to *Ruddigore*, and then Gilbert made a real effort to give Sullivan what he wanted by turning out *The Yeomen of the Guard*, for which Sullivan wrote an excellent score, but in which Gilbert, making desperate efforts to arrive at the poignant and the somber, is workmanlike but not at his best.

Gilbert himself, it seems to me, is successful in achieving an aesthetic effect only in those operas where outlandish combinations produce piquant and surprising contrasts that eventually become resolved: the descent of the Heavy Dragoons upon the aesthetes and love-sick maidens of *Patience*, the intrusion into fairyland, in *Iolanthe*, of the Lord Chancellor and the House of Lords. And in these cases it is hard to tell how much the happy result was a matter of calculation. Gilbert *did* have some instinct for dramatic color; and his charming little drawings show that his characters were not quite all conceived as disputatious two-dimensional monsters; but, if you read the librettos of the operas, without reference to Sullivan's scores, you would hardly be able to imagine, any more than in reading the *Bab Ballads*, that vivifying them by stage production would bring out in them a poetic beauty. There is no color in Gilbert's *writing*: it all comes with the costumes and the settings, and with the brightness of Sullivan's music. The worst operas as aesthetic creations are, in my opinion, *The Mikado* and *The Gondoliers* (admirably solid though the former is as a job of theatrical carpentry), in which a definite national background has no real relevance to either text or music (though Sullivan put into the latter some delightful parodies of Italian opera), the text and the music, as usual, pulling a little against one another. It may be that *Pinafore* is the only point in the series at which the two men are really at one. Here Gilbert approaches Sullivan's prettiness and Sullivan Gilbert's frivolity, and the piece is not complex enough for their divergences to set up a strain.

For years during the period of their first collaboration—as we learn from the biography of Sullivan by his nephew, Herbert Sullivan—Gilbert had been trying to foist upon his partner what he considered a magnificent theme: a magic charm which would convert human beings into the realities of what they pretended to be, one of its effects, by a farfetched and tasteless touch, being the transformation of certain of the characters into a pair of clockwork figures. The composer had fought this off, had had to turn it down again and again. The recurrence, in Sullivan's diary and letters, of his phrase for it, "the lozenge story," comes to suggest an insane obsession on the part of his collaborator to which Sullivan has had to resign himself, a peril which he has learned to evade; and that Gilbert should have thought this idea attractive does show a queer stupidity in him. But when he at last made the break with Sullivan, the librettist's very first act was to exploit this frustrated plot in the incredibly unamusing opera written with Alfred Cellier under the title of *The Mountebanks*. One has only to read its text to appreciate the kind of thing that Sullivan had saved himself and Gilbert from.

After their quarrel and reconciliation, Gilbert and Sullivan did two more operas together: *Utopia, Limited; or The Flowers of Progress* (1893) and *The Grand Duke; or The Statutory Duel* (1896). *The Grand Duke*, written when Gilbert was nearing sixty, is one of his most labored librettos, alternating weary Gilbertianisms with Christmas-pantomime gags of a crudeness that hardly occurs in any of his other librettos. But *Utopia, Limited* is a different matter. The reunion with Sullivan seems to have stimulated him, after the two desolating librettos that he had written for other composers. One wonders why *Utopia* has never been revived by the D'Oyly Carte Company. (The public, when it was first produced, is said to have followed the lead of the Court, who disapproved of the royal drawing-room put on the stage in the Second Act.) Shaw said that he enjoyed the score more than that of any of the other operas, and the libretto, perhaps Gilbert's most ambitious, is, it seems to me, a great deal more amusing than that of either *Princess Ida* or *The Gondoliers*. In this fantasy, a Utopian king, impressed by the glories of England, decides that his country is behind the times and in need of fundamental renovation. He gives his daughters an English education, and he imports six "Flowers of Progress" in the shape of selected representatives of key English institutions: a barrister M.P., a Lord Chamberlain who censors plays, a county councillor who makes municipal improvements, a captain of the First Life Guards, Captain Corcoran of H.M.S. *Pinafore* and Mr. Goldbury, a company promoter— the last of whom reorganizes Utopia as a limited-liability company. Here the satire on contemporary England becomes less elfin and somewhat bolder than in any of the previous pieces. In fact, it leads the way quite plainly for the social-economic comedy of the early nineteen-hundreds. *Utopia* ought, I should think, to be brought into currency again (as *Ruddigore* was so successfully after its relative failure when it was first performed), both as a creditable culmination of the last phase of the partnership and as a link that has been unfairly dropped out of the history of British drama. The other operas have grown so familiar that they are getting to be a bore, and it would be pleasant to hear a fresh one.

April 12, 1947

George Saintsbury: Gourmet and Glutton

IT IS sometimes said of entertaining writers that reading them is like eating peanuts. The literary criticism of George Saintsbury has for a long time had this effect on me. I cannot start one of his books, or even dip into one, without reading more than I meant to, and my appetite still carries me on even after the pleasure has cloyed. I have recently had this experience with the new reprint of *The Peace of the Augustans* in the *World's Classics* series, published by the Oxford Press. This *Survey of Eighteenth Century Literature as a Place of Rest and Refreshment* is in Saintsbury's later and more personal manner, but not so garrulous as the *History of the French Novel*, which came after it, and it would be, I should think, an ideal book with which to begin reading this author. Here you have at their best his easy handling of biography and history, his expert analysis of the technique of writing, his unexpected and witty allusions, his warm and luminous glow and his inexhaustible curiosity.

Reading *The Peace of the Augustans*, I came at last to realize that Saintsbury, besides being a great critic and scholar, was one of the best English *writers* of his time. The spell that he can cast in his more mature work is of a kind that is not common in literary criticism; it is more like the spell of fiction or memoirs—though the critical histories of Saintsbury are not in the least like the work of the great French historian-critics, for Saintsbury had neither Taine's interest in the development of human society nor Renan's in the growth of ideas. What he has done is create an imaginative world composed almost exclusively of books and their makers, with an admixture of foods and wines. In this world, his ostensible occupation is tasting and digesting the authors (as well as the vintages and dinners) and appraising them with scrupulous fairness from the point of view of the enjoyment they afford; but this record becomes an adventure story and a commentary on human experience; and there is even a dramatic element provided by the recurring conflict between Saintsbury's Tory principles and the productions of those of his subjects who hold contrary opinions. The thrill for the reader results from Saintsbury's displays of gallantry in recognizing and applauding the literary merit of writers whose views he abhors; and there are moments when one nearly suspects him of having invented the Tory background—in the same way that a dramatist or novelist arranges contrasting elements—on purpose so that his passion for literature might find itself pitted against this and score unexpected victories over it.

I had been wondering what Saintsbury was like as a man and how he had spent his life, when I came upon the new memorial volume, *A Saintsbury Miscellany*. This selection from his essays and scrapbooks is introduced by "personal portraits" by Oliver Elton, Sir Herbert Grierson and others of Saintsbury's friends, and I expected that it would contain some biographical information that would satisfy my curiosity. One does not, however, find much. There are memoirs of his lectures, his dinners and his conversation, which present him in a sympathetic light, but no real revelation of his character or description of his intimate life. We learn that George Saintsbury, like Thackeray, asked that no life of him or biography of him should be written (rather unfairly, one feels, when he read other people's biographies so avidly and so much enjoyed discussing their personal affairs); and we conclude from certain intimations that the reason was the same as in Thackeray's case: some sort of domestic tragedy that had dislocated and that shadowed his life. This would explain the peculiar voracity with which he fed himself on books. Emotional deprivation sometimes drives people to eating and drinking as a substitute for what has been lost, and this may have been the case with Saintsbury, who certainly loved the pleasures of the table—he liked to write about cookery and wines—and seems to have taken to letters as both a gourmet and something of a glutton. Beginning as a reviewer of current books and a writer of short literary histories of the kind that may be used as textbooks, he gave himself up to literature in a way that was very different from the way of the ordinary scholar, with his tendency toward specialization and his ambition for academic prestige. It was as if he had transferred to literature his whole emotional and moral life, so that presently he appeared as an artist whose contacts were all with books instead of with places and people. One may even say "athletic life," for he has travelled in literature, too, and climbed mountains and done long-distance swimming. Saintsbury must have come as close to reading the whole of English literature as anyone who has ever lived, and he knew French literature almost as well. Academic fashions and categories, conventional assumptions and beaten trails, meant very little to him: he had to explore every inch for himself, see everything with his own eyes and formulate his own opinions.

His thus having the consumption of books for his only serious interest did, however, lead in some ways to a slightly distorted point of view. We find him, for example, in *The Peace of the Augustans* talking as if the enjoyment of literature were somehow a moral matter. He might be justified in this if it were merely a question of acquainting ourselves with the great books of the great writers. But for Saintsbury this is not enough. He seems to want to make us feel that we are under some obligation to gratify the literary palate with everything that can possibly be relished—implying that it is no more than our duty to go all through Dodsley's *Miscellany*, "especially as supplemented later by Pearch," in order to glean some minor poetry, and declaring, after a lengthy review of eighteenth-century periodical literature, that "as one looks over the two score and more little volumes of Chalmers' set, a sacred shame invades [him] at the thought of leaving such a various collection of pastime with the scanty inventory above selected." If an author that he particularly likes has been recently disparaged or attacked, he usually becomes pugnacious, and is quick to suggest that the critic is either a fool or a scoundrel. And he certainly praises too much and praises too many people. While I was reading *The Peace of the Augustans*, I was stimulated by Saintsbury's enthusiasm to look up certain things which I did not know. I had never had much luck with Cowper, and Saintsbury induced me to read two poems, *Yardley Oak* and *The Castaway*, which he extols in the strongest terms; but these seemed to me on just the same level, only a little above mediocrity, as every other serious piece of Cowper's that I had ever tried to read. Then the eye-twinkling and chuckling of this connoisseur over the humor of the satirical verse of Canning, Ellis and Frere in the *Anti-Jacobin Review*, which I had seen only scattered in anthologies, led me to look into the collected volume—only to find it rather disappointing. The merits of the Anti-Jacobins are hardly of such proportions as to warrant this gourmet's delight in them. Here his political prejudice and his snobbery have really for the moment betrayed him—for he becomes a little sickening on the subject of the good family and good breeding of these writers, who, as a matter of fact, in the work that he admires, are not merely reactionary but sometimes stupid and crude. A burlesque of Schiller, *The Rovers*, besides being aggressively Philistine, is slapstick and uninventive.

George Saintsbury's powers of appreciation were limited in one direction in a way that it is hard to account for. In his attitude toward contemporary writing, he practiced a consistent old-fogyism that seems to have no connection with his attitude toward works of the past, in judging which, as I have said, he never depends on conventional views. He does not hesitate either to tell us that a classic like Richardson bores him or, as in the case of George Borrow, to push into prominence a writer who had been rather underrated and neglected. But in regard to anything of importance that had happened since about 1880, he seems to have been not merely cool but hostile, and when he did have a good word for a contemporary, it was usually for someone of the second order: an R. L. Stevenson or a Norman Douglas. He lashed himself into a strange indignation over the movement at the end of the century to introduce form into the English novel. We find in *The Peace of the Augustans* a veritable diatribe on this subject, evidently directed at Henry James. This animus was as much out of harmony with his sensitive feeling for form in verse as it was with his respect for French fiction.

But neither this limitation nor his sometimes exaggerated enthusiasm seriously mars his work; and, in bringing them to notice here, I have merely been making an effort to arrive at an objective view, to correct the bemused condition to which Saintsbury has the power to reduce me. Once you fall under his spell, it will be long before you are troubled by these aspects of him or begin to feel the incompleteness of an entire artistic world of wide scope and huge dimensions that is populated entirely by books.

May 17, 1947

Books of Etiquette and Emily Post

Professor Arthur M. Schlesinger, the Harvard historian, has written an entertaining little treatise called *Learning How to Behave: A Historical Study of American Etiquette Books*. It is curious and rather instructive to look at the development of the United States from the point of view of the literature of etiquette. The first manuals derived from Europe and emphasized deference to rank to the point of, in one case, admonishing the young: "If thy superior be relating a story, say not, 'I have heard it before.' . . . If he tell it not right, snigger not"; but after the Revolution, and especially after the advent of Jackson, the object became not to define class differences but to provide a set of prescriptions which would show anyone how to become a gentleman. The Southerners had, however, based their practice on seventeenth-century guides which helped the planter "to model his life on that of the English landed gentry" and "provided a fairly consistent chart of behavior . . . in emulation of the ancient ideals of Christian chivalry"; and they continued to follow this code. In the period after the Civil War, when the big fortunes were being made, a fresh crop of volumes appeared which had the purpose of orienting the newly rich among the refinements and complications of calling cards and formal dinners. There was an average of five such a year, and this continued through to 1945.

The two greatest publishing successes in the department of etiquette date from the beginning of the nineteen-twenties. At this time, a Miss Lillian Eichler, an advertising copywriter, then eighteen and just out of high school, sold thousands of copies of an *Encyclopedia of Etiquette* by means of a series of advertisements with the caption "What's Wrong with This Picture?" But the book—which had been written in 1901—was by that time, it seems, obsolete (Mr. Schlesinger does not tell us in what respect), for it was returned by "droves of dissatisfied customers." The publisher then proposed to Miss Eichler that she should herself do an up-to-date book, and the result was *The Book of Etiquette*, which between 1921 and 1945 sold over a million copies. In 1922, Emily Post brought out her *Etiquette*, which by 1945 had sold more than two-thirds of a million.

An examination of these two manuals reveals fundamental differences between them and suggests that they have been appealing to two rather different publics. Miss Eichler is practical and comfortable (her book is now frankly called *Today's Etiquette*). She tells you how to teach the children table manners and how to give a dinner without servants. She makes rough tabulations of vintage wines and supplies reliable recipes for half-a-dozen well-known cocktails; she recommends, in a chapter on *The Nature and Meaning of Culture*, that one "read more than one kind of literature: not mystery stories alone, nor light fiction alone," and she lists "nine painters of undisputed glory, with whose work every person of culture should be at least familiar." The precepts are mostly appropriate for anyone of moderate income, and the whole tone is non-invidious. She makes social life sound easy and jolly. But Mrs. Post is another affair. I had had no conception of her extraordinary book till I looked into it recently, fell under its spell and read it almost through. Mrs. Post is not merely the author of a comprehensive textbook on manners: she is a considerable imaginative writer, and her book has some of the excitement of a novel. It has also the snob-appeal which is evidently an important factor in the success of a Marquand or a Galsworthy. (I should explain that the edition I read was the third printing, of 1922.)

Mrs. Post has produced a world which has its characters, its atmosphere, its drama. I was reminded, after reading *Etiquette*, of the late Scott Fitzgerald's once telling me that he had looked into Emily Post and been inspired with the idea of a play in which all the motivations should consist of trying to do the right thing. The element of dramatic conflict would be produced by setting people at cross-purposes through stalemates of good form, from which the only possible rescue would be through the intervention of some bounder as *deus ex machina* to put an end to the sufferings of the gentlefolk who had been paralyzed by Mrs. Post's principles. (There are actually novels by Howells, and even by Henry James, which very nearly fulfill this formula.) For it is true that Mrs. Post has supplied all the materials for such a drama. Her ideal gentleman-clubman and her ideal feminine house guest—described in little essays like the "characters" of La Bruyère or the *Spectator* —are models which can never deviate, and thoroughly priggish figures which would lend themselves to satirical comedy. The "considerate guest," in particular, who is always perfectly sweet to everyone and always wants to do what the others are doing, who pretends to like children and dogs and lets them "climb over her" though she loathes them, could easily be shown as a menace from whom the party would have to be saved by Mrs. Post's hideous villain: "The Guest No One Invites Again."

But Mrs. Post, in providing illustrations, has also invented types that have names, personalities and histories, and that are threaded, like the characters of Proust, in and out all through her book. These figures were originally intended merely as convenient dummies to stand in the places of hosts and guests when she was showing how the right kind of entertaining might be done on various scales by people on different income levels; but they have taken such a hold on the author that they have gratuitously been developed to exemplify, like the groups in Proust, a variety of social milieux. They do, however, all belong to Society, and the author, unlike Miss Eichler, always assumes that the reader wants to belong to Society, too.

At the top of Mrs. Post's structure, from the point of view of a wealth which is combined with "social credentials," stand the Worldlys of Great Estates (run by their butler Hastings) and the Gildings of Golden Hall. The Worldlys are a little difficult, they are constrained by the expensive habits and the inflated self-importance of the rich; but the Gildings are more human and always fun. Of Golden Hall, Mrs. Post writes: "The house is a palace, the grounds are a park. There is not only a long wing of magnificent guest rooms in the house, occupied by young girls or important older people, but there is also a guest annex, a separate building designed and run like the most luxurious country club. . . . Perfectly equipped Turkish and Russian baths in charge of the best Swedish masseur and masseuse procurable . . . a glass-roofed and enclosed riding ring—not big enough for games of polo, but big enough to practise in winter," etc. It was after a party at Golden Hall that Mrs. Toplofty, Bobo Gilding's great-aunt, exclaimed, "How are any of us ever going to amuse any one after *this*? I feel like doing my guest rooms up in moth balls." Bobo Gilding (whose nickname is incidentally explained in a section intended to discourage what Mrs. Post calls conversational "door-slammers": "As for the name 'Bobo,' it's asinine." "Oh, it's just one of those children's names that stick sometimes for life." "Perfect rot. Ought to be called by his name.") —Bobo Gilding, on his side, does not care for his aunt's rather pompous parties, since "entering a drawing-room [for Bobo] was more suggestive of the daily afternoon tea ordeal of his early nursery days than a voluntary act of pleasure." And Mrs. Gilding (who was Lucy Wellborn) "did not care much to go either if none of her particular men friends were to be there. Little she cared to dance the cotillion with old Colonel Bluffington or to go to supper with that odious Hector Newman." Yet old Mrs. Toplofty is by no means dull, for, finding herself once at dinner "next to a man she quite openly despised, [she] said to him with apparent placidity, 'I shall not talk to you— because I don't care to. But for the sake of the hostess I shall say my multiplication tables. Twice one are two, twice two are four—' and she continued on through the tables, making him alternate them with her. As soon as she politely could, she turned to her other companion."

Lucy Gilding "smokes like a furnace and is miserable unless she can play bridge for high stakes." At her wedding, the bridesmaids were dressed "in deep shades of burnt orange and yellow, wood-colored slippers and stockings, skirts that shaded from brown through orange to yellow; yellow leghorn hats trimmed with jonquils, and jonquil bouquets"; and the affair was a great success for everybody except a "distinguished uncle," with whom Mrs. Post frankly sympathizes, who declared: "I did not think it was lovely at all. Every one of the bridesmaids was so powdered and painted that there was not a sweet or fresh face among them."

The Gildings' especial friends are rich young people like the Lovejoys and the Gailys, rich bachelors like Jim Smartlington and Clubwin Doe (the former of whom was elected "with little difficulty" to Clubwin Doe's club, at the same time that young Breezy was kept out by two men who "disliked his 'manner'"). But there are also, in the higher brackets, Mr. and

Mrs. Kindhart. Mrs. Kindhart, unlike Mrs. Worldly, "talks to everyone, everywhere and always." Her "position is as good as Mrs. Worldly's every bit, but perhaps she can be more relaxed." It is the Kindharts who try to be helpful at the catastrophic "bungled dinner" which is given by "you," the reader—the evening when the fire smokes and Mrs. Toplofty issues orders that the logs are to be thrown out into the yard; when the Swedish maid says "Dinner's all ready!" instead of "Dinner is served" and deals the plates out like cards and then stacks them; when the clear soup turns out a "greasy-looking brown" and the hollandaise sauce "a curdled yellow mess"—the evening after which Mrs. Toplofty, Clubwin Doe and the Worldlys and the Gildings, all of whom you invited together, will, as you well know, be telling their friends: "Whatever you do, don't dine with the Newweds unless you eat your dinner before you go, and wear black glasses so no sight can offend you." On that occasion, Mr. Kindhart is the only guest who tries to eat the soup, and Mrs. Kindhart says to you gently: "Cheer up, little girl, it doesn't really matter"—making you know for the first time "to the full how terrible the situation is." (The other guests, on this unfortunate occasion, seem to have fallen a little short of the qualities of delicacy and grace which the author has elsewhere ascribed to the truly well bred.) It was the Kindharts who gave the houseparty at informal Mountain Summit Camp which inspires Mrs. Post to one of her most memorable chapters—that party at which Mr. Kindhart points out after lunch to the guests "a dozen guides who are waiting at the boat-house" and "a small swimming pool which can be warmed artificially" for those who find the lake too cold, but at which the Worldlys strike a false note, for Mr. Worldly insists on bringing his valet, though he well knows that this was not expected, and Mrs. Worldly, at the long pine lunch-table, "looks at her napkin ring as though it were an insect"—till Mrs. Kindhart smiles and says: "I'm sorry, but I told you 'it was roughing it.'"

And then there are the Littlehouses (Mrs. Littlehouse was Sally Titherington), who, when you visit them, may "press you into service as auxiliary nurse, gardener or chauffeur," but whose "personality" is "such that there is scarcely a day in the week when the motors of the most popular of the younger set are not parked at the Littlehouse door." And, on the fringes, such occasional guests as Grace Smalltalk, who *did* write to Mrs. Norman an admirable bread-and-butter letter, and the boring Professor Bugge, who was rather a social problem till he was seated by a clever hostess next to Mrs. Entomoid. In a somewhat different category, not frowned on but not included in the Eastern set, are Mr. and Mrs. Spendeasy Western and Mr. and Mrs. Jameson Greatlake, of 24 Michigan Avenue, Chicago.

But Mrs. Post's real hero and heroine are Mr. and Mrs. Oldname. Mrs. Oldname is "*une dame élégante*"—because, as Mrs. Post tells us, there is no English word to "express the individuality of beautiful taste combined with personal dignity and grace which gives to a perfect costume an inimitable air of distinction." Her tact is unfailing and consummate: to a lady going in to dinner, she will say quietly: "Mr. Traveler, who is sitting next to you at the table, has just come back from two years alone with the cannibals." And "how does Mrs. Oldname walk? One might answer by describing how Pavlowa dances. Her body is perfectly balanced, she holds herself straight, and yet nothing suggests a ramrod. She takes steps of medium length, and, like all people who move and dance well, walks from the hip, not the knee. On no account does she swing her arms, nor does she rest a hand on her hip! Nor, when walking, does she wave her hands about in gesticulation." One of the most telling of the little episodes with which Mrs. Post's commentary is interspersed is her account of a visit to the Oldnames, which has the title *The Small House of Perfection*. "A great friend of the Oldnames, but not a man who went at all into society, or considered whether people had position or not, was invited with his new wife—a woman from another State and of much wealth and discernment—to stay over a weekend at Brook Meadows." She asks her husband what sort of clothes to take, and he tells her that he has never seen Mrs. Oldname "dressed up a bit." The wife wonders whether to pack her cerise satin. The husband thinks it "much too handsome," but the wife decides to put it in. They drive up to a low, white shingled house, and the visitor notices that the flowers bordering the old-fashioned brick walk are "all of one color, all in perfect bloom." "She knew no inexperienced gardener produced that apparently simple approach to a door that has been chosen as frontispiece in more than one book on Colonial architecture. The door was opened by a maid in a silver gray taffeta dress, with organdie collar, cuffs and apron, white stockings and silver buckles on black slippers, and the guest saw a quaint hall and vista of rooms that at first sight might easily be thought 'simple' by an inexpert appraiser." Mrs. Oldname herself was electrifying to the visitor of wealth from another State. To describe her as "simple," exclaims Mrs. Post, "is about as apt as to call a pearl 'simple' because it doesn't dazzle; nor was there an article in the apparently simple living-room that would be refused if it were offered to a museum." The furniture, the appointments, the other guests are filled in with glowing rapture. "That night the bride wore her cerise dress to one of the smartest dinners she ever went down to"; and when later she is alone with her husband she bursts out: "Why in the name of goodness didn't you tell me the truth about these people?" The husband misunderstands: "I told you it was a little house—it was you who insisted on bringing that red dress. I told you it was much too handsome!" "Handsome!" she cries in tears. "I don't own anything half good enough to compare with the least article in this house. That 'simple' little woman, as you call her, would, I think, almost make a queen seem provincial! And as for her clothes, they are priceless—just as everything is in this little gem of a house. Why, the window curtains are as fine as the best things in my trousseau."

There is only one instance on record of anybody's scoring off the Oldnames. Mrs. Oldname had hanging in her dining-room a portrait of a Colonial officer, to which she was rather attached. One day, however, "an art critic, whose knowledge was better than his manners, blurted out, 'Will you please tell me why you have that dreadful thing in this otherwise perfect room?' Mrs. Oldname, somewhat taken aback, answered rather wonderingly: 'Is it dreadful?—Really? I have a feeling of affection for him and his dog!' The critic was merciless. 'If you call a cotton-flannel effigy a dog! And as for the figure, it is equally false and lifeless! It is amazing how anyone with your taste can bear looking at it!' In spite of his rudeness, Mrs. Oldname saw that what he said was quite true, but not until the fact had been pointed out to her. Gradually she grew to dislike the poor officer so much that he was finally relegated to the attic." It will be noted that, though the art critic carried his point, he was still guilty of a grave breach of manners.

The latest edition of Emily Post omits, as she says on the jacket, "certain non-essential customs and old-fashioned ideas," and aims to accommodate itself to the habits of later decades—including even those of the war and post-war young people—when formalities have been going by the board. The chapter, for example, which in the 1922 edition is called *The Chaperon and Other Conventions* is now headed *The Vanished Chaperon and Other Lost Conventions*. But the book is still dominated by the prestige of the Oldnames and the Gildings. Their prestige for Mrs. Post may finally have the effect of making some of her readers sympathetic toward the characters who are awful examples: the Upstarts, Mr. and Mrs. Unsuitable and that touching Mr. Richan Vulgar, who crossed the Atlantic four times a year in order to meet the smart people on shipboard and who, by capturing an innocent celebrity, attracted for a time to his table the Smartlys, the Wellborns and the Lovejoys, only to lose them every one when they found out what he was really like and took to eating their meals on deck. (The story of Mr. Richan Vulgar has been dropped from the new edition, as have also, the Unsuitables and the Upstarts, but a pathetic Miss Nobackground has appeared.) One feels, in fact, something like sadism in the whole approach of Mrs. Post. She likes to humiliate. She cannot tell us how charming Miss Wellborn is or how perfect is Mrs. Oldname's taste without putting in a little incident to show us this polish or grace making somebody else uncomfortable. Mrs. Post's popularity, I think, is partly due to precisely this.

It is obvious that the Gildings and the Oldnames do not themselves need Mrs. Post's book of etiquette; and that the ordinary amiable American, to whom Miss Eichler addresses herself, does not necessarily need to hear about either Great Estates or the Small House of Perfection. But there are people who want to believe in the existence of a social Olympus and who find here the satisfaction that is somehow derived at once from imagining the enjoyment of glamor and power and from immolating oneself before them—since the reader is let in on the lives of the dwellers in these privileged places but is constantly being reminded how desperately he should have to watch his step if he were ever admitted among them.

What you get in Emily Post, for all her concessions to the age's vulgarization, is a crude version of the social ideal to which the mass of Americans aspired after the Civil War: an ideal that was costly and glossy, smart, self-conscious and a little disgusting in a period when even Mrs. Oldname reflected the lavish Gildings in stimulating her visitors to realize that the clothes she wore were "priceless" and her tableware and furniture museum pieces. Today this ideal must be fading with the money that kept it up, but, such as it is, a great many people must still enjoy reading about it. The publishers of Mrs. Post's *Etiquette* have announced that it has sold fifty thousand copies since the beginning of this year: its biggest sale in a decade.

July 19, 1947

A Dissenting Opinion on Kafka

FRANZ KAFKA has been looming on the literary world like the meteorological phenomenon called the Brocken specter: a human shadow thrown on the mist in such a way that it seems monstrous and remote when it may really be quite close at hand, and with a rainbow halo around it. Since the publication in English of *The Trial* in 1937 (*The Castle* came out in 1930 but did not attract much attention), Kafka's reputation and influence have been growing till his figure has been projected on the consciousness of our literary reviews on a scale which gives the illusion that he is a writer of towering stature. New translations of him are constantly appearing, an endless discussion of his writing goes on, and a new collected edition in German is being brought out in New York. This edition, under the imprint of Schocken Books, is in part a reprinting of the old German edition which the war made unavailable, but, when complete, it will include ten or eleven volumes instead of the original six, with two volumes of Kafka's diaries, two of his letters and one or two of his miscellaneous fragments, of all of which only selections were given in a single volume before. We may be proud that this admirably produced and authoritatively edited version of a modern German classic, which was begun in Berlin under Hitler and only finished in Prague on the eve of the German occupation of Czechoslovakia, should thus have been salvaged from the ruins of Central European culture and brought out in the United States. Schocken has also published, both in German and English, *Franz Kafka: A Biography*, by Max Brod, and a selection, in English translation, from Kafka's "stories and reflections" under the title *The Great Wall of China*; and it has announced some further translations. In the meantime, a translation of *Metamorphosis*, one of the most important of Kafka's short stories, has recently been brought out by the Vanguard Press; and *A Franz Kafka Miscellany*, which contains translated scraps of Kafka as well as essays on his work, has been published by the Twice A Year Press. A compilation of essays and memoirs called *The Kafka Problem* has been published by New Directions; and

Kafka's Prayer, an interpretation by Paul Goodman, has just been brought out by Vanguard.

These last two volumes, in the first of which the editor, Mr. Angel Flores, has assembled no less than forty-one pieces by writers of all nationalities, oversaturate and stupefy the reader and finally give rise to the suspicion that Kafka is being wildly overdone. One realizes that it is not merely a question of appreciating Kafka as a poet who gives expression for the intellectuals to their emotions of helplessness and self-contempt but of building him up as a theologian and saint who can somehow also justify for them—or help them to accept without justification—the ways of a banal, bureaucratic and incomprehensible God to sensitive and anxious men. Now, it may make a good deal of difference whether one was born, like the present writer, before the end of the nineteenth century, when stability and progress were taken for granted, instead of in a period when upheaval and backsliding seemed the normal conditions of life; but, with much admiration for Kafka, I find it impossible to take him seriously as a major writer and have never ceased to be amazed at the number of people who can. Some of his short stories are absolutely first-rate, comparable to Gogol's and Poe's. Like them, they are realistic nightmares that embody in concrete imagery the manias of neurotic states. And Kafka's novels have exploited a vein of the comedy and pathos of futile effort which is likely to make "Kafka-esque" a permanent word. But the two of these novels, *The Trial* and *The Castle*, which have become for the cultists of Kafka something like sacred writings, are after all rather ragged performances—never finished and never really worked out. Their themes, as far as Kafka had got, had been developed with so little rigor that Max Brod, when he came to edit them, found mere loose collections of episodes, which he had to piece together as best he could so as to give them a consistent progression, though he was not always able to tell in precisely what order they should come. To compare Kafka, as some of the writers in *The Kafka Problem* do, with Joyce and Proust and even with Dante, great naturalists of personality, great organizers of human experience, is obviously quite absurd. As for the religious implications of these books, they seem to me to be practically nil. I agree with Mr. D. S. Savage, who contributes to *The Kafka Problem* one of its most sensible essays, that the trouble with Kafka was that he could never let go of the world—of his family, of his job, of his yearning for bourgeois happiness—in the interest of divine revelation, and that you cannot have a first-rate saint or prophet without a faith of a very much higher potential than is ever to be felt in Kafka.

All that insulated and eventually nullified the spiritual charge that he carried is indicated in Max Brod's biography. Franz Kafka was the delicate son of a self-made Jewish merchant in the wholesale-women's-wear business in Prague, a vigorous and practical man, who inspired him with fear and respect, and gave him a lifelong inferiority complex. The son was a pure intellectual, who derived from the rabbinical tradition of the mother's side of the family; but he yielded to the insistence of the father and, though at times reduced to thoughts of suicide, he took his place in the drygoods warehouse. His real interest had always been writing, which represented for him not merely an art but also somehow a pursuit of righteousness—he said he regarded it as a form of prayer—and he finally got himself a job in a workers' accident-insurance office, which left him his afternoons free. He wanted, or thought he ought to want, to get married, but his relationship with his father seems to have deprived him of sexual self-confidence. He became engaged to a girl whom he described as "wholesome, merry, natural, robust"; and, after five years of gruelling hesitation, developed tuberculosis, on purpose, in his own opinion, to make it impossible for him to marry. He was by this time, one supposes, too much at home in his isolation to be able to bring himself to the point of taking the risk of trying to get out of it; and he now, at the age of thirty-six, addressed to his father an enormous letter (never yet printed in full), an apologia for his own life, in which he seems to have blamed his failure on him. Later he did get away to Berlin. He had found an intellectual girl who studied Hebrew with him and whom he seems really to have wanted to marry. Her orthodox Chassidic father was forbidden by the rabbi to allow it when Franz confessed that he was not a practicing Jew; but the girl, in revolt against her family tradition, set up housekeeping with him and took care of him. Though he was eager now to work and to live, his disease had left him little time, and, after less than a year of this life, he was dead at forty-one.

The connection of all this with what Kafka wrote is made plain by his friend Max Brod in a book full of understanding. Herr Brod—whom the more metaphysical Kafkians tend to accuse of Philistinism—has, it seems to me, precisely the merit of looking in Kafka's work less for divine than for human meanings. That Kafka was weak-willed, that he was psychologically crippled, Max Brod is quite ready to admit, since he had made it his task during Kafka's life to keep his friend's morale up and make him work. He did stimulate Kafka to write and to have a few of his stories published, but he was very much less successful in his efforts to get him to break with his family. Other people escape from their parents, protests Herr Brod in astonishment and sorrow, so why on earth couldn't Kafka? Why *should* he have allowed his father so to crush and maim his abilities? Why, the reader may second Max Brod, remembering one of Kafka's most effective stories, should this artist have gone on past boyhood accepting the role of cockroach for which, like the hero of *Metamorphosis*, he had been cast by the bourgeois businessman? Well, the cards were stacked against poor Kafka in an overpowering way. His impotence was that of a man constitutionally lacking in vitality and walled in by a whole series of prisons that fitted one into the other like Chinese eggs. There was, first, the strangling father relationship; then the pressure of the tight little group of the Jewish orthodox family; then the constraints of the Jewish community incompletely emerged from the ghetto (Brod points out that the problems of Kafka's heroes are often those of the Jew among semi-alien neighbors—that the wanderer of *The Castle*, for example, is always trying to get himself accepted; he might have added that Joseph K., in *The Trial*, is constantly pursued for some crime which he is not aware of having committed); then the boredom and the spiritual starvation of the writer tied down to business hours—with the impression of hopelessness made on him by the workers who came to his office in the attempt to collect their insurance and who were met by all sorts of evasions and subjected to endless delays ("How modest these men are," he once said to Max Brod. "They come to us and beg, instead of storming the institute and smashing it to little bits."); then the deep-seated inhibitions which seem to have made his love affairs difficult; then the position of the Czechs in the Austrian Empire as an oppressed and somewhat scorned minority; then the privations of a defeated Central Europe, blighted, among other plagues, by the tuberculosis that undermined Kafka. This bewildered and darkened captivity, which may have seemed at the time rather special, was later to become, in Europe, more or less the common lot, and Kafka's fantasies were to gain a validity which could hardly have been foreseen—when, under the rule of the Nazis and the Soviets, men were to find themselves arrested and condemned on charges that had no relation to any accepted code of morals or law, or were driven from place to place to labor or to fight by first one then another inhuman unpetitionable government, which they hadn't the force to defy or the intellect to grasp and disintegrate.

But must we really, as his admirers pretend, accept the plights of Kafka's abject heroes as parables of the human condition? We can hardly feel toward Kafka's father, whose aspect Kafka's God always wears, the same childish awe that Kafka did—especially when the truth is that Kafka himself cannot help satirizing this Father-God as well as his own pusillanimity in remaining in bondage to him. A good deal has been made of the influence on Kafka of the Danish theologian Kierkegaard; but we learn from Max Brod that Kafka was at least equally influenced by Flaubert, and his work is full of a Flaubertian irony which the critics have tended to disregard. There is a story of Kafka's, for example, called *Investigations of a Dog* (included in *The Great Wall of China*), in which a dog is supposed to be inquiring into certain rather puzzling phenomena that are basic to the dog world. Where, he asks, does the food for dogs come from? The conventional explanation—which all right-minded dogs have been taught—is that this food comes out of the earth and is elicited by watering the earth and by singing incantatory hymns and performing ritual dances. Yet, as the scientist-dog has observed, the dogs, when they are invoking food, look not down toward the ground but up. Why *do* they look up, and is this essential? Then there are other unsolved problems: the dogs that roll over in unison and walk on their hind legs to the sound of mysterious music, and the small dandified dogs that seem to float through the air. The point is, of course, that the dogs have had their own reasons for pretending that human beings do not exist. Now, if you read the interpretations of this story which have recently been appearing, you will gather that it is simply an allegory of the relation of man to God—though the analogy does not hold, in view of the fact that the dogs *can* perfectly well see their masters, as man cannot do God, and are dependent on them in a practical way. Kafka remarked of this story, started—and never finished—not long before he died, that it was his *Bouvard et Pécuchet*, by which he must certainly have meant, not merely, as he said, that he thought it was a late work rather lacking in vitality, but also that it had something in common with Flaubert's most contemptuous indictment of the pettiness and ineptitude of the modern world. The sting of Kafka's story resides in the reluctance of the dogs to admit that they are in servitude to men—so that they have all entered into a conspiracy to conceal this fact from themselves, and even their boldest thinker cannot allow himself to find out the secret because it would rob him of his own self-respect. This is much less like an edifying allegory of the relations between God and man than like a Marxist-Flaubertian satire on the parasites of the bourgeoisie.

I do not deny that the enslaver, the master, is often given, in Kafka's stories, a serious theological meaning; but this side is never developed in anything like equal proportion to the ironical self-mocking side. Is the man condemned to death in *The Trial*, and finally convinced of his guilt for some crime which is never named, really either adapted or intended to illustrate Original Sin?—or is Kafka not rather satirizing the absurdities of his own bad conscience? In *The Castle*, there is also self-irony, but, besides this, a genuine wistfulness in K.'s longing to settle down and find a modest place in life for himself. But neither—unless one takes them as parodies of the Calvinist doctrine of Grace—seems to me to possess much interest as the expression of a religious point of view. The Christian of *Pilgrim's Progress* had obstacles to overcome and required moral fortitude to meet them; but all the struggling, such as it is, that is done by Kafka's K. is against an omnipotent and omniscient authority whose power and lights he can never share but to whose will he is doomed to succumb. And Dante, whose religious vision is all an exercise in control and direction, makes even his pagan Ulysses urge his men not to sleep before evening and tells them they were not made "to live like brutes but to follow virile courage and knowledge"; whereas Kafka is at his most characteristic when he is assimilating men to beasts—dogs, insects, mice and apes—which can neither dare nor know. On the other hand, for me, these stories too often forfeit their effectiveness as satires through Kafka's rather meaching compliance, his little-boylike respect and fear in the presence of the things he would satirize: the boring diligence of commercial activity, the stuffiness of middle-class family life, the arid reasonings and tyrannous rigidities of Orthodox Judaism (which have a good deal in common with those of our old-fashioned Puritan Protestantism).

If, however, one puts Kafka beside writers with whom he may properly be compared, he still seems rather unsatisfactory. Gogol and Poe were equally neurotic, in their destinies they were equally unhappy; and if it is true, as Mr. Savage says, that there is present in Kafka's world neither personality nor love, there is no love in either Gogol or Poe, and though there are plenty of personalities in Gogol, the actors of Poe, as a rule, are even less characterized than Kafka's. But, though the symbols that these writers generate are just as unpleasant as Kafka's, though, like his, they represent mostly the intense and painful realization of emotional culs-de-sac, yet they have both certain advantages over Kafka—for Gogol was nourished and fortified by his heroic conception of Russia, and Poe, for all his Tory views, is post-Revolutionary American in his challenging, defiant temper, his alert and curious mind. In their ways, they are both tonic. But the denationalized, discouraged, disaffected, disabled Kafka, though for the moment he may frighten or amuse us, can in the end only let us down. He is quite true to his time and place, but it is surely a time and place in which few of us will want to linger—whether as stunned and hypnotized helots of totalitarian states or as citizens of freer societies, who have relapsed into taking Kafka's stories as evidence that God's law and man's purpose are conceived in terms so different that we may as well give up hope of ever identifying the one with the other.

"One must not cheat anybody," says Kafka, in an aphorism which has been much applauded, "not even the world of its triumph." But what are we writers here for if it is not to cheat the world of its triumph? In Kafka's case, it was he who was cheated and never lived to get his own back. What he has left us is the half-expressed gasp of a self-doubting soul trampled under. I do not see how one can possibly take him for either a great artist or a moral guide.

July 26, 1947

Jean-Paul Sartre: The Novelist and the Existentialist

The Age of Reason is the first novel of Jean-Paul Sartre's to be translated into English. It is the first installment of a trilogy under the general title *The Roads to Freedom*, of which the second installment in translation has been announced for the fall. *The Age of Reason* deals with a group of young people in Paris—*lycée* teachers and students, Bohemians and night-club entertainers—in the summer of 1938. The second novel, *The Reprieve*, which has already appeared in French, carries the same characters along but works them into a more populous picture of what was going on in France during the days of the Munich Conference. The third volume, *The Last Chance*,* has not yet been published in French, so it is impossible at the present time to judge the work as a whole or even to know precisely what the author is aiming at.

The Age of Reason, however, stands by itself as a story. Sartre displays here the same skill at creating suspense and at manipulating the interactions of characters that we have already seen in his plays. His main theme is simply the odyssey of an ill-paid *lycée* teacher who does not want to marry his pregnant mistress and who is trying to raise the relatively large fee required for a competent abortion; but though the author makes this provide a long narrative, in which we follow the hero's every move and in which every conversation is reported in its banal entirety, he stimulates considerable excitement, holds our attention from beginning to end and engineers an unexpected dénouement which has both moral point and dramatic effectiveness. The incidents are mostly sordid, but, if you don't mind this, entertaining. The characters are well observed and conscientiously and intelligently studied, so that the book makes an interesting document on the quality and morale of the French just before their great capitulation. An American reader is struck by the close similarity of these young people,

*There are now to be four volumes instead of three. The third, *La Mort dans L'Âme*, has appeared in French. 1950.

with their irresponsible love affairs, their half-hearted intellectual allegiances and their long drinking conversations, to the same kind of men and girls at the same period in the United States—just as the novel has itself much in common with certain novels that these young people produced. I do not believe, however, that this is the result of imitation by Sartre of the contemporary American novelists whom he is known to admire so much. It is rather that such young people everywhere have come to be more alike, so that the originals for Sartre's Parisians must have been far less specifically Parisian than the Parisians of Balzac or Flaubert or Anatole France or Proust.

It is true, besides, that the writing of the book shows few of the traditional traits that we have been used to in French fiction. It tells the story with a "functional" efficiency, but it is colorless, relaxed, rather flat. It loses little in the English translation, not merely because the translator knows his business, but also because Sartre's style does not put upon him any very severe strain. The conversation is mainly conducted in a monotonous colloquialism of catch-words, where some expression like "*C'est marrant*" does duty for as many emotions as our own ever-recurring "terrific"; and for this Mr. Eric Sutton has been able to find a ready equivalent in a jargon basically British with a liberal admixture of Americanisms.

Of Sartre's imaginative work, I have read, besides this novel, only his plays and a few of his short stories. On this showing, I get the impression of a talent rather like that of John Steinbeck. Like Steinbeck, Sartre is a writer of undeniably exceptional gifts: on the one hand, a fluent inventor, who can always make something interesting happen, and, on the other, a serious student of life, with a good deal of public spirit. Yet he somehow does not seem quite first-rate. A play of Sartre's, for example, such as his recent *Morts sans Sépulture*—which is, I suppose, his best drama so far—affects me rather like *Grapes of Wrath*. Here he has exploited with both cleverness and conviction the ordeal of the French Resistance, as Steinbeck has done that of the sharecroppers; but what you get are a virtuosity of realism and a rhetoric of moral passion which make you feel not merely that the fiction is a dramatic heightening of life but that the literary fantasy takes place on a plane that does not have any real connection with the actual human experience which it is pretending to represent.

I have approached *The Age of Reason* purposely from the point of view of its merits as a novel without reference to the Existentialist philosophy of which Sartre is one of the principal exponents and which the story is supposed to embody. But, with the publication, also, of a translation of a lecture of Sartre's called *Existentialism* and a pamphlet called *What Is Existentialism?* by William Barrett, this demands consideration, too. It should, however, be said that neither of these discussions of the subject provides for the ordinary person the best possible key to Sartre's ideas. The Barrett essay, though very able, is mainly an exposition of the ideas of Martin Heidegger, a contemporary German philosopher, from whom Sartre took some of his prime assumptions, and it presupposes on the part of the reader a certain familiarity with the technical language of philosophy. The lecture by Sartre himself has the special object of defending Existentialism against charges which have been brought against it by the Communists, so that it emphasizes certain aspects of the theory without attempting to state its fundamental principles. It would have been well if the publisher had included a translation of the article called *Présentation*, in which Sartre explained his position in the first number of his magazine, *Les Temps Modernes* (October 1, 1945), and which gives the best popular account I have seen of what this literary school is up to. I can also recommend especially a short summary of the history of Existentialist thought and of its political and social implications— *Existentialism: A New Trend in Philosophy*—contributed by Paul Kecskemeti, a former U.P. foreign correspondent who is also a trained philosopher, to the March, 1947, issue of a magazine called *Modern Review* (published in New York by the American Labor Conference on International Affairs). This study has the unusual merit of not getting so deeply enmeshed in the metaphysical background of Existentialism that it fails to focus clearly on the picture of mankind on the earth which is the most important thing to grasp in a doctrine that is nothing if not realistic.

What is this picture, then? In Sartre's version—to skip alto-

gether the structure of philosophical reasoning on which it is
made to rest and which Sartre has set forth at length in a book
called *L'Etre et le Néant*—it places man in a world without
God (though not all Existentialists are atheists), in which all
the moral values are developed by man himself. Human nature
is not permanent and invariable: it is whatever man himself
makes it, and it changes from age to age. Man is free, beyond
certain limits, to choose what he is to be and do. His life has
significance solely in its relation to the lives of others—in his
actions or refrainings from action: to use a favorite phrase of
Sartre's, the individual must "engage himself."

Now, this conception of man's situation may appear to the
non-religious reader, if he has also the "historical" point of
view, precisely what he has always assumed, and may cause him
to conclude with surprise that he was already an Existentialist
without knowing it. To a Marxist, when he has further discovered that Sartre assigns human beings to the categories of
the social classes almost as relentlessly as Marx, it will be evident that Sartre has borrowed from Marxism, and he may ask
in what way Existentialism is an improvement over Marxism.
In a debate between Sartre and a Marxist, a record of which
follows the printed lecture, the Marxist actually scores rather
heavily. The one advantage, it seems to me, that the doctrine
of Sartre has is that it does away with Dialetical Materialism
and its disguised theological content. There is for Sartre no dialectical process which will carry you straight to salvation if
you get on the proletarian train. He sides with the proletariat,
but intellectual or proletarian has to put up his own battle,
with the odds looking rather against him. Yet Sartre does insist
like a Marxist that every member of modern society belongs to
a social class, and that "every one of his feelings, as well as
every other form of his psychological life, is revelatory of his
social situation." This molding of the individual by class—and
Sartre allows also for the effects of "origin," "milieu," nation-
ality and sexual constitution—produces the limitation on freedom which I mentioned in passing above. One finds oneself in
a situation which one did not make for oneself, but, given that
situation, one can choose various ways of behaving in it. The
bourgeois—with whom Sartre is particularly concerned—can
either go along with his class or rebel against it and try to get

away from it. The Marxist may inquire how this differs from the classical Marxist formulation that "men make their own history, but . . . do not choose the circumstances for themselves," and how Sartre's practical doctrine of man realizing himself through action differs from Marx's conception of testing our ideas through action. To the writer, the conception of a wholly free will seems as naïve as the contrary conception of a wholly mechanistic determinism, and it is surely hardly less naïve to declare, as Sartre appears to do, that we are determined up to a certain point, but that beyond that we can exercise choice. If Marx and Engels, in exploring these problems, are somewhat less schoolmasterishly clear than Sartre, they seem to me, in their tentative way, to give a more recognizable picture than he does of what happens when what we take for the will tries to act on what we take for the world, and of the relation between man and his environment.

But the Existentialist philosophy of Sartre is the reflection of a different age from that which stimulated the activist materialism of Marx, and it has the immense advantages of sincerity and human sympathy over the very peculiar version of Marxism, totalitarian and imperialistic, now exported by the Soviet Union. Let us see it in its historical setting. Mr. Kecskemeti has shown in his essay how the neo-Kantian idealism of the pre-1914 period in Germany, which "admirably expressed the average German's awe in the presence of every kind of expert and official," had to give way, after the first German defeat, which shook this faith in specialized authority, to an effort to find principles of morality in the study of human conduct itself. So, eventually, the Germans got Heidegger. In the same way, Kecskemeti says, the defeat of the French in 1940 deprived them of all they had leaned on: they had at one stroke lost both their great traditions—the tradition of the French Revolution, which collapsed with the Third Republic, and the monarchist-Catholic tradition, which, through Pétain, had sold them out to the invaders. It is characteristic of the French that the destruction of French institutions should have seemed to them a catastrophe as complete as the Flood and caused them to evolve a philosophy which assumes that the predicament of the patriotic Frenchmen oppressed by the German occupation represented the condition of all mankind. They felt imperatively the duty to resist, with no certainty of proving effective, and they had, as Albert Camus has said, to formulate for themselves a doctrine which would "reconcile negative thought and the possibility of affirmative action." Hence the emphasis on the individual—since the Resistance was always an effort of scattered men and women—so different from the emphasis of Marx on the importance of collective action at a time when a great working-class movement was looming and gathering strength. Hence, also, the suffocating atmosphere of corruption, degradation and depression which is a feature of Sartre's work and for which the French Communists, hopped up by the Kremlin to the cocksureness of propaganda, are in the habit of showering him with scorn. But such reproaches have no real validity, either artistic or moral: this atmosphere is Sartre's subject, and he has not allowed it to drug his intelligence or his conscience. It is the climate of the Occupation, and the chief literary achievement of Sartre is to have dramatized the moral poisoning of a France humiliated and helpless, in which people, brooding guiltily or blaming someone else, squabbled horribly, betrayed one another or performed acts of desperate heroism. For, says Sartre, though you cannot appeal to God, you have always a margin of freedom: you can submit, you can kill yourself or you can sell your life dear by resisting. Where this freedom is now to lead Frenchmen since the Germans have been driven out, I do not think that Sartre has yet made clear. Though anti-bourgeois and pro-working-class, he is evidently not an orthodox Communist of the kind who takes his directives from Moscow. One has a little the feeling about him that his basic point of view has been forged, as his material has been supplied, so completely under pressure of the pain and constraint of the collapse and the Occupation that he may never readapt himself to the temper of any new period.

And now how does *The Age of Reason* point the morals of Existentialist principles? Well, if you already know something of the subject, you will recognize some of its concepts turning up in the reflections of the hero as he drearily walks through the Paris streets. And the conflict of classes is there: a seceder from the bourgeoisie, we see this hero, Mathieu, revolving in a lonely orbit but experiencing gravitational pulls from a successful lawyer brother who represents the bourgeoisie, an old friend who has become a Communist and represents the proletariat, and a young girl of Russian émigré parents who represents the old nobility. It is not, however, this central character, so far as this volume takes him, who "engages himself" by a choice: his choices are all of the negative kind. It is the sexual invert Daniel, a neurotic and disconcerting personality, who, exercising free will, resists his suicidal impulses and performs, unexpectedly and for devious reasons, a responsible and morally positive act. Here the difficult "situation" is a matter not of social class but of biological dislocation; and the triumph of Daniel's decision is to be measured by the gravity of his handicap.

Yet it is difficult to see how *The Age of Reason* can have been very profoundly affected by Sartre's Existentialist theory. In such a production of his as his play *Les Mouches*, the dramatist turns academic and rather destroys the illusion by making the characters argue his doctrine; but this novel might perfectly have been written if Sartre had never worked up Existentialism. It does differ from the picture of life presented by the embittered French naturalists after the French defeat of 1871, whose characters were invariably seen as caught in traps of heredity and circumstance and rarely allowed to escape— though Sartre's mood, as in his play *A Huis Clos* (*No Exit*), is sometimes quite close to theirs. But this book does not essentially differ from the novels of other post-naturalistic writers, such as Malraux, Dos Passos and Hemingway, for whom the international socialist movement has opened a door to hope and provided a stimulus to action that were unknown to such a Frenchman as Maupassant or to the Americans who paralleled his pessimism. In Sartre, as in these other writers, you have a study of the mixture in man's nature of moral strength and weakness, and a conviction that, although the individual may not win the stakes he is playing for, his effort will not be lost.

Since *Partisan Review* has published, in the same series as Mr. Barrett's pamphlet, a translation of one of Sartre's long articles, *Portrait of the Anti-Semite*, one should say something about his activity as a journalist. These essays that he contributes to his *Temps Modernes* seem to me among the most interesting work of their kind that has appeared during the current slump in serious periodical writing. In this field, Sartre can be compared only with George Orwell in England; we have nobody so good over here. Mr. Barrett, in an article on Sartre, has complained that he ignores, in his *Portrait*, the Freudian springs of anti-Semitism. It is true that Sartre makes no attempt to explain this phenomenon historically in its political and social connections; but he does pursue with merciless insight at least one of the psychological factors involved: the need of small frustrated people to fake up some inalienable warrant for considering themselves superior to somebody. Sartre's whole essay, in fact, pretends to be nothing else than an elaborate development of this theme. It is no scientific inquiry but an exercise in classical irony, which might almost have been written, we reflect, by one of the more mordant eighteenth-century Encyclopedists. *The Age of Reason* of Sartre's novel is the intellectual maturity of the hero, but the phrase recalls also a period with which Sartre has a good deal in common. In penetrating these enormous editorials that mix comment on current affairs with a philosophy which, whatever its deficiencies, is always clearly and firmly expressed, we are surprised and reassured to find ourselves chewing on something which we might have feared the French had lost. For it is Sartre's great strength in his time that he has managed to remain quite uninfected by the Cocteau-esque Parisian chichi of the interval between the wars. If Existentialism has become, like surrealism, something of a *mouvement à exporter*, no one has probed so shrewdly as Sartre, in one of his articles in *Les Temps Modernes*, the recent attempts of the French to distract the attention of the world from their political and military discredit by exploiting the glory of their writers, or pointed out so boldly the abuses to which this practice may lead. If he sometimes has the air of pontificating, it is probably almost impossible for a French literary man whose influence is being felt to refrain from playing the role of *chef d'école*. And Sartre, bourgeois and provincial, has succeeded in preserving for the French qualities which they very much need and which it is cheering to see still flourish: an industry, an outspokenness and a common sense which are the virtues of a prosaic intelligence and a canny and practical character. This does not, perhaps, necessarily make Sartre a top-flight writer, but, in these articles of *Les Temps Modernes*, it does provide some very good reading.

August 2, 1947

The Musical Glasses of Peacock

Aᴎ ᴏᴍɴɪʙᴜs of Thomas Love Peacock, under the title *The Pleasures of Peacock*, has been brought out by a New York publisher. It is a good thing to have these novels reprinted, and Mr. Ben Ray Redman, who has edited the volume, contributes a well-informed introduction that touches briefly on almost every side of Peacock. But this book has what seems to me the serious defect of being mainly a collection of excerpts. Only two novels are given complete: *Nightmare Abbey* and *Crotchet Castle*. The other five appear merely in selections. Now, it is true that from one point of view Peacock lends himself easily to anthologizing: his plots are not usually important, and his narrative is a loose series of episodes. Yet each of his books as a whole shows the same delicate sense of form as each of the episodes and each of the sentences, and it is a pity to take them to pieces—especially since they are all so short that it was possible, in a thin-paper edition published some years ago, to include the complete novels in one pocket-size volume. It is also rather unfair, it seems to me, to shear off, as Mr. Redman has done, all the quotations that head Peacock's chapters, and to trim away a part of his learned notes. The main text can stand without them, but they do represent the soil out of which that text has grown and help to situate Peacock's mood in an early-nineteenth-century library, where the Greek and Latin classics are mingled with Italian light comedies and the wild folk ballads of Wales. Surely anyone who can care for Peacock would prefer to have him intact.

The Pleasures of Peacock, however, serve to remind us, in any case, of a very fine writer and to offer a pretext for talking about him. We have already seen one revival of Peacock—during the twenties, when J. B. Priestley did a book about him and when Aldous Huxley gave him some vogue by deliberately imitating him. The element that Huxley exploited was the characteristic Peacock symposium: the conversation in a country house, with much passing of port and claret, among highly intellectual guests, each of whom appears as the exponent of some current tendency or doctrine reduced to its simplest terms and carried to its most absurd lengths. This is the critical side of Peacock, for which he is now perhaps most famous because Huxley has seized upon it, injected into it moral earnestness and transposed it into a peevish key. But it is by no means the whole of Peacock, as one can see by comparing him and Huxley. With the later as with the earlier writer, the opinions of the various philosophers more or less cancel one another out; but for Huxley this leads to bitterness and a demand for religious certainties, whereas in Peacock it leads to a final drink and a song in which everyone joins. And this fencing by Peacock's cranks with rigid contradictory ideas—excellent sometimes, of course, but not always remarkably clever—is hardly enough to have preserved him so long. What is it, then, that makes Peacock live? Why is it that Mr. Redman believes that we can still enjoy reading his novels?

Another critic, Mr. Ronald Mason, asked this question three years ago in the English review *Horizon*, and, after discounting almost every source of interest that one may expect to find in a novel, came to the conclusion that Peacock's strength lay mainly in his firmness as a nipper of extremes and in his admirable prose style. Both these merits Peacock certainly had. It was a godsend that in the early nineteenth century, with its seraphic utopianisms, its attitudinizing anti-social romanticisms and its cannibalistic materialisms, one man who had the intelligence to understand and the aesthetic sensibility to appreciate the new movements and the new techniques that were going to people's heads, should have been able to apply to their extravagances a kind of classical common sense; and Peacock's value, as Mr. Mason suggests, should by no means be less today, at a time when extreme ideas are being violently put into practice. As for his style: to the mature reader, whom mere sonority and movement and color do not intoxicate as they did in youth, it seems one of the best in English. Light, lucid, neat and dry, it is as far from the prose of his own period, mossily clogged or grassily luxuriating, as from the showy upholstery of the later age. It redeems him from insipidity at the moments when he is running thinnest; it gives charm to his most telling jokes by slipping them in with a minimum of emphasis. "Nothing superfluous and nothing wanting" was the comment of India House on the papers that won Peacock his job there. If one compares him, particularly, with Thackeray, who liked his work and who is sometimes praised for qualities similar to his, one is struck by the relative coarseness of the texture of the Victorian's writing, with its dilutions and its repetitions, and by the relative commonplaceness of his mind, with its worldly preoccupations and its embarrassing exhibitions of benevolence. When we come to Peacock from this, we are aware of his restraint and distinction, of the spareness and sureness of the pencil which he uses for his prose line-drawings.

This brings us to an aspect of Peacock which Mr. Mason leaves out of account. The fact that Peacock's *imagination* is not vigorous, varied or rich has, I believe, rather kept people from realizing how exquisite his effects sometimes are. It is usual to treat him as a satirist whose power is more or less weakened by his scoring off both sides of every question; but the truth is that Peacock is an artist the aim of whose art is to achieve not merely a weaving of ideas but also an atmosphere —an aroma, a flavor, a harmony. You get closer to what Peacock is trying to do by approaching him through his admiration for Mozart—"There is," he wrote, "nothing perfect in this world except Mozart's music"—than by assimilating him to Lucian or Voltaire. His books are more like light operas than novels (it was quite natural that *Maid Marian* should have been made into one) and the elements of fantasy with which they play—the civilized orangutan of *Melincourt*, who is chivalrous with the ladies, the seven lovely maidens of *Gryll Grange* who keep house for the young man in the tower—as well as the landscapes of mountain streams, the drives and rides in the New Forest, the boating and skating parties, are as important as the conversations. It all makes a delicious music, at the same time sober and gay, in which the words fall like notes from a flute, like progressions on an old-fashioned pianoforte, lighted by slim white candles. In *Gryll Grange*, when we come to the snowstorm, we almost have the illusion that these pale and sifted words of Peacock's are dropping on the page like snowflakes and that they melt away as we read. Even the openings of Peacock's unfinished novels—so sure is his touch on the keyboard to convey us at once to his realm—may be enjoyed as little works in themselves, like the "preludes" of Debussy or Chopin.

It seems to me, too, that the nonchalance of Peacock in dealing with political and moral systems has been given a wrong meaning by his critics—for he is always, in some way, on the *human* side, and he shared the generous ideas of the romantic and utopian generation to an extent that his conservative encomiasts are sometimes reluctant to recognize. I have a suspicion that the relative indifference of the typical Peacockian to *Melincourt* may be partly due to the fact that the hero of this early novel gives expression to such ideas with an eloquence which can almost be called glowing and which suggests real conviction on Peacock's part. The book does go on a little too long, for Peacock has not yet quite found his form; but it is certainly one of his best—with its gentleman anthropoid, its beautiful blue-stocking oread, its forthright and very funny satire on rotten-borough politics and the publishing business, and its admirable discussion, at the end, under the title *The Hopes of the World*, of the future of civilization. Mr. Redman could not have remembered *Melincourt* when he wrote in his introduction in such a way as to give the impression that Peacock's friendship with Shelley is only to be explained on the ground of the attraction of opposites. The creator of the Rousseauist Mr. Forester had no difficulty in sympathizing with the poet's utopian yearnings toward a happier and freer society. It was only that he could not help kidding his friend in the skit of *Nightmare Abbey*—the dry diagnosis of which is a corrective to more impassioned portraits —for the self-delusions of Shelley in his childish relations with women; and that the cool human sympathy I have spoken of compelled him to defend Harriet—in his *Memoirs of Percy Bysshe Shelley*—against the slanders of the Shelley-worshippers.

The mountain-loving Anthelia of *Melincourt* is one of Peacock's most attractive versions of his ideal young Englishwoman—always a strongly positive element in his stories. These girls of his—frank, independent, brave, intelligent and rather intellectual—stand somewhere between the heroines of Shelley and the heroines of Jane Austen. I find them a great deal more attractive, as well as a great deal more convincing, than the women of Victorian fiction. That these latter could not have been found particularly sympathetic by Peacock may be concluded from the unfinished *Cotswold Chace*, in which he is careful to explain that his heroine "wears no crinoline, and, if I might venture to divine, no stays." It is obvious that Peacock's young girls—witty, athletic and fresh—are the mothers of the anti-Victorian goddesses of his son-in-law George Meredith's novels.

The later Peacock was less interested in reformers, less "progressive" and less optimistic. But it is true, as Mr. Redman reminds us, that he had already in the sixties lived long enough to see a great many reforms accomplished but life rendered rather less agreeable than it had been in the early years of the century, and to foresee the mechanical developments— prophesied in *Gryll Grange*—which were to increase men's productive powers and at the same time to reduce them to bondage. When he had retired from his job at India House, he took his family to live in the country, where he spent most of his time with books—though he liked to go to visit Lord Broughton, who, as John Hobhouse, had been Byron's friend and who could give Peacock the good entertainment and the free-ranging conversation with which he had filled his novels. Thackeray met Peacock once in 1850 and called him "a white-headed jolly old worldling"; but he was never really a Thackeray character. He was not worldly in Thackeray's sense. The world he loved was the world of his library—to which he fled when, at the age of eighty, he was warned that the house was on fire, declaring, when they tried to get him out: "By the immortal gods, I will not move!" He was upset when his favorite daughter, who had been educated, on the model of his heroines, both in literature and in outdoor sports and who is said to have been both brilliant and beautiful, married the young George Meredith. Meredith wore a beard, which Peacock could not abide; and, though the young man respected his father-in-law and was influenced in his own work by Peacock's, his ardors, energetic and uneasy, annoyed the old man and made him nervous. It was quite a different thing from Shelley.

Nor did Meredith and his bride get along together. They were both sharp-tongued and self-willed, and they had very little money to live on. They tormented one another unbearably. Mary Meredith, at the end of nine years, ran away to

Capri with another man, but soon came back to die in England. Peacock, then seventy-nine, did not go to her funeral, but he composed for her an epitaph in Latin and Greek, which was never inscribed on her grave. Meredith published soon after, as a commentary on his tragic marriage, the great sequence of sonnets called *Modern Love*, full of self-probings and passionate frustrations of a kind that must have been inconceivable to Peacock; and when one glances back on this mid-century Peacock from the point of view of *Modern Love*, one seems to see an old man in a bottle, whose unshakable poise and calm depend on his not coming out.

For when we look back on Peacock from Meredith's time instead of seeing him in the dawn of the century, he seems to us less mobile and cooler. Peacock's father was a dealer in glassware, and there is sometimes a glint of glassware in the clear, sound and smooth work of Peacock. The editors of the Halliford Edition of Peacock have included in his last novel, *Gryll Grange*, a peculiarly appropriate frontispiece which shows a spun-glass bust of Homer that Peacock had hung in his library. It makes us reflect that the classics in Peacock's hands do a little take on the aspect of having been deftly spun into glass; and his own work may look to us at moments like a fine antique sideboard display, with rows of graceful flower-calyxed goblets all ready for the very best wine—which you will have to buy from somebody else: somebody like Meredith or Shelley. In the meantime, however, Peacock can elicit from them a very pretty music by delicately moistening the rims and rubbing them with the tips of his fingers.

August 23, 1947

Edith Wharton: A Memoir by
an English Friend

Portrait of Edith Wharton, by Percy Lubbock, will be read with fascination by anyone interested in its subject. It is the first important memoir of the novelist that has been published since her death; and it is a literary performance of some distinction—not the usual sketch by a friend, but a real portrait, carefully composed with every brush-stroke studied. The book is, in fact, so very much "written" that the writing sometimes has the effect of obscuring the actualities which the author is trying to describe. Mr. Lubbock, who edited Henry James's letters, is one of James's most faithful disciples, and he here follows the Jamesian procedure of writing around his subject instead of showing it to us directly. He prefers to adumbrate Mrs. Wharton with metaphors or to generalize about her with abstractions rather than tell you what she said and did, how she looked and what she wore; and the result is that we seem to be gazing at her through a kind of sea-mist that never clears and through which we can make out her movements and shape but are unable to scrutinize her features. It is a pleasure to read prose so well worked, in the sense that a tapestry is worked, but, like a tapestry, the book presents a series of somewhat conventionally posed tableaux—Edith Wharton just arrived in England, Edith Wharton in her household in the Faubourg St. Germain, Edith Wharton in Morocco, etc.—which rather lack depth and detail.

The concrete questions that one would have to have answered in order to understand Edith Wharton's career are mostly either ignored or evaded by Mr. Lubbock. Mrs. Wharton was always quite rich. Where did her money come from? Was it her own or was it her husband's? And why did she marry Edward Wharton, with whom she obviously had little in common and was not very much in love? What, precisely, was the matter with him when he became deranged and Mrs. Wharton finally divorced him? Mr. Lubbock tries to put their relationship in as attractive a light as possible, but then he later speaks of Walter Berry, the American lawyer in Paris with whom Edith Wharton's name has always been associated, as "the man she had loved for a lifetime, in youth and age." To what kind of situation had this given rise? There is a legend that Edith Jones's first love was broken up by her mother, who disapproved of it and sent her abroad; and that her first book of poems, which she had secretly had printed, was discovered and destroyed by her family. Is it true? And is it true that she began writing fiction, some years after her marriage, as the result of a nervous breakdown at the suggestion of S. Weir Mitchell, the novelist and neurologist? It has been asserted by persons who should be in a position to know that Edith Wharton had some reason for believing herself to have been an illegitimate child and that her family rather let her down from the point of view of social backing—which would account for the curiously perfunctory, idyllic and unreal way in which she writes of her parents in *A Backward Glance*, as contrasted with her bitter picture, in her novels of old New York, of the cruelty of social convention and the tyranny of the family group, as well as for her preoccupation with the miseries of extramarital love affairs and the problems of young women who have to think about marrying for money and position. The last of these themes, especially—exploited so successfully in *The House of Mirth*—is difficult to account for on the basis of Edith Wharton's being simply the well-born Miss Jones, as is, perhaps, that insistence on her social prerogatives which many who knew her, including Mr. Lubbock, found unnecessary and exaggerated. Of all the conflicts of purpose and the stifled emotions that are expressed in Mrs. Wharton's books, you will find little trace in the figure presented by Mr. Lubbock. Here she is always seen as the hostess or the traveller *de grand luxe*. He intimates that her love for Berry was the source of a good deal of unhappiness, that her perfectly appointed houses and her retinue of clever guests still left her unsatisfied, that her going to live in Europe and breaking her ties with America were a misfortune for her art and her life, and uneasily felt by her as such. But he fails to explain a career which has always appeared rather freakish. The vexed and aggrieved spirit that wrote Edith Wharton's best novels has no part in Mr. Lubbock's portrait, and the novels themselves—for reasons which

Mr. Lubbock does not quite make clear—are mentioned only incidentally.

Mr. Lubbock, however, is not to be blamed. Since he was an old and intimate friend, it was probably impossible for him to go behind his subject's façade less discreetly than he has done; and the fact that he is an Englishman—he has apparently never been in the United States—makes it difficult for him to understand the background and the significance of Edith Wharton's work. What we get from him is a pretty full account of how she behaved in Europe and how she seemed to Europeans. He has added to those we already have a new picture of the literary group—which comes to seem more important as time goes on—that centered around Mrs. Wharton, Henry James and Howard Sturgis, the Anglicized American who wrote *Belchamber*. And he has supplemented his own impressions with those of various other friends, American, English and French, which Mr. Gaillard Lapsley, Edith Wharton's literary executor, has persuaded them to write down at length.

But the American end of the story is largely left a blank. You cannot even see the "port of New York"—it lies beyond the Atlantic and Mr. Lubbock's vision—where Edith Wharton was born, which did as much to mold her mind as Europe (it is precisely one of the functions of Manhattan to blend and to concentrate the influences of the rest of the world), and which—in her sharpness and smartness, her efficiency, her glitter and her cruelty—she so brilliantly reflected in her work. Mr. Lubbock, in his ignorance of America, has made several glaring blunders. When he comes to do a kindly little sketch of the history of American fiction up to what he calls "the uproarious Boston tea party" of the movement that came of age in the twenties, he describes it as if it mainly consisted of or were adequately represented by Hawthorne, Howells and James—a "procession . . . united in their order for all their disparity, marching in honor and sobriety," of which Edith Wharton brings up the rear. Not to attempt to supply the deficiencies of Mr. Lubbock's picture, I will point out that Mrs. Wharton was as much a contributor to the realism of the age that followed hers as she was an inheritor from James, and that a book like *The Custom of the Country* opened the way for novels like *Babbitt* and *Manhattan Transfer*. What she did that these older American writers mentioned by Mr. Lubbock had hardly attempted at all, but that the later writers made their chief business, was draw up a terrific indictment against the new America of money values that, swelling to monstrous proportions during the years after the Civil War, confronted the world at the end of the century. Nor is it true, as Mr. Lubbock asserts, that this later group of writers "cast overboard the wares of the old world," whereas all the earlier ones had been "still of Europe in their art, and in much more than their art, in the climate of their culture, in the style and habit of their thought." Lewis, Dos Passos, Faulkner and Hemingway have obviously owed as much to European writers and European travel as Hawthorne and Howells had done, and if the stories of Sherwood Anderson grew up, like the native grass, without any foreign fertilizer, so had those of Mark Twain, who belonged to the Howells era.

Another error of Mr. Lubbock's appears in connection with his attitude toward Edith Wharton's heroes. We can agree with him that many of these heroes must have been inspired by Walter Berry, and we lack evidence to dispute his contention that Edith Wharton's closest male friend was dry, empty-hearted and worldly, a pretentious and unlikable snob. We certainly get the impression that Mr. Lubbock has a grudge against Berry for encouraging Edith Wharton in her skepticism about religion, and that he would like to believe that, without him, she might at last have accepted the Catholic faith. In any case, Mr. Lubbock believes that Walter Berry, to whom Edith Wharton showed all her work and who sat in judgment on it, was responsible for some of its faults. But he is certainly mistaken in supposing that Mrs. Wharton idealized uncritically those of her characters who were based on Berry. On the contrary, the male type which most conspicuously recurs in her novels is the cultivated intelligent man who cannot bear to offend social convention, the reformer who gets bribed without knowing it in marrying a rich wife, the family man who falls in love with someone more exciting than his wife but doesn't have the courage of his passion; and the treatment of these characters by the author, though outwardly sympathetic, is always well chilled with an irony that has an undercurrent of scorn. It is a phenomenon unfamiliar to Europe, this connoisseur whose culture is sterile, this idealist whose impulses are thwarted, this romantic who cannot act his romance, because, in every one of these roles, he is made helpless by a commercial civilization. But Edith Wharton knew him well, and she never ceased to resent him because he had failed to stand up to the temptations and threats of that civilization and because he had not been strong enough to save from that moneyed world, in which it was even easier for a woman than for a man to be caught, a woman, courageous herself, whom he might have, whom he should have, loved.

Certainly the question of money had been and always remained extremely important for Edith Wharton. Her work is the record of a struggle between wealth and its advantages, on the one hand, and aesthetic and moral values, on the other. (The fortunes of her family, Mr. Lubbock implies, was derived from New York real estate, and insofar as she was dependent on this, she must have found herself in the situation of owing her standard of living to the very extravagances of the speculative and vulgar society which she was constantly castigating.) And for this reason, if her life is to be understood, the facts about it should be brought to light. Her work, I believe, has never been—and was not, even at the time of her greatest success—appreciated or interpreted as it should be; and it is possible that her personal history, which now appears merely puzzling, would provide a dramatic illustration of the tragedy often incurred and the heroism sometimes engendered by a period of American life which imposed upon human beings peculiar and extreme conditions. The papers of Edith Wharton now deposited in the Yale University Library are not, I understand, to be published before 1967, but we may hope to have eventually a biography that will tell the whole of her story and show her in her full dimensions.

October 4, 1947

The Sanctity of Baudelaire

A TRANSLATION by Christopher Isherwood of Baudelaire's *Intimate Journals* was published in England in 1930, with an introduction by T. S. Eliot. It has now been brought out here for the first time, in a somewhat revised text and with an introduction by W. H. Auden instead of the one by Eliot, which in the meantime had been included in the volume of the latter's *Selected Essays* and become one of the principal stimuli for the recent vogue of Baudelaire.

When I speak of Baudelaire's "recent vogue," I do not, of course, mean to imply that his reputation has at any time seriously declined. Baudelaire was one of the greatest of French poets, and has been recognized as such by writers of all periods and many schools. But during the last fifteen years or so, he has been pressed into service by certain elements in the literary world who want to claim him for their own cause, and his career has been shown in a light which falsifies the meaning of his work. Messrs. Eliot, Auden and Isherwood are all, in their several ways, active champions of Christian doctrine. In times of disillusion with politics, it is usual to find a retreat in the direction of traditional religion, and that is what we have been getting lately. Now, Baudelaire, after his exploit of 1848, when he leapt on the barricades and shouted "Down with General Aupick!" (his stepfather), became cynical enough about politics. But this is not enough for Eliot and Auden and Isherwood: they want to have him a good Catholic, too. Eliot and Auden both have attached tremendous importance to the last disjointed entries in his journals, written four or five years before Baudelaire died, in which he alternates programs of diet with desperate expressions of piety. These were dictated, Auden believes, by a "real change of heart." Baudelaire was suffering at the time from the penultimate stage of syphilis. "I have," he wrote at this time, "cultivated my hysteria with delight and terror . . . and today I have received a singular warning. I have felt the wind of the wing of madness pass over me." "To the eye of nature," says Auden, his repentance "was too late. As he spoke, the bird swooped and struck. But, to the eye of the spirit, we are entitled to believe he was in time—for, though the spirit needs time, an instant of it is enough."

But Baudelaire's great book *Les Fleurs du Mal*, the work by which he is known, had been published years before, and, though its poems in praise of Satan and of Peter's denial of Christ are occasionally set off by the brusque descent of disciplinary angels and by favorable references to Jesus, it is hardly a work of piety. I agree with Anatole France (whose critical point of view has become so unfashionable in the present day, with the dogmatisms of unsure people) that "Baudelaire is a very bad Christian. He loves sin and deliciously savors the feeling that he is lost to God. He knows that he is being damned, and thereby he renders to the divine wisdom a tribute which will be counted to him for righteousness, but he is intoxicated by the idea of damnation and his appetite for women goes no further than what is necessary to guarantee that he has definitely forfeited his soul." (So Baudelaire writes in these journals: "For my part, I say: the sole and supreme pleasure in Love lies in the absolute knowledge of doing *evil*. And men and women know, from birth, that in Evil is to be found all voluptuousness.") His references to God, says France, were stimulated by egoism. "In his arrogance he wished to believe that everything he did was important, even his little impurities; so that he wanted them all to be sins that would interest heaven and hell. But at bottom he had only a half-faith. His spirit alone was Christian. His heart and his mind remained empty."

The puritanical side of the Catholic Church had evidently combined with an Oedipus complex to produce in Baudelaire his curious view of love. Is it possible to show that religion contributed much else to his work? He had some sympathy of fellow-feeling for the poor and the ignored and the ill. Yet it is characteristic of him that when he writes his memorable poem about the "bighearted servant" of whom he had been jealous in childhood, he imagines her returning from the grave to weep over his fallen state. This is moving; but so is his satanic pride, and there is a good deal more pride in him than pity. Baudelaire is one of the great modern poets, as Eliot and Auden themselves are poets of at least the first rank. Eliot, in *Ash Wednesday*, can move us when his weakness and chagrin tremble into the accents of prayer; Auden, in his *Christmas Oratorio*, can move us with the spectacle of Joseph and Mary staggered by an Annunciation which seems to be breaking the news of the arrival of a difficult and topflight poet. But are such things as these religion? Are Baudelaire's angels religion? Aren't they rather the literary devices of uncomfortable rationalists who, disgusted by the dullness of democracy, the vulgarity of revolution, have resorted for protection against them to the mythology and animism of childhood? When Baudelaire prayed to Poe (not remarkable for his Christian feeling and rather perfunctory about his faith), as he did in the last entry of his journal; when Eliot and Auden and Isherwood invoke the example of Baudelaire, they are appealing to a passion for literature which has managed to burn pure and intense through suffering and degradation. But what has this to do with the Christian cults for whose rites the churches are built and the parsons and priests ordained?

November 1, 1947

Van Wyck Brooks on the Civil War Period

The Times of Melville and Whitman is the fourth volume in order of appearance in Van Wyck Brooks's history of American literature, but in the chronology of the series it takes its place between the two New England volumes, *The Flowering of New England* and *New England: Indian Summer.* It is not quite so exciting, perhaps, as the volume published just before (chronologically, the first of the series), *The World of Washington Irving*, which revived the intellectual ferment of the period just after the Revolution, but it is distinguished by the same kind of qualities. These two volumes which do not deal with New England seem to me to have a freedom of movement and an exhilaration of spirit, as well as a brilliance of writing, that the New England volumes, remarkable though they are, do not display to the same degree. This is partly because Mr. Brooks has been growing more and more adept and partly because his story in these later-written installments ranges more widely and becomes more varied; but it is also, I believe, partly because the author, being himself a New Yorker, does better when he gets away from New England.

There has always been in American literature a New York tradition as well as a New England one, but it has never been so much talked about precisely because it is less provincial. The New Yorkers, all facing, as it were, in the direction of the mouth of the Hudson, have more easily passed out into the larger world, and the great city in which they have all sojourned has been cosmopolitan and always changing. The New Englanders of the classical generation did derive a certain strength from their relation to small strongly-rooted communities— Cambridge, Concord, Beacon Hill, etc.—but they suffered from the crampedness of these places. The New Yorkers— Irving, Cooper, Melville, Whitman, the Jameses, Edith Wharton, Stephen Crane, John Jay Chapman, Van Wyck Brooks himself—are all men or women of the world in a way that no New Englander is, and they have, most of them, a sense of the country as a whole such as few New Englanders have had. (If one is going in for regional competition, the New Yorkers stand up very well beside Emerson, Hawthorne and Thoreau, the only first-rate New Englanders of the classical age; and they outshine the later New Englanders, from Henry Adams to E. A. Robinson, who mostly did not live in New England.)

This volume of Brooks's history, at any rate, unrolls a lively panorama of the filling-out of the continent between the middle of the century and the eighties. It extends a whole network of literary lines through the South, the Middle West and the Far West, each pegged here and there with the colored pin of some writer of particular note—though a map does not give quite the right metaphor, since the trail is always represented with the scenery, the people, the kinds of life, that the traveller himself saw: Miss Murfree's Tennessee mountaineers, the Illinois and Indiana towns of Joseph Kirkland and Edward Eggleston, the frozen Sierras of John Muir, the stagecoaches, miners and gamblers of Bret Harte and Mark Twain. And you have, also, the long voyages of Melville and the extraordinary wanderings as a folklorist among the American Indians, the European gypsies and the Etruscan Romagnoli of the forgotten Charles Godfrey Leland, one of Mr. Brooks's *trouvailles*. The fluent presentation of all this—which accommodates so much information and keeps straight so many intertwined destinies —is a triumph of the flexibility that Mr. Brooks has developed in applying his method; and these summaries of individual careers are accompanied by the usual formulations, perhaps the most valuable part of the history, of insights into cultural phenomena: the swift fading-out in the South, with the ascendancy of the "cotton snobs," of the Jeffersonian taste and enlightenment, leaving literature in complete discredit and publishing subjected to a censorship imposed by the slaveholding interests in a society without even the town records, without even the private diaries that might allow the nostalgic novelists of the period after the Southern defeat to reconstruct the good old days; the influence of periodical journalism on American writing in general at the time when Stedman wrote that "the worlds before and after the Deluge were not more different than our republics of letters before and after the late war" and that "for ten years the younger generation" had "read nothing but newspapers"; the going-underground, at this time, of our more serious writers for the purpose of escaping the oppression of the twin tyrants of vulgarity and gentility that were established during the reign of commercialism (a tendency which was carried to extreme lengths in Emily Dickinson's secret poems and Henry Adams' unsigned or unpublished writings but which had already manifested itself in the later careers of Whitman and Melville, when the former, retired to Camden, was a prophet without honor and a scandal, and the latter, after the first success of his South Sea island books, had passed into an eclipse so complete that, though he was still alive and writing at the time when Robert Buchanan visited New York in 1885, this English admirer of Melville was unable to find out where he lived); the cult of the common man, to which both Whitman and Melville were dedicated, and the rift between rich and poor, which, widening as the century wore on, was felt to be un-American by the writers of the older generation—with the beginnings in 1861, in the work of Rebecca Harding Davis, of a new kind of realism in fiction dealing with industrial life—the conditions of which, as she said, had an "awful significance we do not see."

What is treated here least satisfactorily—though its effects are thus to some extent allowed for—is the Civil War itself, which, in breaking and embittering the South, in inflating and corrupting the North, left the American republican idealism in a wrecked and demoralized state, dislocating the points of view of writers, Northern and Southern alike, whose training had prepared them for a different kind of world from that with which they were later confronted. Mr. Brooks has shown admirably in Whitman's case his growing dismay and doubt as he lived on after those years of the war that had "trembled and reeled" beneath him; but he is diverted by the scheme of his work from featuring the war as the crisis it was in the development of American society. One feels guilty in complaining at one's ease of a scheme which has enabled the historian to organize so large a body of various and tangled material, but one comes to regret more and more some of the results of his having decided to make two volumes center about New England. For one thing, this has led him to attach to New England, and thus remove from their true frame of reference, writers like Henry James and W. D. Howells whose connection with New England was incidental or who, like Henry

Adams, though born in New England of New England stock, had their real careers somewhere else; and it has also involved him in the awkwardness of covering the war in two different volumes, so that the lives of a Northerner like John De Forest, a Westerner like Ambrose Bierce and a Southerner like Sidney Lanier cannot be considered together in relation to their experience as soldiers; nor can the simultaneous disillusionments with democratic civilization of Henry Adams, of Henry James and of Mark Twain be easily seen as cases of a general shrinking and chill on the part of American idealism.

Another unsatisfactory feature of *The Times of Melville and Whitman* is the discussion of Melville himself. One feels here, too, a certain diffidence about criticizing so large a work, which, in accepting deliberate limitations, has so splendidly justified itself. It has, of course, been one of the conditions of carrying out the program at all that the historian should not treat too elaborately or explore with too much curiosity even the most important or interesting of his individual subjects. Mr. Brooks has handled some difficult cases—Poe in the preceding volume, Whitman and Mark Twain in this—with an intelligence and an expert tact that have managed to summarize these writers without oversimplification, touching on every aspect of their work (he is particularly good with Whitman, who has always been one of his admirations). But in the case of Herman Melville, he seems never to have got into his subject. The situation here is worse even than it was in his treatment of Henry James, for there were certain sides of James that he understood, whereas it can almost be said that he simply passes Melville by—or at least that he sees him only in relation to the national idealism. At the end of the previous volume, the historian told us quite truly that "with Poe another age had opened—intenser, profounder than this" (that is, than Irving's age); but the depths and intensity of Melville, which are surely the most obvious examples of this, he skims over with less insight than he had for Poe's, and when we discover that he has here devoted about the same amount of space to Melville that he had, in the New England volumes, to Oliver Wendell Holmes, we feel that he has let us down. It is possible to agree with Mr. Brooks that Melville did somehow fail to live out his career as a writer, that he always remained something of an amateur; but one cannot admit the implications of Mr. Brooks's theoretical questions as to whether Melville's short stories, "after all . . . would have been recalled at all" if he had not written *Moby Dick* and the three or four books of travel that appeared before it, and as to whether his "metaphysical cogitations . . . were in reality of greater moment than the thoughts of a hundred other men who were obsessed at the time with the conflict of religion and science." Mr. Brooks speaks respectfully of *Moby Dick*, but he sidesteps a real discussion of it in a sentence beginning as follows: "Aside from the innermost meaning of the book—and this seemed clear enough—with what an astonishing skill he sustained the mood"; yet one cannot find out from his chapters on Melville what he supposes this clear meaning to be. The systole and diastole of Melville, the alternations of attraction and repulsion, of ecstatic rapture and horror, that supply the dark fable of *Benito Cereno* as well as that of *Moby Dick*, do not pulse in Mr. Brooks's pages.

Mr. Brooks's *The Ordeal of Mark Twain*, published now twenty-seven years ago, was one of the best of his books. Here he studied Mark Twain in his origins, in his family relations and in his relations with his public, and produced in its tragic closing pages one of the great passages of the American prose-writing of our period—a passionate peroration, which must have set up responsive vibrations in many young American writers who read it. Now, if any American of genius ever went through an ordeal, it was Melville. Precisely what this ordeal consisted of has never, so far as I know, been investigated, and one would have thought that Van Wyck Brooks would have been just the man to do it. But nothing could be further from his procedure with Mark Twain than his way of approaching Melville. He barely mentions Melville's family and marriage, which would make, one imagines, in connection with his wanderings, a gloomy but significant story; and, although Mr. Brooks sticks here to his original version of Mark Twain's career, it is curious to see him resorting to a superficial explanation for Melville's feeling, after writing *Pierre*, that the "thews of a Titan" had been cut in him: simply eyestrain and overwork and a fire at Harper's that destroyed the plates and most of the stock of his books—an explanation that has a disconcerting resemblance to that put forward by Bernard De Voto, Mr. Brooks's implacable antagonist, as an alternative explanation to Brooks's for the pessimism of Mark Twain's later years: simply the failure of Mark Twain's speculations following his early success.

It is the stress of the period one misses. This was the moment of bankruptcies and wounds, of miscarriages, distortions, frustrations. Even the life of a second-rank writer like Cable, homeless between South and North, has an element of strain and waste that does not come through in Mr. Brooks's account of him. If one thinks of it from this point of view, *The Times of Melville and Whitman* seems a little too even and cheerful. But if one thinks of it from the point of view of the distance that Mr. Brooks has already come and the energy he must already have expended, one is amazed that he has still so much to give, that he can still deal so freshly and vividly with so many kinds of subjects, that, at the end of two thousand pages, he is still exerting his spell.

November 29, 1947

An Analysis of Max Beerbohm

THIS reviewer is a little late in getting around to Max Beerbohm's *Mainly on the Air*, which was brought out as long ago as last year; but it may be pleaded that the book itself is not strictly up to date, containing as it does three pieces that first appeared in the early twenties and two that have been published before in earlier volumes of Max's essays. The other pieces, with one or two exceptions, are not—agreeable reading though they make—quite of the author's best. About half of the thin book is made up of B.B.C. broadcasts—three from the thirties, three from the forties—which deal mainly with the London of Max Beerbohm's youth (music halls, glimpses of Gladstone, the old quiet London squares), and most of the non-broadcast pieces are in a similar mild reminiscent vein (top hats and Charterhouse school-days). So the occasion, not important in itself, may conveniently serve as a pretext for a general discussion of the author.

The book has been already so used by Mr. Louis Kronenberger in an admirable little essay called *The Perfect Trifler*, in the *Saturday Review of Literature*. Mr. Kronenberger begins by assuming that Max is already a classic, and he tries to discriminate the qualities that are likely to ensure his permanence. I agree with Mr. Kronenberger that Max Beerbohm is likely to be read much longer than certain of his British contemporaries who at one time attracted as much attention. Chesterton and Belloc, for example, seem today merely literary journalists advertising their barbarous prejudices with the rattle of a coarse verbal cleverness. Their prose is unreadable now, when Max Beerbohm's seems even better than it did when it first appeared. Though I am not much given to rereading books, I have often reread Max Beerbohm, and my respect for his writing has immensely increased since the early nineteen-hundreds, when it was natural to see him as a mere minor sparkler suspended in rather an anomalous position between the constellation of Wilde, Beardsley, Whistler, the *Yellow Book* and the Rhymers' Club, and that of Shaw, Bennett, Wells, Chesterton, Galsworthy and Barrie. But for an expert appreciation of his writing, I refer you to Mr. Kronenberger. What I want to try to do here is go a little behind Max's engaging mask and analyze the point of view which gets expression in his writings and his caricatures, and which it seems to me that Mr. Kronenberger has made to look somewhat simpler than it is.

The truth is that Max is quite complex, and that complexity and the intelligence it generates are what—given his double talent, a complexity in itself—have made him interesting beyond what one might expect from work that seems at first sight so playful. We learn from the memorial volume edited by Max for his half-brother, the actor Sir Herbert Beerbohm Tree, that their father, who was born in Memel, was "of German and Dutch and Lithuanian extraction," and that he "settled in England when he was twenty-three," where he became a successful grain merchant in London and married a lady with an English name. His three sons by this first marriage were sent to be educated in Germany, at the same college where the father had studied. Thereafter one of them went to Cape Colony and decided to spend the rest of his life there, another explored Patagonia and wrote a book on the subject, and the third took to the stage (adopting the name of Tree, derived from the original *baum* of Beerbohm), where he enjoyed, if any actor ever did, a life of fantasy that blithely soared above his actual milieu and era. When, later, their mother died, their father married her sister, and Max was born when his father was sixty-one. (There has always perhaps been about Max something of the *enfant de vieux*, with his frailness, his elfin aspect and that poise and air of experience that caused Wilde to say about him, in his twenties, that he had mastered the secret of perpetual old age.) These are the only data available in regard to Max Beerbohm's antecedents, but they suggest a mixture of foreign with English blood, and an element unassimilated by England that inevitably gravitated away from her. Max himself did not study abroad; he was sent to Charterhouse and Oxford, and seems to have grown up entirely in England; yet, though odd, it did not seem unnatural that, when he married in 1910, this master of English style, who had absorbed so much of Oxford and London, this popular English caricaturist, who had depended on first-hand observation of Parliament, the Court and the theater, should, at the age of thirty-eight, have taken his wife to live in Italy, and should only have returned, under pressure of events, just before the second World War. There had always been perceptible in his work an alien point of view not amenable to English standards.

This alien side of Max Beerbohm declares itself most fully and frankly in the album of drawings called *Rossetti and His Circle*, published in 1922, when Max had lived more than a decade in the country of Rossetti's origins. "Byron, Disraeli, and Rossetti," he explains to us in his preface, "these seem to me the most interesting men that England had in the nineteenth century. . . . To be interesting, a man must be complex and elusive. And I rather fancy it must be a great advantage for him to be born outside his proper time and place." As for the drawings themselves, they are mainly a set of variations on the theme of Rossetti's relation, not to his romantic art, but to the influences of Victorian England that try to distract him from it. You see him—preoccupied, obstinate, brooding, unkempt, ill-dressed—resisting importunity and pressure: the blighting smugness of the academic Jowett, the slick eloquence of the fashionable Leighton, Meredith's self-conscious nature cult, Mill's shy, pale and gentle rationalism, the bohemianism of Sala and Browning's society ladies.

For the alien element in Max is at least as exotic as Rossetti. He says somewhere in his theatrical criticism that the rococo is his favorite style; but this element, when he gives it its head, does not stop with being rococo. In its gemminess, its artificiality, its excrescences of grotesque fancy, it sometimes becomes positively Byzantine. The Englishman in Max, on the other hand, is moderate and unassertive, dominated by common sense—and not merely correct and prosaic, but even occasionally a bit of a Philistine. It was the Byzantine that made him love the nineties and led him to find Beardsley enchanting; it was the Englishman that kept him steady, so that, almost alone of his group, he survived the *fin de siècle* without tragedy, breakdown or scandal—and he walked out of the pages of the *Yellow Book* and into those of the *Saturday Review* as politely and unperturbedly as he might have gone to dine at Simpson's after absinthe at the Café Royal. It was the Byzantine that pricked him to cultivate his early preciosity of style;

the Englishman that taught him the trick, which it has amused him to practise so often, of letting this preciosity down, with deprecating and comic effect, by a descent into the flatly colloquial.

This mixture of contrasting tendencies appears in all Max Beerbohm's work, sometimes with confusing results. In the title of *Zuleika Dobson* there is a simple juxtaposition of the exotic and the British; but in the novel itself the two are entangled in a curious way. I agree with Mr. Kronenberger—though I know we are in a minority—that there is something unsatisfactory and, as he says, "unpalatable" about this book. The trouble, I believe, is due to the fact that in this case the two sets of colors, instead of being blended in a fabric, have got into a kind of snarl. What is the pattern or the point of *Zuleika?* Is it satire or parody or nonsense or what? It is full of amusing things and patches of clever writing, but it has also tiresome stretches of the thought and conversations of characters who do not even have the two-dimensional kind of life—like that of the people of Congreve or Firbank—that is possible within a comic convention. Max Beerbohm may be trying to satirize the admiration of Oxford for a duke, but, just as he frankly himself adores Oxford, so he seems fascinated, less frankly, by his duke, who sets the fashion for all the other undergraduates. (One remembers Max's eulogy of Ouida; and his attitude toward the Duke is closely related to his attitude toward royalty, a subject with which he was preoccupied in his first two collections of essays and to which, in both his writings and his drawings, he has constantly returned. Though he has made a good deal of fun of English monarchs and their households, one feels that he has been somewhat beglamored by them. The waspishness he sometimes displayed at the expense of George V and his family—whom he saluted with satirical verses at the time of the coronation and later caricatured so sharply that a protest from an official source compelled Max to remove certain drawings from one of his exhibitions—seems largely to have been prompted by resentment at their failure to be glamorous enough.) But though it is English to love a duke, the Duke of Dorset projected by Beerbohm is Byzantine and apocalyptic. The hyperbole of magnificence here has its effectiveness, poetic and comic, but it is surely not of Oxford.

The wholesale suicide at the end of the book is also apocalyptic, but it seems to me completely unreal, completely unamusing. An exotic imagination has lost touch with an English subject.

And Max Beerbohm's imagination has in itself never been very strong. It is, in general—to my taste, at any rate—in this department of fairy-tale fantasy that he is usually least successful. Neither *Zuleika* nor *The Happy Hypocrite* is a favorite of mine among his works; and *The Dreadful Dragon of Hay Hill* is perhaps the only really bad thing that he has allowed to get into a book. These stories force unworkable conceits; they get queerly out of range of Max's taste. He is much better when—in *Enoch Soames* or *Not That I Would Boast*—he sticks closer to a real background. Yet this is not enough, with Max, to produce one of his first-rate stories: the feeblest of the *Seven Men* are the ones that are least fantastic. Max's talent for impersonation, extraordinary in its way, is almost exclusively literary—that is, he can give you a poem, a play, a letter, a speech in Parliament, but he is unable to give you people—the heroine of *Zuleika*, for example—whose style can have no basis in reading. When Zuleika begins to talk like a book, she has to explain that she has picked up the habit from a certain Mr. Beerbohm, "who once sat next to me at dinner." The two short stories mentioned above are the virtuoso pieces of a parodist, as is the best thing in *Mainly on the Air*, a portrait of a sententious old fraud called *T. Fenning Dodsworth*; and *Zuleika*, it seems to me, succeeds best when the comedy is verbal, when it arrives at its own kind of parody by exploiting a preciosity that is half burlesque.

There is another set of contrasts in Max's work which should probably be approached in another way. The alien in Max Beerbohm has, one guesses, adapted himself to England at some cost to his better intelligence, but he takes his revenge in indirect ways and at unexpected moments. He has learned the most perfect manners. "Before all things, from first to last," he wrote, or quoted, on the flyleaf of his first book, "I am utterly purposed that I will not offend." Yet his writing is full of hoaxes: he loves to disconcert the reader with bogus historical characters and invented literary references, as he is reported, in private life, to be addicted to such practical jokes as pasting indecent words into the text of John Drinkwater's poems and leaving the book on the night-table of his guest-room.

These irreverent pranks by an imp at the expense of a perfect little gentleman, like the dandiacal aberrations of the foreigner in Max who is bored with his bowler hat, contribute to the series of surprises that are so much more spontaneous in Max's work and so much more piquant, than the mechanical paradoxes of Chesterton or even, sometimes, than the systematic efforts of Shaw to "put the obvious in terms of the scandalous." And Max's digs that have a background of demureness leave, in some cases, real scars. It is true, as Mr. Kronenberger says, that Max Beerbohm, in his later years has been a little in danger of slipping into the role of the professional old fogy. Yet he has not been always a conservative, nor has he always been a gentle "trifler." It was no doubt an exaggeration for Bernard Shaw to say, in 1917, that Max was "the most savage Radical caricaturist since Gillray," and that *Zuleika* was "only his play, not his work." But the series of political cartoons, done during the Boer War and called *The Second Childhood of John Bull*, as well as many of his other drawings between then and the first World War, would go a long way to bear this out. Max gave at that time the impression of being something of a middle-class liberal. In any case, there was sometimes in his caricatures, less often in his writings, an unmistakable accent of anger. His impudence was by no means so childlike as his caricatures of himself, wide-eyed and wispy-limbed, seemed calculated to make one expect; but his animus was never derived from political or moral principle: it was simply an intense dislike of certain vulgarities, stupidities, impostures. What one feels is irrepressible contempt in his drawings of Sir Edward Carson, in his caricature of "Mr. Charles Whibley consoling Mr. Augustine Birrell for the loss of the Education Bill by a discourse on the uselessness of teaching anything whatsoever, sacred or profane, to children of the not aristocratic class," and its effect is none the less deadly because the dig appears to be humorous and made, as it were, in passing.

The series called *Tales of Three Nations*, done in 1923, in which Max cartoons the shifting relations, between Napoleon's time and our twenties, of Germany, France and England, shows a point of view quite free from nationalism and a consistent sympathy with the underdog. He was frightened, however, by the Russian Revolution, and it provoked some of his bitterest pictures. He seems always to have been biassed against Russia, and one suspects that here a British provincialism combined with some Baltic inheritance to produce an unreasonable prejudice. But, aside from the vagaries of the Russians, the turn that things were taking dismayed him. In *A Survey* (1921), he explained, in an epistle to Britannia, that he "used to laugh at the Court and at the persons around it; and this distressed you rather. I never laughed with you at Labour. Labour didn't seem to me quite important enough yet. But Labour is very important now, very strong indeed; as you have found. And I gathered, this year . . . that you thought me guilty of not the very best of taste in failing to bow my knee to your new Baal." In *Observations* (1925), his last volume of topical caricatures, he has a drawing of Civilization wedded to the hideous Industrial System: "You took me for better or wuss in younger and 'appier days, and there'll be no getting away for you from me, ever"; and another, of the Governing Classes booted, bewigged, epauletted and equipped with a silk hat and an umbrella, assailed by a demon-eared Communism brandishing a knife and a torch. It is really the whole modern world that Max Beerbohm despises and dreads; but he has never worked out a consistent line for dealing with contemporary problems. His point of view is instinctively that of the cultivated merchant class. He may admire the feudal nobility, but he is not necessarily sympathetic with them. He prizes the security and freedom of the old-fashioned middle-class gentleman, but he hates all the horrors and rigors, on the masters' side as well as the workers', which have eventually resulted from the system upon which these advantages were based. The difficulties of his position are disarmingly exposed in his essay on servants in *And Even Now*—it appears that he does not like to be waited on and would be glad to see domestic service abolished—in which he calls himself a Tory anarchist.

This is deplorable from the point of view of the man who thinks that "art is a weapon" on one side or other of the class war; but it has not prevented Max Beerbohm from being one of the great critics of his time. Max the critic has a personality somewhat different, though never quite distinct, from Max the storyteller and personal essayist. The writer that emerges, for example, in the two volumes of theatrical notices contributed to the *Saturday Review* has stripped himself, after the pieces of the first few months, of the coyness which Mr. Kronenberger rightly complains of as Max's worst vice. Max tells us that this weekly journalism, which his friends thought a waste of time, actually helped him to improve his writing. In the course of his twelve years of service, he had reduced the arabesques of his earlier style to the sobriety of his later prose; and one meets here, as in no other department of his work, the mind that gives a base to the whole: very flexible, very free from prejudice (he has dropped his undergraduate poses), but completely sure of itself (though he has sometimes to revise his first verdicts), very definite and firm in its judgments, and very direct and courageous in registering unpopular opinions. In its different way, this body of writing is as remarkable as the dramatic criticism of Max's predecessor Shaw—who suggested him to fill his own place on the basis of the young man's attacks on Shaw's *Plays Pleasant and Unpleasant.* Max's caricatures of contemporaries, which are a criticism of public life, also give us the tougher Beerbohm (though, for some reason, the forewords to the albums are sometimes pitched in his coyest lisp). But the field in which his critical faculty is happiest and most at home is that of literature, and here the parodies of *A Christmas Garland*—the most searching, except Proust's, of our time—have their place in a body of comment which has undoubtedly left a deeper imprint than the lightness of its tone ever promised.

It is now a long time, however, since Max Beerbohm the literary critic has played his bright pocket-torch on the present. One gets the impression that Lytton Strachey has been the last contemporary writer in whom he has felt any real interest. One would like to know, by word or picture, what he thinks of T. S. Eliot, Virginia Woolf, Hemingway, Priestley, Maugham. The only ray of light that has reached me on Max's opinion of Joyce has been by way of an anecdote which, since it brings out the discrepancies of our subject, may furnish this piece with an appropriate close. One of the younger English writers had shown Max a copy of *Finnegans Wake*. The veteran of the *Yellow Book* period, who had defended in his earlier days some startling unconventional work, examined this outlandish production; then, "I don't think," he said, "he'll be knighted for that." Max himself *had* just been knighted.

May 1, 1948

The Original of Tolstoy's Natasha

THE PRINCIPAL MODEL for Natasha in Tolstoy's *War and Peace* was his sister-in-law, Tatyana Andreyvna Behrs. She was sixteen when Tolstoy married, a gay, attractive and spirited girl, who was already a great favorite with him. She lived much in the Tolstoy household at Yasnaya Polyana in the country, and her brother-in-law used to tell her that she was paying her way by sitting as a model for him. Later, when she married a young magistrate, she continued to visit the Tolstoys, bringing her family to stay with them in the summer. Her husband died in 1917, and she went to Yasnaya Polyana to live with Tolstoy's daughter Alexandra, on a small pension from the Soviet government. Here, at seventy-five, she set out to write her memoirs, but did not live to bring her story much beyond her marriage in 1867, at the age of twenty-one.

This chronicle has just been translated and brought out for the first time in English under the title *Tolstoy as I Knew Him* and signed with the author's married name, Tatyana A. Kuzminskaya. The original Russian title, here retained as subtitle, *My Life at Home and at Yasnaya Polyana*, describes the contents better, for the book is by no means all about the Tolstoys; it is an autobiography of Tatyana. As such, it is a rewarding document, though not infrequently a boring book. Tatyana-Natasha was writing as a very old lady, on the basis of diaries and letters that date from her remote girlhood. Most of her comments on the literary figures whom she saw at close quarters in her youth—Ostrovsky, Turgenev, Fet and her brother-in-law Leo himself—show no respect for famous names. They are simply the reactions of a woman to various men she has met. At one point, after taking poison over a love affair that was going wrong, she quickly changed her mind about dying when another of her suitors called—received him politely and, going to her mother, begged to be given an antidote. Exercising no sense of selection, she merely writes down all the things that moved her at the moment of their occurrence, in the terms in which they interested her then. None of them seems to have acquired—it is perhaps what one would expect of Natasha—any sort of new significance in the light of her later experience. It is as if the child's passionate "crushes," her vanity in being admired, had been simply relived in memory. Though almost all Tatyana tells you fits perfectly the character created by Tolstoy and though the book is full of other people's testimony to her vivacity and her beauty, the excitement of Natasha is not there. What Tatyana had was evidently overflowing life, not literary ability. She was unable to dramatize herself and what she gives you is a long and slow record of sisters and brothers and parents, uncles and aunts and cousins, nurses and maids and coachmen, protracted visits to country houses and social calls in Moscow (where her father was Court Physician and the Behrses lived in a house at the Kremlin). All the incidents, the most serious and crucial, as well as the most trivial and frivolous, are noted down in the same casual proportions that they had for the young girl at the time. The marriage of a servant, the remodelling of a house, an accident on a dangerous road, a saddle that comes loose at a hunt, a cat that jumps out of the arms of one of the actors in amateur theatricals, are presented on about the same level as the volatile flirtations and engagements, the continual birth of children (in those days people had one a year), and the long illnesses and premature deaths that even the best city doctors could not seem to do much to prevent.

But the most important episode of Tatyana's youth affords a significant insight, much more so than she is aware, into the society to which she belonged and which her brother-in-law so brilliantly depicted. It is an episode typical of their world and yet one for which Tolstoy presents no equivalent in *War and Peace*—a drama that raises a problem which he was only much later to treat. The Natasha of real life had her Anatole Kuragin, as in *War and Peace*—his real name was even Anatole; and her eventual marriage with Kuzminsky seems to have had something in common with Natasha's final acceptance of Pierre. But, in between, had occurred the most serious love affair of her life: her tragically frustrated engagement to Leo Tolstoy's older brother Sergei.

Sergei Tolstoy had been living for years with a gypsy woman named Marya Mikhailovna, by whom he had two children. He had inherited an estate, which he farmed, not far from Yasnaya Polyana, and he lived there with his uncultivated mistress, shutting himself off from social intercourse with the neighbors of his own class. He fell in love with Tatyana and she with him, and he thought he could manage to marry her without telling Marya Mikhailovna. But the news of what was afoot soon reached her, and when her gypsy parents were told, they threatened to sue Sergei and create a public scandal. She was having another baby, which made things very difficult for him. And there was also another difficulty. Two brothers, in Tsarist Russia, were forbidden to marry two sisters unless both ceremonies were performed at the same time—since as soon as one of the marriages had taken place, the in-laws of both the bride and the groom became technically their blood relations. This in itself made the match between Sergei Tolstoy and Tatyana rather a shady transaction: a compliant priest had to be found. (This point is not explained by the editors, with the result that the situation is partly unintelligible to the non-Russian reader.) Sergei began to stay away from Yasnaya Polyana, and when Tatyana grasped the situation, she broke the engagement off, though her disappointment was bitter and the shock had a serious effect on her health. The rest of Sergei's story is not told by Tatyana, but one can find it in *The Tragedy of Tolstoy*, by Tolstoy's daughter Alexandra. Sergei married Marya Mikhailovna and became more and more unsocial. His wife and daughters did all the housework and lived in terror of him. He made it impossible for one of these daughters to see a young man of the local gentry who was in love with her and wanted to marry her, on the ground that he was not well enough educated; and presently another of the daughters, "homely, small, almost a dwarf," ran away with a good-looking cook, who opened a shop with her money, treated her brutally and finally deserted her, leaving her with several children. She died during the Revolution, "alone and unhappy in a faraway village." The third daughter eloped with a Bashkir, who had been brought from the steppes to make kumiss, a fermentation of mare's milk which had been prescribed for her health. She returned the next year, with an undergrown little boy, who had yellow Oriental skin and slanting Oriental eyes. Her father let her live in the house, in a back room as far as possible from his study, but would not see the child. They and Marya Mikhailovna, left alone by Sergei's death, died miserably after the Revolution, when their house, from which they had fled, was burned down and the estate sacked. After the elopement of the second daughter, Sergei had made haste to agree to the marriage of his only remaining child to her insufficiently educated nobleman.

Now, Tatyana could hardly have known at the time that her brother-in-law Leo, who had first accepted her match with Sergei, then applauded her breaking it off, had himself had a serf-girl for a mistress not long before he married her sister. His diaries show how much he had cared for this girl: "I am in love," he declares in one entry, "as I never was before in my life. I have no other thought. I suffer." He has moments of indifference, of revulsion even, but his affection for her seems steadily to grow stronger. "It is getting to be even frightening," he later writes, "how close to me she is. . . . It is not merely the feeling now of a rutting stag, but that of a husband and a wife." He had a son by her, who afterward became coachman for one of his legitimate sons. And in the meantime, by one of those gestures of what he liked to regard as uncompromising honesty that were often so admirably calculated to give pain to other people, he had shown his young wife this diary at a time when his former mistress still sometimes came to the house— with the result that the poor Countess, already of a jealous disposition, was visited by homicidal impulses when she found the woman scrubbing the floors, and even took to disguising herself as a peasant and waylaying her husband about the estate to see whether he were still susceptible to the blandishments of pretty serf-girls. Twenty-seven years after his marriage, Tolstoy tried to write about this love affair, combining it with the story of a similar complication, in which a neighbor, after marrying a jealous wife, had shot his peasant mistress. Tolstoy, in one of his versions of this story, follows the real tragedy; in another, he has the landowner shoot himself. He could not bring himself to publish the piece—to which he gave the title *The Devil*—presumably because, when he showed it to his wife as late as 1909, she was upset by it and made a scene; and it did not appear until after his death.

This situation was evidently a common one. Tolstoy's father, at the age of sixteen, had had an affair with a peasant girl, an affair arranged by his parents themselves; and a son, who was the product of this union, had turned up from time to time to plague the legitimate children. Tolstoy tells of his "strange feeling of consternation when in after years this brother of mine, fallen into destitution and bearing a greater resemblance to my father than any of us, used to beg help of us and was thankful for the ten or fifteen rubles we used to give him." The memory of his own illegitimate family recurred to torment Leo. "I looked at my bare feet," he wrote in his diary of 1909, "and remembered Aksinya [his mistress]—that she is still alive and that they say Ermil is my son, and that I do not beg her forgiveness, have never done penitence, do not repent every hour, and dare to judge others."

D. S. Mirsky, in his *History of Russian Literature*, has truly described *War and Peace* as an "heroic idyll of the Russian nobility," and pointed out that, in spite of the horrors of war and the ineptitudes of civilization, "the general message . . . is one of beauty and satisfaction that the world should be so beautiful." He suggests, I believe correctly, that Tolstoy's penchant for the idyllic is "the opposite pole to his unceasing moral uneasiness." Certainly *War and Peace* is one of the greatest of novels as it is one of the most enchanting. If it is not, as I do not think it is, quite one of the very summits of literature, it is because this idyllic tendency does here get the better of the author at the expense of the conditions of life as he actually knew and lived it. There is in the book, for all its realism, a certain element of the idealization in which we are all disposed to indulge in imagining the lives of our ancestors. In the case of Tolstoy, who had hardly known either his grandparents or his parents, this temptation must have been very strong. In the novel, Prince André and Pierre have their struggles with the problem of the peasantry, but the main problem is expelling the invader, and neither Natasha nor any of the men has to face any human relationship as painful as those in which the real Tatyana and the real Sergei and Leo Tolstoy found themselves involved. The Levin of *Anna Karenina*, which followed *War and Peace*, has to deal in a more direct and drastic way with his relation to the estate he has inherited and with the humans who are part of the estate, as Tolstoy did with Yasnaya Polyana; and immediately after *Anna Karenina*, Tolstoy himself appears in the character of Levin, writing the eloquent *Confession* in which he declares the insufficiency, for the moral life of a man, of property, social position and a comfortable family life, as well as of philosophy and science and the enjoyment and practice of literature. And he later tries to satisfy his moral needs by bringing himself closer to the peasants, on whose work he has always lived and who have given him the leisure to write—eating the same food as they and wearing the same clothes, working the same hours in the fields and mastering their manual skills. It was disturbing, no doubt, to a sensitive man, even after the liberation of the serfs in 1861— which Tatyana, by the way, hardly mentions, so little was it evidently noticeable in the relations of her people with their laborers and servants—to feel that one owed one's education and one's chance to pursue serious interests, as well as one's luxuries and pleasures, to the maintenance of a breed of inferior beings. But to know that one's own blood was mixed with the blood of this breed and to have to watch, in one form or another, the humiliation of one's own children must have been even harder to bear, a constant source of helpless anguish. (A gypsy singer, of course, might represent a higher stratum than that of a simple serf, but the consequences of marrying one, in Sergei's case, turned out to be just about as disastrous as if she had been a serf. When his daughter who eloped with the cook went to her Uncle Leo and asked him to approve this union, on the ground that she was following his doctrine by trying to put herself on a plane with the peasant, he lectured the girl severely, telling her that "no marriage could be happy between people who stood on different levels of development and had no interests in common.")

The emotional effects of this dilemma are not anywhere presented directly either in *War and Peace* or in *Anna Karenina*, though the situation appears in both. In the former, it is idyllic, like everything else. The uncle at whose house the Rostovs spend the night after the hunt has a housekeeper who is also his mistress, but the whole thing is most amiable and comfortable, and when Natasha has done her peasant dance—Tatyana tells us that this incident was derived from a performance of her own—the rosy and plump and good-looking woman sheds a tear or two through her laughter as she perceives that "this slim graceful countess, brought up in velvet and silk, this being so alien to her . . . was able to understand everything about Anisya and Anisya's father and her aunt and her mother, and every Russian in the world." In *Anna Karenina*, a similar situation is presented in a more embarrassing light. When Levin goes with his wife to visit his dying brother, he winces at having her meet the latter's ex-prostitute mistress, with whom he has been living in misery, and he notes, for a fleeting moment, her "expression of eager curiosity" at encountering "that dreadful woman, so incomprehensible to her." It is only later, with *Resurrection*, begun in 1889 and not finished and published till 1899, that Tolstoy comes to grips with this situation. In his youth, he had had an affair with one of his aunt's maids, who had been dismissed for this reason and had come later to a bad end. In the novel, Prince Nekhlyudov finds himself sitting on a jury which has to pass judgment on a girl whom he recognizes as a maid of his aunt's whom he has seduced under similar circumstances and deserted when she was pregnant. She has since become a prostitute and is now implicated in a sordid murder, of which she is completely innocent. At the trial, there is a miscarriage of justice, due partly to the carelessness of the Court but partly to Nekhlyudov's own cowardice, and the girl is condemned to Siberia. Nekhlyudov now brings all his influence to have the decision reversed and makes a vow to expiate his guilt by following her into exile and marrying her. He does get her sentence commuted, and he accompanies the convicts on their journey; but Maslova spares him the final test, for, understanding the undesirability of his spending the rest of his life with her, she marries one of her fellow-prisoners. Nekhlyudov, on the very last pages, happens to pick up a copy of the *New Testament* which has been given him by a travelling evangelist, and is converted to a creed like Tolstoy's own. From that day, for Nekhlyudov, says the author, a new life begins, and "what that new period will come to, time alone will show."

So we never know what happened to Nekhlyudov. It is impossible, from what we have been told of him, to imagine him turning saint or even finding employment that would satisfy his hunger for righteousness. Yet *Resurrection*, though it ends in the air, is not unworthy of its predecessors, and certainly does not deserve the disparagement that it usually gets. It is the novel in which Tolstoy comes closest to the problems of his own life, the only one in which he really grapples with the tragedies of a class-society, as he had seen them at first hand, as he had helped to produce them himself—the only one that gets out into the open such episodes as Tatyana had locked away in her diary. We do know what happened to Tolstoy when he tried to lead a new life: his fanaticisms and his worldly relapses, his absurdities and his desperate death. The story he himself had been living could no more come out satisfactorily than Nekhlyudov's story could. After the period of his first gratification at re-creating his lost parents and in restoring at Yasnaya Polyana the patriarchal family life of which in the preceding generation the continuity had been broken, a malaise which had survived these distractions inescapably asserted itself and came to ache through the whole of his work.

We have seen a somewhat similar preoccupation in the literature of our own South, from the days when George W. Cable was forced to come to live in the North for his boldness in describing the half-colored branches of the prominent white families of New Orleans to the days when the continued anguish of Negro and white relations has inspired those stories of Faulkner's in which neither reader nor author is ever allowed a moment's relief or repose, because the subject admits of no resolution. In Russia, the black-and-white issue was not present to deepen the class distinctions, and it was possible for the landowners in Tolstoy's fiction to contemplate marrying their mistresses, as it was possible for Sergei Tolstoy to remain in serious doubt as to whether it was right for him to put away his gypsy and marry Tatyana. But the strains and the mutilations incurred through these social differences periodically made themselves felt among all those gay parties in country houses, all those balls in St. Petersburg and Moscow, all those jolly affectionate family scenes, all those gallantries of handsome cousins.

August 28, 1948

"The Most Unhappy Man on Earth"

A NEW EDITION of Swift's *Journal to Stella*, edited by
Harold Williams, has been brought out by the Oxford
University Press. The editing of this series of personal letters,
discovered and published after Swift's death, has presented
special problems to scholars. Not only do "the crowded,
minute handwriting, the constant practice of abbreviation, the
frequent scorings and blottings, often," as Mr. Williams says,
"leave the true reading open to difference of opinion"; but the
cipher of Swift's "little language," the curious baby-talk that
he had apparently invented for Stella in her childhood and into
which he still lapses in the journal, written when she was thirty,
has never completely been penetrated. Mr. Williams is not the
first editor who has restudied the difficult texts of those
letters—twenty-five out of sixty-five—of which the originals
survive, and who has attempted to reproduce them accurately,
instead of more or less freely rewriting them or improvising
when in doubt, as was the habit of certain earlier editors. But
he has done on the journal a more thorough job than any of
his predecessors. Unless more original letters turn up, this
must remain the definitive edition. No document needs anno-
tation more, and Mr. Williams has explained everybody and
everything to which Swift refers in his chronicle of his visit to
London in 1710–13, so crowded with dinners and transactions
and interviews with all sorts of people who were after all sorts
of things. The introduction is exact and terse in its unravelling
of a tangled subject; the index is of an unprecedented fullness.

It is only when one compares this edition with the earlier
one included in the best complete set of Swift, that of the old
Bohn's Standard Library, that one becomes aware of the handicaps under which scholarly texts of the classics now come into
circulation. The Bohn edition of the *Journal*, which cost five
shillings, was well-printed in one volume on excellent paper
and in admirably compact form. The portraits, engraved instead of photographed, were not perhaps so faithful to the
originals as they are in Mr. Williams' edition; but the Bohn
edition contained one feature, a gratuitous enrichment of a

popular-priced book, which today appears almost incredible. Instead of rather a dim photograph of one page of one of the letters, which is the best the Oxford Press can do, the old volume had as a frontispiece a most remarkable folded facsimile of all four pages of one, which reproduced the color of the faded ink and the color and texture and watermark of the paper, and which was even sealed with real red sealing wax and stamped with Swift's seal. This must have been done by hand—from 1897, when the volume first appeared, till as late as 1908—for every copy of a book that was going into the common currency of a series not unlike the Modern Library.

But the *Journal to Stella* is essential for anyone who wants to know Swift. I do not think there is any other great writer whose work, for its appreciation, demands, as Swift's does, a fairly close familiarity with the ins and outs of his life. The popularity of *Gulliver's Travels* beyond anything else that Swift wrote is due not to its superiority but simply to the fact that it is the only one of his works on any considerable scale which presents an imaginary picture detached from Swift's own career and the historical background of his time. Swift, with his narrower range, has—in his solitary intensity of passion, his intellectual rigor and strength, his nobility and self-willed idealism, his tragic self-dramatization—something in common with Dante. But Dante got his whole career, personal, political and moral, inside his imaginary picture; Swift, though he, too, got his story told, scattered it in pamphlets and poems, in historical and political essays, in prayers and practical jokes, in epigrams and lampoons, in his correspondence with public men and in his personal letters to Stella.

It is hard to agree with George Saintsbury that this journal is the first modern novel. It shows too little imagination and requires too many notes. Except for the babblings of the little language, themselves of a chilling monotony, what you get is a bare enough record of Swift's habits and business in England —such a diary as, one would think, could not have been very much different if he had kept it for himself alone. Yet here we follow him with something like intimacy for the better part of three years. We see him as he looked to himself; and we feel the unflagging energy of that dynamo of furious emotion, all directed toward power and pride, yet subjected to a discipline so iron that it was impossible for him to be betrayed by any of the ordinary threats or baits. His arrogance imposes itself on us as it did on his contemporaries, because it is backed not merely by brains but also by austere character. We see him arrive in London as the champion of the Irish clergy in their attempt to get their taxes reduced, and we see him effect this purpose and go on to become a public figure, as influential as a great official. We see him as the practical intellect, only half masked, behind the Tory Ministry, equipping it, in a masterly tract, with the arguments that gave it its case for putting an end to the War of the Spanish Succession. And finally, on the collapse of this Ministry, we see him—his patrons afraid of him, chafing against his virtuous tyranny and refusing him the preferment he aims at: a deanery or a canonry which would keep him in England—sent back to the safe distance of Dublin as Dean of St. Patrick's Cathedral. It is a pure drama of personality, not of ideas or political principles. Swift was not even a contemplative man whose observations on life are interesting. His comment, as in *Gulliver's Travels*, written after his return to Ireland, is, couched in impassive prose, primarily a blast of poetic scorn at the animal nature of man. There are in the journal few general reflections, and such as there are are brief, but they may stick in one's head unforgettably, as I find that certain passages have done with me from a reading of more than thirty years back—not because they display Swift's intelligence, but because they show the darkness of his pessimism and the rigidity of his moral nature. "Lord Radnor and I," he writes, "were walking in the Mall this evening; and Mr. Secretary [Henry St. John, later Lord Bolingbroke] met us and took a turn or two, and then stole away, and we both believed it was to pick up some wench; and tomorrow he will be at the cabinet with the Queen: so goes the world." Or "I am just now told that poor dear Lady Ashburnham, the Duke of Ormond's daughter, died yesterday at her country house; the poor creature was with child. She was my greatest favorite; and I am in excessive concern for her loss. I hardly knew a more valuable person on all accounts: you must have heard me tell of her. I am afraid to see the Duke and Duchess; she was naturally very healthy; I am afraid she has been thrown away for want of care. Pray condole with me; 'tis extremely moving.

Her lord's a puppy, and I shall never think it worth my while to be troubled with him, now he has lost all that was valuable in his possession. Yet I think he used her pretty well. I hate life, when I think it exposed to such accidents, and to see so many thousand wretches burdening the earth while such as her die, makes me think God did never intend life for a blessing."

Even in reading the journal, however, one ought to have some acquaintance with Swift's political writing of this period. Mr. Williams has done his best to fill in the political background as well as the personal one. There have lately been two new discoveries of data that might seem to throw light on the origins of Swift and Stella and their relations to one another; but these give rise to two different hypotheses which would appear to be mutually exclusive. Swift and Stella had first known one another, when he was twenty-one and she eight, in the household of Sir William Temple, where Swift lived for ten years as secretary and where Stella grew up as, presumably, the daughter of Sir William's steward and of a woman in the service of his sister. Yet there were rumors that both Stella and Swift were Sir William's illegitimate children. It is surely not credible, in the case of Swift, that he knew himself to be Sir William's son, for his attitude toward Sir William in the journal seems that of a former dependent toward a mildly respected patron, from whose service he has been glad to escape. But it has recently turned out that Sir William Temple's father, Sir John, of whom Swift himself said that he "had been a fast friend to the family," was one of the five persons who authorized, in 1666, the appointment of Swift's supposed father as Steward of the King's Inns in Dublin; and the discoverer of this fact, Mr. Denis Johnston, has concluded, with the support of some other facts, that the mother of Swift at that time had been having a love affair with Sir John, and that Swift, born in 1667 and later assigned to the household of Sir William, was Sir John's illegitimate son. If Stella was Sir William's daughter, Swift would then be her uncle, and this would explain his affectionate relation to her which never became that of lover. But another new piece of evidence, first published and examined by Mr. Maxwell B. Gold in his book *Swift's Marriage to Stella*, seems to bear out the assertions of several persons close to Swift that he did have a marriage ceremony performed a few years after his return from England, though he never consummated the marriage and never saw Stella without someone else present. If he had known himself to be her uncle, it seems unlikely that he would have done even this.

The celebrated anecdote about Swift, first printed by Sir Walter Scott, thus remains as mysterious as ever: "Immediately subsequent to the [marriage] ceremony, Swift's state of mind appears to have been dreadful. Delany [an intimate friend of Swift's], as I have learned from a friend of his relict, being pressed to give his opinion on this strange union, said that about the time it took place, he observed Swift to be extremely gloomy and agitated, so much so that he went to Archbishop King to mention his apprehensions. On entering the library, Swift rushed out with a countenance of distraction, and passed him without speaking. He found the Archbishop in tears, and upon asking the reason he said, 'You have just met the most unhappy man on earth—but on the subject of his wretchedness you must never ask a question.'"

The disease of which Swift died and under which, apparently, his reason gave way has been diagnosed variously as a malady of the ear and as hardening of the arteries of the brain. Krafft-Ebing, whose comment on the case of Swift has been developed by Mr. Gold, thought he suffered from "sexual anaesthesia." But we still have no real idea of what had turned so much of Swift's hunger for love and creative thought into a cold and cruel need to dominate. There is one atrocious entry in the journal in which he boasts to the woman he undoubtedly loved of having interceded with St. John "to hinder a man of his pardon, who is condemned for a rape. The undersecretary was willing to save him, upon an old notion that a woman cannot be ravished; but I told the secretary he could not pardon him without a favorable report from the judge; besides he was a fiddler, and consequently a rogue, and deserved hanging for something else; and so he shall swing. What; I must stand up for the honour of the fair sex? 'Tis true, the fellow had lain with her a hundred times before; but what care I for that? What! must a woman be ravished because she is a whore?" But even more shocking, perhaps, are the last words of the last entry, in reference to a letter of Stella's: "I mightily approve ppt's [Stella's] project of hanging the blind parson—when I read that passage upon Chester walls, as I was coming into town and just received the letter, I said aloud: 'Agreeable B-tch.'"

January 22, 1949

William Faulkner's Reply
to the Civil-Rights Program

WILLIAM FAULKNER'S new novel, *Intruder in the Dust*, is the story of a Negro with white blood who refuses to behave with the submissiveness demanded of his color in the South and has developed so rigid a pride that, even when wrongfully charged with the murder of a white man, he can hardly bring himself to stoop to defend himself against the enemy of his race. The narrative deals with the adventures of the handful of people in the community (the Jefferson, Mississippi, which is the locale of most of Faulkner's fiction) who, having come to respect Lucas' independence, interest themselves in his case and exert themselves to save him from lynching. These champions include a boy of sixteen, who had once been rescued by Lucas when he had fallen through the ice; the boy's uncle, a local lawyer, who has lived abroad and has, to some degree, been able to surmount provincial prejudices; and an old lady of the best local quality, who had grown up with the accused man's dead wife in the relation of mistress and maid. All the happenings are presented from the point of view of the boy. It is his loyalty to the old Negro that leads to the discovery of evidence that the crime has been committed by someone else; and his emergence, under the stimulus of events, out of boyhood into comparative maturity is as much the subject of the book as the predicament of the Negro. The real theme is the relation between the two.

The novel has the suspense and excitement that Faulkner can nearly always create and the disturbing emotional power that he can generate at his best. The earlier Faulkner of *Sanctuary* was often accused of misanthropy and despair, but the truth is that, from *Pylon* on, at any rate, one of the most striking features of his work, and one that sets it off from that of many of his American contemporaries, has been a kind of romantic morality that allows you the thrills of melodrama without making you ashamed, as a rule, of the values which have been invoked to produce them. I do not sympathize with the line of criticism which deplores Faulkner's obstinate persistence in submerging himself in the mentality of the community where he was born, for his chivalry, which constitutes his morality, is a part of his Southern heritage, and it appears in Faulkner's work as a force more humane and more positive than almost anything one can find in the work of even those writers of our more mechanized societies who have set out to defend human rights. *Intruder in the Dust* is one of the most ardent demonstrations of this reconditioned Southern chivalry; and the question that arises in connection with it is not whether it paints too hopeless a picture but, on the contrary, whether it is not too positive, too optimistic—whether the author has not yielded too much to the temptations of the novelist's power to summon for innocence in difficulties the equivalent of the United States Marines.

I shall return to this aspect of *Intruder in the Dust*. In the meantime, it ought to be said that, from the point of view of the writing, this is one of the more snarled-up of Faulkner's books. It is not so bad as *The Bear*, which has pages that are almost opaque. But in his attempt to record the perceptions— the instinctive sensations and the half-formed thoughts—of his adolescent boy, in aiming at prisms of prose which will concentrate the infrared as well as the ultra-violet, he leaves these rays sometimes still invisible, and only tosses into our hands some rather clumsy and badly cut polygons. It would require a good deal of very diligent work and very nice calculation always to turn out the combinations of words that would do what Faulkner wants them to do. His energy, his image-making genius get him where he wants to go about seventy per cent of the time, but when he misses it, he lands in a mess. One cannot object in principle to any of Faulkner's practices: to his shifting his syntax in the middle of a sentence, to his stringing long sequences of clauses together with practically no syntax at all, to his inserting in parenthesis in the middle of a scene (in one case, in the middle of a sentence) a long episode that took place at some other time, to his invention of the punctuation (( )) to indicate a parenthesis within a parenthesis or to his creation of non-dictionary words. He has, at one time or another, justified all these devices. But what is the excuse for writing "the old grunt and groan with some long

familiar minor stiffness so used and accustomed as to be no
longer even an ache and which if they were ever actually cured
of it, they would be bereft and lost"?—a mismanagement of
relatives quite common in the Faulkner of the latest books.
One is willing to give the benefit of the doubt to "regurg,"
"abnegant," "dismatchment," "divinant," "perspicuant," until
one runs into a dictionary word used out of its real meaning,
as in "it's only men who burk at facts"—when one realizes that
Faulkner is not merely coining but groping. It is true that his
new way of writing has enabled him to render impressions
more accurately than he did before: but the passages that
become unintelligible on account of a confusion of pronouns
or that have to be read twice for lack of proper punctuation are
not really the results of an effort to express the hardly express-
ible but the casualties of an indolent taste and a negligent
workmanship that did not appear to the same degree in the
prose—for the most part so steady and clear as well as so tense
and telling—of such a novel as *Light in August*.

One finds here both the vigor of a tradition and the signs of
its current decay. For the writing of Faulkner, too, has a noble
and ancient lineage. Though he echoed, in his earlier novels,
Hemingway and Sherwood Anderson, he belongs, really, not
to their school but to the full-dress post-Flaubert group of
Conrad, Joyce and Proust, whom he has sometimes echoed
since. To their kind of highly complex fiction he has brought
the rich and lively resources, reappearing with amazing freshness, of English lyric verse and romantic prose (as distinguished from what we now call American). This is an advantage
that the Southern writers sometimes have—a contact with the
language of Shakespeare which, if they sidestep the oratorical
Southern verbiage, they may get through their old-fashioned
education. And Faulkner, it must be said, often succeeds as
Shakespeare does—by plunging into the dramatic scene and
flinging down the words and images that flow to the ends of
his fingers. This book, like all his books, is full of passages that
could not have been written if he had sat down and contemplated the object—as Flaubert is said to have done the cabbage
garden by moonlight—instead of allowing himself to be possessed by it. Minor but admirable examples in *Intruder in the
Dust* are the renderings of the impression on the white boy of

the smell of a Negro cabin, with all its social implications, and of the effect of a little frame church that, though lacking a steeple and shabbily patched, speaks to him with the spirit of the Calvinism to which its Scotch-Irish congregation have erected a degenerate shrine. Though he sometimes loses his grasp of language, he has described so many things so well— got out of them so much human meaning! No other of our contemporary novelists, perhaps, can compete with him in this department—for most of the best of them were bred in a world that is based on abstract assumptions, and they cannot help sharing these; whereas, for Faulkner the Mississippian, everything that a man has made wears the aspect of the human agent, and its impact is that of a human meeting.

To be thus out of date, as a Southerner, in feeling and in language and in human relations, may prove, for a novelist, a source of strength. But the weaknesses of Faulkner, also, have their origin in the antiquated community he inhabits, for they result from his not having mastered—I speak of the design of his books as wholes as well as of that of his sentences and paragraphs—the discipline of the Joyces, Prousts and Conrads (though Proust had his solecisms and what the ancients called anacolutha). If you are going to do embroidery, you have to watch every stitch; if you are going to construct a machine, you have to test every part. The technique of the modern novel, with its ideal of technical efficiency, its specialization of means for ends, has grown up in the industrial age, and it has, after all, a good deal in common with the other manifestations of that age. In practicing it so far from such cities as produced the Flauberts, Joyces and Jameses, Faulkner's provinciality, stubbornly cherished and turned into an asset, inevitably tempts him to be slipshod and has apparently made it impossible for him to acquire complete expertness in an art that demands of the artist the closest attention and care.

But *Intruder in the Dust* does not come to us merely as a novel: it also involves a tract. The story is evidently supposed to take place sometime this year or last, and it seems to have been partly inspired by the crisis at the time of the recent war in the relations between whites and Negroes and by the recently proposed legislation for guaranteeing Negro rights. The book contains a kind of counterblast to the anti-lynching bill and to the civil-rights plank in the Democratic platform. The author's ideas on this subject are apparently conveyed, in their explicit form, by the intellectual uncle, who, more and more as the story goes on, gives vent to long disquisitions that seem to become so "editorial" in character that it is difficult to regard them merely as a part of the presentation of the furniture of the uncle's personality. The series may be pieced together as something in the nature of a public message delivered by the author himself. This message, however, suffers from the handicap of being very obscurely expressed. Faulkner, who has shown himself a master at making every possible type of Mississippian talk in his natural idiom, has chosen to couch the uncle's conversations with the boy in a literary prose like his own at its most complicated and non-colloquial—so that it is difficult to reduce what is said to definite propositions. I shall, however, make an attempt to do so.

The point of view, then, seems to be as follows (interpolated comment by the critic):

"The people named Sambo" [the uncle's way of designating the Negroes] have survived the ordeal of slavery and they may survive the ordeal of dictatorship. The capacity for endurance of the Negro is a recurrent theme of Faulkner's, and his respect for their humble persistence is unconsciously but strikingly contrasted here with his attitude toward "the coastal spew of Europe, which this country quarantined unrootable into the rootless ephemeral cities" [as if the Italians, Greeks, Hungarians, Poles, and Czechs had not shown as much tenacity as the Negroes, and as if the Southern Negroes had not been kept alive—that is, encouraged to persist—by the people who had an interest in employing them, just as the immigrants from Europe were].

The Southerners in the United States are the only "homogeneous people." (The New Englander, in his pure and respectable form, crowded back by the coastal spew of Europe, is no longer of real importance.) "We are defending not actually our politics or beliefs or even our way of life, but simply our homogeneity, from a federal government to which, in simple desperation, the rest of this country has had to surrender voluntarily more and more of its personal and private liberty in order to continue to afford the United States." The Negro is homogeneous, too, "except that part of him which is trying to escape not even into the best of the white race but into the second best." The saving remnant of Southerners, such as the characters in the story who rescue old Lucas Beauchamp, should combine with the non-second-rate Negro—the second-rate variety being, by the author's definition, the Negro who demands "not an automobile nor flash clothes nor his picture in the paper, but a little of music (his own), a hearth, not his child but any child [back to Uncle Tom and Uncle Remus!], a God, a heaven which a man may avail himself a little of at any time without having to wait to die [oh, dem golden slippers!], a little earth for his own sweat to fall on among his own green shoots and plants [no large-scale agriculture for Sambo!]." Let the white man give the Negro his rights, and the Negro teach the white man his endurance, and "together we would dominate the United States; we would present a front not only impregnable but not even to be threatened by a mass of people who no longer have anything in common save a frantic greed for money and a basic fear of a failure of national character which they hide from one another behind a loud lipservice to a flag." [The Mississippian may have hold of something here.]

Lucas-Sambo must be defended "from the North and East and West—the outlanders who will fling him decades back not merely into injustice but into grief and agony, and violence, too, by forcing on us laws based on the idea that man's injustice to man can be abolished overnight by police." Any other course of conduct toward the Negro will risk dividing the country. Attempts on the part of the people in other sections of the United States to strengthen the hand of the Negro amount to nothing more than "a paper alliance of theorists and fanatics and private and personal avengers plus a number of others" [including a good many Negroes] against "a con-corded [i.e., solid] South," which is now full of "ignorant people" from other parts of the country, "who fear the color of any skin or shape of nose save their own." Such action will force the many Southerners "who do begrieve Lucas' shameful condition and would improve it" and will eventually abolish it, to ally themselves with all those objectionable elements "with whom we have no kinship whatever, in defense of a principle [the inalienable right to keep the Negro down] which we ourselves begrieve and abhor." They will thus be forced into "the position of the German after 1933, who had no other alternative between being either a Nazi or a Jew, or the present Russian (European, too, for that matter), who hasn't even that, but must be either a Communist or dead." So the Southerners must be allowed, on their own initiative, in their own way, with no intervention by others, to grant the Negro his citizenship. Otherwise—

Otherwise, what? I have been able, I think, up to now, to make Faulkner's argument clear by quoting or paraphrasing his own words, with the addition of a little punctuation; but here I must present you with a chunk of his text without any elucidation, for I cannot be sure what it means: Otherwise "Lucas' equality" cannot "be anything more than its own prisoner inside an impregnable barricade of the direct heirs of the victory of 1861–1865 which probably did more than even John Brown to stalemate Lucas' freedom which still seems to be in check going on a hundred years after Lee surrendered." But, the other side may object: The South will never get around to doing anything for the Negro. Your policy, the South retorts, is dangerous, in any case: it will give rise to "a people divided [Faulkner thus seems to take it for granted that if Washington tries to back the Negroes, it will arouse the whole South to resistance] at a time when history is still showing us that the anteroom to dissolution is division."

But is pressure from outside worth nothing? Has it had no moral effect on the South? It seems to me that this book itself, which rejects outside interference, is a conspicuous sign that it has. The champions of Lucas Beauchamp are shown as rather reluctant, as even, at moments, resentful, in recognizing his rectitude and his dignity, but they do rally to get him cleared. It is true that you have had already, in the title story of *Go Down, Moses*, the same liberal lawyer and decent old maid working together to do the Beauchamps a kindness when their grandson has been executed for murder; but in this new book these white folks of the best old stock come to the rescue of the Negro with a zeal that I do not remember to have seen displayed by the inhabitants of Yoknapatawpha County in any other of Faulkner's books. Young Charles and his young Negro pal are transformed into Boy Scouts. Miss Habersham proves herself a dear gallant old thoroughbred. The uncle is as ironic and delightful as the uncle of the boy next door in E. Nesbit's books about the Bastable children. When this wonderful posse is on the march, they have hair-breadth escapes but get all the breaks. And, in the end, the vulgar upstarts who wanted to see Lucas lynched get into their vulgar cars and turn tail and run away. There has been nothing so exhilarating in its way since the triumphs of the Communist-led workers in the early Soviet films; one is thrilled by the same kind of emotion that one got from some of the better dramatizations of the career of Abraham Lincoln.

This is a new note to come from the South; and it may really represent something more than Faulkner's own courageous and generous spirit, some new stirring of public conscience. In the meantime, in harping on this message, I do not want to divert attention from the genius that produced the book, which sustains, like its predecessors, the polymorphous polychromatic vitality, the poetic truth to experience, of Faulkner's Balzacian chronicle of Yoknapatawpha County. Old Lucas and certain other characters have, as I say, appeared in *Go Down, Moses*, to which *Intruder in the Dust* is, indeed, more or less of a sequel, and the later adventures of Lucas are more interesting if you know his past history as recounted in the earlier volume, and understand his role in the tangle of black-and-white relationships which Faulkner has presented there. This subject of the complicated consequences of the mixture of white with Negro blood has been explored by Faulkner with remarkable intelligence and subtlety and variety of dramatic imagination; and Lucas himself, the black man who embarrasses a set of white relatives by having inherited the strongest traits of a white ancestor common to them all, is one of the author's most impressive creations. Even when the prose goes to pieces, the man and his milieu live.

October 23, 1948

In Memory of Octave Mirbeau

"Dear me, how far from infinite the world is! Talking to my cousin today, I mentioned Octave Mirbeau's name. 'Why, Mirbeau,' she said, 'let me see—that's the son of the doctor at Remalard, the place where we have our estate. I remember that two or three times I lashed him over the head with my whip. He was an impudent little thing as a child—his great idea was to show his bravado by throwing himself under the feet of our horses when we or the Andlaus were out driving.'"

Edmond de Goncourt: Diary,
August 26, 1889

I SHOULD LIKE to take the occasion of the reprint of a very respectable translation by Alvah C. Bessie of Octave Mirbeau's novel, *Le Jardin des Supplices* to look back at a remarkable French writer whose reputation, after his death in 1917, almost immediately evaporated both abroad and in his own country. Mirbeau belonged so much to his period that I may perhaps be pardoned for explaining that I first read him, and almost completely through, at the time of the first World War, and that he will always remain for me an old companion of my experiences of those years. As such a companion, he had perhaps more value than he might have had in other conditions. In the first place, he is at his best when he is describing those wretched French villages, with their doll-bedecked rundown churches, their diseased and deformed inhabitants and their pervasive smell of manure, among which I was then living on more intimate terms than those of the tourist who stares at them from the train and is thrilled by their look of antiquity. It is enough for me to open certain books of Mirbeau to see again their gray walls embedded in mud. In the second place, his favorite theme, the persistence in modern society of predatory and destructive appetites at variance with civilized pretentions, was particularly acceptable then, at a time when it was actually reassuring to read someone who was not trying to convince you that only the Germans had ever been bloodthirsty, who had never even fooled himself with the assumption that our exploiting competitive world was a respectable and reliable affair. And though I saw Mirbeau's faults even then, my opinion of him will always be colored by a certain special affection.

His compatriots, as we trace him through their criticism and journals, seem to have become toward him colder and colder. For Edmond de Goncourt, in the eighties, Mirbeau was a young colleague in the naturalistic movement, who was beginning to show distinguished abilities and who dedicated a novel to him. On André Gide, in the first years of this century, when Gide was an ally of the symbolists by no means enamored of naturalism, Mirbeau made a mixed impression. He responded to Mirbeau's warm indignations and admired some of his work, but complained that "the satirical spirit prevents his having any critical sense." By this time, it had become apparent that Mirbeau repudiated defiantly those versions of the French tradition that were in vogue at the turn of the century. He was not elegant and detached, like the Parnassians, not exquisite like the followers of Mallarmé, and he sometimes made heavy fun of the professional Parisian aesthetes. Nor would he attempt to adjust himself to the demands of a bourgeois audience. He scored against Paul Bourget, in his *Journal d'une Femme de Chambre*, by attributing to his servant-girl heroine a passion for the works of that fashionable novelist but making her conclude, after meeting him once, that, in the eyes of M. Bourget "people didn't begin to have souls below an income of a hundred thousand francs"; and he had none of the quiet discretion in running counter to accepted ideas that caused Anatole France to say of himself that the principal business of his life had been doing up dynamite in bonbon wrappers. He had not even the detachment of the naturalists. He was not only outspoken and tactless: he did not even value the classical "*bon sens français*"—behaved habitually, from the French point of view, intemperately, quixotically, absurdly. A Normand, he was in some ways quite close to the English, who figure in his books in a way that shows a special interest in them—that is, he was blunt, self-willed and not particularly intelligent at the same time that he was subject to moral passion and capable of profound insights and had the courage to give voice to both at the risk of being thought eccentric. In his character as publicist and journalist, in which he played for years a conspicuous role, he was vigorous and audacious. At the time of the Dreyfus case, he went on the stump in the provinces, rousing opinion in Dreyfus' defense; he forfeited by his very first article, in 1889, a job as a newspaper art critic by running down the academic painters and praising Manet and Cézanne; he loved to champion unrecognized writers like Maeterlinck and the seamstress Marguerite Audoux whose work had a lilylike innocence at the opposite pole from his own productions. In politics, he passed at an early stage from fire-breathing royalism to fire-breathing anarchism—the two attitudes having in common a violent hatred of politicians; and remained thereafter consistently pro-worker, anti-bourgeois and anti-clerical. He wrote a labor play, *Les Mauvais Bergers*, produced in 1897, with Sarah Bernhardt and Lucien Guitry, the long heroic speeches of which make very dull reading today, but which differs from most such dramas by its pessimism in regard to the workers' cause; and he created a scandal in 1908 by a play (written with Thadée Natanson), *Le Foyer*, that attacked the philanthropical workshops subsidized by the rich for the relief of the poor.

Nor did the literary cuisine of Mirbeau quite come up to the current French standards. He was always a conscientious workman: his books are never botched or sloppy; he has trained himself with earnest discipline to make the very best of his powers, and he can sometimes write with trenchant lucidity, if rarely with felicitous brilliance. But the seasoning is a little coarse; the ingredients are not well mixed. The flavor is sometimes flat; and there is even a kind of false taste that is calculated to horripilate the French. For example, Mirbeau had a passion for flowers, which he raised and of which he was a connoisseur, but his writing about them—of which there is a good deal in *Le Jardin des Supplices*—combines the botanical and the gaudy in a way that does not conduce to good literature. And his writing about love—exemplified, also, in this book—has similar characteristics. He thus scandalized the bourgeois public and often bored the men of letters, and when he died, his countrymen dropped him. I once talked about him with Jean Cocteau just after the last war. Cocteau expressed surprise that anybody at that late date should be reading Mirbeau at all. "That's a whole generation," he said, "that my generation has skipped." But he approved of *Sébastien Roch*, one of Mirbeau's early books, which had made an impression on me, and suggested that a serious and chronic illness had caused a deterioration in his later work. If you consult the *Histoire de la Littérature Française Contemporaine* by René Lalou, published in 1922, you will find a discussion of Mirbeau, which is almost completely contemptuous and which takes it for granted that his novels are no longer of any interest. Though there are two or three brochures on Mirbeau in various journalistic series dealing with the writers of his period, there is, so far as I know, no reliable biography of him, and it is curiously difficult at the present time even to find out the main facts about his life.

Octave Mirbeau's fiction falls into two groups, quite distinct from one another and with a gap of a decade between them. His first three novels—*Le Calvaire, L'Abbé Jules* and *Sébastien Roch*—were written during the late eighties. All deal more or less with provincial life, and especially with personalities which have become distorted or stunted by not finding their true vocations or appropriate milieux. There is a good deal of original insight—contemporary with Freud's first researches—into the infantile causes of neurosis and the consequences of sexual repression. The first of these books is a study of an unstable young man from the country demoralized by a Parisian cocotte; the second, a strange and repellent tale, is a kind of imaginary memoir which a nephew has written of his uncle: a man of superior abilities, from a bourgeois village background, whose personality has been deformed by his mistake of entering the priesthood—a profession in which his intellectual arrogance, his intractable sensual appetites and his very gift of moral vision make him tragically out of place. *L'Abbé Jules* has vivid flashes when the subject is brought to life dramatically—as when the abbé, returning to his family, frustrated, embittered, forbidding, and hardly condescending to talk to them, examines as if astonished the quilt that they have handed him for a carriage-robe; and both books have a clinical interest: Mirbeau, like Flaubert, was a doctor's son. But the third novel, *Sébastien Roch*, is much better and was to remain probably Mirbeau's best book. This is the story of a gifted boy who is sent away from home to a Jesuit school, where one of the priests seduces him, and who then comes back to his little town, with his emotions in agonized disorder and with no field for the exercise of his talents. He tries to give himself an outlet by writing in a diary and has an awkward love affair with a girl whom he has known since childhood, and, finally, conscripted for the Franco-Prussian War, is unheroically, ridiculously killed. Everyone who has read this book knowing James Joyce's *A Portrait of the Artist as a Young Man* has been struck by parallels between them, in form as well as in content. One would like to know whether Joyce had read *Sébastien Roch*. It is not quite up to the *Portrait*. It has elements of the romantic sentimentality and of the dead mechanical caricature that impair the soundness of all Mirbeau's work. But Mirbeau did his most successful writing in his description of the Breton countryside, and the anguish of adolescence has never been more truthfully treated. If one compares these early stories of Mirbeau with the fiction of his friend Guy de Maupassant, who worked also in the naturalistic tradition, the advantage is not all with the latter. Maupassant has more skill and more style. But such a figure as the conventional wife and mother of Maupassant's *Une Vie* is simply the victim of a melodrama in which the villain is the masculine sex. In *Le Calvaire*, the mother of the hero is a somewhat similar case, but Mirbeau's psychological insight makes it impossible for him to deal in this one-sided pathos, and he shows us that the woman, from a "trauma" of her childhood, has a special predisposition to succumb to such a situation as that later created by her marriage. To the brilliant raconteur of *Boule de Suif*, the war of 1870, again, presents itself mainly in terms of the hatred between Germans and French, whereas with Mirbeau, when he touches on it, the patriotic antagonisms are undercut by a sense of what all men have in common.

Between *Sébastien Roch* of 1889 and *Le Jardin des Supplices* of 1899, Mirbeau published no more fiction; but the first two of his plays were performed, and in the years that immediately followed he wrote half a dozen others. These plays are less interesting than his fiction, but they occupy, in the history of the French theater, an almost unique place. When Bernard Shaw bestowed his accolade on the second-rate Eugène Brieux, accepting him as the great French practitioner of his own peculiar kind of drama, the comedy of social analysis, he might better have selected Mirbeau. Mirbeau's plays are, so far as I know, the only French work of merit that has anything in common with this English school. One of them, *Les Affaires sont les Affaires* (1903), enjoyed an immense success. It was admitted into the repertoire of the Comédie Française at a time when the Comédie produced almost no modern plays, and it continued to be done there for years, thus becoming the only work of Mirbeau's that has been endorsed as a classic, so that it is always well spoken of by such writers as M. Lalou. It is certainly Mirbeau's best play, though not so good as the best of his novels. It suffers from his characteristic fault of introducing incredible monstrosities, against a familiar realistic background, into a story that is meant to be plausible; but such a scene as the conversation between the business man and the ruined marquis is admirable in its confrontation, very similar to such scenes in Shaw, of the spokesmen of two social classes, who expound their opposing roles. And Mirbeau's one-acter *L'Epidémie*, in which a provincial town council declines to do anything about a typhoid epidemic that is killing off the local garrison, till they hear that a bourgeois has died of it, is closer to English satire than to the irony of Anatole France. "Typhoid fever," declares in a quavering voice the oldest member of the council, "is a national institution. Let us not lay impious hands upon our old French institutions"; and, "Let us not," seconds the doctor, "present foreign countries with the deplorable spectacle of a French army beating an ignoble retreat before a few problematical microbes."

Sébastien Roch, the Abbé Jules and the hero of *Le Calvaire* are all subject to a waking delirium—day-dreams in which sexual images are mixed nightmarishly with images of horror—of which Mirbeau sometimes gives descriptions almost as elaborate and solid as his accounts of actual events. The key to most of these fantasies is to be found in Mirbeau's perception that inescapable sexual repression or neurotic emotional impotence may result in sadistic impulses. Now, in the fiction of his second period, he ceases to try to present us with difficult cases of real human beings: it is as if he had allowed these fantasies to take possession of his imagination and to impose themselves upon him as generalized pictures of life. At their soundest, these later novels arrive through distortion at satire; at their worst, they are artistically meaningless, a mere procession of obsessive grotesques.

The first of these books, *Le Jardin des Supplices*, is an epitome of Mirbeau's whole vision after his shift to phantasmagoric mythology from naturalistic observation, and it states the Grand Guignol philosophy which he tries to derive from this vision. The story opens in the noxious atmosphere of corrupt Parisian politics under the Third Republic. A scoundrelly Cabinet Minister, whose future is a toss-up between jail and advancement, is blackmailed by one of his jackals and buys him off by sending him away to Ceylon on a scientific expedition financed by government funds. The object of this expedition is to study marine biology in the Indian Ocean—"to discover the primordial cell," as his chief rather vaguely explains to him, "the protoplasmic initium of organized life, or something of the kind." The lesser scoundrel (who tells the story), pretending to be a great biologist, embarks for the East and meets on the ship a beautiful young English lady named Clara, the daughter of an opium-dealer, who is returning to her home in Canton. She gives the impression of great virtue and dignity, and the impostor falls deeply in love with her. He has retained, unlike his chief, some remnants of moral feeling, and all the idealism of which he is capable comes to life under the influence of his passion. He grows ashamed of his bogus role, of his debauched and dishonest past—cannot bear that he should be deceiving a being whom he so much respects, and one day makes a clean breast to Clara of all the disgraceful truth. To his astonishment, she shows at once, and for the first time in their acquaintance, a vivid interest in him. She had paid no attention to him when she had thought he was a serious scientist, but the idea of his vileness pleases her. She is, it turns out, more corrupt than he: more positively perverse and more formidable. She goes to bed with him immediately in her cabin, and he becomes her abject slave. Instead of getting off at Ceylon, he goes on with Clara to China.

The second half of the novel is devoted to a detailed account of their visit to a Chinese prison. This prison has a magnificent garden, in which the convicts are tortured. The Frenchman is shocked and revolted, but he recognizes in what he sees simply a franker and more elegant version of the kind of thing that is going on, in a disguised and hypocritical way, in the Europe he has left behind. It is in vain that, trying to shut out the garden, he summons his familiar Paris. In a moment of revelation, he identifies these executioners with "all the men and all the women whom I have loved or imagined I loved, little indifferent frivolous souls, on whom is spreading now the ineffaceable red stain," with "the judges, the soldiers, the priests, who everywhere in the churches, the barracks and the temples of justice, are busy at the work of death," and with "the man as individual and the man as mob," and with "the animal, the plant, the element, all nature, in fact, which, urged by the cosmic forces of love, rushes toward murder, in the hope of thus finding beyond life a satisfaction of life's furious desires, which devour it and which gush from it in spurts of dirty froth." Clara, however, is enjoying herself. Among the gorgeous flowers which are a feature of the garden and which seem to grow out of its putrescence and blood, she becomes hysterically excited and later, when they leave the garden, collapses in a fit of convulsions. When she comes to, she seems calmed and purged, and declares that she will never return there, but her Chinese maid assures her lover that she will be back on the next visitor's day. The traveller, though he has given up his mission, has, after all, from one point of view, discovered the secret of life.

It will be seen that *Le Jardin des Supplices* has, in conception, its Swiftian strength. The trouble is that, though the scenes in the garden sometimes verge on a true tragic irony, Mirbeau, where a Swift or a Dante would have kept them under severe control, indulges himself, like his Clara, a little too much in horror. The same kind of wrong exploitation of a promising satirical idea—which Swift, again, would have handled better —appears in the second of these later books, *Le Journal d'une Femme de Chambre*. Here Mirbeau set out to expose the meanness and sordidness of the French bourgeoisie by showing how they look to a servant who goes from one of their households to another. But the book is full of scandalous episodes that are not merely repulsive but also completely unreal. The whole effect is turbid and boring. Almost the only memorable thing in the book is the chapter that describes the humiliations to which women looking for jobs are subjected in employment agencies, and this suffers, like so much else in the later Mirbeau, from systematic exaggeration. The moral of *Le Jardin des Supplices* is repeated by the unlikely conclusion, in which Mirbeau has the victimized *femme de chambre* marry a brutal coachman whose attraction for her is partly due to her believing him to have committed an atrocious murder.

If one has read the contemporary accounts of Mirbeau during the years when he was writing these books, it is quite easy to diagnose the reason—aside from his overindulgence in the salacious aspects of his subjects—that they do not succeed as satires or as what he called some of his plays, "*moralités.*" There is much testimony on the part of those who knew Mirbeau at this period that, however one might like him, his conversation made one uncomfortable, because it consisted so largely of the hair-raisingly implausible stories he would tell about every kind of public figure and about all the people he knew. He was not merely trying to be funny; nor were his stories merely exercises in the expected professional malice of the Parisian literary man. What made his talk disconcerting was that he had evidently fabricated these scandals yet believed them to be actual happenings. (He was, also, it seems, untruthful in his ordinary relations with people.) And his books produce the same effect. In Swift, one feels almost to the end, no matter to what lengths he goes, a sound basis in common sense: he is perfectly well aware that human beings are not really Yahoos and that the poor cannot eat their babies. But Octave Mirbeau does not seem to know when or how much he is deforming reality. The truth is that these stories are a little mad. For all their careful planning and deliberate execution, they represent psychological hypertrophies that are destroying a true sense of the world and preventing the development of the artist. Even the texture of the writing is coarser than that of the early novels. If Mirbeau began by anticipating Freud in the case histories of his early fiction, he took later, in a retrogression, to concocting the kind of nightmare that Freud found it profitable to analyze.

*

Much the best of Mirbeau's later books is the last thing he published, *Dingo*, which appeared in 1913, four years before his death; but, containing no scandalous material, it has never been translated into English and has attained less celebrity than *Le Jardin des Supplices* and *Le Journal d'une Femme de Chambre*. *Dingo*, which is told by the author as if in his own character and which sounds as if it were based on a real experience, is the story of an Australian wild dog that has been sent as a puppy to France and grows up in a small French town: perhaps the most debased and revolting of all Mirbeau's dreadful towns. The animal, more wolf than dog, is handsome, remarkably intelligent and devoted to his master and the family; but as soon as he grows out of puppyhood, he begins killing sheep, fowl and game at a rate that makes him a menace. In all this, however, we are made to see, with a subtlety rare in the later Mirbeau, how the master, without at first quite admitting it even to himself, is deriving a certain satisfaction from these crimes against his neighbors, whom he has gradually come to loathe for their self-righteous pusillanimity and cruelty. On one occasion, when he has gone to visit a family of old friends, whom he supposes himself to like, he vicariously betrays his real scorn of them by doing nothing to prevent the dog from slaughtering their pet sheep, which he associates with their feeble personalities. This dog, at least, is frankly a hunter and loyal to those who have cared for him as well as to a family cat with which he has been brought up. But he becomes more and more of a problem. The master is forced to leave the village; he goes to live in Paris, but here Dingo one day leaps at the throat of a man who is trying to steal him and gives rise to disquieting doubts. Then they travel abroad, but wherever they go, they get into some kind of trouble, and the owner is finally obliged to settle down in the country, at the edge of a large forest, in which the dog is free to roam and where he sometimes disappears for days. While they are living there, the master's wife breaks her ribs in a runaway, and the dog, understanding what has happened, keeps watch day and night in her room, resisting attempts to turn him out and refusing to take any food. He wastes away and dies.

This makes a much better book than my summary may

suggest. *Dingo* and *Sébastien Roch* are Mirbeau's most successful novels. He loved animals, and in his later phase sometimes
wrote about them more satisfactorily than he did about human
beings. André Gide is quite correct in singling out the episode
of the fight between the hedgehog and the viper as one of
the only interesting things in *Les Vingt et un Jours d'un
Neurasthénique*, another of Mirbeau's books of this period,
the Arabian Nights of a nerve sanitarium, which in general
represents an even less appetizing combination of dreariness
with abnormality than *Le Journal d'une Femme de Chambre*.
In *Dingo*, the dog and the cat are splendidly depicted and analyzed, and the humans are more human than usual. The book
has an emotional effect, creates a disturbing suspense. Animal
stories were rather fashionable in the early nineteen hundreds,
but this is one of the most unconventional and one of the most
remarkable, and almost achieves the plane of Tolstoy's wonderful horse story, *Kholstomer*. (Mirbeau, who greatly admired
Tolstoy, is said to have had the dubious reciprocal honor of
being regarded by the latter, in his later years, as the most important living French novelist.) Yet, like everything else of
Mirbeau's, it misses the highest level. Dingo's depredations
are on too enormous a scale. His virtues—he loves the poor
and makes a point of cheering up the unhappy—a little too
sentimental (the Ernest Seton Thompson touch); for Mirbeau
has his great sentimentalities to compensate for his chronic fe-
rocities. And the master's inexhaustible complacence, and the
immunity that both he and the dog enjoy in connection with
Dingo's killings, become rather improbable, too. The element
of fantasy gets in again, and it impairs the interest of the record
of what was evidently a real animal.

And now what about Mirbeau today, when the ferocity of
modern man has demonstrated itself on a scale that even he
had not imagined? Already at the time of the first World War, a
book like *Le Jardin des Supplices* seemed definitely out of date.
Mirbeau did have hold of a terrible truth; and yet, reading the
book, as I did, in a military hospital behind the lines, one realized that the impression made by human pain as a part of one's
daily routine was different from anything felt by a prosperous
pre-war civilian writing at his ease about it (I have not been

able to learn whether Mirbeau actually served in the war of 1870). There was too much Parisian upholstery, too much conventional literature, about *Le Jardin des Supplices*. The characters of Ernest Hemingway, with their bad nerves and their ugly conduct, reflected the cruelty of the time more effectively than Mirbeau's enormities and his rhetorical paroxysms. Brett of *The Sun Also Rises* is the Clara of the later generation, and a more convincing creation. Since then, the indiscriminate bombings of London and Berlin, the death-houses of Dachau and Belsen, the annihilation of Hiroshima, have made Mirbeau and Hemingway both seem somewhat obsolete. Is anyone troubled at present by the idea that human beings are torturing or murdering each other? Don't the bugaboo books of the later Mirbeau, with their mélange of human sympathy and sadism, look today like the slightly cracked fairy-tales of a not ungenial old romantic who was still naïve enough not to take such things for granted?

April 2, 1949

A Revival of Ronald Firbank

NEW DIRECTIONS has brought out an "*Omnibus*" of five of Ronald Firbank's novels: *Valmouth, The Artificial Princess, The Flower Beneath the Foot, Prancing Nigger,* and *Concerning the Eccentricities of Cardinal Pirelli*—with an introduction by Osbert Sitwell, a revised and expanded version of a memoir which has already twice been printed in other volumes. It is a good thing to have Firbank revived. Just before this collection appeared, I had been reading those of his novels that I had not read when they first came out, and these had led me to reread those that I had read. A conviction had been gradually growing on me that he was one of the finest English writers of his period and one of those most likely to become a classic. In England he has been appreciated much better than over here. In America, he was introduced in the twenties by Mr. Carl Van Vechten, but, while Firbank was alive, only three of his ten books were ever published in the United States, and although these had a certain vogue, they figured mainly among the accessories of what was then called "sophistication" and were, I think, more or less confused, through no fault of Mr. Van Vechten's, with Mr. Van Vechten's own novels, which may have been influenced by Firbank but which were not on the same plane of artistic seriousness. Since Firbank's death in 1926, he has hardly been read over here. In England, he has always had a definite position. A collected edition of his work was brought out in a limited edition in 1929, with an essay by Arthur Waley and the memoir by Osbert Sitwell, and the next year a short biography by Ifan Kyrle Fletcher, with reminiscences by Sitwell and others. Both these were imported by Brentano's but aroused little interest in America. E. M. Forster, Cyril Connolly and Evelyn Waugh have all recognized Firbank's genius and written about him.

The story of Firbank himself is as strange and as entertaining, as full of surprising anomalies, as the queer cases presented in his novels. Ronald Firbank's paternal great-grandfather—I rely on Mr. Fletcher's memoir—had been a North of England coal-miner, who could not read or write. The grandfather got himself some schooling, left the mines to do railroad work and had become, by 1866, one of the biggest railroad contractors in England: a self-made man of the ruggedest mold, who would not accept foreign contracts because foreigners did not pay in English gold and who, when offered a loan free of interest, declined it with the remark: "I values at nowt what I gets for nowt." On discovering, in the stable of his eldest son, a fine hunter among the carthorses, he looked at it sourly and said: "Eh, lad!—that won't pull a load o' muck!" This son inherited the business, went into Parliament and was knighted. Mr. Fletcher conveys the impression that Sir Thomas was rather a stuffed shirt. He married the daughter of an Irish clergyman, and their second son was Arthur Annesley Ronald Firbank.

The boy had already from childhood the tendency to catarrh from which he was always to suffer and which finally caused his death. His mother, who had set Sir Thomas to collecting French furniture and porcelain, cultivated the son's sensibilities, coddled him and was always adored by him. (There are a number of striking resemblances between Firbank's personality and Proust's.) Ronald did not last a year at a public school, but he was later sent to France, where he lived in a château and studied French, with the idea of entering the diplomatic service. He published, in 1905, a little book containing two items: one a fairy-tale called *Odette d'Antrevernes*, which exhaled a sickly perfume of the nineties, the other—*A Study in Temperament*—a satirical conversation piece, in which he had found already his characteristic vein. The next year he went to Cambridge but he did not finish.

By this time—rich, shy and fastidious—he had managed to transform himself into something like a nostalgic caricature of the aesthetes of the Beardsley-Wilde period, whose productions, together with those of the *fin de siècle* French poets, provided his chief literary food. He surrounded himself with cut flowers, offered his visitors hothouse peaches, haunted the Russian ballet, wore Chinese and Egyptian rings. When people came to see him, he would sometimes carry on conversations looking out the window with his back turned toward his guests; and even with special friends, he was likely, after a witty beginning, to lapse into incoherent mumbling or to be seized by a *fou rire* which made it impossible for him to finish some anecdote or to go on reading aloud one of his stories. (Proust is said to have behaved in the same way.) When you talked to him, writes one of his college-mates, he was always "writhing about and admiring his hands" like "the portraits of society women by Boldini." On one occasion, when Firbank had been brought to meet some friend of a friend, he refused—no doubt imitating Wilde, who sometimes made similar objections—on the ground that the man was too ugly.

At first glance, you might get the impression that Ronald Firbank had come a very long way from his grandfather, the railroad contractor. Yet the role that Ronald played was deceptive. He had not quite left the old man behind. Though he expressed himself often like a school-girl in a high-pitched slithering voice, though he fidgetted and giggled and drooped, he had sharp powers of observation and a very shrewd sense of values. He was also more practical than people thought. His friends, who had supposed him incapable of travelling from London to Oxford, were surprised when he made journeys without mishap to such faraway places as Haiti and when they learned that he had put down singlehanded a mutiny on the boat on which he had made a trip down the Nile; and they would presently become aware, as he asked them to witness deeds and other legal documents, that he was well able to take care of his business interests. The point was that he was not a weak character but in some ways a very strong one. Harold Nicolson, who evidently had Firbank in mind in the story called *Lambert Orme* in *Some People*—though he transposed Firbank's writings and his later career into somewhat different terms—has dramatized the contrast in Firbank of fortitude and serious purpose with apparent frivolity and softness; but it is characteristic of the difference between Firbank and Nicolson that the latter, always grasping at accepted values, inexpugnably official-minded, should have made Lambert Orme prove his mettle as an officer in the first World War, whereas Firbank had shown his toughness, not by distinguishing himself in the war, but by refusing, as far as possible, to recognize it. It required a good deal of self-confidence to repudiate the public school code, to play the aesthete at that period and to that degree. The preciosity of Firbank's books seems so conscious and calculated that one sometimes suspects him, in fact, of deliberately overplaying this role. V. B. Holland, who knew him at Cambridge, reports that, "seeing him once clad in a sweater and football shorts, I asked him what on earth he had been doing: 'Oh, football,' he replied. 'Rugger or Soccer?' 'Oh, I don't remember'—and a laugh. 'Well, was the ball round or egg-shaped?' 'Oh, I was never near enough to it to see that!' " When the war came, he professed frank loathing of everything connected with it, said he had always found the Germans "most polite." He was called up again and again for medical examinations and questionings by the military authorities, and was finally rejected as physically unfit for service. When, by mistake, he was then called up again, he threatened to sue the War Office for libel and elicited an apology from it. He protested against the war by shutting himself up at Oxford for a period of two years, during which, according to legend, he spoke to nobody but his cleaning woman and the guard on the London train. And for the first time he applied himself to serious writing.

The exhilaration of reading about Firbank is that which we derive from the spectacle—first, perhaps, made popular by Lord Dundreary in that old play *Our American Cousin*—of the apparently silly ass who is really superbly clever, of the sissy who ends by scoring off the world which has been making fun of him. The anecdotes about Ronald Firbank are as amusing as the things in his novels—especially his ostensibly irrelevant remarks, which so often bewildered his companions but left them uneasily wondering whether they didn't mean more than they seemed to. When one of his friends had said, "Good night, Firbank," as he put Ronald into a taxi, "the taxi moved off, but before I had had time to move, there was a violent rattling and banging and the taxi stopped. Firbank leaned out of the window and called to me. 'I wish,' he said, 'you wouldn't call me Firbank; it gives me a sense of goloshes.' " When Sacheverell Sitwell complimented him on his latest novel, *Caprice*, he turned his head away and remarked in a choking voice, "I can't bear calceolarias. Can you?" The technique of his writing is similar. One may have thought, when one first looked at his books in the twenties, that they were foamy improvisations which could be skimmed up in rapid reading. Yet when one tried to run through them, one found oneself pricked by something that queerly impressed; one was aware of artistic seriousness, even if one did not linger to find out what the writer was up to. When one returns to them today, one realizes that Ronald Firbank was one of the writers of his time who took most trouble over their work and who were most singlemindedly devoted to literature. The memoirs of him testify to this. His books are not foolish trifles, scribbled down to get through the boredoms of a languid and luxurious life. They are extremely intellectual, and composed with the closest attention: dense textures of indirection that always disguise point. They have to be read with care, and they can be read again and again, because Firbank has loaded every rift with ore. The effect of his writing is light, but it differs from the flimsier work of the nineties, which, at first sight, it may resemble, in the tension behind it of the effort to find the felicitous or the witty phrase which will render the essence of something. The little dyed twirls of plume and the often fresh sprays of flowers, the half-stifled flutters of laughter and the *fusées* of jewelly fire, have been twisted and tempered in a mind that is capable of concentration. It is a glancing mind but rarely wobbles. Only in the dangling participles with which he sometimes begins his sentences and in a lack of continuity of movement of which I shall speak later does he betray a certain weakness of syntax. But phrase by phrase, sentence by sentence, paragraph by paragraph, chapter by chapter, the workmanship is not merely exact but of a quality for which the craftsman must gratuitously tax himself. It has recently been learned that Beardsley was the child of two generations of jewellers who were also goldsmiths, and, once one knows this, it is quite easy to recognize the influence of the family trade in his clear two-dimensional patterns with their tendril-like ramifications and their delicate scrollings of pin-point lines, in their wreaths and rosettes, their festoons and crests. Perhaps, in a less obvious way, the inheritance of Firbank from old Joseph counts for something here, too. Mr. Fletcher asserts that the grandfather was something of an engineering genius and that his work shows a passion for perfection. Certainly the work of the grandson—decadent though its subject matter usually is—

never fails to live up to the slogan, "I values at nowt what I gets for nowt."

This work of the grandson is also in an old and strong English tradition: it belongs to the school of comedy that had its first great practitioner in Ben Jonson, that was exploited in its purest form by Congreve and the other Restoration dramatists, and that persists through a variety of modifications in Peacock, Gilbert and Aldous Huxley. The true products of this school are at the opposite pole from the hearty and hilarious English humor (though in some writers the two are combined). It is polished and coldly reasoned and rarely admits any kind of idealism. It is occupied with worldly values and if it ever turns its attention to general ideas, it makes mock of them all indiscriminately. Though it sometimes introduces a moralist who is supposed to act as a touchstone in showing up the faults of the other characters, it usually verges on cynicism, and it is always non-romantic and non-sentimental. There is nothing, so far as I know, quite like this English comic tradition in the literature of any other country. Distinguished, unscrupulous, hard; carved, gilded and decorative; planned logically and executed deliberately; of good quality, designed for long wear; intellectual but never intelligent—no people could have developed it but the English. You may feel, when you first approach Firbank, that his talent is too effeminate to claim ancestry from this masculine line; and it is true that a number of his books are occupied almost exclusively with women, and that his writing is full of trailed dots, coy italics and little cries. Yet these latter, always calculated, are really a part of his subject: the mannerisms that go with the habits of his special group and time. You may think that this effete preciosity has little in common with the brutality and elegance of *Love for Love* and *The Way of the World*. Yet the fact that Ronald Firbank is dealing with a later and less lusty phase of the same society as Congreve should not keep us from appreciating that his formal panels are no less finely painted.

Ronald Firbank wrote one play, *The Princess Zoubaroff*, and it affords a useful opportunity to compare his methods and point of view with those of Restoration comedy. The men and women in Wycherley and Congreve are all engaged in chasing one another: they lack sentiment but have vigorous appetites.

The men and women in Firbank, for the most part, have neither sentiment nor keen desires. To them marriage means as little as it does to the characters of Congreve; but the alternative is not a succession of more or less piquant adulteries: it is likely to be an adolescent falling-back on members of their own sexes. Eric and Enid, in *The Princess Zoubaroff*, have been married hardly a week and Enid is still answering congratulatory letters when they visit, at a villa near Florence, another young married couple. Both the husbands and the wives have gone to school together, and they immediately renew old relationships. Enid, who has married to escape from her family and has found marriage disappointing, is perfectly willing for Eric to go away with the husband of her friend on a trip to the Engadine. At the end of the first act, the young woman who has been married the longer conveys to her friend with ominous distaste, "as though she were sickening for the Plague," an intimation that she is going to have a baby. In the next act, the two ladies, with others of the English colony, are recruited by a Russian princess for a sort of Lesbian convent, while the baby is left in the hands of a nurse. The husbands have now been away a long time, and the young women take in with apathy the report of a mountain-climbing accident which may mean that both have been killed. But in the third act the men drift back. They are received without excitement and are themselves very much relieved when they see the wives go off to the Princess's convent. The Scotch nurse at this point gives notice, and the father is left with the baby, whose name he does not even know. His only idea about it is to send it at once to the right kind of school.

This skeleton will bring out the difference between Congreve's men and women and Firbank's. The difference in their literary methods corresponds to the difference in subject. Where the speeches in Congreve are set-pieces, where the scenes have the give-and-take of an energetic well-played game, the dialogue in Firbank is all vague innuendos, gasps and murmurs, light caresses, small digs. Yet as writing it is no less consummate—and much finer than that of Wilde when he is working in the Congreve tradition. Not that Firbank's fluttering absurdities are more skillful than Wilde ringingly turned epigrams; but there is always in the comedies of Wilde an element of conventional theater—of melodrama or simple farce —though in this he is of course running true to the tone of his late-Victorian time. *Lady Windemere's Fan* has passages that might almost have been written by Pinero; *The Importance of Being Ernest* is still not far from *Charley's Aunt*. Firbank's comedy belongs to a society that is as non-moral as the Restoration and quite detached from the middle-class standards that still make themselves felt in Wilde.

One finds also in Firbank, however, besides this durable old English tradition, a certain influence from modern France— notably, I should say, from *Histoire Contemporaine*, Anatole France's Bergeret series. One seems to find the Anatole France formulas both in Firbank's tricks of style and in his presentation of episodes. In the latter connection, Firbank seems also to have reproduced France's faults—for the weakness of his narratives, like the weakness of France's, is a lack of continuous development. One chapter does not lead to another, but each makes a little vignette which, significant and finished though it is, does not always fall into place as part of a coherent scheme.

The point of view in these comedies of Firbank, though they derive from an ancient tradition, is unconventional and very personal. Evelyn Waugh, in his appreciation of Firbank, has explained his own indebtedness to him, and a comparison of these two writers brings out Firbank's peculiar strength. For Evelyn Waugh belongs to the category of social satirists who "castigate the vices" of their time by referring them to old-fashioned virtues which they imagine to have flourished in a previous age. It is possible for a writer of this kind to describe the most fantastic occurrences and the most outrageous behavior, and yet not to antagonize the public, to enjoy, even, a wide popularity, because he reassures the reader by implying an irreproachable standard of stability and respectability. It is the technique of Horace's Augustan odes—a technique which Ronald Firbank could not exploit. He had no real place in English life. He could not invoke old Joseph. His own career and that of his grandfather had not a moment in common. In only one of his novels—*Inclinations*—does Firbank make sound English values assert themselves to the confusion of international decadence. Here a girl from a good county family goes to Greece with a Lesbian novelist, persists in remaining unconscious of the nature of her companion's interest in her, breaks the older lady's heart by running away with an Italian count, returns to her family in England with a baby but without her husband, who is supposed to be looking after his estate but who is suspected of having deserted her, and finally, when family and friends have become completely convinced that the rascally foreigner has let her down, scores again when he duly appears and proves to be not an adventurer but an excellent fellow of limited intelligence and simple tastes like her own. It is a pity that this most satisfactory of Firbank's early books has not been included in this omnibus rather than *The Artificial Princess*, which, good though it is in its way, was Firbank's first longish story, written rather under the influence of Beardsley's *Under the Hill* and not published during Firbank's lifetime. The three novels that followed *The Artificial Princess*—*Vainglory*, *Inclinations* and *Caprice*—are all attempts, most successful in spite of their apparent fanciness, to depict English life and character. Ronald Firbank has caught certain aspects of these as perhaps no one else has done—particularly the English habit of pretending to disregard what is uppermost in people's minds and always talking about something else. In Firbank's next novel, *Valmouth*, he is dealing still with the English scene but has found his own vein of fantasy, and develops in terms of high caricature the theme of the English capacity for carrying on unperturbedly in the presence of the scandalous or the catastrophic.

Thereafter, he abandons England, and we get *The Princess Zoubaroff* (Florence), *Santal* (Algiers), *The Flower Beneath the Foot* (an imaginary European kingdom), *Prancing Nigger* (the West Indies), and *Concerning the Eccentricities of Cardinal Pirelli* (Spain), in which, though the English still figure, they become less and less conspicuous. Yet, free to go where he pleases, with no British conventions to hamper him, Ronald Firbank is not, even now, at ease in his chosen role of well-heeled international drifter. He obviously delights in the humors of *The Princess Zoubaroff*, but this shimmering and chiming comedy leaves a lasting and a disquieting impression. It is really an understatement of the same theme that D. H. Lawrence became violent and shrill about: the biologically sinister phenomenon of a slackening of the interest in mating on the part of the privileged classes of Europe.

Firbank's next book, *Santal*, a very short one, has attracted less attention than any other of his mature writings, but I do not agree with his critics, Mr. Waley and Mr. Forster, that it is altogether without merit. This is his most nearly realistic story, and the only one that is not a comedy. It is Firbank's most direct approach to the personal situation which is reflected by all his work, for it is the story of the religious vocation of an orphaned Arab named Cherif, who, discovering that he has no close ties with the relatives who have taken him in and is incapable of sharing their prosaic interests, sets out on a pilgrimage to a holy man who is supposed to live in the mountains. He finds nothing, his water gives out, and he is left in the barren wilderness reading the Koran and dying of thirst. There were few of Ronald Firbank's contemporaries who could have equalled the writing of such a passage as that which works up to the sentence: "Beneath the pitiless sun all signs of life had vanished, and in the deep of noon the hills looked to ache with light." But Firbank here was under the handicap of having himself been a poor little rich boy, so that it was difficult for him to manage a hero who was supposed to be a poor little poor boy. He could have known little of physical discomforts, and, though he is admirable at describing the landscape, he is unable to conjure up the sensations of a boy riding for days in the desert. Firbank said that, when he was writing *Santal*, he found that the subject bored him and that, reacting from it, his imagination flew to the other extreme and presented him with the luxurious aristocrats of *The Flower Beneath the Foot*, which he could hardly wait to begin. Yet this next book, so funny in its exquisite way, so squirming with court scandal, deals with a similar subject: Laura de Nazianzi, niece of the Mistress of the Robes, "more piquant perhaps than pretty," whose large gray eyes "surveyed the world with a pensive critical glance," is in love with young Prince Yousef of the Kingdom of Pisuerga, whose face, though "handsome to tears," had, "even when he had been a child, lacked innocence," and he apparently returns her love; but for reasons of state he drops her and marries an English princess. Laura enters a convent, and the last turn of the screw for her is that she finds the nuns too much distracted by the excitement of the royal wedding to attend to their religious duties. Laura watches the wedding procession, beating her hands on the broken glass that bristles from the convent wall.

Yet, eventually, we are told, Laura became a saint. This turning to religion from the life of the world is a theme in all Firbank's later books. If you should read *The Flower Beneath the Foot* without knowing Firbank's work well, you might think this was all a joke, that he was merely being silly and witty, as he was in *The Princess Zoubaroff*, about the fashionable aspects of religion. But that was not the case. "I believe that in his early youth," writes one of his friends, Lord Berners, "he had thought of taking Holy Orders. But more than once he had said to me, 'The Church of Rome wouldn't have me and so I laugh at them.'" (He had, however, become a Catholic at Cambridge in 1908.) He strikes one as having nothing to fall back on save his capacity for self-dependence and the discipline imposed by his writing. Art was his only sainthood. He was solitary and must have been lonely, though when someone suggested this, he replied, "I can buy companionship." Though he loves all the gossip of the world he frequents, it is mainly for what he can make of it; and though his work is full of naughty jokes that combine in a startling way a pansy archness with a brutal coarseness, one feels that his interest in sex is also mainly an aesthetic one. From the discrepancies he found in himself—pathetically stunted functions entangled with admirably developed talents, childish inadequacies in personal relations alongside a mature grasp of moral values—he never seems to have had any relief except through the demoralizing comedy and the grotesque pathos of his novels. These novels, in one way or another, like the limericks of Edward Lear, almost always present the eccentric at odds with established society—though established society in Firbank may be itself unconventional and the eccentric, like Laura de Nazianzi, an honest and natural person. The heroines of the early novels—the touching Mrs. Shamefoot of *Vainglory*, who, married to an important public figure and not at all amused by her social set, has concentrated all her longings on having her existence commemorated by a stained-glass window in the local cathedral; Miss Sinquier of *Caprice*, the daughter of a rural dean, who steals the family silver, sells it and blows the money all in, in London—with the aid of hangers-on picked up at the Cafe Royal—on producing *Romeo and Juliet* with herself in the title role, only to be killed after the opening night as the result of catching her foot in a mousetrap and falling through a trap-door in the stage—these are figures of an incredible drollery; but there is something behind them that is not quite funny. Even the Lesbian lady of *Inclinations*, whose frustration is represented by a chapter consisting solely of the exclamation "Mabel!" printed eight times, elicits a certain sympathy. Later on, more and more, the eccentrics become saints. Even Miami of *Prancing Nigger*, who has removed her family from the country to the city and watched the rest of them go to pieces there and who loses her country lover at sea, is last seen as a pious pilgrim on her way to a miraculous shrine. And in the figure of Cardinal Pirelli, Firbank bent all his resources to the creation of his noblest eccentric who is at the same time his strangest saint. The Cardinal, who, having already a dubious reputation, has baptized, out of pity for a childless woman, one of the pups of her favorite dog, comes to present an ecclesiastical problem and soon finds himself shadowed by a Vatican spy who is trying to get something on him. The Cardinal plans a flight from Spain, but on the eve of departure has a fatal stroke in circumstances of the most outrageous scandal. "Now," writes Firbank, "that the ache of life, with its fevers, passions, doubts, its routine, vulgarity, and boredom, was over, his serene, unclouded face was a marvelment to behold. Very great distinction and sweetness was visible there, together with much nobility, and love, all magnified and commingled." (Note here the ache of life that recalls the ache of the hills in the passage quoted from *Santal*.)

Lord Berners, in an account of Firbank's death, says that he was told by a man who lived on the opposite side of a court-yard from Firbank's apartment in Rome, that he had sometimes been wakened at night by the sound of his neighbor's immoderate laughter. Just as his conversation and his reading to friends would sometimes be broken off by paroxysms of mirth that were likely to end in coughing, so even when he was writing alone this uncontrollable laughter would sometimes put an end to his work. So he had been diverted from the sad little story of Cherif to the hilarious but even more harrowing comedy of *The Flower Beneath the Foot*. Ronald Firbank was the poet of the *fou rire*. That is the key to the whole of his work. There is anguish behind it all—and the more ridiculous it is, the better he is expressing this anguish. *The Eccentricities of Cardinal Pirelli* is at once his most preposterous book and the one that has most moral meaning; it combines his most perverse story with his purest and most beautiful writing. He has here expressed his ideal conception, quite heretical but not irresponsible, not lacking in serious intention, of what a Catholic priest might be, and this has enabled him, for the first time, through art, fully to accommodate his imperfections, to triumph over his disabilities. It may be that the dead Cardinal's serenity had been won by him, too, for a moment in the few weeks of life that were left him.

For Firbank himself was to die just after he had finished this novel. On his last visit to England, he told his friends that he had wanted to write a certain number of books, that he had now written them and that he would probably write no more. He was just on the verge of forty and was worrying about his wrinkles. His lungs and heart were in very bad condition, and he had been virtually condemned by the doctor. In Rome he came down with some kind of "chill." He was alone in a rented apartment, where he would not let his friends come to see him, because, he said, the wallpaper was too hideous. He had even sent away his nurse, in the belief that he was getting well. When Ronald Firbank died, Lord Berners was his only friend in Rome. He knew nothing of Firbank's family—his mother had died not long before but he had a sister living—and found the name of his solicitor by chance on a crumpled piece of paper. Not knowing that Firbank was a Catholic, he had him buried in the Protestant Cemetery, curiously but not incongruously, not far from Shelley and Keats. When Osbert Sitwell went to visit the grave, all trace of it had disappeared. The sexton explained that the body had been moved to a Catholic cemetery. Thus, as Sitwell remarks, there was even about Firbank's burial "an inconsequential as well as a tragic element."

December 10, 1949

Paul Rosenfeld: Three Phases

THE DEATH of Paul Rosenfeld has left me not only shocked at the unexpected loss of a friend, but with a feeling of dismay and disgust at the waste of talent in the United States. Paul, when I first knew him—in 1922, I think—was one of the most exciting critics of the "American Renaissance." I had read, while in the army in France, an essay on Sibelius in the *New Republic*, which had had upon me the exhilarating effect that wartime reading sometimes does; and later, when I was back in New York, a longer study on Richard Strauss, a great musical hero of the time, which brought into the writing itself something of the Straussian brilliance but probed with a very sure hand what was specious and vulgar in Strauss. It was the first really searching criticism that I had ever seen of this composer, and both these essays amazed me. They had a kind of fullness of tone, a richness of vocabulary and imagery, and a freedom of the cultural world that were quite different from the schoolmasterish criticism which had become the norm in the United States. *Musical Portraits*, in 1920, the first book that collected these pieces, seemed at the time absolutely dazzling. Paul told me, when I knew him later, that the point when he had felt his maturity was the moment when he had realized with pride that he could turn out as good an article as Huneker; but actually he much surpassed Huneker, who, useful though he was in his role, always remained a rather harried journalist, trying to produce a maximum of copy in order to get money to go abroad. Paul was a serious writer who was working from New York as a base. One had always had the impression that Huneker came in through the back door at Scribner's in a day when the arts were compelled to give precedence to money and gentility, and that there had been something in Bernard Shaw's prophecy that, if he stayed in the United States, he would never be anything but a "clever slummocker"; and one now heard depressing reports that he was old, poor and ill in Brooklyn. But Paul Rosenfeld seemed the spirit of a new and more fortunate age, whose cosmopolitanism was not self-conscious and which did not have to be on the defensive for its catholic interest in art and life. The portraits of Paul's first book dramatized modern music as no criticism had done before; they brought into range a whole fascinating world, united though international, of personality, poetics, texture, mood. Paul Rosenfeld at that time enjoyed a prestige of the same kind as Mencken's and Brooks's, though it was not so widely felt as the former's.

He had inherited a comfortable income, and he built himself at Westport, Connecticut, a small and attractive house, where he lived alone with his work and entertained his friends. The first time I ever saw him, I had not yet met him. It was in Paris sometime in the summer of 1921, and I was dining alone one night in a favorite Italian restaurant, very clean and rather austere—I remember it as always quiet and filled with a clear twilight—to which I had been taken first by somebody during the war and to which I liked to return, ordering almost always the same meal that I had had when I went there first: ravioli and Asti Spumante. A party of three sat down at the table just across from mine, and though I had never seen any of them before, I recognized them soon as Paul Rosenfeld, Sherwood Anderson and Anderson's wife, the sculptress, Tennessee Mitchell. I had heard in New York that Paul was taking the Andersons to Europe, where Anderson had never been, and I observed the party with interest and heard snatches of their conversation. Tennessee Mitchell had the aspect and the manner of a raw-boned prairie woman, and I was touched by Paul's obvious effort to approximate for her benefit to a modestly folksy manner. I was reminded of the incident later when I read in Sherwood Anderson's memoirs that he had sat in the Tuileries one day—he is here apostrophizing himself—with "the tears running from your eyes, because you thought everything around you so beautiful." It was all very typical of the period, and so are my first memories of Paul after I got to know him in New York. I spent a weekend with him once at Westport—sometime in 1922—and read him an article I had just written about T. S. Eliot's *Waste Land* on the occasion of its getting the *Dial* prize. In the city I had been leading at that time rather a frenetic life, and I remember what a relief it was to talk about art with Paul in an atmosphere completely free from the messy dissipation and emotion that were characteristic of the twenties, and for once to get a good night's sleep in a house where everything was quiet and simple. I had that night a delightful dream, which still comes back to me quite distinctly, of little figures that were really alive though much less than life-size, dancing with slow grace to an exquisite Mozartian music which filled me with peace and joy. It was an antidote to the stridencies of the jazz age, which Paul's spirit had managed to exorcise. He loathed jazz in all its raw forms and could only accept it transmuted by the style of a Stravinsky or a Copland.

With his fair reddish hair and mustache, his pink cheeks and his limpid brown eyes, his clothes which always followed with dignity the Brooks-cut college model, his presence, short though he was, had a certain authority and distinction. It was something that made Anderson call him the well-dressed man of American prose. He had a knack of turning pretty little speeches and he was also genuinely considerate in a way that was rare in that era, but he could be forthright when the occasion demanded, and, though naturally candid and warm, he would retire—which always amused me—at a suspicion of imposture or imposition, into a skeptical and ironic reserve. He was, I think, the only man I have known of whom it could truly be said that he possessed a Heinesque wit, and I always thought it a pity that his humor, which contributed so much to the pleasure of being with him, should have figured so little in his essays. (Since writing this, however, I have been looking into one of his later books, *An Hour with American Music*, and I see that it is full of *wit*. It was the humor of exaggeration, to which he sometimes gave rein in his talk, that rarely appeared in his work.)

When I got to know Paul better, we sometimes compared notes about our childhood and education. He had gone to school on the Hudson and had afterwards graduated from Yale, and the latter institution, though he seemed to feel a certain respect for it, had rather oppressed him at the time he had been there; but he had been fortunate in being able to escape to spend his summer vacations in Europe. When he had once found out, he told me, that there existed somewhere else an artistic and social and intellectual world larger and more exciting than anything he had known in America, and that he could always go back to it later, he found that he could endure New Haven, to which he was so ill-adapted, without fears of suffocation. He had grown up in uptown New York in a German-Jewish household, and he had never belonged to any church or been trained in any religion; but he had got from his parents a grounding in the classical German culture, musical and literary. When he went to Europe in summer, he loved to visit a German uncle, who was something of a *bon vivant*. His parents had both died when he was young, and his only close relative was a sister. He never married and, so far as I could see, had no real desire to marry, enjoying the bachelor's life which his moderate means made possible.

His strongest tie was undoubtedly with Stieglitz, toward whom he stood in something like a filial relation; and the group around Stieglitz became for him both family and church. The only traditionally and specifically Jewish trait that ever came, in my intercourse with Paul, as something alien that blocked understanding between us was the quality of his piety toward Stieglitz, whom he accepted and revered as a prophet, unquestioningly obedient to his guidance in the spirit that has been sometimes exemplified by the disciples of Freud and Schoenberg; and his range as a writer on the plastic arts was limited by the exclusiveness of his interest in the work of the Stieglitz group. It was difficult, if not impossible, to persuade him to pay attention to any contemporary American painter who was not a protégé of Stieglitz', and if Stieglitz had excommunicated a refractory or competitive disciple, Paul Rosenfeld, following the official directive, would condemn him, not merely as an artist but as a reprobate who had somehow committed an unpardonable moral treason. He had the tone of the old-fashioned brother whose sister has fallen to shame, or the member of a Communist sect reacting to the name of a heretic.

For the rest, his affectionate and generous nature had to spend itself mainly in the sympathy that he brought to the troubles of his friends and in the tireless encouragement of talent. His judgment here was usually shrewd, his insight often profound; he was tactful and unobtrusive in helping people who needed help, and he did not want thanks in return. His taking the Andersons to Europe is an example that happens to be known of the kind of thing he liked to do, and one has heard of his providing, at a critical time, resources for a now famous composer; but he undoubtedly did more for more people than anyone will ever know. It has remained in my mind that he was present at the deathbed of Randolph Bourne, desperately feeding him with oxygen in the effort to keep him alive. Bourne had been one of the most remarkable of the group that founded the *Seven Arts*. As a hunchback, he was unfit for the services and thus free to repudiate the war as an able-bodied writer could hardly have done so roundly; and the intellectual light and the moral passion, the mastery of self-expression, that led people to forget his deformity as soon as he began to talk, made his friends of that era feel that he was keeping alive spiritual values that might otherwise have gone by the board. "When he died," Paul wrote, "we knew that perhaps the strongest mind of the entire younger generation in America had gone. . . . We see the size of him plainly in the bitter moments in which we realize how vacant the scene has become in the many fields to which he brought the light of his own clear nature!"

II

Paul later sold his house at Westport and took a little corner apartment in an old and elevatorless house on the west side of Irving Place. There, however, he continued to flourish. He liked to give evening parties which were none the less agreeable for their rather old-fashioned character. What was unusual in the dry twenties was that there was very little liquor served: a highball or two or a little punch; and poets read their poetry and composers played their music. One met Ornstein, Milhaud, Varèse; Cummings, Hart Crane and Marianne Moore; the Stieglitzes and all their group; the Stettheimers, Mumford, Kreymborg. One of the images that remains with me most vividly is the bespectacled figure of Copland, at that period gray-faced and lean, long-nosed and rather unearthly, bending above the keyboard as he chanted in a high, cold and passionate voice a poem of Ezra Pound's—*An Immorality*—for which he had written a setting.

In those days I saw a good deal of Paul in a business as well as in a friendly way, for I was working first on *Vanity Fair*, then on the *New Republic*, and Paul wrote a good deal for both. He grew rather stout at this time, and his style betrayed a tendency toward floridity. He felt afterwards, he told me, that his writing, like so many other things during the Boom, had, to its detriment, become somewhat overinflated. My impression is that when people say they do not like Paul Rosenfeld's style, they are thinking of characteristics that only became really rampant in some of his work of this period, and that they have no real acquaintance with his criticism either before or after. As an editor, I had sometimes to struggle with him over the locutions and vocabulary of his essays, and I am fully aware of his faults. He had spent so much time in Europe and he read so much French and German that he could never quite keep his English distinct from his other languages, and habitually wrote *ignore* as if it meant the same thing as *ignorer* and *genial* as if it meant possessing genius. He had also a way of placing adverbs that used to set my teeth on edge, as did some of these adverbs themselves, such as *doubtlessly* and *oftentimes*. There were moments when he *did* overwrite, working himself up into a state of exaltation with romantic Germanic abstractions that sounded a little ridiculous in English. But, going back to his essays today, one is not much bothered by this or even necessarily conscious of it. One finds a body of musical criticism that covers the modern field more completely than one had remembered and that stands up, both as writing and as interpretation, so solidly as to make quite unimportant these minor idiosyncrasies and slips.

There is of course an objection to Paul's writing which is based on disapproval on principle of the romantic and impressionistic school that he enthusiastically represented. In the serious literary journals, a new tone had just been set in the twenties by T. S. Eliot's *The Sacred Wood*, which was spare and terse in style, analytical and logical in treatment. Paul Rosenfeld, who lacked the intellectual instruments for dealing with literary ideas (though he was expert at dealing with musical ones), was somewhat less satisfactory—except when writing of certain kinds of poetry that had something in common with music—on the subject of literature than he was on music and painting; but it was very unjust that this fashion should have prejudiced against him the editors of the kind of magazine on which he most depended for a market. The same tendency appeared in the musical world; and the critics—though less, I think, the composers—complained of his lack of scholarship on the technical side of music. To this a writer who is not a musician can only reply that it seems to him that the moment the critic departs from the technical analysis of a score, he is writing impressionistic criticism; and that Berlioz in his essays on Beethoven's symphonies and Debussy when he is putting on record such an opinion as that Edvard Grieg was a bonbon stuffed with snow are just as much impressionistic critics as Paul Rosenfeld ever was. Berlioz and Debussy, of course, were a great deal more literary and programmatic than the generation of Schoenberg and Stravinsky have liked to be thought to be; but I believe that Paul was right in insisting that every valid work of art owes its power to giving expression to some specific human experience and connecting it with some human ideal. For musicians it must of course be profitable to read the kind of score-by-score study that has been made by Albert Berger, for example, of the development of Aaron Copland; but, as a layman who merely listens to music, I do not see that it is easy to dismiss the interpretations given by Paul of the emotional and social content of the more "abstract" modern composers: Schoenberg and Stravinsky, Bartók and Hindemith. It is just here, where the composer invites it least, that Paul's insight most proves his genius.

All those years we talked much of such matters. The kind of writing I did myself aimed at something rather different from his, and he horrified me once by saying that his idea of good prose was something that was laid on like a thick coat of paint; but we had in common a fundamental attitude and invoked a common cultural tradition, which it is easiest to call humanistic. Among the few things that I really look back upon with anything like nostalgia in the confusion and waste of the twenties are such conversations as those with Paul when we would sit in his corner room, beneath his little collection of Hartleys and O'Keeffes and Marins, surrounded by his shelves full of Nietzsche and Wagner, Strindberg, Shaw and Ibsen, Tolstoy and Dostoevsky, Flaubert, Claudel and Proust, Henry James and Poe, and the English poets that he had read at Yale, or walk back and forth at night between my place and his. He liked New York, was a thorough New Yorker, and—except for a few weeks in the summer, when he would visit the Stieglitzes at Lake George and, as Georgia O'Keeffe once told me, take the same walk every afternoon, or for an occasional out-of-town lecture or concert—he rarely ventured to leave the city. He did visit the Andersons in Virginia, and once got as far as New Mexico—when Georgia O'Keeffe was there—and even saw an Indian corn dance; but it was difficult to make him take an interest in any but the most self-consciously aesthetic aspects of American cultural life. I tried again and again to get him to read such writers as Ring Lardner and Mark Twain, but I never had the least success. When I finally resorted to the device of giving him *Huckleberry Finn* as a Christmas present, he obstinately refused to open it, having learned that Henry James had characterized Mark Twain as a writer for immature minds. I told Paul once later on, when the first liveliness of the twenties was spent, that he would not have lived very differently if he had been the leading music critic of Frankfort, Dresden or Munich; but he protested at once against this. He could never be so free, he said, in Germany—or anywhere else except New York.

III

The depression was disastrous for Paul. His income dwindled almost to nothing; and he was forced to give up Irving Place, moving first to a small apartment on Eleventh Street just off Fifth Avenue, then later to a much less accessible one in the far reaches of West Eleventh Street. The *Dial* suspended publication in 1929; the *New Republic* was in the hands of an editor of whom it might almost be said, as the Nazis said of themselves, that when he heard the word *culture* he reached for his gun. Paul, for the first time in his life, was obliged to resort to real hackwork: little odd jobs and reviews, for which he was not well paid. He developed diabetes and grew thin; and something, I got the impression, went wrong with his personal affairs—though of this I never heard him speak. The staffs and the principal contributors of the *Dial* and the *New Republic*, both non-commercial affairs financed by rich patrons, had been

groups of serious writers who had had lunches and dinners together, where plans and current events were discussed, and
who had been part of Paul's social life as well as a stimulus to
his work. But now, when endowments were drying up, there
was a movement toward the political Left, and such groupings
and common undertakings as the New York "intellectuals" (so
called now rather than "writers" or "artists") continued to go
in for in the thirties, were mostly oriented in the direction of
Communism. Paul intensely disliked all this, and though one
of the great merits of his criticism had been its sure sense of
musical personalities as the reflections of their national and
social backgrounds, he would indignantly deny at this time
that art had anything to do with history. When I argued such
questions with him, I found that "the Artist" meant for him a
being unique and god-like, and that Paul would not admit for
a minute that a philosopher or a scientist or a statesman could
achieve an equal creative importance. On one occasion he was
somehow persuaded to attend an election rally held by the
Communists in Cooper Union, at which there were to be
speeches by writers who had announced that they would vote
for the Communists and who paid their homage to Communism as a literary restorative and bracer in the vein of the new
convert to evangelism or the patent medicine testimonial; but,
seated in a conspicuous place in one of the front rows, he attracted unfavorable attention by pointedly refusing to rise
when the *International* was sung.

   I was deep in Left activities myself, but I always continued
to see him and occasionally went to concerts with him. If you
dined with him in his apartment, he cooked and served the
dinner; and the difficulty was, if you ate out with him in one of
the Greenwich Village restaurants, ever to pay back his hospitality, as he invariably snatched the check and insisted on settling it himself. Even now that he had no regular platform, he
continued to go to concerts and make notes on his impressions of the music and put them away in his files; and he
continued to look for new talent and to acquire new protégés—
though he sometimes had fits of gloom in which he would
declare that American music was an abomination of desolation. He was sharply unsympathetic with the new tendency of
American composers to abandon the abstruse researches into

which they had been led by Schoenberg, the high seasoning and classicizing and virtuosity of abbreviation characteristic of Stravinsky and others, and to try to produce a music that could be heard and enjoyed by bigger audiences than those of the Composers' League. He was shocked, almost personally hurt, when Americans whose work he had thought promising did anything for the radio or Hollywood or published popular books. He expressed his views on this general subject in his essay on Kurt Weill and *Gebrauchsmusik*, in which he asserted that all music was useful, since "all works of musical art express essences and ideas and thus, with their symbols of the inner truth of life, provide the best of bases of social relationships," and that there was of course no reason why composers who "deeply felt the spirit and symbols of social rituals" should not provide these rituals with music—so long as the music provided "conveyed an individual interpretation of the meanings of the ritual" and not merely "general and conventional symbols and a sort of collective expression." He concluded: "Let us by all means have *Gebrauchsmusik*. But let it be the work of artists, not of 'revolutionary' academicians." It will be seen that these considered and formulated views were less severe than his instinctive attitude toward the practice of American composers; and I guessed that this attitude was due to his lately having felt himself a little out of things as well as to disappointment at any evidence that other artists cared anything for popular success.

But it worried me to feel, as time went on, that he was beginning to lose his self-confidence. He had put a good deal of work into the writing of what I gathered from his descriptions was a kind of symphonic novel based on a visit he had made to Rome, but he had decided that his whole conception was vitiated by some moral falsity and he withheld it from publication—which seemed to me a morbid symptom. A healthy writer either knows what he is doing or doesn't discover his error till after he has published the book. The persecution of the Jews by Hitler came later to weigh upon Paul and to become overpoweringly identified with the difficulties he was facing at fifty. The times had not brought to fulfillment that creative and enlightened era of which the sun had seemed to be rising in the days when the *Seven Arts* was founded:

totalitarian states and class pressures were closing down on the artistic élite. The independent American journalism that had flared up for a while in the twenties had given way to the streamlined commercial kind, and the non-commercial magazines were composed for the most part by this time of second-rate academic papers and the commentaries of Talmudic Marxists. Even the *New Yorker*, more liberal and literate than most of the new magazines, and in its own way quite independent, was unable to find a place for Paul: it, too, had a conventional style, which sometimes ran to insipidity through the solicitous care of the editors to eliminate anything unexpected in the way that their writers expressed themselves. It was primarily a humorous weekly and had a department that exploited the absurdities that appeared in other papers, so that they had to be on their guard against writing that might be thought ridiculous. It was one of the most cruel blows of Paul Rosenfeld's later years that the *New Yorker* would not print his articles after asking him, as he assumed, to act as their regular art critic. Paul's prose, as I knew, had its blemishes, but at its best it would have been hopelessly refractory to the *New Yorker* processing mill. There was at that time not a single periodical which would print the work of a writer simply because he knew his subject and wrote about it well. Paul sometimes showed signs of a fear that he had been made the victim of a boycott; and at others was too ready to blame himself. He said to me once that his inheritance from his grandmother had unfitted him to struggle with the world; that he had thrown up his first and only job—as a reporter on a New York paper—when, finding that the work embarrassed him, he had reflected that he did not need a job to live. Certainly he was unfitted for putting himself over or making terms with editors and publishers; no one ever had less sense of business. He never could understand that writing was a commodity like any other, which, from the moment one lacked a patron, had to be sold in a hard-boiled way; and the world came more and more to divide itself for him into two classes, black and white: the negative forces of darkness that were closing down to crush him and the few pure children of light who survived and could heal and save.

I was distressed by him in these latter days and used to

wonder how the circumstances had been combined to undermine so able a man, with the shift in economic conditions, by way of his very virtues even more than by way of his weaknesses. Certainly it was unwise of Paul to have depended as much as he did on the writing of musical criticism. Since he was himself not a musician but a writer, he should not have tied up his talent with the reporting of contemporary concerts. It is impossible for a master of words completely to express himself by merely rendering the effects of some other art; and I have never really understood why Paul did not tackle some bigger subject—a history of American music or a biography of some composer—which would have got him an advance from a publisher and supplied him with a sustaining interest. One might have said the same thing about Huneker; but it is no great comfort to realize that Paul Rosenfeld, in an age which prided itself on its emergence from the Philistinism of Huneker's, should have burned out in much the same way and been left in the same neglect. The burning-out and the public indifference seem somehow to work together. They are an old and depressing story in the American intellectual world.

When I got back to New York from Europe in the autumn of 1945, I spent with Paul a wonderful evening, which, though I may have seen him once or twice afterwards, has left me with a last lively impression that I am extremely glad to have. He was in very much better spirits than he had been during the years of the war. He had received from a foundation a substantial grant to do a book of literary studies; and it seemed to cheer him up to hear talk about Europe again, now that the war was over and the arts might be expected to revive. I told him about my enthusiasm for Benjamin Britten's opera, *Peter Grimes*, which I had heard that summer in London. And both of us were glad to find someone to whom one could express oneself freely about the current state of letters and art. He was angry over his treatment at the hands of one of the highbrow quarterlies, the editor of which had first asked him to be a member of the advisory board and had then refused to print his articles, keeping them, however, for months without letting him know about them. I had had with this same magazine an almost equally annoying experience; and I managed to make Paul laugh by describing to him an essay in which this pedantic editor, in the course of a rigorous analysis of Macbeth's "Out, out, brief candle" speech, conducted in the rigorous spirit of the new "methodological" criticism, had said something like, "We cannot know why Shakespeare has chosen for death the curious adjective *dusty*, but the epithet has a quaint appropriateness that can be felt but hardly explained." We rapidly became so exhilarated, abounding so, as Henry James would say, in our own old sense, affirming our convictions so heartily and making such hilarious fun of the more tiresome of our contemporaries, that we went on till what was for Paul a late hour, walking the autumn streets and stopping off for coffee and beer at Childs' and the Lafayette, almost as if we had been back in the twenties, with the new era of American art just beginning to burst into life between Macdougal Street and Irving Place. Less than a year later, Paul died of a heart attack as he was coming out of a movie, to which he had gone alone.

And now, despite the miseries of his later years, he remains for me, looking back, one of the only sound features of a landscape that is strewn with distortions and wrecks: a being organically moral on whom one could always rely, with a passion for creative art extinguishable only with life. It has worried me to reflect that the rise in morale I thought I had noted in him when I talked to him last was not, after all, to lead to anything, and to remember how unhappy and insecure, how unrewarded, he was at the end. There are tragedies of untimely death which—coming at the end of a man's work or breaking off his career at a crisis—represent a kind of fulfillment. But one can find no justice in Paul's. His death had no dramatic appropriateness; nor was it preceded, I fear, by any very steady serenity. It had been obvious, in view of the interest that had been stimulated in American music, partly through Paul's own efforts, and of the quantity of books about music that were now getting into type, that it was time for a reprinting of Paul's criticism; and the suggestion had been made to two publishers that an omnibus be brought out. But he had not had even this gratification. One can only reassure oneself by remembering that the work he had done was of the kind that pays for itself, because it is done for love, in the desire to give life away, and because it brings, in the doing, elevation and liberation of spirit. To have had thirty years of such work is not the least enviable of destinies; and Paul's best writing bears on every page his triumph and his justification.

1947

UNCOLLECTED REVIEWS

Return of Ernest Hemingway

For Whom the Bell Tolls, by Ernest Hemingway. New York: Charles Scribner's Sons. 471 pages. $2.75.

THIS new novel of Hemingway will come as a relief to those who didn't like "Green Hills of Africa," "To Have and Have Not," and "The Fifth Column." The big game hunter, the waterside superman, the Hotel Florida Stalinist, with their constrained and fevered attitudes, have evaporated like the fantasies of alcohol. Hemingway the artist is with us again; and it is like having an old friend back.

This book is also a new departure. It is Hemingway's first attempt to compose a full-length novel, with real characters and a built-up story. On the eve of a Loyalist attack in the Spanish civil war, a young American who has enlisted on the Loyalist side goes out into country held by the Fascists, under orders to blow up a bridge. He directs with considerable difficulty a band of peasant guerrillas, spends three nights in a cave in their company, blows up the bridge on schedule, and is finally shot by the Fascists. The method is the reverse of the ordinary method in novels of contemporary history, Franz Hoellering's or André Malraux's which undertake a general survey of a revolutionary crisis, shuttling back and forth among various groups of characters. There is a little of this shuttling in "For Whom the Bell Tolls," but it is all directly related to the main action: the blowing-up of the bridge. Through this episode the writer has aimed to reflect the whole course of the Spanish War, to show the tangle of elements that were engaged in it, and to exhibit the events in a larger perspective than that of the emergency of the moment.

In this he has been successful to a degree which will be surprising even to those who have believed in him most. There is in "For Whom the Bell Tolls" an imagination for social and political phenomena such as he has hardly given evidence of before. The vision of this kind of insight is not so highly developed as it is with a writer like Malraux, but it is here combined with other things that these political novels often lack. What

Hemingway presents us with in this study of the Spanish war is not so much a social analysis as a criticism of moral qualities. The *kind* of people people are rather than their social-economic relations is what Hemingway is particularly aware of.

Thus there is here a conception of the Spanish character, very firm and based on close observation, underlying the various social types; and in approaching the role of the Communists in Spain, Hemingway's judgments are not made to fit into the categories of a political line—since he has dropped off the Stalinist melodrama of the days of 1937, a way of thinking certainly alien to his artistic nature—but seem to represent definite personal impressions. The whole picture of the Russians and their followers in Spain—which will put The New Masses to the trouble of immediately denouncing a former favorite at a time when they are already working overtime with so many other denunciations on their hands—looks absolutely authentic. You have the contrast between the exaltation of the converts and recruits of the headquarters of the International Brigade, and the luxury, the insolence and the cynicism of the headquarters of the emissaries of the Kremlin. You have the revolutionary stuffed shirt, André Marty, hero of the 1918 mutiny of the French fleet in the Black Sea, who has been magnified and corrupted in Moscow till he is no longer anything but a mischievous bureaucrat, obsessed with the idea of shooting heretics; and you have the Moscow insider Karkov, cold of head and serious of purpose while he repeats for the sake of conformity the venomous gibberings of Pravda.

You have in the center of the stage the sincere fellow traveler from the States, teacher of Spanish in a Western college; and you have, traced with realism and delicacy, the whole chronicle of his reactions to the Communists, of his relations with the Spaniards he has to work with, and of the operation upon him in Spain of the American influences he brings with him. In the end, realizing fully the military futility of his mission and balked in his effort to save the situation, by the confusion of forces at cross-purposes that are throttling the Loyalist campaign, he is to stick by his gun sustained by nothing but the memory of his grandfather's record as a soldier in the American Civil War. In view of the dramatic declamations on the note of "Look here, upon this picture, and on this!" that the Stalinists were making a year or two ago over the contrast between Dos Passos' attitude and Hemingway's in connection with the Spanish war, it is striking that the hero of "For Whom the Bell Tolls" should end up by cutting a figure not fundamentally so very much different from that of the hero of "The Adventures of a Young Man."

Thus we get down out of the empyrean of Marxist political analysis, where the leaders are pulling the strings for the masses, and see the ordinary people as they come. And we see the actual layout—mile by mile and hill by hill—of the country in which they have to struggle. One of the mostly highly developed of Hemingway's senses is his geographical and strategical vision—what may be called his sense of terrain. It is no doubt from the Western frontier that he has inherited his vivid perception of every tree, every bush, every path, every contour and every stream that go to make up the lay of the land. He derives and he can communicate an excitement from the mere exploration and mastery of country that goes back to Fenimore Cooper; and he has succeeded in getting it into this new novel as he got it into his early stories. We are shown the Spanish conflict in its essential and primitive aspect of groups of imperfectly equipped and more or less groping human beings maneuvering over the surface of the earth.

The novel has certain weaknesses. A master of the concentrated short story, Hemingway is less sure in his grasp of the form of the elaborated novel. The shape of "For Whom the Bell Tolls" is sometimes slack and sometimes bulging. It is certainly quite a little too long. You need space to make an epic of three days; but the story seems to slow up toward the end where the reader feels it ought to move faster; and the author has not found out how to mold or to cut the interior soliloquies of his hero. Nor are the excursions outside the consciousness of the hero, whose point of view comprehends most of the book, conducted with consistent attention to the symmetry and point of the whole.

There is, furthermore, in "For Whom the Bell Tolls" something missing that we still look for in Hemingway. Where the semi-religious exaltation of communism has failed a writer

who had once gained from it a new impetus, a vacuum is created which was not there before and which for the moment
has to be filled. In Hemingway's case, there has poured in a
certain amount of conventional romance. There is in "For
Whom the Bell Tolls" a love story that is headed straight for
Hollywood. The hero falls in with an appealing little girl who
has been captured and raped by the Fascists, who has never
loved before and who wants him to teach her love. She adores
him, lives only to serve him, longs for nothing but to learn his
desires so that she can do for him what he wants, talks of her
identity as completely merged in his. She is as docile as the Indian wives in the early stories of Kipling; and since the dialogue
of the characters speaking Spanish is rendered literally with
its *thees* and *thous* and all the formalities of a Latin language,
the scenes between Robert and Maria have a strange atmosphere of literary medievalism reminiscent of the era of Maurice
Hewlett. Robert keeps insisting to himself on his good fortune
and on the unusualness of his experience in acquiring a girl like
Maria; and, for all the reviewer knows, there may be a few such
cases in Spain. But the whole thing has the too-perfect felicity
of a youthful erotic dream. It lacks the true desperate emotion
of the love affairs in some of Hemingway's other stories. And
in general, though the situation is breathless and the suspense
kept up all through, the book lacks the tensity, the moral
malaise, that made the early work of Hemingway troubling.

But then this early work was, as it were, lyric; and "For Whom
the Bell Tolls" is an effort toward something else, which requires a steady hand. The hero of this new novel is no romantic Hemingway cartoon: his attitude toward his duty and the
danger it involves are studied with more coolness and sobriety
than in the case of perhaps any other of the author's leading
juveniles. The young man is a credible young man who is
shown in his relation to other people, and these other people
are for the most part given credible identities, too. The author
has begun to externalize the elements of a complex personality
in human figures that have a more complete existence than
those of his previous stories.

That he should thus go back to his art, after a period of
artistic demoralization, and give it a larger scope, that, in an

era of general perplexity and panic, he should dramatize the events of the immediate past in terms, not of partisan journalism, but of the common human instincts that make men both fraternal and combative, is a reassuring evidence of the soundness of our intellectual life.

The New Republic, October 28, 1940

Doubts and Dreams: "Dangling Man" and "Under a Glass Bell"

"DANGLING MAN," by Saul Bellow (Vanguard), is the story, told in the form of a diary, of a young Jewish boy in Chicago who throws up a job in a travel bureau expecting to be inducted into the Army, but, owing to various technicalities, is left for a year without being called. In the meantime, he cannot get his job back, and "there is nothing to do but wait, or dangle, and grow more and more dispirited." He lives on his wife's earnings, sits at home and reads the paper, and, though naturally of studious tastes, cannot bring himself to concentrate on anything. He has a love affair in a half-hearted way; then, when it begins to prove a strain, gives it up. He finds himelf getting more and more ill-tempered: he quarrels with his old friends, with his brother, with his wife, and finally comes to blows with his landlord. He has long, brooding dialogues with himself that never come to any conclusion. At last, he cannot stand it any longer and applies to the draft board to he taken, with the result that he is called at once.

And now he is immensely relieved, and everybody feels better about him. Yet the moral situation is ambiguous. From the conventional point of view and from that of his natural instincts as a young man sitting idle during a war, he has of course done the right thing. But his action implies the defeat of other instincts which he had felt to be important. He had not wanted to have to admit that he did not "know how to use his freedom," that he "had no resources—in a word, no character." He had hoped in some way to vindicate the value of the individual even in a crisis where the fate of Western culture seemed to hang on collective enterprise; he had hoped to sustain an example of the independence of the human mind even at a moment when the body had to wait on the orders of the State. But the pressure of the times has compelled his surrender.

This is all there is to the story, but the book is an excellent document on the experience of the non-combatant in time of war. It is well written and never dull—in spite of the dismalness of the Chicago background and the undramatic character of the subject. It is also one of the most honest pieces of testimony on the psychology of a whole generation who have grown up during the depression and the war, and has its affinities with certain other recent books that seem in some cases superficially quite different: the "War Diary" of Jean Malaquais, which shows the same kind of mentality persisting in the conditions of the war itself; "The Journal of Albion Moonlight," by the poet Kenneth Patchen, in which a similar helplessness in face of the war, a similar desperation, is transposed into a delirium of rhetoric; and "So It Doesn't Whistle," by Robert Paul Smith, a novel of the kind of sub-bohemian life, rootless and almost ambitionless, led by young people in big American cities. Most of these writers and the characters in their books have, like the hero of "Dangling Man," passed earlier through a period of Communist thinking. Events have since appeared to prove false the political predictions of the Communists, and the young men have discarded the philosophy without altogether destroying the attitude. They do not much want to defend the status quo, which in the thirties they had learned to distrust, but they cannot refuse the challenge to stand up to the barbarism of the Fascists. In the meantime, their impulses toward artistic creation or intellectual expression are frustrated, bewildered, and soured. The war world and the world at home both seem to present pretty black pictures.

A typical passage in "Dangling Man" shows the hero looking out the window at the winter streets and chimneys of Chicago. It is strikingly similar to Malaquais's thoughts on his companions and his duties in the army:

It was my painful obligation to look and to submit to myself the invariable question: Where was there a particle of what, elsewhere, or in the past, had spoken in man's favor? There could be no doubt that these billboards, streets, tracks, houses, ugly and blind, were related to interior life. And yet, I told myself, there had to be a doubt. There were human lives organized around these ways and houses, and that they, the houses, say, were the analogue, that what men created they also were, through some transcendent means, I could not bring myself to concede. There must be a difference, a quality that eluded me, somehow, a difference between things and persons and even between acts and persons. Otherwise the people who lived here were actually a reflection of the things they lived among. I had always striven to avoid blaming them. Was that not in effect behind my daily reading of the paper? In their businesses and politics, their taverns, movies, assaults, divorces, murders, I tried continually to find clear signs of their common humanity.

The unpublished diary of Anaïs Nin has long been a legend of the literary world, but a project to have it published by subscription seems never to have come to anything, and the books that she has brought out, rather fragmentary examples of a kind of autobiographical fantasy, have been a little disappointing. She has now, however, published a small volume called "Under a Glass Bell," which gives a better impression of her talent.

The pieces in this collection belong to a peculiar genre sometimes cultivated by the late Virginia Woolf. They are half short stories, half dreams, and they mix a sometimes exquisite poetry with a homely realistic observation. They take place in a special world, a world of feminine perception and fancy, which is all the more curious and charming for being innocently international. Miss Nin is the daughter of a Spanish musician, but has spent much of her life in France and in the United States. She writes English, but mostly about Paris, though you occasionally find yourself in other countries. There are passages in her prose which may perhaps suffer a little from an hallucinatory vein of writing which the Surrealists have overdone: a mere reeling-out of images, each of which is designed to be surprising but which, strung together, simply fatigue. In Miss Nin's case, however, the imagery does convey something and is always appropriate. The spun glass is also alive: it is the abode of a secret creature. Half woman, half childlike spirit, she shops, employs servants, wears dresses, suffers the pains of childbirth, yet is likely at any moment to be volatilized into a superterrestrial being who feels things that we cannot feel.

But perhaps the main thing to say is that Miss Nin is a very good artist, as perhaps none of the literary Surrealists is. "The Mouse," "Under a Glass Bell," "Rag Time," and "Birth" are really beautiful little pieces. "These stories," says Miss Nin in a foreword, "represent the moment when many like myself had found only one answer to the suffering of the world: to dream, to tell fairy tales, to elaborate and to follow the labyrinth of fantasy. All this I see now was the passive poet's only answer to the torments he witnessed. . . . I am in the difficult position of presenting stories which are dreams and of having to say: but now, although I give you these, I am awake!" Yet this poet has no need to apolgize: her dreams reflect the torment, too.

The book has been printed by Miss Nin herself and is distributed through the Gotham Book Mart, 51 West Forty-seventh Street. It is well worth the trouble of sending for.

The New Yorker, April 1, 1944

A Novel by Dawn Powell

Dawn Powell's new novel, "My Home Is Far Away" (Scribner), sounds like something between fiction and a memoir. It is the story of three little girls, the children of a travelling salesman in Ohio. Their father is a great fellow when out with the boys and brings home wonderful presents, but spends most of his time on the road, seriously neglects his family, and is always having to look for a new job. The mother dies of tuberculosis and the girls spend some miserable years, during which they are passed around from one relation to another and have a period of living more or less on their own in a room in one of those Western hotels that are part of the railroad station. At last, their father marries again, becomes manager of a furniture store, and, using his wife's money, establishes the family in an ample house and plays the rôle of solid citizen. Now the girls have respectability, but find themselves imprisoned and persecuted by a hateful, neurotic stepmother, who makes their lives more wretched than ever. When the town builds a new high school and it is decided to charge tuition, they find that they will not be allowed to finish their education, and the two oldest girls run away. The second daughter, Marcia, is bright—she has always been so good at her lessons that her teacher thought she was cheating, and she has done so much reading and writing that her relatives say she is "loony." She makes friends with a Chautauqua lecturer, scrapes together a little money, and, relying on his help in the city, slips off to Cleveland alone.

That is all there is to the story, but Dawn Powell has made out of it a chronicle of small-town Middle Western life that is touching without sentimentality and amusing with only rare lapses into caricature and farce. One of the best things that Miss Powell does is her sordid or shabby interiors, such as the railroad hotel and the rooming house which the girls' grandmother keeps in Cleveland—and one remembers the small, intimate New York hotel, with its cocktail-drinking old ladies, which figures in her "Angels on Toast." She gets out of these unpromising backgrounds a humor and a fairy-tale poetry that have something in common with Dickens. The contemporary she most resembles is probably Sinclair Lewis, but she takes human life more calmly, more genially, and less melodramatically. Her quality, however, is all her own: an odd blend of sharp sophistication with something childlike, surprised, and droll—a point of view, in fact, very much like that of the alert, dispossessed little girls in this book.

Miss Powell has so much talent and of a kind that is so uncommon that one is always left rather disgruntled at her not making more of her work than she does. Three of her recent novels—"Angels on Toast" and "A Time to be Born," as well as this latest one—have all been in some ways excellent, but they sound like advanced drafts of books rather than finished productions. It is not only that they are marred by inaccuracies, inconsistencies, and other kinds of careless writing; Miss Powell, in the space of one page, gets her heroine's great-grandmother mixed up with her great-great-grandmother; she uses "phenomena" as if it were singular, she mistakes the meaning of "perquisites;" and she is addicted to such usages as "imbecilic" and "normalcy." These errors might not be important; Scott Fitzgerald in his best work sometimes misused words even more seriously. But her carelessness extends also to the organic life of the story. Miss Powell has a way of resorting, in the latter parts of her novels, to violent and sudden incidents which she needs for the machinery of the action but has not taken the trouble to make plausible; and in the case of this latest novel, these incidents—the death of the grandfather from walking into a third rail and the killing off of another of the characters by an abortion—are particularly unconvincing, owing to the fact that the rest of the narrative seems to run pretty close to experience. Miss Powell has simply not allowed herself time to smooth these gashes and hummocks out. And the whole book, as I say, gives the impression of being merely an all-but-final draft which represents the stage at which the writer has got all his material down but has not yet done the sculptural rehandling which is to bring out its self-consistent contours and set it in a permanent pose.

If we compare "My Home Is Far Away" with the stories of a childhood in Texas in Katherine Anne Porter's "The Leaning Tower," we see the difference between fiction that is interesting because of its implications and satisfying because of its art, and fiction which—though Miss Powell is more lively and can fill in her picture more densely—leaves us feeling that we do not quite know and that the author herself does not know what moral she wants to point with her story or what emotion she wants to convey. This is a genuine disappointment, because Miss Powell, like Marcia in her novel, is a born literary temperament, with an independent point of view that does not lend itself to clichés of feeling, and a life of the imagination that makes writing, for her, an end in itself. She will never be a popular purveyor of the daydreams of feminine fiction. She does not hold up the public for laughter, excitement, or sobs. But, as a writer, she has never yet quite grown up. She appeals to the intelligent reader, but she appeals, again, like the perceptive little girl, who entertains you with breathless dashes of talking but whose vivid improvisations betray, by their falterings and their occasional whoppers, that her imaginative world has not yet been developed to include all of adult experience.

The New Yorker, November 11, 1944

Faintness of the "Age of Thunder" and Power of "The Folded Leaf"

A<small>GE OF</small> T<small>HUNDER</small>," by Frederic Prokosch (Harper), is a story about the adventures of a Frenchman who parachutes into occupied France on a mission to the underground. But when one uses such practical words as "parachute" and "underground" or such a dramatic word as "adventures," one is likely to convey a wholly false impression of the character of Mr. Prokosch's novel. It is a book in which nothing really happens—or rather, in which nothing real happens. Much travelled and multilingual though Mr. Prokosch is, he is incurably American in his conception of Europe as a remote Never-Never land, where life is dreamlike, iridescent, and noble. The result, in "Age of Thunder," is uncomfortable, because the book is simply a flimsy spinning of sentiments, ideas, and symbols, and such brutal immediacies as bombing raids, Nazi tortures, and the ordeals of the French resistance do not seem to belong in the fabric.

These sentiments are, besides, mostly mawkish, the ideas thin, and the symbols trite. The book is really nothing but words, and the only thing that is good in it is the same thing that is good in Mr. Prokosch's rather insubstantial poetry—patches of felicitous words: "The sky was now filled to overflowing with a deep unexplorable blue;" "Under a chestnut tree in the middle of the field stood a shining black mare with her shimmering black foal; the foal dazed and tremulous, fresh from the womb;" "In the intervals of silence the throbbing of frogs grew audible, a sound so low and continual that it perished as pure sound; it lingered on like a fragrance, like a color, like a mood;" "The village square, the stubble around the base of the arches, had grown suddenly alive. It was like the firm line in an engraving beginning to vibrate. The firm kernels of shadow grew uneasy, split, and vanished. Then Jean-Nicolas saw what it was. The rats had emerged. First only a few, only enough to draw a fluid tremor through the ruins. Then more: fifty; a hundred; a thousand." But note here how such solid creatures as horses, frogs, and rats become tenuous at the writer's touch. With human beings, he is, it seems to me, hopeless. He has, at least, to try to do something more with them than exploit them for such quivering phrases, and he falls back on the conventional and even on the cheap. Here is a part of the final message of the book, delivered by one of those wonderful old peasant women that are always saying such deep, wise things for American novelists in Europe: "What will peace bring this time? Peace alone brings nothing. Yes, Monsieur, my mother said it to me and my grandmother before her, and it is still true: we must learn to love one another or die, and that is the only lesson, and there is no other, and that is all there is."

As a whole, the book is high-grade phony.

There is so much of that kind of thing about that it is peculiarly reassuring to read "The Folded Leaf," by William Maxwell (Harper). Mr. Maxwell is not putting on a show for the international literary world, as one feels Mr. Prokosch is; he has no gospel for Europe at war. He does not even have to brush aside the magazine and movie formulas, for he does not hear them humming in his ears. He has fixed upon a segment of experience and has molded it into a work of fiction through a style and a narrative skill which have been learned in the struggle with his subject. "The Folded Leaf" is a quite unconventional study of adolescent relationships—between two boys, with a girl in the offing—in Chicago and in a Middle Western college: very much lived and very much seen. This drama of the immature, with no background more glamorous than middle-class apartments and student fraternity houses, is both more moving and more absorbing than any of the romantic melodramas which have been stimulated by the war.

There are episodes in "The Folded Leaf"—incompletely imagined or dramatized—which sometimes keep it from being quite rounded out. The opening sequence of chapters is perfect: the author alternates between his two heroes, taking us to their respective homes and letting us see inside the minds of both, presenting them in contrast and balance. But from the point where they go to college, though we continue to see Lymie from within—the more sensitive and dependent of the pair—we get rather out of touch with Spud, the athletic and instinctive one, and the girl characters, though carefully sketched, never really find their way into the spotlight with which Lymie and Spud are followed. The end leaves us a little unsatisfied. When the knot of the immediate tangle has been cut by Lymie's attempt at suicide, he tells himself that his adolescence is over and that he is free for a larger world, and the author breaks off the story without quite having been able to persuade us to share Lymie's feeling of confidence. Yet the whole thing has been so real as we read it that we may hardly complain about this. It is almost as if we were merely losing sight, at graduation, of two men we had known in college. We wonder what became of them afterward. There were some things about them that we never knew. But when we look back on them in later years—as we do when we look back on this book—we see new and grave implications in the semi-childish incidents of college life, a contest of impulses and needs which we did not suspect at the time.

Reading "The Folded Leaf," one is reminded of certain American novelists who were working, against the popular taste, in the field of serious social realism at the end of the last century and during the early decades of this. In his effort to deal with young boys on a plane of detached observation as far as possible from the mere sentimentality and humor with which the subject has usually been treated in America, Mr. Maxwell is sometimes quite close to the "Whilomville Stories" of Stephen Crane: he approaches such matters as fraternity initiations and gratuitous schoolboy fights, the traditional customs of childhood, from an anthropological point of view which was also to some extent developed by Crane. And one is also reminded of "Bertram Cope's Year," by Henry B. Fuller, that remarkable novel about students and adults at the University of Chicago, and of Fuller's Chicago novels in general. There is no evidence that Mr. Maxwell has been influenced by these writers, but it occurs to one in connection with the last that there may actually be a special kind of realism which is inevitably imposed upon a Middle Western writer by the landscape and life of his region. This realism may not be at all folksy; it may not be at all raw, like Dreiser's; it may be thoughtful, accomplished, and neat, like the realism of Howells or Fuller.

"The Folded Leaf" is an example of this. With careful, unobtrusive art, Mr. Maxwell has made us feel all the coldness and hardness and darkness of Chicago, the prosaic surface of existence which seems to stretch about one like asphalt or ice. But there are moments when the author breaks away into a kind of poetic reverie that shows he is able to find a way out.

The New Yorker, March 31, 1945

Theodore Dreiser's Quaker and
Graham Greene's Priest

HERE are two novels about religion, one Protestant and one Catholic.

As you read "The Bulwark" (Doubleday) Theodore Dreiser's posthumous novel, you go through all the familiar experience of first groaning over the commonplace characters and the shoddy clichés of the style, then gradually finding yourself won by the candor and humanity of the author, then finally being moved by a powerful dramatic pathos which Dreiser has somehow built up. The people of "The Bulwark," when we start it, seem to be among the least promising that Dreiser has ever tackled: a family of Pennsylvania Quakers, hard-working and poor in the first generation, hard-working and well-to-do in the second, never adventurous, eccentric, or brilliant. Yet, even in its earlier and duller stretches, this is not one of Dreiser's most tedious books. He seems, by the time he wrote it, to have learned to cover ground more quickly. The language, too, is somewhat less oafish than it is in the worst of his work, and, here as elsewhere, the personal voice, the rhythm, carries off the vague and fumbling vocabulary. Yes, we say, when we come to the first love scene, Dreiser is still deeper and purer than most of the people who write so much more cleverly:

It was while they were there seeking to spot a larger darkling fish which she could dip without injuring it that, shaken by her loveliness and her proximity, he began trying to speak to her of her beauty and how much she meant to him. But for the first time in his life he found himself stuttering, unable to get out the words.

"Miss B-Benecia, I mean—"

"Yes, Solon." She turned as if to encourage him. "What is it?" She saw that his lips were pale and his lower lip trembled slightly. "Solon, thee knows thee can say anything to me thee wishes, for I-I—" and then she stopped, as if frightened by her own words.

What bravado on her part, she thought! What unmaidenliness! All of a sudden, at that moment, she felt pale and weak, and actually wanted to run away; only, having seen Solon's lips tremble, she would not let herself do so. Never. For now, as she saw and thought, here was her young Solon, the strong, the honest, the beautiful, and so weak because of his affection for her. And she wished to help him.

And when they have exchanged declarations and confessions, someone comes to interrupt them, and Solon, bending over the water as if looking for fish, says, "They're pretty scary up this way," while Benecia pretends that she has something in her eye.

Solon and Benecia marry, and Solon, who has started in a country store, becomes a banker in Philadelphia, keen, able, and extremely conservative. But Solon and Benecia Barnes have five children who, in the nineteen-twenties, find themselves cramped by their Quaker home and abandon its principles and discipline. Two of the children, a son and a daughter, go in for money and social position; another daughter, who has imagination and aesthetic sensibilities, gravitates to Greenwich Village and lives with an artist, who finally leaves her; another daughter, who is not attractive, becomes assistant to a psychology professor; and the younger boy runs wild, gets arrested, in a scandalous affair, in connection with the death of a girl, and, though he is not directly responsible, kills himself in jail with his penknife. This last incident makes the climax of the book, and the point of the story is that the father, who has seemed to be partly to blame for the difficulties and mistakes of the children, through the drab, constricted life he has imposed upon them—they have always been forbidden to dance, go to the theatre, read novels, and so on—now turns out to be almost unique, in the new American world of fast motorcars and Main Line riches, in being able to withstand the current. Taught that the appetite for money conflicts with the service of God and that the voice of morality is not a convention but something that speaks within, he is proof against the lust for speculation and the blind imitation of one's neighbor that dominated and so debauched the eighteen-nineties and the early nineteen-hundreds. When he discovers that the directors of his bank are loaning money on dubious collateral to concerns in which they have an interest, he quietly gets the federal bank examiner after them and announces his resignation. He has been prompted to take this step partly by the disastrous career of his boy; but, now that the boy is dead and that his wife has died of the shock, and that his other children are lost to him, too, he is tortured by a feeling of guilt. He has to face a new situation, for which the Quaker Church had not prepared him, and yet it is the Quaker faith which comes to his rescue now. He appeals to the "Inner Light" that visits the silence of the Quaker meeting, and he experiences a revelation.

It is interesting and unexpected that the point of view presented in "The Bulwark" should have apparently nothing in common with either Dreiser's early naturalistic materialism or his later combative Communism. When Solon Barnes, in his misery of guilt, finds, in his garden, a beautiful green insect devouring an equally beautiful rosebud, he does not, like the Dreiser of "The Financier," think of "Nature, red in tooth and claw;" he rises, on the contrary, to the realization that "there must be a Creative Divinity, and so a purpose, behind all of this variety and beauty and tragedy of life. For see how tragedy had descended upon him, and still he had faith, and would have." Nor, though (trained to "visit the fatherless and widows") he suffers from his knowledge of the iniquities committed by franchise-grabbing finance capitalism, does he arrive at any conception of what his daughters would have called "social justice." A reading of John Woolman's "Journal" lifts him to a new exaltation of "love and unity with all nature," in which "there was nothing fitful or changing or disappointing —nothing that glowed one minute and was gone the next. This love was rather, as constant as nature itself, everywhere the same, in sunshine or in darkness, the filtered splendor of the dawn, the seeded beauty of the night. It was an intimate relation to the very heart of being." . . .

One morning, as Etta came over to his bedside, he looked up at her and said feebly, "Daughter, what has become of that poor old man who was dying of cancer?"

Grievously startled by this inexplicable inquiry, she had to pause before she could reply, for she was on the verge of tears. Finally she recovered herself enough to ask, "What old man, Father, does thee refer to?"

"Why . . . why . . ." he began, "that poor old man whose son killed himself."

It is thus a very old-fashioned America that reasserts itself in "The Bulwark." One finds even in the writing touches that seem to belong in such old, edifying novels as Dreiser must have read in his childhood. The chapter that tells of Solon's son's suicide is headed, for example:

> Oh what a tangled web we weave,
> When first we practice to deceive!

And the scene at Solon's deathbed is a nineteenth-century deathbed scene, in which the father passes on to his daughters, the psychologist and the Greenwich Villager, the only ones among his children who are able to appreciate what he has to give, the still-living Quaker faith. This seems to be their only hope: they must do with it what they can in the modern world. "If thee does not turn to the Inner Light," he says to one of them, "where will thee go?"

When "The Power and the Glory," by Graham Greene, was first published in the United States, another book with that title was coming out, so that the Graham Greene novel was called "The Labyrinthine Ways." It has now been republished by Viking with the original English title. This book, which is usually a favorite of Mr. Greene's admirers and which I believe the author considers his best, I have found rather disappointing. It is the story of a Catholic village priest under a revolutionary government in Mexico. Though the clergy have been dispossessed and there is actually a price on his head, he persists in remaining in his native State, holding such Masses and administering such sacraments as are possible in his underground life among people who are mostly afraid to hide him. When he has escaped at last to a neighboring State, where he is able to function in freedom, he cannot resist the call to go back in order to confess a criminal whom the authorities had been hunting at the same time as him and whom they have finally captured and wounded—though the priest knows well that the man who has summoned him to this deathbed will betray him and turn him in to the police for ransom.

In "The Power and the Glory," as elsewhere, Mr. Greene is extremely successful in creating a squalid and painful world. He has a palette of sour colors, a repertory of sickening suggestions, a talent for selecting and rubbing in unpleasant details of modern civilization, such as cheap panes of stained glass, inferior dental drills, and insipid correspondence courses, that make good writing and are entirely his own. But the trouble is, it seems to me, that here he has too little to set against them. The canvas is pretty well painted, but the picture is somehow dead. In the case of the wretched peasants, the officials of a godless regime, the middle-class English immigrants, this is appropriate, perhaps, and intentional; but the priest, too, has something of this deadness. He is heroic in a plodding and dogged way, but he is never really made to convey to us the spark of the spiritual life that is needed to vivify this petrified waste. He is always too tired, too drunk, or too scared, and we are not sure that we ever quite believe in him. Nor has the story the suspense of a thriller like the same author's "The Confidential Agent." Dispensing with the excitement of the mystery story, Mr. Greene has not wholly succeeded in creating the higher kind of excitement. His priest who is merely a victim, who is merely pursued and executed, does not stir us with the spiritual passion that ought to be conveyed by the life of a saint.

But if the priest of Graham Greene is less stimulating than Dreiser's Quaker, this is not entirely due, I believe, to the difference that the Protestant faith puts its emphasis on the individual, who has to think and act for himself, whereas the Catholic must put it on the Church, which the individual has merely to obey and to serve. The English Graham Greene, who was born in 1904, has grown up in a less human world than the Middle Western Dreiser, born in 1871. He has grown up in a society that was stiffening in death and dominated by hatred and fear, and the validity of his work derives from its fidelity to the mood of this society. Solon Barnes is of the nineteenth century, and you cannot really shake his self-confidence; Greene's priest belongs to the era between World Wars I and II, and has been reduced to crawling on his belly for spiritual self-preservation while he fights with dogs for bones and keeps his morale up with brandy; and the reader is not even sure that the author has managed to redeem him.

The New Yorker, March 23, 1946

Henry James and Auden in America

IN the autumn of 1904, Henry James returned to the United States, after a residence abroad of nearly twenty-five years. He stayed here ten months and wrote a book about his visit called "The American Scene," which was published in 1907. This book, which seems to have attracted little attention at the time and which has been little read since, has now been republished by Scribner's in an edition which is a startling resuscitation. The old edition was made particularly forbidding by pages that presented dark blocks of small, densely set type; but the new edition has let in the air to Henry James's monumental paragraphs by giving them enough spacing and has brought out the rich phrasing and strong texture of his prose by printing it in large, clear characters. Mr. W. H. Auden has edited the volume and, besides providing a valuable preface, to which I shall return in a moment, has restored to the text a coda which contains one of James's most savage complaints and which, though it appeared in the English edition, was lopped off in the first American one—presumably in order to allow the book to end on a more cheerful note. He has added some earlier American sketches written in 1870 and 1871 and an excellent group of contemporary photographs of buildings and objects described by James.

The result is, as I say, quite astonishing. I had only, hitherto, dipped into "The American Scene," and I discover, on reading it through, that it is different from what I had imagined. This book was written after the long late novels and before the late prefaces and memoirs, and I had ascribed to it the vagueness of impressionism which makes the settings of the former often a little unsatisfactory and the backgrounds in the latter, though charming, a little insubstantial and elusive. But the rendering, in "The American Scene," of James's travels in the United States is magnificently brilliant and solid, and the criticism of the national life shows an incisiveness, a comprehensiveness, a sureness in knowing his way about, a grasp of political and economic factors, that one might not have expected of James returning to Big Business America. It is true, as Mr. Auden says, that he had never approached Europe with anything like the same boldness. In Italy, France, or England, he had always been a "passionate pilgrim," fishing for the picturesque. But, as he tells us, with long residence abroad, the romance and the mystery had evaporated, and America, of which he had been hearing such constant exciting news, had in its turn been coming to seem romantic. This book also bears out the theory that the meagreness of data and the thinness of description that are a feature of the later James have to be blamed on his having cut himself off from his roots in his native country. Certainly, when he did finally return—he had not yet become an English citizen, as he was later to do in his impatience with our policy during World War I—he plunged into the life with a gusto, devoured everything accessible with a voracity, and delivered himself of positive opinions that seem almost to transform the personality of the modest recluse of Lamb House, with his addiction to the crepuscular and the equivocal. One realizes now for the first time, as he was realizing for the first time himself, how very little of America he had seen before. He had never been West or been South. He had known only New York, Newport, and Boston. But he now travelled as far south as Florida and all the way west to California—apparently almost drunk with new discoveries and revelations. (The published volume of "The American Scene" gets him only as far as Florida and does not cover his trip to the West, which he had intended to treat in a separate book. One wonders whether his notes on these travels may not have turned up among the papers which are now being edited at Harvard.)

What is exhilarating and most surprising is the old-fashioned American patriotism which—whether he is indignant or admiring—throbs in every pulse of this book. It would be difficult to see how America, even if it had failed to understand the implications of "The Wings of the Dove," could still have credited James with being an Anglophile after the appearance of "The American Scene," if one did not allow for the shallowness of the criticism and the stupid indifference of the public that marked that whole period in the United States. James explains that the residence abroad of Americans like himself, of small incomes and non-acquisitive tastes, has by this time become merely a matter of having found oneself excreted by a society with whose standards of expenditure one was not in a position to keep up, at the same time that one could not help feeling humiliated at being thrust by it below the salt; and now he returns to the United States with something like an over-mastering homesickness, which makes him want to give it the benefit of every doubt, to hope for the best from all that shocks or repels him. He is not dominated by his wincings and shrinkings from the elements that are alien and vulgar. The flooding in of the new foreign population, though he has to make an effort to accept it, does not horrify him and provoke him to sneers, as it did that professional explorer but professional Anglo-Saxon Kipling. He thinks it a pity that the immigrants should be standardized by barren New York, but he is gratified at the evidence that America has been able to give them better food and clothing. The popular consumption of candy, in contrast to the luxury and privilege that sweets have always been in Europe, seems to please him when he attends the Yiddish theatre.

He is angry over the ravages of big business—the exploitation of real-estate values and the destruction of old buildings and landmarks that followed the Civil War—but he is sufficiently optimistic to hope that the time is arriving when the national taste will have improved to a point where it will check this process. And in the meantime he is struck with awe in the presence of Washington's spirit at Mount Vernon, invokes in the Capital the American eagle as a symbol of the republican idealism, and writes one of the most eloquent and most moving pages to be found in the whole range of his work in celebration of the Concord bridge and the shot heard round the world. It is as if, after the many books which James had written in countries not native to him, under the strain of maintaining an attitude that should be rigorously international, yet addressing himself to an audience that rarely understood what he was trying to do and in general paid little attention to him—it is as if, after a couple of decades of this, his emotions had suddenly been given scope, his genius for expression liberated, and his insight confronted with a field where it could operate without the least diffidence. The truth is the "The American Scene" is one of the best books about modern

America. Scribner's and Mr. Auden are much to be thanked for having dug it up.

This reprinting derives a special interest from the preface by W. H. Auden. Mr. Auden has reversed the procedure of Henry James and T. S. Eliot by coming to live permanently in the United States and becoming an American citizen. He is, I believe, the first important English writer who has deliberately chosen this country and who has succeeded in adapting himself to it. Dickens felt an affinity with America, and Kipling, who had married an American wife, built a house and tried to live in Vermont; but neither, in the long run, could find himself at home in the United States. Dickens, a misfit in England, was made uncomfortable in America in a different way; and the experience of Kipling was disastrous. But Mr. Auden not only seems to have felt, in his reaction against twentieth-century England, that America was in some way appropriate and congenial for him, but even, once actually among us, has lasted through seven years of a period which has certainly not been one of the easiest in our history.

His preface to "The American Scene" is, so far as I know, the first piece of writing in which he has attempted any comparative criticism of conditions in Europe and America, and it confirms the impression one had had, from the remarkable long poems that he has written here, that he *has* got something for his work out of his experience in the United States which is not in the least, as with Kipling it was, a mere new set of theatrical properties: scenery, characters, allusions, and lingo. In his poetry, with its weatherproof base laid so firmly in the English tradition, he has developed a language and an imagery which are not all "Americanized" but which are contemporary-international as those of no other English writer are (just as James, by going to Paris and London, evolved *his* peculiar international language); and he has escaped from what he has called the family atmosphere of public-school and university cliques and the literary world of London. It is true, I believe, that today he can express the situation of moral man in the jaws of mass production, mechanized war, and the first bureaucratic stages of Socialism more clearly and with more intensity

than he did even when he was writing from the point of view
of apprehensive prewar England. It is harder, he says in this
preface, for an American to become a good writer than it is for
a European. He has more odds against him, he is more alone,
but, if he does succeed, he "contributes something unique; he
sees something and says it in a way that no one before him has
said it." It is thus in Auden's pitting himself against the Americanized world rather than in picking up its tone and its aims
that he is showing the influence of America; and if it is true, as
he says in this preface, that the criticism of Eliot and James has
been useful to European culture, it is true, also, that the criticism by Auden of the culture of his adopted country has in this
book made a promising beginning.

The New Yorker, September 28, 1946

CHRONOLOGY

NOTE ON THE TEXTS

NOTES

INDEX

Chronology

1895   Born Edmund Wilson Jr. on May 8 in Red Bank, New Jersey, the only child of Edmund Wilson and Helen Mather Kimball, after a difficult delivery during which his mother was injured by his large head. (Father, son of a Presbyterian minister, was born in Shrewsbury, New Jersey, in 1863. After attending Princeton and Columbia Law School, he began a successful civil and criminal trial practice in 1891. Mother, daughter of a homeopathic physician, was born in Eatontown, New Jersey, in 1865 and attended Abbot Academy in Andover, Massachusetts. She married Edmund Wilson Sr. in 1892. She was interested in outdoor sports and gardening.) Mother calls him "Bunny," since he looks "just like a plum-bun."

1899–1907   Father begins to suffer from morbid hypochondria after his brother dies from Bright's disease. Mother loses much of her hearing. Edmund enters Shrewsbury Academy. Takes nature walks with aunt Laura Kimball; looks up to his uncle Reuel Kimball, pillar of the family and father of his cousin Sandy (Reuel Kimball Jr.), who becomes his inseparable companion. His Wilson grandmother reads him the Old Testament stories that had molded his father. Loves summer family reunions in upstate New York—the old stone house in Talcottville (bought by his father from his mother's relatives), the open countryside with its hills and lofty skies, large dairy farms, and dark rivers: "We fished and swam in the rivers, had all sorts of excursions and games." Develops a lifelong interest in performing magic tricks.

1908   Visits Europe with his family, traveling to Italy, Austria, Bohemia, Germany, France, and England.

1908–10   Father is appointed Attorney General of New Jersey by Republican governor John Franklin Fort and serves until 1914; he will impress Democratic governor Woodrow Wilson (no relation) by his successful prosecution of the corrupt Republican political machine in Atlantic City.

1909–12   Wilson attends the Hill School in Pottstown, Pennsylva-
            nia, where he makes literary friends and begins to think of
            himself as a writer and critic. John A. Lester, an English
            teacher from the Lake District, impresses on him the
            rhetorical trinity of "Lucidity, Force, and Ease"; in a trib-
            ute in *The Triple Thinkers*, Wilson will describe Alfred
            Rolfe, his Greek master, as "the perfect Hellenist" who
            made him feel "that there was . . . something exhilarat-
            ing in the air of the classroom, human, heroic, and shin-
            ing." Writes fiction, satire, and literary essays, for school
            literary magazine. Reads with enthusiasm Hippolyte
            Taine's *History of English Literature* (which he discovers
            in his father's library), Shaw, and Mencken; rejects the
            evangelical Christianity inculcated at Hill.

1912–16   Attends Princeton University. Discovers the American
            classics, including Emerson, Whitman, Mark Twain, and
            Henry James. Serves on the editorial board of the *Nassau
            Literary Magazine* and contributes poems, stories, re-
            views, and editorials. Deeply influenced by professors
            Norman Kemp Smith, a Scottish philosopher who inter-
            prets Kant and Hume, and Christian Gauss, who teaches
            Dante and French literature, seeking to reconcile Neo-
            Classical aesthetic with history and biography. Reads and
            admires the criticism of Sainte-Beuve. Forms friendships
            with John Peale Bishop and F. Scott Fitzgerald. Spends
            summer of 1914 in England, where he begins the series of
            notebooks and journals that he will continue to keep for
            almost six decades, and is in London when war is declared
            on August 4. With Fitzgerald collaborates on *The Evil
            Eye*, a musical comedy presented by Princeton's Triangle
            Club in 1915.

1916–17   After graduation attends summer military camp at Platts-
            burgh, New York, and decides he cannot participate in
            killing "in cold blood." When his father, who has told him
            he will have to support himself, asks about his plans, he
            proposes "to learn something about all the main depart-
            ments of human thought." With help from his father, gets
            job as reporter for the *New York Evening Sun*. Lives at 15
            West 8th Street, New York City. Enlists in U.S. Army Med-
            ical Corps in June, and is sent to France in November 1917.

1918   Serves as an orderly at base hospital in Vittel. After period
            of relative inactivity in which he has time to read and

write ("I have decided to begin the writing of my subsequent books, war or no war," he informs Fitzgerald), begins treating wounded men in June, including burned victims of mustard gas. Treats victims of the flu epidemic; patrols halls to keep crazed patients from jumping out of windows; attends deathbeds and assists an elderly undertaker on his rounds, sometimes piling bodies up "like logs." Shortly before the Armistice, his father gets him transferred to intelligence section at U.S. General Headquarters at Chaumont. Enjoys the company of cynical reporters doing propaganda work.

1919   Reads reports on European political crises, the Allies' rival ambitions, and affairs in revolutionary Russia. Returns to New York in July. Shocked to learn his cousin Sandy has been institutionalized after a nervous breakdown and diagnosed as schizophrenic. Gratified that his father shares his outrage at mass arrests of radicals ordered by U.S. attorney general Mitchell Palmer. Moves into an apartment on West 12th St. Writes steadily and submits work to magazines. Submits a parody to *Vanity Fair*, which attracts the favorable attention of Dorothy Parker; as a result of her recommendation, he is hired to read manuscripts at the magazine. When Parker and Robert Benchley leave the staff in quick succession, Wilson replaces Benchley as managing editor (he will fill the post off and on until 1923). John Peale Bishop joins staff as Wilson's assistant.

1920   Writes a literary column in *Vanity Fair* as well as reviews and essays for *The Dial*, *The New Republic*, and others. Meets John Dos Passos, later to become a close friend, and Edna St. Vincent Millay, whose poetry he promotes in *Vanity Fair*. Writes essay appraising H. L. Mencken. Has first sexual experience with Millay in July 1920 and writes impassioned letters to her: "I suppose all this is pretty casual to you, but it's not to me, as you know." Proposes marriage to Millay during a visit to her in Provincetown; she rejects the offer.

1921   Begins affair with actress Mary Blair, whom he first sees onstage in Eugene O'Neill's *Diff'rent* in February. Has started to drink heavily. Spends summer in France and Italy. Meets Jean Cocteau and Djuna Barnes in Paris.

Writes to Fitzgerald of his hopes "for New York as a cultural center just now—America seems to be actually beginning to express herself in something like an idiom of her own," although "the intellectual and aesthetic manifestations have to crowd their way up and out from between the crevices left by the factories, the office buildings, the apartment houses, and the banks."

1922   *The Undertaker's Garland*, a collection of verse and prose by Wilson and Bishop, is published by Alfred A. Knopf. Writes scores of reviews; topics include *The Waste Land*, *Ulysses*, W. B. Yeats, Edith Wharton, Fitzgerald, and others; also writes sketches of popular culture and the New York scene. Becomes close friend of poet Elinor Wylie, who joins staff of *Vanity Fair*. Lives with Hill classmate and occasional *Vanity Fair* contributor Ted Paramore. Moves in November into a corner room with bath in the same apartment building on University Place where Wylie lives.

1923   Marries Mary Blair, who is pregnant, on February 14. Leaves *Vanity Fair*. Father dies of pneumonia in May. Father's will, made decades earlier, leaves his mother in charge of his estate, so Wilson will be dependent on her to supplement his earnings as editor, critic, and journalist, a situation that leads to strains in their relationship. Lives in Brookhaven, Long Island, with Mary, before they move first to Brooklyn and then to the University Place building, where he rents half a floor. Meets D. H. Lawrence in August and writes an essay on Gertrude Stein in September. Daughter Rosalind Baker Wilson born September 19, 1923.

1924   Wilson's *The Crime in the Whistler Room* is produced by the Provincetown Players in New York, with Mary Blair in the lead role. Travels to California in an unsuccessful effort to persuade to Charlie Chaplin to act in his ballet "Chronkite's Clocks"; during his stay Ted Paramore introduces him to an unhappily married friend, Margaret Canby. Literary friends include E. E. Cummings, Louise Bogan, and Paul Rosenfeld. Wilson writes first American review of Ernest Hemingway's *In Our Time*.

1925   Hired as reviewer and reporter for *The New Republic* (where he will serve as literary editor, 1926–31). Covers New York night-life—theater, vaudeville, movies, music—

as well as literature; publishes essays on Yeats and Henry James; will solicit material for the magazine from writers including E. E. Cummings, Louise Bogan, Allen Tate, Malcolm Cowley, and Ernest Hemingway.

1926   Vacations in New Orleans, where he meets Sherwood Anderson. Separates from Mary Blair; moves to a sparsely furnished room on West 13th Street that will remain his base for several years. Rosalind is by now under the care of Wilson's mother in Red Bank, where he spends weekends. *Discordant Encounters: Plays and Dialogues* published by Albert and Charles Boni.

1927   Begins affair with Frances Minihan, a Ukrainian-American waitress and taxi-dancer whom he meets at the Tango Gardens on 14th Street in February (at a time when her husband is in prison for car theft). Contracts gonorrhea but is cured. Becomes deeply involved with Frances, in a sexual relationship complicated by class differences. Begins to write detailed accounts of their lovemaking in his journals. Responds to execution of anarchists Sacco and Vanzetti in short story "The Men from Rumplemayer's."

1928   Writes essay on Proust for *The New Republic*. Completes a draft of *I Thought of Daisy*, a novel set in Greenwich Village. Becomes a drinking companion of Margaret Canby, who has moved to New York after her divorce, and in April they begin an affair. While Canby is in Paris during the spring, Wilson seduces the poet Léonie Adams, but this affair goes no further. Continues to see Frances Minihan. Takes leave from *The New Republic* in the fall to stay at a beach house near Canby's home in Santa Barbara, where he revises *I Thought of Daisy*. During same period, works on critical study *Axel's Castle*; assures Max Perkins of Scribner's that "popular accounts" of the modernist writers whom he views as emerging from French Symbolism will "persuade people to read them." Shocked by death from a stroke of Elinor Wylie at age 43 in December.

1929   In February, after finishing *I Thought of Daisy*, suffers a nervous collapse marked by acute anxiety and indecision. Spends three and a half weeks at the Clifton Springs Sanitarium in upstate New York; while there begins assembling a collection of his poems, *Poets, Farewell!*, and resumes work on *Axel's Castle*. Scribner's publishes *I Thought of Daisy* in August. Chapters from *Axel's Castle* are serialized in *The New Republic* in the fall and winter. Breaks off affair with Frances Minihan; asks Canby to come east for the winter.

1930   Obtains divorce from Mary Blair in February. Marries Margaret Canby on May 8. Spends summer on Cape Cod with Margaret, Rosalind, and Margaret's son Jimmy in house belonging to Eugene O'Neill. Reads Marx; discusses politics with John Dos Passos, his neighbor on the Cape. In the fall moves with Margaret into a residential hotel on Fifth Avenue. Begins to write political journalism on a regular basis.

1931   *Axel's Castle: A Study in the Imaginative Literature of 1870–1930* published by Scribner's. Publishes "Appeal to Progressives" to "take Communism away from the Communists" in *The New Republic*. Reports on demonstrations, suicides, and other signs of social tension in New York City. Gives up editor's job to crisscross the country as a reporter. Publishes "Detroit Motors," a portrait of the Ford assembly line. Reports on independent radical unions and the case of the Scottsboro Boys; visits with Allen Tate in Tennessee. In the summer Margaret, who has been left behind on these travels, meets him in New Mexico and they go on to Santa Barbara. In "The Jumping-Off Place," he contrasts a luxury hotel in San Diego with a catalog of recent suicides in the city. When he returns east, Margaret remains in California for several months, where she is sometimes despondent.

1932   In February, with Malcolm Cowley, Mary Heaton Vorse, and others, participates in delivery of food and clothing to striking miners in Kentucky. *The American Jitters: A Year of the Slump* published by Scribner's in the spring. Supports Communist presidential candidate William Z. Foster as a protest vote. Drinks heavily and quarrels with Margaret; she goes to California for the summer without him. He works on a play, drinks bathtub gin, and writes political and historical essays; stays on Cape Cod with Rosalind. On two occasions he sees Frances, who wants to be his lover again. Learns on returning to New York in late September that Margaret has died after falling down a flight of stone stairs in Santa Barbara while leaving a party. Flies to California for funeral; wonders if her death could have been a suicide. In lengthy notes begun immediately afterward, remarks: "After she was dead, I loved her." Rents house at 314 East 53rd Street for $50 a month. Visits Jane Addams at Hull House in November and writes an account of Chicago slums.

1933–34 Records impressions of Roosevelt and early New Deal. Spends drunken evening with Fitzgerald and Hemingway in January 1933. Receives visit from T. S. Eliot in May. Resumes affair with Frances. Begins affair with old friend Louise Fort Connor, who is now unhappily married, meeting her occasionally in Chicago, Massachusetts, and New York. Enjoys close literary friendships with Louise Bogan, with whom he reads poetry and studies German, and John Dos Passos, with whom he argues about literature and politics, including developments in the Soviet Union. In 1934 joins editorial board of radical *Modern Monthly*. Conceives a history of revolutionary socialism to be told in terms of personalities. Plans trip to the Soviet Union, funded by a Guggenheim fellowship. Dos Passos enlists the aid of Maxim Gorki to help Wilson obtain a visa, and warns him to avoid political indiscretions in Moscow.

1935 Makes final break with Frances. Leaves for Europe in May; from London sails to Leningrad on Soviet ship, *Berengaria*. After five days in Leningrad, travels to Moscow. Since he is not a member of the Communist Party and is known to associate with American Trotskyites, he is denied permission to work in the Marx-Engels-Lenin Institute. Attends Soviet theatrical productions. Tours collective farm in early June. Meets literary critic D. S. Mirsky (who will be arrested in 1937 and die in the Gulag in 1939). Troubled by cult of Stalin ("This glorification of Stalin is undoubtedly one of the things which affects an American most unpleasantly") and notes: "The atmosphere of fear and suspicion does really become oppressive." Visits Lenin's home in Ulyanovsk, as well as Stalingrad, Rostov-on-Don, Kiev, and Odessa. Becomes ill with scarlet fever while traveling, and is hospitalized for six weeks in chaotic and filthy Odessa hospital, where he is impressed by efficiency and modernity of the Communist Party nurse on the hospital staff and by the dedication of a doctor from the old nobility. Suffers acute kidney attack toward end of stay. Begins studying Russian in order to read Pushkin. Returns to U.S. in October by way of Paris, where he meets André Malraux and James Joyce.

1936   *Travels in Two Democracies*, a collection of reports on the
            United States and the Soviet Union, published by Har-
            court, Brace. To protect Soviet friends he leaves out
            darker aspects of his experience, but his account nonethe-
            less angers the Communists. Stays at rented rooms and in
            Red Bank. Moves in the fall from New York to "Trees,"
            a country house near Stamford, Connecticut, lent to him
            by a literary friend, the heiress Margaret de Silver.

1937   Dismayed by Moscow purge trials and critical of acquain-
            tances who attempt to defend them. Researches early
            utopian socialists for *To the Finland Station*. Publishes a
            play, *This Room and This Gin and These Sandwiches*. In
            September breaks off affair with Louise Connor and an-
            other with Elizabeth Waugh, a married friend on the
            Cape. At a lunch with editors of *Partisan Review* in the
            fall, meets Mary McCarthy (b. 1912), and within a few days
            they become lovers.

1938   Gives lecture at Harvard in January. Wilson and Mc-
            Carthy are married on February 10. He encourages her
            writing. *The Triple Thinkers: Ten Studies of Literature*
            published by Harcourt, Brace in the spring. In June,
            when Mary is two months pregnant, a violent episode (of
            which each will subsequently give very different accounts)
            leads her to spend three weeks in the Payne Whitney Psy-
            chiatric Clinic in New York, diagnosed as suffering from
            anxiety. They move from "Trees" to a house in Stamford.
            Mary enters therapy and resumes writing stories. Visited
            in November by Fitzgerald ("sober, industrious, com-
            pletely transformed") and Sheilah Graham. Son Reuel
            Kimball Wilson born on Christmas Day.

1939   Teaches summer courses at the University of Chicago on
            Dickens and on "Taine and the Marxist texts." Writes two
            long essays on Dickens that will be integrated in *The
            Wound and the Bow*. Meets Saul Bellow in Chicago. Wil-
            son and Mary spend the winter at Truro on Cape Cod.
            She works on her story collection *The Company She Keeps*
            and he on *To the Finland Station*.

1940   *To the Finland Station: A Study in the Writing and Acting
            of History* published in September by Harcourt, Brace.
            Works during the summer at Truro on *The Wound and
            the Bow*; in the fall returns to *The New Republic* as an
            editor. Vladimir Nabokov, newly arrived in the United

States, seeks him out and they begin a long association. Severs ties with *The New Republic* after the magazine's English owner abrogates the editors' independence to urge American intervention in World War II, which Wilson opposes. Fitzgerald, who has been corresponding with Wilson about *To the Finland Station* and his own Hollywood novel, dies on December 21.

1941   Buys a house on Cape Cod, in Wellfleet, with a bank loan and money borrowed from his mother, and moves in with Mary and Reuel during the summer. *The Boys in the Back Room: Notes on California Novelists*, series of essays on writers including John Steinbeck and Nathanael West, is published as a chapbook by Colt Press of San Francisco. *The Wound and the Bow: Seven Studies in Literature* is published by Houghton Mifflin. Edits Fitzgerald's unfinished novel *The Last Tycoon* for publication in October.

1942–43 *Note-Books of Night*, a collection containing memoirs along with romantic and satirical verse, is published by Colt Press in the fall of 1942. Marriage becomes increasingly strained. McCarthy has come to hate Wilson's drinking and spends long periods in New York undergoing psychoanalysis. Wilson helps Nabokov's American career, introducing him to editors and recommending him for reviewing assignments, teaching jobs, and a Guggenheim fellowship. Begins long friendship with Dawn Powell. *The Shock of Recognition*, his anthology documenting the responses of American writers to one another's work, is published by Doubleday in 1943. Works on a novel to be titled "The Story of the Three Wishes" (the only completed segment published in 1998 as *The Higher Jazz*) and on the stories eventually published in *Memoirs of Hecate County*.

1944   In January assumes position as a weekly book reviewer at *The New Yorker*, where most of his work of the next 25 years will first appear. Job enables him to move with Mary to an apartment on Gramercy Park. Their final summer together in Wellfleet is marked by a violent quarrel, after which Wilson promises to stop drinking and for a time keeps his promise. Friendship with Dawn Powell is momentarily chilled when he writes a critical review of her most recent novel, *My Home Is Far Away*, in November. Appalled by wartime propaganda and by Allied bombing campaigns, writes in his journal: "We have arrived now at the same state in which the Germans have been. We are bombing Berlin to cinders, but nobody talks about it."

1945 *The Crack-Up*, a collection of uncollected writings by Fitzgerald, edited by Wilson, is published by New Directions. After quarreling with Wilson in New York, Mary sues for separation and sole custody of Reuel. *New Yorker* editor William Shawn sends Wilson to Europe to survey conditions at the end of the war. Arrives in London in April, and meets many British literary figures, including Graham Greene, George Orwell, Cyril Connolly, Henry Green, and Evelyn Waugh. Is infatuated with young English woman, Mamaine Paget, who becomes a close friend. Visits Italy, where he reports on conditions in Naples, Milan, and Rome. Writes to Nabokov: "The ruined parts of Italy affect me with more repugnance than anything else, I think, that I have ever seen." Meets Ignazio Silone, Alberto Moravia, and George Santayana. Travels to Greece and Crete. After returning home, has brief affair with Anaïs Nin. Custody case comes to trial in September and judge orders a settlement, awarding Mary custody during the school year and Wilson during the summer.

1946 *Memoirs of Hecate County* published by Doubleday. Prosecuted as pornography, the book briefly becomes a bestseller (before being banned in New York and Massachusetts); it earns Wilson $35,000. Meets and falls in love with Elena Mumm Thornton. (Born in France in 1906 to aristocratic German and Russian parents, she is now unhappily married to a Canadian businessman.) After an exhilarating seven-month courtship of letters and irregular meetings, they go to Nevada to obtain divorces, are married on December 10, and then return to the Cape, where she will make a home for him.

1947 *Europe Without Baedeker: Sketches in the Ruins of Italy, France, and England* published by Doubleday. Contracts with Oxford University Press to write a book on American literature "between the Civil War and about 1910," and starts developing materials for it in *The New Yorker*. Enjoys what will become close friendships with W. H. Auden and Isaiah Berlin. Enthusiastically disputes tastes and ideas with Nabokov, exchanging long letters when they are unable to meet. Sends Nabokov a case study from

Havelock Ellis's *Psychology of Sex* of a Ukrainian who despairs of overcoming his love of young girls. Meets Haitian writer Phito Toby-Marcelin, whose fiction he has admired. In September visits Dos Passos in hospital after the car accident in which his wife, Katy, was killed. Mary Blair dies. Visits Zuñi pueblo in New Mexico at the winter solstice and writes detailed account of what he observes there.

1948   Daughter Helen Miranda born February 17. He is disturbed by a visit to Edna Millay at Steepletop, the farm in Austerlitz, New York, where she and Eugen Boissevain have isolated themselves for 20 years: "I reflected in dismay . . . on the tendency of the writers of my generation to burn themselves out or break down."

1949   Spends six weeks in Haiti, November–December, on assignment for *The Reporter*.

1950   *Classics and Commercials: A Literary Chronicle of the Forties*, a collection of book reviews and essays, is published in the fall by Farrar, Straus. Roger Straus becomes his primary publisher; Wilson will no longer have to struggle to get his books into print, and Straus, making loans against Wilson's work, provides a financial arrangement more satisfactory for him than were his mother's sometimes grudging contributions. Edna Millay dies in October.

1951   Wilson's mother dies on February 3, and he inherits the stone house in Talcottville, New York, along with her New Jersey home and a trust fund income of $8,000 a year. His play *The Little Blue Light* is produced in Cambridge, Massachusetts, with Jessica Tandy and Hume Cronyn; the subsequent New York production fails. Christian Gauss dies in November.

1952–53   *The Shores of Light: A Literary Chronicle of the Twenties and Thirties* reintroduces Wilson's earlier reviews to a new generation. Writes essays on Russian classics. In 1952 he spends his first summer at Talcottville since inheriting the house, then goes to Princeton for the winter. Delivers papers on Civil War figures in a seminar established in Gauss's memory (those attending include John Berryman, Saul Bellow, and Leon Edel). Begins studying Hebrew at Princeton Theological Seminary. Jason Epstein, an editor at Doubleday, includes *To the Finland Station* among the initial titles in the new Doubleday Anchor series of paperbacks, to be followed by three more Wilson volumes over the next five years.

1954   *Eight Essays* appears in Anchor Books. *Five Plays* published. Sails to Europe in January; fellow passengers include Jason and Barbara Epstein and Buster Keaton. Spends a week in Paris where he sees Malraux, as he will again later in the year. Teaches American literature at Salzburg seminar in February. In England meets with Cyril Connolly, Angus Wilson, E. M. Forster; travels to Edinburgh where he meets novelist Compton Mackenzie. Visits Max Beerbohm in Italy. Travels to Israel in April for *The New Yorker*. Reads manuscript of *Lolita*, but writes to Nabokov: "I like it less than anything else of yours I have read."

1955   Wilson's account of the Dead Sea Scrolls appears in *The New Yorker*; an expanded version of the *New Yorker* essay is published by Oxford as *The Scrolls from the Dead Sea* and sells well. (Will continue to revise and update the book for the next 12 years.) Immerses himself in Turgenev. Talcottville has become a home to him but not to Elena, who will limit her visits to two weeks in August.

1956   *Red, Black, Blond and Olive: Studies in Four Civilizations: Zuñi, Haiti, Soviet Russia, and Israel*, travel writing that verges on cultural anthropology, is published by Oxford. Publishes a memoir of his father ("The Author at Sixty") in *A Piece of My Mind: Reflections at Sixty*. Anchor Books publishes *A Literary Chronicle* (a selection from *The Shores of Light* and *Classics and Commercials*). Travels to England in July and early August; has second honeymoon in Paris with Elena.

1957   Spends the first of four winters working on the literature of the Civil War era in Harvard's Widener Library. Suffers from gout, a condition he first developed in the early 1940s; has adverse reactions to sulfa drugs when he drinks. Visits the Nabokovs in Ithaca and succeeds in repairing relations with Vladimir, despite tension with Vera Nabokov. "Turgenev and the Life-Giving Drop," his longest literary portrait since his studies of Marx and Dickens, appears in *The New Yorker* in October. Begins a study of the New York Iroquois.

1958   *The American Earthquake: A Documentary of the Twenties and Thirties*, a collection incorporating *The American Jitters* along with other journalistic writings, is published by Anchor Books. Praises Boris Pasternak's *Doctor Zhivago* in "Doctor Life and his Guardian Angel." Visits the Tonawanda and Seneca reservations and becomes a journalistic spokesman on behalf of Indian land rights threatened by development projects. The Internal Revenue Service discovers he has paid no federal income tax between 1946 and 1955, although payments had been withheld by *The New Yorker*, Princeton, and Farrar, Straus; Elena begins sorting through decades of canceled checks and bank statements. Wilson is tried for tax evasion in Utica in November, and is ordered to pay $68,500 in back taxes, penalties, and interest.

1959   Needing money to pay the I.R.S., takes one-year position as Lowell professor at Harvard, lecturing from his Civil War manuscript and giving a seminar on onomatopoeia from the *Aeneid* to Proust and Joyce. Enjoys interacting with visiting writers and intellectuals, including Isaac Bashevis Singer and George F. Kennan.

1960   *Apologies to the Iroquois* published. When a Hungarian translation of his plays arrives at Talcottville from Budapest, begins study of the language with Mary Pcolar, who works in the local drugstore and becomes his driver, typist, and companion. He now polishes his journal as he writes, believing there will be no time to revise it.

1961   *Night Thoughts*, a volume of his collected poems, published. Signs protest against the Bay of Pigs invasion. Attacks both Soviet and American imperialism in the introduction to *Patriotic Gore*, writing: "Whenever we engage in a war or move in on some other country, it is always to liberate somebody." Mortgages Talcottville house and sells his papers to Yale to pay off debts incurred as a result of tax problems.

1962   *Patriotic Gore: Studies in the Literature of the American Civil War* published. *Life* magazine criticizes Wilson's sweeping analogies between Lincoln's historical role and those of Lenin and Bismarck. The book is widely admired by critics and historians; its portraits of Grant, Sherman, Lincoln, Harriet Beecher Stowe, and Justice Holmes are likened by Robert Lowell and Alfred Kazin to Plutarch.

I.R.S. attempts to cut off Wilson's sources of income. Attends a White House dinner for Malraux in May, and has several exchanges with Kennedy; questioned by the President about the view of American wars in *Patriotic Gore*, he suggests that he buy the book. Has what seems a severe heart attack (angina). Writes the first of two self-interviews, dialogues outlining his intellectual world. In September goes to Toronto and Montreal for a study of Canadian literature.

1963   Dispute with the I.R.S. is settled after intervention by Arthur M. Schlesinger, Jr. (then serving as a White House adviser), although Wilson owes collateral payments against future earnings. Publishes *The Cold War and the Income Tax: A Protest*, an account of his experience in which he objects to the use of tax money for nuclear, biological, and chemical weapons. Kennedy adds Wilson's name to the list for his first Medals of Freedom. (When officials from the I.R.S. object, he comments, "This is not an award for good conduct but for literary merit.") Kennedy also expresses interest in Wilson's project, outlined in a 1962 letter to Jason Epstein, to reprint American classics in a series modeled on the French Pléiade. Contributes a second self-interview detailing his tastes in music and the arts to the first issue of *The New York Review of Books*; it is followed by "My Fifty Years with Dictionaries and Grammars." Spends summer in Talcottville, then visits London before going to Paris with Elena and Helen for the late autumn and winter.

1964–65   Visits Rome and Budapest in the spring. Spends a year as a Fellow at the Center for Advanced Studies at Wesleyan. (When an English Department critic pronounces that literature is dead, comments: "How much less, then, should we need criticism?") Publishes *O Canada: An American's Notes on Canadian Culture* and *The Bit Between My Teeth: A Literary Chronicle of 1950–1965*. Criticizes Nabokov's literal translation of Pushkin's *Eugene Onegin* in *The New York Review of Books*; Nabokov in turn dismisses Wilson's critique by ridiculing his grasp of Russian, beginning a series of bitter public exchanges.

1966   *Europe Without Baedeker* reissued, with the addition of "Notes from a European Diary, 1963–1964." Awarded the Emerson-Thoreau Medal of the American Academy of Arts and Letters and the National Medal for Literature.

1967   Publishes *A Prelude: Characters and Conversations from the Early Years of My Life*. Makes cuts in *The Twenties* and interpolates passages of new writing. (Will intermittently work on *The Thirties* until his death. *The Twenties*, *The Thirties*, *The Forties*, *The Fifties*, and *The Sixties* will be posthumously published between 1975 and 1993.) Visits Israel and Jordan, April–May. By now suffers a range of symptoms attributable to emphysema, diabetes, arthritis, shingles, and a disease resembling malaria, caught in Haiti.

1968   "The Fruits of the M.L.A.," a satirical attack on the heavily annotated texts of American classics endorsed by the Modern Language Association, published in *The New York Review of Books*. Receives award of the Aspen Institute of Humanistic Studies ($30,000) at the Waldorf-Astoria (his heart condition prevents him from traveling to the Colorado mountains). In his acceptance speech speaks of Taine's influence in his boyhood, and again attacks the "disgraceful" Vietnam War. Turns from the public world in his journal to chronicle illnesses and recoveries as his health declines.

1969   Publishes *The Dead Sea Scrolls, 1947–1969* (an expanded version of his 1955 book) and *The Duke of Palermo and Other Plays* (with an "Open Letter to Mike Nichols" in which he lists American plays he believes should be revived).

1970   Has a coronary occlusion in New York in March; refuses a pacemaker. Suffers a slight stroke around Christmas.

1971   Publishes *Upstate: Records and Recollections of Northern New York*, which sells unexpectedly well. Exchanges friendly letters with Nabokov, but their reconciliation ends when Nabokov is angered by the account in *Upstate* of Wilson's visit to Ithaca in 1957. Mary McCarthy, with help from James Baldwin, arranges for Wilson to receive the Golden Eagle Award from the International Festival of Books in Nice; he is also awarded the bi-annual Jerusalem Prize, but the prize is transferred to Jorge Luis Borges when Wilson is unable to fulfill the condition of receiving it in person in Jerusalem.

1972   For new edition of *To the Finland Station*, revises portrait of Lenin. Last essays on Russian literature published in *A Window on Russia*. Assembles essays published in *The*

Devils and Canon Barham: Ten Essays on Poets, Novelists and Monsters (1973). Spends winter at Naples, Florida. Has another stroke at Cape Cod in May. Is promised by Roger Straus that his journals will not be censored after his death. Goes to upstate New York for what he reassures Elena will be two weeks. Dictates a last letter to Auden. On June 11 brings the journal up to date after not writing for five months. Dies in the old stone house at Talcottville from a coronary occlusion on the morning of June 12. Buried at Wellfleet June 15.

Note on the Texts

This volume contains three works by Edmund Wilson—*The Triple Thinkers: Twelve Essays on Literary Subjects* (1938; revised edition, 1948), *The Wound and the Bow: Seven Studies in Literature* (1941), and *Classics and Commercials: A Literary Chronicle of the Forties* (1950)—along with six book reviews not collected by Wilson.

The Triple Thinkers was first published by Harcourt, Brace and Company in 1938 with a different subtitle (*Ten Essays on Literary Subjects*) and slightly different contents. In the revised edition of 1948, published by Oxford University Press, Wilson added three essays— "Morose Ben Jonson," "'Mr. Rolfe,'" and "The Historical Interpretation of Literature"—and deleted "The Satire of Samuel Butler." The latter essay was later included in *The Shores of Light: A Literary Chronicles of the Twenties and Thirties* (1952). The text published here is taken from the 1948 Oxford University Press edition.

The Wound and the Bow: Seven Studies in Literature was first published in 1941 by Houghton Mifflin. When the book was reissued in 1947 by Oxford University Press, Wilson took the occasion to make revisions and corrections, and to update the conclusion of the essay on Ernest Hemingway. The text published here is that of the 1947 Oxford University Press edition.

Classics and Commercials: A Literary Chronicle of the Forties was first published in 1950 by Farrar, Straus and Company. In his acknowledgments Wilson notes: "This book contains a selection of my literary articles written during the nineteen-forties. All of them have been revised and some of them considerably rewritten. A few have been brought up to date with postscripts." The text published here is taken from the 1950 Farrar, Straus edition of *Classics and Commercials*.

The six uncollected reviews included here were originally published in the following periodicals:

Return of Ernest Hemingway: *The New Republic*, October 1940.

Doubts and Dreams—"Dangling Man" and "Under a Glass Bell": *The New Yorker*, April 1944.

A Novel by Dawn Powell: *The New Yorker*, November 1944.

Faintness of the *Age of Thunder* and Power of *The Folded Leaf*: *The New Yorker*, March 31, 1945.

Theodore Dreiser's Quaker and Graham Greene's Priest: *The New Yorker*, March 1946.

Henry James and Auden in America: *The New Yorker*, September 1946.

The Dawn Powell review was originally paired with an unrelated review by Wilson of a book by Ronald Knox.

The texts of the original printings chosen for inclusion here are presented without change, except for the correction of typographical errors. Spelling, punctuation, and capitalization are often expressive features and are not altered, even when inconsistent or irregular. The following errors have been corrected: 5.3, 1928; 58.14, grandsons . . .";71.20, genus; 73.13, 15-16, 40, Fitzgerald; 89.17, reçus; 96.4, *trés-joli*; 129.37, "occupying; 143.24, stimulation; 144.18, book.; 149.11, 'the . . . Kings.'; 165.16, It; 190.11, of after; 198.30, set-/ing; 222.20, totaly; 225.22, 226.3, *Cataline*; 230.8, asquiesce; 262.7-8, as as; 292.18, in iciness; 412.6, (1930); 422.29, followd; 462.14, 15, Cleon; 489.38, Mary L.; 490.6, become; 503.3, Engish; 515.35, the; 520.4, Jr.;; 563.7, be; 582.7, Ibsens's; 645.17, Nobokov's; 699.16, jobs; 706.38, where-/ever; 746.20, *No*).; 749.27, on; 758.19, *Rosenkrantz*; 765.23, Chalmer's; 768.35, though; 811.5, it,"; 820.20, crticism; 851.10, ineffacable; 873.30, Varése; 888.35, began.

Notes

In the notes below, the reference numbers denote page and line of this volume (the line count includes headings). No note is made for material included in standard desk-reference books. Quotations from Shakespeare are keyed to *The Riverside Shakespeare*, ed. G. Blakemore Evans (Boston: Houghton Mifflin, 1974). Biographical information beyond that included in the Chronology may be found in Lewis M. Dabney, *Edmund Wilson: A Life in Literature* (Farrar, Straus & Giroux, 2005); Jeffrey Meyers, *Edmund Wilson: A Biography* (Houghton Mifflin, 1995); Edmund Wilson, *The Twenties* (1975), Edmund Wilson, *The Thirties* (1980), *The Forties* (1983), and *The Fifties* (1986, all ed. Leon Edel, Farrar, Straus & Giroux); Edmund Wilson, *The Sixties* (ed. Lewis M. Dabney, Farrar, Straus & Giroux, 1993); Edmund Wilson, *Red, Black, Blond, and Olive: Studies in Four Civilizations* (Oxford University Press, 1956); Edmund Wilson, *A Prelude: Landscapes, Characters and Conversations from the Earlier Years of My Life* (Allen and Unwin, 1967); Elena Wilson, ed., *Letters on Literature and Politics* (Farrar, Straus & Giroux, 1977); Simon Karlinsky, ed., *The Nabokov-Wilson Letters, 1940–1971* (Harper & Row, 1979, 2001); David Castonovo and Janet Groth, *Edmund Wilson: The Man in Letters* (Ohio University Press, 2003).

THE TRIPLE THINKERS

7.2   Paul Elmer More] Paul Elmer More (1864–1937), critical ally of Irving Babbitt and author of *The Shelburne Essays*. See "Notes on Babbitt and More" in *The Shores of Light* (1952).

7.6   Dean Gauss] Christian Gauss (1878–1951), professor of modern languages and Wilson's mentor; dean of Princeton (1925–46). See "Prologue, 1952: Christian Gauss as a Teacher of Literature" in *The Shores of Light*.

9.37   Stuart P. Sherman . . . Seward Collins] Sherman, literary critic (1881–1926) influenced by the New Humanism of Irving Babbitt, author of *On Contemporary Literature* (1917) and *The Genius of America* (1923); Collins (1899–1952), publisher of *The Bookman* (1927–33) and *The American Review* (1933–37), a supporter of Babbitt and More, who in the 1930s identified himself as a fascist.

11.26   Clovis] Frankish king who converted to Christianity in 496.

12.14   Frank Jewett Mather] Professor of art and archaeology at Princeton (1868–1953).

12.37   Oswald Garrison Villard]   Journalist (1872–1949); editor and publisher of *The Nation*.

16.10   Huneker]   James Huneker, American critic (1860–1921), author of *Overtones* (1904), *Iconoclasts* (1905), *Ivory Apes and Peacocks* (1915), and other books that introduced Americans to innovative trends in European literature, art, and music.

20.34   *Biographia Literaria*]   *Biographia Literaria, or Biographical Sketches of My Literary Life and Opinions* (1817) by Samuel Taylor Coleridge.

21.14–15   *Aurora Leigh . . . The Ring and the Book*]   *Aurora Leigh* (1857) and *The Ring and the Book* (1868–69), book-length narrative poems by, respectively, Elizabeth Barrett Browning and Robert Browning.

21.18   Jeremy Taylor]   English churchman (1613–1667); author of *Holy Living* (1650) and *Holy Dying* (1651).

23.27   ἀνήριθμον γέλασμα]   Literally "endless smile," a phrase used by Aeschylus to describe the waves of the ocean.

23.27–28   'daffodils . . . before the swallow dares']   *The Winter's Tale*, IV.iv.118–19.

25.17–18   Maurice de Guérin]   French poet (1810–1839) associated with the Romantic school.

25.36   *La Tentation de Saint Antoine*]   Flaubert's dramatic poem in prose was published in its final version in 1874.

26.16–18   *aethere in alto . . . cadunt*]   Virgil, *Georgics*, IV.78–80: High in the air there is a sound, mixed altogether they heap into a great ball and fall headlong.

26.20–22   'quelquefois les abeilles . . . rebondissantes.']   Sometimes the bees, wheeling in the light, knocked against the windowpanes like bouncing golden balls.—*Madame Bovary*.

26.23–24   *Et iam summa . . . umbrae*]   Virgil, *Eclogues*, I.82–83: And by now, far away, the roof-tops of the farm houses smoke, and greater shadows fall from the high mountains.

26.25–30   'La tendresse . . . sur l'herbe.']   The tenderness of the old days came back to their hearts, abundant and quiet like the flowing river, with as much softness as that conveyed by the odor of the syringas, and cast into their recollections shadows more vast and melancholy than those of the motionless willows that stretched across the grass.—*Madame Bovary*.

26.34–35   *desertaque . . . vacantes*]   Virgil, *Georgics*, III.476: The shepherds' kingdom deserted, far and wide the valleys empty.

26.37–27.1   'Les rues . . . les pavés,']   The streets were deserted. At times a heavy cart passed, shaking the pavement.

27.10–11   'qui ne venaient pas jusqu'à lui]   Which did not reach him.

27.11–12   'tendebantque . . . amore']   *Aeneid*, VI: And reached out longing hands to the far shore.

27.20–21   Louise Colet]   French writer (1810–1870), friend of Flaubert, Musset, and de Vigny.

27.35   Hauptmann]   Gerhart Hauptmann (1862–1946), German writer best known for naturalistic plays such as *The Weavers* (1892).

27.38   Rostand's]   Edmond Rostand (1868–1918), French playwright whose works included *Cyrano de Bergerac* (1896) and *L'Aiglon* (1900).

29.9   Crabbe]   George Crabbe (1754–1832), English poet whose narratives of provincial life were collected in *The Village* (1783), *The Borough* (1810), and other volumes.

29.22   Robinson Jeffers . . . narrative "poems"]   The lengthy verse narratives of Jeffers (1887–1962) include "Tamar" (1924), "Roan Stallion" (1925), and "Cawdor" (1928).

29.25–26   Carl Sandburg . . . *The People, Yes*]   Sandburg's book-length poem was published in 1936.

32.16   Parnassians]   Post-Romantic French poetic group whose members included Leconte de Lisle, Sully Prudhomme, and José-Maria de Heredia.

33.3   Abbé Niles . . . W. C. Handy]   Niles, music critic (1894–1963), an early authority on jazz and blues; Handy (1873–1958), pianist and composer, author of "St. Louis Blues" and "Beale Street Blues."

33.4–5   Professor Kittredge]   George Lyman Kittredge (1860–1941), English professor at Harvard, an authority on Shakespeare and medieval literature.

33.8   Percy's *Reliques*]   *Reliques of Ancient English Poetry* (1765), a collection of traditional Scottish and English poems and ballads edited by Thomas Percy (1729–1811).

35.1   *In Honor of Pushkin*]   Wilson's views on Pushkin can also be found in "Pushkin," written in 1943 and included in *A Window on Russia* (1972).

35.25–26   George Borrow]   English writer, linguist, and traveler (1803–1881), noted for his depiction of gypsy life in *Lavengro* (1851) and *The Romany Rye* (1857). As an agent of the British and Foreign Bible Society, he was resident in St. Petersburg, 1833–35, and made some translations from Russian.

35.29   Lermontov]   Mikhail Lermontov (1814–41), Russian poet, author of the novel *A Hero of Our Time* (1839).

36.34   Cary's translation of Dante]   Henry Francis Cary (1772–1844) published his blank-verse translation of *The Divine Comedy* between 1805 and 1812.

37.11–12   André Chénier] French poet (1762–1794), guillotined during the Revolution.

39.15   Praed] Winthrop Mackworth Praed (1802–1839), English politician known for comic society verse.

40.8   Maurice Baring] British journalist and travel writer (1874–1945), an early western admirer of Russian literature and theater.

45.26   Kalmuck] Kalmyk, a nomadic western Mongolian people who settled on the northwestern shore of the Caspian Sea in the 17th and 18th centuries.

45.28   Sir Charles Grandison] Benevolent gentleman who is the protagonist of Samuel Richardson's novel of the same name, published in 1754.

48.39–49.1   Elizabeth Bennet and Mr. Darcy] Protagonists of Jane Austen's *Pride and Prejudice*.

50.8   Leopardi] Giacomo Leopardi (1798–1837), Italian poet, essayist, and aphorist.

50.10   Beddoes . . . Musset] Thomas Lovell Beddoes (1803–1849), author of poetry and verse dramas on morbid themes, who committed suicide; Alfred de Musset (1810–1857), poet and playwright who largely abandoned writing in his last decades.

50.38   Falconet's] Etienne-Maurice Falconet (1716–1791), French sculptor whose bronze statue of Peter the Great was completed in 1778.

53.9   D. S. Mirsky] Literary historian (1890–1939), author of the English-language *History of Russian Literature* (1927). A friend of Wilson in Moscow in the summer of 1935, Mirsky was arrested by the NKVD in 1937 (at about the time that Wilson translated *The Bronze Horseman*) and died in a forced labor camp.

55.6   GPU] State Political Directorate, the Soviet security police organization from 1922 to 1934, when the state security organization became part of the NKVD.

63.9   *Nescit vox missa reverti*.] The voice sent forth, can never be recalled.

65.18   Manilius] Marcus Manilius, first-century Roman poet, author of *Astronomica*, a long poem on astrology.

65.33   A. W. Verrall . . . Gilbert Murray] Verrall (1951–1912) and Murray (1866–1957), classical scholars and translators of ancient Greek literature.

65.36–37   J. G. Frazer] James G. Frazer (1854–1941), author of *The Golden Bough* (1890–1915).

66.14   Jowett and Mackail] Benjamin Jowett (1817–1893), Oxford professor renowned for translations of Plato, Thucydides, and Aristotle; J. W. Mackail (1859–1945), scholar and translator whose books include *Select Epigrams from the Greek Anthology* (1890) and *Latin Literature* (1895).

66.35–36   'Omnis ab hac cura mens relavata mea est,'] *Tristia*, I.11.1–2: My whole mind is eased by this care.

66.38   'Omnis ab hac cura cura levata mea est.']   All my care is eased by this care.

67.3   'Perditus ac vilis sacci mercator olentis,']   Literally, "ruined and a cheap seller of a fragrant bag."

67.4–5   'Perditus ac similis sacci mercator olentis']   Literally, "ruined and a seller who is like his fragrant bag."

70.15–16   *Lucida tela diei*]   Bright shafts of day.

70.18   Scaliger and Gronovius and Huetius]   Julius Caesar Scaliger (1484–1558), Italian scholar active in the revival of classical studies; Jacobus Gronovius (1645–1716), Dutch classical scholar; Huetius, literary name of Pierre-Daniel Huet (1630–1721), French scholar and ecclesiastic.

70.19   Bentley]   Richard Bentley (1662–1742), classical scholar known for his editions of Horace and Terence.

71.11   *editorum in usum edidit*]   Published for the use of editors.

71.33   *The Grammarian's Funeral*]   Poem by Robert Browning.

71.37–39   the Latin verses . . . which Housman prefixed to his Manilius]   Wilson translated these verses and published them as "Dedication for a Book: A. E. Housman: *Signa pruinosae varantia luce cavernas—*" in *Poets, Farewell!* (1929); it was reprinted in *Night Thoughts* (1961).

73.15   Dodgson]   Charles Lutwidge Dodgson (1832–1898), English classicist and mathematician who as Lewis Carroll published *Alice's Adventures in Wonderland* (1865) and many other works.

73.31   Marius the Epicurean]   Hero of the novel (1878) by Walter Pater.

75.24–25   Taine's *History of English Literature*]   Hippolyte Taine (1828–1893), French historian and literary critic, published his *Histoire de la littérature anglaise* in 1863. See "The Historical Interpretation of Literature" in this volume, in which Wilson shares Flaubert's view of Taine's ostensibly scientific reading of literature through "the moment, the race, and the milieu," but adds, "it was the rabbits he pulled out that saved him."

75.32   La Harpe]   Jean-François de La Harpe (1739–1803), playwright and critic whose *Lycée, ou Course de littérature ancienne et moderne* was published between 1799 and 1805.

78.18   *Un Coeur simple*]   *A Simple Heart*, one of the three novellas comprising Flaubert's *Trois Contes* (1877).

79.15   the Thebaid]   Ancient name for the region of Upper Egypt which was a refuge for early Christian hermits and monks, including St. Pachomius and St. Anthony.

82.30–31   *The Eighteenth Brumaire*]   *The Eighteenth Brumaire of Louis Napoleon* (1852), account by Karl Marx of the coup led by Napoleon's nephew (the future Napoleon III) in 1851.

85.23   The war of 1870]   The Franco-Prussian War.

87.8   Renan and Littré]   Ernest Renan (1823–1892), historian and philosopher, author of *Life of Jesus*; Emile Littré (1801–1881), lexicographer whose four-volume dictionary of the French language was published between 1863 and 1872.

87.24   Saint Vincent de Paul]   Priest (1576–1660) known for his work among the poor and infirm; he founded the Lazarists and the Sisters of Charity, and was canonized in 1737.

99.5   Owen Seaman]   English humorist (1861–1936), editor of *Punch*.

110.14–15   Lord Ormont and his Aminta]   Openly adulterous protagonists of George Meredith's 1894 novel of the same name.

113.9   *Les Trois Mousquetaires* and *The Newcomes*]   *The Three Musketeers* (1844) by Alexandre Dumas; *The Newcomes* (1853–55) by William Makepeace Thackeray.

118.37   Van Wyck Brooks]   Critic and literary historian (1886–1963) whose works included *America's Coming-of-Age* (1915), *The Ordeal of Mark Twain* (1920), and *The Pilgrimage of Henry James* (1925). See "The Pilgrimage of Henry James" in *The Shores of Light* (1952); Brooks's later account of American culture is the subject of "Van Wyck Brooks's Second Phase," "A Picture to Hang in the Library: Brooks's Age of Irving," and "Van Wyck Brooks on the Civil War Period" in the present volume.

123.7   Edmund Gosse]   English man of letters (1849–1928), author of the memoir *Father and Son* (1907).

126.38–39   'Causons, causons, mon bon,']   Let us converse, my good man.

136.34   *Mr. Barnes of New York*]   Novel (1887) by Archibald Clanery Gunter (1847–1907).

138.3   Godkin of the *Post*]   Edwin Godkin (1831–1902), editor of the New York *Evening Post* from 1881 to 1899.

142.17–18   Van Wyck Brooks's recent portrayals]   In *The Flowering of New England* (1936).

150.26–36   But by the later years of the eighties . . . appalling demoralization.] Wilson would use almost the same words when describing his father's hypochondria in "The Author at Sixty" in *A Piece of My Mind* (1956).

155.8   Yasnaya Polyana] Tolstoy's provincial estate.

157.30   Diotima] Diotima of Mantonea, a character in Plato's *Symposium*.

160.6   Balfour, Haldane and Sir Edward Grey] Arthur James Balfour (1848–1930), prime minister of Britain, 1902–5; Viscount Haldane (1856–1928), secretary of state for war, 1905–12, and lord chancellor, 1912–15; Sir Edward Grey (1862–1933), secretary of state for foreign affairs, 1905–16.

160.33   Siegfried Sassoon] English poet and novelist (1886–1967), famous as a war hero who became a protestor against the war; his war experiences were reflected in poems included in *Counter-Attack* (1918) and in the novel *Memoirs of an Infantry Officer* (1930).

162.34   Owen Wister's memoirs of Roosevelt] *Roosevelt: The Story of a Friendship* (1930).

162.38–40   Huysmans . . . a novel, in which were described the rites of the Black Mass] *Là-bas* (*Down There*, 1891).

163.1–2   Alexander Cassatts . . . Weir Mitchells] Alexander Cassatt (1839–1906), president of the Pennsylvania Railroad; George Baer (1842–1914), president of the Reading Company; Silas Weir Mitchell (1829–1914), physician and writer, author of the novel *Hugh Wynne, Free Quaker* (1898). In "The Author at Sixty" in *A Piece of My Mind* (1956), Wilson noted that "Weir Mitchell invented the 'rest cure,' where people got away from their worries. My father spent all of his later years in and out of these sanitariums."

163.3   Coxey's army] Ohio populist politician Jacob Coxey (1854–1951) led a protest march of unemployed men—known as "Coxey's army"—to Washington, D.C., in 1894.

163.4   the Pullman strike] In 1894 a strike by workers in Illinois against the Pullman sleeping car company led to a nationwide boycott of Pullman cars by railway workers led by Eugene V. Debs; federal troops intervened to break the strike, and 13 strikers were killed.

165.1   *Bernard Shaw at Eighty*] In coming to terms with one of the models of his early criticism Wilson draws on seven essays and reviews from 1924 to 1936, including "Bernard Shaw Since the War" (pages 880–84, *Edmund Wilson: Literary Essays and Reviews of the 1920s and 30s*); see also "The Last Phase of Bernard Shaw" in *The Bit Between My Teeth*.

165.15   Henry George] Economist (1839–1897), whose *Progress and Poverty* (1877–79) advocated a single tax levied on land.

166.20–21   Mark Starr] British trade unionist (1894–1985), active in promoting workers' education.

168.29   Childe Harold] Melancholy, disillusioned protagonist of Byron's *Childe Harold's Pilgrimage* (1812–18).

168.30   Don César de Bazan] Hero of the opera of the same name (1872) in four acts by Jules Massenet, based on Victor Hugo's play *Ruy Blas*.

168.30   'Tant pis! C'est moi!'] So much the worse! It is I!

168.39   William Archer] Drama critic (1856–1924) who was the first English translator of the plays of Ibsen.

173.6   Sir Douglas Haig] Haig (1861–1928) was commander in chief of the British Expeditionary Force in France and Flanders, 1915–18.

173.28   Frank Harris] Harris (1856–1931) published *Bernard Shaw* in 1931; he also wrote *Oscar Wilde, His Life and Confessions* (1920).

173.34   John Morley] Statesman and writer (1838–1923), author of biographies of Burke, Voltaire, Rousseau, and others.

175.11   Gaetano Salvemini] Italian socialist politician and historian (1873–1957) who later taught at Harvard.

175.34   Thersites] Greek soldier in *The Iliad* and in Shakespeare's *Troilus and Cressida* who rails bitterly at Agamemnon and Achilles.

180.26   Savoy operas] The series of operettas written by W. S. Gilbert and Arthur Sullivan between 1871 and 1896.

202.36   Lunacharsky] Anatoly Lunacharsky (1875–1933), Bolshevik revolutionary; as Commissar of Enlightenment (1917–29) he led a literacy campaign and was involved in founding the art movement Proletkult.

205.23   Cloître-Saint-Merri] During the republican uprising in Paris against Louis-Philippe, June 5–6, 1832, the insurgents made their final stand around the cloisters of Saint-Merri. (The insurrection of 1832 was later portrayed by Victor Hugo in *Les Misérables*.)

205.32–33   Proust . . . chapter on the death of the novelist Bergotte] Wilson also evokes this passage in *Axel's Castle* and in his 1936 "Letter to the Russians About Hemingway" in *The Shores of Light*.

206.26   Burton Rascoe] Literary critic and columnist (1892–1957), a friend of Wilson.

207.32   misrepresenttation of Sophocles] In "Notes on Babbitt and More" (*The Shores of Light*), Wilson points out how Babbitt turns the Greek for Antigone's "unwritten and unfailing laws of the gods" into "laws unwritten in the heavens."

208.25   Carducci] Giosuè Carducci (1835–1907), Italian poet who won the Nobel Prize in 1906.

209.18   Camille Desmoulins] French revolutionary leader (1760–1794), an associate of Danton, with whom he was executed.

209.22   Alexander Blok's poem, *The Twelve*] Blok (1880–1921) wrote his long poem blending revolutionary and religious imagery in 1918.

212.5   Vincent Sheean] American foreign correspondent (1899–1975), author of the bestselling memoir *Personal History* (1935).

227.14   the current French film] Jonson's play was filmed in 1941 by Maurice Tourneur, in an adaptation by Jules Romains; the cast was headed by Harry Baur and Louis Jouvet.

233.22   Mr. Batch] Comic-strip character created by Jimmy Swinnerton (1875–1974).

237.35   Henry C. Frick] Henry Clay Frick (1849–1919), American industrialist who played a dominant role in the coal and steel industries. See "Frémont and Frick" in *The Shores of Light*.

241.22   *A Blot on the 'Scutcheon*] Browning's verse tragedy was published in 1843.

241.31   *The Autocrat of the Breakfast-Table*] A series of humorous and reflective essays by Oliver Wendell Holmes (1809–1894), originally published in *The Atlantic Monthly*.

241.34–35   *The Wonderful One-Hoss Shay*] "The Deacon's Masterpiece," humorous poem by Oliver Wendell Holmes.

243.24–25   the trial of Orontas in Xenophon] See *Anabasis*, Book One.

245.15–16   the Statue in *Don Giovanni*] The statue of the Commendatore, killed by Don Giovanni, comes to life in the last act to summon him to hell.

252.32   Compton Mackenzie's *Youth's Encounter*] The first volume of the novel *Sinister Street* (1913–14), published in the United States as a separate work.

252.34   'μηδὲν ἄγαν] Nothing in excess.

256.1   *The Historical Interpretation of Literature*] This lecture derives from one of the two courses Wilson taught at the University of Chicago in the summer of 1939, addressing "the social interpretation with Taine and some of the Marxist texts."

256.35   D. S. Mirsky] See note 53.9.

257.2   George Saintsbury] English literary critic and journalist (1845–1933) whose works included *A History of English Prose Rhythm* (1912) and *A History of the French Novel to the Close of the Nineteenth Century* (1917–19). Wilson called him "the sole English literary critic of the late-nineteenth early-twentieth centuries . . . who is really of first-rate stature." See "George Saintsbury's Centenary," pages 715–18, and "George Saintsbury: Gourmet and Glutton," pages 763–66 in this volume.

258.35   Herder]   Johann Gottfried Herder (1744–1803), German critic and poet; his *Ideen zur Geschichte der Menschheit* was published 1784–91.

259.11   Taine]   See "Decline of the Revolutionary Tradition: Taine" in *To the Finland Station* (1940), where Taine is taken as a voice of the bourgeois age.

261.22   *der Dichter*]   The poet.

261.34–35   Franz Mehring]   German socialist (1846–1919), author of *History of German Social Democracy* (1897–98).

263.5–6   the moralizing Russian criticism]   See "Communist Criticism" in *The Shores of Light*.

263.7–8   Belinsky and Chernyshevsky]   Vissarion Belinsky (1811–1848), preeminent Russian literary critic of his era; Nikolai Chernyshevsky (1828–1889), radical critic known for his novel *What Is To Be Done?* (1864).

263.22   Proletcult or Lev or Rapp]   Proletcult ("proletarian culture"), arts movement with ties to constructivism and futurism led by Alexander Bogdanov with support from Anatoly Lunacharsky; Lev, or Lef, avant-garde Soviet literary magazine, *The Left Front of Art*, founded in 1923 by Vladimir Mayakovsky and Osip Brik; RAPP, the Russian Association of Proletarian Writers, founded in 1928, sought to impose a dogmatic "proletarian" style on Soviet literature and severely criticized Boris Pilnyak, Vladimir Mayakovsky, Yevgeny Zamyatin, and other nonconformist writers.

263.23   Count Benckendorff]   Aleksandr Benckendorff (1783–1844) suppressed the 1825 Decembrist uprising and served as chancellor and police chief under Alexander I.

264.13–14   A recent gesture . . . Archibald MacLeish]   See "Archibald MacLeish and the Word" on pages 479–84 in this volume.

THE WOUND AND THE BOW

272.1–2   *I bleed . . . my torn bough!*]   *Pomes Penyeach*, "Tilly," lines 11–12.

275.23   Forster's elaborate memoir]   John Forster (1812–1876), Dickens' lifelong friend and literary executor, author of *The Life of Charles Dickens* (1872–74).

275.24   Ley]   J.W.T. Ley, author of *The Dickens Circle* (1918).

276.5   George Gissing . . . book on Dickens]   *Charles Dickens: A Critical Study* (1898).

281.3   Surtees' *Jorrocks*]   *Jorrocks's Jaunts and Jollities* (1838), humorous, episodic novel by the English editor and sports writer Robert Smith Surtees (1805–1864).

285.15   Lemaître] Frederick Lemaître (1800–1870) was famous for his portrayal of the criminal Robert Macaire, and for such subsequent roles as Cartouche and Vautrin.

285.18–19   Professor Webster] Dr. John Webster, a chemistry professor at Harvard, was tried and hanged in 1850 for the murder and dismemberment of Dr. George Parkman, a prominent Bostonian to whom he owed money.

294.13   Robert Owen] Welsh socialist and utopian reformer (1771–1858), founder of a number of cooperative communities. Wilson portrays Owen at length, and in a different light, in "Origins of Socialism: The Communities of Fourier and Owen" in *To the Finland Station.*

297.19   George Henry Lewes] Philosopher and critic (1817–1878), companion of George Eliot.

297.27   Mrs. Gaskell's industrial studies] Elizabeth Gaskell (1810–1865) dealt with the social problems of the Industrial Revolution in the novels *Mary Barton* (1848) and *North and South* (1855).

297.30   *Gil Blas*] Picaresque romance published in four volumes between 1715 and 1735, by Alain René Lesage (1668–1747).

299.8   the Great Boyg] In Ibsen's *Peer Gynt* (1867), a formless, devouring troll.

304.31   *Noctes Ambrosianae*] Imaginary conversations published in *Blackwood's Edinburgh Magazine* (1822–35), written by John Wilson, James Hogg, and others, and supposed to take place at Ambrose's Tavern in Edinburgh.

322.3   This episode . . . has been hushed up] The British writer Ada Nisbet later sent Wilson a paper on the subject, based on crossed-out pages in Dickens's correspondence that she read with the aid of infrared photography. Wilson assisted in the publication of Nisbet's *Dickens and Ellen Ternan* (1952) and wrote a foreword to the book.

346.22   *The Wide, Wide World*] Bestselling American novel (1850) by Susan Warner, published under the pseudonym Elizabeth Wetherell.

350.27   Walter Besant] Novelist (1836–1901) best known for *All Sorts and Conditions of Men* (1882).

353.19   *Sister Helen*] Ballad by Dante Gabriel Rossetti.

357.24   Chirons] Chiron, wise centaur who was the tutor of Heracles.

362.24   Cyrano de Bergerac] Author and freethinker (1619–1655) whose flamboyant legend was popularized in Edmond Rostand's 1897 play.

364.8 John Hay] Diplomat and writer (1838–1905), ambassador to Great Britain (1897–98) and U.S. secretary of state (1898–1905).

365.6 Angela Thirkell] Thirkell (1890–1961) was also the author of more than 30 novels written as sequels to the Barsetshire novels of Anthony Trollope.

373.8 Dr. Jameson] Leander Starr Jameson (1853–1917), South African physician and colonial administrator. Jameson led an abortive attack on the Transvaal Republic in December 1895 in an attempt to provoke an uprising by English settlers. He was imprisoned for 15 months in England, and later served as prime minister of Cape Colony (1904–8).

375.12 George Moore] Irish novelist and memoirist (1852–1933).

387.2 Meissonier] Jean-Louis-Ernest Meissonier (1815–1891), French painter known for his elaborately detailed battle scenes.

387.18 the Marconi scandals] In 1912 the Asquith government was threatened by allegations that three prominent Liberals, including chancellor of the exchequer David Lloyd George and Sir Rufus Isaacs, the attorney general, had profited from insider trading in shares of the Marconi wireless companies. Although the majority report of a subsequent parliamentary investigating committee found no evidence of wrongdoing, the accusations continued, and included anti-Semitic attacks on Isaacs, his brother Godfrey, the managing director of the English Marconi company, and Herbert Samuel, the minister who had awarded a government contract to Marconi.

390.21 Mrs. Ewing] Juliana Ewing (1841–1885), author of children's stories including *The Brownies and Other Tales* (1870).

391.10 Buchmanite] The American evangelist Frank Buchman (1878–1961) founded an organization, sometimes known as the Oxford Group or Moral Rearmament, that promulgated absolute standards of morality and "the dictatorship of God." See "Saving the Right People and Their Butlers" in *The American Earthquake* (1958).

396.2 *Uncomfortable Casanova*] Originally published as "Casanova" in *The New Republic*, August 1932.

396.5 Havelock Ellis's] Writer and sexologist (1859–1939), author of *Studies in the Psychology of Sex* (1897–1910).

396.6 S. Guy Endore's book] *Casanova: His Known and Unknown Life* (1929).

396.18–19 Rothstein . . . Dapper Don Tourbillon] Arnold Rothstein, New York mobster and bootlegger, a model for Meyer Wolfsheim in *The Great Gatsby*; Nicky Arnstein, partner of Rothstein, a bond thief; Dapper Dan Tourbillon, another conman of the 1920s.

396.21 St. Germain and Cagliostro] Arthur Edward Waite, Count St.

Germain, and Guiseppi Balsamo, who took the name Cagliostro, were famous 18th-century adventurers and charlatans.

400.6   Arthur Symons]   English poet (1865–1945), translator of the memoirs of Casanova

400.32   d'Alembert]   Jean le Rond d'Alembert, 18th-century French
mathematician who co-edited the *Encyclopedia* with Diderot.

401.14   '*par trop cynique*']   Far too cynical.

405.2   *Justice to Edith Wharton*]   See also "Edith Wharton: A Memoir by
an English Friend" on pages 799–803 of the present volume.

405.14   Paul Bourget]   French novelist (1852–1935), author of *The Disciple*
(1889), *Cosmopolis* (1893), and other works.

406.4   Dr. S. Weir Mitchell]   See note 163.1–2.

406.29   Eumenides]   The avenging Furies of Greek mythology.

408.16–17   Clyde Fitch]   Fitch (1865–1909), popular playwright, author of
Captain Jinks of the Horse Marines (1901).

409.13   the Princess de Lamballe]   Marie-Thérèse-Louise, princess of
Lamballe (1749–1792), was Marie Antoinette's closest companion. She was
brutally murdered by a mob during the September massacres of 1792 after refusing to denounce the queen.

415.32   Vesalius]   Andreas Vesalius (1514–1564), anatomist.

415.39   Charles Eliot Norton]   Writer (1827–1908) and professor of art
history at Harvard; his translation of Dante was published 1891–92.

418.2   *Hemingway: Gauge of Morale*]   See "Emergence of Ernest Hemingway" and "The Sportsman's Tragedy" in *The Shores of Light* and "Return
of Ernest Hemingway" on pages 885–89 in this volume.

430.37   Vyshinsky]   Andrei Vyshinsky (1883–1954), prosecutor in the
Moscow trials of the late 1930s.

432.8   Young Pioneers]   A Soviet youth organization for children aged 9
to 14.

432.39   Callot]   Jacques Callot, French painter and engraver (c. 1592–
1635).

434.19   Paul Bunyan]   Giant lumberjack, the hero of a cycle of American
folktales.

437.7   The weaknesses of this book]   Wilson's critical comments
throughout "Hemingway: Gauge of Morale" infuriated Hemingway, and
Scribner's (Hemingway's publishers) broke the contract for *The Wound and
the Bow* rather than offend him.

438.2   *The Dream of H. C. Earwicker*] See "A Guide to *Finnegans Wake*," pages 618–23 in this volume.

451.19   *Erewhon*] Utopian novel (1872) by Samuel Butler.

458.12   Atreidai] The house of Atreus.

459.30   *Candida . . . La Parisienne*] *Candida* (1895), play by George Bernard Shaw; *La Parisienne* (*The Woman of Paris*, 1885), play by Henri Becque.

471.5   Jebb] R. C. Jebb (1841–1905), editor and translator of Sophocles.

472.19   C. M. Bowra] Cecil Maurice Bowra (1898–1971), Oxford classical scholar, author of *Ancient Greek Literature* (1933) and other works.

CLASSICS AND COMMERCIALS

479.4–5   his previous career] See Wilson's satirical poem "The Omelet of A. MacLeish" (1939) in *Night Thoughts* (1961). Parodying *The Hamlet of A. MacLeish* (1928), Wilson has his protagonist, envying the true artists, ask himself: "O when shall I ring with the perilous pain and the fever?"

479.35   Henri Barbusse] French novelist and journalist (1873–1935), author of the World War I novel *Le Feu: Journal d'une escouade* (1916; translated as *Under Fire: The Story of a Squad*).

481.9–10   This skepticism . . . Charles A. Beard] American historian Charles A. Beard (1874–1948), author of some 30 books including *An Economic Interpretation of the Constitution of the United States* (1913) and, with his wife, Mary, *The Rise of American Civilization* (1927). Beard argued that World War I had been fought on behalf of capitalist interests, and he opposed American intervention in World War II.

481.22–23   poem on the "Social Muse," . . . same magazine] "Invocation to the Social Muse" (1932), first published in *The New Republic*. The italicized lines at 481.27–29 are quoted from the poem.

482.33   John Chamberlain] Journalist and book reviewer (1903–1995), whose books included *Farewell to Reform: A History of the Rise, Life, and Decay of the Progressive Mind in America* (1932).

483.19–21   *Dos who saw . . . among you!*] Lines from MacLeish's "Sentiments for a Dedication" (1929).

486.23   Léon Bazalgette] French critic (1873–1928), author of the studies *Walt Whitman, l'homme et son oeuvre* (1908) and *Henry Thoreau, Sauvage* (1914; translated by Van Wyck Brooks as *Henry Thoreau: Bachelor of Nature* in 1924).

487.12   Charles Eliot Norton] See note 415.39.

489.34   *ipsissima verba*] The very words.

489.38   Mary E. Wilkins]   Mary E. Wilkins Freeman (1852–1930), writer whose books include *A New England Nun and Other Stories* (1891) and the novel *Pembroke* (1894).

490.18–19   Vernon Parrington]   American historian and literary critic (1871–1929), author of *Main Currents in American Thought: An Interpretation of American Literature From the Beginnings to 1920* (1927–30).

490.38   *The Peterkin Papers*]   Collection (1880) of humorous children's stories by Lucretia Peabody Hale (1820–1900).

491.6–7   Helen . . . Sill]   Helen Hunt Jackson (1830–1885), American novelist best known for *Ramona* (1884); Thomas Bailey Aldrich (1836–1907), American poet, novelist, and editor, author of *The Story of a Bad Boy* (1869); Charles Dudley Warner (1829–1900), American essayist, novelist, and magazine editor, author (with Mark Twain) of *The Gilded Age* (1873); Edward Rowland Sill (1841–1887), American poet.

493.3–4   visiting Englishman . . . Eric Knight]   I.e., "Richard Hallas" was a pseudonym used by the English writer Eric Knight (1897–1943), a novelist, journalist, and screenwriter, best known for the novels *Lassie Come-Home* (1940) and *This Above All* (1941).

501.37–38   Eddie . . . Crane]   Edgar Guest (1881–1959), folksy poet whose verses in the *Detroit Free Press* were widely syndicated; William Lyon Phelps (1865–1943), longtime Yale professor and popular lecturer; Frank Crane (1861–1928), a minister who became a prolific writer of inspirational newspaper and magazine pieces.

505.27–28   zoöphile fiction of David Garnett]   A woman is transformed into a fox in English writer David Garnett's novel *Lady Into Fox* (1916); *A Man in the Zoo* (1924) tells the story of a man exhibiting himself in a zoo.

514.19   *Boy Meets Girl*]   Bella and Sam Spewack's 1935 play centering on the antics of two screenwriters.

514.33   Gerald Heard]   English writer (1889–1971) who immigrated to the U.S. in 1937 and settled in California. He was interested in spiritualism and the occult; his story collections include *The Great Fog and Other Weird Tales* (1944) and *The Lost Cavern and Other Tales of the Fantastic* (1948).

515.14–15   would-be barbaric tragedies . . . Jeffers]   American poet Robinson Jeffers (1887–1962) wrote long narrative poems such as "Roan Stallion" and "Tamar," which were set against the rugged landscape in and around Carmel, California, where he lived.

516.16   The McNamaras, Mooney and Billings]   The brothers James and John McNamara planted the dynamite bomb that exploded behind the offices of the Los Angeles *Times* on October 1, 1910, resulting in the deaths of 21 people. Labor leaders Thomas Mooney (1882?–1942) and Warren Billings (1893–1972), accused of setting off a bomb during a parade in San

Francisco on July 22, 1916, were convicted in a trial marked by perjury and other irregularities; the case became a cause célèbre, and both men were pardoned in 1939.

517.18   Lautréamont]   Pen name of Isidore Ducasse (1847–1870), French poet, author of the prose poem *Les Chants de Maldoror* (1868–70).

523.12   John Reed . . . Mike Gold]   John Reed (1887–1920), journalist, poet, and political radical, best known for *Ten Days That Shook the World* (1919), an eyewitness account of the Russian Revolution; Michael Gold (1894–1967), journalist, editor of left-wing magazines *Masses* and *New Masses*, playwright, and novelist, author of *Jews Without Money* (1930).

523.22–23   In arguing with Sidney Hook]   An argument between Hook and Eastman as to when revolutionary Marxism had gone wrong, Eastman assigning less of the blame to Lenin than Hook did; Wilson took Eastman's side but disapproved of his polemical manners.

524.11   Sergei Kirov]   Politburo member and Leningrad party chief (1886–1934), who was assassinated in Leningrad on December 1, 1934. Stalin falsely accused his political opponents of conspiring to kill Kirov; allegations that Stalin ordered the assassination remain unproven.

531.11   Jesse Lynch Williams]   Playwright and fiction writer (1871–1929), co-founder (with Booth Tarkington and others) of The Triangle Club, a drama group at Princeton; author of *Princeton Stories* (1895).

532.20   Lionel Johnson]   English poet and critic (1867–1902), one of the members of the Rhymers' Club, whose members included W. B. Yeats and Ernest Dowson.

532.27   *Marius the Epicurean*]   See note 73.31.

533.7–8   invoked by Poe: *Omne tulit punctum, qui miscuit utile dulci*]   Loosely translated, "All praise the man who mixes what is useful and what is pleasing," from Horace, *Ars Poetica*. Poe cited Horace's maxim in a 1842 review of Harry Lorrequer's *Charles O'Malley, The Irish Dragoon*.

533.22   volumes of verse]   *The Tempers* (1913) and *Al Que Quiere!* (1917).

534.22   Duncan Spaeth]   Professor of English (1868–1954) at Princeton; he taught Shakespeare and Romantic poetry.

534.26–27   *The Scholar Gypsy*]   Poem (1853) by Matthew Arnold.

537.26–29   *Rasselas* . . . known."]   See Samuel Johnson, *Rasselas* (1759): "Human life is everywhere a state in which much is to be endured and little to be enjoyed."

544.8   North American Phalanx]   Utopian commune (1843–55) based on the ideas of French socialist thinker Charles Fourier (1772–1837).

544.22   Father Duffy] Francis Patrick Duffy (1871–1932), Catholic priest who served as chaplain of the "Fighting Sixty-Ninth" regiment of the New York National Guard.

547.10   the Barrymores and Mrs. Fiske] Born Herbert Blythe (1847–1905), actor Maurice Barrymore and his wife Georgiana (1856–1893) were popular actors in late-19th-century American theater; their children, John (1882–1942), Lionel (1878–1954), and Ethel (1879–1959), were stars on the stage and in movies; Minnie Maddern Fiske (1865–1932) portrayed Ibsen's heroines in early American productions of his plays.

547.30   George Arliss] English actor and playwright (1868–1946).

549.11   Zimmerwald peace movement] Socialist antiwar movement named for a conference held in the Swiss village of Zimmerwald, near Bern, in September 1915.

549.17   Cheka] The Soviet security police, 1917–22, from *Chrezvychaynaya Kommissiya po bor'be s kontrerevolyutsiey i sabotazhem* (Extraordinary Commission for Combating Counter-Revolution and Sabotage); its successors included the NKVD and KGB. Members of the Soviet security police continued to be known as "chekists" until the collapse of the U.S.S.R. in 1991.

551.4–20   *J'ai cherché . . . ni aimée . . .*] I searched for truth / And I worshiped it, / Sacrificing to it / What I am and what I was / And I die forgotten . . . / Bent under the invisible yoke / Of their misery, / I see them every day resigned and passive / Climbing their Calvary . . . / While my heart embraces / Their infinite suffering / It tightens up in atrocious agony / And beats no more . . . / I die hailing death / Like a traveler arriving in port / After a long crossing / That he neither sought nor loved . . .

552.3   the film] A movie adaptation of Davies' 1941 book *Mission to Moscow*, directed by Michael Curtiz, was released in 1943.

552.16   Kerensky government] Aleksandr Kerensky (1881–1970) became prime minister of the Russian Provisional Government in July 1917 and served until his overthrow by the Bolsheviks in November.

555.16–17   confession by Tukhachevsky] Marshal Mikhail Tukhachevsky (1893–1937) was arrested on May 22, 1937, and falsely accused of involvement in a Trotskyist conspiracy against the government and of spying for Germany. He and seven other Red Army commanders were secretly tried and executed on June 12, 1937. In the film version of *Mission to Moscow*, Tukhachevsky is depicted as confessing in open court at the same time as Nikolai Bukharin, who was publicly tried in March 1938.

556.10–12   *fortiter in re . . . suaviter in modo*] Gentle in manner, strong in practice.

559.27   Henry Luce] American publisher (1898–1967), founder and editor-in-chief of *Time* and *Fortune* magazines, among others.

562.9   Arthur Mizener]   Professor, biographer, and bibliographer (1907–1988). "Thoughts on Being Bibliographed" accompanied Mizener's bibliography of Wilson's writings to 1944 published in *The Princeton University Library Chronicle*.

564.3   James Huneker]   See note 16.10.

564.25–26   *Egoists* and *The Quintessence of Ibsenism*]   Huneker's *Egoists: A Book of Supermen* (1910); Shaw's *The Quintessence of Ibsenism* (1891).

565.11—19   first night of *Hernani* . . . the red vest of Gautier]   When Victor Hugo's play *Hernani* premiered at the Comédie Française in February 1830, a riot broke out between audience members outraged at the play's rejection of classicism and those who supported the romanticism of the play—notably the young poet Théophile Gautier (1811–1872), who wore a red vest to the performance.

568.15   Charley Schwab, Charley Mitchell]   American industrialist Charles Schwab (1862–1939), head of Bethlehem Steel Corporation; Charles E. Mitchell (1877–1955), nicknamed "Sunshine Charley," chairman of National City Bank, who admitted to the Senate Committee on Banking and Currency in 1933 that he paid no income tax in 1929; he was later ordered by the Supreme Court to pay more than $1,000,000 in back taxes. See "Sunshine Charlie" in *The American Earthquake* (1958).

573.2   Wolfe Tone's]   Irish revolutionary (1763–1798), founder of the Society of United Irishmen.

574.9   Ronald Firbank]   English novelist (1886–1926), author of *The Flower Beneath the Foot* (1923) and *Concerning the Eccentricities of Cardinal Pirelli* (1926). See "Firbank and Beckford" in *The Shores of Light* (1952) and "A Revival of Ronald Firbank," pages 856–68 in this volume.

575.19   Charles Boyer]   French actor (1899–1978), star of *Algiers* (1938), *Love Affair* (1939), *All This and Heaven, Too* (1940), and *Gaslight* (1944); during World War II, he was one of the most prominent representatives of the Free French movement in America.

578.17   *This Quarter* . . . *Transition*]   Literary magazines (founded in 1925 and 1927, respectively) that featured experimental modernist writing.

581.36   Moscow Art Theater]   Russia's leading and first artistically innovative theater, founded in 1897 by Konstantin Stanislavsky and Vladimir Nemirovich-Danchenko. See "The Moscow Art Theater" and "Moscow, Athens, and Paris" in *The American Earthquake*.

583.29   Dolores Costello]   American stage and film actress (1905–1979) who was Barrymore's wife from 1928 to 1935.

587.13–14   "I will show . . . dust,"]   From "The Waste Land" (1922).

587.32   Benjamin Jowett]   See note 66.14.

600.16   *Kings Row*] Film (1942) directed by Sam Wood, based on a novel by Henry Bellamann.

600.19   Erich von Stroheim] Austrian-born film director and actor (1885–1957), best known as director of *Greed* (1924); following his performance as a Prussian officer in Jean Renoir's *La Grande Illusion* (1937), he portrayed German villains in several wartime Hollywood films, including *Five Graves to Cairo* (1943) and *The North Star* (1943).

611.11   *Arsenic and Old Lace*] Stage comedy (1941) by Joseph Kesselring that was adapted into a film directed by Frank Capra (released 1944); it tells the story of two elderly spinster sisters who murder men they have taken in as boarders.

611.18   *The Uninvited*] Film (1944) about a haunted English seaside house; it was directed by Lewis Allen and starred Ray Milland, Ruth Hussey, and Donald Crisp.

615 4   Arthur Machen] English writer (1863–1947) of the supernatural and occult who published *The Great God Pan* in 1894; among his other books were *The Hill of Dreams* (1907) and *The Terror* (1917).

620.32   *Jabberwocky*] Nonsense poem by Lewis Carroll from *Through the Looking Glass* (1871).

624.9   Balzac's *Fille aux Yeux d'Or*] The 1835 novella *The Girl with the Golden Eyes*.

624.10   Barbey d'Aurevilly's *Diaboliques*] *Les Diaboliques* (1874), story collection by French writer Jules Barbey d'Aurevilly (1808–1889).

624.11–12   Villiers de l'Isle-Adam's *Axel*] *Axel*, Symbolist play (first produced posthumously in 1890) by the French playwright and fiction writer August Villiers de l'Isle-Adam (1838–1889). See "Axel and Rimbaud" in *Axel's Castle* (1931).

624.12–14   Huysmans' Des Esseintes . . . Durtal] Des Esseintes, protagonist of *A Rebours* (*Against the Grain*, 1884), novel by French writer J. K. Huysmans (1848–1907); Durtal, Huysmans' alter ego in a series of novels including *La-Bas* (*Down There*, 1891), a book dealing with satanism.

624.29–30   *Werther* . . . *La Nouvelle Héloïse*] Novels by Goethe and Rousseau, published in 1774 and 1761.

625.3   Bulwer-Lytton and Ouida] English novelists Edward Bulwer-Lytton (1803–1873) and Ouida, pen name of Marie Louise Ramé (1839–1908).

629.16   Stark Young] Drama critic, playwright, and novelist (1881–1963); a friend of Wilson on the staff of *The New Republic*.

629.27–28   G. B. Stern and Sheila Kaye-Smith] Prolific English novelist and biographer Gladys Bertha Stern (1893–1970); English novelist, poet, and biographer Sheila Kaye-Smith (1887–1956), author of *Joanna Godden* (1922), *The End of the House of Alard* (1923), and many other novels.

632.28 *Evelina . . . Gentlemen Prefer Blondes*] Novel (1778) by English writer Fanny Burney (1752–1840) and collection of linked stories (1925) by American writer Anita Loos (1893–1981).

637.12–13 *The Last Days of Pompeii, Quo Vadis?* and *Ben-Hur*] Novels of Roman antiquity written by English novelist Edward Bulwer-Lytton (1803–1873), Polish novelist Henryk Sienkiewicz (1846–1916), and American novelist, Union general, and politician Lew Wallace (1827–1905), respectively (and published in 1834, 1895, and 1880).

638.11 a clergyman in Kansas] Charles M. Sheldon (1857–1946).

639.20 Gene Stratton-Porter and Harold Bell Wright] Popular novelist Geneva Stratton-Porter (1863–1924), author of *A Girl of the Limberlost* (1909); clergyman and popular novelist Harold Bell Wright (1872–1944), author of *The Shepherd of the Hills* (1907).

640.12–13 Gradgrind . . . utilitarian] Stern father and schoolmaster in Dickens' novel *Hard Times* (1854) who believes that "Facts alone are wanted in this life": "You can only form the minds of reasoning animals upon Facts: nothing else will ever be of service to them."

651.8 Simms] William Gilmore Simms (1806–1870), American novelist and man of letters from South Carolina, author of numerous historical romances in the manner of Scott and Cooper.

651.8 Willis] Nathaniel Parker Willis (1806–1867), journalist and poet, a founding editor of *The Home Journal*.

654.28 Yvor Winters admires this poem of Bryant's] American critic and poet Yvor Winters (1900–1968) called "To a Waterfowl" a "great lyric" in *Maule's Curse: Seven Studies in the History of American Obscurantism* (1938).

657.11–12 Jacques Futrelle . . . Thinking Machine] Professor Augustus S. F. X. Van Dusen, a character also known as the Thinking Machine, was a creation of American writer Jacques Futrelle (1875–1912) and first appeared in the popular story "The Problem of Cell 13," published as a newspaper serial in 1905.

660.20 Jimmy Durante's] American variety entertainer (1893–1980) who sang comic and sentimental songs while accompanying himself on the piano.

663.15 Burton's *Anatomy*] *The Anatomy of Melancholy* (1621) by English writer Robert Burton (1577–1640).

665.3 Gibson girls] The "Gibson Girl" was the image of the fashionable young woman as depicted in the drawings of Charles Dana Gibson (1867–1944).

672.18   Komsomol]   Communist Union of Youth, a Soviet organization for young people aged 14 to 28; many Komsomol activists later became Party members.

673.40   *ci-devant*]   Former.

676.26   the mold . . . has crushed the book.]   See Wilson's meeting with Leonov described in *The Sixties*: "He said that he had survived all those terrible years—'*Ya ochen khitry*' [I am very clever]."

681.20–21   E. Phillips Oppenheim]   Prolific English thriller writer (1886–1946) best known for *The Great Impersonation* (1920).

688.23–25   Albert Bigelow Paine . . . Hollow Tree]   Children's stories by American writer Albert Bigelow Paine (1861–1937) that were collected in *The Hollow Tree* (1898), *The Hollow Tree and Deep Woods Book* (1901), and *Hollow Tree Days and Nights* (1916).

690.15   Krafft-Ebing]   Richard von Krafft-Ebing (1840–1902), German psychiatrist known for his treatise *Psychopathia Sexualis* (1886).

695.18   Benjamin Constant]   French writer and political figure (1767–1830), author of the novel *Adolphe* (1816).

695.25–26   Augustus John . . . memoirs]   Selections from the Welsh artist Augustus John's autobiography (*Chiaroscuro*, 1952) were first published in *Horizon*.

696.15   Chamfort]   Nicolas Chamfort (1741–1794), French writer whose aphorisms were collected in the posthumously published *Pensées, maximes et anecdotes* (1795).

700.11   August Derleth]   American writer (1909–1971) of supernatural fiction, an acolyte of H. P. Lovecraft and founder of the Arkham House publishing company.

706.34   Louis Blanc]   French socialist politician, essayist, and historian (1811–1882).

706.38–39   Edward FitzGerald]   English poet (1809–1883), best known for *The Rubaiyat of Omar Khayyam*, a free translation (1859) of quatrains by the Persian poet (d. 1132?).

710.11   *The Dark Flower*]   Novel (1913) by English writer John Galsworthy (1867–1933).

712.24–25   *The Black Rose* and *The Manatee*]   Bestselling novels of 1945 written by Thomas B. Costain (1885–1965) and Nancy Bruff (b. 1915), respectively.

713.5–6   *1066 and All That*]   Popular comic retelling of English history (1930) by W. C. Sellar (1898–1951) and R. J. Yeatman (1897–1968).

716.32–33   Pigault-Lebrun or Restif de la Bretonne] Charles Antoine Pigault-Lebrun (1753–1835), French novelist and playwright; Nicolas Edmé Restif de la Bretonne (1734–1806), novelist, social reformer, and memoirist, author of the autobiography *Monsieur Nicolas* (1796–97).

717.10   Hogg, Praed, Barham] Scottish writer James Hogg (1770–1835), author of numerous books of poetry and *Private Memoirs and Confessions of a Justified Sinner* (1824); Winthrop Mackworth Praed (1802–1839), English poet of witty and satirical verse; Richard Harris Barham (1788–1845), English clergyman who wrote, under the pseudonym Thomas Ingoldsby, *The Ingoldsby Legends* (1840), a series of humorous tales in verse that Wilson read as an adolescent and returned to in the title essay of *The Devils and Canon Barham* (1973).

717.23   *Liaisons Dangereuses*] *Dangerous Liaisons* (1782), novel by French writer Pierre Choderlos de Laclos (1741–1803), in which two aristocratic libertines who have been taking advantage of purer people end up ruining each other.

721.38–39   at Phoebe and Alice Cary's] Home on East 20th Street in New York City of sisters Alice (1820–1871) and Phoebe Cary (1824–1871), poets who became well known after publishing a jointly written book in 1849.

722.9–10   Jim Fisk . . . Edward Stokes] American capitalist James Fisk, Jr. (1834–1872), partner of Jay Gould, was murdered in Manhattan's Grand Central Hotel by Edward Stokes, a business associate and rival for the affections of Fisk's mistress, actress Josie Mansfield.

722.14–15   Four Hundred . . . Ward McAllister] American socialite (1827–1895), author of *Society as I Have Found It* (1895).

725.22   Compton Mackenzie] Prolific Scottish writer (1883–1972), author of the *Four Winds of Love* tetralogy of novels and his account of his experiences as a soldier and intelligence agent, *Greek Memories* (1932).

729.5–6   Michael Arlen and Katharine Brush] English writer Michael Arlen (1895–1956) and American writer Katharine Brush (1902–1952), authors of light fiction.

734.22–23   Henry Mackenzie's Man of Feeling] The eponymous hero of *The Man of Feeling* (1771) by Scottish writer Henry Mackenzie (1745–1831).

735.5–6   Richard Aldington] English poet, critic, and translator (1892–1962).

736.38   *Patience*] Gilbert and Sullivan operetta (1882) that satirized the Aesthetic movement in England. Its main character, the poet Bunthorne, may have been partly based on Wilde, and the role was associated with Wilde after he was hired to promote the operetta in the United States.

741.32   Maupassant and Swift] Jonathan Swift was incapacitated due to dementia in his last years; French writer Guy de Maupassant suffered from insanity brought on by syphilis and died at the age of 43.

741.38–39 *"Je n'ai rien inventé . . . à mon oreille."*] I have not invented or arranged anything in the last remarks that I cite. Wilde's words are present to my mind, and, I was going to say, to my ear.

747.25 a novel by Ernest Jünger] Most likely *The Storm of Steel: From the Diary of a German Storm-Troop Officer on the Western Front* (1922).

747.40 Hauptmann] See note 27.35.

749.24–25 George Henry Lewes] See note 297.19.

752.35–36 Bayard Taylor] American poet, journalist, and travel writer (1825–1878). Wilson published his long poem "Diversions of the Echo Club" in *The Shock of Recognition*.

758.16 *Le Chapeau de Paille d'Italie*] *An Italian Straw Hat*, farce (1851) by French playwright Eugène Labiche (1815–1888).

767.2 ARTHUR M. SCHLESINGER] American historian (1888–1965), whose books include *The New Deal in Action, 1933–1938* (1939), *Paths to the Present* (1949), and *The American as Reformer* (1950); father of Arthur Schlesinger Jr. (1917–2007).

772.19 Pavlowa] Anna Pavlova (1881–1931), Russian ballerina.

785.33 *Morts sans Sépulture*] Play (1946) by Jean-Paul Sartre, translated into English as *The Victors* by Thornton Wilder and *Men Without Shadows* by Kitty Black.

787.3 *L'Etre et le Néant*] Philosophical work *Being and Nothingness* (1943), one of the cornerstones of existentialism.

790.16 *Les Mouches*] *The Flies* (1943).

791.29 *mouvement à exporter*] Movement for export.

796.31 Harriet] Shelley's first wife Harriet Westbrook, whom Shelley abandoned for Mary Godwin.

808.13 Miss Murfree's Tennessee mountaineers] Published under the pseudonym Charles Egbert Craddock, Mary Murfree's fiction in collections such as *In the Tennessee Mountains* (1884) and *The Mystery of Witch-Face Mountain and Other Stories* (1895) were set in her native state.

808.14–15 Joseph Kirkland . . . Edward Eggleston] Midwest regionalist novelists Joseph Kirkland (1830–1894), author of *Zury: The Meanest Man in Spring County* (1885), and Edward Eggleston (1837–1902), author of *The Hoosier Schoolboy* (1881–82) and *The Graysons* (1888).

808.18–20 the European gypsies . . . Charles Godfrey Leland] Leland (1824–1903), novelist, poet, and essayist, wrote about gypsies in *The English*

Gipsies (1873) and *The Gypsies* (1882), and published the study *Etruscan-Roman Remains in Popular Tradition* in 1892.

808.20   *trouvailles*] Finds.

808.35–39   Stedman . . . newspapers"] The American poet, critic, and editor Edmund Clarence Stedman (1833–1908) made these remarks in an 1873 letter to his friend William Winter, a poet and drama critic.

809.17   Rebecca Harding Davis] American writer (1831–1910), best known as the author of "Life in the Iron Mills" (1861), a story that realistically depicted conditions endured by industrial workers; mother of the novelist and journalist Richard Harding Davis.

810.4   John De Forest] American writer (1826–1906); a Union officer in the Civil War, he published accounts of combat in *Harper's Weekly*, and wrote fiction about the war, including *Miss Ravenel's Conversion from Secession to Loyalty* (1867). See "The Chastening of American Prose Style; John W. De Forest" in *Patriotic Gore* (1962).

812.8   Cable] American novelist George Washington Cable (1844–1925), author of the story collection *Old Creole Days* (1879) and the novel *The Grandissimes: A Story of Creole Life* (1880). See "Novelists of the Post-War South: Albion W. Tourgée, George W. Cable, Kate Chopin, Thomas Nelson Page" in *Patriotic Gore* (1962).

815.20   Jowett] See note 66.14.

815.21   Leighton] English artist Frederic Leighton (1830–1896).

815.23   Sala] English journalist and novelist George Augustus Sala (1828–1895), author of *London in Twice Round the Clock* (1862).

815.37   *Yellow Book . . . Saturday Review*] *The Yellow Book*, English periodical of the 1890s that featured art and writing from Decadent and Aesthetic Movement figures such as Ernest Dowson, Arthur Symons, and Aubrey Bearsdley, who was its art editor; *The Saturday Review*, English periodical published from 1855 to 1938.

818.19   Gillray] English caricaturist and graphic artist James Gillray (1757–1815), best known for his satirical engravings.

820.37   Priestley] English novelist, playwright, and critic J. B. Priestley (1894–1984).

822.27   Ostrovsky] Russian realistic dramatist Aleksandr Ostrovsky (1823–1886).

822.27   Fet] Russian poet Afanasy Fet (1820–1892).

826.15   D. S. Mirsky] See note 53.9.

834.22–23   Krafft-Ebing] See note 690.15.

839.29–33   Faulkner's provinciality . . . closest attention and care.]   Eudora Welty protested this reasoning in a satiric letter to *The New Yorker*, but Faulkner himself wrote to Wilson accepting the critique of his later style.

845.21   Paul Bourget]   See note 405.14.

846.7   Maeterlinck]   Maurice Maeterlinck (1862–1949), Belgian Symbolist poet and playwright who was awarded the Nobel Prize in Literature in 1911.

846.7   Marguerite Audoux]   French novelist (1863–1937), author of *Marie-Claire* (1910), who came from a peasant background and supported herself by working as a seamstress.

849.1   Eugène Brieux]   Realist playwright (1858–1932) whose plays include *The Red Robe* (1900).

854.24   Ernest Seton Thompson]   Ernest Thompson Seton (1860–1946), English-born naturalist who immigrated to Canada as a boy and eventually settled in the United States. Also a writer and artist, he was author of *Wild Animals I Have Known* (1898) and *Lives of the Hunted* (1901).

856.16   Carl Van Vechten]   American novelist, critic, and photographer (1880–1964); his novels include *Peter Whiffle* (1922), *The Blind Bow-Boy* (1923), and *Parties* (1930). Wilson includes him in "the fashionable school of ironic romance" (*The Shores of Light*).

858.1   a *fou rire*]   A fit of uncontrollable laughter.

858.6   Boldini]   Fashionable Italian portrait painter Giovanni Boldini (1845–1931).

859.22   *Our American Cousin*]   Play (1858) by English playwright Tom Taylor (1817–1880).

863.4   Pinero]   English dramatist Arthur Wing Pinero (1855–1934).

863.5   *Charley's Aunt*]   Popular farce (1892) by English playwright Brandon Thomas (1856–1914).

869.24   Huneker]   See note 16.10.

872.13   Stieglitz]   American photographer Alfred Stieglitz (1864–1946), founder of the groundbreaking quarterly journal *Camera Work* and (with Edward Steichen) the gallery known as "291." See "The Stieglitz Exhibition" in *The American Earthquake*.

873.5–6   Randolph Bourne]   American writer and cultural critic (1886–1918).

873.8   *Seven Arts*]   Magazine founded in 1916 by Waldo Frank and James Oppenheim; in its two-year run it featured essays by Bourne as well as Van Wyck Brooks, Paul Rosenfeld, and Sherwood Anderson.

873.29–30   Ornstein, Milhaud, Varèse] Russian-born American pianist and composer Leo Ornstein (1892–2002); French composer Darius Milhaud (1892–1974); French composer Edgard Varèse (1883–1965).

873.31–32   the Stettheimers, Mumford, Kreymborg] American painter Florine Stettheimer (1871–1944) and her sisters Carrie and Ettie; American social and architecture critic Lewis Mumford (1895–1990); American poet and playwright Alfred Kreymborg (1883–1966).

878.9   Kurt Weill . . . Gebrauchsmusik] German-Jewish composer Kurt Weill (1900–1950); Gebrauchsmusik, "music for use," German movement in the 1920s (associated particularly with composer Paul Hindemith) advocating the composition of music for use at specific occasions rather than in the neutral sphere of the concert hall.

UNCOLLECTED REVIEWS

885.20–21   novels of contemporary history . . . Malraux's] Austrian writer Franz Höllering's The Defenders (1941) and French writer André Malraux's La condition humaine (1933; translated as Man's Fate). See "André Malraux" in The Shores of Light.

887.2–3   Stalinists . . . Dos Passos' attitude and Hemingway's] During his visit to Spain in 1937, Dos Passos learned that his friend José Robles, an official in the Republican government, had been secretly shot by the Communist security police for alleged spying. When Dos Passos stated his belief in Robles' innocence, Hemingway argued that he would not have been executed without justification.

887.6–7   "The Adventures of a Young Man."] Dos Passos' novel Adventures of a Young Man (1939).

888.16–17   Maurice Hewlett] English writer (1861–1923), prolific author of historical novels such as The Forest Lovers (1898) and The Life and Death of Richard Yea-and-Nay (1900).

892.34–35   Miss Nin is a very good artist] This review was written before Wilson's brief affair with Nin.

899.31   "Bertram Cope's Year," by Henry B. Fuller] Published in 1919.

903.24   John Woolman's "Journal"] The posthumously published journal of Quaker clergyman and abolitionist John Woolman (1720–1772).

904.6–7   Oh what . . . deceive!] Walter Scott, Marmion (1808), canto 6, introduction, stanza 17.

906.1   Henry James and Auden in America] See "The Ambiguity of Henry James" on pages 90–133 in this volume, "The Pilgrimage of Henry James" and "The Oxford Boys Becalmed" in The Shores of Light, and "W. H. Auden in America" in The Bit Between My Teeth.

Index

957

THE LIBRARY OF AMERICA SERIES

The Library of America fosters appreciation and pride in America's literary heritage by publishing, and keeping permanently in print, authoritative editions of America's best and most significant writing. An independent nonprofit organization, it was founded in 1979 with seed money from the National Endowment for the Humanities and the Ford Foundation.

This book is set in 10 point Linotron Galliard,
a face designed for photocomposition by Matthew Carter
and based on the sixteenth-century face Granjon. The paper
is acid-free lightweight opaque and meets the requirements
for permanence of the American National Standards Institute.
The binding material is Brillianta, a woven rayon cloth made
by Van Heek-Scholco Textielfabrieken, Holland. Compo-
sition by Dedicated Business Services. Printing by
Malloy Incorporated. Binding by Dekker Book-
binding. Designed by Bruce Campbell.